Annual Review of
Psychology

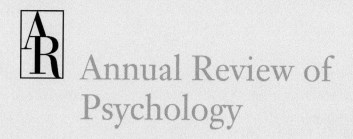

Annual Review of Psychology

Volume 65, 2014

Susan T. Fiske, *Editor*

Princeton University

Daniel L. Schacter, *Associate Editor*

Harvard University

Shelley E. Taylor, *Associate Editor*

University of California, Los Angeles

www.annualreviews.org • science@annualreviews.org • 650-493-4400

Annual Reviews

4139 El Camino Way • P.O. Box 10139 • Palo Alto, California 94303-0139

Annual Reviews
Palo Alto, California, USA

International Standard Serial Number: 0066-4308
International Standard Book Number: 978-0-8243-0265-8
Library of Congress Control Number: 50013143

All Annual Reviews and publication titles are registered trademarks of Annual Reviews.

⊗ The paper used in this publication meets the minimum requirements of American National Standards for Information Sciences—Permanence of Paper for Printed Library Materials, ANSI Z39.48-1992.

Annual Reviews and the Editors of its publications assume no responsibility for the statements expressed by the contributors to this *Annual Review*.

TYPESET BY APTARA
PRINTED AND BOUND BY SHERIDAN BOOKS, INC., CHELSEA, MICHIGAN

Introduction

We owe our science to the public: its tax dollars, its faith in our credibility, and its expectation that we will serve humanity, the planet, and our future. In return for their support, we owe the public our respectful, clear, and timely communication of our sciences. Producing accessible review articles helps to communicate scientific consensus, and Annual Reviews has been leading the way since its inception in 1932 as a nonprofit publisher.

Producing the reviews is not enough, so Annual Reviews communicates in multiple media: electronic and printed text, art and graphics, videos, podcasts, interviews, and social media (Facebook, Twitter, LinkedIn, RSS news feeds, and whatever the next weeks and year bring). What's more, each article becomes it own search engine, linking to the primary literature reviewed. The point is to make the scientific information widely available because it's the least we can do, in recognition of our public support.

Susan T. Fiske, Princeton, New Jersey
Daniel L. Schacter, Cambridge, Massachusetts
Shelley E. Taylor, Los Angeles, California

Annual Review of
Psychology

Volume 65, 2014

Contents

Community Psychology

Subcultures Within Countries

Organizational Climate/Culture

Job/Work Design

Selection and Placement

Personality and Coping Styles

Timely Topics

Indexes

Errata

An online log of corrections to *Annual Review of Psychology* articles may be found at
http://psych.AnnualReviews.org/errata.shtml

Related Articles

From the *Annual Review of Law and Social Science*, Volume 9 (2013)

From the ***Annual Review of Organizational Psychology and Organizational Behavior***, Volume 1 (2014)

From the *Annual Review of Public Health*, Volume 34 (2013)

Stress and Cardiovascular Disease: An Update on Current Knowledge
  Andrew Steptoe and Mika Kivimäki

The Impact of Labor Policies on the Health of Young Children in the Context of
  Economic Globalization
  Jody Heymann, Alison Earle, and Kristen McNeill

Reducing Hospital Errors: Interventions that Build Safety Culture
  Sara J. Singer and Timothy J. Vogus

Searching for a Balance of Responsibilities: OECD Countries' Changing Elderly
  Assistance Policies
  Katherine Swartz

Strategies and Resources to Address Colorectal Cancer Screening Rates and
  Disparities in the United States and Globally
  Michael B. Potter

The Behavioral Economics of Health and Health Care
  Thomas Rice

From the *Annual Review of Sociology*, Volume 39 (2013)

Formations and Formalisms: Charles Tilly and the Paradox of the Actor
  John Krinsky and Ann Mische

The Principles of Experimental Design and Their Application in Sociology
  Michelle Jackson and D.R. Cox

• The New Sociology of Morality
  Steven Hitlin and Stephen Vaisey

Social Scientific Inquiry Into Genocide and Mass Killing: From Unitary Outcome
  to Complex Processes
  Peter B. Owens, Yang Su, and David A. Snow

Interest-Oriented Action
  Lyn Spillman and Michael Strand

Drugs, Violence, and the State
  Bryan R. Roberts and Yu Chen

Healthcare Systems in Comparative Perspective: Classification, Convergence,
  Institutions, Inequalities, and Five Missed Turns
  Jason Beckfield, Sigrun Olafsdottir, and Benjamin Sosnaud

Multiculturalism and Immigration: A Contested Field in Cross-National
  Comparison
  Ruud Koopmans

Sociology of Fashion: Order and Change
  Patrik Aspers and Frédéric Godart

Religion, Nationalism, and Violence: An Integrated Approach
  Philip S. Gorski and Gülay Türkmen-Dervişoğlu

From the *Annual Review of Statistics and Its Application*, Volume 1 (2014)

I Study What I Stink At: Lessons Learned from a Career in Psychology

Robert J. Sternberg

Office of the President, University of Wyoming, Laramie, Wyoming 82071;
email: Robert.sternberg@uwyo.edu

Annu. Rev. Psychol. 2014. 65:1–16

First published online as a Review in Advance on
September 18, 2013

The *Annual Review of Psychology* is online at
http://psych.annualreviews.org

This article's doi:
10.1146/annurev-psych-052913-074851

Keywords

intelligence, creativity, wisdom, leadership, love

Abstract

I describe what I have learned from a rather long career in psychology. My
goal is to aid those younger than I to learn from my experience and avoid my
mistakes. I discuss topics such as the damage that self-fulfilling prophecies
can do, the importance of resilience, the need to overcome fear of failure, the
importance of being flexible in one's goals and changing them as needed, the
relevance of professional ethics, and the need to be wise and not just smart. In
the end, we and our work are forgotten very quickly and one should realize
that, after retirement, it likely will be one's family, not one's professional
network, that provides one's main source of support and comfort.

Contents

INTRODUCTION

I study what I stink at. After 38 years, 1,500 publications, 50 grants, and 13 honorary doctorates in the field, I have learned a lot of lessons from my research, teaching, and writing, and I hope this article will be useful to those at an earlier stage in career than I who might profit in some way from these lessons. Most of the lessons I learned were from my numerous failures.

My goal in this article is not to review my research per se, which I have written about elsewhere over the years of my career (Sternberg 1977, 1985, 1990, 1997b,c, 1998a,b, 2003, 2010; Sternberg et al. 2000, 2011; Sternberg & Lubart 1995). Although I briefly review the trend of my research, my goal rather is to discuss my experience of being in the field and what I have learned from that experience.

I have found the pursuit of psychology just the best way to understand much of what I have tried to do in my life that has not worked out particularly well. Quite simply, in my career, I have generally gotten inspiration by studying things in which I failed. I started studying and writing about intelligence because I did poorly on IQ tests as a child; I started thinking about creativity at a point in my career when I ran out of ideas; I started writing about love when my love life was not doing well; I wrote about thinking styles because of experiences I had had where my way of thinking and learning seemed not to match teachers' expectations; I started studying wisdom because I had given bad advice to a student; I started studying leadership because I most unfairly and grievously lost the election in grade 5 for the vice-presidency of the student council to a kid whose speech was far worse than mine (so I thought); and so forth. Studying my failures has worked for me. I never studied the things I found to be easy, such as writing. I would have made no progress at all in studying those things because I had no insight into what made them hard for others.

If there is a message in this article, it is this: Over the years, I discovered many challenges in my work. The greatest challenge by far has not been in doing research, teaching, or doing administration, but rather in showing resiliency in the face of negative feedback and conquering the fear of failure. If I look back at the students from my Stanford PhD graduate times, it is evident that the ones who succeeded often succeeded by sheer perseverance as much as by anything else.

ELEMENTARY AND JUNIOR HIGH SCHOOL

I had just finished first grade—I would have been 7 years old. I was walking home when an older student accosted me and asked me if I had been promoted. I did not know what the word "promoted" meant. But I did not want the student to know I didn't know. So I said that, no, I had not been promoted. He said he was sorry to hear it. When I got home, I asked my mother what the word meant. I found out, and also found out that I had indeed been promoted. Important lesson: If you don't understand a question, or don't know the answer, don't fake it. You're better off just admitting your ignorance.

My first published article was when I was in sixth grade, when I was 12: It was a review of *Tom Sawyer* for a weekly newspaper for elementary school students called *My Weekly Reader*. The newspaper was circulated all over the United States. Ironically, this earliest piece was probably the most widely circulated piece I have ever written. I learned a lesson from this experience, namely, that even a 12-year-old can do something that is circulated nationally. It made me aware that the world upon which I could have some influence was not limited to Maplewood, New Jersey, or even to the state of New Jersey, which at the time seemed to be most of the world. Kids need to realize that they can speak with a voice that extends way beyond the environments they have experienced.

But my main interest in elementary school was not in literature but rather in psychology. As a child in the early grades, I failed miserably on IQ tests. In the late 1950s, when I went to elementary school, the authorities (at least where I lived) would give IQ tests every couple of years. I'm not sure why. The school psychologist who would come in to administer the tests scared the bejesus out of me. I don't know exactly why. I just thought she looked scary. Perhaps anyone giving such tests would scare me. But as soon as she entered the classroom, I had acquired a conditioned response that resulted in my freezing up. I remember that when taking the tests other children would be turning the page while I still would be on the first problem. Of course I did poorly on the tests. As a result, my teachers in my early elementary school years thought I was stupid; I thought I was stupid; my teachers were happy that they had me pegged as stupid; I was happy that they were happy; and everyone was pretty happy about the whole thing. But each year in early elementary school I did a little worse than I did the previous year.

Then, in fourth grade, I had a teacher, Mrs. Alexa, who, for whatever reason, thought there was more to a child, and to me, than just an IQ score. She made clear to me she expected more of me—that she expected me to become an A student. I really liked Mrs. Alexa. I recall thinking at the time that it was too bad she was so much older than I was—and married. In any case, I wanted to please her, and to my own astonishment, I became an A student. I learned what so many had learned before me, the power of self-fulfilling prophecies (Rosenthal & Jacobson 1968).

Years later, I was invited back to speak at my elementary school in Maplewood. They knew of Mrs. Alexa because I had dedicated my book *Successful Intelligence* (Sternberg 1997b) to her. But Mrs. Alexa was long gone from the school and community. The administrators tried to find her without success. Then, one of the administrators had the bright idea to let her teenage son try to find Mrs. Alexa on the Internet. He succeeded in a matter of minutes, I was told. She was living in New Hampshire. She was invited to come to the event where I would speak, and she accepted. I went to see her in New Hampshire before the event. I didn't recognize her, and it was pretty obvious she didn't remember me, although she said she thought she might. But it was nice to see her, in any case. At least, I'm pretty sure it was she.

When I was in sixth grade, someone came into my classroom and took me out. The purpose, it turned out, was to take me back to a fifth-grade classroom to take that year's IQ test with the fifth-graders. Apparently, they thought the sixth-grade test would be too hard for me. This maneuver on their part had an unexpected consequence, at least for me. Whereas I was petrified when I took the IQ test in the company of my classmates, I found I was much less nervous in the company of fifth-graders, who to me were babies. I, after all, was a sixth-grader, soon to be graduated from elementary school. So I took the test without test anxiety, and oddly enough, after that one success experience, I never was nervous again taking standardized tests. I learned that even with one success experience, one can overcome deeply seated anxieties.

My first major research project was in grade 7, when I was 13. I wanted to understand why I did so poorly on IQ tests. My first research on the topic actually was for my seventh-grade science project. The project involved my creating my own (rather pedestrian) intelligence test. The test, which I called the Sternberg Test of Mental Abilities [I'm sure you've heard of the test, well-known (only to me) by its acronym "STOMA"!], was basically a hodgepodge of kinds of subtests investigators had used over the years. I actually administered this hodgepodge to a bunch of people and discovered that using lots and lots of subtests yielded rank-order scores among people that were not much different from the rank-order scores obtained from using substantially fewer subtests. In other words, I had rediscovered Spearman's (1927) general intelligence, or *g*. Just giving people a lot of tests does not necessarily increase the precision or validity of one's measurement. The issue, I would discover much later, is which tests one chooses to administer.

My project also involved researching the history of intelligence testing. In the course of doing this research, I discovered the Stanford-Binet Intelligence Test in a book in the adult section of the library in my hometown. I thought it would be a useful experience to give the test to some of my classmates.

This aspect of the project was somewhat ill fated. The first person to whom I gave the test was a girl in whom I was romantically interested. I thought that giving her the IQ test would interest her in me. I was wrong. Important lesson here: If you are romantically interested in someone, don't give the person an IQ test. I am very happily married to my wife, Karin, and have never given her an IQ test. I plan to keep it that way.

A person to whom I later gave the IQ test was a friend I had known from Cub Scouts. Unfortunately, he suffered from a serious mental illness. I believe the technical term is that he was a tattletale. He told his mother that I had given him the test. Apparently, being a tattletale is heritable, because she told the junior high school guidance counselor. It appears that being a tattletale also is contagious, because she told the head school system psychologist. He came to my school, called me out of second-period social studies class, and balled me out for 40 minutes, ending with the comment that he personally would burn the book if I ever brought it into school again. He suggested I study intelligence in rats, although I do not think he was offering himself as a subject. There is a lesson there, which most parents and child psychologists know: If you want to discourage a child from pursuing an interest, don't forbid the child to pursue that interest. It makes the interest so much more appealing to the child. I suspect the psychologist sealed my lifelong interest in the topic of intelligence.

My science teacher thought more of my report than the psychologist did: He gave me an A on it. He also defended me from the onslaught. I learned again how a teacher could save a child from feeling destroyed.

In grade 11, we had to do an independent project in physics. My grades had shown a pretty steady trajectory. The first marking period I got an A−, the second one a B+, the third one a B, and I think you get the idea. I wondered why my performance in physics was flagging. We were taking what was supposed to be an innovative course, called PSSC physics, but I found it to be close to incomprehensible. So I created a physics aptitude test, which basically measured two kinds of skills—quantitative reasoning and mechanical reasoning. I came to realize that I was good at the former but rather poor at the latter. And as the physics course progressed, it involved more and more mechanics. The physics teacher was impressed and gave me an A on the project, although it did not save my grade in physics.

The next summer, at age 17, I was admitted to a National Science Foundation program at Roswell Park Memorial Institute in Buffalo, New York. It is a cancer institute, and I chose to be in the biostatistics department because I was interested in statistics. But I ended up being something of a misfit. So I gave up on biostatistics, learned to program in FORTRAN, and wrote a program that would score the physics aptitude test if the test were administered on what I believe were called "port-a-punch" cards. You punched out your answers on a computer card. (What young person today even knows that computers used to read cards through a card reader?) Amazingly, my now-former physics teacher allowed me to administer the test to students in physics, and I found that it predicted grades with a validity coefficient in the 60s, which was pretty darn impressive. I saw that, even as a high school student, I could create a test that actually worked.

The summer after that, the summer of 1968, I was ready for something new, so I wrote to the Psychological Corporation, a testing company in New York, modestly asking that they hire me for the summer. They were intrigued and asked me to come to New York for an interview. I did. They interviewed me and also gave me an ability test. They hired me. They paid me a royal $100 a week. I was delighted. I spent the summer there, working on a variety of projects, but mostly on the Miller Analogies Test, a high-level test used for graduate admissions. The next summer, 1969, I worked there again. The work I did became the basis for a book I later wrote in graduate school when I was short on money, *How to Prepare for the Miller Analogies Test* (Sternberg 1974). It was my first published book. The book is still in print, entering its eleventh edition. Sadly, this less-than-monumental volume is the most successful book I have ever written, at least in terms of going into successive editions.

THE COLLEGE YEARS AT YALE

I was going to need a scholarship to go to college. My brother Paul and I are first-generation high school graduates. My father dropped out of high school in the Depression; my mother had to leave Vienna, in a hurry, in 1938. My mother was very supportive of my going to college; my father, from whom my mother was divorced, had checked out (I never saw him except at my own instigation) and would have been happy for me to take over his button business in a second-floor walk-up in Newark, New Jersey. Fortunately, I received a National Merit Scholarship, so I was able to go to college. I went to Yale in part because I was led to believe it had a strong psychology department.

My career as a psychologist got off to a rotten start. I took introductory psychology my freshman year. I was eager still to find out why I had done so poorly on IQ tests as a child. My first test was a series of short essays. I realized as I was writing them that I was not sure exactly what was expected. What I did not realize was how the writing would be scored. The teacher expected us to make 10 points that he had in mind for each essay. He graded us on the number of points we made and then averaged the scores. Just before Thanksgiving, he handed out the test papers in descending order. As each student got his or her paper, he or she could leave. In this way, all the 150 or so students in the class could see who the smart ones were and who the not-so-smart ones were. He handed out the 10s, the 9s, then the 8s. By the time he got to the 7s, I figured my paper must have gotten out of order: It seemed inconceivable to me that I could have gotten lower than a 7. Finally he handed me my paper with a 3 on it. He commented to me that there was a famous Sternberg in psychology (Saul Sternberg, mentioned again later in this article) and that it was obvious there would not be another one. I ended up with a C in the course, which the professor referred to as a "gift," and decided to major in math. After failing the midterm exam in a course on real analysis, and being told by the professor to drop the course, I returned to psychology. My C in intro psych was now looking pretty good. I did much better in later courses and ended up graduating with highest honors in psychology. Three decades or so later I was president of the American Psychological Association (APA) and commented to the psychologist who was president the year before—Phil Zimbardo—that it was ironic the president of APA had gotten a C in introductory psychology. He responded that he, too, had gotten a C.

I learned several important lessons from this experience. First, the skills one needs to succeed in introductory psychology courses are not the same as, and are only weakly overlapping with, the ones needed to succeed in the field. Second, teachers tend to teach (*a*) the way they were taught and (*b*) the way they optimally would like to learn. But the way they teach is not always a good fit to diverse students' styles of learning, and unfortunately, some of the students who could be most successful in the field may be taught in ways that never allow them to go on to career success. Third, teachers are sometimes too quick to give up on students. The ones they give up on may be the ones who, someday, will be able to make more of a difference to the field than the teachers themselves.

After my freshman year, I went back to work at the Psychological Corporation. I asked for a raise, but they did not want to give me one. Finally, they consented to give me a raise from $100 to $105. Had they given me the raise right away, I would have been delighted. But by then I was so pissed off at them that I decided that this summer would be my last summer there. I learned a lesson from that, too, which has served me well as an administrator: Don't go out of your way to antagonize employees on whose goodwill you depend.

As a college sophomore, I did a study that showed that if you gave students taking a mental test reminders of how much of their allotted time was remaining, the psychometric properties of the test improved relative to those for a group in which students were not given such information. I tried to get the paper published but did not succeed. So I later used it as an appendix in a book I wrote, *Writing the Psychology Paper*, as an example of how to write a paper. The paper was well written but somewhat vacuous. In retrospect, the lesson I learned is that it is not enough to write a paper well—you really want to have some important message to write about. Duh.

I needed a job. The jobs available sounded boring, such as working in the dining hall or sorting records in a dean's office. So I wrote to Henry (Sam) Chauncey, Jr., the director of Admissions and Financial Aid Policy at Yale, and asked if he would meet with me to consider hiring me. The meeting took place, and I was hired. I spent my next few years doing part-time admissions research.

In the end, I published a couple of articles in *College and University* (Sternberg 1972, 1973) based upon research I had done in the Yale undergraduate admissions office. In one piece, I showed that Yale could cut the number of applicants it carefully reviewed by 40% by employing a "decision rule," which was 98% accurate in predicting admit and reject decisions for the top and the bottom of the admissions pool. Using the rule would enable admissions officers to spend more time on the applicants for whom decisions were more difficult—those in the middle of the pool. The second article, a cost-benefit analysis of the Yale admissions office interview, showed that the interview was pretty close to useless in the admissions decision process but was beneficial because applicants liked it and thought they performed much better than they actually did on it. So we kept it, if for no other reason than that it was a good public relations tool. To this day, as an administrator, I have to think both about the substantive value of what we do in a university and its public relations value.

In my junior year, I took a laboratory course with a professor on human information processing. I really liked the course a lot and got an A. I had great relations with the professor, who was very supportive of me, my work, and my ambition to pursue a career in psychology. Here's what's odd. The professor was the same one who had given me a C in the introductory course and told me there was a famous Sternberg in psychology and it looked like there wouldn't be another one. What had changed? Really, the way he taught the course. The freshman intro course was basically a memorize-the-book, memorize-the-lectures type of course. I never have been very good at that type of course. The junior-year course was a lab course that emphasized more creative research work. So I did much better. The lesson? What you learn from a student in a course you teach is not how smart the student is but rather how well the student's way of learning matches the way you teach. Teachers should be hesitant to draw conclusions about students' abilities unless they teach to a variety of ability patterns and learning styles.

In my senior year at Yale, I worked with Endel Tulving. He was a fantastic advisor. I did some work on what was called negative transfer in part-whole and whole-part free recall and some work on the measurement of subjective organization in free recall. The latter work resulted in an article with Tulving that we submitted to *Psychological Bulletin*. We had written a methodological article that we thought provided a novel and useful way of measuring subjective organization in free recall—that is, the extent to which the output of a free-recall task is organized rather than random. The article was summarily rejected by the editor at the time, Richard Herrnstein. For me, it was quite depressing because it was one of my earliest papers and I (presciently) foresaw a career of one rejection after another. Later, in writing another paper, I asked Tulving how I should cite the article that had been rejected. Without skipping a beat, he said, "Cite it as 'rejected by *Psychological Bulletin*.'" At the time, I was stunned by his response. I was just starting my career, and I could not imagine why, at that time or, for that matter, at any time, I would want to advertise that my paper had been rejected. I later better came to understand his message—that we had ideas in which we took pride, and regardless of what the reviewers and editors thought, we should still take pride in them. The article was later published in the journal when the next editor took charge (Sternberg & Tulving 1977). Not all so many years later, I was editor of the journal!

The most important lesson I learned from Tulving is that just because a lot of people believe something, it doesn't mean it is true (see Tulving & Madigan 1970, Tulving & Thomson 1973).

THE GRADUATE SCHOOL YEARS AT STANFORD

I arrived at Stanford for graduate school and proudly showed my new advisor, Gordon Bower, a project I had done as an undergraduate. I was very proud of the paper I had written and asked him for comments. I figured this was a good way for him to see what a brilliant student he had acquired. A week or two later he handed the paper back to me and merely commented that the parts he had not liked, he had crossed out. I looked at the paper and discovered he had crossed out almost the whole thing. I later concluded he was right—the paper really wasn't very good. He had been kind in not just coming out and telling me that.

My first-year project with Gordon Bower at Stanford was on negative transfer in part-whole and whole-part free recall (Sternberg & Bower 1974). The project was based on some of my (unpublished) undergraduate research with Endel Tulving on the same topic. The project was quite successful in one sense and not very successful in another. The success was that, after the article based upon the research was published, research in the area pretty much stopped. The bad news, I later learned, is that it is actually bad to close down an area—there is nothing to do in it anymore!

My main interest was not really in memory but rather in intelligence. I was still trying to figure out why I had done poorly on IQ tests. At the end of my first year, I met Tulving at the Center for Advanced Study in the Behavioral Sciences. A group of his colleagues at the Center joined us. They asked me what I was doing in my research. I told them about my successful first-year project but also told them that I was not sure what I was going to do next. I still remember their pitying looks. They seemed to be thinking, "The poor guy—he had one idea and flamed out immediately thereafter."

I thought I wanted to do something with intelligence, and with analogies in particular. Thus, when Barron's Educational Series, Inc. asked me to write a book on analogies, I accepted. I have written or edited over 100 books, but regrettably, my most successful book has been that one I wrote in graduate school, *How to Prepare for the Miller Analogies Test* (Sternberg 1974). I wrote it partly for the money, obviously. As a graduate student, I needed that money. But I was also hoping it would give me ideas about how to study analogies.

I did end up studying analogies and intelligence for my dissertation, but the ideas did not come from writing that book. Rather, they came from looking at materials that my wife (at the time) was using in her work as an elementary school mathematics specialist. The materials were called "People Pieces," and they were tiles with schematic pictures of people that varied in four dimensions—height (tall or short), weight (fat or thin), color (blue or red), and sex (male or female). I realized I could systematically manipulate these features and create analogies out of them. In this way, I could scientifically study the psychological bases of reaction times in solving analogies based on the pieces.

The dissertation took the better part of my second and third years at Stanford, which were my last years there. I went through the whole two years having no idea how the data would come out. Finally, when the data all were collected, I analyzed the data and found that none of the mathematical models I had proposed accounted particularly well for the data. I was chagrined. But then I studied the residuals and found that with just one slight modification of the models, the prediction of response times was excellent. This experience also taught me a valuable lesson: It ain't over 'til it's over! If the data don't look right at first, make sure that you understand and analyze the data in the best possible way before concluding there is little or nothing there. Had I not carefully looked at residuals of the data from the model, I would have thought the project had failed.

THE FACULTY YEARS AT YALE

My dissertation came out successfully, and after three years I left Stanford to return to Yale as an assistant professor. I submitted a book manuscript based on my long dissertation (it was over 750 pages long) to Larry Erlbaum, who had just recently started Lawrence Erlbaum, Inc. He sent the book out for review and got two reviews. One was fairly short and fairly positive. The other was 17 single-spaced pages long and devastating. I figured that was the end of that. The person who wrote it was very famous in the field and obviously did not like my take on it. To my amazement, Erlbaum told me that, despite the review, he still fully intended to publish the book. He told me to make the revisions I thought were warranted and to ignore the rest. I did, and he published the book (Sternberg 1977), which later became a citation classic. I learned that just because work is negatively reviewed, it is not necessarily bad.

One thing I learned early in my career is the value of collaboration. Most of my written work has been collaborative—with graduate students, postdoctoral fellows, faculty members, and others. I could have accomplished relatively little in my career without collaborators. I have had many notably successful collaborations, such as with Janet Davidson, Elena Grigorenko, Linda Jarvin, James Kaufman, Todd Lubart, David Preiss, Karin Sternberg, Richard Wagner, Wendy Williams, and Li-fang Zhang, among others. The list of collaborators goes on, and I would have had little success in writing without these joint efforts.

One of the weirder experiences I had during my assistant professor years was with the *Journal of Experimental Psychology: General*. I submitted an article on our work on response-time and error-rate models of linear syllogistic reasoning (i.e., solution of problems such as John is taller than James; James is taller than Joseph; who is shortest?) I got back two reviews, which were generally quite favorable. However, one review suggested I lengthen the paper, whereas the other review suggested I shorten the paper. The editor, a famous experimental psychologist, wrote back that he had to reject the paper because one reviewer suggested I lengthen it, the other suggested I shorten it, and I obviously could not do both. Duh! He seemed unable to make the decision for himself. I wrote a protest and he eventually accepted the paper.

I have thought a great deal about the peer-review process in editorial as well as grant decisions. I once received a review of an article I wrote in which the referee suggested I find some other line of work more consistent with my limited level of mental abilities. My receiving this review reflected two extraordinary events: the first was that the referee would have written such a savage remark, and the second was that the journal editor would send the review to me.

I shrugged the review off, even finding it mildly amusing. As someone who then had been writing articles for 25 years, I was used to nasty *ad hominem* remarks. This one was worse than most, but probably not the absolute worst I had seen to that point (or subsequently). And I even have seen published critiques of my and others' work where the primary goal of the critic seemed to be character assassination rather than scientific exchange. It is important, in academia, never to take things personally.

When I was an assistant professor, I received excellent advice from my mentors, advice that, in combination with my own, I have attempted to pass on to the next generation. One of the best pieces of advice I received was from Wendell Garner, my mentor when I was a junior faculty member. He told me that, as psychologists, we ultimately are judged by the positive contributions we make. Indeed, if one thinks of great psychologists in any field of endeavor, they are known primarily not for their critiques but rather for their new and useful ideas. As a field, we need to set better examples for our colleagues and for the next generation by exerting positive rather than negative leadership and, most importantly, by being civil to those with whom we interact.

Very early in my career, I received a phone call inviting me to collaborate with the Ministry for the Development of Intelligence in Venezuela on a project for developing a program to enhance the intelligence of Venezuelan college students. The grant we received enabled us to spend several years developing a program that was to be administered to the college students (Sternberg 1986a). But then the party in power lost the next election, and the subsequent administration mocked and cut off the funding for these projects. The program was later published as a book (*Intelligence Applied*; Sternberg 2006), now in a new edition (and published as *Applied Intelligence*; Sternberg et al. 2008). I learned how easy it is to have one's funding cut off when the government, or a corporation, finds further funding of the work to be inconvenient.

Although most of my work has been scientific, I also have done some textbooks, some of which died after a few editions (e.g., Sternberg 1995), and some of which have persevered through many editions (e.g., Sternberg & Sternberg 2012). Writing textbooks is a different art from writing scientific articles. It is extremely hard. You need to write in a way that will engage people much younger and less knowledgeable than you. Moreover, there is tremendous pressure to dumb down the material—more so in recent years than in years further past. But if you succeed in getting a contract and producing the book, you may find it greatly rewarding to know that students have learned psychology from your own textbook. In my own case, textbooks were motivated partly by my desire to produce a better textbook than what was out there, partly by my excitement about writing for a student audience, and partly by my need for money to pay for my kids' college. My "better" idea was to teach psychology using principles of my theory of successful intelligence.

When an article (or book manuscript) is rejected, one never knows for sure whether it is because it is really bad—or because it is really good. I usually would take reviews seriously, ignoring personal comments, and then resubmit. Sometimes, the second and then the third journal would reject the work. I would usually conclude after three go-arounds that either my ideas were not so good or that I had not succeeded in writing about them in a way that persuaded other people that they were good, however good or bad they might be. Sometimes I would put the article in the proverbial file drawer until I could figure out a way to present the ideas more effectively.

Once, I went through this process and got three rejections of an article. I put it away and then forgot about it. Ten years later, I was cleaning out some file drawers and found the article. I reread it and felt, as I had ten years before, that it was a good article. I resubmitted it to a strong journal, making no changes at all. Within a few months, I got a response. The reviews were very positive but pointed out that my citations were all at least ten years old. I updated the references, and the article was accepted (Sternberg 1997a).

A lot of my ideas about creativity were crystallized in our investment theory of creativity (Sternberg & Lubart 1995). It was Endel Tulving who served as a role model for the theory. We argued that creative people are creative by virtue of an attitude toward life—they are people who defy the crowd. People often are afraid to defy the crowd, however, because of external pressures to conform, which then lead them to pressure themselves to conform.

Things did not always go so well. Another article that I submitted was rejected by a couple of journals, and the ideas were ridiculed as naïve and ill conceived. I gave up on the article. A few years later, the article was published—by someone else. That is, someone else did essentially the same research, got it published, and also got many citations to the work. In that case, I think I was ahead of the times, and when one is ahead of the times, ideas are often not appreciated.

I should add that not everything that goes into the file drawer is worth publishing—ever. During my first year, I did some research in perception, which I thought showed that Wendell Garner's theory of perception was incorrect. I was in an awkward position, because he was a senior faculty member in my own department and a mentor to me. I showed him the paper, and he did not think much of it. I submitted it, and it was rejected, but I planned to resubmit it. Then I was invited to give a colloquium at Bell Labs. I presented the work. In the audience was my namesake, Saul Sternberg, to whom I am not related, to my knowledge, in any way. He asked a question about the work, and I immediately realized that he had pointed out a fatal flaw in the work: The results suffered from a statistical artifact, which rendered them worthless. It was one of the most embarrassing experiences in my professional career and one from which I learned that sometimes one's own confidence in one's own work can be severely misplaced.

In my third year I got a phone call from a professor I knew at another institution. He asked me what his institution would have to do to recruit me to come to that institution. I told him that at Yale very few assistant professors got tenure—at the time it was about 10%—and so the big issue for me was tenure. He told me that would be no problem. We agreed to be in touch. Still a naïve 28-year-old, I told the chair of my department, at the time Bill Kessen, that I had received a tenure offer from that institution. Yale formed a committee to consider me for tenure. Things went badly downhill from there. I did not hear back from the other institution for a long time. In the meantime, a full professor at Yale left Yale to go to that other institution. I should have realized that his departure did not bode well for me. I eventually called another professor I knew at that institution, who said that, well, I did not have a tenure offer, but more like a 90% tenure offer. He said they would invite me to give a talk. I told Kessen that what I had thought was a tenure offer had turned out to be only a 90% offer. He asked me to keep him informed. Eventually the other department did invite me to give a talk, and almost no one came. I went through the visit without even meeting the head of the department, certainly a bad sign. I never heard back from them. I eventually called the department head, who told me that I was not going to receive a tenure offer from them. I was mortified. I went back to Kessen and told him that the 90% offer was now a 0% offer. He asked me to write a letter asking that my name be withdrawn from consideration for tenure. I felt that writing such a letter would be incredibly embarrassing. I delayed and thought and thought about how I could turn things around. I even went to interview at one other place but didn't much like it. One day, while I was jogging, I had an insight. There was absolutely nothing I could do to turn the situation around. I had to write the letter. I did. I can remember few times in my life when I have been so embarrassed. I expected my colleagues at Yale to treat me poorly after that, but in fact they were very kind. I was grateful and stayed. I learned that in academia, if you don't have anything in writing, you don't have anything!

The next year, they did a search for the tenure slot vacated by the colleague who had left to go to the institution that never came through for me. I was now 29 years old. Yale had a fixed-slot tenure system. There was no actual tenure track. One could be tenured only if someone else resigned or retired. Anyway, Yale eventually offered the slot to Bill Estes, who was 60. He went to Harvard. So the slot was open again the following year. I became a candidate once again.

Several assistant professors were being considered at the same time for tenure at Yale. Once I was in the office of one of them and noticed his calendar out on his desk. He had dinner engagements with pretty much all the full professors in the department. I found myself thinking that I had really blown it. I didn't know that that was part of the deal in getting tenure. That colleague was acting kind of strangely toward me. One day I went to see him and said that I hoped we could remain friends even though we both were being considered for the same slot. He said we couldn't. We didn't talk a whole lot after that. I got the slot. And I learned that life is too short to take things personally. It's not worth getting into a personal tiff over everyone with whom you compete or have differences because that will eventually be almost everyone you know. I have had some colleagues who went after me in a serious way. Taking things personally is a sure way to be left with no friends at all and to wreck one's health as well.

Wendell Garner, the next chair of the department, taught me many lessons during my years at Yale, one of the most important of which was the need to stand up for what one believes in. During my fifth year at Yale, when I was being considered again for the senior position, scuttlebutt reached my ears suggesting that some of the referees who had been consulted on my work were not so positive about it because it was on intelligence, and they believed that intelligence was a rather dumpy area of study within psychology. According to the gossip I heard, they were suggesting that Yale instead give the position to someone writing about a more prestigious field, perhaps thinking, reasoning, or problem solving. I spoke to Garner and asked him what I should do. I somewhat bitterly pointed out that I could have done exactly the same work and called it something else— thinking, reasoning, or problem solving—and then perhaps I would not be in the pickle I was in. He stared me in the eye and said that I was right in my concern: My work in the field of intelligence might indeed cost me my job. But if it did, I would find another job. He pointed out that, when I had come to Yale, my goal had been to make a meaningful difference to the field of intelligence. That I had done. That was my mission—my reason for being in psychology—and so that was what I had to do. It was a good lesson to learn early in my career. Garner also repeated to me some advice he had once gotten from Michael Posner, who had told him that the hardest articles to get published are one's worst ones, because they are bad, but also one's best and most creative ones, because they threaten the existing order.

Not long thereafter, I decided to start studying love (see, e.g., Sternberg 1986b). I was in a failing relationship, so it was time again to study something I was failing at. I published a few articles, thinking that people would be impressed with my versatility. Instead, I started getting comments such as that perhaps I had run out of ideas about intelligence, or maybe I was getting soft in the head, or perhaps I wanted to be a TV star like Dr. Ruth (or, years later, Dr. Phil), or maybe my love life had gone sour (which it had). I got quite a bit of flack. I learned that people tend to put you in a box. If you start writing about something new, it makes them uncomfortable. Yet to continue to grow as a scholar, that is precisely what you need to do.

For most of my career, if someone had told me that they thought I would become a dean, I would have suggested he or she get his or her head examined. But after 30 years at Yale, I left. It was not an easy decision. But a number of factors combined to lead me to make the change at a time when many other scholars are counting the years to retirement.

First, I had been writing for 30 years and found myself feeling increasingly frustrated. I had never had the success with trade (popular) books that some of my colleagues had, and perhaps as a result, I felt that my writing was producing little change in the world. I had set out to reform admissions, instruction, and assessment, none of which had happened or even looked to be close on the horizon. Indeed, in those days of George W. Bush as president and the No Child Left Behind Act in the schools, I felt I was further away from realizing change than I ever had been before. I looked forward at perhaps 15 more years doing science and writing articles, and what I saw depressed me. I felt that the trajectory I was on was not going to lead to any significant change in society. Some writers succeed in changing the world—I clearly hadn't.

Second, a really important grant proposal I had written was turned down. My collaborators and I had done an assessment project that had yielded really great results. It was called the Rainbow Project (Sternberg & Rainbow Proj. Collab. 2006). But the commercial outfit that funded us, upon seeing the results, cut off our funding. There are various interpretations as to why they might have done so. One is that we threatened them commercially. Another is that the work was not very good, despite the enormous attention it received and despite its having been published as the lead article in the leading journal in the field. A third was the explanation the commercial outfit gave us—that the work could never be upscaled and made to work with large numbers of participants. I had gone into psychology to make a difference to the world, and now I felt the testing company wanted to make sure I didn't make that difference. I wanted to prove that upscaling was possible and that my ideas about admissions could make the difference to the world I hoped for.

Third, I had not much liked what I had seen in observing some of my senior colleagues during my years at Yale. My feeling about an academic career was that one spends the first 20 or 30 years trying to claw to the top or wherever one can get, and then after that, one tries desperately to hang on to whatever position one has obtained, only practically inevitably to feel one letting go, finger by finger, of the precipice on which one is hanging. I thought that by becoming a dean and remaining at the same time a professor, I might be able to start on a new trajectory, metaphorically climbing a new mountain.

Finally, in 2003 I served as president of the APA. I had been reluctant to run because I never saw myself as much of a big-time leader or even candidate for a basically political position. But I thought I had a mission—to unify psychology (Sternberg 2004b)—and the presidency of APA seemed to be the way to achieve that mission. When I ran, I initially was able to endure doing something I thought I stank at—running a campaign—by imagining I was only playacting being a candidate. Eventually I became the candidate whose role I playacted and forgot I was playacting. My experience as APA president convinced me I could do administration and, to my surprise, I really liked it.

One would like to say that, as the years go on, one's career gets easier. I think this is partially right. In my experience, the trajectory is curvilinear, as I imply above. At first, one is on a rising trajectory. But as the field moves on, it is difficult to change oneself as quickly as the field changes. I had noticed this earlier in my career—some people got stuck and seemed not to be able to change with the world. Earlier on, I had noticed this in others. As the years went by, I noticed it in myself.

I had early on developed a three-part theory of intelligence, and then a three-part theory of love, and then a three-part theory of creativity. At that point, I had three theories with three parts. People began to ask me why three of my theories had three parts. I thought about the question deeply, not to mention profoundly, and answered that I could think of three reasons my theories had three parts. I was stuck. The theory of leadership that I have developed is called WICS, which stands for wisdom, intelligence, and creativity, synthesized. I have graduated to a four-part theory!—sort of.

So I think things get a little easier and then get a lot harder later in a career. It is a constant challenge to renew oneself and not allow oneself to get stale. The rejections don't stop in one's later years—at least, they have not for me. I have probably had more articles rejected than anyone

I know, although almost all of them were eventually published. What has changed is the thickness of my skin: I have grown used to rejections and take them much more lightly than I did when I was younger.

THE DEANSHIP YEARS AT TUFTS

Becoming a dean is undoubtedly not the right thing for everyone, but it was the right thing for me. My research operation has been smaller, and I have been publishing less, but it is still more than most academics publish. Moreover, the nature of my writing has changed to some extent. I have become much more concerned with writing about issues as they pertain to colleges and universities, in general. It has been a chance for me to apply the concepts about which I wrote before to a larger academic context (e.g., Sternberg 2010a).

I encountered one major challenge as a dean that I had not encountered before. When I would write anything pertaining to the university, I had to be super careful about what I said. As a professor, you can tell any story you want about what you do, so long as it is veridical. In contrast, administrators can't all be telling different stories about their university. They need a more or less common story. At Tufts, the president wanted very much to control the message. I chafed at this, but it was his prerogative to control that message.

At Tufts, we instituted the Kaleidoscope Project (Sternberg 2010b), which was an upscaling of the Rainbow Project. We measured creative, analytical, practical, and wisdom-based skills in our applicants who chose to participate, roughly one-third of them. The results were excellent: We improved prediction of academic and extracurricular performance over SAT and high school grade point average. And I showed that it was indeed possible to upscale the Rainbow Project we did at Yale.

THE PROVOSTSHIP YEARS AT OKLAHOMA STATE

Tufts was not quite the right place for me. In the end of my term at Yale, I had begun to feel that the place was a bit elitist as well as elite, and I had gone to Tufts hoping that it would be different. It was different, but not really in that way. There is nothing wrong with being elitist, I suppose, but it was not a good fit to a guy who was a first-generation high school graduate whose research had always been about the breadth and modifiability of abilities and about access. It almost felt as though the underpinnings of the universities I had been at were at odds with my core beliefs in my research and my life.

Oklahoma State is a land-grant university that emphasizes access, service to the state and the nation, and the development of ethical leaders who make a positive, meaningful, and enduring difference to the world. I had a wonderful time during my three years as a provost at Oklahoma State. I also published like a madman, but in different outlets from those to which I had been accustomed. Now I was publishing mostly in higher-ed periodicals, and mostly about my thoughts on education [e.g., Sternberg (2010b) on the land-grant mission; Sternberg (2012b) on how our meritocracy has become fractured through the way we admit students].

At Oklahoma State, we instituted an admissions project, Panorama, that was an expansion of the project on admissions, Kaleidoscope, we had done at Tufts. We once again found it to be highly successful in selecting students for admission who were not only analytically smart but also creatively and practically smart and wise.

The greatest lesson I learned at Oklahoma State was how differently diverse constituencies see the role a university should play in society. Professors often tend to take their views as definitive, but

I was working with the legislature, major donors, alumni, students, businesses, and others beside professors, and all had vastly different conceptions of what we as a university ought to be doing.

THE PRESIDENCY AT THE UNIVERSITY OF WYOMING

I reached age 62 and realized that if I ever were to be a university president, my time was running out. And I really wanted to apply my ideas about psychology applied to education in an entire university setting. So I became a candidate in a few searches, but the place to which my wife and I really wanted to go, without question, was the University of Wyoming. I loved its being a land-grant institution committed to excellence, and Karin loved that it is situated in the Rocky Mountains. Both of us thought Laramie, Wyoming, would be a great place to raise what now were two-year-old triplets. I've just arrived and so far our expectations are more than met. We love it here! And it is indeed a chance to apply my ideas about education. What I probably had not realized, however, is how intensely political the context is in which a public university president operates. Almost as much so as the presidency of APA.

If there is one thing I have learned in administration, it is never to cover up a university's screwups, or one's personal ones either. In the course of one's career, one will make mistakes, some of them serious. The temptation is to cover them up. The problem is that then one has two issues to deal with—the initial screwup and then the cover-up. And my experience is that the career killer is almost never the initial mistake—it's the cover-up.

FINAL THOUGHTS

I believe the issue of fit is important not just for administrators but also for all scholars (Sternberg 2004a). Yale was a great fit for me in the 30 years I was there. Had I been in another institution, I might not equally have flourished. But I also saw scholars, especially junior faculty, ground down by a system that was highly competitive, that dismissed most of its junior faculty, and that required very high visibility and impact nationally and internationally. It was a great fit for me for 30 years, but then it wasn't. It was time to move on. It is hugely important that one find a job where the kind of science one does and the kinds of writing one does are valued. I needed to be in a place that shared my view that the purpose of higher education is to produce ethical leaders who will make the world a better place (Sternberg 2013).

One can help find fit by finding great mentors. In this regard, I have been very lucky. Endel Tulving at Yale taught me the importance of defying the crowd—of being willing to take contrarian positions, even though writing about them would inspire conflict and sometimes animosity. Gordon Bower at Stanford taught me the importance of having an audience and of writing appropriately for different audiences. Wendell Garner taught me the value of integrity in all I did. As a dean, Jamshed Bharucha, our provost, taught me the importance of seeing things from perspectives that seem strange and often just plain wrong. As a provost, Burns Hargis, our president, taught me how to operate an academic institution in a political context. One's writing will be far more insightful and just plain wise if one can find mentors who broaden and deepen one's thinking about the issues on which one writes.

One final warning: When I was young, I wanted to be like my mentors—Endel Tulving, Gordon Bower, and Wendell Garner. All were internationally famous experimental psychologists, all were elected to membership in the National Academy of Sciences, and all won practically every award there was to win. As the years went by, I felt like I was falling further and further behind on their path. I became more and more despondent. Eventually, though, I realized that I had not exactly fallen behind on their path; rather, I had taken a different path. We are "successfully intelligent" to the extent we optimize becoming the person we can be. None of us can be someone else. Find your own dreams and realize them; don't settle for someone else's, no matter how appealing they may be.

When I was younger, I admired the people who wrote until they dropped. I remembered B. F. Skinner giving a talk at APA, writing an article based on it, and then dropping dead. I thought this was just the greatest thing. Now I see things differently. I wonder if they could not find anything else in their later years that made life worth living. I believe I have, and when the time comes, I will look forward to other challenges and opportunities to renew myself. I hope to write for a long time, but not until I drop dead. I've got other things I hope to do, and they await me down the line. And I have learned that if you want to be immortal, don't count on your work to achieve immortality (Sternberg 2012a). For the most part, psychologists' work, and the psychologists themselves, start to be forgotten no later than the day they announce they are going to retire. For me, my immortality is through my beloved wife and five children, and their children, and the children the generation thereafter. That's good enough for me—more than good enough!

DISCLOSURE STATEMENT

The author is not aware of any affiliations, memberships, funding, or financial holdings that might be perceived as affecting the objectivity of this review.

LITERATURE CITED

Rosenthal R, Jacobson L. 1968. *Pygmalion in the Classroom: Teacher Expectation and Pupils' Intellectual Development*. New York: Holt, Rinehart & Winston

Spearman C. 1927. *The Abilities of Man*. New York: Macmillan

Sternberg RJ. 1972. A decision rule to facilitate the undergraduate admissions process. *Coll. Univ.* 48:48–53

Sternberg RJ. 1973. Cost-benefit analysis of the Yale admissions office interview. *Coll. Univ.* 48:154–64

Sternberg RJ. 1974. *How to Prepare for the Miller Analogies Test*. Woodbury, NY: Barron's Educ. Ser.

Sternberg RJ. 1977. *Intelligence, Information Processing, and Analogical Reasoning: The Componential Analysis of Human Abilities*. Hillsdale, NJ: Erlbaum

Sternberg RJ. 1985. *Beyond IQ: A Triarchic Theory of Human Intelligence*. New York: Cambridge Univ. Press

Sternberg RJ. 1986a. *Intelligence Applied: Understanding and Increasing Your Intellectual Skills*. San Diego, CA: Harcourt Brace Jovanovich

Sternberg RJ. 1986b. A triangular theory of love. *Psychol. Rev.* 93:119–35

Sternberg RJ. 1990. *Metaphors of Mind*. New York: Cambridge Univ. Press

Sternberg RJ. 1995. *In Search of the Human Mind*. Orlando, FL: Harcourt Brace Coll. Publ.

Sternberg RJ. 1997a. Construct validation of a triangular love scale. *Eur. J. Soc. Psychol.* 27(3):313–35

Sternberg RJ. 1997b. *Successful Intelligence*. New York: Plume

Sternberg RJ. 1997c. *Thinking Styles*. New York: Cambridge Univ. Press

Sternberg RJ. 1998a. *Cupid's Arrow*. New York: Cambridge Univ. Press

Sternberg RJ. 1998b. *Love Is a Story*. New York: Oxford Univ. Press

Sternberg RJ. 2003. *Wisdom, Intelligence, and Creativity Synthesized*. New York: Cambridge Univ. Press

Sternberg RJ. 2004a. *Psychology 101$\frac{1}{2}$: The Unspoken Rules for Success in Academia*. Washington, DC: Am. Psychol. Assoc.

Sternberg RJ. 2004b. Unifying the field of psychology. In *Unity in Psychology: Possibility or Pipedream?*, ed. RJ Sternberg, pp. 3–14. Washington, DC: Am. Psychol. Assoc.

Sternberg RJ. 2006. *Intelligence Applied*. San Diego, CA: Academic

Sternberg RJ. 2010a. *College Admissions for the 21st Century*. Cambridge, MA: Harvard Univ. Press

Sternberg RJ. 2010b. Defining a great university. *Inside High. Ed.* **http://www.insidehighered.com/views/ 2010/11/29/sternberg**

Sternberg RJ. 2012a. Becoming immortal: genes, memes, and dreams. *Psychologist* 25(9):688–89

Sternberg RJ. 2012b. Our fractured meritocracy. *Chron. High. Educ.* Dec. 12. **http://chronicle.com/blogs/conversation/2012/12/12/our-fractured-meritocracy/**

Sternberg RJ. 2013. Character development: putting it into practice in admissions and instruction. *J. Coll. Charact.* 14(3):253–58

Sternberg RJ, Bower GH. 1974. Transfer in part-whole and whole-part free recall: a comparative evaluation of theories. *J. Verbal Learn. Verbal Behav.* 13:1–26

Sternberg RJ, Forsythe GB, Hedlund J, Horvath J, Snook S, et al. 2000. *Practical Intelligence in Everyday Life.* New York: Cambridge Univ. Press

Sternberg RJ, Jarvin L, Grigorenko EL. 2011. *Explorations of the Nature of Giftedness.* New York: Cambridge Univ. Press

Sternberg RJ, Kaufman JC, Grigorenko EL. 2008. *Applied Intelligence.* New York: Cambridge Univ. Press

Sternberg RJ, Lubart TI. 1995. *Defying the Crowd: Cultivating Creativity in a Culture of Conformity.* New York: Free Press

Sternberg RJ, Rainbow Proj. Collab. 2006. The Rainbow Project: enhancing the SAT through assessments of analytical, practical and creative skills. *Intelligence* 34(4):321–50

Sternberg RJ, Sternberg K. 2012. *Cognitive Psychology.* Belmont, CA: Cengage. 6th ed.

Sternberg RJ, Tulving E. 1977. The measurement of subjective organization in free recall. *Psychol. Bull.* 84:539–56

Tulving E, Madigan SA. 1970. Memory and verbal learning. *Annu. Rev. Psychol.* 21:437–84

Tulving E, Thomson D. 1973. Encoding specificity and retrieval processes in episodic memory. *Psychol. Rev.* 80:352–73

Oxytocin Pathways and the Evolution of Human Behavior

C. Sue Carter

Department of Psychiatry, University of North Carolina School of Medicine, Chapel Hill, North Carolina 27599; and Department of Psychology, Northeastern University, Boston, Massachusetts 02115; email: sue_carter@med.unc.edu

Annu. Rev. Psychol. 2014. 65:17–39

First published online as a Review in Advance on September 19, 2013

The *Annual Review of Psychology* is online at http://psych.annualreviews.org

This article's doi:
10.1146/annurev-psych-010213-115110

Keywords

vasopressin, social behavior, neocortex, autonomic nervous system

Abstract

This review examines the hypothesis that oxytocin pathways—which include the neuropeptide oxytocin, the related peptide vasopressin, and their receptors—are at the center of physiological and genetic systems that permitted the evolution of the human nervous system and allowed the expression of contemporary human sociality. Unique actions of oxytocin, including the facilitation of birth, lactation, maternal behavior, genetic regulation of the growth of the neocortex, and the maintenance of the blood supply to the cortex, may have been necessary for encephalization. Peptide-facilitated attachment also allows the extended periods of nurture necessary for the emergence of human intellectual development. In general, oxytocin acts to allow the high levels of social sensitivity and attunement necessary for human sociality and for rearing a human child. Under optimal conditions oxytocin may create an emotional sense of safety. Oxytocin dynamically moderates the autonomic nervous system, and effects of oxytocin on vagal pathways, as well as the antioxidant and anti-inflammatory effects of this peptide, help to explain the pervasive adaptive consequences of social behavior for emotional and physical health.

Contents

OVERVIEW

Humans have a history of within-species aggression, abuse, and warfare, which continues to this day. However, we also are the primate species that relies most strongly for its survival on social intelligence and social communication (Hrdy 2009).

In the absence of social interactions, humans typically cannot reproduce, thrive, or even survive. Without formal training, most humans nurture their children, care for the infirm, and share joy in the accomplishments of others. How does this happen and why?

The purpose of this review is to examine the hypothesis that the mammalian neuropeptide, oxytocin, had a permissive role in the evolution of the human nervous system and continues to play a central role in the expression of the high levels of sociality that are essential to contemporary human behavior. Specifically, I propose that in humans our large cortex, high levels of social cognition, and complex social interactions and social bonds could not have evolved without the physiological and behavioral functions of oxytocin.

Of particular relevance to the evolution and expression of primate sociality are selective social interactions, which in turn rely on social sensitivity, cognition, and communication (Seyfarth & Cheney 2012). Oxytocin is at the core of the anatomical and physiological substrates for mammalian reproduction. The mammalian brain and pelvis can be physically remodeled by the actions of oxytocin. Oxytocin is permissive for birth and is probably of special importance to species, including primates, in which infants have large heads. Oxytocin helps to protect the brain from hypoxia, especially during birth (Khazipov et al. 2008). Through lactation and prolonged periods of postnatal nurture and later social interactions, oxytocin shapes the physical development of the human neocortex as well as social learning. Oxytocin present during the perinatal period can tune the central nervous system, potentially supporting adaptive patterns of physiology and behavior in later life. Oxytocin also helps to regulate the autonomic nervous system, with consequences for sensory, visceral, metabolic, and smooth motor systems. Throughout the lifespan oxytocin may increase social sensitivity and modulate reactivity to stressors. Oxytocin can encourage emotional states that allow optimal development and the social use of others during periods of stress and restoration. Oxytocin protects and heals tissues and has therapeutic consequences that are only now being discovered.

The actions of oxytocin are tightly interwoven with a genetically related and structurally similar neuropeptide, vasopressin. Vasopressin influences the functions of oxytocin, and vice versa, in part because these peptides are capable of binding to each other's receptors. In contrast to oxytocin, vasopressin has been associated with mobilization, anxiety, and defensive behaviors, but also the formation of selective social bonds. Interactions between oxytocin and vasopressin are difficult to study and are not discussed in detail here. However, the dynamic interplay between these two peptides and a host of other molecules, such as dopamine (Aragona & Wang 2009, Young et al. 2011) and endogenous opioids (Burkett et al. 2011), supports social behaviors, especially in the face of challenge.

Characterized initially as a "female reproductive hormone," it is now clear that oxytocin has effects in both sexes (Lee et al. 2009). Vasopressin may be of particular importance in males but also has functions in females. However, at least some of the effects of these peptides differ between males and females (Carter 2007, Carter et al. 2009a, De Vries & Panciza 2006, Taylor et al. 2010). Sex differences in the actions of oxytocin and vasopressin, especially in early life, may be fundamental to sex differences in behavior, although this is not currently well studied.

Dozens of recent papers have documented the importance of oxytocin, especially in the context of genetic variations. Polymorphisms and epigenetic modification of receptors in the oxytocin pathways contribute to both individual differences in social behavior and the management of challenge across the life cycle. In addition, studies of the effects of intranasal oxytocin are offering a new perspective on the role of oxytocin in human behavior. The importance of oxytocin also is supported by the success of new therapies in which this peptide is used for the treatment of maladaptive social behaviors and physical dysfunctions. Those findings are not described here but are detailed in many excellent reviews, such as those of Ebstein et al. (2012), Feldman (2012), Lee et al. (2009), MacDonald & Feifel (2013), and Meyer-Lindenberg et al. (2011).

THE EVOLVED BIOCHEMISTRY OF SOCIAL BEHAVIOR

The need to interact with others of their own species is not unique to vertebrates. Reliance on others and positive social interactions appeared early and often in the course of evolution. For example, asexual bacteria reproduce more successfully and produce complex biological structures in the presence of others (Ingham & Ben Jacob 2008). Social behavior and the benefits of sociality are considered central to evolution. However, genetic pathways for eusociality, such as the social systems seen in colonies of bees and termites, have evolved several times in insects. In fact, the genetic systems responsible for social behavior in insects appear to reflect the actions of an "accelerated" form of evolution (Woodard et al. 2011).

Social behaviors are likely to have multiple genetic and physiological origins and substrates. Thus, whether a common genetic core underlies the tendency toward sociality across or among vertebrates and invertebrates remains to be determined. Even in nematodes, oxytocin-like molecules regulate a series of interactive behaviors and social interactions necessary for successful mating (Garrison et al. 2012). The patterns of peptide-stimulated behaviors described in nematodes appear to be strikingly similar to those seen in vertebrates. Furthermore, the subcellular signaling properties of the class of molecules to which oxytocin belongs are associated with behavioral phenotypes that are consistent among widely divergent animals (Yamashita & Kitano 2013).

There is strong evidence that a suite of molecules with properties necessary for fundamental functions—such as the regulation of water and minerals, immunity and metabolism—have been repeatedly repurposed for various functions. In multicellular animals, neural and endocrine systems coordinate physiology with the demands of the physical and social environment. The genes responsible for oxytocin-like peptides are believed to have evolved more than 700 million years ago (Donaldson & Young 2008), initially regulating cellular processes, such as water balance and homeostasis, that defend cells from dehydration. In the course of mammalian evolution these versatile molecules acquired a host of new functions, including the regulation of complex social behaviors (Goodson et al. 2012).

The developmental importance of oxytocin must be appreciated in the context of the phylogeny and anatomy of the nervous system. The evolution of mammalian physical traits was concurrent with the evolution of oxytocin and its role in mammalian development. Why or how this occurred is not known. However, unique anatomical changes appear to have accompanied the eventual evolution of the human nervous system, with our exceptionally large neocortex, permitting the capacity for language and human social cognition. Possible roles for oxytocin in the development and expression of the human nervous system are detailed below.

OXYTOCIN PATHWAYS

Physiological and Anatomical Characteristics of the Oxytocin System

Oxytocin is a 9 amino acid peptide hormone composed of a 6 amino acid ring and a 3 amino acid tail. At least some of the functions of oxytocin may be explained by the dynamic biological properties of the sulfur bonds that create the ring in oxytocin and that allow the oxytocin molecule to form temporary and long-lasting unions with other chemical entities (Martin & Carter 2013). The now well-established capacity of oxytocin to play a role in social bonds (Carter et al. 2008) appears to be built upon the chemistry of this remarkable molecule, which itself forms bonds throughout the body.

Oxytocin is not a classical neurotransmitter, i.e., limited to local actions by crossing a synapse between an axon and dendrite for its effects. Rather, oxytocin appears to be released from the neuronal soma, axons, and dendrites, acting broadly in the nervous system as a neuromodulator. Upon release, oxytocin may flow through neural tissue by a process termed volume transmission (Neumann & Landgraf 2012). For example, there is evidence that oxytocin from the paraventricular nucleus (PVN) of the hypothalamus can reach the central amygdala via anatomical "expressways," allowing this molecule to quickly modulate emotional functions of the amygdala and brain stem (Stoop 2012). In the presence of oxytocin, avoidance or fear may be replaced by approach and positive emotional states (Carter 1998).

The cells that synthesize oxytocin are most concentrated in hypothalamic, midline neurons. In particular the PVN and supraoptic nuclei of the hypothalamus contain large cells expressing high levels of oxytocin, with separate cells expressing vasopressin (Gainer 2012). The exceptionally large magnocellular neurons, which synthesize oxytocin and vasopressin, also extend processes to the posterior pituitary gland.

The PVN is a major site of convergence and integration for neural communication relating to stress, affective disorders, and cardiovascular regulation, with effects on the hypothalamic-pituitary-adrenal (HPA) axis and autonomic function (Herman 2012). Oxytocin is colocalized in a subset of neurons in the PVN with major adaptive or stress hormones, such as corticotropin-releasing hormone (CRH), which regulates the HPA axis and which also has been implicated in some of the detrimental effects of chronic stress (Aguilera et al. 2008). Oxytocin may be co-released with CRH as an adaptive response to a variety of challenges, both positive and negative (Carter et al. 2008, Neumann & Landgraf 2012).

Oxytocin can be released in a coordinated fashion, within the brain and at the posterior pituitary, into the general circulation (Neumann & Landgraf 2012). It is likely that the ability of oxytocin to have exceptionally broad and synchronized behavioral and physiological consequences is related to this capacity for movement throughout the brain and body (Stoop 2012).

Oxytocin is produced tonically. In typical humans basal levels of oxytocin vary among individuals, but in plasma oxytocin, levels are notably consistent across time (Dai et al. 2012, Gouin et al. 2010, Weisman et al. 2013). Oxytocin also can be released as pulses, thus promoting muscle contractions in tissues such as the uterus and mammary gland, especially when these tissues are steroid primed.

The pulsatile release of oxytocin neurons may be related to the plasticity of the hypothalamic cells (Theodosis 2002). In adult rats, oxytocin-synthesizing neurons undergo physical transformations in response to hormonal and social stimulation. During pregnancy, birth, and lactation, and perhaps under other conditions such as dehydration or sexual stimulation (Carter 1992), glial processes that normally separate the oxytocin-containing neurons are retracted, allowing electrical coupling and then the pulsatile release of oxytocin. Vasopressin-containing neurons typically do not show this form of plasticity and pulsatile release. Furthermore, oxytocin-producing cells are sensitive to oxytocin itself; thus, a form of autocrine feedback regulates the functions of oxytocin-producing cells. Stimulation of the oxytocin system may feed forward to release more oxytocin, and in some cases administration of oxytocin appears to enhance the synthesis of endogenous oxytocin in the central nervous system (Grippo et al. 2012).

Oxytocin may be available at high levels in blood and brain. The messenger RNA for oxytocin has been reported in rats to be the most abundant transcript in the hypothalamus (Gautvik et al. 1996), possibly translating into very high concentrations of the oxytocin peptide in the brain. Oxytocin also is found in abundance in blood, as measured by an antibody-based enzyme immunoassay (Carter et al. 2007, Kramer et al. 2004). It has been suggested that these high levels are measurement artifacts caused by the binding of antibodies to nonhormonal components of blood (Szeto et al. 2011). However, recent studies using mass spectrometry, widely accepted as the gold standard for determining peptide levels, support the hypothesis that oxytocin is truly abundant in blood but is sequestered by binding to other molecules in plasma. Thus, measurement methodologies that commonly involve extraction of other molecules in blood, such as albumin, may discard the majority of the oxytocin and greatly underestimate the abundance of oxytocin (Martin & Carter 2013).

Levels of oxytocin in blood and brain vary across species (Kramer et al. 2004). Furthermore, individual differences in oxytocin are common, and these have been related to individual traits, including social behavior (Gouin et al. 2010) and some of the novel patterns of behaviors associated with schizophrenia (Rubin et al. 2011). In Williams syndrome, dramatic individual differences in both oxytocin and social behavior also were detected and are associated with a unique behavioral phenotype (Dai et al. 2012).

Vasopressin: Adaptation and Survival in a Hostile Environment?

Vasopressin is genetically and structurally related to oxytocin, with only two amino acids distinguishing the two molecules. Both oxytocin and vasopressin evolved by duplication from a common ancestral molecule, presumed to be vasotocin (Goodson et al. 2012). Vasopressin's functions may be closer to the more primitive functions of the molecules from which these peptides arose (Albers 2012).

The biological actions of vasopressin, which include water conservation, probably facilitated survival and the transition to terrestrial living, and may have been co-opted across evolution to regulate defensive behaviors and aggression (Ferris 2008, Frank & Landgraf 2008). Vasopressin is critical to social adaptation in a demanding world, with a behavioral profile that is associated with attachment to and defense of self, family, and other members of our social networks (Carter 1998).

For example, vasopressin plays an important role in the selective sociality necessary for pair bond formation (Carter 1998, Winslow et al. 1993). However, many of the functions of vasopressin differ from those of oxytocin (Carter & Porges 2013, Neumann & Landgraf 2012, Stoop 2012). For example, in maternal behavior oxytocin is critical to nursing and important to nurturing (Pedersen 1997), whereas vasopressin has been implicated in maternal aggression (Bosch & Neumann 2012) and paternal defense of the young (Kenkel et al. 2012, 2013). Some aspects of vasopressin's functions within the nervous system are sexually dimorphic, with possible implications for sex differences in the tendency to show defensive behaviors and for disorders, such as autism, that are male biased (reviewed in Carter 2007, Carter et al. 2009a).

In the socially monogamous prairie voles, the development of pair bonds is associated with a preference for the familiar partner and other family members, and concurrently the emergence of potentially lethal aggression toward outsiders (Carter et al. 1995). Either vasopressin or oxytocin can facilitate the general tendency toward social contact in prairie voles. However, in that species both oxytocin and vasopressin appear to be necessary for selective sociality and pair bonding (Cho et al. 1999) and possibly male parental behavior (Kenkel et al. 2012). Mate guarding and aggression toward strangers in prairie vole males appear to rely primarily on vasopressin (Winslow et al. 1993). Thus, the behavioral motif of vasopressin-like molecules is strongly associated with defensiveness and survival (Albers 2012).

Vasopressin also may synergize with CRH (Aguilera et al. 2008) to increase stress reactivity, anxiety, and repetitive behaviors, such as territorial marking in rodents (Ferris 2008). Vasopressin also has been associated with defensive aggression and emotional dysregulation (Albers 2012, Coccaro et al. 1998). Some of the effects of vasopressin are opposite to those of oxytocin, and both hormones are probably critical for optimal reproduction and survival (Carter 1998, Carter & Porges 2013, Neumann & Landgraf 2012). However, in general vasopressin is associated with stress and arousal. Because vasopressin is important in defensive behaviors (Winslow et al. 1993), it also is possible that vasopressin can lower the threshold to aggression (Ferris 2008).

Vasopressin elevates blood pressure and has been implicated in cardiovascular disease as well as posttraumatic stress disorder (PTSD) (Wentworth et al. 2013). This peptide is synthesized in brain regions that regulate biological rhythms and may play a role in sleep disturbances and insomnia—perhaps contributing to disorders such as PTSD. It is plausible that oxytocin is protective against PTSD (Olff 2012), possibly through its capacity to counteract some of the hyperarousal associated with vasopressin.

Sex differences in the management of stressful experiences may be at least partially influenced by vasopressin (Carter 1998, Taylor et al. 2000). The synthesis of vasopressin is androgen dependent, especially in the medial amygdala and bed nucleus of the stria terminalis, from which it is released into the lateral septum (De Vries & Panzica 2006). We have speculated that this sexually dimorphic central axis may be of particular relevance to sex differences in male-biased disorders such as autism (Carter 2007).

Receptors for Oxytocin and Vasopressin

Although beyond the scope of this review, it is useful to understand that the functions of oxytocin and vasopressin depend on their capacity to bind to specific receptors. The expression of receptors for oxytocin and vasopressin are modulated by both genetic and epigenetic processes, which are only now becoming apparent (Ebstein et al. 2012, Gregory et al. 2009). Only one oxytocin receptor has been described, the gene for which (*OXTR*) is located on chromosome 3p24–26 (Gimpl & Fahrenholz 2001). The *OXTR* gene encodes a G-protein-coupled receptor with a seven-transmembrane domain. The same oxytocin receptor is present in neural tissue and in other parts of the body, such as the uterus and breast.

Three receptor subtypes have been identified for vasopressin. Of these, the vasopressin receptor 1a (V1a), which is found in the brain, has been associated with social behavior, especially in males, as well as the regulation of responses to stressors, blood pressure, and other cardiovascular functions. The V1b receptor has been implicated in endocrine and behavioral responses to stressors and aggression (Stevenson & Caldwell 2012). The V2 receptor is localized to the kidney and does not appear to be involved in behavior.

Receptors for both oxytocin and vasopressin are abundant in areas of the nervous system that regulate social, emotional, and adaptive behaviors including the amygdala, the HPA axis, and the autonomic nervous system. Both individual and species differences in V1a receptor distributions have been identified. Among the sources of these differences are species-typical genetic variations in the promoter region of the gene for the V1a receptor (Hammock & Young 2005). The oxytocin receptor also shows species differences in expression, which may be of considerable relevance to species differences in social behavior and emotion regulation.

BEHAVIORAL AND NEUROBIOLOGICAL CONSEQUENCES OF OXYTOCIN

Mammalian Reproduction and Parenting Shape the Nervous System

Mammalian behavior is particularly dependent on selective social interactions. Young mammals are supported by the mother or other caretakers during gestation, birth, and the postpartum period (Hrdy 2009). During the prenatal and postpartum periods, mammalian offspring are emotionally and physiologically tuned by these caretakers (Feldman 2012). Much of the mammalian neocortex develops postnatally, during a period when offspring are nourished by milk and reliant on maternal behavior and other aspects of group living (Hrdy 2009). In humans the maturation of the neocortex occurs over an exceptionally long period, with some processes extending into the fourth decade of life (Rakic 2009, Somel et al. 2013). Mechanisms that maintain relationships and social support over the lifetime of an individual may be especially important in humans, allowing time for learning a large repertoire of social and cognitive behaviors, and for the acquisition of an extensive social network.

A biological prototype for mammalian sociality, and especially selective social bonds, can be found in the mother–infant interaction and lactation (Carter 1998). Lactation is unique to mammals and relies on oxytocin (among other hormones). The neurobiological substrates for gestation, birth, and lactation allowed the emergence in mammals of an increased brain size. In humans the brain continues to mature well into adulthood (Somel et al. 2013).

Gestation, lactation, and high levels of maternal behavior provide nurture for offspring. The mammalian birth process accommodates the enlarged primate nervous system, while increased parental investment is necessary to nourish and protect the immature offspring and to support the elaboration of the primate nervous system (Keverne 2013). Furthermore, lactation—especially frequent and nocturnal nursing—has the capacity to suppress maternal ovarian function. Whether oxytocin is directly involved in lactational amenorrhea is not well studied, but this is plausible since oxytocin has been directly implicated in ovulation (Niswender et al. 2007). Because lactational suppression of ovulation can be contraceptive, it contributes to spacing births, with indirect consequences for resource allocation. Mothers who are gestating or rearing fewer babies can contribute more to the physical, emotional, and cognitive development of a given offspring. Oxytocin also is present in human milk, which also may serve as a form of social and hormonal communication between mother and baby. The lactating mother, with increased potential to release oxytocin, also has reduced reactivity to stressors (Carter & Altemus 1997). These adaptations increase maternal behavioral flexibility in the face of the demands of child rearing and also can modify the behavior and physiology of the infant (Zhang & Meaney 2010), with consequences that vary according to environmental demands and with the history of the mother.

Much of the neocortex develops postnatally, during a period when offspring are supported by maternal behavior and milk. Among humans living in foraging societies, other group members play critical roles in caring for and provisioning offspring (Hrdy 2009). Social bonds are especially important to selectively direct social behavior toward familiar others, who are often family members or sexual partners. In turn, cohesion of the family or social group facilitates successful reproduction and fitness, which has been documented in modern nonhuman primates living in nature (Seyfarth & Cheney 2012, 2013).

Maternal oxytocin acts as a signaling mechanism between the mother and fetus. Of particular importance to cortical and hippocampal functioning is gamma-aminobutyric acid (GABA). Maternal oxytocin released during birth triggers a switch in GABA signaling in the fetal brain from excitatory to inhibitory. Inhibitory GABA is necessary for cognitive functions. In vivo administration of an oxytocin antagonist before delivery prevents this switch of GABA activity in fetal neurons and aggravates the severity of hypoxic episodes (Tyzio et al. 2006). Maternal oxytocin apparently inhibits fetal neurons and concurrently increases their resistance to hypoxia, which can serve to protect cortical tissue during birth. The birth-related surge in oxytocin also helps to regulate the synchronization of the fetal hippocampal neurons, possibly facilitating the transition from prenatal to postnatal life (Crepel et al. 2007, Khazipov et al. 2008). Such changes have long-term consequences for emotional and cognitive functions and the growth of the nervous system.

Placental gestation and live birth are critical to mammalian brain development. The placenta is regulated by the maternal genome, providing an early source of nutrition for the fetus and giving the mother further opportunity to influence the size of her offspring (Keverne 2013). Mice in which the gene for oxytocin or its receptor is genetically disrupted are still capable of birth. However, in primates or other mammals with a large cranium, oxytocin may have a special importance by creating the strong contractions needed to expel the fetus from the uterus. Delivering a large baby, which involves prenatal maternal investment, cervical stimulation, and the release of oxytocin, as well as stress and pain, may increase the attachment between the mother and offspring. As one example, the success of precocial mammals such as sheep, whose infants must follow the mother immediately following birth, depends on high levels of cortical-motoric maturation as well as selective attachment to the mother, who is the infant's source of food and protection (Keverne 2013). In addition, oxytocin may serve to protect both mother and infant from pain (or from the memory of pain) associated with childbirth (Mazzuca et al. 2011), thus further promoting attachment. Emerging evidence also indicates that maternal oxytocin may protect a mother from postpartum depression (Stuebe et al. 2013).

In socially monogamous or communal species, care of the young often extends beyond the maternal-infant unit (Hrdy 2009). In this context it is useful to note that interacting with an infant can release oxytocin in adult males, including humans (Feldman 2012) and prairie voles (Kenkel et al. 2012). In turn, the release of oxytocin in males by stimuli from the infant could facilitate coping with the complex needs of the infant. For example, when reproductively naive males are exposed to an infant, they quickly enter a physiological state characterized by activation of both the sympathetic and parasympathetic nervous systems. This somewhat novel physiological state, which probably depends on interactions between oxytocin and vasopressin, allows the simultaneous appearance of nurture and protective forms of social behavior (Kenkel et al. 2013).

Oxytocin and Love

Although research is actually rather meager, there has been a popular acceptance of oxytocin as the "hormone of love" (reviewed in Carter & Porges 2013). Nonetheless, within the past decade, research in animals, including humans, has confirmed and extended the general conclusions drawn from research in rodents (Carter 1998).

The initial stages of falling in love with a new partner may include excitement and arousal (Fisher et al. 2006). Oxytocin has been implicated in social attention and eye gaze (Guastella & MacLeod 2012), which often are critical in early stages of relationship formation. The initial stages in a passionate relationship, as well as the experience of sexual arousal and orgasm, could draw upon the apparent capacity of oxytocin, and presumably also vasopressin, to permit increased sympathetic arousal without parasympathetic retraction (Carter 1992, Kenkel et al. 2013, Norman et al. 2011).

Inherent in most definitions of love are social communication, feelings of empathy, and a sense of reciprocal trust. Results from computerized games and other forms of behavioral paradigms have implicated oxytocin in trust (Kosfeld et al. 2005), empathy (Carter et al. 2009b), cooperation (Hurlemann et al. 2010, Rilling et al. 2012) and neural activation in brain regions associated with sociality (Jack et al. 2012). Oxytocin may mediate the buffering effects of positive relationships and modulate reactivity to stressful experiences. In general, oxytocin tends to support a sense of safety and social behaviors characterized by "immobility without fear" (Porges 1998, p. 852). Thus, the capacity to be close to and sensitive to others, which is typical of loving relationships, can be supported by oxytocin's behavioral effects.

Key to positive relationships between adults are selective social behaviors and social bonds. Studies originally conducted in prairie voles revealed that oxytocin was capable of facilitating social contact as well as selective social preferences in both sexes (Cho et al. 1999, Williams et al. 1994). In prairie voles, mating facilitated the onset of pair bonding (Williams et al. 1992), a behavior that was later shown to be dependent on oxytocin (Williams et al. 1994). In the prairie vole model, access to both oxytocin and vasopressin receptors appears necessary for pair bonding to emerge, whereas either oxytocin or vasopressin alone facilitates nonselective sociality (Cho et al. 1999, Young et al. 2011). Whether human social behavior and attachments can be formed in the absence of oxytocin or vasopressin is not known.

Oxytocin is released in response to a variety of experiences and stimuli and under various circumstances, both positive and negative (Carter 1992, Dai et al. 2012, Feldman 2012). Attachments and social bonds also form under many different kinds of conditions. These and many other studies leave little doubt that oxytocin plays a central role in the social behaviors that lie at the heart of the human experience of love. However, it is likely that vasopressin also plays a major role in emotional and visceral experiences.

Other Emotionally Powerful Social Behaviors

Powerful positive social behaviors and experiences may be built upon the primal functions of oxytocin and vasopressin. For example, social and emotional cohesion appears to be biologically based. In fact, humans are so deeply interwoven with and dependent upon others of our own species that we may fail to recognize the fundamental nature of social behavior. Hofer (1987), on the basis of his studies of the development of the maternal and infant dyad, concluded that regulators of physiology were embedded in social behavior. Hofer's concept of "hidden regulators" focused on the benefits of proximity. However, other forms of interaction, including those encoded as cognitive experiences, can mediate human behavior. The importance of hidden regulators to emotional states of course is not limited to mothers and infants.

Humans gain pleasure from working together. We share the emotions of others and can experience emotional contagion (Hatfield et al. 1994). We experience emotional elation from playing team sports and from observing the triumphs of others (Pepping & Timmermans 2012). Experiencing the physical and emotional consequences of the feelings of others may encourage humans to emulate the virtuous behavior of others, including the expression of positive social behaviors and social cohesion (Koh & Fredrickson 2010).

Healthy humans are more capable than other apes of vicariously experiencing and responding to the emotional states and experiences of others. Studies of empathy have often focused on negative emotional states or the pain of others (Decety 2011). However, it is also possible to measure behavioral and neural changes as a function of "witnessing acts of moral beauty" in others—a process that has been termed moral elevation (Englander et al. 2012, p. 1). Experiencing "other praising emotions," including admiration, gratitude, and elevation, can be accompanied by a novel set of experiences and emotional responses, which are differentiated experimentally from more conventional positive emotions such as joy and amusement (Algoe & Haidt 2009). Hints regarding the biological basis of moral elevation come from the phenomenology of this behavior, which includes autonomic shifts such as chills or tearing.

Moral elevation has a particularly interesting effect on the nervous system as measured by neural imaging. Neural synchronization (within a subject) of midline brain regions occurred during videos known to elicit moral elevation (Englander et al. 2012). Among the brain regions activated by moral-elevation videos were the medial prefrontal cortex and insula. These same brain areas have been implicated in self-referential and interoceptive processes and may regulate autonomic responses. Synchrony in these brain regions did not consistently occur during videos depicting admiration or neutral (i.e., nonemotional) stimuli. It is likely that highly emotional responses, including moral elevation, are supported by a common underlying neurophysiology—possibly including those responses associated with falling in love. Oxytocin has been implicated in moral elevation by the fact that lactating women express milk during elevating experiences (Silvers & Haidt 2008). However, whether this is cause or effect, or both, is not known.

Positive experiences also can change pain thresholds, possibly in part through actions of oxytocin. For example, social laughter can raise pain thresholds (Dunbar et al. 2012). In the latter study, reduced sensitivity to pain during social laughter was attributed to possible changes in endogenous opioids, although biochemical measures of opioids (or oxytocin) were not taken. However, in other human experiences, including birth, lactation (Brunton & Russell 2010), and early development (Mazzuca et al. 2011), oxytocin has been implicated in both pain regulation and events that may create pain. Oxytocin dynamically interacts with endogenous opioids (Burkett et al. 2011), and this interaction has broad implications for human behavior.

Oxytocin and Coping with the Stress of Life

Oxytocin is a component of the capacity of the mammalian body to manage the response to challenge. Animal research suggests that acute stressors, especially of high intensity, can release oxytocin in both sexes (Neumann & Landgraf 2012, Pournajafi-Nazarloo et al. 2013). In the face of a severe challenge, oxytocin could initially support an increase in arousal and activation of the sympathetic nervous system and other components of the HPA system. A large pulse of oxytocin also might activate vasopressin receptors, further supporting mobilization and potentially defensive responses. The arousal-enhancing effects of oxytocin, and presumably the release of oxytocin, may differ widely among individuals and are likely influenced by social history and context (Bartz et al. 2011).

In the face of chronic stress, the anti-stress effects of oxytocin may take precedence, permitting a more passive form of coping and immobility without fear (Porges 1998). In addition, sex differences are commonly observed in the capacity of oxytocin or vasopressin to influence stress management. Oxytocin appears to be a component of a more social or passive coping strategy, whereas vasopressin may permit active and mobilized coping strategies (reviewed in Carter 2007; Taylor et al. 2000, 2010).

Behavioral, physiological, and anatomic data from rodents (Kenkel et al. 2013) and humans (Grewen & Light 2011) suggest that the antistress effects of chronic oxytocin downregulate the sympathetic nervous system while supporting the protective and restorative functions of the vagal systems.

As one behavioral example, individuals with higher levels of parasympathetic activity showed more rapid increases in self-described positive emotions and a sense of connectedness (Koh & Fredrickson 2010). These and other findings suggest that oxytocin has effects on the regulation of emotion, the mammalian autonomic nervous system, homeostasis, coping, and healing, helping to explain the important consequences of the presence or absence of social engagement and attachment. Oxytocin and social support have been implicated in human wound healing (Gouin et al. 2010) and are protective against cardiovascular dysfunction. Oxytocin may act to protect or repair tissue (Karelina & DeVries 2011). Oxytocin also has antioxidant and anti-inflammatory properties across the lifespan and even in tissue models in vitro (Gutkowska & Jankowski 2012, Szeto et al. 2008). These adaptive properties of oxytocin further help to explain the capacity of loving relationships and psychological safety to protect and heal in the face of stress and adversity.

The Effects of Oxytocin Treatments Are Not Always Prosocial

Recent human research, particularly studies conducted in individuals with a history of personal adversity, suggest that in some contexts exogenous oxytocin can have asocial or negative consequences (Bartz et al. 2011), including increasing the perception of threat in the presence of individuals from other social groups (De Dreu 2012). Recent evidence from studies in mice indicates that oxytocin, through localized actions on the oxytocin receptor, can enhance fear conditioning (Guzmán et al. 2013). In some cases negative effects of oxytocin, especially when seen following exogenous oxytocin treatments, could reflect in part the capacity of oxytocin, especially at high doses, to dynamically interact with the vasopressin receptor. In large amounts, oxytocin may stimulate the vasopressin receptor, functioning like vasopressin and enhancing defensive or aggressive responses (see the previous discussion on this point). Aggressive or defensive responses to out-group members are consistent with the behavioral effects of vasopressin found in male prairie voles (Winslow et al. 1993).

It is also possible that the actions of oxytocin differ depending on activity in other neuroendocrine systems, such as those regulated by sex steroids, opioids, catecholamines, or inflammatory cytokines. Support for this notion comes from studies of the factors that regulate oxytocin during birth (Brunton & Russell 2010) and the prevalence of sex differences emerging from the literature on the actions of oxytocin in humans and other mammals (Carter 2007; Taylor et al. 2000, 2010).

Another example of the apparently paradoxical effects of high levels of oxytocin is seen in Williams syndrome (Dai et al. 2012). This genetic condition, caused by deletion of ~28 genes, is associated with a behavioral phenotype that includes high levels of gregariousness and a tendency to approach strangers but also high levels of anxiety in nonsocial contexts. Endogenous oxytocin, as well as vasopressin, measured in blood varies widely between individuals with this condition. Oxytocin levels were correlated positively with approach to strangers, but high levels of oxytocin also were associated with maladaptive social behaviors in everyday life, in part because individuals with Williams syndrome can be too trusting. Whether this atypical behavioral phenotype can be directly attributed to oxytocin, vasopressin, or—more likely—interactions between these peptides, remains to be determined.

There also is increasing evidence that the effects of exposure to exogenous oxytocin are not necessarily associated with increases in positive sociality. In prairie voles a single low-dose oxytocin injection given on the first day of life facilitated pair-bond formation in adulthood. However, high doses of oxytocin had the opposite consequences, producing animals that preferred an unfamiliar partner (Bales et al. 2007b). Repeated exposure to oxytocin early in life in pigs also disrupted subsequent social behavior, under some conditions producing piglets that were less capable than normal animals of appropriate and reciprocal social interactions (Rault et al. 2013). Oxytocin given intranasally to prairie voles during adolescence also did not reliably facilitate social behavior and, once again, at some doses disrupted the tendency of this species to show a partner preference (Bales et al. 2013). It is possible that effects such as these also might represent interactions between systems that rely on both oxytocin and vasopressin.

Consequences of Isolation May Be Mediated Through Oxytocin

In the context of the shared physiology among social and emotional behaviors, it is not surprising that social interactions and isolation have powerful physiological consequences. Individuals with a perceived sense of social support are more likely to avoid or survive illness and have longer lives than otherwise similar people who live alone, especially those who experience a sense of loneliness (Cacioppo et al. 2006).

Experiments in animals provide an opportunity to examine in more depth the physiological consequences of the absence of a social partner. Highly social mammals, including prairie voles, offer useful models for examining the biology of social separation and isolation because they share with humans the capacity to form long-lasting social relationships (Carter et al. 1995). Prairie voles also have a human-like autonomic nervous system, with high levels of parasympathetic vagal activity and a dependence on social behavior for emotion regulation (Grippo et al. 2007, 2009). Because the autonomic nervous system mediates many of the consequences of social interactions (Kenkel et al. 2013), the response of prairie voles to their social environment offers a rodent model for examining mechanisms through which peptides, including oxytocin, regulate reactions to the social environment.

As one example, in prairie voles isolation from a partner for a few weeks produced significant increases in several behavioral measures of depression and anxiety. Isolated animals were less exploratory, showed increases in anhedonia (indexed by a loss of preference for sweet liquids), and were more likely to show immobility in response to a stressor—in this case possibly immobility with fear (Porges 1998). In prairie voles, separation from a partner, followed by prolonged isolation, is associated with increases in heart rate, decreases in parasympathetic function, and increases in behavioral reactivity to stressors, such as the presence of a social intruder. Following a 5-minute social stressor (an intruder), isolated prairie voles required an average of more than 15 hours for heart rate to return to baseline. In contrast, animals living in sibling pairs required about 2.5 hours for their heart rate to recover. In the absence of a social partner, oxytocin increased in female (but not male) prairie voles (Grippo et al. 2007). Elevated oxytocin may be protective against the negative consequences of isolation, which include reductions in the expression of the oxytocin receptor (Pournajafi-Nazarloo et al. 2013). However, these findings in voles suggest a possible hormonal advantage for females—at least in comparison to males—in the capacity to cope with isolation. Experiments with female voles revealed that oxytocin injections over a period of weeks were capable of reversing the cardiac and behavioral effects of isolation, including protecting against the increases in heart rate and reductions in vagal tone that typically accompany isolation (Grippo et al. 2009).

In postmenopausal women, increases in oxytocin also have been associated with gaps in social relationships (Taylor et al. 2006). Releasing oxytocin may be a component of a self-regulatory process that helps mammals deal with isolation or other stressful experiences. These hormonal responses also might facilitate social engagement or relationships, functions that could be especially adaptive in females who under some circumstances may be less able than males to live alone (Taylor et al. 2010). However, it cannot be assumed that males and females use oxytocin pathways in identical ways. Research on the functions of oxytocin and vasopressin in emotional responses and coping holds promise for understanding sex differences in social behavior in a more general sense.

ANATOMICAL, PHYSIOLOGICAL, AND GENETIC EFFECTS OF OXYTOCIN

Genetic and Epigenetic Variation

Oxytocin pathways are influenced by genetic variations and may be epigenetically tuned by social experiences and exposure to hormones. For example, mounting evidence indicates that genetic and epigenetic variations in the *OXTR* gene can predict individual differences in behavior, physiology, and even brain anatomy (Ebstein et al. 2012, Meyer-Lindenberg et al. 2010, Tost et al. 2010). Genetic variations in the *OXTR* gene, indexed by single-nucleotide polymorphisms, were originally related to autism spectrum disorders (variant rs2254298 G > A) (Jacob et al. 2007). Another variant (rs53676 G > A) has been associated with behavior and brain activity in the context of social cues (Ebstein et al. 2012). Studies of this kind are leading to a new awareness of the behavioral importance of oxytocin pathways.

The *OXTR* gene can be silenced via DNA methylation, thus reducing the expression of the oxytocin receptor. Functional relationships between methylation of the *OXTR* gene and behavior have been detected in autism (Gregory et al. 2009). However, within a population with autistic traits, those individuals with the highest levels of methylation were the least behaviorally impaired (S. Jacob & J. Connelly, personal communication). Thus, in at least some cases, methylation of the *OXTR* gene has been associated with beneficial consequences. In humans, methylation status of the *OXTR* gene also has been shown to predict neural responses to ambiguous social stimuli (Jack et al. 2012). Additional research is needed, but these findings suggest that epigenetic methylation of the *OXTR* gene may be one component of an adaptive strategy, possibly downregulating the oxytocin receptor but also encouraging, through negative feedback, upregulation of the synthesis of the oxytocin peptide.

Oxytocin pathways may be particularly susceptible to modification in early life. It is well established that neonatal social experiences and exposure to hormones can have lifelong consequences for behavior (Carter et al. 2009a). Both social experiences and exposure to the oxytocin peptide around the time of birth appear to epigenetically tune the expression of the oxytocin receptor.

Data from both behavior and measures of peptide receptors suggest that a single exposure to exogenous oxytocin in early life may be capable of producing dose-dependent changes in behavior in adulthood (Carter et al. 2009a). Low—but not high—doses of exogenous hormone facilitated pair bonding as well as the expression of endogenous oxytocin (Bales et al. 2007b). Low doses of oxytocin in early life also inhibited the expression of the V1a receptor in adulthood (Bales et al. 2007a). The enduring consequences of these treatments may reflect the capacity of early exposure to oxytocin to epigenetically regulate the *OXTR* gene.

Oxytocin and the Development of the Human Neocortex

The primate nervous system developed across the course of evolution, with physical adaptations that were critical to permit human behavior, including cognition and speech. It is possible that the diverse physiological mechanisms of action of oxytocin allowed the elaboration of the human nervous system. The role of oxytocin in this process is poorly understood but may be approximated by understanding certain features of the development and evolution of the cortex.

The human brain is two to three times larger than that of related primates, including chimpanzees (Keverne 2013, Somel et al. 2013). This difference is due primarily to increases in cortical tissue, especially neurons located in association areas such as the prefrontal cortex. Creating a physiological and anatomical environment that allowed the extreme encephalization seen in humans appears to have drawn on several of the novel properties of oxytocin.

The origins of the neocortex have been traced to the reptilian ancestor of early mammals and depend on delicately balanced developmental processes (Rakic 2009). During development the cells of the neocortex differentiate, migrate, enlarge, and in some cases undergo cell death (including apoptosis). The human neocortex originates from progenitor cells in the ventricular and subventricular zones of the embryonic brain. Following paths laid by transient radial glia, neuronal cells that will become the neocortex migrate toward the surface of the brain, in most cases bypassing earlier cells. The result is formation of the distinct cytoarchitectural layers of the laminar neocortex permitting specialization of the brain for functions including speech and complex cognitions. Differences in the abundance of progenitor cells between mice and primates can be detected prior to the differentiation of the cortex. For example, it has been estimated by Rakic (2009, p. 726) that fewer than "7 extra rounds of cell division in the progenitor cells at an early embryonic stage would be sufficient to create the 1,000 fold difference in total cortical surface area that differentiates the brains of mice from those of humans." Thus, initially subtle developmental events may have allowed the eventual evolution of the human neocortex.

Oxytocin, Encephalization, and Social Behavior

Oxytocin encourages encephalization and cognition indirectly through social behavior. Neuroendocrine events, including those that were dependent on oxytocin, apparently support the prolongation of infant care and slow maturation of the human nervous system. This provides humans with an extended period for social learning, the development of an extended network of selective relationships, and cultural intelligence. Species differences in mammalian brain size among primates have been related to the appearance of social bonding, and it has been proposed that social relationships and bonds supported the evolution of the cortex (Dunbar 2009, Seyfarth & Cheney 2012, Shultz & Dunbar 2010). Social support within and beyond the family also may have permitted the evolution of human intelligence (Hrdy 2009). Furthermore, it has been proposed by anatomists that the human nervous system is a product of adaptations for sociality (Adolphs 2009). Perhaps these relationships are regulated in part by differences in the availability of oxytocin or variations in other components of the oxytocin pathways.

Oxytocin May Directly Foster Encephalization

Oxytocin has the capacity to remodel the bodily tissues. Oxytocin can influence cellular growth, death or motility, inflammation, or differentiation, although the most complete work in this area has been done in the heart (Gutkowska & Jankowski 2012). In rodents, apoptosis in heart tissue can be inhibited by oxytocin and especially by the precursor or "fetal" form of oxytocin.

Emerging evidence indicates that oxytocin also has direct effects on brain development. Oxytocin has been shown to reduce apoptosis and to promote adult neurogenesis (Leuner et al. 2012). Systematic analyses of the role of oxytocin in neocortical development are lacking. However, it is plausible that variations in oxytocin might facilitate neocortical growth by encouraging undifferentiated stem cells to grow into cortical cells (Gutkowska & Jankowski 2012) or by inhibiting the programmed destruction of brain cells. Together these processes would synchronize neocortical development to the physical demands of mammalian reproduction. Furthermore, it has been shown in tissue slices from rats that the synchronous firing of cortical cells is facilitated in the presence of oxytocin acting via effects on the GABA system (Crepel et al. 2007). Thus, both the anatomy and functional physiology of the developing mammalian brain could be sculpted by changes in oxytocin pathways.

Oxytocin, Oxygen, and the Growth of the Neocortex

In the transition from reptiles to mammals, and especially to primates, sophisticated autonomic systems emerged that are capable of concurrently supporting social behavior and the physiological demands of the expanding and oxygen-hungry mammalian cortex (Porges 2011). Cortical function is serviced by autonomic processes that originate in the brain stem. The role of the brain stem in cortical function is easily detected. When oxygen is no longer available, following damage to the brain stem or autonomic nervous system, consciousness is lost, typically followed by death. However, under normal conditions the entire brain, including cortical, subcortical, and autonomic pathways, is necessary to coordinate dynamic social behaviors, such as social cognition and social communication, with basic bodily functions, including survival and reproduction.

Critical to primate social engagement and communication are the bones, muscles, and nerves of the face and head, including the larynx, pharynx, and middle ear (Porges 2011). These structures and the nerves that innervate them form a system that permits social engagement and communication. The muscles of the mammalian face and head also are regulated in part by the autonomic nervous system, which in turn is influenced by oxytocin (Grippo et al. 2009, Quintana et al. 2013). Therefore it is not surprising that functions of the face, such as facial emotions and eye gaze, can be influenced by oxytocin (Guastella & MacLeod 2012).

The autonomic effects of oxytocin are context dependent and are not simple (Porges 2011). However, growing evidence suggests that oxytocin regulates both sympathetic and vagal branches of the autonomic nervous system (Kenkel et al. 2013). The PVN is a major regulatory center for autonomic functions (Herman 2012). The PVN of the hypothalamus synthesizes oxytocin but also responds to oxytocin. Lower brain stem structures, such as the dorsal motor nucleus of the vagus, also have high concentrations of oxytocin receptors. In addition, most—if not all—of the visceral target organs of the autonomic nervous system, such as the heart and digestive and immune systems, contain receptors for oxytocin and may also locally synthesize oxytocin (Gimpl & Fahrenholz 2001, Welch et al. 2009).

Developmental factors that regulate the capacity of the brain and skull to expand also are indirect determinants of human behavior (Porges 2011). The face and head arise embryologically from ancient gill arches. The detachment from the skull of the middle-ear bones occurred in the evolutionary transition from reptiles to mammals. It is detached middle-ear bones that are used to detect high-frequency sounds, and these bones also provide the definitive fossil evidence that a given species is a mammal (Manley 2010). The developmental and evolutionary detachment of the middle-ear bones also allowed the expansion and elaboration of the face, skull, and neocortex. A possible direct role for oxytocin in skull development has not to our knowledge been reported. However, oxytocin receptors are found in bone, and oxytocin has been implicated in bone growth and remodeling of other bony structures. In fact, oxytocin levels tend to be low in osteoporosis, possibly contributing to the loss of bone flexibility with age (Breuil et al. 2011). Cellular functions of oxytocin often involve the regulation of calcium. Therefore, it is plausible, but not proven, that oxytocin plays a role in the structure of the mammalian skull, helping to make room for the expansion of the human neocortex.

Oxytocin: The War Between the Sexes and Cortical Growth

Live birth puts restrictions on the physical size of an infant, especially the head. A large baby with an expanded neocortex is a physical burden for the mother. In primates, infants are gestated, nursed, and carried for months or years. Reproductive restrictions are further increased in bipedal primates, since mothers must give birth through a pelvic girdle adapted for upright locomotion. Thus, the capacity of the mother to regulate offspring development, especially the size of the neocortex, could be critical to both her survival and reproductive success (Keverne 2013). At the same time, the father's genome may be better served by larger offspring. As originally proposed by Haig (2011), this asymmetrical parental regulation of fetal growth creates a genetic war between the sexes. The weapons for this war include dueling genes and hormones that regulate the growth of the fetal neocortex and skull. Oxytocin is likely to be one of those hormones.

Through a process known as genomic imprinting, the expression of a subset of genes that is of particular relevance to growth and development can be epigenetically determined by one parent versus the other. This is accomplished by selective silencing of one of a pair of alleles for a given gene, allowing the other allele to dominate. Research in mice by Keverne (2013) and his associates showed that the matrilineal germ line contains cells that will become the neocortex, whereas progenitor cells that will become the hypothalamus originate in the father's genome. The primary source of oxytocin is from the hypothalamus, in neurons that are regulated by paternally expressed genes that are susceptible to genomic imprinting.

One paternally expressed gene, known as Peg3, plays a critical role in the development of the hypothalamus as well as the placenta (Broad et al. 2009, Champagne et al. 2009). Evidence for the importance of the Peg3 protein comes from experiments in which the Peg3 gene was inactivated. In the absence of Peg3 gene expression, females had a reduced number of hypothalamic oxytocin neurons, lower reproductive success, and specific reductions in the growth of the offspring that survived. Peg3 gene mutant mothers also were less attentive to their young, showing increased indications of anxiety and aggression (Keverne 2013). Thus, at least in mice, a single gene, the expression of which can be genetically influenced by the father and epigenetically regulated by the mother, has a major role in the synthesis of oxytocin.

Genomic imprinting or epigenetic silencing of the paternal allele of the Peg3 gene allows the maternal genome to dominate the development of the fetus. Although the genes that produce cells synthesizing oxytocin may originate in the father, it is the mother who determines the expression of these genes and thus the size of her offspring at birth.

At the same time, the mother also assumes the burden of providing food and nurture to her offspring, regulating continued cortical development in what can be an extended postnatal period. Oxytocin also has been implicated in food intake and metabolic efficiency (Chaves et al. 2013). Thus, the maternal endocrine environment affects and potentially "programs" the morphology of her offspring.

A long period of dependence on the mother (or other caretakers) characterizes most primates, especially humans. The slow maturation of the nervous system, possibly paced by the maternal genome, also increases the developmental significance of selective social interactions and long-term attachments. The capacity of a mother (or other caretakers) to maintain a lasting attachment to an offspring is essential to permit the full expression of the traits associated with human sociality and human cognition. As mentioned above, lactation, maternal behavior, and social bonding are functions that rely on oxytocin. If the processes observed in mice apply to humans, then it may be the mother who regulates the timing and eventually the extent of the cortical and bodily development of her offspring as well as the availability of hypothalamic oxytocin. Each of these would have lasting consequences for brain function and behavior.

SUMMARY

Oxytocin is a powerful molecule with a unique and unusually broad profile of biological and behavioral effects. Oxytocin acts upon receptors and tissues that are ancient and have evolved many functions (Ebstein et al. 2012, Garrison 2012, Meyer-Lindenberg et al. 2011, Yamashita & Kitano 2013). Understanding this system provides a window into the evolution and epigenetics of the human brain (Keverne 2013).

Abundant evidence indicates that individual differences in experience, with effects on health and behavior across the lifecycle, are shaped by caretaker-offspring interactions (Zhang & Meaney 2010). The nervous system seems to be especially sensitive in early life to the presence or absence of peptides, such as oxytocin (Carter et al. 2009a) and vasopressin (Stribley & Carter 1999, Zhang et al. 2012), with epigenetic consequences that may help to explain individual differences in behavior and coping strategies. Although beyond the scope of this review, there is now little doubt of the epigenetic importance of oxytocin and vasopressin (Carter et al. 2009a). Thus, medical manipulations or even rearing procedures that may influence these hormones, especially in early life, should be applied with caution (Harris & Carter 2013).

Throughout vertebrate evolution, the effects of oxytocin-like molecules have been integral to survival and reproduction. In modern humans, the functions of oxytocin facilitate birth and both directly and indirectly influence brain anatomy, allowing the elaboration of the human neocortex and thus cognition and language. The mammalian brain and body are physically remodeled by the presence of oxytocin. Oxytocin plays a role in sensory, autonomic, integrative, visceral, and motor systems. It helps to tune the emotional nervous system in early life. Oxytocin may help to provide a sense of safety or trust. Oxytocin protects and directly heals tissue, with therapeutic consequences that are only now being discovered. Simply put, I suggest here that *Homo sapiens*, with their high level of dependence on social behavior and cognition, could not have evolved without oxytocin.

DISCLOSURE STATEMENT

The author is not aware of any affiliations, memberships, funding, or financial holdings that might be perceived as affecting the objectivity of this review.

ACKNOWLEDGMENTS

This review is strongly influenced by the generous conceptual input and insights of Stephen Porges. I am also grateful for insights and encouragement from Sarah Hrdy. Meetings organized by the Fetzer Institute created a context from which this review emerged. Studies from the author's laboratories were primarily sponsored by the National Institutes of Health, especially the NICHD and NIMH. Support is gratefully acknowledged from many colleagues and students whose ideas and data inform the perspective offered here. For convenience, examples used here draw heavily from research that originated in my laboratory. However, many other excellent studies and reviews provided inspiration for the hypotheses generated here.

LITERATURE CITED

Adolphs R. 2009. The social brain: neural basis of social knowledge. *Annu. Rev. Psychol.* 60:693–716

Aguilera G, Subburaju S, Young S, Chen J. 2008. The parvocellular vasopressinergic system and responsiveness of the hypothalamic pituitary adrenal axis during chronic stress. *Prog. Brain Res.* 170:29–39

Albers HE. 2012. The regulation of social recognition, social communication and aggression: vasopressin in the social behavior neural network. *Horm. Behav.* 61:283–92

Algoe SB, Haidt J. 2009. Witnessing excellence in action: the "other-praising" emotions of elevation, gratitude and admiration. *J. Posit. Psychol.* 4:105–27

Aragona BJ, Wang Z. 2009. Dopamine regulation of social choice in a monogamous rodent species. *Front. Behav. Neurosci.* 3:15

Bales KL, Perkeybile AM, Conley OG, Lee MH, Guoynes CD, et al. 2013. Chronic intranasal oxytocin causes long-term impairments in partner preference formation in male prairie voles. *Biol. Psychiatry* 74:180–88

Bales KL, Plotsky PM, Young LJ, Lim MM, Grotte N, et al. 2007a. Neonatal oxytocin manipulations have long-lasting, sexually dimorphic effects on vasopressin receptors. *Neuroscience* 144:38–45

Bales KL, van Westerhuyzen JA, Lewis-Reese AD, Grotte ND, Lanter JA, Carter CS. 2007b. Oxytocin has dose-dependent developmental effects on pair bonding and alloparental care in female prairie voles. *Horm. Behav.* 49:355–42

Bartz JA, Zaki J, Bolger N, Ochsner KN. 2011. Social effects of oxytocin in humans: context and person matter. *Trends Cogn. Sci.* 15:301–9

Bosch OJ, Neumann ID. 2012. Both oxytocin and vasopressin are mediators of maternal care and aggression in rodents: from central release to sites of action. *Horm. Behav.* 61:293–303

Breuil V, Amri EZ, Panaia-Ferrari P, Testa J, Elabd C, et al. 2011. Oxytocin and bone remodeling: relationships with neuropituitary hormones, bone status and body composition. *Joint Bone Spine* 78:611–15

Broad KD, Curley JP, Keverne EB. 2009. Increased apoptosis during brain development underlies the adult behavioral deficits seen in mice lacking a functional paternally expressed gene 3 (*Peg3*). *Dev. Neurobiol.* 69:314–25

Brunton PJ, Russell JA. 2010. Endocrine induced changes in brain function during pregnancy. *Brain Res.* 1364:198–215

Burkett JP, Spiegel LI, Inoue K, Murphy AZ, Young LJ. 2011. Activation of μ-opioid receptors in the dorsal striatum is necessary for adult social attachment in monogamous prairie voles. *Neuropsychopharmacology* 36:2200–10

Cacioppo JT, Hughes ME, Waite LJ, Hawkely LC, Thisted RA. 2006. Loneliness as a specific risk factor for depressive symptoms: cross-sectional and longitudinal analysis. *Psychol. Aging* 21:140–51

Carter CS. 1992. Oxytocin and sexual behavior. *Neurosci. Biobehav. Rev.* 16:131–44

Carter CS. 1998. Neuroendocrine perspectives on social attachment and love. *Psychoneuroendocrinology* 23:779–818

Carter CS. 2007. Sex differences in oxytocin and vasopressin: implications for autism spectrum disorders? *Behav. Brain Res.* 176:170–86

Carter CS, Altemus M. 1997. Integrative functions of lactational hormones in social behavior and stress management. *Ann. N. Y. Acad. Sci.* 807:164–74

Carter CS, Boone EM, Pournajafi-Nazarloo H, Bales KL. 2009a. The consequences of early experiences and exposure to oxytocin and vasopressin are sexually dimorphic. *Dev. Neurosci.* 31:332–41

Carter CS, DeVries AC, Getz LL. 1995. Physiological substrates of monogamy: the prairie vole model. *Neurosci. Biobehav. Rev.* 19:303–14

Carter CS, Grippo AJ, Pournajafi-Nazarloo H, Ruscio MG, Porges SW. 2008. Oxytocin, vasopressin and social behavior. *Prog. Brain Res.* 170:331–36

Carter CS, Harris J, Porges SW. 2009b. Neural and evolutionary perspectives on empathy. In *The Social Neuroscience of Empathy*, ed. J Decety, W Ickes, pp. 169–82. Cambridge, Mass.: MIT Press

Carter CS, Porges SW. 2013. The biochemistry of love: an oxytocin hypothesis. *EMBO Rep.* 14:12–16

Carter CS, Pournajafi-Nazarloo H, Kramer KM, Ziegler TW, White-Traut R, et al. 2007. Oxytocin: behavioral associations and potential as a salivary biomarker. *Ann. NY Acad. Sci.* 1098:312–22

Champagne FA, Curley JP, Swaney WT, Hasen NS, Keverne EB. 2009. Paternal influence on female behavior: the role of *Peg3* in exploration, olfaction, and neuroendocrine regulation of maternal behavior of female mice. *Behav. Neurosci.* 123:469–80

Chaves VE, Tilelli CQ, Brito NA, Brito MN. 2013. Role of oxytocin in energy metabolism. *Peptides* 45:9–14

Cho MM, DeVries AC, Williams JR, Carter CS. 1999. The effects of oxytocin and vasopressin on partner preferences in male and female prairie voles (*Microtus ochrogaster*). *Behav. Neurosci.* 113:1071–80

Crepel V, Aronov D, Jorquera I, Represa A, Ben-Ari Y, Cossart R. 2007. A parturition-associated nonsynaptic coherent activity pattern in the developing hippocampus. *Neuron* 54:105–20

Coccaro EP, Kavoussi RJ, Hauger RL, Cooper TB, Ferris CF. 1998. Cerebrospinal fluid vasopressin levels: correlates with aggression and serotonin function in personality-disorder subjects. *Arch. Gen. Psychiatry* 55:708–14

Dai L, Carter CS, Ying J, Bellugi U, Pournajafi-Nazarloo H, Korenberg JR. 2012. Oxytocin and vasopressin are dysregulated in Williams syndrome, a genetic disorder affecting social behavior. *PLoS ONE* 7(6):e38513

De Dreu CK. 2012. Oxytocin modulates cooperation within and competition between groups: an integrative review and research agenda. *Horm. Behav.* 61:419–28

De Vries GJ, Panzica GC. 2006. Sexual differentiation of central vasopressin and vasotocin systems in vertebrates: different mechanisms, similar endpoints. *Neuroscience* 138:947–55

Decety J. 2011. The neuroevolution of empathy. *Ann. N. Y. Acad. Sci.* 1231:3–45

Donaldson ZR, Young LJ. 2008. Oxytocin, vasopressin, and the neurogenetics of sociality. *Science* 322:900–4

Dunbar RIM. 2009. The social brain hypothesis and its implication for social evolution. *Ann. Human Biol.* 36:562–72

Dunbar RIM, Baron R, Frangou A, Pearce E, van Leeuwen JC, et al. 2012. Social laughter is correlated with an elevated pain threshold. *Proc. R. Soc. B* 279:1161–67

Ebstein RP, Knafo A, Mankuta D, Chew SH, Lai PS. 2012. The contributions of oxytocin and vasopressin pathway genes to human behavior. *Horm. Behav.* 61:359–79

Englander ZA, Haidt J, Morris JP. 2012. Neural basis of moral elevation demonstrated through inter-subjective synchronization of cortical activity during free-viewing. *PLoS ONE* 7(6):e39384

Feldman R. 2012. Oxytocin and social affiliation in humans. *Horm. Behav.* 61:380–91

Ferris CF. 2008. Functional magnetic resonance imaging and the neurobiology of vasopressin and oxytocin. *Prog. Brain Res.* 170:305–20

Fisher HE, Aron A, Brown LL. 2006. Romantic love: a mammalian brain system for mate choice. *Philos. Trans. R. Soc. B* 361:2173–86

Frank E, Landgraf R. 2008. The vasopressin system—from antidiuresis to psychopathology. *Eur. J. Pharmacol.* 583:226–42

Gainer H. 2012. Cell-type specific expression of oxytocin and vasopressin genes: an experimental odyssey. *J. Neuroendocrinol.* 24:528–38

Garrison JL, Macosko EZ, Bernstein S, Pokala N, Albrecht DR, Bargmann CI. 2012. Oxytocin/vasopressin-related peptides have an ancient role in reproductive behavior. *Science* 338:540–43

Gautvik KM, deLecea L, Gautvik VT, Danielson PE, Tranque P, et al. 1996. Overview of the most prevalent hypothalamus-specific mRNAs, as identified by directional tag PCR subtraction. *Proc. Natl. Acad. Sci. USA* 93:8733–38

Gimpl G, Fahrenholz F. 2001. The oxytocin receptor system: structure, function and regulation. *Physiol. Rev.* 81:629–83

Goodson JL, Kelly AM, Kingsbury MA. 2012. Evolving nonapeptide mechanisms of gregariousness and social diversity. *Horm. Behav.* 61:239–50

Gouin JP, Carter CS, Pournajafi-Nazarloo H, Glaser R, Malarkey WB, et al. 2010. Marital behavior, oxytocin, vasopressin and wound healing. *Psychoneuroendocrinology* 35:1082–90

Gregory SG, Connelly JJ, Towers AJ, Johnson J, Biscocho D, et al. 2009. Genomic and epigenetic evidence for oxytocin receptor deficiency in autism. *BMC Med.* 7:62

Grewen KM, Light KC. 2011. Plasma oxytocin is related to lower cardiovascular and sympathetic reactivity to stress. *Biol. Psychol.* 87:340–49

Grippo AJ, Gerena D, Huang J, Kumar N, Shah M, et al. 2007. Social isolation induces behavioral and neuroendocrine disturbances relevant to depression in female and male prairie voles. *Psychoneuroendocrinology* 32:966–80

Grippo AJ, Pournajafi-Nazarloo H, Sanzenbacher L, Trahanas DM, McNeal N, et al. 2012. Peripheral oxytocin administration buffers autonomic but not behavioral responses to environmental stressors in isolated prairie voles. *Stress* 15:149–61

Grippo AJ, Trahanas DM, Zimmerman RR II, Porges SW, Carter CS. 2009. Oxytocin protects against negative behavioral and autonomic consequences of long-term social isolation. *Psychoneuroendocrinology* 34:1542–53

Guastella AJ, MacLeod C. 2012. A critical review of the influence of oxytocin nasal spray on social cognition in humans: evidence and further directions. *Horm. Behav.* 61:410–18

Gutkowska J, Jankowski M. 2012. Oxytocin revisited: its role in cardiovascular regulation. *J. Neuroendocrinol.* 24:599–608

Guzmán YF, Tronson NC, Jovesevic V, Sato K, Guedea AL, et al. 2013. Fear-enhancing effects of septal oxytocin receptors. *Nat. Neurosci.* 16:1185–87

Haig D. 2011. Genomic imprinting and evolutionary psychology of human kinship. *Proc. Natl. Acad. Sci. USA* 108:10878–85

Hammock EA, Young LJ. 2005. Microsatellite instability generates diversity in brain and sociobehavioral traits. *Science* 308:1630–34

Harris JC, Carter CS. 2013. Therapeutic interventions with oxytocin: current status and concerns. *J. Am. Acad. Child Adolesc. Psychiatry.* In press

Hatfield E, Cacioppo JT, Rapson RL. 1994. *Emotional Contagion.* Cambridge, UK: Cambridge Univ. Press

Herman JP. 2012. Neural pathways of stress integration: relevance to alcohol abuse. *Alcohol Res.* 34:441–47

Hofer MA. 1987. Early social relationships: a psychobiologist's view. *Child Dev.* 58:633–47

Hrdy SB. 2009. *Mothers and Others: The Evolutionary Origins of Mutual Understanding.* Cambridge, MA: Belknap Press, Harvard Univ. Press

Hurlemann R, Patin A, Onur OA, Cohen MX, Baumgartner T, et al. 2010. Oxytocin enhances amygdala-dependent, socially reinforced learning and emotional empathy in humans. *J. Neurosci.* 30:4999–5007

Ingham CJ, Ben Jacob E. 2008. Swarming and complex pattern formation in *Paenibacillus vortex* studied by imaging and tracking cells. *BMC Microbiol.* 8:36

Jack A, Connelly JJ, Morris JP. 2012. DNA methylation of the oxytocin receptor gene predicts neural response to ambiguous social stimuli. *Front. Hum. Neurosci.* 6:280

Jacob S, Brune CW, Carter CS, Leventhal B, Lord C, Cook EH Jr. 2007. Association of the oxytocin receptor gene (*OXTR*) in Caucasian children and adolescents with autism. *Neurosci. Lett.* 417:6–9

Karelina K, DeVries AC. 2011. Modeling social influences on human health. *Psychosom. Med.* 73:67–74

Kenkel W, Paredes J, Yee JR, Pournajafi-Nazarl KL, Carter CS. 2012. Exposure to an infant releases oxytocin and facilitates pair-bonding in male prairie voles. *J. Neuroendocrinol.* 24:874–86

Kenkel WM, Paredes J, Lewis GF, Yee JR, Pournajafi-Nazarloo H, et al. 2013. Autonomic substrates of the response to pups in male prairie voles. *PLoS ONE.* 8:e69965

Keverne EB. 2013. Significance of epigenetics for understanding brain development, brain evolution and behaviour. *Neuroscience.* In press. doi:10.1016/j.neuroscience.2012.11.0

Khazipov R, Tyzio R, Ben-Ari Y. 2008. Effects of oxytocin on GABA signalling in the foetal brain during delivery. *Prog. Brain Res.* 170:243–57

Kob BE, Fredrickson BL. 2010. Upward spirals of the heart: Autonomic flexibility, as indexed by vagal tone, reciprocally and prospectively predicts positive emotions and social connectedness. *Biol. Psychol.* 85:432–36

Kosfeld M, Heinrichs M, Zak PJ, Fischbacher U, Fehr E. 2005. Oxytocin increases trust in humans. *Nature* 435:673–76

Kramer KM, Cushing BS, Carter CS, Wu J, Ottinger MA. 2004. Sex and species differences in plasma oxytocin using an enzyme immunoassay. *Can. J. Zool.* 82:1194–200

Lee J-H, Macbeth AH, Pagani JH, Young WS. 2009. Oxytocin: the great facilitator of life. *Prog. Neurobiol.* 88:127–51

Leuner B, Caponiti JM, Gould E. 2012. Oxytocin stimulates adult neurogenesis even under conditions of stress and elevated glucocorticoids. *Hippocampus* 22:861–68

MacDonald K, Feifel D. 2013. Helping oxytocin deliver: considerations in the development of oxytocin-based therapeutics for brain development. *Front. Neurosci.* 7:35

Manley GA. 2010. An evolutionary perspective on middle ears. *Hear. Res.* 263:3–8

Martin WL, Carter CS. 2013. Oxytocin and vasopressin are sequestered in plasma. In 10th *World Congress of Neurohypophyseal Hormones Abstracts*, Bristol, UK

Mazzuca M, Minlebaev M, Shakirzyanova A, Tyzio R, Taccola G, et al. 2011. Newborn analgesia mediated by oxytocin during delivery. *Front. Cell Neurosci.* 5:3

Meyer-Lindenberg A, Domes G, Kirsch P, Heinrichs M. 2011. Oxytocin and vasopressin in the human brain: social neuropeptides for translational medicine. *Nat. Rev. Neurosci.* 12:524–38

Neumann ID, Landgraf R. 2012. Balance of brain oxytocin and vasopressin: implications for anxiety, depression and social behaviors. *Trends Neurosci.* 35:649–59

Niswender GD, Davis TL, Griggith RJ, Bogan RL, Monser K, et al. 2007. Judge, jury and executioner: the auto-regulation of luteal function. *Soc. Reprod. Fertil. Suppl.* 64:191–206

Norman GJ, Cacioppo JT, Morris JS, Malarkey WB, Berntson GG, DeVries AC. 2011. Oxytocin increases autonomic cardiac control: moderation by loneliness. *Biol. Psychol.* 86:174–80

Olff M. 2012. Bonding after trauma: on the role of social support and the oxytocin system in traumatic stress. *Eur. J. Psychotraumatol.* doi:10.3402/ejpt.v3i0.18597

Pedersen CA. 1997. Oxytocin control of maternal behavior: regulation by sex steroids and offspring stimuli. *Ann. N. Y. Acad. Sci.* 807:126–45

Pepping GJ, Timmermans EJ. 2012. Oxytocin and the biopsychology of performance in team sports. *Sci. World J.* 2012:567363

Porges SW. 1998. Love: an emergent property of the mammalian autonomic nervous system. *Psychoneuroendocrinology* 23:837–61

Porges SW. 2011. *The Polyvagal Theory: Neurophysiological Foundations of Emotions, Attachment, Communication and Self-Regulation.* New York: Norton

Pournajafi-Nazarloo H, Kenkel W, Mohsenpour SR, Sanzenbacher L, Saadat H, et al. 2013. Exposure to chronic isolation modulates receptors mRNAs for oxytocin and vasopressin in the hypothalamus and heart. *Peptides* 43:20–26

Quintana DS, Kemp AH, Alvares GA, Guastella AJ. 2013. A role for autonomic cardiac control in the effects of oxytocin on social behavior and psychiatric illness. *Front. Neurosci.* 7:48

Rakic P. 2009. Evolution of the neocortex: a perspective from developmental biology. *Nat. Rev. Neurosci.* 10:724–35

Rault J-L, Carter CS, Garner JP, Marchant-Forde JN, Richert BT, Lay DC Jr. 2013. Repeated intranasal oxytocin administration in early life dysregulates the HPA axis and alters social behavior. *Physiol. Behav.* 112–113:40–48

Rilling JK, DeMarco AC, Hackett PD, Thompson R, Ditzen B, et al. 2012. Effects of intranasal oxytocin and vasopressin on cooperative behavior and associated brain activity in men. *Psychoneuroendocrinology* 37:447–61

Rubin LH, Carter CS, Drogos L, Jamadar R, Pournajafi-Nazarloo H, et al. 2011. Sex-specific associations between peripheral oxytocin and positive emotion perception in schizophrenia. *Schizophr. Res.* 30:266–70

Seyfarth RM, Cheney DL. 2012. The evolutionary origins of friendship. *Annu. Rev. Psychol.* 63:153–77

Seyfarth RM, Cheney DL. 2013. Affiliation, empathy and the origins of theory of mind. *Proc. Natl. Acad. Sci. USA* 110(Suppl. 2):10349–56

Shultz S, Dunbar R. 2010. Encephalization is not a universal macroevolutionary phenomenon in mammals but is associated with sociality. *Proc. Natl. Acad. Sci. USA* 107:21582–86

Silvers JA, Haidt J. 2008. Moral elevation can induce nursing. *Emotion* 8:291–95

Somel M, Liu X, Khaitovich P. 2013. Human brain evolution: transcripts, metabolites and their regulators. *Nat. Rev. Neurosci.* 14:112–27

Stevenson EL, Caldwell HK. 2012. The vasopressin 1b receptor and the neural regulation of social behavior. *Horm. Behav.* 61:277–82

Stoop R. 2012. Neuromodulation by oxytocin and vasopressin. *Neuron* 76:142–59

Stribley JM, Carter CS. 1999. Developmental exposure to vasopressin increases aggression in adult prairie voles. *Proc. Natl. Acad. Sci. USA* 96:12601–4

Stuebe AM, Grewen K, Meltzer-Brody S. 2013. Association between maternal mood and oxytocin response to breastfeeding. *J. Womens Health* 22:352–61

Szeto A, McCabe PM, Nation DA, Tabak BA, Rossetti MA, et al. 2011. Evaluation of enzyme immunoassay and radioimmunoassay methods for the measurement of plasma oxytocin. *Psychosom. Med.* 73:393–400

Szeto A, Nation DA, Mendez AJ, Dominguez-Bendala J, Brooks LG, et al. 2008. Oxytocin attenuates NADPH-dependent superoxide activity and IL-6 secretion in macrophages and vascular cells. *Am. J. Physiol. Endocrinol. Metabol.* 295:E1495–501

Taylor SE, Gonzaga GC, Klein LC, Hu P, Greendale GA, Seeman TE. 2006. Relation of oxytocin to psychological stress responses and hypothalamic-pituitary-adrenocortical axis activity in older women. *Psychosom. Med.* 68:238–45

Taylor SE, Klein LC, Lewis BP, Gruenewald TL, Gurung RA, Updegraff JA. 2000. Biobehavioral responses to stress in females: tend-and-befriend, not fight-or-flight. *Psychol. Rev.* 107:411–29

Taylor SE, Saphire-Bernstein S, Seeman TE. 2010. Are plasma oxytocin in women and plasma vasopressin men biomarkers of distressed pair-bond relationships? *Psychol. Sci.* 21:3–7

Theodosis DT. 2002. Oxytocin-secreting neurons: a physiological model of morphological neuronal and glial plasticity in the adult hypothalamus. *Front. Neuroendocrinol.* 23:101–35

Tost H, Kolachana B, Hakimi S, Lemaitre H, Verchinski BA, et al. 2010. A common allele in the oxytocin receptor gene (OXTR) impacts prosocial temperament and human hypothalamic-limbic structure and function. *Proc. Natl. Acad. Sci. USA* 107:13936–41

Tyzio R, Cossart R, Khalilov I, Minlebaev M, Hubner CA, et al. 2006. Maternal oxytocin triggers a transient inhibitory switch in GABA signaling in the fetal brain during delivery. *Science* 314:1788–92

Weisman O, Zagoory-Sharon O, Schneiderman I, Gordon I, Feldman R. 2013. Plasma oxytocin distributions in a large cohort of women and men and their gender-specific associations with anxiety. *Psychoneuroendocrinology* 38:694–701

Welch MG, Tamir H, Gross KJ, Chen J, Anwar M, Gershon MD. 2009. Expression and developmental regulation of oxytocin (OT) and oxytocin receptors (OTR) in the enteric nervous system (ENS) and intestinal epithelium. *J. Comp. Neurol.* 512:256–70

Wentworth BA, Stein MB, Redwine LS, Xue Y, Taub PR, et al. 2013. Post-traumatic stress disorder: a fast track to premature cardiovascular disease. *Cardiol. Rev.* 21:16–22

Williams JR, Catania K, Carter CS. 1992. Development of partner preferences in female prairie voles (*Microtus ochrogaster*): the role of social and sexual experience. *Horm. Behav.* 26:339–49

Williams JR, Insel TR, Harbaugh CR, Carter CS. 1994. Oxytocin administered centrally facilitates formation of a partner preference in female prairie voles. *J. Neuroendocrinol.* 6:247–50

Winslow JT, Hastings N, Carter CS, Harbaugh CR, Insel TR. 1993. A role for central vasopressin in pair bonding in monogamous prairie voles. *Nature* 365:545–48

Woodard SH, Fischman BJ, Venkat A, Hudson ME, Varala K, et al. 2011. Genes involved in convergent evolution of eusociality in bees. *Proc. Natl. Acad. Sci. USA* 108:7472–77

Yamashita K, Kitano T. 2013. Molecular evolution of the oxytocin-oxytocin receptor system in eutherians. *Mol. Phylogenet. Evol.* 67:520–28

Young KA, Gobrogge KL, Liu Y, Wang Z. 2011. The neurobiology of pair bonding: insights from a socially monogamous rodent. *Front. Neuroendocrinol.* 32:53–69

Zhang L, Hernandez VS, Liu B, Medina MP, Nava-Kopp AT, et al. 2012. Hypothalamic vasopressin system regulation by maternal separation: its impact on anxiety in rats. *Neuroscience* 215:135–48

Zhang TY, Meaney MJ. 2010. Epigenetics and the environmental regulation of the genome and its function. *Annu. Rev. Psychol.* 61:439–66

Gene-Environment Interaction

Stephen B. Manuck[1] and Jeanne M. McCaffery[2]

[1]Department of Psychology, University of Pittsburgh, Pittsburgh, Pennsylvania 15260;
email: manuck@pitt.edu

[2]Department of Psychiatry and Human Behavior, The Miriam Hospital, and Warren Alpert School of Medicine at Brown University, Providence, Rhode Island 02903;
email: jeanne_mccaffery@brown.edu

Annu. Rev. Psychol. 2014. 65:41–70

The *Annual Review of Psychology* is online at
http://psych.annualreviews.org

This article's doi:
10.1146/annurev-psych-010213-115100

Keywords

behavioral genetics, heritability, diathesis-stress, differential susceptibility, vantage sensitivity, gene-environment correlation

Abstract

With the advent of increasingly accessible technologies for typing genetic variation, studies of gene-environment (G × E) interactions have proliferated in psychological research. Among the aims of such studies are testing developmental hypotheses and models of the etiology of behavioral disorders, defining boundaries of genetic and environmental influences, and identifying individuals most susceptible to risk exposures or most amenable to preventive and therapeutic interventions. This research also coincides with the emergence of unanticipated difficulties in detecting genetic variants of direct association with behavioral traits and disorders, which may be obscured if genetic effects are expressed only in predisposing environments. In this essay we consider these and other rationales for positing G × E interactions, review conceptual models meant to inform G × E interpretations from a psychological perspective, discuss points of common critique to which G × E research is vulnerable, and address the role of the environment in G × E interactions.

Contents

INTRODUCTION

Universally acknowledged in principle, gene-environment (G × E) interaction presently appears to divide scientists as much as it binds a duality of nature and nurture. On the one hand, putative G × E interactions affecting behavior are now published by the handful monthly, extending to virtually all topics of psychological science and appearing regularly in journals of cognition; development; personality and psychopathology; health psychology; and social, cognitive, and affective neuroscience. The recent emergence of these literatures is abetted by increasingly accessible technologies for typing genetic variation, and undoubtedly also by the opportunities they afford to engage fundamental questions of heredity and environment that have variously intrigued, provoked, and inflamed psychology for a century. Yet, as enthusiastically as many psychologists embrace the prospect that genes moderate an environment's stamp or that some genetic effects on behavior may be conditioned by predisposing circumstance, others find the whole enterprise plagued with weaknesses, including inflated claims, genetic naïveté and woolly-headed biologizing, statistical inadequacies, rampant replication failures, publication bias, and a curious preoccupation with a small collection of dubious gene polymorphisms. It is not surprising then to see much G × E literature dismissed wholesale, as in a recent analysis of G × E studies of psychiatric disorders that attributed "most or even all" G × E findings to likely type I errors (Duncan & Keller 2011), or to read another refer to the sometimes uneasy alliance of psychology and molecular genetics by admonishing investigators to "play nice in the sandbox" of G × E research (Dick 2011, p. 401). Such controversy aside, the proliferation of G × E literature in recent years coincides with dampening expectations of rapid progress in identifying genes of direct association with psychological traits and disorders (phenotypes). In this context, we introduce G × E interaction here as one of several hypotheses offered to explain why discovered genetic variants have so far accounted for only a small portion of heritable variation in behavioral phenotypes. We then consider other rationales for positing G × E interactions, discuss prevailing conceptual models of G × E interaction in psychology, and highlight key areas of critique of G × E literature. In closing, we consider the role of the environment in G × E interaction, and in particular, how environmental influences are expressed and what implications pervasive gene-environment correlations have for interpreting G × E research.

PROGRESS IN GENE DISCOVERY

As the Human Genome Project neared completion of a first draft of the genome in 2000, a doyen of behavioral genetics, Robert Plomin, predicted psychology might soon be "awash" in genes (Plomin & Crabbe 2000). Thirteen years on, Plomin amended his forecast in light of unanticipated delays in gene discovery (Plomin 2013). These were not delays due to want of effort, as the intervening years saw a succession of methods deployed to locate genetic variation underlying heritable behaviors. The first approach was linkage analysis, which had already been applied for a number of years. Linkage analysis seeks variants of DNA sequence (markers) that co-occur with the presence of a disease or disordered condition in pedigreed families containing affected and unaffected members. Such co-occurrence, or co-inheritance, places the marker in proximity to a causal genetic variant, but because only a few hundred markers are commonly used, positive linkage signals may still be many, perhaps millions, of base-pairs (units of DNA sequence) distant from the responsible gene. Linkage analysis identified chromosomal regions associated with hundreds of Mendelian disorders that, like Huntington disease, are caused by single mutations. When extended to complex disorders, such as schizophrenia, bipolar disorder, or major depression, however, few replicated linkage signals emerged (Freitag 2007, Kendler 2011, Riley & Kendler 2006). This result directed attention to a major drawback of linkage analysis, namely its ability to detect only variants with large effects, and these were often limited to a select number of family pedigrees. The lack of success suggested, too, that many disorders may conform better to a polygenic model of inheritance, entailing many genes, each of small effect (Risch & Merikangas 1996).

A second approach, capable of detecting even modest associations, targets specific genes based on their suspected relevance to the phenotype of interest. Not surprisingly, in behavioral studies such "candidate genes" often encode components of neurotransmission, neuroendocrine function, or related cellular processes lying in plausible biological pathways. The aim of this approach is to determine whether the level of a quantitative trait or the presence of a disorder associates above chance with one or another variant (allele) of a known gene polymorphism or with a particular combination of alleles of multiple polymorphisms within the same gene (haplotypes). Unlike linkage analyses, candidate gene studies typically test for association in samples of unrelated individuals and often emphasize functional variation, such as promoter variants that affect the transcriptional efficiency of genes or base-pair substitutions in gene coding regions (exons) that alter the amino acid sequence of a protein.

Among notable successes are the discovery of a major risk allele for late-onset Alzheimer's disease in the gene encoding the lipid transport molecule, apolipoprotein E (*APOE*) (Poirier et al. 1993), and genetic variation in the ethanol-metabolizing enzyme, alcohol dehydrogenase 1B (*ADH1B*), which modulates risk for alcohol dependence and related medical sequelae (e.g., Bierut et al. 2012, Li et al. 2011). These and similar findings encouraged many psychologists to include molecular variation in their own research, with much of this work focusing on a limited number of candidate gene polymorphisms that could be genotyped at feasible cost and added to existing protocols. With the accumulation of studies, it became apparent that, unlike the two examples cited above, many candidate associations fare poorly in replication. The first polymorphism prominently related to a human personality trait, novelty seeking, was a widely studied variant of the dopamine D4 receptor (*DRD4*) (Ebstein et al. 1996). Although this finding attracted much attention, the association proved equivocal in later research (e.g., Kluger et al. 2002, Munafo et al. 2008b), and weak or similarly inconclusive findings have emerged in meta-analyses of other highly cited candidate gene associations for personality and psychopathology, health-related behaviors, and cognition (e.g., Barnett et al. 2008; Chabris et al. 2012; Gyekis et al. 2013; Mandelman & Grigorenko 2012; Munafo et al. 2005, 2009b; Vassos et al. 2013). Nor is the replication problem limited to studies of behavioral phenotypes; a review of over 160 early candidate gene associations in diverse medical conditions found the vast majority of attempted replications unsuccessful (Hirschhorn et al. 2002). Although several explanations have been posited, including underpowered studies, heterogeneous or poorly measured phenotypes, and dilution of effects by unknown or untested moderators, the poor reproducibility of many candidate gene associations has lessened enthusiasm for this approach, at least among geneticists (Munafo 2006).

Another limitation of the candidate gene study is its reliance on a prior hypothesis, which narrows the search space for genetic variation to components of prevailing biological models and, hence, rarely nominates more than a handful of the estimated 20,000 to 25,000 human genes. And by prioritizing coding sequences and adjacent regions, candidate gene studies neglect large expanses of the genome that do not code for protein. Until recently, these regions were largely dismissed as uninformative, but such DNA may harbor abundant functional elements, such as sequences encoding untranslated RNA transcripts that can exert regulatory influences on far distant genes (Ecker 2012, Mendes et al. 2006).

Ultimately, sequencing entire genomes should reveal all sources of genetic variation among individuals, yet even with steeply declining costs, whole-genome sequencing may not gain wide feasibility for some time (Durbin et al. 2010). Until then, and for several years now, the most powerful method of gene discovery is the genome-wide association (GWA) study. GWA studies use DNA microarrays (chips) containing probes for hundreds of thousands or, typically now, a million or more single-nucleotide polymorphisms (SNPs) that tag common variation across the genome. Unlike the candidate gene approach, but similar to linkage analysis, GWA studies require no mechanistic hypotheses and therefore have the potential to identify genes implicating previously unrecognized biological pathways. Also, even small genetic effects can be detected in GWA studies, although the enormous number of SNPs tested for association demands very large samples and stringent statistical thresholds to adjust for multiple testing. Despite these hurdles, GWA studies have found novel loci (locations of DNA sequence) related to many complex physical traits and disorders, often well replicated and sustained on meta-analytic review (Visscher et al. 2012a).

One early success was the discovery in 2007 of the fat mass and obesity-associated *FTO* gene, which contains a SNP whose minor (less-frequent) allele is associated with a >20% increased risk of obesity and ~2- to 3-pound-higher body weight (e.g., Frayling et al. 2007, Willer et al. 2009). When treated as a candidate gene in studies of eating habits, the *FTO* risk allele also predicted a variety of behaviors relevant to obesity, including greater caloric intake and fat consumption (e.g., Cecil et al. 2008), more frequent eating episodes (McCaffery et al. 2012), and insensitivity to satiety-related cues (Wardle et al. 2009). An additional 31 SNPs, plus *FTO*, were also found to be associated with body mass index (BMI) in a recent study of 250,000 individuals, although *FTO* alone accounted for one-third of the variance in BMI attributable to all SNPs, and all loci together accounted for only about 1.5% of variance in BMI (Speliotes et al. 2010). In another example, GWA studies identified nearly a dozen blood pressure–associated SNPs (Levy et al. 2009, Newton-Cheh et al. 2009), and yet again, little of the total variance (~1%) can be explained by the aggregate of discovered variants. In other instances, GWA-identified loci account for a somewhat larger proportion of phenotypic variation. About 10% of the variance in height was predicted by 180 loci of genomewide significance (i.e., surviving correction for multiple testing) in a sample of over 180,000 individuals (Lango Allen et al. 2010), and about 50 loci similarly account for around 10% of risk for type 2 diabetes (Visscher et al. 2012a). It is also noteworthy that, except in a few instances such as the *APOE* risk allele for Alzheimer's disease, most reported candidate gene associations have not replicated in GWA studies (e.g., Bosker et al. 2011, Siontis et al. 2010).

GWA studies of behavioral phenotypes are not as plentiful as those of physical attributes and diseases, nor are their study samples typically as large or the number of significant loci detected as numerous (Visscher et al. 2012b). In the largest psychiatric GWA study to date, which included approximately 60,000 cases and controls, Smoller and colleagues (2013) sought variants of shared association across five disorders: autism spectrum disorder, attention deficit-hyperactivity disorder, bipolar disorder, major depressive disorder, and schizophrenia. Their analysis showed evidence of common genetic contribution across several adult-onset psychiatric phenotypes and implicated calcium channel pathways as a potential mechanism. Nonetheless, identified SNPs from this and prior studies typically account for a maximum of 3% to 6% of the variance in diverse behavioral disorders (e.g., Anney et al. 2012, Major Depress. Disord. Work. Group Psychiatr. GWAS Consort. et al. 2013, Psychiatr. GWAS Consort. Bipolar Disord. Work. Group 2011, Saccone et al. 2010, Schizophr. Psychiatr. GWAS Consort. 2011, Smoller et al. 2013, Sullivan et al. 2012). Similarly, few GWA signals have emerged for general cognitive abilities in either children or adults (e.g., Benyamin et al. 2013, Davies et al. 2011, Docherty et al. 2010) or, aside from *APOE*, for cognitive decline with aging (e.g., De Jager et al. 2012). Finally, a few GWA studies have examined major personality traits (e.g., de Moor et al. 2012, Service et al. 2012, Terracciano et al. 2010, van den Oord et al. 2008, Verweij et al. 2010), but again show only sporadic associations. Also, most of these reflect nominal (not genomewide) significance, rarely replicate in independent samples, and in no instance account for more than about 1% of variance in the associated trait.

The Missing Heritability

Do the limitations of linkage analysis, equivocal candidate gene associations, and so-far limited yield on GWA studies signal fundamental problems in gene detection or merely obstacles in the path of discovery? With respect to GWA studies at least, proponents might argue that GWA not only is suited to identifying most common variants for complex traits and disorders, but in fact has achieved much already. By one recent estimate, GWA studies have found over 2,000 phenotype-associated loci since 2007, nearly all previously unknown and providing as many new targets for biological investigation (Visscher et al. 2012a). To the point that GWA studies tend only to find variants of small effect, aggregating top GWA "hits" into multilocus composites, or genetic risk scores, can amplify phenotype prediction and has shown some utility in clinical research. For instance, a genetic risk score composed of 13 SNPs derived from GWA studies of myocardial infarction and coronary heart disease modestly predicted incident coronary disease and atherosclerosis in the Framingham Heart Study (Thanassoulis et al. 2012), and a composite of the BMI-associated variants identified by Speliotes et al. (2010) predicted rapid juvenile growth and later obesity in a longitudinally studied birth cohort (Belsky et al. 2012).

Still, the phenotypic variance accounted for by all SNPs of genomewide significance is minimal for nearly all outcomes and rarely exceeds 10% (Manolio et al. 2009). This proportion is even lower for behavioral traits and disorders, where 5% or less of the variance is commonly explained and only a handful of SNPs have been identified with robust significance (Plomin 2013). In contrast, biometric family studies (e.g., twin studies) typically show genetic influences accounting for 30% to 50% of individual differences in most behavioral traits (Turkheimer 2000). Specific cognitive abilities have somewhat greater genetic variance, and in some psychopathologies, such as schizophrenia and autism, genetic liability may reach 80% or 90% (Plomin et al. 2008). How is it that these genetic effects can be so appreciable and yet the sum of SNPs detected in GWA studies explains only a fraction of heritable differences among individuals? Where is the remaining genetic variation? This question is widely known as the problem of the "missing heritability" (Maher 2008).

Where Is the Missing Heritability?

Several possibilities have been prominently discussed. First, many phenotype-associated loci may be of small effect size and difficult to isolate individually. A recently developed quantitative method, labeled genomewide complex trait analysis, permits estimation of the collective actions of all loci genotyped on GWA arrays (Lee et al. 2011, Yang et al. 2011) and has shown much heritable variation captured in their cumulative effects. Basically, this approach quantifies the genetic relatedness of paired combinations of subjects in a GWA sample using all genotyped SNPs, then asks how strongly this index of genetic similarity covaries with pairwise similarity in the study phenotype. Genetic variation estimated by this technique explained 30% to 40% of the variance in schizophrenia and bipolar disorder (Visscher et al. 2012b), around 30% of the variance in major depression (Lubke et al. 2012), 40% to 50% of individual differences in intelligence (Chabris et al. 2012, Davies et al. 2011, Plomin et al. 2012); 20% of variation in smoking-related phenotypes (Lubke et al. 2012), and ~4% to 12% of the variance in various personality traits (Verweij et al. 2012, Vinkhuyzen et al. 2012). These estimates, even the smallest, far exceed the sum of individual GWA-identified SNPs for corresponding traits and disorders and suggest that many, probably thousands, of variants of extremely small effect underlie much of the heritable variation in these phenotypes. The fact that they elude detection in traditional GWA analyses follows from their tiny effect sizes, which only the statistical power afforded by enormous study samples could accommodate. Hence, it is not surprising that most GWA studies of behavior yield few "hits" of genomewide significance, and virtually all conclude with a plea for ever larger samples.

Still, estimates of heritability are generally larger in traditional twin and family studies than those cited above from genomewide trait analysis. This suggests there is genetic variation not tagged by the million and more SNPs now genotyped on DNA microarrays. Because their intent is to encompass common variation, commercial chips usually emphasize SNPs for which the frequency of the less prevalent allele (the minor allele frequency) is >5%, although more recent arrays may include SNPs with a minor allele frequency as low as 1% to 2%. But SNPs of very low minor allele frequency (e.g., <0.05%) are not well captured, leading to the hypothesis that some heritable variation might be carried by rare causal variants, many of which could exert moderate or large effects but require extensive DNA sequencing to identify (Cirulli & Goldstein 2010, Manolio et al. 2009).

Other genetic influences could reside in structural variants of DNA that are also poorly tagged on existing microarrays. In one class of structural variation, called copy number variants, large genomic segments are duplicated a varying number of times, and some copy number variants have been associated with schizophrenia, autism, and mental retardation (Conrad et al. 2010, Sullivan et al. 2012). These often have large effects (in schizophrenia, for instance, odds ratios range from 3 to >20), but because they are also extremely rare, account for little variance overall (Sullivan et al. 2012, Visscher et al. 2012b). Another reason heritability estimates may be larger in twin modeling, compared to genomewide analysis from SNP arrays, is that twin studies reflect both additive and nonadditive genetic variance, which includes genetic dominance and gene-gene interactions (epistasis). Although estimated nonadditive genetic effects in twin studies tend to be small for most behavioral phenotypes, it is possible that some of the genetic variance eluding GWA detection lies in interactions among genes (Plomin 2013). Hence, the so-called missing heritability may be attributed to a combination of causes, including a very large number of common variants of very small effect size, rare variants to which GWA studies are insensitive, additionally rare structural variations, and perhaps some gene-gene interaction.

Is There a Role for G × E Interaction?

Yet a further possibility is that some or much genetic variation is expressed conditionally, as a function of environmental factors to which some, but not all, individuals are exposed (Manolio et al. 2009, Plomin 2013, Sullivan et al. 2012, Uher 2008). This implies a statistical interaction between defined genotypes and differing environmental exposures—molecular G × E interaction, or more accurately, genotype-environment interaction. Such interactions would tend to dilute genetic "main effects" if exposure to a predisposing environment is limited in a study population and if the genetic variation examined has little effect outside that environment. Conversely, genetic effects might be detected more readily if sought in samples enriched for key environmental exposures. Although often mentioned only briefly in commentaries on missing heritability, the idea that genetic influences vary over diverse environments is not new and has been studied in animal models for many years (Plomin et al. 2008).

The earliest prominent behavioral studies of human G × E interactions were rooted conceptually in the diathesis-stress model of disease risk, which dates from the early 1960s. This model hypothesizes genetic vulnerabilities to mental disorders that are expressed when susceptible individuals encounter life adversities. G × E interactions have attracted interest elsewhere as well, as in agricultural genetics, where their experimental study informs the commercial viability of new genetic strains under varying soil and climate conditions (Crossa 2012), as well as in cancer genetics, where heritable variation and lifestyle are likely entwined in the origins of most common cancers (Hunter 2005), and in environmental genetics, where exposure rates for major toxins (pollution, chemical exposures) vary across populations (e.g., Thomas 2010a). Thus, in addition to their possible contribution to gene discovery, G × E interactions may be pursued with a variety of aims—to test conceptual models of development and disease risk, define boundaries of genetic and environmental influences, and identify individuals most susceptible to risk exposures or most amenable to preventive and therapeutic interventions.

Another reason to posit G × E interaction is suggested by Uher (2009), who notes that common psychopathologies, such as major depression and anxiety disorders, confer a small reproductive disadvantage. Even a slight reduction in fertility would ordinarily suffice to remove a harmful genetic variant through negative selection, so that the persistence of such alleles and their associated disorders presents a paradox. The pressure of selection will be relaxed, but not eliminated, if many persons carrying a risk allele do not experience the disorder, as would happen if the disorder's occurrence requires both the risk allele and exposure to a predisposing, and possibly infrequent, environmental "pathogen." Moreover, if the same genotype bestows a benefit in other environments or in circumstances prevailing at other times, and if this confers reproductive advantage, the implicated allele could persist in the population indefinitely. Such G × E interactions would be consistent, too, with evidence of strong environmental risk factors and with observed regional and temporal differences in incidence rates of these disorders.

The same is not likely to explain persistence of more severe mental disorders, however, such as schizophrenia, bipolar disorder, and autism, which are far less prevalent, have very high heritability, and profoundly depress reproductive fitness (Power et al. 2013). Instead, these disorders may reflect a chance aggregation of deleterious alleles that are of recent origin, rare, and subject to strong negative selection. The rate at which new mutations arise may be sufficient to offset the rate at which existing ones are selected against (termed mutation-selection balance), so that these disorders endure at stable, but low, frequencies over time. That these disorders show limited variation in incidence across geographic regions and cultures and are more likely to occur with a later paternal age (which increases risk of acquiring new mutations) are consistent with this hypothesis, as are the related discoveries of several rare structural variants (e.g., copy number variants), some of which appear to have arisen de novo in affected individuals (Sullivan et al. 2012, Visscher et al. 2012b). Altogether, the foregoing arguments suggest different pathways to different psychopathologies and anticipate that G × E interactions will figure prominently in the most common of these disorders (Uher 2009).

LATENT VARIABLE G × E INTERACTION

Heritability estimates reflect the proportion of phenotypic variation due to genetic differences among individuals of a given population, as seen at a particular time and in a particular environment or range of environments. Elsewhere, or in a different mix of environments, a trait's heritability may be either greater or smaller, and even if the same, whatever genetic variation predicts trait variability in one environment might differ in another. In a twin study of stress-elicited physiological responses, for instance, several cardiovascular measurements (e.g., heart rate, blood pressure) were obtained while study participants sat at rest and during performance of frustrating cognitive and psychomotor tasks (De Geus et al. 2007). The twin analyses revealed two kinds of genetic effects: those common to cardiovascular measurements obtained both at rest and under stress, and new genetic variation that emerged only during stress. The latter indicates a gene × stress (G × E) interaction in which some genes modulate cardiovascular reactions under stress but do not affect variation in the same parameters at rest. This finding suggests, too, that discovering specific genes contributing to cardiovascular regulation will benefit from observations made in multiple environments, including those that perturb resting-state functioning. The same may be anticipated for other phenotypes as well, when genetic variances are imperfectly correlated across different environments (De Geus et al. 2007).

The preceding example involved behavioral testing in two distinct settings, whereas most biometric family studies are blind to the environments participants experience. Instead, effects of heredity and environment are inferred alone from phenotypic differences and similarities among persons who vary in genetic relatedness or rearing background (Plomin et al. 2008). The correlation of a trait (phenotype) among identical twins reared in different families, for instance, sets an upper limit on heritability, since they share all genetic variation and are raised in unrelated (uncorrelated) environments. Conversely, any difference between the phenotypic correlation and unity (i.e., the difference from a coefficient of 1.0) reflects dissimilarity between identical cotwins resulting from their individual, or unique, experiences (termed nonshared environment), plus any error of measurement. In another comparison, phenotypic correlations among paired siblings reared in the same family, but where one or both were adopted (genetically unrelated), denote similarities of phenotype attributable to their shared family environments. Since the latter inference does not rely on measuring actual attributes of the shared environment, though, these effects could reflect any factor on which families differ, such as parenting styles, socioeconomic status, diet, or neighborhood characteristics.

The logic underlying these inferences is less obvious when extended to the bulk of reported twin studies, where cotwins share genetic variation and are also raised in the same family. Yet because identical and fraternal (dizygotic) twins differ in their genetic relatedness by an average of 50% (and assuming that identical and fraternal twins experience their shared environments equally), the total phenotypic variance can be partitioned algebraically into genetic and environmental components. In these analyses, structural equations are commonly used to relate observed phenotypes to latent (unobserved) genetic and environmental determinants and to test competing models in which additive and nonadditive genetic components, and shared and nonshared environmental parameters, are added or removed to identify a best-fitting model. These analyses are insensitive, however, to any differences in genetic effects that might occur over an unmeasured gradient of shared environmental experience (e.g., warm or harsh parenting), as these will be concealed in the estimate of additive genetic variance. Recognizing this limitation, advances in twin structural modeling have been introduced recently that permit the incorporation of measured environmental variables, thus allowing estimation of environmentally moderated genetic influences (Purcell 2002). Such latent variable G × E interaction has now been shown for several behavioral phenotypes.

In one example, the heritability of trait positive and negative emotionality among late adolescents varied by quality of parental relationships, namely the degree of positive regard experienced by study participants (Krueger et al. 2008). The proportion of trait variation due to genetic influences differed about twofold over a range of ± 2 standard deviations in parental positive regard, from strong genetic effects at the high end of positive regard to much weaker effects at the low end of this distribution. Likewise, heritable differences in childhood IQ have been found to vary from ~10% to 70% over a gradient of low to high childhood socioeconomic status in the United States (Turkheimer et al. 2003). This finding has replicated in most other US studies of childhood IQ but not in studies of European cohorts or of predominantly postadolescent samples (reviewed in Hanscombe et al. 2012). These discrepancies await elucidation but may reflect national differences in educational and family support services affecting disadvantaged youth and, in relation to older study cohorts, further moderation by known age-related changes in genetic effects on cognitive abilities.

Cultural and institutional factors that proscribe or channel personal conduct, such as social norms, regulations, or legal restrictions and prohibitions, might also act to restrict genetic influences on behavior, whereas their absence may allow for a wider expression of genetic differences among individuals (Shanahan & Hofer 2005). Variation in such social control might explain why patterns of alcohol use appear to be less heritable in persons with a religious upbringing (Koopmans et al. 1999) and among those living in rural or more stable communities (Dick et al. 2001, Rose et al. 2001) and why stronger genetic effects on adolescent drinking are seen where peer substance use is prevalent or parental monitoring deficient (Dick et al. 2007a,b). Similarly with respect to cigarette smoking, the heritability of daily smoking among adolescents and young adults is lowest where cigarette taxes are high, tobacco products are not easily obtained, and cigarette advertising is restricted (Boardman 2009).

A third health-related behavior, physical activity, also interacts with latent genetic variation in predicting adiposity, with stronger genetic effects on BMI in sedentary individuals than among the more physically active (e.g., McCaffery et al. 2009, Mustelin et al. 2009). These findings, and other literatures showing genetic effects to vary by environment, suggest that some or much associated molecular variation will likewise interact with environmental factors (Dick 2011). For instance, shortly after discovery of the BMI-associated *FTO* gene, *FTO* susceptibility alleles were found related to adiposity more strongly in persons of sedentary (versus active) lifestyle (e.g., Andreasen et al. 2008, Kilpelainen et al. 2011). Although the earliest of these studies preceded evidence of activity-dependent variation in the heritability of BMI, other latent variable G × E findings would also suggest the likelihood of interactions involving specific genotypes and environmental moderators (Dick et al. 2009, Latendresse et al. 2011).

CHALLENGES OF G × E RESEARCH

Having good reason to posit G × E interactions doesn't assure their discovery, and investigators differ on how best to pursue G × E research with measured genotypes and in their interpretations of existing evidence. Like candidate gene studies generally, G × E findings have been challenged for limited replication and vulnerability to publication bias. In addition, tests of interactions are susceptible to scaling artifacts, and inadequate statistical power may undermine the reliability of many reported G × E results. In discussing several of these concerns, we suggest that some seemingly contentious issues in this field may partly reflect differences of approach between two disciplines with a shared interest in G × E research, statistical genetics and psychology.

A "Main Effect" Predicate for G × E Research?

Some disagreement surrounds what prior evidence is needed to advance a G × E hypothesis, and particularly, whether a polymorphism suggested for G × E must already demonstrate association with the outcome of interest (that is, exert a main effect on the study phenotype). Consider two examples. The first is the aforementioned interaction of *FTO* with level of physical activity, in which effects of *FTO* genotype on adiposity are greatest among people who are least physically active (Kilpelainen et al. 2011). In the second, a variant of the gene encoding brain-derived neurotrophic factor (*BDNF*) was recently associated with poorer working memory performance among midlife men and women, and here too, only among those who are least physically active (Erickson et al. 2013). These two interactions are analogous but forwarded on different grounds. *FTO* was selected as a candidate for G × E after GWA studies found it related to adiposity, and physical activity was selected as a moderator because it is known to variably affect body weight. In the second example, Erickson et al. (2013) cite several observations in nominating *BDNF* as a candidate for G × E research on cognition. These include widespread expression of BDNF in the brain, which supports neuronal and synaptic function; polymorphic variation in the *BDNF* gene, encoding substitution of a methionine (Met) for valine (Val) amino acid in the BDNF protein; and an inconsistent literature associating the *BDNF* Met allele with deficits in episodic and working memory performance, in which heterogeneity of effect sizes suggested possible stratification by unmeasured moderators (Mandelman & Grigorenko 2012). Additionally, extended exercise improves cognitive function and increases serum BDNF levels in humans, and physical activity improves learning and memory in rodent models, mediated by enhanced BDNF production and secretion (summarized in Erickson et al. 2013). Together, these observations suggested that physical activity may benefit cognitive functioning through a BDNF mechanism, and to that extent, such effects might differ in magnitude with functional variation in the *BDNF* gene.

Thus, in the example of *BDNF*, the rationale for positing a G × E interaction draws on multiple streams of evidence—from neurogenetics, experimental neuroscience, and studies in physical training—to postulate a common pathway linking genotype, activity level, and cognition. It is theoretically grounded and hypothesis driven in a way many psychologists would find familiar. In this instance, justification is also undeterred by the equivocal literature on *BDNF* main effects and thus differs from the GWA-based G × E approach exemplified by the interaction of *FTO* and physical activity. When the first of the *FTO* G × E studies were published, little was known about the function of *FTO* or how it might affect relevant metabolic processes, so that only the fact that *FTO* exerted a main effect on obesity risk nominated it for G × E interaction. Understandably so, since GWA is an atheoretical approach to gene discovery that is meant to find phenotype-associated genetic variation without regard to known functionality or prior biological plausibility. But beyond that, some statistical geneticists elevate the gene "main effect" to a predicate for G × E investigation, arguing that only genetic variants of "compelling association" in GWA studies most warrant interrogation for interaction with environmental exposures (Psychiatr. GWAS Consort. Steer. Comm. 2009). Others invoke the lack of a marginal main effect as well to critique candidate gene G × E studies, which often exploit polymorphisms of absent or checkered main effect histories (Risch et al. 2009). Of course, this reasoning also negates a key argument for G × E studies, that gene associations may be amplified, and therefore more readily detected, when examined in the context of predisposing environments (Caspi et al. 2010, Dick 2011, Moffitt et al. 2006). Moffitt et al. (2006) aptly framed this negation as a logical paradox, where a G × E interaction impedes its own discovery by weakening the genetic main effect on which its investigation is dependent.

Our point is not to discount direct effects of genetic variation but instead to suggest limitations imposed when insisting that they precede G × E consideration. Another limitation is the paucity of "compelling" associations found for behavioral phenotypes in GWA studies, which generates few candidates to probe for G × E interaction. On the other hand, GWA-inspired G × E interactions, when found, are as cogent as hypothesis-driven findings, and like GWA studies generally, have the added potential to identify novel biological mechanisms. GWA-derived multilocus composites can be exploited in G × E research as well. For instance, high parental negativity and a chaotic home environment were found recently to accentuate effects of a ten-SNP genetic risk score on children's mathematical abilities (Docherty et al. 2011). And finally, many genetic epidemiologists do not adhere dogmatically to the marginal genetic main effect as a predicate for G × E research but embrace G × E interaction as a possible aid in gene discovery and to elucidate variability in responses to common environmental risk factors (Thomas 2010b).

Scaling and Models

In an early G × E experiment, Krafka (1920) reported that the number of facets in the compound eye of *Drosophila* varied inversely with manipulated rearing temperature and that temperature affected facet number more strongly in one genetic strain than in another. Some years later, this experiment became the subject of a controversy between the statistician, Ronald Fisher, and embryologist, Lancelot Hogben. To puncture Hogben's enthusiasm for G × E effects on development, Fisher argued that interactions can be artifacts of the metrics used in their analysis and showed that expressing facet number logarithmically removed the interaction from Krafka's data. As interpreted by Tabery (2008), Fisher was motivated to dismiss G × E interactions from prior studies of strain and soil effects on crop variation, where such interactions were not prominent, and perhaps also by the eugenic social biology he espoused, where conditional genetic effects would impede eugenic selection to improve human "stock." Notwithstanding that Fisher made his case by transforming a variable of absolute scale (a counted object, no less), the proper scale of measurement for many behavioral variables is unknown. Can we confidently assume, for instance, that twice the score on a trait anxiety scale denotes twice the level of an anxious disposition or that severity of a mental disorder tracks with a simple count of symptoms? Sensitivity of a G × E interaction to scaling effects will vary by phenotype and moderator and may be greatest for ordinal interactions in which the influence of one predictor (e.g., an environmental exposure) varies by degree, but not direction, with the level of another (e.g., genotype) (Thomas 2010a). Whatever the prevalence of scale-dependent effects, though, confidence in a G × E interaction will be enhanced if shown for measurements having different metric properties as well as for different indicators of the same construct (Dick 2011, Hyde et al. 2011, Moffitt et al. 2006).

In addition to scaling artifacts, how an interaction is tested for deviation from main effects can affect the likelihood of its detection. For instance, if an interaction is modeled as the product of relative risks conferred by two predisposing factors, as commonly done in predicting diagnostic status for a disorder, the bar on claiming an interaction is set higher than if it is modeled as a departure from additive risks. Which is the more appropriate model for testing interactions cannot be adjudicated on statistical grounds and is a perennial source of controversy in epidemiology (Rothman et al. 2008). Another complicating factor is the potential for erroneous G × E findings when logistic regression is used for analysis of categorical outcomes (Kendler 2011). This was shown by Eaves (2006), for instance, when dichotomizing variables of continuous distribution for analysis as binary outcomes in G × E simulations produced a high rate of spurious interactions. On the other hand, model-dependent differences also may be overstated, as G × E interactions on the multiplicative and additive models are similar when one or both predictors are independently weak, which has generally been true for genetic main effects (Uher 2008, 2011).

Power, Replication, and Publication Bias

Statistical power and replication woes stalk G × E interaction as aggressively as they do GWA and candidate-gene association studies (Munafo & Flint 2009). Rules of thumb abound, as that G × E interactions require samples four times larger than are needed to find genetic main effects or that G × E research requires samples in the thousands (for candidate genes) or tens of thousands (for GWA studies) (Thomas 2010b). Power to detect a G × E interaction can vary by a number of factors, including effect size, distribution of genotypes, quality of measurement, proximity of the phenotype to biological actions of the implicated gene, and rates of exposure to the environmental moderator. With respect to the latter, if a risk allele affects a study phenotype in environment A and not in environment B, an associated G × E interaction will be most readily observed when samples are drawn equally from the two environments. If sampled from A or B alone, however, the interaction cannot be seen at all for lack of variance in the moderating environments. Thus, an underlying biological interaction that involves a causal genetic variant with environmentally modulated phenotypic effects may or may not be observed as a statistical interaction at the population level, depending on the distribution of environmental exposures sampled (Rutter 2010; Uher 2008, 2011; Uher & McGuffin 2008).

Nor is a genetic main effect necessarily easier to detect than an interaction. Caspi et al. (2010) modeled power to identify an ordinal G × E of moderate effect size in simulations involving samples of 1,000 individuals, with genotypes of equal frequency and varying exposure rates for a nominal environmental moderator. With very low exposure, neither a genetic main effect nor the G × E interaction is readily detected. Power to identify the main effect exceeds that of the interaction when a majority of individuals are exposed to the "predisposing" environment, and yet the reverse holds at lesser, but nontrivial, exposure rates. Power is also qualified by variation in the distribution of genotypes and recedes as minor alleles become less common. Of course, observational studies are necessarily constrained by the population frequencies of genetic variants and by naturally occurring variability in environmental exposures. Experimental studies, such as laboratory-based paradigms or randomized clinical trials, offer enhanced power to test G × E hypotheses and allow causal inferences not permitted in correlational designs (Thomas 2010a,b; Uher 2011; van IJzendoorn et al. 2011). Here, exposure rate is controlled by random assignment to study conditions and, if participants are selected from a pool of previously genotyped individuals, distribution of genotypes can be equalized as well (Caspi et al. 2010). Finally, power to detect G × E interactions should increase when either the phenotype or environmental moderator is measured with heightened precision (van der Sluis et al. 2010) or, as in neuroimaging and psychophysiological protocols, when dependent variables reflect intermediate behavioral or biological processes that genetic differences may influence more directly than distal phenotypes, such as complex traits and disorders (Hariri 2009, Hyde et al. 2011).

Inadequate statistical power is one reason a true $G \times E$ interaction might not be observed or a previously reported $G \times E$ may fail to replicate. Obviously, replication is essential to the credibility of any finding, although the aims of successor studies may vary and do not always conduce to exact replication. At present, meta-analysis is our preferred arbiter of valid findings, requiring multiple studies of comparable method and outcome that claim to test the same hypothesis. Comparability can be ambiguous, though, in the sense that two measured variables might be equivalent in one frame of reference, but not another. Consider that there are many adversities of early childhood, such as material privation, family discord, emotional neglect, or physical and sexual abuse. If early adversity is indexed by childhood abuse in an initial $G \times E$ study predicting a later psychopathology, a subsequent study using a different indicator of adversity (e.g., insensitive parenting) might be represented variously as a direct replication, a replication attempt of trivial difference (e.g., due to working from a different set of available measurements), or a deliberate attempt to probe the boundaries of childhood experiences pertinent to this $G \times E$ interaction. How it is framed will inform our interpretation of the second study's positive or negative outcome. And from the perspective of $G \times E$ hypotheses grounded in a theoretical framework, the interpretation of a particular interaction will also draw on a consilience of observations by other methodologies that more broadly confirm predictions from an underlying construct (Caspi et al. 2010).

That said, the essential importance of replication cannot be gainsaid, and it is sobering that a recent survey of $G \times E$ studies in psychiatric research found only about one-quarter of studies following up 10 original $G \times E$ findings to have replicated successfully (Duncan & Keller 2011). These authors interpreted the poor replication rate as indicative of editorial biases favoring publication of novel $G \times E$ findings and cited other ways in which publication bias may generate a skewed literature. These include less frequent replication among later studies; instances of cryptic $G \times E$ replication, in which an analogous, but previously untested, $G \times E$ finding is reported beside a failure to confirm the original interaction; and a preponderance of smaller, poorly powered studies among "successful" replications. These are not unique to $G \times E$ studies, of course, nor definitive, as the enhanced power of larger studies, for instance, can be offset if accompanied by weaker measurements of environment or outcome. Still, the centrality of replication means that finding robust $G \times E$ interactions requires meeting the challenge of their repeated observation.

PSYCHOLOGICAL MODELS OF $G \times E$ INTERACTION

Psychology got a head start on $G \times E$ interaction when, 50 years ago, Meehl (1962) hypothesized a genetic vulnerability to schizophrenia, a single "schizogene" that predisposed individuals to the fully expressed disorder when co-occurring with ambivalent and inconsistent maternal parenting. Later theorizing posited multiple genetic influences, different environmental risk factors, and extension of the framework to other mental disorders to form the diathesis-stress model of psychopathology (Monroe & Simons 1991, Zuckerman 1999). Until recently, support rested on family studies, as when "latent" genetic liability is inferred among twins from differences in twin-pair zygosity and in cotwin diagnostic status along a continuum from low (fraternal cotwin, unaffected) to high (identical cotwin, affected) risk. High genetic risk defined in this manner, for instance, was shown to magnify effects of maltreatment on children's risk for conduct problems (Jaffee et al. 2005) and of stressful life events on women's risk for major depression (Kendler et al. 1995). Now the same $G \times E$ hypotheses are routinely tested on the molecular level as interactions between specific genotypes and the same environmental moderators (Caspi et al. 2002, 2003).

The diathesis-stress (or vulnerability) model reflects a predominant interest in disorders of functioning and their etiologies, yet genetic variation is potentially just as relevant to positive outcomes, beneficial traits, and responses to interventions intended to enhance competent functioning. We have labeled as vantage sensitivity a form of G × E interaction in which benefits accrued in a favorable environment are likewise modulated by genetic variation (Sweitzer et al. 2013), and this model is formalized in further treatment by Pluess & Belsky (2013). On a third model, now commonly referred to as differential susceptibility, some genetic variation is thought to portend both greater vulnerability to adversity and an increased responsiveness to advantage, rather than valenced sensitivity to environments that are either, and specifically, adverse or propitious. This potential for disordinal (or cross-over) interactions has been wedded to theoretical frameworks in developmental psychology that posit variability in individuals' responsiveness to environmental influences that can be either positive or negative (Belsky & Pluess 2009, Boyce & Ellis 2005). In the following sections, we discuss some considerations pertinent to each of the three models.

Diathesis-Stress (Vulnerability) Model

The bulk of G × E research comports with this model, if only because most investigators have focused on genetic influences moderated by adversities. The range of studied phenotypes is broad, including major psychopathologies and personality traits; children's cognitive and social development; physiological responses to naturally occurring stressors, life events, or trauma; and, in experimental studies, behavioral, autonomic, or neuroendocrine reactions to acute psychological challenges, as well as neural responses to threat-related cues in brain circuitries of emotion processing (Hariri 2009, Hyde et al. 2011, Manuck & McCaffery 2010). Much of this research, particularly that addressed to distal behavioral traits and disorders, has so far produced only small literatures, often of just a few studies. Thus, it is difficult presently to gauge the strength of individual findings, and given the diversity of study outcomes, problematic to aggregate over topical literatures that share only a common interpretive framework. Notable exceptions are two studies describing genotype-dependent environmental influences on risk for antisocial behavior and depression, respectively, in a longitudinally studied birth cohort (Caspi et al. 2002, 2003). Now cited over 8,000 times, these two studies largely kick started the current era of psychological research on G × E interactions, and the literatures they generated now include over 80 replication attempts or attempted extensions of the initial studies as well as ancillary literatures of mechanistic interest.

Monoamine oxidase-A, childhood adversity, and antisocial behavior. In the first study, exposure to maltreatment in childhood, such as physical or sexual abuse, maternal rejection, or harsh physical punishment, predicted later male aggressive and antisocial behaviors, and this association varied by genotype of a promoter polymorphism in the gene encoding the degradative enzyme monoamine oxidase-A (*MAOA*) (Caspi et al. 2002). Effects of maltreatment on boys' later conduct problems, antisocial disposition, and violent offending were greater in individuals with an *MAOA* variant of lesser transcriptional efficiency (low-activity *MAOA* genotype) than among those carrying an alternate (high-activity) allele. The interaction was corroborated in a majority of initial replication reports involving other male samples recruited from nonpatient populations and was confirmed in an early meta-analysis of eight studies (Taylor & Kim-Cohen 2007). Since then many additional reports have been published, including further studies of early maltreatment, studies examining other environmental moderators (e.g., socioeconomic disadvantage, peer deviance, parenting styles, maternal prenatal smoking), and studies of females. In a recent meta-analysis of 27 independent studies, childhood maltreatment was again found to presage antisocial outcomes more strongly in males of low-activity, relative to high-activity, *MAOA* genotype ($P = 0.0000008$) (Byrd & Manuck 2013). The interaction did not extend to the aggregate of other early-life adversities, and in females, high-activity *MAOA* genotype predicted greater antisocial behavior in those who were also maltreated, but only weakly and inconsistently. In sum, *MAOA* variation appears to moderate effects of childhood adversity on males' aggressive and antisocial behaviors, specifically among studies that, like the initial report, targeted boys' early experiences of abuse, neglect, or other ill treatment.

The serotonin transporter gene, life stress, and depression. In the second influential study, both recent stressful life events and childhood maltreatment predicted later depression more strongly in young adults carrying the short (S) variant of a length polymorphism in the regulatory region of the serotonin transporter gene (5-HTTLPR) relative to individuals homozygous for the long (L) allele (Caspi et al. 2003). As with the prior study on *MAOA* variation and antisocial behavior, many investigators quickly attempted replication of this key early $G \times E$ finding, and several narrative and meta-analytic reviews followed. Two prominently reported meta-analyses, published in 2009, failed to confirm the interaction of 5-HTTLPR and life events on depression (Munafo et al. 2009a, Risch et al. 2009). Subsequent commentaries pointed to several limitations of these analyses, noting that they included only a small number of relevant investigations, over-sampled from studies of negative outcome, excluded maltreatment studies and those exploiting exposures to a common stressor, and with respect to studies of enumerated life events, relied disproportionately on self-report inventories (which are subject to recall biases and other reporting inaccuracies) rather than contextually sensitive interviews or objective indicators of stress (Rutter et al. 2009, Uher & McGuffin 2010). In a further meta-analysis that included all available literature, Karg et al. (2011) confirmed the interaction of 5-HTTLPR genotype and life stress exposures on depression and depressive symptomatology across 54 published studies ($P = 0.00002$). Consistent with the critiques of earlier reviews, stratified analyses showed variation across studies of differing methodology. The interaction was robust in studies of childhood maltreatment, in cohorts exposed to a common stressor, and in studies with objective measures of stress exposure or assessing life events by structured interview. In contrast, 5-HTTLPR genotype interacted only marginally with self-reported life events.

As replicable examples of environmentally moderated genetic vulnerability (diathesis stress), it is not surprising that these two seminal studies have continued to inspire wide interest in $G \times E$ interactions. Their interpretation is further informed by related literatures studying the same genetic variation via other methodologies. For instance, persons of low-activity *MAOA* genotype may perform more poorly on tests of executive processing (e.g., working memory, attentional control) with diminished engagement of frontal brain regions supporting these processes, indicating a possible deficit in inhibitory control underlying the restraint of aggressive and antisocial impulses (e.g., Byrd & Manuck 2013, Cerasa et al. 2008, Enge et al. 2011, Fan et al. 2003, Meyer-Lindenberg et al. 2006). With respect to 5-HTTLPR, a variety of evidence suggests that the S-allele heightens sensitivity to stress. This is seen in cognition, as an increased vigilance, or attentional bias, toward negative emotional stimuli (Pergamin-Hight et al. 2012); in peripheral physiology, as heightened cortisol reactivity to acute psychological stressors (Miller et al. 2013); and on neuroimaging, as enhanced reactivity to threat-related stimuli in the amygdala, accompanied by altered neural coupling with prefrontal regulatory regions (Drabant et al. 2012, Hariri et al. 2005, Munafo et al. 2008a). These and other observations from human and animal research are consistent with the hypothesis that these polymorphisms provide a genetic substrate for individual differences in sensitivity to life adversities.

Vantage Sensitivity

The notion that genetic variation might also moderate positive effects of exposure to salutary environments is not so much a novel concept as a logical complement to the diathesis-stress (vulnerability) framework. And although observational studies of naturally occurring adversities dominate G × E research on mental disorders and other problematic behaviors, intervention studies and studies of health-promoting behaviors more commonly illustrate vantage sensitivity. As an example, nicotinic receptor gene variations associated with frequency of smoking in a community sample were recently found to predict successful abstinence among individuals assigned to active treatment arms of a smoking cessation trial, relative to placebo-treated controls (Chen et al. 2012). Similarly, several developmental studies have found benefits of favorable environmental exposures moderated by variation in *DRD4*. Children carrying the 7-repeat variant of a common *DRD4* length polymorphism were more likely to exhibit prosocial behaviors, such as donating to a charity or sharing with others, when prompted experimentally or with increasing maternal positivity than were those of alternate *DRD4* genotype (Bakermans-Kranenburg & van IJzendoorn 2011, Knafo 2009, Knafo et al. 2011). Likewise, treatment to enhance maternal sensitivity and effective parenting preferentially reduced oppositional behavior in children with externalizing problems among those carrying the 7-repeat allele (Bakermans-Kranenburg & van IJzendoorn 2008). Although these studies offer evidence consistent with vantage sensitivity, it is noteworthy that some of the same genes that moderate positive outcomes in positive environments, like *DRD4*, are likewise prominent among G × E studies of risk incurred in adverse environments and thus also contribute to evidence for the differential susceptibility hypothesis (Pluess & Belsky 2013).

Differential Susceptibility

Some authors have found it peculiar that reported G × E interactions for mental disorders seldom involve genetic variants for which reliable main effects are found, either in the G × E studies themselves or in very large GWA investigations, and while acknowledging that cross-over interactions could accommodate the absence of a genetic main effect, view this possibility as unlikely (Boffetta et al. 2012, Risch et al. 2009). Conversely, we have noted Uher's argument that an allele conferring risk for a disorder associated with even a small reproductive disadvantage will tend to be removed by negative selection, so that persistence of the risk allele would seem to require compensating benefit at other times or in other circumstances (Uher 2009). This implies a disordinal interaction between the gene polymorphism and whatever environmental factors condition its cost and benefit. This is also the pattern of interaction defining differential susceptibility, which grew out of theorizing on individual differences in developmental plasticity. Belsky and colleagues (1991) proposed a theory of socialization that identified differences in developmental outcomes as conditional adaptations to rearing environments containing cues to either good or poor future life prospects and, at the same time, allowed for heritable variation in individuals' sensitivity to these cues. By this account, behavioral outcomes may differ most appreciably ("for better or for worse") across a gradient of favorable to unfavorable environments in persons who are genetically most susceptible to such influences (i.e., differential susceptibility) (Belsky & Pluess 2009). In related theorizing, Boyce & Ellis (2005) independently postulated individual differences in children's responsiveness to varying environmental "contexts" but were less explicit regarding a genetic origin of these differences (Ellis et al. 2011).

Consistent with its provenance in developmental psychology, the differential susceptibility framework has sought support from child and adolescent studies. Across multiple cohorts, for instance, youth carrying the 5-HTTLPR S-allele showed greater positive affect when experiencing supportive parenting and less positive affect with unsupportive parenting than did counterparts of alternate genotype (Hankin et al. 2011). This finding is reminiscent of the first clear demonstration of differential susceptibility, in which young adults who were homozygous for the 5-HTTLPR S-allele reported greater depressive symptomatology if reared in an adverse family environment or experiencing recent stressful life events and less depressive symptomatology if raised in supportive families or experiencing positive events, relative to those carrying the L-allele (Taylor et al. 2006). In another example, adults with the *DRD4* 7-repeat allele discounted future rewards more steeply if raised in socioeconomically stressed families and less steeply if reared in more advantaged circumstances, compared to like-reared study participants lacking the 7-repeat variant (Sweitzer et al. 2013).

These and other recent studies illustrate differential susceptibility as a reversal of allelic association across an environmental gradient in individuals of the same cohort. A second source of evidence comes from literatures testing G × E interactions separately on vulnerability and vantage sensitivity models for the same genetic variation. In the preceding section, we cited studies in which children exposed to positive parenting or prosocial experimental manipulations experienced more favorable outcomes if carrying the *DRD4* 7-repeat allele. In other studies and against a variety of developmental adversities (e.g., parenting deficiencies, maternal insensitivity, low socioeconomic status), the 7-repeat allele was associated with unfavorable child outcomes, such as disorganized infant attachment, heightened sensation seeking, and various externalizing behaviors (Bakermans-Kranenburg & van IJzendoorn 2006, Nobile et al. 2007, Sheese et al. 2007, Van IJzendoorn & Bakermans-Kranenburg 2006). In a meta-analysis of these and other child studies of dopamine system polymorphisms, genotype-dependent positive outcomes proved significant in positive environments, as did negative outcomes in adverse environments (Bakermans-Kranenburg & van IJzendoorn 2011). A similar conclusion was supported (albeit limited to white participants) on a meta-analysis of interactions involving 5-HTTLPR variation, as seen across 30 child and adolescent studies of behavioral and psychiatric outcomes, when effect sizes were again combined separately among investigations of either positive or negative environmental exposures (van IJzendoorn et al. 2012).

A challenge for the differential susceptibility model is to explain how a reversal of allelic association across favorable and unfavorable environments might occur. One obvious possibility would involve genetic influences on fundamental psychological processes that target no particular outcome but may be exploited to disparate effects in differing environments. For instance, the attentional bias toward negative emotional stimuli predicted by the 5-HTTLPR S-allele has been shown for positive stimuli as well (Fox et al. 2011). Thus, 5-HTTLPR variation might contribute to differences in individuals' sensitivity to external stimuli generally rather than vigilance directed toward the detection of threat alone (Pluess & Belsky 2013). Alternatively, a genetic variant could have multiple phenotypic effects (termed pleiotropy) that dispose to outcomes of differing valence, with environmental factors promoting the dominance of one over the other. Here, too, the 5-HTTLPR might serve as an example, as the S-allele has been related not only to indicators of heightened emotionality but also to better performance on certain cognitive tasks, such as reversal learning and attentional set-shifting (reviewed in Homberg & Lesch 2011). Conceivably, the first of these might be expressed preferentially in adverse environments and the second in circumstances advantaging competent cognitive functioning. A similar argument is offered by Sweitzer et al. (2013) with respect to *DRD4* variation, in which pleiotropic effects of the 7-repeat allele on both reward sensitivity and higher executive processes differentially affect risk-related decision making, modulated by early environmental influences on developing brain circuitries of regulatory control.

Despite positive evidence, the generality of differential susceptibility remains uncertain. Because few investigators have explicitly hypothesized disordinal G × E effects, some cited findings are supported only by visual inspection of plotted interaction terms rather than formal testing for bidirectional allelic associations. Recent papers have drawn attention to this deficiency and offered recommendations for distinguishing differential susceptibility from other forms of interaction, as by examining "regions of significance" or calculating the proportion of the interaction explained on either side of the crosspoint on the environmental axis (Roisman et al. 2012). A related risk in claiming evidence of differential susceptibility is the greater power to detect crossover interactions in standard regression models, owing to reduced, or absent, main effect variance. This suggests that spurious G × E interactions in underpowered samples are more likely to be attributed to differential susceptibility than to G × E models positing ordinal interactions (Dick 2011). Other limitations of current work on differential susceptibility include a restricted focus on just a few monoamine-regulating genes, principally in the serotonin and dopamine systems, and a paucity of literature outside of developmental research.

Plasticity Alleles?

One danger of framing G × E findings in psychological terms is the temptation to attribute purpose to genetic variants whose only actions are biological and distant from predicted phenotypes. Terms like vulnerability and vantage sensitivity are more accurately evaluative characterizations that label G × E interactions by the valence of their outcomes and environmental moderators, and even then require a consensual frame of reference. Many other such models might be conceived as well. For instance, the same pattern of interaction that comports with diathesis-stress (vulnerability) could also define a resilience model, in which persons possessing a protective genotype are spared undesired outcomes commonly occasioned by an adverse environmental exposure (Pluess & Belsky 2013). A related difficulty, also of terminology, attends a distinction now often made between so-called vulnerability alleles and alleles implicated in differential susceptibility, which are said to confer plasticity (e.g., Belsky et al. 2009). We suggest this distinction may be misleading, since all G × E interactions reflect genotype-dependent variation in phenotypic response to varying environmental conditions, or plasticity. Interpreting G × E interactions from a "reaction norm" perspective, which unites the several G × E models within a familiar biological framework, demonstrates this point (Manuck 2010).

A reaction norm refers to the range of phenotypic variation observable across different environments in individuals of the same genotype. For illustration, the lines drawn in **Figure 1** depict the reaction norms of three genotypes, *a*, *b*, and *c*. Each reaction norm denotes variation in an unnamed phenotype (on the ordinate) as a function of a hypothetical environmental variable (on the abscissa). Genotype *a* exhibits greater plasticity than either *b* or *c* because it produces a broader range of phenotype values across the gradient of environmental variation. The reaction norms of genotypes *b* and *c* are equivalently shallow and thus parallel, but *b* is displaced upward along the ordinate to yield a higher average phenotype than genotype *c*; this difference reflects a genetic main effect (G). Finally, a G × E interaction exists when two or more reaction norms differ in slope, indicating that their respective genotypes occasion different phenotypic responses over an identical range of environments (Stearns 1992). If the environmental factor in the figure were an index of good to poor parenting and the phenotype a measure of poor psychosocial adjustment, the interaction of *a* and *c* would exemplify the diathesis-stress (vulnerability) model and that of *a* and *b*, differential susceptibility.

What then distinguishes the psychological models of G × E interaction? It cannot be that differential susceptibility requires an allele of a particular quality, plasticity, that is lacking in the diathesis-stress model, since the reaction norm of genotype *a* is both constant and compatible with interactions involving either *b* or *c*. And if plasticity (great or small) is a property possessed of all genotypes, and all G × E interactions entail allele-specific differences in phenotypic plasticity, it is also true that the magnitude of such differences need not differ between the various interaction models. Rather, what distinguishes the disordinal interactions of differential susceptibility from

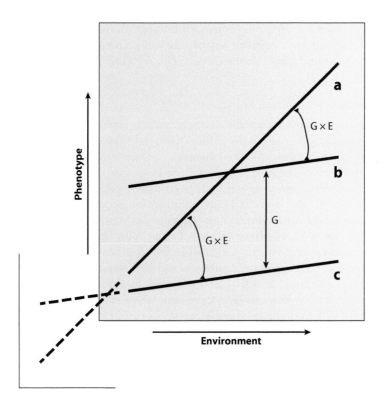

Figure 1

Reaction norms of three hypothetical genotypes: *a*, *b*, and *c*. Dashed lines depict hypothetical extension of reaction norms *a* and *c*. Abbreviations: G, genetic main effect; G × E, gene-environment interaction. Adapted from Manuck (2010).

ordinal interactions of the diathesis-stress (vulnerability) model is simply that, in differential susceptibility, different genotypes produce identical phenotypes at an intermediate location along an environmental gradient. If a phenotype of the same value is produced instead at either end of the gradient, the interaction is one of diathesis-stress or vantage sensitivity. Nonetheless, the form of the interaction is not the same as the conditions that give rise to it, and true disordinal interactions may well be overlooked in studies sampling from restricted ranges of phenotype or environment (Belsky & Pluess 2009). If the axes depicted in **Figure 1** capture only a portion of their natural ranges and could be extended meaningfully (dashed lines), for instance, the reaction norms of genotypes *a* and *c* would ultimately cross over to reveal an otherwise unrecognized instance of differential susceptibility.

THE ENVIRONMENT IN G × E INTERACTION

In this article, we have briefly reviewed the recent—and to some, frustrating—history of attempts to identify genetic variants underlying heritable variation in behavior; outlined some of the reasons offered in explanation of the "missing heritability," and among these, highlighted the possibility of prevalent G × E interactions; summarized points of common critique to which G × E research is vulnerable; and overviewed various conceptual frameworks that inform the interpretation of G × E interactions from a psychological perspective. Most of our discussion has focused on the genetic component of G × E interaction and has taken at face value whatever environmental parameter partnered in a given G × E finding or literature. In this concluding section, we turn to the environmental component explicitly, with two questions in mind: What does the environment do, and how truly "environmental" is the E in G × E interaction?

What Does the Environment Do?

In the most prosaic sense and perhaps also the most common, environments may simply afford (or impede) opportunities for the expression of behavioral propensities to which genotypes conduce. This was implicit, for instance, in several examples of latent variable G × E interactions cited previously, where heritable influences on smoking or alcohol use varied by religious upbringing (Koopmans et al. 1999), community attributes (e.g., urban/rural) (Dick et al. 2001, Rose et al. 2001), legal restrictions (Boardman 2009), peer substance use, or parental monitoring (Dick et al. 2007a,b). Some of these environmental variables have also been shown to moderate effects of individual polymorphisms on behavior (e.g., Dick et al. 2009, Latendresse et al. 2011). Other environmental factors prominently implicated in G × E interactions involve impactful experiences, like childhood abuse, that evoke strong emotional and physiological reactions. Recent evidence suggests that such responses affect biological pathways that intersect with genetic influences, acting even to affect the expression of genes themselves. These effects can either be transitory and contemporaneous with environmental exposures or, via certain genomic modifications, persist over much, or all, of the life span.

The first step in the expression of a gene (i.e., the transcription of DNA into RNA) happens when various transcription factors bind to gene regulatory sequences. In a behavioral context, this may occur when experiences are transduced into patterns of centrally mediated neuroendocrine or neural output (e.g., hormone release, neurotransmission) that then activate receptors and intracellular signaling cascades culminating in the transcriptional control of genes. The protein produced by a targeted gene might also vary in amino acid sequence owing to polymorphic variation in a coding region, in which case a G × E interaction could result when an environmental event first promotes gene transcription (by activating transcription factors) and the transcribed gene then yields a protein of varying structure due to a difference in genotype. DNA variation can also occur in regulatory sequences, suggesting that effects of a transcription factor on gene expression may itself vary by genotype of a polymorphism in the gene's regulatory region. An interesting example is a functionally active regulatory SNP in the gene encoding the inflammatory cytokine, interleukin-6 (IL-6). IL-6 is a marker of risk for diseases linked to inflammation, and levels of IL-6 are elevated in association with a variety of psychosocial and sociodemographic adversities (Miller et al. 2009). In a study of older adults, recently widowed individuals showed higher plasma IL-6 levels than nonbereaved counterparts if homozygous for a variant (the G-allele) of an upstream regulatory SNP labeled *IL6* -174G/C (Schultze-Florey et al. 2012). Among those carrying the alternate C-allele, bereavement did not increase IL-6 levels. Additionally, the stress-sensitive neurotransmitter, norepinephrine, is known to enhance *IL6* expression by activating a proximal transcription factor (GATA1), and like the effect of bereavement on IL-6 levels, the ability of norepinephrine to stimulate GATA1-mediated *IL6* transcription is mitigated in the presence of the *IL6* -174C allele (Cole et al. 2010). Thus, "stress" may augment *IL6* expression through activation of a transcription factor that is itself modulated by polymorphic variation in the *IL6* gene, which suggests a mechanism for genotype-dependent stressor effects on inflammatory responses. More generally, these experiments illustrate how neurotransmitters, hormones, and genetic variation might converge to influence gene expression and give rise to G × E interactions.

A gene can be expressed only if it is accessible to the transcription apparatus of the cell, and accessibility of the DNA is regulated by a number of biochemical processes. Collectively, these processes define the epigenome, a term meaning "above the genome" and referring to various chemical modifiers that inhibit or allow gene transcription without altering the DNA's nucleotide sequence. The study of variation in gene expression caused by these mechanisms is called epigenetics, and epigenetic mechanisms have attracted interest in part because the ways in which they regulate transcriptional control can persist through successive cycles of cell replication to affect gene expression over protracted periods. One type of epigenetic modification, methylation, occurs when a methyl group (a carbon and three hydrogen atoms) attaches to a cytosine nucleotide of DNA. An effect of this addition is to interfere with the binding of transcription factors to regulatory sequences and thus usually to repress or silence gene expression. In contrast, low levels of methylation ordinarily permit gene transcription. A second epigenetic mechanism involves modifications of chromatin structure. Chromatin is a complex of DNA and histone proteins, in which DNA is wrapped tightly around the histones and, in this conformation, is inaccessible to transcription factors. Conversely, transcriptional activity is enabled when, by acetylation, histones are bound less tightly to DNA. These and other epigenetic modifications of DNA play critical roles in developing organisms, providing a mechanism for the differentiation and maintenance of tissue-specific cells. That some epigenetic changes to DNA can be induced (or even reversed) during life, as catalyzed by various enzymes such as DNA methyltransferase and demethyltransferase, suggests that environmental exposures such as those experienced in early development can exert long-lasting biological and behavioral influences through an epigenetic mechanism.

Elegant experimental studies have shown deficiencies of early rearing to effect lifelong behavioral alterations in laboratory animals via epigenetic modifications of the hypothalamic-pituitary-adrenal system (Champagne & Mashoodh 2009, Meaney 2010), although relatively little research has yet been done in humans or in relation to G × E. One exception is recent work relevant to posttraumatic stress disorder (PTSD), which was previously predicted by an interaction of early childhood trauma with polymorphic variation in *FKBP5*, a protein involved in the regulation of glucocorticoid receptor binding and function (Binder et al. 2008, Xie et al. 2010). In follow-up work, Klengel and colleagues (2013) found exposure to trauma in early life to be associated with demethylation of DNA proximal to a glucocorticoid response element in *FKBP5*, an effect that was specific to persons carrying one of the *FKBP5* variants previously linked to risk of PTSD. The associated demethylation increases *FKBP5* expression, thereby suppressing responses to cortisol in glucocorticoid-sensitive tissues and increasing glucocorticoid resistance in individuals with the *FKBP5* risk allele. These findings may be relevant to the pathophysiology of PTSD, and in this instance, corroborative studies in hippocampal cells suggest that patterns of methylation in the brain parallel those first observed in peripheral blood cells. Other work will surely follow on epigenetic mechanisms of environmental influences and their potential interaction with genetic variation; already, commercial arrays are available to simultaneously assess the methylation status of hundreds of thousands of genes (Pan et al. 2012). How pervasive behaviorally relevant epigenetic effects may eventually turn out and, given expected heterogeneity of epigenetic modifications across tissues, how generalizable findings may prove elsewhere when based on cells conveniently sampled from blood will largely determine the explanatory scope of these newly recognized mechanisms. Until then, the limited current work in this area may be best seen as promissory.

The E in G × E Research

It is reassuring that new biological understandings may bring gene and environment together in a swirl of molecular interplay to undergird statistical G × E associations at the population level, however few examples we have at hand. At the same time, there is a conundrum at the heart of much G × E literature that obscures interpretation. If the boundary between heredity and environment can seem to erode when environments act, in part, to affect gene expression (even of the genes that convey heritable variation), it is weakened in a more fundamental sense if environmental exposures are themselves subject to genetic influence. And there is abundant evidence of such gene-environment correlations (rGEs). These may occur when individuals select environmental experiences guided by their heritable dispositions (active rGE) or create aspects of the environments they experience, as through the reactions they elicit in others (evocative rGE). And in a family context, phenotype and environment may be correlated due to shared genetic variation among related individuals (passive rGE) (Plomin et al. 2008). Importantly, twin studies document genetic influences on nearly all categories of environmental exposures, including stressful life events; traumatic (life-threatening) events; divorce; adverse parenting environments; socioeconomic position; peer group relations; work and classroom environments; and exposures to smoking, drugs, and alcohol; as well as protective resources such as the availability of confidants and engagement in social networks (reviewed in Kendler & Baker 2007, Manuck & McCaffery 2010). Effect sizes are generally modest to moderate but may be underestimated due to arbitrary reporting intervals that imperfectly capture stable individual differences in exposure rates. When measured on just two occasions, for example, genetic factors accounted for over 60% of variability in reported life events and social integration—two sentinel markers of environmental adversity and resources in G × E research (Foley et al. 1996, Kendler 1997).

To the extent rGE is present, an ostensible G × E interaction may partly reflect an interaction of measured genotypes with unrecognized genetic variation in the environmental moderator (G × G interaction). It also occasions the peculiar circumstance in which one scientist's environment (e.g., smoking, parenting, social support) is another's heritable phenotype. And although G × E investigators often document a null association between study genotypes and key environmental exposures, this alone cannot exclude potential confounding by rGE, since other genetic variation not included in the analysis may associate with the environmental factor. As a consequence, much G × E research undoubtedly harbors cryptic rGE and, when unacknowledged, suggests tacit acceptance of variables that are not explicitly genetic as environmental—a sort of methodological environmentalism. Obviously, these interpretive problems do not apply to studies of experimentally manipulated environmental exposures, such as randomized clinical trials and studies of responses to laboratory challenges (Uher 2008, van IJzendoorn et al. 2011). And to be sure, some investigators have employed creative methods to address rGE confounding. For instance, Caspi et al. (2003) found depression to be predicted by the interaction of 5-HTTLPR genotype with stressful life events that were experienced before, but not after, outcome assessment. This suggests an absence of rGE confounding, on the assumption that genetic effects on event exposures should be constant over time. In addition, quantitative (twin) genetic studies can potentially distinguish environmental effects that are causal from those associated with correlated genetic variation (Kendler et al. 1999). Yet, analogous claims cannot be made for the bulk of G × E studies, which typically enroll population or case-control samples of unrelated participants and employ measurement protocols precluding causal inference.

Maybe the more interesting question is not whether the environments studied in G × E research are purely environmental in origin, but why this seems to matter. G × E interaction was born, in part, as a rhetorical truce in the nature/nurture debate of the early- and mid-twentieth century (Cravens 1988). It was not generally expressed then in terms of statistical interaction among codependent processes, as treated here, but as an inchoate sense of coacting factors that, once acknowledged, allowed proponents of each side to go their separate ways (albeit with occasional flare-ups). And perhaps behavioral genetics itself, with its heritability and two kinds of environmentality (shared, nonshared), inadvertently reinforces popular notions of the essential separateness of gene and environment. Against this background, an interaction confounded by rGE might well seem to lack the implications of a true G × E finding. Yet what is the implication, if not confirming a proposition predicated on a frayed dichotomy? If heritable influences contribute to interindividual variability in as many categories of experience as rGE literature documents, finding the pure environment (and hence pure G × E interaction) in a natural population may be akin to verifying Newton's first law of motion from everyday experiences in a world possessed of atmosphere, friction, and gravity. As a practical matter, too, genetic variance in environmental exposures does not preclude environmental interventions to alleviate their ill consequences. And recognizing that, for instance, adversities of early rearing may have a heritable component is no more an argument against interventions to redress such circumstances than is the observation that, by genotype, some children may be protected from adversity. In view of the extent of demonstrated rGE, it seems reasonable to assume that most dimensions of measured experience will have both environmental and genetic determinants, and most G × E studies will not be able to partition genetic and environmental influences on their environmental moderators. With this in mind, we think it useful to acknowledge the interpretive limitations of most nonexperimental G × E inter-actions and recommend adopting a slightly different terminology, one that refers more modestly to interactions between genes and environmental exposures, where exposures denote experiences that may be attributable to a variety of undetermined causes. Finally, relinquishing pure G × E interaction as the grail of G × E research may encourage interest in a broader expanse of potential gene-exposure (G × E_{exp}) interactions affecting behavior, such as those moderated by complexly determined experiences, dispositions, abilities, attitudes, and affective states.

DISCLOSURE STATEMENT

The authors are not aware of any affiliations, memberships, funding, or financial holdings that might be perceived as affecting the objectivity of this review.

ACKNOWLEDGMENTS

Preparation of this manuscript was supported, in part, by NIH grants PO1 HL040962 (S.B.M.) and UO1 DK056992-11S1 (J.M.M.).

LITERATURE CITED

Andreasen CH, Stender-Petersen KL, Mogensen MS, Torekov SS, Wegner L. 2008. Low physical activity accentuates the effect of the *FTO* rs9939609 polymorphism on body fat accumulation. *Diabetes* 57(1):95–101

Anney R, Klei L, Pinto D, Almeida J, Bacchelli E, et al. 2012. Individual common variants exert weak effects on the risk for autism spectrum disorders. *Hum. Mol. Genet.* 21(21):4781–92

Bakermans-Kranenburg MJ, van IJzendoorn MH. 2006. Gene-environment interaction of the dopamine D4 receptor (*DRD4*) and observed maternal insensitivity predicting externalizing behavior in preschoolers. *Dev. Psychobiol.* 48(5):406–9

Bakermans-Kranenburg MJ, van IJzendoorn MH. 2008. Experimental evidence for differential susceptibility: dopamine D4 receptor polymorphism (*DRD4 VNTR*) moderates intervention effects on toddlers' externalizing behavior in a randomized control trial. *Dev. Psychol.* 44:293–300

Bakermans-Kranenburg MJ, van IJzendoorn MH. 2011. Differential susceptibility to rearing environment depending on dopamine-related genes: new evidence and a meta-analysis. *Dev. Psychopathol.* 23(1):39–52

Barnett JH, Scoriels L, Munafo MR. 2008. Meta-analysis of the cognitive effects of the catechol-O-methyltransferase gene Val158/108Met polymorphism. *Biol. Psychiatry* 64:137–44

Belsky DW, Moffitt TE, Houts R, Bennett GG, Biddle AK, et al. 2012. Polygenic risk, rapid childhood growth, and the development of obesity: evidence from a 4-decade longitudinal study. *Arch. Pediatr. Adolesc. Med.* 166(6):515–21

Belsky J, Jonassaint C, Pluess M, Stanton M, Brummett B, Williams R. 2009. Vulnerability genes or plasticity genes? *Mol. Psychiatry* 14(8):746–54

Belsky J, Pluess M. 2009. Beyond diathesis stress: differential susceptibility to environmental influences. *Psychol. Bull.* 135(6):885–908

Belsky J, Steinberg L, Draper P. 1991. Childhood experience, interpersonal development, and reproductive strategy: and evolutionary theory of socialization. *Child Dev.* 62(4):647–70

Benyamin B, Pourcain B, Davis OS, Davies G, Hansell NK, et al. 2013. Childhood intelligence is heritable, highly polygenic and associated with FNBP1L. *Mol. Psychiatry.* In press

Bierut LJ, Goate AM, Breslau N, Johnson EO, Bertelsen S, et al. 2012. *ADH1B* is associated with alcohol dependence and alcohol consumption in populations of European and African ancestry. *Mol. Psychiatry* 17(4):445–50

Binder EB, Bradley RG, Liu W, Epstein MP, Deveau TC, et al. 2008. Association of FKBP5 polymorphisms and childhood abuse with risk of posttraumatic stress disorder symptoms in adults. *JAMA* 299(11):1291–305

Boardman JD. 2009. State-level moderation of genetic tendencies to smoke. *Am. J. Public Health* 99(3):480–86

Boffetta P, Winn DM, Ioannidis JP, Thomas DC, Little J, et al. 2012. Recommendations and proposed guidelines for assessing the cumulative evidence on joint effects of genes and environments on cancer occurrence in humans. *Int. J. Epidemiol.* 41(3):686–704

Bosker FJ, Hartman CA, Nolte IM, Prins BP, Terpstra P, et al. 2011. Poor replication of candidate genes for major depressive disorder using genome-wide association data. *Mol. Psychiatry* 16:516–32

Boyce WT, Ellis BJ. 2005. Biological sensitivity to context: I. An evolutionary-developmental theory of the origins and functions of stress reactivity. *Dev. Psychopathol.* 17(2):271–301

Byrd AL, Manuck SB. 2013. *MAOA*, childhood maltreatment and antisocial behavior: meta-analysis of a gene-environment interaction. *Biol. Psychiatry.* In press

Caspi A, Hariri AR, Holmes A, Uher R, Moffitt TE. 2010. Genetic sensitivity to the environment: the case of the serotonin transporter gene and its implications for studying complex diseases and traits. *Am. J. Psychiatry* 167(5):509–27

Caspi A, McClay J, Moffitt TE, Mill J, Martin J, et al. 2002. Role of genotype in the cycle of violence in maltreated children. *Science* 297(5582):851–54

Caspi A, Sugden K, Moffitt TE, Taylor A, Craig IW, et al. 2003. Influence of life stress on depression: moderation by a polymorphism in the 5-HTT gene. *Science* 301(5631):386–89

Cecil JE, Tavendale R, Watt P, Hetherington MM, Palmer CN. 2008. An obesity-associated *FTO* gene variant and increased energy intake in children. *N. Engl. J. Med.* 359(24):2558–66

Cerasa A, Gioia MC, Fera F, Passamonti L, Liguori M. 2008. Ventro-lateral prefrontal activity during working memory is modulated by MAO A genetic variation. *Brain Res.* 1201:114–21

Chabris CF, Hebert BM, Benjamin DJ, Beauchamp J, Cesarini D, et al. 2012. Most reported genetic associations with general intelligence are probably false positives. *Psychol. Sci.* 23(11):1314–23

Champagne FA, Mashoodh R. 2009. Genes in context: gene-environment interplay and the origins of individual differences in behavior. *Curr. Dir. Psychol. Sci.* 18(3):127–31

Chen LS, Baker TB, Piper ME, Breslau N, Cannon DS. 2012. Interplay of genetic risk factors (*CHRNA5-CHRNA3-CHRNB4*) and cessation treatments in smoking cessation success. *Am. J. Psychiatry* 169(7):735–42

Cirulli ET, Goldstein DB. 2010. Uncovering the roles of rare variants in common disease through whole-genome sequencing. *Nat. Rev. Genet.* 11(6):415–25

Cole SW, Arevalo JM, Takahashi R, Sloan EK, Lutgendorf SK, et al. 2010. Computational identification of gene-social environment interaction at the human *IL6* locus. *Proc. Natl. Acad. Sci. USA* 107(12):5681–86

Conrad DF, Pinto D, Redon R, Feuk L, Gokcumen O, et al. 2010. Origins and functional impact of copy number variation in the human genome. *Nature* 464(7289):704–12

Cravens H. 1988. *The Triumph of Evolution: The Heredity-Environment Controversy, 1900–1941.* Baltimore, MD: Johns Hopkins Univ. Press

Crossa J. 2012. From genotype × environment interaction to gene × environment interaction. *Curr. Genomics* 13(3):225–44

Davies G, Tenesa A, Payton A, Yang J, Harris SE, et al. 2011. Genome-wide association studies establish that human intelligence is highly heritable and polygenic. *Mol. Psychiatry* 16:996–1005

De Geus EJ, Kupper N, Boomsma DI, Snieder H. 2007. Bivariate genetic modeling of cardiovascular stress reactivity: Does stress uncover genetic variance? *Psychosom. Med.* 69(4):356–64

De Jager PL, Shulman JM, Chibnik LB, Keenan BT, Raj T, et al. 2012. A genome-wide scan for common variants affecting the rate of age-related cognitive decline. *Neurobiol. Aging* 33(5):1017.e1–15

de Moor MH, Costa PT, Terracciano A, Krueger RF, de Geus EJ, et al. 2012. Meta-analysis of genome-wide association studies for personality. *Mol. Psychiatry* 17:337–49

Dick DM. 2011. Gene-environment interaction in psychological traits and disorders. *Annu. Rev. Clin. Psychol.* 7:383–409

Dick DM, Latendresse SJ, Lansford JE, Budde JP, Goate A, et al. 2009. Role of *GABRA2* in trajectories of externalizing behavior across development and evidence of moderation by parental monitoring. *Arch. Gen. Psychiatry* 66(6):649–57

Dick DM, Pagan JL, Viken R, Purcell S, Kaprio J, et al. 2007a. Changing environmental influences on substance use across development. *Twin Res. Hum. Genet.* 10(2):315–26

Dick DM, Rose JL, Viken R, Kaprio J, Koskenvuo M. 2001. Exploring gene-environment interactions: socioregional moderation of alcohol use. *J. Abnorm. Psychol.* 110:625–32

Dick DM, Viken R, Purcell S, Kaprio J, Pulkkinen L, Rose RJ. 2007b. Parental monitoring moderates the importance of genetic and environmental influences on adolescent smoking. *J. Abnorm. Psychol.* 116(1):213–18

Docherty SJ, Davis OSP, Kovas Y, Meaburn EL, Dale PS, et al. 2010. A genome-wide association study identifies multiple loci associated with mathematics ability and disability. *Genes Brain Behav.* 9:234–47

Docherty SJ, Kovas Y, Plomin R. 2011. Gene-environment interaction in the etiology of mathematical ability using SNP sets. *Behav. Genet.* 41:141–54

Drabant EM, Ramel W, Edge MD, Hyde LW, Kuo JR, et al. 2012. Neural mechanisms underlying 5-HTTLPR-related sensitivity to acute stress. *Am. J. Psychiatry* 169(4):397–405

Duncan LE, Keller MC. 2011. A critical review of the first 10 years of candidate gene-by-environment interaction research in psychiatry. *Am. J. Psychiatry* 168:1041–49

Durbin RM, Abecasis GR, Altshuler DL, Auton A, Brooks LD, et al. 2010. A map of human genome variation from population-scale sequencing. *Nature* 467:1061–73

Eaves LJ. 2006. Genotype × environment interaction in psychopathology: fact or artifact? *Twin Res. Hum. Genet.* 9(1):1–8

Ebstein RP, Novick O, Umansky R, Priel B, Osher Y, et al. 1996. Dopamine D4 receptor (D4DR) exon III polymorphism associated with the human personality trait of novelty seeking. *Nat. Genet.* 12(1):78–80

Ecker JR. 2012. ENCODE explained. *Nature* 489:52–55

Ellis BJ, Boyce WT, Belsky J, Bakermans-Kranenburg MJ, van IJzendoorn MH. 2011. Differential susceptibility to the environment: an evolutionary-neurodevelopmental theory. *Dev. Psychopathol.* 23(1):7–28

Enge S, Fleischhauer M, Lesch KP, Reif A, Strobel A. 2011. Serotonergic modulation in executive functioning: linking genetic variations to working memory performance. *Neuropsychologia* 49(13):3776–85

Erickson KI, Banducci SE, Weinstein AM, MacDonald AW, Ferrell RE, et al. 2013. The brain-derived neurotrophic factor Val66Met polymorphism moderates an effect of physical activity on working memory performance. *Psychol. Sci.* 24:1770–79

Fan J, Fossella J, Sommer T, Wu Y, Posner MI. 2003. Mapping the genetic variation of executive attention onto brain activity. *Proc. Natl. Acad. Sci. USA* 100(12):7406–11

Foley DL, Neale MC, Kendler KS. 1996. A longitudinal study of stressful life events assessed at interview with an epidemiological sample of adult twins: the basis of individual variation in event exposure. *Psychol. Med.* 26(6):1239–52

Fox E, Zougkou K, Ridgewell A, Garner K. 2011. The serotonin transporter gene alters sensitivity to attention bias modification: evidence for a plasticity gene. *Biol. Psychiatry* 70(11):1049–54

Frayling TM, Timpson NJ, Weedon MN, Zeggini E, Freathy RM, et al. 2007. A common variant in the *FTO* gene is associated with body mass index and predisposes to childhood and adult obesity. *Science* 316(5826):889–94

Freitag CM. 2007. The genetics of autistic disorders and its clinical relevance. *Mol. Psychiatry* 12(1):2–22

Gyekis JP, Yu W, Dong S, Wang H, Qian J, et al. 2013. No association of genetic variants in *BDNF* with major depression: a meta- and gene-based analysis. *Am. J. Med. Genet. B* 162B:61–70

Hankin BL, Nederhof E, Oppenheimer CW, Jenness J, Young JF, et al. 2011. Differential susceptibility in youth: evidence that 5-HTTLPR × positive parenting is associated with positive affect "for better and worse." *Transl. Psychiatry* 1:e44

Hanscombe KB, Trzaskowski M, Haworth CM, Davis OS, Dale PS, Plomin R. 2012. Socioeconomic status (SES) and children's intelligence (IQ): In a UK-representative sample SES moderates the environmental, not genetic, effect on IQ. *PLoS ONE* 7(2):e30320

Hariri AR. 2009. The neurobiology of individual differences in complex behavioral traits. *Annu. Rev. Neurosci.* 32:225–47

Hariri AR, Drabant EM, Munoz KE, Kolachana BS, Mattay VS, et al. 2005. A susceptibility gene for affective disorders and the response of the human amygdala. *Arch. Gen. Psychiatry* 62(2):146–52

Hirschhorn JN, Lohmueller K, Byrne E, Hirschhorn K. 2002. A comprehensive review of genetic association studies. *Genet. Med.* 4(2):45–61

Homberg JR, Lesch KP. 2011. Looking on the bright side of serotonin transporter gene variation. *Biol. Psychiatry* 69(6):513–19

Hunter DJ. 2005. Gene-environment interactions in human diseases. *Nat. Rev. Genet.* 6(4):287–98

Hyde LW, Bogdan R, Hariri AR. 2011. Understanding risk for psychopathology through imaging gene-environment interactions. *Trends Cogn. Sci.* 15(9):417–27

Jaffee SR, Caspi A, Moffitt TE, Dodge KA, Rutter M, et al. 2005. Nature × nurture: genetic vulnerabilities interact with physical maltreatment to promote conduct problems. *Dev. Psychopathol.* 17(1):67–84

Karg K, Burmeister M, Shedden K, Sen S. 2011. The serotonin transporter promoter variant (5-HTTLPR), stress, and depression meta-analysis revisited: evidence of genetic moderation. *Arch. Gen. Psychiatry* 68(5):444–54

Kendler KS. 1997. Social support: a genetic-epidemiologic analysis. *Am. J. Psychiatry* 154(10):1398–404

Kendler KS. 2011. A conceptual overview of gene-environment interaction and correlation in a developmental context. In *The Dynamic Genome and Mental Health*, ed. KS Kendler, S Jaffee, D Romer, pp. 5–28. New York: Oxford Univ. Press

Kendler KS, Baker JH. 2007. Genetic influences on measures of the environment: a systematic review. *Psychol. Med.* 37(5):615–26

Kendler KS, Karkowski LM, Prescott CA. 1999. Causal relationship between stressful life events and the onset of major depression. *Am. J. Psychiatry* 156(6):837–41

Kendler KS, Kessler RC, Walters EE, MacLean C, Neale MC, et al. 1995. Stressful life events, genetic liability, and onset of an episode of major depression in women. *Am. J. Psychiatry* 152(6):833–42

Kilpelainen TO, Qi L, Brage S, Sharp SJ, Sonestedt E. 2011. Physical activity attenuates the influence of FTO variants on obesity risk: a meta-analysis of 218,166 adults and 19,268 children. *PLoS Med.* 8(11):e1001116

Klengel T, Mehta D, Anacker C, Rex-Haffner M, Pruessner JC, et al. 2013. Allele-specific *FKBP5* DNA demethylation mediates gene-childhood trauma interactions. *Nat. Neurosci.* 16(1):33–41

Kluger AN, Siegfried Z, Ebstein RP. 2002. A meta-analysis of the association between *DRD4* polymorphism and novelty seeking. *Mol. Psychiatry* 7(7):712–17

Knafo A. 2009. *Prosocial development: the intertwined roles of children's genetics and their parental environment.* Presented at Bienn. Meet. Soc. Res. Child Dev., Denver, Colo.

Knafo A, Israel S, Ebstein RP. 2011. Heritability of children's prosocial behavior and differential susceptibility to parenting by variation in the dopamine receptor D4 gene. *Dev. Psychopathol.* 21(1):53–67

Koopmans JR, Slutske WS, van Baal GC, Boomsma DI. 1999. The influence of religion on alcohol use initiation: evidence for genotype × environment interaction. *Behav. Genet.* 29(6):445–53

Krafka J. 1920. The effect of temperature upon facet number in the bar-eyed mutant of *Drosophila. J. Gen. Physiol.* 2(5):445–64

Krueger RF, South S, Johnson W, Iacono W. 2008. The heritability of personality is not always 50%: gene-environment interactions and correlations between personality and parenting. *J. Personal.* 76(6):1485–522

Lango Allen H, Estrada K, Lettre G, Berndt SI, Weedon MN, et al. 2010. Hundreds of variants clustered in genomic loci and biological pathways affect human height. *Nature* 467:832–38

Latendresse SJ, Bates JE, Goodnight JA, Lansford JE, Budde JP, et al. 2011. Differential susceptibility to adolescent externalizing trajectories: examining the interplay between *CHRM2* and peer group antisocial behavior. *Child Dev.* 82(6):1797–814

Lee SH, Wray NR, Goddard ME, Visscher PM. 2011. Estimating missing heritability for disease from genome-wide association studies. *Am. J. Hum. Genet.* 88(3):294–305

Levy D, Ehret GB, Rice K, Verwoert GC, Launer LJ, et al. 2009. Genome-wide association studies of blood pressure and hypertension. *Nat. Genet.* 41(6):677–87

Li D, Zhao H, Gelernter J. 2011. Strong association of the alcohol dehydrogenase 1B gene (*ADH1B*) with alcohol dependence and alcohol-induced medical diseases. *Biol. Psychiatry* 70(6):504–12

Lubke GH, Hottenga JJ, Walters R, Laurin C, de Geus EJ, et al. 2012. Estimating the genetic variance of major depressive disorder due to all single nucleotide polymorphisms. *Biol. Psychiatry* 72:707–9

Maher B. 2008. Personal genomes: the case of the missing heritability. *Nature* 456:18–21

Major Depress. Disord. Work. Group Psychiatr. GWAS Consort., Ripke S, Wray NR, Lewis CN, Hamilton SP, et al. 2013. A mega-analysis of genome-wide association studies for major depressive disorder. *Mol. Psychiatry* 18(4):497–511

Mandelman SD, Grigorenko EL. 2012. *BDNF* Val66Met and cognition: all, none, or some? A meta-analysis of the genetic association. *Genes Brains Behav.* 11(2):127–36

Manolio TA, Collins FS, Cox NJ, Goldstein DB, Hindorff LA, et al. 2009. Finding the missing heritability of complex diseases. *Nature* 461:747–53

Manuck SB. 2010. The reaction norm in gene × environment interaction. *Mol. Psychiatry* 15:881–82

Manuck SB, McCaffery JM. 2010. Genetics of stress: gene-stress correlation and interaction. In *Handbook of Behavioral Medicine: Methods and Applications*, ed. A Steptoe, pp. 455–78. New York: Springer

McCaffery JM, Papandonatos GD, Bond DS, Lyons MJ, Wing RR. 2009. Gene × environment interaction of vigorous exercise and body mass index among male Vietnam-era twins. *Am. J. Clin. Nutr.* 89(4):1011–18

McCaffery JM, Papandonatos GD, Peter I, Huggins GS, Raynor HA, et al. 2012. Obesity susceptibility loci and dietary intake in the Look AHEAD Trial. *Am. J. Clin. Nutr.* 95(6):1477–86

Meaney MJ. 2010. Epigenetics and the biological definition of gene × environment interactions. *Child Dev.* 81(1):41–79

Meehl PE. 1962. Schizotaxia, schizotypy, schizophrenia. *Am. Psychol.* 12:827–38

Mendes Soares LM, Valcarcel J. 2006. The expanding transcriptome: the genome as the "Book of Sand." *EMBO J.* 25:923–31

Meyer-Lindenberg A, Buckholtz JW, Kolachana B, Hariri AR, Pezawas L. 2006. Neural mechanisms of genetic risk for impulsivity and violence in humans. *Proc. Natl. Acad. Sci. USA* 103(16):6269–74

Miller G, Chen E, Cole SW. 2009. Health psychology: developing biologically plausible models linking the social world and physical health. *Annu. Rev. Psychol.* 60:501–24

Miller R, Wankerl M, Stalder T, Kirschbaum C, Alexander N. 2013. The serotonin transporter gene-linked polymorphic region (5-HTTLPR) and cortisol stress reactivity: a meta-analysis. *Mol. Psychiatry.* 18:1018–24

Moffitt TE, Caspi A, Rutter M. 2006. Measured gene-environment interactions in psychopathology. *Perspect. Psychol. Sci.* 1:5–27

Monroe SM, Simons AD. 1991. Diathesis-stress theories in the context of life-stress research: implications for the depressive disorders. *Psychol. Bull.* 110:406–25

Munafo MR. 2006. Candidate gene studies in the 21st century: meta-analysis, mediation, moderation. *Genes Brain Behav.* 5(Suppl. 1):3–8

Munafo MR, Brown SM, Hariri AR. 2008a. Serotonin transporter (5-HTTLPR) genotype and amygdala activation: a meta-analysis. *Biol. Psychiatry* 63(9):852–57

Munafo MR, Clark T, Flint J. 2005. Does measurement instrument moderate the association between the serotonin transporter gene and anxiety-related personality traits? A meta-analysis. *Mol. Psychiatry* 10:415–19

Munafo MR, Durrant C, Lewis G, Flint J. 2009a. Gene × environment interactions at the serotonin transporter locus. *Biol. Psychiatry* 65(3):211–19

Munafo MR, Flint J. 2009. Replication and heterogeneity in gene × environment interaction studies. *Int. J. Neuropsychopharmacol.* 12(6):727–29

Munafo MR, Timpson NJ, David SP, Ebrahim S, Lawlor DA. 2009b. Association of the *DRD2* gene Taq1A polymorphism and smoking behavior: a meta-analysis and new data. *Nicotine Tob. Res.* 11(1):64–76

Munafo MR, Yalcin B, Willis-Owen SA, Flint J. 2008b. Association of the dopamine D4 receptor (*DRD4*) gene and approach-related personality traits: meta-analysis and new data. *Biol. Psychiatry* 63(2):197–206

Mustelin L, Silventoinen K, Pietilainen K, Rissanen A, Kaprio J. 2009. Physical activity reduces the influence of genetic effects on BMI and waist circumference: a study in young adult twins. *Int. J. Obes.* 33(1):29–36

Newton-Cheh C, Johnson T, Gateva V, Tobin MD, Bochud M. 2009. Genome-wide association study identifies eight loci associated with blood pressure. *Nat. Genet.* 41(6):666–76

Nobile M, Giorda R, Marino C, Carlet O, Pastore V, et al. 2007. Socioeconomic status mediates the genetic contribution of the dopamine receptor D4 and serotonin transporter linked promoter region repeat polymorphisms to externalization in preadolescence. *Dev. Psychopathol.* 19(4):1147–60

Pan H, Chen L, Dogra S, Teh AL, Tan JH, et al. 2012. Measuring the methylome in clinical samples: improved processing of the Infinium Human Methylation450 BeadChip Array. *Epigenetics* 7(10):1173–87

Pergamin-Hight L, Bakermans-Kranenburg MJ, van IJzendoorn MH, Bar-Haim Y. 2012. Variations in the promoter region of the serotonin transporter gene and biased attention for emotional information: a meta-analysis. *Biol. Psychiatry* 71(4):373–79

Plomin R. 2013. Child development and molecular genetics: 14 years later. *Child Dev.* 84(1):104–20

Plomin R, Crabbe J. 2000. DNA. *Psychol. Bull.* 126(6):806–28

Plomin R, DeFries JC, McClearn GE, McGuffin P. 2008. *Behavioral Genetics*. New York: Worth. 5th ed.

Plomin R, Haworth CM, Meaburn EL, Price TS, Wellcome Trust Case Control Consort., Davis OS. 2012. Common DNA markers can account for more than half of the genetic influence on cognitive abilities. *Psychol. Sci.* 24(4):562–68

Pluess M, Belsky J. 2013. Vantage sensitivity: individual differences in response to positive experiences. *Psychol. Bull.* 139:901–16

Poirier J, Davignon J, Bouthillier D, Kogan S, Bertrand P, Gauthier S. 1993. Apolipoprotein E polymorphism and Alzheimer's disease. *Lancet* 342(8873):697–99

Power RA, Kyaga S, Uher R, MacCabe JH, Langstrom N, et al. 2013. Fecundity of patients with schizophrenia, autism, bipolar disorder, depression, anorexia nervosa, or substance abuse versus their unaffected siblings. *JAMA Psychiatry* 70(1):22–30

Psychiatr. GWAS Consort. Bipolar Disord. Work. Group. 2011. Large-scale genome-wide association analysis of bipolar disorder identifies a new susceptibility locus near *ODZ4*. *Nat. Genet.* 43(10):977–83

Psychiatr. GWAS Consort. Steer. Comm. 2009. A framework for interpreting genome-wide association studies of psychiatric disorders. *Mol. Psychiatry* 14(1):10–17

Purcell S. 2002. Variance components models for gene-environment interaction in twin analysis. *Twin Res.* 5(6):554–71

Riley B, Kendler KS. 2006. Molecular genetic studies of schizophrenia. *Eur. J. Hum. Genet.* 14(6):669–80

Risch N, Herrell R, Lehner T, Liang KY, Eaves L. 2009. Interaction between the serotonin transporter gene (5-HTTLPR), stressful life events, and risk of depression: a meta-analysis. *JAMA* 301(23):2462–71

Risch N, Merikangas K. 1996. The future of genetic studies of complex human diseases. *Science* 273:1516–17

Roisman GI, Newman DA, Fraley RC, Haltigan JD, Groh AM, Haydon KC. 2012. Distinguishing differential susceptibility from diathesis-stress: recommendations for evaluating interaction effect. *Dev. Psychopathol.* 24(2):389–409

Rose RJ, Dick DM, Viken RJ, Kaprio J. 2001. Gene-environment interaction in patterns of adolescent drinking: regional residency moderates longitudinal influences on alcohol use. *Alcohol Clin. Exp. Res.* 25(5):637–43

Rothman KJ, Greenland S, Lash TL, eds. 2008. *Modern Epidemiology*. Philadelphia, PA: Kluwer. 3rd ed.

Rutter M. 2010. Gene-environment interplay. *Depress. Anxiety* 27:1–4

Rutter M, Thapar A, Pickles A. 2009. Gene-environment interactions: biologically valid pathway or artifact? *Arch. Gen. Psychiatry* 66(12):1287–89

Saccone NL, Schwantes-An TH, Wang JC, Grucza RA, Breslau N. 2010. Multiple cholinergic nicotinic receptor genes affect nicotine dependence risk in African and European Americans. *Genes Brain Behav.* 9(7):741–50

Schizophr. Psychiatr. GWAS Consort. 2011. Genome-wide association study identifies five new schizophrenia loci. *Nat. Genet.* 43(10):969–76

Schultze-Florey CR, Martinez-Maza O, Magpantay L, Breen EC, Irwin MR, et al. 2012. When grief makes you sick: Bereavement induced systemic inflammation is a question of genotype. *Brain Behav. Immun.* 26(7):1066–71

Service SK, Verweij KJ, Lahti J, Congdon E, Ekelund J, et al. 2012. A genome-wide meta-analysis of association studies of Cloninger's Temperament Scales. *Transl. Psychiatry* 2:e116

Shanahan MJ, Hofer SM. 2005. Social context in gene-environment interactions: retrospect and prospect. *J. Gerontol. B Sci. Soc. Sci.* 60(Spec. No. 1):65–76

Sheese BE, Voelker PM, Rothbart MK, Posner MI. 2007. Parenting quality interacts with genetic variation in dopamine receptor D4 to influence temperament in early childhood. *Dev. Psychopathol.* 19(4):1039–46

Siontis KC, Patsopoulos NA, Ioannidis JP. 2010. Replication of past candidate loci for common diseases and phenotypes in 100 genome-wide association studies. *Eur. J. Hum. Genet.* 18:832–37

Smoller JW, Kendler K, Craddock N. 2013. Identification of risk loci with shared effects on five major psychiatric disorders: a genome-wide analysis. *Lancet* 381(9875):1371–79

Speliotes EK, Willer CJ, Berndt SI, Monda KL, Thorleifsson G, et al. 2010. Association analyses of 249,796 individuals reveal 18 new loci associated with body mass index. *Nat. Genet.* 42(11):937–48

Stearns S. 1992. *The Evolution of Life Histories.* New York: Oxford Univ. Press

Sullivan PF, Daly MJ, O'Donovan M. 2012. Genetic architectures of psychiatric disorders: the emerging picture and its implication. *Nat. Rev. Genet.* 13:537–51

Sweitzer MM, Halder I, Flory JD, Craig AE, Gianaros PJ, et al. 2013. Polymorphic variation in the dopamine D4 receptor predicts delay discounting as a function of childhood socioeconomic status: evidence for differential susceptibility. *Soc. Cogn. Affect. Neurosci.* 8:499–508

Tabery J. 2008. R.A. Fisher, Lancelot Hogben, and the origin(s) of genotype-environment interaction. *J. Hist. Biol.* 41(4):717–61

Taylor A, Kim-Cohen J. 2007. Meta-analysis of gene-environment interactions in developmental psychopathology. *Dev. Psychopathol.* 19:1029–37

Taylor SE, Way BM, Welch WT, Hilmert CJ, Lehman BJ, Eisenberger NI. 2006. Early family environment, current adversity, the serotonin transporter promoter polymorphism, and depressive symptomatology. *Biol. Psychiatry* 60(7):671–76

Terracciano A, Sanna S, Uda M, Deiana B, Usala G, et al. 2010. Genome-wide association scan for five major dimensions of personality. *Mol. Psychiatry* 15:647–56

Thanassoulis G, Peloso GM, Pencina MJ, Hoffmann U, Fox CS, et al. 2012. A genetic risk score is associated with incident cardiovascular disease and coronary artery calcium: the Framingham Heart Study. *Circ. Cardiovasc. Genet.* 5:113–21

Thomas D. 2010a. Methods for investigating gene-environment interactions in candidate pathway and genome-wide association studies. *Annu. Rev. Public Health* 31:21–36

Thomas D. 2010b. Gene-environment-wide association studies: emerging approaches. *Nat. Rev. Genet.* 11(4):259–72

Turkheimer E. 2000. Three laws of behavior genetics and what they mean. *Curr. Dir. Psychol. Sci.* 9(5):160–64

Turkheimer E, Haley A, Waldron M, D'Onofrio B, Gottesman II. 2003. Socioeconomic status modifies heritability of IQ in young children. *Psychol. Sci.* 14(6):623–28

Uher R. 2008. Forum: the case for gene-environment interactions in psychiatry. *Curr. Opin. Psychiatry* 21(4):318–21

Uher R. 2009. The role of genetic variation in the causation of mental illness: an evolution-informed framework. *Mol. Psychiatry* 14(12):1072–82

Uher R. 2011. Gene-environment interactions. In *The Dynamic Genome and Mental Health*, ed. KS Kendler, SR Jaffee, D Romer, pp. 29–58. New York: Oxford Univ. Press

Uher R, McGuffin P. 2008. The moderation by the serotonin transporter gene of environmental adversity in the aetiology of mental illness: review and methodological analysis. *Mol. Psychiatry* 13(2):131–46

Uher R, McGuffin P. 2010. The moderation by the serotonin transporter gene of environmental adversity in the etiology of depression: 2009 update. *Mol. Psychiatry* 15(1):18–22

van den Oord EJ, Kuo PH, Hartmann AM, Webb BT, Moller HJ, et al. 2008. Genomewide association analysis followed by a replication study implicates a novel candidate gene for neuroticism. *Arch. Gen. Psychiatry* 65(9):1062–71 van der Sluis S, Verhage M, Posthuma D, Dolan CV. 2010. Phenotypic complexity, measurement bias, and poor phenotypic resolution contribute to the missing heritability problem in genetic association studies. *PLoS ONE* 5(11):E13929

van IJzendoorn MH, Bakermans-Kranenburg MJ. 2006. DRD4 7-repeat polymorphism moderates the association between maternal unresolved loss or trauma and infant disorganization. *Attachment Hum. Dev.* 8(4):291–307

van IJzendoorn MH, Bakermans-Kranenburg MJ, Belsky J, Beach S, Brody G, et al. 2011. Gene-by-environment experiments: a new approach to finding the missing heritability. *Nat. Rev. Genet.* 12(12):881

van IJzendoorn MH, Belsky J, Bakermans-Kranenburg MJ. 2012. Serotonin transporter genotype 5HTTLPR as a marker of differential susceptibility? A meta-analysis of child and adolescent gene-by-environment studies. *Transl. Psychiatry* 2(8):e147

Vassos E, Collier DA, Fazel S. 2013. Systematic meta-analyses and field synopsis of genetic association studies of violence and aggression. *Mol. Psychiatry.* Epub ahead of print. doi:10.1038/mp.2013.31

Verweij KJ, Yang J, Lahti J, Veijola J, Hintsanen M, et al. 2012. Maintenance of genetic variation in human personality: testing evolutionary models by estimating heritability due to common causal variants and investigating the effect of distant inbreeding. *Evolution* 66(10):3238–51

Verweij KJ, Zietsch BP, Medland SE, Gordon SD, Benyamin B, et al. 2010. A genome-wide association study of Cloninger's temperament scales: implications for the evolutionary genetics of personality. *Biol. Psychiatry* 85:306–17

Vinkhuyzen AA, Pedersen NL, Yang J, Lee SH, Magnusson PK, et al. 2012. Common SNPs explain some of the variation in the personality dimensions of neuroticism and extraversion. *Transl. Psychiatry* 2:e102

Visscher PM, Brown MA, McCarthy MI, Yang J. 2012a. Five years of GWAS discovery. *Am. J. Hum. Genet.* 90:7–24

Visscher PM, Goddard ME, Derks EM, Wray NR. 2012b. Evidence-based psychiatric genetics, AKA the false dichotomy between common and rare variant hypotheses. *Mol. Psychiatry* 17:474–85

Wardle J, Llewellyn C, Sanderson S, Plomin R. 2009. The *FTO* gene and measured food intake in children. *Int. J. Obes.* 33(1):42–45

Willer CJ, Speliotes EK, Loos RJ, Li S, Lindgren CM. 2009. Six new loci associated with body mass index highlight a neuronal influence on body weight regulation. *Nat. Genet.* 41(1):25–34

Xie P, Kranzler HR, Poling J, Stein MB, Anton RF. 2010. Interaction of *FKBP5* with childhood adversity on risk for post-traumatic stress disorder. *Neuropsychopharmacology* 35(8):1684–92

Yang J, Lee SH, Goddard ME, Visscher PM. 2011. GCTA: a tool for genome-wide complex trait analysis. *Am. J. Hum. Genet.* 88(1):76–82

Zuckerman M, ed. 1999. *Vulnerability to Psychopathology: A Biosocial Model*. Washington, DC: Am. Psychol. Assoc.

The Cognitive Neuroscience of Insight

John Kounios[1] and Mark Beeman[2]

[1]Department of Psychology, Drexel University, Philadelphia, Pennsylvania 19102;
email: john.kounios@gmail.com

[2]Department of Psychology, Northwestern University, Evanston, Illinois 60208;
email: mjungbee@northwestern.edu

Annu. Rev. Psychol. 2014. 65:71–93

The *Annual Review of Psychology* is online at
http://psych.annualreviews.org

This article's doi:
10.1146/annurev-psych-010213-115154

Keywords

attention, cognitive enhancement, creativity, hemispheric asymmetry,
problem solving

Abstract

Insight occurs when a person suddenly reinterprets a stimulus, situation, or
event to produce a nonobvious, nondominant interpretation. This can take
the form of a solution to a problem (an "aha moment"), comprehension of a
joke or metaphor, or recognition of an ambiguous percept. Insight research
began a century ago, but neuroimaging and electrophysiological techniques
have been applied to its study only during the past decade. Recent work
has revealed insight-related coarse semantic coding in the right hemisphere
and internally focused attention preceding and during problem solving. Individual differences in the tendency to solve problems insightfully rather
than in a deliberate, analytic fashion are associated with different patterns of
resting-state brain activity. Recent studies have begun to apply direct brain
stimulation to facilitate insight. In sum, the cognitive neuroscience of insight is an exciting new area of research with connections to fundamental
neurocognitive processes.

Contents

INTRODUCTION

In an article in the *Annual Review of Astronomy and Astrophysics*, William Wilson Morgan (1988) summarized several of the groundbreaking scientific contributions he made over his long career. One of these was the discovery of the structure of the Milky Way galaxy. What isn't obvious from his article is how he came to make this discovery (Sheehan 2008).

In 1951, Morgan had been calculating the distances of OB associations, which are groups of hot, bright stars. OB associations are considered "star nurseries" because these stars are young. One evening, he finished his work for the night and started to walk home from the Yerkes Observatory. He glanced up at the sky to observe the stars that he had been studying and had what he called a "flash inspiration . . . a creative intuitional burst": These stars are organized in a three-dimensional, strand-like structure. Galaxies come in a variety of forms, but he knew that in spiral galaxies OB associations reside in the galactic arms. Morgan understood that the strand-like form was a galactic arm and that he had directly apprehended the spiral structure of the Milky Way, a realization that he substantiated with data that he presented at a conference a few months later.

Morgan's breakthrough realization was an insight, colloquially known as an "aha moment"—a sudden, conscious change in a person's representation of a stimulus, situation, event, or problem (Kaplan & Simon 1990). Awareness of this kind of representational change, though abrupt, takes place after a period of unconscious processing (van Steenburgh et al. 2012). Because insights are largely a product of unconscious processing, when they emerge, they seem to be disconnected from the ongoing stream of conscious thought. In contrast, analytic thought is deliberate and conscious and is characterized by incremental awareness of a solution (Smith & Kounios 1996).

Although Morgan's insight was literally on a cosmic scale, the phenomenon of insight, in a more modest guise, is a common experience that occurs in perception, language comprehension, problem solving, and other domains of cognition (van Steenburgh et al. 2012). It is therefore of interest to ask what happened in Morgan's brain and in the brains of many other people when they have had an insight. This article reviews relevant cognitive neuroscience research and an emerging theoretical framework that is progressing toward an answer to this question. Before describing this work, we circumscribe the insight phenomenon to specify the domain of this review.

WHAT IS INSIGHT?

Insight is often defined as a sudden change in or the formation of a concept or other type of knowledge representation, often leading to the solution of a problem. These changes are thought to have certain attributes. For example, insights are frequently accompanied by a burst of emotion, including a highly positive surprise at either the content or manner of the realization. In contrast, analytic solutions are not typically accompanied by an emotional response except perhaps for a sense of satisfaction resulting from completing the task. However, though not an unusual concomitant, a conscious emotional response is not a necessary feature of insight. Participants in many studies have solved dozens of verbal puzzles with insight (e.g., Jung-Beeman et al. 2004, Smith & Kounios 1996) without reports of multiple bursts of emotion.

Another feature is that insights often break an impasse or mental block produced because a solver initially fixated on an incorrect solution strategy or strong but ultimately unhelpful associations of a problem. The breaking of an impasse is accompanied by the reinterpretation or restructuring of a problem to reveal a new, often simple, solution or solution strategy. Some researchers implicitly consider problem restructuring and the breaking of an impasse to be defining features of insight (e.g., Cranford & Moss 2012). However, this view excludes prominent types of insights, such as those that occur (*a*) when the solution suddenly intrudes on a person's awareness when he or she is not focusing on any solution strategy, (*b*) when an insight pointing to a solution occurs while a person is actively engaged in analytic processing but has not yet reached an impasse, and (*c*) when a person has a spontaneous realization that does not relate to any explicitly posed problem. We therefore do not consider the breaking of an impasse to be a precondition for insight.

Thus, there are a number of potential definitions of insight, depending on which combination of features one selects. Very narrowly defined, insight could be thought of as a sudden solution to a problem preceded by an impasse and problem restructuring and followed by a positive emotional response. In contrast, the broadest definition of insight is the common nonscientific one in which an insight is any deep realization, whether sudden or not. Within cognitive psychology and cognitive neuroscience, inconsistency exists concerning what we consider to be a basic criterion for insight, namely, suddenness. For example, a number of purported insight studies do not specifically isolate and focus on solutions that occurred suddenly (e.g., Luo & Niki 2003, Wagner et al. 2004).

Another broad use of the term insight can be found in clinical psychology, in which insight refers to self-awareness, often of one's own symptoms, functional deficits, or other kind of predicament. The clinical and nonscientific uses of the term do not require suddenness of realization or any accompanying emotional response. Indeed, in clinical psychology, the lack of an emotional response could itself be considered a symptom signifying a lack of insight.

The issue of defining insight is not an exercise in pedantry. When insight is defined too broadly, it includes so many diverse, loosely related phenomena that it becomes virtually impossible for researchers to draw general conclusions. For example, one recent review of cognitive neuroscience research on creativity and insight lumps together widely diverse studies characterized by a variety of definitions, assumptions, experimental paradigms, empirical phenomena, analytical methods, and stages of the solving process (and inconsistent experimental rigor). Unsurprisingly, because of such indiscriminate agglomeration, that review failed to find much consistency across studies, leading the authors to pronounce a negative verdict on the field (Dietrich & Kanso 2010). In contrast, going to the other extreme by adopting an overly narrow definition of insight can lead one to miss important large-scale generalizations that cut across particular experimental paradigms.

Thus, progress in studying insight can be facilitated or enhanced by "carving nature at its joints" and adopting a middle-path definition of insight to guide the selection of empirical phenomena and the development of experimental paradigms for its study. Specifically, we define insight as any sudden comprehension, realization, or problem solution that involves a reorganization of the elements of a person's mental representation of a stimulus, situation, or event to yield a nonobvious or nondominant interpretation. Insights are not confined to any particular domain of understanding, but we do not include all sudden realizations within this definition. For example, the reading of an isolated word starts with unconscious processing followed by a sudden conscious realization of the word's meaning. But this is not an insight, because it doesn't involve reorganizing a mental representation to arrive at a nonobvious or nondominant interpretation. Insights may be especially salient when they follow an impasse, but impasse is not a necessary precondition for insight; otherwise, spontaneous sudden realizations would be excluded because they are not associated with an explicit problem whose solution is blocked by another idea. Insights are often accompanied by surprise and a positive burst of conscious emotion, but we do not consider these to be defining features because individual insights in a sequence of insights, as occur in many experimental studies, don't all elicit such conscious affective responses. (Of course, this doesn't exclude the possibility that all insights may be accompanied by unconscious affective responses; cf. Topolinski & Reber 2010.) Phenomena such as impasse and emotion play important roles in problem solving and are worthy of study. However, isolating the core processes of insight is a prerequisite for investigating it. To accomplish this, we adopt a "Goldilocks" approach— neither too much nor too little—and argue that this strategy can, and has, enabled progress in understanding insight's neurocognitive substrates.

It is also critical to recognize that insight involves several component processes working together and unfolding over time. Experimental paradigms that emphasize one process over another will reveal different parts of this network. Such results may appear complex but actually paint a richer picture of insight, just as studying encoding and retrieval, or implicit and explicit learning, paints a more complete picture of how the brain supports memory.

SCOPE OF THE REVIEW

This review discusses the current state of cognitive neuroscience research on insight. Though we also discuss selected behavioral cognitive studies that inform the neuroscientific framework we describe, we do not provide an overall review of the relevant cognitive literature here. Recent reviews of the cognitive literature are available elsewhere (e.g., van Steenburgh et al. 2012). Moreover, our discussion of neuroscientific studies is not exhaustive. We focus on those that meet several methodological criteria.

The first desideratum is that a study must demonstrably isolate the insight phenomenon. Some studies present problems to participants and simply assume that the solutions are the result of insight rather than analytical thought. However, as described below, many types of problems can be solved by either insight or analysis (Bowden et al. 2005). Therefore, with some exceptions, we do not discuss studies that do not demonstrate that participants' solutions were, in fact, a product of insight. One exception to this criterion is studies that use classic insight problems, such as the Nine-Dot Problem, that have been used by researchers for many decades and for which a consensus has been tacitly reached—though perhaps not yet with sufficient justification—that solutions to these problems are usually achieved by insight (e.g., Chi & Snyder 2012).

A number of studies examine brain activity when people recognize rather than generate solutions (e.g., Ludmer et al. 2011, Luo et al. 2011, Metuki et al. 2012). People may feel a sense of insight upon recognizing solutions, but these postsolution recognition processes differ from the processes responsible for generating the solutions. Once people see a solution word, they can perform a directed semantic memory search to connect the solution to the problem rather than an open-ended search for associations that might lead to the solution. Although solution recognition is itself interesting, it differs from pure insight.

A second criterion is that a candidate study must use an appropriate control or comparison condition. For example, in studies that use remote associates problems or anagrams, insight solutions can be directly compared to analytic solutions for the same type of problem because this comparison controls for all factors except for the cognitive solving strategy—insight versus analytic processing—that is the factor of primary interest. We therefore do not focus on studies that directly compare neural activity for sets of problems that differ in complexity, solving duration, visual content, working-memory load, and so forth (e.g., Aziz-Zadeh et al. 2013, Sheth et al. 2008) because differences in cognitive strategy are confounded with these ancillary factors. We wish to highlight how insight solving differs from analytic solving when other factors are held relatively constant.

Other studies are not discussed here due to methodological issues that cannot be addressed on a study-by-study basis in an article of this scope, such as problematic baselining of neural activity (e.g., Sandkühler & Bhattacharya 2008). Another type of methodological issue involves the integration over time of functional magnetic resonance imaging (fMRI) signal. One study attempted to use both subjective (self-report) and objective measures to distinguish insight from analytic solving (Aziz-Zadeh et al. 2009). Unfortunately, the objective measure was speed of solution: It was assumed that fast solutions were achieved with insight and slow solutions were achieved analytically. Not only is this assumption questionable, it also completely confounds the experimental contrast with the duration of solving effort. Because fMRI signal is integrated over time—the longer an area is active, the more the measured signal will increase—it is very sensitive to such confounds. Thus, it is impossible to know which effects were real and which were confound related.

It is important to note that the studies that are not discussed here due to methodological issues are not entirely uninformative. However, careful consideration must be given to each of these issues in the context of interpreting the results.

COGNITIVE PSYCHOLOGY OF INSIGHT

Much of the cognitive psychology research on insight done over the past three decades aimed to clarify the relationship between insightful and analytic thought (Sternberg & Davidson 1995). Early gestalt studies distinguished insight and analysis almost solely on the basis of the informal conscious experience of a problem solution emerging suddenly versus gradually. To extend this research, cognitive psychologists attempted to uncover more formal evidence to distinguish these two types of processing. A prominent example is a pioneering series of studies done by Janet Metcalfe during the 1980s. For example, Metcalfe & Wiebe (1987) focused on metacognitive characteristics of insight such as participants' feelings of "warmth" (i.e., closeness to solution) while working on insight and analytic problems. Participants reported a gradual increase in feelings of warmth leading up to analytic solutions, but little or no warmth preceding insights until shortly before they solved the problem. Moreover, insight problems that were accompanied by feelings of warmth usually elicited incorrect solutions.

Metcalfe & Wiebe's (1987) study was groundbreaking in showing a behavioral difference between insight and analytic solving beyond factors that differentially affected solution rates for these two types of problems. However, because Metcalfe's study sampled participants' feelings only once every 15 seconds, it did not directly address one of the central characteristics thought to distinguish insight and analytic solving, namely, the suddenness of solution. Rather, her procedure was designed to examine changes over time in participants' feelings about their closeness to solution.

However, it is possible to measure the accrual of solution information with higher temporal resolution using the speed-accuracy decomposition procedure (Kounios et al. 1987, Meyer et al. 1988). This technique revealed no discernable partial response information preceding the solution when people solve insight-like anagrams (Smith & Kounios 1996). Thus, insight solving occurs in a discrete transition from a state of no conscious information about the solution to the final complete solution, with no intermediate states. In contrast, for similar speed-accuracy decomposition studies of other (noninsight) tasks, such as lexical decision, semantic verification, short-term recognition memory, and long-term recognition memory, people show evidence of substantial partial information (Smith & Kounios 1996). This finding objectively validated the conscious experience of the abruptness of insight.

The conscious experience of insight directly relates to unconscious processing that precedes it. When people solve problems (anagrams), they solve better and experience their solutions as more insight-like when, prior to solution, solution-related words are presented to them subliminally (Bowden 1997). The fact that a subliminal prime can spark a later insight supports the hypothesis that insight solutions are preceded by substantial unconscious processing rather than spontaneously generated. Similarly, when people respond to solution words before solving a problem, the amount of semantic priming for solution words—an index of related unconscious processing—is directly related to how they experience the recognition of the solution. Specifically, people show more solution priming when they recognize solution words with a feeling of sudden insight than when they recognize the words without an insight experience (Bowden & Jung-Beeman 2003b).

These studies are also notable for a methodological innovation. Much of the insight literature compares performance on so-called insight problems with performance on analytic problems, a distinction based largely on researchers' intuitions or introspections about sudden versus gradual solution. This phenomenological difference had rarely been measured and quantified in a rigorous way. Furthermore, applying the monikers "insight" and "analytic" to specific problems assumes that all participants will always solve insight problems insightfully and analytic problems analytically—hardly a safe assumption. To put insight research on a firmer empirical foundation, Bowden (1997) developed a procedure for soliciting participants' trial-by-trial judgments of whether a solution had been derived by insight or analysis. This technique has been validated by subsequent studies that have shown that the number of insight solutions and analytic solutions to a series of problems varies independently as a function of factors such as mood (Subramaniam et al. 2009) and meaningfully with respect to cognitive strategies (Kounios et al. 2008) and brain activations (Jung-Beeman et al. 2004, Kounios et al. 2006, Subramaniam et al. 2009). The insight judgment procedure has thus provided a foundation for subsequent neuroimaging studies of insight because it allows researchers to isolate the insight phenomenon by controlling for ancillary differences between problems that were solved insightfully and analytically (Bowden et al. 2005, Kounios & Beeman 2009).

The development of short problems solvable by insight (Bowden & Jung-Beeman 2003a) has also proved useful in later neuroscience studies. Early studies of insight typically posed a small number of complex problems to participants. Most participants take many minutes to solve such problems, when they are able to solve them. However, neuroimaging and electrophysiological methods require many trials to accurately record brain activity. An alternative approach uses a relatively large number of structurally identical verbal problems, called remote associates problems, modeled after one type of problem developed by Mednick for his remote associates test of creativity (Mednick 1962). Bowden & Jung-Beeman (2003a) developed a set of compound remote associates problems that consist of three words (e.g., pine, crab, sauce). The participant's task is to think of a single solution word (apple) that will form a compound or familiar phrase with each of the three problem words (pineapple, crabapple, applesauce).

Remote associates problems are well suited to neuroimaging and electrophysiological studies. Large numbers of these problems have been developed, allowing for neuroimaging and electrophysiological studies with a sufficient number of trials per condition. Other types of short problems can serve this function as well. For example, anagrams have also been used with the insight judgment procedure (Bowden 1997, Kounios et al. 2008).

NEURAL BASIS OF INSIGHT

Hemispheric Asymmetry

Much of the research on the neural basis of insight has been framed by hemispheric differences, namely, that the right hemisphere contributes relatively more to insight solving than to analytic solving, whereas the left hemisphere contributes more to analytic solving than to insight solving. This hypothesis particularly influenced the experimental methods and predictions of early cognitive neuroscience studies of insight. For instance, several studies used visually lateralized probe words to detect and compare semantic processing in the hemispheres while participants worked on remote associates problems. On trials for which participants failed to solve problems within a time limit, they still showed semantic priming for the solution words by responding to solution word probes more quickly than to unrelated word probes. Importantly, this solution priming was especially pronounced when the solution word probes were presented to the left visual field, thus being directed initially to the right hemisphere (Beeman & Bowden 2000, Bowden & Beeman 1998). Furthermore, enhanced priming in the right hemisphere occurred only when participants reported that they recognized a solution word probe with a feeling of insight (Bowden & Jung-Beeman 2003b).

This rightward asymmetry of insight processing was predicted (Bowden & Beeman 1998) on the basis of prior evidence of right hemisphere involvement in integrating distant semantic relations in language input (e.g., St George et al. 1999) as well as a theoretical framework that describes the right hemisphere as engaging in relatively coarser semantic coding than the left hemisphere (Jung-Beeman 2005). This framework incorporates neuropsychological and neurological evidence of subtle comprehension deficits following right hemisphere brain damage with neuroanatomical findings of asymmetric neuronal wiring.

According to the coarse semantic coding framework, when readers or listeners encounter a word or concept, they activate a semantic field related to the word: a subset of features, properties, and associations of that word. Evidence suggests that the left hemisphere strongly activates a relatively smaller semantic field of features, those most closely related to the dominant interpretation or the current context; in contrast, the right hemisphere weakly activates a relatively broader semantic field, including features that are distantly related to the word or context (Chiarello 1988, Chiarello et al. 1990). Despite some obvious limitations, coarser semantic coding in the right hemisphere has one big advantage: The less sharply each word's meaning is specified, the more likely it is to connect to other words and concepts. This is a key ingredient for drawing inferences (Virtue et al. 2006, 2008), extracting the gist (St George et al. 1999), comprehending figurative language (Mashal et al. 2008), and for insight.

The coarse semantic coding notion is more than a metaphor. Rather, it potentially links asymmetric semantic processing to asymmetric brain wiring. Aside from some size asymmetries in particular regions of cortex (such as Broca's area and Wernicke's area), lateralized cytoarchitectonic differences also influence how neurons integrate inputs (for a review, see Hutsler & Galuske 2003). In brief, pyramidal neurons collect inputs through their dendrites. Differences in synaptic distributions along dendrites influence the type of inputs that cause these pyramidal neurons to fire. The range of cortical area over which neurons collect inputs could be termed their input fields. In association cortices in or near language-critical areas, such as Wernicke's area, Broca's area, and the anterior temporal cortex, right hemisphere neurons have larger input fields than do left hemisphere neurons (e.g., Jacob et al. 1993, Scheibel et al. 1985, Seldon 1981). Specifically, right hemisphere pyramidal neurons have more synapses overall and especially more synapses far from the cell body. This indicates that they have larger input fields than corresponding left hemisphere pyramidal neurons. Because cortical connections are spatially organized, the right hemisphere's larger input fields collect more differentiated inputs, perhaps requiring a variety of inputs to fire. The left hemisphere's smaller input fields collect highly similar inputs, likely causing the neuron to respond best to somewhat redundant inputs. Outputs from neurons appear to show similar asymmetry; for example, axons in superior temporal cortex are longer in the right hemisphere than in the left hemisphere, favoring more integrative processing in the right hemisphere (Tardif & Clarke 2001).

These neuroanatomical asymmetries could contribute to the right hemisphere's bias to engage in coarser semantic coding and the left hemisphere's bias to engage in finer (i.e., less coarse) semantic coding. As previously noted (Jung-Beeman 2005), there is a huge gap between descriptions of dendritic branching and modes of language processing or problem solving. However, the asymmetries that exist in neuronal wiring almost certainly influence information processing, and the asymmetries that indisputably exist in language processing must have some neuroanatomical basis. The coarser semantic coding framework attempts to bridge that gap. In so doing, it also provides an avenue for future research on the relationship between neural microcircuitry and higher cognitive functions.

Neural Correlates of Insight Solving

Further specification of the neural bases of insight can be achieved through neuroimaging studies. These studies have identified a number of distinct components of insight and have generally supported the idea that the right hemisphere contributes relatively more to insight than to analytic solving.

One early neuroimaging study of insight isolated neural correlates of the insight experience with both fMRI and high-density EEG in separate experiments matched as closely as possible for procedure (Jung-Beeman et al. 2004). EEG has excellent temporal resolution but limited spatial resolution. It is therefore good at circumscribing a neural process in time. fMRI has excellent spatial resolution but limited temporal resolution and is therefore best suited to localize a neural event in space. Together these techniques were able to isolate insight's neural correlates in both space and time. This combination of methods was crucial, because fMRI's power to localize insight-related neural activity would have been less informative without knowing whether these neural correlates occurred before, after, or at the moment of solution. A neural correlate of the insight experience itself would have to occur at, or immediately prior to, the moment of conscious awareness of a solution.

At the moment when people solve problems by insight, relative to solving identical problems by analytic processing, EEG shows a burst of high-frequency (gamma-band) EEG activity over the right temporal lobe, and fMRI shows a corresponding change in blood flow in the medial aspect of the right anterior superior temporal gyrus (Jung-Beeman et al. 2004) (**Figure 1**). In the initial fMRI experiment, this right temporal area was the only area exceeding strict statistical thresholds, but weak activity was detected in other areas, including bilateral hippocampus and

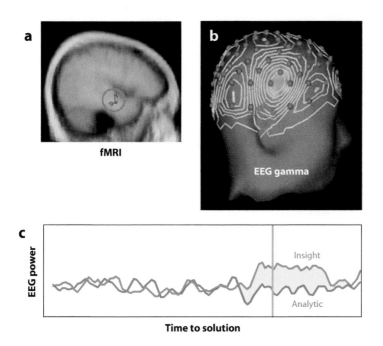

Figure 1

Neural correlates of insight. (*a*) Insight-related blood oxygen–level dependent (BOLD) activity in the right anterior superior temporal gyrus recorded by functional magnetic resonance imaging (fMRI). (*b*) Insight-related gamma-band oscillatory activity recorded by electroencephalogram (EEG) over the anterior right temporal lobe. (*c*) Time course of insight- and analysis-related gamma-band EEG power recorded at a right anterior electrode. The vertical gray line marks the point in time at which participants made a bimanual button press to indicate that they had solved a problem. EEG power leading up to insight and analytic solutions diverges at approximately 300 ms before the bimanual button press. Taking into consideration that a button press requires about 300 milliseconds to initiate and execute (Smith & Kounios 1996), the insight-related burst of gamma activity occurred at approximately the time at which the solution to the problem became available to participants. Adapted from Jung-Beeman et al. (2004), with permission.

parahippocampal gyri and anterior and posterior cingulate cortex. In a later replication with more participants and stronger imaging methods (Subramaniam et al. 2009), the same network of areas all far exceeded critical statistical threshold, with the right anterior temporal region again being the strongest. The close spatial and temporal correspondence of the fMRI and EEG results obtained by Jung-Beeman et al. suggested that they were produced by the same underlying brain activation. This right temporal brain response was identified as the main neural correlate of the insight experience because (*a*) it occurred at about the moment when participants realized the solution to each of these problems, (*b*) the same region is involved in other tasks demanding semantic integration (St George et al. 1999); and (*c*) gamma-band activity has been proposed to be a mechanism for binding information as it emerges into consciousness (Tallon-Baudry & Bertrand 1999). Alternative interpretations of this finding were rejected based on considerations of timing, functional neuroanatomy, etc.

The burst of gamma-band EEG activity in the right temporal lobe was not unexpected, given earlier visual half-field studies (Beeman & Bowden 2000, Bowden & Beeman 1998, Bowden & Jung-Beeman 2003b). However, the EEG results revealed another, totally unexpected, finding. The insight-related gamma-band activity was immediately preceded by a burst of alpha-band activity (10 Hz) measured over right occipital cortex (Jung-Beeman et al. 2004) (see **Figure 2**).

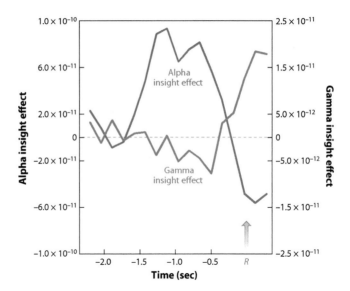

Figure 2

The time course of the insight effect. Alpha power (9.8 Hz at right parietal-occipital electrode PO8) and gamma power (39 Hz at right temporal electrode T8) for the insight effect (i.e., correct insight solutions minus correct noninsight solutions, in v^2). The left y-axis shows the magnitude of the alpha insight effect (*purple line*); the right y-axis applies to the gamma insight effect (*green line*). The x-axis represents time (in seconds). The gray arrow and R (at 0.0 sec) signify the time of the button-press response. Note the transient enhancement of alpha on insight trials (relative to noninsight trials) prior to the gamma burst.

Alpha-band oscillations reflect neural inhibition; occipital alpha reflects inhibition of visual inputs, that is, sensory gating (Jensen & Mazaheri 2010). It appears likely that the preinsight alpha burst reflects transient sensory gating that reduces noise from distracting inputs to facilitate retrieval of the weakly and unconsciously activated solution represented in the right temporal lobe (Jung-Beeman et al. 2004; cf. Wu et al. 2009). This idea is analogous to the common behavior of closing or averting one's eyes to avoid distractions that would otherwise interfere with intense mental effort.

The discovery of transient sensory gating immediately preceding the insight-related burst of gamma-band activity suggested a promising research strategy. Previous behavioral research had demonstrated the discrete, all-or-nothing nature of insight solutions (Smith & Kounios 1996). On the other hand, visual hemifield solution-priming studies showed that insight, though consciously abrupt, is preceded by unconscious processing, primarily in the right hemisphere (e.g., Bowden & Beeman 1998). So, an insightful solution is a discrete phenomenon in terms of its availability to awareness, but it is preceded by unconscious neural precursors. It should therefore be possible to trace these neural precursors backward in time from the gamma burst at the moment of insight to reveal the brain mechanisms that unfold to produce an insight.

Preparation for Insight

Before people even start to tackle a problem, their state of mind—and their brain activity—predisposes them to solve either by insight or analytic processing. Participants' neural activity, assessed with both EEG and fMRI during a task-free preparation phase prior to each remote associates problem, shows that such predispositions do occur: Distinct patterns of neural activity precede problems that people eventually solve by insight versus those that they solve by analysis

(Kounios et al. 2006). EEG showed that preparation for analytic solving involves increased neural activity (i.e., decreased alpha-band activity) measured over visual cortex, hypothesized to reflect outward focus of attention directed to the computer monitor on which the next problem in the sequence was to be displayed. Both EEG and fMRI revealed that preparation for insight solving involves activation of the anterior cingulate and bilateral temporal cortices. The temporal lobe activation suggests that cortical regions involved in lexical and semantic processing are prepared to respond. Previous research implicates anterior cingulate cortex in monitoring other brain regions for conflicting action tendencies (Botvinick et al. 2004). Kounios et al. (2006) expanded on this notion of conflicting action tendencies to propose that the anterior cingulate's role in problem solving is to detect the activation of conflicting solution possibilities or strategies. If the anterior cingulate is sufficiently activated at the time a problem is presented, then it can detect the weak activation of nondominant solution possibilities, enabling attention to switch to one of these weakly activated ideas. Switching attention to a nonobvious solution brings the idea to awareness as an insight. However, when the anterior cingulate is relatively deactivated prior to the presentation of a problem, attention is dominated by the more obvious associations and solution possibilities afforded by the problem.

Thus, the transient state of one's attentional focus, varying from trial to trial, helps to determine the range of potential solutions that a person is prepared to consider when a problem is presented: Outwardly directed attention coupled with low anterior cingulate activity focuses processing on the dominant features or possibilities of a situation; inwardly directed attention and high anterior cingulate activity heightens sensitivity to weakly activated remote associations and long-shot solution ideas.

One important, but unresolved, issue is to what extent such preparatory activity is under voluntary control and to what extent spontaneous shifts of attention may be involved. Kounios et al. (2006) found no evidence of any trial-to-trial sequential clusters of insight or analytic solutions that would suggest slow spontaneous shifts of attention. However, this kind of analysis would not be capable of showing attention shifts on a timescale shorter than the duration of a single trial (i.e., approximately 10 sec.). Identifying any neural correlates of possible strategic or spontaneous attention shifts is therefore an important focus for future investigations. Progress in elucidating the role of attention shifts would suggest practical techniques for controlling or enhancing cognitive style.

Resting-State Brain Activity and Individual Differences

Given that transient shifts in attention influence whether people solve by analysis or by insight, do any longer-lasting states or traits influence this preparatory activity and the corresponding predisposition to solve by insight or analysis? One approach is to examine whether individual differences in resting-state brain activity while people have no task to perform or any particular expectation about what will follow may influence their subsequent problem-solving style. In one study, we recorded participants' resting-state EEGs before tasking them with solving a series of anagrams (Kounios et al. 2008). Participants were classified as high insight or low insight based on the proportion of problems they solved with insight. These groups exhibited different patterns of resting-state EEGs, suggesting that the insightful and analytic cognitive styles have their origins in, or are at least related to, distinct patterns of resting-state neural activity. The differences between these patterns highlighted two general phenomena.

Insightful individuals show greater right hemisphere activity at rest, relative to analytic individuals, consistent with the idea of insight-related right hemisphere bias described above. The fact that an insight-related hemispheric difference can be found in the resting state suggests that the functional hemispheric asymmetry occurring during problem solution (Jung-Beeman et al.

2004) may have its origin in structural hemispheric differences among people, such as the cytoar-chitectonic differences described above (Jung-Beeman 2005) or in asymmetries of structural or functional connectivity.

Insightful individuals also showed greater diffuse activation of visual cortex compared to an-alytical individuals, even when resting-state EEGs were measured while participants' eyes were closed (Kounios et al. 2008). This finding mirrors earlier behavioral research showing that highly creative individuals tend to have diffuse attention when at rest or when cognitive resources are not dominated by a task (e.g., Ansburg & Hill 2003, Carson et al. 2003).

Resting-state EEG can be perturbed by stimuli but otherwise is relatively stable; in fact, be-havioral genetics studies show that individual differences in resting-state EEG have a substantial genetic loading largely attributable to individual differences in gray matter and white matter volume (Smit et al. 2012). It is not yet known whether insight-related individual differences in resting-state EEG are a subset of the genetically loaded individual differences in EEG or brain volume, but if so, this would be a promising avenue of investigation into the stability and origins of cognitive style.

Studies of insight-related resting-state brain activity may also provide a link to recent so-cial psychological research on construal level. According to construal level theory, psychological "distance"—thinking about things that are far away in space or time, or about people that are different from oneself—engages abstract thinking (Trope & Liberman 2010). Based on this idea, Förster et al. (2004) predicted that priming people to think about the distant future would bias them to think abstractly, which in turn would induce a person to think more insightfully and creatively; conversely, priming people to think about the near future would bias them to think concretely and therefore analytically. Their studies supported these predictions: Participants primed by asking them to think about the distant future subsequently did better on insight and creativity tasks; those asked to think about the near future did better on analytic tasks. These results are particularly interesting because construal-level priming may influence task-related cognition by transiently al-tering the resting-state brain activity from which task-related brain activity emerges. A potentially fruitful line of research would be to examine how various types of priming might influence the ten-dency to solve problems insightfully or analytically by imposing transient changes in resting-state brain activity.

Thus, distinct patterns of neural activity are associated with insight versus analytic solving at the moment of insight, in the last two seconds leading up to that moment, in the preparation phase prior to presentation of a problem, and even in resting-state brain activity of individuals who tend to solve by insight contrasted with those who tend to solve analytically. These findings objectively substantiate an abundance of behavioral evidence that indicates insight solving differs from analytic solving and that these solving styles result from different tunings of the network of brain areas involved in problem solving. Moreover, the specific areas associated at each distinct stage of solving (or preparation) help inform theories of how insight is different from analysis. Compared to analytic solving, insight requires greater input from and integration of relatively coarser semantic processing of right hemisphere temporal areas, greater sensitivity to competing responses in cognitive control mechanisms supported by the anterior cingulate cortex, and a relative emphasis on internal processing and de-emphasis on external stimuli.

ATTENDING IN, OUT, AND AROUND

A prominent theme in insight and creativity research is the role that attention deployment plays in cognitive style. Though a number of behavioral studies have observed that highly creative individuals have diffuse attention, taken as a whole, neuroimaging and electrophysiological studies of insight suggest that attention plays a more nuanced role. Neural activity during the preparatory phase suggests that attention can also be focused outwardly on external objects or inwardly on internal knowledge in memory (see Chun et al. 2011), which influences the likelihood that people will solve with insight (Kounios et al. 2006, Wegbreit et al. 2012).

Occipital alpha-band EEG activity reflects visual cortex inhibition that protects fragile internal processing from potentially interfering or distracting perceptual inputs (Ray & Cole 1985). Levels of occipital alpha during the different phases leading up to the solution of a problem suggest that (*a*) during the resting state, insightful individuals have more externally oriented attention than do analytical individuals (Kounios et al. 2008); (*b*) during the preparation phase prior to the presentation of a problem that will be solved by insight, there is greater internal focus of attention (Kounios et al. 2006); and (*c*) just before the emergence of an insight, there is another brief burst of inward focus (Jung-Beeman et al. 2004).

Thus, the notion that insight is associated with diffuse attention appears to be an oversimplification. Insightful individuals may generally have more diffuse and outwardly directed attention, but successful insight solving involves transiently redirecting attention inwardly during the preparation for and solving of a problem. It therefore appears that the tendency to solve problems insightfully is associated with broad perceptual intake as the default mode of resting-state attention deployment, coupled with the tendency to focus inwardly in preparation for, and during, solving. In contrast, analytical people's resting-state attention is less outwardly focused during the resting state and less inwardly directed during preparation and solving.

FACTORS THAT INFLUENCE THE LIKELIHOOD OF INSIGHT

Understanding the factors that can increase or reduce the likelihood of experiencing insight is important for both theoretical and practical reasons. Besides contributing toward the development of a theoretical model of insight, understanding these factors also suggests strategies for its enhancement outside the laboratory. Here we focus on the interrelated factors of mood, attention, and cognitive control.

Mood

Positive affect enhances insight and other forms of creativity, both when the mood occurs naturally and when it is induced in the laboratory (e.g., Ashby et al. 1999, Isen et al. 1987). Though some aspects of creative production may be impeded by positive mood or aided by other moods such as depression (Verhaeghen et al. 2005), insight and related processes seem to benefit from greater positive mood (or reduced anxiety) either when participants enter the lab in a relatively positive mood or after they watch funny film clips (H. Mirous & M. Beeman, manuscript submitted; Subramaniam et al. 2009). Facilitation of insight by positive mood has also been demonstrated in the workplace, as documented by diaries and self-reports (Amabile et al. 2005).

Mood influences other cognitive abilities that are related to insight and creativity. For example, positive mood facilitates intuition, the ability to make decisions or judgments about stimuli without conscious access to the information or processes influencing their behavior. When people are working on remote associates problems, they show better-than-chance judgment about whether individual problems are solvable before they are able to state the solution; such intuitive judgments are improved after people recall happy autobiographical events and are impeded after recalling sad autobiographical events (Bolte et al. 2003).

Finding or intuiting the presence of a solution to a remote associates problem requires a person to access weak associations of the problem words because the solution is typically not a strong associate of all three problem words. Thus, the presentation of the problem will evoke only weak activation of the solution's representation. Positive mood seems to broaden the scope of semantic processing to make such weak associations more accessible (Isen & Daubman 1984, Isen et al. 1985). For instance, the amplitude of the N400 component of the event-related potential (ERP) is inversely proportional to the relatedness of a word to its semantic context (Kounios 1996), and N400 semantic relatedness effects are modulated by mood. When a positive mood is induced, target words that loosely fit their semantic context elicit a smaller N400 than when the participant is in a neutral mood (Federmeier et al. 2001). This indicates that a positive mood makes a word seem less incongruent with its semantic context. Additionally, when people listen to stories that imply specific causal events without stating them explicitly, they show sensitivity to semantic information that is related to the implicit inference. Specifically, they read or respond to probe words that are related to an implicit inference more quickly than they read or respond to unrelated probe words. Such inference-related priming normally occurs earlier and more strongly for words presented to the right hemisphere (left visual field) than for words presented to the left hemisphere (right visual field) (Beeman et al. 2000). But people show stronger inference-related priming to inference-related words presented in the middle of the visual field while listening to stories after watching funny film clips than after watching emotionally neutral films; they show no inference-related priming after watching scary film clips that induce anxiety (H. Mirous & M. Beeman, manuscript submitted).

Recently it has also been argued that the relation between broad associations and positive mood is bidirectional, making it possible to induce a positive mood by instructing or otherwise inducing participants to process remote associations (Bar 2009, Brunyé et al. 2013). According to this idea, a positive mood both facilitates insight and is enhanced by it. This shows deep integration of cognitive and affective processes and relates to many everyday behaviors, such as peoples' enjoyment of verbal puzzles, especially those with surprising solutions.

The fact that people engage in coarser semantic coding when they are in a positive mood compared to when they are in neutral or anxious mood raises the possibility that positive mood may selectively activate right hemisphere semantic processing. However, as of yet, there is no evidence to support this hypothesis. For example, the neuroimaging study of insight and mood by Subramaniam et al. (2009) found no evidence of lateralized differences in brain activity that were attributable to mood.

Mood and Attention

A more likely hypothesis is that mood influences the likelihood of insight by modulating attention or cognitive control, which in turn modulates semantic processing. For example, anxiety narrows the scope of attention by eliciting excessive focus on the center of one's field of vision—which usually includes the source of the threat—to the exclusion of peripheral information (Easterbrook 1959). From the evolutionary standpoint, this makes great sense: Early humans spotting a lion on the African savannah would not want to be distracted by less important stimuli. In contrast, positive mood appears to broaden attention. It increases the perception and utilization of global and peripheral perceptual features at the expense of the local details of complex stimuli by spatially broadening the "spotlight" of attention (Gasper & Clore 2002). For example, in a task that requires participants to respond to a centrally located target stimulus and disregard other stimuli that flank it, a positive mood increases both facilitation and interference of target processing attributable to the flanking stimuli (Rowe et al. 2007). Beyond visual processing, positive mood seems to broaden the processing of novel and varied stimuli, stimulating exploratory behavior (Fredrickson & Branigan 2005).

Models of Attention

One possibility is that mood affects the balance between two brain systems: an anterior attention network that maintains top-down control over perceptual processing in the service of goals and a posterior network involved in bottom-up attentional capture by salient stimuli. According to attentional control theory, anxiety shifts the balance away from the top-down system toward the bottom-up system (Derakshan & Eysenck 2009), leading to enhanced distractibility by task-irrelevant stimuli, especially threatening stimuli (Bar-Haim et al. 2007). This view suggests that anxiety shifts attention toward external stimuli and away from internal representations, states, and goals; positive affect may have the opposite effect.

In practice, attentional control theory makes predictions that are similar to those of the spotlight model of attention. Moreover, it links positive mood with internally focused attention in a way that is consistent with research implicating both of these factors in preparation for insight (Kounios et al. 2006, Subramaniam et al. 2009). Attentional control theory is therefore a promising direction for future insight research.

One important question is why changes in the breadth of perceptual attention due to mood and other factors should be related to changes in the breadth or narrowness of thought to include or exclude remote associations, what Rowe et al. (2007) called conceptual attention. Rowe et al. demonstrated that a positive mood both increases the breadth of visual attention to include stimuli that flank a target and enhances performance on remote associates problems that, as noted, require access to distant associations of the problem words. Rowe et al. (2007) argued that perceptual and conceptual attention are closely linked.

Current attention theory can be expanded to include both phenomena. The biased competition model of attention characterizes the neural computations subserving vision as a process of competition between the representations of the stimuli in the visual field (Desimone 1998). This competition can be biased to favor a particular stimulus by a variety of factors, including externally driven (bottom-up) and internally driven (top-down) processes. Such biasing is manifested as an increase in the neural activity subserving one of the representations.

A similar mechanism may underlie the conceptual processing that occurs during problem solving. According to this idea, the presentation of a problem activates a number of associations in a person's memory. Dominant associations are strongly activated; nondominant ones are weakly activated. All of these associations compete for processing resources, though under normal circumstances, the dominant associations win the competition for further processing. However, top-down mechanisms can bias this competition toward weak associations by actively selecting nondominant representations; by expanding the scope of attention to boost activation of nondominant representations; or, simply, by not suppressing the less dominant associations when the dominant ones capture the spotlight. Dominant associations are already as activated as they can be, so expanding the scope of attention would benefit weak associations more than it would do for strong ones giving weak associations a greater opportunity to capture attention and spark an insight. Bottom-up processes can also bias the competition between ideas. Stimuli in the surrounding environment that are related to the solution can intervene to bias processing toward a weak association by acting as a hint that triggers an insight (Bowden 1997, Seifert et al. 1995). Thus, the biased competition model may be generalized to explain the role of conceptual attention in problem solving by insight.

Cognitive Control

Other research has focused on the role of cognitive control, especially the ability to maintain or switch between different thoughts, actions, and goals. People often focus on a task or goal to shield it from distraction. In other cases, especially in creative tasks, people need to flexibly switch between different processes, associations, or goals. These two functions, task shielding and task switching, appear to be in direct competition: The need for flexible switching demands relaxation of task shielding and leaves processing open to distraction (Dreisbach 2012). Positive affect enhances task switching but yields increased distractibility (Dreisbach & Goschke 2004).

As noted above, preparation for insight involves increased activity in the anterior cingulate during the preparatory period preceding a problem (Kounios et al. 2006). Anterior cingulate activation is hypothesized to be a sign that problem solvers are sensitized to competing, nondominant associations that they can switch to, resulting in an insight. When a person is in a positive mood, the preparation period shows stronger anterior cingulate activation than occurs for people not in a positive mood. In fact, the anterior cingulate was found to be the only brain area whose activation varies with mood, preparation for insight versus analytic processing, and later insight versus analytic solving (Subramaniam et al. 2009).

The anterior cingulate has long been recognized as a critical component of the cognitive control network. One hypothesis, backed up by substantial evidence, is that this brain region monitors other regions for competing action tendencies or stimulus representations (Kerns et al. 2004, Weissman et al. 2005). It has been proposed to be an interface between emotion and cognition (Allman et al. 2001, Bush et al. 2000, Lane et al. 1998) in part because some (ventral) regions of the cingulate are important for emotional processing (Mayberg et al. 1999).

Another brain area implicated in insight-related cognitive control is prefrontal cortex. Considerable evidence supports the idea that prefrontal cortex exerts control over other brain regions in response to input from the anterior cingulate signaling the presence of cognitive conflict (Miller & Cohen 2001). According to this idea, modulation of insight solving due to changes in anterior cingulate activity should be mediated, at least in part, by control signals originating in prefrontal cortex that limit the range of possibilities that a person considers when working on a problem. This limiting function is ordinarily helpful because it focuses the solver on a small number of the most viable solution paths to avoid computational overload. However, it can be a hindrance when a person tries to solve a problem whose solution lies on a nonobvious solution path. In support of this idea, patients with damage to lateral prefrontal cortex were better able to solve matchstick insight problems than were healthy control participants (Reverberi et al. 2005).

STIMULATING INSIGHT

One limitation of neuroimaging and electrophysiological studies is that they are inherently correlational—they don't directly show that the recorded patterns of brain activity cause the measured changes in behavior or experience. But the advent of brain stimulation techniques now affords the opportunity to treat brain activity as an independent variable rather than a dependent one.

Recent efforts have applied one brain-stimulation technique, transcranial direct current stimulation (tDCS), to attempt to enhance insight solving. Two recent studies have yielded promising results (Chi & Snyder 2011, 2012). Researchers tested the hemispheric hypothesis of insight by applying facilitatory (anodal) stimulation to right frontal-temporal cortex and inhibitory (cathodal) stimulation to left frontal-temporal cortex. This pattern of stimulation, but not the reverse hemispheric pattern, significantly enhanced solution rates for the nine-dot problem and for an insight matchstick problem. This stimulation protocol yielded especially dramatic enhancement for the classic nine-dot problem, increasing the solution rate from 0% to 40%. Additional studies have found that stimulation interfering with left dorsolateral prefrontal cortex facilitates solving compound remote associates problems (Metuki et al. 2012) or flexibly generating unusual uses for objects (Chrysikou et al. 2013). These studies suggest that such tasks benefit from the release of cognitive control that would otherwise maintain focus on fine semantic coding in the left hemisphere; however, neither of these studies specifically contrasted insight versus analytic performance.

Such stimulation studies are encouraging initial efforts that provide striking support for the claim that insight depends relatively more on right than on left temporal lobe processes. They also raise the alluring possibility that someday brain stimulation techniques will be refined to the point at which individuals grappling with difficult problems may have the option of donning a "thinking cap" that will increase their ability to find solutions. However, it should be kept in mind that these early studies—similar to other groundbreaking studies—raise as many questions as they answer. For example, this stimulation protocol simultaneously stimulated right frontal-temporal cortex and inhibited left frontal-temporal cortex (Chi & Snyder 2012). It is not yet known whether it was the right frontal-temporal stimulation, the left frontal-temporal inhibition, or the combination of the two that facilitated solving these insight problems. Moreover, it is not yet known whether this tDCS protocol actually increased the probability that participants solved these problems insightfully or whether it increased the probability that they solved the problems analytically. As we have noted, most problems can be solved by either strategy. The fact that researchers have considered the nine-dot and matchstick-type problems to be insight problems doesn't preclude the possibility that they can be solved analytically. These studies did not assess the strategies that their participants employed, so all that is known is that the solution rates for these problems increased rather than how or why they increased. Thus, much foundational work must be done before tDCS can be considered a realistic possibility for adaptively modifying people's cognitive strategies.

Pharmacological intervention is another route to insight enhancement. To date, we are aware of no studies that use drugs to attempt selective facilitation of insight solving. However, the recent demonstration that alcohol can enhance insight, but not analytic, solving of remote associates problems shows that pharmacological promotion of insight is achievable (Jarosz et al. 2012).

FUTURE DIRECTIONS

Neuroimaging and electrophysiological techniques have begun to reveal neural substrates of insight that were invisible to behavioral research. This has led to progress in understanding how insight emerges from more basic cognitive mechanisms. Technologies for stimulating insightful thought are becoming available, including intervention by direct brain stimulation.

Nevertheless, from our current vantage point, it is important to keep in mind that the surface has barely been scratched. Research has shown that multiple component processes and corresponding neural substrates are involved, and some of these are susceptible to subtle shifts in attention, mood, and other factors. Refined methods will expand on the research we have described and contribute new findings from connectivity and network analyses. And one can only guess what will be uncovered by future studies of insight-related individual differences in neuroanatomy, cytoarchitectonics, and genetics. The psychopharmacology of insight and creativity, currently virtually unexplored, holds out the promise of contributing both to our scientific understanding of insight and to methods for enhancing it. Further research will reveal the limits and applicability of brain stimulation, neurofeedback, and cognitive training techniques for enhancing insight and, more generally, influencing and optimizing cognitive styles to suit different circumstances. The study of insight began in the early twentieth century, but a century from now, researchers may look back at the early twenty-first century as the beginning of a golden age of insight research.

SUMMARY POINTS

1. Insight is any sudden comprehension, realization, or problem solution that involves a reorganization of the elements of a person's mental representation of a stimulus, situation, or event to yield a nonobvious or nondominant interpretation. Insight is sudden, but it is preceded by substantial unconscious processing.

2. Some critical components of insight are preferentially associated with the right cerebral hemisphere. Insight culminates with a sharp increase in neural activity in the right anterior temporal lobe at the moment of insight.

3. Insights are immediately preceded by a transient reduction of visual inputs that apparently reduce distractions and boost the signal-to-noise ratio of the solution.

4. Neural activity immediately before the presentation of an expected problem predicts whether that problem will be solved by insight or analytically. Such preparation for insight involves inwardly directed attention; preparation for analysis involves outwardly directed attention.

5. Resting-state neural activity biases later processing to favor insight or analytical problem solving.

6. Positive mood facilitates insight by increasing attentional scope to include weakly activated solution possibilities.

7. Direct stimulation of right frontal-temporal cortex coupled with inhibition of left frontal-temporal cortex enhances solving of insight problems.

8. Cognitive neuroscience methods have contributed exciting new results and theories of insight; nevertheless, insight research is still in a very early stage. Continuing applications of new methods, paradigms, and models hold much promise for additional substantial progress.

FUTURE ISSUES

1. How and when can insight be facilitated? People often ask how they can foster more insightful thinking, even though in many situations and for many problems, analytic processing would be more effective. At the least, problems must be deeply analyzed [what Graham Wallas (1926) termed immersion] before an insight solution can be achieved. So the question becomes when insight should be facilitated. We suggest that the right time to facilitate insight is when semantic integration processes activate the representation of a potential solution to a level just below the threshold for consciousness, setting the stage for an aha moment. Thus, honing intuition to sense the presence of a subthreshold solution may be the first step toward facilitating insight. At this time, inducing a positive mood and broadening attention through various means, and not directly focusing on the problem, is likely to increase the chance of achieving insight.

2. What individual differences in attention or cognitive control are most conducive to insight? Recent work shows that while in the resting state and not engaged in any task, individuals who tend to solve by insight deploy attention differently from individuals who are more analytic. What is the best way to characterize this pattern of differences? Do high-insight individuals deploy attention externally at rest and internally during solving? Or do they just deploy their attention in a less-focused manner? Do these differences primarily occur in bottom-up attention or primarily in top-down attention and cognitive control? How tightly coupled are insight-related individual differences in visual cortex and those in the anterior cingulate? Do individual differences in insightfulness have a genetic basis?

3. How do individual differences in processes that support insight interact? In general, positive mood facilitates insight by encouraging broader or less selective attention. However, a greater tendency or ability to solve problems with insight may also be associated with individual differences in other factors that cause broad associative thinking, such as schizotypy (Folley & Park 2005). It is possible that for individuals who typically think more broadly, anxiety would facilitate solving by focusing their attention to harness their broader associative processes toward a useful solution.

4. How does insight problem solving relate to other creative behavior? Insight is considered a critical facet of creative cognition. However, creativity is a highly complex behavior. Although aspects of creativity may be entirely unrelated, others are likely linked, perhaps sharing similar patterns of attention. How do insight, intuitive decision making, divergent thinking, and creative achievement relate to each other, and to attention and cognitive control?

DISCLOSURE STATEMENT

The authors are not aware of any affiliations, memberships, funding, or financial holdings that might be perceived as affecting the objectivity of this review.

ACKNOWLEDGMENTS

Preparation of this article and some of the research described therein was supported by National Science Foundation grant 1144976 to J.K. and John Templeton Foundation grant 24467 to M.B.

LITERATURE CITED

Allman J, Hakeem A, Erwin JM, Nimchinsky E, Hof P. 2001. The anterior cingulate cortex: the evolution of an interface between emotion and cognition. *Ann. N. Y. Acad. Sci.* 935:107–17

Amabile TM, Barsade SG, Mueller JS, Staw BM. 2005. Affect and creativity at work. *Adm. Sci. Q.* 50:367–403

Ansburg PI, Hill K. 2003. Creative and analytic thinkers differ in their use of attentional resources. *Personal. Individ. Differ.* 34:1141–52

Ashby FG, Isen AM, Turken U. 1999. A neuropsychological theory of positive affect and its influence on cognition. *Psychol. Rev.* 106:529–50

Aziz-Zadeh L, Kaplan JT, Iacoboni M. 2009. "Aha!": the neural correlates of verbal insight solutions. *Hum. Brain Mapp.* 30:908–16

Aziz-Zadeh L, Liew S-L, Dandekar F. 2013. Exploring the neural correlates of visual creativity. *Soc. Cogn. Affect. Neurosci.* 8: 475–80

Bar M. 2009. A cognitive neuroscience hypothesis of mood and depression. *Trends Cogn. Sci.* 13:456–63

Bar-Haim Y, Lamy D, Pergamin L, Bakermans-Kranenburg MJ, van IJzendoorn MH. 2007. Threat-related attentional bias in anxious and nonanxious individuals: a meta-analytic study. *Psychol. Bull.* 133:1–24

Beeman MJ, Bowden EM. 2000. The right hemisphere maintains solution-related activation for yet-to-be-solved problems. *Mem. Cogn.* 28:1231–41

Beeman MJ, Bowden EM, Gernsbacher MA. 2000. Right and left hemisphere cooperation for drawing predictive and coherence inferences during normal story comprehension. *Brain Lang.* 71:310–36

Bolte A, Goschke T, Kuhl J. 2003. Emotion and intuition: effects of positive and negative mood on implicit judgments of semantic coherence. *Psychol. Sci.* 14:416–21

Botvinick MM, Cohen JD, Carter CS. 2004. Conflict monitoring and anterior cingulate cortex: an update. *Trends Cogn. Sci.* 8:539–46

Bowden EM. 1997. The effect of reportable and unreportable hints on anagram solution and the aha! experience. *Conscious. Cogn.* 6:545–73

Bowden EM, Beeman MJ. 1998. Getting the right idea: Semantic activation in the right hemisphere may help solve insight problems. *Psychol. Sci.* 9(6):435–40

Bowden EM, Jung-Beeman M. 2003a. Normative data for 144 compound remote associate problems. *Behav. Res. Methods* 35(4):634–39

Bowden EM, Jung-Beeman M. 2003b. Aha! Insight experience correlates with solution activation in the right hemisphere. *Psychon. Bull. Rev.* 10:730–37

Bowden EM, Jung-Beeman M, Fleck J, Kounios J. 2005. New approaches to demystifying insight. *Trends Cogn. Sci.* 9(7):322–28

Brunyé TT, Gagnon SA, Paczynski M, Shenhav A, Mahoney CR, Taylor HA. 2013. Happiness by association: Breadth of free association influences affective states. *Cognition* 127:93–98

Bush G, Luu P, Posner MI. 2000. Cognitive and emotional influence in anterior cingulate cortex. *Trends Cogn. Sci.* 4:215–22

Carson SH, Peterson JB, Higgins DM. 2003. Decreased latent inhibition is associated with increased creative achievement in high-functioning individuals. *J. Personal. Soc. Psychol.* 85:499–506

Chi RP, Snyder AW. 2011. Facilitate insight by non-invasive brain stimulation. *PLoS ONE* 6(2):e16655

Chi RP, Snyder AW. 2012. Brain stimulation enables the solution of an inherently difficult problem. *Neurosci. Lett.* 515:121–24

Chiarello C. 1988. Lateralization of lexical processes in the normal brain: a review of visual half-field research. In *Contemporary Reviews in Neuropsychology*, ed. HA Whitaker, pp. 36–76. New York: Springer-Verlag

Chiarello C, Burgess C, Richards L, Pollock A. 1990. Semantic and associative priming in the cerebral hemispheres: some words do, some words don't . . . sometimes, some places. *Brain Lang.* 38:75–104

Chrysikou EG, Hamilton RH, Coslett HB, Datta A, Bikson M, Thompson-Schill SL. 2013. Noninvasive transcranial direct current stimulation over the left prefrontal cortex facilitates cognitive flexibility in tool use. *Cogn. Neurosci.* 4:81–89

Chun MM, Golomb JD, Turk-Browne NB. 2011. A taxonomy of external and internal attention. *Annu. Rev. Psychol.* 62:73–101

Cranford EA, Moss J. 2012. Is insight always the same? A protocol analysis of insight in compound remote associate problems. *J. Probl. Solving* 4(2):128–53

Derakshan N, Eysenck MW. 2009. Anxiety, processing efficiency, and cognitive performance: new developments from attentional control theory. *Eur. Psychol.* 14:168–76

Desimone R. 1998. Visual attention mediated by biased competition in extrastriate visual cortex. *Philos. Trans. R. Soc. Lond. B* 353:1245–55

Dietrich A, Kanso R. 2010. A review of EEG, ERP, and neuroimaging studies of creativity and insight. *Psychol. Bull.* 136:822–48

Dreisbach G. 2012. Mechanisms of cognitive control: the functional role of task rules. *Curr. Dir. Psychol. Sci.* 21:227–31

Dreisbach G, Goschke T. 2004. How PA modulates cognitive control: reduced perseveration at the cost of increased distractibility. *J. Exp. Psychol.: Learn. Mem. Cogn.* 30(2):343–53

Easterbrook JA. 1959. The effect of emotion on cue utilization and the organization of behavior. *Psychol. Rev.* 66:183–201

Federmeier KD, Kirson DA, Moreno EM, Kutas M. 2001. Effects of transient, mild mood states on semantic memory organization and use: an event-related potential investigation in humans. *Neurosci. Lett.* 305:149–52

Folley BS, Park S. 2005. Verbal creativity and schizotypal personality in relation to prefrontal hemispheric laterality: a behavioral and near-infrared optical imaging study. *Schizophr. Res.* 80:271–82

Förster J, Friedman RS, Liberman N. 2004. Temporal construal effects on abstract and concrete thinking: consequences for insight and creative cognition. *J. Personal. Soc. Psychol.* 87:177–89

Fredrickson B, Branigan C. 2005. Positive emotions broaden the scope of attention and thought-action repertoires. *Cogn. Emot.* 19:313–32

Gasper K, Clore GL. 2002. Attending to the big picture: mood and global versus local processing of visual information. *Psychol. Sci.* 13:34–40

Hutsler J, Galuske RA. 2003. Hemispheric asymmetries in cerebral cortical networks. *Trends Neurosci.* 26:429–35

Isen AM, Daubman KA. 1984. The influence of affect on categorization. *J. Personal. Soc. Psychol.* 47:1206–17

Isen AM, Daubman KA, Nowicki GP. 1987. Positive affect facilitates creative problem solving. *J. Personal. Soc. Psychol.* 52:1122–31

Isen AM, Johnson MM, Mertz E, Robinson GF. 1985. The influence of positive affect on the unusualness of word associations. *J. Personal. Soc. Psychol.* 48:1413–26

Jacob R, Schall M, Scheibel AB. 1993. A quantitative dendritic analysis of Wernicke's area in humans. II. Gender, hemispheric, and environmental factors. *J. Comp. Neurol.* 327:97–111

Jarosz AF, Colflesh GJ, Wiley J. 2012. Uncorking the muse: Alcohol intoxication facilitates creative problem solving. *Conscious. Cogn.* 21:487–93

Jensen O, Mazaheri A. 2010. Shaping functional architecture by oscillatory alpha activity: gating by inhibition. *Front. Hum. Neurosci.* 4:186

Jung-Beeman M. 2005. Bilateral brain processes for comprehending natural language. *Trends Cogn. Sci.* 9:512–18

Jung-Beeman M, Bowden EM, Haberman J, Frymiare JL, Arambel-Liu S, et al. 2004. Neural activity when people solve verbal problems with insight. *PLoS Biol.* 2(4):e97

Kaplan CA, Simon HA. 1990. In search of insight. *Cogn. Psychol.* 22:374–419

Kerns JG, Cohen JD, MacDonald AW III, Cho RY, Stenger VA, Carter CS. 2004. Anterior cingulate, conflict monitoring and adjustments in control. *Science* 303:1023–26

Kounios J. 1996. On the continuity of thought and the representation of knowledge: Electrophysiological and behavioral time-course measures reveal levels of structure in semantic memory. *Psychon. Bull. Rev.* 3:265–86

Kounios J, Beeman M. 2009. The Aha! moment. The cognitive neuroscience of insight. *Curr. Dir. Psychol. Sci.* 18(4):210–16

Kounios J, Fleck JI, Green DL, Payne L, Stevenson JL, et al. 2008. The origins of insight in resting-state brain activity. *Neuropsychologia* 46(1):281–91

Kounios J, Frymiare JL, Bowden EM, Fleck JI, Subramaniam K, et al. 2006. The prepared mind: Neural activity prior to problem presentation predicts subsequent solution by sudden insight. *Psychol. Sci.* 17(10):882–90

Kounios J, Osman AM, Meyer DE. 1987. Structure and process in semantic memory: new evidence based on speed–accuracy decomposition. *J. Exp. Psychol.: Gen.* 116:3–25

Lane RD, Reiman EM, Axelrod B, Yun L, Holmes A. 1998. Neural correlates of emotional awareness: evidence of an interaction between emotion and attention in the anterior cingulate cortex. *J. Cogn. Neurosci.* 10:525–35

Ludmer R, Dudai Y, Rubin N. 2011. Uncovering camouflage: Amygdala activation predicts long-term memory of induced perceptual insight. *Neuron* 69:1002–14

Luo J, Li W, Fink A, Jia L, Xiao X, et al. 2011. The time course of breaking mental sets and forming novel associations in insight-like problem solving: an ERP investigation. *Exp. Brain Res.* 212:583–91

Luo J, Niki K. 2003. Function of hippocampus in "insight" of problem solving. *Hippocampus* 13:316–23

Mashal N, Faust M, Hendler T, Jung-Beeman M. 2008. Hemispheric differences in processing the literal interpretation of idioms: converging evidence from behavioral and fMRI studies. *Cortex* 44:848–60

Demonstrates that schizotypes show more creativity than normal control participants in a divergent thinking task.

Mayberg HS, Liotti M, Brannan SK, McGinnis S, Mahurin RK, et al. 1999. Reciprocal limbic-cortical function and negative mood: converging PET findings in depression and normal sadness. *Am. J. Psychiatry* 156:675–82

Mednick S. 1962. The associative basis of the creative process. *Psychol. Rev.* 69(3):220–32

Metcalfe J, Wiebe D. 1987. Intuition in insight and noninsight problem solving. *Mem. Cogn.* 15(3):238–46

Metuki N, Sela T, Lavidor M. 2012. Enhancing cognitive control components of insight problem solving by anodal tDCS of the left dorsolateral prefrontal cortex. *Brain Stimul.* 5:110–15

Meyer DE, Irwin DE, Osman AM, Kounios J. 1988. The dynamics of cognition and action: mental processes inferred from speed-accuracy decomposition. *Psychol. Rev.* 95:183–237

Miller EK, Cohen JD. 2001. An integrative theory of prefrontal cortex function. *Annu. Rev. Neurosci.* 24:167–202

Morgan WW. 1988. A morphological life. *Annu. Rev. Astron. Astrophys.* 26:1–10

Ray WJ, Cole HW. 1985. EEG alpha activity reflects attentional demands, and beta activity reflects emotional and cognitive processes. *Science* 228:750–52

Reverberi C, Toraldo A, D'Agostini S, Skrap M. 2005. Better without (lateral) frontal cortex? Insight problems solved by frontal patients. *Brain* 128:2882–90

Rowe G, Hirsch JB, Anderson AK. 2007. Positive affect increases the breadth of attentional selection. *Proc. Natl. Acad. Sci. USA* 101:383–88

Sandkühler S, Bhattacharya J. 2008. Deconstructing insight: EEG correlates of insightful problem solving. *PLoS ONE* 3(1):e1459

Scheibel AB, Fried I, Paul L, Forsythe A, Tomiyasu U, et al. 1985. Differentiating characteristics of the human speech cortex: a quantitative Golgi study. In *The Dual Brain: Hemispheric Specialization in Humans*, ed. DF Benson, E Zaidel, pp. 65–74. New York: Guilford

Seifert CM, Meyer DE, Davidson N, Patalano AL, Yaniv I. 1995. Demystification of cognitive insight: opportunistic assimilation and the prepared-mind hypothesis. In *The Nature of Insight*, ed. R Sternberg, JE Davidson, pp. 65–124. Cambridge, MA: MIT Press

Seldon HL. 1981. Structure of human auditory cortex. II. Cytoarchitectonics and dendritic distributions. *Brain Res.* 229:277–94

Sheehan W. 2008. W. W. Morgan and the discovery of the spiral arm structure of our galaxy. *J. Astron. Hist. Herit.* 11:3–21

Sheth BR, Sandkuhler S, Bhattacharya J. 2008. Posterior beta and anterior gamma oscillations predict cognitive insight. *J. Cogn. Neurosci.* 21:1269–79

Smit DJ, Boomsma DI, Schnack HG, Hulshoff Pol HE, de Geus EJ. 2012. Individual differences in EEG spectral power reflect genetic variance in gray and white matter volumes. *Twin Res. Hum. Genet.* 15:384–92

Smith RW, Kounios J. 1996. Sudden insight: all-or-none processing revealed by speed–accuracy decomposition. *J. Exp. Psychol.: Learn. Mem. Cogn.* 22(6):1443–62

St George M, Kutas M, Martinez A, Sereno MI. 1999. Semantic integration in reading: engagement of the right hemisphere during discourse processing. *Brain* 122:1317–25

Sternberg RJ, Davidson JE. 1995. *The Nature of Insight*. Cambridge, MA: MIT Press

Subramaniam K, Kounios J, Parrish TB, Jung-Beeman M. 2009. A brain mechanism for facilitation of insight by positive affect. *J. Cogn. Neurosci.* 21:415–32

Tallon-Baudry C, Bertrand O. 1999. Oscillatory gamma activity in humans and its role in object representation. *Trends Cogn. Sci.* 3:151–62

Tardif E, Clarke S. 2001. Intrinsic connectivity of human auditory areas: a tracing study with DiI. *Eur. J. Neurosci.* 13:1045–50

Topolinski S, Reber R. 2010. Gaining insight into the "aha" experience. *Curr. Dir. Psychol. Sci.* 19:402–5

Trope Y, Liberman N. 2010. Construal-level theory of psychological distance. *Psychol. Rev.* 117:440–63

van Steenburgh J, Fleck JI, Beeman M, Kounios J. 2012. Insight. In *The Oxford Handbook of Thinking and Reasoning*, ed. K Holyoak, R Morrison, pp. 475–91. New York: Oxford Univ. Press

Verhaeghen P, Joormann J, Khan R. 2005. Why we sing the blues: the relation between self-reflective rumination, mood, and creativity. *Emotion* 5:226–32

Virtue S, Haberman J, Clancy Z, Parrish T, Jung-Beeman M. 2006. Neural activity of inferences during story comprehension. *Brain Res.* 1084:104–14

Virtue S, Parrish T, Beeman M. 2008. Inferences during story comprehension: cortical recruitment affected by predictability of events and working memory capacity. *J. Cogn. Neurosci.* 20:2274–84

Wallas G. 1926. *The Art of Thought*. New York: Harcourt Brace

Wagner U, Gais S, Haider H, Verleger R, Born J. 2004. Sleep inspires insight. *Nature* 427(6972):352–55

Wegbreit E, Suzuki S, Grabowecky M, Kounios J, Beeman M. 2012. Visual attention modulates insight versus analytic solving of verbal problems. *J. Probl. Solving* 4(2):artic. 5

Weissman DH, Gopalakrishnan A, Hazlett CJ, Woldorff MG. 2005. Dorsal anterior cingulate cortex resolves conflict from distracting stimuli by boosting attention toward relevant events. *Cereb. Cortex* 15:229–37

Wu L, Knoblich G, Wei G, Luo J. 2009. How perceptual processes help to generate new meaning: an EEG study of chunk decomposition in Chinese characters. *Brain Res.* 1296:104–12

Describes a theory of stages leading to insight or "illumination"; immersion in the facts of a problem is the first stage.

Color Psychology: Effects of Perceiving Color on Psychological Functioning in Humans

Andrew J. Elliot[1] and Markus A. Maier[2]

[1]Department of Clinical and Social Sciences in Psychology, University of Rochester, Rochester, New York 14627; email: andye@psych.rochester.edu

[2]Department of Psychology, University of Munich, Munich 80802, Germany; email: markus.maier@psy.lmu.de

Annu. Rev. Psychol. 2014. 65:95–120

First published online as a Review in Advance on June 26, 2013

The *Annual Review of Psychology* is online at http://psych.annualreviews.org

This article's doi: 10.1146/annurev-psych-010213-115035

Keywords

hue, achievement, attraction, consumer, food

Abstract

Color is a ubiquitous perceptual stimulus that is often considered in terms of aesthetics. Here we review theoretical and empirical work that looks beyond color aesthetics to the link between color and psychological functioning in humans. We begin by setting a historical context for research in this area, particularly highlighting methodological issues that hampered earlier empirical work. We proceed to overview theoretical and methodological advances during the past decade and conduct a review of emerging empirical findings. Our empirical review focuses especially on color in achievement and affiliation/attraction contexts, but it also covers work on consumer behavior as well as food and beverage evaluation and consumption. The review clearly shows that color can carry important meaning and can have an important impact on people's affect, cognition, and behavior. The literature remains at a nascent stage of development, however, and we note that considerable work on boundary conditions, moderators, and real-world generalizability is needed before strong conceptual statements and recommendations for application are warranted. We provide suggestions for future research and conclude by emphasizing the broad promise of research in this area.

Contents

INTRODUCTION

Humans encounter the world as a colorful place. Color is perceived on essentially every object that we view in daily life; it is even present in our dreams (Rechtschaffen & Buchignani 1992). Those with normal color vision experience a vast and rich chromatic palette, with estimates reaching up to 2.3 million discernable colors (Linhares et al. 2008) that may be seen together in an "almost infinite" number of possible combinations (Hård & Sivik 2001, p. 4). Color considerations emerge regularly in our decision making and conversation, as we choose which color clothes to wear, pick a color for our new car or computer, and comment on the color of our friend's skin, hair, or makeup. Popular opinions abound on the nature of color associations and on presumed influences of color on our feelings, aesthetic judgments, and beyond.

A considerable amount of scientific research has been conducted on many aspects of color. There are robust, well-developed literatures focused on the way that color is defined and modeled (i.e., color physics), on the way that the eye and brain process color stimuli (i.e., color physiology and neuroscience), on the way that color terms are represented in language (i.e., color linguistics and categorization), and on various practical issues such as color reproduction, color deficiency, and color appearance phenomena (e.g., illusions, synesthesia). Surprisingly, there is no comparably robust, well-developed literature on the effects of color perception on psychological functioning in humans. However, research activity in this area has surged in the past decade, and a number of noteworthy theoretical ideas and empirical findings have emerged. The time is right for a review of this research.

Several *Annual Review of Psychology* (ARP) articles have been written on color. Until 1989, each of these reviews was entitled "Color Vision" and focused on color physics and physiology. In 1989, an article entitled "Essay Concerning Color Constancy" was published in ARP, but here again the focus was on basic properties of color perception. The same is true for the two other color-focused ARP articles that have appeared since 1989, the 1994 article "Color Appearance: On Seeing Red or Yellow or Green or Blue" and the 2008 article "Color in Complex Scenes." An article with "color psychology" in the title has yet to appear in ARP. Our focus in the present review is on a subset of color psychology, namely, the influence of perceiving color on psychological functioning in humans. Even this subset of color psychology is too broad for a single review; thus, we focus primarily on effects of color perception on downstream affective, cognitive, and behavioral responding in two fundamentally important domains of daily life: achievement contexts and affiliation/attraction contexts.

HISTORICAL CONTEXT (PRE-TWENTY-FIRST CENTURY)

Theoretical Work

Scholarly interest in the link between color and psychological functioning may be traced back to the German poet and polymath Johann Wolfgang von Goethe. In his classic work "Theory of Colors," Goethe (1810/1967) offered intuition-based speculation on the influence of color perception on emotional experience. Colors were categorized as "plus colors" or "minus colors." Plus colors, namely, yellow, red-yellow, and yellow-red, were thought to induce positive feelings such as lively, aspiring, and warm, whereas minus colors, namely, blue, red-blue, and blue-red, were said to induce negative feelings such as restless, anxious, and cold.

Goethe's speculations were expanded on in the twentieth century by psychiatrist Kurt Goldstein. Goldstein (1942) integrated Goethe's ideas with his own clinical observations in proposing that color perception produces physiological reactions in the body that are overtly manifest in people's emotions, cognitive focus, and motor behavior. Red and yellow were posited to be stimulating, to prompt an outward focus, and to produce forceful action, whereas green and blue were posited to be relaxing, to encourage an inward focus, and to produce calm and stable action. Goldstein's ideas were vaguely formulated, and subsequent researchers have tended to read his ideas through the lens of wavelength and arousal. Specifically, longer wavelength colors such as red and orange are thought to be experienced as arousing or warm, whereas shorter wavelength colors such as green and blue are thought to be experienced as relaxing or cool (Nakashian 1964). The experiential states induced by wavelength are presumed to influence performance on achievement tasks, with longer, relative to shorter, wavelength colors inducing states that impair performance on complex tasks but facilitate performance on simple tasks (Stone & English 1998).

Similar to Goldstein, Ott (1979) proposed that color directly produces physical reactions in the body that are manifest in observable behavior. He posited that pink and orange light have an endocrine-based weakening effect on muscle functioning, whereas blue has an endocrine-based strengthening effect on muscle functioning. Others have offered theoretical statements focused on learned associations to color and their possible influence on affective, cognitive, and behavioral responding. For example, Frank & Gilovich (1988) proposed that black is associated with negative concepts such as evil and death and prompts people to behave more aggressively toward others, accordingly. In similar fashion, Soldat et al. (1997) proposed that red is associated with happiness and blue is associated with sadness, and that these colors lead to information processing and behavior consistent with these emotions. Finally, much of the pre-twenty-first-century writing on color and psychological functioning focused on applied questions per se (e.g., Does the color on an office wall influence worker productivity? What colors are most fashionable? What colors enhance the taste of food?), with little or no interest in or reliance on theoretical considerations.

Methodological Issues

Conducting scientific research on color requires attending to the fact that color varies on multiple attributes. In most experimental research, the most important of these attributes to attend to are hue, lightness, and chroma (Fairchild 2005). Hue is wavelength and is what most people think of when they hear the word "color." Lightness is similar to brightness and is essentially the white-to-black property of the color. Chroma is similar to saturation and is essentially the intensity or vividness of the color (Fairchild 2005). Each of these color attributes may have an influence on psychological functioning (Camgöz et al. 2004), so only one of them should be allowed to vary in a well-controlled experiment. Failure to control for nonfocal color attributes leads to a confounded design and results that are essentially impossible to interpret (Valdez & Mehrabian 1994). That is, if more than one color attribute varies at the same time, it is not possible to determine if an obtained result is due to the color attribute of central interest or to one or more of the other color attributes. In addition to varying on hue, lightness, and chroma, color also varies on perceived typicality—the degree to which a color is seen as a standard representation of its category. Although not as important as controlling for the multidimensionality of color stimuli, equating colors on perceived typicality bolsters the rigor of empirical work on color.

Unfortunately, the majority of the extant research on color and psychological functioning conducted pre-twenty-first century failed to systematically attend to the multidimensionality (and perceived typicality) of color stimuli. Many investigators likely selected colors that appeared (to their eyes) to be reasonable exemplars of color categories without pilot testing this assumption; others simply picked colors from unsystematic popular sets that were readily available (e.g., Milton Bradley color papers) or picked colors by visually matching (i.e., "eyeballing") them to systematic sets without independent verification. In addition to this critical flaw, many of the studies conducted during this time also contained other methodological problems such as failing to keep the experimenter blind to the hypothesis, failing to exclude color-deficient participants, and failing to present the color stimuli in a time-controlled manner. In light of these issues, it should come as little surprise that much of the research conducted in this era yielded inconsistent findings that were largely unsupportive of hypotheses. Also in light of these issues, we have refrained from reviewing the details of this literature herein, referring the reader instead to reviews by Whitfield & Wiltshire (1990), Valdez & Mehrabian (1994), and Elliot & Maier (2012). Given the centrality of the hypothesized relation between wavelength and arousal, however, we offer a brief summary statement on empirical work testing this relation. Simply put, many studies have been conducted, but they have primarily produced null results; this is particularly the case for experiments utilizing rigorous methods (Kaiser 1984, Suk & Irtel 2010, Valdez & Mehrabian 1994).

RECENT THEORETICAL ADVANCES AND METHODOLOGICAL CONSIDERATIONS

Theoretical Advances

In the past decade, the primary theoretical advances in the area of color and psychological functioning have shared a common feature: They have sought to ground color effects in biology, drawing on parallels between human and nonhuman responding to color stimuli. The germ of these ideas has been present for quite some time and noted by a number of different scholars (Darwin 1872, Ellis 1900, Humphrey 1976). However, these new theoretical frameworks contain additional insights and conceptual statements informed by contemporary knowledge from multiple disciplines and afford the generation of clear and precise hypotheses that can be put to direct empirical test. These frameworks have focused primarily, but by no means exclusively, on the color red.

Hill & Barton (2005) highlighted the signal function of red in competitive interactions in human and nonhuman animals. In many animals, including primates, red coloration in aggressive encounters is a testosterone-based indictor of dominance in males; the alpha male shows the most prominent red. Likewise, in humans, testosterone surges in aggressive encounters produce visible reddening of the face, whereas fear produces pallor. This link between red and dominance may transfer from physiological processes to artificial stimuli such as sport jerseys (for analogs in the wild, see Healey et al. 2007, Pryke 2009). If so, wearing red in aggressive competitions such as boxing should function as a dominance signal and lead to enhanced performance attainment.

Other theorists have focused on the signal value of skin coloration in affiliative interaction and attraction in human and nonhuman animals. Changizi and colleagues (2006) argue that trichromatic color vision evolved to allow primates to detect subtle color changes on the skin based on underlying blood flow. These skin color modulations reflect the emotion, state, or condition of the perceived conspecific, and visual sensitivity to these modulations is thus extremely useful in interpersonal interaction. Our visual systems detect modulations in both the oxygenation of hemoglobin (along a red-green axis) and concentration of hemoglobin (along a blue-yellow axis), and these modulations are associated with specific shifts in coloration. Greater oxygenation produces more red and less green coloration, whereas greater concentration produces more blue and less yellow coloration. Thus, color vision enables perceivers to discern, among other things, when a date is becoming sexually aroused (more oxygenation-based redness) or an elderly parent is becoming sick (more concentration-based blueness). Likewise, Stephen and colleagues (2009b) draw parallels between human and nonhuman signal coloration in positing that facial skin coloration carries cues that perceivers use to judge the attractiveness, health, and dominance of conspecifics. They propose that the redness and yellowness of skin promote positive perceptions: Redness (due to blood oxygenation) is thought to reflect cardiovascular wellness, and yellowness (due to carotenoids) is thought to reflect fruit and vegetable consumption. Fink and colleagues (2006) contend that the homogeneity of skin color, beyond hue per se, influences perceptions of the attractiveness, health, and age of faces.

In their color-in-context theory, Elliot & Maier (2012) focus on both biologically based and learned sources of color meanings and effects. Some color effects are thought to represent inherent tendencies to interpret and respond to color in a manner similar to that observed in our nonhuman primate relatives. Other color effects are thought to be rooted in the repeated pairing of color and particular concepts, messages, and experiences; over time, these pairings create strong and often implicit color associations such that the mere perception of the color evokes meaning-consistent affect, cognition, and behavior. Furthermore, it is likely that some color-meaning links, especially those that are observed across time and culture, are a product of the cognitive reinforcement and shaping (via social learning) of an initial biologically engrained predisposition. Such higher-order learning may be responsible for reinforcing and extending the applicability of color-meaning links beyond natural bodily processes (based in blood physiology) to objects in close proximity to the body (e.g., clothes) and even objects in the broader environment (e.g., signs and signals). Thus, a red dress may carry sexual meaning, much like the red of sexual excitation on the face and upper chest. Critically, color meanings and effects are posited to be context specific. The same color can have different and even opposite meanings and effects in different contexts. For example, red is hypothesized to have a negative meaning (failure) and aversive implications (avoidance motivation) in achievement contexts, but it is hypothesized to have a positive meaning (sexual receptivity or status) and appetitive implications (sexual desire) in mating contexts.

Methodological Considerations

As noted in the Methodological Issues section above, to avoid confounding hue, lightness, and chroma in an experiment, it is imperative to vary only one attribute at a time. In the past decade, researchers have begun to address this issue of color control with much greater regularity by implementing a variety of different techniques. These techniques vary considerably in their effectiveness, ease of use, and flexibility of application.

One approach that has been adopted quite frequently is to use a computer software program to select colors to be printed or displayed on a computer monitor. Many software programs such as Photoshop include a function that allows the user to insert numerical values for hue, lightness, and chroma (or similar attributes) based on the metric of a particular color model. Unfortunately, the software program, computer monitor, and printer are typically not calibrated and thus do not produce color in the same way. The upshot is that the resultant color output is typically discrepant from the color values entered into the computer program; this discrepancy can be trivial or considerable, but, importantly, its extent is unknown. Given this problem, this approach to color control is not a good option; it is certainly better than no control at all, but data obtained via this method must be interpreted cautiously.

A second approach that may be employed is to select pre-existing color samples within a well-validated model such as the Munsell color system or the Natural Color System. These systems provide arrays of color chips that are systematically arranged according to uniform perceptual spacing for hue, lightness, and chroma (or similar attributes). Color chips may be selected that vary on one attribute but are the same on the other two attributes. Although this approach affords tight experimental control, it is limited to the specific color combinations provided in the material sets of each system. In addition, and more importantly, the color chips themselves must be used as stimuli to fully exploit the rigor of the approach, and this greatly limits the ways in which color can be presented (e.g., it can't be presented on a monitor or superimposed onto a picture of an object for printing). Accordingly, this approach is not well suited to many types of research on color and psychological functioning.

A third approach is to use a spectrophotometer to create color stimuli. A spectrophotometer is a device that assesses color at the spectral level; it provides objective numeral values for hue, lightness, and chroma (or similar attributes) and does so taking into account different types of environments (e.g., direct sunlight or cool white fluorescent lighting) and observer viewing angles. Using a spectrophotometer, the color attributes of a given stimulus are assessed and then adjusted to select target values that vary on only one attribute. Color may be assessed in a range of formats, be it printed, presented on a computer monitor, or present on a physical object. This combination of accuracy and flexibility makes the spectrophotometer approach ideal.

The one limitation of the spectrophotometer approach is that it does not take into account variability in color perception across individuals. A technique commonly used in psychophysical research that does account for this variability is the minimally distinct border method. In this approach, two adjacent hues are presented on a computer monitor, and participants' task is to adjust the lightness or chroma of one of the hues until they become the same on this attribute. Although this approach allows tight experimental control, there are several limitations to employing this method in research on color and psychological functioning: It can only be used when presenting color on a computer monitor, it draws explicit attention to color stimuli (making research on implicit effects impossible), and it can only be used with participants who are able to complete the minimally distinct border task.

We think the use of a spectrophotometer is the optimal method for controlling color in research on color and psychological functioning. It is objective, flexible, and adaptable, and it yields data that are sufficiently accurate for anything except, perhaps, psychophysical research. Although it does not control for individual differences in color perception, this variation is like any other individual difference in that it merely adds unsystematic variance to the design that is randomly dispersed across conditions.

In the following empirical review, we focus primarily on work that has used one of the aforementioned forms of color control, including a good deal of work that has utilized the spectrophotometer method. We think the move toward more rigorous control of color stimuli is an important factor contributing to the improved clarity and consistency of the empirical yield during the past decade and is an important reason for the current resurgence of research in this area.

One final methodological issue should be noted, and that concerns conducting color research on web platforms such as the popular Mechanical Turk (MTurk). Color presentation is device dependent. The color values selected and inputted by an investigator for use in an MTurk experiment will be presented to participants in myriad different ways because participants will be viewing the color stimuli on myriad different computer monitors. Given that color matching is impossible in this instance, it seems prudent to limit color research to one of two possibilities, accordingly: (a) comparison of one chromatic color to a white control condition (in which case color control is not possible anyway) or (b) use of color words rather than color stimuli. Even the former possibility must carry an important caution: Participants will view the presented color stimuli at myriad different angles, and perceived color can vary considerably as a function of viewing angle. For example, an experimenter-intended red may indeed look red when viewed by participants straight on, but may look washed out or even pinkish when viewed from even a moderate angle.

In the following, we review the empirical research on color and psychological functioning from the past decade, focusing primarily on work relevant to achievement and affiliation/attraction contexts. We limit our review to articles published in peer-reviewed journal articles and papers published in edited volumes or conference proceedings.

EMPIRICAL FINDINGS: COLOR EFFECTS ON PSYCHOLOGICAL FUNCTIONING

Color in Achievement Contexts

Competitive sport performance. Hill & Barton (2005) used data from four combat sports (e.g., boxing, tae kwon do) in the 2004 Olympics to test their proposal that red functions as a dominance cue in human competitions and enhances performance accordingly. Their results showed that competitors randomly assigned to red relative to blue sportswear were more likely to win the competition; this was particularly the case with male competitors (Barton & Hill 2005) and with competitors of relatively equal ability. Ilie et al. (2008) extended this finding to performance on a multiplayer first-person shooter video game, finding that red teams win more virtual matches than blue teams. Attrill et al. (2008) analyzed more than 50 years of archival data from elite English soccer leagues and found a performance advantage for teams wearing red relative to others colors. Subsequent research testing for a red advantage in soccer and rugby leagues in England and other countries has yielded mixed results. Piatti et al. (2012) found the red effect in the Australian National Rugby League but also found evidence that it was primarily driven by the top teams in the league. Allen & Jones (2013) found the red advantage in the English Premier League with more recent data than those examined by Attrill et al. (2008), but they also found that this effect did not hold for home games with team ability held constant. Red was not found to boost team performance in archival analyses of elite soccer leagues in Germany, Poland, and Spain (Garcia-Rubio et al.

2011, Kocher & Sutter 2008, Szmajke & Sorokowski 2006), and the National Hockey League in North America (Caldwell & Burger 2011). These data suggest that the red effect may be present in some countries but not others, perhaps as a function of culture-specific learned associations to red that run counter to, and weaken the influence of, any inherent meaning. Likewise, the strength of the red effect may vary as a function of team versus one-on-one competition (Kocher & Sutter 2008) or collaborative versus combat sport. For example, red may have a stronger effect in combat sports where direct physical dominance is the aim, and the red of blood, both spilled and drained from the face of a frightened opponent, is more visible and salient.

Although less studied, some evidence from one-on-one combat sports such as judo suggests that wearing blue may convey a performance advantage over wearing white (Matsumoto et al. 2007, Rowe et al. 2005). However, reanalyses of such data have revealed that this effect may be partially or entirely due to confounding factors (e.g., inclusion of repechage rounds; Dijkstra & Preenen 2008). Black and white have been examined as achromatic colors that have associations with aggression (black) or its absence (white), and that, accordingly, may influence either players' aggressiveness or referees' perceptions of aggressiveness in competitive sport. The data appear to be mixed, but the most recent, and perhaps methodologically strongest, research yielded supportive evidence (see Caldwell & Burger 2011, Tiryaki 2005, Webster et al. 2012).

The mechanism to account for the red effect posited by Hill & Barton (2005) is that wearing red enhances one's dominance, aggressiveness, and testosterone, which facilitates competitive outcomes. That the red effect has been found to be most prominent with males (Barton & Hill 2005) is consistent with this account, as are several studies linking wearing red or being affiliated with red (relative to chromatic or achromatic controls) to perceiving oneself as more dominant, intimidating, threatening, aggressive, and powerful (Feltman & Elliot 2011, Ten Velden et al. 2012) and exhibiting a higher heart rate, higher testosterone, and greater preperformance strength (Dreiskaemper et al. 2013, Farrelly et al. 2013; although see also Hackney 2006). Independent of the influence of wearing red, viewing red on an opponent may also exert an influence. A number of studies have yielded results that are ambiguous regarding this wearing/viewing distinction, showing that a target presented in red is perceived to be more dominant, aggressive, brave, competitive, and more likely to win a competition (Little & Hill 2007, Sorokowski & Szmajke 2007) or demonstrating a general association between red and anger or aggression (Bagchi & Cheema 2013; Fetterman et al. 2011, 2012; Guéguen et al. 2012; Tharangie et al. 2009, 2011; Young et al. 2013). Other research has clearly differentiated viewing red from wearing red and found that opponents wearing red are perceived to be more dominant, intimidating, competitive, and assertive (Feltman & Elliot 2011, Greenlees et al. 2008, Ten Velden et al. 2012; although see also Furley et al. 2012). In a particularly elegant series of studies, Ten Velden et al. (2012) showed that playing with red (relative to blue) poker chips increased participants' experienced dominance and led to increased betting behavior, whereas the opposite perceptions and behavior were observed for participants playing against an opponent using red (relative to blue) chips. Other explanations have also been offered for the red effect, namely that the influence of red is due to its greater visibility (for relevant findings, see Rowe et al. 2005) or to referee bias favoring those wearing red (for relevant findings, see Hagemann et al. 2008). It should be noted that all of these explanations may have merit and may be seen as complementary rather than conflicting.

Individual cognitive and motor performance. Elliot and colleagues (2007) proposed that viewing red in an achievement context can undermine performance on challenging tasks that require mental manipulation and flexibility. They posited that red is associated with failure and danger and evokes avoidance motivation in such contexts, which impedes performance attainment. Their experimental studies indicated that individuals who viewed red before or during anagram, analogy, and math tasks performed worse than those who viewed green or achromatic control colors. Subsequent research has also observed this red effect using additional chromatic controls and additional types of challenging cognitive tasks (e.g., verbal reasoning, working memory, attentional interference, creativity, and language proficiency; Elliot et al. 2011, Gnambs et al. 2010, Ioan et al. 2007, Jung et al. 2011b, Lichtenfeld et al. 2009, Maier et al. 2008, Yamazaki & Eto 2011). Some experiments have found evidence that the red effect may be particularly or only present for males in some instances (Gnambs et al. 2010, Ioan et al. 2007), and others have not found the effect with some control conditions (Jung et al. 2011b, Lichtenfeld et al. 2012, Mehta & Zhu 2009, Yamazaki 2010) or with ambient color (i.e., color painted on an office wall; Küller et al. 2009). Some experiments have yielded evidence suggesting that viewing blue or green may be particularly beneficial for creative performance (Lichtenfeld et al. 2012, Mehta & Zhu 2009; cf. Küller et al. 2009) and that yellow may be detrimental for certain types of challenging cognitive tasks (Kumi et al. 2013, Yamazaki 2010), but these questions have received only a modicum of empirical attention. In a related vein, Akers et al. (2012) found that viewing green (relative to red or gray) during a cycling task led to less perceived exertion during the task.

Avoidance motivation can facilitate performance on basic, detail-oriented cognitive tasks that require minimal mental manipulation or flexibility (Friedman & Förster 2010), and, accordingly, Mehta & Zhu (2009) offered and found evidence to support the proposal that red facilitates performance on such tasks (e.g., proofreading; cf. Küller et al. 2009). Other experiments have found that red can facilitate performance on an overlearned motor task (Larionescu & Pantelimona 2012), a target-shooting task (Sorokowski & Szmajke 2011), and an immediate-response basic strength task (Elliot & Aarts 2011); some have found that red can undermine performance on a goal-directed motor movement task (Williams et al. 2011) and a delayed-response basic strength task (Payen et al. 2011). Other factors, beyond task type, also warrant consideration as boundary conditions and moderators of the influence of red on cognitive performance. For example, the red effect may vary as a function of the difficulty level of the task, the degree to which ability evaluation is made salient or social in the achievement setting, and the extent to which the individual's ability level, sex, or culture make ability evaluation threatening. Moderately challenging tasks, moderately evaluative contexts, and moderately reactive individuals would seem most likely to exhibit the red effect, whereas ceiling or floor effects may weaken or eliminate the effect in other instances (for an illustration regarding sex moderation, see Gnambs et al. 2010). Furthermore, ambient color may not be sufficient to produce an effect, or prolonged exposure to color may lead to habituation over time (Küller et al. 2009).

In terms of the mechanism(s) responsible for the red effect on performance, several studies have demonstrated that red is implicitly associated with failure and danger in achievement situations (Mehta & Zhu 2009, Moller et al. 2009, Rutchick et al. 2010). For example, Rutchick et al. (2010) showed that participants are more likely to complete word stems with failure-relevant words (e.g., fai_ as "fail" rather than "fair") when using a red (relative to black) pen. Interestingly, teachers are evaluated more negatively when they grade students' work using red versus aqua ink (Dukes & Albanesi 2013). Some research suggests that red may even carry negative valence by default, as red has been linked to negative content and affective experience in situations where no ability evaluation or content is present (Chien 2011b, Diehl et al. 2011, Genschow et al. 2012, Gerend & Sias 2009, Magee 2012, Moller et al. 2009, Piotrowski & Armstrong 2012; although see Chien 2011a). Viewing red in achievement situations prior to or during task engagement has been shown to evoke avoidance motivation and behavior in a number of studies using a variety of different indicators: local relative to global processing, selecting easy rather than moderately difficult tasks, walking more slowly to an evaluative event, knocking fewer times on the door of a testing room, moving physically away from an ability test, less risky investment decision making, decreased heart rate variability, and right relative to left frontal cortical activation (Elliot et al. 2007, 2009, 2011; Gillebaart et al. 2012; Kliger & Gilad 2012; Lichtenfeld et al. 2009; Maier et al. 2008; Meier et al. 2012; Mehta & Zhu 2009; Rutchick et al. 2010; Shavit et al. 2013; Tanaka & Tokuno 2011). Data supporting the role of avoidance motivation as a mediator of the link between red and performance have been reported in Lichtenfeld et al. (2009), Maier et al. (2008), and Mehta & Zhu (2009). Furthermore, Mehta & Zhu (2009) documented approach motivation, operationalized as focusing on speed over accuracy, as a mediator of their observed positive effect of blue on creative performance.

High school and college teachers sometimes print alternate forms of quizzes or exams on different colored paper to ensure that students receiving the same form do not sit in close proximity to each other during the evaluative event. Several studies have been conducted to determine the fairness of this procedure (i.e., whether color or lack of color conveys a performance advantage). The results are mixed. A few studies have found that students perform better on exams printed on standard white paper relative to primary colors; white versus pastel colors have tended to produce null results (Clary et al. 2007, Fordham & Hayes 2009, Meyer & Bagwell 2012, Skinner 2004, Tal et al. 2008). Colored exams are unusual, and the white advantage that sometimes emerges may be a function of distraction due to novelty (Skinner 2004). In interpreting these studies it is important to bear in mind that they have been driven primarily by applied concerns and have not attended to basic methodological issues such as experimenter blindness or controlling nonhue attributes. One additional applied question that has received attention is whether adding color (of any sort) to cognitive tasks helps children with learning disabilities such as attention deficit-hyperactivity disorder to concentrate and perform better. Imhof (2004) found support for this possibility (see also controversial research on colored overlays and reading behavior in children with disabilities, overviewed in Henderson et al. 2013 and Wilkins 2003).

Color in Affiliation/Attraction Contexts

Color on the skin. Stephen, Perrett, and colleagues have conducted a program of research designed to test their theoretical proposals (described in the section Recent Theoretical Advances and Methodological Considerations) regarding relations between various properties of facial skin color and perceived health and attractiveness. In their research, participants have either added color to faces to enhance a target characteristic or they have rated faces or made forced choices between faces with regard to a target characteristic. This research has revealed that faces that are redder (presumably due to blood perfusion), yellower (presumably due to carotenoids), and lighter are rated as healthier and more attractive (Coetzee et al. 2012; Re et al. 2011; Stephen & McKeegan 2010; Stephen et al. 2009a, 2011, 2012a,b; Whitehead et al. 2012). Some data suggest that these relations may be particularly strong for own-race judgments (Stephen et al. 2012b). The links between redness or lightness and these characteristics are occasionally not observed (Coetzee et al. 2012, Stephen et al. 2012b), and the links between yellow and health and between lightness and health seem particularly prominent for female faces (Stephen et al. 2009a,b).

An experiment by Stephen et al. (2012a) focused specifically on women viewing men's faces found that women put more red on men's faces to make them more aggressive, dominant, and attractive; the relation was stronger for aggressiveness than dominance than attractiveness, a pattern that may reflect a tradeoff between the costs of selecting an aggressive mate and the benefits of selecting a dominant and attractive mate. Stephen et al. (2009a) showed that perceivers not only view redder (i.e., blood colored) facial skin as more healthy, but they also consider oxygenated blood color (brighter red) relative to deoxygenated blood color (bluish red) as a sign of better health. Stephen & McKeegan (2010) examined color contrast of the lips, relative to the rest of the face, and found that perceivers view greater redness, less blueness, and more lightness contrast to be more attractive; this was especially so for female targets for the redness and blueness contrasts (cf. Stephen et al. 2009a). Johns et al. (2012) tested whether the link between enhanced redness and attractiveness is present for women's genitalia; no significant effect was observed. Two studies have tested whether women's facial skin becomes redder during the most fertile phase of their ovulation cycle. One study found supportive evidence (Oberzaucher et al. 2012), whereas the other did not (Samson et al. 2011).

Given that the relations observed in this body of work are presumed to be due to mate preference and selection processes, it is surprising that perceiver sex by target sex interactions have not emerged when tested. Additional research on this lack of sex specificity is needed. It would also be interesting to see if location of facial coloration moderates the observed relations and whether dynamic displays of facial redness have a different influence than static displays. For example, perceiving a slight increase in facial redness may be particularly likely to increase health and attractiveness ratings relative to a slight decrease or a static, average, degree of red coloration. An added benefit of such research is that the color manipulations could be instantiated in extremely subtle fashion, without conscious awareness or knowledge that the experiment involved the manipulation of color.

Fink and colleagues have conducted a number of studies testing their proposal that homogeneous facial skin color distribution (i.e., more even skin color) negatively predicts perceptions of age and positively predicts perceptions of health and attractiveness. These studies have yielded supportive results (Coetzee et al. 2012, Fink et al. 2006, Fink & Matts 2007, Matts et al. 2007, Samson et al. 2010). Fink et al. (2008) even demonstrated that perceivers look more often and longer at a face with homogeneous skin color. Most of these studies have examined skin color distribution for female targets, but two recent experiments have found the same pattern for male targets as well—more homogeneous facial skin color leads to lower perceptions of age and higher perceptions of health and attractiveness (Fink et al. 2012a,b). More detailed analyses focusing independently on the homogeneity of specific chromophores have found that both homogeneous hemoglobin and homogeneous melanin negatively predict age and positively predict health and attractiveness (Fink et al. 2012a, Matts et al. 2007). It is in these more detailed analyses that a subtle sex difference emerges: For women targets, the homogeneity of melanin is a stronger predictor of perceived age, health, and attractiveness, whereas for male targets, the homogeneity of hemoglobin is a stronger predictor of these characteristics. A recent study by Oberzaucher et al. (2012) found that women's facial skin homogeneity was greater during the most fertile phase of their ovulation cycle. As with the research on skin color per se, the relations observed are presumed to be due to mate preference and selection processes, but perceiver sex effects have not emerged. Subsequent work would do well to explore this issue.

Extended color stimuli. Color may not only have an influence on attraction when displayed directly on the skin, but it may also impact attraction when seen in close proximity to a person of the opposite sex. Indeed, in a series of experiments, Elliot & Niesta (2008) found that men rate women as more attractive and sexually desirable when the women are viewed within a red picture border or in red clothing. Subsequent research has also found support for this extended red effect on perceived attractiveness or attraction (Elliot et al. 2013b; Guéguen 2012a; Jung et al. 2011a,b; Pazda et al. 2012, 2013; Roberts et al. 2010; Schwarz & Singer 2013), although a few experiments have not found the effect with some measures (Schwarz & Singer 2013), some control conditions (Jung et al. 2011b, Roberts et al. 2010), or at all (Purdy 2009). Several experiments have shown that the effect is not limited to perceptions but may be observed in actual behavior. Specifically, researchers, especially Guéguen and colleagues, have demonstrated that men are more likely to contact a woman displaying red on a dating website (Guéguen & Jacob 2013b), tip waitresses in red more generously (Guéguen & Jacob 2012, 2013a), are more likely to approach a woman at a bar wearing red lipstick (Guéguen 2012c), are more likely to pick up a woman hitchhiker wearing red (Guéguen 2012b), ask more intimate questions of and sit closer to a woman in red (Niesta Kayser et al. 2010), and walk more quickly to an interview on dating conducted by a woman in red (Meier et al. 2012). Research on the sex-specificity of the red effect is equivocal with regard to perceptions of attractiveness (see Elliot & Niesta 2008, Roberts et al. 2010), but it seems clear that the effect is specific to men with regard to actual behavior (Guéguen 2012b; Guéguen & Jacob 2012, 2013a). Both men and women rate women wearing color cosmetics (which include red) as more attractive than those not so adorned (Etcoff et al. 2011, Guéguen & Jacob 2011, Huguet et al. 2004, Smith et al. 2006; for complementary behavioral findings with male perceivers, see Guéguen 2008, Guéguen & Jacob 2011, Jacob et al. 2009). Interestingly, Burtin et al. (2011) demonstrated that women rate themselves as more attractive when wearing red, relative to blue, perhaps reflecting women's knowledge of men's preferences. Black, like red, has been shown to facilitate perceptions of attractiveness (either directly or indirectly) for men viewing women in the few experiments that have examined this question (Pazda et al. 2013, Roberts et al. 2010); however, this black effect does not appear to translate to men's actual behavior toward women (Guéguen 2012b; Guéguen & Jacob 2013a,b).

Some experiments have found that the red effect is limited to men rating younger (but not older) women (Schwarz & Singer 2013) and to culturally appropriate expressions of attraction (Elliot et al. 2013). Another possible moderator that warrants—but has yet to receive—attention is the attractiveness level of the female target. Red is unlikely to bolster the attractiveness of an already highly attractive woman due to a ceiling effect (a "10" is a "10" regardless), but the more interesting question is whether red facilitates attractiveness for unattractive females. One possibility is that men's immediate, subcortically driven response in this instance is appetitive but that this immediate response is overridden (perhaps even to the point of derogation) upon additional cortically driven appraisal. Type of clothing may also serve a moderating role, as a sexy dress might again produce a ceiling effect that minimizes or eliminates the influence of red; the strongest effect may be on more mundane apparel such as everyday shirts or dresses.

With regard to mediation of the red effect, Guéguen (2012a) and Pazda et al. (2012) posited that men perceive a woman in red to be more sexually receptive and that this in turn facilitates their perceptions of her attractiveness and sexual desirability. In support of this proposal, Guéguen (2012a) demonstrated that men rate women wearing red as more sexually receptive, and Pazda et al. (2012, 2013) showed that this influence of red on perceived sexual receptivity accounts for the effect of red on perceived attractiveness and sexual desirability. Pazda et al. (2013) also found that black (as well as red, unexpectedly; although see also Liang et al. 2010) enhances women's perceived fashionableness and showed that black (as well as red, again, unexpectedly) influences perceived attractiveness via its influence on perceived fashionableness.

In a series of experiments, Roberts et al. (2010) demonstrated that the red effect observed for men viewing women is also present for women viewing men. Specifically, they showed that women rate men wearing a red shirt (relative to white and several chromatic colors) as more attractive. Elliot et al. (2010) found this same effect of red (relative to white and several chromatic colors) on both perceived attractiveness and attraction, with color displayed on picture borders as well as shirts. Elliot & Maier (2013) also found evidence of this red effect in a pilot study and observed a supportive, but not quite significant, trend in a subsequent experiment. Meier et al. (2012) showed that women walk more quickly to an interview on dating conducted by a man wearing a red shirt. Research has yet to emerge on women's actual behavior when interacting with a man in red; such work is likely to require careful attention to social norms and conventions (that vary by country) regarding the appropriateness of women taking the initiative in intersexual interactions. Research on the sex specificity of the red effect is equivocal, as some work suggests that it is specific to women viewing men, whereas other work suggests that it may generalize across sex (see Elliot et al. 2010, Roberts et al. 2010). In a set of experiments, Burtin et al. (2011) showed that men perceived themselves to be more attractive when wearing a red, relative to blue, shirt. Roberts et al. (2010) found that the faces of men photographed while wearing red are rated as more attractive, even when no color is made visible to the rater. Black (and sometimes blue), like red, has been shown to facilitate women's attractiveness to men in the few studies that have examined this relation (Roberts et al. 2010).

Other findings from the extant research point to possible moderators of this red effect. Wartenberg et al. (2011) found that women viewing a man in a red, relative to blue, shirt perceived him to be more attractive, but only if he was of the same race. Roberts et al. (2010) conducted an intriguing experiment in which they photographed men in a red or white shirt; they showed women both these original pictures and adjusted pictures, with red superimposed on the initial white picture and white superimposed on the initial red picture. They found the red effect overall but also found that the adjusted pictures had novel and potentially informative effects (e.g., men photographed in red but shown in white were viewed as particularly attractive, perhaps due to the juxtaposition of a confident red-induced facial expression and a humble white shirt). Women's cycle status is another possible moderator worthy of consideration, as women may be most attracted to men in red when they are most fertile (for relevant links between dominance cues and cycle status, see Penton-Voak et al. 1999). Furthermore, women may only find men in a particular type of red attractive: Intense, vivid red may cue aggression, and light, pinkish red may cue femininity, both to the detriment of women's attractiveness judgments and attraction. The optimal red for women may be one that is strong enough to evoke attraction without also cuing aggression (for discussion on women's preference for dominant but warm and trustworthy men, see Jensen-Campbell et al. 1995). The broader literature on sexuality indicates that the factors influencing women's attraction to men are much more complex and variegated than those influencing men's attraction to women (Buss 2008, Moore 2010), and this will likely prove true regarding women's perceptions of and responses to male red.

With regard to mediation of the red effect, Elliot et al. (2010) posited that women perceive a man in red to be higher in status and that this in turn facilitates their perceptions of his attractiveness and sexual desirability. Elliot et al. (2010) found support for the link between red and status perceptions (for a comparable finding, see Stephen et al. 2012a) and for status perceptions as a mediator of the red-attractiveness relation. Contrary to expectations, they did not find that status perceptions directly mediated the red–sexual desirability relation; instead, they found an indirect mediational process whereby perceived attractiveness mediates the link between perceived status and sexual desirability.

Use of color in sexual signaling. Research indicates that women convey sexual interest to men through a variety of overt and covert means, including flirtation, provocative body posturing, and wearing revealing clothing (Givens 1978, Grammer et al. 2005). Men tend to interpret red clothing on a woman as a sexual signal (Guéguen 2012a), but an independent question is whether women actually use red in this way or not. Elliot & Pazda (2012) found that women indeed use red clothing to signal sexual intent on dating websites. In one study, they showed that women who indicated an interest in casual sex on their web profile were more likely to display red (but not black, blue, or green) on their profile picture than women who did not indicate an interest in casual sex. In another study, they found that women on a website overtly dedicated to facilitating short-term sexual relations were more likely to display red (but not black, blue, or green) on their profile picture than women on a website expressly dedicated to facilitating long-term relationships. Elliot et al. (2013a) showed that women expecting to converse with an attractive man (relative to an unattractive man, an attractive woman, or an average woman) were more likely to choose to wear red (relative to green or blue) for the conversation. They additionally found that women's choice of red was positively related to perceived attractiveness and status only when they expected to converse with an attractive man. Beall & Tracy (2013) found that women at peak fertility were more likely to wear red or pink clothing (but not other colored clothing) than women not at peak fertility. Guéguen (2012d) found that women wear more color cosmetics when near the midpoint of their cycle. Subsequent research would do well to explore the culture-based boundary conditions for women's use of red as a sexual signal. It is likely that in cultures with conservative norms or customs regarding women's assertiveness, only some women (e.g., those high in sociosexuality) may feel comfortable using red in this way or may constrain this use of red to particular settings (e.g., nightclubs) or relational contexts (e.g., preexisting intimate relationships). Research has yet to examine men's use of red in sexual signaling, and this too should be added to the empirical agenda.

BROAD CONCLUSIONS AND HIGHLIGHTS FROM OTHER RESEARCH AREAS

Broad Conclusions

The empirical work that we have reviewed clearly indicates that color can carry meaning and have an important influence on affect, cognition, and behavior in achievement and affiliation/attraction contexts. Red, especially, has been shown to be a critical color in this regard. This should come as no surprise, as red has long been identified as a unique, special color. Ellis (1900), for example, commenced his prescient essay "The Psychology of Red" with the following: "Among all colors, the most poignantly emotional tone undoubtedly belongs to red" (p. 365). Many things in biology, culture, and language point to the poignancy and prominence of red. Red is the color of blood and, therefore, the color of life and (when spilled) death. Dynamic variation in visible blood flow on the face and body of a conspecific communicates critical, adaptation-relevant information, from the pallor of fear, to the flush of sexual interest or arousal, to the florid crimson of anger and imminent aggression (Changizi 2009). More static individual differences in visible blood flow are indicative of cardiac health or illness (Stephen et al. 2011). Red is the color of ripe fruit, and vivid red (especially against a green background) allows such ripe fruit to be detected from afar (Regan et al. 2001). Red is the color of many aposematic (warning) signals conveyed on the bodies of poisonous insects and reptiles (Stevens & Ruxton 2012). Red is regarded by anthropologists to have been the first chromatic color used in symbolic fashion in interpersonal communication, and the use of red ochre in prehistoric cave painting is thought to be the first use of chromatic color in art (Henshilwood et al. 2009). Red is a term that appears in all or nearly all lexicons, and red is the first chromatic term to emerge in most of these languages (Kay & Maffi 1999). Given all of this, the contemporary use of red in signs (e.g., alarms, sirens), symbols (e.g., hearts, crosses), and sayings (e.g., "in the red," "roll out the red carpet") seems fitting, and the preponderance of red effects observed in the current literature is sensible.

Although red is clearly special and has garnered the majority of research attention, a few other colors have been examined in recent research as well. Conceptually, blue and green seem reasonable candidates for consideration, as they both have positive links in the natural realm (e.g., blue sky and water, green foliage and vegetation) and both have been shown to be associated with positive content [blue, e.g., openness, peace (Kaya & Epps 2004, Mehta & Zhu 2009); green, e.g., calmness, success (Clarke & Costall 2008, Moller et al. 2009)]. In the literature that we reviewed, a few studies have yielded preliminary evidence that one or both of these colors may have positive implications for performance or experience during task engagement in some instances. Yellow, like red, is linked to aposematism in insects and reptiles (Stevens & Ruxton 2012) and is commonly used to indicate caution in signage and brake lights. A few studies have hinted that yellow may have inimical implication for performance outcomes. Achromatic black and white tend to carry general negative and positive connotations, respectively (Lakens et al. 2012). The extant research suggests that black may be linked to greater, and white to lesser, aggression in competitive sport, and black may facilitate perceptions of fashionableness and attractiveness in the affiliation domain. Each of these nascent possibilities warrants further empirical consideration.

Another clear take-home message from the literature that we have reviewed is that color meanings and, therefore, color effects are context specific. The same color can have different meanings in different contexts, leading to different implications. For example, the extant literature shows that red carries negative, threatening meaning when seen on an opponent or test of ability and evokes avoidance-relevant affect, cognition, and behavior; but red carries positive, appetitive meaning when seen on a potential mate and facilitates approach-relevant responding. Importantly, context may be physical as well as psychological; color is typically viewed on an object as well as within a psychological context, and the object on which a color is viewed can influence its meaning and valence. Thus, red on a woman's T-shirt may be viewed as sexy and appealing, but the same red on the entirety of a woman's business suit may be seen as unfashionable and garish. When context cues are absent, it is possible that some colors have default associations, especially the most basic color terms in language (i.e., white, black, and red; Kay & Maffi 1999). For example, red may carry the meaning of danger (or potential danger) by default, with a clearly appetitive context (e.g., mating) needed to prompt positive associative content (see Genschow et al. 2012, Maier et al. 2013). Color and context, be it psychological or physical, are integrated together to produce meaning at an early, rudimentary stage of visual processing that requires no intention or awareness (Castelhano & Henderson 2008, Zachar et al. 2008). As such, color can act as an "implicit affective cue," influencing psychological functioning in a subtle, nonconscious fashion (Friedman & Förster 2010). Most work on color has neglected to attend to the issue of context moderation, and we believe that careful consideration of this issue holds great promise for advancing theory and research in this area.

Highlights from Other Research Areas

The literature on color psychology is vast. Indeed, the literature on the influence of color on psychological functioning is itself expansive, and this required us to conduct our review of the extant research in a selective fashion. There are many other interesting bodies of work emerging in this area, and in the following we briefly touch on a few highlights, focusing primarily on research in the areas of consumer behavior and food/beverage evaluation and consumption.

It is taken as an undeniable fact by marketers, advertisers, and graphic artists that color influences consumer behavior (Paul & Okan 2011). One line of research in this area focuses on atmospherics, addressing issues such as the influence of building, store, and website color on drawing consumers in, keeping them engaged, and enhancing their shopping experience. Blue appears to be a highly positive color in this regard, as blue stores and websites are rated as more relaxing, less crowded, and even more trustworthy (Alberts & van der Geest 2011, Gorn et al. 2004, Lee & Rao 2010, Yüksel 2009). Another focus in this area is on the role that color plays in company and brand identity and recognition. Color is often an integral aspect of logos and product packaging (e.g., Coca Cola red, IBM blue, Cadbury purple) and is presumed to be used in shaping image/personality and facilitating reflexive purchasing behavior (Hynes 2009). The most commonly utilized color in logos of major companies is blue (Labrecque & Milne 2013), which has been linked to high perceptions of competence in this context (Labrecque & Milne 2012). Color norms have been shown to emerge for certain product categories, and deviations from these norms have been found to be beneficial in some categories (e.g., entertainment) but harmful when there is a dominant market leader (e.g., fast food; Labrecque & Milne 2013). A third line of research in this area focuses on the effect of color on consumers' evaluations of and purchasing intentions toward products. Consumers have been shown to prefer unusual color descriptions of products (e.g., Coke red, Kermit green; Miller & Kahn 2005), and male consumers have been shown to perceive greater savings when product prices are presented in red rather than black (Puccinelli et al. 2013). Consumers also desire that the color of a product match its intended use or purpose. Specifically, they prefer blue for products that are functional or associated with water, and prefer red for products that are luxury items or are associated with status, such as a sports car (Bottomley & Doyle 2006, Hanss et al. 2012, Ngo et al. 2012). On a general note, several researchers caution against making broad, global statements about color in the area of consumer behavior because consumer attitudes and behaviors are presumed to be influenced by context-free color preferences that vary by country, race, sex, and age (Aslam 2006, Chebat & Morrin 2007, Funk & Ndubisi 2006).

Another active area of research focuses on the influence of color on our experience and intake of food and drink. One line of work in this area focuses on the link between food/beverage color and flavor perception, with researchers drawing an important distinction between flavor identification and flavor intensity (Spence et al. 2010). Regarding identification, people have been found to have strong expectations regarding color-flavor links such that they expect, for example, red drinks to taste like strawberry or cherry and green drinks to taste like lime, mint, or apple (Shankar et al. 2010; Zampini et al. 2007, 2008). Violations of these expectations of "appropriate" color-flavor associations can lead to difficulty in taste discrimination. With regard to intensity, the empirical yield is more equivocal. Some experiments have found color effects consistent with color-flavor expectations (e.g., brown M&Ms are perceived to be more chocolaty than green; Hoegg & Alba 2007, Kappes et al. 2006, Shankar et al. 2009, Zellner & Durlach 2008), but many others have failed to find these types of effects (for reviews, see Shankar et al. 2010, Spence et al. 2010). Another line of research in this area focuses on the effect of tableware color on both flavor perception and food and beverage consumption. A few researchers have found red effects in this domain, showing, for example, that coffee is perceived to be warmer when served in a red cup (Guéguen & Jacob 2013c), that popcorn taken from a red bowl is perceived to be sweeter (Harrar et al. 2011), and that people eat less snack food from a red plate and drink less soda from a red-labeled cup (Genschow et al. 2012; see also Geier et al. 2012 for a related finding that could also be interpreted in terms of a red-stop association). Piqueras-Fiszman & Spence (2012) found that hot chocolate was rated as more chocolaty and better when consumed from orange- or dark-cream-colored cups, and Ross et al. (2009) found that red wine was perceived to have a better flavor when it was served in a blue glass. In Piqueras-Fiszman et al. (2012), people given strawberry mousse on a white (relative to black) plate rated it as sweeter, more intense, and tastier; Van Ittersum & Wansink (2011) found that people served themselves less food when putting red-sauced pasta on a white plate and white-sauced pasta on a red plate (relative to color-match conditions). These latter effects are likely due to a perceptual effect of color contrast, independent of color associations.

FUTURE DIRECTIONS

Throughout our empirical review we have made ongoing mention of specific issues in need of further research attention. Here we pull back from the specifics to offer broader suggestions regarding directions for future research. We highlight three foci: the source of color effects, overlooked conceptual issues, and methodological considerations.

Color meanings, and therefore color effects on psychological functioning, are clearly a function of social learning (i.e., the repeated pairing of color and particular concepts, messages, and experiences over time and multiple repetition). The provocative proposal being advanced in the contemporary literature is that at least some color meanings and effects are also a function of biology. Theorists have drawn conceptual parallels between human and nonhuman animals' responses to and uses of color, and data have been acquired that are consistent with such parallels. An important next step for this literature, however, is to put this question of biological basis to more direct empirical test. Several methods are available to address this question; we briefly note three herein that have started to receive some research attention in this and related literatures. First, the degree to which the same color effect emerges across culturally distinct countries around the globe (including culturally isolated populations) may be examined (Norenzayan & Heine 2005). Convergence across countries/populations would suggest that the effect represents a human universal, likely grounded in biology (see Elliot et al. 2013). Second, for color effects involving women's sexuality, ovulation cycle effects may be examined (Gangestad & Thornhill 1998). To the extent that women naturally or behaviorally display more red mid-cycle, for example, it would suggest a biological basis for observed red effects in this domain (see Beall & Tracy 2013, Guéguen 2012d). Third, the degree of involvement of the two neural subsystems that underlie human color vision—L-M ("red-green") and S-(L+M) ("blue-yellow") cone-opponent processes—may be examined for a given effect (Hurlbert & Ling 2007). To the extent that variation in the two cone-opponent processes accounts for an affective, cognitive, or behavioral response, a biological basis is likely operative (for related work, see Taylor et al. 2013). It is important to reiterate that biological and environmentally based explanations of color effects are not mutually exclusive, and their interplay is complex. Any biological influence would take place in the context of highly impactful social learning histories and cultural norms that may support and extend, or may stifle or even countervail, inherent propensities (Elliot & Maier 2012).

Subsequent research on color and psychological functioning would do well to extend its reach to other, heretofore largely overlooked, content areas. One such area is that of color and emotion perception. Changizi et al. (2006) posit that a primary reason for the emergence of color vision in primates was the facilitation of emotional communication via color on the face. Research is needed to test implications of this provocative proposal. For example, from this perspective it seems reasonable to hypothesize that color-deficient individuals (typically male) would be less adept at navigating emotion-relevant social interactions. Another largely overlooked area is that of the influence of nonhue color attributes on psychological functioning. The vast majority of the research conducted to date has focused on hue, with a bit of attention paid to lightness in achromatic colors (Lakens et al. 2012, Meier et al. 2004, Sherman & Clore 2009). Lightness with regard to chromatic colors, as well as chroma, has been largely ignored (for exceptions, see Camgöz et al. 2004, Suk & Irtel 2010). A third overlooked area is the influence of psychological functioning on color perception. Again, nearly all of the research conducted to date has either focused on color-meaning associations or the influence of color on psychological functioning. The opposite direction of causality has been greatly understudied (although see Fetterman et al. 2011, Mitterer et al. 2009, Sherman et al. 2012).

From a methodological standpoint, the literature on color and psychological functioning has seen several improvements in the past decade, which are likely responsible for the current resurgence of interest and empirical activity. However, the need for improvement remains in several areas, three of which we briefly note. First, controlling for nonfocal color attributes is undoubtedly the most important of the recent methodological improvements, but implementation of this advance remains inconsistent. Some continue to select color stimuli unsystematically, and many rely on computer software programs for color control which, as we detailed previously, is problematic. Controlling color attributes at the spectral level (using prematched stimuli or a spectrophotometer) is necessary to conduct truly rigorous color research. Second, much of the extant research on color and psychological functioning, like much of the research in experimental psychology in general, is underpowered. Greater rigor is needed with regard to statistical power, as more highly powered samples provide more stable and accurate estimates of population effect sizes. Third, the majority of research in this area has been conducted with university undergraduates (an attribute shared with much of the research in experimental psychology in general). Research utilizing samples with greater diversity in terms of age, education level, and socioeconomic status would be welcomed.

We close this section with a broader word on generalizability and application. The research that we have reviewed in this article has clearly demonstrated that color *can* have an influence on psychological functioning. However, the research remains at a nascent stage of development, and considerable work is needed to determine boundary conditions for and moderators of the observed effects before strong statements about robustness and real-world application are justified. Furthermore, most of the research to date has utilized tightly controlled laboratory experiments that present individuals with a single color on carefully prepared stimuli in a relatively distraction-free environment. The degree to which color effects are observed when individuals encounter a welter of colors on diverse stimuli in the bustle of everyday life remains a largely open question (for promising early returns, see Beall & Tracy 2013, Elliot & Pazda 2012, Guéguen 2012b). Color effects are provocative and media friendly, which can impel the urge to move quickly from initial empirical demonstration to conclusions about real-world implications. We think it best to resist this urge, opting instead to allow the evidence to accumulate and the literature to mature before definitive statements and real-world recommendations are offered.

CONCLUDING REMARKS

Color is a complex construct studied in multiple ways by scholars across multiple disciplines. Theory and empirical work linking color to psychological functioning have been relatively slow to emerge, but the past decade has seen considerable development. Our review herein has necessarily been selective, given the breadth of research in this area, but a clear take-home message is that color is about more than aesthetics—it can carry important information and can have an important influence on people's affect, cognition, and behavior. Research in this area holds promise not only to yield interesting and provocative findings regarding color per se, but also to produce important insights into the nature of attention and perception, interpersonal communication, and the biology-culture interface more generally.

DISCLOSURE STATEMENT

The authors are not aware of any affiliations, memberships, funding, or financial holdings that might be perceived as affecting the objectivity of this review.

LITERATURE CITED

Akers A, Barton J, Cossey R, Gainsford P, Griffin M, Micklewright D. 2012. Visual color perception in green exercise: positive effects of mood on perceived exertion. *Environ. Sci. Technol.* 46:8661–66

Alberts W, van der Geest TM. 2011. Color matters: color as trustworthiness cue in Web sites. *Tech. Commun.* 58:149–60

Allen MS, Jones MV. 2013. The home advantage over the first 20 seasons of the English Premier League: effects of shirt colour, team ability, and time trends. *Int. J. Sport Exerc. Psychol.* In press

Aslam MM. 2006. Are you selling the right colour? A cross-cultural review of colour as a marketing cue. *J. Mark. Commun.* 12:15–30

Attrill MJ, Gresty KA, Hill RA, Barton RA. 2008. Red shirt colour is associated with long-term success in English football. *J. Sport Sci.* 26:577–82

Bagchi R, Cheema A. 2013. The effect of red background color on willingness-to-pay: the moderating role of selling mechanism. *J. Consum. Res.* 39:947–60

Barton RA, Hill RA. 2005. Reply. *Nature* 437:E10

Beall AT, Tracy JL. 2013. Women are more likely to wear red or pink at peak fertility. *Psychol. Sci.* 24:1837–41

Bottomley PA, Doyle JR. 2006. The interactive effects of colors and products on perceptions of brand logo appropriateness. *Mark. Theory* 6:63–83

Burtin L, Kaluza A, Klingenberg M, Straube J, Utecht C. 2011. *Red shirt, nice flirt! How red influences the perception of self-attractiveness.* Paper presented at Empiriepraktikumskongress, Univ. Jena, Ger.

Buss D. 2008. *Evolutionary Psychology: The New Science of the Mind.* Boston, MA: Allyn & Bacon. 3rd ed.

Caldwell DF, Burger JM. 2011. On thin ice: Does uniform color really affect aggression in professional hockey? *Soc. Psychol. Personal. Sci.* 2:306–10

Camgöz N, Yener C, Guvenc D. 2004. Effects of hue, saturation, and brightness: part 2. *Color Res. Appl.* 29:20–28

Castelhano MS, Henderson JM. 2008. The influence of color on the perception of scene gist. *J. Exp. Psychol: Learn. Mem. Cogn.* 34:660–75

Changizi M. 2009. *The Vision Revolution.* Dallas, TX: Benbella

Changizi MA, Zhang Q, Shimojo S. 2006. Bare skin, blood and the evolution of primate colour vision. *Biol. Lett.* 2:217–21

Chebat JC, Morrin M. 2007. Colors and cultures: exploring the effects of mall décor on consumer perceptions. *J. Bus. Res.* 60:189–96

Chien YH. 2011a. Message framing and color combination in the perception of medical information. *Psychol. Rep.* 108:667–72

Chien YH. 2011b. Use of message framing and color in vaccine information to increase willingness to be vaccinated. *Soc. Behav. Personal.* 39:1063–72

Clarke T, Costall A. 2008. The emotional connotations of color: a qualitative investigation. *Color Res. Appl.* 33:406–10

Clary R, Wandersee J, Schexnayder E. 2007. Does the color-coding of examination versions affect college science students' test performance? Counter claims of bias. *J. Coll. Sci. Teaching* 37:40–47

Coetzee V, Faerber SJ, Greeff JM, Lefevre CE, Re DE, Perrett DI. 2012. African perceptions of female attractiveness. *PLoS ONE* 7:e48116

Darwin C. 1872. *The Expression of the Emotions in Man and Animals.* London: John Murray

Diehl JJ, Wolf J, Herlihy L, Moller AC. 2011. Seeing red: color selection as an indicator of implicit social conceptions about the autism spectrum. *Disabil. Stud. Q.* 31:1–14

Dijkstra PD, Preenen PT. 2008. No effect of blue on winning contests in judo. *Proc. Biol. Sci.* 275:1157–62

Dreiskaemper D, Stauss B, Hagemann N, Buesch D. 2013. Influence of red jersey color on physical parameters in combat sports. *J. Sport Exerc. Psychol.* 35:44–49

Dukes RL, Albanesi H. 2013. Seeing red: quality of an essay, color of the grading pen, and student reactions to the grading process. *Soc. Sci. J.* 50:96–100

Elliot AJ, Aarts H. 2011. Perception of the color red enhances the force and velocity of motor output. *Emotion* 11:445–49

Elliot AJ, Greitemeyer T, Pazda AD. 2013a. Women's use of red clothing as a sexual signal in intersexual interaction. *J. Exp. Soc. Psychol.* 49:599–602

Elliot AJ, Maier MA. 2012. Color-in-context theory. *Adv. Exp. Soc. Psychol.* 45:61–126

Elliot AJ, Maier MA. 2013. The red-attractiveness effect, applying the Ioannidis and Trikalinos (2007a) test, and the broader scientific context: a reply to Francis 2013. *J. Exp. Soc. Psychol.: Gen.* 142:297–300

Elliot AJ, Maier MA, Binser MJ, Friedman R, Pekrun R. 2009. The effect of red on avoidance behavior in achievement contexts. *Personal. Soc. Psychol. Bull.* 35:365–75

Proposes and provides evidence for a social-emotional function to color vision.

Proposes and reviews research on a context-based theory of color and psychological functioning.

Elliot AJ, Maier MA, Moller AC, Friedman R, Meinhardt J. 2007. Color and psychological functioning: the effect of red on performance in achievement contexts. *J. Exp. Psychol.: Gen.* 136:154–68

Elliot AJ, Niesta D. 2008. Romantic red: Red enhances men's attraction to women. *J. Personal. Soc. Psychol.* 95:1150–64

Elliot AJ, Kayser DN, Greitemeyer T, Lichtenfeld S, Gramzow RH, et al. 2010. Red, rank, and romance in women viewing men. *J. Exp. Psychol.: Gen.* 139:399–417

Elliot AJ, Payen V, Brisswalter J, Cury F, Thayer J. 2011. A subtle threat cue, heart rate variability, and cognitive performance. *Psychophysiology* 48:1340–45

Elliot AJ, Pazda AD. 2012. Dressed for sex: red as a female sexual signal in humans. *PLoS ONE* 7:e34607

Elliot AJ, Tracy JL, Pazda AD, Beall A. 2013b. Red enhances women's attractiveness to men: first evidence suggesting universality. *J. Exp. Soc. Psychol.* 49:165–68

Ellis H. 1900. The psychology of red. *Pop. Sci. Mon.* 57:365–75

Etcoff NL, Stock S, Haley LE, Vickery SA, House DM. 2011. Cosmetics as a feature of the extended human phenotype: modulation of the perception of biologically important facial signals. *PLoS ONE* 6:e25656

Overviews basic principles of color science.

Fairchild MD. 2005. *Color Appearance Models*. New York: Wiley. 2nd ed.

Farrelly D, Slater R, Elliott H, Walden H, Wetherell M. 2013. Competitors who choose to be red have higher testosterone levels. *Psychol. Sci.* In press

Feltman R, Elliot AJ. 2011. The influence of red on perceptions of dominance and threat in a competitive context. *J. Sport Exerc. Psychol.* 33:308–14

Fetterman AK, Robinson MD, Gordon RD, Elliot AJ. 2011. Anger as seeing red: perceptual sources of evidence. *Soc. Psychol. Personal. Sci.* 2:311–16

Fetterman AK, Robinson MD, Meier BP. 2012. Anger as "seeing red": evidence for a perceptual association. *Cogn. Emot.* 26:1445–58

Fink B, Bunse PJ, Matts BJ, D'Emiliano D. 2012a. Visible skin colouration predicts perception of male facial age, health, and attractiveness. *Int. J. Cosmet. Sci.* 34:307–10

Links homogeneity of facial skin color distribution to evaluation of female targets.

Fink B, Grammer K, Matts PJ. 2006. Visible skin color distribution plays a role in the perception of age, attractiveness, and health in female faces. *Evol. Hum. Behav.* 27:433–42

Fink B, Matts PJ. 2007. The effects of skin colour distribution and topography cues on the perception of female age and health. *J. Eur. Acad. Dermatol.* 22:493–98

Fink B, Matts PJ, D'Emiliano D, Bunse L, Weege B, Röder S. 2012b. Colour homogeneity and visual perception of age, health, and attractiveness of male facial skin. *J. Eur. Acad. Dermatol.* 26:1486–92

Fink B, Matts PJ, Klingenberg H, Kuntze S, Weege B, Grammer K. 2008. Visual attention to variation in female facial skin color distribution. *J. Cosmet. Dermatol.* 7:155–61

Fordham DR, Hayes DC. 2009. Worth repeating: Paper color may have an effect on student performance. *Iss. Account. Educ.* 24:187–94

Frank MG, Gilovich T. 1988. The dark side of self- and social perception: black uniforms and aggression in professional sports. *J. Personal. Soc. Psychol.* 54:74–85

Friedman RS, Förster J. 2010. Implicit affective cues and attentional tuning: an integrative review. *Psychol. Bull.* 136:875–93

Funk D, Ndubisi NO. 2006. Colour and product choice: a study of gender roles. *Manag. Res. News* 29:41–52

Furley P, Dicks M, Memmert D. 2012. Nonverbal behavior in soccer: the influence of dominant and submissive body language on the impression formation and expectancy of success of soccer players. *J. Sport Exerc. Psychol.* 34:61–82

Gangestad SW, Thornhill R. 1998. Menstrual cycle variation in women's preference for the scent of symmetrical men. *Proc. Biol. Sci.* 265:927–33

Garcia-Rubio MA, Picazo-Tadeo AJ, González-Gómez. 2011. Does a red shirt improve sporting performance? Evidence from Spanish football. *Appl. Econ. Lett.* 18:1001–4

Geier A, Wansink B, Rozin P. 2012. Red potato chips: Segmentation cues can substantially decrease food intake. *Health Psychol.* 31:398–401

Genschow O, Reutner L, Wänke M. 2012. The color red reduces snack food and soft drink intake. *Appetite* 58:699–702

Gerend MA, Sias T. 2009. Message framing and color priming: how subtle threat cues affect persuasion. *J. Exp. Soc. Psychol.* 45:999–1002

Gillebaart M, Förster J, Rotteveel M. 2012. Mere exposure revisited: the influence of growth versus security cues on evaluations of novel and familiar stimuli. *J. Exp. Psychol.: Gen.* 141:699–714

Givens DB. 1978. The nonverbal basis of attraction: flirtation, courtship, and seduction. *Psychiatrie* 41:346–59

Gnambs T, Appel M, Batinic B. 2010. Color red in web-based knowledge testing. *Comput. Hum. Behav.* 26:1625–31

Goethe W. 1810/1967. *Theory of Colours.* **London: Frank Cass**

Goldstein K. 1942. Some experimental observations concerning the influence of colors on the function of the organism. *Occup. Ther. Rehabil.* 21:147–51

Gorn GJ, Chattopadhyay A, Sengupta J, Tripathi S. 2004. Waiting for the web: how screen color affects time perception. *J. Mark. Res.* 41:215–25

Grammer K, Renninger L, Fischer B. 2005. Disco clothing, female sexual motivation, and relationship status: Is she dressed to impress? *J. Sex Res.* 41:66–74

Greenlees I, Leyland A, Thelwell R, Filby W. 2008. Soccer penalty takers' uniform colour and pre-penalty kick gaze affect the impressions formed of them by opposing goalkeepers. *J. Sport Sci.* 26:569–76

Guéguen N. 2008. The effects of women's cosmetics on men's approach: an evaluation in a bar. *N. Am. J. Psychol.* 10:221–28

Guéguen N. 2012a. Color and women attractiveness: when red clothed women are perceived to have more intense sexual intent. *J. Soc. Psychol.* 152:261–65

Guéguen N. 2012b. Color and women hitchhikers' attractiveness: Gentlemen drivers prefer red. *Color Res. Appl.* 37:76–78

Guéguen N. 2012c. Does red lipstick really attract men? An evaluation in a bar. *Int. J. Psychol. Stud.* 4:206–9

Guéguen N. 2012d. Makeup and menstrual cycle: Near ovulation, women use more cosmetics. *Psychol. Rec.* 62:1–8

Guéguen N, Jacob C. 2011. Enhanced female attractiveness with use of cosmetics and male tipping behavior in restaurants. *J. Cosmet. Sci.* 62:283–90

Guéguen N, Jacob C. 2012. Lipstick and tipping behavior: when red lipstick enhances waitresses' tips. *Int. J. Hosp. Manag.* **31:1333–35**

Guéguen N, Jacob C. 2013a. Clothing color and tipping: Gentlemen patrons give more tips to waitresses with red clothes. *J. Hosp. Tour. Res.* In press

Guéguen N, Jacob C. 2013b. Color and cyber-attractiveness: Red enhances men's attraction to women's internet personal ads. *Color Res. Appl.* 38:309–12

Guéguen N, Jacob C. 2013c. Coffee cup color and evaluation of a beverage's "warmth quality." *Color Res. Appl.* In press

Guéguen N, Jacob C, Lourel M, Pascual A. 2012. When drivers see red: car color frustrators and drivers' aggressiveness. *Aggress. Behav.* 38:166–69

Hackney AC. 2006. Testosterone and human performance: influence of the color red. *Eur. J. Appl. Physiol.* 96:330–33

Hagemann N, Strauss B, Leißing J. 2008. When the referee sees red. *Psychol. Sci.* 19:769–771

Hanss D, Böhm G, Pfister HR. 2012. Active red sports car and relaxed purple-blue van: Affective qualities predict color appropriateness for car types. *J. Consum. Behav.* 11:368–80

Hård A, Sivik L. 2001. A theory of colours in combination: a descriptive model related to the NCS colour-order system. *Color Res. Appl.* 26:4–28

Harrar V, Piqueras-Fiszman B, Spence C. 2011. There's more to taste in a coloured bowl. *Perception* 40:880–82

Healey M, Uller T, Olsson M. 2007. Seeing red: morph-specific contest success, and survival rates, in a colour-polymorphic agamid lizard. *Anim. Behav.* 73:337–41

Henderson LM, Tsogka N, Snowling MJ. 2013. Questioning the benefits that coloured overlays can have for reading in students with and without dyslexia. *J. Res. Spec. Educ. Needs* 13:57–65

Henshilwood C, d'Errico F, Watts I. 2009. Engraved ochres from the Middle Stone Age levels at Blombos Cave, South Africa. *J. Hum. Evol.* 57:27–47

Hill RA, Barton RA. 2005. Red enhances human performance in contests. *Nature* **435:293**

Hoegg J, Alba JW. 2007. Taste perception: more than meets the tongue. *J. Consum. Res.* 33:490–98

Huguet P, Croizet J-C, Richetin J. 2004. Is "what has been cared for" necessarily good? Further evidence for the negative impact of cosmetics use on impression formation. *J. Appl. Soc. Psychol.* 34:1752–71

Early speculative theorizing on color and psychological functioning.

Links extended color displays to real-world behavioral responding.

Documents parallels between human and nonhuman response to color.

Humphrey N. 1976. The colour currency of nature. In *Colour for Architecture*, ed. T Porter, B Mikellides, pp. 95–98. London: Studio-Vista

Hurlbert AC, Ling Y. 2007. Biological components of sex differences in color preference. *Curr. Biol.* 17:R623–25

Hynes N. 2009. Colour and meaning in corporate logos: an empirical study. *Brand Manag.* 16:545–55

Ilie A, Ioan S, Zagrean L, Moldovan M. 2008. Better to be red than blue in virtual competition. *Cyberpsychol. Behav.* 11:375–77

Imhof M. 2004. Effects of color stimulation on handwriting performance of children with ADHD without and with additional learning disabilities. *Eur. Child Adolesc. Psychol.* 13:191–98

Ioan S, Sandulache M, Avramescu S, Ilie A, Neacsu A, et al. 2007. Red is a distractor for men in competition. *Evol. Hum. Behav.* 28:285–93

Jacob C, Guéguen N, Boulbry G, Ardicioni R. 2009. Waitresses' facial cosmetics and tipping: a field experiment. *Int. J. Cosmet. Sci.* 29:188–90

Jensen-Campbell LA, Graziano WG, West S. 1995. Dominance, prosocial orientation, and female preferences: Do nice guys really finish last? *J. Personal. Soc. Psychol.* 68:427–40

Johns SE, Hargrave LA, Newton-Fisher NE. 2012. Red is not a proxy signal for female genitalia in humans. *PLoS ONE* 7:e34669

Jung I, Kim M, Han K. 2011a. The influence of an attractive female model on male users' product ratings. *KHCI Conf. Proceed.*, Seoul, South Korea

Jung I, Kim M, Han K. 2011b. Red for romance, blue for memory. *HCI Int.: Posters Extended Abstr. Commun. Comput. Inf. Sci.* 173:284–88. Berlin: Springer

Kaiser PK. 1984. Psychological response to color: a cultural review. *Color Res. Appl.* 9:29–36

Kappes SM, Schmidt SJ, Lee SY. 2006. Color halo/horns and halo-attribute dumping effects within descriptive analysis of carbonated beverages. *J. Food Sci.* 71:S590–95

Kay P, Maffi L. 1999. Color appearance and the emergence and evolution of basic color lexicons. *Am. Anthropol.* 101:743–60

Kaya N, Epps HH. 2004. Relationship between color and emotion: a study of college students. *Coll. Stud. J.* 38:396–405

Kliger D, Gilad D. 2012. Red light, green light: color priming in financial decisions. *J. Sociol. Econ.* 41:738–45

Kocher MG, Sutter M. 2008. Shirt colour and team performance in football. In *Myths and Facts About Football: The Economics and Psychology of the World's Greatest Sport*, ed. P Andersson, P. Ayton, C Schmidt, pp. 125–130. Cambridge, UK: Cambridge Sch. Publ.

Küller R, Mikellides B, Janssens J. 2009. Color, arousal, and performance—a comparison of three experiments. *Color Res. Appl.* 34:141–52

Kumi R, Conway CM, Limayem M, Goyal S. 2013. Learning in color: how color and affect influence learning outcomes. *IEEE Trans. Prof. Commun.* 56:2–15

Labrecque LI, Milne GR. 2012. Exciting red and competent blue: the importance of color in marketing. *J. Acad. Mark. Sci.* 40:711–27

Labrecque LI, Milne GR. 2013. To be or not to be different: Exploration of norms and benefits of color differentiation in the marketplace. *Mark. Lett.* 24:165–76

Lakens D, Semin GR, Foroni F. 2012. But for the bad, there would not be good: grounding valence in brightness through shared relational structures. *J. Exp. Psychol.: Gen.* 141:584–94

Larionescu AM, Pantelimona M. 2012. The influence of colour on the efficacy of basketball throws. *Ann. Univ. Galaţi* 1452:82–85

Lee S, Rao VS. 2010. Color and store choice in electronic commerce: the explanatory role of trust. *J. Electr. Commer. Res.* 11:110–26

Liang CC, Chen K, Ho C. 2010. A study of color emotion for plastic eyewear. *New World Situat. New Dir. Concurr. Eng.* 3:147–62

Lichtenfeld S, Elliot AJ, Maier MA, Pekrun R. 2012. Fertile green: Green facilitates creative performance. *Personal. Soc. Psychol. Bull.* 38:784–97

Lichtenfeld S, Maier MA, Elliot AJ, Pekrun R. 2009. The semantic red effect: processing the word red undermines intellectual performance. *J. Exp. Soc. Psychol.* 45:1273–76

Linhares JM, Pinto PD, Nascimento SM. 2008. The number of discernable colors in natural scenes. *J. Opt. Soc. Am. A* 25:2918–24

Little AC, Hill R. 2007. Attribution to red suggests special role in dominance signaling. *J. Evol. Psychol.* 5:161–68

Magee RG. 2012. Impression formation online: how web page colors can interact with physical temperature. *J. Media Psychol.* 24:124–33

Maier MA, Elliot AJ, Lee B, Lichtenfeld S, Barchfeld P, et al. 2013. Red and impression formation in the job application context. *Motiv. Emot.* 37:389–401

Maier MA, Elliot AJ, Lichtenfeld S. 2008. Mediation of the negative effect of red on intellectual performance. *Personal. Soc. Psychol. Bull.* 34:1530–40

Matsumoto D, Konno J, Hata S, Takeuchi M. 2007. Blue judogis may bias competition outcomes. *Res. J. Budo* 39:1–7

Matts PJ, Fink B, Grammer K, Burquest M. 2007. Color homogeneity and visual perception of age, health, and attractiveness of female facial skin. *J. Am. Acad. Dermatol.* 57:977–84

Mehta R, Zhu RJ. 2009. Blue or red? Exploring the effect of color on cognitive task performance. *Science* 323:1226–29

Meier BP, D'Agostino PR, Elliot AJ, Maier MA, Wilkowski BM. 2012. Color in context: Psychological context moderates the influence of red on approach- and avoidance-motivated behavior. *PLoS ONE* 7:e40333

Meier BP, Robinson MD, Clore GL. 2004. Why good guys wear white. *Psychol. Sci.* 15:82–87

Meyer MJ, Bagwell J. 2012. The non-impact of paper color on exam performance. *Iss. Account. Educ.* 27:691–706

Miller EG, Kahn BE. 2005. Shades of meaning: the effect of color and flavor names on consumer choice. *J. Consum. Res.* 32:86–92

Mitterer H, Horschig JM, Müsseler J, Majid A. 2009. The influence of memory on perception: it's not what things look like, it's what you call them. *J. Exp. Psychol.: Learn. Mem. Cogn.* 35:1557–62

Moller AC, Elliot AJ, Maier MA. 2009. Basic hue-meaning associations. *Emotion* 9:898–902

Moore MM. 2010. Human nonverbal courtship behavior—a brief historical review. *J. Sex Res.* 47:171–80

Nakashian JS. 1964. The effects of red and green surroundings on behavior. *J. Gen. Psychol.* 70:143–62

Ngo MK, Piqueras-Fiszman B, Spence C. 2012. On the colour and shape of still and sparkling water: insights from online and laboratory-based testing. *Food Qual. Prefer.* 24:260–68

Niesta Kayser D, Elliot AJ, Feltman R. 2010. Red and romantic behavior in men viewing women. *Eur. J. Soc. Psychol.* 40:901–8

Norenzayan A, Heine SJ. 2005. Psychological universals: What are they and how can we know? *Psychol. Bull.* 135:763–84

Oberzaucher E, Katina S, Schmehl S, Holzleitner I, Mehu-Blantar I. 2012. The myth of hidden ovulation: shape and texture changes in the face during the menstrual cycle. *J. Evol. Psychol.* 10:163–75

Ott JW. 1979. The dual function of the eyes. *South. J. Optom.* 21:8–13

Paul S, Okan A. 2011. Response to color: literature review with cross-cultural marketing perspective. *Int. Bull. Bus. Adm.* 11:34–41

Payen V, Elliot AJ, Coombes SA, Chalabaev A, Brisswalter J, Cury F. 2011. Viewing red prior to a strength test inhibits motor output. *Neurosci. Lett.* 495:44–48

Pazda AD, Elliot AJ, Greitemeyer T. 2012. Sexy red: Perceived sexual receptivity mediates the red-attraction relation in men viewing women. *J. Exp. Soc. Psychol.* 48:787–90

Pazda AD, Elliot AJ, Greitemeyer T. 2013. Perceived sexual receptivity and fashionableness: separate paths linking red and black to perceived attractiveness. *Color Res. Appl.* In press

Penton-Voak IS, Perrett DI, Castles DL, Kobayashi T, Burt DM, et al. 1999. Menstrual cycle alters face preference. *Nature* 399:741–42

Piatti M, Savage DA, Torgler B. 2012. The red mist? Red shirts, success and team sports. *Sport Soc.* 15:1209–27

Piotrowski C, Armstrong T. 2012. Color red: implications for applied psychology and marketing. *Psychol. Educ. Interdisc. J.* 49:55–57

Piqueras-Fiszman B, Alcaide J, Roura E, Spence C. 2012. Is it the plate or is it the food? Assessing the influence of the color (black or white) and shape of the plate on the perception of food placed on it. *Food Qual. Prefer.* 24:205–8

Links multiple colors to psychological functioning and shows meditational processes.

Piqueras-Fiszman B, Spence C. 2012. The influence of the color of the cup on consumers' perceptions of a hot beverage. *J. Sens. Stud.* 27:324–31

Pryke SR. 2009. Is red an innate or learned signal of aggression and intimidation? *Anim. Behav.* 78:393–98

Puccinelli NM, Chandrashekaran R, Grewal D, Suri R. 2013. Are men seduced by red? The effect of red versus black prices on price perceptions. *J. Retail.* 89:115–25

Purdy MA. 2009. The influence of the amygdala and color on judgments of attractiveness. *UNC-Ashville J.* (Dec.)

Re DE, Whitehead RD, Xiao D, Perrett DI. 2011. Oxygenated-blood colour change thresholds for perceived facial redness, health, and attractiveness. *PLoS ONE* 6:e17859

Rechtschaffen A, Buchignani C. 1992. The visual appearance of dreams. In *The Europsychology of Sleep and Dreaming*, ed. J Antrobus, M Bertini, pp. 143–55. Hillsdale, NJ: Erlbaum

Regan BC, Julliot C, Simmen B, Viénot F, Charles-Dominique P, Mollon JD. 2001. Fruits, foliage, and the evolution of primate colour vision. *Phil. Trans. R. Soc. Lond. B* 356:220–83

Roberts SC, Owen RC, Havlicek J. 2010. Distinguishing between perceiver and wearer effects in clothing color-associated attributions. *Evol. Psychol.* 8:350–64

Ross CF, Bohischeid J, Weller K. 2008. Influence of visual masking technique on the assessment of 2 red wines by trained and consumer assessors. *J. Food Sci.* 73:S279–85

Rowe C, Harris JM, Roberts SC. 2005. Seeing red? Putting sportswear in context. *Nature* 437:E10

Rutchick AM, Slepian ML, Ferris BD. 2010. The pen is mightier than the word: object priming of evaluative standards. *Eur. J. Soc. Psychol.* 40:704–8

Samson N, Fink B, Matts PJ. 2010. Interaction of skin color distribution and skin surface topography cues in the perception of female facial age and health. *J. Cosmet. Dermatol.* 10:78–84

Samson N, Fink B, Matts PJ. 2011. Does a woman's skin color indicate her fertility level? *Swiss J. Psychol.* 70:199–202

Schwarz S, Singer M. 2013. Romantic red revisited: Red enhances men's attraction to young, but not menopausal women. *J. Exp. Soc. Psychol.* 49:161–64

Scott IML, Pound N, Stephen ID, Clark AP, Penton-Voak IS. 2010. Does masculinity matter? The contribution of masculine face shape to male attractiveness in humans. *PLoS ONE* 5:e13585

Shankar MU, Levitan CA, Prescott J, Spence C. 2009. The influence of color and label information on flavor perception. *Chem. Percept.* 2:53–58

Shankar MU, Levitan CA, Spence C. 2010. Grape expectations: the role of cognitive influences in color-flavor interactions. *Conscious. Cogn.* 19:380–90

Shavit T, Rosenboim M, Cohen C. 2013. Does the color of feedback affect investment decisions? *Int. J. Appl. Behav. Econ.* 2:15–26

Sherman GD, Clore GL. 2009. White and black are perceptual symbols of moral purity and pollution. *Psychol. Sci.* 20:1019–25

Sherman GD, Haidt J, Clore GL. 2012. The faintest speck of dirt: Disgust enhances the detection of impurity. *Psychol. Sci.* 23:1506–14

Skinner NF. 2004. Differential test performance from differently colored paper: White paper works best. *Teach. Psychol.* 31:111–13

Smith MJ, Perrett DI, Jones BC, Cornwell RE, Moore FR, et al. 2006. Facial appearance is a cue to estrogen levels in women. *Proc. Biol. Sci.* 273:135–40

Soldat AS, Sinclair RC, Mark MM. 1997. Color as an environmental processing cue: External affective cues can directly affect processing strategy without affecting mood. *Soc. Cogn.* 15:55–71

Sorokowski P, Szmajke A. 2007. How does the "red win" effect work? The role of sportswear colour during sports competitions. *Pol. J. Appl. Psychol.* 5:71–79

Sorokowski P, Szmajke A. 2011. The influence of the "red win" effect in sports: a hypothesis of erroneous perception of opponents dressed in red—preliminary test. *Hum. Mov.* 12:367–73

Spence C, Levitan CA, Shankar MU, Zampini M. 2010. Does food color influence taste and flavor perception in humans? *Chem. Percept.* 3:68–84

Stephen ID, Coetzee V, Law Smith M, Perrett DI. 2009a. Skin blood perfusion and oxygenation colour affect perceived human health. *PLoS ONE* 4:e5083

Stephen ID, Coetzee V, Perrett DI. 2011. Carotenoid and melanin pigment coloration affect perceived human health. *Evol. Hum. Behav.* 32:216–27

Stephen ID, Law Smith MJ, Stirrat MR, Perrett DI. 2009b. Facial skin coloration affects perceived health of human faces. *Int. J. Primatol.* 30:845–57

Stephen ID, McKeegan AM. 2010. Lip colour affects perceived sex typicality and attractiveness of human faces. *Perception* 39:1104–10

Stephen ID, Oldham FH, Perrett DI, Barton RA. 2012a. Redness enhances perceived aggression, dominance and attractiveness in men's faces. *Evol. Psychol.* 10:562–72

Stephen ID, Scott IML, Coetzee V, Pound N, Perrett DI, Penton-Voak IS. 2012b. Cross-cultural effects of color, but not morphological masculinity, on perceived attractiveness of men's faces. *Evol. Hum. Behav.* 33:260–67

Stevens M, Ruxton GD. 2012. Linking the evolution and form of warning coloration in nature. *Proc. Biol. Sci.* 279:417–26

Stone NJ, English AJ. 1998. Task type, posters, and workspace color on mood, satisfaction, and performance. *J. Environ. Psychol.* 18:175–85

Suk HJ, Irtel H. 2010. Emotional response to color across media. *Color Res. Appl.* 35:64–77

Szmajke A, Sorokowski P. 2006. Permitted support in sport: the influence of sportsmen's outfit colour on competitions in sport. *Med. Sport* 10:119–22

Tal IR, Akers KG, Hodge GK. 2008. Effect of paper color and question order on exam performance. *Teach. Psychol.* 35:26–28

Tanaka A, Tokuno Y. 2011. The effect of the color red on avoidance motivation. *Soc. Behav. Personal.* 39:287–88

Taylor C, Clifford A, Franklin A. 2013. Color preferences are not universal. *J. Exp. Psychol.: Gen.* In press

Ten Velden FS, Baas M, Shalvi S, Preenen PTY, De Dreu CKW. 2012. In competitive interaction, displays of red increase actors' competitive approach and perceivers' withdrawal. *J. Exp. Soc. Psychol.* 48:1205–8

Tharangie KGD, Althaff Irfan CM, Yamada K, Marasinghe A. 2011. Appraisal and guideline to utilize colours in interactive learning environments based on Kansei engineering. *Int. J. Biometrics* 3:285–99

Tharangie KGD, Althaff Irfan CM, Young IM, Nomura S, Yamada K, Marasinghe A. 2009. Colour interaction, psychological functioning and Kansei measurement method. *J. Med. Inform. Technol.* 13:223–28

Tiryaki ME. 2005. Assessing whether black uniforms affect the decisions of Turkish soccer referees: Is finding of Frank and Gilovich's study valid for Turkish culture? *Percept. Mot. Skills* 100:51–57

Valdez P, Mehrabian A. 1994. Effects of color on emotions. *J. Exp. Psychol.: Gen.* 123:394–409

Van Ittersum K, Wansink B. 2011. Plate size and color suggestibility: the Delboeuf illusion's bias on serving and eating behavior. *J. Consum. Res.* 39:215–28

Wartenberg W, Höpfner T, Potthast P, Mirau A. 2011. If you wear red on a date, you will please your mate. *Proc. Empiriepraktikumskongress, 6th*, Aug. 7, pp. 26–27. Univ. Jena, Ger.

Webster DG, Urland GR, Correll J. 2012. Can uniform color cause aggression? Quasi-experimental evidence from professional ice hockey. *Soc. Psychol. Personal. Sci.* 3:274–81

Whitehead RD, Ozakinci G, Perrett DI. 2012. Attractive skin coloration: harnessing sexual selection to improve diet and health. *Evol. Psychol.* 10:842–54

Whitfield TW, Wiltshire TJ. 1990. Color psychology: a critical review. *Genet. Soc. Gen. Psychol. Monogr.* 116:385–411

Wilkins A. 2003. *Reading Through Colour*. Chichester, UK: Wiley

Williams CK, Grierson LE, Carnahan H. 2011. Colour-induced relationship between affect and reaching kinematics during a goal-directed aiming task. *Exp. Brain Res.* 212:555–61

Yamazaki AK. 2010. An analysis of background-color effects on the scores of a computer-based English test. *Lect. Notes Comput. Sci.* 6277:630–36

Yamazaki AK, Eto K. 2011. A preliminary examination of background-color effects on scores of computer-based English grammar testing using near-infrared spectroscopy. *Lect. Notes Comput. Sci.* 6883:31–39

Young SG, Elliot AJ, Feltman R, Ambady N. 2013. Red enhances the processing of facial expressions of anger. *Emotion* 13:380–84

Yüksel A. 2009. Exterior color and perceived retail crowding: effects on tourists' shopping quality inferences and approach behaviors. *J. Qual. Assur. Hosp. Tour.* 10:233–54

Links facial skin coloration to evaluation of male and female targets.

Highlights the importance of controlling for nonfocal color attributes in color research.

Zachar G, Schrott A, Kabai P. 2008. Context-dependent prey avoidance in chicks persists following complete telencephalectomy. *Brain Res. Bull.* 76:289–92

Zampini M, Sanabria D, Phillips N, Spence C. 2007. The multisensory perception of flavor: assessing the influence of color cues on flavor discrimination responses. *Food Qual. Prefer.* 18:975–84

Zampini M, Wantling E, Phillips N, Spence C. 2008. Multisensory flavor perception: assessing the influence of fruit acids and color cues on the perception of fruit-flavored beverages. *Food Qual. Prefer.* 19:335–43

Zellner DA, Durlach P. 2008. Effect of color on expected and experienced refreshment, intensity, and liking of beverages. *Am. J. Psychol.* 116:633–47

Human Infancy . . . and the Rest of the Lifespan

Marc H. Bornstein

Child and Family Research, *Eunice Kennedy Shriver* National Institute of Child Health and Human Development, National Institutes of Health, Public Health Service, Bethesda, Maryland 20892; email: Marc_H_Bornstein@nih.gov

Annu. Rev. Psychol. 2014. 65:121–58

First published online as a Review in Advance on September 13, 2013

The *Annual Review of Psychology* is online at http://psych.annualreviews.org

This article's doi: 10.1146/annurev-psych-120710-100359

Keywords

infancy, infant effects, stability, prediction

Abstract

Human infancy has been studied as a platform for hypothesis and theory testing, as a major physiological and psychological adjustment, as an object of adults' effects as well as a source of effects on adults, for its comparative value, as a stage of life, and as a setting point for the life course. Following an orientation to infancy studies, including previous reviews and a discussion of the special challenges infants pose to research, this article focuses on infancy as a foundation and catalyst of human development in the balance of the life course. Studies of stability and prediction from infancy illustrate the depth and complexity of modern research on infants and provide a long-awaited reply to key philosophical and practical questions about the meaningfulness and significance of infancy.

Contents

HUMAN INFANCY

He who . . . considers things in their first growth and origin . . . will obtain the clearest view of them.
(Aristotle 350 BCE/2000, book one, part two)

Human infancy has always offered a certain romantic and simultaneously enigmatic attraction: All of us have been infants, yet perceptions, thoughts, and feelings of our infancy are seemingly lost to us. Infants are irresistible to our senses, engaging of our intellect, and moving to our emotions. Infants are completely dependent and under our care, and the results of our actions toward them become embodied in them. Infancy represents a beginning in which much is invested theoretically, psychologically, and personally. Formal studies of infancy have largely concerned delineating the status of different characteristics (constructs, structures, functions, and processes) in early life. Focusing on characteristics so close to the start, investigators of infancy are also naturally concerned with how biological and experiential forces fuse to shape our origins as well as the unfolding course of future development.

Infancy encompasses only a fraction of the average person's expected lifespan, but infancy is characterized by remarkable physiological, physical, and psychological changes, many of which are evident even on casual observation. Within this brief period, the child's length and weight multiply, and the child changes from an immature being unable to move his or her limbs in a coordinated manner to one who can purposefully control complicated sequences of muscle contractions and flexions necessary to grasp and walk, and from an unintelligible babbler to a sentient being who can verbalize needs and wishes with abundant clarity.

As the baby grows into the child, and the child eventually into the adult, exploring and explaining what transforms as the individual develops from infancy to maturity, and what remains stable and predicts the future person, have constituted challenging tasks to philosophy, biology, and psychology. A reply to them is the principal aim of this *Annual Review of Psychology* article.

DEFINITION, HISTORY, CHALLENGE, AND ORIENTATION

What is an infant? What were the origins of infancy studies? The period of life called infancy is somewhat ambiguous and arbitrary; however, the Latinate root of infant, *in + fans* (nonspeaker), ties the definition to a psychosocial event, i.e., the onset of language, rather than to physical characteristics, weaning or walking, educational requirements, or vagaries of legal opinion. For purposes of this review, infancy encompasses roughly the first year of postnatal life.

In response to a note on language acquisition by Taine (see Kessen 1965), Charles Darwin (1877) published in the English journal *Mind* "A Biographical Sketch of an Infant." The notes that constituted this account of the first years of his firstborn son William Erasmus (Doddy) had been recorded in notebooks almost 40 years earlier. Darwin's foremost roles in the origins and descent of comparative psychology generally, of developmental science specifically, and of infant studies particularly are by now legendary (Lerner et al. 2011). In the years following Darwin's publication, a plethora of "baby biographies" appeared, and infancy studies blossomed (Bornstein et al. 2013a).

Previous Reviews

Landmark reviews and integrations of the infancy literature to date include Kessen and colleagues' (1970) overview in Mussen's third edition of Carmichael's *Manual of Child Psychology*, entitled "Human Infancy: A Bibliography and Guide." Their survey approach appended more than 2,000 references to works on infants appearing to that time. Stone and colleagues' (1973) *The Competent Infant* built on the efforts of Kessen and coworkers, excerpting important original works. Haith & Campos (1977) updated the bibliography in their "Human Infancy" article with copious additional references in the first *Annual Review of Psychology* (*ARP*) article on infancy, and Hay's (1986) *ARP* review organized progress in infancy studies to roughly a quarter-century ago. Since then much has happened, and infants have grown up. Articles, essays, chapters, monographs, and books on infancy have appeared at an ever-quickening pace. Notable periodic compilations focused on academic approaches to infancy (not trade books) include Haith & Campos's (1983) *Handbook of Child Psychology: Infancy and Developmental Psychobiology*, Osofsky's (1987) *Handbook of Infant Development*, and Rosenblith's (1992) *In the Beginning: Development from Conception to Age Two*; they have been supplanted by more contemporary treatments, including Fogel's (2007) *Infancy: Infant, Family, and Society*, Bremner & Wachs's (2010) *Handbook of Infant Development*, and Bornstein et al.'s (2014) *Development in Infancy: A Contemporary Introduction*. Several scientific journals such as *Infancy*, the *Infant Mental Health Journal*, and *Infant Behavior and Development*, to name a few, are now devoted exclusively to infancy and enjoy robust publication; of course, infant studies also prominently populate a host of other academic periodicals in psychology and allied disciplines. These trends validate Haith & Campos's (1977) salutation that the "allocation of a whole chapter in the *Annual Review of Psychology* to 'Infancy' is only one of many indications that the field has come into its own" (p. 251).

Thus, the literature in infancy is reviewed periodically, but not previously from the perspective that is advanced here. This review looks at infancy as a setting point in the life course. It has not been possible to do so before now because appropriate longitudinal data on the same participants collected in one study beginning in infancy and extending forward had not yet reached a critical mass.

Challenges of Studying Infants

How much we have learned about infant behavior and development in approximately the last half-century is testimony to the ingenuity, patience, and persistence of researchers in meeting and overcoming the formidable challenges posed by infants themselves. First and foremost, infants are by definition nonverbal (but not, of course, noncommunicative), and they are also, especially in the early months of life, motorically incompetent, emotionally labile, and subject to rapid fluctuations in behavioral state. Unlike adults, infants are not motivated to perform for researchers. Other problems too vex investigators, such as infants' short attention spans and their limited response repertoires.

Yet infants are also important and attractive to study, for a host of reasons spelled out immediately below, not the least of which is their role in the balance of the lifespan, the principal subject here. The impediments infants present have stimulated researchers to develop strategies geared to overcome various communication barriers that naturally but infelicitously separate infants from the rest of us. Through intense appeal and decades of rigorous investigation, infants have slowly divulged their many secrets. This glimpse into the heretofore private world of infancy, and what it portends for the future, constitutes one of the notable achievements of modern developmental science.

Seven Types of Infancy Studies

Infants contribute to psychological inquiry in the "magical number seven" (Miller 1956) major ways. Here, I touch on six of the seven types very briefly and then dwell on the seventh in detail. Each type merits extended treatment, which is not possible within the confines of an *ARP* article. Amplification of one illustrates the breadth and depth of all.

First, infancy provokes enduring philosophical, juridical, and social disputes and questions, and it therefore has been the subject of continuing theoretical interest. Because infancy is a period of life that precedes the onset and influence of (many) experiences, for example, traditional nature-nurture debates have turned to infants. A principal task of infancy is radical adaptation from the secure comfort of the intrauterine environment to the kaleidoscopic extrauterine universe. Second, therefore, infancy is a major physiological and psychological adjustment. Third, adults wield extraordinary and nearly limitless control over infants in part because infancy is a period of both helplessness and plasticity. Aside from genetic bequest, caregivers exercise continuing and powerful influence over infants in their roles as ministrators, socializers, and educators. Fourth, however, human infants are equally powerful stimuli to adults. Infants inspire song, poetry, literature, humor, art, and articles in the *Annual Review of Psychology*. It is only for heuristic purposes that the otherwise inextricable mutuality between infants and adults into "effects on" and "effects of" can be separated. Transactions rule life: the level at which parents pitch the complexity of speech to their infant depends on the infant's display of understanding, and infants' comprehension depends on the complexity of speech addressed to them. Fifth, infancy is a natural arena for comparison of human abilities, behaviors, and development relative to newborns of other species, and because many sorts of experimentation with human infants fall outside of ethical bounds, comparative animal models of infancy are common. Sixth, infancy appears to be a distinct stage of life, based on biological, cognitive, and social data, and so is meritorious of study in its own right. Infants do not speak, whereas children do; infants creep and crawl, whereas children walk and run. Many outstanding developmental theorists—including Freud, Piaget, Erikson, and Werner—have championed stage theories of development, and all have identified infancy as one. Finally, but not least important, infancy has been studied as a basis of stability in development and prediction of the future life course.

STABILITY AND PREDICTION FROM INFANCY

The concept of development is most readily associated with change (Block & Block 2006a; Kagan 1976, 1998; Wohlwill 1973). As the child rapidly grows from the infant, changes in many developmental characteristics are prominent and observable. The measured values of characteristics plotted across age define their developmental functions, and the species-general developmental function of many characteristics (from height to language) is discontinuous (Emmerich 1964).

The other side of the developmental coin to change is consistency, manifest as continuity and stability. In actuality, consistency may be more parsimonious and orderly than change, and many characteristics of human development remain (more or less) consistent over time or connect in regular ways to later points in development. Consistency *qua* continuity describes maintenance of the group mean level of a characteristic over time; consistency *qua* stability describes maintenance in the ranks of individuals in a group with respect to the expression of a characteristic over time (Bornstein & Bornstein 2008, Hartmann et al. 2011). Thus, a stable characteristic is one that some individuals demonstrate at a relatively high level at time 1 (infancy) and again at a relatively high level at time 2 (maturity). Stability has many variations and interpretations. Homotypic stability expresses maintenance of rank order status on an identical characteristic from time 1 to time 2 (e.g., vocabulary size at 12 months and at 12 years). Heterotypic stability or predictive validity expresses maintenance of rank order status between two related, but not identical, characteristics. The two may be related because they share the same underlying process (e.g., vocabulary size at 12 months and reading ability at 12 years both reflect language). Stability and prediction share their side of the developmental coin.

A fundamental conceptual issue that has framed debates in theory and research across the history of developmental science has concerned stability and prediction. What do individual differences in infants tell us about the human being's future development? The terms "seeds," "precursors," "potentials," and "anlagen" are commonly applied to constructs, structures, functions, and processes in infants that foretell later characteristics. This review deliberates on questions of stability and prediction from infancy.

Why and How Developmental Science Is Concerned with Stability and Prediction from Infancy

Why. The long-term significance of infancy has engendered intense dispute between two polar theoretical stances. Some authorities rail against so-called infant determinism and contend that infancy is not particularly important because the status of the infant or experiences in infancy have little (if any) long-term significance. That is, infant characteristics and experiences leave no irreversible signs on people's lives but are supplanted later in development. This position emphasizes discontinuities and instabilities between infancy and maturity: Infancy is disconnected from the balance of the life course, and infant characteristics and experiences are peripheral or ephemeral or inconsequential in the sense that they exert little or no enduring effect (Bruer 2002, Clarke & Clarke 2000, Kagan 1998, Lewis 1997). Empirical support for this point of view typically consists of failures to find lagged associations between the same or different characteristics in infancy and maturity and demonstrations of the recovery of functioning from early adversity or deprivation, as well as failures of early experiences or interventions to show sustained effects.

However, others theorists contend that infancy is part of a seamless and united lifeline and that characteristics and experiences in infancy are not only important in themselves but are also crucial to later life. For these theorists, biological functioning, intellectual predilections, personality inclinations, and social orientations in infancy set enduring patterns. Arguments for the specialness of infancy in these ways derive from a diverse and impressive array of theoretical starting points, including psychoanalysis, behaviorism, constructivism, ethology, neuropsychology, attachment, and systems theory. For example, Freud (1940/1949) focused attention on infancy, suggesting that the ways babies are treated establish lifelong personality traits, and Erikson (1963) theorized that the resolutions of developmental crises in infancy have implications for the way the person negotiates successive stages of development. For theorists like Watson, Skinner, Dollard, and Miller, learning in infancy is important because it occurs first and promotes easy and rapid later learning. They asserted that early and simpler behavior patterns underlie later and more complex ones. Piaget (1970) likewise opined that advanced developmental capacities build on elementary ones of very early life, all the way back to infancy. For their part, ethologists and embryologists from Lorenz and Tinbergen to Gottlieb emphasized the lifelong legacy of infant experiences (as in sensitive periods; Bornstein 1987, 1989). Bowlby, Ainsworth, and their successors (Sroufe et al. 2005) in turn theorized that attachment experiences and classification in infancy augur future cognitive development, personality, and social relationships. Furthermore, modern systems theorists contend that development consists of hierarchically organized characteristics that incorporate earlier emerging ones (Lewontin 2005). Finally, contemporary life-course theory brackets human development as extending from the prenatal period and infancy to maturity and death. Understanding development requires examining characteristics and experiences over long periods of time to capture how later life depends on early life trajectories (Elder 1998, Elder et al. 2015).

Infancy has therefore held a certain significance for those interested in stability and prediction, even when the characteristics and long-term effects of experiences from infancy are neither obvious nor direct. Developmental science generally carries three burdens—description, explanation, and prediction. Of these, prediction is the most thorny and problematic (as many a homespun philosopher has quipped: "Prediction is difficult, especially if it's about the future"). However, prediction from infancy has many vital purposes and benefits, its moral and ethical consequences notwithstanding. To put their ambit and value most succinctly, stability and prediction deepen psychological understanding, open the possibility of individual assessment, and lead to greater economy of decision making and more efficacious distribution of resources. These are theoretically worthy as well as highly practical goals.

Stability and prediction are also important constructs for developmental science per se. In interpreting the theoretical significance of a characteristic, it is essential to determine whether the characteristic represents something enduring in individuals or is better viewed as linked to a particular developmental time point or context, with few or no future implications. Knowledge about which characteristics are stable or predictive, beginning when, and over what periods of time, is foundational in the study of development.

Findings of stability and prediction tell us about the nature and overall ontogenetic course of a characteristic. Whether individuals maintain their order on some characteristic, or a characteristic is predictive through time, informs not only about individual variation but contributes to understanding of the origins, nature, and future of that characteristic as well. Is past performance the best predictor of future performance? Insofar as a characteristic is stable or predictive, we know that individuals who do well or poorly with respect to that characteristic at one time are likely to do well and poorly again later. Moreover, stable and predictive early characteristics tend to shape later emerging ones. Infants who know more words at 1 year tend to know more words at 2 years, and 2-year-olds who know more words may be at a long-term advantage because knowing more words speeds learning to read, improves verbal comprehension, and eventuates in more advanced written language skills (Marchman & Fernald 2008).

Stability and prediction are also meaningful because characteristics with such attributes in childhood signal developmental status to other people, thereby affecting the child's environment and likely his or her own development. Interactants often adjust their expectations and behaviors to match another's consistent characteristics (as when adults modify their language to harmonize with the language of a child). On the basis of stability and prediction, infants actively contribute to their own development.

Finally, most developmental scientists believe that individuals understand the world in unique ways that reflect their unique persons, interactions, and experiences. This perspective depends (in part, at least) on stable tendencies and capacities in the individual. In a nutshell, developmentalists are broadly interested in how characteristics manifest themselves in infancy and the developmental course of those characteristics—their stability and prediction through time. Characteristics that are stable or predictive in ontogeny are informative as to the nature of those characteristics per se as well as the individuals who possess them.

How. Historically, reports of stability and prediction have relied on simple or zero-order lagged correlations and regression analyses, comparing infants' performance early in life with their performance years later as children, adolescents, or even adults. However, the statistical armamentarium for estimating stability and prediction across time has grown increasingly sophisticated with the addition of latent growth curve modeling (Asendorpf & van Aken 1999, Blaga et al. 2009, Bridgett et al. 2009, Bridgett & Mayes 2011, Hill-Soderlund & Braungart-Rieker 2008, Pasco Fearon & Belsky 2011), path analyses (Bornstein et al. 2006, LaBuda et al. 1986), hierarchical linear modeling (Bada et al. 2007, Shafir et al. 2006), and hazard functions (Frank et al. 2011). For temporally distal developmental processes, moreover, tests of indirect paths between predictors and criteria are sometimes more sensitive, powerful, and theoretically appropriate than tests of simple direct relations (Shrout & Bolger 2002). A developmental cascade, for example, defines a longitudinal relation in which a characteristic at time 1 is uniquely associated with another characteristic at time 2 separate from other intrapersonal and extrapersonal factors (Masten & Cicchetti 2010). In cumulative processes, which refer to the growing implications of earlier characteristics or experiences for later outcomes, early individual differences are magnified in prediction (DiPrete & Eirich 2006). That is, in some cases the linear model may be inadequate to the task of assessing stability or prediction, and other statistical techniques may be more appropriate for multilevel longitudinal analysis (Bergman et al. 2003, Collins & Sayer 2001, Little et al. 2000).

Duncan et al. (2006) usefully described a continuum for evaluating the methodological rigor of studies such as those aimed at stability and prediction. At the popular end of the spectrum are correlational designs that analyze simple associations between measures in infancy and later outcomes, with few adjustments for confounding factors, and so this kind of research likely suffers from various biases. At the rare end are experiments in which infants are randomly assigned to treatment conditions and followed longitudinally; experiments can provide unbiased estimates of prediction (and, of course, are more appropriate to prediction than to stability). Between these extremes fall studies that employ techniques to reduce various biases (e.g., such as omitted variables using fixed effects and instrumental variables regression) and natural experiments. Despite the burgeoning literature documenting stability and prediction (reviewed below), it is necessary to be cautious in drawing strong conclusions because to date few studies have employed research designs or analytic methods that effectively and comprehensively address threats to internal validity. Increasingly, however, researchers are opting for designs and analyses that seriously address biases from diverse sources.

Furthermore, empirical studies of stability and prediction usually settle for data from only two assessment waves. However, it is less than desirable to discern patterns of stability and prediction from two assessments (i.e., whether stability and prediction stabilize at a nonzero value or approach zero in the limit). Following the logic in Fraley and colleagues (2012b), a significant relation between measurements of some characteristic at time 1 and the same or a different characteristic at time 2 would seem to indicate that the characteristic is stable or predictive. However, conclusions about stability or prediction would vary depending on the resultant coefficient at other developmental waves. Suppose, on the one hand, that stability and prediction maintained to times

3, 4, and 5. This pattern would suggest that stability and prediction are enduring. Suppose, on the other hand, that stability or prediction attenuated at times 3, 4, or 5; that is, as the temporal interval increased, stability or prediction approached 0.00 in the limit. This pattern would suggest that although the time 1 characteristic may play a role in the time 2 characteristic, the association eventually tempers, indicating that longer-term stability or prediction may be trifling. The two patterns have contrasting consequential implications (McCartney & Rosenthal 2000).

Long-Term Stability and Prediction from Infancy

The infancy literature is replete with studies of stability and prediction assessments confined *within* the first year of life (e.g., Artzi et al. 2011, Beebe et al. 2010, Bridgett et al. 2009, Fish 2001, Ruddy & Bornstein 1982), and developmental science more generally abounds with studies that evaluate and substantiate stability and prediction *after* infancy (e.g., Asendorpf & van Aken 2003, Casey et al. 2011, Caspi 2000, Dennissen et al. 2007, Gao et al. 2010a, Guerin et al. 1997, Martinez-Torteya et al. 2009, Reese et al. 2010). Notably, Bloom (1964) suggested that 50% of an adult intelligence is developed by 4 years of age, basing this conclusion on the strong statistical correlation between IQ at 4 years and IQ at 17 years. The Fels Longitudinal Study reported that IQ at 3 years predicted attained education and occupational status after 26 years (McCall 1977). Block & Block (2006b) observed that preschool children who were relatively more anxious, indecisive, and prone to guilt were more likely to endorse conservative values at age 23. Many reports now extend from childhood or adolescence well into late life (Ashby & Schoon 2012, Benson & Elder 2011, Casey et al. 2011, Gao et al. 2010b, Kell et al. 2013). Among the oldest active longitudinal studies, with birth years extending from 1903 to the 1920s, was Terman's on a sample of talented children: By the 1990s, investigators who continued this project had completed 13 waves of data spanning 70 years (Crosnoe & Elder 2004, Holahan et al. 1995, Shanahan & Elder 2002). Notably, however, previous long-term longitudinal studies typically began in adolescence and often assumed that what had transpired before—in the first years of life—was of little consequence.

Because long-term longitudinal research generally was rare, and research beginning in infancy was almost absent, it was not possible previously to answer questions about stability and prediction from infancy. This is unfortunate, because knowing more about which aspects of humanity are stable or predictive is (as argued above) vital to a full understanding of the nature and process of development. Now, however, examples from multiple domains have begun to populate the life-course literature, and they reveal pervasive stabilities and predictions from the first year of life (or even before; DiPietro et al. 2002) to childhood, adolescence, and adulthood. To animate the discussion and broaden generalizations, the following sections illustrate stability and prediction from biological, physical, and motor domains of development; from perceptual, cognitive, and communicative domains of development; and from emotion, temperament, and social domains of development. Infant experiences are also considered. Most are recent efforts, but where available, each section begins with reference to classical studies from the 1960s to the 1970s. In which domains of development are characteristics preserved from infancy? Several, it turns out.

Biological, Physical, and Motor Development

Interest in stability and prediction in biology was reinvigorated when events occurring in early postnatal (or even prenatal) life were traced and found to have long-lasting effects on behavior and health. Barker and his colleagues in the 1980s unearthed an association between low birth weight and ischemic heart disease in adulthood (Barker & Osmond 1986). The so-called Barker Hypothesis identified the general importance of early determinants of adult disease. Since the

1980s, a wealth of data has been published showing an inverse association between infant size at birth and adult blood pressure, type 2 diabetes, heart disease, and enhanced response to stress (Barker et al. 2002, Hales et al. 1991, Huxley et al. 2000, Jones et al. 2006, Phillips et al. 2005). More generally, this line of research has led to articulation of the developmental origins of health and disease paradigm (Barker 1998, Bateson et al. 2004, Gluckman & Hanson 2006).

A frequent design encountered in the biological literature consists of between-group comparisons of "treatment" children, adolescents, or adults versus controls, where the treatment (preterm versus full term, toxin exposed versus nonexposed) happened in the first year of life, or sometimes earlier. Publications appear periodically as successive waves of data collection are completed (Corapci et al. 2006, Gahagan et al. 2009, Geva et al. 2009, Hane et al. 2010, Lorenz et al. 2009, McAnulty et al. 2010, Paradise et al. 2007, van Baar et al. 2006). The deduction is that any mature differences between the groups are ascribable to continuing infancy (or prenatal) characteristics or experiences (rather than any intervening factor or experience). These studies concern themselves with an eclectic variety of outcomes, linking different biological, physical, or motor characteristics in the first year of life to many different later criteria. For example, preterm infants, relative to term infants, later in life show anatomical differences in the brain structure; are at increased risk of diabetes and heart disease; are more likely to display impaired motor skills, higher heart rate, attention and cognition problems, delayed language, lower IQs, and developmental and learning disabilities; and experience increased problems in social and academic functioning (Aziz et al. 2012; Bhutta et al. 2002; Caravale et al. 2005; Foster-Cohen et al. 2007; Gayraud & Kern 2007; Kerkhof et al. 2012; Mewes et al. 2006; Phillips & Barker 1997; Saigal 2000; Saigal et al. 2000; Salt & Redshaw 2006; Sansavini et al. 2006; Schothorst & van Engeland 1996; Shenkin et al. 2004; Spassov et al. 1994; Taylor et al. 2000a,b; van de Weijer-Bergsma et al. 2008; Woodward et al. 2004). Children born before 26 weeks gestation and followed until age 6 years experience higher rates of cognitive impairment in comparison with their classmates (Marlow et al. 2005). Smaller babies also grow up to be sadder adults: Birth weight has been linked to both depression and anxiety over 40 years (Colman et al. 2007). Long-term follow-up studies show that preterm infants (even those without medical disabilities) as adults have lower educational attainment and income, are less likely to establish a family, and are more likely to receive Social Security benefits (Moster et al. 2008). Infancy is also a particularly vulnerable period, for example to malnutrition, and growth problems forecast poor cognitive and social functioning in middle childhood and adolescence (Grantham-McGregor & Fernald 1997, Guerrant et al. 1999, Kar et al. 2008). Pre- and postnatal exposure to various toxins, such as polychlorinated biphenyls (PCBs), and drugs, such as cocaine, also has been shown to have adverse behavioral and emotional effects, for example in decreased sustained activity and high-level play and increased withdrawn and depressed behavior, aggression, and emotional reactivity (Lai et al. 2002, Mayes et al. 1997, Perera et al. 2012, Vreugdenhil et al. 2002, Yu et al. 1991).

A more straightforward approach in these domains has been to assess a hormonal or autonomic or central nervous system characteristic in infancy and relate it directly to the same or another (related) characteristic later in development. The diversity is striking. Higher levels of testosterone at 3 months of age predict greater penile growth in early childhood (Boas et al. 2006). Heart rate (HR), heart rate variability (HRV), and parasympathetic control measured in the first year of life are stable up to 5 years (Bar-Haim et al. 2000, Bornstein & Suess 2000, Calkins & Keane 2004). Skin conductance activity in typically developing 1-year-olds predicts mother-rated aggressive behavior problems at age 3 years (Baker et al. 2013). Thus, hormones and measures of autonomic function during infancy carry through to multiple measures of physical, autonomic, and behavior characteristics in childhood and later. Together, these results provide evidence of early postnatal origins of more mature development.

Likewise, cortical evoked response potentials (ERPs) in the first year of life predict children's later language, cognitive, and socioemotional development (van der Feest 2010). Infants who show less neural activity to phonemic nonnative contrasts at age 7.5 months have larger vocabularies at 24 months, suggesting that infants who are more attuned to the sounds in their language are better at learning words (Kuhl 2009); auditory ERPs of English-exposed American infants in response to both Spanish and English voicing contrasts at 11 months of age predict the number of words children produce at 18 through 30 months of age (Kuhl & Rivera-Gaxiola 2008; see also Garcia-Sierra et al. 2011, Rivera-Gaxiola et al. 2005); auditory ERPs at 6 and 9 months predict language at 3 and 4 years (Choudhury & Benasich 2011); and a discriminant function analysis of the brain waves of newborns predicts the classification of 8-year-old children into normal- and low-language performance groups with about 80% accuracy (Molfese 2000). Brain electrical activity at age 8 months also predicts working memory at age 4.5 years (Wolfe & Bell 2007). Stability in frontal brain activity asymmetry at 10 months of age predicts higher externalizing and internalizing behaviors as rated by mothers at 2.5 years of age (Smith & Bell 2010), and infants with right frontal electroencephalography (EEG) asymmetry show higher levels of anxiety and less ability to regulate their emotions in middle childhood (Hannesdottir et al. 2010).

Magnetic resonance imaging (MRI) can be used to measure the sizes of brain structures, and these measures in young infants also predict later language abilities (Ortiz-Mantilla et al. 2010). Functional MRI (fMRI) studies allow precise localization of brain activity and show remarkable similarity in the structures responsive to language in infants and adults (Dehaene-Lambertz et al. 2002, 2006).

A related characteristic shown to be predictive in the long term is physical status of the infant. Low birth weight (<2 kg) is predictive of motor problems at age 16 years (Whitaker et al. 2006); height and head circumference at 1 year predict IQ and neurodevelopmental outcomes at 9 and 10 years (Fattal-Valevski et al. 2009); and being small for gestational age has an independent effect on 16-year full-scale IQ, controlling for other pre- and postnatal risk factors (Lorenz et al. 2009). Small-for-gestational-age newborns have higher HR and lower HRV than do newborns adequate for gestational age; babies born with low birth weight have lower HRV in childhood and adulthood as compared to babies born with normal weight; and those born preterm have higher HR at 18 to 24 years as compared with normal controls (Aziz et al. 2012, Kerkhof et al. 2012, Phillips & Barker 1997, Spassov et al. 1994).

Even infantile colic (excessive crying in an otherwise healthy baby classically defined by Wessel criteria as at least three hours of crying at least three days a week for three weeks; Wessel et al. 1954) appears to be associated with migraines in children ages 6 to 18 years (Gelfand et al. 2012, Guidetti et al. 1984). Other early childhood periodic syndromes (benign paroxysmal vertigo or benign paroxysmal torticollis) are thought to be expressions of genes that later in life also manifest as migraine (Giffin et al. 2002).

An initiator, Gesell (1937) reported patterns of individuality and consistency in motor behavior from the first to the fifth year of life. Movement and coordination between ages 1.5 and 4.5 months are consistent with the later female advantage in finer motor skill and male advantage in gross motor activity (Piek et al. 2002). Movement at age 4 months predicts motor and cognitive status at 2 years (Rose-Jacobs et al. 2004); motor control at age 3 months predicts parent-reported attention problems at 8 years (Friedman et al. 2005); manipulative skill at 4 months (Kohen-Raz 1967) predicts eye-hand coordination as assessed by the Beery Developmental Test of Visual Motor Integration (VMI) at 5 years (Siegel 1983a); activity at 5 months predicts attention and play after 1 year (Tamis-LeMonda & Bornstein 1993); psychomotor status at 6 months predicts developmental profiles at 2 years (McCall et al. 1972); and motor control at 3 months predicts attention at 8 years (Friedman et al. 2005). A large-scale ($N = 374$) normative prospective

14-year longitudinal multivariate multisource controlled study showed that infants who were more motorically mature and who explored more actively at 5 months of age achieved higher levels of academic achievement at 14 years through conceptually related and age-appropriate measures of psychometric intelligence at ages 4 and 10 years and academic achievement at 10 years. This developmental cascade applied equally to girls and boys and was independent of children's behavioral adjustment and social competence; mothers' supportive caregiving, verbal intelligence, education, and parenting knowledge; and the material home environment (Bornstein et al. 2013b).

Similarly, the Bayley Scales Psychomotor Development Index (PDI) in the first year of life predicts expressive language at 2 years (Siegel 1981), 3 years (Siegel 1979), and 4 years (Siegel 1982), and the McCarthy General Cognitive Index at 6 years (Siegel 1983a); the PDI at 4 months of age predicts VMI at age 6 (Siegel 1989); and the PDI at 8 months and motor development at 1 year predict intellectual level at age 7 (Broman 1989).

Perceptual, Cognitive, and Communicative Development

A second developmental domain in which long-term stabilities and predictions are being documented includes perception, cognition, and communicative functions in the first year of life. Neonatal look duration relates to selective attention at age 12 years (Sigman et al. 1991), and ocular reaction time to targets in a visual expectation paradigm at age 3.5 months relates to ocular reaction time at age 4.5 years (Dougherty & Haith 1997). Visual exploratory behavior at 3 months predicts novelty seeking at age 15 years (Laucht et al. 2006, Schwartz et al. 2011). Perceiving a unique face in an anomalous social experience (still-face) at age 5 months predicts face recognition at 1.5 years (Bornstein et al. 2004). Despite years of visual input being available to both hemispheres following corrective surgery for congenital cataracts that blocked all patterned input to both the left and right eyes in infancy, people later show impaired face processing in the right but not the left hemisphere (Le Grand et al. 2003). Long-term perceptual effects are not restricted to vision: Infants who nursed for 6 weeks from mothers who had placed a balm with a distinctive odor on their nipples retained a representation of the odor for at least 18 months after they had stopped nursing (Allam et al. 2010), and 6.5-month-olds sitting in a dark room who reached out on hearing a sound from the space in front of them reached out again when they returned to the lab and the sounds were played for them two years later (Keen & Berthier 2004); in both instances, infants without the early experience did not react.

Studies of stability in cognition have demonstrated consistencies as well. Six-month-olds' performance in an action interpretation task predicts their performance on theory of mind tasks at 4 years (Aschersleben et al. 2008). Infant information-processing abilities in the first six months of life in three domains (attention, speed, and memory) relate to language and executive functions (working memory, inhibition, and shifting) at age 1.8 (Dixon & Smith 2008), age 4 (Courage et al. 2004, Cuevas & Bell 2013), and age 11 years (Rose et al. 2012); academic achievement at age 14 years (Bornstein et al. 2012); span of apprehension and intelligence at age 18 years (Sigman et al. 1997); and IQ and academic achievement at age 21 years (Fagan et al. 2007); even after contributions of biological and psychological third variables have been partialed (Bornstein et al. 2012, Laucht et al. 1994).

The Bayley Scales are often interpreted as a general measure of infant cognition. The Bayley Scales Mental Development Index administered at 4 to 12 months predicts Reynell Developmental Language Scales performance at 2, 3, and 4 years (Siegel 1979, 1981, 1982, 1983a,b, 1985a,b), and administered at 3 months predicts the Stanford-Binet at 3 years, the McCarthy Scales of Children's Abilities at 4 years, and the Wechsler Preschool and Primary Scale of Intelligence at 4, 5, and 6 years (Wilson 1978).

Infants in the first year of life do not command much in the way of verbal abilities per se; however, some speaking patterns we acquire early appear to last a lifetime (Flege 1991). Longitudinal studies demonstrate stability and prediction from a variety of early preverbal skills to measures of later language. Indian infants adopted by American families and only exposed to English relearn Indian-dialect phonemes more quickly than do American children who had never heard the Indian phonemes (Singh et al. 2011). Speech perception at age 6 months predicts language acquisition (word understanding, word production, and phrase understanding) at 2 years (Fernald et al. 2006, Tsao et al. 2004), and speech discrimination at 6 months predicts phonemic awareness scores at age 5 years (Cardillo 2010). Speech processing performance (segmenting words from fluent speech) before age 12 months predicts language assessed at 6 years (Newman et al. 2006). The trajectory of learning to discriminate vowels between 7 and 11 months predicts children's language abilities and preliteracy skills at age 5 years, an association that holds regardless of socioeconomic status as well as the level of children's language skills at 18 and 24 months of age (Cardillo Lebedeva & Kuhl 2009). Infants' early phonetic perception (Kuhl et al. 2005, 2008; Tsao et al. 2004), their pattern-detection skills for speech (Newman et al. 2006), mismatch responses to native-language sounds (Kuhl et al. 2008), and processing efficiency for words (Fernald et al. 2006) have all been linked to advanced later language abilities. Studies of communication skills and expressive vocabulary at 8 and 12 months also show predictive relations to mother-reported child symbolic use of objects at 2 years (Bornstein et al. 1999, Reilly et al. 2009), and 12-month-olds' vocabulary as measured by the CDI predicts their verbal IQ at age 4 (Blaga et al. 2009, Domsch et al. 2009). Finally, 3-month-old boys' differential vocalizations to their mothers versus a stranger predicts cognitive and academic functioning at 12 years, high school grade-point average and SAT scores, and education completed by age 28 (Roe 2001).

Emotion, Temperament, and Social Development

A third developmental domain of long-term study includes evaluations of emotions, temperament, and social interactions in the first year as predictive of child, adolescent, or adult criteria. Emotions are normally thought to be transient and fleeting. In consequence, emotions per se might not be expected to cast a long shadow. Nonetheless, low approach behaviors and poor inhibitory control at age 4 months have been linked to internalizing behaviors at 4 years (He et al. 2010), 3- to 4-month-olds' emotional distress in response to unfamiliar objects predicts behavioral inhibition or shyness at ages 7 and 14 years (Meili-Dworetzki & Meili 1972), and 3- to 4-month-olds who cry during experiments are more likely to be fearful and anxious adolescents (Ohr et al. 2006). Institutionalized care beyond age 1 year appears to undermine emotion identification and labeling in 4- to 5-year-olds (Camras et al. 2006).

Thomas, Chess, and colleagues (1963, 1970) followed children at regular intervals from infancy to young adulthood to try to understand the temperamental origins of later behavioral disorders. Their findings suggest that some aspects of early temperament have long-term consequences. For example, the majority (70%) of difficult infants in their sample manifested behavior problems later in life (Thomas et al. 1970). Temperamental difficultness, irritability, and negativity themselves appear to be stable from the first year (Rothbart & Bates 2006). Four-month-olds' behavioral inhibition, an infant temperamental style characterized by distress to novelty, predicts social wariness at age 7 years (as moderated by maternal negative personality; Degnan et al. 2008). In more normal bands of temperament, mother as well as father reports of activity level, smiling and laughter, distress to limitations, and fear at age 6 months foretell behavioral adjustment at 5.5 years (Komsi et al. 2006), and temperamental exuberance in 4-month-olds predicts 5-year-olds' externalizing and surgency (Degnan et al. 2011).

In one longitudinal study, 4-month-olds were classified as either high or low in reactivity (depending on levels of motor activity and distress in response to auditory, olfactory, and visual stimuli) and were then examined at 14 and 21 months (Kagan et al. 1994), 4.5 years (Kagan et al. 1998), and 7 years of age (Kagan et al. 1999). Temperamental reactivity was stable over time. Moreover, children classified as highly reactive in infancy were more likely to react fearfully to novel stimuli at ages 14 and 21 months than were children classified as unreactive; by 4.5 years, highly reactive children showed less spontaneity and sociability with adults; and by 7 years, highly reactive children were more likely to behave anxiously than were nonreactive children. Highly reactive infants had become shy and anxious at 15 years of age (Kagan 2013), and fMRI examinations at 21 years in the same sample revealed that previously inhibited children showed more amygdala activity than did previously uninhibited children when looking at novel as opposed to familiar faces (Schwartz et al. 2003).

Infants' expressions of smiling and laughter predict their anticipatory eagerness about upcoming positive events at age 7 (Rothbart 1988, Rothbart et al. 2000). Parent-reported infant reactivity to sensory stimulation at 10 months is related to social inhibition at 2 years (Andersson et al. 1999), and fear (distress to novelty) in infancy is associated with increased latency to approach later in childhood (Rothbart & Mauro 1990). In early-adopted children followed from infancy to adolescence, temperament was found to be stable (Jaffari-Bimmel et al. 2006), and physical aggression, as reported by mothers and fathers, in a sample of children initially recruited at 12 months was moderately stable one year later (Alink et al. 2006). Infant activity level predicts positive emotionality, and higher anger/frustration and low soothability-falling reactivity, at age 7; infants who show a short latency to grasp objects at 6.5, 10, and 13.5 months show high levels of positive anticipation and impulsivity as well as high anger-frustration and aggression at age 7 (Rothbart et al. 2000). Putnam et al. (2008) reported stability for fine-grained scales and factor-level temperamental dimensions from the Infant Behavior Questionnaire-Revised to the Early Childhood Behavior Questionnaire to the Children's Behavior Questionnaire.

Temperamentally difficult 1-year-olds who experience negative and intrusive mothering show externalizing behavior at 3 years (Belsky et al. 1998); similarly, infants who are temperamentally difficult and experience harsh parental reactions as 4-year-olds show externalizing behavior in adolescence (Bates et al. 1995).

Social anxiety disorder (SAD) causes the experience of intense fear and distress in social situations. Chronis-Tuscano and her colleagues (2009) investigated whether behavioral inhibition, a temperamental disposition to withdraw from unfamiliar social interactions, was an early sign of SAD. They measured temperament at ages 4 months, 24 months, 4 years, and 7 years. When the children were between the ages of 14 and 16 years, they were assessed for SAD. Onset for SAD was normally after 7 years. Temperament proved relatively stable from infancy to adolescence, and infants who showed early stable and high maternal-reported behavioral inhibition were most likely to show SAD by 14 to 16 years of age.

Across domains, temperament at 8 months predicts working memory at 4.5 years (Wolfe & Bell 2007), exuberance in infancy (vigorous motor activity, babbling, and smiling) predicts sociability and risk taking at 5 years (Lahat et al. 2012), hyperreactivity in the first months of life predicts periodic syndromes at 10–11 years (Guidetti et al. 1984), and reactivity at 4 months correlates with ventromedial prefrontal structural brain differences at 18 years (Schwartz et al. 2010).

The social status and social interaction style of infants have also been found to predict later development. In this area, infants' attachment status (usually measured around or just after the child is 1 year old) has been the focus of many follow-on longitudinal investigations. Developmentalists have been drawn to infant attachment, especially because of reasoning that the security of the infant's early relationships influences the ways in which the person relates to others during life after infancy (Bowlby 1969, van IJzendoorn 2005). Main & Cassidy (1988) reported a high degree of stability between 12-month attachment assessments in the "strange situation" and 6-year assessments, and meta-analysis confirms that attachment status is moderately stable across (at least) the first 19 years of life (Fraley 2002).

Expectations of its developmental spreading effects are borne out in studies that show that quality of infant attachment predicts later social relationships with siblings and peers (Furman & Lanthier 2002, Garner 2006, Ladd & Pettit 2002, Volling 2003, Zimmermann et al. 2001). Indeed, different attachment types predict a variety of developmental outcomes. Secure infant-mother attachments at 12 months are associated with more accurate perception of emotion in faces (Steele et al. 2008) and superior problem-solving abilities in diverse stressful and challenging contexts into the preschool years (Sroufe et al. 2005). Babies with secure (type B) attachments to their mothers are later more cooperatively playful when interacting with a friendly stranger and more popular and socially competent in their peer group in elementary school (Sroufe et al. 2005). The quality of infant attachments also predicts school children's perceptions of their relationships with teachers, underscoring both the long-lasting and broad impact of infant attachment status (Howes et al. 1998; NICHD Early Child Care Res. Netw. 2005, 2006). For its part, insecure attachment in infancy, in particular the disorganized/disoriented classification, predicts antisocial behavior in childhood (Jaffari-Bimmel et al. 2006), posttraumatic stress disorder symptoms at 8.5 years (MacDonald et al. 2008), externalizing behaviors at 12 years (Pasco Fearon & Belsky 2011), and compromised parent-adolescent relationships and increased likelihood of deviant behavior among youth (Allen et al. 1998). A core assumption of attachment theory is that individual differences in adult attachment styles emerge from individuals' developmental histories (Hazan & Shaver 1987, Mikulincer & Shaver 2007). An age-18 follow-up of the National Institute of Child Health and Human Development (NICHD) Study of Early Child Care and Youth Development, a longitudinal investigation that tracked a cohort of children and their parents from birth, reported that individual differences in adult attachment styles could be traced to variations in infants' care-giving environments in combination with other factors (Fraley et al. 2013). Infant attachment security is associated with the security of participants' romantic relationships in young adulthood (Roisman et al. 2005). Adults who classify themselves as secure are more likely to describe their early experiences with their parents as being affectionate, caring, and loving (Hazan & Shaver 1987), whereas adults who classify themselves as insecure are more likely to describe their parents as cold or rejecting (Collins & Read 1990).

Attachment classification is not the only long-term social style predictor from infancy. It has been recognized for some time that early (age 3 months) infant participation in interactions with their mothers predicts their later (6-year-old) intelligence (Coates & Lewis 1984), as infants' stimulation of maternal responsiveness affects their own later development (Bornstein et al. 2008, Tamis-LeMonda et al. 1996, Vibbert & Bornstein 1989). Other socioemotional factors in infants appear to be predictive as well. For example, differences in infants' perception of intentional agency at 12 months predict their understanding of others' theory of mind, mental states, and beliefs as 4-year-olds (Yamaguchi et al. 2009). Infants' interactions at 7 months predict their expressive and productive vocabulary at 14 months (Lundén & Silvén 2011). Infants whose mothers show positive responses at age 12 months have higher IQ as measured by the Wechsler Preschool and Primary Scale of Intelligence at 4 years (Pearson et al. 2011), and fathers' diverse vocabulary in interactions with their infants at 6 months predicts children's communication skills at 15 months, after adjusting for infant developmental level at 6 months and other confounders (Pancsofar & Vernon-Feagans 2010). Noll & Harding (2003) found that when mothers respond to their 12- to 47-month-olds' object play in an "options-promoting" manner (encouraging, affirming, and/or expanding on the child's activities), their children later engaged in higher levels of symbolic play. Socially at-risk mothers who received nurse visitations prenatally and postnatally had 15-year-olds who were relatively protected on a host of criminal and antisocial behaviors (Olds et al. 1998). Parents who endorse more egalitarian parenting attitudes at age 1 month are more likely to have children who are liberal in their ideologies at age 18 years (Fraley et al. 2012a).

Infants' extrafamilial social experiences are likewise predictive of later development. Infants who experience longer hours of child care, based on average hours per week since 1 month of age, are rated by caregivers at 4.5 years as showing more problem behaviors, even when extensive family covariates and other child care dimensions are included as covariates (NICHD Early Child Care Res. Netw. 1998, 2003a,b). Infant child care hours continue to predict outcomes through high school, showing modest associations with self-reports of risk taking and impulsivity (Belsky et al. 2007), and the effects of early child care on cognitive and social functioning appear to persist through age 15 (Vandell et al. 2010). Similar patterns of associations between hours of infant care and child problem behaviors have been reported in other studies conducted in the United States (Loeb et al. 2007) as well as in Canada (Côté et al. 2008) and the United Kingdom (Neighb. Nurs. Initiat. Res. Team 2007).

Reciprocally, clinical levels of maternal depression when children are between 3 months and 3 years of age are associated with aggression and antisocial behaviors at 5 to 8 years of age (Wright et al. 2000). Indeed, as pointed out previously, more severe social deprivation in infancy appears to exert untoward effects on later development. Beckett and colleagues (2006) and Kreppner and colleagues (2007) compared multiple cognitive and socioemotional outcomes in 11-year-olds initially reared in Romanian institutions categorized as socially depriving but adopted out of Romania into the United Kingdom prior to 2 years of age with samples of noninstitutionalized children adopted from Romania and nondeprived within-U.K. early (before the age of 6 months) adoptees. By the age of 11 years, Romanian children adopted in the United Kingdom before 6 months of age largely caught up when compared to within-country U.K. adoptees, and more so than Romanian children placed into adoptive homes after age 6 months. For example, their mean IQ score at 11 years exceeded 90. Children adopted before 12 months of age are as securely attached as their nonadopted peers, whereas children adopted after their first birthday show less attachment security than do nonadopted children (van den Dries et al. 2009). The sequelae of deprivation in infancy are still present in some children at age 11, as evidenced in their quasi-autism (problems in social reciprocity and communication, unusual and circumscribed interests), disinhibited attachment (lack of clear differentiation between familiar and unfamiliar adults), inattention/overactivity (both at home and at school; many attention deficit–hyperactivity disorder diagnoses), and cognitive impairment (poor academic achievement). Sheridan and colleagues (2012) used structural MRI and EEG to examine brain structure and function in typically developing children in Romania exposed to institutional rearing and children previously exposed to institutional rearing but then randomized to a high-quality foster care intervention to evaluate whether placement in an improved environment mitigates the effects of institutional rearing on neural structure. Children with histories of institutional rearing had smaller cortical gray matter volume than did never-institutionalized children. Cortical white matter for children placed in foster care did not differ from never-institutionalized children but was smaller for children not randomized to foster care. Other complementary research shows that institutionalized children possess larger amygdalae than do noninstitutionalized children (Tottenham et al. 2010).

Within an adopted sample, current executive functioning is associated with measures of early deprivation after controlling for IQ, with less time spent in the birth family before placement in an institution and lower quality of physical/social care in institutions predicting poorer executive functioning performance (Hostinar et al. 2012). Effects of deprivation in infancy are broad:

Hearing-impaired infants identified for fitting with cochlear implants before age 6 months test with better language skills at age 2 years than do children identified just a few months later (Yoshinaga-Itano et al. 1998).

In Bronfenbrenner's bioecological model, the macrosystem is acknowledged to exert effects on development (Bronfenbrenner & Morris 2006). Infancy is apparently vulnerable to macrosystem forces. For example, economic conditions in early life (such as business cycles) have far-reaching consequences for individual mortality rates (van den Berg et al. 2009): Being born during a recession is associated with an increase in the mortality rate after the first year of life. Birth-year (but not subsequent) family income is negatively associated with adult body mass index among low-income families (Ziol-Guest et al. 2009); likewise, immune-mediated chronic diseases play a role in associations between poverty in the prenatal year through age 2 (but not between ages 3 and 5 years or between ages 6 and 15 years) and in limitations on activities of daily living, hypertension, and arthritis and in adult productivity between ages 30 and 41 (Ziol-Guest et al. 2012). Duncan et al. (2015) learned that family income in the period from age 0 to 2 years had larger beneficial effects on adolescents' completed schooling and adults' college attendance than did later family income. Generally speaking, economic disadvantage in very early childhood is linked to worse overall health status and higher rates of mortality in adulthood (Case et al. 2005), and early family indigence is linked to heightened risk for several chronic diseases in adulthood (R.C. Johnson & R.F. Schoeni, unpublished manuscript, as reported in Duncan et al. 2015): By age 50, individuals who experienced poverty in early childhood were 46% more likely to have asthma, 75% more likely to be diagnosed with hypertension, 83% more likely to have been diagnosed with diabetes, 2.25 times more likely to have experienced a stroke or heart attack, and 40% more likely to have been diagnosed with heart disease in comparison with individuals whose family incomes were 200% of the poverty line or greater.

Illustrative Long-Term Longitudinal Epidemiological Projects

The foregoing summaries recount stability and prediction literatures from infancy that have developed around specific topics in specific studies. A number of large-scale multivariate epidemiological longitudinal efforts also have been initiated that have or will adventitiously address issues in stability and prediction from infancy. Among the most notable is the Dutch Hunger Winter study. Near the end of World War II, western (but not northern or eastern) Holland endured a food blockade that provided an unhappy but significant natural experiment in infant development and long-term public health. Unlike other famines, the Dutch Hunger Winter struck during a precisely circumscribed time and place and in a society that keeps comprehensive and meticulous health records of its population. As a result, researchers could identify children who were malnourished during different specific ontogenetic periods and follow their development periodically well into adulthood. Relative to those children who received proper nutrition, malnourished fetuses and infants suffered more nervous system congenital abnormalities as well as increased risk of schizophrenia in maturity (Hoek et al. 1998, 1999).

Other notable long-term longitudinal multivariate epidemiological investigations from infancy include the Helsinki Birth Cohort (1934–1944) study in men now reaching old age (Tuovinen et al. 2012); cohorts in the United Kingdom marked by birthdates of 1946, 1958, 1970, and 2000 (the Millennium National Longitudinal Study), all scheduled to be followed into the later years of life (Ferri et al. 2003); the US National Longitudinal Survey of Youth, which has followed a sample of individuals born in the 1950s and 1960s and their offspring (Blau 1999); the Panel Study of Income Dynamics that has followed a nationally representative sample of US children since 1968 (Duncan et al. 2010); the Dunedin Study from New Zealand, which has continuously observed children

Table 1 Longitudinal epidemiological studies from infancy to maturity

Name	Enrollment		Country/topic	URL
	Year	N		
Some general studies				
Kauai[a]	1955	600	Hawaii	https://www.ncjrs.gov/App/publications/Abstract.aspx?id=122798
Solna[b]	~1955	212	Sweden	http://www.oru.se/English/Research/Old-research-pages/Research-projects/project/School-of-Law-Psycology-and-Social-work/The-Solna-study/
Dunedin[c]	1972–1973	>1,000	New Zealand	http://dunedinstudy.otago.ac.nz/studies/main-study/description
Minnesota[d]	1975	267	United States	http://www.cehd.umn.edu/icd/research/parent-child/
CFRS, NICHD[e]	1988	400+	United States + cross-cultural	http://www.cfr.nichd.nih.gov/index.html
ALSPAC[f]	1991–1992	>14,000	United Kingdom	http://www.bristol.ac.uk/alspac/
ECLS-B[g]	1998–1999	14,000	United States	http://nces.ed.gov/ecls/birth.asp
LSAC[h]	1999–2000	>10,000	Australia	http://flosse.fahcsia.gov.au/fahcsia-help/doku.php?id=the_surveys#hilda
Gen R[i]	2002–2006	9,778	The Netherlands	http://www.generationr.nl/het-onderzoek.html
Some specific studies				
ATP[j]	1982–1983	2,443	Temperament	http://www.aifs.gov.au/atp/about/about.html
LLAS[k]	1987	160	Adoption	http://www.socialsciences.leiden.edu/educationandchildstudies/childandfamilystudies/research/adoption-and-foster-care-pearl-agp.html
SECCYD[l]	1991	1,364	Child care	http://www.nichd.nih.gov/research/supported/seccyd/overview.cfm#participants
Jyväskylä[m]	1993–1996	410	Dyslexia	https://www.jyu.fi/ytk/laitokset/psykologia/huipputtutkimus/en/research/JLD_main/JLD

Note: General studies are multivariate epidemiological efforts; specific studies are designed to examine a specific topic.
Footnotes: [a]The Children of Kauai, [b]Solna Study, [c]Dunedin Multidisciplinary Health and Development Study, [d]Minnesota Longitudinal Study of Risk and Adaptation, [e]Child and Family Research Section, National Institute of Child Health and Human Development, [f]Avon Longitudinal Study of Parents and Children (Children of the 90s), [g]Early Childhood Longitudinal Study-Birth Cohort, [h]Longitudinal Study of Australian Children, [i]Generation R Study, [j]Australian Temperament Project, [k]Leiden Longitudinal Adoption Study, [l]Study of Early Child Care and Youth Development (NICHD), [m]Jyväskylä Longitudinal Study of Dyslexia.

born from 1972 to 1973; the Carolina Abecedarian Project in the United States, which began in the 1970s with predominantly African American families with 3-month-olds; the Cebu Longitudinal Health and Nutrition Survey in the Philippines, which began with a cohort of Filipino women who gave birth between 1983 and 1984; the Avon Longitudinal Study of Parents and Children in the United Kingdom, which followed all 1991–1992 births in that district; and the NICHD Study of Early Child Care and Youth Development, which recruited families in 1991 from research sites around the United States. **Table 1** presents a representative sampling of such studies.

Desiderata

Stability and prediction from infancy are compelling and long-standing topics of philosophical, biological, psychological, and clinical interest. Should we take these emerging long-term stability and predictive validity data from infancy at face value? In evaluating their merit as well as designing the studies of tomorrow and assessing reports that will appear in the future, several considerations warrant attention.

Baby biographies of the late-nineteenth and early-twentieth centuries that followed on Darwin provided a wealth of ideas about infants, and the evidence developed from those baby biographies had two important implications. First, they showed that infants of different ages were competent at different tasks, and second, they revealed considerable individual variation among infants. The question that naturally arose was whether individual differences in infants were transient or consequential. Stability and prediction alike intimate their meaningfulness. Among the perennial and far-reaching questions about human ontogeny, the issue looms large of what connections (if any) obtain between early individual differences and later life.

In practice, stability and prediction effects and their sizes depend on what variables are considered, the way they are measured and when, the length of time between initial and criterion measurements, which analyses are used, which kinds of infants or families living in which circumstances are studied, whether background variables are statistically controlled, and so forth. The penultimate section of this review explores some of these critical desiderata.

Longitudinal methodology. In the past, cross-sectional designs prevailed in developmental study, and investigations that followed individuals over their lives were rare, essentially excluding longitudinal data. In consequence, life course study has been late in arriving to the scholarly developmental literature (Elder et al. 2015). The fortuitous expansion of long-term longitudinal studies, coupled with conceptual and methodological advances, has generated new knowledge about ontogenetic stability and prediction. There is today, moreover, substantial appreciation of the benefits of longitudinal data (Ferri et al. 2003, Hauser 2009, Phelps et al. 2002), which Butz & Torrey (2006) referred to as one of the greatest innovations of twentieth-century social science. Even still, most of this growing literature is correlational, and there are far fewer studies that rely on quasi-experimental designs or use rigorous analysis of longitudinal ones.

Cause, source, and covariates. An association between the same characteristic early and late, or between different characteristics early and late, forges a lagged link that is suggestive but not determinative of a causal connection between the two. Moreover, stability and prediction presuppose, but do not prove, that the stable or predictive characteristic is in the individual. It could be that other endogenous or even exogenous variables theoretically carry or mediate lagged associations.

Stability between infancy and maturity might depend, in part or in whole, on stability in the child's environment: stability in how significant people interact with the child or in the physical surroundings they provide. For example, one characteristic (easy temperament) at time 1 in infancy could relate to the same or to another characteristic (open personality) at time 2 in maturity because of stability in the individual characteristic or because some environmental characteristic (parents who support well-being) is stable. Individuals inherit a species-typical genome and a species-typical environment. Species-universal conditions constrain development—they limit the contexts in which genes will be expressed—and thus an individual's life course. For the most part, naturalistic circumstances favor environmental stability, and children are reared in stable material and social environments (Holden & Miller 1999); thus, consistent experiences across (at least) early development are likely. For example, observer ratings of maternal sensitivity in parent–child relationships correlate across multiple assessment waves ranging from early infancy to age 15 (Fraley et al. 2012b). The likelihood of stability and predictive validity is enhanced when environmental contexts remain relatively stable. Of importance to the interpretation of stability and prediction, beyond temporal ordering, is therefore the control of continuing environmental supports to stability and prediction.

Similarly, inclusion and elimination of other third-variable common causes that could mediate observed links is requisite to apt interpretation. If third variables mediate stability or prediction, once the contribution of the common cause is removed, individual stability or prediction should attenuate. For this reason, third variables are increasingly being taken into account through the application of partial correlations (Lozoff et al. 1991), hierarchical regression approaches (Rose-Jacobs et al. 2009), or other statistical maneuvers. Path analysis modeling makes it possible to reduce the influence of key confounds and initial covariances because it allows control for spurious effects related to covariances between the infant and other exogenous factors. Structural equation modeling is often also employed to assess stabilities and predictions controlling for other variables, and here the use of latent variables capitalizes on the shared contributions of different approaches, allows for measurement of a characteristic to vary (appropriately) across time while retaining comparability, and permits purer representations of characteristics because variance arising from sources unique to particular indicators that is not accounted for by the factor is relegated to its error term (Bentler 1995, Bentler & Wu 1995, Bollen 1989, Kline 1998).

Prediction failures. Bell and colleagues (1965) examined relations between low birth weight and incidence of disease or deformity at age 10 years; they found no relation. Kagan and colleagues (1978) showed 2-year-olds distinctive and unusual pictures, which children failed to recognize as 10-year-olds. Some studies produce mixed or inconclusive stability or prediction. In essence, it could be that there actually is little or no stability or prediction from infancy. However, it would be invalid to accept this null hypothesis about human development before examining measures that redress a raft of alternative explanations for null results. The want of a connection between a characteristic in infancy and later life could be attributable to several different possibilities (such as the measurement instrument or the measure) or correlations may be misleading if development follows a progression of discrete stages) or if the range of scores at either anchor age is truncated (Smolak & Levine 1984) or if the experience is brief, unimportant, or not meaningful (Kagan 2013).

Of course, some development may seem discontinuous. New abilities emerge that often qualitatively differ from anything preceding. Do all early attainments qualify as precursors to later ones? Are nonverbal gestures precursors to language? Is the newborn's stepping reflex a precursor to walking?

Moreover, there are many reasons to expect null or small associations between infancy and maturity. One reason is that individual differences in maturity are influenced by concurrent experiences. For example, daily-diary study indicates that variation in adult attachment patterns reflects contemporaneous experiences in interpersonal relationships (La Guardia et al. 2000, Pierce & Lydon 2001). The likelihood that early status or experience plays a role in shaping later individual differences has to be judged in the context of understanding that later variance can result from more proximate cause. Likewise, environments are subject to change. Furthermore, all mature characteristics are likely a function of a number of factors. To the extent that multiple factors contribute to variation in the mature phenotype, the explanatory power of any one relative to the rest is diminished (Ahadi & Diener 1989, Strube 1991).

Independent variables and dependent variables. Stability and prediction depend crucially on the infant variable, the criterion variable, and the fit between the two. This admonition has several constituents. First, to be valuable and meaningful, a characteristic observed in an infant needs to be reliable, meaning that observed one day, the characteristic ought to be similar to that observed in the same infant a short time later. Otherwise, the characteristic would not constitute a reliable index of the infant. Statistically speaking, unreliability places inexorable limits on predictive validity (Cohen et al. 2003). (Similarly, it is unreasonable to expect an early experience to predict later to a greater degree than it predicts subsequent assessments of itself.) Additionally, a characteristic may not be stable at one point in the life course but may stabilize at a later age.

Second, use of a single infant variable may underestimate the true effect on a mature criterion. Generally, the less information that is available, the lower the stability estimate (Hartmann et al. 2011). Colombo and colleagues (1988, 2004) showed that the predictive validity of infant performance is improved by combining or aggregating items or tasks. Because the effects of individual differences can be expected to accumulate across development, focus on a single predictive index measured at a single point in time may underestimate its true contribution. Focus on a single outcome variable measured at a single point in time may likewise underestimate stability and prediction in development (Caspi et al. 1989, Rutter & Rutter 1993).

Third, in considering infant variables, it may be critical to distinguish between performance and competence because one may predict better than the other. Relatively rapid development also makes it difficult to determine which performance is more representative of the baby and therefore predictive: optimal performance, average performance, or minimal performance.

Last, across time the same measures (that assess homotypic stability) are (usually) more highly related than are different measures (that assess heterotypic stability or prediction). Thus, homotypic stability may represent liberal (upper-bound) estimates that are augmented because of shared source and method variance, practice effects, and the like, whereas heterotypic stability may represent conservative (lower-bound) estimates because of the variance introduced by differences in assessment instruments and procedures used at different times. Greater stability might be expected between variables that conceptually relate than between those that do not. (Similarly, whether assessments are made across consistent or inconsistent contexts may make a difference: The former enhance stability, and the latter attenuate stability; Bornstein et al. 1999.) Finally, although surface manifestations of characteristics change over the life course, some latent variable of surface variables might reflect an enduring individual difference (Bornstein & Putnick 2012).

Timing. Different patterns of stability and prediction could emerge depending on the ages at which individuals are initially and terminally assessed, and concomitantly longitudinal effects are a complex function of the interval between assessments. Measures taken early in development are (usually) less highly predictive than are measures taken later in development (Asendorpf 1992, McGrew & Knopik 1993) because people are thought to become increasingly consistent in relation to one another as they age (Roberts & DelVecchio 2000), and so stabilities tend to increase with increasing age. Furthermore, the shorter the interassessment interval, normally the higher the stability estimate, a phenomenon sometimes called the Guttman (1954) "simplex" (Conley 1984).

Both catch-up and sleeper effects moderate stability and prediction. Catch-up effects define situations where a relation between time 1 and time 2 may hold, but not between time 1 and time 3 (Wilson 1978). For example, compared to infants born at term, very-low-birth-weight infants show deficits in reading comprehension at age 9 years that no longer obtain at 15 years (Samuelsson et al. 2006). Reciprocally, sleeper effects define situations in which a relation between time 1 and time 2 may not hold but may emerge between time 1 and time 3 (Betancourt et al. 2011, Bridgett & Mayes 2011). For example, infants who were born during the Dutch Hunger Winter and experienced chronic malnutrition in their first trimester in utero manifested elevated rates of schizophrenia, which did not emerge until late in development (Hoek et al. 1999, Roseboom et al. 2006).

Developmental research has primarily focused attention on micro timescales to assess normative ontogenetic patterning. Less attention has been focused on longer timescales to explore stability and prediction, and even less has been done to explore development in terms of very long timescales (our concern here). Comprehensive explanations in development need to consider all timescale perspectives.

Sample. Sample size and composition moderate stability and prediction. Small samples may lack the power to detect existing associations that large samples possess. Homogenous samples may harbor associations that are masked by diverse samples (Bornstein et al. 2013b). In some subsamples, stability and prediction may be smaller, and in other subsamples, they may be larger. Loss of follow-up over time (attrition) may introduce bias, as stability and prediction apply only to those individuals who survive longitudinal study.

Effect size. Effect size (like the correlation coefficient, which is often the main statistic used to authenticate the relation between infant scores and mature scores) quantifies stability or prediction. Stability and prediction effect sizes tend to be small to modest. However, judgments of the importance of an effect are subjective. As many theoreticians and empiricists have emphasized, small effect sizes can be meaningful, as for example from a public health perspective (Abelson 1985; Ahadi & Diener 1989; Cortina & Landis 2009; Prentice & Miller 1992; Rosenthal & Rubin 1982, 1983; Vacha-Haase & Thompson 2004; Yeaton & Sechrest 1981). The correlation coefficient, moreover, is subject to the nature of the distribution and does not necessarily provide useful information about individual cases. Lack of heterogeneity in the distribution of scores (restriction of range) at either anchor age can attenuate correlation, and failure to examine individual patterns may account for the apparent lack of stability or predictability.

Theory. Stability and prediction need to be interpreted taking into consideration assumptions of a field. Background theory, classical research, and even the temporal distance of the relation can create a situation in which any nonzero effect reasonably supports conclusions about stability and prediction. That is, importance is at least partly a function of whether stability or prediction is expected at all. Theory and empiricism once established the strong expectation of no stability or predictive validity of mental development from infancy (Bayley 1949), and the implications of this position were far-reaching for the nature of infancy and conceptions of mental development. To be meaningful, new predictive data may need only fail to disconfirm such expectations. In the field of stability and prediction from infancy, small effects can represent impressive support, and showing that stability or prediction holds under unlikely and unexpected circumstances can be as striking as (or, in some cases, more striking than) showing that one or the other accounts for a great deal of variance. The fact that an effect survives a stringent test, as in the inclusion of multiple controls, is additionally probative.

Direct and indirect effects. Some stability or prediction effects are direct, and others are indirect. Direct effects may be evidenced by associations between independent variables and dependent variables. Indirect effects play theoretically appealing and essential roles, as in developmental cascades, but may be more elusive and challenging to detect than direct effects. They are also destined to be small mathematically due to the statistical fact that, as the number of intervening variables in an indirect effect increases, the magnitude of the overall indirect effect decreases. (The indirect effect is the product of path coefficients leading from an independent variable through intervening variable(s) to a criterion variable.)

Weaknesses and strengths of the literature. On the one hand, longitudinal study is subject to design flaws. Reusing the same measures, a good thing for strict assessments of stability, can capitalize on practice effects and shared method variance, a bad thing for conclusions. Similarly, the use of the same reporters or testers at different ages capitalizes on shared source variance that may inflate stability correlations, and staff members who are familiar with participants may carry over their familiarity from one testing session to another. Most stability and prediction reports do not indicate whether testers are masked (but see Rose-Jacobs et al. 2004, 2011). On the other hand, the stability and prediction literature doubtlessly suffers the "file drawer" problem, it being unlikely that nonsignificant findings have been published (Rosenthal 1979).

Mechanisms. Considerations of stability and prediction often do not speak to the specific mechanisms through which each occurs, but they should. The assessment and demonstration of stability or prediction constitute the (important) descriptive phase of investigation, and either may obtain even if specific developmental processes remain unspecified. However, clarifying mechanisms of stability and prediction will constitute an important next wave in future research. Ultimate criteria for success in developmental science turn on how well we can explain and understand processes underlying individual functioning and development and on how well we can predict.

Overview

On first observation, newborns and infants often appear disorganized and erratic. At a given moment, babies seem to be constantly moving their eyes, hands, and feet without apparent purpose. Over longer periods, they appear to shift randomly and unpredictably between sleep and alertness. However, infants are not quite so irregular and unpredictable. Close and consistent inspection reveals that infants are regular in many ways and their systems cycle in detectable patterns. Indeed, infant activity is organized at fast, medium, and slow rhythms. Some actions regularly cycle at high frequencies, perhaps once or more every second. Heartbeats, breathing, and sucking exemplify fast biological rhythms that maintain life, and kicking and rocking illustrate other fast-cycling behaviors. General movements of the body cycle at intermediate rates, on the order of once every minute or two. States of waking, quiet sleep, and active sleep cycle at low frequencies in periods of up to 24 hours. By observing activity over extended times and carefully decomposing it, it is possible to detect regularity underlying infants' seeming randomness. A snapshot of the infant at any one time captures the simultaneous and independent cycling of several complex rhythms. In short, apparent irregularity is only just that, apparent, and much infant behavior is characterized by underlying regularity.

Macken & Barton (1979) wished to know how infants acquire the voicing contrast in American English word-initial stop consonants, and so they recorded the speech of four monolingual children at two-week intervals, beginning in infancy. They then submitted recordings of infants' spontaneous speech to two kinds of analyses: transcriptions by trained phoneticians and instrumental analysis. The human judges divided infant data into three general stages: (1) the child has no contrast, (2) the child has a contrast but one that falls within the adult perceptual boundaries and thus is presumably not perceptible to adults, and (3) the child has a contrast that resembles the adult contrast. Some Stage 2 contrasts that children maintained went unnoted by the transcribers and were presumably not perceptible to adults. However, spectrograms with high temporal resolution and scale magnification revealed a statistically significant number of distinct phonemically voiceless stop productions. In short, judgments of adults did not capture significant facts about the child's language production where spectrographic analysis provided insight. Speech contrasts that infants had learned and were maintaining would not have been detected by parents or other adults, and it might have taken up to another year before the children's productions improved to the point where the contrasts that the infants were making were perceived by adults. These two homilies impart pointed lessons for understanding stability and prediction from infancy. Not the least, methods and measures applied today that fail to substantiate preservation in development leave open the possibility that methods and measures applied tomorrow may reverse current conclusions.

Development is governed by genetic and biological factors in combination with experiences and environmental influences. Thus, developmental stability and prediction of any characteristic are attributable to endogenous factors that transact exogenous ones. Biological forces generally tend to reinforce homeostasis in the individual. Moreover, the consistent social network in which development normally transpires also contributes to stability and prediction. Thus, individual ↔ environmental relational processes actually tilt to promote stability and prediction in development. Contrary to first blush, stability and prediction in development are expectable.

That said, even the strongest stability or prediction coefficient one could practically expect to see, say $r = 0.90$, leaves substantial common variance unaccounted for, ≈20%. Here, theoretical perspective comes into play. Focusing on instability and prediction failures would lead to the singular but limited view that development is disorderly; focusing on stability and prediction risks overlooking necessary adaptability and change in the developing organism. Despite stability and prediction, children can and do alter over time in their status relative to one another. The lifespan perspective in developmental science specifies that human beings are open systems, and the plastic nature of psychological functioning ensures both stability and instability across the life course. Both confer advantage. Many developmental processes are Janus-like, with both stable and unstable, continuous and discontinuous aspects. Infant status does not fix a child's health or height, perceptiveness or personality. To be stable or predictable does not mean to be immutable or impervious to experience or adaptation. Like stability, adaptation is an identifying characteristic of development, and children change in both their relative standing and mean level on every characteristic as they grow.

The mature status of each aspect of a person is influenced by contemporary circumstances and by expectations of the future, but it is also affected by prenatal and infancy status and experiences and, in some instances, by circumstances of prior generations (Elder et al. 2015). Interdisciplinary life-course study, coupled with the progress of long-term longitudinal research, is occupying increasing attention, as the precursors to mature status are explored among early sensitive periods, cascades, cumulative effects, and other temporal associations that extend over decades (Bauldry et al. 2012, Bornstein 1989, Kuh & Ben-Schlomo 2004).

Long-term studies of stability and prediction are identifying relations between late-life adaptation and the earliest phases of lifespan development. Although this article has documented links between early and later life, those links require reinforcement as much as reassessment, and there is much more to learn. Important efforts should start with refinement, replication, and reflection.

CONCLUSIONS

...The childhood shews the man... (John Milton 1671/1960, "Paradise Regained," book 4, line 220)

A key goal of contemporary developmental science is mapping temporal trajectories from early characteristics to mature phenotypes. Many developmentalists have maintained that different stages of life vary qualitatively, that infancy stands apart from the balance of the life course, and that development from infancy is unstable and noncontinuous. However, the "blooming, buzzing confusion" of infancy cloaks order (James 1890, p. 488). Some relations between infancy and maturity may be obscured because they are displaced in time, and others may go unnoticed because surface manifestations of different characteristics at different developmental periods appear unrelated. We now know too that much of development consists of hierarchically organized abilities that subsume one another. An implication of contemporary relational systems perspectives is that earlier emerging characteristics in development lay foundations for and so likely exert impact on later-appearing characteristics.

A central issue in developmental study is evaluation of forces bound up in ontogenetic advance. Central to understanding developmental advance is recognizing the contributions of the individual, experience, and their transactions. Individuals contribute to their own development, and we are increasingly aware that people are agents in their own lives. The emerging literature in stability and prediction indicates that infants bring substantial variation in their individuality to their own long-term development.

Stability and predictive validity in development from infancy have several noteworthy implications. First, they have meaning for developmental science in terms of more adequately describing the growth of individuals. Second, they have significance for more completely understanding the nature of diverse biological and psychological phenomena. Through elucidation of stability and prediction, infancy studies can lead to insights that have significance for psychology as a whole. Studies of stability and prediction between infancy and maturity are therefore important to theory building; they are equally important to understanding clinical populations. Third, because there are threads of stability and prediction from infancy, measures in infancy might one day serve as screening tools for early detection of later (risk) status, and so infancy has implications for the identification, prevention, and treatment of disorders. The emerging critical mass of data on stability and prediction overturn the argument that infancy is not meaningful in itself and that it is unrelated to later life. Early childhood exposure to microorganisms that are common in the natural environment adjusts the immune system so that even disadvantaged adults living under unhealthy conditions in low- and middle-income countries have lower blood concentrations of proteins that signal inflammations, which portend cancer, diabetes, and heart disease (McDade 2012). The contemporary life-course perspective on human development supports some stability and prediction, even from the prenatal period.

The developmental changes that take place during the first year of life are as dramatic—or more dramatic—than any others in the human lifespan. The most remarkable involve the changing shape and capacity of the body; the complexity of the nervous system; the dawning of sensory and perceptual capacities; the increasing abilities to make sense of, understand, and master things in the world; the achievement of communication; the emergence of characteristic personal styles; and the formation of specific social bonds. At no other time is development so fast-paced or thoroughgoing in so many different spheres of life. Yet, at the core of the infant, and later the toddler, child, adolescent, and adult, is the same individual, and some stability and predictability from infancy—whatever their dynamic endogenous and exogenous origins—can be supposed.

Deconstructing infancy studies in this way contributes to elaborating and to explaining infancy *qua* a dimension of human fascination and intellectual significance. The ineffable romance of infancy may haunt us in many ways, but in other ways we now see more clearly that infancy contributes concretely to our understanding ourselves. The fact that infants are unvolitional, uncooperative, unstable, nonverbal, and motorically inept once warded off all but philosophical speculation about them. Developmental scientists have finally overcome infants' formidable and intractable posture to extract information of all sorts from and about them. In recent years, a revolution has taken place in infancy studies, fueled by technological and methodological advances. We now know a great deal about babies' perceptions, thoughts, and feelings. Taken together, longitudinal studies are coming to bind infancy more tightly to the tapestry of lifespan development. Longitudinality is a social science Hubble telescope (Butz & Torrey 2006).

Infancy is the first phase of life lived outside the womb, and the characteristics developed and acquired then help to forge a foundation for the balance of the life course; some individual differences in infancy may endure, at least in part, and they are certainly those that later experiences build on or modify. Infancy is only one phase in the lifespan, however, and so our physical development, nervous system maturity, motor capacities, perceptual abilities, cognitive competencies, and personalities and social styles are also shaped by development and experiences after infancy. Living is to experience consequential and life-altering events. The start does not fix the course or outcome of development, but it clearly exerts an impact on both. Ascribing certain prospects to the future may be unachievable, but the longitudinal literature from infancy is starting to reveal enduring effects that we should not ignore or dismiss. The future may not be an utterly random bet. "At first the infant..." Shakespeare has Jacques recite in *As You Like It*. Infancy introduces the part and also sets the stage for the unfolding drama that is to follow.

DISCLOSURE STATEMENT

The author is not aware of any affiliations, memberships, funding, or financial holdings that might be perceived as affecting the objectivity of this review.

ACKNOWLEDGMENTS

Work on this article was supported by the Intramural Research Program of the NIH, NICHD. I thank A. Dovidio, H. Simon, and D.L. Putnick.

LITERATURE CITED

Abelson R. 1985. A variance explanation paradox: when a little is a lot. *Psychol. Bull.* 97:129–33

Ahadi S, Diener E. 1989. Multiple determinants and effect sizes. *J. Personal. Soc. Psychol.* 56:398–406

Alink LR, Mesman J, van Zeijl J, Stolk M, Juffer F, et al. 2006. The early childhood aggression curve: development of physical aggression in 10- to 50-month-old children. *Child Dev.* 77:954–66

Allam DE, Soussignan R, Patris B, Marlier L, Schaal B. 2010. Long-lasting memory for an odor acquired at the mother's breast. *Dev. Sci.* 13:849–63

Allen JP, Moore C, Kuperminc G, Bell K. 1998. Attachment and adolescent psychosocial functioning. *Child Dev.* 69:1406–19

Andersson K, Bohlin G, Hagekull B. 1999. Early temperament and stranger wariness as predictors of social inhibition in 2-year-olds. *Br. J. Dev. Psychol.* 17:421–34

Aristotle. 350 BCE (2000). *Politics*, transl. B. Jowett. New York: Dover

Artzi M, Ben Sira L, Bassan H, Gross-Tsur V, Berger I, et al. 2011. Brain diffusivity in infants with hypoxic-ischemic encephalopathy following whole body hypothermia: preliminary results. *J. Child Neurol.* 26:1230–36

Aschersleben G, Hofer T, Jovanovic B. 2008. The link between infant attention to goal-directed action and later theory of mind abilities. *Dev. Sci.* 11:862–68

Asendorpf JB. 1992. Beyond stability: predicting inter-individual differences in intra-individual change. *Eur. J. Personal.* 6:103–17

Asendorpf JB, van Aken MAG. 1999. Resilient, overcontrolled, and undercontrolled personality prototypes in childhood: replicability, predictive power, and the trait-type issue. *J. Personal. Soc. Psychol.* 77:815–52

Asendorpf JB, van Aken MAG. 2003. Validity of big five personality judgments in childhood: a 9 year longitudinal study. *Eur. J. Personal.* 17:1–17

Ashby JD, Schoon I. 2012. Living the dream? A qualitative retrospective study exploring the role of adolescent aspirations across the life span. *Dev. Psychol.* 48:1694–706

Aziz W, Schlindwein FS, Wailoo M, Biala T, Rocha FC. 2012. Heart rate variability analysis of normal and growth restricted children. *Clin. Auton. Res.* 22:91–97

Bada HS, Das A, Bauer CR, Shankaran S, Lester B, et al. 2007. Impact of prenatal cocaine exposure on child behavior problems through school age. *Pediatrics* 119:348–59

Baker E, Shelton KH, Baibazarova E, Hay DF, van Goozen SH. 2013. Low skin conductance activity in infancy predicts aggression in toddlers 2 years later. *Psychol. Sci.* 24:1051–56

Bar-Haim Y, Marshall PJ, Fox NA. 2000. Developmental changes in heart period and high-frequency heart period variability from 4 months to 4 years of age. *Dev. Psychobiol.* 37:44–56

Barker DJP. 1998. *Mothers, Babies, and Health in Later Life*. Edinburgh, UK: Churchill Livingstone

Barker DJP, Eriksson JG, Forsén T, Osmond C. 2002. Fetal origins of adult disease: strength of effects and biological basis. *Int. J. Epidemiol.* 31:1235–39

Barker DJP, Osmond C. 1986. Infant mortality, childhood nutrition, and ischaemic heart disease in England and Wales. *Lancet* 1:1077–81

Bates JE, Pettit GS, Dodge KA. 1995. Family and child factors in stability and change in children's aggressiveness in elementary school. In *Coercion and Punishment in Long Term Perspectives*, ed. J McCord, pp. 124–38. New York: Cambridge Univ. Press

Bateson P, Barker D, Clutton-Brock T, Deb D, D'Udine B, et al. 2004. Developmental plasticity and human health. *Nature* 430:419–21

Bauldry S, Shanahan MJ, Boardman JD, Miech RA, Macmillan R. 2012. A life course model of self-rated health through adolescence and young adulthood. *Soc. Sci. Med.* 75:1311–20

Bayley N. 1949. Consistency and variability in the growth of intelligence from birth to eighteen years. *J. Genet. Psychol.* 75:165–96

Beckett C, Maughan B, Rutter M, Castle J, Colvert E, et al. 2006. Do the effects of early severe deprivation on cognition persist into early adolescence? Findings from the English and Romanian adoptees study. *Child Dev.* 77:696–711

Beebe B, Jaffe J, Markese S, Buck K, Chen H, et al. 2010. The origins of 12-month attachment: a microanalysis of 4-month mother-infant interaction. *Attach. Hum. Dev.* 12:3–141

Bell DA, Taylor WC, Dockrell WB. 1965. A ten year follow-up of low birth weight infants: intellectual functioning. *Alberta J. Educ. Res.* 11:220–25

Belsky J, Hsieh K, Crnic K. 1998. Mothering, fathering, and infant negativity as antecedents of boys' externalizing problems and inhibition at age 3 years: differential susceptibility to rearing experience? *Dev. Psychopathol.* 10:301–19

Belsky J, Vandell D, Burchinal M, Clarke-Stewart KA, McCartney K, et al. 2007. Are there long-term effects of early child care? *Child Dev.* 78:681–701

Benson JE, Elder GH. 2011. Young adult identities and their pathways: a developmental and life course model. *Dev. Psychol.* 47:1646–57

Bentler PM. 1995. *EQS Structural Equations Program Manual*. Encino, CA: Multivar. Softw.

Bentler PM, Wu EJC. 1995. *EQS for Windows User's Guide*. Encino, CA: Multivar. Softw.

Bergman LR, Magnusson D, El-Khouri BM. 2003. *Studying Individual Development in an Interindividual Context: A Person-Oriented Approach. Volume 4 of Paths Through Life*. Mahwah, NJ: Erlbaum

Betancourt LM, Yang W, Brodsky NL, Gallagher PR, Malmud EK, et al. 2011. Adolescents with and without gestational cocaine exposure: longitudinal analysis of inhibitory control, memory and receptive language. *Neurotoxicol. Teratol.* 33:36–46

Bhutta AT, Cleves MA, Casey PH, Cradock MM, Anand KJS. 2002. Cognitive and behavioral outcomes of school-aged children who were born preterm: a meta-analysis. *JAMA* 288:728–37

Blaga OM, Shaddy DJ, Anderson CJ, Kannass K, Little TD, Colombo J. 2009. Structure and continuity of intellectual development in early childhood. *Intelligence* 27:106–13

Blau DM. 1999. The effect of income on child development. *Rev. Econ. Stat.* 81:261–76

Block J, Block JH. 2006a. Venturing a 30-year longitudinal study. *Am. Psychol.* 61:315–27

Block J, Block JH. 2006b. Nursery school personality and political orientation two decades later. *J. Res. Personal.* 40:734–49

Bloom BS. 1964. *Stability and Change in Human Characteristics*. New York: Wiley

Boas M, Boisen K, Virtanen H, Kaleva H, Kaleva M, et al. 2006. Postnatal penile length and growth rate correlate to serum testosterone level: a longitudinal study of 1962 normal boys. *Eur. J. Endocrinol.* 154:125–29

Bollen KA. 1989. *Structural Equations with Latent Variables*. New York: Wiley

Bornstein MH, ed. 1987. *Sensitive Periods in Development: Interdisciplinary Perspectives*. Hillsdale, NJ: Erlbaum

Bornstein MH. 1989. Sensitive periods in development: structural characteristics and causal interpretations. *Psychol. Bull.* 105:179–97

Bornstein MH, Arterberry ME, Lamb ME. 2014. *Development in Infancy: A Contemporary Introduction*. New York: Psychol. Press

Bornstein MH, Arterberry ME, Mash C. 2004. Long–term memory for an emotional interpersonal interaction occurring at 5 months of age. *Infancy* 6:407–16

Bornstein MH, Bornstein L. 2008. Psychological stability. In *International Encyclopedia of Social Sciences*, Vol. 8, pp. 74–75. Detroit, Mich.: Macmillan Ref.

Bornstein MH, Hahn CS, Bell C, Haynes OM, Slater A, et al. 2006. Stability in cognition across early childhood: a developmental cascade. *Psychol. Sci.* 17:151–58

Bornstein MH, Hahn CS, Suwalsky JTD. 2013a. Physically developed and exploratory young infants contribute to their own long-term academic achievement. *Psychol. Sci.* In press

Bornstein MH, Hahn CS, Wolke D. 2012. Systems and cascades in cognitive development and academic achievement. *Child Dev.* 84:154–62

Bornstein MH, Jager J, Putnick DL. 2013b. Sampling in developmental science: situations, shortcomings, solutions, and standards. *Dev. Rev.* In press

Bornstein MH, Putnick DL. 2012. Stability of language in childhood: a multiage, multidomain, multimeasure, and multisource study. *Dev. Psychol.* 48:477–91

Bornstein MH, Suess PE. 2000. Child and mother cardiac vagal tone: continuity, stability, and concordance across the first 5 years. *Dev. Psychol.* 36:54–65

Bornstein MH, Tamis-LeMonda CS, Hahn C-S, Haynes OM. 2008. Maternal responsiveness to very young children at three ages: longitudinal analysis of a multidimensional modular and specific parenting construct. *Dev. Psychol.* 44:867–74

Bornstein MH, Tamis-LeMonda CS, Haynes OM. 1999. First words in the second year: continuity, stability, and models of concurrent and predictive correspondence in vocabulary and verbal responsiveness across age and context. *Infant Behav. Dev.* 22:65–85

Bowlby J. 1969. *Attachment and Loss: Attachment*. New York: Basic Books

Bremner JG, Wachs TD, eds. 2010. *The Wiley-Blackwell Handbook of Infant Development*. Malden, Mass.: Wiley-Blackwell. 2nd ed.

Bridgett DJ, Gartstein MA, Putnam SP, McKay T, Iddins E, et al. 2009. Maternal and contextual influences and the effect of temperament development during infancy on parenting in toddlerhood. *Infant Behav. Dev.* 32:103–16

Bridgett DJ, Mayes LC. 2011. Development of inhibitory control among prenatally cocaine exposed and non-cocaine exposed youths from late childhood to early adolescence: the effects of gender and risk and subsequent aggressive behavior. *Neurotoxicol. Teratol.* 33:47–60

Broman SH. 1989. Infant physical status and later cognitive development. In *Stability and Continuity in Mental Development*, ed. MH Bornstein, NA Krasnegor, pp. 45–62. Mahwah, NJ: Erlbaum

Bronfenbrenner U, Morris PA. 2006. The bioecological model of human development. In *Handbook of Child Psychology*. Vol. 1: *Theoretical Models of Human Development*, ed. RM Lerner, W Damon, pp. 793–828. New York: Wiley

Bruer J. 2002. *The Myth of the First Three Years*. New York: Free Press

Butz WP, Torrey BB. 2006. Some frontiers in social science. *Science* 312:1898–900

Calkins SD, Keane SP. 2004. Cardiac vagal regulation across the preschool period: stability, continuity, and implications for childhood adjustment. *Dev. Psychobiol.* 45:101–12

Camras LA, Perlman SB, Wismer-Fries AB, Pollack S. 2006. Post-institutionalized Chinese and Eastern European children: heterogeneity in the development of emotion understanding. *Int. J. Behav. Dev.* 3:193–99

Caravale B, Tozzi C, Albino G, Vicari S. 2005. Cognitive development in low risk preterm infants at 3–4 years of life. *Arch. Dis. Child. Fetal Neonatal* 90:F474–79

Cardillo GC. 2010. *Predicting the predictors: individual differences in longitudinal relationships between infant phonetic perception, toddler vocabulary, and preschooler language and phonological awareness*. PhD dissert., Univ. Wash.

Cardillo Lebedeva GC, Kuhl PK. 2009. Individual differences in infant speech perception predict language and pre-reading skills through age 5 years. Presented at *Annu. Meet. Soc. Dev Behav. Pediatr.*, Portland, OR

Case A, Fertig A, Paxson C. 2005. The lasting impact of childhood health and circumstances. *J. Health Econ.* 24:365–89

Casey BJ, Somerville LH, Gotlib IH, Ayduk O, Franklin NT, et al. 2011. Behavioral and neural correlates of delay of gratification 40 years later. *Proc. Natl. Acad. Sci. USA* 108:14998–5003

Caspi A. 2000. The child is father of the man: personality continuities from childhood to adulthood. *J. Personal. Soc. Psychol.* 78:158–72

Caspi A, Bem DJ, Elder GH. 1989. Continuities and consequences of interactional styles across the life course. *J. Personal.* 57:375–406

Choudhury N, Benasich AA. 2011. Maturation of auditory evoked potentials from 6 to 48 months: prediction to 3 and 4 year language and cognitive abilities. *Clin. Neurophysiol.* 122:320–38

Chronis-Tuscano A, Degnan KA, Pine DS, Perez-Edgar K, Henderson HA, et al. 2009. Stable early maternal report of behavioral inhibition predicts lifetime social anxiety disorder in adolescence. *J. Am. Acad. Child Adolesc. Psychiatry* 48:928–35

Clarke AM, Clarke ADB. 2000. *Early Experience and the Life Path*. London: Kingsley

Coates DL, Lewis M. 1984. Early mother-infant interaction and infant cognitive status as predictors of school performance and cognitive behavior in six-year-olds. *Child Dev.* 55:1219–30

Cohen J, Cohen P, West SG, Aiken LS. 2003. *Applied Multiple Regression/Correlation Analysis for the Behavioural Sciences*. Mahwah, NJ: Erlbaum. 3rd ed.

Collins LM, Sayer AG, eds. 2001. *New Methods for the Analysis of Change*. Washington, DC: Am. Psychol. Assoc.

Collins NL, Read SJ. 1990. Adult attachment, working models, and relationship quality in dating couples. *J. Personal. Soc. Psychol.* 58:644–63

Colman I, Ploubidis GB, Wadsworth MEJ, Jones PB, Croudace TJ. 2007. A longitudinal typology of symptoms of depression and anxiety over the life course. *Biol. Psychiatry* 62:1265–71

Colombo J, Mitchell DW, Horowitz FD. 1988. Infant visual attention in the paired-comparison paradigm: test-retest and attention-performance relations. *Child Dev.* 59:1198–210

Colombo J, Shaddy DJ, Richman WA, Maikranz JM, Blaga OM. 2004. The developmental course of habituation in infancy and preschool outcome. *Infancy* 5:1–38

Conley JJ. 1984. The hierarchy of consistency: a review and model of longitudinal findings on adult individual differences in intelligence, personality and self-opinion. *Personal. Individ. Differ.* 5:11–25

Corapci F, Radan AE, Lozoff B. 2006. Iron deficiency in infancy and mother-child interaction at 5 years. *J. Dev. Behav. Pediatr.* 27:371–78

Cortina JM, Landis RS. 2009. When small effect sizes tell a big story, and when large effect sizes don't. In *Statistical and Methodological Myths and Urban Legends*, ed. CE Lance, RJ Vandenberg, pp. 287–308. New York: Taylor & Francis

Côté SM, Borge AI, Geoffroy MC, Rutter M, Tremblay RE. 2008. Nonmaternal care in infancy and emotional/behavioral difficulties at 4 years old: moderation by family risk characteristics. *Dev. Psychol.* 44:155–68

Courage ML, Howe ML, Squires SE. 2004. Individual differences in 3.5-month-olds' visual attention: What do they predict at 1 year? *Infant Behav. Dev.* 27:19–30

Crosnoe R, Elder GH. 2004. From childhood to the later years: pathways of human development. *Res. Aging* 26:623–54

Cuevas K, Bell MA. 2013. Infant attention and early childhood executive function. *Child Dev.* In press

Darwin CR. 1877. A biographical sketch of an infant. *Mind* 2:286–94

Degnan KA, Calkins SD, Keane SP, Hill-Soderlund AL. 2008. Profiles of disruptive behavior across early childhood: contributions of frustration reactivity, physiological regulation, and maternal behavior. *Child Dev.* 79:1357–76

Degnan KA, Hane AA, Henderson HA, Moas OL, Reeb-Sutherland BC, Fox NA. 2011. Longitudinal stability of temperamental exuberance and social-emotional outcomes in early childhood. *Dev. Psychol.* 47:765–80

Dehaene-Lambertz G, Dehaene S, Hertz-Pannier L. 2002. Functional neuroimaging of speech perception in infants. *Science* 298:2013–15

Dehaene-Lambertz G, Hertz-Pannier L, Dubois J, Meriaux S, Roche A, et al. 2006. Functional organization of perisylvian activation during presentation of sentences in preverbal infants. *Proc. Natl. Acad. Sci. USA* 103:14240–45

Dennissen JAJ, Asendorpf JB, van Aken MAG. 2007. Childhood personality predicts long-term trajectories of shyness and aggressiveness in the context of demographic transitions in emerging adulthood. *J. Personal.* 76:1–33

DiPietro JA, Bornstein MH, Costigan KA, Pressman EK, Hahn C-S, et al. 2002. What does fetal movement predict about behavior during the first two years of life? *Dev. Psychobiol.* 40:358–71

DiPrete T, Eirich G. 2006. Cumulative advantage as a mechanism for inequality: a review of theoretical and empirical developments. *Annu. Rev. Sociol.* 32:271–97

Dixon WE Jr, Smith PH. 2008. Attentional focus moderates habituation-language relationships: Slow habituation may be a good thing. *Infant Child Dev.* 17:95–108

Domsch H, Lohaus A, Thomas H. 2009. Prediction of childhood cognitive abilities from a set of early indicators of information processing capabilities. *Infant Behav. Dev.* 32:91–102

Dougherty TM, Haith MM. 1997. Infant expectations and reaction time as predictors of childhood speed of processing and IQ. *Dev. Psychol.* 33:146–55

Duncan GE, Duncan SC, Strycker LA, Okut H, Hix-Small H. 2006. *Recent Methodological and Statistical Advances: A Latent Variable Growth Modeling Framework*. New York: Cambridge Univ. Press

Duncan GJ, Magnuson K, Votruba-Drzal E. 2015. Children and socioeconomic status. See Lerner 2015. In press

Duncan GJ, Ziol-Guest KM, Kalil A. 2010. Early-childhood poverty and adult attainment, behavior, and health. *Child Dev.* 81:306–25

Elder GH. 1998. The life course as developmental theory. *Child Dev.* 69:1–12

Elder GH, Shanahan MJ, Jennings JM. 2015. Human development in time and place. See Lerner 2015. In press

Emmerich W. 1964. Continuity and stability in early social development. *Child Dev.* 35:311–32

Erikson E. 1963. *Childhood and society*. New York: Norton

Fagan JF, Holland CR, Wheeler K. 2007. The prediction, from infancy, of adult IQ and achievement. *Intelligence* 35:225–31

Fattal-Valevski A, Toledano-Alhadef H, Leitner Y, Geva R, Eshel R, Harel S. 2009. Growth patterns in children with intrauterine growth retardation and their correlation to neurocognitive development. *J. Child Neurol.* 24:846–51

Fernald A, Perfors A, Marchman VA. 2006. Picking up speed in understanding: speech processing efficiency and vocabulary growth across the 2nd year. *Dev. Psychol.* 42:98–116

Ferri E, Bynner J, Wadsworth M, eds. 2003. *Changing Britain, Changing Lives: Three Generations at the Turn of the Century*. London: Inst. Educ., Univ. London

Fish M. 2001. Attachment in low-SES rural Appalachian infants: contextual, infant, and maternal interaction risk and protective factors. *Infant Ment. Health J.* 22:641–64

Flege JE. 1991. Age of learning affects the authenticity of voice-onset time (VOT) in stop consonants produced in a second language. *J. Acoust. Soc. Am.* 89:395–411

Fogel A. 2007. *Infancy: Infant, Family, and Society*. Cornwall-on-Hudson, NY: Sloan Publ.

Foster-Cohen S, Edgin JO, Champion PR, Woodward LJ. 2007. Early delayed language development in very preterm infants: evidence from the MacArthur-Bates CDI. *J. Child Lang.* 34:655–75

Fraley RC. 2002. Attachment stability from infancy to adulthood: meta-analysis and dynamic modeling of developmental mechanisms. *Personal. Soc. Psychol. Rev.* 6:123–51

Fraley RC, Griffin BN, Roisman GI, Belsky J. 2012a. Developmental antecedents of political ideology: a longitudinal investigation from birth to age 18 years. *Psychol. Sci.* 23:1425–31

Fraley RC, Roisman GI, Booth-LaForce C, Owen MT, Holland AS. 2013. Interpersonal and genetic origins of adult attachment styles: a longitudinal study from infancy to early adulthood. 104:817–38

Fraley RC, Roisman GI, Haltigan JD. 2012b. The legacy of early experiences in development: formalizing alternative models of how early experiences are carried forward over time. *Dev. Psychol.* 49:109–26

Frank DA, Rose-Jacobs R, Crooks D, Cabral HJ, Gerteis J, et al. 2011. Adolescent initiation of licit and illicit substance use: impact of intrauterine exposures and post-natal exposure to violence. *Neurotoxicol. Teratol.* 33:100–9

Freud S. 1940/1949. *An Outline of Psycho-Analysis.* New York: Norton

Friedman AH, Watamura SE, Robertson SS. 2005. Movement-attention coupling in infancy and attention problems in childhood. *Dev. Med. Child Neurol.* 47:660–65

Furman W, Lanthier R. 2002. Parenting siblings. In *Handbook of Parenting: Children and Parenting,* ed. MH Bornstein, vol. 1, pp. 165–88. Mahwah, NJ: Erlbaum. 2nd ed.

Gahagan S, Yu S, Kaciroti N, Castillo M, Lozoff B. 2009. Linear and ponderal growth trajectories in well-nourished, iron-sufficient infants are unimpaired by iron supplementation. *J. Nutr.* 139:2106–12

Gao Y, Raine A, Venables PH, Dawson ME, Mednick SA. 2010a. Association of poor childhood fear conditioning and adult crime. *Am. J. Psychol.* 167:56–60

Gao Y, Raine A, Venables PH, Dawson ME, Mednick SA. 2010b. Reduced electrodermal fear conditioning from ages 3 to 8 years is associated with aggressive behavior at age 8 years. *J. Child Psychol. Psychiatry* 51:550–58

Garcia-Sierra A, Rivera-Gaxiola M, Percaccio CR, Conboy BT, Romo H, et al. 2011. Bilingual language learning: an ERP study relating early brain responses to speech, language input, and later word production. *J. Phon.* 39:546–57

Garner PW. 2006. Prediction of prosocial and emotional competence from maternal behavior in African American preschoolers. *Cult. Divers. Ethnic Minor. Psychol.* 12:179–98

Gayraud F, Kern S. 2007. Influence of preterm birth on early lexical and grammatical acquisition. *First Lang.* 27:159–73

Gelfand AA, Thomas KC, Goadsb PJ. 2012. Before the headache: infant colic as an early life expression of migraine. *Neurology* 79:1392–96

Gesell A. 1937. Motor disability and mental growth. *Psychol. Record* 1:87–94

Geva R, Yosipof R, Eshel R, Leitner Y, Fattal-Valevski A, Harel S. 2009. Readiness and adjustments to school for children with intrauterine growth restriction (IUGR): an extreme test case paradigm. *J. Except. Child.* 75:211–30

Giffin NJ, Benton S, Goadsby PJ. 2002. Benign paroxysmal torticollis of infancy: four new cases and linkage to CACNA1A mutation. *Dev. Med. Child Neurol.* 44:490–93

Gluckman P, Hanson M. 2006. The developmental origins of health and disease: an overview. In *Developmental Origins of Health and Disease,* ed. P Gluckman, M Hanson, pp. 1–5. London: Cambridge Univ. Press

Grantham-McGregor SM, Fernald LC. 1997. Nutritional deficiencies and subsequent effects on mental and behavioral development in children. *Southeast Asian J. Trop. Med. Public Health* 28:50–68

Guerin DW, Gottfried AW, Thomas CW. 1997. Difficult temperament and behavior problems: a longitudinal study from 1.5 to 12 years. *Int. J. Behav. Dev.* 21:71–90

Guerrant DI, Moore SR, Lima AA, Patrick PD, Schorling JB, Guerrant RL. 1999. Association of early childhood diarrhea and cryptosporidiosis with impaired physical fitness and cognitive function four–seven years later in a poor urban community in northeast Brazil. *Am. J. Trop. Med. Hyg.* 61:707–13

Guidetti V, Ottaviano S, Pagliarini M. 1984. Childhood headache risk: warning signs and symptoms present during the first six months of life. *Cephalalgia* 4:237–42

Guttman L. 1954. A new approach to factor analysis: the radex. In *Mathematical Thinking in the Social Sciences,* ed. PF Lazarsfeld, pp. 258–349. Glencoe, IL: Free Press

Haith MM, Campos JJ. 1977. Human infancy. *Annu. Rev. Psychol.* 28:251–93

Haith MM, Campos JJ, eds. 1983. *Handbook of Child Psychology: Infancy and Developmental Psychobiology.* New York: Wiley

Hales CN, Barker DJ, Clark PM, Cox LJ, Fall C, et al. 1991. Fetal and infant growth and impaired glucose tolerance at age 64. *BMJ* 303:1019–22

Hane AA, Henderson HA, Reeb-Sutherland BC, Fox NA. 2010. Ordinary variations in human maternal caregiving in infancy and biobehavioral development in early childhood: a follow-up study. *Dev. Psychobiol.* 52:558–67

Hannesdottir DK, Doxie J, Bell MA, Ollendick TH, Wolfe CD. 2010. A longitudinal study of emotion regulation and anxiety in middle childhood: associations with frontal EEG asymmetry in early childhood. *Dev. Psychobiol.* 52:197–204

Hartmann DP, Pelzel KE, Abbott CB. 2011. Design, measurement, and analysis in developmental research. In *Developmental Science: An Advanced Textbook*, ed. MH Bornstein, ME Lamb, pp. 109–97. New York: Psychol. Press. 6th ed.

Hauser RM. 2009. The Wisconsin Longitudinal Study: designing a study of the life course. In *The Craft of Life Course Research*, ed. GH Elder Jr, JZ Giele, pp. 29–50. New York: Guilford

Hay DF. 1986. Infancy. *Annu. Rev. Psychol.* 37:135–61

Hazan C, Shaver PR. 1987. Romantic love conceptualized as an attachment process. *J. Personal. Soc. Psychol.* 52:511–24

He J, Degnan KA, McDermott JM, Henderson HA, Hane AA, et al. 2010. Anger and approach motivation in infancy: relations to early childhood inhibitory control and behavior problems. *Infancy* 15:246–69

Hill-Soderlund AL, Braungart-Rieker JM. 2008. Early individual differences in temperamental reactivity and regulation: implications for effortful control in early childhood. *Infant Behav. Dev.* 31:386–97

Hoek HW, Brown AS, Susser E. 1998. The Dutch famine and schizophrenia spectrum disorders. *Soc. Psychiatry Epidemiol.* 33:373–79

Hoek HW, Brown AS, Susser ES. 1999. The Dutch famine studies: prenatal nutritional deficiency and schizophrenia. In *Prenatal Exposures in Schizophrenia. Progress in Psychiatry*, ed. ES Susser, AS Brown, JM Gorman, pp. 135–61. Washington, DC: Am. Psychiatr. Assoc.

Holahan CK, Sears RR, Cronbach LJ. 1995. *The Gifted Group in Later Maturity*. Stanford, CA: Stanford Univ. Press

Holden GW, Miller PC. 1999. Enduring and different: a meta-analysis of the similarity in parents' child rearing. *Psychol. Bull.* 125:223–54

Hostinar CE, Stellern SA, Schaefer C, Carlson SM, Gunnar MR. 2012. Associations between early life adversity and executive function in children adopted internationally from orphanages. *Proc. Natl. Acad. Sci. USA* 109:17208–12

Howes C, Hamilton CE, Phillipsen LC. 1998. Stability and continuity of child-caregiver and child-peer relationships. *Child Dev.* 69:418–26

Huxley RR, Shiell AW, Law CM. 2000. The role of size at birth and postnatal catch-up growth in determining systolic blood pressure: a systematic review of the literature. *J. Hypertens.* 18:815–31

Jaffari-Bimmel N, Juffer F, van IJzendoorn MH, Bakermans-Kranenburg MJ, Mooijaart A. 2006. Social development from infancy to adolescence: longitudinal and concurrent factors in an adoption sample. *Dev. Psychol.* 42:1143–53

James W. 1890. *The Principles of Psychology*. New York: Henry Holt

Jones A, Godfrey KM, Wood P, Osmond C, Goulden P, Phillips DI. 2006. Fetal growth and the adrenocortical response to psychological stress. *J. Clin. Endocrinol. Metab.* 91:1868–71

Kagan J. 1976. Emergent themes in human development. *Am. Sci.* 64:186–96

Kagan J. 1998. *Three Seductive Ideas*. Cambridge, Mass.: Harvard Univ. Press

Kagan J. 2013. *The Human Spark*. New York: Basic Books

Kagan J, Arcus D, Snidman N, Feng WY, Hendler J, Greene S. 1994. Reactivity in infants: a cross-national comparison. *Dev. Psychol.* 30:342–45

Kagan J, Lapidus DR, Moore M. 1978. Infant antecedents of cognitive functioning. *Child Dev.* 49:1005–23

Kagan J, Snidman N, Arcus D. 1998. Childhood derivatives of high and low reactivity in infancy. *Child Dev.* 69:1483–93

Kagan J, Snidman N, Zentner M, Peterson E. 1999. Infant temperament and anxious symptoms in school age children. *Dev. Psychopathol.* 11:209–24

Kar BR, Rao SL, Chandramouli BA. 2008. Cognitive development in children with chronic protein energy malnutrition. *Behav. Brain Funct.* 4:1–31

Keen RE, Berthier NE. 2004. Continuities and discontinuities in infants' representation of objects and events. *Adv. Child Dev. Behav.* 32:243–79

Kell HJ, Lubinski D, Benbow CP. 2013. Who rises to the top? Early indicators. *Psychol. Sci.* 24:648–59

Kerkhof GF, Breukhoven PE, Leunissen RW, Willemsen RH, Hokken-Koelega AC. 2012. Does preterm birth influence cardiovascular risk in early adulthood? *J. Pediatr.* 161:390–96.e1

Kessen W. 1965. *The Child*. New York: Wiley

Kessen W, Haith MM, Salapatek PH. 1970. Human infancy: a bibliography and guide. In *Carmichael's Manual of Child Psychology*, ed. P Mussen, pp. 287–445. New York: Wiley

Kline RB. 1998. *Principles and Practice of Structural Equation Modeling*. New York: Guilford

Kohen-Raz R. 1967. Scalogram analysis of some developmental sequences of infant behaviors as measured by the Bayley Infant Scale of Mental Development. *Genet. Psychol. Monogr.* 76:3–21

Komsi N, Räikkönen K, Pesonen A, Heinonen K, Keskivaara P, et al. 2006. Continuity of temperament from infancy to middle childhood. *Infant Behav. Dev.* 29:494–508

Kreppner JM, Rutter M, Beckett C, Castle J, Colvert E, et al. 2007. Normality and impairment following profound early institutional deprivation: a longitudinal follow-up into early adolescence. *Dev. Psychol.* 43:931–46

Kuh D, Ben-Shlomo Y. 2004. *A Life Course Approach to Chronic Disease Epidemiology*. New York: Oxford Univ. Press. 2nd ed.

Kuhl P, Rivera-Gaxiola M. 2008. Neural substrates of language acquisition. *Annu. Rev. Neurosci.* 31:511–34

Kuhl PK, Conboy BT, Coffey-Corina S, Padden D, Rivera-Gaxiola M, Nelson T. 2008. Early phonetic perception as a pathway to language: new data and native language magnet theory, expanded (NLM-e). *Philos. Trans. R. Soc. B* 363:979–1000

Kuhl PK, Conboy BT, Padden D, Nelson T, Pruitt J. 2005. Early speech perception and later language development: implications for the "critical period." *Lang. Learn. Dev.* 1:237–64

Kuhl PK. 2009. Linking infant speech perception to language acquisition. In *Infant Pathways to Language*, ed. J Colombo, P McCardle, L Freund, pp. 213–44. New York: Psychol. Press

LaBuda MC, DeFries JC, Plomin R, Fulker DW. 1986. Longitudinal stability of cognitive ability from infancy to early childhood: genetic and environmental etiologies. *Child Dev.* 57:1142–50

Ladd GW, Pettit GD. 2002. Parents and children's peer relationships. In *Handbook of Parenting. Practical Parenting*, ed. MH Bornstein, vol. 5, pp. 269–309. Mahwah, NJ: Erlbaum. 2nd ed.

La Guardia JG, Ryan RM, Couchman CE, Deci EL. 2000. Within-person variation in security of attachment: a self-determination theory perspective on attachment, need fulfillment, and well-being. *J. Personal. Soc. Psychol.* 79:367–84

Lahat A, Degnan KA, White LK, McDermott JM, Henderson HA, et al. 2012. Temperamental exuberance and executive function predict propensity for risk taking in childhood. *Dev. Psychopathol.* 24:847–56

Lai T, Liu X, Guo YL, Guo N, Yu M, et al. 2002. A cohort study of behavioral problems and intelligence in children with high prenatal polychlorinated biphenyl exposure. *Arch. Gen. Psychiatry* 59:1061–66

Laucht M, Becker K, Schmidt MH. 2006. Visual exploratory behavior in infancy and novelty seeking in adolescence: two developmentally specific phenotypes of DRD4? *J. Child Psychol. Psychiatry* 47:1143–51

Laucht M, Esser G, Schmidt M. 1994. Contrasting infant predictors of later cognitive functioning. *J. Child Psychol. Psychiatry* 35:649–62

Le Grand R, Mondloch CJ, Maurer D, Brent HP. 2003. Expert face processing requires visual input to the right hemisphere during infancy. *Nat. Neurosci.* 6:1108–12

Lerner RM, ed. 2015. *Ecological Settings and Processes in Developmental Systems. Handbook of Child Psychology and Developmental Science*, Vol. 4, ed. MH Bornstein, T Leventhal. Hoboken, NJ: Wiley. 7th ed. In press

Lerner RM, Lewin-Bizan S, Warren AEA. 2011. Concepts and theories of human development. In *Developmental Science: An Advanced Textbook*, ed. MH Bornstein, ME Lamb, pp. 3–49. New York: Psychol. Press. 6th ed.

Lewis M. 1997. *Altering Fate: Why the Past Does Not Predict the Future*. New York: Guilford

Lewontin R. 2005. *The Triple Helix*. Cambridge, MA: Harvard Univ. Press

Little TD, Schnabel KU, Baumert J, eds. 2000. *Modeling Longitudinal and Multilevel Data: Practical Issues, Applied Approaches, and Specific Examples*. Mahwah, NJ: Erlbaum

Loeb S, Bridges M, Bassok D, Fuller B, Rumberger RW. 2007. How much is too much? The influence of preschool centers on children's social and cognitive development. *Econ. Educ. Rev.* 26:52–66

Lorenz JM, Whitaker AH, Feldman JF, Yudkin PL, Shen S, et al. 2009. Indices of body and brain size at birth and at the age of 2 years: relations to cognitive outcome at the age of 16 years in low birth weight infants. *J. Dev. Behav. Pediatr.* 30:535–43

Lozoff B, Jimenez E, Wolf AW. 1991. Long-term developmental outcome of infants with iron deficiency. *N. Engl. J. Med.* 325:687–94

Lundén M, Silvén M. 2011. Balanced communication in mid-infancy promotes early vocabulary development: effects of play with mother and father in mono- and bilingual families. *Int. J. Biling.* 15:535–59

MacDonald HZ, Beeghly M, Grant-Knight W, Augustyn M, Woods RW, et al. 2008. Longitudinal association between infant disorganized attachment and childhood posttraumatic stress symptoms. *Dev. Psychopathol.* 20:493–508

Macken MA, Barton D. 1979. The acquisition of the voicing contrast in English: a study of voice-onset time in word-initial stop consonants. *J. Child Lang.* 7:41–74

Main M, Cassidy J. 1988. Categories of response to reunion with the parent at age 6: predictable from infant attachment classifications and stable over a 1-month period. *Dev. Psychol.* 24:415–26

Marchman VA, Fernald A. 2008. Speed of word recognition and vocabulary knowledge in infancy predict cognitive and language outcomes in later childhood. *Dev. Sci.* 11:F9–16

Marlow N, Wolke D, Bracewell MA, Samara M. 2005. Neurologic and developmental disability at six years of age after extremely preterm birth. *N. Engl. J. Med.* 352:9–19

Martinez-Torteya C, Bogat A, von Eye A, Levendosky AA. 2009. Resilience among children exposed to domestic violence: the role of risk and protective factors. *Child Dev.* 80:562–77

Masten AS, Cicchetti D. 2010. Developmental cascades. *Dev. Psychopathol.* 22:491–95

Mayes LC, Feldman R, Granger RH, Haynes OM, Bornstein MH, Schottenfeld R. 1997. The effects of polydrug use with and without cocaine on mother-infant interaction at 3 and 6 months. *Infant Behav. Dev.* 20:489–502

McAnulty GB, Butler SC, Bernstein JH, Als H, Duffy FH, Zurakowski D. 2010. Effects of the newborn individualized developmental care and assessment program (NIDCAP) at age 8 years: preliminary data. *Clin. Pediatr.* 49:258–70

McCall RB. 1977. Childhood IQ's as predictors of adult educational and occupational status. *Science* 197:482–83

McCall RB, Hogarty PS, Hurlburt N. 1972. Transitions in infant sensorimotor development and the prediction of childhood IQ. *Am. Psychol.* 27:728–48

McCartney K, Rosenthal R. 2000. Effect size, practical importance, and social policy for children. *Child Dev.* 71:173–80

McDade TW. 2012. Early environments and the ecology of inflammation. *Proc. Natl. Acad. Sci. USA* 109:17281–88

McGrew KS, Knopik SN. 1993. The relationship between the WJ-R Gf-Gc cognitive clusters and writing achievement across the life-span. *Sch. Psychol. Rev.* 22:687–95

Meili-Dworetzki G, Meili R. 1972. *Grundlagen individueller Persönlichkeitsunterschiede: Ergebnisse einer Längsschnittuntersuchung mit zwei Gruppen von der Geburt bis zum 8. und 16. Altersjahr [Foundations of individual personality differences: Results of a longitudinal study with two cohorts from birth to the 8th and 16th year of age].* Berne, Ger.: Huber

Mewes AU, Hüppi PS, Als H, Rybicki FJ, Inder TE, et al. 2006. Regional brain development in serial magnetic resonance imaging of low-risk preterm infants. *Pediatrics* 118:23–33

Mikulincer M, Shaver PR. 2007. Attachment, group- related processes, and psychotherapy. *Int. J. Group Psychother.* 57:233–45

Miller GA. 1956. The magical number seven, plus or minus two: some limits on our capacity for processing information. *Psychol. Rev.* 63:81–97

Milton J. 1671/1960. Paradise regained. In *The Complete Poetical Works of John Milton*, ed. L Amiel. New York: Univers. Class.

Molfese DL. 2000. Predicting dyslexia at 8 years of age using neonatal brain responses. *Brain Lang.* 72:238–45

Moster D, Lie RT, Markestad T. 2008. Long-term medical and social consequences of preterm birth. *N. Engl. J. Med.* 359:262–73

Neighb. Nurs. Initiat. Res. Team. 2007. *National Evaluation of the Neighbourhood Nurseries Initiative: Integrated Report.* London: Dep. Educ. Skills

Newman R, Ratner NB, Jusczyk AM, Jusczyk PW, Dow KA. 2006. Infants' early ability to segment the conversational speech signal predicts later language development: a retrospective analysis. *Dev. Psychol.* 42:643–55

NICHD Early Child Care Res. Netw., ed. 2005. *Child Care and Child Development.* New York: Guilford

NICHD Early Child Care Res. Netw. 1998. Early child care and self-control, compliance, and problem behavior at twenty-four and thirty-six months. *Child Dev.* 69:1145–70

NICHD Early Child Care Res. Netw. 2003a. Does quality of child care affect child outcomes at age 4(1/2)? *Dev. Psychol.* 39:451–69

NICHD Early Child Care Res. Netw. 2003b. Does amount of time spent in child care predict socioemotional adjustment during the transition to kindergarten? *Child Dev.* 74:976–1005

NICHD Early Child Care Res. Netw. 2006. Child-care effect sizes for the NICHD Study of Early Child Care and Youth Development. *Am. Psychol.* 61:99–116

Noll LM, Harding CG. 2003. The relationship of mother-child interaction and the child's development of symbolic play. *Infant Ment. Health J.* 24:557–70

Ohr PS, Feingold J, Fagen JW. 2006. Predicting adolescent anxiety ratings from infant behavioral style in response to expectancy violation. *Appl. Dev. Sci.* 10:147–56

Olds D, Henderson CR, Cole R, Eckenrode J, Kitzman H, et al. 1998. Long-term effects of nurse home visitation on children's criminal and antisocial behavior: 15-year follow-up of a randomized controlled trial. *JAMA* 280:1238–44

Ortiz-Mantilla S, Choe MS, Flax J, Grant PE, Benasich AA. 2010. Associations between the size of the amygdala in infancy and language abilities during the preschool years in normally developing children. *Neuroimage* 49:2791–99

Osofsky JD. 1987. *Handbook of Infant Development.* New York: Wiley. 2nd ed.

Pancsofar N, Vernon-Feagans L. 2010. Fathers' early contributions to children's language development in families from low-income rural communities. *Early Child. Res. Q.* 25:450–63

Paradise JL, Feldman HM, Campbell T, Dollaghan CA, Rockette HE, et al. 2007. Tympanostomy tubes and developmental outcomes at 9 to 11 years of age. *N. Engl. J. Med.* 356:248–61

Pasco Fearon RM, Belsky J. 2011. Infant-mother attachment and the growth of externalizing problems across the primary-school years. *J. Child Psychol. Psychiatry* 52:782–91

Pearson RM, Heron J, Melotti R, Joinson C, Stein A, et al. 2011. The association between observed non-verbal maternal responses at 12 months and later infant development at 18 months and IQ at 4 years: a longitudinal study. *Infant Behav. Dev.* 34:525–33

Perera F, Vishnevetsky J, Herbstman J, Calafat A, Xiong W, et al. 2012. Prenatal bisphenol A exposure and child behavior in an inner-city cohort. *Environ. Health Perspect.* 120:1190–94

Phelps E, Furstenberg FF Jr, Colby A, eds. 2002. *Looking at Lives: American Longitudinal Studies of the Twentieth Century.* New York: Sage Found.

Phillips DI, Barker DJ. 1997. Association between low birthweight and high resting pulse in adult life: Is the sympathetic nervous system involved in programming the insulin resistance syndrome? *Diabet. Med.* 14:673–77

Phillips DI, Goulden P, Syddall HE, Sayer AA, Dennison EM, et al. 2005. Fetal and infant growth and glucose tolerance in the Hertfordshire Cohort Study: a study of men and women born between 1931 and 1939. *Diabetes* 54:S145–50

Piaget J. 1970. Piaget's theory. In *Carmichael's Manual of Child Psychology*, ed. PH Mussen, pp. 703–32. New York: Wiley

Piek JP, Gasson N, Barrett N, Case I. 2002. Limb and gender differences in the development of coordination in early infancy. *Hum. Mov. Sci.* 21:621–39

Pierce T, Lydon J. 2001. Global and specific relational models in the experience of social interactions. *J. Personal. Soc. Psychol.* 80:613–31

Prentice DA, Miller DT. 1992. When small effects are impressive. *Psychol. Bull.* 112:160–64

Putnam SP, Rothbart MK, Gartstein MA. 2008. Homotypic and heterotypic continuity of fine-grained temperament during infancy, toddlerhood and early childhood. *Infant Child Dev.* 17:387–405

Reese E, Jack F, White N. 2010. Origins of adolescents' autobiographical memories. *Cogn. Dev.* 25:352–67

Reilly S, Bavin EL, Bretherton L, Conway L, Eadie P, et al. 2009. The Early Language in Victoria Study (ELVS): a prospective, longitudinal study of communication skills and expressive vocabulary development at 8, 12 and 24 months. *Int. J. Speech Lang. Pathol.* 11:344–57

Rivera-Gaxiola M, Silva-Pereyra J, Kuhl PK. 2005. Brain potentials to native and non-native speech contrasts in 7- and 11-month-old American infants. *Dev. Sci.* 8:162–72

Roberts BW, DelVecchio WF. 2000. The rank-order consistency of personality traits from childhood to old age: a quantitative review of longitudinal studies. *Psychol. Bull.* 126:3–25

Roe KV. 2001. Relationship between male infants' vocal responses to mother and stranger at three months and self-reported academic attainment and adjustment measures in adulthood. *Psychol. Rep.* 89:255–58

Roisman GI, Collins WA, Sroufe LA, Egeland B. 2005. Predictors of young adults' representations of and behavior in their current romantic relationship: prospective tests of the prototype hypothesis. *Attach. Hum. Dev.* 7:105–21

Rose SA, Feldman JF, Jankowski JJ. 2012. Implications of infant cognition for executive functions at age 11. *Psychol. Sci.* 23:1345–55

Roseboom T, de Rooij S, Painter R. 2006. The Dutch famine and its long-term consequences for adult health. *Early Hum. Dev.* 82:485–91

Rose-Jacobs R, Cabral H, Beeghly M, Brown ER, Frank DA. 2004. The Movement Assessment of Infants (MAI) as a predictor of two-year neurodevelopmental outcome for infants born at term who are at social risk. *Pediatr. Phys. Ther.* 16:212–21

Rose-Jacobs R, Soenksen S, Appugliese DP, Cabral HJ, Richardson MA, et al. 2011. Early adolescent executive functioning, intrauterine exposures and own drug use. *Neurotoxicol. Teratol.* 33:379–92

Rose-Jacobs R, Waber D, Beeghly M, Cabral H, Appugliese D, et al. 2009. Intrauterine cocaine exposure and executive functioning in middle childhood. *Neurotoxicol. Teratol.* 31:159–68

Rosenblith JF. 1992. *In the Beginning: Development from Conception to Age Two.* Newbury Park, Calif.: Sage

Rosenthal R. 1979. The file drawer problem and tolerance for null results. *Psychol. Bull.* 86:638–41

Rosenthal R, Rubin DB. 1982. A simple, general purpose display of magnitude of experimental effect. *J. Educ. Psychol.* 74:166–69

Rosenthal R, Rubin DB. 1983. A note on percent of variance explained as a measure of the importance of effects. *J. Appl. Soc. Psychol.* 9:395–96

Rothbart MK. 1988. Temperament and the development of inhibited approach. *Child Dev.* 59:1241–50

Rothbart MK, Bates JE. 2006. Temperament. In *Handbook of Child Psychology: Cognition, Perception, and Language*, ed. D Kuhn, RS Siegler, series ed. W Damon, vol. 2, pp. 99–166. Hoboken, NJ: Wiley. 6th ed.

Rothbart MK, Derryberry D, Hershey K. 2000. Stability of temperament in childhood: laboratory infant assessment to parent report at seven years. In *Temperament and Personality Development Across the Life Span*, ed. VJ Molfese, DL Molfese, pp. 85–119. New York: Psychol. Press

Rothbart MK, Mauro JA. 1990. Temperament, behavioral inhibition, and shyness in childhood. In *Handbook of Social and Evaluation Anxiety*, ed. H Leitenberg, pp. 139–60. New York: Plenum

Ruddy MG, Bornstein MH. 1982. Cognitive correlates of infant attention and maternal stimulation over the first year of life. *Child Dev.* 53:183–88

Rutter M, Rutter M. 1993. *Developing Minds: Challenge and Continuity Across the Life Span.* New York: Basic Books

Saigal S. 2000. Follow-up of very low birthweight babies to adolescence. *Sem. Neonatol.* 5:107–18

Saigal S, Hoult L, Streiner D, Stoskopf B, Rosenbaum P. 2000. School difficulties at adolescence in a regional cohort of children who were extremely low birth weight. *Pediatrics* 105:325–31

Salt A, Redshaw M. 2006. Neurodevelopmental follow-up after preterm birth: follow up after two years. *Early Hum. Dev.* 82:185–97

Samuelsson S, Finnström O, Flodmark O, Gäddlin P, Leijon I, Wadsby MA. 2006. Longitudinal study of reading skills among very-low-birthweight children: Is there a catch-up? *J. Pediatr. Psychol.* 319:967–77

Sansavini A, Guarini A, Alessandroni R, Faldella G, Giovanelli G, Salvioli G. 2006. Early relations between lexical and grammatical development in very immature Italian preterms. *J. Child Lang.* 33:199–216

Schothortst PF, van Engeland H. 1996. Long-term behavioral sequelae of prematurity. *J. Am. Acad. Child Adolesc. Psychiatry* 35:175–83

Schwartz C, Kunwar PS, Greve DN, Kahan J, Snidman NC, Bloch RB. 2011. A phenotype of early infancy predicts reactivity of the amygdala in male adults. *Mol. Psychiatry* 17:1042–50

Schwartz CE, Kunwar PS, Greve DN, Moran LR, Viner JC, et al. 2010. Structural differences in adult orbital and ventromedial prefrontal cortex predicted by infant temperament at 4 months of age. *Arch. Gen. Psychiatry* 67:78–84

Schwartz CE, Wright CI, Shin LM, Kagan J, Whalen PJ, et al. 2003. Differential amygdala response to novel versus newly familiar neutral faces: a functional MRI probe developed for studying inhibited temperament. *Biol. Psychiatry* 53:854–62

Shafir T, Angulo-Barroso R, Calatroni A, Jimenez E, Lozoff B. 2006. Effects of iron deficiency in infancy on patterns of motor development over time. *Hum. Mov. Sci.* 25:821–38

Shanahan MJ, Elder GH. 2002. *History, Agency, and the Life Course.* Lincoln: Univ. Neb. Press

Shenkin SD, Starr JM, Deary IJ. 2004. Birth weight and cognitive ability in childhood: a systematic review. *Psychol. Bull.* 130:989–1013

Sheridan MA, Fox NA, Zeanah CH, McLaughlin KA, Nelson CA. 2012. Variation in neural development as a result of exposure to institutionalization early in childhood. *Proc. Natl. Acad. Sci. USA* 109:12927–32

Shrout PE, Bolger N. 2002. Mediation in experimental and nonexperimental studies: new procedures and recommendations. *Psychol. Methods* 7:422–45

Siegel LS. 1979. Infant perceptual, cognitive, and motor behaviours as predictors of subsequent cognitive and language development. *Can. J. Psychol.* 33:382–95

Siegel LS. 1981. Infant tests as predictors of cognitive and language development at two years. *Child Dev.* 52:545–57

Siegel LS. 1982. Early cognitive and environmental correlates of language development at 4 years. *Int. J. Behav. Dev.* 5:433–44

Siegel LS. 1983a. Correction for prematurity and its consequences for the assessment of the very low birth weight infant. *Child Dev.* 54:1176–88

Siegel LS. 1983b. The prediction of possible learning disabilities in preterm and full-term children. In *Infants Born at Risk: Physiological, Perceptual, and Cognitive Processes*, ed. T Field, A Sostek, pp. 295–315. New York: Grune & Stratton

Siegel LS. 1985a. Biological and environmental variables as predictors of intellectual functioning at 6 years. In *The At-Risk Infant: Psycho/Socio/Medical Aspects*, ed. S Harel, N Anastasiow, pp. 65–73. Baltimore, MD: Brooks

Siegel LS. 1985b. At risk index to predict learning problems in preterm and fullterm children. In *Early Identification of Children at Risk: An International Perspective*, ed. WK Frankenburg, RN Emde, JW Sullivan, pp. 231–44. New York: Plenum

Siegel LS. 1989. A reconceptualization of prediction from infant test scores. In *Stability and Continuity in Mental Development*, ed. MH Bornstein, NA Krasnegor, pp. 89–103. Hillsdale, NJ: Erlbaum

Sigman M, Cohen SE, Beckwith L. 1997. Why does infant attention predict adolescent intelligence? *Infant Behav. Dev.* 20:133–40

Sigman M, Cohen SE, Beckwith L, Asarnow R, Parmelee AH. 1991. Continuity in cognitive abilities from infancy to 12 years of age. *Cogn. Dev.* 6:47–57

Singh L, Liederman J, Mierzejewski R, Barnes J. 2011. Rapid reacquisition of native phoneme contrasts after disuse: You do not always lose what you do not use. *Dev. Sci.* 14:949–59

Smith CL, Bell MA. 2010. Stability in infant frontal asymmetry as a predictor of toddlerhood internalizing and externalizing behaviors. *Dev. Psychobiol.* 52:158–67

Smolak L, Levine MP. 1984. The effects of differential criteria on the assessment of cognitive-linguistic relationships. *Child Dev.* 55:973–80

Spassov L, Curzi-Dascalova L, Clairambault J, Kauffmann F, Eiselt M, et al. 1994. Heart rate and heart rate variability during sleep in small-for-gestational age newborns. *Pediatr. Res.* 35:500–5

Sroufe LA, Egeland B, Carlson EA, Collins WA. 2005. *The Development of the Person: The Minnesota Study of Risk and Adaptation from Birth to Adulthood.* New York: Guilford

Steele H, Steele M, Croft C. 2008. Early attachment predicts emotion recognition at 6 and 11 years. *Attach. Human Dev.* 4:379–93

Stone LJ, Smith HT, Murphy LB. 1973. *The Competent Infant: Research and Commentary*. New York: Basic Books

Strube MJ. 1991. Multiple determinants and effect size: a more general method of discourse. *J. Personal. Soc. Psychol.* 61:1024–27

Tamis-LeMonda CS, Bornstein MH. 1993. Antecedents of exploratory competence at one year. *Infant Behav. Dev.* 16:423–39

Tamis-LeMonda CS, Bornstein MH, Baumwell L, Damast AM 1996. Responsive parenting in the second year: specific influences on children's language and play. *Early Dev. Parent.* 5:173–83

Taylor HG, Klein N, Hack M. 2000a. School-age consequences of birth weight less than 750 g: a review and update. *Dev. Neuropsychol.* 17:289–321

Taylor HG, Klein N, Minich NM, Hack M. 2000b. Verbal memory deficits in children with less than 750 g birth weight. *Child Neuropsychol.* 6:49–63

Thomas A, Chess S, Birch H. 1970. The origins of personality. *Sci. Am.* 223:102–9

Thomas A, Chess S, Birch HG, Hertzig M, Korn S. 1963. *Behavioral Individuality in Early Childhood*. New York: N.Y. Univ. Press

Tottenham N, Hare TA, Quinn BT, McCarry TW, Nurse M, et al. 2010. Prolonged institutional rearing is associated with atypically large amygdala volume and difficulties in emotion regulation. *Dev. Sci.* 13:46–61

Tsao F, Liu H, Kuhl PK. 2004. Speech perception in infancy predicts language development in the second year of life: a longitudinal study. *Child Dev.* 75:1067–84

Tuovinen S, Räikkönen K, Kajantie E, Henriksson M, Leskinen JT, et al. 2012. Hypertensive disorders in pregnancy and cognitive decline in the offspring up to old age. *Neurology* 79:1578–82

Vacha-Haase T, Thompson B. 2004. How to estimate and interpret various effect sizes. *J. Couns. Psychol.* 51:473–81

van Baar AL, Ultee K, Boudewijn Gunning W, Soepatmi S, de Leeuw R. 2006. Developmental course of very preterm children in relation to school outcome. *J. Dev. Phys. Disabil.* 18:273–93

van de Weijer-Bergsma E, Wijnroks L, Jongmans MJ. 2008. Attention development in infants and preschool children born preterm: a review. *Infant Behav. Dev.* 31:333–51

van den Berg GJ, Lindeboom M, Lopez M. 2009. Inequality in individual mortality and economic conditions earlier in life. *Soc. Sci. Med.* 69:1360–67

van den Dries L, Juffer F, van IJzendoorn MH, Bakermans-Kranenburg MJ. 2009. Fostering security? A meta-analysis of attachment in adopted children. *Child Youth Serv. Rev.* 31:410–21

van der Feest SVH. 2010. Review of the book: *Early Language Development. Bridging Brain and Behavior*, by AD Friederici, G Thierry. *J. Child Lang.* 37:217–28

van IJzendoorn MH. 2005. Attachment in social networks: toward an evolutionary social network model. *Hum. Dev.* 48:85–88

Vandell DL, Belsky K, Burchinal M, Vandergrift N, Steinberg L, NICHD Early Child Care Res. Netw. 2010. Do effects of early child care extend to age 15 years? Results from the NICHD Study of Early Child Care and Youth Development. *Child Dev.* 81:737–56

Vibbert M, Bornstein MH 1989. Specific associations between domains of mother-child interaction and toddler referential language and pretense play. *Infant Behav. Dev.* 12:163–84

Volling BL. 2003. Sibling relationships. In *Well-Being: Positive Development Across the Life Course. Crosscurrents in Contemporary Psychology*, ed. MH Bornstein, L Davidson, CLM Keyes, KA Moore, pp. 205–20. Mahwah, NJ: Erlbaum

Vreugdenhil H, Slijper F, Mulder F, Weisglas-Kuperus N. 2002. Effects of perinatal exposure to PCBs and dioxins on play behavior in Dutch children at school age. *Environ. Health Perspect.* 110:A593–98

Wessel MA, Cobb JC, Jackson EB, Harris GS Jr, Detwiler AC. 1954. Paroxysmal fussing in infancy, sometimes called colic. *Pediatrics* 14:421–35

Whitaker H, Feldman J, Lorenz J, Shen S, McNicholas F, et al. 2006. Motor and cognitive outcomes in nondisabled low-birth-weight adolescents: early determinants. *Arch. Pediatr. Adolesc. Med.* 160:1040–46

Wilson RS. 1978. Synchronies in mental development: an epigenetic perspective. *Science* 202:939–48

Wohlwill JF. 1973. *The Study of Behavioral Development*. New York: Academic

Wolfe CD, Bell MA. 2007. The integration of cognition and emotion during infancy and early childhood: regulatory processes associated with the development of working memory. *Brain Cogn.* 65:3–13

Woodward L, Mogridge J, Wells N, Scott W, Inder TE. 2004. Can neurobehavioral examination predict the presence of cerebral injury in the very low birth weight infant? *J. Dev. Behav. Pediatr.* 25:326–34

Wright CA, George TP, Burke R, Gelfand DM, Teti DM. 2000. Early maternal depression and children's adjustment to school. *Child Study J.* 30:153–68

Yamaguchi M, Kuhlmeier VA, Wynn K, vanMarle K. 2009. Continuity in social cognition from infancy to childhood. *Dev. Sci.* 12:746–52

Yeaton W, Sechrest L. 1981. Meaningful measures of effect. *J. Consult. Clin. Psychol.* 49:766–67

Yoshinaga-Itano C, Sedey AL, Coulter DK, Mehl AL. 1998. Language of early- and later-identified children with hearing loss. *Pediatrics* 102:1161–71

Yu M, Hsu C, Gladen BC, Rogan WJ. 1991. In utero PCB/PCDF exposure: relation of developmental delay to dysmorphology and dose. *Neurotoxicol. Teratol.* 13:195–202

Zimmermann P, Maier M, Winter M, Grossmann KE. 2001. Attachment and emotion regulation of adolescents during joint problem-solving with a friend. *Int. J. Behav. Dev.* 25:331–42

Ziol-Guest K, Duncan GJ, Kalil A. 2009. Early childhood poverty and adult body mass index. *Am. J. Public Health* 99:527–32

Ziol-Guest K, Duncan GJ, Kalil A, Boyce WT. 2012. Early childhood poverty, immune mediated disease processes, and adult productivity. *Proc. Natl. Acad. Sci. USA* 109:17289–93

Bullying in Schools: The Power of Bullies and the Plight of Victims

Jaana Juvonen[1] and Sandra Graham[2]

[1]Department of Psychology, [2]Department of Education, University of California, Los Angeles, California 90095; email: j_juvonen@yahoo.com

Annu. Rev. Psychol. 2014. 65:159–85

First published online as a Review in Advance on August 5, 2013

The *Annual Review of Psychology* is online at http://psych.annualreviews.org

This article's doi: 10.1146/annurev-psych-010213-115030

Keywords

aggression, emotional distress, school context, social cognitions, social dominance, social stigma

Abstract

Bullying is a pervasive problem affecting school-age children. Reviewing the latest findings on bullying perpetration and victimization, we highlight the social dominance function of bullying, the inflated self-views of bullies, and the effects of their behaviors on victims. Illuminating the plight of the victim, we review evidence on the cyclical processes between the risk factors and consequences of victimization and the mechanisms that can account for elevated emotional distress and health problems. Placing bullying in context, we consider the unique features of electronic communication that give rise to cyberbullying and the specific characteristics of schools that affect the rates and consequences of victimization. We then offer a critique of the main intervention approaches designed to reduce school bullying and its harmful effects. Finally, we discuss future directions that underscore the need to consider victimization a social stigma, conduct longitudinal research on protective factors, identify school context factors that shape the experience of victimization, and take a more nuanced approach to school-based interventions.

Contents

INTRODUCTION

Highly publicized school shootings and suicides by victims of chronic peer abuse have increased public concern about bullying. Although violent reactions to bullying are rare, awareness of peer maltreatment has generated a large body of research that allows us to better understand both the motives underlying bullying and its effects on victims. These studies, published largely since the late 1990s (Stassen Berger 2007), rely on two complementary research orientations: the American research tradition focusing on childhood aggression (e.g., Parke & Slaby 1983) and the Scandinavian research tradition illuminating the effects of aggressive behaviors on other children (Lagerspetz et al. 1982; Olweus 1978, 1993). Focusing on individual differences, the largely American studies provide insights into the social cognitions and relationships of bullies compared with their well-adjusted peers. In contrast, the Scandinavian research, stemming from a phenomenon known as mobbing, in which a group turns against one person (Olweus 1978), highlights the plight of victims as well as the group dynamics that encourage and maintain bullying behaviors.

In an effort to bridge these two traditions, we review the current research on both bullying perpetration and victimization. The review is divided into six sections. In the first section we define bullying and review its prevalence and the stability of bullying and victimization trajectories over time. The second section is devoted to bullying perpetration; we discuss the forms and functions of bullying as a subcategory of aggression in an effort to understand the motives and social-cognitive mechanisms underlying the behavior. Turning to the plight of the victim in the third section, we review research on risk factors and the consequences of victimization, underscoring the cyclical processes between the two. After reviewing some of the social-cognitive and biological mechanisms that help account for the distress of victims, we examine in the fourth section the ways in which contexts (specifically, the school environment and electronic communication context) give rise to bullying and amplify the distress of the victim. In the fifth section we briefly review the main intervention approaches designed to reduce bullying in schools before considering future directions for research in the sixth and final section.

Definition and Prevalence of Bullying

Bullying involves targeted intimidation or humiliation. Typically, a physically stronger or socially more prominent person (ab)uses her/his power to threaten, demean, or belittle another. To make the target or victim feel powerless, the bully can resort to a number of aggressive behaviors (Olweus 1993, Smith & Sharp 1994). However, bullying entails more than aggression: It captures a dynamic interaction between the perpetrator and the victim. The power imbalance between the two parties distinguishes bullying from conflict. Although definitions of bullying frequently specify that it needs to be repeated (e.g., Olweus 1993), it is not clear that repetition is a required component, inasmuch as a single traumatic incident can raise the expectation and fear of continued abuse.

Bullying takes place among young children as well as adults in a variety of settings, but most of the research focuses on children and youth in schools (e.g., Juvonen & Graham 2001). Survey data indicate that approximately 20–25% of youths are directly involved in bullying as perpetrators, victims, or both (e.g., Nansel et al. 2001). Large-scale studies conducted in Western nations suggest that 4–9% of youths frequently engage in bullying behaviors and that 9–25% of school-age children are bullied (Stassen Berger 2007). A smaller subgroup of youths who both bully and are bullied (bully-victims) has also been identified (e.g., Nansel et al. 2001).

Stability of Bullying and Victimization

Developmental psychologists have assumed some degree of temporal stability in bullying and victimization, although more is known about perpetration of bullying than about victimization. Several large, multinational studies have examined the stability of aggression from early childhood through adolescence (Dodge et al. 2006). With repeated assessments over many years and advances in methods for modeling developmental trajectories, these studies have identified latent classes of individuals who vary in terms of the stability of aggressive behaviors.

In one of the most comprehensive studies to date, six longitudinal data sets from Canada, New Zealand, and the United States were used to examine developmental trajectories of aggressive youth (Broidy et al. 2003). On the basis of samples comprising more than 5,000 boys and girls, all of the databases had comparable aggression measures, including items that capture bullying from middle childhood (ages 5–7) through at least adolescence. Robustly identified across all of the data sets was a class of chronically aggressive youths, representing 5–10% of the samples. Classes of increasing and decreasing aggression trajectories were also identified, a finding that underscores the instability of aggression over time. These discontinuous classes were less robust, and their size varied from 15% to 60% across the different longitudinal data sets. Assuming that a subset of aggressive youths in these multinational studies were bullies, it seems reasonable to conclude that a small percentage of youths, less than 10%, are likely to be chronic bullies throughout childhood. The most consistent evidence regarding the discontinuous trajectories documents desistance from physical aggression over time, suggesting that many childhood bullies "age out" of their tendency to physically intimidate others by adolescence. However, we do not know whether physical aggression is replaced by others forms of bullying.

Comparable longitudinal research examining the stability of victims of bullying across childhood and adolescence does not exist. Most victimization studies that address stability are relatively short term, usually spanning one or two years (e.g., Hanish & Guerra 2002, Juvonen et al. 2000), with a few extending to four or five years (e.g., Kochenderfer-Ladd & Wardrop 2001). Not surprisingly, stability coefficients are stronger when there is a shorter time interval between assessments (e.g., from the beginning to the end of a school year). Even within one school year, however, the stability estimates range from one-third (Juvonen et al. 2000) to approximately one-half (e.g., Fox & Boulton 2006).

Only a few studies of peer victimization have employed a latent class approach in which trajectories of victimization can be modeled, and none has aggregated data across multiple data sets. In one study of young adolescents, three latent classes were identified on the basis of self-reported experiences with bullying across three years of middle school: a frequently victimized class, a sometimes victimized class, and a nonvictimized class (Nylund et al. 2007). At the beginning of middle school, membership in these three classes was fairly evenly distributed: 20% of students were in the highly victimized class, 37% in the sometimes victimized class, and 43% in the nonvictimized class. By spring of eighth grade, only approximately 5% of students were in the victimized class, whereas the percentage of students in the nonvictimized class had increased to almost 70%. Hence, going from being the youngest to the oldest students in their schools, and transitioning from early to middle adolescence, was accompanied by a decline in experiences of victimization.

In summary, longitudinal research on bullying perpetration and victimization indicates more instability than stability. A host of changing factors, such as school transitions, probably contribute to the flux. However, this instability does not necessarily mean that bullying has no lasting effects. Although many temporarily victimized youths may subsequently appear adjusted, some of the symptoms and increased sensitivity to maltreatment persist after bullying has stopped (Rudolph et al. 2011). It is also important to consider the overlap among bully and victim groups over time. In one of the few studies that examined the co-occurrence of bullying and victimization longitudinally, 9% of the sample students who had reputations as bullies during childhood developed reputations as victims by adolescence, whereas approximately 6% who were childhood victims in the eyes of peers had become bullies three years later (Scholte et al. 2007). Thus, bullying perpetration and victimization are probably more dynamic than previously assumed.

FORMS AND FUNCTIONS OF BULLYING BEHAVIORS

Bullying takes many forms, ranging from name-calling and physical attacks to spreading of malicious rumors and sending embarrassing pictures online. Disentangling the "whats" from the "whys" of such behaviors, Little et al. (2003) maintain that any one form of aggression can be used for different purposes. For example, whereas a physical attack may capture a reaction to provocation, physical aggression can also be used proactively to intimidate a peer (see also Prinstein & Cillessen 2003). Although distinctions between different functions of aggressive behaviors are challenging to assess empirically, the conceptual differentiations help shed light on the motives underlying bullying behaviors. Before discussing these functions, we first review research on the forms of bullying—a topic that has received considerable empirical attention.

Direct and Indirect Forms of Bullying

Most forms of bullying can be classified as direct or indirect (Feshbach 1969, Lagerspetz et al. 1988). In contrast to direct confrontation (e.g., physical aggression, threats, name-calling), indirect tactics include spreading of rumors, backstabbing, and exclusion from the group. In other words, the indirect forms frequently involve relational manipulation (Crick & Grotpeter 1995). Whereas the direct forms of bullying often involve intimidating, humiliating, or belittling someone in front of an audience, the indirect forms are designed to damage the targets' social reputation or deflate their social status while concealing the identity of the perpetrator (Björkqvist et al. 1992). That is, the bully is able to use the peer group as a vehicle for the attack (Xie et al. 2002) when relying on relationally indirect tactics.

Although one might expect a developmental progression from direct confrontation to reliance on indirect forms of aggression, inasmuch as the latter requires more sophisticated social understanding and skills (Rivers & Smith 1994), a recent meta-analysis of more than 100 studies did not reveal any reliable age differences in the use of direct versus indirect tactics (Card et al. 2008). This conclusion may be somewhat misleading, however, because some forms of aggression (e.g., the most covert tactics, such as spreading of rumors) are simply not studied among young children. Additionally, the lack of age differences between direct and indirect forms of aggression might simply reflect the heterogeneity of the types of behaviors that are grouped together. For example, although both name-calling and physical aggression are considered direct forms of aggression, only physical bullying is known to decreases with age (e.g., Brame et al. 2001).

Compared with age differences in preference for particular forms of aggression, gender differences have prompted a much livelier debate (e.g., Underwood 2003). Ideas of gendered forms of aggression are popular inasmuch as physical aggression is associated with males, whereas relational forms of aggression are considered to be the domain of females (hence the labels mean girls, queen bees, and alpha girls). What is the research evidence for such gender differences? If the question is whether boys are more physically aggressive than girls, the answer is a resounding "yes." At every age group and across races/ethnicities, social classes, cultures, and national boundaries, boys are more likely than girls to engage in physical forms of bullying such as hitting, kicking, and shoving (Archer 2004, Card et al. 2008, Dodge et al. 2006). Even the most physically aggressive girls are rarely as aggressive as the most physically aggressive boys (Broidy et al. 2003).

If boys are more physically aggressive, then are girls more relationally aggressive than boys? The answer to this question is more equivocal. Beginning in the 1980s with research by Finnish developmental psychologists (e.g., Lagerspetz et al. 1988), followed by the seminal research of Crick and colleagues in the United States (e.g., Crick & Grotpeter 1995; see review in Crick et al. 2007), researchers have documented that relational forms of inflicting harm on others (e.g., excluding a person from the group or spreading rumors to tarnish someone's reputation) were tactics more commonly employed by girls than by boys. Because girls were thought to value relationships more than boys, behaviors that harmed those relationships should be an especially effective form of aggression for them (Coyne, Nelson & Underwood 2011). Additionally, from an evolutionary perspective, girls who attack the reputations of other girls would be in a better position to compete for males (e.g., Artz 2005).

Two comprehensive meta-analyses conducted during the past decade (Archer 2004, Card et al. 2008) and one narrative review (Archer & Coyne 2005) have called into question popular beliefs about gender and relational aggression. Although girls use more relational than physical aggressive behaviors, there are no strong differences between the two genders in the use of relational aggression. Boys are just as likely as girls to enact behaviors that damage the reputation of peers or engage in exclusionary tactics. By middle adolescence, relational aggression probably becomes the norm for both genders as it becomes less socially acceptable for individuals to physically aggress against their peers (Archer & Coyne 2005). Moreover, the different forms of aggression are highly correlated. The meta-analysis by Card et al. (2008) reported an average correlation of $r = 0.76$ between direct and indirect forms, which means that approximately half of the variance in these two forms of aggression is shared.

In summary, bullying takes many forms. The indirect forms of bullying require considerable social insight compared with the direct and overt tactics that include name-calling and physical aggression. Although one might assume that these forms would vary developmentally, the only reliable difference is that physical aggression decreases with age. Robust gender differences are also documented only for physical aggression. Indirect forms of aggression that typically involve manipulation of relationships do not show a reliable gender difference, although girls who desire to aggress against their peers are likely to use relational tactics.

Bullying and Social Dominance

Why do youths resort to any form of aggression to bully their peers? Early studies suggested that childhood aggression stems from a lack of social skills or that aggressive behaviors reflect a budding antisocial personality (e.g., Olweus 1978). However, there is substantial evidence suggesting that indirect forms of aggression, in particular, demand sophisticated social skills (Björkqvist et al. 2000, Sutton et al. 1999) and that most bullies do not turn into violent adults because bullying behaviors are often short-lived (Broidy et al. 2003, Loeber & Hay 1997). To understand why some youths resort to bullying, even if temporarily, it is therefore critical to consider the motives and the possible social function(s) underlying the behaviors.

When bullying is defined as a form of instrumental behavior, researchers acknowledge that bullies are not necessarily lacking social skills or the ability to regulate emotions. Rather, there is evidence suggesting that bullies are cold and calculating, often lacking empathy (Gini et al. 2007, Jolliffe & Farrington 2006) and resorting to coercive strategies to dominate and control the behavior of peers (Ojanen et al. 2005, Pellegrini et al. 1999). Indeed, bullies score high when asked how important it is to be visible, influential, and admired (Salmivalli et al. 2005, Sijtsema et al. 2009).

Not only do bullies strive to dominate, they also frequently have high social status. Beginning in elementary school, some aggressive children are considered to be popular (Rodkin et al. 2006). By early adolescence, peer-directed hostile behaviors are robustly associated with social prominence or high status (e.g., Adler & Adler 1998, Parkhurst & Hopmeyer 1998). These findings are consistent with ethological research demonstrating that aggression is a way to establish a dominant position within a group (e.g., Hinde 1974). Hence, bullying perpetration can be considered a strategic behavior that enables youths to gain and maintain a dominant position within their group (Hawley 1999, Juvonen et al. 2012; also see Eder 1985, Merten 1997).

If bullying behaviors are more temporary than stable and indeed reflect desires to be powerful and prominent, then bullying should peak during times of social reorganization and uncertainty. Indeed, status enhancement is particularly important during early adolescence, which coincides with a transition from elementary school to middle school (LaFontana & Cillessen 2010). Not only do bullying behaviors increase during this developmental phase (Espelage et al. 2001, Pellegrini & Long 2002), but there is a particularly robust association between aggressive behaviors and social prominence after the transition to the new school (e.g., Cillessen & Borch 2006; Cillessen & Mayeux 2004). The establishment of a social hierarchy may be adaptive not only for the one who desires to be powerful, but also for the larger collective. A dominance hierarchy allows youths to navigate the social scene more safely as they learn how to align themselves and establish their position in the hierarchy (Juvonen & Galván 2008).

Taken together, bullying behaviors are not only proactive or instrumental forms of aggression, but they appear to be guided by social dominance motives that peak at times of social reorganization associated with transitions. On the basis of the current evidence, it is difficult to determine whether these transitions involve mainly environmental changes (e.g., larger schools, increased anonymity) or whether the combination of environmental and developmental (e.g., pubertal) changes is involved in the creation of social hierarchies based on aggression.

Inflated Self-Views and Social-Cognitive Biases of Bullies

In light of the positive relation between aggression and high social status, it should come as no surprise that many aggressive youths have high and even inflated perceptions of themselves (e.g., Cairns & Cairns 1994, Hymel et al. 1993). For example, aggressive elementary school students overestimate their competencies not only in terms of their peer status but in terms of academic and athletic domains as well (Hymel et al. 1993). Moreover, peer-identified bullies rate themselves lower on depression, social anxiety, and loneliness than do youths who are socially adjusted (Juvonen et al. 2003).

There are multiple explanations for why aggressive youths, and bullies in particular, display (unrealistically) positive self-views. One set of explanations pertains to their information-processing biases. For example, one meta-analytic review shows strong support for a hostile attribution bias in aggressive youths (De Castro et al. 2002). This attributional bias to perceive ambiguous situations as reflecting hostile peer intent (Dodge 1993) may account for bullies' lack of emotional distress. They can maintain their positive self-views by blaming and aggressing against others instead of accepting personal responsibility for negative events (Weiner 1995).

It is also important to realize that the social feedback bullies receive from peers is more positive than negative. Youths rarely challenge bullies by intervening when witnessing bullying incidents (e.g., O'Connell et al. 1999), although most condemn bullying behaviors (Boulton et al. 2002, Rigby & Johnson 2006). Moreover, when bullying incidents take place, some bystanders reinforce the bullies by smiling and laughing (Salmivalli et al. 1998). Although peers typically do not personally like those who bully others, they are still likely to side with the bully in part to protect their social status, reputation, and physical safety (Juvonen & Galván 2008, Salmivalli 2010).

The research described in this section indicates that bullies think highly of themselves on the basis of the social feedback they receive. This favorable social feedback, combined with hostile attributional bias, allows bullies to feel good about themselves and perhaps to discount the harm they inflict on others. When peers do not challenge bullies' aggressive behaviors, bullying is maintained and even reinforced by the peer collective.

PLIGHT OF VICTIMS

Not surprisingly, victims of bullying display numerous adjustment problems, including depressed mood and anxiety (e.g., Hawker & Boulton 2000), psychosomatic problems (e.g., headaches and stomachaches; Gini & Pozzoli 2009), and academic difficulties (e.g., Nakamoto & Schwartz 2010). However, due to the correlational nature of this research, it is not clear whether bullying experiences cause these adjustment problems or whether signs of maladjustment make victims easy targets.

Victim Subtypes

Bullying is rarely targeted randomly. To understand what factors increase the risk of being bullied, it is useful to consider which type of reactions might be rewarding for bullies. In other words, who makes a "safe" target in making the bully feel powerful? Olweus (1993) described the most typical group of victims as submissive victims: those who are anxious, insecure, and sensitive (e.g., those who often cry in response to bullying). This profile of submissive victims has received subsequent support from longitudinal studies showing that internalizing problems (e.g., Hodges & Perry 1999, Hodges et al. 1999) and, specifically, lack of confidence in social interactions (Egan & Perry 1998, Salmivalli & Isaacs 2005) increase the risk of being bullied. The unfolding of this sequence was particularly well demonstrated in an observational study that relied on a paradigm in which youths with peer relationship problems (a history of rejection by classmates) were exposed to a new set of peers in the context of contrived play groups. Boys who submitted to peers' hostile behaviors became increasingly targeted across subsequent play sessions (Schwartz et al. 1993). Consequently, they also became more withdrawn, providing evidence for cyclical processes between risk factors and consequences of victimization.

In addition to submissive victims, Olweus (1993) identified another group of chronic targets: provocative victims who resort to aggression, much like bullies. Perry et al. (1990) labeled the aggression displayed by these targets as ineffectual, suggesting that their failed attempts to retaliate against more-powerful bullies did not stop the bullying. Hence, these individuals may also make easy targets whose emotional response is rewarding for bullies. Members of this group, frequently labeled bully-victims or aggressive victims in subsequent studies, appear to have emotion regulation and attention problems akin to attention deficit and hyperactivity disorders (e.g., Bettencourt et al. 2012). When compared with bullies and victims, the comorbid bully-victim group shares some of the plight of victims (e.g., moderate levels of distress, high level of peer rejection) but not any of the social benefits associated with the high social status of bullies (Juvonen et al. 2003). Given that reactively aggressive victims constitute a particularly stable group of targeted youths (Camodeca et al. 2002), bully-victims may indeed represent a distinct risk group whose developmental trajectories continue to be problematic (also see Burk et al. 2010).

Individual and Social Risk Factors

In addition to specific psychological characteristics that might encourage a bully to target a specific youth, several nonbehavioral characteristics increase the risk of being bullied. For example, obesity (Pearce et al. 2002) and off-time pubertal maturation (Nadeem & Graham 2005, Reynolds & Juvonen 2010) place youths at elevated risk of peer ridicule and intimidation. Additionally, children with disabilities (Son et al. 2012) and LGBT (lesbian, gay, bisexual, and transgender) youths (e.g., Katz-Wise & Hyde 2012) are much more likely to be bullied compared with their "typical" peers. Thus, any condition or characteristic that makes youths stand out from their peers increases the likelihood of them being bullied.

Research on rejected social status (i.e., being disliked and avoided) shows that any nonnormative behaviors or physical characteristics that set a child apart from the group place them at risk of being shunned by their group. Wright et al. (1986) adopted the label social misfit to describe individuals whose social behavior deviates from group norms. In a study of boys living in cottages while attending summer camp for youths with behavior problems, aggressive boys were rejected in cabins where verbal threats and hitting were low-frequency behaviors, whereas withdrawn boys were rejected in cabins where aggression was normative (Wright et al. 1986). These findings have been replicated in other experimental studies (Boivin et al. 1995) as well as in large-scale classroom contexts (Stormshak et al. 1999). Although the lack of fit between an individual and a group is likely to increase the risk of rejection within the group, it appears that the marginal social status, in turn, increases the risk of prolonged or more severe peer victimization because these youths are unlikely to be supported or defended by any group members.

Interpersonal risk factors can contribute to increased risk of peer victimization in a few different ways. For example, emotional or behavioral problems may elicit bullying especially when the targets are lower in social status (Hodges et al. 1999). Adolescents suffering from depression are likely to be bullied because they have difficulties in establishing friendships (Kochel et al. 2012). Marginal social status (Buhs et al. 2006) and lack of friends (e.g., Hodges & Perry 1999) may also function as independent risk factors for peer victimization over time (Hodges et al. 1999, Kochenderfer & Ladd 1997). Although peers, even close friends, do not necessarily stand up for victims of bullying, emotional support from a friend plays a critical role in how victims are affected by being bullied. For example, one recent study shows that although bullied youths are more likely to have internalizing problems over time, those victims who report receiving emotional support from a friend are protected (Yeung et al. 2012).

Taken together, individual risk factors (e.g., obesity, disabilities, LGBT status) that set a youth apart from the group (norm) increase the risk of bullying, especially in the absence of friends or when rejected by the group. However, when an obese child or a sexual minority youth has friends or is accepted by classmates, the chances of being bullied are decreased. Even just one friend can protect against being bullied and the degree to which victimized youth feel distressed (Hodges et al. 1999, Hodges & Perry 1999).

Cyclical Processes and Consequences of Peer Victimization

Many factors that place youths at risk of victimization (e.g., internalizing problems, lack of social connections) can also be considered consequences of peer victimization. To address the question of directionality, the authors of a recent meta-analysis computed effect sizes for two sets of studies: those in which internalizing problems were considered antecedents of subsequent peer victimization (11 studies) and those in which changes in internalizing problems were examined as consequences of victimization (15 studies). The effect sizes for the first set of studies ranged from $r = -0.05$ to 0.20, whereas those for the second set of studies ranged from $r = 0.04$ to 0.41 (Reijntjes et al. 2010). Although the effects are somewhat stronger when internalizing symptoms are considered to be consequences of bullying experiences, the effect sizes do not statistically differ. Thus, the relationships between peer victimization and internalizing problems are reciprocal, probably reflecting cyclical processes over time.

Unless the reciprocal and possibly cyclical processes can be interrupted, victims of bullying are likely to manifest psychosocial difficulties later in life. In one of the most recent long-term longitudinal studies examining psychiatric outcomes in a large community sample across preadolescence to early adulthood, victims and bully-victims displayed elevated rates of psychiatric disorders in young adulthood (Copeland et al. 2013). Even when childhood psychiatric problems and earlier family hardships were controlled for, victims continued to have a higher prevalence of various anxiety-related disorders. Bully-victims, in turn, were at elevated risk of adult depression in addition to specific phobias and panic disorders. On the basis of additional evidence, bully-victims also appeared to be at the highest risk of suicide-related behaviors (Winsper et al. 2012).

Thus, the evidence suggests that victims of bullying are emotionally distressed both concurrently and over time. Even single incidents of bullying are related to increases in daily levels of anxiety (Nishina & Juvonen 2005). Although the associations between internalizing distress and victimization are likely to be cyclical, it is critical to understand the mediating mechanisms that account for the links between victimization and adjustment problems. In the following section, we turn to investigations that examine the underlying processes between peer victimization and psychosocial difficulties, as well as academic and health problems.

Mediating Mechanisms Underlying Psychosocial Problems

To understand reactions to negative social experiences, it is useful to consider the recipients' or targets' causal perceptions (attributions) of why they are mistreated. By relying on hypothetical scenarios of bullying encounters in which the participant is asked to take the perspective of a victim (Graham & Juvonen 1998), middle-school students who were identified as victims of bullying by their peers were more likely to endorse attributions for bullying that were internal and uncontrollable by them (e.g., "I would not be picked on if I were a cooler kid," "Kids do this to me because they know I won't get them into trouble"). Capturing characterological self-blame (Janoff-Bulman 1979), such attributions partly accounted for the concurrent association between the victim's reputation and level of emotional distress. When examining similar associations over time, another study found that self-blame exacerbated the effects of victimization on internalizing problems (Perren et al. 2013).

Whereas self-blame may help account for why submissive victims are socially anxious and depressed, other-blame can in turn help explain why some victims of bullying want to retaliate in response to being bullied. Indeed, hostile attributions of negative peer intent partly account for why bullied youths experience increased externalizing problems over time (Perren et al. 2013). Thus, subjective interpretations of why victims are bullied enable us to understand the underlying mechanisms that account for or intensify the associations between bullying experiences and both internalizing and externalizing problems (Prinstein et al. 2005).

Mechanisms Underlying School Difficulties and Health Problems

Just as attributions help us comprehend how and why bullied youths display different types of psychosocial difficulties, such problems can in turn help us explain why bullied youths do not do well in school (e.g., Espinoza et al. 2013). Researchers are aware that victims of bullying are likely to be absent from school and to receive low grades from teachers (e.g., Juvonen et al. 2011). Testing a meditational model, Nishina et al. (2005) found that the association between earlier bullying experiences and subsequent school functioning (higher rates of absenteeism and lower grades) can be partly accounted for by emotional distress and somatic complaints. In other words, not only may victimized youths feel anxious, they may also suffer from headaches and other physical ailments that prevent them from coming to school.

An increasing number of studies document that victims of bullying indeed suffer from health problems (for a meta-analysis, see Gini & Pozzoli 2009). A possible physiological pathway by which peer victimization may give rise to health problems implicates the hypothalamic-pituitary-adrenal axis. By examining salivary cortisol samples, one study showed that peer victimization predicted poor health outcomes and that during a stress test victims had altered cortisol levels compared with their nonvictimized peers (Knack et al. 2011). Specifically, higher cortisol immediately after the stressor and lower cortisol 30 min after the stressor were associated with more health problems. These findings suggest that the association between peer victimization and poor physical health can be explained partly by differences in reactivity to stress detected at the neuroendocrine level.

Recent neuroimaging studies have, in turn, explored the underlying neural mechanisms associated with victimization in the form of social exclusion. College students who were led to believe that they were excluded by two others when playing an electronic ball-tossing game (*Cyberball*) showed increased activity in the dorsal anterior cingulate cortex (dACC) compared with those who continued to be included in the game. Moreover, increased dACC activity was associated with more self-reported feelings of stress following *Cyberball* (Eisenberger et al. 2003). The dACC is the same region that is activated when individuals experience physical pain. Studies with 12- and 13-year-old adolescents that used the same paradigm reported more activity in the subgenual anterior cingulate cortex (subACC) (Masten et al. 2011). Given that the subACC is a region associated with affective processes, the results suggest that adolescents have particular difficulty handling the negative emotions associated with social exclusion (see review in Eisenberger 2012). Increased subACC activity following social exclusion in the study on adolescents was also associated with increases in depression 1 year later (Masten et al. 2011). These neuroimaging studies further demonstrate the ways in which the physiological responses of victims of bullying can help us understand their emotional and physical pain.

The above reviewed studies present solid evidence that peer victimization predicts increased adjustment difficulties and health problems over time (e.g., Arseneault et al. 2006), although many symptoms and victimization are likely to be cyclically related over time. In addition to social-cognitive mechanisms (specifically attributions about one's plight as a victim), physiological mechanisms, including neuroendocrine reactions to stress and neural mechanisms in response to social pain, can help explain the level of emotional distress. Emotional and physical stress, in turn, can help account for why victims of bullying often also struggle academically.

BULLYING IN CONTEXT: CYBERSPACE AND SCHOOLS

Thus far we have not said very much about the different contexts in which bullying takes place. Most bullying research is carried out in schools, where youths interact daily with their peers. Yet the online environment that so dominates the lives of today's youths is also a frequent context for peer abuse. In this section we first consider the relatively new topic of bullying in cyberspace. We then turn to factors in the school context that are related to increased rates of bullying and a heightened sense of vulnerability when victimized.

Cyberbullying

Labeled as cyberbullying, electronically mediated bullying involves texting via cell phone; emailing or instant messaging; or posting messages on social networking sites and in chat rooms. Much like bullying in general, cyberbullying can be either direct (i.e., threats or nasty messages are sent to the target) or indirect (i.e., malicious comments, pictures, and private messages are spread much like rumors). Although there are similarities between cyberbullying and other types of bullying in terms of bully-victim overlap and the emotional distress associated with such experiences (e.g., Kowalski et al. 2012), particular contextual features make cyberbullying distinct. Two of the unique features of electronic bullying are its speed and spread: Degrading messages can quickly reach not only the target, but also a vast number of other individuals (Patchin & Hinduja 2006, Ybarra & Mitchell 2004). Another feature associated with cyberbullying is anonymity. When screen names (that can be easily created and changed) are used to send instant messages or to take part in discussions in chat rooms, the identity of the perpetrator can be easily concealed. Such a sense of anonymity, combined with very limited social controls (i.e., monitoring), makes it easy to send a hostile message or post embarrassing pictures of someone (e.g., Slonnje et al. 2013). Because the lack of social cues in online communication also encourages greater self-disclosure (Mesch 2009), cyberspace may provide particularly fertile grounds for bullying. Such questions about the unique features of the online environment have yet to be explored in the cyberbullying literature, which thus far comprises mainly descriptive studies.

The School Context

Bullying is largely studied as a school-based phenomenon, but it is surprising how little empirical research has directly examined school factors as the context for peer victimization. Many student misbehaviors are related to school characteristics, including school size, urbanicity, teacher quality, disciplinary practices, and percentage of ethnic minority students (Gottfredson 2001). However, these school context correlates are inconsistently related to bullying behavior (Bradshaw et al. 2009, Payne & Gottfredson 2004). Probably the most consistent school context correlate of bullying is school climate. To the degree that students do not feel accepted, supported, respected, and treated fairly in their schools, bullying is more of a problem (Bradshaw et al. 2009, Payne & Gottfredson 2004). In the following sections we highlight research on other school context factors that have been more uniquely linked to students becoming the victim of bullying.

Racial/ethnic diversity. A good deal of bullying research is conducted in urban schools where multiple ethnic groups are represented, but very little of that research has systematically examined ethnicity-related context variables such as the racial/ethnic composition of schools (Graham 2006). In part to address this void, one study examined sixth-grade students' experiences of vulnerability at school—defined as perceived victimization, feeling unsafe, feeling lonely, and having low self-worth—in 99 classrooms and 10 middle schools that varied in ethnic diversity (Juvonen et al. 2006). This study documented that greater ethnic diversity at both the classroom and school levels was related to a lower sense of vulnerability among Latino and African American students, including less self-reported victimization. The authors argued that power relations may be more balanced in ethnically diverse schools with multiple ethnic groups and that shared power, in turn, reduces incidents of bullying. (Recall the definition of bullying as a power imbalance.) Although a few studies have examined peer victimization in different ethnic groups (e.g., Hanish & Guerra 2000; also see Graham et al. 2009b), to our knowledge this is the first study to document the buffering effects of greater ethnic diversity.

Organization of instruction. In the school violence literature, the use of academic tracking has been associated with more disruptive behavior on the part of students who are grouped for instruction in low-ability tracks (e.g., Gottfredson 2001). The general argument has been that students who are exposed to a less demanding curriculum and to more deviant peers are at greater risk of antisocial behavior. There is no comparable literature documenting effects of the organization of instruction on the experience of victimization. However, one recent study examined the role of academic teaming in middle school on students' victimization experiences (L. Echols, manuscript submitted). Academic teaming is the practice of grouping students into smaller learning communities for instruction (Thompson & Homestead 2004). Students in these teams often share the majority of their academic classes, limiting their exposure to the larger school community. Although the social and academic benefits of teaming practices have been highlighted in the literature (e.g., Mertens & Flowers 2003), recent analyses suggest that teaming increased (rather than decreased) the experience of victimization for students who were not well liked by their peers (L. Echols, manuscript submitted). In other words, socially vulnerable adolescents who reside within small collectives may have few opportunities to redefine their social identities and instead become increasingly stigmatized.

Deviation from classroom norms. Previous sections of this article reviewed the psychological consequences of being the target of peer abuse. Many victims feel lonely, depressed, and socially anxious, and they tend to blame themselves for their harassment experiences. An important school context factor that may exacerbate these victim-maladjustment linkages is the extent to which victims deviate from the norms of their classroom. Like social misfits (Wright et al. 1986), victims might feel especially bad when they differ from most other students in their classroom.

Two recent studies on victimization and classroom norms are consistent with a social misfit analysis. Focusing on first graders, one study found that elevated levels of victimization and emotional problems were reported by those residing in classrooms where most students got along well and were kind to one another (Leadbeater et al. 2003). To the extent that the first graders' own ratings were high in perceived victimization and deviated from the classroom norm, students were judged by their teachers to be depressed and sad. Similarly, a study of middle-school students documented that the relationship between victimization and social anxiety was strongest when sixth-grade students resided in classrooms that were judged by the their teachers to be orderly rather than disorderly (Bellmore et al. 2004). In this case the more orderly classrooms were those in which students on average scored low on teacher-rated aggression. In both studies, a positive classroom norm (prosocial conduct, high social order) resulted in worse outcomes for victims who deviated from those norms.

The above-described middle-school study also reported that victimization was more predictive of loneliness and social anxiety for students who were members of the majority ethnic group in their classroom (Bellmore et al. 2004). Being a victim when one's own ethnic group holds the numerical balance of power can be a particularly painful example of deviation from the norm. The evidence suggests that victims who are members of the majority ethnic group are more likely to endorse self-blaming attributions ("It must be *me*"), and self-blame, in turn, predicts adjustment difficulties (Graham et al. 2009a). Not only does more diversity with multiple ethnic groups that share the balance of power protect against victimization (Juvonen et al. 2006), but such diversity may also foster enough attributional ambiguity to ward off self-blaming tendencies (S. Graham & A.Z. Taylor, manuscript in preparation).

Thus, research on schooling as a context for bullying is still relatively recent. In the research reviewed we highlight context factors that predict victimization, such as low racial/ethnic diversity and academic teaming for instruction. With regard to the psychological consequences of bullying, we review research on the degree to which victims of bullying in particular classroom settings deviate from the local norms. The first-grade victim in a classroom where most peers are prosocial or the sixth-grade victim in a classroom where most of the students are from his or her ethnic group might have particular adjustment difficulties. A plausible mechanism is that victims who deviate from the norm are particularly vulnerable to self-blaming attributions.

INTERVENTIONS TO PREVENT AND REDUCE BULLYING IN SCHOOL

What can be done to prevent bullying? What works to get rid of it once it has been detected? As public awareness of the serious consequences of school bullying has increased, more attention than ever has been directed toward interventions that can provide answers to these questions. If we had been writing this article 10 years ago, the prevention/intervention literature would have been relatively sparse. For example, in 2001 we coedited one of the first comprehensive books on school bullying (Juvonen & Graham 2001), and that volume did not contain a single chapter on intervention. Today there is a growing international literature on school-based interventions; articles on intervention programs have been included in several edited volumes (e.g., Jimerson et al. 2009, Smith et al. 2004). Some of the programs involve the whole school, whereas others target at-risk individuals (typically bullies). Certain programs focus on prosocial skill building, whereas others rely on the punishment of undesirable behavior (e.g., zero-tolerance policies). The database of empirical studies is sufficiently large to have prompted at least three research syntheses within the past decade (Baldry & Farrington 2007, Smith et al. 2004, Vreeman & Carroll 2007). These syntheses have focused primarily on universal or schoolwide bullying interventions as opposed to targeted programs for bullies and victims, but we outline both types of approaches in the following sections.

Schoolwide Interventions

A schoolwide approach targets all students, their parents, and adults within the school, including administrators, teachers, and staff. Such programs operate under the assumptions that bullying is a systemic social problem and that finding a solution is the collective responsibility of everyone in the school. Systemic prevention requires changing the culture of the whole school rather than (or in addition to) focusing on the behavior of individuals or groups directly involved in bullying incidents.

Most schoolwide programs have their roots in the approach prescribed in the Olweus Bullying Prevention Program (OBPP) developed by Olweus (1993) in Norway. This approach requires increased awareness of the nature of the problem, heightened monitoring, and systematic and consistent responses to incidents of bullying. For example, students are asked to create their own rules about bullying, and they are provided with information about strategies for dealing with bullying and opportunities for classroom discussions about their experiences. Teachers and school staff receive training that includes strategies for preventing problems associated with bullying. Common across all program participants is knowledge of the school's rules about bullying, including what behaviors constitute bullying and what consequences students and staff will face if they engage in those behaviors. Evaluations of OBPP in Norway revealed decreases in self-reported bullying and victimization, decreases in teachers' and students' reports of other students' bullying, and increases in students' perceptions of a positive school climate (Olweus 1993). The success of OBPP in Norway fueled efforts to implement similar schoolwide programs in both Europe and the United States.

Two recent meta-analyses (Merrell & Isava 2008, Smith et al. 2004) and two narrative analyses (Baldry & Farrington 2007, Vreeman & Carroll 2007) of research on these Olweus-inspired antibullying programs provide evidence of the effectiveness of schoolwide approaches. Unfortunately, the effects are modest at best. When considering the reductions in incidents of bullying, only approximately one-third of the school-based interventions included in the Merrell & Isava (2008) meta-analysis showed any positive effects.

Several explanations have been offered for these disappointing findings. First, there is inconsistency in the degree to which the programs conformed to many of the principles of good intervention research, such as random assignment to treatment and control groups, careful monitoring of treatment fidelity, and appropriate intervals between pretests and posttests (Ryan & Smith 2009). Second, most interventions relied heavily on student self-reports of bullying—as target, perpetrator, or witness. Because whole-school approaches are designed to raise awareness of bullying, this increased consciousness might result in elevated reports of bullying, which could then mask treatment effects (Smith et al. 2004). Third, the Olweus intervention was implemented in Norwegian schools, where the norm is small classrooms, well-trained teachers, and relatively homogeneous student populations. An intervention developed in that setting may not be easily portable to other school contexts with very different organizational structures, student demographics, and staff buy-in (Limber 2011). Research on decision making about program adoption reveals that many teachers and administrators in American schools are reluctant to embrace whole-school interventions because they believe either that there is not enough time and space in the curriculum or that developing antibullying attitudes is primarily the responsibility of parents (Cunningham et al. 2009).

It would be premature to conclude that whole-school interventions are not effective inasmuch as some of the more recent programs not included in the previous reviews are showing promising results. One noteworthy program is KiVa, an acronym for *kiusaamista vastaan*, translated from Finnish as "against bullying" (Kärnä et al. 2011). Developed and implemented in Finland, KiVa differs from the Olweus program in its specific focus on bystanders or witnesses to bullying. KiVa aims to develop among bystanders more empathy for victims and strategies to help victims when they are being harassed. A second noteworthy program is WITS (Walk Away, Ignore, Talk It Out, and Seek Help), developed in Canada (Leadbeater & Sukhawathanakul 2011). Focusing on the early grades, WITS raises awareness of the problem of school bullying and then teaches first- to third-grade students a set of social skills to help them resolve interpersonal conflicts. Although both KiVa and WITS have documented reductions in school bullying in Finland and Canada, respectively, neither has yet been evaluated in American schools. A third noteworthy recent program, and one that did originate in the United States, is Steps to Respect (Frey et al. 2009). Implemented during the elementary-school grades in the Pacific Northwest, Steps to Respect is unique in terms of its attention to relational aggression (e.g., gossip, ostracism) and the use of playground observation methods to assess changes in bullying behavior. With more rigorous experimental designs, manualized treatment, multiple informants, and long-term follow-up, all three of these programs are representative of a more current group of whole-school interventions that conform more closely to principles of good preventive interventions.

Targeted Interventions

Unlike schoolwide approaches that address the needs of everyone, a targeted intervention approach focuses on the 10–15% of youths who are involved in bullying incidents as bullies or victims, although research has concentrated almost exclusively on perpetrators rather than victims. The best known of these interventions emerge from the childhood aggression literature and are designed to address the dysfunctional thoughts and behaviors of the children who aggress against others. As described above, a dysfunctional thought pattern characteristic of some aggressive youths—many of whom are also bullies—is a hostile attributional bias, or the tendency to believe that peers are intentionally causing them harm, particularly in ambiguous situations (Dodge et al. 2006). Hostile attributional bias may be only one part of a larger set of deficits that interfere with adaptive social information processing. For example, Crick & Dodge (1994) proposed a five-step social-cognitive model that has become very influential in the bullying intervention literature. In that model, the information processing difficulties of bullies begin when they inaccurately interpret social cues associated with ambiguous peer provocation (e.g., someone is pushed while waiting in line and it is unclear why) and continue as they formulate goals, access from memory a repertoire of possible behavioral responses (e.g., "Should I retaliate or just ignore it?"), and finally choose a response.

One of the most extensive aggression interventions that includes social information-processing skills is Fast Track (e.g., Conduct Probl. Prev. Res. Group 2011). Begun in 1991 at four sites across the United States, Fast Track identified a sample of 890 kindergarten children at risk of conduct problems on the basis of parent and teacher reports. These children were then randomly assigned to either an intervention group or a no-treatment control group. Those in the intervention group participated in a year-long curriculum in first through fifth grades with weekly meetings that included training in social information processing, social problem solving, emotional understanding, communication, and self-control. The social-cognitive component was accompanied by individualized academic tutoring as needed, and there was a parent-training component as well. Intervention activities continued to tenth grade but were individualized in middle school and high school. Intervention participants showed improved social-cognitive skills and fewer conduct problems from the early elementary grades; remarkably, positive gains remained after the intervention ended (i.e., twelfth grade) for boys who were most at risk of conduct problems at entry into the Fast Track (Conduct Probl. Prev. Res. Group 2011).

Fast Track is a unique intervention because of its multiple components and longitudinal design. It is more of a demonstration project showing the potential of good intervention science than a program that could be easily implemented by individual schools. However, other short-term and more streamlined social-cognitive interventions for aggressive boys have also reported improvements in both social information-processing skills and behavior. Examples of these targeted approaches are Brainpower (Hudley & Graham 1993) for elementary school–age boys and the Coping Power Program (Lochman & Wells 2004) for boys transitioning to middle school. Whether the short-term effects of these programs are maintained over time is not known.

No comparable interventions exist to alter the maladaptive social cognitions (attributional biases) of victims. Recall that victims are more likely to blame themselves for their harassment experiences ("It must be *me*") and that self-blaming attributions are related to mental health difficulties (Graham & Juvonen 1998). Thus, one intervention strategy might be to alter the victims' maladaptive thoughts about the causes of their plight. What more adaptive attribution might replace self-blame? In some cases change efforts might target behaviors (e.g., "I was in the wrong place at the wrong time"). The goal would be to help victimized youths recognize that there are responses in their repertoire to prevent future encounters with harassing peers. External attributions can also be adaptive because they protect self-esteem (Weiner 1995). Knowing that others are also victims or that there are some aggressive youths who randomly single out unsuspecting targets can help lessen the victims' tendency to feel humiliated because of self-blame (Nishina & Juvonen 2005). The idea of altering dysfunctional causal thoughts about oneself to produce changes in affect and behavior has produced a rich empirical literature on attribution therapy in educational and clinical settings (Wilson et al. 2002). There is no reason that the guiding assumption of that research cannot be applied to alleviating the plight of victims of bullying. Such an approach could be embedded in the context of a universal intervention program.

The schoolwide bullying prevention approach and the targeted intervention approach, although complementary, represent different schools of thought, and each has advantages and disadvantages. The schoolwide programs aim to build resiliency in all children and to create a more supportive school climate. As critiques of these programs have shown, how one determines that the school climate has actually changed for the better can be challenging. The targeted programs focus on the small number of youths at risk of negative outcomes. Whether or not the intervention has been successful is therefore easier to determine. However, because they rely on accurate identification, targeted interventions need to take into account what we know about the (in)stability of bully and victim status over time. Therefore, interventionists need to be aware of the possibility of false positives if identification is made at a single point in time. Interventionists must also guard against the risk of harmful (iatrogenic) effects that sometimes occur when youths with similar problems are aggregated together for treatment (Dodge et al. 2006).

Fidelity and sustainability, two important components of good interventions (Flay et al. 2005), are likely to be differentially achieved in the whole-school versus targeted approaches. Fidelity, or the consistency with which all of the components of the intervention are implemented, is probably easier to achieve in targeted approaches because there are fewer people, both adults (trainers) and children, to keep track of. With multiple activities at multiple levels involving multiple stakeholders, it is more difficult to monitor treatment fidelity in schoolwide programs, and indeed, that is one explanation for the disappointing findings in many of those interventions (Ryan & Smith 2009). However, sustainability may be easier to achieve in schoolwide programs. Systemic changes in individual students and adults at the classroom, school, and community levels are needed to build a foundation for long-term prevention of bullying. With the exception of Fast Track, most targeted interventions are imported from the outside, are implemented by the researchers, and are usually too short-lived to achieve the stakeholder buy-in needed to sustain them. Rarely are they powerful enough by themselves to maintain behavior change in individual children in the long term.

CONCLUSIONS AND FUTURE DIRECTIONS

Proposing future directions for research on school bullying requires that we distinguish between what the field already knows with much certainty—that is, what issues and complexities have already been resolved—and what issues, challenges, and complexities would benefit from continuing or new research. For example, the field probably does not need more studies in which the primary research goal is to document gender differences in rates of physical and relational bullying. Because the different forms of bullying (physical, verbal, and relational; or direct and indirect) tend to be highly correlated in research, there may be only limited theoretical payoff of more studies that seek to identify the unique correlates of each form.

On the basis of our understanding of school bullying as reviewed in this article, we suggest four directions for future research. None of the proposed directions can be discussed in detail, and surely they reflect our biases. We offer them as food for thought to enrich the study of bullying in schools.

Longitudinal Research on Victimization

Because the childhood aggression literature has a long history in both American and international research, that field has benefited from numerous longitudinal studies from multiple sites around the world that have identified the trajectories of aggressive children and the long-term risk factors associated with such behavior (Dodge et al. 2006). Consensus has emerged in longitudinal studies about the ways to assess aggressive behavior and the critical developmental periods that would need to be captured. These agreements have made it possible to aggregate data sets across multiple sites, yielding a robust picture of continuities and discontinuities in childhood aggression trajectories (e.g., Broidy et al. 2003). In part because American researchers did not begin to seriously study peer victimization before the 1990s, the field does not have a comparable multisite, multinational longitudinal literature on the trajectories of victims of bullying. Such studies are sorely needed. We know that the plight of the victim is a real one—socially, emotionally, physically, and academically—and that the underpinnings of that plight are biological, psychological, and contextual. What we do not know is why the experiences of victimization fluctuate over time, whether victim trajectories may decline developmentally (much like physically aggressive youths seem to "age out"), and what the undisputed long-term consequences of peer abuse are. Answers to these questions can be achieved only with collaborative longitudinal studies that cast a wide empirical net across age, time, setting, and measurement.

Victimization as Social Stigma

In this article we do not extensively discuss the individual characteristics of youths that put them at risk of victimization. Given space limitations, we mention almost in passing that youths who are ethnic or sexual minorities, are obese, or have mental and physical disabilities might be most at risk. A 2011 report on school bullying by the US Commission on Civil Rights confirms these as risk factors. After examining a compendium of school district data, legal briefs, and testimony of experts, the Commission concluded that "...bullying based on students' identities—such as their sex, race, ethnicity or national origin, disability, sexual orientation or gender identity, or religion—can be particularly damaging. Unfortunately these forms of bullying are all too common in American schools" (US Comm. Civ. Rights 2011, p. 8).

If these stigmatized social identities are among the major causes of victimization, it is surprising how unconnected the empirical literatures addressing these stigmas remain. For example, there is a growing literature on the experience of school-based racial discrimination during adolescence, but most of that research has evolved from the adult racial discrimination literature, drawing few parallels to peer victimization research (Benner & Graham 2013). Similarly, childhood obesity research is largely found in the child health literature, despite knowledge that obese youths are often targets of peer harassment (e.g., Pearce et al. 2002); and research on bullying of LBGT youths, although increasing (e.g., Toomey et al. 2010), has not been well informed by the peer relations literature. Furthermore, none of the bullying interventions that we review herein specifically targeted any of these stigmatized groups.

We would like to see much more cross-fertilization between these separate social identity literatures and the school bullying literature. For example, are the correlates and mediating mechanisms associated with the plight of the victim the same in each of these stigmatized identities, or are they qualitatively different? Should schoolwide or targeted interventions be developed and tailored to each type of social stigma, or should the more general approaches in the bullying literature be expected to improve the plight of all victims, regardless of their stigmatized identity? Does it make a difference for the effectiveness of targeted intervention if an individual has multiple stigmatized identities that are experienced simultaneously (e.g., the ethnic minority boy who is LGBT)? We have no definitive answers to these questions. However, we believe that a more integrated developmental approach to social stigma—understanding commonalities and differences across particular identities and bringing this understanding to bear on intervention research—will move the bullying literature closer to addressing some of the most powerful social stressors of childhood and adolescence.

School Context Matters

Most bullying takes place at school and among schoolmates. Yet as our review shows, researchers know surprisingly little about the characteristics of schools that promote or protect against bullying by one's peers. One contextual characteristic that we believe to be particularly understudied is the racial/ethnic composition of classrooms and schools. A great deal of American bullying research is conducted in urban schools where multiple ethnic groups are represented, but not much of that research has examined the role that ethnicity plays in the experience of victimization. We do not think that ethnic group per se is the critical variable, given that there is no consistent evidence in the literature that any one ethnic group is more or less likely to be the target of bullying (Graham et al. 2009b). Rather, the more important context variable is whether ethnic groups are the numerical majority or minority in their school. Numerical minority group members appear to be at greater risk of victimization because they have fewer same-ethnicity peers to help ward off potential bullies (Hanish & Guerra 2002); youths who are victims as well as members of the majority ethnic group may suffer the most because they deviate from the norms of their group to be powerful (Bellmore et al. 2004); and ethnically diverse classrooms may reduce rates of victimization because the numerical balance of power is shared among many groups (Juvonen et al. 2006).

We view these studies as a useful starting point for a much fuller exploration of the ways in which school ethnic diversity can be a protective factor. Among the possible new directions for this research are the role of cross-ethnic friendships as sources of support and the degree to which students with stigmatized identities experience more acceptance and less harassment in ethnically diverse schools. Today's multiethnic urban schools are products of the dramatic changes in the racial/ethnic composition of the school-aged population in just a single generation. They are ideal settings in which to test hypotheses about the role of ethnic diversity in shaping the experience of victimization. Additionally, examination of ethnic diversity can provide some important insights into protective factors that may also apply to other forms of diversity (e.g., students with disabilities, sexual minority youths).

Our review of the plight of the victim suggests the need for more studies on the degree to which schools are organized to be sensitive to developmental periods when youths may be most at risk. The middle-school transition, for example, appears to be a particularly vulnerable period in part because social dominance hierarchies become reconfigured and reestablished very quickly. We are struck by how little of the middle-school transition literature addresses bullying even though it is known to peak during these years. As we note above, some of the instructional practices that are designed to be both academically and socially supportive during transitions, such as small learning communities and academic teaming, may actually be risky for youths with reputations as victims (L. Echols, manuscript submitted). We would like to see a more systematic analysis by bullying researchers of other presumably sound pedagogical practices in schools that could be disadvantageous for youths at risk of victimization.

Designing Interventions That Work

The schoolwide intervention literature is large and increasing, but in some respects it is disappointing. Many of the programs simply do not work. Evaluations of these programs show that part of the problem is methodological; too many studies do not conform to good principles of prevention and intervention research. An important future direction is that interventions be designed with random assignments to treatment and control conditions, manualized treatments, careful attention to fidelity and dosage, multiple outcome measures, and longitudinal follow-up. The KiVa program that we introduce in our intervention section has many of these qualities and is showing promising results in Finnish schools (Kärnä et al. 2011). Strong school-based interventions should also address mediating and moderating mechanisms (Why does the treatment work, and for whom?). Our review identifies important social-cognitive mediators, such as attributions for victimization, and moderators, such as chronicity of abuse and the ethnic diversity of one's school, that could be included and examined in the next generation of school-based interventions.

Although interventions that take a whole-school approach are here to stay, we do not want to lose sight of the plight of the victims and a more nuanced approach to intervention that better acknowledges their plight. We conclude with three examples of what such an approach might entail. First, we know that school transitions are risky times for most youths, but especially for victim-prone youths whose negative experiences might spike during those times. Preventive interventions that offer victims special support to navigate these turbulent transitions would be worthwhile. The buffering effect of even one friendship is well documented in the victimization literature, and these underutilized findings could be incorporated into a preventive approach. Second, most schoolwide interventions or even targeted interventions for bullies focus on changing direct forms of physical aggression and verbal aggression such as name-calling and insults. Our review also underscores that indirect forms of victimization such as social ostracism and cybertactics are particularly insidious because they can go undetected for long periods. A challenge for interventionists is to figure out a way to incorporate cyberbullying and other more covert forms of harassment that are not easily detected. Third, the social hierarchy literature reminds us to what extent popular and dominant youths control peer norms and the degree to which bystanders are unwilling to stand up to the bully or come to the aid of the victim. Intervention approaches that can harness the influence of these powerful youths toward more prosocial goals and norms are especially needed (for a recent example of such an approach, see Paluck & Shepherd 2012). It may not be necessary to take a top-down approach to schoolwide intervention if we can penetrate social norms and raise collective responsibility by working directly with the youth who most directly shape peer norms.

IMPLICATIONS FOR INTERVENTION

Popular and dominant bullies control the peer norms and the degree to which bystanders are unwilling to come to the aid of the victim. It may be necessary to penetrate social norms and raise collective responsibility by working directly with the youths who most directly shape peer norms.

SUMMARY POINTS

1. Bullying perpetration and victimization are more unstable than stable, yet little is known about what accounts for the discontinuous trajectories of bullies or victims.

2. Bullying is likely to be motivated by social dominance that peaks at times of social reorganization associated with environmental (e.g., school) transitions.

3. The social prominence of bullies and their tendency to blame others partly explain their (overly) positive self-views, whereas bystander reinforcement explains why it is difficult to intervene with bullying behaviors.

4. Victims' reactions or responses to bullying (internalizing problems giving rise to submissive responses versus externalizing behaviors giving rise to hostile retaliation) may partly account for the continuous victim trajectories.

5. Unless youths have friends or are well accepted by their peers, individual risk factors (e.g., obesity, disabilities, LGBT status) that indicate a deviation from the group norm increase the likelihood of being bullied.

6. When victims of bullying deviate from the group norms, they are particularly vulnerable because of their self-blaming attributions.

7. Peer victimization predicts increased adjustment difficulties and health problems over time; social-cognitive mechanisms (specifically attributions about one's plight as a victim) as well as physiological mechanisms, including neuroendocrine reactions to stress and neural mechanisms in response to social pain, can help explain emotional and physical health problems.

8. Fidelity of implementation is a challenge facing schoolwide antibullying interventions, whereas targeted intervention effects are difficult to sustain.

FUTURE ISSUES

1. A multisite, multinational longitudinal literature on the trajectories of victims of bullying is needed to explain how the experiences of victimization fluctuate over time, how some children recover from their plight, and what the undisputed long-term consequences of peer abuse are.

2. Investigators should connect research on bullying with studies conducted on discrimination of potentially stigmatized groups based on sex, race, ethnicity or national origin, disability, sexual orientation or gender identity, and religion to understand the similarities among them and the unique features and consequences of each.

3. School contextual factors (e.g., ethnic composition of schools, organizational and instructional practices) that can protect youths from bullying and alleviate the social or physical pain associated with victimization experiences should be examined.

4. Researchers should further develop rigorously evaluated interventions in light of the most current research evidence on bullying and victimization that take into account the discrete features of contexts (e.g., school or online) in which bullying and victimization unfold and try to target the most insidious forms of bullying that are difficult for outsiders to detect.

DISCLOSURE STATEMENT

The authors are not aware of any affiliations, memberships, funding, or financial holdings that might be perceived as affecting the objectivity of this review.

LITERATURE CITED

Adler PA, Adler P. 1998. *Peer Power: Preadolescent Culture and Identity*. New Brunswick, NJ: Rutgers Univ. Press

Archer J, Coyne SM. 2005. An integrated review of indirect, relational, and social aggression. *Personal. Soc. Psychol. Rev.* 9:212–30

Archer J. 2004. Sex differences in aggression in real-world settings: a meta-analytic review. *Rev. Gen. Psychol.* 8:291–322

Arseneault L, Walsh E, Trzesniewski K, Newcombe R, Caspi A, Moffitt TE. 2006. Bullying victimization uniquely contributes to adjustment problems in young children: a nationally representative cohort study. *Pediatrics* 118:130–38

Artz S. 2005. To die for: violent adolescent girls' search for male attention. In *The Development and Treatment of Girlhood Aggression*, ed. D Pepler, K Madsen, C Webster, K Levene, pp. 135–60. Mahwah, NJ: Erlbaum

Baldry AC, Farrington DP. 2007. Effectiveness of programs to prevent school bullying. *Vict. Offenders* 2:183–204

Bellmore A, Witkow M, Graham S, Juvonen J. 2004. Beyond the individual: the impact of ethnic diversity and behavioral norms on victims' adjustment. *Dev. Psychol.* 40:1159–72

Benner AD, Graham S. 2013. The antecedents and consequences of racial/ethnic discrimination during adolescence: Does the source of discrimination matter? *Dev. Psychol.* 49:1602–13

Bettencourt A, Farrell A, Liu W, Sullivan T. 2012. Stability and change in patterns of peer victimization and aggression during adolescence. *J. Clin. Child Adolesc.* 27:1–13

Björkqvist K, Österman K, Kaukiainen A. 2000. Social intelligence − empathy = aggression? *Aggress. Viol. Behav.* 5:191–200

Björkqvist K, Österman K, Lagerspetz KMJ. 1994. Sex differences in covert aggression among adults. *Aggress. Behav.* 20:27–33

Boivin M, Dodge KA, Coie JD. 1995. Individual-group behavioral similarity and peer status in experimental play groups of boys: the social misfit revisited. *J. Personal. Soc. Psychol.* 69:269–79

Boulton MJ, Trueman M, Flemington I. 2002. Associations between secondary school pupils' definitions of bullying, attitudes towards bullying, and tendencies to engage in bullying: age and sex differences. *Educ. Stud.* 28:353–70

Bradshaw CP, Sawyer AL, O'Brennan LM. 2009. A social disorganization perspective on bullying-related attitudes and behaviors: the influence of school context. *Am. J. Commun. Psychol.* 43:204–20

Brame B, Nagin DS, Tremblay RE. 2001. Developmental trajectories of physical aggression from school entry to late adolescence. *J. Child Psychol. Psychiatry* 42:503–12

Broidy LM, Nagin DS, Tremblay RE, Bates JE, Brame B, et al. 2003. Developmental trajectories of childhood disruptive behaviors and adolescent delinquency: a six-site, cross-national study. *Dev. Psychol.* 39:222–45

Buhs ES, Ladd GW, Herald SL. 2006. Peer exclusion and victimization: processes that mediate the relation between peer group rejection and children's classroom engagement and achievement? *J. Educ. Psychol.* 98:1–13

Burk LR, Armstrong JM, Park J-H, Zahn-Waxler C, Klein MH, Essex MJ. 2010. Stability of early identified aggressive victim status in elementary school and associations with later mental health problems and functional impairments. *J. Abnorm. Child Psychol.* 39:225–38

Cairns RB, Cairns BD. 1994. *Lifelines and Risks: Pathways of Youth in Our Time*. New York: Cambridge Univ. Press. 218 pp.

Camodeca M, Goossens FA, Terwogt MM, Schuengel C. 2002. Bullying and victimization among school-age children: stability and links to proactive and reactive aggression. *Soc. Dev.* 11:332–45

Card NA, Stucky BD, Sawalani GM, Little TD. 2008. Direct and indirect aggression during childhood and adolescence: a meta-analytic review of gender differences, intercorrelations, and relations to maladjustment. *Child Dev.* 79:1185–229

Cillessen AHN, Borch C. 2006. Developmental trajectories of adolescent popularity: a growth curve modelling analysis. *J. Adolesc.* 29:935–59

Cillessen AHN, Mayeux L. 2004. From censure to reinforcement: developmental changes in the association between aggression and social status. *Child Dev.* 75:147–63

Conduct Probl. Prev. Res. Group. 2011. The effects of the Fast Track preventive intervention on the development of conduct disorder across childhood. *Child Dev.* 82:331–45

Copeland WE, Wolke D, Angold A, Costello EJ. 2009. Adult psychiatric outcomes of bullying and being bullied by peers in childhood and adolescence. *JAMA* 70:419–26

Coyne SM, Nelson DA, Underwood M. 2011. Aggression in children. In *The Wiley-Blackwell Handbook of Childhood Cognitive Development*, ed. PK Smith, CH Hart, pp. 491–509. Oxford, UK: Wiley. 2nd ed.

Crick NR, Dodge KA. 1994. A review and reformulation of social information processing mechanisms in children's social adjustment. *Psychol Bull.* 115:74–101

Crick NR, Grotpeter JK. 1995. Relational aggression, gender, and social-psychological adjustment. *Child Dev.* 66:710–22

Crick NR, Ostrov JM, Kawabata Y. 2007. Relational aggression and gender: an overview. In *The Cambridge Handbook of Violent Behavior and Aggression*, ed. DJ Flannery, AT Vazsonyi, ID Waldman, DJ Flannery, AT Vazsonyi, ID Waldman, pp. 245–59. Cambridge, UK: Cambridge Univ. Press

Cunningham C, Vaillancourt T, Rimas H, Deal K, Cunninghm L, et al. 2009. Modeling the bullying prevention program preferences of educators: a discrete choice conjoint experiment. *J. Abnorm. Child Psychol.* 37:929–43

De Castro BO, Veerman JW, Koops W, Bosch JD, Monshouwer HJ. 2002. Hostile attribution of intent and aggressive behavior: a meta-analysis. *Child Dev.* 73:916–34

Dodge KA, Coie JD, Lynam D. 2006. Aggression and antisocial behavior in youth. In *Handbook of Child Psychology: Social, Emotional, and Personality Development*, ed. W Damon, RL Lerner, N Eisenberg, pp. 710–88. Hoboken, NJ: Wiley. 6th ed.

Dodge KA, Dishion TJ, Lansford JE. 2006. *Deviant Peer Influence in Programs for Youth*. New York: Guilford

Dodge KA. 1993. Social-cognitive mechanisms in the development of conduct disorder and depression. *Annu. Rev. Psychol.* 44:559–84

Eder D. 1985. The cycle of popularity: interpersonal relations among female adolescents. *Sociol. Educ.* 58:154–65

Egan SK, Perry DG. 1998. Does low self-regard invite victimization? *Dev. Psychol.* 34:299–309

Eisenberger NI, Lieberman MD, Williams KD. 2003. Does rejection hurt? An fMRI study of social exclusion. *Science* 5643:290–92

Eisenberger NI. 2012. The pain of social disconnection: examining the shared neural underpinnings of physical and social pain. *Neuroscience* 13:421–34

Espelage DL, Bosworth K, Simon TR. 2001. Short-term stability and prospective correlates of bullying in middle-school students: an examination of potential demographic, psychosocial, and environmental influences. *Violence Vict.* 16:411–26

Presents a definitive review of research on gender differences in various forms of aggression.

Espinoza G, Gonzales NA, Fuligni AJ. 2013. Daily school peer victimization experiences among Mexican American adolescents: associations with psychosocial, physical and school Adjustment. *J. Youth Adolesc.* In press

Feshbach ND. 1969. Sex differences in children's modes of aggressive responses toward outsiders. *Merrill Palmer Q.* 15:249–58

Flay BR, Biglan A, Boruch RF, González Castro F, Gottfredson D, Kellam S, et al. 2005. Standards of evidence: criteria for efficacy, effectiveness, and dissemination. *Prev. Sci.* 6:151–75

Fox CL, Boulton MJ. 2006. Longitudinal associations between submissive/nonassertive social behavior and different types of peer victimization. *Violence Vict.* 21:383–400

Frey KS, Hirschstein MK, Edstrom LV, Snell JL. 2009. Observed reductions in school bullying, nonbullying aggression, and destructive bystander behavior: a longitudinal evaluation. *J. Educ. Psychol.* 101:466–81

Gini G, Albiero P, Benelli B, Altoè G. 2007. Does empathy predict adolescents' bullying and defending behavior? *Aggress. Behav.* 33:467–76

Gini G, Pozzoli T. 2009. Association between bullying and psychosomatic problems: a meta-analysis. *Pediatrics* 123:1059–65

Gottfredson DC. 2001. *Schools and Delinquency.* Cambridge, UK: Cambridge Univ. Press

Graham S, Bellmore A, Nishina A, Juvonen J. 2009a. "It must be *me*": ethnic diversity and attributions for victimization in middle school. *J. Youth Adolesc.* 38:487–99

Graham S, Juvonen J. 1998. Self-blame and peer victimization in middle school: an attributional analysis. *Dev. Psychol.* 34:587–38

Graham S, Taylor AZ, Ho AY. 2009b. Race and ethnicity in peer relationship research. In *Handbook of Peer Interactions, Relationships, and Groups*, ed. KH Rubin, WM Bukowski, B Laursen, pp. 294–413. New York: Guilford

Graham S. 2006. Peer victimization in school: exploring the ethnic context. *Curr. Dir. Psychol. Sci.* 15:317–20

Hanish LD, Guerra NG. 2000. Predictors of peer victimization among urban youth. *Soc. Dev.* 9:521–43

Hanish LD, Guerra NG. 2002. A longitudinal analysis of patterns of adjustment following peer victimization. *Dev. Psychopathol.* 14:69–89

Hawker DSJ, Boulton MJ. 2000. Twenty years' research on peer victimization and psychosocial maladjustment: a meta-analytic review of cross-sectional studies. *J. Child Psychol. Psychiatry* 41:441–55

Hawley P. 1999. The ontogenesis of social dominance: a strategy-based evolutionary perspective. *Dev. Rev.* 19:97–132

Hinde RA. 1974. *Biological Bases of Human Social Behaviour.* New York: McGraw-Hill

Hodges EVE, Boivin M, Vitaro F, Bukowski WM. 1999. The power of friendship: protection against an escalating cycle of peer victimization. *Dev. Psychol.* 35:94–101

Hodges EVE, Perry DG. 1999. Personal and interpersonal antecedents and consequences of victimization by peers. *J. Personal. Soc. Psychol.* 76:677–85

Hudley C, Graham S. 1993. An attributional intervention with African American boys labeled as aggressive. *Child Dev.* 64:124–38

Hymel S, Bowker A, Woody E. 1993. Aggressive versus withdrawn unpopular children: variations in peer and self-perceptions in multiple domains. *Child Dev.* 64:879–96

Janoff-Bulman R. 1979. Characterological and behavioral self-blame: inquiries into depression and rape. *J. Personal. Soc. Psychol.* 35:1798–809

Jimerson SR, Swearer SM, Espelage DL. 2009. *Handbook of Bullying in Schools: An International Perspective.* New York: Routledge

Jolliffe D, Farrington DP. 2006. Examining the relationship between low empathy and bullying. *Aggress. Behav.* 32:540–50

Juvonen J, Galván A. 2008. Peer influence in involuntary social groups: lessons from research on bullying. In *Understanding Peer Influence in Children and Adolescents*, ed. MJ Prinstein, KA Dodge, pp. 225–44. New York: Guilford

Juvonen J, Graham S, Schuster MA. 2003. Bullying among young adolescents: the strong, the weak, and the troubled. *Pediatrics* 112:1231–37

Juvonen J, Graham S. 2001. *Peer Harassment in School: The Plight of the Vulnerable and Victimized.* New York: Guilford

Represents one of the first edited volumes by American researchers on peer victimization in schools.

Juvonen J, Nishina A, Graham S. 2000. Peer harassment, psychological adjustment, and school functioning in early adolescence. *J. Educ. Psychol.* 92:349–59

Juvonen J, Nishina A, Graham S. 2006. Ethnic diversity and perceptions of safety in urban middle schools. *Psychol. Sci.* 17:393–400

Juvonen J, Wang Y, Espinoza G. 2011. Bullying experiences and compromised academic performance across middle school grades. *J. Early Adolesc.* 31:152–73

Juvonen J, Wang Y, Espinoza G. 2013. Physical aggression, spreading of rumors, and social prominence in early adolescence: reciprocal effects supporting gender similarities? *J. Early Adolesc.* In press

Kärnä A, Voeten M, Little T, Poskiparta E, Kaljonen A, Salmivalli C. 2011. A large scale evaluation of the KiVa anti-bullying program: grades 4–6. *Child Dev.* 82:311–30

Katz-Wise SL, Hyde JS. 2012. Victimization experiences of lesbian, gay, and bisexual individuals: a meta-analysis. *J. Sex Res.* 49:142–67

Knack JM, Jensen-Campbell LA, Baum A. 2011. Worse than sticks and stones? Bullying is associated with altered HPA axis functioning and poorer health. *Brain Cogn.* 77:183–90

Kochel KP, Ladd GW, Rudolph KD. 2012. Longitudinal associations among youth depressive symptoms, peer victimization, and low peer acceptance: an interpersonal process perspective. *Child Dev.* 83:637–50

Kochenderfer BJ, Ladd GW. 1997. Victimized children's responses to peers' aggression: behaviors associated with reduced versus continued victimization. *Dev. Psychopathol.* 9:59–73

Kochenderfer-Ladd B, Wardrop JL. 2001. Chronicity and instability of children's peer victimization experiences as predictors of loneliness and social satisfaction trajectories. *Child Dev.* 72:134–51

Kowalski RM, Morgan CA, Limber SP. 2012. Traditional bullying as a potential warning sign of cyberbullying. *Sch. Psychol. Int.* 33:505–19

LaFontana KM, Cillessen AHN. 2010. Developmental changes in the priority of perceived status in childhood and adolescence. *Soc. Dev.* 19:130–47

Lagerspetz KMJ, Björkqvist K, Berts M, King E. 1982. Group aggression among school children in three schools. *Scand. J. Psychol.* 23:45–52

Lagerspetz KMJ, Björkqvist K, Peltonen T. 1988. Is indirect aggression typical of females? Gender differences in aggressiveness in 11- to 12-year-old children. *Aggress. Behav.* 14:403–14

Leadbeater B, Hoglund W, Woods T. 2003. Changing contexts? The effects of a primary prevention program on classroom levels of peer relational and physical victimization. *J. Community Psychol.* 31:397–418

Leadbeater BJ, Sukhawathanakul P. 2011. Multi-component programs for reducing peer victimization in early elementary school: a longitudinal evaluation of WITS primary program. *J. Community Psychol.* 39:606–20

Limber SP. 2011. Development, evaluation, and future directions of the Olweus bullying prevention program. *J. Sch. Violence* 10:71–87

Little T, Henrich C, Jones S, Hawley P. 2003. Disentangling the "whys" from the "whats" of aggressive behaviour. *Int. Behav. Dev.* 27:122–33

Lochman JE, Wells KC. 2004. The coping power program for preadolescent boys and their parents: outcome effects at the 1-year follow up. *J. Consult. Clin. Psychol.* 72:571–78

Loeber R, Hay D. 1997. Key issues in the development of aggression and violence from childhood to early adulthood. *Annu. Rev. Psychol.* 48:371–410

Masten CL, Eisenberger NI, Borofsky LA, McNealy K, Pfeifer JH, Dapretto M. 2011. Subgenual anterior cingulate responses to peer rejection: a marker of adolescents' risk for depression. *Dev. Pathopsychol.* 23:283–92

Merrell K, Isava D. 2008. How effective are school bullying intervention programs? A meta-analysis of intervention research. *Sch. Psychol. Q.* 23:26–42

Merten DE. 1997. The meaning of meanness: popularity, competition, and conflict among junior high school girls. *Sociol. Educ.* 70:175–91

Mertens SB, Flowers N. 2003. Middle school practices improve student achievement in high poverty schools. *Middle Sch. J.* 35:33–43

Mesch GS. 2009. Parental mediation, online activities, and cyberbullying. *Cyber Psychol. Behav.* 12:387–93

Nadeem E, Graham S. 2005. Early puberty, peer victimization, and internalizing symptoms in ethnic minority adolescents. *J. Early Adolesc.* 25:197–222

Nakamoto J, Schwartz D. 2010. Is peer victimization associated with academic achievement? A meta-analytic review. *Soc. Dev.* 19:221–42

Nansel TR, Overpeck M, Pilla RS, Ruan W, Simons-Morton B, Scheidt P. 2001. Bullying behaviors among US youth: prevalence and association with psychosocial adjustment. *JAMA* 285:2094–100

Nishina A, Juvonen J, Witkow MR. 2005. Sticks and stones may break my bones, but names will make me feel sick: the psychosocial, somatic, and scholastic consequences of peer harassment. *J. Clin. Child Adolesc.* 34:37–48

Nishina A, Juvonen J. 2005. Daily reports of witnessing and experiencing peer harassment in middle school. *Child Dev.* 76:435–50

Nylund K, Bellmore A, Nishina A, Graham S. 2007. Subtypes, severity, and structural stability of peer victimization: What does latent class analysis say? *Child Dev.* 78:1706–22

O'Connell P, Pepler D, Craig W. 1999. Peer involvement in bullying: insights and challenges for intervention. *J. Adolesc.* 22:437–52

Ojanen T, Grönroos M, Salmivalli C. 2005. An interpersonal circumplex model of children's social goals: links with peer-reported behavior and sociometric status. *Dev. Psychol.* 41:699–710

Olweus D. 1978. *Aggression in the Schools: Bullies and Whipping Boys.* New York: Hemisphere Publ.

Olweus D. 1993. *Bullying at School: What We Know and What We Can Do.* Oxford, UK/Cambridge, Mass.: Blackwell

Paluck LE, Shepherd H. 2012. The salience of social referents: a field experiment on collective norms and harassment behavior in a school social network. *J. Personal. Soc. Psychol.* 103:899–915

Parke RD, Slaby RG. 1983. The development of aggression. *Handb. Child Psychol.* 4:547–641

Parkhurst JT, Hopmeyer A. 1998. Sociometric popularity and peer-perceived popularity: two distinct dimensions of peer status. *J. Early Adolesc.* 18:125–44

Patchin JW, Hinduja S. 2006. Bullies move beyond the schoolyard a preliminary look at cyberbullying. *Youth Violence Juv. Justice* 4:148–69

Payne AA, Gottfredson DC. 2004. Schools and bullying: school factors related to bullying and school-based interventions. In *Bullying: Implications for the Classroom*, ed. CE Sander, GD Phye, pp. 159–76. San Diego: Elsevier

Pearce MJ, Boergers J, Prinstein MJ. 2002. Adolescent obesity, overt and relational peer victimization, and romantic relationships. *Obesity* 10:386–93

Pellegrini AD, Bartini M, Brooks F. 1999. School bullies, victims, and aggressive victims: factors relating to group affiliation and victimization in early adolescence. *J. Educ. Psychol.* 91:216–24

Pellegrini AD, Long JD. 2002. A longitudinal study of bullying, dominance, and victimization during the transition from primary school through secondary school. *Br. J. Dev. Psychol.* 20:259–80

Perren S, Ettekal I, Ladd G. 2013. The impact of peer victimization on later maladjustment: mediating and moderating effects of hostile and self-blaming attributions. *J. Child Psychol. Psychiatry* 54:46–55

Perry DG, Williard JC, Perry LC. 1990. Peers' perceptions of the consequences that victimized children provide aggressors. *Child Dev.* 61:1310–25

Prinstein MJ, Cheah CSL, Guyer AE. 2005. Peer victimization, cue interpretation, and internalizing symptoms: preliminary concurrent and longitudinal findings for children and adolescents. *J. Clin. Child Adolesc.* 34:11–24

Prinstein MJ, Cillessen AH. 2003. Forms and functions of adolescent peer aggression associated with high levels of peer status. *Merrill Palmer Q.* 49:310–42

Reijntjes A, Kamphuis JH, Prinzie P, Telch MJ. 2010. Peer victimization and internalizing problems in children: a meta-analysis of longitudinal studies. *Child Abuse Negl.* 34:244–52

Reynolds BM, Juvonen J. 2010. The role of early maturation, perceived popularity, and rumors in the emergence of internalizing symptoms among adolescent girls. *J. Youth Adolesc.* 40:1407–22

Rigby K, Johnson B. 2006. Expressed readiness of Australian schoolchildren to act as bystanders in support of children who are being bullied. *Educ. Psychol.* 26:425–40

Rivers I, Smith PK. 1994. Types of bullying behaviour and their correlates. *Aggress. Behav.* 20:359–68

Rodkin PC, Farmer TW, Pearl R, Acker RV. 2006. They're cool: social status and peer group supports for aggressive boys and girls. *Soc. Dev.* 15:175–204

Describes the first successful whole-school bullying intervention.

Rudolph KD, Troop-Gordon W, Hessel ET, Schmidt JD. 2011. A latent growth curve analysis of early and increasing peer victimization as predictors of mental health across elementary school. *J. Clin. Child Adolesc. Psychol.* 40:111–22

Ryan W, Smith JD. 2009. Antibullying programs in schools: How effective are evaluation practices? *Prev Sci.* 10:248–59

Salmivalli C, Isaacs J. 2005. Prospective relations among victimization, rejection, friendlessness, and children's self- and peer-perceptions. *Child Dev.* 76:1161–71

Salmivalli C, Lagerspetz K, Björkqvist K, Österman K, Kaukiainen A. 1998. Bullying as a group process: participant roles and their relations to social status within the group. *Aggress. Behav.* 22:1–15

Salmivalli C, Ojanen T, Haanpää J, Peets K. 2005. "I'm OK but you're not" and other peer-relational schemas: explaining individual differences in children's social goals. *Dev. Psychol.* 41: 363–75

Presents a current review of research on the multiple roles involved in bullying episodes.

Salmivalli C. 2010. Bullying and the peer group: a review. *Aggress. Viol. Behav.* 15:112–20

Scholte RHJ, Engels RCME, Overbeek G, Kemp RAT, Haselager GJT. 2007. Stability in bullying and victimization and its association with social adjustment in childhood and adolescence. *J. Abnorm. Child Psychol.* 35:217–28

Schwartz D, Dodge KA, Coie JD. 1993. The emergence of chronic peer victimization in boys' play groups. *Child Dev.* 64:1755–72

Sijtsema JJ, Veenstra R, Lindenberg S, Salmivalli C. 2009. Empirical test of bullies' status goals: assessing direct goals, aggression, and prestige. *Aggress. Behav.* 35:57–67

Slonnje R, Smith PK, Frisen A. 2013. The nature of cyberbullying, and strategies for prevention. *Comput. Hum. Behav.* 29:26–32

Smith J, Schneider B, Smith P, Ananiadou K. 2004. The effectiveness of whole-school antibullying programs: a synthesis of evaluation research. *Sch. Psychol. Rev.* 33:547–60

Smith P, Sharp S. 1994. *School Bullying: Insights and Perspectives.* New York: Routledge

Describes successful bullying interventions from around the world.

Smith PK, Pepler D, Rigby K. 2004. *Bullying in Schools: How Successful Can Interventions Be?* Cambridge, UK: Cambridge Univ. Press

Son E, Parish SL, Peterson NA. 2012. National prevalence of peer victimization among young children with disabilities in the United States. *Child. Youth Serv. Rev.* 34:1540–45

Stassen Berger K. 2007. Update on bullying at school: science forgotten? *Dev. Rev.* 27:90–126

Stormshak EA, Bierman KL, Bruschi C, Dodge KA, Coie JD. 1999. The relation between behavior problems and peer preference in different classroom contexts. *Child Dev.* 70:169–82

Sutton J, Smith PK, Swettenham J. 1999. Bullying and "theory of mind": a critique of the "social skills deficit" view of anti-social behaviour. *Soc. Dev.* 8:117–27

Thompson K, Homestead ER. 2004. 30 years of advocating for young adolescents: middle school students and parents through the 1970s, 1980s, and 1990s. *Middle Sch. J.* 35:56–56

Toomey RB, Ryan C, Diaz RM, Card NA, Russell ST. 2010. Gender-nonconforming lesbian, gay, bisexual, and transgender youth: school victimization and young adult psychosocial adjustment. *Dev. Psychol.* 46:1580–89

Underwood MK. 2003. *Social Aggression Among Girls.* New York: Guilford

US Comm. Civ. Rights. 2011. *Peer-to-Peer Violence + Bullying: Examining the Federal Response.* Washington, DC: US Comm. Civ. Rights

Vreeman RC, Carroll AE. 2007. A systematic review of school-based interventions to prevent bullying. *Arch. Pediatr. Adolesc. Med.* 161:78–88

Weiner B. 1995. *Judgments of Responsibility: A Foundation for a Theory of Social Conduct.* New York: Guilford

Wilson T, Damiani M, Shelton N. 2002. Improving the academic performance of college students with brief attributional interventions. In *Improving Academic Achievement: Impact of Psychological Factors on Education*, ed. J Aronson, pp. 91–110. New York: Academic

Winsper C, Lereya T, Zanarini M, Wolke D. 2012. Involvement in bullying and suicide-related behavior at 11 years: a prospective birth cohort study. *J. Am. Acad. Child Adolesc. Psychiatry* 51:271–82

Wright JC, Giammarino M, Parad HW. 1986. Social status in small groups: individual-group similarity and the social "misfit." *J. Personal. Soc. Psychol.* 50:523–36

Xie H, Swift DJ, Cairns BD, Cairns RB. 2002. Aggressive behaviors in social interaction and developmental adaptation: a narrative analysis of interpersonal conflicts during early adolescence. *Soc. Dev.* 11:205–24

Ybarra ML, Mitchell KJ. 2004. Online aggressor/targets, aggressors, and targets: a comparison of associated youth characteristics. *J. Child Psychol. Psychiatry* 45:1308–16

Yeung Thompson RS, Leadbeater BJ. 2013. Peer victimization and internalizing symptoms from adolescence into young adulthood: building strength through emotional support. *J. Res. Adolesc.* 23:290–303

Is Adolescence a Sensitive Period for Sociocultural Processing?

Sarah-Jayne Blakemore[1] and Kathryn L. Mills[1,2]

[1] Institute of Cognitive Neuroscience, University College London, London, WC1N 3HT United Kingdom; email: s.blakemore@ucl.ac.uk

[2] Child Psychiatry Branch, National Institute of Mental Health, Bethesda, Maryland 20892

Annu. Rev. Psychol. 2014. 65:187–207

First published online as a Review in Advance on September 6, 2013

The *Annual Review of Psychology* is online at http://psych.annualreviews.org

This article's doi:
10.1146/annurev-psych-010213-115202

Keywords

social cognition, mentalizing, adolescent brain development, risk taking, plasticity, sensitive period

Abstract

Adolescence is a period of formative biological and social transition. Social cognitive processes involved in navigating increasingly complex and intimate relationships continue to develop throughout adolescence. Here, we describe the functional and structural changes occurring in the brain during this period of life and how they relate to navigating the social environment. Areas of the social brain undergo both structural changes and functional reorganization during the second decade of life, possibly reflecting a sensitive period for adapting to one's social environment. The changes in social environment that occur during adolescence might interact with increasing executive functions and heightened social sensitivity to influence a number of adolescent behaviors. We discuss the importance of considering the social environment and social rewards in research on adolescent cognition and behavior. Finally, we speculate about the potential implications of this research for society.

Contents

OVERVIEW

Adolescence is often defined as the period between the onset of puberty and the achievement of relative self-sufficiency. Therefore the beginning of adolescence is largely defined by a biological event, whereas the end of adolescence is often defined socially. Adolescence is particularly protracted in humans compared with other species (Bogin & Smith 1996). Behavioral changes and improvements in cognitive skills in adolescence have been reported for millennia, including by Aristotle (Ross 1925). Recently, with the advent of brain imaging technologies, we have begun to understand changes occurring in the brain during this period of life (Casey et al. 2008). This review highlights research on adolescent social cognitive development, which paints a picture of adolescence as a period of heightened sensitivity to sociocultural signals in the environment. This framework addresses the social contextual factors and motivations that might influence behavior during adolescence. We propose that social context and social acceptance play a pivotal role in adolescence because they influence the majority of adolescent-typical behaviors. This review integrates research across neuroscience and psychology within the framework that adolescents' health and well-being are influenced through interacting with their environment (Call et al. 2002). We also discuss potential implications of basic research on adolescence for society.

DEFINING ADOLESCENCE AS A SENSITIVE PERIOD FOR SOCIAL PROCESSING

The period of adolescence begins with the physical, cognitive, and social changes occurring with the onset of puberty. The adults that emerge from adolescence must be equipped to navigate the

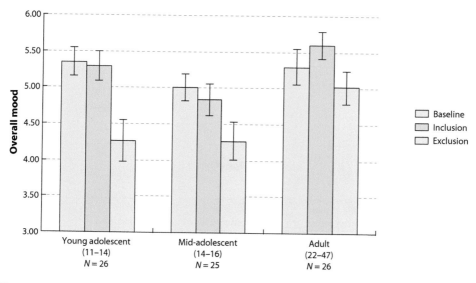

Figure 1

Adolescents are hypersensitive to the negative consequences of social exclusion. In this study, young adolescents (11–14 years), mid-adolescents (14–16 years), and adults (22–47 years) first completed baseline measures of mood. They then played the *Cyberball* online ball game and were either included or excluded by the other players in the game. After each run (inclusion and exclusion), participants completed measures of mood again. The graph shows overall mood ratings for each group under each condition. Mood was lowered by the social exclusion condition, compared with baseline and inclusion, particularly strongly in the two adolescent groups. Adapted from Sebastian et al. (2010).

social complexities of their community. It has been proposed that adolescence is a time of particular cultural susceptibility (Choudhury 2010, Fiske 2009) and that the impact of puberty on the brain makes adolescents particularly sensitive to their social environments (Crone & Dahl 2012, Peper & Dahl 2013). Adolescents go through a period of social reorienting where the opinions of peers become more important than those of family members (Larson & Richards 1991, Larson et al. 1996). Adolescents aged 13 to 17 years reported that peer evaluations affect their feelings of social or personal worth and that peer rejection indicates their unworthiness as an individual (O'Brien & Bierman 1988). Although the adolescents and children aged 10 to 13 years similarly felt that peers provided companionship, stimulation, and support, the younger group did not indicate that peer acceptance impacted self-evaluation. The authors suggest that increasing abilities to form abstract representations, as well as increasing motivation for peer acceptance, might account for the influence of peers on self-evaluations in adolescence. These self-reported accounts of the importance of peer acceptance are supported by the results of a behavioral study investigating the effects of social exclusion in the lab. After being excluded by other players in an online game called *Cyberball*, young and mid-adolescents (11–16 years) reported lowered overall mood, and young adolescents (11–14 years) reported higher state anxiety, compared with adults (Sebastian et al. 2010). Thus, it appears that the desire to be accepted by one's peers, and avoidance of social rejection, is particularly acute in adolescence and might drive adolescent behavior (**Figure 1**).

Mental health disorders often have an onset in adolescence (Kessler et al. 2005) (**Figure 2**). The heightened vulnerability to psychiatric conditions during adolescence has been proposed to relate to genetically preprogrammed neural development at the same time as new stresses and challenges emerge in the environment (Andersen & Teicher 2008, Leussis & Andersen 2008). Stress exposure, including social stress, during adolescence may be longer lasting and qualitatively

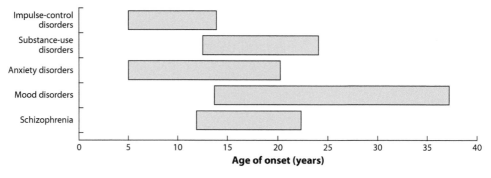

Figure 2

The ranges of onset age for common psychiatric disorders. The graph is based on the results of a nationally representative epidemiological survey of mental disorders and demonstrates that most individuals diagnosed with a mental disorder show the beginnings of the illness in late childhood or in adolescence. Adapted from Paus et al. (2008) with data from Kessler et al. (2005).

Hypothalamic-pituitary-adrenal (HPA) axis: major part of the neuroendocrine system that controls reactions to stress and regulates many body processes

Glucocorticoid: a steroid hormone that is produced by the adrenal cortex of animals

different from stress exposure at other periods of life, possibly due to the interaction between the developing hypothalamic-pituitary-adrenal (HPA) axis and glucocorticoids (for review, see McCormick et al. 2010). One reason why adolescents show increased sensitivity to stress-induced levels of glucocorticoids is the increase in glucocorticoid regulation in the human prefrontal cortex (Perlman et al. 2007). This neural change, which increases from infancy through childhood and adolescence, might make adolescents more vulnerable to psychiatric illnesses (Perlman et al. 2007). Rodent studies indicate that social stress induced by isolation can have long-lasting impacts (see sidebar Possible Consequences of Social Isolation in Adolescence). Exposure to social isolation during adolescence increases the likelihood of depressive-like behaviors as well as alterations in the structure of the prefrontal cortex (Leussis & Andersen 2008). The long-lasting effects of stress in adolescence include disrupted social and reproductive behavior. For example, male rats exposed to chronic social instability stress during adolescence were, in adulthood, more anxious and less socially interactive (Green et al. 2012), showed deficits across many sexual behaviors (McCormick et al. 2013), and had lower plasma testosterone concentrations than rats not exposed to social stressors during adolescence (McCormick et al. 2013). There is also evidence from studies on hamsters that adolescence is a period of increased sensitivity to the organizational

POSSIBLE CONSEQUENCES OF SOCIAL ISOLATION IN ADOLESCENCE

A recent study found that rats socially isolated during early adolescence were faster at remembering drug-associated contextual stimuli than rats that were not socially isolated during early adolescence or rats that were socially isolated during late adolescence (Whitaker et al. 2013). The socially isolated rats showed enhanced synaptic plasticity in an area of the brain involved in reward-based learning and addictive behaviors, and their drug-associated memories were harder to extinguish (Whitaker et al. 2013). Importantly, later resocialization of the rats isolated during early adolescence did not reverse the neural changes. This study suggests that early adolescence is a sensitive period for social signals and that social isolation during this time can change neural mechanisms involved in acquiring and maintaining drug-associated cues, possibly increasing vulnerability to addictive behaviors (Whitaker et al. 2013). Although the study involved rodents, the impact of social isolation on adolescent health and life trajectories likely applies to humans. If so, the consequences of social exclusion can be so great that mechanisms and behaviors promoting peer acceptance are considered adaptive.

effects of testosterone, which in turn affects adult reproductive behavior (Schulz et al. 2009). These and many other animal studies (reviewed in Toledo-Rodriguez & Sandi 2011) show that stress exposure during adolescence has a significant impact on the adult. Mild stress exposure during the pubertal transition in rats (postnatal days 28–42) increases risk-taking and novelty-seeking behavior and decreases anxious behavior in later adolescence (postnatal days 45–51), suggesting that stress experienced during puberty motivates the rats to hasten independence-building behaviors (Toledo-Rodriguez & Sandi 2011).

Although much evidence for adolescence as a sensitive period for social processing comes from rodent studies, there is evidence that socioenvironmental conditions experienced during human adolescence can impact attitudes toward health and reproduction in young adulthood (Brumbach et al. 2009). Adolescents within socially unpredictable environments not only experienced decreased physical and mental health in the short term but also adopted faster life history strategies in young adulthood, such as decreased health, less sexual restrictedness, and less resource-accruing potential (Brumbach et al. 2009). Further human studies are needed to investigate whether the adolescent brain is particularly sensitive to cues from the social environment or lack thereof.

SOCIAL COGNITIVE DEVELOPMENT

Social cognition refers to the ability to make sense of the world through processing signals generated by members of the same species (Frith 2008). Social cognitive processes include basic perceptual processes such as face processing (Farroni et al. 2005), biological motion detection (Pelphrey & Carter 2008), and joint attention (Carpenter et al. 1998)—all of which rapidly develop from birth (see Baillargeon et al. 2010). Other social cognitive processes are more complex, such as understanding others' mental states (Blakemore et al. 2007), social emotional processing (Burnett et al. 2009), and negotiating complex interpersonal decisions (Crone 2013). Recent neuroimaging and behavioral studies have shown that these skills continue to develop past childhood and throughout adolescence (reviewed in Apperly 2010, Blakemore 2012).

Social Cognitive Development in Adolescence

Until recently, there was a shortage of studies looking into social cognitive abilities after childhood, as it was generally assumed that these abilities were already mature by mid-childhood in typically developing children. Most paradigms have been designed to investigate social cognition (in particular, theory of mind) in young children and result in ceiling effects after mid-childhood (Apperly 2010).

One of the first studies to investigate neurotypical changes in social cognitive behavior in adolescence showed the ability to integrate the perspectives and intentions of others when making fairness considerations continues to improve (Güroğlu et al. 2009). The authors of this study suggested that the rewarding nature of peer relationships during adolescence could affect social decision-making processes. Another study demonstrated that online social cognitive skills improve across adolescence (Dumontheil et al. 2010a). Participants aged 7 to 27 years were tested on their ability to take the perspective of another person when making decisions. Their paradigm adapted a referential communication task in which participants are instructed to move objects around a set of shelves by a director, who cannot see some of the objects that the participant can see. Adults frequently make mistakes in this type of trial, in which the participant needs to take account of the director's perspective in order to guide decisions (Keysar et al. 2000, 2003). As an added control, Dumontheil et al. (2010a) included a condition in which the director is gone and participants have to follow a nonsocial rule ("ignore objects with a grey background") when following the (otherwise)

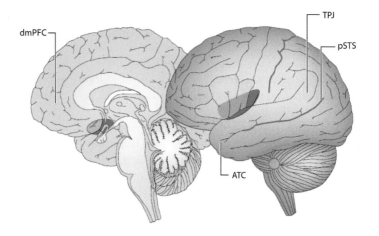

Figure 3

Mentalizing network: areas of the brain that may be sensitive to social cognitive processes necessary to navigate the adolescent social environment. Regions on the lateral surface of the brain that are involved in social cognition include the dorsal medial prefrontal cortex (dmPFC) and temporoparietal junction (TPJ), which are involved in thinking about mental states; the posterior superior temporal sulcus (pSTS), which is involved in observing faces and biological motion; and anterior temporal cortex (ATC), which is involved in applying social knowledge. Adapted from Blakemore (2008).

same instructions as in the director condition. Although accuracy improved until mid-adolescence in both conditions, accuracy in the director condition continued to improve after mid-adolescence. This suggests that the ability to use another's perspective to guide decisions continues to develop beyond the establishment of abilities recruited in the control condition (e.g., working memory, response inhibition). This improvement may be due to increased motivation to take account of another's perspective as well as improved integration of social cognition and cognitive control systems (Dumontheil et al. 2010a). Introspective awareness of one's performance on a perceptual task also improves across adolescence, following a trajectory similar to mentalizing (Weil et al. 2013). This finding that self-awareness increases during adolescence might have implications for how adolescents integrate their own self-judgments with peer evaluations.

SOCIAL BRAIN NETWORK

It has been proposed that social cognition has been so fundamental to the survival and reproductive fitness of various primate species that primate brains include regions specialized for social cognitive processes (Brothers 2002, Rushworth et al. 2013). Although this idea remains contentious, there exists a network of brain regions consistently involved in social cognitive processes (Adolphs 2009, Frith 2007). Mentalizing (theory of mind), the process of mental state attribution, has been associated with a network of brain regions including the dorsal medial prefrontal cortex (dmPFC), temporoparietal junction (TPJ), posterior superior temporal sulcus (pSTS), and anterior temporal cortex (ATC) (**Figure 3**). Together, this set of regions is sometimes called the social brain network. The mentalizing tasks that recruit these regions use stimuli such as animated shapes (Castelli et al. 2000), cartoon stories (Brunet et al. 2000, Gallagher et al. 2000), and written stories (Fletcher et al. 1995) designed to elicit the representation of mental states. Although the coactivation of these regions has been demonstrated in many social cognitive neuroimaging experiments, the individual contributions of these anatomically distinct regions to social cognitive processes are debated.

Mentalizing: the ability to understand other people's behavior and actions in terms of underlying mental states

Electrophysiological and functional magnetic resonance imaging (fMRI) studies consistently report the involvement of the pSTS in the perception of biological motion and eye gaze (Puce & Perrett 2003) and in grasping the intentionality and appropriateness of biological motion (Pelphrey et al. 2004). It may be that the pSTS is involved in decoding complex social gestures conveyed through eye gaze and body movement. The TPJ, while in close anatomical proximity to the pSTS, is involved in different aspects of social cognition. It is suggested that the TPJ is activated specifically in situations when one is inferring the mental states of others rather than just information known about another (Saxe & Kanwisher 2003, Saxe et al. 2009). In contrast, dmPFC is activated in multiple conditions: when inferring the mental states of others, when reflecting on knowledge of another's traits, and when reflecting on the traits of oneself (Frith 2007). Frith (2007) has proposed that the underlying similarity between tasks that activate the dmPFC is their involvement in handling communicative intentions, which requires a second-order representation of mental state, whether our own or another's. A combination of lesion, nonhuman primate, and fMRI studies has prompted researchers to theorize the involvement of the ATC in applying social knowledge (Olson et al. 2013) and processing social scripts (Frith 2007, Frith & Frith 2003).

Some of the strongest evidence linking areas of the mentalizing brain network to adaptations to the social environment comes from primate studies. In macaques, the size of an individual's social group is associated with both the structure and function of homologous brain areas involved in social cognition (Sallet et al. 2011). Macaques housed in more complex social environments had greater gray matter volume in the temporal cortex and rostral prefrontal cortex, and higher-ranking male macaques had greater gray matter volume in similar regions after controlling for network size, weight, and age (Sallet et al. 2011). These studies support the idea of the existence of a mentalizing brain network as well as the idea that this network exists in nonhuman primates (Rushworth et al. 2013).

Structural Development

The cerebral cortex in humans is formed during a well-defined developmental period. Anatomical studies of postmortem human brain tissue provided some of the first evidence that the brain undergoes profound changes in anatomy across the first decades of life (Petanjek et al. 2011, Webb et al. 2001, Yakovlev & Lecours 1967). However, MRI studies over the past 20 years have illuminated how and when the human brain develops. Neuroimaging methods, such as structural MRI, have enabled the investigation of these anatomical changes in the living human brain across development. Structural MRI studies have consistently shown continuing neuroanatomical development in gray matter and white matter (Brain Dev. Coop. Group 2012, Giedd et al. 1999, Sowell et al. 2003, Tamnes et al. 2013), with association cortices reducing in gray matter volume across adolescence and white matter increasing into adulthood. Until recently, most structural MRI studies of the developing brain have examined gray and white matter volumes in relatively large regions. Gray matter volume itself is the product of cortical thickness and surface area, which are influenced by distinct genetic (Panizzon et al. 2009, Winkler et al. 2010), evolutionary (Rakic 1995), and cellular (Chenn & Walsh 2002) processes, in addition to being phenotypically distinct (Winkler et al. 2010). Gray matter volume is more highly correlated with, and genetically and environmentally related to, surface area than with cortical thickness (Winkler et al. 2010). Differences in surface area are pronounced across species, whereas cortical thickness is highly conserved in comparison (Hill et al. 2010, Rakic 1995).

Areas within the mentalizing network continue to develop in gray matter volume, cortical thickness, and surface area across adolescence before relatively stabilizing in the early twenties (Mills et al. 2013). In a study using a large sample of individuals with at least two brain scans between ages 7 and 30 years, we examined the structural developmental trajectories of the mentalizing brain network. Gray matter volume and cortical thickness in medial Brodmann area 10 (a proxy for dmPFC), TPJ, and pSTS decreased from childhood into the early twenties, whereas the ATC increased in gray matter volume until adolescence and in cortical thickness until early adulthood. Surface area for each region followed a cubic trajectory, reaching a peak in late childhood or early adolescence before decreasing into the early twenties (Mills et al. 2013). This protracted development demonstrates that areas of the brain involved in deciphering the mental states of others are still maturing from late childhood into early adulthood.

The underlying mechanisms associated with a reduction in gray matter volume are still debated (Paus et al. 2008, Poldrack 2010), and to date no studies have tested the relationship between developmental changes in underlying cellular or synaptic anatomy and structural MRI measures. Despite these limitations, it is thought that reductions in gray matter volume might reflect synaptic reorganization and/or increases in white matter integrity (Paus et al. 2008). Histological studies of postmortem human brain tissue support the idea that the prefrontal cortex continues to undergo synaptic pruning across adolescence (Huttenlocher & Dabholkar 1997, Petanjek et al. 2011). White matter generally increases in volume and integrity across adolescence and into young adulthood (Lebel et al. 2008, Lenroot et al. 2007). The developmental changes in white matter are thought to provide evidence for an extended period of myelination of connections between association cortices, which has been found in histological studies (Yakovlev & Lecours 1967).

Functional Development of the Social Brain Network in Adolescence

A number of fMRI studies show functional changes across adolescence in the brain networks associated with social cognition, including face processing, mentalizing, peer evaluation, and peer influence. We discuss these studies below.

Face processing. Understanding the mental states of others by processing facial expressions is a crucial skill and is one that continues to develop across adolescence (McGivern et al. 2002). Recruitment of the prefrontal cortex during face-processing tasks increases between childhood and adolescence and then decreases between adolescence and adulthood (reviewed in Blakemore 2008). Brain systems supporting detection and interpretation of communicative signals from face processing also show age-related changes from childhood to adulthood, perhaps due to changing cognitive strategies (Cohen Kadosh et al. 2013a,b).

Recent longitudinal neuroimaging studies are beginning to provide evidence of changes in neural responses to social stimuli such as faces between childhood and adolescence. As participants transitioned from late childhood (~10 years) to adolescence (~13 years), they showed greater neural activity in the ventral striatum and ventromedial PFC while looking at facial displays (Pfeifer et al. 2011). The ATC was the only area to show a longitudinal change in preference for emotional facial displays. This study correlated longitudinal changes in ventral striatal activity with decreasing susceptibility (i.e., increasing resistance) to peer influence, demonstrating that heightened subcortical reactivity in socioemotional situations might indicate better emotion-regulation capacities (Pfeifer et al. 2011). In addition, pubertal status during early adolescence was related to increased neural recruitment of the amygdala, hippocampus, and ATC when participants looked at affective facial stimuli (i.e., happy, sad, angry faces) (Moore et al. 2012).

Mentalizing. Many fMRI studies that use mentalizing report decreases in dmPFC recruitment between adolescence and adulthood (reviewed in Blakemore 2008, 2012). These studies have used a variety of tasks that require mental state attribution, such as understanding irony (Wang et al.

2006), thinking about social emotions such as guilt (Burnett et al. 2009), understanding intentions (Blakemore et al. 2007), understanding emotions from photographs of eyes (Moor et al. 2012), and thinking about the preferences and dispositions of oneself or a fictitious story character (Pfeifer et al. 2009). In some studies, higher activity in more posterior regions, such as the pSTS/TPJ (Blakemore et al. 2007), and in the ATC (Burnett et al. 2009), was observed in adults as compared to adolescents. These changes in functional recruitment have been hypothesized to reflect changes in neurocognitive strategy and/or neuroanatomy (Blakemore 2008).

In an adapted version of the Director task (Apperly et al. 2010, Dumontheil et al. 2010a), areas of the mentalizing brain network were engaged when participants had to use social cues to select an appropriate action in a communicative context (Dumontheil et al. 2012). Although both adults and adolescents recruited the dmPFC when the social cues were needed to accurately perform the task, adolescents also recruited the dmPFC when social cues were not needed. The authors suggest that this engagement of the dmPFC in social conditions, even when social signals are irrelevant, may reflect the use of brain regions involved in mentalizing even when they are not necessary during adolescence.

Adolescents also show developmental changes in sensitivity to the perspectives of others. In an fMRI study, young adolescents (12 to 14 years), older adolescents (15 to 17 years), and emerging adults (18 to 22 years) completed a social exchange game in which participants were the second player in an investment game (van den Bos et al. 2011). These participants were first given an amount of money by an anonymous first player, which they could divide equally between themselves and the first player (reciprocate) or keep most for themselves (defect). Participants' ability to understand the intentions of the first player was also measured by comparing trials on which the first player stood to lose a large amount of money by trusting the second player with trials where the first player stood to lose a relatively small amount of money. Older adolescents and emerging adults were more likely to reciprocate when the first player stood to lose more money, whereas the younger adolescents did not differentiate, supporting the idea that the ability to understand the intentions of others increases into adulthood. The recruitment of the left TPJ when participants were shown that the first player trusted them increased with age, and this level of activation correlated with participants' sensitivity to the first player's intentions. All participants showed greater recruitment in the dmPFC when making self-oriented choices (defecting), but only young adolescents engaged this region when making reciprocal choices. This heightened activation in the dmPFC for reciprocal choices decreased between early and late adolescence and remained stable into early adulthood, possibly reflecting a shift away from engaging in social interactions from an egocentric perspective (van den Bos et al. 2011).

Social emotion. Social emotions—such as guilt, embarrassment, shame, and pride—require representing another's mental state, whereas basic emotions such as fear and disgust do not. Because adolescence is a period of increased sensitivity to peer evaluation, there may be changes in how social emotions are processed. One fMRI study investigated changes in neural recruitment during a social emotional task between adolescence (11 to 18 years) and adulthood (23 to 32 years) (Burnett et al. 2009). Participants were instructed to read sentences describing social or basic emotion scenarios. Adolescents recruited the dmPFC more than adults when reading social emotional sentences relative to basic emotion sentences. In contrast, adults recruited the left ATC more than did adolescents when reading social emotional sentences relative to basic emotion sentences (Burnett et al. 2009).

A more recent study investigated the influence of puberty on social emotion processing in adolescence (Goddings et al. 2012). In a sample of 42 female adolescents (11 to 13 years), levels of pubertal hormones (testosterone, estradiol, and dehydroepiandrosterone) were related to ATC recruitment during social emotional processing. Whereas activity in the left ATC was positively correlated with hormone levels (irrespective of age), activity in the dmPFC was negatively correlated with chronological age (irrespective of hormone levels), providing evidence for a dissociation between puberty- and age-related changes in neural function during adolescence (Goddings et al. 2012).

Conformity: changes in valuation to match the group

Peer evaluation. There are a number of fMRI investigations of experimentally manipulated social exclusion using the *Cyberball* task. This task involves participants playing a game of "catch" with two other players under the guise that they are playing with real peers over the Internet. However, the other players are actually preprogrammed to include or exclude the participant. In one study, recruitment of the mPFC during exclusion relative to inclusion was associated with greater self-reported susceptibility to peer influence in adolescents but not in adults (Sebastian et al. 2011). This study also found age-related differences in right ventrolateral PFC (vlPFC) recruitment during exclusion conditions, with adults recruiting right vlPFC more than adolescents. Another fMRI study using the *Cyberball* task specifically in a group of adolescents aged 12 to 13 years found recruitment of the right vlPFC during exclusion conditions was negatively correlated with self-reported measures of distress following exclusion (Masten et al. 2009). Together, these studies suggest the vlPFC plays a role in regulating distress following social exclusion and that this region is still developing functionally between adolescence and adulthood. Healthy adolescents who display heightened activity in an area of the brain called the subgenual anterior cingulate cortex while being excluded from peers in *Cyberball* were more likely to show an increase in depressive symptoms during the following year (Masten et al. 2011).

Prompted by research linking good peer relationships to well-being, Masten and colleagues examined how 12- to 13-year-olds respond to witnessing peer rejection in an online game (Masten et al. 2010). Participants first completed a self-reported measure of trait empathy before participating in an fMRI task where they witnessed peer exclusion in a game of *Cyberball*. Afterward, they were asked to write a letter to the rejected player as a measure of prosocial behavior. Activity in the mentalizing network was related to observed exclusion compared to observed inclusion. Although recruitment of the dmPFC and ATC appeared to be related to self-reported trait empathy, only the anterior insula showed a positive correlation with prosocial behavior. Together, these findings suggest that young adolescents recruit the mentalizing network more while witnessing peer rejection than in a situation where peers are being treated equally.

Peer influence. Peer influence on conformity shows a curvilinear pattern between middle childhood and late adolescence, reaching a peak in early adolescence (Berndt 1979). The popularity rankings of a given song influence how much adolescents like it (Berns et al. 2010). In an fMRI task, adolescents aged 12 to 17 years listened to and rated the likeability of short music clips, first without knowing the popularity of the song and then after receiving its popularity ranking. Adolescents' change in song evaluation correlated with increased recruitment of the anterior insula and ACC, which the authors suggest may reflect the anxiety of having preferences that are dissimilar to those of others.

The presence of peers affects how likely adolescents are to take risks in a driving game. Adolescents (13 to 16 years), young adults (18 to 22 years), and adults (24+ years) took around the same number of driving risks when alone, whereas the adolescents took significantly more in the presence of their friends (Gardner & Steinberg 2005). In contrast, peers had no impact on risk taking in adults and had an intermediate effect on risk taking in youths (Gardner & Steinberg 2005) (see **Figure 4**). In an fMRI version of this task, in the peers-present condition two friends communicated with the participant (who was in the MRI scanner) over an intercom (Chein et al.

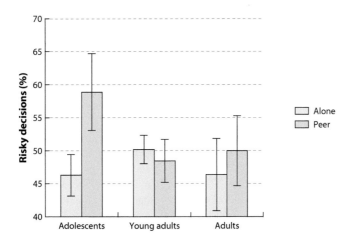

Figure 4

Risky behavior in adolescents, young adults, and adults when alone or when being watched by peers. This graph illustrates the average percentage of risky decisions for adolescent, young adult, and adult participants when playing the Stoplight task alone and with a peer audience. Adapted from Chein et al. (2011).

2011). Adults aged 24 to 29 years showed higher activity in lateral PFC than did adolescents aged 14 to 18 years or younger adults aged 19 to 22 years when they had to make critical decisions in the driving game, both when alone and when peers were present. Relative to both groups of adults, adolescents showed increased recruitment of the ventral striatum and orbitofrontal cortex during the driving decisions with peers compared to when alone.

Social context modulates risk attitudes adopted by adolescents (Engelmann et al. 2012). Relative to adults, adolescents showed greater risk-adverse behavior after receiving expert advice, and this effect is modulated by increased engagement of the dorsolateral PFC by adolescents during valuation in the presence of advice (Engelmann et al. 2012). The authors suggest enhanced inhibitory and cognitive control processes may underlie the effect of social context on risky decision making in adolescents.

THE SOCIAL ENVIRONMENT DURING ADOLESCENCE AND EMERGING BEHAVIORS AND COGNITIONS

Characteristic behaviors of adolescence, such as heightened self-consciousness, mood variability, novelty seeking, risk taking, and peer orientation, are fundamental to the successful transition into a stable adult role. Here we discuss changes in the social environment during adolescence as well as how emerging behaviors and cognitions are involved in the successful navigation of these environments.

Changes in Social Environment

The adolescent social environment is different from the child and adult social environments in many ways. In many school systems, the transition from primary to secondary school occurs around the onset of puberty, which may place children into new environments without the same peers, in a different structure of learning, and at the bottom of the age hierarchy. Adolescents are also exposed to novel situations that they were unlikely to encounter as children, which might play a role in the increased risky decision making seen in the transition from childhood to adolescence.

Risky Decision Making

Adolescents are stereotypically known for their engagement in risky behaviors. There is experimental evidence supporting the idea that, while in laboratory settings, adolescents are more likely than children and adults to make risky decisions in "hot" contexts (Blakemore & Robbins 2012). Experimental evidence from risky decision making and probabilistic reward paradigms mostly supports the hypothesis that adolescents are biased to taking risks due to overactive reward-related circuitry (i.e., ventral striatum) (Ernst et al. 2006, Van Leijenhorst et al. 2010). Probabilistic reward paradigms in laboratory experiments on risk taking often involve gambling tasks. Children and adolescents show adult levels of probability estimation and reward evaluation during one such gambling task, suggesting that heightened risky decision making in adolescents is probably not related to a change in risk perception (Van Leijenhorst et al. 2008). When asked in a laboratory setting to estimate the risks of negative outcomes to some risky behaviors, adolescents actually overestimate risks (Reyna & Farley 2006). Adolescents also rate the potential reward to be gained as very high, which may make the perceived benefits outweigh the perceived risk (Reyna & Farley 2006). Social and contextual cues can bias the way adolescents perceive the risk involved in certain behaviors (Reyna 2008, Reyna & Adam 2003, Reyna & Farley 2006). Although risky decision making during adolescence is often framed as maladaptive and unavoidable, this perspective leaves out many key features of risky decision making, including the fact that the outcome can be positive and that some risky decision making is necessary in development and throughout life. A recent report highlights the benefits of asking "What's in it for the adolescent?" when studying risky behavior and risky decision making in adolescence (Ellis et al. 2012). We propose that some rewards gained by risky behaviors are social in nature, such as peer acceptance or the avoidance of social exclusion, and that this is a potential major driver of risky behavior, in particular in adolescence, when social acceptance is especially important. (see **Figure 5**).

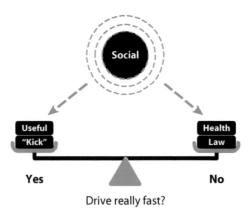

Figure 5

Illustration of some of the factors that influence certain risky decisions. In a scenario in which the individual is making a choice whether or not to drive very fast, multiple factors might weigh in, such as the potential outcome of injury (health), being arrested (law), arriving somewhere in less time (useful), and getting a subjective feeling of pleasure from the experience ("kick"). Above this "seesaw" is another potential factor that could weigh on either side of the decision process, which is made up of social factors (e.g., family, teachers, peers). The potential of peer acceptance/rejection could weigh on either side of the seesaw depending on the peers, and the weight of the factor (indicated by dashed lines) could vary on the basis of the individual and the developmental stage.

Executive Functions

Cognitive abilities such as processing speed, voluntary response suppression, delay discounting, future planning, and working memory all mature into adolescence (Luna et al. 2004, Steinberg et al. 2009). Developmental improvements in executive functions likely influence—and are influenced by—social cognitive processing during adolescence. Developmental neuroimaging studies show correlations between the protracted development of the prefrontal cortex and maturing cognitive and behavioral abilities during adolescence, such as manipulating multiple items in mind (Crone et al. 2006b), suppressing reflexive behavior (Luna et al. 2001), relational reasoning (Dumontheil et al. 2010b), future planning (Kaller et al. 2012), and delay discounting (Costa Dias et al. 2013). Successful emotion regulation in early adolescence (10 to 13 years) is impacted by the adolescent's sensitivity to rejection as well as situational factors of the emotional stimuli. Compared with older adolescents and adults (14 to 23 years), young adolescents found it harder to regulate their emotions when presented with social affective stimuli compared to nonsocial affective stimuli (Silvers et al. 2012).

The ability to consider future consequences of actions continues to improve across adolescence (Crone & van der Molen 2004), which might impact how adolescents interact in social situations. Both young adolescents (12 to 14 years) and older adolescents (16 to 18 years) showed heart rate slowing after erring on a task-switching task, which might indicate an increasing ability to monitor performance (Crone et al. 2006a). The ability to monitor one's performance in social situations likely affects the overall success of the interaction. Developmental fMRI studies suggest that distinct neural systems develop at different rates across childhood and adolescence and that these age-related changes in regions involved in feedback processing may underlie behavioral differences in flexible performance adjustment (Crone et al. 2008). A qualitative shift in neural recruitment during feedback-based learning is seen in early adolescence, possibly reflecting the increasing influence of negative feedback on behavioral adjustment (van Duijvenvoorde et al. 2008). The changes in the processing of feedback in adolescence have implications for successful social communication; however, further studies are needed to use integrative tasks to test directly the influence of gradually improving executive functions on social cognition.

> **Executive functions:** a set of cognitive processes that regulate, control, and manage other cognitive processes
>
> **Acculturation:** adaptation to the mainstream culture of where one has immigrated

IMPLICATIONS FOR SOCIETY

Is the Human Brain Particularly Sensitive to Social Signals During Adolescence?

This review has focused on evidence from the psychology and neuroscience literatures to support the view of adolescence as a period particularly sensitive to social environmental cues. However, two further lines of evidence need to be acquired to support this theory: (*a*) the brain during adolescence (more than in childhood and adulthood) is particularly susceptible to social environmental cues, and (*b*) changes in the brain during adolescence reflect particular susceptibility to social environmental cues (more than other types of stimuli). That is, are our brains organized in such a manner that reflects our ancestors navigating increasingly complex social environments, or foraging in increasingly unstable climates? Similarly, is the protracted development of the mentalizing brain network reflective of the need for later acculturation into one's society and culture? Acculturation, or adaptation to the mainstream culture of where one has immigrated, occurs more rapidly at younger ages (1 to 15 years) (Cheung et al. 2011), suggesting that the sensitive period for cultural learning is not adolescent specific but instead that cultural sensitivity may begin to close during adolescence. Perhaps the cognitive and behavioral abilities that emerge during adolescence enhance social signals or allow them to be more easily integrated.

Educational Implications

Adolescence represents a period of brain development during which environmental experiences—including teaching—can and do profoundly shape the developing brain. If early childhood is seen as a major opportunity—or a sensitive period—for teaching, so too might adolescence. It is only recently that teenagers have been routinely educated in the West. In many countries a large proportion of teenagers have no access to secondary school education. And yet the adolescent brain is malleable and adaptable—this is an excellent opportunity for learning and creativity. Risk taking in an educational context is a vital skill that enables progress and creativity. Although some adolescents use risk taking to achieve great things, many are worried about taking risks in the context of learning. The heightened risk taking in this age group should be harnessed for learning and creativity.

A prevailing view in adolescent research is that certain behaviors are desirable (e.g., long-term planning), and certain behaviors are undesirable (e.g., risk taking). Although long-term planning can help many individuals attain high-quality and stable adult lives, other external factors may prevent individuals from attaining this goal despite their using long-term planning (Ellis et al. 2012). In certain situations, taking a risk might actually be more likely to give the individual a chance to obtain the preferred outcome. The research described above emphasizes the role of contextual cues in influencing adolescent behaviors. A shift from treating adolescent behaviors, especially risk-taking behaviors, in isolation to a model that integrates social environmental cues might enhance our understanding of adolescent behaviors and improve interventions. What is sometimes seen as the problem with adolescents—risk taking, poor impulse control, self-consciousness, and so forth—is actually reflective of brain changes that provide an excellent opportunity for education and social development.

Adolescence is a time of opportunity for learning new skills and forging an adult identity. Research on brain development suggests that adolescence might represent a period of relatively high neural plasticity, in particular in brain regions involved in executive function and social cognition. The research on the brain basis of social development in adolescence might have implications for "when to teach what" and could inform both curriculum design and teaching practice with the aim of ensuring that classroom activities exploit periods of neural plasticity that facilitate maximal learning.

Legal Implications

Developmental neuroscience has already affected legal proceedings in United States by calling into question the sentencing procedures applied to adolescents (see Steinberg 2013), and many developmental scientists are still struggling with questions of culpability during an age of relative brain immaturity (Cauffman & Steinberg 2000, Steinberg 2009, Steinberg & Scott 2003). Although the discussion on culpability and the brain is ongoing, evidence from multiple fields supports the need for special consideration in prosecuting and punishing adolescents. Twenty years ago, Terrie Moffitt presented evidence supporting the idea that the majority of adolescents who engage in criminal behavior will do so during adolescence and at no other period of their life (Moffitt 1993). Such problem behaviors have also been shown to decrease without formal training (Chamberlain & Moore 1998). Further, interventions that segregate adolescents engaging in problem behaviors into groups can actually be harmful (Dishion & Tipsord 2011, Dishion et al. 2012, Ellis et al. 2012). The social augmentation hypothesis suggests that peer exclusion in adolescence can lead to neuroanatomical shifts in reward sensitivity, therefore making the adolescent more susceptible to peer influence (Dishion et al. 2012). The research reviewed in this article would support this speculative hypothesis, and future work will need to integrate measures of social exclusion and peer influence with neuroimaging paradigms, as some have already begun to do (Peake et al. 2013).

Psychology and intervention research provide a strong argument for reducing situations in which high-risk behaviors such as gang affiliation and crime are rewarded through positive peer responses (Dishion & Tipsord 2011). The capacity for change is reflected in the extended neuroanatomical and functional development of the human brain. By understanding and harnessing the plasticity of the brain during adolescence, legal interventions might better prevent reoffending and promote prosocial behavior. It is important that these interventions take into account not only the adolescent but also the influences of the social and physical environments in which the adolescent finds him or herself. Evidence from neuroscience and psychology studies shows that the social environment during adolescence has a profound impact on life course trajectories, and it is necessary to attempt to change the adolescent engaging in criminal behaviors as well as the social environment that may promote such behaviors.

Social Implications

A consequence of research on adolescence might be a change in how adolescents are perceived, including how adolescents perceive themselves, the period of adolescence and what can be expected, and how adolescents interpret their experiences in the world. Research on adolescent brains and behaviors has penetrated multiple media outlets and is a perennial topic that receives much attention. One study has investigated how adolescents understand and feel about research on the adolescent brain (Choudhury et al. 2012). The participating adolescents in this study felt that although research on the adolescent brain is necessary and important, the model of the adolescent brain as an explanation for adolescent behavior is insufficient (Choudhury et al. 2012). Interestingly, participants were less interested in how neuroscience could influence how they understand themselves and more interested in how research on the adolescent brain could influence the perspectives of adults (Choudhury et al. 2012). They pointed out the potential for neuroscience research to perpetuate stereotypes or combat stereotypes, depending on how adults incorporate research in their understanding of adolescence (Choudhury et al. 2012).

Adolescents are sensitive to the signals within their social environment, and these signals can impact how likely they are to invest in the future. A recent report suggested that adolescents perceive their risk of dying soon as higher than it actually is (Fischhoff et al. 2010). This perception may impact the likelihood of engaging in behaviors reflecting a faster life history strategy, although this has not been directly tested. Indeed, the authors voice similar concerns in the first sentence of the report: "Adolescents' willingness to prepare for the future depends, in part, on their confidence in living long enough to get a return on that investment" (Fischhoff et al. 2010). Perceived threats and crime expectations in the environment, but not actual experience with violence, correlated with mortality judgments (Fischhoff et al. 2010). Larger social structures have consequences for the health of adolescents, with factors such as inequality and poverty reducing adolescent health (Viner et al. 2012).

CONCLUSION

In the present review, we have discussed research that describes adolescence as a period of biological and social transition. Neuroimaging and behavioral studies in humans, and neuroanatomical and behavioral studies in animals, have demonstrated that the social brain and social cognition undergo a profound period of development in adolescence. As such, adolescence might represent a sensitive period for the processing and acquisition of sociocultural knowledge.

SUMMARY POINTS

1. Areas of the brain involved in understanding the mental states of others continue to develop structurally and functionally across adolescence.

2. Adolescence might represent a period of enhanced sensitivity to social signals in the environment, and these signals might influence an adolescent's life course trajectory by motivating certain behaviors.

3. Studies of adolescent behaviors would benefit from measuring social influences.

4. Adults can have a large impact on the social cognitive development and life course trajectories of adolescents by creating and maintaining the structures of social environments.

FUTURE ISSUES

1. How can we better define the transition period between adolescence and adulthood? What factors influence this transition, and are there differential outcomes in health, reproduction, and quality of life between those who transition at different ages?

2. Do heritability studies support the theory that areas of the mentalizing brain network are particularly sensitive to social environmental cues during adolescence?

3. How does research on adolescent brain development influence adolescents' self-perception and health?

4. How many abilities that develop during adolescence are related to navigating the social environment?

5. How does risk taking in adolescence relate to social status and the social context?

6. How do individual differences, such as gender, personality, and resistance to peer influence, affect the developing adolescent brain?

DISCLOSURE STATEMENT

The authors are not aware of any affiliations, memberships, funding, or financial holdings that might be perceived as affecting the objectivity of this review.

ACKNOWLEDGMENTS

The authors thank A.L. Goddings, R.M. Walford, and S. Burnett Heyes for their help with this review. Support for K.L.M. came from the National Institutes of Mental Health Graduate Partnership Program. Support for S.J.B. came from the Royal Society and the Leverhulme Trust. S.J.B. is funded by a Royal Society University Research Fellowship.

LITERATURE CITED

Adolphs R. 2009. The social brain: neural basis of social knowledge. *Annu. Rev. Psychol.* 60:693–716

Andersen SL, Teicher MH. 2008. Stress, sensitive periods and maturational events in adolescent depression. *Trends Neurosci.* 31:183–91

Apperly IA. 2010. *Mindreaders: The Cognitive Basis of "Theory of Mind."* New York: Psychol. Press

Apperly IA, Carroll DJ, Samson D, Humphreys GW, Qureshi A, Moffitt G. 2010. Why are there limits on theory of mind use? Evidence from adults' ability to follow instructions from an ignorant speaker. *Q. J. Exp. Psychol.* 63:1201–17

Baillargeon R, Scott RM, He Z. 2010. False-belief understanding in infants. *Trends Cogn. Sci.* 14(3):110–18

Berndt TJ. 1979. Developmental changes in conformity to peers and parents. *Dev. Psychol.* 15:608–16

Berns GS, Capra CM, Moore S, Noussair C. 2010. Neural mechanisms of the influence of popularity on adolescent ratings of music. *NeuroImage* 49:2687–96

Blakemore S-J. 2008. The social brain in adolescence. *Nat. Rev. Neurosci.* 9:267–77

Blakemore S-J. 2012. Development of the social brain in adolescence. *J. R. Soc. Med.* 105:111–16

Blakemore S-J, Den Ouden H, Choudhury S, Frith C. 2007. Adolescent development of the neural circuitry for thinking about intentions. *Soc. Cogn. Affect. Neurosci.* 2:130–39

Blakemore S-J, Robbins TW. 2012. Decision-making in the adolescent brain. *Nat. Neurosci.* 15:1184–91

Bogin B, Smith BH. 1996. Evolution of the human life cycle. *Am. J. Human Biol.* 8:703–16

Brain Dev. Coop. Group. 2012. Total and regional brain volumes in a population-based normative sample from 4 to 18 years: the NIH MRI Study of Normal Brain Development. *Cereb. Cortex* 22:1–12

Brothers L. 2002. The social brain: a project for integrating primate behavior and neurophysiology in a new domain. In *Foundations in Social Neuroscience*, ed. JT Cacioppo, GG Berntson, R Adolphs, CS Carter, RJ Davidson, MK McClintock, BS McEwen, MJ Meaney, DL Schacter, EM Sternberg, SS Suomi, SE Taylor, pp. 367–85. Cambridge, MA: MIT Press

Brumbach BH, Figueredo AJ, Ellis BJ. 2009. Effects of harsh and unpredictable environments in adolescence on development of life history strategies: a longitudinal test of an evolutionary model. *Hum. Nat.* 20:25–51

Brunet E, Sarfati Y, Hardy-Baylé MC, Decety J. 2000. A PET investigation of the attribution of intentions with a nonverbal task. *NeuroImage* 11:157–66

Burnett S, Bird G, Moll J, Frith C, Blakemore S-J. 2009. Development during adolescence of the neural processing of social emotion. *J. Cogn. Neurosci.* 21:1736–50

Call KT, Riedel AA, Hein K, McLoyd V, Petersen A, Kipke M. 2002. Adolescent health and well-being in the twenty-first century: a global perspective. *J. Res. Adolesc.* 12:69–98

Carpenter M, Nagell K, Tomasello M. 1998. Social cognition, joint attention, and communicative competence from 9 to 15 months of age. *Monogr. Soc. Res. Child Dev.* 63:i–vi, 1–143

Casey BJ, Getz S, Galvan A. 2008. The adolescent brain. *Dev. Rev.* 28:62–77

Castelli F, Happé F, Frith U, Frith C. 2000. Movement and mind: a functional imaging study of perception and interpretation of complex intentional movement patterns. *NeuroImage* 12:314–25

Cauffman E, Steinberg L. 2000. (Im)maturity of judgment in adolescence: why adolescents may be less culpable than adults. *Behav. Sci. Law* 18:741–60

Chamberlain P, Moore KJ. 1998. Models of community treatment for serious offenders. In *Social Programs That Work*, ed. J Crane, pp. 258–76. Princeton, NJ: Sage Found.

Chein J, Albert D, O'Brien L, Uckert K, Steinberg L. 2011. Peers increase adolescent risk taking by enhancing activity in the brain's reward circuitry. *Dev. Sci.* 14:F1–10

Chenn A, Walsh CA. 2002. Regulation of cerebral cortical size by control of cell cycle exit in neural precursors. *Science* 297:365–69

Cheung BY, Chudek M, Heine SJ. 2011. Evidence for a sensitive period for acculturation: younger immigrants report acculturating at a faster rate. *Psychol. Sci.* 22:147–52

Choudhury S. 2010. Culturing the adolescent brain: What can neuroscience learn from anthropology? *Soc. Cogn. Affect. Neurosci.* 5:159–67

Choudhury S, McKinney KA, Merten M. 2012. Rebelling against the brain: public engagement with the "neurological adolescent." *Soc. Sci. Med.* 74:565–73

Cohen Kadosh K, Johnson MH, Dick F, Cohen Kadosh R, Blakemore S-J. 2013a. Effects of age, task performance, and structural brain development on face processing. *Cereb. Cortex* 23:1630–42

Cohen Kadosh K, Johnson MH, Henson RN, Dick F, Blakemore S-J. 2013b. Differential face-network adaptation in children, adolescents and adults. *NeuroImage* 69:11–20

Costa Dias TG, Wilson VB, Bathula DR, Iyer SP, Mills KL, et al. 2013. Reward circuit connectivity relates to delay discounting in children with attention-deficit/hyperactivity disorder. *Eur. Neuropsychopharmacol.* 23:33–45

Crone EA. 2013. Considerations of fairness in the adolescent brain. *Child Dev. Perspect.* 7:97–103

Crone EA, Dahl RE. 2012. Understanding adolescence as a period of social-affective engagement and goal flexibility. *Nat. Rev. Neurosci.* 13:636–50

Crone EA, Somsen RJM, Zanolie K, Van der Molen MW. 2006a. A heart rate analysis of developmental change in feedback processing and rule shifting from childhood to early adulthood. *J. Exp. Child Psychol.* 95:99–116

Crone EA, Van der Molen MW. 2004. Developmental changes in real life decision making: performance on a gambling task previously shown to depend on the ventromedial prefrontal cortex. *Dev. Neuropsychol.* 25:251–79

Crone EA, Wendelken C, Donohue S, Van Leijenhorst L, Bunge SA. 2006b. Neurocognitive development of the ability to manipulate information in working memory. *Proc. Natl. Acad. Sci. USA* 103:9315–20

Crone EA, Zanolie K, Van Leijenhorst L, Westenberg PM, Rombouts SA. 2008. Neural mechanisms supporting flexible performance adjustment during development. *Cogn. Affect. Behav. Neurosci.* 8:165–77

Dishion TJ, Ha T, Véronneau M-H. 2012. An ecological analysis of the effects of deviant peer clustering on sexual promiscuity, problem behavior, and childbearing from early adolescence to adulthood: an enhancement of the life history framework. *Dev. Psychol.* 48:703–17

Dishion TJ, Tipsord JM. 2011. Peer contagion in child and adolescent social and emotional development. *Annu. Rev. Psychol.* 62:189–214

Dumontheil I, Apperly IA, Blakemore S-J. 2010a. Online usage of theory of mind continues to develop in late adolescence. *Dev. Sci.* 13:331–38

Dumontheil I, Hillebrandt H, Apperly IA, Blakemore S-J. 2012. Developmental differences in the control of action selection by social information. *J. Cogn. Neurosci.* 24:2080–95

Dumontheil I, Houlton R, Christoff K, Blakemore S-J. 2010b. Development of relational reasoning during adolescence. *Dev. Sci.* 13:F15–24

Ellis BJ, Del Giudice M, Dishion TJ, Figueredo AJ, Gray P, et al. 2012. The evolutionary basis of risky adolescent behavior: implications for science, policy, and practice. *Dev. Psychol.* 48:598–623

Engelmann JB, Moore S, Monica Capra C, Berns GS. 2012. Differential neurobiological effects of expert advice on risky choice in adolescents and adults. *Soc. Cogn. Affect. Neurosci.* 7:557–67

Ernst M, Pine DS, Hardin M. 2006. Triadic model of the neurobiology of motivated behavior in adolescence. *Psychol. Med.* 36:299–312

Farroni T, Johnson MH, Menon E, Zulian L, Faraguna D, Csibra G. 2005. Newborns' preference for face-relevant stimuli: effects of contrast polarity. *Proc. Natl. Acad. Sci. USA* 102:17245–50

Fischhoff B, Bruine de Bruin W, Parker AM, Millstein SG, Halpern-Felsher BL. 2010. Adolescents' perceived risk of dying. *J. Adolesc. Health* 46:265–69

Fiske ST. 2009. *Handbook of Neuroscience for the Behavioral Sciences.* New York: Wiley

Fletcher PC, Happé F, Frith U, Baker SC, Dolan RJ, et al. 1995. Other minds in the brain: a functional imaging study of "theory of mind" in story comprehension. *Cognition* 57:109–28

Frith CD. 2007. The social brain? *Philos. Trans. R. Soc. Lond. Ser. B Biol. Sci.* 362:671–78

Frith CD. 2008. Social cognition. *Philos. Trans. R. Soc. Lond. Ser. B Biol. Sci.* 363:2033–39

Frith U, Frith CD. 2003. Development and neurophysiology of mentalizing. *Philos. Trans. R. Soc. Lond. Ser. B Biol. Sci.* 358:459–73

Gallagher HL, Happé F, Brunswick N, Fletcher PC, Frith U, Frith CD. 2000. Reading the mind in cartoons and stories: an fMRI study of "theory of mind" in verbal and nonverbal tasks. *Neuropsychologia* 38:11–21

Gardner M, Steinberg L. 2005. Peer influence on risk taking, risk preference, and risky decision making in adolescence and adulthood: an experimental study. *Dev. Psychol.* 41:625–35

Giedd JN, Blumenthal J, Jeffries NO, Castellanos FX, Liu H, et al. 1999. Brain development during childhood and adolescence: a longitudinal MRI study. *Nat. Neurosci.* 2:861–63

Goddings A-L, Burnett Heyes S, Bird G, Viner RM, Blakemore S-J. 2012. The relationship between puberty and social emotion processing. *Dev. Sci.* 15:801–11

Green MR, Barnes B, McCormick CM. 2012. Social instability stress in adolescence increases anxiety and reduces social interactions in adulthood in male Long-Evans rats. *Dev. Psychobiol.* doi: 10.1002/dev.21077

Güroğlu B, van den Bos W, Crone EA. 2009. Fairness considerations: increasing understanding of intentionality during adolescence. *J. Exp. Child Psychol.* 104:398–409

Hill J, Inder T, Neil J, Dierker D, Harwell J, Van Essen D. 2010. Similar patterns of cortical expansion during human development and evolution. *Proc. Natl. Acad. Sci. USA* 107:13135–40

Huttenlocher PR, Dabholkar AS. 1997. Regional differences in synaptogenesis in human cerebral cortex. *J. Comp. Neurol.* 387:167–78

Kaller CP, Heinze K, Mader I, Unterrainer JM, Rahm B, et al. 2012. Linking planning performance and gray matter density in mid-dorsolateral prefrontal cortex: moderating effects of age and sex. *NeuroImage* 63:1454–63

Kessler RC, Berglund P, Demler O, Jin R, Merikangas KR, Walters EE. 2005. Lifetime prevalence and age-of-onset distributions of DSM-IV disorders in the National Comorbidity Survey Replication. *Arch. Gen. Psychiatry* 62:593–602

Keysar B, Barr DJ, Balin JA, Brauner JS. 2000. Taking perspective in conversation: the role of mutual knowledge in comprehension. *Psychol. Sci.* 11:32–38

Keysar B, Lin S, Barr DJ. 2003. Limits on theory of mind use in adults. *Cognition* 89:25–41

Larson R, Richards MH. 1991. Daily companionship in late childhood and early adolescence: changing developmental contexts. *Child Dev.* 62:284–300

Larson RW, Richards MH, Moneta G, Holmbeck G, Duckett E. 1996. Changes in adolescents' daily interactions with their families from ages 10 to 18: disengagement and transformation. *Dev. Psychol.* 32:744–54

Lebel C, Walker L, Leemans A, Phillips L, Beaulieu C. 2008. Microstructural maturation of the human brain from childhood to adulthood. *NeuroImage* 40:1044–55

Lenroot RK, Gogtay N, Greenstein DK, Wells EM, Wallace GL, et al. 2007. Sexual dimorphism of brain developmental trajectories during childhood and adolescence. *NeuroImage* 36:1065–73

Leussis MP, Andersen SL. 2008. Is adolescence a sensitive period for depression? Behavioral and neuroanatomical findings from a social stress model. *Synapse* 62:22–30

Luna B, Garver KE, Urban TA, Lazar NA, Sweeney JA. 2004. Maturation of cognitive processes from late childhood to adulthood. *Child Dev.* 75:1357–72

Luna B, Thulborn KR, Munoz DP, Merriam EP, Garver KE, et al. 2001. Maturation of widely distributed brain function subserves cognitive development. *NeuroImage* 13:786–93

Masten CL, Eisenberger NI, Borofsky LA, McNealy K, Pfeifer JH, Dapretto M. 2011. Subgenual anterior cingulate responses to peer rejection: a marker of adolescents' risk for depression. *Dev. Psychopathol.* 23:283–92

Masten CL, Eisenberger NI, Borofsky LA, Pfeifer JH, McNealy K, et al. 2009. Neural correlates of social exclusion during adolescence: understanding the distress of peer rejection. *Soc. Cogn. Affect. Neurosci.* 4:143–57

Masten CL, Eisenberger NI, Pfeifer JH, Dapretto M. 2010. Witnessing peer rejection during early adolescence: neural correlates of empathy for experiences of social exclusion. *Soc. Neurosci.* 5:496–507

McCormick CM, Green MR, Cameron NM, Nixon F, Levy MJ, Clark RA. 2013. Deficits in male sexual behavior in adulthood after social instability stress in adolescence in rats. *Horm. Behav.* 63:5–12

McCormick CM, Mathews IZ, Thomas C, Waters P. 2010. Investigations of HPA function and the enduring consequences of stressors in adolescence in animal models. *Brain Cogn.* 72:73–85

McGivern RF, Andersen J, Byrd D, Mutter KL, Reilly J. 2002. Cognitive efficiency on a match to sample task decreases at the onset of puberty in children. *Brain Cogn.* 50:73–89

Mills KL, Lalonde F, Clasen LS, Giedd JN, Blakemore S-J. 2013. Developmental changes in the structure of the social brain in late childhood and adolescence. *Soc. Cogn. Affect. Neurosci.* In press

Moffitt TE. 1993. Adolescence-limited and life-course-persistent antisocial behavior: a developmental taxonomy. *Psychol. Rev.* 100:674–701

Moor BG, Macks ZA, Güroglu B, Rombouts SA, Molen MW, Crone EA. 2012. Neurodevelopmental changes of reading the mind in the eyes. *Soc. Cogn. Affect. Neurosci.* 7:44–52

Moore WE 3rd, Pfeifer JH, Masten CL, Mazziotta JC, Iacoboni M, Dapretto M. 2012. Facing puberty: associations between pubertal development and neural responses to affective facial displays. *Soc. Cogn. Affect. Neurosci.* 7:35–43

O'Brien SF, Bierman KL. 1988. Conceptions and perceived influence of peer groups: interviews with preadolescents and adolescents. *Child Dev.* 59:1360–65

Olson IR, McCoy D, Klobusicky E, Ross LA. 2013. Social cognition and the anterior temporal lobes: a review and theoretical framework. *Soc. Cogn. Affect. Neurosci.* 8:123–33

Panizzon MS, Fennema-Notestine C, Eyler LT, Jernigan TL, Prom-Wormley E, et al. 2009. Distinct genetic influences on cortical surface area and cortical thickness. *Cereb. Cortex* 19:2728–35

Paus T, Keshavan M, Giedd JN. 2008. Why do many psychiatric disorders emerge during adolescence? *Nat. Rev. Neurosci.* 9:947–57

Pelphrey KA, Carter EJ. 2008. Charting the typical and atypical development of the social brain. *Dev. Psychopathol.* 20:1081–102

Pelphrey KA, Morris JP, McCarthy G. 2004. Grasping the intentions of others: the perceived intentionality of an action influences activity in the superior temporal sulcus during social perception. *J. Cogn. Neurosci.* 16:1706–16

Peper JS, Dahl RE. 2013. Surging hormones—brain-behavior interactions during puberty. *Curr. Dir. Psychol. Sci.* 22:134–39

Perlman WR, Webster MJ, Herman MM, Kleinman JE, Weickert CS. 2007. Age-related differences in glucocorticoid receptor mRNA levels in the human brain. *Neurobiol. Aging* 28:447–58

Petanjek Z, Judaš M, Šimic G, Rasin MR, Uylings HBM, et al. 2011. Extraordinary neoteny of synaptic spines in the human prefrontal cortex. *Proc. Natl. Acad. Sci. USA* 108:13281–86

Pfeifer JH, Masten CL, Borofsky LA, Dapretto M, Fuligni AJ, Lieberman MD. 2009. Neural correlates of direct and reflected self-appraisals in adolescents and adults: when social perspective-taking informs self-perception. *Child Dev.* 80:1016–38

Pfeifer JH, Masten CL, Moore WE 3rd, Oswald TM, Mazziotta JC, et al. 2011. Entering adolescence: resistance to peer influence, risky behavior, and neural changes in emotion reactivity. *Neuron* 69:1029–36

Poldrack RA. 2010. Interpreting developmental changes in neuroimaging signals. *Hum. Brain Mapp.* 31:872–78

Puce A, Perrett D. 2003. Electrophysiology and brain imaging of biological motion. *Philos. Trans. R. Soc. Lond. Ser. B Biol. Sci.* 358:435–45

Rakic P. 1995. A small step for the cell, a giant leap for mankind: a hypothesis of neocortical expansion during evolution. *Trends Neurosci.* 18:383–88

Reyna VF. 2008. A theory of medical decision making and health: fuzzy trace theory. *Med. Decis. Making* 28:850–65

Reyna VF, Adam MB. 2003. Fuzzy-trace theory, risk communication, and product labeling in sexually transmitted diseases. *Risk Anal.* 23:325–42

Reyna VF, Farley F. 2006. Risk and rationality in adolescent decision making: implications for theory, practice, and public policy. *Psychol. Sci. Public Interest* 7:1–44

Ross WD. 1925. *Ethica Nicomachea.* Transl. WD Ross. London: Oxford Univ. Press

Rushworth MF, Mars RB, Sallet J. 2013. Are there specialized circuits for social cognition and are they unique to humans? *Curr. Opin. Neurobiol.* 23:1–7

Sallet J, Mars RB, Noonan MP, Andersson JL, O'Reilly JX, et al. 2011. Social network size affects neural circuits in macaques. *Science* 334:697–700

Saxe R, Kanwisher N. 2003. People thinking about thinking people. The role of the temporo-parietal junction in "theory of mind." *NeuroImage* 19:1835–42

Saxe RR, Whitfield-Gabrieli S, Scholz J, Pelphrey KA. 2009. Brain regions for perceiving and reasoning about other people in school-aged children. *Child Dev.* 80:1197–209

Schulz KM, Zehr JL, Salas-Ramirez KY, Sisk CL. 2009. Testosterone programs adult social behavior before and during, but not after, adolescence. *Endocrinology* 150:3690–98

Sebastian C, Viding E, Williams KD, Blakemore S-J. 2010. Social brain development and the affective consequences of ostracism in adolescence. *Brain Cogn.* 72:134–45

Sebastian CL, Tan GC, Roiser JP, Viding E, Dumontheil I, Blakemore S-J. 2011. Developmental influences on the neural bases of responses to social rejection: implications of social neuroscience for education. *NeuroImage* 57:686–94

Silvers JA, McRae K, Gabrieli JD, Gross JJ, Remy KA, Ochsner KN. 2012. Age-related differences in emotional reactivity, regulation, and rejection sensitivity in adolescence. *Emotion* 12:1235–47

Sowell ER, Peterson BS, Thompson PM, Welcome SE, Henkenius AL, Toga AW. 2003. Mapping cortical change across the human life span. *Nat. Neurosci.* 6:309–15

Steinberg L. 2009. Adolescent development and juvenile justice. *Annu. Rev. Clin. Psychol.* 5:459–85

Steinberg L. 2013. The influence of neuroscience on US Supreme Court decisions about adolescents' criminal culpability. *Nat. Rev. Neurosci.* 14:513–18

Steinberg L, Graham S, O'Brien L, Woolard J, Cauffman E, Banich M. 2009. Age differences in future orientation and delay discounting. *Child Dev.* 80:28–44

Steinberg L, Scott ES. 2003. Less guilty by reason of adolescence: developmental immaturity, diminished responsibility, and the juvenile death penalty. *Am. Psychol.* 58:1009–18

Tamnes CK, Walhovd KB, Dale AM, Ostby Y, Grydeland H, et al. 2013. Brain development and aging: overlapping and unique patterns of change. *NeuroImage* 68C:63–74

Toledo-Rodriguez M, Sandi C. 2011. Stress during adolescence increases novelty seeking and risk taking behavior in male and female rats. *Front. Behav. Neurosci.* 5:17

van den Bos W, Van Dijk E, Westenberg M, Rombouts SA, Crone EA. 2011. Changing brains, changing perspectives: the neurocognitive development of reciprocity. *Psychol. Sci.* 22:60–70

van Duijvenvoorde ACK, Zanolie K, Rombouts SARB, Raijmakers MEJ, Crone EA. 2008. Evaluating the negative or valuing the positive? Neural mechanisms supporting feedback-based learning across development. *J. Neurosci.* 28:9495–503

Van Leijenhorst L, Westenberg PM, Crone EA. 2008. A developmental study of risky decisions on the cake gambling task: age and gender analyses of probability estimation and reward evaluation. *Dev. Neuropsychol.* 33:179–96

Van Leijenhorst L, Zanolie K, Van Meel CS, Westenberg PM, Rombouts SARB, Crone EA. 2010. What motivates the adolescent? Brain regions mediating reward sensitivity across adolescence. *Cereb. Cortex* 20:61–69

Viner RM, Ozer EM, Denny S, Marmot M, Resnick M, et al. 2012. Adolescence and the social determinants of health. *Lancet* 379:1641–52

Wang AT, Lee SS, Sigman M, Dapretto M. 2006. Developmental changes in the neural basis of interpreting communicative intent. *Soc. Cogn. Affect. Neurosci.* 1:107–21

Webb SJ, Monk CS, Nelson CA. 2001. Mechanisms of postnatal neurobiological development: implications for human development. *Dev. Neuropsychol.* 19:147–71

Weil LG, Fleming SM, Dumontheil I, Kilford EJ, Weil RS, et al. 2013. The development of metacognitive ability in adolescence. *Conscious. Cogn.* 22:264–71

Whitaker LR, Degoulet M, Morikawa H. 2013. Social deprivation enhances VTA synaptic plasticity and drug-induced contextual learning. *Neuron* 77:335–45

Winkler AM, Kochunov P, Blangero J, Almasy L, Zilles K, et al. 2010. Cortical thickness or grey matter volume? The importance of selecting the phenotype for imaging genetics studies. *NeuroImage* 53:1135–46

Yakovlev PA, Lecours IR. 1967. The myelogenetic cycles of regional maturation of the brain. In *Regional Development of the Brain in Early Life*, ed. A Minkowski, pp. 3–70. Oxford, UK: Blackwell

Psychological Research on Retirement

Mo Wang[1] and Junqi Shi[2]

[1]Department of Management, Warrington College of Business Administration, University of Florida, Gainesville, Florida 32611; email: mo.wang@warrington.ufl.edu

[2]Department of Management, Lingnan (University) College, Sun Yat-sen University, Guangzhou 510275, China; email: shijq3@mail.sysu.edu.cn

Annu. Rev. Psychol. 2014. 65:209–33

First published online as a Review in Advance on June 7, 2013

The *Annual Review of Psychology* is online at http://psych.annualreviews.org

This article's doi: 10.1146/annurev-psych-010213-115131

Keywords

retirement, retirement planning, retirement decision making, retirement adjustment, bridge employment

Abstract

Retirement as a research topic has become increasingly prominent in the psychology literature. This article provides a review of both theoretical development and empirical findings in this literature in the past two decades. We first discuss psychological conceptualizations of retirement and empirical operationalizations of retirement status. We then review three psychological models for understanding the retirement process and associated antecedents and outcomes, including the temporal process model of retirement, the multilevel model of retirement, and the resource-based dynamic model for retirement adjustment. We next survey the empirical findings regarding how various individual attributes, job and organizational factors, family factors, and socioeconomic context are related to the retirement process. We also discuss outcomes associated with retirement in terms of retirees' financial well-being, physical well-being, and psychological well-being.

Contents

INTRODUCTION

Given the rapid aging of the population and labor force, employee retirement has been an important element in political, socioeconomic, and human resource areas. As a result, there is a vast and diverse body of literature on retirement, both within academic circles and in the popular press. In fact, a Google Scholar search in January 2013, using the key word retirement yielded 1,220,000 hits. Within the psychology literature, using the same key word in the PsycINFO database yielded 6,857 hits, whereas limiting the search to only peer-reviewed journal articles still yielded 4,580 hits. In the 1970s there were only 207 peer-reviewed articles for the key word retirement, according to PsycINFO. In the 1980s the count rose to 535, in the 1990s to 687, and then in the 2000s it ballooned to 2,019. Thus, it is clear that retirement is a popular topic for researchers both within and outside psychology and that it is becoming more prominent in the psychology literature.

Due to the breadth and depth of psychological research on retirement, we must place several bounds on this review. First, as is the tradition of the *Annual Review of Psychology*, we purposely orient our review with a recency bias, where we consider newer and current topics to a greater degree than older ones. This is particularly important because as socioeconomic phenomena, the forms and processes of retirement evolve as the societal structures (e.g., labor force structure, population structure, societal culture, and economic structure) change over time (Szinovacz 2013). Second, although most of our citations are relatively recent, we attempt to strike a balance by linking traditional contributions of retirement research, especially theoretical perspectives, to the current literature. Finally, our bibliography is selective rather than exhaustive, and we orient our review to provide a critical discussion of the current status of research that aims to inspire future research.

In organizing this review, we first discuss various psychological conceptualizations of retirement, including both process-oriented conceptualizations and status-oriented empirical operationalizations. We then discuss three recent psychological models for understanding the retirement process and its antecedents and outcomes, including the temporal process model of retirement, the multilevel model of retirement, and the resource-based dynamic model for retirement adjustment. We next examine how various individual attributes, job and organizational factors, family factors, and socioeconomic context are related to the retirement process. We also review research on retirement outcomes in terms of retirees' financial well-being, physical well-being, and psychological well-being.

PSYCHOLOGICAL CONCEPTUALIZATION OF RETIREMENT

As noted by Denton & Spencer (2009), retirement has been defined in various ways by different researchers, largely depending on the research questions being addressed and the researcher's disciplinary background. In this review, following the psychological perspective laid out by Shultz & Wang (2011), we define retirement as an individual's exit from the workforce, which accompanies decreased psychological commitment to and behavioral withdrawal from work. This definition allows us to emphasize retirement as both a psychological process in conceptualization and a life status in empirical operationalization. This definition is also consistent with the argument made by life-stage developmental theorists (e.g., Levinson & Levinson 1996) that retirement is a life stage that not only corresponds to decreased levels of physical activities and productivities but also involves lowered stress and less responsibility to others in day-to-day life.

Retirement as Decision Making

In psychological research, retirement has often been conceptualized as a decision-making process, which emphasizes that when workers decide to retire, they make a motivated choice to decrease their psychological commitment to work and behaviorally withdraw from work-related activities (Adams et al. 2002, Feldman 1994, Shultz & Wang 2007, Wang et al. 2008). Essentially, this conceptualization hypothesizes that after workers make the decision to retire, their work activities should monotonically decline over time, and other life activities, such as family- and community-related activities, would increase (e.g., Wang & Shultz 2010). This conceptualization also highlights the importance of the retirement decision as a major life event and illustrates some normative motivations for people to retire, such as health issues; family care needs; attitudes toward one's job, employer, and career; and desires for leisure pursuits (e.g., Chevalier et al. 2013, Shultz et al. 1998).

When conceptualizing retirement as decision making, researchers have typically relied on the informed decision-making approach to conduct their investigations. This approach assumes that older workers make their retirement decisions based on information they have regarding their own characteristics and their work and nonwork environment. In other words, older workers are expected to search and weigh the relevant information and evaluate the overall utility of retirement before they reach the decision about retirement. Following this general approach, theoretical mechanisms that have been applied to study the retirement decision-making process include rational choice theory, image and role theory, theory of planned behavior, and expectancy theory. Specifically, rational choice theory has been used to tie older workers' financial status as well as the external economic environment to their retirement decisions. It views the retirement decision as a result of comparing the financial resources accumulated and financial resources needed in retirement (Laitner & Sonnega 2013). Rationally, workers will retire only when they feel that their accumulated financial resources, as well as the forecast of future economic conditions, would allow them to support their consumption needs in retirement.

Both image theory and role theory have been used to link workers' demographic status, work experience, marital life, type of industries, and productivity to their retirement decision making (e.g., Adams et al. 2002, Mears et al. 2004). In particular, all of these factors are related to how people perceive themselves and their roles in the larger societal context, which creates comparison standards for workers to evaluate whether the action of retirement matches their self-images or roles. If the match is achieved, then the decision will be made to retire (Brougham & Walsh 2007).

The theory of planned behavior has been used to link workers' retirement decision to their attitudes toward their jobs, employers, careers, and retirement, as well as the workplace norms (e.g., Adams & Beehr 1998, Shultz et al. 2003, Zhan et al. 2013). The general premise of this theory highlights the importance of workers' attitudes toward retirement and its alternative—continuing working—in influencing their retirement decisions. It also emphasizes the role of perceived social pressure to retire in influencing an individual's retirement decision.

Finally, expectancy theory has been used to link workers' productivity, job characteristics, health status, and subjective life expectancy to their retirement decisions (e.g., Karpansalo et al. 2004, Shultz & Wang 2007, van Solinge & Henkens 2010). Specifically, this theory argues that when retirees perceive low expectancy for reaching good productivity or receiving rewards from their work (due to their health status, job characteristics, or skills and abilities), they are more likely to retire instead of continuing to work.

As noted by Wang & Shultz (2010), one limitation of the decision-making conceptualization of retirement is that not all retirement decisions are voluntary (e.g., Gallo et al. 2000, Szinovacz & Davey 2005, van Solinge & Henkens 2007). As such, the theoretical utility of this conceptualization depends on the extent to which the retirement decision is indeed a result of motivated choice. Therefore, the voluntariness of the retirement decision could be viewed as a boundary condition for applying the informed decision-making approach to studying the retirement decision-making process.

Retirement as an Adjustment Process

Retirement can also be conceptualized as an adjustment process that incorporates both the retirement transition (i.e., from employment to retirement) and postretirement trajectory (i.e., postretirement development in life) (Wang 2007; Wang et al. 2009, 2011). In particular, this conceptualization emphasizes that it is not the decision to retire but rather the characteristics of the retirement transition process embedded in this decision that are of most importance (van Solinge & Henkens 2008). Therefore, conceptualizing retirement as an adjustment process focuses on investigating the fine-grained nature of retirement (e.g., the timing of the retirement, the previous preparation for the retirement, the resources available in retirement, and the amount of activity change resulting from the retirement) (Szinovacz 2003). Further, this conceptualization recognizes retirement as a longitudinal developmental process characterized by adjustment, which provides a more realistic depiction of retirement (Wang et al. 2011).

When conceptualizing retirement as an adjustment process, researchers most frequently use three theories. In particular, the life course perspective considers retirement as a transition in the course of the lifespan and argues that a person's individual history (e.g., how people dealt with previous transitions, their work and leisure habits, and previous workforce participation patterns;

Appold 2004, Carr & Kail 2013, Orel et al. 2004, von Bonsdoff et al. 2009) and attributes (e.g., demographics, health and financial status, and transition-related abilities and skills; Donaldson et al. 2010, Griffin & Hesketh 2008, Wang 2007) influence the pathways he/she takes to accomplish the transition. The general premise is that if an individual has cultivated a flexible style in dealing with life transitions, is less socially integrated with work, and has the attributes that help facilitate the transition, the person will be more likely to prepare well for the transition, engage in the transition with better timing, and achieve better outcomes from the transition (van Solinge & Henkens 2008, Wang et al. 2011). Further, the life course perspective also highlights that the experience of life transitions and the posttransition development are contingent on the specific contexts in which the transition occurs, such as older workers' job-associated statuses and roles (e.g., preretirement job attitudes, job characteristics, and career standings; Wang 2007, Wang et al. 2008, Zhan et al. 2013), as well as social context (e.g., social network, family structure, and marital life; Reitzes & Mutran 2004, Szinovacz & Davey 2004, Wang 2007). Finally, the life course perspective predicts a positive developmental trajectory in retirees' postretirement life, which is characterized by gradually decreased psychological and physical demands (Pinquart & Schindler 2007, Wang 2007).

Continuity theory emphasizes human beings' general tendency to maintain consistency in life patterns over time and to accommodate changes and transitions without the experience of a stressful disruption (Atchley 1999). Consequently, continuity theory predicts that only severe difficulty in maintaining general life patterns would lead to undesirable transition quality and unsuccessful adjustment to retirement. Empirical studies have shown that such severe difficulty may be associated with declines in health and financial status (e.g., Gallo et al. 2000, Wang 2007) and functional capacity change (e.g., Shultz & Wang 2007) during retirement transition and can be countered with bridge employment (e.g., Kim & Feldman 2000, Zhan et al. 2009), retirement planning (Taylor-Carter et al. 1997), and transferability of skills (Spiegel & Shultz 2003).

Role theory emphasizes retirement as triggering a role transition, which may weaken or eliminate work roles, such as the worker role, the organizational member role, and the career role, while strengthening the family member role and the community member role (Barnes-Farrell 2003). Further, role theory argues that the role transition can lead to either positive or negative adjustment consequences, depending on whether the role transition is desirable or matches the individual's values and goals (e.g., Adams et al. 2002, Wang 2007). Applying role theory, empirical studies have examined the impact of role stressors (e.g., Lin & Hsieh 2001), role identities (e.g., Taylor et al. 2007), and values and goals (e.g., Shultz et al. 1998) on retirement transition and adjustment.

Retirement as a Career Development Stage

In the past 20 years, accompanying technology development and pension system reform, there has been a continuous trend for workers to move away from the traditional linear career progression (Wang et al. 2013). As such, instead of viewing retirement as a career exit, it can be conceptualized as a late-career development stage that recognizes the continued potential for growth and renewal of careers in people's retirement life (Wang et al. 2013, Wang & Shultz 2010). This conceptualization is consistent with the protean career model, which argues that careers are controlled by workers themselves and focus on the worker's personal values and goals (e.g., Kim & Hall 2013). Specifically, this conceptualization pays great attention to how retirees may align their career goals with their work and leisure activities in retirement life and emphasizes examining unique factors that are associated with retirees' career potential and career pursuit, which may inform retirees' workforce participation activities and patterns after they retire. Thus, the research question considered by conceptualizing retirement as a career development stage centers on retirees' agency efficacy in career pursuit (e.g., Jex et al. 2007, Post et al. 2013).

Applying this conceptualization, empirical studies have shown that at the individual level, factors that influence one's career capacity, such as physical aging (e.g., Gobeski & Beehr 2008, Wang et al. 2008), cognitive aging (e.g., Wang & Chen 2006), and experience and expertise (e.g., Kim & Feldman 2000), may impact retirees' further career engagement and development. At the job level, issues such as keeping up with technology demands at work (Spiegel & Shultz 2003), searching for desirable job characteristics (Adams & Rau 2004, Rau & Adams 2005), and coping with job stressors (Elovainio et al. 2005, Shultz et al. 2010) have been shown to influence retirees' career pursuit. Finally, at the organizational level, factors such as organizational climate related to age bias and discrimination (Posthuma & Campion 2009), organizational downsizings (Gallo et al. 2000), and age-related managerial accommodations (Zappala et al. 2008) have also been associated with retirees' career pursuit. It is important to recognize that factors that may influence younger workers' career pursuits are not necessarily the same as those that may influence older workers' and retirees' career pursuits (Kim & Hall 2013, Wang et al. 2013). For example, to retirees, job security is often a minor concern when they choose to continue work part time (Morrow-Howell & Leon 1988).

Empirical Operationalization of Retirement

In the psychology literature, although retirement has often been conceptualized as one of three psychological processes we reviewed above, empirical studies have operationalized retirement status in multiple different ways. In fact, Ekerdt (2010, p. 70) has noted, "The designation of retirement status is famously ambiguous because there are multiple overlapping criteria by which someone might be called retired, including career cessation, reduced work effort, pension receipt, or self-report." Recently, Denton & Spencer (2009) identified eight different common ways that researchers from across the globe measured retirement status: (*a*) nonparticipation in the labor force, (*b*) reduction in hours worked and/or earnings, (*c*) hours worked or earnings below some minimum cutoff, (*d*) receipt of retirement/pension income, (*e*) exit from one's main employer, (*f*) change of career or employment later in life, (*g*) self-assessed retirement, and (*h*) some combination of the previous seven. Not surprisingly, psychologists, who are more likely to study individual-level phenomena, are most likely to choose to operationalize retirement status via self-report and self-assessment (Shultz & Wang 2011). Nevertheless, it is important for researchers to realize that operationalizing retirement in different ways may yield dramatically different findings, and it is possible to have mismatch between the conceptualization of retirement and the operationalization of retirement, rendering difficulty in interpreting research findings.

For example, if a researcher conceptualizes retirement as a decision made with the intention to withdraw from the workforce, it may be best to measure retirement via self-assessment but not via receipt of retirement/pension income. This is because a person may be eligible to receive retirement/pension income but still be engaged in some form of employment and have no intention of exiting the workforce. Similarly, it may not be ideal to use nonparticipation in the labor force or hours worked as indicators of retirement status because older workers may cease their participation in the workforce or cut down their work hours involuntarily. As such, these indices may not sufficiently capture the active withdrawal intention from the workforce that the researcher aims to operationalize. However, if a researcher wishes to study changes in retirees' financial statuses as a result of decision making and how these changes may be associated with changes in their health statuses, then using receipt of retirement/pension income as a measure of retirement status may provide a more accurate and relevant operationalization that could generate policy implications.

Further, if a researcher wishes to study how retirement-related human resource management practices influence retirees' career-related choices (e.g., conceptualizing retirement as a career development stage), then the exit from one's organization may be used as the more relevant operationalization of retirement status. Finally, following Wang et al. (2013), we recommend that researchers accommodate the specific features of the person's retirement (e.g., paid work hours, nature of the employment, and amount of pension/social security received) in their inquiries to better capture the heterogeneity of retirement in their operationalization.

PSYCHOLOGICAL MODELS FOR UNDERSTANDING RETIREMENT

In this section, we focus our review on three psychological models that clarify the retirement process and its antecedents and outcomes. They are the temporal process model of retirement, the multilevel model of retirement, and the resource-based dynamic model for retirement adjustment. In particular, the temporal process model of retirement provides a heuristic description of the retirement process itself, characterizing the retirement process as including three different phases that gradually unfold. The multilevel model of retirement provides a systematic and structural approach for searching and examining potential antecedents that can be used to understand and predict the retirement process. Finally, the resource-based dynamic model for retirement adjustment offers a coherent theoretical framework for understanding outcomes of the retirement process.

The Temporal Process Model of Retirement

The temporal process model of retirement argues that the retirement process usually consists of three broad and sequential phases: retirement planning, retirement decision making, and retirement transition and adjustment (Shultz & Wang 2011, Wang & Shultz 2010). In particular, the process typically starts with a somewhat distal preretirement preparation and planning phase (i.e., retirement planning), as individuals begin to envision what their retirement might entail and begin discussing those plans with friends, family members, and colleagues. Through this process, retirement planning helps in generating more accurate expectations for retirement life as well as mobilizing and organizing resources to serve the needs of the individual in the coming retirement. In particular, Taylor-Carter et al. (1997) categorize retirement planning into financial and cognitive planning. The goal of financial planning is to find a balance between revenue income and revenue expenditure that allows the individual to maintain a desired lifestyle in retirement (Hershey et al. 2013).

Although there often are social security and employer-provided pension funds for retirees to some degree, the focus of financial planning for retirement is on private savings. McCarthy (1996) argues that there are six steps in financial planning for retirement: collecting personal financial data, defining goals, identifying problems, planning, implementing the plan, and monitoring and revising the plan. Many challenges exist for the individual during financial planning because of varying levels of motivation to save for retirement across the lifespan and a fluctuating economic environment for investing (Hershey et al. 2013). Regarding cognitive planning for retirement, according to Adams & Rau (2011), the goal is to address four key questions: What will I do? How will I afford it? Where will I live? Who will I share it with? Answering these questions requires the individual to gather large amounts of information about the current situation (e.g., amount of current funds or current state of health) as well as to use cognitive skills to make predictions about possible futures (e.g., community involvement or working state of a spouse; Leung & Earl 2012, Wang 2007). Previous research has demonstrated that retirement planning in both financial and cognitive ways is crucial for structure, social interaction, and maintaining a standard of living into retirement (Hershey et al. 2013).

Next, as retirement becomes more proximal, one enters the retirement decision-making phase. Consistent with the informed decision-making approach we reviewed previously, during this phase, one has to weigh the values of work and leisure over time against individual circumstances to make the retirement decision. Some researchers have attempted to further specify the retirement decision-making phase into smaller stages. For example, Feldman & Beehr (2011) focused on capturing the thought-change process concerning retirement decision making and categorized the retirement decision-making phase into three stages: imagining the possibility, assessing when it is time to let go of the job, and putting concrete plans into action at present. These three stages characterize a cognitive process that first brainstorms possible futures, then considers the past experiences at work, and finally uses the compiled information to take steps toward retirement in the present (Feldman & Beehr 2011).

Sometimes the individual may also face the decision of whether to retire early. Early retirement has been defined as exiting the workforce before an individual is eligible for receiving social security benefits and/or pension (Damman et al. 2011, Feldman 1994, Kim & Feldman 1998). As such, in the United States, early retirement is usually operationalized as retiring before age 62 (i.e., the earliest one can start receiving social security benefits). Recently, Feldman (2013) argued that one's status of early retirement is at least partly subjective as well. In other words, whether a person retires early also depends on whether retirement happens at an age that is younger than one's expected retirement age (Potocnik et al. 2010). This subjective component for defining early retirement has become more and more prominent, given that continuous technology advancement and health care improvement have allowed people to work longer, even after they take early retirement incentives (e.g., Kim & Feldman 2000). This subjective definition also emphasizes the role of perceived person-environment fit in making early retirement decisions, as people who perceive poor person-environment fit with their work are more likely to exit the workforce early (Armstrong-Stassen et al. 2012, Feldman 2013, Herrbach et al. 2009).

Finally, as individuals make the transition from full-time worker to retiree, they enter the phase of retirement transition and adjustment. The most prominent component of this adjustment process involves changes in daily activity. Retirees have many options for how to spend their time after entering retirement, including leisure activities, volunteer work, and various forms of paid work (Adams & Rau 2011). Leisure activities are characterized by enjoyment, novelty, relaxation, companionship, aesthetic appreciation, and intimacy, including talking to or visiting friends and family, involvement in clubs and organizations, religious activity, physical activity such as exercise and sports, and hobby activity such as gardening and arts and crafts (Nimrod et al. 2009). Volunteer work can involve caring for one's family members as well as formally volunteering outside the home in business and civic organizations (Dosman et al. 2006, Kaskie et al. 2008).

Paid work following retirement is commonly referred to as bridge employment, which is defined as the pattern of labor force participation exhibited by older workers as they leave their career jobs and move toward complete labor force withdrawal (Feldman 1994, Wang et al. 2009). Recent studies have documented the high prevalence of engagement in bridge employment among retirees. For example, Brown and colleagues (2010) showed that over 20% of workers age 50 and older who reported themselves as being retired were also working for pay at the same time, which suggests a much higher prevalence rate for retirees to take bridge jobs. They also found that 75% of workers aged 50 and older expect to have a paid job during retirement. Similarly, Giandrea et al. (2009), using the Health and Retirement Study data from 1998 through 2006, found that among those aged 51 to 56 in 1998, 64% moved to a bridge job prior to exiting the labor force completely. Many financial factors could motivate an individual to seek further work after retirement, such as an increasing age to qualify for social security benefits, a decline of traditional defined benefit plans in favor of defined contribution plans (such as 401k plans), and improved labor market earnings (Cahill et al. 2013). Individuals may also try to mitigate and adapt to the lifestyle change in retirement by continuing workforce participation (Wang & Shultz 2010).

Bridge employment can take many different forms. When the work hours in bridge employment are reduced, compared to the preretirement job, the bridge job operates in the form of phased retirement, which has been shown to help retirees ease into their retirement (Wang et al. 2009). From the organizational perspective, one can continue working for one's preretirement employer or for a different employer full time or part time when entering retirement (Zhan et al. 2013). This organization-based bridge employment decision has received increasing research attention because more and more organizations are facing the pressure of a labor force shortage as baby boomers start to enter their retirement (Wang & Shultz 2010). As such, retaining retired workers through bridge jobs may help organizations to maintain flexible access to a skilled and experienced workforce. From the career perspective, bridge employment can also take two forms: career bridge employment, in which the individual works in the same industry or field as the individual's career job, and bridge employment in a different field (Wang et al. 2008). Previous research (e.g., Wang et al. 2008) suggests that a psychological attachment to the career and incentives given by companies to retain their skilled labor force make it likely that an individual will keep working in the form of career bridge employment, whereas a need to change working conditions contributes to bridge employment in a different field. Both forms of bridge employment can also be the result of a lack of retirement planning (Wang et al. 2008).

Summary. Using the temporal process model to describe and understand the retirement process allows researchers to investigate retirement as it unfolds over time from one phase to another. The general unfolding sequence established by this model helps researchers to further examine the interdependence among these retirement phases (e.g., how these stages influence one another and how they together influence the long-term adjustment outcomes of retirement; Shultz & Wang 2011). However, it is important to note that this temporal process is not homogeneous across individuals. Within the broad phases are smaller and shorter segments that individuals go through as they approach retirement, transition through the retirement decision-making process, and begin life as a self-designated retiree. Thus, researchers often focus on a specific phase of the retirement process in a given study, all the while realizing that they are studying just one piece of the larger retirement puzzle. In addition, this process is unlikely to go smoothly for all retirees. Some older individuals enter retirement experiencing ambivalence, anxiety, fear, depression, and a deep feeling of loss. As research summarized by Brown and colleagues (1996) and O'Rand (2003) shows, disabled individuals, individuals from traditionally disadvantaged race and ethnic groups, those from lower social classes, undocumented immigrants, the economically needy, individuals who have never worked, and the chronically unemployed will approach retirement planning, decision making, and transition and adjustment processes with vastly different experiences and perspectives. Thus, this temporal process model of retirement reinforces the need to examine the unique psychological dynamics that individuals face as they transition through their own retirement process.

The Multilevel Model of Retirement

The multilevel model of retirement originated from the sociological perspective that views retirement as a multilevel phenomenon (Szinovacz 2013). Specifically, at the societal or macrolevel, retirement can be conceived as an institution, reflecting cultural norms and societal values and their manifestation in diverse support systems for retirees. The mesolevel consists of retirement policies and cultures reinforced at the organizational level, manifested in the explicit forms of specific organizational policies relating to benefits, retirement age, and other supports for older workers and retirees, as well as in the implicit forms of retirement images and expectations that are propagated by the organization or in the work environment. At the microlevel, retirement manifests as an individual's own pathway for exiting the workforce, emphasizing retirement plans, decisions, and postretirement activities and behaviors, largely as we reviewed previously in the temporal process model of retirement.

Applying this multilevel model of retirement to psychological research points to the importance of considering variables from various levels to understand the individual retirement process. In particular, this multilevel model of retirement reveals that one's behaviors and actions throughout the retirement process are not only influenced by the individual-level variables (i.e., the microlevel variables) but also shaped by the larger context of their retirement (i.e., the macro- and mesolevel variables). Therefore, the multilevel model of retirement can serve as a general theoretical framework for searching and examining potential antecedents that can be used to understand and predict the retirement process. In the sections that follow, we rely on this model to guide our review of empirical findings on antecedents of the retirement process.

According to Szinovacz (2013), at the macrolevel the contexts that may impact the individual retirement process include characteristics of retirement support systems, cultural values and social norms about retirement, and economic and labor market conditions. For example, the eligible age for receiving social security has profound impact on retirement planning and retirement decision making because it provides a concrete timeline for workers to evaluate their proximity to entering retirement life (Ekerdt et al. 2001). Further, cultural values that encourage retirement and view it as a voluntary and desirable transition are likely to shape positive attitudes toward retirement, facilitating retirement planning and early retirement decisions (Hershey et al. 2007). Similarly, social norms for retirement timing could impact retirement decision making across different work environments and cohorts (Mermin et al. 2007). It is also important to note that the gender and family norms embedded in social security benefits (e.g., spouse allowance, length-of-marriage requirements for divorces, and not recognizing homosexual partnerships) have direct consequences for retirement-related behaviors in certain populations (e.g., older minority women; Angel et al. 2007). Finally, older workers' economic context can play an important role in the retirement process. Specifically, a poor economy and high unemployment rates are likely to discourage older workers from remaining in the labor market, whereas a robust economy and low unemployment rates may be positively related to retirees' likelihood of returning to work after retirement (Munnell et al. 2008).

At the mesolevel, the contexts that may influence individual retirement processes include the work context (i.e., organizational and job factors) and the nonwork life context (i.e., family and social network factors). In particular, the relevant organizational and job factors may include age- and retirement-related human resource practices, workplace ageism, job characteristics, and job- and career-related attitudes. For example, following the rational choice approach, the availability and the form of the pension plan offered by the organization (i.e., defined benefit versus defined distribution) are expected to shape people's retirement decision making through influencing their financial resources (Laitner & Sonnega 2013, Szinovacz 2013). Further, human resource policies that accommodate older workers' needs (e.g., flexible work schedule) and counter workplace ageism may both serve to retain older workers and attract them to bridge employment in the same organization (Wang & Shultz 2010). Undesirable work conditions, such as high physical and cognitive demands, are likely to push older workers to retire (Shultz et al.

1998), whereas positive attitudes toward one's job, organization, and career are likely to keep older workers from completely exiting the workforce (Zhan et al. 2013).

The family and social network factors that may influence the individual retirement process include social support, marital and dependent-care situations, and spouse's working situations. Following the life course perspective, the life transition processes of individuals (e.g., retirement) are closely linked to their significant others (Wang & Shultz 2010). Specifically, family members and friends may influence one's retirement planning, retirement decision, and postretirement activities through lending their material and immaterial support, offering anchoring points and role modeling opportunities, and providing a desirable social context that can substitute for the relations at work (Szinovacz 2013). Further, some individuals may postpone retirement until their children are no longer dependent on them, whereas others may retire early to take care of grandchildren or dependents with illness (Brown & Warner 2008). Finally, the spouse's working situation may influence an individual's retirement planning and decision making because people typically would like to time their retirement together to ease leisure-activity planning and social adjustment (Curl & Townsend 2008).

At the microlevel, variables that may influence the individual retirement process include individual attributes (e.g., demographics, health and financial conditions, knowledge and skills, personality, and needs and values), employment history, and attitudes toward retirement. Following the life course perspective, individual attributes and employment history form the immediate personal context of the life transition process. For example, the cumulative advantage/disadvantage theory (O'Rand 2003) indicates that individuals from lower-socioeconomic-status groups not only accumulate less human capital (e.g., knowledge and skills) early in life but also are more subject to health problems. These early disadvantages tend to increase financial and health-risk exposure in adulthood, whereas advantage opens expanded opportunities. Therefore, a person's retirement process is likely influenced by the cumulative life experiences stemming from his/her individual attributes and consequent employment history (Szinovacz & Davey 2005, van Solinge & Henkens 2007). Further, an individual's attitudes toward retirement are probably the most proximal predictors of retirement-related behaviors. According to the theory of planned behavior, positive attitudes toward retirement will be associated with engagement in retirement planning and will facilitate one's decision to retire (Shultz et al. 2003).

The Resource-Based Dynamic Model for Retirement Adjustment

The resource-based dynamic model for retirement adjustment focuses on explaining retirement adjustment as a longitudinal process during which retirees' levels of adjustment may fluctuate as a function of individual resources and changes in these resources (Wang et al. 2011). Therefore, this model directs research attention to the underlying mechanism through which retirement has its impact on retirees' well-being rather than focusing on the absolute good or bad impact of retirement on retirees. As such, this model can be used as a unified theoretical framework to study various outcomes of retirement (e.g., retirees' financial, physical, and psychological well-being) as well as the factors that drive those outcomes.

Specifically, resources can be broadly defined as the total capability an individual has to fulfill his or her centrally valued needs. In a review of different types of resources studied in previous retirement research, Wang (2007) suggested that this total capability may include one's physical resources (e.g., muscle strength; Jex et al. 2007), cognitive resources (e.g., processing speed and working memory; Wang & Chen 2006), motivational resources (e.g., self-efficacy; Dendinger et al. 2005), financial resources (e.g., salary and pension; Damman et al. 2011), social resources (e.g., social network and social support; Kim & Feldman 2000), and emotional resources (e.g., emotional stability and affectivity; Blekesaune & Skirbekk 2012). It is expected that the ease of retirement adjustment is the direct result of the individual's access to these resources. On the one hand, when people have more resources to fulfill the needs they value in retirement, they will experience less difficulty in adjusting to retirement. On the other hand, decreases in retirees' resources will have adverse effects on retirement adjustment.

Following this resource perspective, variation in well-being along the retirement adjustment process can be viewed as a result of resource changes. In other words, if compared to the reference point (e.g., the beginning of the retirement adjustment), a retiree's total resources do not change significantly (e.g., due to successfully maintaining prior lifestyles and activities), he or she may not experience significant change in well-being. If a retiree's total resources significantly decrease compared to the reference point (e.g., due to losing a major income source), he or she may experience negative change in well-being. Further, compared to the reference point, if an individual's retirement enables him or her to invest significantly more resources (e.g., due to gaining cognitive resources that were previously occupied by a stressful job) in fulfilling centrally valued needs, he or she may experience a positive change in well-being. As such, this theoretical framework has the flexibility to accommodate a variety of longitudinal patterns for retirement adjustment, which significantly enriches the understanding of individual differences in the longitudinal process of retirement adjustment (Wang 2007, Wang et al. 2013).

Moreover, using resource change as the mechanism to explain variation in retirement adjustment, this theoretical framework can also be applied to consider the factors that may influence retirement adjustment quality (e.g., Carr & Kail 2013, Kubicek et al. 2011, Wang et al. 2011). In particular, researchers may focus on examining antecedents that have a direct impact on different types of resources. This theorizing offers a large scope of antecedents that could influence various retirees' resources in the adjustment process, including variables from the macrolevel (e.g., societal norms and government policies), organizational level (e.g., organizational climate and human resource practices), job level (e.g., job conditions), household level (e.g., marital quality), and individual level (e.g., health behaviors and psychological resilience). As such, adopting the resource-based dynamic perspective may lead to a more comprehensive and fruitful examination of different factors that influence retirement adjustment.

Finally, compared to traditional theories for retirement adjustment (e.g., life course perspective, continuity theory, and role theory), this resource-based dynamic model also provides new opportunities to understand the turning point that connects two different trends in the retirement adjustment process. For example, following this model, one may hypothesize that certain individual differences (e.g., openness to change, goal orientation in retirement, and need for structure) may impact retirees' motivational resources, and certain environmental factors (e.g., family support, community cohesiveness, and unemployment rate in the local labor market) may impact retirees' financial and social resources. In turn, these resources may predict how fast the turning points will be reached for retirees who experience negative change first but positive change in their well-being later. This is because these individual differences and environment factors all facilitate retirees obtaining more resources, which makes them more likely to switch from the downward trend to the upward trend. Therefore, in future studies, applying this resource-based dynamic perspective may further improve our understanding of the form and nature of the retirement process.

ANTECEDENTS OF THE RETIREMENT PROCESS

In this section, we review empirical findings regarding antecedents of the retirement process. Based on the temporal process model reviewed previously, we focus on antecedents related to retirement planning, retirement decision making, and postretirement activities. In particular, we follow the multilevel model of retirement and organize our review of antecedents into categories of individual attributes, job and organizational factors, family factors, and socioeconomic contexts.

Individual Attributes

Among individual attributes, various demographics have been associated with the retirement process. For example, regarding gender effect on the retirement process, Glass & Kilpatrick (1998) showed that men were more likely not only to save more for retirement, but also to invest in more aggressive financial mechanisms. Hershey et al. (2002) found that men were more likely to have specific concrete retirement goals (e.g., buy a motor home and travel to Alaska), whereas women reported more general and abstract goals (e.g., be happy). Davis (2003) found that male retirees were more likely than female retirees to engage in career bridge employment than full retirement.

Regarding the age effect on the retirement process, a recent study by Phua & McNally (2008) showed that younger and older men's attitudes toward retirement planning were somewhat different. Younger men were much less likely to be saving for retirement, and they also made a much stronger distinction between preretirement planning and financial planning for retirement, whereas older men saw these two forms of planning as more closely aligned. Further, Ekerdt et al. (2001) found that the closer the perceived proximity of retirement was, the more motivated workers were to engage in both formal and informal retirement planning activities. Age has also been repeatedly demonstrated to be one of the strongest predictors of individuals' decisions to retire: The older the individual is, the more likely it is that the individual will retire (e.g., Adams & Rau 2004, Kim & Feldman 2000, Wang et al. 2008). Davis (2003) and Wang et al. (2008) further found that younger retirees were more likely than older retirees to engage in bridge employment in a different field than in full retirement. On the other hand, Loi & Shultz (2007) found that younger retirees were more motivated to seek bridge employment opportunities than older retirees for financial reasons, whereas older retirees were more motivated than younger retirees to seek jobs with more flexible schedules.

Education is related to postretirement activities. Highly educated people typically have more capacity and options in maintaining their life patterns because of their professional knowledge and/or skills. For example, Kim & DeVaney (2005) found that retirees who had college degrees were more likely to engage in bridge employment than were those who did not have college degrees. Similarly, Wang et al. (2008) found that retirees who received more years of education were more likely to engage in bridge employment than in full retirement.

Previous studies have examined the predictive effect of health on retirement decision making and consistently found that employees who are healthy are likely to continue to stay employed, whereas those employees with health problems are more likely to retire (e.g., Shultz & Wang 2007, Szubert & Sobala 2005). Health problems also prompt perceptions of untimely and involuntary retirement (Szinovacz & Davey 2005, van Solinge & Henkens 2007). Kim & Feldman (2000) and Wang et al. (2008) also found that retirees who had better health were more likely to engage in bridge employment than in full retirement.

Citing a 2004 AARP report, Taylor & Geldhauser (2007) note that older workers from lower income brackets (household income lower than $40,000) are less likely than those from higher income brackets (household income higher than $100,000) to engage in informal and formal retirement planning. Financial status consistently predicts retirement decisions as well. Specifically, those with more accumulated financial resources and higher perceptions of their adequacy are more likely to retire (Gruber & Wise 1999). However, when it comes to bridge employment, the relationship is rather complicated. For example, Wang et al. (2008) found that retirees' total wealth did not predict the likelihood that retirees would engage in career bridge employment versus full retirement. This suggests that financial motivation may not be a primary driving force for people to engage in career bridge employment versus full retirement. However, Wang et al. (2008) did find that retirees who had better financial conditions were less likely to engage in bridge employment in a different field than to pursue full retirement. This is consistent with Kim & Feldman's (2000) finding that an individual's salary at retirement was negatively related to the amount of work a retiree did in bridge employment.

Regarding the effect of personal needs and values, Shultz et al. (1998) found that retirees who valued leisure activities (e.g., travel and hobbies) and spending time with family were more likely to voluntarily retire. Further, Adams & Rau (2004) found that that retirees' work ethic was negatively related to their pursuit of bridge employment opportunities. Perhaps people with greater work ethic might be more prepared for retirement and might feel it to be their "just reward" for their years of hard work. It has been shown that retirees who had generative motives (i.e., working for teaching and sharing knowledge with the younger generation) were more likely to take bridge employment than full retirement (Dendinger et al. 2005). Davis (2003) also found that retirees who had higher entrepreneurial orientations were more likely to engage in career bridge employment than in full retirement, whereas retirees who had more desire to pursue a new career were more likely to engage in bridge employment in a different field than in full retirement.

Regarding the effect of personality on the retirement process, Lockenhoff and colleagues (2009) found that individuals low in conscientiousness retired earlier than those who were high in conscientiousness. Robinson et al. (2010) found that neuroticism was related to a negative view of retirement circumstances, whereas conscientiousness was related to a more positive perception of the retirement decision. A recent study by Blekesaune & Skirbekk (2012) demonstrated some interesting interaction effects between personality and gender in predicting disability-related retirement. Specifically, they found that neuroticism increased the risk for women to take disability-related retirement, whereas openness increased such risk for men. Further, agreeableness and extraversion decreased the risk for disability-related retirement for men. The mechanisms behind these interaction effects were still unclear.

Older workers' attitudes toward retirement also play important roles in shaping the retirement process. Kim & Moen (2001) reported that in the preretirement stage, unfavorable attitudes toward retirement were associated with the absence of retirement planning and failure to seek information about retirement. Ekerdt et al. (2001) also found that ambivalent attitudes about the timing and form of retirement were related to uncertainty in making retirement decisions. Finally, Adams & Rau (2004) found that retirees' negative attitude toward retirement was positively related to their search for bridge employment opportunities.

Job and Organizational Factors

Numerous studies have shown that the characteristics of one's preretirement job have important implications for the retirement process. For example, both Lin & Hsieh (2001) and Elovainio et al. (2005) reported that those who perceived their jobs as being stressful and having higher workloads intended to retire early. Similarly, research on blue-collar workers in Poland (Szubert & Sobala 2005) indicated that demanding work conditions (e.g., heavy lifting at work) were related to increased risks for leaving the workforce before the nationally mandated age of retirement. Further, Wang et al. (2008) and Gobeski & Beehr (2008) found that workers in stressful jobs (e.g., jobs with greater physical and psychological demands) were more likely to take bridge employment in a different field than to take career bridge employment or full retirement.

Job and career attitudes have also been shown to be critical for the retirement process. For example, researchers reported that those who report simply "being tired of work" were more likely to decide to retire (e.g., Bidwell et al. 2006). On the other hand, Adams and his colleagues (e.g., Adams & Beehr 1998, Adams et al. 2002) showed that one's organizational commitment and career attachment were negatively related to the decision to retire. Wang et al. (2008) found that retirees who had higher job satisfaction at preretirement jobs were more likely to engage in career bridge employment than in bridge employment in a different field or in full retirement, whereas Kim & Feldman (2000) showed that retirees with longer job tenure were more likely to engage in bridge employment than in full retirement.

Organizational policies and workplace norms with regard to older workers and retirement are important to the retirement process as well. In particular, the retirement benefit packages offered by the employer, such as pension and health insurance, have profound influence on the retirement process. For example, Kim & Feldman (1998) found that both lower salary and higher pension benefits were significantly related to early retirement decisions. Munnell and colleagues (2004) also found that pension coverage increased the probability of actual retirement, and this effect was more pronounced for individuals with defined benefit plans than for those with defined contribution plans. Regarding the effect of health insurance coverage, Mermin et al. (2007) showed that individuals whose employers provided health insurance coverage after retirement expected to retire earlier and also did in fact retire earlier than those whose employers covered only current workers.

Further, Settersten & Hagestad (1996) reported that workplace norms regarding appropriate retirement ages produce pressures on older workers with regard to their retirement preferences and plans. Specifically, they found that individuals who were behind schedule with regard to their career advancement or who had plateaued in their careers or jobs were more likely to feel pressure from the organization to retire. On the other hand, Rau & Adams (2005) found that human resource practices such as scheduling flexibility and equal employment opportunity targeted to older workers increased the desirability of potential bridge employment opportunities for retirees.

Family Factors

Several family factors may influence the retirement process. First, family members can play an important part in retirement planning, either through involvement in or influence on each other's retirement plans. Such involvement in planning activities is evident from studies showing that spouses often influence each other's retirement decisions as well as each other's financial preparation for retirement (e.g., Henkens & van Solinge 2002). For example, risk aversion in the allocations in defined contribution plans is related to risk aversion of the spouse (Bernasek & Shwiff 2001). There is also evidence that spouses coordinate their pension decisions and opt for similar rather than diversified investments (Shuey 2004).

Second, events in families' lives may serve as anchor points for individuals' retirement decision making. For example, spouses may time their retirement in relation to that of their partner (Curl & Townsend 2008, Henkens 1999), and one spouse's retirement may accelerate the retirement transition of the other spouse (Pienta 2003). Nevertheless, the impact of marital status on the retirement process is less straightforward. Although some studies showed that older workers who were married were more likely to retire than those who were not married (Henkens 1999, Henkens & van Solinge 2002), other studies showed that marital status and marital quality were not related to retirement decisions (e.g., Wang et al. 2008). Further, Davis (2003) found that married retirees were less likely to engage in bridge employment than those who were not married. The effect of marital status may partly depend on the spouse's working status. Specifically, retirees who had working spouses were less likely to take early retirement (Kim & Feldman 1998) but were more likely to spend longer hours working on their bridge employment (Kim & Feldman 2000). Given that there have been relatively fewer studies investigating this type of antecedent on retirement decision making and bridge employment, it is too early to draw conclusions about these effects.

Third, the care needs of family members may also influence the retirement process. Studies have shown that some parents may postpone retirement until their children are no longer dependent on them, whereas others may retire early to care for dependent children or grandchildren (e.g., Brown & Warner 2008). Kim & Feldman (2000) also found that having dependent children was positively related to retirees' engagement in bridge employment. Further, illness of spouses or care needs of parents may prompt individuals to retire earlier than planned and to perceive such retirements as forced rather than wanted (Szinovacz & Davey 2004, 2005).

Socioeconomic Context

Different countries often endorse different social institutions for retirement support. Therefore, across different societies, older workers may exhibit different retirement planning behaviors. For example, Hershey et al. (2007) examined the psychological and cross-cultural precursors to financial planning for older workers in the United States and the Netherlands. They found that Dutch workers were less involved in retirement planning activities and had lower levels of goal clarity for retirement planning than did US workers. This is not surprising given that the majority of older Dutch workers are still covered by guaranteed defined benefit pension plans, whereas the vast majority of US organizations now offer more volatile and uncertain defined contributions plans.

Another important component of the social institution for retirement support is health care coverage for older adults. Research has shown that raises in Medicare eligibility age would lead employees without employer health insurance beyond retirement to further delay their retirement transition (French & Jones 2004). A similar impact on retirement decision making is expected for any increases in the social security eligibility age (Mermin et al. 2007).

Although Munnell et al. (2008) found that a robust local economy and low unemployment levels were positively related to retirees' likelihood of returning to work after retirement, there is very little research on socioeconomic infrastructures that may affect retirement behaviors or postretirement lifestyles. Given that some older workers have care responsibilities either for frail spouses or for parents (Szinovacz & Davey 2004, 2005), it would be important to investigate whether the local availability of care agencies, day care centers for the elderly, or even nursing homes influence retirement behaviors. As far as postretirement lifestyles are concerned, local infrastructures can constrain retirees' leisure pursuits or their involvement in volunteer activities, and such constraints may in turn influence retirees' decisions on whether to remain in the area or move to another location (Adams & Rau 2011).

RETIREMENT OUTCOMES

In this section, we review psychological research on the major outcomes associated with retirement. These outcomes include financial well-being, physical well-being, and psychological well-being in retirement. They are often studied as indicators of adjustment to retirement life (Wang 2012). However, it is important to recognize that retirement as a single life event is rarely the cause of these outcomes. Rather, as suggested by the resource-based dynamic model for retirement adjustment reviewed previously, the resource-related factors or changes associated with the retirement process are driving these outcomes (Wang et al. 2011). As such, our review focuses on identifying various factors embedded in the retirement process (e.g., individual attributes, preretirement job and organizational factors, family factors, retirement transition factors, and postretirement activities) that may influence these outcomes.

Financial Well-Being

A retiree's financial well-being can be defined as the extent to which the person feels satisfied with his/her financial status and is able to maintain effective financial functioning (e.g., receive stable income that will fully cover his/her expenses; Wang 2012). Among various individual attributes that influence financial well-being in retirement, financial literacy is the one that receives the most attention. The dozens of investigations that have been carried out on financial literacy during the past two decades have revealed that the extent and veracity of one's domain-specific knowledge in finance is related to financial well-being after retirement (for a review, see Lusardi 2011). Another important individual attribute that influences financial well-being in retirement is how clear a person is regarding his/her financial goals after retirement. A recent investigation of nearly 1,500 New Zealanders revealed that the clarity of one's financial goals was moderately correlated with perceived financial preparedness (Noone et al. 2010). Similarly, Stawski and colleagues (2007) found financial goal clarity regarding retirement life to be predictive of perceived financial well-being.

Not surprisingly, engagement in preretirement financial planning has been repeatedly documented to lead to better financial well-being in retirement. Specifically, financial planning is associated with increased saving for retirement, improved budgeting, and established long-term investment plans (Hershey et al. 2007). Further, people who receive additional financial incentives to retire (e.g., taking early retirement incentives or redundancy packages) are often more likely to be financially better off when entering retirement (Quick & Moen 1998).

People's preretirement job experience is related to their financial well-being in retirement as well. Specifically, people who have more disrupted preretirement career paths (e.g., changing jobs multiple times, having periods of unemployment) are less likely to receive as much social security or pensions as those who have more stable career paths, which in turn undermines their financial well-being in retirement (Glass & Kilpatrick 1998, O'Rand 2003). In fact, this is one of the reasons why women and people with lower levels of education are often financially worse off in retirement (Wang & Shultz 2010). In addition, unemployment right before retirement also poses a risk to retirees' financial well-being because it is often harder for older adults to find jobs that offer the amount of salary that is comparable to what they had before they were laid off (Pinquart & Schindler 2007). Therefore, they may have to dip into their savings before entering retirement, which creates financial pressure later in retirement.

The number of dependents and costs related to dependent care often jeopardize people's financial well-being in retirement. The more dependents the retiree has and the more cost incurred due to the dependent(s), the more likely financial well-being in retirement will suffer (Marshall et al. 2001). Further, for retirees who are in poor financial situations, working after retirement often provides additional income for their retirement, thus easing their financial difficulty (Quinn 2010). However, it is also known that retirees often seek bridge employment opportunities because of financial hardship (Cahill et al. 2013). Therefore, the causal relationship between bridge employment and financial well-being is still unclear.

Physical Well-Being

Following the contemporary wellness perspective adopted by the public health literature, a retiree's physical well-being can be defined as the extent to which there is absence of physical diseases (e.g., heart disease and cancer) and functional limitations (e.g., the lack of capability to handle daily life and engage in social activities; Jex et al. 2007, Zhan et al. 2009). It is not surprising that retirees' preretirement health status is most predictive of their physical well-being in retirement (Zhan et al. 2009). This is consistent with the notion that genetic and allostatic factors (i.e., the accumulated cost for our body to adapt to the changing social and physical environments in which we live) are the dominant causes of major diseases (Wang & Shultz 2010). Further, healthy behaviors and habits, such as exercise, healthy diet, absence of drug and alcohol dependence, and hygiene, are important for maintaining physical well-being in retirement (Wang 2012).

Job-related physical demands have been documented as a factor related to physical well-being in retirement. People who retire from highly demanding physical jobs are more likely to experience worse cardiovascular health when they enter retirement, although over time it may improve (Tuomi et al. 1991). Health insurance in retirement is also related to physical well-being. Retirees typically enjoy better physical well-being when their health insurance offers more extensive service coverage and they incur lower out-of-pocket costs (Stanton 2006). In addition, retirees with better quality and consistency of health care are also more likely to have better physical well-being in retirement (Singh 2006).

Among postretirement activities, research has unequivocally shown that retirees who engaged in bridge employment and voluntary work had fewer major diseases and functional limitations than retirees who chose full retirement (Cahill et al. 2013, Dave et al. 2008). In fact, it has been found that engaging in bridge employment showed no differential effects on individuals' physical well-being as compared to continuing work without official retirement (Zhan et al. 2009). This suggests that physical and/or cognitive activities in working help to maintain retirees' physical health.

Psychosocial Well-Being

A retiree's psychological well-being can be defined as the extent to which the person is generally content with his/her psychological states and enjoys effective psychological functioning (Wang 2012). Using nationally representative longitudinal data from the US Health and Retirement Study and the growth mixture modeling technique, Wang (2007) showed that over an eight-year period of retirement transition and adjustment, about 70% of retirees experienced minimum psychological well-being changes, about 25% of retirees experienced negative changes in psychological well-being during the initial transition stage but showed improvements afterward, and about 5% of retirees experienced positive changes in psychological well-being. These findings were further corroborated by Pinquart & Schindler (2007), who used a nationally representative sample of German retirees from the German Socioeconomic Panel Study. Specifically, Pinquart & Schindler (2007) found that during retirement transition and adjustment, about 75% of German retirees experienced trivial changes in life satisfaction, about 9% of German retirees experienced a significant decrease in their life satisfaction during the initial transition stage but showed stable or increasing life satisfaction thereafter, and about 15% of German retirees experienced a significant increase in their life satisfaction. Although the proportion estimates for subpopulations were not entirely the same across American and German retirees, both studies support the multiple-pathway nature of retirement transition and adjustment, suggesting that retirees' psychological well-being does not follow a uniform pattern of transition and adjustment.

Retirees' work role identity has been shown to be negatively related to retirees' psychological well-being (e.g., Quick & Moen 1998, Reitzes & Mutran 2004). In particular, retirees who strongly identify themselves with their work roles are often more likely to experience decreases in psychological well-being when entering retirement. Further, people who retire from jobs that involve high levels of work stress, psychological and physical demands, job challenges, and job dissatisfaction are more likely to enter retirement with low levels of psychological well-being (Quick & Moen 1998, van Solinge & Henkens 2008, Wang 2007). Finally, people who experienced unemployment right before retirement are also more likely to enter retirement with low levels of psychological well-being (Marshall et al. 2001, Pinquart & Schindler 2007).

Married retirees usually enjoy better psychological well-being than single or widowed retirees (Pinquart & Schindler 2007), but this beneficial effect disappears when their spouses are still working (Wang 2007). Retirees with happier marriages (Szinovacz & Davey 2004, Wang 2007) and fewer dependents to support (Kim & Feldman 2000, Marshall et al. 2001) are more likely to achieve better psychological well-being as well. Finally, and not surprisingly, losing a partner during the retirement transition had a negative impact on psychological well-being (van Solinge & Henkens 2008).

Among retirement transition-related factors, the voluntariness of the retirement (Reitzes & Mutran, 2004; Shultz et al. 1998; van Solinge & Henkens 2007, 2008) and retirement planning (Petkoska & Earl 2009, Reitzes & Mutran 2004, Wang 2007) have been shown to be positively related to retirees' psychological well-being. People who retire earlier than expected or planned are more likely to experience decreased psychological well-being entering retirement (Quick & Moen 1998, Wang 2007). Further, people who retire for health reasons are more likely to experience decreased psychological well-being, whereas those who retire to become engaged in leisure or other non-work-related activities and those who receive financial incentives or redundancy payouts are more likely to experience better psychological well-being in retirement (Quick & Moen 1998).

Among postretirement activities, bridge employment (Kim & Feldman 2000, Wang 2007, Zhan et al. 2009), volunteer work (Dorfman & Douglas 2005, Kim & Feldman 2000), and leisure activities (Dorfman & Douglas 2005) are all beneficial to retirees' psychological well-being. Further, when retirees work for generative reasons (i.e., working for teaching and sharing knowledge with the younger generation), they are more likely to experience improved psychological well-being (Dendinger et al. 2005). Finally, retirees' anxiety associated with maintaining their social status and contacts via social activities was negatively related to retirement satisfaction (van Solinge & Henkens 2007, 2008).

Consequences of Financial, Physical, and Psychological Well-Being in Retirement

In reviewing the literature regarding the consequences of physical, financial, and psychological well-being in retirement, it is important to note that these wellness states influence each other to a significant extent. For example, retirees' health problems have important implications for their financial well-being because they are likely to lead to higher levels of health care costs and to limit retirees' ability to work to achieve an additional source of income (Shultz & Wang 2007). Further, problems in physical health and daily functions are likely to limit retirees' social activity and exchange with the environment, which in turn negatively impacts their psychological well-being (Pinquart & Schindler 2007, Quick & Moen 1998, van Solinge & Henkens 2008, Wang 2007).

Similarly, retirees' financial well-being could influence their physical health as well as psychological well-being. Specifically, financial well-being is closely related to retirees' life quality, such as nutrition intake, living conditions, choice of leisure activities, and health care quality (Taylor & Geldhauser 2007). Further, lack of financial well-being often manifests as a source of chronic stress, leading to anxiety and feelings of helplessness for retirees (Pinquart & Schindler 2007, Reitzes & Mutran 2004), which may increase the risk of cardiovascular episodes (Li et al. 2007).

Retirees' lack of psychological well-being often manifests as a risk factor for them to engage in maladaptive coping behaviors. For example, a lower level of adjustment to retirement is associated with increased alcohol use (e.g., Perreira & Sloan 2001). Therefore, retirees' psychological well-being has important implications for their physical health. In addition, a lower level of adjustment to retirement often decreases retirees' self-efficacy regarding managing their retirement, which in turn compromises effective goal setting for maintaining and improving financial well-being (Kim et al. 2005).

Finally, retirees' financial, physical, and psychological well-being have important influences on their longevity and mortality (Tsai et al. 2005). They also influence retirees' work-related behaviors. For example, Wang et al. (2008) found that (*a*) retirees who had better physical health and experienced less psychological stress were more likely to engage in career bridge employment than in full retirement, (*b*) retirees who had better physical health and financial conditions were more likely to engage in bridge employment in a different field than in full retirement, and (*c*) retirees who had better financial conditions and experienced less psychological stress were more likely to engage in career bridge employment than in bridge employment in a different field.

CONCLUSION

As this review has shown, psychological research on retirement has already established viable conceptualizations for studying the psychological nature of retirement. In addition, recent theoretical models have provided comprehensive frameworks for understanding the retirement process as well as its antecedents and outcomes. Nevertheless, empirical investigations have just started to operationalize these theoretical models, and more thorough examinations of components of the retirement process are warranted. Moving forward, we expect psychological research on retirement to take a more interdisciplinary approach, accumulate more knowledge about causal relationships, and provide more careful consideration about the research context at macro-, meso-, and microlevels.

DISCLOSURE STATEMENT

The authors are not aware of any affiliations, memberships, funding, or financial holdings that might be perceived as affecting the objectivity of this review.

LITERATURE CITED

Adams GA, Beehr TA. 1998. Turnover and retirement: a comparison of their similarities and differences. *Pers. Psychol.* 51:643–65

Adams GA, Prescher J, Beehr TA, Lepisto L. 2002. Applying work-role attachment theory to retirement decision-making. *Int. J. Aging Hum. Dev.* 54:125–37

Adams GA, Rau BL. 2004. Job seeking among retirees seeking bridge employment. *Pers. Psychol.* 57:719–44

Adams GA, Rau BL. 2011. Putting off tomorrow to do what you want today: planning for retirement. *Am. Psychol.* 66:180–92

Angel JL, Jimenénez MA, Angel RJ. 2007. The economic consequences of widowhood for older minority women. *Gerontologist* 47:224–34

Appold SJ. 2004. How much longer would men work if there were no employment dislocation? Estimates from cause-elimination work life tables. *Soc. Sci. Res.* 33:660–80

Armstrong-Stassen M, Schlosser F, Zinni D. 2012. Seeking resources: predicting retirees' return to their workplace. *J. Manag. Psychol.* 27:615–35

Atchley RC. 1999. Continuity theory, self, and social structure. In *Families and Retirement*, ed. CD Ryff, VW Marshall, pp. 145–58. Newbury Park, CA: Sage

Barnes-Farrell JL. 2003. Beyond health and wealth: attitudinal and other influences on retirement decision-making. In *Retirement: Reasons, Processes, and Results*, ed. GA Adams, TA Beehr, pp. 159–87. New York: Springer

Bernasek A, Shwiff S. 2001. Gender, risk, and retirement. *J. Econ. Issues* 35:345–56

Bidwell J, Griffin B, Hesketh B. 2006. Timing of retirement: including delay discounting perspective in retirement model. *J. Vocat. Behav.* 68:368–87

Blekesaune M, Skirbekk V. 2012. Can personality predict retirement behavior? A longitudinal analysis combining survey and register data from Norway. *Eur. J. Aging* 9:199–206

Brougham RR, Walsh DA. 2007. Image theory, goal incompatibility, and retirement intent. *Int. J. Aging Hum. Dev.* 63:203–29

Brown M, Aumann K, Pitt-Catsouphes M, Galinsky E, Bond JT. 2010. *Working in Retirement: A 21st Century Phenomenon.* Boston, MA: Fam. Work Inst., Sloan Cent. Aging Work Boston Coll.

Brown MT, Fukunaga C, Umemoto D, Wicker L. 1996. Annual review, 1990–1996: social class, work, and retirement behavior. *J. Vocat. Behav.* 49:159–89

Brown TH, Warner DF. 2008. Divergent pathways? Racial/ethnic differences in older women's labor force withdrawal. *J. Gerontol. B Psychol. Sci. Soc. Sci.* 63B:S122–34

Cahill KE, Giandrea MD, Quinn JE. 2013. Bridge employment. See Wang 2013, pp. 293–310

Carr DC, Kail BL. 2013. The influence of unpaid work on the transition out of full-time paid work. *Gerontologist* 53:92–101

Chevalier S, Fouquereau E, Gillet N, Demulier V. 2013. Development of the Reasons for Entrepreneurs' Retirement Decision Inventory (RERDI) and preliminary evidence of its psychometric properties in a French sample. *J. Career Assess.* 21:572–86

Curl AL, Townsend AL. 2008. Retirement transitions among married couples. *J. Workplace Behav. Health* 23:89–107

Damman M, Henkens K, Kalmijn M. 2011. The impact of midlife educational, work, health, and family experiences on men's early retirement. *J. Gerontol. B Psychol. Sci. Soc. Sci.* 66:617–27

Dave D, Rashad I, Spasojevic J. 2008. The effects of retirement on physical and mental health outcomes. *South. Econ. J.* 75:497–523

Davis MA. 2003. Factors related to bridge employment participation among private sector early retirees. *J. Vocat. Behav.* 63:55–71

Dendinger VM, Adams GA, Jacobson JD. 2005. Reasons for working and their relationship to retirement attitudes, job satisfaction and occupational self-efficacy of bridge employees. *Int. J. Aging Hum. Dev.* 61:21–35

Denton F, Spencer B. 2009. What is retirement? A review and assessment of alternative concepts and measures. *Can. J. Aging* 28:63–76

Donaldson T, Earl JK, Muratore AM. 2010. Extending the integrated model of retirement adjustment: incorporating mastery and retirement planning. *J. Vocat. Behav.* 77:279–89

Dorfman LT, Douglas K. 2005. Leisure and the retired professor: occupation matters. *Educ. Gerontol.* 31:343–61

Dosman D, Fast J, Chapman S, Keating N. 2006. Retirement and productive activity in later life. *J. Fam. Econ. Issues* 27:401–19

Ekerdt DJ. 2010. Frontiers of research on work and retirement. *J. Gerontol. B Psychol. Sci. Soc. Sci.* 65:69–80

Ekerdt DJ, Hackney J, Ko;loski K, DeViney S. 2001. Eddies in the stream: the prevalence of uncertain plans for retirement. *J. Gerontol. B Psychol. Sci. Soc. Sci.* 56:S162–70

Elovainio M, Forma P, Kivimaki M, Sinervo T, Sutinen R, Laine M. 2005. Job demands and job control as correlates of early retirement thoughts in Finnish social and health care employees. *Work Stress* 19:84–92

Feldman DC. 1994. The decision to retire early: a review and conceptualization. *Acad. Manag. Rev.* 19:285–311

Feldman DC. 2013. Feeling like it's time to retire: a fit perspective on early retirement decisions. See Wang 2013, pp. 280–92

Feldman DC, Beehr TA. 2011. A three-phase model of retirement decision making. *Am. Psychol.* 66:193–203

French E, Jones JB. 2004. *The effects of health insurance and self-insurance on retirement behavior.* Work. Pap. WP2004-12. Chestnut Hill, MA: Cent. Retire. Res. Boston Coll.

Gallo WT, Bradley EH, Siegel M, Kasl S. 2000. Health effects of involuntary job loss among older workers: findings from the Health and Retirement Survey. *J. Gerontol. B Psychol. Sci. Soc. Sci.* 55:S131–40

Giandrea MD, Cahill KE, Quinn JF. 2009. Bridge jobs: a comparison across cohorts. *Res. Aging* 31:549–76

Glass JC, Kilpatrick BB. 1998. Gender comparisons of baby boomers and financial preparation for retirement. *Educ. Gerontol.* 24:719–45

Gobeski KT, Beehr TA. 2008. How retirees work: predictors of different types of bridge employment. *J. Organ. Behav.* 37:401–25

Griffin B, Hesketh B. 2008. Post-retirement work: the individual determinants of paid and volunteer work. *J. Occup. Organ. Psychol.* 81:101–21

Gruber J, Wise DA. 1999. Social security and retirement around the world. *Res. Labor Econ.* 18:1–40

Henkens K. 1999. Retirement intentions and spousal support: a multiactor approach. *J. Gerontol. B Psychol. Sci. Soc. Sci.* 54:S63–73

Henkens K, van Solinge H. 2002. Spousal influences on the decision to retire. *Int. J. Sociol.* 32:55–74

Herrbach O, Mignonac K, Vandenberghe C, Negrini A. 2009. Perceived HRM practices, organizational commitment, and voluntary early retirement among late-career managers. *Hum. Resour. Manage.* 48:895–915

Hershey DA, Henkens K, Van Dalen HP. 2007. Mapping the minds of retirement planners. *J. Cross-Cult. Psychol.* 38:361–82

Hershey DA, Jacobs-Lawson JM, Austin JT. 2013. Effective financial planning for retirement. See Wang 2013, pp. 402–30

Hershey DA, Jacobs-Lawson JM, Neukam KA. 2002. The influence of aging and gender on workers goals for retirement. *Int. J. Aging Hum. Dev.* 55:163–79

Jex S, Wang M, Zarubin A. 2007. Aging and occupational health. See Shultz & Adams 2007, pp. 199–224

Karpansalo M, Manninen P, Kauhanen J, Lakka T, Salonen J. 2004. Perceived health as a predictor of early retirement. *Scand. J. Work Environ. Health* 30:287–292

Kaskie B, Imhof S, Cavanaugh J, Culp K. 2008. Civic engagement as a retirement role for aging Americans. *Gerontologist* 48:368–77

Kim H, DeVaney SA. 2005. The selection of partial or full retirement by older workers. *J. Fam. Econ. Issues* 26:371–94

Kim J, Kwon J, Anderson EA. 2005. Factors related to retirement confidence: retirement preparation and workplace financial education. *Financ. Couns. Plann. Educ.* 16:77–89

Kim JE, Moen P. 2001. Is retirement good or bad for subjective well-being? *Curr. Dir. Psychol. Sci.* 10:83–86

Kim N, Hall DT. 2013. Protean career model and retirement. See Wang 2013, pp. 102–16

Kim S, Feldman DC. 1998. Healthy, wealthy, or wise: predicting actual acceptances of early retirement incentives at three points in time. *Pers. Psychol.* 51:623–42

Kim S, Feldman DC. 2000. Working in retirement: the antecedents of bridge employment and its consequences for quality of life in retirement. *Acad. Manag. J.* 43:1195–210

Kubicek B, Korunka C, Raymo JM, Hoonakker P. 2011. Psychological well-being in retirement: the effects of personal and gendered contextual resources. *J. Occup. Health Psychol.* 16:230–46

Laitner J, Sonnega A. 2013. Economic theories of retirement. See Wang 2013, pp. 136–51

Leung CSY, Earl JK. 2012. Retirement Resources Inventory: construction, factor structure and psychometric properties. *J. Vocat. Behav.* 81:171–82

Levinson DJ, Levinson JD. 1996. *The Seasons of a Woman's Life.* New York: Knopf

Li Y, Aranda M, Chi I. 2007. Health and life satisfaction of ethnic minority older adults in mainland China: effects of financial strain. *Int. J. Aging Hum. Dev.* 64:361–79

Lin T, Hsieh A. 2001. Impact of job stress on early retirement intention. *Int. J. Stress Manag.* 8:243–47

Lockenhoff CE, Terracciano A, Costa PT Jr. 2009. Five-factor model personality traits and the retirement transition: longitudinal and cross-sectional associations. *Psychol. Aging* 24:722–28

Loi J, Shultz K. 2007. Why older adults seek employment: differing motivations among subgroups. *J. Appl. Gerontol.* 26:274–89

Lusardi A. 2011. *Americans' financial capability.* Pension Res. Counc. Work. Pap. 2011–02, Natl. Bur. Econ. Res., Cambridge, MA

Marshall VW, Clarke PJ, Ballantyne PJ. 2001. Instability in the retirement transition: effects on health and well-being in a Canadian study. *Res. Aging* 23:379–409

McCarthy JT. 1996. *Financial Planning for a Secure Retirement.* Brookfield, WI: Int. Found. Empl. Benefit Plans. 2nd ed.

Mears A, Kendall T, Katona C, Pashley C, Pajak S. 2004. Retirement intentions of older consultant psychiatrists. *Psychiatr. Bull.* 28:130–32

Mermin GBT, Johnson RW, Murphy D. 2007. Why do boomers plan to work longer? *J. Gerontol. B Psychol. Sci. Soc. Sci.* 62:S286–94

Morrow-Howell N, Leon J. 1988. Life-span determinants of work in retirement years. *Int. J. Aging Hum. Dev.* 27:125–40

Munnell AH, Soto M, Triest RK, Zhivan NA. 2008. *Do state economics or individual characteristics determine whether older men work?* IB #8-13. Cent. Retire. Res. Boston Coll., Chestnut Hill, MA

Munnell AH, Triest RK, Jivan NA. 2004. *How do pensions affect expected and actual retirement ages?* Work. Pap. 2004-270. Cent. Retire. Res. Boston Coll., Chestnut Hill, MA

Nimrod G, Janke M, Kleiber D. 2009. Expanding, reducing, concentrating and diffusing: activity patterns of recent retirees in the United States. *Leis. Sci.* 31:37–52

Noone JH, Stephens C, Alpass F. 2010. The Process of Retirement Planning Scale (PRePS): development and validation. *Psychol. Assess.* 22:520–31

O'Rand A. 2003. Cumulative advantage and gerontological theory. *Annu. Rev. Gerontol. Geriatr.* 22:14–30

Orel NA, Ford RA, Brock C. 2004. Women's financial planning for retirement: the impact of disruptive life events. *J. Women Aging* 16:39–53

Perreira KM, Sloan FA. 2001. Life events and alcohol consumption among mature adults: a longitudinal analysis. *J. Stud. Alcohol* 62:501–8

Petkoska J, Earl JK. 2009. Understanding the influence of demographic and psychological variables on retirement planning. *Psychol. Aging* 24:245–51

Pienta AM. 2003. Partners in marriage: an analysis of husbands' and wives' retirement behavior. *J. Appl. Gerontol.* 22:340–58

Pinquart M, Schindler I. 2007. Changes of life satisfaction in the transition to retirement: a latent-class approach. *Psychol. Aging* 22:442–55

Post C, Schneer JA, Reitman F, Ogilvie D. 2013. Pathways to retirement: a career stage analysis of retirement age expectations. *Hum. Relat.* 66:87–112

Posthuma RA, Campion MA. 2009. Age stereotypes in the workplace: common stereotypes, moderators, and future research directions. *J. Manag.* 35:158–88

Potocnik K, Tordera N, Peiro JM. 2010. The influence of the early retirement process on satisfaction with early retirement and psychological well-being. *Int. J. Aging Hum. Dev.* 70:251–73

Phua VC, McNally JW. 2008. Men planning for retirement: changing meaning of preretirement planning. *J. Appl. Gerontol.* 27:588–608

Quick HE, Moen P. 1998. Gender, employment, and retirement quality: a life course approach to the differential experiences of men and women. *J. Occup. Health Psychol.* 1:44–64

Quinn JF. 2010. Work, retirement, and the encore career: elders and the future of the American workforce. *Generations* 34:45–55

Rau BL, Adams GA. 2005. Attracting retirees to apply: desired organizational characteristics of bridge employment. *J. Organ. Behav.* 26:649–60

Reitzes DC, Mutran EJ. 2004. The transition into retirement: stages and factors that influence retirement adjustment. *Int. J. Aging Hum. Dev.* 59:63–84

Robinson O, Demetre J, Corney R. 2010. Personality and retirement: exploring the links between the Big Five personality traits, reasons for retirement and the experience of being retired. *Personal. Individ. Differ.* 48:792–97

Settersten RA Jr, Hagestad G. 1996. What's the latest: cultural age deadlines for educational and work transitions. *Gerontologist* 36:602–13

Shuey KM. 2004. Worker preferences, spousal coordination, and participation in an employer-sponsored pension plan. *Res. Aging* 26:287–316

Shultz KS, Adams GA, eds. 2007. *Aging and Work in the 21st Century*. Mahwah, NJ: Erlbaum

Shultz KS, Morton KR, Weckerle JR. 1998. The influence of push and pull factors on voluntary and involuntary early retirees' retirement decision and adjustment. *J. Vocat. Behav.* 53:45–57

Shultz KS, Taylor MA, Morrison RF. 2003. Work related attitudes of Naval officers before and after retirement. *Int. J. Aging Hum. Dev.* 57:259–74

Shultz KS, Wang M. 2007. The influence of specific health conditions on retirement decisions. *Int. J. Aging Hum. Dev.* 65:149–61

Shultz KS, Wang M. 2011. Psychological perspectives on the changing nature of retirement. *Am. Psychol.* 66:170–79

Shultz KS, Wang M, Crimmins E, Fisher G. 2010. Age differences in the demand-control model of work stress: an examination of data from 15 European countries. *J. Appl. Gerontol.* 29:21–47

Singh S. 2006. Perceived health among women retirees. *Psychol. Stud.* 51:166–70

Spiegel PE, Shultz KS. 2003. The influence of preretirement planning and transferability of skills on Naval officers' retirement satisfaction and adjustment. *Mil. Psychol.* 15:285–307

Stanton MW. 2006. *The High Concentration of U.S. Health Care Expenditures.* Research in Action, Issue 19. AHRQ Publ. No. 06–0060. Agency Healthc. Res. Qual., Rockville, MD. **http://www.ahrq.gov/ research/findings/factsheets/costs/expriach/index.html**

Stawski RS, Hershey DA, Jacobs-Lawson JM. 2007. Goal clarity and financial planning activities as determinants of retirement savings contributions. *Int. J. Aging Hum. Dev.* 64:13–32

Szinovacz ME. 2003. Contexts and pathways: retirement as institution, process, and experience. In *Retirement: Reasons, Processes, and Results*, ed. GA Adams, TA Beehr, pp. 6–52. New York: Springer

Szinovacz ME. 2013. A multilevel perspective for retirement research. See Wang 2013, pp. 152–73

Szinovacz ME, Davey A. 2004. Honeymoons and joint lunches: effects of retirement and spouse's employment on depressive symptoms. *J. Gerontol. B Psychol. Sci. Soc. Sci.* 59:P233–45

Szinovacz ME, Davey A. 2005. Predictors of perceptions of involuntary retirement. *Gerontologist* 45:36–47

Szubert Z, Sobala W. 2005. Current determinants of early retirement among blue collar workers in Poland. *Int. J. Occup. Med. Environ. Health* 18:177–84

Taylor MA, Geldhauser HA. 2007. Low-income older workers. See Shultz & Adams 2007, pp. 25–50

Taylor MA, Shultz KS, Morrison RF, Spiegel PE, Greene J. 2007. Occupational attachment and met expectations as predictors of retirement adjustment of naval officers. *J. Appl. Soc. Psychol.* 37:1697–725

Taylor-Carter MA, Cook K, Weinberg C. 1997. Planning and expectations of the retirement experience. *Educ. Gerontol.* 23:273–88

Tsai SP, Wendt JK, Donnelly RP, de Jong G, Ahmed FS. 2005. Age at retirement and long term survival of an industrial population: prospective cohort study. *Br. Med. J.* 331:995–98

Tuomi K, Järvinen E, Eskelinen L, Ilmarinen J, Klockars M. 1991. Effect of retirement on health and work ability among municipal employees. *Scand. J. Work Environ. Health* 17(Suppl. 1):75–81

van Solinge H, Henkens K. 2007. Involuntary retirement: the role of restrictive circumstances, timing, and social embeddedness. *J. Gerontol. B Psychol. Sci. Soc. Sci.* 62:S295–303

van Solinge H, Henkens K. 2008. Adjustment to and satisfaction with retirement: two of a kind? *Psychol. Aging* 23:422–34

van Solinge H, Henkens K. 2010. Living longer, working longer? The impact of subjective life expectancy on retirement intentions and behavior. *Eur. J. Public Health* 20:47–51

von Bonsdoff ME, Shultz KS, Leskinen E, Tansky J. 2009. The choice between retirement and bridge employment: a continuity theory and life course perspective. *Int. J. Aging Hum. Dev.* 69:79–100

Wang M. 2007. Profiling retirees in the retirement transition and adjustment process: examining the longitudinal change patterns of retirees' psychological well-being. *J. Appl. Psychol.* 92:455–74

Wang M. 2012. Health, fiscal, and psychological well-being in retirement. In *The Oxford Handbook of Work and Aging*, ed. J Hedge, W Borman, pp. 570–84. New York: Oxford Univ. Press

Wang M. 2013. *The Oxford Handbook of Retirement.* New York: Oxford Univ. Press

Wang M, Adams GA, Beehr TA, Shultz KS. 2009. Career issues at the end of one's career: bridge employment and retirement. In *Maintaining Focus, Energy, and Options Through the Life Span*, ed. SG Baugh, SE Sullivan, pp. 135–62. Charlotte, NC: Inf. Age Publ.

Wang M, Chen Y. 2006. Age differences in attitude change: influences of cognitive resources and motivation on responses to argument quantity. *Psychol. Aging* 21:581–89

Wang M, Henkens K, van Solinge H. 2011. Retirement adjustment: a review of theoretical and empirical advancements. *Am. Psychol.* 66:204–13

Wang M, Olson D, Shultz K. 2013. *Mid and Late Career Issues: An Integrative Perspective.* New York: Psychol. Press

Wang M, Shultz K. 2010. Employee retirement: a review and recommendations for future investigation. *J. Manag.* 36:172–206

Wang M, Zhan Y, Liu S, Shultz K. 2008. Antecedents of bridge employment: a longitudinal investigation. *J. Appl. Psychol.* 93:818–30

Zappalá S, Depolo M, Fraccaroli F, Guglielmi D, Sarchielli G. 2008. Postponing job retirement? Psychosocial influences on the preference for early or late retirement. *Career Dev. Int.* 13:150–67

Zhan Y, Wang M, Liu S, Shultz KS. 2009. Bridge employment and retirees' health: a longitudinal investigation. *J. Occup. Health Psychol.* 14:374–89

Zhan Y, Wang M, Yao X. 2013. Domain specific effects of commitment on bridge employment decisions: the moderating role of economic stress. *Eur. J. Work Organ. Psychol.* 22:362–75

Adoption: Biological and Social Processes Linked to Adaptation

Harold D. Grotevant and Jennifer M. McDermott

Department of Psychology, University of Massachusetts Amherst, Massachusetts 01003;
email: hgroteva@psych.umass.edu, mcdermott@psych.umass.edu

Annu. Rev. Psychol. 2014. 65:235–65

First published online as a Review in Advance on
September 6, 2013

The *Annual Review of Psychology* is online at
http://psych.annualreviews.org

This article's doi:
10.1146/annurev-psych-010213-115020

Keywords

children, context, development, families, neuroendocrine system, risk

Abstract

Children join adoptive families through domestic adoption from the
public child welfare system, infant adoption through private agencies, and
international adoption. Each pathway presents distinctive developmental
opportunities and challenges. Adopted children are at higher risk than the
general population for problems with adaptation, especially externalizing,
internalizing, and attention problems. This review moves beyond the
field's emphasis on adoptee–nonadoptee differences to highlight biological
and social processes that affect adaptation of adoptees across time. The
experience of stress, whether prenatal, postnatal/preadoption, or during the
adoption transition, can have significant impacts on the developing neuroendocrine system. These effects can contribute to problems with physical
growth, brain development, and sleep, activating cascading effects on social,
emotional, and cognitive development. Family processes involving contact
between adoptive and birth family members, co-parenting in gay and
lesbian adoptive families, and racial socialization in transracially adoptive
families affect social development of adopted children into adulthood.

Contents

INTRODUCTION

Adoption involves the legal transfer of parental rights and responsibilities from a child's birth parents to adults who will raise the child (Reitz & Watson 1992). Within this broad definition, adoptions vary according to characteristics of the adopted child (age and health at placement, whether placed alone or with siblings); characteristics of the adoptive parents (single or two parent, same sex or heterosexual, same or different race or nationality from the child); the circumstances leading to adoption (desire for a better future for the child, abandonment, removal following maltreatment); and the adoption intermediary (private agency, public child welfare system, independent placement between individuals).

Because of this heterogeneity of arrangements, adoption has been of interest to those in many disciplines beyond psychology, including anthropology, communications, cultural studies, genetics, history, medicine, social work, and sociology. Most psychological research on adoption has focused on the growth of adopted children from birth to maturity, revealing extraordinary diversity among adopted persons and their developmental contexts (Brodzinsky & Palacios 2005). This review, the first on adoption to appear in the *Annual Review of Psychology*, begins with a sketch of the diverse topics studied in the field, setting the stage for our primary focus on the biological and social processes that affect the adaptation of adopted persons over time.

Research focusing on outcomes for adopted persons covers a broad range of topics, including (*a*) physical development; (*b*) self-esteem and identity; (*c*) cognitive outcomes such as IQ, school performance, and specific abilities; (*d*) psychological adjustment, including mental health and psychopathology; and (*e*) relationships with parents (including attachment), peers, and romantic partners. Although some outcome-oriented research simply examines differences between adopted and nonadopted persons, these lines of research increasingly examine mediating processes and moderating factors that affect adaptation across a range of outcome domains (Palacios

& Brodzinsky 2010). Especially promising work is focusing on neuroendocrine processes and related issues such as stress, sensitive periods, plasticity, and resilience (Nelson et al. 2011).

Parenting and family relationships also receive considerable attention in the study of adoption (e.g., Brodzinsky & Pinderhughes 2002), especially issues such as prospective parents' motivation for adoption, parenting behavior, parent-child communication about adoption, cultural socialization and preparation of children for encountering bias (in the case of transracial or international adoption), and special issues encountered by same-sex parents and single parents. Recognition that adoption may involve contact with the child's birth relatives has spurred work on contact (or openness) between the child's adoptive and birth families (Grotevant et al. 2013) and on relational processes such as emotional distance regulation (Grotevant 2009).

Intersections beyond the family, such as with the Internet (Howard 2012) or with institutions such as schools, psychological services, and the child welfare system (Palacios 2009) can also profoundly affect the development of adopted persons. In addition, stigmatized societal attitudes about adoption and geopolitical debates about international and transracial adoption provide context for individual and family development (Gibbons & Rotabi 2012). These debates about attitudes and values become played out in policy discussions about the best interests of children at the agency, local, national, and international levels and in discussions about how best to prepare prospective adoptive parents and provide adoption-competent clinical services.

The topics reflected in the literature on the psychology of adoption have arisen from two directions. The first has emerged from practical concerns about the health and adjustment of adopted children and their families. This emphasis, primarily from clinical psychology, social work, and pediatrics, has focused on the development and testing of prevention and intervention strategies for identified adoption-related issues (e.g., Juffer et al. 2005). The second direction has emerged from the view of adoption as a natural experiment that can shed light on the nature-nurture debate or answer questions about the impact of early adverse experience on development (e.g., Haugaard & Hazan 2003, Lipscomb et al. 2012). Both directions are reflected in this review.

This review takes an integrative developmental approach, acknowledging the transactional pathways that connect developmental contexts and early experiences with biological and social processes that influence behavior and adaptation over time (see **Figure 1**). We begin by

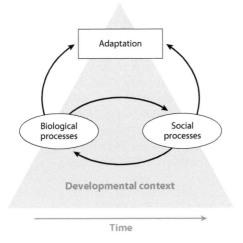

Figure 1

Interplay of biological and social processes as they influence behavior and adaptation over time.

considering three major pathways to adoption: domestic adoption of children from the public child welfare system, domestic adoption of children (usually infants) through private agencies and intermediaries, and international adoption. These pathways often provide strikingly different early experiences and developmental contexts that shape later developmental pathways in predictable ways. First, we provide an overview of the literature focused on developmental outcomes for children and adolescents. Building on the suggestion of Palacios & Brodzinsky (2010) that adoption research must better address processes of development, we next review the burgeoning body of work on the biological and social processes that mediate the connections between adoption and outcomes. Finally, implications of this body of work for practice and future research are discussed. Because adoption involves a legal relationship, it must be considered within the societal and historical contexts in which the relevant laws and policies are situated. Therefore, the specific legal and policy issues raised in this review focus primarily on domestic and international adoptions taking place in the United States.

THREE PATHWAYS TO ADOPTION

It is very difficult to generalize about adoption, because children have highly varied experiences between birth and placement with an adoptive family. Even within the three pathways described below, children's experiences vary in duration and intensity. Nevertheless, knowing about the three pathways highlights key experiences and risks that children may encounter prior to adoption, which in turn set the stage for future developmental challenges. Understanding trends affecting these three pathways to adoption is also important for identifying future needs of the adoptive population. Other formal and informal adoption and adoption-like arrangements (e.g., stepparent adoption, informal kinship care, kinship foster care, child circulation) are beyond the scope of this review. Informative discussions about these distinctive pathways as well as the history of adoption may be found in Boswell (1988), Carp (2002), Charles et al. (2012), Herman (2008), and van IJzendoorn & Juffer (2006).

Domestic Adoption from the Public Child Welfare System

Over 400,000 children in the United States are currently in foster care, and 104,236 of them were waiting to be adopted at the end of fiscal year (FY) 2011 (Child. Bur. 2012). The mean age of these waiting children when they were removed from their parents was 5.0 years, but they ranged in age from infancy to 17 years. Many children adopted from the public child welfare system experienced years of abuse or neglect prior to removal from their families, and some experienced further trauma while in the foster care system (Groza et al. 2005). In FY 2011, 50,516 children were adopted with public agency involvement, at the average age of 6.4 years. Ninety percent of these children received an adoption subsidy provided by the government to help adoptive parents meet their children's special needs. Most were adopted by married couples (68%) or single women (27%). Most were adopted by a foster parent (54%) or relative (31%) who already knew them; only 15% were adopted by a nonrelative (Child. Bur. 2012).

Domestic Infant Adoption Through Private Agencies and Intermediaries

Accurate statistics about children adopted domestically in the United States through private agencies or intermediaries rather than through the public child welfare system are not available; however, the best estimate is that approximately 14,000 such children are adopted per year, mostly as infants (Child Welf. Inf. Gatew. 2005). Although the 14,000 nonrelative placements are sometimes called "voluntary relinquishments," the term "voluntary" may be a misnomer; many of these placements occur because the child's expectant parents feel they are not able to raise the child on their own and have no choice but to place for adoption. Outside the United States, formal (legal) domestic adoptions by nonrelatives are rare, either because of a social and financial safety net that makes it possible for single parents to raise their children (as in many Western European countries; e.g., Hoksbergen & ter Laak 2005) or because of cultural values that prioritize blood ties (as in many Asian countries; e.g., McGinnis 2006).

International Adoption

Over one million children were adopted worldwide across national boundaries between the end of World War II and the present, typically from poorer to wealthier countries (Selman 2009). The United States is home to many of these children; adoptions into the United States from other countries rose steadily from FY 1999 ($N=15,719$) to 2004 ($N=22,991$), but since have declined steadily (FY 2011 $N=9,319$) (US Dep. State 2012). The countries of origin sending the most children to the United States in FY 2009 through 2011 were China, Ethiopia, and Russia, although the top countries of origin change periodically in response to geopolitical considerations and the impact of international regulations (US Dep. State 2012). The children may have lived with their birth family, in an orphanage, and/or with a foster family before adoption. Standards of care vary considerably across these preadoptive placements; variations in quality and duration of early care have consequences for later developmental outcomes (Miller 2012).

DEVELOPMENTAL OUTCOMES

A recent review of psychological research on adoption by Palacios & Brodzinsky (2010) traced increasing maturity in the psychological study of adoption in the movement from (*a*) studies comparing adopted and nonadopted children across a host of psychological outcomes, to (*b*) studies detailing children's postadoption recovery following early adversity, and (*c*) studies focusing on processes influencing adoption outcomes. The authors urged further study of the processes underlying between-group differences and recovery following adversity; these processes are the primary focus of this review.

To varying degrees, the three pathways to adoption expose children to negative experiences such as teratogenic prenatal environments, institutionalization, separation from birth parents, and maltreatment. Demographic trends in the pathways to adoption suggest that over the next decade, as the mix of US adoptions shifts away from domestic infant and international adoption toward adoption from the child welfare system, the needs of children and their adoptive families for support and intervention will increase. Understanding the biological and social processes that influence the likelihood of adaptive or maladaptive developmental trajectories for adopted children will make important contributions to the well-being of these children and their families.

Although the vast majority of adopted children develop within the typical range (Palacios & Brodzinsky 2010), some negative outcomes are evident among adopted children who experienced significant early adversity or trauma prior to placement. These children tend to exhibit high rates of externalizing behavior problems (such as aggression, oppositional behavior, and conduct problems) as well as internalizing behavior problems (such as anxiety and depression) and attention problems, including attention deficit–hyperactivity disorder (ADHD) (Juffer et al. 2011). Even among children who have not experienced early adversity, patterns of initial positive adjustment followed by later problem behaviors and socioemotional difficulties during the middle childhood and teen years have emerged (Hawk & McCall 2010). However, these patterns represent group trends, and the trajectories of individual children vary greatly depending upon a number of pre- and post-adoption factors.

A primary outcome focus in adoption studies has been the prevalence of internalizing and externalizing behaviors, both of which have consequences for children's peer relations and social development. The extensive Adoption Meta-Analysis Project (Adoption MAP) at Leiden University (Juffer & van IJzendoorn 2005, 2007; van den Dries et al. 2009; van IJzendoorn & Juffer 2006; van IJzendoorn et al. 2005) examined outcome differences between adopted and nonadopted persons and revealed higher levels of externalizing and internalizing behaviors among adoptees than nonadopted controls ($d = 0.24$ and 0.16, respectively) and fewer externalizing and internalizing problems among international than domestic adoptees ($d = 0.10$ and 0.07, respectively), but among international adoptees, those who experienced extreme deprivation showed more serious externalizing behaviors than those who had not experienced such deprivation ($d = 0.17$). Collectively, the effect sizes for these patterns are small and support the notion that early experience prior to adoption confers risk for internalizing and externalizing issues for some but not all children.

Hawk & McCall (2010) reexamined these Adoption MAP findings with a more narrow review of 18 studies that all used the behavior problem scales of the Child Behavior Checklist, comparing postinstitutionalized (PI) international adoptees with nonadopted controls; some studies also included noninstitutionalized international adoptees. Consistent with Juffer & van IJzendoorn (2005), they found that PI internationally adopted children generally showed higher levels of internalizing, externalizing, and attention problems than did nonadopted children or the noninstitutionalized adoptees. Moreover, when accounting for the different ages at which children were assessed, older PI children scored higher on internalizing than did younger PI children. Notably, some problems emerged or became more severe during adolescence, and later-adopted children showed worse outcomes than early-adopted children.

Employing an innovative design to study attention problems, Lindblad et al. (2010) used linked data from the Swedish national health statistics register and prescription drug register to compare use of medication prescribed for ADHD in full population cohorts of internationally adopted children ($N = 16,134$) and nonadopted children ($N = 1,326,090$). Rates of prescribed medication were higher for adopted children in comparison to nonadoptees, and the odds ratios were particularly high for adoptees from regions where preadoption conditions are generally poor, including Eastern Europe, Middle East/Africa, and Latin America. Later age of adoption also increased the risk for attention problems.

Taken together, these data highlight the considerable challenges facing some adopted children and families while acknowledging significant heterogeneity of preadoption experiences for both international and domestic adoptees. Multiple factors (genetic, prenatal, preplacement, adoptive family, societal context) contribute to developmental trajectories among adopted children. The complex transactional influences of these multiple factors across time contribute to the difficulty of predicting developmental outcomes for individual children.

Methodological issues in this area are also considerable. Take for instance children's age at adoption, a measure that has frequently been used as an indicator of a child's exposure to potentially damaging environments. In the large Adoption MAP, differences were not found as a function of age of adoption, regardless of whether the cutoff point used for early versus late was 12 months or 24 months. However, Hawk & McCall (2011) found elevated levels of internalizing, externalizing, and attention problems among children assessed as adolescents who had been adopted from Russia after 18 months of age. These patterns did not emerge among the earlier-adopted children. These analyses were complicated by the different cutoff points used for age of adoption in different studies. Hawk and McCall concluded that their results were consistent with the possibility of a sensitive period between 6 and 12 months (on the early side) and 18 and 24 months (on the later side), such that significant deprivation experienced between those ages predicted a higher likelihood of later behavior problems. Age of adoption effects in the English and Romanian Adoption study (ERA) (Rutter & Sonuga-Barke 2010) also differed in time period, such that children adopted after 6 months (rather than 18) showed subsequent problems in adjustment. In general, research suggests that children for whom institutional rearing ends no later than 6 months of age fare better than those for whom deprivation continues or the deprivation occurs later (Zeanah et al. 2011).

Nonetheless, it is important to note that sensitive period findings among PI children also depend on factors beyond age such as experience prior to institutionalization, severity of the institutionalization, age at assessment (e.g., Merz & McCall 2010), and the developmental domain being examined (Zeanah et al. 2011). According to Hawk & McCall (2011), contrasting findings about age of adoption may reflect the more extreme impact of the extensive deprivation experienced by the children in Romania in the 1990s in comparison to the primarily socioemotional deprivation experienced by the children in Russia. Differences such as these are likely to be obscured in large meta-analyses or other reviews.

Taken together, these findings highlight some of the methodological challenges in this area and suggest that age of adoption is an imperfect proxy for early experience. Understanding age of adoption effects requires knowledge of early contexts and experiences to which children were exposed. Although findings at the behavioral level are generally consistent with our rapidly expanding knowledge of underlying neurological development, there are cases in which the associations between neural development and behavioral measures are unclear. Further research incorporating both neural and behavioral measures will be necessary in order to develop more precise statements about sensitive periods linked to experience prior to adoption (Zeanah et al. 2011).

In respect to social development, there is a striking paucity of research on positive outcomes or strengths of adopted children; this stands in sharp contrast to the large literature on problem behavior and psychopathology. Several factors have contributed to this imbalance: the origins of much of the adoption literature in clinical practice, where higher risk for problem behaviors among adopted children has long been noted; funding streams that prioritize problematic outcomes; and the general emphasis in psychological research on identifying group differences (see Palacios & Brodzinsky 2010).

However, there are many adopted children who successfully exhibit similar if not elevated levels of social skills compared to nonadopted peers (Sharma et al. 1996, Tan & Camras 2011). Thus far, differences in processing of socioemotional information (Camras et al. 2006, Wismer Fries & Pollak 2004) and aberrant social behavior in the form of disinhibited social approach (Bruce et al. 2009b) have emerged primarily in cases where children were adopted from institutionalized care settings. Among internationally adopted children, both poor social skills and higher rates of disinhibited social approach are markers for risk of being bullied by peers in adolescence (Raaska et al. 2012).

However, PI children also have the capacity to display appropriate socioemotional skills in forming attachment relationships (Smyke et al. 2009) and can distinguish familiar and unfamiliar faces (Moulson et al. 2009). Such mixed patterns of socioemotional behavior call for further investigations of the associations between socioemotional skill preservation among adopted children and potential interactions with other cognitive regulatory factors that influence social outcomes. Among adopted children who have not experienced early adversity, multiple questions remain unanswered regarding the presence and function of social and emotion-regulation skills at different time points across development. Relatively little research has examined specific skills underlying social competence with peers in domestic or internationally adopted children. However, Palacios et al. (2012) found that children growing up in institutions (rather than adoptive families) did more poorly than the adopted and community comparison children on several measures of social competence and peer relations. The adopted children were more similar to the community comparison children than to the children in the protective institutions. Social competence was positively associated with adaptive developmental outcomes, underscoring the need to understand linkages across biological, cognitive, and social domains.

The need to better understand mechanisms underlying differences in developmental outcomes is relevant for both internationally and domestically adopted children. Specifically, increased knowledge of biological and social processes that shape trajectories for adopted children will allow for more targeted interventions to address specific areas of vulnerability. Although, as depicted in **Figure 1**, underlying biological and social processes are intertwined throughout development, for the purpose of discussion they are each given emphasis in the separate sections below. Nevertheless, at a microlevel, one could consider specific mechanisms by which the child's biological functioning can influence, and in turn be impacted by, social experiences preceding adoption or the transition to an adoptive family with adjustment to new caregivers. At a macrolevel, social processes involved in creating and maintaining adoptive families across a range of diverse family structures, or social processes involved in maintenance of healthy communication between a child's birth and adoptive parents, could also activate changes in a child's biological processes. Detailed discussion of these biological and social processes occurs in separate sections in this review; however, it is highly probable that these processes can and do interact at various points to independently and jointly contribute to developmental outcomes for adopted individuals over time. Consideration of such interactions may further promote work that has just begun to explore areas of overlap in these processes in an effort to elucidate the best adoption practices to benefit long-term child outcomes.

BIOLOGICAL PROCESSES AND COGNITIVE FUNCTIONS

Biological Processes

Stress reactivity. Stress reactivity influences a number of biological processes that may be involved in adaptation for adopted children. Situated throughout the central nervous system and periphery of an organism, the stress system is responsible for maintaining stability of internal function and is activated when normal functioning is at risk or perceived to be at risk (Chrousos 2009). Activation of this system generates a multifaceted neuroendocrine response involving the hypothalamic-pituitary-adrenal (HPA) axis. Among the most prominent functions of the HPA axis is the production of stress-related hormones known as glucocorticoids (Herman & Cullinan 1997). These hormones have a vast and pervasive impact throughout the body and are involved in both mounting and terminating the stress response (Sapolsky et al. 2000). Under typical circumstances, the activation and deactivation of the stress system is a normal and necessary function. When continually taxed, either hyper- or hypoactivation of the stress system ensues, and both of these conditions contribute to a host of problematic outcomes. Thus, for children experiencing early adversity, what starts as a protective feature of the body's typical response to a stressor can ultimately initiate long-standing and serious issues in a child's development (Charmandari et al. 2003).

Implications for adopted children. Although many adopted children have tolerable experiences of stress, it is also the case that adopted children may experience acute or chronic stress prior to adoption, during the adoption process, and at various time points postadoption. In particular, the experience of childhood adversity prior to adoption (e.g., separation from caregivers, neglect, or maltreatment) can significantly impact a child's stress system (for a review, see Gunnar et al. 2006) and have cascading effects on later developmental processes and outcomes. In the realm of adoption, improved assessments of children's early experiences can illuminate specific ways in which neuroendocrine processes mediate links between early experiences and a broad array of physical, cognitive, and socioemotional outcomes. Research is steadily growing in respect to the former two domains, which established links between altered function of the stress response system and physical growth and cognitive function; however, there is a serious need for studies that explore neuroendocrine function in adopted individuals across a wide range of socioemotional scenarios including parent-child interactions, in peer contexts, and at various time points throughout childhood and adolescence. Intervention work aimed at normalizing stress reactivity in infants and toddlers in foster care demonstrates the importance of caregiver responsiveness to children's emotional needs (Attachment and Biobehavioral Catch-up Intervention; Dozier et al. 2008), and projects such as the Early Growth and Development Study (Leve et al. 2007, 2013b) have begun intensive efforts to utilize measures of stress reactivity in relation to adoption outcomes over time. Yet, to date, a large portion of the adoption literature examining stress reactivity has focused on children adopted following the extreme experience of orphanage care. Thus, the following sections highlight the substantial literature on adopted children who experienced early adversity, with an emphasis on a subset of biological processes—physical growth, brain development, and sleep—and the cognitive functions impacted by these processes.

Physiological growth: Body and brain. Current evidence points to a strong influence of the stress system response on basic growth patterns (for a review, see Johnson & Gunnar 2011). Although less clearly studied, there are hints of cascading problems across the cognitive and even the socioemotional realm based on physiological differences that may be tied to patterns of early stress reactivity. A prominent physiological outcome resulting from extensive exposure to early life stress is altered growth patterns in height, weight, and head circumference.

Body growth. Beyond growth delays based on nutritional deficiencies, the association between children's experience of early adversity and growth failure is influenced by the stress system's activation of the HPA axis. Activation of the HPA axis generates corticotropin-releasing hormone that subsequently reduces appetite and suppresses growth hormones (Dautzenberg et al. 2001, Romero et al. 2009). Miller & Hendrie (2000) estimate that for every two to three months of institutionalized care, children lose approximately one month of linear growth. In an extensive review of 33 studies of internationally adopted children (van IJzendoorn et al. 2007), substantial lags in height, weight, and head circumference were evident at the time of adoption. However, children who were placed before 12 months of age had smaller delays in these parameters as well as significant catch-up in height and weight (but not head circumference) when assessed eight years post adoption. Conversely, later age of placement was associated with less physical catch-up (van IJzendoorn et al. 2007). Thus, among internationally adopted children, particularly those experiencing early deprivation in institutions, adoption appears to produce significant change in trajectories of physical growth.

The Bucharest Early Intervention Project (BEIP), the first randomized clinical trial of high-quality foster care as an intervention for social deprivation associated with institutionalization, revealed similar improvement in growth patterns (Zeanah et al. 2003). Prior to randomization, institutionalized children showed significantly lower scores on all physical growth parameters in comparison to the never-institutionalized group. However, when children were placed into high-quality foster care, they exhibited near-normal levels of height and weight (but not head circumference) after 12 months (Johnson et al. 2010). Physical catch-up was greater if the child was placed in the new environment by 12 months, and higher caregiving quality (especially positive regard and sensitivity) predicted catch-up in height and weight (Johnson et al. 2010).

Despite patterns of apparent growth catch-up in childhood, longitudinal data from the English and Romanian Adoption Study (ERA) (for details, see Rutter et al. 2010) reveal that children who were older than 6 months of age when adopted from the extreme conditions in Romanian orphanages can also exhibit growth deficiencies in adolescence. Given this later-emerging pattern of physical development, growth advances during childhood may be best categorized as growth spurts (Sonuga-Barke et al. 2010). Of note, the growth deficiency observed during adolescence was only statistically significant for girls. Therefore, early chronic stress exposure may evoke capped trajectories of growth among children experiencing early deprivation, possibly through mechanisms driving earlier pubertal onset (Sonuga-Barke et al. 2010).

Brain development. Another key physiological outcome in relation to children's experience of early adversity is structural differences in brain development that may substantially influence cognitive, as well as social and emotional, functioning. Indirect evidence for associations between brain development and maladaptive outcomes was evident in several studies of children experiencing early psychosocial deprivation. Findings from the ERA study suggest that head circumference, an indirect measure of brain growth, might mediate the effect of institutional deprivation on deprivation-specific psychological patterns (Kreppner et al. 2010). Similarly, the BEIP has shown that patterns of brain activity, assessed via electroencephalogram (EEG), mediate the association between the experience of institutionalization and ADHD symptoms at 5 years of age (McLaughlin et al. 2010). These EEG differences in brain activity are hypothesized to indicate a developmental delay in cortical maturation and correspond to patterns of ADHD in noninstitutionalized children (Shaw et al. 2007). Similarly, specific perturbations in EEG power distribution among PI toddlers have been linked to disinhibited social approach during the preschool age range (Tarullo et al. 2011). This pattern underscores that deviations in brain development associated with early adversity can also impact social skills that may strongly contribute to developmental outcomes.

More recently, the use of magnetic resonance imaging has allowed for direct assessment of brain growth linked to early adversity. A recent review on the effects of child maltreatment on brain structure highlights a common pattern of deficits in total brain volume linked to decreased amount of both white and gray matter, which represent neural connections and neuron volume, respectively, across a number of regions (Hart & Rubia 2012). Decreased brain volume is associated with lower potential for processing power and thus can impact higher-order cognitive functions (Nelson 2007). A similar pattern of both gray and white matter reduction among PI children was found in children assessed during adolescence in the ERA study (Mehta et al. 2009). In the BEIP, children (8–11 years old) who had previously experienced institutionalization also had smaller cortical gray matter volume compared to Romanian children who had never been institutionalized. However, placement into a foster care intervention was associated with increased cortical white matter relative to children not randomized to foster care, indicating neural plasticity in white matter and demonstrating the potential for catch-up to never-institutionalized peers (Sheridan et al. 2012).

Another study of PI children using diffusion tensor imaging also demonstrated reduced brain volumes based on both gray and white matter deficits. This technology further revealed compromised integrity of white matter tracts that serve to connect different regions of the brain among previously institutionalized as compared to never-institutionalized children (Eluvathingal et al. 2006). These results, along with other work tracking changes in brain electrical activity over time (Vanderwert et al. 2010), highlight long-lasting alterations in the neural development in the brain among children experiencing institutionalization.

In addition to whole-brain volumetric differences, children who have experienced early adversity such as maltreatment, trauma, or neglect have volumetric differences in limbic structures including the amygdala and the hippocampus. More specifically, the amygdala processes emotional information and is associated with behavioral control, whereas the hippocampus plays a central role in learning and memory. Among PI children, two studies have found increased amygdala volume (Mehta et al. 2009, Tottenham et al. 2010), whereas one has found no difference between previously institutionalized and never-institutionalized children (Sheridan et al. 2012). Data on amygdala volumes among maltreated children with posttraumatic stress disorder (PTSD) and controls also vary, in that some studies have reported no differences (De Bellis et al. 1999, 2001; Woon & Hedges 2008), whereas other work found decreased amygdala volumes (Carrión et al. 2001). In part, these contrasting findings may result from differences in analytical approaches to processing imaging data with different comparisons being employed in different studies. Additionally, the previously mentioned studies also varied in the homogeneity of the populations being assessed in terms of early experience or age (Hart & Rubia 2012).

Similar patterns of conflicting results have also emerged from studies examining change in the hippocampus associated with early life stress in children. Several reports indicate no change in this region due to maltreatment (De Bellis et al. 1999, 2001) or institutionalized care (Mehta et al. 2009, Tottenham et al. 2010). In contrast, one study of children with PTSD found increases in hippocampal volume compared to children without PTSD (Tupler & De Bellis 2006), whereas another study found reductions in hippocampal volume due to PTSD approximately one year after a baseline assessment (Carrión et al. 2007). Additional work is needed to discern the precise circumstances that contribute to specific types of change in brain structure and function among children experiencing early adversity prior to adoption.

Implications for adoption outcomes. It is important to note that equivocal research results stem from a range of factors related to early developmental contexts. Combined, the findings suggest that differences in the development of certain brain regions may depend on numerous factors including the nature and extent of the stressor, age of placement, remediating factors after adoption and age of assessment. Much of the imaging work related most directly to adoption has come from children in foster care (with an emphasis on the hippocampus and amygdala); however, a number of additional brain regions have been identified as potentially vulnerable to early adversity in childhood including the cerebellum (Bauer et al. 2009), the prefrontal cortices (Carrión et al. 2009, Hanson et al. 2012, Richert et al. 2006), and the parietal lobes (De Bellis et al. 2002). Deficits in these brain areas have been tied to impaired social, emotional, and behavioral regulation. The full range and depth of these deficits due to early adversity, as well as the potential for recovery with placement into enriched environments via adoption, are still being explored.

A number of unanswered questions remain about the associations between altered developmental growth trajectories and longitudinal effects on cognitive, social, and emotional outcomes. In respect to brain development, surprisingly few links have emerged between neural measures and behavioral data. This pattern highlights the need for exploring associations outside of task-specific measures collected at the same time as neural data. Along these lines, recent work from the BEIP revealed connections between neural reactivity, attachment status, and social skills in peer interactions among children placed into the foster care intervention (Almas et al. 2012). Specifically, children who received the intervention earlier exhibited enhanced cortical maturity (i.e., higher levels of alpha power) compared to children who were placed into the intervention later. Moreover, this neural pattern moderated relations between early attachment security and measures of social skills with peers in middle childhood (Almas et al. 2012). These findings support prior literature reporting difficulties in attachment formation and peer relations among children experiencing early psychosocial deprivation (Erol et al. 2010, Roy et al. 2004). They also highlight how stress during sensitive periods can impact the development of neural mechanisms that contribute to social function in respect to early attachment patterns and to later, more complex, social interactions with peers during middle childhood and adolescence.

Additional work is needed exploring the potential for changes in brain structure or function as new social bonds are formed between adopted children and their parents in cases where early adversity is not a factor. Greater insight on the neural correlates of the bonding process at various age points in development may help illuminate specific physiological mechanisms by which adoption contributes to positive developmental outcomes across emotional, social, and cognitive domains. For example, recent work examining neural correlates of bonding in infants and foster mothers demonstrated associations between the affiliative neuropeptide, oxytocin, and foster mother expressions of delight toward their infant (Bick et al. 2013). Furthermore, as the bonding process unfolded over several months, oxytocin became predictive of foster mothers' neural reactivity to images of their foster infant (Bick et al. 2013). This work highlights the feasibility of investigating biomarkers of the bonding processes in the context of alloparental care.

Sleep. Beyond alterations in physical growth, stressful experiences can also have a significant negative impact on children's sleep patterns and their subsequent cognitive, emotional, and behavioral function (Aronen et al. 2000, Steenari et al. 2003). Studies in nonadopted children have found that arousal linked to acute stress (e.g., caregiver transitions) and the presence of chronic stress (e.g., alertness due to anxiety about prior traumas) are associated with greater difficulty initiating and maintaining sleep (Dahl 1996, Sadeh 1996). Among children in foster care who have experienced trauma, bedtime may be particularly stressful in a manner beyond general child fears of the dark due to lack of trust of caregivers and negative associations with abuse (Dozier 2005, Tininenko et al. 2010).

Several studies examining children internationally adopted from China or Cambodia note sleep problems as a prominent adjustment difficulty (Rettig & McCarthy-Rettig 2006, Tan et al. 2007) despite comparable, or better, functioning on other developmental outcomes in comparison with nonadopted children. Specific types of sleep problems for these internationally adopted children include longer periods of night waking, talking or crying in one's sleep, nightmares, and problems initiating sleep (Tan et al. 2007). Moreover, sleep challenges may be especially prominent in the early transition to a new adoptive family as children shift sleeping environments (sometimes time zones as well) and must adjust to the expectations and interactions with their new caregivers (Miller 2005).

Given the links between impaired sleep and behavior problems, interventions for foster children should place a strong emphasis on factors that correspond to mitigation of sleep issues such as foster parent stress level, attachment relationship quality, and the formation of a warm and contingent caregiving environment (see Tininenko et al. 2010). One intervention that emphasizes these factors has demonstrated more positive sleep patterns in children. Specifically, children in the foster care intervention had earlier bedtimes, shorter time to fall asleep, and longer time in bed compared to children in regular foster care programs and low-income children in non-foster-care homes. Family stress has previously been demonstrated as a potent precursor to sleep issues in nonadopted children (Bell & Belsky 2008), and recent data in both adopted and non-adopted children reveal associations between marital instability and childhood sleep problems (Mannering et al. 2011).

Implications for adoption outcomes. Although it has been proposed that various aspects of sleep may be resistant to influences of stress, the long-term consequences of sleep disturbances early in childhood are poorly understood even among nonadopted children. Current evidence suggests that difficulties in respect to quantity and quality of sleep are linked with heightened negative affect (Mikoteit et al. 2013), decreased flexibility in response to challenging situations among young children (Berger et al. 2012), and risk for anxiety and depression among adolescents (Gregory & Sadeh 2012). Further work is needed in adopted children that focuses on connections between sleep patterns and cognitive function and how the transition to adoption, as well as later reflections on being adopted, may play a role in sleep quality and developmental outcomes. Given the strong associations between sleep patterns and behavioral and emotional regulation, it is imperative to understand best practices for promoting sleep when adopted children transition into their new family environment.

Cognitive Functions

Intelligence. Beyond the physical realm, activation and refinement of the stress system can have significant consequences on children's cognitive function. In respect to intelligence, Adoption MAP examined school performance (based on 55 studies) and IQ scores (based on 48 studies) of adopted children in comparison to (*a*) their birth siblings or peers who remained behind in their original environment and (*b*) nonadopted children in the adoptees' new environment (van IJzendoorn et al. 2005). Adopted children scored higher on IQ tests and performed better in school than did comparison children who remained behind; the adoptees did not differ in IQ from the comparison children in their new environments, but they did not perform as well in school and sometimes developed learning problems (van IJzendoorn et al. 2005). Age at adoption moderated the effect for school achievement; children adopted after their first birthday did more poorly in school. The authors attributed these effects to the often dramatic changes the children experienced with adoption as they moved into cognitively enriching environments.

Among previously institutionalized children, the BEIP found that patterns of improved IQ were somewhat sustained throughout early childhood, but the improvements were particularly prominent for children placed earlier into a foster care intervention and for those who remained in this placement through their eighth year of life (Fox et al. 2011). Similar patterns have been reported in internationally adopted children. Namely, children who are in foster care or who are adopted at young ages generally exhibit higher IQ scores than do PI children (Loman et al. 2009).

Executive functions. A number of cognitive factors that direct goal-oriented behavior comprise executive functions. At the core of executive functioning are the components of inhibitory control, the manipulation of information in working memory, and the capacity for flexible attention shifting (Zelazo et al. 2003). Deficits in executive functions are prominent among children experiencing early adversity. Among maltreated children, difficulty engaging executive functions emerges in neutral (Bruce et al. 2009a, Pears et al. 2012) and affectively laden contexts (Shackman et al. 2007). PI children also exhibit global deficits across a range of executive function skills (Bruce et al. 2009b, Colvert et al. 2008) with the degree of impairment tied to duration of exposure to adversity such that children who spent longer in institutionalized care have more severe deficits in executive function skills (Colvert et al. 2008, Pollak et al. 2010). Additionally, less time with the birth family and lower quality of care in the institution are also associated with poorer executive function in preschool-aged children one year after adoption (Hostinar et al. 2012). Exposure to adversity is thought to negatively impact the development of the prefrontal circuitry that underlies executive functioning with evidence of links between these factors emerging in studies using a range of imaging techniques including event-related potentials (Loman et al. 2013, McDermott et al. 2012), functional magnetic resonance imaging (Hanson et al. 2012, Tottenham et al. 2011), positron emission tomography (Chugani et al. 2001), and diffusion tensor imaging (Eluvathingal et al. 2006).

Inhibitory control. In respect to specific executive function skills, patterns of inhibitory control difficulties are prevalent in PI children in early and middle childhood, with the severity of impairment linked to age of adoption. Namely, the younger a child is removed from institutional care and adopted, the better the performance on inhibitory control (Colvert et al. 2008, Jacobs et al. 2010). Deficits in inhibitory control have also emerged among children in the BEIP study and among PI children adopted into the United States (Loman et al. 2013, McDermott et al. 2013). Moreover, links between impaired inhibitory control and perturbed social development have been found among previously institutionalized children. Specifically, children experiencing early psychosocial deprivation have an increased prevalence of disinhibited social approach, or abnormal approach behavior toward adults who are not their caregivers, and this type of behavior is associated with lower inhibitory control skills (Bruce et al. 2009b). Thus the ability to regulate social behavior may depend in part on adequate development of executive functioning skills such as inhibitory control.

Working memory. Impairments in working memory among children adopted from institutions have emerged on paired-associate learning tasks, spatial working memory, and episodic memory (Bos et al. 2009, Pollak et al. 2010). In a study by Güler and colleagues (2012), associations between physiological indices of attention allocation (i.e., event-related potentials) predicted memory performance among the PI group of children. Pollak et al. (2010) studied timing of early adversity in school-aged children by comparing children who had experienced prolonged institutionalization prior to adoption, brief institutionalization (two months or less) prior to adoption, and rearing in their families of birth. The PI children performed worse than children in the other two groups on measures of spatial working memory, memory for faces, visual attention, and paired-associate learning, suggesting delayed maturation of specific aspects of frontal circuitry and possibly reduced connectivity between frontal cortex and other regions of the brain. In a related study, Desmarais and colleagues (2012) found that spatial working memory skills mediated the effect between PI status and sentence comprehension.

Although not directly examined in the context of adoption studies, research on children experiencing trauma and subsequent PTSD also reports poorer memory performance (De Bellis et al. 2010) that may be driven by deficits in hippocampal activity (Carrión et al. 2010). These patterns have substantial implications for children entering adoption via the foster care system or via international adoption from countries with limited caregiving resources, as an extensive body of research indicates that early adversity impacts the neural circuitry for executive function skills (for reviews, see Dawson et al. 2000, De Bellis 2005, Hughes 2011).

Response monitoring. Because many adopted children experience foster care prior to adoption, studies of foster children are also potentially informative. Using an electrophysiological measure of response monitoring that identifies information about a sequence of cognitive processes, Bruce and colleagues (2009a) found that maltreated children in foster care performed more poorly than did foster children receiving an intervention or nonmaltreated children. Similar patterns of enhanced response monitoring are evident in PI children in high-quality foster care or adopted into stable families (Loman et al. 2013, McDermott et al. 2012) and suggest that despite continued issues with executive functioning and, in particular, attention problems, children placed into enriched environments after experiencing early deprivation have the capacity to capitalize on compensatory processes driven by prefrontal neural circuitry.

Implications for adoption outcomes. New directions in executive function research among typically developing populations are focusing on the precise caregiving mechanisms that enhance child performance on key executive function skills in toddlerhood (Bernier et al. 2010). Parenting interventions aimed at increasing executive function skills would hold significant implications for adopted children who may have experienced early adversity. Although work in adoption samples has indicated a strong presence of heritability for general cognitive skills (e.g., Plomin & DeFries 1985), as well as specific skills such as inhibitory control (Leve et al. 2013a), such work has primarily focused on early ages of assessment. Moreover, little work has explored executive functions in domestically adopted children as compared with internationally adopted children.

Future Directions in Research on Biological Processes

Much work remains to be done before a full understanding of how biological processes affected by deprivation or maltreatment exert their influence on specific cognitive functions. Longitudinal work that incorporates the earliest possible assessment of contextual experience, even prenatal experience, is well poised to illuminate additional mechanisms (i.e., epigenetics) through which biological processes such as stress reactivity shape later cognitive outcomes. Additionally, work is needed to uncover the factors that contribute to maintenance of cognitive advances among children adopted from adverse early experiences. Ultimately, investigations highlighting biological processes may illuminate mechanistic pathways through which early experience has cascading effects on adaptive and maladaptive patterns of outcomes throughout the lifespan. It is also likely that there are fluctuating levels of interaction between biological and social processes across time and contexts. Novel approaches to incorporating elements of biological processes may advance understanding in several areas of social processes and vice versa.

SOCIAL PROCESSES

The following sections examine social processes linked to developmental outcomes for adopted children in three contexts that have raised concerns about best practices and the best interests of the child: (*a*) contexts in which there is contact between adoptive and birth family members, (*b*) contexts in which children are adopted by lesbian or gay parents, and (*c*) contexts in which children have been adopted transracially. In each case, the developmental outcomes under investigation primarily reflect risks hypothesized to be associated with growing up in such contexts. Within contexts involving birth and adoptive family contact, outcomes have typically focused on adjustment (usually reflecting internalizing and externalizing problem behavior), identity, and parent-child relationships. For children adopted by lesbian and gay parents, outcomes under study have included gender role development as well as adjustment. Studies involving transracial adoption have typically focused on identity, especially racial and ethnic identity. Because each of these lines of work originated in concerns about potentially harmful effects on children, outcomes typically focus on problems rather than strengths. More research focusing on positive behaviors of adopted children is strongly needed.

Contact Between Adoptive and Birth Family Members

Background. Although adoption involves the legal transfer of parental rights and responsibilities from birth to adoptive parents, adoptions are increasingly involving the possibility for contact between the child's adoptive and birth relatives; arrangements involving contact are often referred to as open adoptions (Grotevant 2012). In open adoptions, contact can vary widely in its medium (letters, emails, photos, face-to-face meetings, Facebook, Skype), frequency, intensity, and participants; all of these dimensions of contact can change over time. Open adoptions occur most frequently in domestic infant placements but are increasingly occurring in adoptions from the child welfare system (Neil et al. 2011) and international adoptions (Scherman 2012).

The contemporary movement toward open adoptions began in the 1970s, when several influential social forces converged. The number of infants available for adoption had declined as a result of access to reliable contraception and legal abortion and the reduced stigma associated with parenting outside marriage. Staff at some adoption agencies believed that the option for expectant mothers to have contact with their children after placement could make them more willing to consider making an adoption plan. Interest in biological connection and kinship was stimulated by discoveries about the importance of genetics in promoting health and by media attention to kinship through landmark films such as *Roots*. Energized by the human rights movements of the 1960s, adopted persons claimed the right to possess full and accurate information about themselves, such as the identity of their birth parents and family history information that might bear on their health and that of their children (for a more detailed history of open adoption, see Carp 1998).

Questions under investigation. Early experiments with openness split the adoption practice community into two camps: (*a*) those who argued that open adoption should become standard practice because the secrecy of closed adoptions had been harmful to all parties involved (e.g., Pannor & Baran 1984) and (*b*) those who countered that children in open adoptions would be confused about who their "real" parents were, leading to identity confusion and later adjustment problems; that adoptive parents' sense of entitlement to be the child's full parents would suffer; and that birth mothers would never be able to resolve their loss over the adoption because they would be reminded of it upon every contact (e.g., Kraft et al. 1985). Despite strongly held opinions about openness, little research was available to guide practice and policy. Currently, two primary sets of questions are being investigated by researchers focusing on openness (Grotevant 2012). First, what are the effects of different contact arrangements on adopted children, adoptive parents, and birth parents? Second, how do adoptive kinship networks that experience contact manage the complexities of their relationships?

New insights about social processes. Several studies have examined links between birth family contact and children's adjustment outcomes, especially externalizing disorders. No direct connection has been found between contact and externalizing (e.g., Brodzinsky 2006, Grotevant et al. 2011, Neil 2009). However, Grotevant et al. (2011) found that the family's satisfaction with contact (rather than the existence of contact itself) predicted less externalizing behavior in adolescence and that the effect persisted into emerging adulthood. How participants make meaning of their contact appears to have more impact on adjustment than the presence or absence of contact. Satisfaction with contact arrangements was higher in open than in closed adoptions for adopted children and their adoptive parents, both during adolescence (Grotevant et al. 2007) and emerging adulthood (Farr et al. 2013).

Many adoption professionals have hypothesized that contact with birth relatives would have a positive impact on identity development, since adoptees have real relationships with birth family members that provide direct access to genealogical and genetic information and grounding for development of their sense of self as an adopted person (e.g., Grotevant & Von Korff 2011). Von Korff & Grotevant (2011) found that the frequency of adoption-related conversations in adoptive families mediated the association between contact with birth relatives and adoptive identity development during adolescence and emerging adulthood. Discussions about relationships with birth relatives and contact logistics contributed to the construction of a coherent adoptive identity. Such discussions are rare in families with closed adoptions, since there is no contact to manage and little new information to discuss.

Although, within a sample of infant adoptions, satisfaction with the presence or absence of contact arrangements tended to be higher for all parties when contact was taking place (e.g., Grotevant et al. 2007), feelings about contact also depended on the dynamics of the relationships with the child's birth relatives. For example, Grotevant (2009) proposed that the process of emotional distance regulation underlies the dynamics of contact; differences in each individual's comfort in engaging in new relationships must be bridged in a dynamic process involving connection and separateness over time. Successful relationships in such complex family situations hinge on participants' flexibility, communication skills, and commitment to the relationships. Although these skills can be learned and supported, circumstances may also exist such that one or more parties to the adoption may be unable or unwilling to participate in contact.

Neil & Howe (2004) proposed a transactional model of contact, positing that the quality of the contact would be influenced by the psychological strengths and limitations of the parties directly involved. Qualitative analysis of interviews with those participating in contact in "complex" cases (often when the child had been adopted following removal from the birth family because of maltreatment) revealed that important considerations included building relationships, understanding each person's role, navigating family boundaries, coping with the "strangeness" of the contact meetings, and dealing with complex feelings (Neil et al. 2011).

Contact has been studied most in domestic private adoptions in which birth parents often play active roles in selecting the child's adoptive parents. Less is known about the contact outcomes and relational issues that arise in adoptions from the child welfare system, where children were removed from their parents because of maltreatment (but see Neil 2012, Neil et al. 2011), or in international adoptions, where cultural norms in the child's country of origin concerning adoption and the placement of children may be very different from those in the child's country of adoption (Roby & Matsumura 2002). Contact is increasingly occurring in both of these settings, and further research on those situations is needed.

Adoption by Lesbian and Gay Parents

Background. Lesbian and gay individuals and couples have long filled the roles of adoptive parents, but the lack of legal recognition of their relationship has led many of them to adopt as single persons. More recently, lesbian and gay couples in some jurisdictions have been explicitly permitted by law to adopt children (Appell 2012), and they are doing so in increasing numbers (Brodzinsky et al. 2012). This trend reflects changing public attitudes about the acceptability of lesbian and gay relationships, as seen in the growing legalization of same-sex marriage. Adoption by lesbian and gay couples has been viewed by some as an opportunity to find adoptive homes for the large number of children in the public child welfare children waiting for permanent families (Brodzinsky 2011). Currently, over 50% of lesbian and gay adoptive couples have adopted children from the public system (Brodzinsky 2011); nevertheless, only about half of the children available for adoption through the public system are placed for adoption in any given year (Child. Bur. 2012).

Questions under investigation. Adoption professionals and policymakers have asked whether lesbian and gay couples can provide safe and secure homes for adopted children, and whether children raised by same-sex parents fare as well as those who have a mother and a father. Concerns typically revolve around adjustment/mental health, attachment, gender role development, and sexual orientation. Until the recent surge of research on lesbian and gay adoption, opinions based on broader attitudes about sexual orientation and the definition of family have driven practice and policy decisions. However, two current longitudinal research programs (i.e., Farr & Patterson 2013, Goldberg & Smith 2011) are adding substantive research-based evidence to the discussion.

New insights about social processes. Both the Farr and Goldberg projects employ comparative designs (including lesbian, gay, and heterosexual couples), but both also focus on social processes that might account for differences that arise. Some research has focused on prospective parents' pathways to adoption (e.g., Downing et al. 2009), and other work has focused on outcomes for parents, such as stress and depression (Goldberg & Smith 2011). However, the work most relevant to practice and policy addresses outcomes for the children. Since openly acknowledged lesbian and gay adoption is a relatively new phenomenon, the children in these studies are still young, and longitudinal follow-ups will be required to examine longer-term outcomes more commonly associated with adolescence or young adulthood (e.g., identity, sexual orientation). Nevertheless, some findings about young children are emerging.

In the first wave of Farr's longitudinal study (Farr et al. 2010), the children were between 13 and 72 months of age (mean = 36). No differences were found between families headed by lesbian, gay, or heterosexual couples on children's internalizing, externalizing, or total behavior problems as measured by the Achenbach Child Behavior Checklist (parent report) or Teacher Report Form (teacher report). Also, no differences were found in children's gender role behavior. However, parenting stress (which did not differ by couple type) was significantly associated with children's internalizing, externalizing, and total behavior problems (Farr et al. 2010). On the other hand, supportive co-parenting, demonstrated in videotaped parent-child interaction, was associated with better child adjustment (Farr & Patterson 2013). These studies highlight the importance of moving beyond family type comparisons to focusing on family and parenting processes as predictors of child outcomes.

Goldberg et al. (2012) examined gender-typed play behavior in young children adopted by lesbian, gay, and heterosexual parents. Play preferences were assessed by parent report of child play activities in a sample of 2- to 4-year-old adopted children who were the oldest in the family. Play preferences of young children in families headed by same-gender couples were less gender-stereotyped than were play preferences in families headed by heterosexual couples. This tendency was more evident in lesbian couple families than in gay couple families. Future observational research is needed to examine the social processes underlying these differences.

Longitudinal research following these children and families through adolescence is critically important and needs to reflect the changing developmental demands facing children at different ages. It also needs to reflect the community contexts in which the families live, since prior research has shown that state-level policies that are discriminatory or hostile to lesbian and gay populations are associated with the presence of psychiatric disorders among lesbian and gay adults (Hatzenbuehler et al. 2009, 2010). Because parental adjustment difficulties could negatively affect parenting stress and interactional processes, children growing up in such contexts could be at risk. Future research should also include examination of transracial adoption and open adoption, since many lesbian and gay couples adopt transracially and have contact with the child's birth relatives (Farr & Patterson 2009, Goldberg 2009, Goldberg et al. 2011).

Cultural Socialization and Preparation for Bias in Transracially Adoptive Families

Background. Adoptions are considered transracial when the racial, ethnic, or cultural origin of the child differs from that of the child's parent(s). According to the nationally representative National Survey of Adoptive Parents, approximately 40% of U.S. adoptions are transracial, but this figure varies by type of adoption. Approximately 21% of private domestic adoptions, 28% of adoptions from foster care, and 84% of international adoptions are transracial; most transracial placements involve white parents adopting children of color (Vandivere et al. 2009).

Practice recommendations about transracial adoption have evolved alongside shifting societal attitudes about race, culture, and difference. In the early days of transracial adoption (1950s for international adoptions and 1960s for domestic transracial adoptions), parents were advised to take a colorblind approach to raising their adopted children, de-emphasizing the importance of race and racial differences (e.g., Lee et al. 2006) in order to support the integration of the child into the family. During that era, America was viewed as a cultural melting pot in which old ethnic and cultural identities ideally became subordinated to a new American identity.

Views have changed dramatically since then, shifting from the ideal of the melting pot society to one that acknowledges cultural diversity and the fact that race indeed matters. The reality is that children of color in the United States, regardless of adoptive status, experience racism and discrimination ranging from subtle microaggressions to blatant attacks (Fisher et al. 2000). Despite this understanding, white parents who endorse colorblindness do not discuss racism in advance of their child's experiencing it; adopted children raised by such parents have to navigate a racialized world on their own (Samuels 2009).

Questions under investigation. As with other new forms of adoption (including open adoptions and adoption by gay or lesbian parents), questions have been raised about the effects of transracial adoption on children. The broadest concerns have been raised about identity (especially with regard to race, ethnicity, and culture); adjustment (usually operationalized in terms of internalizing or externalizing behavior problems); and ultimately, the ability to function effectively as an adult person of color in a race-conscious society. These outcomes are potentially interrelated. The adoption literature contains many first-person accounts of transracially adopted young adults whose lack of clarity about their racial/cultural identity as a person of color created challenges for their finding their place in society (e.g., Trenka et al. 2006). These accounts, including blogs, videos, and memoirs, often link difficulty finding one's place culturally with significant adjustment challenges such as depression (e.g., Lee 2008).

New insights about social processes. Most social process research on transracial adoption has examined socialization practices that promote the development of racial/ethnic/cultural identity and the ability of transracially adopted persons to function effectively as adult members of their cultural groups. A major review of parents' ethnic-racial socialization practices (Hughes et al. 2006) revealed two distinctive processes: (a) cultural socialization (CS), defined as "parental practices that teach children about their racial or ethnic heritage and history; that promote cultural customs and traditions; and that promote children's cultural, racial, and ethnic pride" (p. 749), and (b) preparation for bias (PB), described as "parents' efforts to promote their children's awareness of discrimination and prepare them to cope with it" (p. 756). Vonk et al. (2010) distinguished among CS activities that were more distal (e.g., reading books, attending cultural events); more intermediate (e.g., learning the language, visiting the country of origin); and more personal (e.g., living in an integrated neighborhood, having friendships with persons of the child's race, exposure to social justice issues). Their analysis of data from the National Survey of Adoptive Parents revealed that the CS strategies used most frequently by transracially adoptive parents (both domestic and international) involved little actual contact with people of the children's race; in contrast, the strategies that required the greatest integration and most personal impact (e.g., living in diverse neighborhoods) occurred least frequently.

Several studies have also examined factors influencing parents' use of CS and PB strategies. In a sample of white adoptive mothers raising children of Korean and Chinese descent, mothers' personal connections to Asian Americans enhanced the likelihood that they would use CS and PB strategies (Johnston et al. 2007). Parents who cited the positive value of cultural socialization (Thomas & Tessler 2007) or who scored low on a scale of colorblindness (Lee et al. 2006) were also more likely to use CS and PB strategies. Use of CS and PB strategies was also enhanced under certain ecological conditions, such as larger size of the Asian population in the family's county of residence (Thomas & Tessler 2007).

Children's experiences of discrimination (as reported by their parents) were predictive of problem behaviors in both children and adolescents adopted transracially from Latin America and among children adopted from Asia (Lee 2010). These postadoption experiences were as predictive of problem behaviors as were indicators of preadoption adversity (Lee 2010).

Do parental socialization practices serve protective functions against such negative outcomes? Leslie et al. (2013) found that racial socialization (combining elements of CS and PB) of adolescents did moderate the link between experiences of discrimination and perceived stressfulness of the experience. At high levels of discrimination, racial socialization served a protective function in moderating the perception of stress; at low levels of discrimination, racial socialization had little impact on stress.

Other studies have examined links between cultural socialization practices and adoption outcomes. Canadian adopted youth who were knowledgeable about their Romanian cultural heritage displayed more positive adoption identities and were more communicatively open about adoption than were youth who were less familiar with their cultural background (Le Mare & Audet 2011). Korean adoptees who engaged in cultural activities during young adulthood (ages 18 to 21) scored higher on measures of ethnic identity than did their peers who did not engage in such activities (Song & Lee 2009).

Most of the research linking cultural socialization practices with adoption outcomes has been cross-sectional and has relied on self-report questionnaires or interviews administered to adoptive parents and/or their youth. Consequently, this line of work is subject to all the limitations inherent in cross-sectional and self-report research strategies. Kim et al. (2013) have been among the few to examine CS practices engaging multiple informants and using interaction data in addition to self-reports. They videotaped 30 families with an adolescent adopted from South Korea talking about how race and ethnicity were discussed or negotiated in their family. They also asked parents and adolescents to report on the degree to which cultural socialization practices were used by the parents. Parents reported more extensive use of CS practices than their adolescents said their parents used. From the interaction videos, 9 families were coded as acknowledging racial and ethnic differences (race and ethnicity had an effect on the family), 6 rejected differences, and 15 showed discrepant views of the adolescent and parents. Interestingly, only adolescents' reports of their parents' engagement in cultural socialization were consistent with the coding of the family interaction. This study demonstrates the importance of obtaining views of multiple respondents and corroborating them with multiple research methods.

From a methodological standpoint, the study of transracial adoption will benefit from longitudinal, multi-informant designs that incorporate observational as well as self-report methods. Knowledge in this area will also be advanced by studies that involve mixed qualitative and quantitative methods to insure that participants' actual and perceived experiences are being fully registered. These studies also underscore the importance of obtaining data relevant to the lived experience of the adopted persons themselves.

Conceptually, it will be important for future work to extend beyond a unidirectional socialization model of parental influence. Most studies assume that parents' values about cultural competence and their own cultural skills drive the process. However, it may be that children's experiences in the community affect parental behavior (e.g., Vashchenko et al. 2012) or that some parents wait for their children to take the lead in requesting culturally based activities (e.g., Bebiroglu & Pinderhughes 2012). Family dynamics regarding cultural participation will be important to trace as they change over time, as will influences of siblings, peers, community norms, and the media. Finally, studies of transracial adoption include those of US black children adopted by white families as well as internationally adopted children of color (primarily Asian or Latino) adopted by white families. Although both family situations share certain challenges, research and theory should also take into account the distinctive racial and ethnic dynamics that apply to specific populations.

CONCLUSIONS AND IMPLICATIONS FOR PRACTICE

Until recently, the psychological study of adoption has been dominated by research examining differences between groups of adopted and nonadopted persons and by studies examining resilience in children who have experienced significant preadoption deprivation. Missing from both lines of research has been a focus on the processes that mediate between adoption status and developmental outcomes (Palacios & Brodzinsky 2010). This article has reviewed recent work examining biological and social processes contributing to the understanding of developmental trajectories for adopted persons, from childhood into adulthood.

Varied professionals (such as those involved in the placement of adopted children, preparation of adoptive parents, education and support of adopted children and families, and psychological or medical treatment of children postadoption) need research-based information to guide their work. The research reviewed in this article suggests several important implications for practice.

The literature on developmental processes highlights the need for early assessment and screening of children prior to placement so that services can be tailored to children's risks and needs. After placement, adoptive parents require accurate information about their children's backgrounds and support for successful parenting based on their children's histories. Furthermore, because children's needs are not always fully apparent at placement, postadoption services and subsidies should be available on an as-needed basis rather than only around the time of adoption.

More generally, knowledge of adoption has matured to the point where there is a clear need for a substantial clinical training specialization that is informed about adoption. Adoption-competent mental health practice must be responsive to the burgeoning research literature on the development of adopted children and the dynamics of adoptive families (Cent. Adoption Support Educ. 2012). This should involve general understanding of adoption (including the pathways through which children join their adoptive families) as well as specific knowledge about topics such as trauma, the applicability of neuroscience to adoption, birth family contact, transracial adoption, adoption by lesbian and gay parents, and other contemporary issues facing adoptive families and their children.

As the general public becomes more aware of the significance of neuroendocrine processes in development, there is a need for accurate translation of research findings for nonspecialists, so that results are not inappropriately oversimplified or overgeneralized. Much remains to be done to push translational neuroscience research fully into the realm of clinical application; however, with careful thought and a cautious approach, this is an area that holds strong potential for supporting the continued development of interventions for adoptive families whose children struggle with issues associated with early adversity.

SUMMARY POINTS

1. Children join adoptive families through three primary paths: domestic adoption from the public child welfare system, domestic infant adoption through private agencies or intermediaries, and international adoption. Each pathway presents distinctive developmental opportunities and challenges.

2. Adopted children are at higher risk than the general population for problems with adaptation, especially those involving externalizing, internalizing, and attention problems, yet the majority of adopted children develop within the typical range.

3. Each child's developmental trajectory is shaped by biological and social processes that are the subject of significant current research interest.

4. The experience of stress, whether prenatally, postnatally/preadoption, during the adoption transition, or during adolescence, can have a significant impact on the developing neuroendocrine system and can contribute to problems with physical growth, brain development, and sleep; these problems can have cascading effects on social, emotional, and cognitive developmental outcomes.

5. Effects of contact between adoptive and birth family members on adoptee adjustment depend on the ability of the adoptive and birth parents to establish and maintain mutually satisfying relationships.

6. Family processes, such as parenting stress and supportive co-parenting, operate similarly in families with lesbian, gay, and heterosexual parents. Adopted children raised by lesbian and gay parents do not differ in adjustment, on average, from children raised by heterosexual parents.

7. A significant proportion of children are adopted by parents whose racial background differs from that of the child. Racial identity of children of color adopted by white parents is promoted in families that acknowledge race and culture, support the development of racial pride, and prepare children to deal with bias they will encounter in a race-conscious society.

FUTURE ISSUES

1. Advances in understanding the neurobiological sequelae of deprivation will require methods that can pinpoint possible mechanisms that might be implicated in developmental outcomes. This will require a thoughtful approach to assessment, careful selection of comparison groups, and choice of appropriate control variables.

2. Further longitudinal research is needed at the intersection of biological and social processes in order to trace the cascading effects of early experience on development. Examples of intersection include tracing biological processes during the transition to adoption, such as sleep patterns, and examining the impact on cognitive function and vulnerability for academic difficulties, internalizing issues, and externalizing problems.

3. Additional context-oriented assessments of emotion regulation skills and peer interactions will help characterize both the strengths and challenges of adopted children in the domain of social development. Such assessments need to occur at various time points throughout development as children progress through increasingly complex social realms from early childhood through adolescence.

4. Additional well-validated and developmentally sensitive measures are needed to address adoption-specific outcomes and processes such as family communication, self-concept and identity, and issues unique to specific family structures (such as transracially adoptive families, lesbian and gay adoptive families, and families with open adoptions).

5. Although quantitative and qualitative traditions are well established in adoption research, there is a need for more mixed-method projects that integrate, within the same study, insights from qualitative and quantitative approaches. The goal should be to capitalize on the strengths of psychometrically validated measures, observational measures, and first-person accounts of adopted persons while continually cross-validating conclusions across data sources.

6. The field needs better theories and methods that can acknowledge the complex family situations in which adopted children grow up as well as the sequence and combination of birth, foster, and adoptive families in which any particular child might reside over time.

7. Practitioners need the benefit of well-designed, cost-effective, validated interventions that are sensitive to the issues (e.g., transition from birth to adoptive family, maintaining contact with birth families, handling special needs of the adopted child) encountered by foster and/or adopted children.

8. Cross talk needs to be facilitated between researchers focusing on biological and social processes, with an emphasis on research that attempts to integrate these processes from the earliest feasible stages.

DISCLOSURE STATEMENT

The authors are not aware of any affiliations, memberships, funding, or financial holdings that might be perceived as affecting the objectivity of this review.

ACKNOWLEDGMENTS

Preparation of this review was supported in part by the Rudd Family Foundation Chair in Psychology at the University of Massachusetts Amherst. The authors thank Rachel Farr, Philip Fisher, Quade Yoo Song French, Jesús Palacios, and Gretchen Miller Wrobel for their comments on an earlier draft of the manuscript.

LITERATURE CITED

Almas AN, Degnan KA, Radulescu A, Nelson CA, Zeanah CH, Fox NA. 2012. Effects of early intervention and the moderating effects of brain activity on institutionalized children's social skills at age 8. *Proc. Natl. Acad. Sci. USA* 109(Suppl. 2):17228–31

Appell AR. 2012. Legal issues in lesbian and gay adoption. In *Adoption by Lesbians and Gay Men*, ed. DM Brodzinsky, A Pertman, pp. 36–61. New York: Oxford Univ. Press

Aronen ET, Paavonen EJ, Fjällberg M, Soininen M, Törrönen J. 2000. Sleep and psychiatric symptoms in school-age children. *J. Am. Acad. Child Adolesc. Psychiatry* 39(4):502–8

Bauer PM, Hanson JL, Pierson RK, Davidson RJ, Pollak SD. 2009. Cerebellar volume and cognitive functioning in children who experienced early deprivation. *Biol. Psychiatry* 66(12):1100–6

Bebiroglu N, Pinderhughes EE. 2012. Mothers raising daughters: new complexities in cultural socialization for children adopted from China. *Adoption Q.* 15(2):116–39

Bell BG, Belsky J. 2008. Parents, parenting, and children's sleep problems: exploring reciprocal effects. *Br. J. Dev. Psychol.* 26(4):579–93

Berger RH, Miller AL, Seifer R, Cares S, Lebourgeois MK. 2012. Acute sleep restriction effects on emotion responses in 30- to 36-month-old children. *J. Sleep Res.* 21:235–46

Bernier A, Carlson SM, Whipple N. 2010. From external regulation to self-regulation: early parenting precursors of young children's executive functioning. *Child Dev.* 81(1):326–39

Bick J, Grasso D, Dozier M, Bernard K, Simons R. 2013. Foster mother–infant bonding: associations between foster mothers' oxytocin production, electrophysiological brain activity, feelings of commitment, and caregiving quality. *Child Dev.* 84:826–40

Bos KJ, Fox N, Zeanah CH, Nelson CA. 2009. Effects of early psychosocial deprivation on the development of memory and executive function. *Front. Behav. Neurosci.* 3:16

Boswell J. 1988. *The Kindness of Strangers: The Abandonment of Children in Western Europe from Late Antiquity to the Renaissance*. Chicago: Univ. Chicago Press

Brodzinsky DM. 2006. Family structural openness and communication openness as predictors in the adjustment of adopted children. *Adoption Q.* 9(4):1–18

Brodzinsky DM. 2011. Expanding resources for children III: research-based best practices in adoption by gays and lesbians. New York: Donaldson Adopt. Inst. **http://adoptioninstitute.org/publications/2011_10_Expanding_Resources_BestPractices.pdf**

Brodzinsky DM, Green R-J, Katuzny K. 2012. Adoption by lesbians and gay men: what we know, need to know, and ought to do. In *Adoption by Lesbians and Gay Men*, ed. DM Brodzinsky, A Pertman, pp. 233–54. New York: Oxford Univ. Press

Brodzinsky DM, Palacios J. 2005. *Psychological Issues in Adoption: Research and Practice*. Westport, CT: Praeger

Brodzinsky DM, Pinderhughes EE. 2002. Parenting and child development in adoptive families. In *Handbook of Parenting*: Vol.1: *Children and Parenting*, ed. MH Bornstein, pp. 279–311. Mahwah, NJ: Erlbaum

Bruce J, McDermott JM, Fisher PA, Fox NA. 2009a. Using behavioral and electrophysiological measures to assess the effects of a preventive intervention: a preliminary study with preschool-aged foster children. *Prev. Sci.* 10(2):129–40

Bruce J, Tarullo AR, Gunnar MR. 2009b. Disinhibited social behavior among internationally adopted children. *Dev. Psychopathol.* 21:157–71

Camras LA, Perlman SB, Wismer Fries AB, Pollak SD. 2006. Post-institutionalized Chinese and Eastern European children: heterogeneity in the development of emotion understanding. *Int. J. Behav. Dev.* 30(3):193–99

Carp E. 1998. *Family Matters: Secrecy and Disclosure in the History of Adoption*. Cambridge, Mass.: Harvard Univ. Press

Carp E. 2002. *Adoption in America: Historical Perspectives*. Ann Arbor: Univ. Mich. Press

Carrión VG, Weems CF, Reiss AL. 2007. Stress predicts brain changes in children: a pilot longitudinal study on youth stress, posttraumatic stress disorder, and the hippocampus. *Pediatrics* 119(3):509–16

Carrión VG, Haas BW, Garrett A, Song S, Reiss AL. 2010. Reduced hippocampal activity in youth with posttraumatic stress symptoms: an fMRI study. *J. Pediatr. Psychol.* 35(5):559–69

Carrión VG, Weems CF, Eliez S, Patwardhan A, Brown W, et al. 2001. Attenuation of frontal asymmetry in pediatric posttraumatic stress disorder. *Biol. Psychiatry* 50(12):943–51

Carrión VG, Weems CF, Watson C, Eliez S, Menon V, Reiss AL. 2009. Converging evidence for abnormalities of the prefrontal cortex and evaluation of midsagittal structures in pediatric posttraumatic stress disorder: an MRI study. *Psychiatry Res.* 172(3):226–34

Cent. Adoption Support Educ. 2012. *What Does Adoption Competency Mean?* Baltimore, MD: Cent. Adoption Support Educ. **http://www.adoptionsupport.org/Adoption_Competency.pdf**

Charles P, Maza P, Shuman M, Flango V, Swope H. 2012. *Adoption and foster care data: issues and trends.* Presented at 38th Annu. Conf. North Am. Counc. Adopt. Child., Washington, DC

Charmandari E, Kino T, Souvatzoglou E, Chrousos GP. 2003. Pediatric stress: hormonal mediators and human development. *Horm. Res.* 59:161–79

Child. Bur., US Dep. Health Hum. Serv. 2012. *The AFCARS report: preliminary FY 2011 estimates as of July 2012. No. 19.* Washington, DC: US Dep. Health Hum. Serv. **http://www.acf.hhs.gov/sites/default/files/cb/afcarsreport19.pdf**

Child Welf. Inf. Gatew. 2005. *Voluntary relinquishment for adoption.* Washington, DC: Child Welf. Inf. Gatew. **https://http:www.childwelfare.gov/pubs/s_place.pdf**

Chrousos GP. 2009. Stress and disorders of the stress system. *Nat. Rev. Endocrinol.* 5(7):374–81

Chugani HT, Behen ME, Muzik O, Juhász C, Nagy F, Chugani DC. 2001. Local brain functional activity following early deprivation: a study of postinstitutionalized Romanian orphans. *NeuroImage* 14(6):1290–301

Colvert E, Rutter M, Kreppner J, Beckett C, Castle J, et al. 2008. Do theory of mind and executive function deficits underlie the adverse outcomes associated with profound early deprivation? Findings from the English and Romanian adoptees study. *J. Abnorm. Child Psychol.* 36(7):1057–68

Dahl RE. 1996. The impact of inadequate sleep on children's daytime cognitive function. *Semin. Pediatr. Neurol.* 3(1):44–50

Dautzenberg FM, Kilpatrick GJ, Hauger RL, Moreau J. 2001. Molecular biology of the CRH receptors—in the mood. *Peptides* 22(5):753–60

Dawson G, Ashman SB, Carver LJ. 2000. The role of early experience in shaping behavioral and brain development and its implications for social policy. *Dev. Psychopathol.* 12:695–712

De Bellis MD. 2005. The psychobiology of neglect. *Child Maltreat.* 10(2):150–72

De Bellis MD, Hall J, Boring AM, Frustaci K, Moritz G. 2001. A pilot longitudinal study of hippocampal volumes in disorder. *Biol. Psychiatry* 50:305–9

De Bellis MD, Hooper SR, Woolley DP, Shenk CE. 2010. Demographic, maltreatment, and neurobiological correlates of PTSD symptoms in children and adolescents. *J. Pediatr. Psychol.* 35(5):570–77

De Bellis MD, Keshavan MS, Clark DB, Casey BJ, Giedd JN, et al. 1999. Developmental traumatology part II: brain development. *Biol. Psychiatry* 45:1271–84

De Bellis MD, Keshavan MS, Frustaci K, Shifflett H, Iyengar S, et al. 2002. Superior temporal gyrus volumes in maltreated children and adolescents with PTSD. *Biol. Psychiatry* 51(7):544–52

Desmarais C, Roeber BJ, Smith ME, Pollak SD. 2012. Sentence comprehension in postinstitutionalized school-age children. *J. Speech Lang. Hear. Res.* 55:45–54

Downing J, Richardson H, Kinkler L, Goldberg A. 2009. Making the decision: factors influencing gay men's choice of an adoption path. *Adoption Q.* 12(3):247–71

Dozier M. 2005. Challenges of foster care. *Attachment Hum. Dev.* 7(1):27–30

Dozier M, Peloso E, Lewis E, Laurenceau JP, Levine S. 2008. Effects of an attachment based intervention on the cortisol production of infants and toddlers in foster care. *Dev. Psychopathol.* 20:845–59

Eluvathingal TJ, Chugani HT, Behen ME, Juhász C, Muzik O, et al. 2006. Abnormal brain connectivity in children after early severe socioemotional deprivation: a diffusion tensor imaging study. *Pediatrics* 117(6):2093–100

Erol N, Simsek Z, Munir K. 2010. Mental health of adolescents reared in institutional care in Turkey: challenges and hope in the twenty-first century. *Eur. Child Adolesc. Psychiatry* 19:113–24

Farr RH, Forssell S, Patterson C. 2010. Parenting and child development in adoptive families: Does parental sexual orientation matter? *Appl. Dev. Sci.* 14(3):164–78

Farr RH, Grant-Marsney HA, Musante DS, Grotevant HD, Wrobel GM. 2013. Adoptees' contact with birth relatives in emerging adulthood. *J. Adolesc. Res.* In press

Farr RH, Patterson CJ. 2009. Transracial adoption by lesbian, gay, and heterosexual couples: Who completes transracial adoptions and with what results? *Adoption Q.* 12(3):187–204

Farr RH, Patterson CJ. 2013. Coparenting among lesbian, gay, and heterosexual couples: associations with adopted children's outcomes. *Child Dev.* 84:1226–40

Fisher CB, Wallace SA, Fenton RE. 2000. Discrimination distress during adolescence. *J. Youth Adolesc.* 29(6):679–95

Fox NA, Almas AN, Degnan KA, Nelson CA, Zeanah CH. 2011. The effects of severe psychosocial deprivation and foster care intervention on cognitive development at 8 years of age: findings from the Bucharest Early Intervention Project. *J. Child Psychol. Psychiatry* 52(9):919–28

Gibbons JL, Rotabi KS. 2012. *Intercountry Adoption: Policies, Practices, and Outcomes*. Burlington, VT: Ashgate Publ. 389 pp.

Goldberg AE. 2009. Heterosexual, lesbian, and gay preadoptive parents' preferences about child gender. *Sex Roles* 61(1–2):55–71

Goldberg AE, Kashy DA, Smith JZ. 2012. Gender-typed play behavior in early childhood: adopted children with lesbian, gay, and heterosexual parents. *Sex Roles.* 67:503–15

Goldberg AE, Kinkler LA, Richardson HB, Downing JB. 2011. Lesbian, gay, and heterosexual couples in open adoption arrangements: a qualitative study. *J. Marriage Fam.* 73(2):502–18

Goldberg AE, Smith JZ. 2011. Stigma, social context, and mental health: lesbian and gay couples across the transition to adoptive parenthood. *J. Couns. Psychol.* 58(1):139–50

Gregory AM, Sadeh A. 2012. Sleep, emotional and behavioral difficulties in children and adolescents. *Sleep Med. Rev.* 16:129–36

Grotevant HD. 2009. Emotional distance regulation over the life course in adoptive kinship networks. See Wrobel & Neil 2009, pp. 295–316

Grotevant HD. 2012. What works in open adoption. In *What Works in Child Welfare*, ed. PA Curtis, G Alexander, pp. 309–28. Washington, DC: Child Welf. Leag. Am.

Grotevant HD, McRoy RG, Wrobel GM, Ayers-Lopez S. 2013. Contact between adoptive and birth families: perspectives from the Minnesota/Texas Adoption Research Project. *Child Dev. Perspect.* 7:193–98

Grotevant HD, Rueter M, Von Korff L, Gonzalez C. 2011. Post-adoption contact, adoption communicative openness, and satisfaction with contact as predictors of externalizing behavior in adolescence and emerging adulthood. *J. Child Psychol. Psychiatry* 52(5):529–36

Grotevant HD, Von Korff L. 2011. Adoptive identity. In *Handbook of Identity Theory and Research*, ed. SJ Schwartz, K Luyckx, VL Vignoles, pp. 585–601. New York: Springer

Grotevant HD, Wrobel GM, Von Korff L, Skinner B, Newell J, et al. 2007. Many faces of openness in adoption: perspectives of adopted adolescents and their parents. *Adoption Q.* 10(3–4):79–101

Groza V, Houlihan L, Wood ZB. 2005. Overview of adoption. In *Child Welfare for the 21st Century*, ed. GP Mallon, PM Hess, pp. 432–51. New York: Columbia Univ. Press

Güler OE, Hostinar CE, Frenn KA, Nelson CA, Gunnar MR, Thomas KM. 2012. Electrophysiological evidence of altered memory processing in children experiencing early deprivation. *Dev. Sci.* 15(3):345–58

Gunnar MR, Fisher PA, Early Exp. Stress Prev. Netw. 2006. Bringing basic research on early experience and stress neurobiology to bear on preventive interventions for neglected and maltreated children. *Dev. Psychopathol.* 18(3):651–77

Hanson JL, Chung MK, Avants BB, Rudolph KD, Shirtcliff EA, et al. 2012. Structural variations in prefrontal cortex mediate the relationship between early childhood stress and spatial working memory. *J. Neurosci.* 32(23):7917–25

Hart H, Rubia K. 2012. Neuroimaging of child abuse: a critical review. *Front. Hum. Neurosci.* 6:52

Hatzenbuehler ML, Keyes KM, Hasin DS. 2009. State-level policies and psychiatric morbidity in lesbian, gay, and bisexual populations. *Am. J. Public Health* 99(12):2275–81

Hatzenbuehler ML, McLaughlin KA, Keyes KM, Hasin DS. 2010. The impact of institutional discrimination on psychiatric disorders in lesbian, gay, and bisexual populations: a prospective study. *Am. J. Public Health* 100(3):452–59

Haugaard JJ, Hazan C. 2003. Adoption as a natural experiment. *Dev. Psychopathol.* 15(4):909–26

Hawk BN, McCall RB. 2010. CBCL behavior problems of post-institutionalized international adoptees. *Clin. Child Fam. Psychol. Rev.* 13(2):199–211

Hawk BN, McCall RB. 2011. Specific extreme behaviors of postinstitutionalized Russian adoptees. *Dev. Psychol.* 47(3):732–38

Herman E. 2008. *Kinship by Design: A History of Adoption in the Modern United States*. Chicago: Univ. Chicago Press

Herman JP, Cullinan WE. 1997. Neurocircuitry of stress: central control of the hypothalamo-pituitary-adrenocortical axis. *Trends Neurosci.* 20(2):78–84

Hoksbergen R, ter Laak J. 2005. Changing attitudes of adoptive parents in Northern European countries. See Brodzinsky & Palacios 2005, pp. 27–46

Hostinar CE, Stellern SA, Schaefer C, Carlson SM, Gunnar MR. 2012. Associations between early life adversity and executive function in children adopted internationally from orphanages. *Proc. Natl. Acad. Sci. USA* 109(Suppl.):17208–12

Howard JA. 2012. *Untangling the Web: The Internet's Transformative Impact on Adoption*. New York: Donaldson Adopt. Inst. **http://adoptioninstitute.org/publications/2012_12_UntanglingtheWeb.pdf**

Hughes C. 2011. Changes and challenges in 20 years of research into the development of executive functions. *Infant Child Dev.* 20:251–71

Hughes D, Rodriguez J, Smith EP, Johnson DJ, Stevenson HC, Spicer P. 2006. Parents' ethnic-racial socialization practices: a review of research and directions for future study. *Dev. Psychol.* 42(5):747–70

Jacobs E, Miller LC, Tirella LG. 2010. Developmental and behavioral performance of internationally adopted preschoolers: a pilot study. *Child Psychiatry Hum. Dev.* 41(1):15–29

Johnson DE, Gunnar MR. 2011. Growth failure in institutionalized children. *Monogr. Soc. Res. Child Dev.* 76(4):92–126

Johnson DE, Guthrie D, Smyke AT, Koga SF, Fox NA, et al. 2010. Growth and associations between auxology, caregiving environment, and cognition in socially deprived Romanian children randomized to foster versus ongoing institutional care. *Arch. Pediatr. Adolesc. Med.* 164(6):507–16

Johnston KE, Swim JK, Saltsman BM, Deater-Deckard K, Petrill SA. 2007. Mothers' racial, ethnic, and cultural socialization of transracially adopted Asian children. *Fam. Relat.* 56:390–402

Juffer F, Bakermans-Kranenburg MJ, van IJzendoorn MH. 2005. The importance of parenting in the development of disorganized attachment: evidence from a preventive intervention study in adoptive families. *J. Child Psychol. Psychiatry* 46(3):263–74

Juffer F, Palacios J, Le Mare L, Sonuga-Barke E, Tieman W, et al. 2011. Development of adopted children with histories of early adversity. *Monogr. Soc. Res. Child Dev.* 76(4):31–61

Juffer F, van IJzendoorn M. 2005. Behavior problems and mental health referrals of international adoptees. *J. Am. Med. Assoc.* 293(20):2501–15

Juffer F, van IJzendoorn MH. 2007. Adoptees do not lack self-esteem: a meta-analysis of studies on self-esteem of transracial, international, and domestic adoptees. *Psychol. Bull.* 133(6):1067–83

Kim OM, Reichwald R, Lee R. 2013. Cultural socialization in families with adopted Korean adolescents: a mixed-method, multi-informant study. *J. Adolesc. Res.* 28(1):69–95

Kraft AD, Palombo J, Mitchell DL, Woods PK, Schmidt AW, Tucker NG. 1985. Some theoretical considerations on confidential adoptions part III: the adopted child. *Child Adolesc. Soc. Work J.* 2(3):139–53

Kreppner J, Kumsta R, Rutter M, Beckett C, Castle J, et al. 2010. Developmental course of deprivation-specific psychological patterns: early manifestations, persistence to age 15, and clinical features. *Monogr. Soc. Res. Child Dev.* 75(1):79–101

Le Mare L, Audet K. 2011. Communicative openness in adoption, knowledge of culture of origin, and adoption identity in adolescents adopted from Romania. *Adoption Q.* 14(3):199–217

Lee B, dir. 2008. *Adopted*. New York: Point Made Films. Motion pict., 80 min.

Lee RM. 2010. Parental perceived discrimination as a postadoption risk factor for internationally adopted children and adolescents. *Cult. Divers. Ethn. Minor. Psychol.* 16(4):493–500

Lee RM, Grotevant HD, Hellerstedt WL, Gunnar MR. 2006. Cultural socialization in families with internationally adopted children. *J. Fam. Psychol.* 20(4):571–80

Lee RM, Seol KO, Sung M, Miller MJ. 2010. The behavioral development of Korean children in institutional care and international adoptive families. *Dev. Psychol.* 46(2):468–78

Leslie LA, Smith JR, Hrapczynski KM, Riley D. 2013. Racial socialization in transracial adoptive families: Does it help adolescents deal with discrimination stress? *Fam. Relat.* 62(1):72–81

Leve LD, Degarmo DS, Bridgett DJ, Neiderhiser JM, Shaw DS, et al. 2013a. Using an adoption design to separate genetic, prenatal, and temperament influences on toddler executive function. *Child Dev.* 49(6):1045–57

Leve LD, Neiderhiser JM, Ge X, Scaramella LV, Conger RD, et al. 2007. The Early Growth and Development Study: a prospective adoption design. *Twin Res. Hum. Genet.* 10(1):84–95

Leve LD, Neiderhiser JM, Shaw DS, Ganiban J, Natsuaki MN, Reiss D. 2013b. The Early Growth and Development Study: a prospective adoption study from birth through middle childhood. *Twin Res. Hum. Genet.* 16(1):412–23

Lindblad F, Weitoft GR, Hjern A. 2010. ADHD in international adoptees: a national cohort study. *Eur. Child Adolesc. Psychiatry* 19(1):37–44

Lipscomb ST, Leve LD, Shaw DS, Neiderhiser JM, Scaramella LV, et al. 2012. Negative emotionality and externalizing problems in toddlerhood: overreactive parenting as a moderator of genetic influences. *Dev. Psychopathol.* 24(1):167–79

Loman MM, Johnson AE, Westerlund A, Pollak SD, Nelson CA, Gunnar MR. 2013. The effect of early deprivation on executive attention in middle childhood. *J. Child Psychol. Psychiatry* 54(1):37–45

Loman MM, Wiik KL, Frenn KA, Pollak SD, Gunnar MR. 2009. Postinstitutionalized children's development: growth, cognitive, and language outcomes. *J. Dev. Behav. Pediatr.* 30:426–34

Mannering AM, Harold GT, Leve LD, Shelton KH, Shaw DS, et al. 2011. Longitudinal associations between marital instability and child sleep problems across infancy and toddlerhood in adoptive families. *Child Dev.* 82(4):1252–66

McDermott JM, Troller-Renfree S, Vanderwert R, Nelson CA, Zeanah CH, Fox NA. 2013. Psychosocial deprivation, executive functions, and the emergence of socio-emotional behavior problems. *Front. Hum. Neurosci.* 77:167

McDermott JM, Westerlund A, Zeanah CH, Nelson CA, Fox NA. 2012. Early adversity and neural correlates of executive function: implications for academic adjustment. *Dev. Cogn. Neurosci.* 2(Suppl. 1):S59–66

McGinnis HA. 2006. Korea and adoption. In *The Praeger Handbook of Adoption*, ed. KS Stolley, VL Bullough, pp. 370–78. Westport, CT: Praeger

McLaughlin KA, Fox NA, Zeanah CH, Sheridan MA, Marshall P, Nelson CA. 2010. Delayed maturation in brain electrical activity partially explains the association between early environmental deprivation and symptoms of attention-deficit/hyperactivity disorder. *Biol. Psychiatry* 68(4):329–36

Mehta MA, Golembo NI, Nosarti C, Colvert E, Mota A, et al. 2009. Amygdala, hippocampal and corpus callosum size following severe early institutional deprivation: the English and Romanian Adoptees Study pilot. *J. Child Psychol. Psychiatry* 50(8):943–51

Merz E, McCall R. 2010. Behavior problems in children adopted from psychosocially depriving institutions. *J. Abnorm. Child Psychol.* 38(4):459–70

Mikoteit T, Brand S, Beck J, Perren S, Von Wyl A, et al. 2013. Visually detected NREM stage 2 sleep spindles in kindergarten children are associated with current and future emotional and behavioral characteristics. *J. Sleep Res.* 22:129–36

Miller LC. 2005. Immediate behavioral and developmental considerations for internationally adopted children transitioning to families. *Pediatr. Clin. North Am.* 52(5):1311–30, vi–vii

Miller LC. 2012. Medical status of internationally adopted children. In *Intercountry Adoption: Policies, Practices, and Outcomes*, ed. JL Gibbons, KS Rotabi, pp. 187–98. Burlington, Vt.: Ashgate Publ.

Miller LC, Hendrie NW. 2000. Health of children adopted from China. *Pediatrics* 105(6):e76

Moulson MC, Westerlund AF, Fox NA, Zeanah CH, Nelson CA. 2009. The effects of early experience on face recognition: an event-related potential study of institutionalized children in Romania. *Child Dev.* 80(4):1039–56

Neil E. 2009. Post-adoption contact and openness in adoptive parents' minds: consequences for children's development. *Br. J. Soc. Work* 39(1):5–23

Neil E. 2012. Making sense of adoption: integration and differentiation from the perspective of adopted children in middle childhood. *Child. Youth Serv. Rev.* 34(2):409–16

Neil E, Cossar J, Jones C, Lorgelly P, Young J. 2011. *Supporting Direct Contact After Adoption.* London: Br. Assoc. Adoption Foster.

Neil E, Howe D. 2004. Conclusions: a transactional model for thinking about contact. In *Contact in Adoption and Permanent Foster Care*, ed. E Neil, D Howe, pp. 224–54. London: Br. Assoc. Adoption Foster.

Nelson CA. 2007. A neurobiological perspective on early human deprivation. *Child Dev. Perspect.* 1(1):13–18

Nelson CA, Bos K, Gunnar MR, Sonuga-Barke EJS. 2011. The neurobiological toll of early human deprivation. *Monogr. Soc. Res. Child Dev.* 76(4):127–46

Palacios J. 2009. The ecology of adoption. See Wrobel & Neil 2009, pp. 71–95

Palacios J, Brodzinsky D. 2010. Adoption research: trends, topics, outcomes. *Int. J. Behav. Dev.* 34(3):270–84

Palacios J, Moreno C, Román M. 2013. Social competence in internationally adopted and institutionalized children. *Early Child. Res. Q.* 28:357–65

Pannor R, Baran A. 1984. Open adoption as standard practice. *Child Welf.* 63(3):245–50

Pears KC, Fisher PA, Bruce J, Kim HK. 2012. Early elementary school adjustment of maltreated children in foster care: the roles of inhibitory control and caregiver involvement. *Child Dev.* 81:1550–64

Plomin RC, DeFries JC. 1985. A parent-offspring adoption study of cognitive abilities in early childhood. *Intelligence* 9:341–56

Pollak SD, Nelson CA, Schlaak MF, Roeber BJ, Wewerka SS, et al. 2010. Neurodevelopmental effects of early deprivation in postinstitutionalized children. *Child Dev.* 81(1):224–36

Raaska H, Lapinleimu H, Sinkkonen J, Salmivalli C, Matomäki J, et al. 2012. Experiences of school bullying among internationally adopted children: results from the Finnish Adoption (FINADO) study. *Child Psychiatry Hum. Dev.* 43:592–611

Reitz M, Watson KW. 1992. *Adoption and the Family System.* New York: Guilford

Rettig MA, McCarthy-Rettig K. 2006. A survey of the health, sleep, and development of children adopted from China. *Health Soc. Work* 31(3):201–7

Richert KA, Carrión VG, Karchemskiy A, Reiss AL. 2006. Regional differences of the prefrontal cortex in pediatric PTSD: an MRI study. *Depress. Anxiety* 23:17–25

Roby J, Matsumura S. 2002. If I give you my child, aren't we family? A study of birthmothers participating in Marshall Islands–U.S. adoptions. *Adoption Q.* 5(4):7–31

Romero LM, Dickens MJ, Cyr NE. 2009. The Reactive Scope Model—a new model integrating homeostasis, allostasis, and stress. *Horm. Behav.* 55(3):375–89

Roy P, Rutter M, Pickles A. 2004. Institutional care: associations between overactivity and lack of selectivity in social relationships. *J. Child Psychol. Psychiatry* 45:866–73

Rutter M, Sonuga-Barke EJ. 2010. X. Conclusions: overview of findings from the ERA study, inferences, and research implications. *Monogr. Soc. Res. Child Dev.* 75:212–29

Rutter M, Sonuga-Barke EJ, Castle J. 2010. I. Investigating the impact of early institutional deprivation on development: background and research strategy of the English and Romanian Adoptees (ERA) study. *Monogr. Soc. Res. Child Dev.* 75:1–20

Sadeh A. 1996. Stress, trauma and sleep in children. *Child Adolesc. Psychiatr. Clin. North Am.* 5(3):685–700

Samuels GM. 2009. "Being raised by white people": navigating racial difference among adopted multiracial adults. *J. Marriage Fam.* 71:80–94

Sapolsky RM, Romero LM, Munck AU. 2000. How do glucocorticoids influence stress responses? Integrating permissive, suppressive, stimulatory, and preparative actions. *Endocr. Rev.* 21(1):55–89

Scherman R. 2012. Openness and intercountry adoption in New Zealand. In *Intercountry Adoption: Policies, Practices, and Outcomes*, ed. JL Gibbons, KS Rotabi, pp. 283–92. Burlington, Vt.: Ashgate Publ.

Selman P. 2009. From Bucharest to Beijing: changes in countries sending children for international adoption 1990 to 2006. See Wrobel & Neil 2009, pp. 41–70

Shackman JE, Shackman AJ, Pollak SD. 2007. Physical abuse amplifies attention to threat and increases anxiety in children. *Emotion* 7(4):838–52

Sharma AR, McGue MK, Benson PL. 1996. The emotional and behavioral adjustment of United States adopted adolescents: part 1: an overview. *Child. Youth Serv. Rev.* 18(1–2):83–100

Shaw P, Eckstrand K, Sharp W, Blumenthal J, Lerch JP, et al. 2007. Attention-deficit/hyperactivity disorder is characterized by a delay in cortical maturation. *Proc. Natl. Acad. Sci. USA* 104(49):19649–54

Sheridan MA, Fox NA, Zeanah CH, McLaughlin KA, Nelson CA. 2012. Variation in neural development as a result of exposure to institutionalization early in childhood. *Proc. Natl. Acad. Sci. USA* 109(32):12927–32

Smyke AT, Zeanah CH, Fox NA, Nelson CA. 2009. A new model of foster care for young children: the Bucharest Early Intervention Project. *Child Adolesc. Psychiatr. Clin. North Am.* 18:721–34

Song SL, Lee RM. 2009. The past and present cultural experiences of adopted Korean American adults. *Adoption Q.* 12(1):19–36

Sonuga-Barke E, Schlotz W, Rutter M. 2010. Physical growth and maturation following early severe institutional deprivation: Do they mediate specific psychopathological effects? *Monogr. Soc. Res. Child Dev.* 75(1):143–66

Steenari M-R, Vuontela V, Paavonen EJ, Carlson S, Fjallberg M, Aronen ET. 2003. Working memory and sleep in 6- to 13-year-old schoolchildren. *J. Am. Acad. Child Adolesc. Psychiatry* 42(1):85–91

Tan TX, Camras LA. 2011. Social skills of adopted Chinese girls at home and in school: parent and teacher ratings. *Child. Youth Serv. Rev.* 33:1813–21

Tan TX, Dedrick RF, Marfo K. 2007. Factor structure and clinical implications of child behavior checklist/1.5–5 ratings in a sample of girls adopted from China. *J. Pediatr. Psychol.* 32(7):807–18

Tarullo AR, Garvin MC, Gunnar MR. 2011. Atypical EEG power correlates with indiscriminately friendly behavior in internationally adopted children. *Dev. Psychol.* 47:417–31

Thomas KA, Tessler RC. 2007. Bicultural socialization among adoptive families: Where there is a will, there is a way. *J. Fam. Issues* 28(9):1189–219

Tininenko JR, Fisher PA, Bruce J, Pears KC. 2010. Sleep disruption in young foster children. *Child Psychiatry Hum. Dev.* 41(4):409–24

Tottenham N, Hare TA, Millner A, Gilhooly T, Zevin JD, Casey BJ. 2011. Elevated amygdala response to faces following early deprivation. *Dev. Sci.* 14(2):190–204

Tottenham N, Hare TA, Quinn BT, McCarry TW, Nurse M, et al. 2010. Prolonged institutional rearing is associated with atypically large amygdala volume and difficulties in emotion regulation. *Dev. Sci.* 13(1):46–61

Trenka J, Oparah JC, Shin SY. 2006. *Outsiders Within: Writing on Transracial Adoption.* Cambridge, Mass.: South End Press

Tupler LA, De Bellis MD. 2006. Segmented hippocampal volume in children and adolescents with posttraumatic stress disorder. *Biol. Psychiatry* 59(6):523–29

US Dep. State Bur. Consul. Aff. 2012. *Intercountry Adoption.* Washington, DC: US Dep. State. **http:// adoption.state.gov**

van den Dries L, Juffer F, van IJzendoorn MH, Bakermans-Kranenburg MJ. 2009. Fostering security? A meta-analysis of attachment in adopted children. *Child. Youth Serv. Rev.* 31(3):410–21

Vanderwert RE, Marshall PJ, Nelson CA, Zeanah CH, Fox NA. 2010. Timing of intervention affects brain electrical activity in children exposed to severe psychosocial neglect. *PLoS ONE* 5(7):e11415

Vandivere S, Malm K, Radel L. 2009. *Adoption USA: A Chartbook Based on the 2007 National Survey of Adoptive Parents.* Washington, DC: US Dep. Health Hum. Serv. **http://aspe.hhs.gov/hsp/09/ nsap/chartbook/index.cfm**

van IJzendoorn MH, Bakermans-Kranenberg MJ, Juffer F. 2007. Plasticity of growth in height, weight, and head circumference: meta-analytic evidence of massive catch-up after international adoption. *J. Dev. Behav. Pediatr.* 28:334–43

van IJzendoorn MH, Juffer F. 2006. The Emanuel Miller Memorial Lecture 2006: adoption as intervention. Meta-analytic evidence for massive catch-up and plasticity in physical, socio-emotional, and cognitive development. *J. Child Psychol. Psychiatry* 47(12):1228–45

van IJzendoorn MH, Juffer F, Poelhuis CWK. 2005. Adoption and cognitive development: a meta-analytic comparison of adopted and nonadopted children's IQ and school performance. *Psychol. Bull.* 131(2):301–16

Vashchenko M, D'Aleo M, Pinderhughes EE. 2012. "Just beyond my front door": public discourse experiences of children adopted from China. *Am. J. Community Psychol.* 49(1–2):246–57

Von Korff L, Grotevant HD. 2011. Contact in adoption and adoptive identity formation: the mediating role of family conversation. *J. Fam. Psychol.* 25(3):393–401

Vonk ME, Lee J, Crolley-Simic J. 2010. Cultural socialization practices in domestic and international transracial adoption. *Adoption Q.* 13(3–4):227–47

Wismer Fries AB, Pollak SD. 2004. Emotion understanding in postinstitutionalized Eastern European children. *Dev. Psychopathol.* 16(2):355–69

Woon FL, Hedges DW. 2008. Hippocampal and amygdala volumes in children and adults with childhood maltreatment-related posttraumatic stress disorder: a meta-analysis. *Hippocampus* 18(8):729–36

Wrobel G, Neil E, eds. 2009. *International Advances in Adoption Research for Practice*. Chichester, UK: Wiley-Blackwell

Zeanah CH, Gunnar MR, McCall RB, Kreppner J, Fox NA. 2011. Sensitive periods. *Monogr. Soc. Res. Child Dev.* 76(4):147–62

Zeanah CH, Nelson CA, Fox NA, Smyke AT, Marshall P, et al. 2003. Designing research to study the effects of institutionalization on brain and behavioral development: the Bucharest Early Intervention Project. *Dev. Psychopathol.* 15(4):885–907

Zelazo PD, Müller U, Frye D, Marcovitch S, Argitis G, et al. 2003. The development of executive function in early childhood. *Monogr. Soc. Res. Child Dev.* 68(3):vii–137

RELATED RESOURCES

British Association for Adoption and Fostering: **http://baaf.co.uk**

Child Welfare Information Gateway, Children's Bureau, US Department of Health and Human Services: **http://childwelfare.gov**

Donaldson Adoption Institute: **http://adoptioninstitute.org**

North American Council on Adoptable Children: **http://nacac.org**

Rudd Adoption Research Program, University of Massachusetts Amherst: **http://psych.umass.edu/ruddchair**

US Department of State, Intercountry Adoption: **http://adoption.state.gov**

Combination Psychotherapy and Antidepressant Medication Treatment for Depression: For Whom, When, and How

W. Edward Craighead[1,2] and Boadie W. Dunlop[1]

[1]Department of Psychiatry and Behavioral Sciences and [2]Department of Psychology, Emory University, Atlanta, Georgia 30322; email: ecraigh@emory.edu, bdunlop@emory.edu

Annu. Rev. Psychol. 2014. 65:267–300

First published online as a Review in Advance on September 13, 2013

The *Annual Review of Psychology* is online at http://psych.annualreviews.org

This article's doi: 10.1146/annurev.psych.121208.131653

Keywords

major depressive disorder, CBT, antidepressant medications, combination treatment, mechanisms of therapeutic change, neurobiology of depression change

Abstract

Major depressive disorder (MDD) is among the most frequent and debilitating psychiatric disorders. Efficacious psychotherapy and antidepressant medications have been developed, and two-thirds of depressed patients respond to single-modality treatment; however, only about one-third of patients remit to single-modality treatments with no meaningful differences in outcomes between treatment types. This article describes the major clinical considerations in choosing between single-modality or combination treatments for MDD. A review of the relevant literature and meta-analyses provides suggestions for which treatment to use for which patient and when each treatment or combination should be provided. The review summarizes the moderators of single-modality and combination-treatment outcomes. We describe models of mechanisms of treatment efficacy and discuss recent treatment-specific neurobiological mechanisms of change.

Contents

INTRODUCTION

Major depressive disorder (MDD) is among the most prevalent and debilitating of psychiatric problems affecting about 1 in 6 women and 1 in 10 men over the life span (Kessler et al. 2005). MDD negatively impacts an individual's quality of life and produces impairments in role functioning (Wells et al. 1989). MDD is a leading cause of family dysfunction and death from suicide (Arató et al. 1988, Rich et al. 1988), and it contributes to increased risk of morbidity and mortality from diabetes, cardiovascular disease, and stroke (Barth et al. 2005, Egede 2006, Loeb et al. 2012). MDD reduces productivity and is a major health expense, thereby becoming a societal and economic problem. It is the fourth leading cause of disability worldwide, and by 2020 it is projected to be second only to ischemic heart disease as a cause of disability (Murray & Lopez 1997). By 2030, MDD is expected to be the largest worldwide contributor to disease burden (World Health Organ. 2004).

Although highly variable across studies, the average age of onset for initial depressive episodes is late adolescence or emerging adulthood; the majority of individuals who will experience MDD will have done so by early adulthood (Hankin & Abramson 1999, Kessler et al. 2005). MDD is also a recurrent disorder, and it frequently becomes a chronic problem. For example, Lewinsohn et al. (1999; see also Fergusson & Woodward 2002) found that ~45% of adolescents who suffer an episode of MDD experience a recurrence by age 24, and Rohde and colleagues (2012) found that cumulatively among the same group ~50% had a subsequent depressive episode by age 30. Episodes in which full criteria for MDD are present continuously for 2 years or more are considered chronic; about 30% of depressed individuals in the community and 50% of those who are in treatment suffer from chronic depression (Klein & Black 2013, Mueller et al. 1999, Waraich et al. 2004). The duration of MDD episodes is also highly variable; estimates of the average time to spontaneous recovery range from 5 months to 13 months (Angst et al. 2003, Lewinsohn et al. 1999). Risk factors for the development of MDD include positive family history for a mood disorder, early life trauma, prior anxiety disorders, and substance abuse (see Ritschel et al. 2013).

MDD as defined by current nosologies [e.g., *Diagnostic and Statistical Manual of Mental Disorders, 5th Edition* (DSM-5; APA 2013)] is a heterogeneous syndrome, with multiple likely etiologies and pathological forms. As shall become apparent, this heterogeneity contributes strongly to the variable response to treatment observed in clinical trials of treatments for depression.

CURRENT TREATMENTS FOR MDD

Antidepressant medications (ADM) and psychotherapies are the two primary outpatient treatments for MDD. Various forms of stimulation treatments (e.g., transcranial magnetic stimulation, deep brain stimulation, vagus nerve stimulation, electroconvulsive therapy) exist for patients who do not respond to ADM or psychotherapy, but stimulation treatments are not well studied as forms of combination treatment and are not discussed further in this review (Kennedy & Giacobbe 2007).

Antidepressant Medications

Although the first antidepressants were identified through serendipitous discovery, more recent developments in pharmacology are driven by current understandings of the biological functions of neurotransmitter systems within the central nervous system. There are several ADM classes, which are categorized by their structural or functional relationships. No antidepressant class or individual medication has consistently proven to be superior to others for the treatment of MDD (APA 2010). Thus, recommendations for first-line ADM treatments for MDD are based primarily on tolerability and safety rather than on efficacy. Selective serotonin reuptake inhibitors (SSRIs), serotonin-norepinephrine reuptake inhibitors (SNRIs), bupropion, or mirtazapine are considered first-line antidepressants (APA 2010). Owing to their greater health risks, tricyclic antidepressants and monoamine oxidase inhibitors are generally used only after first-line agents fail. Treatment with ADM should be sustained for at least 4–8 weeks prior to determining efficacy. The goal of treatment is essentially to eliminate depressive symptoms; dosage is increased every 2–4 weeks (unless side effects prevent further increases) until either that goal is achieved or the FDA maximum recommended dose is reached (APA 2010).

DSM-5 (APA 2013) identifies several clinical subtypes of MDD, including those characterized by melancholic, atypical, or psychotic features. Standard of care for MDD with psychotic features (i.e., episodes characterized by hallucinations, delusions, or catatonia) includes medication treatment with antipsychotics or electroconvulsive therapy. Beyond depression with psychotic features, there currently are no reliable clinical or biological measures to match individual patients to specific treatments to maximize outcomes.

Psychotherapies for MDD

Psychological treatments for MDD are derived from the theoretical constructs about the nature of the disorder and the psychological factors that permit its persistence. Evidence-based psychotherapies for the acute treatment of MDD include Beck's eponymous cognitive-behavioral therapy (CBT; Beck et al. 1979), interpersonal therapy (IPT; Klerman et al. 1984), and behavioral activation (BA; Jacobson et al. 2001). Other forms of psychotherapy with some support for efficacy in MDD include behavioral marital therapy (Beach et al. 1990), problem-solving focused therapy (e.g., Nezu et al. 2013), and short-term psychodynamic psychotherapy (Driessen et al. 2010). All these therapies are short term, educational, and fairly directive, and they typically comprise 16–20 sessions over 12–16 weeks. Although CBT has been more extensively evaluated and is discussed more thoroughly in this article, there is minimal empirical evidence to support the choice of one treatment over another; therefore, the decision of which treatment to use is typically based on therapist competence, therapist availability, marital status, and patient preference.

TREATMENT OUTCOMES FOR MDD

Outcome Definitions

The most widely accepted outcome target in the treatment of MDD is remission, in which a patient has returned to the pre-episode level of functioning and has no or only a few mild and infrequently experienced residual depressive symptoms. In clinical trials, remission is defined most often as a rating scale score below a certain threshold, most commonly a Hamilton Depression Rating Scale (HDRS; Hamilton 1960) 17-item total score of ≤ 7. Some studies use alternative rating scales, such as the Montgomery Åsberg Depression Rating Scale (MADRS; Montgomery & Åsberg 1979), the Quick Inventory of Depressive Symptoms (QIDS; Rush et al. 2003), or the Beck Depression Inventory-II (BDI-II, or a self-report measure; Beck et al. 1996). One important caveat regarding the clinical trial definitions of remission is that these cutoffs were arrived at by consensus (Frank et al. 1991); likewise, subsequent analyses suggest that these thresholds may not accurately or adequately reflect functional recovery (Dunlop et al. 2012b, Zimmerman et al. 2012).

Another commonly used outcome measure is response, typically defined as a 50% or more decrease from the baseline score on a rating scale. Response reflects clear improvement with treatment, but it does not imply that full remission has been achieved. Response short of remission is generally an unsatisfactory outcome because the presence of ongoing significant symptoms at the end of treatment is the strongest predictor of future depressive episodes (Judd et al. 2000, Paykel et al. 1995). A return to a full depressive episode within two months of the end of an episode is termed a relapse, whereas such an episode occurring more than two months after remission or response is considered a recurrence, denoting a new major depressive episode. Consequently, maintaining remission for at least two months is referred to as recovery (Frank et al. 1991). The validity of these distinctions has been questioned (Rush et al. 2006), but they are noted here because they are important concepts for interpreting treatment and relapse-prevention trials discussed below.

Efficacy of Single-Modality Treatments

Only about one-third of individuals with MDD seek and receive treatment of any type, and members of minority groups are particularly unlikely to seek or receive depression treatment (Gonzalez et al. 2010). Among those who do receive treatment, evidence-based psychotherapies and ADM are equally efficacious, on average (APA 2013, Cuijpers et al. 2008, Gelenberg et al. 2010, Khan et al. 2012, Spielmans et al. 2011). The data for head-to-head trials of psychotherapy alone versus medication alone are not included in this review; they have been extensively reviewed by others (Cuijpers et al. 2008, Spielmans et al. 2011). The outcome data from individual clinical trials of treatments for MDD are highly variable. Nevertheless, reviews and meta-analyses consistently conclude that regardless of the form of treatment, about two-thirds of all patients with MDD will show a positive response to an active treatment in a clinical trial, but only 30–40% of treated patients with MDD will achieve remission (e.g., DeRubeis et al. 2005b).

The overwhelming majority of clinical trials for MDD involve strict inclusion and exclusion criteria that may reduce generalizability of the results to clinical practice. Four common exclusions used in studies of adults with MDD are (*a*) presence of psychotic symptoms; (*b*) presence of clinically significant suicidal ideation; (*c*) mild severity, typically identified as a screening-visit score below a threshold on a depression rating scale; and (*d*) a medical illness that may interfere with treatment or impair response to treatment. Many studies also exclude individuals with psychiatric comorbidities, such as concurrent substance abuse, eating disorders, and certain anxiety disorders (e.g., obsessive compulsive disorder). Community, nonresearch protocol patients seeking treatment often fall into one or more of these exclusion categories, which may limit extension of these research findings to treatment selection in routine clinical care. Many measured and unmeasured factors contribute to variability in results between trials, and these are discussed in greater detail below. Although considered in the most sophisticated meta-analyses, these preceding factors severely limit the conclusions that can be reached and the clinical practice implications derived from those reports. The conclusions that investigators do reach are further limited by the small sample sizes in most of the individual clinical trials and the redundant inclusion of those same small trials in extant meta-analytic studies.

More recently, clinical scientists have shown increasing concern about the degree of placebo response in clinical trials, an effect that may lead to an exaggerated expectation of benefit in community clinical settings (Dunlop et al. 2012d). Placebo response identified in clinical trials is a multifaceted phenomenon, capturing elements of expectation, time and attention, spontaneous recovery, and regression to the mean effects (Frank & Frank 1991). Patients in clinical trials, particularly those evaluating ADM versus placebo, are provided substantially more contact with a treatment team than is observed in routine clinical practice; thus patients assigned to placebo in clinical trials may experience substantial benefit. For psychotherapy treatments, competence of treatment delivery may be greater in clinical trials, which employ specifically trained therapists, than the level of clinical competence provided in community settings. Thus, for both ADM and psychotherapeutic treatments there are significant concerns regarding the generalizability of clinical trial results.

In summary, the aggregated data reported in the higher-quality meta-analytic studies and qualitative reviews support a consistent conclusion. Namely, single-modality treatments for MDD produce essentially identical outcomes regardless of the treatment given, though some individuals benefit specifically from one form of treatment and not another (McGrath et al. 2013). Although two-thirds of patients show a clinical response, only about one-third of treated MDD patients achieve remission.

Concerns with Single-Modality Treatments

Using ADM and psychotherapy as monotherapies can present significant problems and limitations. For example, each of the ADMs has side effects, and these frequently affect the willingness of patients to complete a course of the medicine. The medications can be expensive, especially when they must be maintained over a long time period, such as in the treatment of chronic depression. Both these factors as well as other variables (e.g., patient's disorganization) result in lower-than-effective adherence to prescribed medical regimens. Furthermore, up to 20% of patients taking ADM for two years will experience a depressive recurrence (Hansen et al. 2008, Kocsis et al. 2007), a phenomenon known as depressive recurrence on antidepressant therapy (DRAT) or "poop out" (Dunlop 2013). Finally, even very effective ADM have a high relapse rate, exceeding 50%, even if a medication is taken as a maintenance treatment for 12–15 months (Hollon et al. 2005a).

Likewise, there are issues related to delivery of short-term evidence-based psychotherapies. For example, when a psychotherapy does not produce a remission, patients frequently experience a resulting demoralization and may be unlikely to seek further treatment; thus, the MDD continues and likely worsens. In contrast to the fairly common aphorism, "at least psychotherapy doesn't hurt patients," the demoralized patient does suffer as a result of ineffective treatment (Craighead et al. 2013a). Even though a clinical trial may show that a specific treatment (e.g., CBT or IPT) is efficacious for MDD, these evidence-based therapies are not very well disseminated, thus limiting the availability of evidence-based treatments in much of the United States. Limited dissemination also leads many therapists to claims that they conduct evidence-based therapy, but in fact, they may have had very minimal, if any, formal training in the therapy that is purportedly being delivered. Consequently, psychotherapy may be incompetently delivered (e.g., CBT; DeRubeis et al. 2005b), resulting in poorer clinical outcomes than reported in clinical trials. In a recent study, 10–15% of community psychotherapy providers produced negative outcomes (actual deterioration) among their patients (Kraus et al. 2011).

Evidence-based therapies need to be disseminated and delivered in a manner functionally equivalent to those evaluated in the clinical trials that support their effectiveness. For example, after reviewing the relevant literature, the National Health Service in England adopted CBT as the first-line treatment for MDD. They have invested more than £400 million to train 6,000 therapists who will be competent in CBT (Cent. Ment. Health et al. 2012).

The greatest concern with all the monotherapies (both ADM and psychotherapies) was previously summarized; namely, only 30–40% of treated MDD patients remit with a monotherapy when treatment is offered under ideal conditions with competent professionals. Despite these concerns, each approach to treatment has its positive aspects. For example, ADM generally produce faster treatment effects (Keller et al. 2000), and psychotherapy (at least CBT) seems to confer more enduring maintenance of positive outcomes (Craighead et al. 2007, Hollon et al. 2005a). As we discuss below, the positive effects of the two treatments have influenced researchers and practitioners to consider treatment combinations in an effort to enhance their overall clinical effectiveness.

COMBINATION TREATMENTS FOR MDD

Overview

As noted above, failure to achieve full recovery from MDD is the strongest predictor of a future, recurrent episode, so improvement in short-term treatment outcomes and prevention of depressive relapses and recurrences are greatly needed. Over the past 30 years, many studies have examined the efficacy of combined medication and psychotherapy in the acute treatment of MDD and the effect of combination therapy on maintenance of wellness. Outcomes from combination versus single-modality treatment trials are mixed, although the overall weight of evidence supports combination as superior (see **Table 1**). However, a key clinical challenge that remains to be solved is to identify which individuals require combination treatment to achieve and maintain recovery from MDD.

The remainder of this article summarizes the state of knowledge about the efficacy of combination treatment for MDD, identifies the limitations of the current knowledge base, and suggests directions for future research. The following questions are addressed: Does combination treatment for MDD produce superior short-term outcomes relative to single treatments? Do combination treatments for MDD produce protection against relapse/recurrence? Should combination treatment be administered concurrently from the beginning of treatment, sequentially if response to the initial treatment is inadequate, or in combination after a trial of monotherapy? Of the large clinical trials evaluating combination treatments for MDD, which important limitations affect the internal validity and generalizability of results to impact clinical care of depressed patients?

Strategies for Combination Treatments

Practitioners can utilize three strategies to employ monotherapies in combination to treat MDD. First, the treatments may be employed concurrently from the beginning of treatment. Second, the treatments may be employed sequentially: Either ADM or psychotherapy is offered first, and the other is added to augment the first if the monotherapy fails or is only partially successful. Finally, ADM and therapy may be offered within stepped treatment, which when conceptually driven is referred to as clinical staging (see McGorry et al. 2010). Within the clinical staging model, a combination of decisions regarding the patient's stage of the disorder is used to guide the treatment process. Clinical staging occurs most frequently when ADM is used initially to treat an individual's debilitating depressive symptoms; the treatment effects may be fairly rapid, and then a psychosocial intervention is added to address the remaining symptoms and problems in daily life (e.g., marital conflict, cognitive distortions, social interactions). A clear demonstration of this process occurs when deep brain stimulation (Ramirez et al. 2013) alleviates a patient's most severe depressive symptoms, but some combination of evidence-based therapy (e.g., behavioral activation and dialectical behavior therapy) is needed to teach living skills to the chronically depressed patient. Below, we note that data regarding neural impacts of clinical interventions augur for a clinical staging approach to combination treatments.

Rationale for Combination Treatments

There are at least three different conceptualizations of the mechanisms by which combined treatment may produce better outcomes than individual treatment.

Additive model. At a study level, some individuals remit only with medication, and others remit only with psychotherapy (in addition to those who will remit to neither and those who will remit to either) (Schatzberg et al. 2005). Thus, by simple addition, the proportion of remitters in a combined-therapy condition will be greater than the proportion of those treated with a monotherapy because some of those who will not have remitted to one of the monotherapies will have remitted to the other monotherapy. This effect produces higher rates of remission in the combined treatment. At an individual level, additive effects may be important, particularly for the goal of achieving remission. One of the monotherapies may produce benefit but leave certain symptoms unaddressed (i.e., a response but not a remission). One example of this additive model

Table 1 Large randomized trials comparing single-modality treatments with combination treatment for acute treatment of major depressive disorder

Author (year)	Design	Patients	% Chronic MDE	Mean HDRS	Arms (N)	Duration (weeks)	Medication	Dropouts	Remission definition	Remission rate
Keller et al. (2000)	Randomize from start	Recruited outpatients with MDD; depressive symptoms ≥2 years HDRS 24: ≥20	35	26.9 (24-item)	ADM (220) CBASP (216) ADM + CBASP (226)	12	Nefazodone	ADM: 26% CBASP: 24% ADM + CBASP: 21%	HDRS ≤8 at weeks 10 and 12 for completers or at final visit for dropouts	ADM: 29% CBASP: 33% ADM + CBASP: 48% $p < 0.001$ for combination versus either ADM or CBASP alone
de Jonghe et al. (2001)	Randomize from start	Consecutive outpatients with MDD HDRS 17: >14	18	20.4	ADM (57) ADM + SPSP (72)	24	Fluoxetine, amitriptyline, moclobemide, sequentially	ADM: 42% ADM + SPSP: 18%	HDRS <8	ADM: 22.8% ADM + SPSP: 43.1% $p = 0.02$
de Jonghe et al. (2004)	Randomize from start	Consecutive outpatients with MDD HDRS 17: 12–24	15	18.1	SPSP (106) SPSP + ADM (85)	24	Various	SPSP: 29% SPSP + ADM: 23%	HDRS <8	SPSP: 32.1% SPSP + ADM: 42.4% $p = 0.14$
Schramm et al. (2007)	Randomize from start	Inpatients with MDE as part of MDD or BP II HDRS 17: ≥16	36	23.5	ADM (61) ADM + IPT (63)	5	Serrtraline, amitriptyline, or amitriptyline-N-oxide	ADM: 15% ADM + IPT: 16%	HDRS <8	ADM: 34% ADM + IPT: 49% $p = 0.105$

Blom et al. (2007)	Randomize from start	Clinically referred outpatients with MDD HDRS 17: ≥14	n.r.	21.4	ADM (47) IPT (50) ADM + IPT (49) IPT + PBO (47)	12–16	Nefazodone	ADM: 36.2% IPT: 32% ADM + IPT: 32.7% IPT + PBO: 25.5%	HDRS ≤8	19.3% overall Remission OR for ADM + IPT versus ADM: 3.22 (1.02–10.12, $p = 0.045$) Remission OR for ADM + IPT versus IPT or IPT + PLA: n.s.
Lesperance et al. (2007)	Randomize from start	Recruited outpatients with MDD and coronary artery disease HDRS 24: ≥20	22	22.8	ADM + CM (75) IPT + PBO + CM (75) ADM + IPT + CM (67) PBO + CM (67)	12	Citalopram	ADM + CM: 13% IPT + PBO + CM: 21% ADM + IPT + CM: 12% PBO + CM: 30%	HDRS 24 ≤8	ADM + CM: 36% IPT + PBO + CM: 21% ADM + IPT + CM: 36% PBO + CM: 23% IPT versus PBO: $p = $ n.s. ADM versus PBO: $p = 0.01$
Kocsis et al. (2009)	Randomize after nonremission with prospective ADM for 12 weeks	Recruited outpatients with MDD; depressive symptoms ≥2 years No min. HDRS	58	19.3 (24-item)	ADM (94) ADM + CBASP (195) ADM + BSP (189)	12	Various	ADM: 17% ADM + CBASP: 13% ADM + BSP: 14%	HDRS 24 <8 and ≥50% decrease from BL	ADM: 39.5% ADM + CBASP: 38.5% ADM + BSP: 31.0% $p = $ n.s.

Abbreviations: ADM, antidepressant medication; BL, baseline; BP, bipolar disorder; BSP, brief supportive therapy; CBASP, cognitive behavioral analysis system of psychotherapy; CM, clinical management; HDRS, Hamilton Depression Rating Scale; IPT, interpersonal therapy; MDD, major depressive disorder; MDE, major depressive episode; n.r., not reported; n.s., not significant; OR, odds ratio; PBO, placebo; SPSP, short psychodynamic supportive psychotherapy.

in an individual is a case in which medication reduces sadness, suicidal ideation, and insomnia but leaves persisting anhedonia and guilt, which may be resolved through CBT. Through addressing these residual symptoms, combination treatment may convert a nonremitter to remitter status.

Synergistic model. In synergies, effects that could not be achieved by either individual intervention are possible only when methods are used together. For example, ADM improve hippocampal function through increased cell survival and dendritic growth (Encinas et al. 2006). Because the hippocampus is crucial for new learning, patients with severe hippocampal dysfunction from their depression may require biological enhancement of hippocampal function to be able to utilize CBT. Similarly, highly anergic patients may require a medication to allow them to "get over the hump" to engage in rewarding activities that are a key component of BA. In both cases, the two treatments are required to make synergistic, meaningful gains. Alternatively, based on the partial or full completion of CBT, patients who need ADM but, for any number of reasons, might refuse medication initially may, as a result of CBT, experience a cognitive change that results in the patient recognizing the need to take ADM. The cognitive change in this example works synergistically to facilitate the acceptance of ADM by patients who need the medications but otherwise might refuse them. This synergy differs from the simpler additive model and the straightforward enhancement of adherence to medications.

Adherence model. Although a more prosaic point, adherence to treatment is crucial to the success of both ADM and psychotherapy treatments. Psychotherapy can enhance adherence to ADM dosing through educational and motivational impacts. Conversely, patients who may be at risk for missing therapy appointments owing to anergia or who cannot complete homework assignments owing to concentration deficits may be aided in these tasks through medication effects.

In addition to these three models for improved outcomes during acute treatment, combination treatment may have effects on the long-term course of MDD. Specifically, combination treatment may provide better protection against relapse and recurrence after remission.

Considerations for Interpreting Combination-Treatment Study Outcomes

Combination-treatment studies are challenging to implement and susceptible to a variety of internal and external validity threats that require consideration. **Table 2** highlights potential sources of bias in trials that compare the benefits of one modality of treatment versus the other or of a combination treatment versus a single-modality treatment.

Sample selection and treatment preferences present particularly knotty issues in evaluating the efficacy of psychotherapy in combination trials. Because all patients in clinical trials are volunteers, a significant potential for selection bias exists. For example, there appears to be great variability among the patient samples enrolled in different trials, and this variability can also occur between sites in the same trial (DeRubeis et al. 2005a). Many trials have not examined patient preference prior to randomization, and some studies show high rates of patient refusal to start a treatment to which they have been randomized, indicating the presence of strong patient preferences (de Jonghe et al. 2001, 2004; Dimidjian et al. 2006). Matching patients to their treatment preference may have sizeable effects on outcomes, so differential preference rates in a randomized trial may impact results unless patients who would refuse a particular treatment are prospectively excluded from participation. This aspect of clinical trials has received inadequate attention in trial design and interpretation.

The pharmacotherapy arm in a clinical trial may not reflect real-world clinical practice. Specifically, patients receiving medication only in clinical trials may still receive significant amounts of

Table 2 Considerations for acute studies of combination versus individual treatments for major depressive disorder (MDD)

Question	Concern
Was the psychotherapy arm an evidence-based form of treatment for MDD?	Use of psychotherapies not proven to be effective in the treatment of MDD may underestimate benefits.
Was pharmacotherapy administered in a manner consistent with standard clinical care?	1. Was pharmacotherapy dosed adequately? 2. Was an early switch to an alternative medication allowed for patients unable to tolerate the initial medication?
Were adequate control conditions present for both the pharmacotherapy and the psychotherapy arms?	1. Including a pill-placebo arm but no control form of psychotherapy distorts expectation bias against medication. 2. Wait-list controls provide no meaningful expectation of improvement and do not represent an adequate control for psychotherapy.
Was the clinic setting of the study generally known for expertise in providing only one form of treatment?	1. Substantial sampling bias may arise from studies performed in locations where patients expect one particular form of treatment. 2. Study investigators' allegiance to specific forms of treatment may have substantial effects on study outcomes.
Was the trial's duration adequate to allow for the emergence and detection of the benefits of combination treatment?	Trials of less than 12 weeks' duration may not allow adequate time for the benefits of monotherapy with psychotherapy to emerge nor for medication-induced remission to occur.
Were the rates of early termination and refusal of randomization assignment different between the treatment arms?	High rates of dropout from one treatment arm may indicate a study sample biased against that form of treatment.
Was the study powered adequately?	1. Conclusions of "no benefit" from combination treatment may arise from an inadequate power to detect statistically significant change. 2. Conclusions of "benefit" from combination treatment may reflect chance results in small samples.
Were treatment preferences assessed prior to randomization?	Trial outcomes may be affected by expectancy. Samples of patients in which there is a strong preference for one treatment over another may not reflect usual clinical practice.

time with the prescribing physician, including the provision of some aspects of supportive therapy (Dunlop & Vaughan 2010). It is, therefore, possible that combination treatment may be more efficacious in clinical trials than in real-world settings, where pharmacotherapy visits may be very brief "med-check" appointments. Conversely, clinical trials involving psychotherapy typically incorporate well-trained therapists, who can easily communicate with the trial pharmacotherapists. Such valuable aspects of psychotherapy provision may not apply in many real-world settings, consequently resulting in an overestimation of the value of combined treatment in actual clinical practice.

Expectation biases are another potential problem in multiarmed clinical trials, in which one of the arms is a placebo pill. In such trials, patients assigned to a medication condition do not know whether they are receiving an active treatment. In contrast, psychotherapy control conditions are not typically presented to patients as "placebo psychotherapy," but rather they are represented as an effective form of psychotherapy, with extensive description of the treatment. In particular, more severely depressed or impaired patients may be particularly unwilling to enroll in trials involving potential assignment to placebo medication. In contrast, a wait-list condition provides no benefits from attention or hope, and it is also an inadequate control condition for psychotherapy.

Finally, the singular focus on depression rating scale changes as the measure of outcome can lead investigators to overlook other important clinical outcomes that may emerge from combined treatment, specifically improvements in quality of life and functioning. A review of 12 naturalistic studies of ADM-treated MDD patients followed for at least 10 years found that longitudinal changes in depressive symptoms were not accompanied by changes in patients' psychosocial functioning (Hughes & Cohen 2009). Individual studies examining patients with chronic forms of depression have found that combination treatment significantly improved quality of life over medication monotherapy (Greenberg 1999, Molenaar et al. 2007, von Wolff et al. 2012). Acknowledging this oversight in prior work and incorporating appropriate measures of these constructs are essential as MDD combination-treatment outcome research progresses. Indeed, an exclusive focus on depressive symptomatology as compared with other domains of functioning may overlook the greatest benefit of added psychotherapy in combination treatment.

Limitations of Meta-Analysis

Meta-analysis is considered the preferred method to evaluate treatment outcomes across studies, and it can be employed to overcome design concerns that may affect individual studies. Several meta-analyses have examined various aspects of the efficacy of combined versus single-modality treatments for MDD. Meta-analysis is a powerful technique to identify mean effect sizes and to compare outcomes quantitatively across a broad range of studies, particularly when many small studies have been conducted, as is the case in the acute treatment of MDD. Meta-analysis, however, has several important limitations.

Specifically, studies included in a meta-analysis should be sufficiently similar in design to produce a meaningful estimate of effect size for an actual clinical intervention (Higgins & Green 2011, Lieberman et al. 2005). Heterogeneity in trial design factors listed in **Table 2** may be differentially valued by those conducting meta-analyses; these discrepant evaluations across investigators may result in differing conclusions based on different meta-analyses. For studies of MDD combination treatment, several issues require particular consideration to determine whether the studies included in a meta-analysis are similar enough in design to produce valid results. First, although the additive and synergistic models of the benefits of combination treatment imply that combination treatment should be superior to either treatment delivered singly, it is possible that combination therapy is superior to medication-only treatment but not superior to psychotherapy alone. Alternatively, combination therapy might be superior to psychotherapy only but may not improve medication-treatment outcomes. Thus, meta-analyses ideally would be performed for all combination-treatment studies with two sensitivity analyses, specifically evaluating the benefit of combination therapy versus ADM alone and combination therapy versus psychotherapy alone.

Second, investigators need to define an adequate form of each treatment. For medication, underdosing or not allowing a switch for medication intolerance reflects an inadequate representation of regular psychopharmacologic practice. For experimental psychotherapy conditions the question is even more complex: (*a*) What is considered an efficacious psychotherapy? Should only evidence-based forms of psychotherapy be included, or should all forms of counseling be included? Any form of psychotherapy may provide benefit to patients through the shared effects common to all therapies, but additional benefit may arise for some patients specifically from the evidence-based treatments. (*b*) What is considered an adequate psychotherapy dose (i.e., number and duration of sessions)? (*c*) How much experience do therapists need to be considered adequate to provide competent clinical practice? Failure to consider adequacy of treatments may bias meta-analyses toward null findings or toward evidence of positive effects, depending on the specific studies included, a decision not infrequently made in an arbitrary fashion.

A third consideration is the need for a measure of publication bias, such as a funnel plot or using Duval and Tweedie's trim and fill procedure (Duval & Tweedie 2000). For various reasons, small studies with positive results are more likely to be published than are small studies with negative results. Without considering the presence of this bias, meta-analyses may falsely conclude that efficacy exists, owing to the absence of negative unpublished results from small studies. In one meta-analysis controlling for publication bias of studies of psychological treatments for MDD, the mean effect size estimate was reduced from 0.67 to 0.42 (Cuijpers et al. 2010a).

In sum, the previously reviewed issues dramatically affect the outcomes of meta-analyses. Thus, when interpreting the meaning of a meta-analysis, individuals must review the selection criteria for studies included in the analyses. The inclusion of many small studies with weak selection criteria and poor methodological implementation, even if the results are statistically significant, can render the outcome of a meta-analysis clinically and scientifically inconsequential.

EFFICACY OF COMBINATION TREATMENTS: ACUTE EFFECTS

Medication Alone versus Combined Treatments

Meta-analyses of ADM versus combination treatment have consistently found small benefits from combination treatment over ADM alone. The broadest meta-analysis (Cuijpers et al. 2009a) of 25 studies, which included studies of all forms of depressive disorders, found an effect size of Cohen's $d = 0.31$. Importantly, the benefit of combination treatment was driven exclusively by studies of patients with MDD ($d = 0.40$), with no effect seen in studies of dysthymia ($d = 0.00$). A meta-analysis limited to 16 trials treating MDD, including a total of 1,842 patients, found a remission rate of 33% for medication monotherapy versus 44% for combination treatment (Pampallona et al. 2004). The odds ratio for remission with combination treatment was 1.86 [95% confidence interval (CI): 1.38–2.52]. This analysis also suggested greater benefit for combination therapy for studies employing treatment durations greater than 12 weeks; this effect was due partly to a smaller percentage of patients dropping out of the combined treatment condition compared to the monotherapy treatment condition in the longer studies. From these analyses, the number needed to treat (NNT) with combination therapy to gain one additional remission over medication monotherapy is 8–9. This NNT is comparable to the NNT of 7 for SSRIs versus placebo to achieve remission in clinical trials of MDD (Arroll et al. 2009).

To delineate the specific benefit of ADM versus that of the placebo effect of a pill, Cuijpers and colleagues (2010b) conducted a meta-analysis comparing the combination of psychotherapy with either active ADM or a placebo pill. The effect size for combination treatment with ADM over pill placebo was only $d = 0.25$ (95% CI: 0.03–0.46). Again, however, the studies included in that analysis included very diverse groups of patients (many studies compared medically ill or substance-abusing patients), so comparability with other meta-analyses is limited.

One large clinical trial that failed to find benefit from combination treatment over ADM alone was the Research Evaluating the Value of Augmenting Medication with Psychotherapy (REVAMP) (Kocsis et al. 2009). In this trial, chronically depressed patients who failed to remit after 12 weeks of treatment with a single ADM were randomly assigned to augmentation with (*a*) cognitive behavioral analysis system of psychotherapy (CBASP), (*b*) brief supportive therapy, or (*c*) a medication change (either a switch to a second ADM or a two-drug combination). Because the trial was enriched with medication nonremitters, investigators might have expected it to be particularly likely to show the benefit of the psychotherapy addition to ADM. However, no meaningful difference was found among the three treatment approaches on any efficacy measure. There was a potential for selection bias in this trial versus other combination-treatment trials because the patients entering REVAMP knew they would all be initially treated with ADM monotherapy, and few study participants desired psychotherapy treatment alone (Steidtmann et al.

2012). In the only other large trial permitting adjustments in the pharmacotherapy condition, the combination of short psychodynamic supportive therapy with adjustable pharmacotherapy was superior to pharmacotherapy alone (de Jonghe et al. 2001). The sample for that trial was highly psychotherapy preferring; 32% of the patients refused randomization to the ADM monotherapy arm versus only 13% who refused combination. Thus, it remains uncertain whether the combination of psychotherapy plus ADM is superior to algorithmically determined and maximized ADM treatment.

Psychotherapy Alone versus Combined Treatments

A maximally inclusive recent meta-analysis reported a small overall effect size (Cohen's $d = 0.35$; 95% CI: 0.25–0.45, $p < 0.001$) in the change in depression severity favoring combined treatment versus psychotherapy alone (Cuijpers et al. 2009b). This meta-analysis incorporated studies that employed any form of psychological intervention and patients with any form of depressive disorder, which included studies limited to specific subgroups (such as medically ill subjects). Within combination treatments, non-CBT therapies produced significantly larger effect sizes than did studies using CBT as the psychotherapy, which suggests that medication produces a bigger contribution to outcomes for studies that employ non-CBT therapies. Although many factors may have contributed to this finding, one important interpretation may be that CBT has larger antidepressive effects than do other psychotherapies; thus, CBT may leave less room for improvement with ADM cotreatment than other psychotherapies. There was no evidence of publication bias in the overall analysis, but many of the included studies were not of high quality. Similarly, Cuijpers et al. (2009b) found essentially no benefit to psychotherapy combined with SSRIs ($d = 0.10$), but slightly larger effects were found when psychotherapy was combined with tricyclic antidepressants ($d = 0.35$) or other antidepressants ($d = 0.47$).

A meta-analysis of studies limited to patients with MDD treated in psychiatric specialty settings and using a formal psychotherapeutic treatment also found benefit for combined treatment over psychotherapy alone (de Maat et al. 2007). In the seven included studies, dropout rates were equal between the combined therapy and psychotherapy alone treatment groups. The intent-to-treat analyses found a 12% greater remission rate for combined treatment over psychotherapy (46% versus 34%, respectively; $p < 0.00007$), reflecting a relative risk for remission of 1.32 (95% CI: 1.12–1.56). The remission rate difference was larger and statistically significant only in the moderately depressed, not the mildly depressed patients. Similarly, statistical significance in remission rates was present in the chronically depressed but not nonchronically depressed patients. Whether evaluating combination therapy against medication or psychotherapy alone, results consistently indicate that patients with chronic forms of MDD are most likely to receive enhanced acute benefits from combination treatment (Friedman et al. 2004, von Wolff et al. 2012).

Summary of Acute-Phase Combination Treatments for MDD

Considering these meta-analyses together, we conclude that for the treatment of MDD, combination treatment is superior to ADM alone and probably superior to psychotherapy alone, with the possible exception of CBT. There is little evidence showing that combination therapy is superior to ADM or psychotherapy alone in mild cases of MDD. In contrast, for dysthymia, a chronic form of low-grade depression, the addition of psychotherapy does not enhance treatment with ADM alone. Combination treatment has more rapid effects than does psychotherapy alone. Combination treatment has not definitively proven superior to pharmacotherapy administered in an adjustable manner, at least for patients willing to start treatment with ADM monotherapy. There are, however, nearly as many completed meta-analyses as there are high-quality, adequately powered studies; the field currently needs additional adequately powered investigations rather than more meta-analyses. Indeed, the field critically needs research studies that employ new designs that investigate which treatments or combinations of treatments work for which patients under which conditions. This approach was posed in principle by Paul (1969, p. 62) over 40 years ago, and it seems to be finding its fruition in recent depression research using contemporary approaches to study personalized medicine.

EFFICACY OF COMBINATION TREATMENTS: PREVENTION OF RELAPSE/RECURRENCE

Repeated depressive episodes are the rule rather than the exception in patients with MDD. At least 75% of MDD patients will experience multiple depressive episodes across the life span (Hughes & Cohen 2009, Judd 1997, Mueller et al. 1999); thus, identifying best practices to maintain wellness and prevent recurrence after recovery from a depressive episode is of great importance. There is growing recognition that the mechanisms involved in recovering and maintaining recovery from a depressive episode may differ from those involving an episode's initiation (Post 1992, Segal et al. 2002, Sheets et al. 2013). Conceptualizing MDD in this manner suggests that different intervention strategies may be needed during periods of acute-phase treatment versus those of maintenance treatment, at least for some subsets of depressed patients.

Both CBT and IPT have demonstrated efficacy in preventing recurrence following successful acute psychotherapy treatment (Dobson et al. 2008, Frank et al. 2007, Hollon et al. 2005a, Vittengl et al. 2007), though some studies have found IPT to be less efficacious than medication when ADM are continued through the maintenance phase (Frank et al. 1990, Reynolds et al. 1999). Such enduring effects of psychotherapy in the absence of ongoing sessions suggest that psychotherapy treatments change risk factors for recurrence in a manner that treatment with acute ADM does not (Hollon et al. 2006).

Design Issues During Maintenance-Phase Interventions

Studies examining the protective effects of combination treatment in preventing depressive relapses or recurrences differ in important design characteristics. The specific design issues that have implications for interpreting results and considering how to employ combination treatments most effectively to prevent relapse and recurrence are (*a*) maintenance versus discontinuation of the ADM employed during the acute phase; (*b*) the degree of residual depressive symptoms present at the beginning of the follow-up period; and (*c*) whether the combination treatment being evaluated was applied during the acute-treatment phase or sequentially after remission had been achieved with a single-modality treatment.

An important consideration in relapse/recurrence prevention studies is whether ADM are continued during the maintenance phase. ADM treatment that is efficacious during acute treatment protects against recurrence when it is continued during maintenance treatment, but discontinuing ADM during maintenance increases recurrence risk (Hollon et al. 2005a); risk of recurrence is even greater for patients with chronic or recurrent episodes (Keller et al. 1998, 2007). The current standard of care for psychopharmacologic management of most patients with recurrent MDD recovered with ADM is to maintain ADM indefinitely at the same dose used to achieve recovery (APA 2010). Several head-to-head maintenance comparisons of psychotherapy alone versus medication alone indicate psychotherapy is clearly superior in protecting against relapse if ADM is discontinued (Blackburn et al. 1986; Hollon et al. 1992, 2005a; Kovacs et al. 1981;

Simons et al. 1986), though some studies did not find this effect (Perlis et al. 2002, Shea et al. 1992). When ADM are maintained during follow-up, the data are more mixed; some studies still indicate a benefit for CBT (Hollon et al. 2005a, Simons et al. 1986), whereas others indicate no difference between treatment conditions (Evans et al. 1992, Frank et al. 1990).

The degree of recovery from depression required for patients to enter a trial's maintenance phase is another important consideration. The greater the presence of residual symptoms is after treatment for a major depressive episode, the more elevated the risk is for depressive recurrence compared with patients who achieve a full remission (Judd et al. 2000, Paykel et al. 1995, Thase et al. 1992). Any differential levels of residual symptoms within the experimental conditions in a maintenance-phase combination trial may produce a bias in any observed differential outcomes (Karp et al. 2004).

Finally, the timing of the provision of the combination treatment is of great importance. Combination treatment can be provided from the outset of treatment, or the two treatment components can be added sequentially. Some studies of combination treatment reporting maintenance-phase outcomes simply added a naturalistic follow-up phase, with or without ADM continuation, to a study designed to examine the acute-phase efficacy of combination treatment. Thus, the trial's primary aim was not to evaluate prevention of recurrence, but rather short-term improvements (Evans et al. 1992, Maina et al. 2009, Miller et al. 1989), and the maintenance phase of the studies was simply an add-on.

One of the most important threats to the validity of naturalistic follow-up of trials involving combination treatment from the outset is the "differential sieve" phenomenon (Klein 1996). The differential sieve problem arises when only responders or remitters to an acute-phase treatment enter into the follow-up phase. By not considering all subjects who start treatment, the potential for differential retention makes maintenance studies vulnerable to bias because patients at high risk for relapse (i.e., most severely depressed or more difficult to treat) may be more likely to enter the maintenance phase in one arm of a trial than in a comparator arm (Dunlop et al. 2012b, Evans et al. 1992). For example, if a combination-treatment arm can push a greater proportion of higher-risk patients into remission than the monotherapy arm does, then during follow-up there will be a bias for greater relapses in the combination arm because it will have retained a higher proportion of greater at-risk patients at the beginning of the maintenance phase. This concern is partially alleviated if equal proportions of the patients in each condition from the acute-treatment phase enter the follow-up phase; however, there could still be differential mixtures of at-risk and less-at-risk patients, owing to differential patterns of acute response. In essence, a more powerful acute-phase treatment can appear less effective than a comparator in maintenance treatment owing to features of the patients it helps. Although little evidence indicates that treatment responders differ from nonresponders in clinically meaningful ways, selection bias may still emerge from unmeasured important factors (Hollon et al. 2006).

Design Improvements for Maintenance-Phase Interventions

Stronger evidence for the value of combined treatment to prevent recurrence can be gleaned from trials incorporating randomized discontinuation of components of a combined treatment provided to all patients from the outset of treatment. Patients achieving remission with combined treatment are randomly assigned to discontinue either the psychotherapy or the ADM (blinded switch to placebo), neither, or both after maintaining stable remission through a treatment consolidation phase of several months. This design allows investigators to identify the relative importance of treatment components for long-term stability. Two large trials of combined tricyclic ADM plus IPT reached similar conclusions; namely, the best results through maintenance occur when both aspects of treatment are continued, and maintenance of ADM alone has a greater effect on preventing recurrence than does IPT alone among MDD patients initially treated with combination therapy (Frank et al. 1990, Reynolds et al. 1999).

Sequential treatment designs provide another strong form of evidence for the role of combined treatment. In this design, patients are randomized to additional treatment in a maintenance phase. Mindfulness-based cognitive behavior therapy (MBCT) is a manualized, group-based, eight-session, skills-training form of CBT (Teasdale et al. 2000), which can be added after patients have achieved remission with ADM treatment. A meta-analysis of six similarly designed MBCT versus treatment as usual or placebo trials found consistent, similar effect sizes in prevention of recurrence (Piet & Hougaard 2011). Other studies of patients fully remitting (Bockting et al. 2005) or partially remitting (Fava et al. 1996, 1998; Paykel et al. 1999) to ADM monotherapy have demonstrated the efficacy of a subsequent course of CBT in preventing recurrences. Only one study has failed to find a benefit on relapse prevention from adding CBT to ADM therapy for patients in remission (Perlis et al. 2002). This study was unique because at the same time that CBT was added, the fluoxetine doses for all remitted patients were doubled. This dose increase, combined with the relatively brief follow-up period of 28 weeks, resulted in very few recurrences during the study. In summary, the efficacy of CBT and MBCT in preventing MDD recurrence represents one of the strongest and most robust findings in the area of combination treatment of MDD.

Mechanisms of Combination Relapse Prevention

Researchers do not know how treatment with CBT reduces relapse in medication-treated patients with residual symptoms. In the relevant studies, there is a minimal change in symptom burden between patients who do and do not receive CBT for relapse prevention, which suggests that reduction of symptoms does not explain CBT's positive effect (Scott et al. 2000). This effect may be obtained because of the change in cognitive processing and resultant schema change (à la Beck's model of CBT); improvement of positive coping mechanisms, perhaps via developing compensatory skills for poor coping patterns (Persons 1993); an increase in self-efficacy through internalization of positive life experiences; or an increased ability to employ adaptive metacognitive views of one's cognitions and emotions (Teasdale 1997). The positive coping interpretation receives support from the efficacy of problem-solving treatment for minor depression, which directly targets an avoidant coping style, thought to contribute to maintenance of depressive states (Oxman et al. 2008), and the metacognitive viewpoint receives support from the MBCT data (see Segal et al. 2002).

The sustained benefits of cognitively informed psychotherapy treatments in preventing recurrence may be most applicable for patients who have experienced a greater number of lifetime episodes of MDD. Patients with three or more prior episodes demonstrate benefits of MBCT, whereas patients with two or fewer episodes have not shown significant benefit from this treatment (Ma & Teasdale 2004, Teasdale et al. 2000). Similarly, the addition of an 8-session course of CBT prevented recurrence in patients with ≥5 prior episodes among patients in remission and those maintained on treatment as usual (Bockting et al. 2005). In patients with more frequent episode recurrence, mindfulness and cognitive interventions may act to disrupt the learned associations between negative thinking patterns and depressive episodes or may interrupt ruminative thought processes that may lead to depressed mood states (Segal et al. 2002). One must remember, however, that the enduring effects of monotherapy CBT have been obtained with treatment-naïve patients as well as with those who have had recurrent episodes. Thus, a final conclusion regarding the mechanisms by which the enduring effects of sequentially combined ADM and CBT operate cannot currently be reached. As we note later, the enduring effects of CBT may emerge for a specific subset of patients regardless of whether CBT is conducted alone or in combination with ADM.

Summary of Maintenance-Phase Combination Treatments for MDD

Combination treatment extends time to recurrence or relapse in MDD patients fully or partially remitting to acute-phase treatment. For patients who receive combination treatment during the acute phase, the best long-term outcomes occur if both components of treatment continue through the maintenance phase. Discontinuing ADM after its use in an acute-phase treatment carries the greatest risk for recurrence. Thus, patients who receive combination treatment from the outset will have a better prognosis if psychotherapy is discontinued, rather than discontinuing ADM. Patients receiving initial treatment with ADM monotherapy are less likely to experience a recurrence if they complete a short course of CBT after improving; this benefit is particularly clear for patients with recurrent depression or those who continue to have residual depressive symptoms upon completion of ADM acute treatment.

IMPROVING APPLICATIONS OF COMBINATION TREATMENT

Overview

The question of whether combination treatment for MDD is superior to single-modality treatment is inextricably bound with the following issue: Should combined treatment be administered concurrently for all patients, or should it be given sequentially for those patients who do not remit to the initial treatment? The primary advantage for concurrent initial treatment is a shortened time to remission. Within the sequential approach, in which patients must first demonstrate inability to remit from a single treatment, there is a period of 2–3 months lost while administering an insufficiently effective treatment. The concurrent approach incurs greater financial costs in the short run, owing to the greater intensity of treatment, though this concern may be obviated if long-term costs are reduced through decreased relapse rates.

No controlled studies have explicitly compared concurrent versus sequential treatments. However, Frank and coworkers studied two consecutive cohorts of women treated with IPT, with medication added either concurrently from the start of treatment or sequentially for nonremitters to IPT monotherapy. They found significantly higher remission rates in the sequentially treated patients (79%) compared with the concurrently treated cohort (66%, $p = 0.02$). This difference was even more pronounced in the more severely depressed (HDRS $\geq$ 20) women (81% versus 58%, respectively; $p < 0.02$) (Frank et al. 2000). The criteria for participation were similar between the two trials, but there were important differences between the studies, including the type of antidepressant used and the amount of IPT provided. Although these data are suggestive, conclusive evidence requires trials specifically designed to compare concurrent and sequential approaches.

A theoretical risk of administering combined treatment is the potential interference of one treatment with another. The relief provided by medication may reduce motivation to engage in psychotherapy (Rounsaville et al. 1981). Other interference effects may arise from patients' psychological interpretation of sources of benefit. Specifically, patients may attribute gains in treatment solely to medication effects, thereby diminishing their sense of self-efficacy in managing depressive symptoms. Relevant potential concerns have emerged from the anxiety disorders literature, in which combination treatment led to worse long-term outcomes than did treatment with CBT alone (Barlow et al. 2000). This negative interaction may arise from mood-state or context-dependent learning effects, in which extinction learning and coping skills learned in psychotherapy when experiencing reduced levels of anxiety (due to medication treatment) are not fully accessible in higher-level states present after medication has been discontinued (Bouton et al. 2006). Such detrimental effects may be less likely to occur with the effective treatments for MDD, which do not depend as much on the more exposure learning-based methods employed to treat anxiety.

Moderators of Outcomes with Combination Treatment: Which Patients Need Combination Treatment?

Routine provision of combination treatment to all depressed patients is not warranted, given the increased cost of combination therapy and that many patients improve with a single-modality treatment. Thus, there is a great need to identify the individuals for whom combination treatment is necessary to achieve remission and sustain recovery. Efforts are increasing to identify predictor variables that can match individual patients to the treatment modality that will provide the best chance for remission. Predictors of outcome may be prognostic (i.e., nonspecifically indicating likelihood of outcome, regardless of treatment modality) or prescriptive (specifically indicating better outcomes with one form of treatment over another) (Fournier et al. 2009). Sociodemographic and clinical variables are the most frequently replicated predictors to date, although efforts to identify biomarkers of treatment outcomes are currently the focus of great interest.

Sociodemographic and clinical moderators. Several demographic characteristics nonspecifically predict poor outcomes from MDD treatment. The strongest of these is low socioeconomic status, which is consistently associated with lower likelihood of remission (Lorant et al. 2003). The consistency of this finding across multiple large studies suggests socioeconomic status should be included as a covariate in all outcomes analyses from clinical trials. Other well-replicated nonspecific predictors of poor outcome to monotherapies include older age (Fournier et al. 2009, Hirschfeld et al. 1998, Sotsky et al. 1991, Thase et al. 1997) and lower intelligence and/or limited education (Dunkin et al. 2000, Haaga et al. 1991, Trivedi et al. 2006).

Researchers have proposed several clinical factors as prescriptive variables to indicate the need for specific treatments. Factors that could indicate the need for combination treatment are best derived from study designs that compare a combination-treatment arm with both a medication arm and a psychotherapy arm. Without individual arms for each modality, it is impossible to know whether any identified predictor of outcome is specific to the combination treatment or simply a predictor for the extra component added to the combination. Unfortunately, very few studies have compared combination treatment individually against each modality. A second approach for identifying individuals who need combination treatment may be derived from prognostic factors of poor outcome in head-to-head psychotherapy versus ADM single-modality trials; factors that are associated with poor outcome to both monotherapies may indicate the need for more intensive, combined treatment.

The best-replicated clinical factor predictive of outcome is MDD chronicity, which predicts poorer response across treatment modalities (Blom et al. 2007, Fournier et al. 2009, Joyce et al. 2002, Sotsky et al. 1991, Thase et al. 1994, Trivedi et al. 2006). Whether comparing combination against ADM or psychotherapy alone, study results consistently indicate that patients with more chronic MDD are most likely to receive enhanced acute benefits from combination treatment (Friedman et al. 2004, von Wolff et al. 2012). A recent meta-analysis limited to patients with chronic depression (including dysthymia and chronic MDD) found a benefit ratio (i.e., a risk ratio for positive end points) for remission of 1.25 (0.97–1.61) for combination therapy over ADM monotherapy (von Wolff et al. 2012). However, by combining both dysthymia and chronic MDD into one meta-analysis, this benefit ratio likely underestimated the value of combined treatment for chronic MDD. Several large studies of combination therapy versus ADM alone for dysthymia have failed to find benefit for combination treatment (Browne et al. 2002, de Mello et al. 2001, Markowitz et al. 2005, Ravindran et al. 1999). Indeed, von Wolff and colleagues (2012) found that for depressive symptoms in patients with dysthymia, the benefit ratio of combined treatment versus ADM alone was 0.95. In contrast, for studies limited to chronic MDD, the benefit ratio was 4.0 in favor of combination treatment.

There is a little evidence indicating that more severely depressed patients (HDRS >20) benefit more from acute combination treatment than from ADM monotherapy (Cuijpers et al. 2009). Gender has also not consistently predicted outcomes to different treatment modalities. Recent adverse life events have been associated with superior outcomes for CBT over ADM (Fournier et al. 2009) and to poorer response in an ADM-only trial (Mazure et al. 2000).

Patient preference is often used to match patients to treatment, although in clinical trials the value of preference in predicting outcome is mixed. Some randomized trials of psychotherapy versus ADM have required patients, including those with personal treatment preferences, to be willing to start randomized treatment; these studies have found that preference is not associated with outcome (Dunlop et al. 2012c, Kwan et al. 2010, Leykin et al. 2007). Attrition rates between patients matched and mismatched by treatment preference are variable across trials; mismatch predicts greater dropout rates in some trials (Kwan et al. 2010, Raue et al. 2009), but not others (Dunlop et al. 2012c, Kocsis et al. 2009, Leykin et al. 2007). These variable findings indicate the crucial contribution of how the informed consent process is performed, particularly the discussion around randomization and the patient's willingness to start the treatment regardless of preference. More generally, patients preferring ADM over psychotherapy or combination treatment have higher rates of attrition (Dunlop et al. 2012c, Steidtmann et al. 2012), which may stem from beliefs about causes of their depression (Dunlop et al. 2012c, Steidtmann et al. 2012) or from practical factors related to treatment (e.g., preference for ADM may derive from time or travel constraints, which may contribute to attrition).

Two large combination trials of treatments for chronic MDD have evaluated patient preference as a predictor (Kocsis et al. 2009, Steidtmann et al. 2012). In both trials, the majority of patients entering the trial preferred combination therapy rather than monotherapy treatment. In the nefazodone/CBASP trial, matching to treatment preference strongly predicted remission among the few patients who preferred a monotherapy over combination (Kocsis et al. 2009). In the REVAMP trial, patients indicated their preference for combination therapy or a monotherapy at the beginning of the initial medication-only phase; this preference did not associate with outcomes among the ADM nonremitters randomized to a 12-week course of combination treatment (CBASP or brief supportive therapy plus ADM) or ADM adjustment only (Steidtmann et al. 2012). These differing results speak to the importance of how trial design factors may influence the sample of MDD patients included in trials.

Childhood maltreatment is associated with poorer outcomes to treatment with medication or combined treatment for MDD (Nanni et al. 2012). Among chronically ill patients, patients reporting early childhood adversity, including parental loss, physical or sexual abuse, and neglect, improved significantly more with combination CBASP plus nefazodone over nefazodone alone, though the combination therapy was not superior to CBASP alone (Nemeroff et al. 2003), indicating that ADM did not add to the treatment outcomes. Childhood adversity also predicted poorer outcomes to the initial medication monotherapy phase in the REVAMP trial (Klein et al. 2009). Again, these results need further study by enrolling patients on the basis of early abuse and then randomizing them to treatments to determine if abuse history is an actual specific marker of treatment outcomes.

Higher levels of anxiety (or the presence of a comorbid anxiety disorder) typically predict poorer outcomes of treatment for MDD (Fava et al. 2008, Souery et al. 2007) or longer time to remission (Frank et al. 2011). Studies of combination-therapy versus monotherapy treatments have not reported differential outcomes by type of treatment among anxious patients. However, among patients with a comorbid anxiety disorder, anxiety symptoms improved considerably more among chronically depressed patients who received combination nefazodone and CBASP compared with those who received CBASP alone; of note, the combination was not superior to nefazodone alone for anxiety symptoms (Ninan et al. 2002). Some studies comparing psychotherapy versus ADM or their combination allow the concurrent use of benzodiazepines to treat insomnia or anxiety (Frank et al. 2011), which acts to reduce the likelihood of finding differences between treatment conditions.

Because greater medical disease burden is a poor prognostic factor for MDD treatment (Iosifescu et al. 2003), combination treatment may have particular value in depressed medically ill patients. However, in the single large controlled trial of combination treatment performed in patients with coronary artery disease and MDD, citalopram plus IPT was not superior to citalopram plus clinical management; both arms achieved remission rates of 36% (Lesperance et al. 2007).

Brain-based moderators. Although chronicity is currently the best clinical marker to identify which patients need combination treatment to remit from a major depressive episode, many patients in a chronic or recurrent episode achieve remission with a single-modality treatment. Several methods are being investigated to better stratify patients into subgroups to identify the individuals who will need ADM, psychotherapy, or combination treatment to achieve remission (Dunlop et al. 2012a). Neuroimaging, including positron emission tomography (PET) and functional magnetic resonance imaging (fMRI), is at the forefront of these methods, but other methods are also under investigation (Kemp et al. 2008).

ADM and psychotherapy have been shown to act via different mechanisms in the brain to achieve their treatment effects (DeRubeis et al. 2005b). A wide variety of studies employing neuroimaging have been performed in efforts to determine the neurological basis for change with single-modality treatments, but no studies have specifically examined the effects of combined treatment versus those of a monotherapy. Nevertheless, understanding the biological mechanisms by which different single-modality treatments work may contribute to the rational use of combination treatment in the future.

Neuroimaging has greatly enhanced our understanding of brain function in depressed patients (Price & Drevets 2011). Symptoms of depression such as changes in appetite, sleep, and energy are likely mediated in part through hypothalamic regions. Negative emotional experience (sadness and anxiety) is thought to involve the amygdala, insula, and subgenual cingulate cortex. Anhedonia and motivation are mediated largely by processing between the ventral tegmentum and ventral striatum regions, and the basal ganglia are important for psychomotor speed. Cognitive functions such as attention, working memory, and decision making are performed via processing in prefrontal regions, including the dorsolateral prefrontal cortex and anterior cingulate cortex. These various brain regions are connected within networks of activity, and the regions reflect nodes within a network. However, a complete delineation of the scope and function of these networks has not yet been described. One emerging conceptualization proposes that in a depressive episode excessive negative emotion processing in the limbic regions may impact other nodes in the network, driving cognition toward negative thoughts (pessimism, guilt, worthlessness) and disrupting attentional systems (Wang et al. 2012); nevertheless, the directionality of network activation is not currently clearly articulated.

A commonly referenced heuristic for understanding how psychotherapy and ADM differentially impact these networks in MDD is the top-down versus bottom-up distinction (Ochsner et al. 2009). In this model, ADMs modify neurotransmitter activity to diminish activity in limbic brain regions, including the amygdala, insula, subgenual cingulate cortex (Broadman Area 25), and hippocampus, thereby reducing negative emotional states and freeing cortical regions from negative bias. However, other data indicate that at least some antidepressants may have direct effects on cortical function, which is not surprising given the diffuse distribution of serotonin and norepinephrine pathways within the brain (Deutch & Roth 2009, Fu et al. 2004).

Psychotherapy approaches, except perhaps for BA, are proposed to act through top-down mechanisms, implying that through actions of cognitive networks, excessive negative limbic activity can be decreased. There are reciprocal connections between limbic regions and cortical regions such as the anterior cingulate cortex and the orbitofrontal cortex. These regions exist within networks that reciprocally or unidirectionally transmit information for processing. Thus, mood may be regulated through acting on these networks at accessible nodes. The nodes are generally considered limbic for medication, whereas they are more cognitive for psychotherapy (see Ochsner et al. 2009 for a more detailed discussion).

Although the networks important for regulating mood have not been completely identified, this model opens the possibility that neuroimaging may reveal different patterns of abnormal activity and, thus, indicate the specific need for an ADM or psychotherapeutic intervention. This model suggests that specific single-modality interventions may ultimately function most effectively when a specific pattern of neural connectivity has been identified and a treatment that focuses on that pattern is employed; this approach would maximize the efficacy of that monotherapy. However, some individuals' maladaptive patterns may be such that combination interventions are necessary to correct the dysfunctional neural pathways associated with their MDD. The goal of improved outcomes through combinations of different forms of treatment complements the model of bottom-up and top-down mechanisms of action of medication and psychotherapy treatments. It is important to recognize that although the model may be appealing, biological evidence of its validity is scant and the model has been explored in only a few, unreplicated studies.

Most neuroimaging studies of predictors of treatment response to date have explored single modality forms of treatment. Very few neuroimaging studies have examined changes with ADM versus psychotherapy treatments (Brody et al. 2001, Goldapple et al. 2004, Kennedy et al. 2007, Siegle et al. 2012), and even fewer used a randomized design (Kennedy et al. 2007). Outcome markers in these studies have generally reflected response or remission versus nonresponse to any treatment (Konarski et al. 2009) rather than differential biomarkers that could guide selection of one treatment over another.

Most reported findings of outcome prediction need replication in independent samples. Nonspecific predictors of positive outcomes, such as greater resting-state activity in the pre- and peri-genual anterior cingulate cortex (Mayberg et al. 1997), need to be distinguished from the specific therapeutic effect of a treatment versus nonspecific placebo effects of time, expectation, and clinical attention. For CBT, assessment of limbic (amygdala, subgenual cingulate) reactivity to negative mood challenge, and regulation of negative emotions by dorsolateral, ventrolateral, and anterior cingulate cortices, may indicate which patients may benefit from CBT treatment (Siegle et al. 2012, Wager et al. 2008). Some evidence suggests that patients who demonstrate the greatest differences from healthy controls on emotion-processing tasks may be least likely to benefit from CBT (Ritchey et al. 2011, Siegle et al. 2012). Significant hypoactivity of the dorsolateral prefrontal cortex may indicate a need for ADM treatment, potentially representing an inability to activate nodes necessary for emotion regulation (Fales et al. 2009, Fu et al. 2004, Kennedy et al. 2001).

Neuroimaging may also be valuable for identifying individuals at risk for recurrent MDD. In a subset of unmedicated patients with MDD in remission, greater recall for negatively valenced self-referent words was associated with greater amygdala activation over healthy controls during a sad mood induction task (Ramel et al. 2007). Similarly, remitted MDD patients who demonstrated activation of the medial prefrontal cortex (relative to visual cortex activation) while watching sad film clips had higher rates of major depressive episode recurrence over 18 months of follow-up (Farb et al. 2011). Approaches such as these may help identify which depressed patients will likely benefit from maintenance ADM or a specific course of CBT for relapse prevention.

Only recently has neuroimaging been used to predict differential response to psychotherapy or ADM. In a PET resting-state study, Mayberg and coworkers (McGrath et al. 2013) identified several brain regions that differentially predicted remission and nonresponse among patients randomly assigned to treatment with CBT or ADM. In particular, hypoactivity in the anterior insula (relative to whole-brain metabolism) predicted remission with CBT and nonresponse with ADM, whereas hyperactivity in this region predicted remission to ADM and nonresponse to CBT. The better response to ADM in insula-hyperactive individuals was not absolute; several of these patients also did not respond to ADM. This finding conforms with the results of a meta-analysis of neuroimaging studies of MDD treatment, in which greater activity in the anterior insula predicted lower likelihood of response to both ADM and CBT treatments (Fu et al. 2013). That the insula could serve a predictive role in MDD treatment selection is credible on the basis of its significant role in several processes that are disrupted in MDD, including interoception, emotional self-awareness, decision making, cognitive control, and integration of emotionally important social information (Craig 2009, Critchley 2005, Farb et al. 2012).

Enthusiasm for these neuroimaging findings needs to be tempered with the recognition that, to date, all biological predictor studies have identified potential prescriptive factors through post hoc analyses. Proof of their utility in clinical decision making will require prospective randomized trials in which patients are stratified, using the potential predictors, into treatment conditions. Until such data are generated, the best approach to matching individual patients to treatments is to compare across studies for factors found to associate with outcomes in retrospective analyses.

FUTURE DIRECTIONS

Future studies of combination treatments for MDD should prioritize identifying the individuals who require combined treatment to recover and maintain wellness, rather than documenting the average effects of combination therapy (i.e., employ a personalized medicine approach to treating MDD). In light of expense, inconvenience, and insignificant additional gain for many patients, application of combined treatment needs to be reserved for individuals most at risk of incomplete benefit from a monotherapy or who possess the biological and psychological characteristics most predictive of benefit from combination treatment. More precise identification of these factors should be the primary focus of future research efforts.

Patient treatment preferences, beliefs about depression etiology, and treatment effects and risks must be evaluated prior to randomization but after completion of the informed consent process; this process may involve substantial provision of new information for participants. For effectiveness trials, which aim to mimic real-world clinical practice, all patients should be randomized, regardless of whether their treatment assignment would affect their intent to complete the trial. For efficacy trials, or trials examining biological or other moderators of outcomes, patients should be asked directly by senior research personnel during the consent process whether they are willing to accept randomization and start treatment, regardless of their preferences; patients who do not agree (i.e., plan to drop out if they are not randomized to their preference) should be terminated from the study prior to randomization.

Previous treatment experiences should be recorded to the degree possible. Studies routinely exclude patients who have failed to respond to the psychotherapy evaluated in that particular trial. However, the exclusion should apply to patients who have received that form of treatment, regardless of prior response. Similarly for medication, trials typically exclude patients who have not responded to treatment with the ADM used in the trial. However, failure to respond to one SSRI may predict failure to respond to another, so the exclusion should be based on failure to respond to the class of medications rather than on failure to respond to the individual agent.

Placebo control arms are not necessary for trials aiming solely to identify the efficacy of combined treatment. However, such trials should include arms for each of the two individual treatments comprising the combination treatment in order to minimize selection bias for patients seeking a particular form of treatment. Studies examining biological or psychological mediators of outcome would benefit from the use of placebo arms to isolate the shared and specific mediators of change in patients who benefit from treatment.

Outcomes should be broadened to include measures beyond symptom reduction. Specifically, measures of work, family, quality of life, and social function should be included to identify whether broader effects of combined treatment occur. Within symptom-reduction measures, outcomes can vary substantially, depending on whether a self-report scale or clinician-rated scale is used. Self-report measures of depression severity typically show higher rates of remission to treatment than do clinician-administered scales (Dunlop et al. 2010, 2011; Trivedi et al. 2006). However, clinical global impression scales may overestimate improvement compared with a patient's assessment (de Jonghe et al. 2001, Rush et al. 2005). Future determinants of remission should likely involve a blending of self- and clinician-rated scales (Uher et al. 2008).

CONCLUSIONS

Single-modality treatments for MDD produce essentially identical results, on average, though clearly some individuals benefit specifically from one form of treatment and not another. Only about one-third of monotherapy patients achieve remission of MDD, whereas about two-thirds show a clinical response. This finding has led to studies regarding the clinical outcomes of combination treatments.

For acute treatment of MDD, there is little evidence that combination therapy is superior to ADM or psychotherapy alone in mild cases of MDD. Combination treatment for MDD demonstrates its greatest advantage over single-modality treatment in patients with chronic MDD. Patients with recurrent forms of MDD likely benefit from a course of CBT-based treatment after improvement with ADM monotherapy. A simplified treatment algorithm for these recommendations is displayed in **Figure 1**.

Combination treatment extends time to recurrence or relapse in MDD patients fully or partially remitting during acute-phase treatment. For patients who receive combination treatment during the acute phase, the best long-term outcomes occur if both components of treatment continue through the maintenance phase. Discontinuing ADM after its use in an acute-phase treatment carries the greatest risk for recurrence. Patients receiving initial treatment with ADM monotherapy are less likely to experience a recurrence if they complete a short course of CBT after improving; this benefit is clear, particularly for patients with recurrent depression or those who continue to have residual depressive symptoms upon completion of acute treatment.

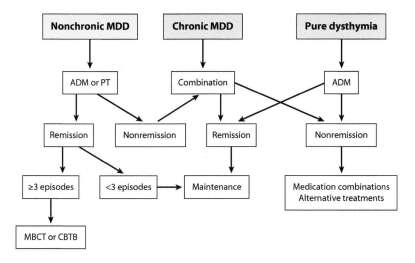

Figure 1

Evidence-based treatment algorithm for depressive disorders. For nonchronic MDD, monotherapy treatment with either ADM or psychotherapy is appropriate, with combination treatment indicated if the monotherapy treatment fails to produce remission. For chronic MDD, combination treatment is indicated from the start of treatment. For both forms of MDD, remitting patients with highly recurrent illness (≥3 lifetime episodes) may benefit from additional sessions of MBCT or CBTB directed toward relapse prevention. Patients with dysthymia should initially be treated with ADM, progressing to combination treatments if remission is not attained. Abbreviations: ADM, antidepressant medication; CBTB, cognitive behavior therapy with booster sessions; MBCT, mindfulness-based cognitive therapy; MDD, major depressive disorder; PT, psychotherapy.

Great promise is offered by the identification of baseline markers that differentially predict remission to individual or combination treatments. Further work needs to identify markers of maintenance of effects achieved during acute treatment.

DISCLOSURE STATEMENT

Dr. Craighead is a board member of Hugarheill ehf, an Icelandic company dedicated to the prevention of depression, and he receives book royalties from John Wiley & Sons. He is a consultant to the George West Mental Health Foundation that oversees Skyland Trail, a residential treatment facility in Atlanta, Georgia. Dr. Dunlop has received honoraria for consulting work performed for Bristol- Myers Squibb, MedAvante, Pfizer, and Roche. He has received research support from AstraZeneca, Bristol-Myers Squibb, Evotec, Forest, GlaxoSmithKline, Novartis, Ono Pharmaceuticals, Pfizer, Takeda, and Transcept.

ACKNOWLEDGMENTS

The authors acknowledge the support of NIH grant MH-080880 (W.E.C.) and MH-086690 (B.W.D.) as well as the support of grants (W.E.C.) from the Brock Family Foundation and the Realan Foundation. The authors express their appreciation to Linda W. Craighead, Jacqueline Larson, and Allison Meyer for reading earlier versions of this manuscript and to Jacqueline Larson for assistance in the technical preparation of the manuscript.

LITERATURE CITED

Am. Psychiatr. Assoc. (APA). 2010. *Practice Guideline for the Treatment of Patients with Major Depressive Disorder.* Arlington, VA: APA. 3rd ed.

Am. Psychiatr. Assoc. (APA). 2013. *Diagnostic and Statistical Manual of Mental Disorders.* Washington, DC: APA. 5th ed.

Angst J, Gamma A, Sellaro R, Lavori PW, Zhang H. 2003. Recurrence of bipolar disorders and major depression. A life-long perspective. *Eur. Arch. Psychiatry Clin. Neurosci.* 253:236–40

Arató M, Demeter E, Rihmer Z, Somogyi E. 1988. Retrospective psychiatric assessment of 200 suicides in Budapest. *Acta Psychiatr. Scand.* 77(4):454–56

Arroll B, Elley CR, Fishman T, Goodyear-Smith FA, Kenealy T, et al. 2009. Antidepressant versus placebo for depression in primary care. *Cochrane Database Syst. Rev.* 3:CD007954

Barlow DH, Gorman JM, Shear MK, Woods SW. 2000. Cognitive-behavioral therapy, imipramine, or their combination for panic disorder: a randomized controlled trial. *JAMA* 283:2529–36

Barth J, Paul J, Härter M, Bengel J. 2005. Inpatient psychotherapeutic treatment for cardiac patients with depression in Germany: short-term results. *Psychosoc. Med.* 2:1–8

Beach SRH, Sandeen EE, O'Leary KD. 1990. *Depression in Marriage: A Model for Etiology and Treatment.* New York: Guilford

Beck AT, Rush AJ, Shaw BF, Emery G. 1979. *Cognitive Therapy of Depression.* New York: Guilford

Beck AT, Steer RA, Brown GK. 1996. *Manual for the Beck Depression Inventory–II.* San Antonio, TX: Psychol. Corp.

Blackburn I, Eunson K, Bishop S. 1986. A two-year naturalistic follow-up of depressed patients treated with cognitive therapy, pharmacotherapy and a combination of both. *J. Affect. Disord.* 10(1):67–75

Blom MB, Spinhoven P, Hoffman T, Jonker K, Hoencamp E, et al. 2007. Severity and duration of depression, not personality factors, predict short term outcome in the treatment of major depression. *J. Affect. Disord.* 104:119–26

Bockting CH, Schene AH, Spinhoven P, Koeter MW, Wouters LF, et al. 2005. Preventing relapse/recurrence in recurrent depression with cognitive therapy: a randomized controlled trial. *J. Consult. Clin. Psychol.* 73(4):647–57

Bouton ME, Westbrook RF, Corcoran KA, Maren S. 2006. Contextual and temporal modulation of extinction: behavioral and brain mechanisms. *Biol. Psychiatry* 60:352–60

Brody AL, Saxena S, Stoessel P, Gillies LA, Fairbanks LA, et al. 2001. Regional brain metabolic changes in patients with major depression treated with either paroxetine or interpersonal therapy: preliminary findings. *Arch. Gen. Psychiatry* 58(7):631–40

Browne G, Steiner M, Roberts J, Gafni A, Byrne C, et al. 2002. Sertraline and/or interpersonal psychotherapy for patients with dysthymic disorder in primary care: 6-month comparison with longitudinal 2-year follow-up of effectiveness and costs. *J. Affect. Disord.* 68:317–30

Cent. Ment. Health, Dep. Health, Mind, NHS Confed. Ment. Health Netw., et al. 2012. *No Health Without Mental Health: Implementation Framework.* London: Dep. Health, Natl. Health Serv. **https://www.gov.uk/government/uploads/system/uploads/attachment_data/file/216870/No-Health-Without-Mental-Health-Implementation-Framework-Report-accessible-version.pdf**

Craig DB. 2009. How do you feel–now? The anterior insula and human awareness. *Nat. Rev. Neurosci.* 10(1):59–70

Craighead WE, Craighead L, Ritschel L, Zagoloff A. 2013a. Behavior therapy and cognitive-behavioral therapy. In *Handbook of Psychology*, Vol. 8: *Clinical Psychology*, pp. 291–319. Hoboken, NJ: Wiley. 2nd ed.

Craighead WE, Miklowitz DJ, Craighead LW, eds. 2013b. *Psychopathology: History, Diagnosis, and Empirical Foundations.* New York: Wiley

Craighead WE, Sheets ES, Brosse AL, Ilardi SS. 2007. Psychosocial treatments for major depressive disorder. In *A Guide to Treatments That Work*, ed. PE Nathan, JM Gorman, pp. 289–307. New York: Oxford Univ. Press. 3rd ed.

Critchley HD. 2005. Neural mechanisms of autonomic, affective, and cognitive integration. *Comp. Neurol.* 493(1):154–66

Cuijpers P, Dekker J, Hollon SD, Andersson G. 2009a. Adding psychotherapy to pharmacotherapy in the treatment of depressive disorders in adults: a meta-analysis. *J. Clin. Psychiatry* 70(9):1219–29

Cuijpers P, Smit F, Bohlmeijer E, Hollon SD, Andersson G. 2010a. Efficacy of cognitive-behavioural therapy and other psychological treatments for adult depression: meta-analytic study of publication bias. *Br. J. Psychiatry* 196(3):173–78

Cuijpers P, van Straten A, Andersson G, van Oppen P. 2008. Psychotherapy for depression in adults: a meta-analysis of comparative outcome studies. *J. Consult. Clin. Psychol.* 76(6):909–22

Cuijpers P, van Straten A, Hollon SD, Andersson G. 2010b. The contribution of active medication to combined treatments of psychotherapy and pharmacotherapy for adult depression: a meta-analysis. *Acta Psychiatr. Scand.* 121(6):415–23

Cuijpers P, van Straten A, Warmerdam L, Andersson G. 2009b. Psychotherapy versus the combination of psychotherapy and pharmacotherapy in the treatment of depression: a meta-analysis. *Depress. Anxiety* 26(3):279–88

de Jonghe F, Hendriksen M, van Aalst G, Kool S, Peen J, et al. 2004. Psychotherapy alone and combined with pharmacotherapy in the treatment of depression. *Br. J. Psychiatry* 185(1):37–45

de Jonghe F, Kool S, van Aalst G, Dekker J, Peen J. 2001. Combining psychotherapy and antidepressants in the treatment of depression. *J. Affect. Disord.* 64:217–29

de Maat S, Dekker J, Schoevers R, de Jonghe F. 2007. Relative efficacy of psychotherapy and combined therapy in the treatment of depression: a meta-analysis. *Eur. Psychiatry* 22(1):1–8

de Mello MF, Myczcowisk LM, Menezes PR. 2001. A randomized controlled trial comparing moclobemide and moclobemide plus interpersonal psychotherapy in the treatment of dysthymic disorder. *J. Psychother. Pract. Res.* 10(2):117–23

DeRubeis RJ, Hollon SD, Amsterdam JD, Shelton RC, Young PR, et al. 2005a. Cognitive therapy versus medications in the treatment of moderate to severe depression. *Arch. Gen. Psychiatry* 62(4):409–16

DeRubeis RJ, Siegle GJ, Hollon SD. 2005b. Cognitive therapy versus medication for depression: treatment outcomes and neural mechanisms. *Nat. Rev. Neurosci.* 9(10):788–96

Deutch AY, Roth RH. 2009. Neurochemical systems in the central nervous system. In *Neurobiology of Mental Illness*, ed. DS Charney, EJ Nestler, pp. 12–28. New York: Oxford Univ. Press. 3rd ed.

Dimidjian S, Hollon SD, Dobson KS, Schmaling KB, Kohlenberg RJ, et al. 2006. Randomized trial of behavioral activation, cognitive therapy, and antidepressant medication in the acute treatment of adults with major depression. *J. Consult. Clin. Psychol.* 74(4):658–70

Dobson KS, Hollon SD, Dimidjian S, Schmaling KB, Kohlenberg RJ, et al. 2008. Randomized trial of behavioral activation, cognitive therapy, and antidepressant medication in the prevention of relapse and recurrence in major depression. *J. Consult. Clin. Psychol.* 76:468–77

Driessen E, Cuijpers P, de Maat SCM, Abbass AA, de Jonghe F, Dekker JJM. 2010. The efficacy of short-term psychodynamic psychotherapy for depression: a meta-analysis. *Clin. Psychol. Rev.* 30:25–36

Dunkin JJ, Leuchter AF, Cook IA, Kasl-Godley JE, Abrams M, Rosenberg-Thompson S. 2000. Executive dysfunction predicts nonresponse to fluoxetine in major depression. *J. Affect. Disord.* 60(1):13–23

Dunlop BW. 2013. Depressive recurrence on antidepressant treatment (DRAT): 4 next step options. *Curr. Psychiatry* 12(5):54–55

Dunlop BW, Binder EB, Cubells JF, Goodman MG, Kelley ME, et al. 2012a. Predictors of remission in depression to individual and combined treatments (PReDICT): study protocol for a randomized controlled trial. *Trials* 13:106

Dunlop BW, Holland P, Bao W, Ninan PT, Keller MB. 2012b. Recovery and subsequent recurrence in patients with recurrent major depressive disorder. *J. Psychiatr. Res.* 46(6):708–15

Dunlop BW, Kelley ME, Mletzko TC, Velasquez CM, Craighead WE, Mayberg HS. 2012c. Depression beliefs, treatment preference, and outcomes in a randomized trial for major depressive disorder. *J. Psychiatr. Res.* 46(3):375–81

Dunlop BW, Li T, Kornstein SG, Friedman ES, Rothschild AJ, et al. 2010. Correlation between patient and clinician assessments of depression severity in the PREVENT study. *Psychiatry Res.* 177:177–83

Dunlop BW, Li T, Kornstein SG, Friedman ES, Rothschild AJ, et al. 2011. Concordance between clinician and patient ratings as predictors of response, remission and recurrence in major depressive disorder. *J. Psychiatr. Res.* 45:96–103

Dunlop BW, Thase ME, Wun CC, Fayyad R, Guico-Pabia CJ, et al. 2012d. A meta-analysis of factors impacting detection of antidepressant efficacy in clinical trials: the importance of academic sites. *Neuropsychopharmacology* 37(13):2830–36

Dunlop BW, Vaughan CL. 2010. Survey of investigators' opinions on the acceptability of interactions with patients participating in clinical trials. *J. Clin. Psychopharmacol.* 30:323–27

Duval S, Tweedie R. 2000. Trim and fill: a simple funnel-plot-based method of testing and adjusting for publication bias in meta-analysis. *Biometrics* 56:455–63

Egede LE. 2006. Disease-focused or integrated treatment: diabetes and depression. *Med. Clin. North Am.* 90(4):627–46

Encinas JM, Vaahtokari A, Enikolopov G. 2006. Fluoxetine targets early progenitor cells in the adult brain. *Proc. Natl. Acad. Sci. USA* 103:8233–38

Evans MD, Hollon SD, DeRubeis RJ, Piasecki JM, Grove WM, et al. 1992. Differential relapse following cognitive therapy and pharmacotherapy for depression. *Arch. Gen. Psychiatry* 49(10):802–8

Fales CL, Barch DM, Rundle MA, Mintun MA, Mathews J, et al. 2009. Antidepressant treatment normalizes hypoactivity in dorsolateral prefrontal cortex during emotional interference processing major depression. *J. Affect. Disord.* 112:206–11

Farb NAS, Anderson AK, Bloch RT, Segal ZV. 2011. Mood linked responses in medial prefrontal cortex predict relapse in patients with recurrent unipolar depression. *Biol. Psychiatry* 70(4):366–72

Farb NAS, Segal ZV, Anderson AK. 2012. Attentional modulation of primary interoceptive and exteroceptive cortices. *Cereb. Cortex* 23(1):114–26

Fava GA, Grandi S, Zielezny M, Rafanelli C, Canestrari R. 1996. Four-year outcome for cognitive behavioral treatment of residual symptoms in major depression. *Am. J. Psychiatry* 153(7):945–47

Fava GA, Rafanelli C, Grandi S, Conti S, Belluardo P. 1998. Prevention of recurrent depression with cognitive behavioral therapy: preliminary findings. *Arch. Gen. Psychiatry* 55(9):816–20

Fava M, Rush AJ, Alpert JE, Balasubramani GK, Wisniewski SR, et al. 2008. Difference in treatment outcome in outpatients with anxious versus nonanxious depression: STAR*D report. *Am. J. Psychiatry* 165(3):342–51

Fergusson DM, Woodward LJ. 2002. Mental health, educational, and social role outcomes of adolescents with depression. *Arch. Gen. Psychiatry* 59:225–31

Fournier JC, DeRubeis RJ, Shelton RC, Hollon SD, Amsterdam JD, Gallop R. 2009. Prediction of response to medication and cognitive therapy in the treatment of moderate to severe depression. *J. Consult. Clin. Psychol.* 77(4):775–87

Frank E, Cassano GB, Rucci P, Thompson WK, Kraemer HC, et al. 2011. Predictors and moderators of time to remission of major depression with interpersonal psychotherapy and SSRI pharmacotherapy. *Psychol. Med.* 41(1):151–62

Frank E, Grochocinski VJ, Spanier CA, Buysse DJ, Cherry CR. 2000. Interpersonal psychotherapy and antidepressant medication: evaluation of a sequential treatment strategy in women with recurrent major depression. *J. Clin. Psychiatry* 61(1):51–57

Frank E, Kupfer DJ, Buysse DJ, Swartz HA, Pilkonis PA, et al. 2007. Randomized trial of weekly, twice-monthly, and monthly interpersonal psychotherapy as maintenance treatment for women with recurrent depression. *Am. J. Psychiatry* 164:761–67

Frank E, Kupfer DJ, Perel JM, Cornes C, Jarrett DB, et al. 1990. Three-year outcomes for maintenance therapies in recurrent depression. *Arch. Gen. Psychiatry* 47:1093–99

Frank E, Prien RF, Jarrett RB, Keller MB, Kupfer DJ, et al. 1991. Conceptualization and rationale for consensus definitions of terms in major depressive disorder. Remission, recovery, relapse, and recurrence. *Arch. Gen. Psychiatry* 48:851–55

Frank JD, Frank JB. 1991. *Persuasion and Healing: A Comparative Study of Psychotherapy.* Baltimore, MD: Johns Hopkins Univ. Press. 3rd ed.

Friedman MA, Detweiler-Bedell JB, Leventhal HE, Horne R, Keitner GI, Miller IW. 2004. Combined psychotherapy and pharmacotherapy for the treatment of major depressive disorder. *Clin. Psychol. Sci. Pract.* 11(1):47–68

Fu CHY, Steiner H, Costafreda SG. 2013. Predictive neural markers of clinical response in depression: a meta-analysis of functional and structural neuroimaging studies of pharmacological and psychological therapies. *Neurobiol. Dis.* 52:75–83

Fu CHY, Williams SC, Cleare AH, Brammer MJ, Walsh ND et al. 2004. Attenuation of the neural response to sad faces in major depression by antidepressant treatment: a prospective, event-related functional magnetic resonance imaging study. *Arch. Gen. Psychiatry* 61:877–89

Gelenberg AJ, Freeman MP, Markowitz JC, Rosenbaum JF, Thase ME, et al. 2010. *Practice Guideline for the Treatment of Patients with Major Depressive Disorder.* Arlington, VA: Am. Psychiatr. Assoc. 3rd ed.

Goldapple K, Segal Z, Garson C, Lau M, Bieling P, et al. 2004. Modulation of cortical-limbic pathways in major depression: treatment-specific effects of cognitive behavior therapy. *Arch. Gen. Psychiatry* 61(1):34–41

González HM, Vega WA, Williams DR, Tarraf W, West BT, Neighbors HW. 2010. Depression care in the United States: too little for too few. *Arch. Gen. Psychiatry* 67(1):37–46

Greenberg RP. 1999. Common psychosocial factors in psychiatric drug therapy. In *The Heart and Soul of Change: Common Factors in Effective Psychotherapy, Medicine, and Human Services,* ed. MA Hubble, BL Duncan, S Miller, pp. 297–328. Washington, DC: Am. Psychiatr. Assoc.

Haaga DA, DeRubeis RJ, Stewart BL, Beck AT. 1991. Relationship of intelligence with cognitive therapy outcome. *Behav. Res. Ther.* 29(3):277–81

Hamilton M. 1960. A rating scale for depression. *J. Neurol. Neurosurg. Psychiatry* 23:56–62

Hankin BL, Abramson LY. 1999. Development of gender differences in depression: description and possible explanations. *Ann. Med.* 31(6):372–79

Hansen R, Gaynes B, Thieda P, Gartlehner G, Deveaugh-Geiss A, et al. 2008. Meta-analysis of major depressive disorder relapse and recurrence with second-generation antidepressants. *Psychiatr. Serv.* 59(10):1121–30

Higgins JPT, Green S, eds. 2011. *Cochrane Handbook for Systematic Reviews of Interventions,* Version 5.1.0 (updated March 20, 2011). Cochrane Collab. **http://www.cochrane-handbook.org**

Hirschfeld RM, Russell JM, Delgado PL, Fawcett J, Friedman RA, et al. 1998. Predictors of response to acute treatment of chronic and double depression with sertraline or imipramine. *J. Clin. Psychiatry* 59(12):669–75

Hollon SD, DeRubeis RJ, Seligman MEP. 1992. Cognitive therapy and the prevention of depression. *Appl. Prev. Psychol.* 1(2):89–95

Hollon SD, DeRubeis RJ, Shelton RC, Amsterdam JD, Salomon RM, et al. 2005a. Prevention of relapse following cognitive therapy versus medications in moderate to severe depression. *Arch. Gen. Psychiatry* 62(4):417–22

Hollon SD, Jarrett RB, Nierenberg AA, Thase ME, Trivedi M, Rush AJ. 2005b. Psychotherapy and medication in the treatment of adult and geriatric depression: which monotherapy or combined treatment? *J. Clin. Psychiatry* 66(4):455–68

Hollon SD, Stewart MO, Strunk D. 2006. Enduring effects for cognitive behavior therapy in the treatment of depression and anxiety. *Annu. Rev. Psychol.* 57:285–315

Hughes S, Cohen D. 2009. A systematic review of long-term studies of drug treated and non-drug treated depression. *J. Affect. Disord.* 118:9–18

Iosifescu DV, Nierenberg AA, Alpert JE, Smith M, Bitran S, et al. 2003. The impact of medical comorbidity on acute treatment in major depressive disorder. *Am. J. Psychiatry* 160(2):2122–27

Jacobson NS, Martell CR, Dimidjian S. 2001. Behavioral activation treatment for depression: returning to contextual roots. *Clin. Psychol. Sci. Pract.* 8(3):255–70

Joyce PR, Mulder RT, Luty SE, Sullivan PF, McKenzie JM, et al. 2002. Patterns and predictors of remission, response and recovery in major depression treated with fluoxetine or nortriptyline. *Aust. N. Z. J. Psychiatry* 36(3):384–91

Judd LL. 1997. The clinical course of unipolar major depressive disorders. *Arch. Gen. Psychiatry* 52:989–91

Judd LL, Paulus MJ, Schettler PJ, Akiskal HS, Endicott J, et al. 2000. Does incomplete recovery from first lifetime major depressive episode herald a chronic course of illness? *Am. J. Psychiatry* 157(9):1501–4

Karp JF, Buysse DJ, Houck PR, Cherry C, Kupfer DJ, Frank E. 2004. Relationship of variability in residual symptoms with recurrence of major depressive disorder during maintenance treatment. *Am. J. Psychiatry* 161:1877–84

Keller MB, Kocsis JH, Thase ME, Gelenberg AJ, Rush AJ, et al. 1998. Maintenance phase efficacy of sertraline for chronic depression: a randomized controlled trial. *JAMA* 280:1665–1672

Keller MB, McCullough JP, Klein DN, Arnow B, Dunner DL, et al. 2000. A comparison of nefazodone, the cognitive behavioral-analysis system of psychotherapy, and their combination for the treatment of chronic depression. *N. Engl. J. Med.* 342(20):1462–70

Keller MB, Trivedi MH, Thase ME, Shelton RC, Kornstein SG, et al. 2007. The Prevention of Recurrent Episodes of Depression with Venlafaxine for Two Years (PREVENT) study: outcomes from the 2-year and combined maintenance phases. *J. Clin. Psychiatry* 68(8):1246–56

Kemp AH, Gordon E, Rush AJ, Williams LM. 2008. Improving the prediction of treatment response in depression: integration of clinical, cognitive, psychophysiological, neuroimaging and genetic measures. *CNS Spectr.* 13(12):1066–86

Kennedy SH, Evans KR, Krüger S, Mayberg HS, Meyer JH, et al. 2001. Changes in regional brain glucose metabolism measured with positron emission tomography after paroxetine treatment of major depression. *Am. J. Psychiatry* 158(6):899–905

Kennedy SH, Giacobbe P. 2007. Treatment resistant depression—advances in somatic therapies. *Ann. Clin. Psychiatry* 19(4):279–87

Kennedy SH, Konarski JZ, Segal ZV, Lau MA, Bieling PJ, et al. 2007. Differences in brain glucose metabolism between responders to CBT and venlafaxine in a 16-week randomized controlled trial. *Am. J. Psychiatry* 164(5):778–88

Kessler RC, Berglund P, Demler O, Jin R, Merikangas KR, Walters EE. 2005. Lifetime prevalence and age-of-onset distributions of DSM-IV disorders in the National Comorbidity Survey Replication. *Arch. Gen. Psychiatry* 62(6):593–602

Khan A, Faucett J, Lichtenberg P, Kirsch I, Brown WA. 2012. A systematic review of comparative efficacy of treatments and controls for depression. *PLoS ONE* 7(7):e41778

Klein DF. 1996. Preventing hung juries about therapy studies. *J. Consult. Clin. Psychol.* 64(1):81–87

Klein DN, Arnow BA, Barkin JL, Dowling F, Kocsis JH, et al. 2009. Early adversity in chronic depression: clinical correlates and response to pharmacotherapy. *Depress. Anxiety* 26:701–10

Klein DN, Black SR. 2013. Persistent depressive disorder. Major depression. See Craighead et al. 2013b, pp. 334–55

Klerman GL, Weissman MM, Rounsaville BJ, Chevron ES. 1984. *Interpersonal Psychotherapy of Depression.* New York: Basic Books

Kocsis JH, Leon AC, Markowitz JC, Manber R, Arnow B, et al. 2009. Patient preference as a moderator of outcome for chronic forms of major depressive disorder treated with nefazodone, cognitive behavioral analysis system of psychotherapy, or their combination. *J. Clin. Psychiatry* 70(3):354–61

Kocsis JH, Thase ME, Trivedi MH, Shelton RC, Kornstein SG, et al. 2007. Prevention of recurrent episodes of depression with venlafaxine ER in a 1-year maintenance phase from the PREVENT Study. *J. Clin. Psychiatry* 68(7):1014–23

Konarski JZ, Kennedy SH, Segal ZV, Lau MA, Bieling PJ, et al. 2009. Predictors of nonresponse to cognitive behavioural therapy or venlafaxine using glucose metabolism in major depressive disorder. *J. Psychiatry Neurosci.* 34(3):175–80

Kovacs M, Rush A, Beck AT, Hollon SD. 1981. Depressed outpatients treated with cognitive therapy or pharmacotherapy: a one-year follow-up. *Arch. Gen. Psychiatry* 38(1):33–39

Kraus DR, Castonguay L, Boswell JF, Nordberg SS, Hayes JA. 2011. Therapist effectiveness: implications for accountability and patient care. *Psychother. Res.* 21(3):267–76

Kwan BM, Dimidjian S, Rizvi SL. 2010. Treatment preference, engagement, and clinical improvement in pharmacotherapy versus psychotherapy for depression. *Behav. Res. Ther.* 48(8):799–804

Lesperance F, Frasure-Smith N, Koszycki D, Laliberte M-A, van Zyl LT, et al. 2007. Effects of citalopram and interpersonal psychotherapy on depression in patients with coronary artery disease. *JAMA* 297:367–79

Lewinsohn PM, Rohde P, Klein DN, Seeley JR. 1999. Natural course of adolescent major depressive disorder: I. Continuity into young adulthood. *J. Am. Acad. Child Adolesc. Psychiatry* 38:56–63

Leykin Y, DeRubeis RJ, Gallop R, Amsterdam JD, Shelton RC, Hollon SD. 2007. The relation of patients' treatment preferences to outcome in a randomized clinical trial. *Behav. Ther.* 38(3):209–17

Lieberman JA, Greenhouse J, Hamer RM, Krishnan KR, Nemeroff CB, et al. 2005. Comparing the effects of antidepressants: consensus guidelines for evaluating quantitative reviews of antidepressant efficacy. *Neuropsychopharmacology* 30(3):445–60

Loeb DF, Ghushchyan V, Huebschmann AG, Lobo IE, Bayliss EA. 2012. Association of treatment modality for depression and burden of comorbid chronic illness in a nationally representative sample in the United States. *Gen. Hosp. Psychiatry* 34(6):588–97

Lorant V, Deliège D, Eaton W, Robert A, Philippot P, Ansseau M. 2003. Socioeconomic inequalities in depression: a meta-analysis. *Am. J. Epidemiol.* 157:98–112

Ma SH, Teasdale JD. 2004. Mindfulness-based cognitive therapy for depression: replication and exploration of differential relapse prevention effects. *J. Consult. Clin. Psychol.* 72(1):31–40

Maina G, Rosso G, Bogetto F. 2009. Brief dynamic therapy combined with pharmacotherapy in the treatment of major depressive disorder: long-term results. *J. Affect. Disord.* 114:200–7

Markowitz JC, Kocsis JH, Bleiberg KL, Christos PJ, Sacks M. 2005. A comparative trial of psychotherapy and pharmacotherapy for 'pure' dysthymic patients. *J. Affect. Disord.* 89:167–75

Mayberg HS, Brannan SK, Mahurin RK, Jerabek PA, Brickman JS, et al. 1997. Cingulate function in depression: a potential predictor of treatment response. *Neuroreport* 8:1057–61

Mazure CM, Bruce ML, Maciejewski PK, Jacobs SC. 2000. Adverse life events and cognitive-personality characteristics in the prediction of major depression and antidepressant response. *Am. J. Psychiatry* 157(6):896–903

McGorry PD, Nelson B, Goldstone S, Yung AR. 2010. Clinical staging: a heuristic and practical strategy for new research and better health and social outcomes for psychotic and related mood disorders. *Can. J. Psychiatry* 55(8):486–96

McGrath CL, Kelley ME, Holtzheimer PE, Dunlop BW, Craighead WE, et al. 2013. Toward a neuroimaging treatment selection biomarker for major depressive disorder. *JAMA Psychiatry* 70:821–29

Miller IW, Norman WH, Keitner GI. 1989. Cognitive-behavioral treatment of depressed inpatients: six- and twelve-month follow-up. *Am. J. Psychiatry* 146:1274–79

Molenaar PJ, Dekker J, Van R, Hendricksen M, Vink A, Schoevers RA. 2007. Does adding psychotherapy to pharmacotherapy improve social functioning in the treatment of outpatient depression? *Depress. Anxiety* 24:553–62

Montgomery SA, Åsberg M. 1979. A new depression scale designed to be sensitive to change. *Br. J. Psychiatry* 134:382–89

Mueller TI, Leon AC, Keller MB, Solomon DA, Endicott J, et al. 1999. Recurrence after recovery from major depressive disorder during 15 years of observational follow-up. *Am. J. Psychiatry* 156:1000–6

Murray CJL, Lopez AD. 1997. Global mortality, disability, and the contribution of risk factors: Global Burden of Disease Study. *Lancet* 349:1436–42

Nanni V, Uher R, Danese A. 2012. Childhood maltreatment predicts unfavorable course of illness and treatment outcome in depression: a meta-analysis. *Am. J. Psychiatry* 169(2):141–51

Nemeroff CB, Heim CM, Thase ME, Klein DN, Rush AJ, et al. 2003. Differential responses to psychotherapy versus pharmacotherapy in patients with chronic forms of major depression and childhood trauma. *Proc. Natl. Acad. Sci. USA* 100(24):14293–96

Nezu AM, Nezu CM, D'Zurilla TJ. 2013. *Problem-Solving Therapy*. New York: Springer

Ninan PT, Rush AJ, Crits-Christoph P, Kornstein SG, Manber R, et al. 2002. Symptomatic and syndromal anxiety in chronic forms of major depression: effect of nefazodone, cognitive behavioral analysis system of psychotherapy, and their combination. *J. Clin. Psychiatry* 63(5):434–41

Ochsner KN, Ray RR, Hughes B, McRae K, Cooper JC, et al. 2009. Bottom-up and top-down processes in emotion generation: common and distinct neural mechanisms. *Psychol. Sci.* 20(11):1322–31

Oxman TE, Hegel MT, Hull JG, Dietrich AJ. 2008. Problem-solving treatment and coping styles in primary care for minor depression. *J. Consult. Clin. Psychol.* 76(6):933–43

Pampallona S, Bollini P, Tibaldi G, Kupelnick B, Munizza C. 2004. Combined pharmacotherapy and psychological treatment for depression: a systematic review. *Arch. Gen. Psychiatry* 61(7):714–19

Paul GL. 1969. Behavior modification research: design and tactics. In *Behavior Therapy: Appraisal and Status*, ed. CM Franks, pp. 29–62. New York: McGraw-Hill

Paykel ES, Ramana R, Cooper Z, Hayhurst H, Kerr J, Barocka A. 1995. Residual symptoms after partial remission: an important outcome in depression. *Psychol. Med.* 25(6):1171–80

Paykel ES, Scott J, Teasdale JD, Johnson AL, Garland A, et al. 1999. Prevention of relapse in residual depression by cognitive therapy: a controlled trial. *Arch. Gen. Psychiatry* 56(9):829–35

Perlis RH, Nierenberg AA, Alpert JE, Pava J, Matthews JD, et al. 2002. Effects of adding cognitive therapy to fluoxetine dose increase on risk of relapse and residual depressive symptoms in continuation treatment of major depressive disorder. *J. Clin. Psychopharmacol.* 22(5):474–80

Persons JB. 1993. Outcome of psychotherapy for unipolar depression. In *Handbook of Effective Psychotherapy*, ed. TR Giles, pp. 305–23. New York: Plenum

Piet J, Hougaard E. 2011. The effect of mindfulness-based cognitive therapy for prevention of relapse in recurrent major depressive disorder: a systematic review and meta-analysis. *Clin. Psychol. Rev.* 31:1032–40

Post RM. 1992. Transduction of psychosocial stress into the neurobiology of recurrent affective disorder. *Am. J. Psychiatry* 149:999–1010

Price JL, Drevets W. 2011. Neural circuits underlying the pathophysiology of mood disorders. *Trends Cogn. Sci.* 16(1):61–71

Ramel W, Goldin PR, Eyler LT, Brown GG, Gotlib IH, McQuaid JR. 2007. Amygdala reactivity and mood-congruent memory in individuals at risk for depressive relapse. *Biol. Psychiatry* 61(2):231–39

Ramirez CL, Ritschel LA, Mayberg HS. 2013. *Adjunctive treatment with behavioral activation to enhance functional recovery following deep brain stimulation for depression.* Poster accepted for presentation at Assoc. Behav. Cogn. Ther., Nov., Nashville, TN

Raue PJ, Schulberg HC, Heo M, Klimstra S, Bruce ML. 2009. Patients' depression treatment preferences and initiation, adherence, and outcome: a randomized primary care study. *Psychiatr. Serv.* 60(3):337–43

Ravindran AV, Anisman H, Merali Z, Charbonneau Y, Telner J, et al. 1999. Treatment of primary dysthymia with group cognitive therapy and pharmacotherapy: clinical symptoms and functional impairments. *Am. J. Psychiatry* 156(10):1608–17

Reynolds CF III, Frank E, Perel JM, Imber SD, Cornes C, et al. 1999. Nortriptyline and interpersonal psychotherapy as maintenance therapies for recurrent major depression: a randomized controlled trial in patients older than 59 years. *JAMA* 281:39–45

Rich CL, Fowler RC, Fogarty LA, Young D. 1988. San Diego Suicide Study: III. Relationships between diagnoses and stressors. *Arch. Gen. Psychiatry* 45(6):589–92

Ritchey M, Dolcos F, Eddington KM, Strauman TJ, Cabeza R. 2011. Neural correlates of emotion processing in depression: changes with cognitive behavioral therapy and predictors of treatment response. *J. Psychiatr. Res.* 45(5):577–87

Ritschel LA, Gillespie CF, Arnarson EO, Craighead WE. 2013. Major depression. See Craighead et al. 2013b, pp. 285–333

Rohde P, Lewinsohn PM, Klein DN, Seeley JR, Gau JM. 2012. Key characteristics of major depressive disorder occurring in childhood, adolescence, emerging adulthood, and adulthood. *Clin. Psychol. Sci.* 1:41–53

Rounsaville BJ, Klerman GL, Weissman MM. 1981. Do psychotherapy and pharmacotherapy for depression conflict? Empirical evidence from a clinical trial. *Arch. Gen. Psychiatry* 38:24–29

Rush AJ, Kraemer HC, Sackeim HA, Fava M, Trivedi MH, et al. 2006. Report by the ACNP Task Force on response and remission in major depressive disorder. *Neuropsychopharmacology* 31(9):1841–53

Rush AJ, Trivedi MH, Carmody TJ, Ibrahim HM, Markowitz JC, et al. 2005. Self-reported depressive symptom measures: sensitivity to detecting change in a randomized, controlled trial of chronically depressed, non-psychotic outpatients. *Neuropsychopharmacology* 30:405–16

Rush AJ, Trivedi MH, Ibrahim HM, Carmody TJ, Arnow B, et al. 2003. The 16-item Quick Inventory of Depressive Symptomatology (QIDS) Clinician Rating (QIDS-C) and Self-Report (QIDS-SR): a psychometric evaluation in patients with chronic major depression. *Biol. Psychiatry* 54:573–83

Schatzberg AF, Rush AJ, Arnow BA, Banks PLC, Blalock JA, et al. 2005. Chronic depression. Medication (nefazodone) or psychotherapy (CBASP) is effective when the other is not. *Arch. Gen. Psychiatry* 62(5):513–20

Schramm E, van Calker D, Dykierek P, Lieb K, Kech S, et al. 2007. An intensive treatment program of interpersonal psychotherapy plus pharmacotherapy for depressed inpatients: acute and long-term results. *Am. J. Psychiatry* 164(5):768–77

Scott J, Teasdale JD, Paykel ES, Johnson AL, Abbott R, et al. 2000. Effects of cognitive therapy on psychological symptoms and social functioning in residual depression. *Br. J. Psychiatry* 177:440–46

Segal ZV, Williams JG, Teasdale JD. 2002. *Mindfulness-Based Cognitive Therapy For Depression: A New Approach To Preventing Relapse*. New York: Guilford

Shea MT, Elkin I, Imber SD, Sotsky SM, Watkins JT, et al. 1992. Course of depressive symptoms over follow-up. Findings from the National Institute of Mental Health Treatment of Depression Collaborative Research Program. *Arch. Gen. Psychiatry* 49(10):782–87

Sheets ES, Craighead LW, Brosse AL, Hauser M, Madsen JW, Craighead WE. 2013. Prevention of recurrence of major depression among emerging adults by a group cognitive-behavioral/interpersonal intervention. *J. Affect. Disord.* 147:425–30

Siegle GJ, Thompson WK, Collier A, Berman SR, Feldmiller J, et al. 2012. Toward clinically useful neuroimaging in depression treatment. *Arch. Gen. Psychiatry* 69(9):913–24

Simons AD, Murphy GE, Levine JL, Wetzel RD. 1986. Cognitive therapy and pharmacotherapy for depression: sustained improvement over one year. *Arch. Gen. Psychiatry* 43:43–48

Sotsky SM, Glass DR, Shea MT, Pilkonis PA, Collins JF, et al. 1991. Patient predictors of response to psychotherapy and pharmacotherapy: findings in the NIMH Treatment of Depression Collaborative Research Program. *Am. J. Psychiatry* 148(8):997–1008

Souery D, Oswald P, Massat I, Bailer U, Bollen J, et al. 2007. Clinical factors associated with treatment resistance in major depressive disorder: results from a European multicenter study. *J. Clin. Psychiatry* 68:1062–70

Spielmans GI, Berman MI, Usitalo AN. 2011. Psychotherapy versus second-generation antidepressants in the treatment of depression: a meta-analysis. *J. Nerv. Ment. Dis.* 199(3):142–49

Steidtmann D, Manber R, Arnow BA, Klein DN, Markowitz JC, et al. 2012. Patient treatment preference as a predictor of response and attrition in treatment for chronic depression. *Depress. Anxiety* 29(10):896–905

Teasdale JD. 1997. The relationship between cognition and emotion: the mind-in-place in mood disorders. In *Science and Practice of Cognitive Behavior Therapy*, ed. DM Clark, CG Fairburn, pp. 67–93. Oxford, UK: Oxford Univ. Press

Teasdale JD, Segal ZV, Williams JM, Ridgeway VA, Soulsby JM, Lau MA. 2000. Prevention of relapse/recurrence in major depression by mindfulness-based cognitive therapy. *J. Consult. Clin. Psychol.* 68(4):615–23

Thase ME, Buysse DJ, Frank E, Cherry CR, Cornes CL, et al. 1997. Which depressed patients will respond to interpersonal psychotherapy? The role of abnormal EEG sleep profiles. *Am. J. Psychiatry* 154(4):502–9

Thase ME, Reynolds CF, Frank E, Simon AD. 1994. Response to cognitive-behavioral therapy in chronic depression. *J. Psychother. Pract. Res.* 3(3):204–14

Thase ME, Simons AD, McGeary J, Cahalane JF, Hughes C, et al. 1992. Relapse after cognitive behavior therapy of depression: potential implications for longer courses of treatment. *Am. J. Psychiatry* 149(8):1046–52

Trivedi MH, Rush AJ, Wisniewski SR, Nierenberg AA, Warden D, et al. 2006. Evaluation of outcomes with citalopram for depression using measurement-based care in STAR*D: implications for clinical practice. *Am. J. Psychiatry* 163(1):28–40

Uher RR, Farmer AA, Maier WW, Rietschel MM, Hauser JJ, et al. 2008. Measuring depression: comparison and integration of three scales in the GENDEP study. *Psychol. Med.* 38(2):289–300

Vittengl JR, Clark LA, Dunn TW, Jarrett RB. 2007. Reducing relapse and recurrence in unipolar depression: a comparative meta-analysis of cognitive-behavioral therapy's effects. *J. Consult. Clin. Psychol.* 75(3):475–88

von Wolff A, Hölzel LP, Westphal A, Härter M, Kriston L. 2012. Combination of pharmacotherapy and psychotherapy in the treatment of chronic depression: a systematic review and meta-analysis. *BMC Psychiatry* 12:61

Wager TD, Barrett LF, Bliss-Moreau E, Lindquist K, Duncan S, et al. 2008. Prefrontal-subcortical pathways mediating successful emotion regulation. *Neuron* 59:1037–50

Wang L, Hermens DF, Hickie IB, Lagopoulos J. 2012. A systematic review of resting-state functional-MRI studies in major depression. *J. Affect. Disord.* 142:6–12

Waraich P, Goldner EM, Somers JM, Hsu L. 2004. Prevalence and incidence studies of mood disorders: a systematic review of the literature. *Can. J. Psychiatry* 49(2):124–38

Wells KB, Stewart A, Hays RD, Burnam MA, Rogers W, et al. 1989. The functioning and well-being of depressed patients. Results from the Medical Outcomes Study. *JAMA* 262(7):914–19

World Health Organ. (WHO). 2004. *Global Burden of Disease: 2004 update*. Geneva: WHO. **http://www.who.int/healthinfo/global_burden_disease/GBD_report_2004update_full.pdf**

Zimmerman M, Martinez J, Attiullah N, Friedman M, Toba C, et al. 2012. Further evidence that the cutoff to define remission on the 17-item Hamilton Depression Rating Scale should be lowered. *Depress. Anxiety* 29(2):159–65

Sport and Nonsport Etiologies of Mild Traumatic Brain Injury: Similarities and Differences

Amanda R. Rabinowitz,[1] Xiaoqi Li,[2] and Harvey S. Levin[2]

[1]Department of Neurosurgery, University of Pennsylvania School of Medicine, Philadelphia, Pennsylvania 19104; email: rabinowitz.a@gmail.com

[2]Physical Medicine and Rehabilitation Alliance, Baylor College of Medicine and the University of Texas-Houston Medical School, Houston, Texas 77030

Annu. Rev. Psychol. 2014. 65:301–31

First published online as a Review in Advance on September 11, 2013

The *Annual Review of Psychology* is online at http://psych.annualreviews.org

This article's doi: 10.1146/annurev-psych-010213-115103

Keywords

concussion, neuropsychology, diffuse axonal injury, neuroimaging

Abstract

Mild traumatic brain injury (mTBI) has recently gained appreciation as a significant public health problem, which has highlighted just how little is known about its proximal and long-term effects. A major challenge in the study of mTBI is the heterogeneity of the condition. Research on mTBI has historically separated sport and nonsport etiologies, and the extent to which research from one of these samples translates to the other is unclear. This review examines the literature on mTBI, with a focus on comparing sport and nonsport etiologies with regard to the latest research on biomechanics, pathophysiology, neurocognitive effects, and neuroimaging. Issues of particular relevance to sports injuries, such as exercise, repetitive injuries, subconcussive blows, and chronic injury effects, are also reviewed.

Contents

INTRODUCTION

Mild traumatic brain injury (mTBI) has recently gained appreciation as a major public health problem, in large part due to the tragic deaths of high-profile athletes who sustained sports concussions and/or repetitive subconcussive head impacts and had evidence of neuropathology at autopsy (McKee et al. 2009). This new focus has highlighted just how little is known about the proximal and long-term effects of these injuries. A major challenge in the study of mTBI is the heterogeneity of the condition. Although the majority of individuals with mTBI recover without complication, a significant minority experience immediate and long-term consequences that severely interfere with their quality of life. Because patients vary widely with regard to injury etiology, it is very difficult to generalize research findings to a particular case. This causes much uncertainty and confusion for both patients and healthcare providers.

Research on mTBI has historically separated sport and nonsport etiologies—with samples including either exclusively participants with sports-related injuries or patients with mixed etiologies presenting for treatment. The extent to which research from one of these samples translates to the other remains an open question. In general, the evidence suggests that sports-related concussions are associated with less disability and more rapid recovery than are concussions in nonathletes caused by falls, motor vehicle accidents, or other mechanisms. However, despite relatively better short-term outcomes, athletes may be more vulnerable to the deleterious long-term effects of mTBI because they are often subjected to repetitive trauma and greater levels of physical exertion during recovery.

This review examines the literature on mTBI, with a focus on comparing sport and nonsport etiologies. We hope that this comparison will help elucidate the possibly distinct pathophysiological and neuroreparative processes at play in mTBI and suggest risk and resiliency factors for persistent dysfunction. We compare etiologies with regard to the latest research on biomechanics, pathophysiology, neurocognitive effects, and neuroimaging. We also review issues of particular relevance to sports injuries, such as physical exertion, repetitive injuries, subconcussive blows, and chronic injury effects.

TERMINOLOGY

Some have argued that concussion is a distinct disease entity from mTBI (McCrory et al. 2013). However, the terms are sometimes used interchangeably. Most agree that concussion represents a form of mTBI. Typically, the term "concussion" is used to refer to mTBIs that cause no more than transient disruption of function. We acknowledge that there is a wide spectrum of pathophysiological severity associated with the mild brain injuries that receive a concussion or mTBI diagnosis. However, current diagnostic criteria and consensus definitions allow for considerable overlap between the two classifiers. Within this review, both terms are used. For the most part, our choice of terms reflects how samples were characterized by the studies cited.

SIGNIFICANCE

Over one million concussions occur annually in the United States (Faul et al. 2010), and concussions account for over 1% of all US emergency department visits (Bazarian et al. 2005). Many of these injuries occur as a result of athletic participation. The Centers for Disease Control and Prevention estimates that approximately 300,000 sports-related concussions occur annually (Thunnan et al. 1998). This figure may represent a substantial underestimate because as many as half of sports-related concussions go unreported (McCrea et al. 2004).

These injuries exert a significant toll on patients and society. Concussions lead to cognitive, emotional, and somatic symptoms that interfere with academic and job performance. Furthermore, many patients go on to experience persistent dysfunction. It has been reported that more than one-third of patients in prospective studies did not resume work by three months after their injury (Boake et al. 2005), and lingering cognitive complaints are reported by as many as 15% of patients one year postinjury (Røe et al. 2009). However, the accuracy of the 15% estimate has been called into question, with some noting that rates of persisting problems vary across samples, and the true incidence of poor outcomes is likely to be much less than the rates observed in retrospective studies that may oversample patients with complicated recoveries (Iverson 2005). Furthermore, poor association between long-term symptoms and early neurological findings has led many to believe that persistent symptomatology may be more related to psychological and contextual factors than underlying neuronal dysfunction (Ponsford et al. 2012, Williams et al. 2010). However, it is also possible that early neurological signs are not sufficiently sensitive to the neuropathology underlying long-term symptoms.

Meta-analyses of neuropsychological outcomes in mTBI suggest that mild impairment up to three months postinjury is typical for patients from the general population (Belanger et al. 2005) but unusual for athletes, who tend to show full recovery within 10 days postsports concussion (Belanger & Vanderploeg 2005). Plausible hypotheses for this observed difference include explanations at the biomechanical, physiological, and psychological levels. In general, the biomechanical forces at play in most sports-related head injuries may cause less severe traumatic forces in comparison with other common injury mechanisms (i.e., motor vehicle crashes and falls). Relatedly, athletes' physical attributes, such as well-developed neck musculature, may help minimize rotational acceleration forces exerted on the brain. Regarding physiological factors, a higher preinjury level of physical fitness may protect athletes from neuronal injury. It could also be the case that properly timed physical activity promotes recovery. Furthermore, athletes may be less likely to have comorbidities that complicate recovery—such as chronic medical conditions, substance use disorders, or psychiatric diagnoses such as posttraumatic stress disorder (PTSD). Finally, athletes' high motivation to return to their sport may lead them to minimize symptoms, thus obscuring persistent dysfunction in this population.

Although those with sports-related injuries appear to enjoy better acute outcomes, this group may be at risk for chronic problems. Research on retired professional football players has shown an association between recurrent concussion and late-life cognitive dysfunction (Guskiewicz et al. 2005) and depression (Guskiewicz et al. 2007a). Evidence also exists of long-term neurological disturbance in athletes who played at the university level, with one study demonstrating signs of impairment on electrophysiological and behavioral measures more than three decades after injury (De Beaumont et al. 2009). It is commonly assumed that athletes' exposure to repetitive injuries confers risk for neurological symptoms later in life, although poor acute-injury management and genetic factors are also thought to play a role.

BIOMECHANICS OF MILD TRAUMATIC BRAIN INJURY

Biomechanics is the study of biological systems, such as the brain, in response to physical forces. Mechanical forces can damage the brain directly, as an immediate consequence of deformation and strain, or they can lead to delayed damage by initiating physiological processes that result in cell dysfunction or death. Many different head motions can occur in response to a motor vehicle crash or a head-to-head collision on a football field. If you consider that tremendous variety in combination with the distinct musculoskeletal and neuroanatomical attributes of each individual, it becomes clear that the biomechanical characteristics of each head injury are unique.

Despite the heterogeneity of concussion biomechanics, researchers have endeavored to model injury thresholds that delineate the mechanical loadings associated with different levels of brain injury. Organized sports, particularly football, have provided a rich source of data for studying brain injury mechanics. Some researchers have employed a combination of video analysis and dummy impact reconstruction to estimate angle, speed, and player kinematics associated with injuries (Meaney & Smith 2011). A recent innovation in this research now allows for mechanical data to be collected during the course of athletic participation. Helmets with embedded accelerometers are now being used to study real-time injury mechanics. One of these systems is the Head Impact Telemetry (HIT) system (Simbex LLC, Lebanon, New Hampshire), which has been employed in the study of Division I university football players (Duma et al. 2005, Guskiewicz et al. 2007b).

Researchers have used the methods described above to estimate injury tolerance levels, that is, the likelihood that an individual will sustain a concussion at an impact of a given magnitude. Some have proposed that impacts of $90\,g$ linear acceleration sustained for 9 milliseconds (ms) or longer are sufficient to produce mTBI (Ono & Kanno 1996). However, more recent research using real-time recordings from helmet-embedded accelerometers suggests a more complex picture. Guskiewicz et al. (2007b) reported concussions sustained at much lower levels of linear acceleration (as low as $60\,g$), and other work from this group has revealed that athletes can undergo impacts greater than $90\,g$ without any signs of neurological dysfunction (McCaffrey et al. 2007).

The extent to which sports-related impacts may differ biomechanically from other mechanisms of concussive injury is currently unknown. However, the study of sports impacts has revealed that the relationship between impact forces and injury is not direct but rather appears to be moderated by other factors that are not currently well understood. However, certain features of sports impacts could serve as speculative mechanisms for possible differences in the biomechanical profiles of sports and nonsports-related concussions. Athletes in high-impact sports, e.g., football and hockey, wear helmets and other protective gear that may buffer the effects of collision on the brain. However, evidence suggests that helmets do not have a significant effect on angular accelerations—the type of acceleration that is thought to contribute most to concussion (King et al. 2003). It should be noted that helmets are effective at protecting against cranial fractures and more severe brain injuries.

In many cases, it is likely that an athlete's training and agility protect her or him against more severe brain injuries. Athletes who participate in contact sports are trained to absorb impacts to the head with their bulkier shoulders and torsos in order to minimize angular accelerations. In many cases, though certainly not all, an athlete may see a hit coming and adjust his or her body posture appropriately. In contrast, motor vehicle accidents generally are completely unanticipated and transpire within mere milliseconds of the motorist's awareness. Furthermore, musculoskeletal attributes, such as well-developed neck and shoulder muscles, can protect the head against high rotational accelerations. In fact, women's relatively less bulky neck musculature has been put forward as a factor that may explain why females in comparison with males appear to be more susceptible to concussion in sports that are popular among both genders, such as soccer (Barnes et al. 1998).

The influence of training, preparedness, and musculoskeletal characteristics on injury biomechanics has yet to be systematically evaluated in sports-related concussion. The new technological advance of helmet accelerometer telemetry holds tremendous promise to elucidate the biomechanical properties of injurious and noninjurious sports impacts. Notably, however, helmet telemetry is not easily applied to sports that do not require helmets but still have a high risk of concussion, such as women's soccer (Covassin et al. 2003). In fact, because football and ice hockey have received the most research attention, there is a great risk of neglecting the unique biomechanical characteristics of head injuries in women's sports. This is an important focus for future research.

PATHOPHYSIOLOGY OF MILD TRAUMATIC BRAIN INJURY

The acute symptoms of concussion are believed to arise as a result of transient neurochemical and neurometabolic changes initiated by the biomechanical strains discussed above. This neurochemical and neurometabolic cascade has been extensively reviewed elsewhere (Giza & Hovda 2001). Briefly, immediately following head trauma, biomechanical forces lead to disruption of neuronal membranes, axonal stretching, and the opening of voltage-gated ion channels. Uncontrolled ion flux across the membrane causes excitatory neurotransmitters, such as glutamate, to bind to cell receptors, causing further depolarization as potassium leaves and calcium enters neurons. In order to restore membrane potential, the sodium potassium pump must go into overdrive, transporting potassium into and sodium out of the cell. This is an energy-expensive process, requiring increased use of adenosine triphosphate—the neuron's currency for electrochemical transport. In order to fuel this process, glucose metabolism dramatically increases. At the same time, cerebral blood flow decreases, by as much as 50% of normal volume in experimental animal models. Hence, concussion creates a state of hypermetabolism and hyperglycolysis while, simultaneously, cerebral blood flow is decreased and glucose availability in the brain is diminished. This has been referred to as an "energy crisis" in the brain (Giza & Hovda 2001).

This model of concussion pathophysiology has been applied as a framework for understanding the emergence and recovery of concussion symptoms. Animal work suggests that chemical and metabolic levels return to normal within 10 days of injury (Hovda et al. 1995). This time frame is appealing because it maps nicely onto the 10-day recovery curve for neuropsychological consequences of sports-related concussion (Belanger & Vanderploeg 2005). Furthermore, the brain's increased need for energy in the period immediately following concussion provides explanations for other clinical observations, for example, the apparent increased vulnerability to reinjury in the days following an initial injury (Guskiewicz et al. 2003, McCrea et al. 2009) and symptom exacerbation with physical exertion in some patients (Leddy et al. 2010, Solomon 2007). These findings and clinical observations have been used as the rationale for concussion management consensus guidelines (McCrory et al. 2013).

As we have noted, much of the research on neurochemical and neurometabolic consequences of concussion is based on a fluid percussive injury model in rodents. Although this research has provided valuable insight into TBI pathophysiology, these models are limited by important differences between real-life and experimental injury mechanisms, as well as considerable differences in anatomy and physiology across species. Hence, it is important to validate pathophysiological theories in human samples. At least one human study provides support for changes in glucose metabolism following TBI. Bergsneider and colleagues (2001) used [^{18}F]fluorodeoxyglucose positron emission tomography to assess the temporal pattern and correlation of functional and metabolic recovery in patients with mild, moderate, and severe TBI. This study revealed reduced metabolism following both mild and severe TBI that persisted for several weeks in most cases. Notably, this represents a longer time period than the window for metabolic disruption observed in experimental injury studies. However, this time frame is more consistent with neuropsychological recovery from mTBI within the general population (Belanger et al. 2005). Surprisingly, the investigators found no correlation between cerebral metabolism and measures of functional disability, such as cognitive performance.

Although the neurometabolic and neurochemical mechanisms discussed above provide plausible explanations for certain clinical phenomena—emergence and recovery of acute concussion symptoms, increased concussion vulnerability following injury, and symptom exacerbation with exertion—other observations from clinical practice and research are not well explained by this pathophysiological process, for example, persisting symptoms in a subset of patients (Røe et al. 2009) as well as emerging clinical evidence of long-term neuropathological consequences of mTBI (McKee et al. 2009). Although there is not strong evidence of a causal link between mTBI and long-term clinical outcomes, these observations suggest the possibility of enduring neuropathological changes in a subset of patients.

Recent research supports a mechanism for persistent neuronal injury following mTBI. Direct mechanical injury to neurons is a prominent feature of moderate and severe TBI (Adams et al. 1989). Trauma can lead to contusion, hemorrhage, and diffuse axonal injury (DAI). Contusion and hemorrhage are rare in concussions. However, axons are particularly vulnerable to mechanical injury due to their viscoelastic properties; hence, axonal pathology is prevalent across TBI severity levels (Adams et al. 1989, Smith et al. 2003). Support for DAI in concussion comes from research on a porcine TBI model that uses a rotational acceleration injury mechanism with parameters akin to those related to concussion in humans. Histopathological studies of these animals revealed multifocal axonal pathology (Browne et al. 2011). The clinical relevance of this model provides strong support for axonal injury in concussion. A growing body of human neuroimaging research also provides indirect evidence of concussion-related axonal pathology by demonstrating abnormal water diffusivity in neuronal white matter (Bazarian et al. 2007, Bigler & Bazarian 2010, Mayer et al. 2010, Niogi et al. 2008, Wilde et al. 2008).

DAI may also play a role in protracted clinical outcome. Mounting evidence suggests that axonal damage triggers a progressive neurodegenerative process that is associated with Alzheimer's disease pathology (Johnson et al. 2010, Smith et al. 2003). These findings have begun to elucidate a potential link between history of head trauma and deleterious long-term emotional, cognitive, and behavioral changes (McKee et al. 2009).

NEUROIMAGING FINDINGS IN MILD TRAUMATIC BRAIN INJURY

Although conventional neuroimaging techniques are known to be insensitive to concussion neuropathology, a number of novel approaches have begun to elucidate the immediate and long-term effects of concussion on the brain.

Diffusion Tensor Imaging

Diffusion tensor imaging (DTI) has garnered significant attention as a technique for examining damage to the brain's white matter tracts.

Whereas gray matter is made up of neuron cell bodies, the brain's white matter is primarily composed of axons. This tissue appears white because of the fatty myelin sheaths that cover many axon fibers. Functionally related gray matter regions are connected by collections of axons that serve to transmit information from one part of the brain to another. Hence, coherent bundles of white matter make up the communicative infrastructure of the human brain. DTI is a magnetic resonance imaging technique that measures the diffusion of water in tissues. Because myelin sheaths and axonal membranes constrain the movement of water molecules, the diffusion properties of water can be used to estimate the integrity of white matter tracts. Anisotropic diffusion refers to the tendency for water molecules to diffuse more rapidly along the direction of an axon. This property measured by fractional anisotropy (FA) ranges from 0 to 1 and characterizes the extent to which water molecules are constrained. An FA value of 0 represents free diffusion in a perfect sphere, whereas an FA of 1 represents maximal anisotropic diffusion, i.e., diffusion in one direction. Although FA is the most commonly reported DTI index, other indices may be clinically relevant, such as mean diffusivity (MD), radial diffusivity, and axial diffusivity.

Because of axons' particular vulnerability to mechanical stretch injury, mTBI is considered by many to be a white matter disorder. Hence, DTI is a promising tool for investigating mTBI neuropathology in vivo. However, changes in FA are challenging to interpret because both increased and decreased FA in injured individuals has been reported (Bigler & Bazarian 2010). It has been argued that elevated FA is related to inflammatory responses, such as axonal swelling (Niogi et al. 2008) or cytotoxic edema (Bazarian et al. 2007), whereas lower FA values may reflect axonal degeneration (Lipton et al. 2009).

DTI research has revealed a pattern of white matter changes associated with mTBI, suggesting that specific white matter pathways are particularly vulnerable to traumatic damage. DTI abnormalities are particularly prevalent in frontal pathways such as the anterior corona radiata, and temporal tracts such as the uncinate fasciculus (Bazarian et al. 2007, Bigler & Bazarian 2010, Lipton et al. 2009, Mayer et al. 2010, Niogi et al. 2008, Wilde et al. 2008). Research examining DTI outcomes in selected samples of patients with chronic mTBI symptoms has revealed decreased FA, suggestive of white matter loss (Chappell et al. 2006, Kraus et al. 2007, Lipton et al. 2009, Niogi et al. 2008). Interestingly, some of these studies have also uncovered correlations between DTI indices and objective measures of dysfunction, such as cognitive test performance (Kraus et al. 2007, Lipton et al. 2009, Niogi et al. 2008). However, retrospective studies are somewhat limited by their cross-sectional methodology. As noted previously, the vast majority of mTBI patients recover from their injuries. Cross-sectional studies are ill suited to evaluate the extent to which DTI indices predict persistent dysfunction in mTBI patients.

Research on acute mTBI has also uncovered evidence of FA abnormality, with some studies reporting increased FA in acute mTBI patients as compared with controls (Bazarian et al. 2007, Wilde et al. 2008). One study examined DTI outcomes in patients within weeks after mTBI (mean time since injury = 12 days) and followed them up to five months postinjury. This study found increased FA during the subacute injury phase, which partially normalized by the chronic injury phase (Mayer et al. 2010). Notably, evidence seems to suggest that mTBI has a phase-dependent effect on FA, with patients in the acute phase exhibiting increased FA, suggestive of cytotoxic edema, and patients with chronic mTBI deficits demonstrating reduced FA, suggestive of white matter degeneration. Further research is necessary to determine the extent to which acute increase of FA predicts chronically reduced FA. Other studies have not confirmed this finding but rather reported lower FA or no difference as compared with controls (Levin et al. 2010, Zhang et al. 2010). This might be due to the heterogeneity of injury or a fluctuating level of FA within the first two weeks of injury.

A handful of studies have examined DTI in athlete samples. One group of investigators imaged athletes with persisting concussion symptoms one month postinjury and found that MD was sensitive to differences between concussed patients and controls (Cubon et al. 2011). In contrast, FA did not distinguish between concussed patients and control participants; however, FA was sensitive to group differences between patients with moderate to severe TBI and controls. The comparison of concussed patients with controls revealed increased MD, suggestive of decreased white matter integrity in left hemisphere thalamo-cortical, fronto-occipital, and temporal-occipital pathways (Cubon et al. 2011). Another innovative study examined pre- and postseason DTI in high school football and hockey players. Only one athlete from the small sample sustained a concussion during the course of the season. However, this athlete exhibited the greatest pre-postseason change in FA and MD values. The authors also reported that members of the athlete group, who were presumably exposed to subconcussive impacts, exhibited greater FA and MD changes than did nonathlete control participants (Bazarian et al. 2012).

Taken together, the current DTI literature seems to indicate that concussion causes white matter changes and particularly affects long white matter tracts involving frontal and temporal brain regions. MD may be more sensitive than FA to milder forms of injury associated with athlete samples. Within days to weeks of concussion, increased FA may reflect acute inflammatory responses, such as cytotoxic edema. Furthermore, at least some mTBI patients demonstrate chronic DTI abnormalities characterized by reduced FA. FA reductions are thought to imply white matter degeneration and hence could serve as an in vivo marker of DAI (Huisman et al. 2004). Research demonstrating correlations between chronic FA reductions and cognitive test performance suggests that DAI may be an underlying cause of chronic mTBI dysfunction. Notably, DTI may underestimate the true level of neuropathology because a measured voxel size is much larger than an individual nerve fiber. This leads to poor characterization of the white matter fibers that may be most susceptible to DAI—that is, fibers that cross, merge, or fan.

Task-Related Functional Magnetic Resonance Imaging

Functional magnetic resonance imaging (fMRI) is another promising neuroimaging technique for studying mTBI-related neuropathology. Task-related designs are the most common application of fMRI. These experiments examine patterns of brain activation during execution of a cognitive task and typically compare the blood-oxygen-level-dependent (BOLD) response in injured and healthy participants. The BOLD response is determined by cerebral blood flow, blood volume, and the ratio of deoxyhemoglobin to oxyhemoglobin. Cerebral blood flow responds to the energy demands of neurons as they fire, and hence the BOLD hemodynamic response can serve as a proxy for neuronal activity. However, it is important to note that the BOLD response is an indirect measure of neuronal functioning. It lags neuronal activation by 1–2 seconds and is subject to vascular factors that may be unrelated to neuronal activity (Logothetis 2008). Despite these limitations, fMRI has many advantages and remains a popular method for studying the thinking brain. It is safe, noninvasive, and has adequate resolution for rendering both spatial and temporal neuronal dynamics. In the study of mTBI, task-related fMRI designs have been used to uncover increased neuronal activity (hyperactivation) and decreased neuronal activity (hypoactivation) in injured brains as they perform cognitive tasks.

Hypoactivation in mTBI has been reported by a handful of studies. One study examined auditory orienting in a group of mTBI patients within three weeks of their injuries. Behavioral results revealed poorer performance on the auditory attention tasks for mTBI patients as compared to control participants. This performance deficit was accompanied by hypoactivation throughout the auditory attention network (Mayer et al. 2009). In the sports concussion literature, one study examined a group of symptomatic elite male athletes who had sustained a sports-related concussion between 1 and 14 months previously. Behaviorally, concussed athletes did not differ significantly from controls in their performance of a working memory task. However, concussed athletes demonstrated hypoactivation in the prefrontal cortex and anterior cingulate gyrus (Chen et al. 2004), areas thought to be critically involved in working memory (Petrides 1991). Additionally, the authors noted that concussed athletes exhibited a more widely distributed pattern of activation, suggesting less efficient use of neural resources (Chen et al. 2004). Another study from this group reported a relationship between hypoactivation of frontal brain regions and self-reported postconcussion symptoms (Chen et al. 2007).

Other fMRI work has demonstrated task-related hyperactivation in mTBI patients. One study examined brain activation during attention (Stroop), working memory (n-back), and motor tasks in mTBI patients 18–40 days postinjury. Behaviorally, the mTBI group performed more poorly than controls on cognitive tasks. Neuroimaging results revealed hyperactivation in relevant brain regions during execution of n-back and Stroop. Additionally, the mTBI group showed activation in brain regions outside of the working memory network as memory load increased to the highest level of task difficulty (3-back) (Smits et al. 2009). In this sample, severity of postconcussion symptoms was associated with hyperactivation during task performance, suggesting that increased task-related neuronal activity could serve as a marker of mTBI neuropathology. McAllister and colleagues (2001) also examined the brain's response to increased working memory demands on the n-back task. Although behavioral performance did not differ between mTBI and control groups, they found differences in the pattern of brain activation related to increased cognitive processing demands. Healthy control participants demonstrated increased activation for each increase in cognitive processing load (e.g., from 1-back to 2-back and from 2-back to 3-back). In contrast, mTBI patients demonstrated a disproportionate increase in activation as the task difficulty increased from low to moderate difficulty (1-back to 2-back) but very little increase as the task progressed to the highest load condition (2-back to 3-back) (McAllister et al. 2001).

At first blush, the literature on task-related fMRI abnormalities associated with mTBI appears inconsistent. Is mTBI characterized by increased or decreased neuronal activity? A closer examination of the research findings offers some clarification, as it appears that the relationship between brain activation and mTBI is moderated by the location of neuronal activation. In general, when hypoactivation is reported, it is typically found in brain regions thought to be critically implicated in the experimental task (Chen et al. 2004, Mayer et al. 2009). In contrast, when hyperactivation is reported, there is typically a greater spatial distribution of activity across brain regions (Chen et al. 2004, McAllister et al. 2001, Smits et al. 2009). Taken together, these findings suggest that mTBI may be characterized by disruption to task-related functional networks, resulting in less efficient recruitment of neural resources. Hillary and colleagues (Hillary 2008, Hillary et al. 2006) have noted that activation in a more widely distributed anatomical network is associated with cognitive challenge in both healthy individuals and those with brain disease. Specifically, they argue that activation of right dorsolateral prefrontal cortex may be directly proportional to the relative task difficulty for each participant. Hence, group differences in patterns of activation may be due to a lower tolerance for task difficulty in patients (Hillary 2008, Hillary et al. 2006).

Functional Connectivity

Over the past decade, investigators have become interested in the activity of the brain during rest. Resting-state fMRI examines the BOLD signal while a person is awake and lying quietly with eyes closed (Raichle et al. 2001). This paradigm has some advantages over the event-related designs discussed above, which require a subject to engage in a specific task. In event-related designs, the BOLD signal is influenced by both neurophysiological and behavioral contributions. Brain activity during rest is less likely to be confounded by interindividual or time-dependent differences in behavioral performance. Hence, resting-state measures hold promise as more reliable indices of underlying brain activity. However, resting-state fMRI studies, similar to task-dependent fMRI studies, are limited by the indirect relationship between neuronal activity and the BOLD signal.

Some researchers have used resting-state fMRI data to measure the functioning of the brain's networks by examining coherent activation of spatially distributed brain regions. This analytic technique, called functional connectivity analysis, attempts to capture intercommunication between anatomically distinct regions of the brain to achieve a specific function. Of these resting-state networks, the default mode network (DMN) has received the most attention. The DMN includes the precuneus/posterior cingulate cortex; medial prefrontal cortex; and medial, lateral, and inferior parietal cortex (for review, see Broyd et al. 2009). Researchers have noted that the DMN is active during rest but is deactivated during goal-oriented tasks (Raichle et al. 2001). The DMN is thought to mediate passive mental activities; however, its precise function is poorly understood.

Functional connectivity analyses provide a promising window into mTBI neuropathology. Research has demonstrated that functionally synchronous networks map onto the structure of white matter pathways that connect brain regions (van den Heuvel et al. 2009). Hence, changes in the connectivity of these networks may reflect damage or disruption to these white matter structures, such as DAI. Studies of functional connectivity in mTBI patients have demonstrated signs of reduced connectivity in the DMN within the semiacute injury phase (<3 weeks postinjury). Interestingly, in this sample, DMN connectivity indices were more sensitive to mTBI than was cognitive test performance (Mayer et al. 2011). In the sports concussion literature, a recent study found reduced number and strength of DMN connections in asymptomatic athletes who had been cleared for return to play by their team physician (a mean of 10 days postinjury) (Johnson et al. 2012a).

Network disruption in mTBI is probably not specific to the DMN. Evidence suggests that other brain networks are also affected. Another study of mTBI patients with persistent symptoms (ranging from 3 to 53 days postinjury) found evidence of increased thalamic resting-state network connectivity and decreased thalamic network symmetry in patients with mTBI as compared with healthy controls. Thalamic connectivity abnormalities were correlated with self-reported symptoms and cognitive deficits on neuropsychological tests (Tang et al. 2011). Another study took an independent component analysis approach to identify 15 distinct functional networks (Stevens et al. 2012). Voxelwise group comparisons found abnormal mTBI-related functional connectivity in each of the 15 networks identified. Furthermore, connectivity abnormalities were correlated with symptom severity for nearly each resting state network. Interestingly, abnormalities were characterized by both deficits and enhancements in regional connectivity. The authors speculated that abnormal enhancements may reflect a compensatory response (Stevens et al. 2012).

Electrophysiology

Just as in fMRI research, electrophysiological measures can be examined during rest or in response to a specific event. One method for investigating neuroelectrophysiology is to measure event-related potentials (ERPs). ERPs refer to the series of positive and negative deflections in ongoing electroencephalogram measured on the scalp, which are time locked to a stimulus presentation or behavioral response. This technique is well suited for detection of mTBI-related circuit disruption because of its excellent temporal resolution and sensitivity to subtle disruptions in cognitive functions typically affected by mTBI, such as attention and speeded processing.

ERP studies have revealed mTBI-related abnormalities in both acute and protracted stages using both visual and auditory modalities. One of the best-known cognitive ERP tasks is the oddball paradigm. This design involves presentation of two categories of stimuli; one occurs frequently and the other rarely. The appearance of the rare stimulus is associated with a strong, positive wave (referred to as P3) over central and parietal electrodes at 300 to 600 ms following the stimulus presentation. The P3 component is thought to reflect the amount of attention allocated in the task or the degree and quality of information processing, i.e., volitional aspects of attention (Broglio et al. 2011).

The majority of cognitive ERP studies have evaluated patients during the chronic injury stage (i.e., greater than one month, and in many cases greater than one year, postinjury). One study examined a sample of participants who had sustained an mTBI within the five years prior to the examination. Although the majority of participants denied persistent cognitive problems, neuropsychological testing revealed mild impairments in memory and attention. Furthermore, ERP findings indicated increased negativity of the putative "O-wave" or "reorienting negativity" in the injured group (Potter et al. 2001). Another study evaluated well-functioning university students an average of 6.4 years after sustaining an mTBI (mixed etiologies) and found significantly reduced P3 amplitude despite equivalent behavioral performance on most oddball performance indices and all neuropsychological tests (Segalowitz et al. 2001).

An interesting study by Lachapelle and colleagues provides some indication that neuroelectric abnormalities may predict functional disability. This study evaluated symptomatic participants who had sustained motor vehicle–related injuries (Lachapelle et al. 2008). Results revealed that mTBI participants showed delayed ERP latencies as compared with uninjured controls. Furthermore, ERP latency abnormality upon admission was a significant predictor of inability to return to work at the end of treatment, suggesting that these measures could serve as meaningful predictors of mTBI functional outcome (Lachapelle et al. 2008).

Research from the sports concussion literature has shown that mTBI is associated with moderate to large decreases in ERP components related to stimulus acquisition (P3 amplitude) and cognitive processing speed (P3 latency). In many cases, ERP abnormalities are demonstrated in the absence of self-reported symptoms or impaired performance on neuropsychological tests, suggesting that these measures may be more sensitive to concussion-related neuropathology than the commonly used clinical indicators (for a review, see Broglio et al. 2011).

One study examined ERPs during an auditory oddball task in a group of symptomatic concussed athletes in the subacute injury phase, a mean of 10 weeks postinjury. Results revealed that both symptomatic and asymptomatic concussed athletes demonstrated reduced amplitude and prolonged latency of the P3 component relative to controls, despite equivalent behavioral performance (Gosselin et al. 2006). Another study examined a different electrophysiological outcome, motor-evoked potentials (MEPs) obtained through transcranial magnetic stimulation in acutely concussed college athletes assessed on days 1, 3, 5, and 10 postconcussion. Findings demonstrated decreased MEP amplitude ratios and prolonged MEP latencies as compared with noninjured controls over the 1- to 10-day postinjury period (Livingston et al. 2010). Other work by this group found that MEP abnormalities persisted after neurocognitive deficits and symptoms had resolved (Livingston et al. 2012).

Further evidence of ERP abnormalities in the absence of self-reported symptoms comes from a very intriguing study of athletes with remote history sports-related concussion (30 years or more since their most recent concussion) (De Beaumont et al. 2009). This study found that concussed former athletes differed from uninjured control athletes on both behavioral and neuroelectric measures. Behaviorally, concussed individuals demonstrated bradykinesia and poorer memory and executive functioning. On electrophysiological assessment, the concussed group exhibited significantly delayed and attenuated P3 component during an auditory oddball paradigm and significantly prolonged cortical silent period in response to transcranial magnetic stimulation (De Beaumont et al. 2009).

Investigators have also used electroencephalogram to examine functional connectivity. Results from these studies support the notion that mTBI causes reduced neuronal coherence in both acute and chronic stages of the disease (Kumar et al. 2009, Marquez de la Plata et al. 2011, Slobounov et al. 2011). Some have offered DAI as a speculative mechanism underlying these effects.

The current neuroimaging literature strongly suggests that both structural and functional changes related to mTBI affect at least a subset of patients and can persist far beyond the acute injury stage. Furthermore, neurophysiological changes appear to persist in the absence of clinical abnormalities—specifically, self-reported symptoms and neuropsychological deficits. Notably, this mounting body of research is somewhat at odds with standard clinical wisdom and even the latest consensus guidelines, which have considered concussion a transient disruption of neuronal functioning (McCrory et al. 2013, Moser et al. 2007). Although sports concussions are generally characterized by a less severe clinical presentation, neurophysiological findings from this population are remarkably consistent with studies of general mTBI samples, suggesting that similar pathophysiological processes are at play.

NEUROPSYCHOLOGY OF MILD TRAUMATIC BRAIN INJURY

Many mTBI patients complain, at least during the first two to four weeks, of cognitive problems such as memory difficulties, trouble with concentration, and mental slowing. For this reason, neurocognitive test performance has been used as an objective marker of concussion-related dysfunction in a variety of clinical applications, such as sports concussion management (Barth et al. 1989, Guskiewicz et al. 2004), and litigation (Murrey & Starzinski 2007). Traditional neuropsychological tests have the most empirical support for their reliability and validity as measures of neurocognitive functioning (Ellemberg et al. 2009). However, a number of computerized test batteries designed specifically for the assessment of mTBI have recently gained popularity and offer more precise electronic measurement of reaction or processing time.

Over the past 30 years, mTBI patients have been evaluated in many studies with comprehensive neuropsychological batteries that assess a wide variety of functions, such as attention, processing speed, executive functions, verbal fluency, memory acquisition, delayed memory, language, visuospatial functions, and motor functions. This body of literature provides strong evidence that mTBI causes acute deficits in information processing speed, learning, memory, attention, and executive functioning (Belanger & Vanderploeg 2005, Levin et al. 1987, Vanderploeg et al. 2005).

However, whether mTBI produces persistent cognitive dysfunction remains controversial, with some arguing that chronic cognitive problems are better accounted for by psychological or contextual factors (Bryant & Harvey 1999, Marsh & Smith 1995, McCrea et al. 2012).

Research findings on the chronic neurocognitive effects of mTBI are somewhat mixed. One prospective study included patients from three medical centers and found that acute cognitive deficits associated with mTBI largely resolved by one to three months postinjury (Levin et al. 1987). Another excellent study conducted by Ponsford and colleagues (2011) followed 123 mTBI patients and 100 matched trauma controls presenting to the emergency department of a major adult trauma center. This study found that there were no differences between mTBI and trauma control patients in cognitive test performance upon initial presentation to the emergency department. However, mTBI patients performed more poorly than controls on cognitive tests at one week and three months later. The mTBI group was also more likely to report continued cognitive problems and difficulty with activities of daily living. There were no group differences in psychiatric symptoms (Ponsford et al. 2011).

A recent meta-analysis of 25 studies previously examined in prior meta-analytic reviews included 2,834 mTBI patients and 2,057 control participants. The results of this study suggest that the neuropsychological effects of mTBI fully remit within three months of injury (Rohling et al. 2011). An earlier meta-analysis of this literature examined moderators of neuropsychological effects. This review included 39 studies composed of 1,463 patients and 1,119 controls, and it found that study design was a significant moderator of the duration of cognitive deficits. In unselected and prospective samples, cognitive impairments resolved within three months of injury. However, clinic-based samples and samples including participants involved in litigation demonstrated more severe and persistent cognitive dysfunction (Belanger et al. 2005).

Prospective, longitudinal designs comparing an unselected group of mTBI patients to an appropriate control group mitigate many confounds associated with studies that enroll chronic patients attending clinics or that use other sampling methods that may lead to selection bias. Cross-sectional studies selecting patients on the basis of current symptoms are not representative of the general mTBI population and hence cannot be used to estimate the effects of mTBI on cognitive functioning. In contrast, longitudinal studies that recruit patients acutely postinjury allow for within-subject comparisons and are best suited to examine the course of mTBI recovery. A control group is necessary in order to account for noninjury contributions to variation in cognitive outcomes over time, such as repeated exposure to tests, the passage of time, physical maturation/aging, or other individual-difference variables. Yet the question of what is an appropriate control group for studies of mTBI is unresolved.

Most studies recruit healthy uninjured individuals as a control group. Uninjured control samples are limited because they differ from patients with regard to factors that can influence cognition, such as posttraumatic stress from injury or hospitalization (Bryant & Harvey 1999) and risk factors that predispose to injury. For this reason, some investigators have proposed the use of orthopedically injured trauma patients (Ponsford et al. 2011). This comparison group would allow investigators to control for posttrauma stress as well as risk factors that predispose to injury, including pre-existing behavioral problems, subtle learning disabilities, and family variables (Iverson et al. 2005; Stancin et al. 1998, 2001). For these reasons, orthopedic controls would be an advantageous control group for mTBI studies. However, this methodological option is not without its limitations. It is possible that a significant number of trauma control patients sustain occult brain injuries at the time of trauma that go undiagnosed in the context of more obvious injuries. Hence, it is possible that comparisons with injured control groups underestimate the cognitive effects of brain injury. The use of two control groups—orthopedically injured and healthy uninjured—may be the most rigorous approach for evaluating the neurocognitive effects of mTBI.

Neuropsychology of Sports-Related Concussion

Research on the neuropsychological consequences of sports-related concussion has taken a different methodological approach that exploits the advantages inherent in working with the athlete population. Athletes can be evaluated prior to the start of an athletic season in order to obtain a preinjury measure of their cognitive functioning. Barth and colleagues (1989) at the University of Virginia developed the Sports as a Laboratory Assessment Model to better characterize the neuropsychological impact of concussion and the trajectory of recovery. This group was the first to conduct preconcussion (baseline) neuropsychological assessments on athletes. This method allows for the impact of the injury to be assessed directly (as change from baseline performance) rather than simply inferred on the basis of between-group comparisons (Barth et al. 1989).

An objective measure of athletes' premorbid cognitive abilities provides an ideal comparison standard for postconcussion assessment and research. In the time since Barth's seminal 1989 study, a number of studies have been published that evaluate the neurocognitive effect of sports concussion, either with or without baseline testing. A meta-analysis of this literature (Belanger & Vanderploeg 2005) included 21 studies involving 790 sports concussion cases and 2,014 control cases. The results showed that the overall acute effect of sports concussion on cognitive test performance ($d = 0.49$) was comparable to that observed in nonathletes. Effects were greatest for delayed memory, memory acquisition, and global cognitive functioning. Studies that used athletes' baseline performance as the basis of comparison demonstrated markedly smaller effects than studies comparing concussed and control groups, presumably due to practice effects associated with repeated exposure to the test battery (Belanger & Vanderploeg 2005).

The literature on the neurocognitive effects of sports concussion diverges from that on the effects of general mTBI. Specifically, the sports concussion literature suggests that, at the aggregate level, no cognitive effects of concussion persist beyond 7 to 10 days postinjury (Belanger & Vanderploeg 2005). Notably, this recovery timeline is more consistent with the animal research characterizing the neurometabolic cascade following mTBI (Giza & Hovda 2001).

Baseline cognitive testing provides clinicians and researchers with a coveted opportunity for test interpretation; the advantages of using an athlete's baseline assessment results as the point of comparison for determining injury impact are clear. In fact, there is near consensus that preinjury baseline assessment is best practice for sports concussion management (Barth et al. 1989, Guskiewicz et al. 2004, Van Kampen et al. 2006). However, some authors have drawn attention to issues that complicate straightforward pre-postinjury test comparisons (Bailey et al. 2006, Ragan & Kang 2007, Randolph et al. 2005). Furthermore, a recent study with a large sample of concussed athletes ($N > 200$) demonstrated that the proportion of participants who declined from baseline on the Immediate Post-Assessment of Concussion Test (ImPACT) was no greater than the number who would be expected to decline based on chance alone (Echemendia et al. 2012).

As mentioned above, practice effects may benefit athletes' postinjury performance and result in findings that underestimate postconcussion cognitive deficits. Other questions remain regarding the reliability of cognitive tests across the time frame that typically transpires between baseline and postconcussion assessment (Ragan & Kang 2007, Randolph 2011). Effort toward testing is another issue that could influence research findings on the cognitive effects of sports concussion. Those who work with athletes have been quick to note that an athlete's approach to testing can be dramatically different during the baseline and postconcussion assessments. Athletes postconcussion are often highly motivated to return to play and eager to demonstrate to the assessor that they are functioning well. This level of motivation may be far greater than what is typically seen in other settings in which neuropsychological tests are administered. In contrast, at baseline, some athletes may be less engaged in cognitive testing. They may view the testing session as a nuisance or an imposition.

Suboptimal motivation during baseline testing could lead to invalid conclusions regarding the athlete's true level of premorbid functioning. In fact, data presented by Bailey and colleagues (2006) demonstrate that some athletes exhibit markedly improved performance postconcussion relative to their baseline scores. This strongly suggests that, for some athletes, the baseline assessment underrepresents their true premorbid abilities.

Experimental Measures of Cognitive Functioning

Some have called into question the appropriateness of traditional neuropsychological tests as measures of mTBI-related cognitive deficits. Most tests were designed to detect gross cognitive changes, such as those associated with severe brain injuries and neurological diseases (Collie & Maruff 2003). Hence, many traditional tests may not be sensitive to the more subtle cognitive changes associated with concussion. Some have proposed novel test paradigms for the evaluation of cognitive consequences of mTBI. A few investigators have pursued impaired eye movements as a potential marker of concussion-related dysfunction. Eye movements rely on a complex network involving cortical and subcortical structures as well as the cerebellum. Hence, measures of oculo-motor tracking are potentially sensitive to an underlying cause of mTBI dysfunction—disruptions of the brain's white matter connections.

A few studies have used eye-tracking technology to assess oculomotor functioning. One study compared visual tracking synchronization and diffusion tensor imaging in a small group of subjects with postconcussion syndrome (PCS) and controls. They found that gaze error variability was significantly correlated with mean FA values in white matter tracks that may be particularly vulnerable to mTBI (anterior corona radiate and genu of the corpus callosum) (Maruta et al. 2010). Another study compared 36 mTBI patients with persistent dysfunction (diagnosed with PCS) to 36 mTBI patients demonstrating good recovery (controls) at three to five months postinjury on re-flexive, anti-, and self-paced saccades; memory-guided sequences; and smooth pursuit. They found that the PCS group performed more poorly than controls on antisaccades, self-paced saccades, memory-guided sequences, and smooth pursuit (Heitger et al. 2009). Furthermore, analysis of covariance revealed that eye-movement outcomes were largely independent of group differences in depression and estimated intellectual ability (Heitger et al. 2009).

Other work has used more easily administered low-technology assessments of eye tracking. The King-Devick test requires subjects to read a series of single-digit numbers aloud from left to right on three test cards. Performance is based on the total time that it takes subjects to complete the number naming task and relies on rapid eye movements and saccades (Oride et al. 1986). Researchers in one study administered this test to a group of boxers and mixed martial arts fighters pre- and postbout (Galetta et al. 2011a). Results revealed that King-Devick performance was significantly worse for those fighters who experienced head trauma during their match. Those with loss of consciousness exhibited the greatest declines from their prebout functioning. Another study conducted by the same group examined King-Devick performance as a rapid sideline screening tool in collegiate athletes (Galetta et al. 2011b). All athletes were administered the test preseason to obtain a preinjury baseline. Ten athletes sustained a concussion during the course of their athletic season and were readministered the King-Devick test immediately postinjury. Group-level results revealed significant declines from baseline performance, with all except one athlete exhibiting worse performance.

Performance variability is another experimental index of cognitive dysfunction that has been applied to the study of mTBI. The field of psychology has historically been dominated by measures of central tendency. Intraindividual variability has typically been disregarded as error, instability, and noise. However, a new and growing literature on performance variability has already amassed impressive evidence suggesting that fluctuations in cognitive performance reflect more than random error and measurement unreliability and, in fact, are often negatively correlated with mean levels of performance (Hultsch & MacDonald 2004).

Investigators examining intraindividual inconsistencies in cognitive performance have operationalized performance variability in a number of ways. Some work has used intraindividual standard deviations taken from multiple trials within a single task, whereas other studies have considered variability in performance on the same task on separate occasions. A few investigators have taken a cross-domain approach to intraindividual variability by examining within-person inconsistency in performance across different neuropsychological tests administered as part of a neuropsychological test battery (Holtzer et al. 2008, Schretlen et al. 2003). One study of 72 collegiate athletes and 42 athletically active control participants examined the influence of sports-related concussion on cross-domain variability. A subset of athletes demonstrated preinjury cognitive performance that was characterized by a high level of intraindividual variability. These high-variability athletes were more likely to demonstrate increased variability postconcussion, whereas low-variability athletes exhibited a pattern of performance similar to that demonstrated by controls tested twice, suggesting practice effects (Rabinowitz & Arnett 2013).

It is quite possible, and even likely, that traditional measures of cognitive functioning fail to fully characterize the cognitive consequences of mTBI. There is a high prevalence of cognitive complaints immediately following mTBI that is not always borne out on objective measures of cognitive dysfunction. Furthermore, neuroimaging findings suggest that there is neurological dysfunction in the absence of deficits on neuropsychological tests. For these reasons, experimental indices of cognitive functioning, like those discussed above, are appealing. However, it is important to temper enthusiasm for early promising findings because these measures may not be as psychometrically sound as traditional assessment methods and have typically been evaluated in relatively small groups of patients.

Computerized Testing

Computerized test batteries for assessment of mTBI have gained popularity in recent years (Schatz & Zillmer 2003). Most of these test batteries focus on the cognitive domains that appear to be most sensitive to mTBI, namely, attention, memory, processing speed, and reaction time. The Im-PACT tool has become widely used in athletic organizations (Lovell et al. 2000). It includes tests of verbal and visual memory, reaction time, and psychomotor processing speed. The Automated Neuropsychological Assessment Metrics, employed by the US military, tests working memory, mental arithmetic, visuospatial processing, and sustained attention (Kabat et al. 2001). CogSport is another computerized battery that assesses simple reaction time, complex reaction time, working memory, and efficiency of new learning (Collie et al. 2003). The HeadMinder Concussion Resolution Index is a more targeted assessment that measures simple and complex reaction time and processing speed (Erlanger et al. 1999).

Computerized testing paradigms offer a number of advantages. The use of computer-administered tests reduces the time and complexity demands associated with traditional neuropsychological testing. Test instructions and timing of stimulus presentation are standardized to a greater degree than can be achieved with paper-and-pencil test administration. Furthermore, computerized tests more accurately record reaction times and facilitate analysis of response patterns (Schatz & Zillmer 2003). Additionally, the computerized batteries designed for mTBI assessment have accounted for some of the unique requirements for testing the sports-related concussion population. Specifically, most of the test batteries include many alternate forms in order to support baseline testing and serial postinjury assessment (Schatz & Zillmer 2003).

Although computerized batteries have increased the ease and efficiency of test administration, research evidence suggests that these instruments may have inadequate reliability (Broglio et al. 2007). An accepted minimal standard for test-retest reliabilities for clinical decision making is 0.70 (Mayers & Redick 2012). Test-retest reliability studies for the ImPACT, one of the most commonly used computerized measures, have been mixed. In a validation study of the ImPACT, the authors reported acceptable levels of reliability (0.65–0.86) in healthy controls tested 1 to 13 days apart (Iverson et al. 2003). However, other investigators have found much lower test-retest reliability coefficients when using longer test-retest intervals, more typical of the amount of time that passes between baseline and postconcussion assessment. For example, one study tested 76 healthy controls 45 days apart and reported test-retest reliability coefficients ranging from 0.23 to 0.38 (Broglio et al. 2007). Another study used an even lengthier test-retest interval of approximately two years and found test-retest correlations on the ImPACT ranging from 0.30 to 0.60 in 95 athletes (Schatz 2010).

PHYSICAL ACTIVITY AND MILD TRAUMATIC BRAIN INJURY

One of the most striking differences between athletic samples and general mTBI samples is pre- and postinjury level of physical activity. Considerable evidence indicates that physical exertion interacts with acute concussion pathophysiology. Animal research suggests that mTBI triggers a neurometabolic response that places a high energy demand on the brain as homeostasis is restored (Giza & Hovda 2001). Hence, competing demands on the system in the form of physical or mental exertion are believed to compromise restorative processes (Silverberg & Iverson 2013). This finding is supported by patient reports of symptom exacerbation with exertion (Leddy et al. 2010, Solomon 2007). There is general consensus among clinicians that mTBI patients should rest until they are asymptomatic (McCrory et al. 2013). However, some have questioned the rationale behind complete rest during postconcussion management (Silverberg & Iverson 2013), noting that exertion causes postconcussion-like symptoms in mTBI patients with remote injuries, at time points for which we would expect the neurometabolic cascade to have fully resolved, and in healthy adults without a history of mTBI (Alla et al. 2010, Griesbach 2011).

Other animal research suggests that exercise promotes neuroplasticity following brain injury; however, animals that are allowed to exercise too soon after injury do not demonstrate these exercise-induced benefits (Griesbach et al. 2004). An abundance of indirect evidence also supports a positive role of exercise in mTBI recovery (Schneider et al. 2013). For example, research has linked exercise with improved cognitive functioning (Castelli et al. 2007), greater hippocampal volumes and better memory (Chaddock et al. 2010), and improved sleep quality (Brand et al. 2010) as well as reductions of depression, anxiety, fatigue, and headache symptoms (Edmonds et al. 2004, Herring et al. 2010, Lockett & Campbell 1992, Mead et al. 2009). Furthermore, concussed athletes are accustomed to frequent exercise, and the cessation of regular physical activity on its own is associated with many postconcussion-like symptoms (Mondin et al. 1996).

Although the literature concerning the effects of exercise on recovery from mTBI is methodologically weak, retrospective correlational data provide some evidence that both over- and underactivity are related to prolonged concussion symptoms. One study retrospectively assigned concussed students to one of two groups based on their self-reported activity levels (Majerske et al. 2008). Students who reported moderate levels of physical and cognitive exertion experienced better outcomes than those with minimal or high levels of activity. Of course, because students were not randomly assigned to activity conditions, causality cannot be implied from the Majerske study. Another study examined the effect of prescribed cognitive and physical rest on concussion symptoms (Moser et al. 2012). This study demonstrated a benefit of rest regardless of whether it was initiated within the acute injury phase (1–7 days), the subacute injury phase (8–30 days), or the chronic injury phase (greater than one month postinjury). However, this study has significant limitations. Specifically, patients were not randomly assigned to groups but rather all patients were initiated on the rest protocol immediately upon presentation to the clinic, and group membership was determined retrospectively based on when the patients sought treatment. Furthermore, the investigators did not compare outcomes with a no-treatment or placebo control group. Hence, rival hypotheses such as the passage of time, the placebo effect, and the Hawthorne effect cannot be ruled out.

A recent review on the effects of rest and physical activity following sports-related concussion included three studies evaluating the benefits of rest and three articles evaluating the benefits of exercise, one of which was a case study (Schneider et al. 2013). The authors concluded that the current state of the literature was extremely limited, and methodologically rigorous studies evaluating the effects of rest and treatment following concussion were warranted. However, there is some indication that rest may be of benefit initially, whereas low-level exercise may be of benefit postacutely. However, the proper timing for initiating activity is currently unknown (Schneider et al. 2013).

POSTTRAUMATIC STRESS

It was previously thought that disturbed consciousness protected TBI victims from PTSD (Sbordone & Liter 1995). It is now clear that PTSD can occur after TBI and is, in fact, quite common (Bryant et al. 2000, Williams et al. 2002b). This high co-occurrence of posttraumatic stress symptoms and mTBI poses a challenge for those disentangling the effects of each disorder because both produce markedly similar symptoms, such as cognitive dysfunction, emotional disturbance, and functional disability (Bryant 2008, Vasterling et al. 2009).

The most obvious factor linking PTSD and mTBI is the experience of a traumatic event. Memories of trauma, even if incomplete, can trigger development of PTSD symptoms. The extent and duration of altered consciousness can influence the coherence of memory for the trauma (Sbordone & Liter 1995). This suggests that less severe brain injuries (i.e., mTBIs) will be more likely to produce PTSD symptoms than severe brain injuries associated with prolonged loss of consciousness, a hypothesis that has some support in the literature (Belanger et al. 2009).

Memory for a traumatic event is not sufficient to produce PTSD. An individual's event-related attributions are a key factor in the development of psychological distress following trauma (Delahanty et al. 1997, Williams et al. 2002a). Stressful events that are interpreted as uncontrollable are more likely to lead to negative psychological outcomes (Kushner et al. 1993). For example, in a study of non-brain-injured survivors of motor vehicle accidents, those who blamed their accidents on others were more distressed than those who attributed responsibility for the accident to themselves (Delahanty et al. 1997). Another study examined PTSD symptoms in 66 survivors of severe TBI and found that external attributions for the cause of trauma predicted the severity of PTSD symptoms (Williams et al. 2002a).

Research from rodent models of brain injury suggests that physiological factors may also play a role in the development of PTSD symptoms following mTBI. One study found that rats subjected to a fluid percussion injury (FPI) exhibited a more pronounced stress response in the week following injury as compared with sham-injured rats (Griesbach et al. 2011). Another study conducted by the same group found that brain-injured rats exhibited increased fear conditioning and greater generalization of the fear response to novel stimuli, which was associated with decreased gamma-aminobutyric acid inhibition of the amygdala (Reger et al. 2012). This research indicates that we cannot assume that mTBI and PTSD are spuriously related to each other via a lurking third variable—namely trauma. Rather, mTBI may have a causal influence on the development of PTSD via effects on stress physiology and altered fear conditioning. Furthermore, PTSD symptoms may prolong mTBI symptoms. Another animal study suggests that the presence of stress may interfere with neural repair processes, as injured rats exposed to postinjury stress showed decreased levels of brain-derived neurotrophic factor (Griesbach et al. 2012).

Studies of PTSD and mTBI patients in the veteran population have demonstrated that the effect of mTBI on psychological, medical, and functional outcomes is nonsignificant after controlling for PTSD and depression (Hoge et al. 2008, Meares et al. 2008). These findings have led some to question whether mTBI contributes to prolonged dysfunction or if persistent problems are fully attributable to psychological distress (Bryant 2008). Other researchers report similar findings from the study of nonveteran mTBI samples and have hypothesized that stress and poor psychological adjustment contribute to the maintenance of mTBI symptoms (Ponsford et al. 2000). However, statistically controlling for PTSD symptoms cannot address the question of whether mTBI patients with and without PTSD would differ from each other if they did not have PTSD (Miller & Chapman 2001). Furthermore, the likelihood that both disorders share not only symptoms but also neural processes renders attempts to disentangle their components extremely complex (for a thorough discussion of the limitations of covariance analysis, see Miller & Chapman 2001).

The influence of PTSD on mTBI symptoms and recovery is germane to a discussion of differences between sport and nonsport TBI. The majority of sports-related brain injury mechanisms may be inherently less stressful than other mTBI etiologies, such as motor vehicle accidents, falls, or assaults. Athletes are more psychologically prepared for the possibility of head trauma and may feel as though they have greater control over the likelihood of injury by virtue of their athletic training. Furthermore, there may be psychologically protective personality traits that are more prevalent among athletes. These contextual and psychological factors may cause reduced incidence of emotional distress and PTSD among those with sports-related concussion relative to those with nonsport mTBIs. Given the likely direct influence of PTSD symptoms on postconcussion-like symptoms and a possible effect of stress on prolonging mTBI recovery (Griesbach et al. 2012), stress responses may play a significant role in the relatively shorter recovery times observed in athletes.

ISSUES OF PARTICULAR RELEVANCE TO SPORTS-RELATED BRAIN INJURY

Athletes represent a unique population of mTBI patients. Athletes who are studied at the college or professional level have typically accumulated many years of experience in their sport, which often amounts to numerous exposures to concussive and subconcussive head trauma. This has led many experts to speculate that athletes are more vulnerable to the deleterious long-term effects of mTBI.

Repetitive Injuries

Investigations of the impact of repetitive mTBI on neurological functioning have predominantly focused on athletes, who are at greatest risk for exposure to multiple injuries. This research has demonstrated that a positive history of prior concussions puts athletes at increased risk for future concussions (Guskiewicz et al. 2000), which has led to the common assumption that mTBI triggers a pathological process that decreases concussion threshold and worsens the severity of subsequent concussive injuries. Some research findings have supported these claims. A study of electrophysiological outcomes in junior hockey players demonstrated that athletes with three or more concussions exhibited prolonged latency of the P3 response as compared to those with no concussion history (Gaetz et al. 2000). Research on symptoms and neuropsychological outcomes has shown that athletes who experienced three or more concussions exhibit more severe acute symptoms, long-term cognitive deficits, and increased depression as compared to athletes who have sustained a single concussion (Collins et al. 2002; Guskiewicz et al. 2003, 2005, 2007a; Iverson et al. 2004). However, other studies have failed to find evidence of cumulative concussion effects on neuropsychological functioning or symptom reporting (Iverson et al. 2006, Macciocchi et al. 2001). Discrepancies in the literature may be partially explained by small sample sizes and poor reliability of self-reported concussion history.

Animal research has been valuable in elucidating the biological mechanisms that may underlie cumulative concussion effects. One study subjected rats to one, three, or five FPIs or sham injuries spaced five days apart (Shultz et al. 2012). Rats in the repeated FPI conditions displayed significantly worse short- and long-term cognitive impairments. Furthermore, neuropathological analysis revealed increased short- and long-term neuroinflammation and cortical damage associated with repeated injuries. Another study, utilizing a clinically relevant rotational acceleration mTBI model in neonatal swine, found that there was a greater distribution of diffuse axonal injury in animals subjected to two injuries as compared to those subjected to one injury (Raghupathi et al. 2004). Although these models are informative, animals in these studies are subjected to multiple injuries with interinjury intervals ranging from minutes (Raghupathi et al. 2004) to days (Shultz et al. 2012), which represents considerably shorter between-injury intervals than what humans typically experience.

Repetitive impacts to the head that do not produce a concussion have been referred to as subconcussive blows. There is much speculation about the role of subconcussive impacts on acute and chronic neurological functioning in athletes. Indirect evidence of a relationship between subconcussive forces and neurological impairment comes from reports of increased risk of chronic neurological impairment in individuals exposed to contact sports for long durations or at high levels of competition (Rabadi & Jordan 2001). By contrast, studies examining acute neurocognitive outcomes in nonconcussed athletes exposed to subclinical levels of head trauma have generally failed to support this claim (McCrory 2003, Miller et al. 2007).

The methodological advance of helmet-embedded accelerometers (e.g., the HIT system) has only recently made the relationship between biomechanical forces and neurological impairment accessible to research. Early findings have been mixed. One study of 46 college football players found that repetitive subconcussive impacts sustained over a single season did not result in impaired performance on neuropsychological tests (Gysland et al. 2012). However, a study of 24 high school football players found a subset of athletes with no clinically observed signs of concussion who exhibited cognitive impairment and altered activation of the dorsolateral prefrontal cortex evidence on fMRI (Talavage et al. 2013). Membership in this group was also associated with a significantly higher numbers of head collisions. Another study of 214 Division 1 college varsity football and hockey players found that poorer postseason cognitive performance was associated with higher scores on several head impact exposure metrics, suggesting that repetitive impacts over the course of one athletic season may have neurocognitive effects (McAllister et al. 2012). Although neurological dysfunction in these samples could be due to subconcussive impacts, it is also quite possible that at least some players in these studies were in fact concussed and simply failed to report their symptoms.

Long-Term Impairment

It has long been known that moderate to severe TBI is associated with increased risk for dementia later in life. Martland (1928) was the first to describe the role of TBI in progressive neurological dysfunction when he characterized chronic neuropathology in boxers, known as dementia pugilistica. For decades the idea that a similar process might affect other athletes subjected to chronic, repetitive head trauma, such as football and hockey players, went unappreciated. Recently, the relationship between mTBI and progressive neuropathology has garnered much attention, mainly due to postmortem evidence of degenerative neuropathology in high-profile professional football and hockey players (McKee et al. 2009). Chronic traumatic encephalopathy (CTE) has now replaced dementia pugilistica as the term to describe this condition. CTE is currently understood as a progressive neurodegenerative disorder triggered by repetitive head trauma and characterized by brain atrophy and tau pathology (McKee et al. 2009). This disorder is suspected to cause mid-life cognitive dysfunction, emotional dysregulation, and motoric disturbance (Gavett et al. 2011).

The neuropathological and clinical characterization of CTE has been based on relatively few cases (McKee et al. 2009, 2013), and issues such as its cause, incidence, neuropathological features, and clinical presentation remain controversial (McCrory 2011, Smith et al. 2013). For example, the behavioral correlates of CTE neuropathology are, as yet, impossible to characterize, given the significant ascertainment bias in the extant research. Families of individuals exhibiting behavioral and cognitive impairments are more likely to submit the brains of their deceased loved-ones for study than are the families of normally functioning individuals. Additionally, in many of the identified cases, clinical symptoms are confounded by drug and alcohol abuse (McKee et al. 2013). Furthermore, the notion that CTE is caused by repetitive head injury has been questioned. Evidence comparing postmortem brains from long-term survivors of TBI with tissue from uninjured age-matched controls demonstrated that neurofibrillary tangles and amyloid-β were rare in control tissue but were abundant and widely distributed in one-third of TBI patients (Johnson et al. 2012b). These findings suggest that a single injury may be sufficient to produce CTE-like neuropathology. Furthermore, there is some doubt that tauopathy is the principal pathological feature of TBI-related neurodegeneration, with some arguing that chronic TBI produces a "polypathology" characterized by amyloid-β, tau, and TDP-43 pathologies; loss of white matter integrity; neuronal loss; and neuroinflammation (Smith et al. 2013).

Other research evidence supports an association between head injury and neurological dysfunction later in life. Guskiewicz and colleagues (2005) administered questionnaires querying general health and memory complaints to a large cohort of retired professional football players. Players who reported three or more concussions during their athletic careers had a fivefold prevalence of mild cognitive impairment diagnosis and a threefold prevalence of self-reported memory problems, suggesting that the onset of dementia may be initiated by repetitive head trauma. A subsequent report from this study also indicated increased risk of lifetime depression diagnosis associated with repeated concussion (Guskiewicz et al. 2007a). However, the strength of this research is limited by its self-reported methodology.

Methodologically rigorous research on chronic mTBI-related neurodegeneration has been hindered by the fact that CTE pathology can only be quantified by postmortem histopathological analysis. However, a recent study was able to detect deposition of tau in living retired football players using a positron emission tomography imaging technique (Small et al. 2013). This exciting work compared five retired football players with histories of mood and cognitive symptoms with five control participants matched for age, sex, education, and body mass index. They found greater evidence of tauopathy in the subcortical and limbic brain areas of football retirees as compared with controls (Small et al. 2013). Although the sample size is small, these initial findings lend support to the self-report and histopathological studies discussed above. Most importantly, these findings suggest that positron emission tomography imaging may represent an important methodological advance in our ability to elucidate the link between brain trauma and progressive neurological dysfunction.

Notably, nearly all of the research on chronic dysfunction related to repetitive head trauma has been conducted in athletes, who are at higher risk of repetitive injuries than are individuals in the general population. Yet other populations are at risk for repetitive brain injuries, specifically military veterans, and evidence of CTE has been reported among this group (McKee et al. 2013). However, in the group of veterans studied, 86% were also athletes, and hence it is difficult to know if nonathletes are regularly exposed to levels of head trauma associated with the development of a neurodegenerative syndrome. Nevertheless, as indicated previously, a single TBI might be sufficient to trigger neurodegenerative processes (Johnson et al. 2010).

DISCUSSION

The remarkable heterogeneity in mTBI outcomes is currently poorly understood. This poses a great challenge to clinicians hoping to provide prognostic information and counsel their patients. Although injury etiology itself would not be expected to produce distinct clinical conditions, etiology can serve as a proxy for other factors that have great bearing on mTBI dysfunction and recovery, i.e., biomechanics, pathophysiology, and psychological and environmental factors that promote risk and resiliency.

Three general hypotheses exist that may account for the observed differences in clinical presentation following mTBI: (*a*) Sports-related mTBI may be associated with a lower level of injury due to less severe biomechanical loads in comparison to those associated with other mTBI mechanisms, (*b*) athletes may experience less dysfunction and more rapid recovery at the same level of injury because of their personal physiological and psychological characteristics, and (*c*) athletes may be less likely to report symptoms and more likely to return to their regular activities despite similar levels of impairment and recovery trajectories. Although there is some support for each of these hypotheses, the complex interplay among pathophysiological, psychological, and environmental influences on mTBI dysfunction and recovery is still poorly understood.

In general, patients with sports-related mTBI may differ considerably from patients with other mTBI mechanisms with regard to pathophysiological, psychological, and environmental disease-moderating factors. Our current understanding of the different biomechanical properties associated with distinct injury mechanisms is incomplete because of the heterogeneity of individual anatomy and injury conditions. So the possibility remains that injuries produced by sports are associated with less severe biomechanical loads on the brain. Hence, comparing sports concussions to other mTBI cases might be comparing apples to oranges. However, it is now known that athletes in contact sports are regularly subjected to forces and rotations sufficient to produce mTBI (Gusckiewicz et al. 2007a, McCaffrey et al. 2007), and evidence from neuroimaging suggests similar patterns of neuronal disruption for sports and nonsports mTBI.

Athletes may also differ from nonathletes in important risk and protective factors that influence the clinical manifestation of mTBI. The athletic population may have a lower incidence of preexisting psychiatric comorbidities. Athletes also may be less susceptible to postinjury PTSD symptoms because they are more psychologically prepared for the likelihood of sustaining a head injury. The return-to-play incentive may be far more powerful than return to work or school. Hence, athletes' motivation to recover may lead to improved postinjury outcomes, minimization of symptoms despite incomplete recovery, or a combination of both. Athletes are more likely to exercise in the subacute period following their injury, which may promote or interfere with recovery depending on the timing of initiation. Unfortunately, the proper timing of postinjury exercise is not yet known. Finally, athletes are more likely to experience multiple mTBIs and subconcussive impacts.

Important methodological considerations must be kept in mind when reading the mTBI literature. Researchers examining sports-related concussion recruit patients from the sideline rather than the emergency department or clinic. Not all mTBI patients seek treatment. Hence, it is likely that sports-related concussion samples are skewed toward a lower level of injury than what is seen in most emergency department and clinic presenting samples. However, one study compared patients with sports and nonsports mTBI from the same setting and found that sports mTBI patients exhibited less functional disability than patients whose mTBI was the result of a motor vehicle accident (Ponsford et al. 2000). Furthermore, research on the neuropsychological effects of sports-related concussion often compares athletes' postinjury performance to their own baseline rather than to a control group. Practice effects, sandbagging, and highly motivated postinjury test performance may lead to underestimates of neurocognitive effects in this population. Additionally, time postinjury varies considerably across mTBI studies. Because of the accessibility of patients, sports-related concussions can be evaluated within minutes, and patients presenting to the emergency department can be evaluated within hours; in contrast, clinic-based samples may not be seen until weeks or months after an injury. Studies conducted in these settings are each sampling distinct spectra of mTBI as a clinical phenomenon.

Finally, many studies are limited by crude methods of assessing injury severity and recovery. Biomechanical data have only recently become available and only for a very small subset of sports injuries. The initial level of injury is difficult to determine, and self-report is often the only method for assessing injury characteristics, such as loss of consciousness and posttraumatic amnesia. However, the development of new serum biomarkers sensitive to brain injury may improve the quantification of acute injury severity (R. Siman, N. Giovannone, G. Hanten, E.A. Wilde, S.R. McCauley, J.V. Hunter, X. Li, H.S. Levin, and D.H. Smith, manuscript submitted; Siman et al. 2009). Traditional neuropsychological tests may not be sensitive to subtle cognitive deficits. Furthermore, no validated in vivo measures of mTBI pathophysiology currently exist. However, there is great promise for the future of this field, as novel research programs are currently addressing each of the aforementioned limitations.

CONCLUSIONS

Multiple factors lead to differences in clinical presentation between sports and nonsports mTBI. It is likely that sports-related concussion studies include some patients with lower levels of injury. However, we do not believe that this completely explains differences in research findings, as athletes in contact sports frequently experience impacts sufficient to produce mTBI, and neuroimaging examination suggests that they exhibit similar patterns of cerebral dysfunction when they are concussed. Athletes may experience less dysfunction and more rapid recovery at the same level of injury as a result of the psychological and environmental protective factors discussed above. Because of the tremendous motivation to return to play, athletes may also underreport symptoms and prematurely return to their regular activities, thus creating the impression that athletes recover more quickly than they actually do.

In this review we have identified some of the factors that influence mTBI presentation. Age at injury and genetic factors are also important patient characteristics that influence disease severity and recovery but are outside of the purview of the present review. The direct and interactive effects of pathophysiological, psychological, and environmental factors that may influence the clinical manifestation of mTBI should be examined in future research. Large studies that sample multiple injury etiologies from the same type of setting are best equipped to characterize differences and similarities between sports and nonsports mTBI. We recommend the use of multiple modalities to fully characterize effects of mTBI on neuronal functioning. Specifically, the most valuable contributions to the field will be made by longitudinal prospective studies integrating serum biomarkers, multimodal neuroimaging, psychological functioning, and both traditional and experimental assessments of cognition.

DISCLOSURE STATEMENT

The authors are not aware of any affiliations, memberships, funding, or financial holdings that might be perceived as affecting the objectivity of this review.

ACKNOWLEDGMENTS

The authors' research was supported by Mild Traumatic Brain Injury and Diffuse Axonal Injury NINDS Grant P01 NS056202 awarded to Douglas Smith, M.D., and Neurobehavioral Outcome of Head Injury in Children NINDS Grant NS-21889 awarded to Gerri Hanten, Ph.D. and Harvey Levin, Ph.D.

LITERATURE CITED

Adams JH, Doyle D, Ford I, Gennarelli T, Graham D, McLellan D. 1989. Diffuse axonal injury in head injury: definition, diagnosis and grading. *Histopathology* 15:49–59

Alla S, Sullivan SJ, McCrory P, Schneiders AG, Handcock P. 2010. Does exercise evoke neurological symptoms in healthy subjects? *J. Sci. Med. Sport* 13:24–26

Bailey CM, Echemendia RJ, Arnett PA. 2006. The impact of motivation on neuropsychological performance in sports-related mild traumatic brain injury. *J. Int. Neuropsychol. Soc.* 12:475–84

Barnes BC, Cooper L, Kirkendall DT, McDermott TP, Jordan BD, Garrett WE. 1998. Concussion history in elite male and female soccer players. *Am. J. Sports Med.* 26:433–38

Barth JT, Alves WM, Ryan TV, Macciocchi SN, Rimel RW, et al. 1989. Mild head injury in sports: neuropsychological sequelae and recovery of function. In *Mild Head Injury*, ed. HS Levin, HM Eisenberg, AL Benton, pp. 257–75. New York: Oxford Univ. Press

Bazarian JJ, McClung J, Shah MN, Ting Cheng Y, Flesher W, Kraus J. 2005. Mild traumatic brain injury in the United States, 1998–2000. *Brain Inj.* 19:85–91

Bazarian JJ, Zhong J, Blyth B, Zhu T, Kavcic V, Peterson D. 2007. Diffusion tensor imaging detects clinically important axonal damage after mild traumatic brain injury: a pilot study. *J. Neurotrauma* 24:1447–59

Bazarian JJ, Zhu T, Blyth B, Borrino A, Zhong J. 2012. Subject-specific changes in brain white matter on diffusion tensor imaging after sports-related concussion. *Magn. Reson. Imaging* 30:171–80

Belanger HG, Curtiss G, Demery JA, Lebowitz BK, Vanderploeg RD. 2005. Factors moderating neuropsychological outcomes following mild traumatic brain injury: a meta-analysis. *J. Int. Neuropsychol. Soc.* 11:215–27

Belanger HG, Kretzmer T, Yoash-Gantz R, Pickett T, Tupler LA. 2009. Cognitive sequelae of blast-related versus other mechanisms of brain trauma. *J. Int. Neuropsychol. Soc.* 15:1–8

Belanger HG, Vanderploeg RD. 2005. The neuropsychological impact of sports-related concussion: a meta-analysis. *J. Int. Neuropsychol. Soc.* 11:345–57

Bergsneider M, Hovda DA, McArthur DL, Etchepare M, Huang S-C, et al. 2001. Metabolic recovery following human traumatic brain injury based on FDG-PET: time course and relationship to neurological disability. *J. Head Trauma Rehab.* 16:135–48

Bigler ED, Bazarian JJ. 2010. Diffusion tensor imaging. *Neurology* 74:626–27

Boake C, McCauley SR, Levin HS, Pedroza C, Contant CF, et al. 2005. Diagnostic criteria for postconcussional syndrome after mild to moderate traumatic brain injury. *J. Neuropsychiatry Clin. Neurosci.* 17:350–56

Brand S, Gerber M, Beck J, Hatzinger M, Pühse U, Holsboer-Trachsler E. 2010. High exercise levels are related to favorable sleep patterns and psychological functioning in adolescents: a comparison of athletes and controls. *J. Adolesc. Health* 46:133–41

Broglio SP, Ferrara MS, Macciocchi SN, Baumgartner TA, Elliott R. 2007. Test-retest reliability of computerized concussion assessment programs. *J. Athl. Train.* 42:509

Broglio SP, Moore RD, Hillman CH. 2011. A history of sport-related concussion on event-related brain potential correlates of cognition. *Int. J. Psychophysiol.* 82:16–23

Browne KD, Chen XH, Meaney DF, Smith DH. 2011. Mild traumatic brain injury and diffuse axonal injury in swine. *J. Neurotrauma* 28:1747–55

Broyd SJ, Demanuele C, Debener S, Helps SK, James CJ, Sonuga-Barke EJ. 2009. Default-mode brain dysfunction in mental disorders: a systematic review. *Neurosci. Biobehav. Rev.* 33:279–96

Bryant RA. 2008. Disentangling mild traumatic brain injury and stress reactions. *N. Engl. J. Med.* 358:525–27

Bryant RA, Harvey AG. 1999. Postconcussive symptoms and posttraumatic stress disorder after mild traumatic brain injury. *J. Nerv. Ment. Dis.* 187:302–5

Bryant RA, Marosszeky JE, Crooks J, Gurka JA. 2000. Posttraumatic stress disorder after severe traumatic brain injury. *Am. J. Psychiatry* 157:629–31

Castelli DM, Hillman CH, Buck SM, Erwin HE. 2007. Physical fitness and academic achievement in third- and fifth-grade students. *J. Sport Exerc. Psychol.* 29:239

Chaddock L, Erickson KI, Prakash RS, Kim JS, Voss MW, et al. 2010. A neuroimaging investigation of the association between aerobic fitness, hippocampal volume, and memory performance in preadolescent children. *Brain Res.* 1358:172–83

Chappell MH, Uluğ AM, Zhang L, Heitger MH, Jordan BD, et al. 2006. Distribution of microstructural damage in the brains of professional boxers: a diffusion MRI study. *J. Magn. Reson. Imaging* 24:537–42

Chen J, Johnston K, Frey S, Petrides M, Worsley K, Ptito A. 2004. Functional abnormalities in symptomatic concussed athletes: an fMRI study. *NeuroImage* 22:68–82

Chen J-K, Johnston KM, Collie A, McCrory P, Ptito A. 2007. A validation of the post concussion symptom scale in the assessment of complex concussion using cognitive testing and functional MRI. *J. Neurol. Neurosurg. Psychiatry* 78:1231–38

Collie A, Maruff P. 2003. Computerised neuropsychological testing. *Br. J. Sports Med.* 37:2–3

Collie A, Maruff P, Makdissi M, McCrory P, McStephen M, Darby D. 2003. CogSport: reliability and correlation with conventional cognitive tests used in postconcussion medical evaluations. *Clin. J. Sport Med.* 13:28–32

Collins MW, Lovell MR, Iverson GL, Cantu RC, Maroon JC, Field M. 2002. Cumulative effects of concussion in high school athletes. *Neurosurgery* 51:1175–81

Covassin T, Swanik CB, Sachs ML. 2003. Sex differences and the incidence of concussions among collegiate athletes. *J. Athl. Train.* 38:238

Cubon VA, Putukian M, Boyer C, Dettwiler A. 2011. A diffusion tensor imaging study on the white matter skeleton in individuals with sports-related concussion. *J. Neurotrauma* 28:189–201

De Beaumont L, Theoret H, Mongeon D, Messier J, Leclerc S, et al. 2009. Brain function decline in healthy retired athletes who sustained their last sports concussion in early adulthood. *Brain* 132:695–708

Delahanty DL, Herberman HB, Craig KJ, Hayward MC, Fullerton CS, et al. 1997. Acute and chronic distress and posttraumatic stress disorder as a function of responsibility for serious motor vehicle accidents. *J. Consult. Clin. Psychol.* 65:560–67

Duma SM, Manoogian SJ, Bussone WR, Brolinson PG, Goforth MW, et al. 2005. Analysis of real-time head accelerations in collegiate football players. *Clin. J. Sport Med.* 15:3–8

Echemendia RJ, Bruce JM, Bailey CM, Sanders JF, Arnett PA, Vargas G. 2012. The utility of post-concussion neuropsychological data in identifying cognitive change following sports-related MTBI in the absence of baseline data. *Clin. Neuropsychol.* 26:1077–91

Edmonds M, McGuire H, Price J. 2004. Exercise therapy for chronic fatigue syndrome. *Cochrane Database Syst. Rev.* 3:CD003200

Ellemberg D, Henry LC, Macciocchi SN, Guskiewicz KM, Broglio SP. 2009. Advances in sport concussion assessment: from behavioral to brain imaging measures. *J. Neurotrauma* 26:2365–82

Erlanger D, Feldman D, Kutner K. 1999. *Concussion Resolution Index.* New York: Headminder Inc.

Faul M, Xu L, Wald M, Coronado V. 2010. *Traumatic Brain Injury in the United States: Emergency Department Visits, Hospitalizations, and Deaths.* Atlanta, GA: Cent. Dis. Control Prev.

Gaetz M, Goodman D, Weinberg H. 2000. Electrophysiological evidence for the cumulative effects of concussion. *Brain Inj.* 14:1077–88

Galetta KM, Barrett J, Allen M, Madda F, Delicata D, et al. 2011a. The King-Devick test as a determinant of head trauma and concussion in boxers and MMA fighters. *Neurology* 76:1456–62

Galetta KM, Brandes LE, Maki K, Dziemianowicz MS, Laudano E, et al. 2011b. The King-Devick test and sports-related concussion: study of a rapid visual screening tool in a collegiate cohort. *J. Neurol. Sci.* 309:34–39

Gavett BE, Stern RA, McKee AC. 2011. Chronic traumatic encephalopathy: a potential late effect of sport-related concussive and subconcussive head trauma. *Clin. Sports Med.* 30:179–88, xi

Giza CC, Hovda DA. 2001. The neurometabolic cascade of concussion. *J. Athl. Train.* 36:228–35

Gosselin N, Thériault M, Leclerc S, Montplaisir J, Lassonde M. 2006. Neurophysiological anomalies in symptomatic and asymptomatic concussed athletes. *Neurosurgery* 58:1151–61

Griesbach GS. 2011. Exercise after traumatic brain injury: is it a double-edged sword? *Phys. Med. Rehab.* 3:S64–S72

Griesbach GS, Hovda D, Molteni R, Wu A, Gomez-Pinilla F. 2004. Voluntary exercise following traumatic brain injury: brain-derived neurotrophic factor upregulation and recovery of function. *Neuroscience* 125:129–40

Griesbach GS, Hovda DA, Tio DL, Taylor AN. 2011. Heightening of the stress response during the first weeks after a mild traumatic brain injury. *Neuroscience* 178:147–58

Griesbach GS, Vincelli J, Tio DL, Hovda DA. 2012. Effects of acute restraint-induced stress on glucocorticoid receptors and brain-derived neurotrophic factor after mild traumatic brain injury. *Neuroscience* 120:393–402

Guskiewicz KM, Bruce SL, Cantu RC, Ferrara MS, Kelly JP, et al. 2004. Recommendations on management of sport-related concussion: summary of the National Athletic Trainers' Association position statement. *Neurosurgery* 55:891–95

Guskiewicz KM, Marshall SW, Bailes J, McCrea M, Cantu RC, et al. 2005. Association between recurrent concussion and late-life cognitive impairment in retired professional football players. *Neurosurgery* 57:719–26

Guskiewicz KM, Marshall SW, Bailes J, McCrea M, Harding HP Jr, et al. 2007a. Recurrent concussion and risk of depression in retired professional football players. *Med. Sci. Sports Exerc.* 39:903–9

Guskiewicz KM, McCrea M, Marshall SW, Cantu RC, Randolph C, et al. 2003. Cumulative effects associated with recurrent concussion in collegiate football players. *J. Am. Med. Assoc.* 290:2549–55

Guskiewicz KM, Mihalik JP, Shankar V, Marshall SW, Crowell DH, et al. 2007b. Measurement of head impacts in collegiate football players: relationship between head impact biomechanics and acute clinical outcome after concussion. *Neurosurgery* 61:1244–53

Guskiewicz KM, Weaver NL, Padua DA, Garrett WE. 2000. Epidemiology of concussion in collegiate and high school football players. *Am. J. Sports Med.* 28:643–50

Gysland SM, Mihalik JP, Register-Mihalik JK, Trulock SC, Shields EW, Guskiewicz KM. 2012. The relationship between subconcussive impacts and concussion history on clinical measures of neurologic function in collegiate football players. *Ann. Biomed. Eng.* 40:14–22

Heitger MH, Jones RD, Macleod A, Snell DL, Frampton CM, Anderson TJ. 2009. Impaired eye movements in post-concussion syndrome indicate suboptimal brain function beyond the influence of depression, malingering or intellectual ability. *Brain* 132:2850–70

Herring MP, O'Connor PJ, Dishman RK. 2010. The effect of exercise training on anxiety symptoms among patients: a systematic review. *Arch. Intern. Med.* 170:321–31

Hillary FG. 2008. Neuroimaging of working memory dysfunction and the dilemma with brain reorganization hypotheses. *J. Int. Neuropsychol. Soc.* 14:526–34

Hillary FG, Genova HM, Chiaravalloti ND, Rypma B, DeLuca J. 2006. Prefrontal modulation of working memory performance in brain injury and disease. *Hum. Brain Mapp.* 27:837–47

Hoge CW, McGurk D, Thomas JL, Cox AL, Engel CC, Castro CA. 2008. Mild traumatic brain injury in US soldiers returning from Iraq. *New Engl. J. Med.* 358:453–63

Holtzer R, Verghese J, Wang C, Hall CB, Lipton RB. 2008. Within-person across-neuropsychological test variability and incident dementia. *J. Am. Med. Assoc.* 300:823–30

Hovda D, Lee S, Smith M, Von Stuck S, Bergsneider M, et al. 1995. The neurochemical and metabolic cascade following brain injury: moving from animal models to man. *J. Neurotrauma* 12:903–6

Huisman TA, Schwamm LH, Schaefer PW, Koroshetz WJ, Shetty-Alva N, et al. 2004. Diffusion tensor imaging as potential biomarker of white matter injury in diffuse axonal injury. *Am. J. Neuroradiol.* 25:370–76

Hultsch DF, MacDonald SWS. 2004. Intraindividual variability in performance as a theoretical window onto cognitive aging. In *New Frontiers in Cognitive Aging*, ed. RA Dixon, L Backman, LG Nilsson, pp. 65–88. London: Oxford Univ. Press

Iverson GL. 2005. Outcome from mild traumatic brain injury. *Curr. Opin. Psychiatry* 18:301–17

Iverson GL, Brooks B, Lovell M, Collins M. 2006. No cumulative effects for one or two previous concussions. *Br. J. Sports Med.* 40:72–75

Iverson GL, Gaetz M, Lovell MR, Collins MW. 2004. Cumulative effects of concussion in amateur athletes. *Brain Inj.* 18:433–43

Iverson GL, Lange RT, Franzen MD. 2005. Effects of mild traumatic brain injury cannot be differentiated from substance abuse. *Brain Inj.* 19:11–18

Iverson GL, Lovell MR, Collins MW. 2003. Interpreting change on ImPACT following sport concussion. *Clin. Neuropsychol.* 17:460–67

Johnson B, Zhang K, Gay M, Horovitz S, Hallett M, et al. 2012a. Alteration of brain default network in subacute phase of injury in concussed individuals: resting-state fMRI study. *NeuroImage* 59:511–18

Johnson VE, Stewart W, Smith DH. 2010. Traumatic brain injury and amyloid-β pathology: a link to Alzheimer's disease? *Nat. Rev. Neurosci.* 11:361–70

Johnson VE, Stewart W, Smith DH. 2012b. Widespread tau and amyloid-β pathology many years after a single traumatic brain injury in humans. *Brain Pathol.* 22:142–49

Kabat MH, Kane RL, Jefferson AL, DiPino RK. 2001. Construct validity of selected Automated Neuropsychological Assessment Metrics (ANAM) battery measures. *Clin. Neuropsychol.* 15:498–507

King AI, Yang KH, Zhang L, Hardy W, Viano DC. 2003. *2003 Intl. IRCOBI Conf. Biomech. Impact*, pp. 1–12. Bron, Fr.: IRCOBI Secr.

Kraus MF, Susmaras T, Caughlin BP, Walker CJ, Sweeney JA, Little DM. 2007. White matter integrity and cognition in chronic traumatic brain injury: a diffusion tensor imaging study. *Brain* 130:2508–19

Kumar S, Rao SL, Chandramouli BA, Pillai SV. 2009. Reduction of functional brain connectivity in mild traumatic brain injury during working memory. *J. Neurotrauma* 26:665–75

Kushner MG, Riggs DS, Foa EB, Miller SM. 1993. Perceived controllability and the development of post-traumatic stress disorder (PTSD) in crime victims. *Behav. Res. Ther.* 31:105–10

Lachapelle J, Bolduc-Teasdale J, Ptito A, McKerral M. 2008. Deficits in complex visual information processing after mild TBI: electrophysiological markers and vocational outcome prognosis. *Brain Injury* 22:265–74

Leddy JJ, Kozlowski K, Donnelly JP, Pendergast DR, Epstein LH, Willer B. 2010. A preliminary study of subsymptom threshold exercise training for refractory post-concussion syndrome. *Clin. J. Sports Med.* 20:21–27

Levin HS, Mattis S, Ruff RM, Eisenberg HM, Marshall LF, et al. 1987. Neurobehavioral outcome following minor head injury: a three-center study. *J. Neurosurg.* 66:234–43

Levin HS, Wilde E, Troyanskaya M, Petersen NJ, Scheibel R, et al. 2010. Diffusion tensor imaging of mild to moderate blast-related traumatic brain injury and its sequelae. *J. Neurotrauma* 27:683–94

Lipton ML, Gulko E, Zimmerman ME, Friedman BW, Kim M, et al. 2009. Diffusion-tensor imaging implicates prefrontal axonal injury in executive function impairment following very mild traumatic brain injury. *Radiology* 252:816–24

Livingston SC, Goodkin HP, Hertel JN, Saliba EN, Barth JT, Ingersoll CD. 2012. Differential rates of recovery after acute sport-related concussion: electrophysiologic, symptomatic, and neurocognitive indices. *J. Clin. Neurophysiol.* 29:23–32

Livingston SC, Saliba EN, Goodkin HP, Barth JT, Hertel JN, Ingersoll CD. 2010. A preliminary investigation of motor evoked potential abnormalities following sport-related concussion. *Brain Inj.* 24:904–13

Lockett DM, Campbell JF. 1992. The effects of aerobic exercise on migraine. *Headache* 32:50–54

Logothetis NK. 2008. What we can do and what we cannot do with fMRI. *Nature* 453:869–78

Lovell M, Collins M, Podell K, Powell J, Maroon J. 2000. *ImPACT: Immediate Post-Concussion Assessment and Cognitive Testing*. Pittsburgh, PA: NeuroHealth Syst.

Macciocchi SN, Barth JT, Littlefield L, Cantu RC. 2001. Multiple concussions and neuropsychological functioning in collegiate football players. *J. Athl. Train.* 36:303–6

Majerske CW, Mihalik JP, Ren D, Collins MW, Reddy CC, et al. 2008. Concussion in sports: postconcussive activity levels, symptoms, and neurocognitive performance. *J. Athl. Train.* 43:265–74

Marquez de la Plata CD, Garces J, Shokri Kojori E, Grinnan J, Krishnan K, et al. 2011. Deficits in functional connectivity of hippocampal and frontal lobe circuits after traumatic axonal injury. *Arch. Neurol.* 68:74–84

Marsh NV, Smith MD. 1995. Post-concussion syndrome and the coping hypothesis. *Brain Inj.* 9:553–62

Martland H. 1928. Dementia pugilistica. *J. Am. Med. Assoc.* 91:1103–7

Maruta J, Suh M, Niogi SN, Mukherjee P, Ghajar J. 2010. Visual tracking synchronization as a metric for concussion screening. *J. Head Trauma Rehab.* 25:293–305

Mayer AR, Ling J, Mannell MV, Gasparovic C, Phillips JP, et al. 2010. A prospective diffusion tensor imaging study in mild traumatic brain injury. *Neurology* 74:643–50

Mayer AR, Mannell MV, Ling J, Elgie R, Gasparovic C, et al. 2009. Auditory orienting and inhibition of return in mild traumatic brain injury: a FMRI study. *Hum. Brain Mapp.* 30:4152–66

Mayer AR, Mannell MV, Ling J, Gasparovic C, Yeo RA. 2011. Functional connectivity in mild traumatic brain injury. *Hum. Brain. Mapp.* 32:1825–35

Mayers LB, Redick TS. 2012. Clinical utility of ImPACT assessment for postconcussion return-to-play counseling: psychometric issues. *J. Clin. Exp. Neuropsychol.* 34:235–42

McAllister TW, Flashman LA, Maerlender A, Greenwald RM, Beckwith JG, et al. 2012. Cognitive effects of one season of head impacts in a cohort of collegiate contact sport athletes. *Neurology* 78:1777–84

McAllister TW, Sparling MB, Flashman LA, Guerin SJ, Mamourian AC, Saykin AJ. 2001. Differential working memory load effects after mild traumatic brain injury. *NeuroImage* 14:1004–12

McCaffrey MA, Mihalik JP, Crowell DH, Shields EW, Guskiewicz KM. 2007. Measurement of head impacts in collegiate football players: clinical measures of concussion after high- and low-magnitude impacts. *Neurosurgery* 61:1236–43

McCrea M, Guskiewicz K, Randolph C, Barr WB, Hammeke TA, et al. 2012. Incidence, clinical course, and predictors of prolonged recovery time following sport-related concussion in high school and college athletes. *J. Int. Neuropsychol. Soc.* 19:22–33

McCrea M, Hammeke T, Olsen G, Leo P, Guskiewicz K. 2004. Unreported concussion in high school football players: implications for prevention. *Clin. J. Sport Med.* 14:13–17

McCrea MA, Iverson GL, McAllister TW, Hammeke TA, Powell MR, et al. 2009. An integrated review of recovery after mild traumatic brain injury (MTBI): implications for clinical management. *Clin. Neuropsychol.* 23:1368–90

McCrory P. 2011. Sports concussion and the risk of chronic neurological impairment. *Clin. J. Sport Med.* 21:6–12

McCrory P, Meeuwisse WH, Aubry M, Cantu B, Dvořák J, et al. 2013. Consensus statement on concussion in sport: the 4th International Conference on Concussion in Sport held in Zurich, November 2012. *Br. J. Sport. Med.* 47:250–58

McCrory PR. 2003. Brain injury and heading in soccer: head to ball contact is unlikely to cause injury but head to head contact might. *Br. Med. J.* 327:351–52

McKee AC, Cantu RC, Nowinski CJ, Hedley-Whyte ET, Gavett BE, et al. 2009. Chronic traumatic encephalopathy in athletes: progressive tauopathy following repetitive head injury. *J. Neuropathol. Exp. Neurol.* 68:709–35

McKee AC, Stein TD, Nowinski CJ, Stern RA, Daneshvar DH, et al. 2013. The spectrum of disease in chronic traumatic encephalopathy. *Brain* 136:43–64

Mead GE, Morley W, Campbell P, Greig CA, McMurdo M, Lawlor DA. 2009. Exercise for depression. *Cochrane Database Syst. Rev.* 3:CD004366

Meaney DF, Smith DH. 2011. Biomechanics of concussion. *Clin. Sports Med.* 30:19–31

Meares S, Shores EA, Taylor AJ, Batchelor J, Bryant RA, et al. 2008. Mild traumatic brain injury does not predict acute postconcussion syndrome. *J. Neurol. Neurosur. Psychiatry* 79:300–6

Miller GA, Chapman JP. 2001. Misunderstanding analysis of covariance. *J. Abnorm. Psychol.* 110:40–48

Miller JR, Adamson GJ, Pink MM, Sweet JC. 2007. Comparison of preseason, midseason, and postseason neurocognitive scores in uninjured collegiate football players. *Am. J. Sports Med.* 35:1284–88

Mondin GW, Morgan WP, Piering PN, Stegner AJ. 1996. Psychological consequences of exercise deprivation in habitual exercisers. *Med. Sci. Sports Exerc.* 28:1199–203

Moser RS, Glatts C, Schatz P. 2012. Efficacy of immediate and delayed cognitive and physical rest for treatment of sports-related concussion. *J. Pediatr.* 161:922–26

Moser RS, Iverson GL, Echemendia RJ, Lovell MR, Schatz P, et al. 2007. Neuropsychological evaluation in the diagnosis and management of sports-related concussion. *Arch. Clin. Neuropsychol.* 22:909–16

Murrey G, Starzinski D. 2007. *The Forensic Evaluation of Traumatic Brain Injury: A Handbook for Clinicians and Attorneys.* Boca Raton, FL: CRC Press

Niogi S, Mukherjee P, Ghajar J, Johnson C, Kolster R, et al. 2008. Extent of microstructural white matter injury in postconcussive syndrome correlates with impaired cognitive reaction time: a 3T diffusion tensor imaging study of mild traumatic brain injury. *Am. J. Neuroradiol.* 29:967–73

Ono K, Kanno M. 1996. Influences of the physical parameters on the risk to neck injuries in low impact speed rear-end collisions. *Accid. Anal. Prev.* 28:493–99

Oride M, Marutani J, Rouse M, DeLand P. 1986. Reliability study of the Pierce and King-Devick saccade tests. *Am. J. Optom. Physiol. Opt.* 63:419–24

Petrides M. 1991. Functional specialization within the dorsolateral frontal cortex for serial order memory. *Proc. Biol. Sci.* 246:299–306

Ponsford J, Cameron P, Fitzgerald M, Grant M, Mikocka-Walus A. 2011. Long-term outcomes after uncomplicated mild traumatic brain injury: a comparison with trauma controls. *J. Neurotrauma* 28:937–46

Ponsford J, Cameron P, Fitzgerald M, Grant M, Mikocka-Walus A, Schönberger M. 2012. Predictors of postconcussive symptoms 3 months after mild traumatic brain injury. *Neuropsychology* 26:304–13

Ponsford J, Willmott C, Rothwell A, Cameron P, Kelly AM, et al. 2000. Factors influencing outcome following mild traumatic brain injury in adults. *J. Int. Neuropsychol. Soc.* 6:568–79

Potter DD, Bassett MR, Jory SH, Barrett K. 2001. Changes in event-related potentials in a three-stimulus auditory oddball task after mild head injury. *Neuropsychologia* 39:1464–72

Rabadi MH, Jordan BD. 2001. The cumulative effect of repetitive concussion in sports. *Clin. J. Sport Med.* 11:194–98

Rabinowitz AR, Arnett PA. 2013. Intraindividual cognitive variability before and after sports-related concussion. *Neuropsychology* 27:481–90

Ragan B, Kang M. 2007. Measurement issues in concussion testing. *Athlet. Ther. Today* 12:2–6

Raghupathi R, Mehr MF, Helfaer MA, Margulies SS. 2004. Traumatic axonal injury is exacerbated following repetitive closed head injury in the neonatal pig. *J. Neurotrauma* 21:307–16

Raichle ME, MacLeod AM, Snyder AZ, Powers WJ, Gusnard DA, Shulman GL. 2001. A default mode of brain function. *Proc. Natl. Acad. Sci. USA* 98:676–82

Randolph C. 2011. Baseline neuropsychological testing in managing sport-related concussion: Does it modify risk? *Curr. Sports Med. Rep.* 10:21–26

Randolph C, McCrea M, Barr WB. 2005. Is neuropsychological testing useful in the management of sport-related concussion? *J. Athl. Train.* 40:139–52

Reger ML, Poulos AM, Buen F, Giza CC, Hovda DA, Fanselow MS. 2012. Concussive brain injury enhances fear learning and excitatory processes in the amygdala. *Biol. Psychiatry* 71:335–43

Røe C, Sveen U, Alvsåker K, Bautz-Holter E. 2009. Post-concussion symptoms after mild traumatic brain injury: influence of demographic factors and injury severity in a 1-year cohort study. *Disabil. Rehabil.* 31:1235–43

Rohling ML, Binder LM, Demakis GJ, Larrabee GJ, Ploetz DM, Langhinrichsen-Rohling J. 2011. A meta-analysis of neuropsychological outcome after mild traumatic brain injury: re-analyses and reconsiderations of Binder et al. 1997, Frencham et al. 2005, and Pertab et al. 2009. *Clin. Neuropsychol.* 25:608–23

Sbordone RJ, Liter JC. 1995. Mild traumatic brain injury does not produce post-traumatic stress disorder. *Brain Inj.* 9:405–12

Schatz P. 2010. Long-term test-retest reliability of baseline cognitive assessments using ImPACT. *Am. J. Sports Med.* 38:47–53

Schatz P, Zillmer EA. 2003. Computer-based assessment of sports-related concussion. *Appl. Neuropsychol.* 10:42–47

Schneider KJ, Iverson GL, Emery CA, McCrory P, Herring SA, Meeuwisse WH. 2013. The effects of rest and treatment following sport-related concussion: a systematic review of the literature. *Br. J. Sport Med.* 47:304–7

Schretlen DJ, Munro CA, Anthony JC, Pearlson GD. 2003. Examining the range of normal intraindividual variability in neuropsychological test performance. *J. Int. Neuropsychol. Soc.* 9:864–70

Segalowitz SJ, Bernstein DM, Lawson S. 2001. P300 event-related potential decrements in well-functioning university students with mild head injury. *Brain Cogn.* 45:342–56

Shultz SR, Bao F, Omana V, Chiu C, Brown A, Cain DP. 2012. Repeated mild lateral fluid percussion brain injury in the rat causes cumulative long-term behavioral impairments, neuroinflammation, and cortical loss in an animal model of repeated concussion. *J. Neurotrauma* 29:281–94

Silverberg ND, Iverson GL. 2013. Is rest after concussion "the best medicine?" Recommendations for activity resumption following concussion in athletes, civilians, and military service members. *J. Head Trauma Rehab.* 28:250–59

Siman R, Toraskar N, Dang A, McNeil E, McGarvey M, et al. 2009. A panel of neuron-enriched proteins as markers for traumatic brain injury in humans. *J. Neurotrauma* 26:1867–77

Slobounov S, Gay M, Zhang K, Johnson B, Pennell D, et al. 2011. Alteration of brain functional network at rest and in response to YMCA physical stress test in concussed athletes: RsFMRI study. *NeuroImage* 55:1716–27

Small GW, Kepe V, Siddarth P, Ercoli LM, Merrill DA, et al. 2013. PET scanning of brain tau in retired National Football League players: preliminary findings. *Am. J. Geriatr. Psychiatry* 21:138–44

Smith DH, Johnson VE, Stewart W. 2013. Chronic neuropathologies of single and repetitive TBI: substrates of dementia? *Nat. Rev. Neurol.* 9:211–21

Smith DH, Meaney DF, Shull WH. 2003. Diffuse axonal injury in head trauma. *J. Head Trauma Rehab.* 18:307–16

Smits M, Dippel DW, Houston GC, Wielopolski PA, Koudstaal PJ, et al. 2009. Postconcussion syndrome after minor head injury: brain activation of working memory and attention. *Hum. Brain Mapp.* 30:2789–803

Solomon GS. 2007. A comment on "exertion" after sports-related concussion. *J. Neuropsychiatry Clin. Neurosci.* 19:195–96

Stancin T, Kaugars AS, Thompson GH, Taylor HG, Yeates KO, et al. 2001. Child and family functioning 6 and 12 months after a serious pediatric fracture. *J. Trauma Acute Care Surg.* 51:69–76

Stancin T, Taylor HG, Thompson GH, Wade S, Drotar D, Yeates KO. 1998. Acute psychosocial impact of pediatric orthopedic trauma with and without accompanying brain injuries. *J. Trauma Acute Care Surg.* 45:1031–38

Stevens MC, Lovejoy D, Kim J, Oakes H, Kureshi I, Witt ST. 2012. Multiple resting state network functional connectivity abnormalities in mild traumatic brain injury. *Brain Imaging Behav.* 6:293–318

Talavage TM, Nauman E, Breedlove EL, Yoruk U, Dye AE, et al. 2013. Functionally-detected cognitive impairment in high school football players without clinically-diagnosed concussion. *J. Neurotrauma.* In press

Tang L, Ge Y, Sodickson DK, Miles L, Zhou Y, et al. 2011. Thalamic resting-state functional networks: disruption in patients with mild traumatic brain injury. *Radiology* 260:831–40

Thunnan DJ, Branche CM, Sniezek JE. 1998. The epidemiology of sports-related traumatic brain injuries in the United States: recent developments. *J. Head Trauma Rehabil.* 13:1–8

van den Heuvel MP, Mandl RC, Kahn RS, Pol H, Hilleke E. 2009. Functionally linked resting state networks reflect the underlying structural connectivity architecture of the human brain. *Hum. Brain Mapp.* 30:3127–41

Van Kampen DA, Lovell MR, Pardini JE, Collins MW, Fu FH. 2006. The "value added" of neurocognitive testing after sports-related concussion. *Am. J. Sports Med.* 30:1630–35

Vanderploeg RD, Curtiss G, Belanger HG. 2005. Long-term neuropsychological outcomes following mild traumatic brain injury. *J. Int. Neuropsychol. Soc.* 11:228–36

Vasterling JJ, Verfaellie M, Sullivan KD. 2009. Mild traumatic brain injury and posttraumatic stress disorder in returning veterans: perspectives from cognitive neuroscience. *Clin. Psychol. Rev.* 29:674–84

Wilde E, McCauley S, Hunter J, Bigler E, Chu Z, et al. 2008. Diffusion tensor imaging of acute mild traumatic brain injury in adolescents. *Neurology* 70:948–55

Williams WH, Evans JJ, Needham P, Wilson BA. 2002a. Neurological, cognitive and attributional predictors of posttraumatic stress symptoms after traumatic brain injury. *J. Trauma. Stress* 15:397–400

Williams WH, Evans JJ, Wilson BA, Needham P. 2002b. Brief report: prevalence of post-traumatic stress disorder symptoms after severe traumatic brain injury in a representative community sample. *Brain Inj.* 16:673–79

Williams WH, Potter S, Ryland H. 2010. Mild traumatic brain injury and postconcussion syndrome: a neuropsychological perspective. *J. Neurol. Neurosur. Psychiatry* 81:1116–22

Zhang K, Johnson B, Pennell D, Ray W, Sebastianelli W, Slobounov S. 2010. Are functional deficits in concussed individuals consistent with white matter structural alterations: combined FMRI & DTI study. *Exp. Brain Res.* 204:57–70

The Psychology of Change: Self-Affirmation and Social Psychological Intervention

Geoffrey L. Cohen[1] and David K. Sherman[2]

[1]Graduate School of Education, Department of Psychology, and (by courtesy) Graduate School of Business, Stanford University, Stanford, California 94305; email: glc@stanford.edu

[2]Department of Psychological & Brain Sciences, University of California, Santa Barbara, California 93106; email: david.sherman@psych.ucsb.edu

Annu. Rev. Psychol. 2014. 65:333–71

The *Annual Review of Psychology* is online at http://psych.annualreviews.org

This article's doi:
10.1146/annurev-psych-010213-115137

Keywords

health, intervention, relationships, self-affirmation, stereotype threat

Abstract

People have a basic need to maintain the integrity of the self, a global sense of personal adequacy. Events that threaten self-integrity arouse stress and self-protective defenses that can hamper performance and growth. However, an intervention known as self-affirmation can curb these negative outcomes. Self-affirmation interventions typically have people write about core personal values. The interventions bring about a more expansive view of the self and its resources, weakening the implications of a threat for personal integrity. Timely affirmations have been shown to improve education, health, and relationship outcomes, with benefits that sometimes persist for months and years. Like other interventions and experiences, self-affirmations can have lasting benefits when they touch off a cycle of adaptive potential, a positive feedback loop between the self-system and the social system that propagates adaptive outcomes over time. The present review highlights both connections with other disciplines and lessons for a social psychological understanding of intervention and change.

Contents

INTRODUCTION

In the 1940s, despite war shortages in finer meats and produce, many American homemakers refused to purchase inferior but more abundant foods even when pressured with patriotic appeals. But when Kurt Lewin (1997/1948) brought homemakers together in small groups to talk about obstacles to serving the recommended foods—thus creating a new group norm around the desired behavior—their purchase patterns changed. In the U.S. Civil Rights era, prejudice was widespread, and opposition to equal rights proved tenacious in many quarters. But when Milton Rokeach (1973) threatened Americans' conception of themselves as compassionate—with a brief insinuation that they valued their own freedom more than the freedom of others—their support for civil rights strengthened in a lasting way.

Today many social problems afflict society—inequalities in education, health, and economic outcomes; political polarization; and intergroup conflict. But these social problems share a psychological commonality with the historical cases described above. The commonality is the notion that barriers and catalysts to change can be identified and that social psychological interventions can bring about long-term improvement.

This review has two purposes. First it looks at threats to, and affirmations of, the self as barriers and catalysts to change. Threats and affirmations arise from the self's fundamental motive: to be morally and adaptively adequate, good and efficacious. How people maintain the integrity of the self, especially when it comes under threat, forms the focus of self-affirmation theory (Steele 1988; see also Aronson et al. 1999, Sherman & Cohen 2006). We provide an overview of self-affirmation theory and review research in three areas where the theory has yielded impactful self-affirmation interventions: education, health, and interpersonal and intergroup relationships.

Self-integrity: the perception of oneself as morally and adaptively adequate

A second purpose of this review is to address questions related to the psychology of change raised by self-affirmation research. Increasingly, social psychological research demonstrates the potential for brief interventions to have lasting benefits (Cohen & Garcia 2008, Garcia & Cohen 2012, Walton & Cohen 2011, Wilson 2011, Yeager & Walton 2011). These interventions help people to adapt to long-term challenges. For example, a series of 10-minute self-affirming exercises, which prompt people to write about core personal values, raised minority student achievement in public schools, with effects that persisted for years (Cohen et al. 2006, 2009; Sherman et al. 2013). How is this possible? How and when do social psychological interventions such as self-affirmation spark lasting positive change? An impactful intervention acts like almost any formative experience. It works not in isolation but rather like a turning point in a story, an event that sets in motion accumulating consequences (Elder 1998). Timely interventions can channel people into what we refer to as a cycle of adaptive potential. This is a series of reciprocally reinforcing interactions between the self-system and the social system that propagates adaptive outcomes over time (cf. Elder 1974, Wilson 2011). The self acts; the social system reacts; and the cycle repeats in a feedback loop (Caspi & Moffitt 1995). We discuss lessons for intervention and for a social psychological understanding of change.

Cycle of adaptive potential: a positive feedback loop between the self-system and the social system that propagates adaptive outcomes over time

Psychological threat: the perception of environmental challenge to one's self-integrity

The Pervasive Psychology of Self-Defense

Key to understanding the effects of affirmation is psychological threat, the perception of an environmental challenge to the adequacy of the self. Whether people see their environment as threatening or safe marks a dichotomy that runs through research not only on self-affirmation but also on attachment, stress, and coping (see Worthman et al. 2010). Psychological threat represents an inner alarm that arouses vigilance and the motive to reaffirm the self (Steele 1988). Although psychological threat can sometimes trigger positive change (Rokeach 1973, Stone et al. 1994), it can also impede adaptive coping. People may focus on the short-term goal of self-defense, often at the cost of long-term learning. Like a distracting alarm, psychological threat can also consume mental resources that could otherwise be marshaled for better performance and problem solving. Thus, psychological threat can raise a barrier to adaptive change.

Major life events, such as losing one's job or receiving a medical diagnosis, can obviously give rise to psychological threat. But the self-integrity motive is so strong that mundane events can threaten the self as well and instigate defensive responses to protect it (Sherman & Cohen 2006). When people make trivial choices, such as between two similarly appealing music albums, they tend to defensively rationalize their selection (Steele et al. 1993). When partisans encounter evidence that challenges their political views, they tend to reflexively refute it (Cohen et al. 2007). When sports fans see their favorite team suffer a defeat, they experience it partly as their own and increase their consumption of unhealthy comfort foods (Cornil & Chandon 2013; see also Sherman & Kim 2005). When people confront petty insults, they sometimes turn to violence and even homicide to reassert an image of personal strength and honor in the minds of others (Cohen et al. 1996; see also Baumeister et al. 1996). Although the objective stakes of many of these situations seem low, the subjective stakes for the self can be high. That everyday events can bring about feelings of threat and trigger extreme responses attests to the power and pervasiveness of the self-integrity motive.

Greenwald (1980) likened the self to a totalitarian regime that suppresses and distorts information to project an image of itself as good, powerful, and stable. However, unlike a totalitarian regime, people can be self-critical. They sometimes denigrate themselves more than outside observers do and believe that others judge them more harshly than they actually do (e.g., Savitsky et al. 2001). People can feel guilty for events they have little control over (Doosje et al. 2006). Although they can spin idealized fantasies of their abilities, they can also give accurate self-appraisals at moments of truth (Armor & Sackett 2006). Storyteller rather than totalitarian regime seems an apt metaphor for the self. The self has a powerful need to see itself as having integrity, but it must do so within the constraints of reality (Adler 2012, Kunda 1990, Pennebaker & Chung 2011, Wilson 2011). The goal is not to appraise every threat in a self-flattering way but rather to maintain an overarching narrative of the self's adequacy. A healthy narrative gives people enough optimism to "stay in the game" in the face of the daily onslaught of threats, slights, challenges, aggravations, and setbacks.

Successful social psychological interventions help individuals access this narrative process through two avenues (see also Wilson 2011). One avenue is to encourage people to appraise a difficult circumstance in a hopeful and nondefensive way that, in turn, sustains the perceived adequacy of the self. Helping trauma victims make sense of their experiences promotes health (Pennebaker & Chung 2011); helping students to interpret mistakes as an opportunity for growth rather than evidence of incompetence improves their academic performance (Dweck 2008, Walton & Cohen 2011, Wilson & Linville 1982, Yeager et al. 2014); and helping parents to see their infants' cries in a more sympathetic and less defensive light reduces abuse (Bugental et al. 2002). A second avenue for intervention focuses on changing not people's appraisal of a specific challenge but their appraisal of themselves. The present review addresses this second avenue and the theory that it proceeds from, self-affirmation theory.

Self-Affirmation Theory

The postulate that people are motivated to maintain self-integrity rests at the center of self-affirmation theory (Steele 1988; see also Sherman & Cohen 2006). Self-integrity is a sense of global efficacy, an image of oneself as able to control important adaptive and moral outcomes in one's life. Threats to this image evoke psychological threat (see Steele 1988, Sherman & Cohen 2006). Three points about this motive merit emphasis.

First, the motive is to maintain a global narrative of oneself as a moral and adaptive actor ("I am a good person"), not a specific self-concept (e.g., "I am a good student") (cf. Aronson 1969). With time, people may commit themselves to a particular self-definition (e.g., parent, teacher). However, the self can draw on a variety of roles and identities to maintain its perceived integrity. Such flexibility can be adaptive. People can flexibly define success in a way that puts their idiosyncratic strengths in a positive light, establishing a reliable but realistic basis for self-integrity (Dunning 2005). The flexibility of the self-system can also promote adaptation, especially in dynamic social systems. Lower animals have relatively simple goals that they try to meet. A mouse unable to forage for food would be a failure. But humans have a unique ability to adapt to a vast range of circumstances. For children and adults, the flexibility of the self-system may foster adaptation to the wide array of challenges they face across cultures and over the lifespan (Worthman et al. 2010).

Second, the motive for self-integrity is not to be superior or excellent, but to be "good enough," as the term "adequate" implies—to be competent enough in a constellation of domains to feel that one is a good person, moral and adaptive. An implication for intervention is that, to affirm the self, an event need foster only a sense of adequacy in a personally valued domain, not a perception of overall excellence.

Third, the motive for self-integrity is not to esteem or praise oneself but rather to act in ways worthy of esteem or praise. Having people praise themselves (e.g., "I am lovable") tends to backfire among those who seem to need the praise most, low-self-esteem individuals, in part because these "affirmations" lack credibility (Wood et al. 2009). People want not simply praise but to be praiseworthy, not simply admiration but to be admirable, according to the values of their group or culture (Smith 1759/2011; see also Leary 2005). An implication for intervention is that rewards and praise are secondary to opportunities for people to manifest their integrity through meaningful acts, thoughts, and feelings.

Although the flexibility of the self-system can be adaptive, it can also prove costly when people cannot find constructive avenues to achieve self-integrity. The self may then seek out alternative domains in which to invest itself. A disadvantaged student may want to succeed in school but, distrustful that society will reward his or her efforts, find other niches to exert control and gain respect; this is one explanation for the draw of gang membership and violent behavior (Matsuda et al. 2013). However, the flexibility of the self-system can also be harnessed for positive ends. People can import into a threatened domain the sense of personal integrity that they feel in another. Thus they can sustain a global sense of adequacy while adaptively confronting a specific threat. For a wide range of challenges, this is what self-affirmation interventions enable people to do.

What Are Self-Affirmations?

A self-affirmation is an act that demonstrates one's adequacy (Steele 1988; see also G.L. Cohen & J. Garcia, manuscript in preparation). Although big accomplishments such as winning a sports contest can obviously affirm one's sense of adequacy, small acts can do so as well. Examples of events that although small from the perspective of an outsider can be subjectively "big" (Yeager & Walton 2011) include a stressed employee who cares for his children or merely reflects on the personal importance of his family; an ill resident of a nursing home who enacts a small measure of control over daily visitations (Schulz 1976); and a lonely patient who, receiving a personal note from her doctor, realizes that others care for her (Carter et al. 2013). Even small inputs into the self-system can have large effects, because a healthy self-system is motivated to maintain integrity and generate affirming meanings (Steele 1988; see also Sherman & Cohen 2006). Many events in a given day are seen as relevant to the self in some way and this enables people to continually refresh their sense of adequacy. But there are times when sources of self-affirmation may be few, or threats to the self may run especially high. Times of high need can be identified, making possible well-timed self-affirmation interventions. Stressful transitions and choice points, for example, mark such timely moments. Self-affirmations given at these times can help people navigate difficulties and set them on a better path. Their confidence in their ability to overcome future difficulties may grow and thus bolster coping and resilience for the next adversity, in a self-reinforcing narrative (Cohen et al. 2009).

Self-affirmations bring about a more expansive view of the self and its resources. They can encompass many everyday activities. Spending time with friends, participating in a volunteer group, or attending religious services anchor a sense of adequacy in a higher purpose. Activities that can seem like distractions can also function as self-affirmations. Shopping for status goods (Sivanathan & Pettit 2010) or updating one's Facebook page (Toma & Hancock 2013) afford culturally prescribed ways to enact competence and adequacy. For people who value science, simply donning a white lab coat can be self-affirming (see Steele 1988).

Although many inductions of self-affirmation exist, the most studied experimental manipulation has people write about core personal values (McQueen & Klein 2006; cf. Napper et al. 2009). Personal values are the internalized standards used to evaluate the self (Rokeach 1973). People first review a list of values and then choose one or a few values most important to them. The list typically excludes values relevant to a domain of threat in order to broaden people's focus beyond it. To buffer people against threatening health information, health and rationality might be excluded from the list. Among patients with chronic illness, values related to family might be avoided insofar as they remind patients of the burden they worry they place on relatives (see Ogedegbe et al. 2012). People then write a brief essay about why the selected value or values are important to them and a time when they were important. Thus, a key aspect of the affirmation intervention is that its content is self-generated and tailored to tap into each person's particular valued identity (Sherman 2013). Often people write about their relationships with friends and family, but they also frequently write about religion, humor, and kindness (Reed & Aspinwall 1998).

Table 1 provides excerpts from affirmation essays written by adolescents and adults in research studies. As the examples illustrate, completing a values affirmation is not typically an act

Self-affirmation: an act that manifests one's adequacy and thus affirms one's sense of global self-integrity

Values affirmation intervention: an activity that provides the opportunity to assert the importance of core values, often through writing exercises

Table 1 Excerpts from affirmation essays

Middle school participants
Dance is important to me, because it is my passion, my life. My second home is the dance studio, my second family is my dance team. My family and friends are so important to me, even more than dance. My family, I can't live without them. My friends, I am my real self around them (and my sister). I can be silly, goofy, and weird and they don't care, they accept me for who I am. . . . And for being creative, I LOVE being creative in dance. When I'm dancing or making a dance it takes me to another place.
Being creative is important to me all the time, because I can use things different kinds of ways and look at things differently. For example, if I can combine the color of the clothes I'll wear or make different kinds of use for the things I have. . . . Being with my family is what makes me happy because only your family understands you better than anyone and you can be yourself no matter what and they would never criticize you. With my friends it's not always the same we can fight sometimes or cry but it's what friendships are for so you should enjoy the moment and be happy with them.
If I didn't have my family, I [wouldn't] be raised right and if I didn't have my friends I would be a boring person. If I didn't have my religion, I wouldn't know what to do, I would be lost.
Music is important to me because it gives me a way to express myself when I'm mad, happy, or sad. I also think family and friends are important because everything, like money, fame, happiness mean nothing if you don't have loved ones to share it with. My friends and family are important because I love them to death and they make me who I am. I also think religious values are very important because if you don't know what you believe in anybody can tell you anything and you'll believe it.
Politics is another really important thing to me because I love politics and I some day want to become a corporate lawyer and to later become the first black president.

College participants
How can one get by without friendship or family? I know I couldn't, I need that support, at times it can feel like the only thing I have that's real. At other times I don't need it, but love and comfort from relationships is something that is always nice. . . . I was stuck in Keystone this winter and had no [way] of getting back home, I felt helpless . . . I didn't know what to do, so I called a friend and they drove 2 hours out of their way to come help me out, without even thinking twice, without that friend I would of had one bad night. Not the end of the world no, but when in need I fall back on my support, friends and family, without that support I would never stop falling.
My relationship with my family is very important to me because it is my parents and brother who helped push me to be who I am today. Without them, I probably wouldn't have the patience and motivation to have applied for this university and be successful here. Whenever I have a problem, it is my family I can go to to help me through it. My friends are also very important. If I didn't have the strong loving relationship with my friends from home, I wouldn't be who I am today. My new friends that I have made [here] are also a big part in my life because they make me smile every day.
My religious values are the foundation of my life; they guided me, helped me, and strengthened me in every aspect of my life. I have always had a strong faith which has taught me to love others and led me to be a better person. I've found that I enjoy life to a greater extent, worry less, and smile more than my friends who don't have religious values. I believe this is because my faith has taught me to be grateful for everything I have, to trust that everything will be fine, and to enjoy every day as if it were the last.
For me the sense of humor of someone is the most important thing. Every time someone makes me laugh it gives me comfort and happiness. I think having a good sense of humor is the best quality that a person can have. It does not matter if a person is good looking or not if they can make others laugh. Every time I meet someone I care if they have a good sense of humor or if they are funny. That is why most of my friends are always laughing, because we all like to make jokes and laugh together. I even think that laughing, making jokes and having a good sense of humor is what keeps us together as friends. Furthermore, our sense of humor is what makes us unique as a group of friends.

of self-aggrandizement (consistent with Crocker et al. 2008, Shnabel et al. 2013). Rather, it is a psychological time-out (Lyubomirsky & Della Porta 2010): a moment to pull back and regain perspective on what really matters. As one college student wrote, "How can one get by without friendship or family? I know I couldn't, I need that support, at times it can feel like the only thing I have that's real." Although the physical act of writing this essay is momentary, it can bring to mind a lifelong source of strength. As **Table 1** also illustrates, people often affirm themselves by writing about their connections to other people and to purposes and projects outside themselves

(Shnabel et al. 2013; see also Crocker et al. 2008). Against this broadened conception of the self in the world, a particular threat that confronts a person feels less dire.

Understanding the Effects of Self-Affirmation

Before focusing on self-affirmation interventions in education, health, and interpersonal and intergroup relations, we summarize how affirmations affect psychology to create a moment of potential change. Then we discuss how and when that change persists.

The psychology of self-affirmation. First, affirmations remind people of psychosocial resources beyond a particular threat and thus broaden their perspective beyond it (Sherman & Hartson 2011). Under normal circumstances, people tend to narrow their attention on an immediate threat (e.g., the possibility of failure), a response that promotes swift self-protection and, in the face of acute dangers, survival (e.g., the fight-or-flight response) (see Pratto & John 1991, Tugade & Fredrickson 2004). But when self-affirmed, people can see the many ordinary stressors of daily life in the context of the big picture (Schmeichel & Vohs 2009, Wakslak & Trope 2009). A specific threat and its implications for the self thus command less vigilance. Nonaffirmed participants saw a psychologically threatening stimulus—a live but securely caged tarantula—as physically closer to them than it actually was, but self-affirmed participants estimated its distance accurately, as though the affirmation psychologically distanced the threat from the self (Harber et al. 2011).

Second, because a threat is seen in the context of an expansive view of the self, it has less impact on psychological well-being (Cohen et al. 2009, Cook et al. 2012, Sherman et al. 2013). Among self-affirmed minority students in a field experiment, a low classroom grade exerted less influence on their long-term sense of belonging in school than it did for their nonaffirmed peers (Cook et al. 2012). Likewise, when college students were self-affirmed, their attention was less absorbed by ruminative thoughts about past failure (Koole et al. 1999).

Third, affirmations foster an approach orientation to threat rather than avoidance. If a threat is seen as important and addressable (Vohs et al. 2013), affirmations make it less likely that people will shrink away from the threat or deny its importance to themselves. Self-affirmed participants in one study asserted that the threatening domain was *more* important to them than did nonaffirmed participants (Cohen et al. 2007, study 1; see also Koole et al. 1999). People can thus better deal with the threat in a constructive way, rather than spend mental energy on avoidance, suppression, and rationalization (see Koole et al. 1999, Taylor & Walton 2011). For example, self-affirmed participants were less likely to shun threatening health information that could benefit them (e.g., Klein & Harris 2009, van Koningsbruggen et al. 2009; see also Taylor & Walton 2011). Self-affirmed participants also showed greater attention to their errors on a cognitive task, as indexed by error-related negativity, a neural signal of the brain's error-detection system (Legault et al. 2012). This pattern suggests greater engagement among affirmed individuals in learning from their mistakes.

Affirmations lift psychological barriers to change through two routes: the buffering or lessening of psychological threat and the curtailing of defensive adaptations to it.

Buffering against threat. Self-affirmations can reassure people that they have integrity and that life, on balance, is okay in spite of an adversity before them. Social relationships appear to have this kind of power. When people were put in a stressful situation, such as receiving mild electric shocks, those who felt they had social support in their lives, or those who simply had the chance to see a picture of a loved one, experienced less fear, threat, and pain (e.g., Master et al. 2009; see also Cacioppo & Patrick 2008). Likewise, when people were put under intense social evaluation—giving an impromptu speech in front of a judgmental audience—those who had reflected on an important personal value no longer displayed an elevation in the stress hormone cortisol (Creswell et al. 2005). Neither social support nor values affirmation eliminated the stressor. Rather they placed it in a larger context of "things that truly matter for my adequacy." Less encumbered by psychological threat, self-affirmed people can better marshal their cognitive resources to meet the demands of the task at hand, for example, solving more creative problems under pressure (Creswell et al. 2013) or exerting self-control in a depleting situation (Schmeichel & Vohs 2009).

Reducing defensiveness. Self-affirmations also reduce defensive responses, adaptations to protect the self from threat (for a review, see Sherman & Cohen 2006). These include the self's strategies of spin control, such as denying responsibility for failure and taking selective credit for success. Defensive responses also include various behavioral adaptations, such as denigrating others to affirm the self, and engaging in denial, rumination, and even heavy drinking and other chemically induced escapes (Steele et al. 1981) that help people to cope with threats to self. Such defensive adaptations serve as a psychological immune system (Gilbert et al. 1998). Although these defenses protect self-integrity in the short term, they can undermine growth and prove self-defeating in the long term. One way that self-affirmations promote change is by curbing defensive reactions. Studies show that defensive denial, bias, and distortion in one domain are lessened by affirmations of self-integrity in another. For example, self-affirmed individuals were more open to a scientific report linking their behavior to cancer risk (Sherman et al. 2000).

In summary, affirmations help people to maintain a narrative of personal adequacy in threatening circumstances. They thus buffer individuals against threat and reduce defensive responses to it. The effect is catalytic. Forces that would otherwise be suppressed by psychological threat—such as cognitive aptitude or persuasive evidence—are unleashed.

Cycles of Adaptive Potential: How Social Psychological Processes Such as Self-Affirmation Propagate Through Time

The review so far has described the psychology of the affirming moment. But several of the intervention studies to be discussed find that the effects of self-affirming writing activities can persist, for instance improving the grades of at-risk minority students years later (Cohen et al. 2009, Sherman et al. 2013). In fact, social psychology has established that brief interventions can have large and long-term effects when they address key psychological processes, as pioneered in the studies of Lewin and Rokeach described in the introductory section of this review (for reviews, see Ross & Nisbett 2011, Wilson 2011). In some cases, the effects of the intervention even grow. Time does not necessarily weaken the influence of the past, but can, it seems, preserve and strengthen it. A key feature of these interventions is that their effectiveness depends on the point in the process in which they are introduced. For example, if teachers are led to expect certain incoming students in their classroom to bloom intellectually, they elicit stronger performance from those students (Rosenthal 1994). But the effects of this "high expectations" intervention disappear if it is delivered only a short time after teachers have met their students and begun to form their own impressions of them (for a meta-analysis, see Raudenbush 1984).

Like any formative experience, a successful intervention is not an isolated event but rather a turning point in a process (see Elder 1998). When well-timed and well-situated, it touches off a series of reciprocally reinforcing interactions between the self-system and the social system (see **Figure 1**). A positive feedback loop between these two powerful systems can drive adaptive outcomes over time. We refer to this as a cycle of adaptive potential, because it increases the actor's potential to achieve adaptive outcomes. The cycle can take over and propagate adaptive outcomes

Defensive adaptations: adaptations aimed at protecting self-integrity by reducing psychological threat or its effects, including cognitive adaptations (e.g., self-serving biases) and behavioral adaptations (e.g., self-handicapping, alcohol consumption)

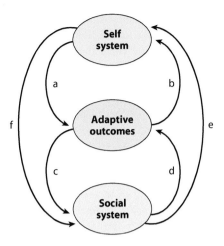

Figure 1

Cycle of adaptive potential, a positive feedback loop between the self-system and the social system that promotes adaptive outcomes over time. Examples of paths include Path a: as a result of being self-affirmed, the person (e.g., athlete, student) achieves more adaptive outcomes (e.g., better performance); Path b: as a result of performing better, the person feels more self-affirmed; Path c: because the person performs better, others (e.g., coaches, teachers) expect more of him/her; Path d: expecting more, others in the social system draw out better performance from the person; Path e: others in the social system affirm the person's self through positive feedback, rewards, etc.; Path f: the person alters the social system through paths other than adaptive outcomes (e.g., by seeking opportunities for practice or by selecting challenging courses).

long after the intervention has receded in time and memory (Caspi & Moffitt 1995, Walton & Cohen 2011, Wilson 2011).

Three principles explain how and when processes propel themselves through time in cycles of adaptive potential (Cohen et al. 2012, Garcia & Cohen 2012, Yeager & Walton 2011). First, because of recursion, the output of a process such as self-affirmation can cycle back as its input, thus perpetuating itself (Cohen et al. 2009, Wilson & Linville 1982). Better performance may affirm the self, leading to still better performance, further affirming the self, and so on, as improvement maintains or even builds on itself. Second, because of interaction, the output of a process can interact with other processes in the environment. For example, if self-affirmed students perform better, they may find themselves held to higher expectations by their teachers or placed in a higher track, which could raise their performance further and open new opportunities. An early advantage can thus channel people into subsequent experiences that perpetuate and broaden the advantage. For long-term effects to occur, a process need not recur, as in recursion, but can instead feed into altogether different processes. Indeed, many social environments abound with change processes (G.L. Cohen & J. Garcia, manuscript in preparation). For instance, schools and cultures produce massive change, as when they transform a kindergartner into an educated, civilized adult. An intervention need not create new processes but may simply interface with these existing ones. Effects then reverberate through the interconnected forces in a social system (Caspi et al. 1987; Caspi & Moffitt 1995; Elder 1974, 1998; Lewin 1997/1948; Wilson 2011). Because of recursion and interaction, the benefits of an intervention can maintain themselves through the progressive accumulation of their own consequences (see Caspi et al. 1987).

Third, because of subjective construal, an intervention can trigger an enduring shift in perception (Sherman et al. 2013; see also Ross & Nisbett 2011, Wilson 2011). Even if the objective environment remains constant, the subjective experience of it may change. For example,

Recursive process: a process in which the output feeds back as an input

Interactive process: a process in which the output serves as an input to an altogether different process in a system

Subjective construal: the actor's subjective perception; even if the objective environment remains constant, the subjective experience of it can be changed through intervention

Latino American middle school children who affirmed core values saw instances of racial threat as unrelated to their likelihood of success in school (Sherman et al. 2013). When affirmed, people tend to narrate adversity as an isolated event rather than an indictment of their adequacy (Cohen et al. 2009). Approach, rather than avoidance, becomes more likely, as does problem solving over giving up. As these personal styles take hold, individuals may construe themselves as the kind of person who can overcome difficulties, an identity that can then guide their behavior (cf. Freedman & Fraser 1966). Their narrative of personal adequacy may strengthen, which may bolster coping with the next adversity, further strengthening the narrative, in a repeating cycle. An intervention may thus have lasting effects by changing the way people filter information about themselves and their environment.

To illustrate these principles, consider the parable of the professional hockey player. Given the many influences on a child's likelihood of becoming a professional hockey player, it seems surprising that birth date has a sizable impact (Gladwell 2008; for a recent comprehensive test, see Addona & Yates 2010). Children with a birthday that falls soon after the cut-off date for entry into this age-based sport have an advantage. As the oldest in their cohort, they tend to be bigger and more adept than other children, and they may stand out as more talented as a result. Their environment may be more affirming; they may score more, be given more opportunities to practice, and be recruited to higher-caliber teams. These experiences affirm the children and strengthen their self-confidence, love for the sport, and identity as a hockey player, which can fuel their desire to practice and improve, evoking further affirmation and opportunity, in a repeating interactive cycle (**Figure 1**). Analogous to affirmation interventions, a birthdate is not the sole cause of children's athletic fate. It is a trigger for a series of iterative interactions between the child and a powerful system of athletic socialization that allocates more resources to higher performers. The parable of the professional hockey player illustrates how recursion, interaction, and subjective construal can turn a variable with no intrinsic causal power into a life-altering influence by putting a person on a cycle of adaptive potential.

Like a fortuitous event, even a brief intervention can have a lasting impact if it is appropriately situated and timed. It can then trigger a positive cycle or interrupt a negative one (Wilson & Linville 1982). Indeed, the three domains where affirmation has had lasting benefit—education, health, and relationships—are ones where problems emerge from a slow-moving accumulation of costs. Each domain abounds with recursive, interactive processes that carry forward the influence of timely experiences, both for ill and for good.

The influence of recursion, interaction, and subjective construal, and the affirmation interventions that tap into these processes, were tested using randomized experiments, many in field settings such as schools and health care centers. The interventions did not eliminate the problems under study and, of course, were not expected to do so. But they did lead to positive and in some cases lasting changes in academic performance, health, and the quality of interpersonal and intergroup relations.

AFFIRMATION INTERVENTIONS

Education

Students want to think positively of themselves. But the daily stressors of school—tests, grades, peer relations—can threaten their sense of personal adequacy. School can be especially threatening for members of historically marginalized groups such as African Americans and Latino Americans (Steele 2010). They may worry that they could be seen through the lens of a negative stereotype rather than accorded respect and judged on their merits. Such vigilance is understandable and even adaptive given the current and historical significance of race in America (Steele 2010, Walton & Cohen 2011). Race, gender, immigration status, and other group memberships can thus give rise to a repeated threat for entire groups in academic and work settings. As hundreds of studies have shown, social identity threat—awareness that one could be devalued on the basis of one's group—can be stressful and undermine learning and performance (Inzlicht & Schmader 2011, Steele 2010, Steele et al. 2002). Even if an African American and a white student work in the same classroom and receive similar instruction, their subjective experience may differ. For the African American student, the prospect of being stereotyped as intellectually limited can render the classroom more threatening.

Policy changes and education reform that eliminate this "threat in the air" are of paramount importance (Steele 2010). Even partial closure of the achievement gap would make a large difference in the lives of many children and their families. Promisingly, lab studies demonstrate that affirmations can improve the performance of students working under the specter of a negative stereotype (Martens et al. 2006, Shapiro et al. 2012, Taylor & Walton 2011).

But in contrast to the lab, in real-world academic and work settings, social identity threat is not acute but chronic (Cohen & Garcia 2008, Garcia & Cohen 2012, Yeager & Walton 2011). It recurs in a multitude of daily experiences, such as learning new material, taking a test, getting help, and making friends. Imagine an African American student who enters middle school with trepidation, uncertain of whether he belongs and will be accepted by peers and teachers. He wants to achieve academically. But, in the first week of school, he is called on by his teacher for his perspective as a "black student." Aware of being stereotyped, the student may feel that his fears have been confirmed, and he may learn less and perform worse on the next exam. The student's sense of threat may then increase, harming performance further, in a recursive process that strengthens with time. Increasingly subtle events may trigger perceived threat, with more mental energy spent on vigilance rather than learning. If teachers fail to grasp the invisible forces at work, they may see the student as limited, give him less support, and hold him to a lower standard. These could exacerbate threat and undermine performance further.

However, a moment of validation at a threatening transition could improve a trajectory (Cohen et al. 2009, Yeager & Walton 2011). If an affirmed student performed better early in an academic transition, this could trigger a cascade of positive effects—greater self-confidence in the student, higher expectations from the teacher—all of which could further affirm the student, relax vigilance, and benefit performance, in a cycle of adaptive potential. Or, more modestly, a downward cycle might be slowed or averted.

Educational interventions. The first set of randomized field experiments tested the effectiveness of values affirmation in lifting the achievement of African Americans (Cohen et al. 2006, 2009) and Latino Americans (Sherman et al. 2013; for additional published replications, see Bowen et al. 2012, Harackiewicz et al. 2014, Miyake et al. 2010, Woolf et al. 2009). The research took place at three middle schools with students in early adolescence, a key transition marked by feelings of inadequacy and a quest for identity. Too many adolescents take a wrong turn and find themselves ensnared in negative trajectories with lifelong consequences (Eccles et al. 1991, Moffitt et al. 2011). The schools were racially mixed such that roughly half the students were minority, that is, African American or Latino American depending on the school, and roughly half were white. Although the schools were located in middle-class neighborhoods, most minority students at one site came from socioeconomically disadvantaged families (Sherman et al. 2013, study 1), an important population given the widening socioeconomic gap in achievement (Reardon 2011). Critically, in the experiments featured here, the academic environments provided material and human resources to help students succeed, and indeed, some had undertaken initiatives to advance

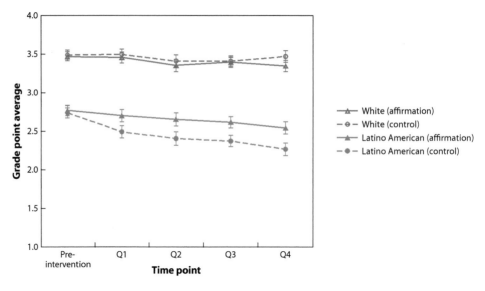

Figure 2

Performance across the school year as a function of ethnicity and affirmation condition, with means and error terms adjusted for baseline covariates and grade level. Middle school students completed a series of writing exercises related to either their most important value in the affirmation condition or an unimportant value/neutral topic in the control condition. Abbreviation: Q, quarter. Adapted from Sherman et al. (2013), study 1.

the learning of underrepresented students. Thus, the social system was "ready" to respond and reinforce better student performance once it occurred.

Each student was randomly assigned to complete either values affirmation exercises or control exercises [for methodological details, see Cohen et al. 2006, 2009 (supplementary materials); Sherman et al. 2013]. These were distributed by teachers as regular in-class assignments two to five times over the year. Each took roughly 10 minutes to complete (see **Table 1** for sample essays). Although students likely expected teachers to read their essays, teachers knew neither students' condition assignments nor the content of their essays. Because early outcomes matter more in a recursive process, the interventions were given early in the year, typically the fourth week of school. In most cases the exercises occurred right before an in-class exam so that their psychological effects could be immediately channeled into better performance rather than decay before they could affect a key outcome. Because novel rather than repetitive experiences have more emotional impact (Lyubomirsky & Della Porta 2010), the nature of the exercises was varied throughout the year.

Students' official grades were tracked for the next one to three years. The values affirmation intervention significantly improved the grade point average (GPA) of the identity-threatened groups, African American students in one school (Cohen et al. 2006, 2009) and Latino American students in two others (Sherman et al. 2013), in their core courses (English, math, social studies, and science). For instance, the affirmation halved the percentage of African American students who received a D or F in the first term of the course in which the intervention was given (Cohen et al. 2006). Because the intervention benefited ethnic minority students but not white students, it closed the achievement gap. The closure corresponded to roughly 30% for Latino and African American students at two school sites (Cohen et al. 2009; Sherman et al. 2013, study 2) and 22% for economically disadvantaged Latino American students at another (see **Figure 2**) (Sherman et al. 2013, study 1).

The intervention's effects persisted and improved students' trajectory through the rest of middle school. Two years later, affirmed African Americans and Latino Americans continued to earn higher GPAs than their nonaffirmed peers (Cohen et al. 2009, Sherman et al. 2013). At one site where high school records were available, the intervention effect persisted into a third year, when most students progressed into high school (Sherman et al. 2013, study 1). Students appeared to carry the benefits with them into a new environment.

The affirmation did not boost GPA but rather slowed its decline. The downward trend common among middle school students (Eccles et al. 1991) proved less steep among affirmed minorities. As a result, the performance trajectories of affirmed and nonaffirmed students tended to diverge with time (see **Figure 2**). This pattern is consistent with the notion that the intervention interrupted a recursive cycle in which threat and poor performance fed on one another and worsened outcomes over time. Also suggestive of a recursive process, the most threatened subgroup, those who would be most undermined by threat and its accumulating consequences, derived the greatest lasting benefit from affirmation. For example, among African American students, those who at baseline had a history of poor performance and felt most unsure of their belonging at school showed almost a full grade point benefit in GPA (Cook et al. 2012, study 1). These were the students whose academic potential was most inhibited by psychological threat. Put differently, the intervention benefit was not diffuse but concentrated among the most threatened, and sometimes hardest to reach, subgroup.

Would values affirmation help close the social-class achievement gap (Reardon 2011)? A randomized field experiment that disentangled the effect of student social class from the effect of student race found that it could (Harackiewicz et al. 2014). It focused on first-generation college students, over 90% of whom were white. These students came from families where neither parent had received a four-year college degree, a proxy for low socioeconomic status. Students with poor socioeconomic backgrounds can face extra stress in college because of financial worries and a sense of not fully belonging on campus (Stephens et al. 2012). For these students, two in-class values affirmations improved their grades in an introductory biology course. It cut the achievement gap between them and their more financially advantaged peers in the course by 50%. Remarkably, first-generation students also proved more likely to enroll in the second course in the biology sequence if they had been in the affirmation condition (86% did so) rather than in the control condition (66% did so). In another study with low-income middle school students, the standard affirmation did not affect students' initial grades, but it did prevent a drop in grades over the course of the year (Bowen et al. 2012).

Values affirmation has also helped another group of students who contend with social identity threat: female college students enrolled in introductory physics, a gateway science course (Miyake et al. 2010). Women who had been randomly assigned to complete values affirmation exercises in their class performed better on their course exams and earned higher grades than did those who completed control exercises. Once again, the greatest benefit accrued to the most threatened subgroup: in this context, women who wondered relatively more if gender stereotypes about science ability might be true[1]. Together, the results of these field experiments suggest that affirmation removed a barrier that prevented the full expression of students' potential (Walton & Spencer 2009).

---

[1]Another affirmation intervention with an ethnically heterogeneous sample of medical students in England found mixed effects, improving the performance of all students on their clinical evaluations and undermining the performance of white students on a written examination (Woolf et al. 2009). However, at least two issues limit interpretability. First, it was unclear whether identity threat contributed to the performance of the ethnic minority sample, a heterogeneous group consisting primarily of Asian Indian, Pakistani, and Bangladeshi participants. Second, procedural changes made the affirmation evaluative in nature. Students' instructors evaluated their essays as "suitable" or "not suitable" for submission to each student's portfolio of learning. A few essays were singled out to be discussed in students' tutorials. Beyond unblinding instructors to students' condition assignment, the evaluative and public nature of the activity may have compromised its ability to be affirming.

Self-affirmation processes bear not only on underperformance but also on bullying and aggression. Young adolescents completed either affirmation or control tasks in school, with outcomes measured several weeks or months after the intervention (Thomaes et al. 2009). Affirmation lessened the extent to which students with grandiose self-views, a risk factor for aggression, reacted to threat (i.e., a drop in their self-esteem) by hitting, name calling, rumor spreading, or committing other antisocial acts as assessed by their classmates. In another field experiment, self-affirmation increased prosocial behavior among students with a history of antisocial behavior, as assessed by their teachers (Thomaes et al. 2012). In summary, psychological threat contributes not only to underperformance but also to bullying and aggression, important problems that have proved difficult to change. And timely self-affirmations can help remedy them.

Understanding the longevity of affirmation effects. How do affirmation intervention effects persist over long periods of time, as they did in these studies? Recursion, interaction, and subjective construal can channel people into a cycle of adaptive potential.

Feeling affirmed, a student may perform better on the next classroom test, and performing better, the student may feel more affirmed, in a recursive process that lifts the student's trajectory and eventually becomes a continual source of self-affirmation. In one series of studies, much of the effect of affirmation on second-year grades was mediated by its effect on first-year grades, suggesting that early strong performance begot later strong performance (Cohen et al. 2009, Harackiewicz et al. 2014). Also consistent with a recursive process was the finding that randomized "affirmation boosters" in the second year did not increase the affirmation's benefit. The processes that the intervention set in motion in the first year sufficed to explain its continuing effect in the second year (Cohen et al. 2009).

A cycle of adaptive potential is, by definition, interactive. Academic institutions teem with processes that recognize, reinforce, and provide resources for student success. By interacting with these processes, an intervention can trigger consequences that have causal power unto themselves. For example, a student who excels early in the year may be seen by teachers as having greater potential. The positive effects of high teacher expectancies on student performance (Rosenthal 1994) may then take hold and propel the intervention effect through time (see Yeager & Walton 2011). Indeed, fewer minority students were placed in their school's remedial track or retained in grade in the affirmation condition (3%) than in the control condition (9%); affirmed minorities also took more advanced math courses (Cohen et al. 2009). When self-affirmed minority students performed better, the system reacted by categorically reshaping their academic experience. Deflection from failure channels such as remediation and entry into success channels such as advanced placement courses can shape students' academic trajectory (Grubb 2009, Steele 2010). The consequences of the intervention can thus break free of their origin and propagate change through time.

Beyond recursion and interaction, subjective construal can fuel a cycle of adaptive potential. Feeling affirmed and achieving more, students may become more hopeful. They may narrate adversity in a more optimistic light. Consistent with this, several findings suggest that self-affirmed minorities were more likely to see adversity as an isolated event rather than a threat to self (see Cook et al. 2012; Sherman et al. 2013, study 2). Among nonaffirmed minority students, a poor grade or a stressful day predicted a lower sense of belonging in school and a higher sense of racial threat (see Cook et al. 2012, Sherman et al. 2013). Each adversity seemed to raise anew the question of whether they belonged (Walton & Cohen 2011). Indeed, over two years, minority students saw their sense of belonging in school fall, as if successive adversities reinforced the narrative that they did not belong (Cook et al. 2012). Likewise, among nonaffirmed first-generation college students, uncertainty about whether they "had the right background" for their course grew over the semester (Harackiewicz et al. 2014). But for self-affirmed students, these effects vanished. They did not question their belonging. Self-affirmed minority students also displayed lower cognitive accessibility of the racial stereotype, suggesting that they were less likely to filter classroom experience through the lens of race (Cohen et al. 2006). To the extent that they were less vigilant to racial cues, they may have had more mental resources for performance and learning (Taylor & Walton 2011). Although the intervention was brief, its effects were repeatedly relived in subjective experience.

In summary, affirmation interventions can trigger a series of reciprocally reinforcing interactions between the self-system and the social system that foster students' adaptive potential over time.

Health

Most people want to think of themselves as healthy, so it can be threatening to confront evidence that challenges that assessment. Illness, frailty, and the prospect of death represent some of the most powerful challenges to adaptive adequacy (see Greenberg et al. 1997). Health-related threats can take many forms: evidence that one's diet puts one at risk for heart disease; a screening that reveals a vulnerability to cancer. Even a visit to the doctor's office can be stressful (Havranek et al. 2012). The effect can run in the reverse direction too. Prolonged stress can have serious health costs that bring a person to the doctor's office (Sapolsky 2004, Sterling 2004, Taylor 2010). Self-affirmation interventions will not cure serious illness, but they can catalyze the impact of other positive health-related forces, such as health information, postoperative care regimens, and a person's goal to live a healthful life.

Like education outcomes, health outcomes are also driven by recursive, interactive processes. For example, stress and illness can exacerbate one another in a vicious cycle (Sapolsky 2004). Failure to achieve a health goal may lead people to give up prematurely, worsening health (see Logel & Cohen 2012, Vohs et al. 2013). Because these processes depend on continual feedback loops, timely interventions could break a negative cycle and perhaps spark a positive one.

Research in this area uses the two routes of affirmation influence. One route uses affirmation to reduce defensive rejection of threatening health information, the other to buffer people against the effects of stress.

Reducing defensiveness. For many diseases, simple preventive steps, such as smoking cessation or diet change, would save a profound number of lives if practiced on a large scale.

But imagine a middle-aged man whose doctor tells him that his diet puts him at risk for heart disease and diabetes. Rather than admit to his dietary misdeeds, he may deploy defensive biases that shield the self from blame but also block change (Sherman & Cohen 2006). He might denigrate the evidence of a link between fat intake and heart disease or assure himself that drugs will undo the damage. Rationalizing the threat away, he persists in his behavior. Persisting in his behavior, he embraces his rationalization more, increasing resistance to change.

However, timely self-affirmation can open people up to threatening health information. With their self-integrity less on trial, self-affirmed individuals can better confront threatening information and evaluate it in a manner less tethered to their needs for self-integrity (Klein et al. 2011). This effect has been confirmed in many studies (for reviews, see Harris & Epton 2009, 2010; Sherman & Hartson 2011).

Affirmation has increased openness to information about the life-threatening habit of smoking. Tobacco-related illness in the United States causes more deaths than HIV, car accidents, alcohol and illegal drug use, suicides, and murders combined (CDC 2012). One study presented smokers with graphic antismoking cigarette advertisements (Harris et al. 2007). Relative to participants in a control condition, participants who first completed a self-affirmation—listing their desirable qualities—saw the advertisements as more distressing, expressed greater confidence in their ability to stop smoking, and had a stronger motivation to quit. This effect on motivation persisted one week later.

When affirmed, people are also more likely to take the first steps toward positive behavioral change. Another study focused on smokers low in socioeconomic status, the demographic group with the highest rate of smoking (Armitage et al. 2008). Among affirmed participants, 59% took leaflets about how to quit smoking, compared with only 37% of nonaffirmed participants. In yet another study, people at risk for diabetes defensively rejected information about their health risk. They declined the opportunity for a diabetes screening test, even though taking the test presumably would have helped them to acquire medical advice that could improve their health and perhaps even prolong their lives (van Koningsbruggen & Das 2009). However, providing them with the opportunity to reflect on important values before reviewing the information decreased their denigration of the health message and increased their likelihood of agreeing to take a screening test (see also Howell & Shepperd 2012). Other small behavioral wins from self-affirmation have been documented, such as increases in the number of college students purchasing condoms after watching an AIDS education video (Sherman et al. 2000).

Two insights arise from this research. First, affirmation enables more balanced information processing. Without the self on trial, people are better able to evaluate evidence on its merits (Correll et al. 2004, Klein et al. 2011). Thus, affirmation does not produce change by itself but enables change to occur if evidence warrants it. Second, echoing the findings in education, affirmation promotes change among people under consistent psychological threat—people whose behavior puts them at risk for a health condition and who thus have cause to feel that their self-integrity is under threat (e.g., Griffin & Harris 2011, Harris & Napper 2005, van Koningsbruggen & Das 2009; cf. Klein & Harris 2009).

Although three null findings have been published (Dillard et al. 2005, Fry & Prentice-Dunn 2005, Zhao et al. 2012)[2], on the whole the research paints a picture of the affirmed mind as an open mind (Correll et al. 2004). Whether the moment of openness then prompts enduring changes in behavior, however, hinges on other factors.

Overcoming barriers to long-term behavior change. The effects of affirmation on attitude and motivation tend to persist, even one month later (Harris et al. 2007, Harris & Napper 2005). But long-term effects on behavior have been mixed (Harris & Epton 2010). In one positive study, drinkers at a bar completed a brief affirmation—selecting and copying an affirming statement that incorporated an implementation intention for how to deal with threat (e.g., by prompting participants to write "If I feel threatened or anxious, then I will think about the things I value about myself")—while others completed a standard affirmation, reflecting on acts of kindness (Armitage et al. 2011). All participants then read a message that summarized the medical risks of alcohol consumption. Relative to a control condition, both affirmations reduced consumption of alcohol, as assessed by self-reports on a validated measure one month later. Between the two time points, the percentage of participants drinking within healthful government-recommended levels jumped

---

[2]In two of these null reports, the authors raise questions about whether their manipulations successfully instantiated affirmation because of either a novel affirmation method (Dillard et al. 2005) or failed manipulation checks for the majority of participants (Fry & Prentice-Dunn 2005). In two of the reports (Dillard et al. 2005, Zhao et al. 2012), the null result may be due to low statistical power, as the key comparisons, though not statistically significant, were in the predicted direction such that affirmation led to more openness to threatening health messages among those for whom the message was most relevant. By chance alone, periodic null effects would occur in a large set of studies. It is also possible that the effects of affirmation depend on hidden moderators not assessed in these studies. For example, in Griffin & Harris (2011), affirmation effects were moderated by trait defensiveness.

by an average of 32 percentage points in the affirmation conditions, more than double the change observed in the control condition.

However, in some studies, affirmed participants fail to make the behavioral changes that they predict they will (Harris et al. 2007, Harris & Napper 2005, Reed & Aspinwall 1998; for a review, see Harris & Epton 2010). Indeed, changes in attitude and motivation seldom suffice for long-term behavioral change (Lewin 1997/1948, Ross & Nisbett 2011). For many health-risk behaviors such as smoking, many people want to stop but are unable to do so (CDC 2012).

Behavior change not only has value in its own right but also helps to trigger changes in self-construal that carry forward intervention effects. Once people act in a healthful way, they may see themselves as a person who cares about health and then behave in ways congruent with that identity (Freedman & Fraser 1966). To achieve long-term benefits with an affirmation, it may be essential to ensure early behavioral wins. These wins also help to convince people that behavior change is possible, a key condition for affirmation-induced change to occur (see Vohs et al. 2013).

Two strategies to promote long-term behavior change, and spur a cycle of adaptive potential, have received suggestive support. One encourages people to form realistic, concrete plans for how to implement their new health-related goals in specific situations (Gollwitzer & Sheeran 2006). One study had college students review a report about the need to eat fruits and vegetables (Epton & Harris 2008). The report provided easy-to-implement steps to incorporate these foods into their diets (e.g., "Add extra vegetables to your pizza"). Although speculative, this may have been a critical aspect of the intervention. When self-affirmed, participants ate more portions of fruits and vegetables over the following week, as assessed by a validated daily diary instrument.

A second strategy to promote long-term behavior change reinstates affirmation at the choice point, when the risk behavior occurs. Because affirmations help people postpone short-term gratifications for the sake of long-term goals (Schmeichel & Vohs 2009), and reduce stress that people might otherwise manage by drinking and smoking (Steele et al. 1981), it may be important to time affirmations to moments of greatest vulnerability (O. Fotuhi, S. Spencer, G.T. Fong, & M.P. Zanna, manuscript in preparation). For example, incorporating a specific implementation intention into the affirmation may be effective ("If I feel tempted to drink alcohol, then I will think about the things I value about myself") (cf. Armitage et al. 2011). Two recent unpublished studies used a recurring physical cue to keep the self-affirming value salient after participants left the laboratory: a bracelet given to participants, inscribed with the words, "Remember the values" (O. Fotuhi, S. Spencer, G.T. Fong, & M.P. Zanna, manuscript in preparation), and a key chain with a secret compartment that contained a slip of paper on which participants had written a phrase related to their most important value (G.M. Walton, C. Logel, J.M. Peach, S.J. Spencer, M.P. Zanna, manuscript under review). Another technique has people write about a value they share with a close other who supports their health goal (O. Fotuhi, S. Spencer, G.T. Fong, & M.P. Zanna, manuscript in preparation). By mentally pairing a value with their health goal in this way, smokers may be more likely to call to mind their value when they are tempted to smoke. Interventions that used these tactics to increase the adhesiveness of a single affirmation yielded long-term improvements in smoking cessation (O. Fotuhi, S. Spencer, G.T. Fong, & M.P. Zanna, manuscript in preparation) and GPA (G.M. Walton, C. Logel, J.M. Peach, S.J. Spencer, M.P. Zanna, manuscript under review).

Buffering against stress. Stress, especially when chronic, can threaten the integrity of the self (Keough & Markus 1998). Indeed, stress often arises from events that call into question people's sense of adaptive adequacy, their perceived ability to meet the demands on them (see Sherman & Cohen 2006). Given this, values affirmations may help buffer people against stress by allowing them to anchor their sense of adequacy in another domain where it is less subject to question.

Physiological evidence of the stress-buffering effect of affirmation was found among college undergraduates facing a real-world stressor—the midterm exam that they had singled out as most stressful (Sherman et al. 2009; see also Creswell et al. 2005). Students in the treatment condition completed two values affirmations before this midterm exam, whereas students in the control condition completed neutral writing exercises. By the morning of their midterm, nonaffirmed students showed a marked increase in epinephrine, as measured by urinary catecholamines, hormones involved in the fight-or-flight response. Affirmed students did not show an increase in epinephrine. Once again, the stress-reduction effect of the intervention was concentrated among the most threatened: students worried about being disliked and seen as unintelligent.

Stress can harm health, especially when it is prolonged (Sapolsky 2004, Sterling 2004, Taylor 2010). Chronic stressors at sensitive periods can keep the stress system on alert for threat even years later, a risk factor for cardiovascular disease (see Miller et al. 2009). This vigilance can create a self-fulfilling prophecy wherein the expectation of threat readies people to perceive it, thereby reinforcing the expectation of threat in a recursive loop that imposes an increasingly heavy toll on health (Miller et al. 2009). Vigilance may help explain why various afflictions—poor sleep, obesity, hypertension, heart disease—cluster among distressed populations (Sterling 2004; see also Walton & Cohen 2011).

Interventions can promote health if they target the psychological "ringleader," perceived threat (see Cacioppo & Patrick 2008). The most effective way to do so is to change the social environment—classrooms, work, home, society—so that it better provides everyday opportunities to manifest adequacy, such as through meaningful work and civic engagement (Sterling 2004). But short of this, timely interventions that assuage threat at sensitive periods can help.

One study focused on women with early-stage (stage I and II) breast cancer (Creswell et al. 2007, a reanalysis of Stanton et al. 2002). The original study found that expressive writing, in which patients reflected on their thoughts and feelings about their experience with breast cancer, reduced self-reported illness symptoms at a three-month follow-up, relative to writing about facts about cancer and treatment (for a review of expressive writing interventions, see Pennebaker & Chung 2011). Content analyses suggested that the active ingredient in women's essays was the act of affirming the self. Patients who affirmed important values, such as relationships or religion, or who reflected on valued personal qualities benefited most. Consistent with the stress-buffering effects of self-affirmation, self-affirming writing was associated with less subjective distress immediately after the writing exercises. By helping patients to see themselves as people with adaptive adequacy in spite of their illness, or even because of their ability to cope with it, the writing exercise seemed to lessen the stress of chronic illness and thus improved long-term health. People benefited from the expressive writing not so much because it led them to reappraise their cancer but because it helped them to reappraise themselves. As a cancer survivor said when reflecting on this research, "This process of self-affirmation allowed me to find the strength and sense of self to keep getting back up" (Norris 2008).

The role of self-affirmation as a buffer against stress and illness is highlighted in a study that used a novel "meaning-making affirmation" (see Keough & Markus 1998). It encouraged participants to extract a value-relevant meaning from their daily experience. College students completed self-affirming writing exercises every other day on ten occasions during their winter break. Participants wrote about their day's experiences and put them into perspective with respect to their most important value. They thus assigned a self-affirming meaning to what they might otherwise construe as a hassle or stressor. For instance, they might see driving a sibling to work as an expression of the value they place on family. Relative to a writing control group, self-affirmed students reported less stress and better health, as assessed by a composite measure of illness, physical symptoms, and health center visits. As evidence that the exercises helped students to integrate stressors into a self-affirming narrative, those who benefited most were students who reported the greatest number of daily hassles that implicated their self-worth (Keough & Markus 1998).

The stress-buffering effects of self-affirmation can improve objective health outcomes by interrupting negative cycles (Logel & Cohen 2012). Stress can undermine self-control, which can increase the likelihood that one will fail to meet health-related goals, which can increase stress further, in a repeating cycle. One study recruited women concerned with their weight. Consistent with the effects of stress on self-control, preoccupation with one's weight predicts distress, poor eating, lack of exercise, and—ironically—weight gain (Haines et al. 2007, Logel & Cohen 2012). More generally, psychological threat can increase appetite for sugary and high-fat comfort foods (see Cornil & Chandon 2013, Sterling 2004). Before being weighed and having their height and waistline measured, participants completed a standard values affirmation or control exercise (Logel & Cohen 2012). Approximately 2.5 months later, affirmed participants had lost more weight than nonaffirmed participants. They also had lower body mass index (BMI) and a smaller waist circumference, a health factor independent of BMI. Affirmation produced these effects, the authors speculated, because it buffered women against weight-related stress and thus helped them to tap into psychological resources to meet their weight-related goals (see also Schmeichel & Vohs 2009). Consistent with this speculation, affirmation both improved women's working memory performance—needed to maintain focus on long-term goals—and strengthened the association between better memory and weight loss. Once people begin to achieve important health goals, they may feel more affirmed and receive more affirming feedback from others, each of which could reinforce the change and carry it forward through time.

Field experiments on patients with chronic health conditions. The February 2012 issue of *Archives of Internal Medicine* featured a series of large randomized trials that found benefits of an affirmation-informed intervention for at-risk individuals on a medical regimen. Medical treatment poses many stressors, such as pain, aversive medical procedures, and separation from loved ones. Severe or prolonged stress can interfere with treatment and recovery (Kiecolt-Glaser et al. 1998).

In the studies, all patients received a standard behavioral intervention to promote recovery from their health problem. Patients in the treatment condition were also encouraged to reflect on core values and proud moments whenever they encountered situations that made it difficult to follow their medical regimen, and to remind themselves of small and often value-relevant events that made them feel good, such as a beautiful sunset. In one study, affirmation increased prescribed medication use among hypertensive African Americans, from 36% to 42% at a 12-month follow-up (Ogedegbe et al. 2012). Another study focused on patients who had undergone an intervention for a heart condition, for whom physical exercise marks a key step in recovery (Peterson et al. 2012). The percentage of patients who achieved the recommended level of physical activity rose from 37% in the control condition to 55% in the affirmation condition. In a third study on young asthma patients, affirmation had a null effect on physical activity, although a positive effect emerged among young patients who had had a serious medical episode that required hospitalization or intensive care and who thus presumably faced the greatest psychological threat (Mancuso et al. 2012).

In these studies, the intervention also contained a positive mood component (e.g., patients received happiness-inducing gifts in the mail), so it is unclear whether affirmation or positive mood drove the effects. However, a randomized double-blind field experiment tested whether a pure affirmation intervention could reduce patients' stress in their interactions with their health care provider and thus promote better patient-physician communication (Havranek et al. 2012). Poor communication between patients and their physicians contributes to patient nonadherence to prescribed care, a major health problem (Zolnierek & DiMatteo 2009). Approximately half of patients fail to adhere to their doctor's regimens for treatment or for prevention of illness (Sabaté 2003). Moreover, because accurate diagnosis hinges on patients' ability to talk candidly about their condition, it is essential to find ways to promote better communication between patients and their physicians.

Communication tends to be less open and more strained when the patient and physician have different racial backgrounds, for instance, when a minority patient meets with a white doctor. Such race discordances predict poorer patient-physician communication, a cause of racial disparities in compliance and health care (see Havranek et al. 2012). Although many factors contribute to this problem, Havranek and colleagues (2012) speculated that social identity threat played a role. Minority patients may worry that their doctor could stereotype them as uninformed or unintelligent, a concern that may be fueled by the cold, awkward, or rushed demeanor of their doctor. The patient's unease and the doctor's demeanor may reciprocally reinforce one another, increasing tension and distrust. But perhaps a values affirmation at the beginning of this interaction might put the patient at ease. The patient might then feel more empowered to take control of the interaction, and the quality of the exchange might improve.

African American patients with a clinical diagnosis of hypertension participated in the study. Most were socioeconomically disadvantaged. Patients were randomly assigned to complete either a standard values affirmation task or a control task at their health care clinic immediately prior to their appointment with a white health care provider. Patients remained unaware of the rationale for the activity, and health care providers remained unaware of the condition assignments of their patients. Each meeting between patient and provider was audiotaped. As assessed by an established coding protocol, the communications between the patient and the provider proved superior among affirmed patients than among nonaffirmed patients. Affirmed patients gave and requested more information about their medical condition. Their interactions evinced greater attentiveness, warmth, and respect, and less depression and distress. Indeed, the aspects of the exchange that affirmation improved are predictive of patients' adherence to their doctors' prescribed care (see Havranek et al. 2012).

As in other domains, affirmation acts as a catalyst in the health domain. It allows people to take advantage of the opportunities for improvement available in a medical regimen or persuasive information, and to deal more adaptively with stress. Many of the health-based affirmations also seem to encourage a habit of self-affirming in challenging circumstances, which may help explain the longevity of their effects. If success occurs at a timely moment, it can set in motion a cycle of adaptive potential that benefits long-term health.

Intergroup Conflict and Interpersonal Relationships

People want to have rewarding relationships, and most want to resolve disagreements equitably. But these motives are sometimes compromised by the competing motive to maintain self-integrity. Because our social worth affects our sense of self-worth (Leary 2005), people may be especially sensitive to perceived threats in their relationships. This vulnerability can cause a harmful defensive style. Affirmation interventions can ease this defensiveness and put the relationship on a better course. Indeed, affirmations have been shown to lessen defensive behavior in interpersonal and intergroup encounters and to promote trust, compromise, and closeness (see also Crocker et al. 2008).

Conflict. When people are affirmed in valued domains unrelated to a dispute, they are more open to otherwise identity-threatening political information and less intransigent in negotiations (for a review, see Cohen 2012). Among people in Israel and Bosnia, historically conflict-ridden areas, self-affirmed participants were more likely to acknowledge wrongdoings inflicted by their group on the other side and to support reparations to those harmed (Čehajić-Clancy et al. 2011). After viewing presidential debates on the eve of the 2008 election, affirmed Democrats and Republicans were less partisan in their evaluations of Barack Obama's debate performance, and 10 days after the election, previously affirmed Republicans thought that President Obama would govern in a more balanced and objective fashion (Binning et al. 2010). Arab American men were able to induce prejudiced people to consider their perspective of being unfairly treated in the wake of 9/11 when they first asked them self-affirming questions, such as, "When were you really creative?" (Stone et al. 2011). Affirmation—induced in this case by the target of prejudice and not a third-party experimenter or interventionist—increased openness to a stigmatized other.

In negotiation, affirmation can lessen the escalation of commitment often observed as partisans' identity becomes bound to the positions they advocate (Sivanathan et al. 2008). When affirmed, people are less likely to derogate concessions offered by adversaries in a negotiation (Ward et al. 2011). In a negotiation over abortion rights, participants whose commitment to their political views had been made salient proved responsive to affirmation. When affirmed, they made more compromises in a negotiation over abortion legislation, and they left the negotiation with stronger trust of the advocate on the other side of the issue (Cohen et al. 2007). Affirmation seems to provide reassurance that a social or political identity, one that would otherwise fix people's evaluations and negotiation positions, is but one of many valued identities. In conflicts where downward spirals of accusation and counteraccusation can escalate into aggression (Kennedy & Pronin 2008), the improved trust and open-mindedness brought about by affirmation holds promise for improved relations.

Relationships. Relationships are so recursive and dynamic, and so intertwined with our sense of self and well-being, that self-affirmation interventions could make a difference in relational matters. One of the strongest predictors of marital distress is defensiveness (Gottman 2011). In arguments, unhappy couples often sink into a mire of reciprocal retaliation. Each person's defensiveness evokes a response in kind from the other, a downward spiral of tit-for-tat that is not only mathematically predictable, consistent with a recursive cycle, but also predictive of early divorce. By contrast, happy couples seem to escape these recursive cycles by parrying with a surprising moment of affirmation—a disarming compliment, an assurance of regard, a bit of shared humor. Indeed, this pattern of disarming affirmation proved among the strongest predictors of marital stability and happiness (Gottman 2011). Such affirming gestures seem especially beneficial for people who feel insecure in their relationships (Overall et al. 2013). Observational studies thus suggest that reducing threat can lessen defensiveness and help couples resolve disagreements constructively (see also Murray et al. 2006).

But can one experimentally introduce such a turning point in a relationship? Although the body of research is not yet as voluminous as in education and health, studies suggest that the answer is yes. In one study, a standard affirmation reduced the defensive distancing strategies that low-self-esteem people in long-term relationships use to regulate the risk of losing the affection of their partner (Jaremka et al. 2011). After a standard relationship threat induction—thinking about personal traits they wanted to keep secret from their partner—affirmed low-self-esteem participants proved less prone to derogate their partner and to contemplate relationship-sabotaging behaviors such as starting arguments. Relational insecurity can also lead people to adopt a distant but self-protective social demeanor, which can evoke rejection from others, deepening insecurity, in a "self-fulfilling prophecy of social rejection" (Stinson et al. 2011, p. 1145). This negative spiral can be interrupted, and a positive trajectory fostered, through values affirmation. When affirmed, relationally insecure participants not only felt more confident in the regard of their family and romantic partners, but also behaved with greater ease and positivity in an interaction with a stranger several weeks later (Stinson et al. 2011).

Small positive shifts in how people construe their relationships can accumulate into enduring changes in the narratives people craft about themselves and their relationships. These in turn can promote warmer relationships, provide further affirmation, and trigger a cycle of adaptive potential that could have far-reaching effects on trust, well-being, and health (Cacioppo & Patrick 2008). More modestly, such shifts may enable couples to break free of downward cycles. Such recursive possibilities received support in a series of studies that tested a novel intervention (Marigold et al. 2007, 2010; see also Finkel et al. 2013). It aimed to encourage low-self-esteem participants to draw self-affirming meanings that, ordinarily, seem to elude them. College students in romantic relationships were instructed to think of a time when their partner complimented them and, in a subtly presumptive prompt, "explain why your partner admired you . . . what it meant to you and its significance for your relationship." Relative to various control conditions, including one that asked participants only to recall the compliment, the intervention led low-self-esteem participants to feel more secure both in their relationship and about themselves. They were more confident in their partner's affection for them, more optimistic about the future of their relationship, and expressed a more positive sense of personal worth. The intervention's effect on relationship security and quality persisted two weeks later. It also seemed to trigger a shift in the actual quality of participants' relationships. At the end of two weeks, affirmed participants reported that their partners had acted more supportively and less critically toward them (Marigold et al. 2007). There was also some evidence that their partners, in turn, saw them as less harsh and critical (Marigold et al. 2010).

The role of self-affirmation processes in negotiations between real-world stakeholders and among people in long-term, committed relationships will, we hope, prove an exciting area of future research.

IMPLICATIONS, QUALIFICATIONS, AND QUESTIONS

Values affirmations can improve grades for students in a lasting way, open people up to threatening health information, reduce sympathetic nervous system activation during stressors, lead overweight people to lose weight, increase patients' compliance with treatment regimens, and improve intergroup and interpersonal relations. Its versatility reflects the pervasiveness of psychological threat in social life. That brief writing exercises could have wide-ranging and long-term benefits may seem nonintuitive. But it is plausible when seen in context. For a person who feels threatened, such as a minority student worried about the transition to middle school, an early moment to manifest personal adequacy in the classroom can provide a psychological foothold. In the context of a powerful social system such as school, designed to reinforce positive change, an affirmation can nudge a motivated but underperforming student away from failure in a lasting way. Below we highlight the main ideas and implications of affirmation and its utility as a centerpiece in intervention.

Lessons

The self is both a barrier and a catalyst to social change. People want to learn, grow, be healthy, and have rewarding relationships, but psychological threat can impede their ability to do so. By helping people to situate threats into a narrative of global adequacy, affirmations turn down the inner alarm of psychological threat. They thus lessen stress and self-protective defenses. Less encumbered, people can make better use of the resources for performance and growth in their social environment, in their relationships, and in themselves. Self-affirmation processes also suggest when environmental stressors may harm long-term health—when they threaten self-integrity—and how interventions can lessen their cumulative costs (Keough & Markus 1998, Logel & Cohen 2012, Miller et al. 2009).

Social psychological processes such as self-affirmation can propagate over time. The effects of self-affirmation interventions can persist for a long time. For example, effects on academic grades and health outcomes have endured months and years after the commencement of the intervention (e.g., Cohen et al. 2009, Harackiewicz et al. 2014, Logel & Cohen 2012, Miyake et al. 2010, Ogedegbe et al. 2012, Sherman et al. 2013). Social psychological interventions such as affirmation can channel people onto a cycle of adaptive potential (**Figure 1**). A positive feedback loop between the self-system and the social system carries the intervention's effects through time to improve the actor's adaptive outcomes. More modestly, such interventions can interrupt a failure trajectory (Wilson & Linville 1982).

Any experience can have persistent effects if it hitches a person to processes that propel outcomes through time. Three principles explain how and when this occurs. Because of subjective construal, an experience or intervention can bring about a lasting shift in perception. Self-affirmed individuals narrate adversity in a manner that better maintains the adequacy of the self and helps them to adaptively engage with threats; this narrative can build on itself over time (Cohen et al. 2009, Cook et al. 2012, Sherman et al. 2013, Wilson 2011). For intervention effects to last, they may need to bring about a long-term shift in subjective construal, the beliefs and schemas that filter experience: an optimistic outlook, openness to challenge, and a self-construal as a person who belongs and can succeed in new settings (for a discussion, see Ross & Nisbett 2011). Without cultivating a lasting shift in the way people construe themselves or their social world, an intervention's impact may fade after it ends, as people slide back to their old habits, seek the familiar, and avoid challenges that would promote their continued growth (Caspi & Moffitt 1995). For example, Schulz & Hanusa (1978) found strong initial health benefits of an intervention that increased elderly nursing home residents' sense of control over their lives. But after the intervention ended, its benefits vanished and treated residents' health worsened. Residents may have come to construe their greater control as temporary and dependent on an external agent rather than based in their own agency. Other examples of disappointing interventions include the Cambridge-Somerville youth program (McCord 1978; see Ross & Nisbett 2011), which provided substantial material and social resources to at-risk juveniles. Such resources may be necessary for change to occur, but not sufficient.

Because of recursion, a process such as self-affirmation can feed off its own consequences (Cohen et al. 2009, Wilson 2011). Self-affirmed individuals may achieve better outcomes, which in turn can reaffirm them and promote better outcomes, in a cycle that sustains itself. Because of the interaction between the person and the social environment, different processes can feed off one another's effects. Achieving better outcomes, self-affirmed individuals may evoke positive responses from teachers or friends, which in turn may evoke even better outcomes from them. Their social world may change, and a new current of processes may then propel their advantage. Affirmed students may be placed in more demanding courses (see Cohen et al. 2009) and come to befriend peers who set a norm for higher achievement (cf. Alwin et al. 1991). Not only may they be shaped by their environment, but they may shape it; with fewer underperformers in a classroom, the teacher might be better able to teach and reach more children. To paraphrase Caspi & Moffitt (1995), the person acts; other variables react; and the person reacts back in iterative interactions—a cycle illustrated in the parable of the professional hockey player described previously.

An understanding of the interdependencies in a system can improve intervention. For instance, in one study variation, teachers were permitted to read their students' affirmation essays

(Bowen et al. 2012). Relative to a standard affirmation and a control condition, teacher awareness increased student grades. Teachers who read the essays may have felt more connected to their students and treated them more attentively, thus fueling the recursive processes initiated by the affirmation in the student. An intervention need not introduce new processes but can instead act as a triggering mechanism for existing ones.

Because of subjective construal, recursion, and interaction, the benefits of an intervention can carry forward through time and can accumulate. They can also widen in scope if they foster assets that promote wide-ranging advantages (Masten & Cicchetti 2010). For example, an intervention that bolstered students' sense of belonging benefited not only their grades but also their self-reported well-being and health three years later (Walton & Cohen 2011). But not all intervention effects persist. And the system can respond in ways that undo intervention effects, if, for example, a teacher raises the curve in response to improved grades (see Garcia & Cohen 2012, Heckman et al. 1998). To make an intervention effect stick, it is necessary to understand the key processes at work in the system. When an intervention occurs at the right time and place and to the persons who need it, what would otherwise be a transient happenstance, such as writing about an important value, becomes a turning point.

Three methodological lessons follow from the importance of time, recursion, and interaction (see Bronfenbrenner 1977, Lewin 1943). First, experimentally manipulated interventions can reveal much about the recursive and interactive processes at work in a system (Lewin 1997/1948). The long-term effects of an affirmation on middle school minority students underscored the recursive, interactive processes that turn early performance outcomes in school into enduring advantages and disadvantages (Cohen et al. 2009, Sherman et al. 2013). Second, because recursive processes take time to develop, a full understanding of them requires longitudinal research, not just the freeze-frame of a short-term measure (Lewin 1943; e.g., Obradović et al. 2010). A single assessment would have failed to capture the downward trend in performance and belonging of middle school minority students and how these constructs fluctuate together for them. A wide-angle temporal lens also pinpoints the time and place a problem emerges and thus when and with whom to intervene (e.g., Cook et al. 2011). A corollary is that the effect of an intervention may take time to occur (Pennebaker & Chung 2011, Schulz & Hanusa 1978) or persist longer than expected (Green & Shachar 2000). Third, because a process interacts with the system in which it occurs, field studies provide a necessary supplement to lab studies. This is not simply because field studies can test the robustness of a process, its signal in the noise of the real world. It is because social systems contain variables that interact with the process and affect its manifestation (Paluck 2009). For example, a school may transform a psychological effect into a structural reality—as when self-affirmed children earn higher grades and are then admitted into more advanced courses (Cohen et al. 2009). "Rigor is not reductionism" sums up these methodological implications.

New trajectories can transform the psychology of the actor. Over time the cumulative advantages of an intervention or formative experience can transform the actor. For instance, months after the intervention had commenced, affirmed minority students had a more robust identity as a person who belongs in school and were resilient to ongoing threats (Cohen et al. 2009, Cook et al. 2012, Sherman et al. 2013; see also Walton & Cohen 2011). Affirmed students experienced many of the same stressors and slights as others but without the detrimental impact that nonaffirmed students experienced. Their experiences throughout the school year made the affirmed and nonaffirmed increasingly dissimilar, as their felt belonging in school diverged with time (Cook et al. 2012). Because affirmed students lived in a subjectively less threatening world, they may have been more emboldened to seize opportunities to transform their circumstances. Self-affirmed children took more advanced courses in math, which suggests that they put themselves on a positive trajectory (Cohen et al. 2009; see also Yeager & Walton 2011). That agents can initiate their own trajectories, and transform themselves in the process, seems key to understanding how and when early influences lead to divergent outcomes. For example, people place themselves in social environments—friendships, marriages, jobs—that can reinforce their beliefs, values, and identity for a lifetime (Alwin et al. 1991, Caspi & Moffitt 1995). A continuity between humans and lower animals is suggested by a study with genetically identical mice in which small early differences in roaming activity became self-reinforcing, compounding over time into large differences in behavior and brain structure (Freund et al. 2013). Cumulative consequences of small initial differences, whether due to chance, personality, or an intervention, can transform the actor.

Timing matters. A major determinant of the effectiveness of an intervention is timeliness. Any resource can provide a bridge to better outcomes if timed to key transitions and choice points (Elder 1998; see also Bronfenbrenner 1977). The importance of timeliness is evident even at the small temporal scale of the laboratory study. Affirmations reduced defensiveness when they occurred either before the presentation of threatening information or soon after. But once participants had engaged in defensive rationalization, the affirmation could not undo it (Critcher et al. 2010; see also Briñol et al. 2007). In some respects, a social psychological intervention is like an engineered coincidence. It places in close proximity three events that otherwise might seldom co-occur: a positive influence, a challenge, and an immediate chance to change. A smoker is affirmed, receives threatening health information, then has the opportunity to assert a commitment to quit.

Over large time scales, early outcomes matter more because their consequences can compound (Cohen et al. 2009, Sherman et al. 2013, Wilson 2011). Not only can early effects magnify in recursive loops, but a small effect can add up into a large one if it repeatedly recurs. Just as small but consistent advantages in baseball batting averages compound into large differences in success over a season or career, a small but consistent advantage in student test performance will compound into a sizable increase in cumulative GPA (Abelson 1985, Cohen et al. 2006). In a field experiment, affirmation benefited minority students' classroom grades more if it took place in the first week of school, before any drop in performance and its ensuing psychological toll, than if it took place at the standard time a few weeks later (Cook et al. 2012). Strikingly, the effect of early timing on first-term class grades equaled the effect of the presence versus absence of the intervention in previous research (Cohen et al. 2006). The beginning of a process, like the beginning of a story, sets the stage for what follows and marks an ideal time to intervene.

Interventions such as affirmation may also have larger benefits if timed to the onset of key developmental transitions. Adolescence, the ascension to college, and entry into gateway courses represent sensitive periods that are often threatening, unpredictable, and stressful—an opportune circumstance for an affirmation. People are often impressionable at such transitions, and their experiences in them can fix the starting point of a recursive process (see Alwin et al. 1991, Elder 1998). As life-course theorists have noted, the outcome of an early life transition can give rise to a chain of advantages or disadvantages that shapes the outcomes of later transitions (Elder 1998). Finally, early experiences anchor people's expectations for threat or safety in an environment (Miller et al. 2009, Worthman et al. 2010). Once formed, such foundational beliefs can filter subsequent experience and prove difficult to undo (cf. Ross & Nisbett 2011). When African Americans performed poorly early in the school year, they suffered a drop in their sense of academic belonging and did not recoup it even if their grades later improved (Cook et al. 2012). Affirmed African Americans, however, were buffered against the effects of early adversity. Transitions thus represent both points of vulnerability and windows of opportunity (Anderson 2003). It is easier to control a process in its germinal stages. But once a process has accumulated its full consequences, it may have a momentum that is hard to halt.

Interventions are more impactful if they take into account the psychological landscape of social problems. Social problems have a psychological side that, if not addressed, will limit the effectiveness of reforms. Improvements in school curriculum may produce little gain if students find the classroom threatening rather than safe. Health campaigns may yield disappointing results if they arouse defensiveness. A sound peace proposal could meet with rejection if adversaries stake their identity on prevailing over the other side. To the extent that financial distress can imprint on children a view of the world as threatening and requiring vigilance, interventions later in life may need to assure them that their school or work environment is a safe place where they belong and good things eventually happen (Chen & Miller 2012, Harackiewicz et al. 2014).

Not only can psychological threat suppress the benefits of structural reforms and institutions. It can also hide the successful impacts that they have already achieved. When social psychological interventions raise the performance of minority undergraduates, this suggests that the collegiate programs that promoted their recruitment and retention were successful, as the performance of students begins to reflect their acquired aptitude (Steele 2010, Walton & Spencer 2009). Together, structural reforms and psychological interventions can synergize each other's effects and reduce the gap between where people are and what they can achieve in a variety of domains (Garcia & Cohen 2012, Yeager & Walton 2011).

Moderators and Boundary Conditions

Social psychological interventions like affirmation are not panaceas but catalysts (Yeager & Walton 2011). Affirmation lifts a barrier, psychological threat, that would otherwise block the impact of positive forces in the person or the situation. Indeed, in all the problem domains discussed, psychological threat stands in tension with hidden positive forces, such as the desire and ability to learn, to be healthy, and to have rewarding relationships. By tipping the balance of forces, affirmation unleashes "previously unrealized behavioral potentials," especially for those on the cusp of change (Bronfenbrenner 1977, p. 528). The forces in tension are key. As with almost any intervention, the effectiveness of affirmation thus depends on prior conditions or moderators.

Resources for growth. For affirmation to afford benefits, there must be forces to impel improvement once psychological threat is lifted. Affirmation will afford little benefit if the motivation and ability to improve are absent. Without resources for growth, affirmation may even trigger disengagement (see Vohs & Schmeichel 2013). These resources may either reside latent in the person (e.g., cognitive ability inhibited by stress) or be scaffolded by the environment (e.g., information about health risk behavior). Intervention "cocktails" that combine affirmation with programs to boost motivation and skills may thus yield the greatest benefit. In a sense, the effect of affirmation reveals less about its intrinsic power and more about the potentials untapped in a person or an environment. Likewise, benefits will tend to persist more in contexts that reinforce the change. Without an attentive teacher, a partner in peace, or an interested romantic partner, an initial improvement will be like a spark without kindling. Conversely, even a small improvement can sum into large consequences if the environment repeatedly reinforces the desired behavior, as many institutions are designed to do. To use an evolutionary analogy, a small increase in the length of a finch's beak may seem trivial, but it is not if it enables the finch to eat more seeds.

Situational- and individual-based differences in psychological threat. For affirmations to yield benefit, psychological threat must be a significant impediment to improvement. In the absence of threat, affirmation has different effects. It may increase self-confidence and resistance to change (Briñol et al. 2007). In contexts where psychological threat contributes little to outcomes relative to other factors such as a dysfunctional school or neighborhood violence, little benefit of the standard affirmation would be expected. Moreover, most studies focus on domains where self-protective responses are harmful (e.g., resisting health information) and affirmation thus prompts a more adaptive response. But sometimes threat and defensiveness foster adaptive outcomes (e.g., Rokeach 1973, Stone et al. 1994). In such cases affirmation should lead to negative effects. When the salient identity was being an open-minded negotiator, affirmation led people to be more closed-minded (Cohen et al. 2007). Affirmation is a tool to unleash potentials suppressed by threat, positive or negative.

At the dispositional level, people who are under threat benefit most from affirmation. One of the best ways to make predictions about the effect of affirmation is to identify whether a threat response occurs at baseline. People with low self-esteem and those who feel insecure in their relationships seem at particular risk. So do people who experience social identity threat in a setting (Steele 2010). But dispositional moderators may vary by context. Low-self-esteem participants act more defensive in some contexts (Jaremka et al. 2011), whereas high-self-esteem people act more defensive in others (Landau & Greenberg 2006; see also Aronson 1969). Another key source of individual differences in responsiveness to affirmation is the ability to generate self-affirming meanings spontaneously (see Pietersma & Dijkstra 2012). High-self-esteem people seem to do this more readily in romantic relationships and thus benefit less from affirmation (Marigold et al. 2007). More generally, the ability to create affirming events, reminders, or meanings seems to contribute to well-being and health. For instance, among adolescents burdened with household responsibilities, those who saw themselves as fulfilling valued social roles such as "good son or daughter" had lower levels of C-reactive protein and other markers of cardiovascular risk (Fuligni et al. 2009).

Types of values and affirmations. Because affirmations work, in part, by putting a threat in the context of the big picture, affirmations that focus people on narrow self-centered values (e.g., power, status) or on sources of integrity conditional on meeting external standards (e.g., approval) tend to be less effective than affirmations that focus people on values that transcend themselves (e.g., compassion, service to others) or on less conditional sources of integrity (e.g., being loved) (Burson et al. 2012, Schimel et al. 2004). Indeed, many affirmation essays focus on unconditional sources of integrity, often from social relationships (Crocker et al. 2008, Shnabel et al. 2013). As one middle school student wrote, "I can't live without [my family]. My friends, I am my real self around them ... I can be silly ... and they don't care, they accept me for who I am" (**Table 1**). Although speculative, one reason for the effectiveness of affirmation interventions is that people may seldom spontaneously affirm themselves in this way at moments of threat. Instead they may adopt a tunnel-vision focus on the threat and lose sight of what really matters. They may try to affirm themselves in the same domain as the threat, which can increase defensiveness (Blanton et al. 1997, Sivanathan et al. 2008), or seek affirmation in extrinsic areas such as financial success and status rather than in the intrinsic sources of integrity cultivated by values affirmations (Schimel et al. 2004; see also Nickerson et al. 2003).

Awareness of self-affirmation processes. As with many interventions, subtlety may be important to the effectiveness of affirmation (Sherman et al. 2009; see also Robinson 2010, Yeager & Walton 2011). For example, students are unaware that the "writing exercises" that teachers provide them are intended to reduce stress and social identity threat. If they were aware of the purpose, they might see the affirmation as a means to an end, robbing it of its intrinsic appeal. Unlike many interventions, affirmation is also "wise" in the sense that it does not suggest to the beneficiaries that they are being singled out as in need of help, a message that can be threatening (Cohen et al. 1999, Steele 2010, Yeager et al. 2014). Indeed, when participants are told that the affirmation is expected to benefit them, or simply led to see a connection between it and the outcome measure, its impact decreases (Sherman et al. 2009, Silverman et al. 2012). However, the benefits of self-affirmation can be restored even when people are aware of its expected impact if they are given a choice about whether to affirm or not (Silverman et al. 2012). When given a choice, people may construe the writing exercise not as a threatening act of control or stigmatization but rather as a tool to achieve agency over their well-being.

Affirmation interventions are not only subtle but also indirect. People often affirm themselves on values remote from the threatening domain rather than directly relevant to it. As self-affirmation theory suggests, a threat derives its power from the challenge it poses to global self-integrity (Steele 1988). For this reason, interventions need not resolve a specific threat to remedy its effects. People can find anchorage for self-integrity in domains beyond the threat. In a variety of areas, in fact, indirect approaches to a behavioral or psychological problem seem to work as well as, and some-times even better than, frontal assaults on it. From increasing happiness to reducing loneliness and depression, from preventing teen pregnancy and academic failure to reducing childhood obesity, many successful interventions do not directly confront the problem. Instead, they bring people to-gether around positive, value-relevant activities such as meditation, extracurricular activities, and volunteer work (Creswell et al. 2012, Lyubomirsky & Della Porta 2010, Robinson 2010, Schreier et al. 2013, Wilson 2011). Although these activities do not directly address the difficulty, they help to remedy it nonetheless.

Connections With Other Research Areas

Resilience. One connection concerns the adaptive systems that foster human resilience. The out-comes in self-affirmation research overlap with the outcomes in resiliency research—stress reactiv-ity, information processing, and self-regulation. The core areas typically affirmed—relationships, family, and spiritual and religious values—dovetail with the hot spots for intervention in resilience research (Masten & Obradović 2006). Affirmation also promotes adaptive processes that resemble the strategies of the resilient. These include constructively orienting to errors (Legault et al. 2012), regulating negative emotions while maintaining a focus on big-picture goals (Creswell et al. 2005, Schmeichel & Vohs 2009), which is similar to a "shift-and-persist" strategy that characterizes people resilient to early adversity (Chen & Miller 2012), and perhaps marshaling into cognitive reappraisal processes, in which higher cortical regions of the brain are recruited to downregulate threat and fear (see Ochsner et al. 2002). With time, these adaptive tendencies may give rise to interpersonal assets, as suggested by research on the resilient. With negative emotions kept at bay, the resilient tend to be good-natured rather than ill-tempered and defensive. This can help them retain the support of family, friends, and coworkers through the lifespan (Caspi & Moffitt 1995, Lyubomirsky & Della Porta 2010) and attract the interest of a role model (Chen & Miller 2012). Psychological assets beget social assets.

In a study of men and women resilient to the stresses of the Great Depression, Elder (1974) saw in them an "adaptive, competent self." Rather than being preoccupied with "matters of self-defense," "inclined to withdraw in adverse situations, and defensive," the resilient had acquired assets that echo the effects of self-affirmation (Elder 1974, pp. 247, 249): a sense of "personal worth ... inner security" (p. 11), "an active coping orientation to the environment," an ability to control stress, a "capacity for sustaining effort and relationships, even in the face of obstacles," "flexibility in the ability to learn and grow from mistakes," "the resilience to rise above setbacks," and a faith in their ability to adapt adequately to changing circumstances (p. 247). By meeting adversity, these individuals became better prepared for new challenges, in a cycle of adaptive potential (Elder 1974).

Social ties. Research on self-affirmation and research on social ties can inform each other. Some of the effects of self-affirmation may arise from the protective effects of subjective connectedness (Cacioppo & Patrick 2008, Taylor 2007). Much "self" affirmation seems to be "social" affirmation. Most people choose to affirm themselves in the domain of relationships (e.g., Creswell et al. 2007). They seem better buffered when they write about why their values make them closer to others (e.g., "I feel part of a team when I play music with my band") (Shnabel et al. 2013) and focus on their positive feelings for others (Crocker et al. 2008). At first glance, the social aspect of affirmation seems contrary to a motive for self-integrity. However, the self draws its integrity from the social world (Leary 2005). As Solomon Asch (1954) wrote, "The ego is not dedicated solely to its own enhancement ... [but] needs and wants to be concerned with its surroundings, to bind itself to others, and to work with them" (p. 320).

Social ties may derive some of their benefit from self-affirmation processes. For example, social support benefits mental health not only because it helps people to manage stressors (Taylor 2007) but also because it provides opportunities to participate in pleasurable, value-laden activities and conversations, as when two music students talk about their favorite band (Lakey & Orehek 2011). Though they do not remedy a specific stressor, these acts may bolster people's sense of global adequacy and thus their well-being and resiliency. In one intriguing study, writers lived longer if their autobiographies referred to a greater number of positive social roles (e.g., mother, neighbor, colleague) (Pressman & Cohen 2007). From a self-affirmation perspective, reference to a broader range of social roles in one's life story reflects a broader pool of affirmational resources to draw on in difficult times.

Links to other interventions. Affirmation may be an invisible component of successful interventions and practices in a variety of disciplines. Some forms of behavioral activation therapy, effective in treating depression, have patients articulate their values and set concrete behavioral goals for living them out (e.g., for the value of good parenting, a goal might be "taking a walk with my daughter once a week"), breaking ruminative cycles (Lejuez et al. 2001). In motivational interviewing, a clinical intervention to change health behavior, counselors encourage clients to affirm their self-identified goals and values (Ehret et al. 2014). Effective well-being interventions have people participate in value-relevant activities such as practicing random acts of kindness (Lyubomirsky & Della Porta 2010). The positive impact of volunteer work on adolescents' health and school achievement may arise from the chance it gives teenagers to craft an identity based on constructive social values (Schreier et al. 2013; see also Allen & Philliber 2001, Wilson 2011). Likewise, expressive writing interventions (Pennebaker & Chung 2011) and narratives of personal agency (Adler 2012) can help people salvage from hardship a sense of purpose and global adequacy. Imaginary acts of self-transformation can bolster a sense of adequacy and thus help people to cope with challenging circumstances. For example, among preschool children, wearing a Superman cape tripled the number who sacrificed a short-term pleasure for the sake of obtaining a more prized reward later (Karniol et al. 2011, study 1). By cognitively transforming into Superman, children could envision themselves as a competent agent, able to manage a difficult situation, and they could thus perform in a way that better achieved their goal. Finally, the motive for self-integrity can be channeled into socially constructive behavior. In one intervention, official voter turnout increased with a short pre-election survey that presented the act of voting as an affirmation of identity (e.g., "How important is it to you to be a *voter* in tomorrow's election?") rather than an isolated behavior (e.g., "How important is it to you to *vote* in tomorrow's election?") (Bryan et al. 2011).

More generally, affirmation is not simply a paper-and-pencil manipulation but rather an act that manifests one's adequacy. The theoretical principles behind affirmation, not any specific practice, is what we hope people take from this review and use to guide efforts at purposeful change. These principles seem harnessed in a variety of success stories. Anecdotally, teachers report that having underprivileged children write about their troubles and relate them to larger social values improves their engagement with school (Freedom Writ. & Gruwell 1999). Similarly, expert tutors, among the most effective of educational "interventions," often begin the tutoring session by asking students about their hobbies, friends, and families. The tutors tune in to students' emotional state, and they provide subtle but well-timed gestures of encouragement that interrupt downward spirals of demoralization and establish a psychological safety zone that helps children confront challenges (Lepper & Woolverton 2001). Likewise, many effective doctors see their patients as whole people with goals and lives, not bodies with disease (Verghese et al. 2011). Indeed, one psychiatric intervention reduced the number of suicide reattempts simply by sending former patients timely postcards inquiring into their well-being (see Carter et al. 2013). To an outsider, such practices can seem insignificant at best and inefficient at worst. But from the perspective of people under threat, a self-affirming act can be a timely sign of their adequacy in the wider world.

CONCLUSION

Self-affirmation theory began with the question of how people cope with threats to the self (Steele 1988). It has spurred a more general account of the change process: how and when people adapt adequately to threatening circumstances, how interventions can foster this adaptation, and when these new adaptations stick. A developmentally informed social psychology addresses these topics and speaks to the problem of stability and change. Although social psychology has long demonstrated the malleability of human behavior (Ross & Nisbett 2011), other traditions have shown the striking continuity of personality over time (e.g., Caspi et al. 1987, Caspi & Moffitt 1995). For example, the finding that children's performance on laboratory self-control tasks can be boosted by situational intervention (e.g., Karniol et al. 2011) seems to clash with the finding that childhood variation on such self-control measures predicts health, wealth, employment, and crime decades later (Moffitt et al. 2011). The contradiction resolves itself when we realize that "persistent doesn't equal permanent" (Sapolsky 2010, p. xxvi). Persistent can be fragile. Outcomes that seem set in stone may in fact be the repeating output of dynamic processes. At timely moments the processes can be redirected to prompt lasting adaptive change (Wilson 2011).

In Raymond Carver's story, *A Small, Good Thing*, a baker gives delicious cinnamon rolls to a couple whose child has just died (Carver 1989). The baker says to the stricken couple, "Eating is a small, good thing in a time like this." Of course, his gift to them is not so small after all, in part because it is given at precisely the right moment. A little help with a financial aid form for college, some health advice from a friend, a word of encouragement from a mentor, a conversation with a stranger, and other seemingly random events can change a life and even the course of history. But such events need not be left to chance alone. Social psychology can help locate the right place and the right time for a small, good thing to happen.

FUTURE ISSUES

1. Some people may affirm themselves spontaneously. Indeed, some people try to turn almost any writing exercise into a self-affirming one. What are the effects of these self-generated affirmations? How do they differ from the experimentally induced affirmations? And how can researchers capture the spontaneous affirmation process and its effects in everyday life?

2. Affirmations tend to yield concentrated rather than diffuse effects, because they typically benefit the people for whom a threat in a given context is most salient and acute. Understanding this heterogeneity is important, as it can help to "reverse engineer" which individuals and groups are most under threat in a given setting.

3. Insofar as the benefits of values affirmation and other social psychological interventions result from carefully conducted research by trained experimental social psychologists, how best should practitioners, policy makers, and researchers work together to scale up such interventions? This seems a particularly challenging issue given that attention to local conditions, personalization of the intervention materials, considerations of timing and other theoretical principles can be difficult to maintain in the scaling-up process.

4. Jamie Pennebaker and Cindy Chung (2011) wrote, "If you are expecting a clean and simple explanation for the effectiveness of writing, we have some very bad news: There is no single reason that explains it" (p. 426). The same notion applies to the effects of self-affirmations. Yet some lessons have emerged related to how and when self-affirmation interventions prompt lasting change. Future research should examine a range of mechanisms and mediators at different levels of analysis, including the neural activity of the affirmed mind, the content of the writing exercises, and the recursive processes and feedback mechanisms that affirmation catalyzes. Longitudinal experiments will be particularly useful to capture the multiple processes that propagate effects over time.

DISCLOSURE STATEMENT

The authors are not aware of any affiliations, memberships, funding, or financial holdings that might be perceived as affecting the objectivity of this review.

ACKNOWLEDGMENTS

We thank Sarah Wert, Heejung Kim, Kevin Binning, Stephanie Reeves, and Amy Petermann for assistance and thoughtful comments on earlier drafts, and Julio Garcia, Claude Steele, Gregory Walton, David Yeager, Lee Ross, Emily Pronin, David Creswell, Kody Manke, and Shannon Brady for helpful discussions. Preparation of this manuscript was supported by grants NSF DRL-1109548 and NIH 5R01HD055342-04 to G.L.C.

LITERATURE CITED

Abelson RP. 1985. A variance explanation paradox: when a little is a lot. *Psychol. Bull.* 97:129–33

Addona V, Yates PA. 2010. A closer look at the relative age effect in the National Hockey League. *J. Quant. Anal. Sports* 6(Artic. 9):1–17

Adler JM. 2012. Living into the story: agency and coherence in a longitudinal study of narrative identity development and mental health over the course of psychotherapy. *J. Personal. Soc. Psychol.* 102:367–89

Allen JP, Philliber S. 2001. Who benefits most from a broadly targeted prevention program? Differential efficacy across populations in the Teen Outreach Program. *J. Community Psychol.* 29:637–55

Alwin DF, Cohen RL, Necomb TM. 1991. *Political Attitudes Over the Life Span: The Bennington Women After Fifty Years.* Madison: Univ. Wis. Press

Anderson SL. 2003. Trajectories of brain development: point of vulnerability or window of opportunity. *Neurosci. Biobehav. Rev.* 27:3–18

Armitage CJ, Harris PR, Arden MA. 2011. Evidence that self-affirmation reduces alcohol consumption: randomized exploratory trial with a new, brief means of self-affirming. *Health Psychol.* 30:633–41

Armitage CJ, Harris PR, Hepton G, Napper L. 2008. Self-affirmation increases acceptance of health-risk information among UK adult smokers with low socioeconomic status. *Psychol. Addict. Behav.* 22:88–95

Armor DA, Sackett AM. 2006. Accuracy, error, and bias in predictions for real versus hypothetical events. *J. Personal. Soc. Psychol.* 91:583–600

Aronson E. 1969. The theory of cognitive dissonance: a current perspective. In *Advances in Experimental Social Psychology*, ed. L Berkowitz, 4:1–34. New York: Academic

Aronson J, Cohen GL, Nail PR. 1999. Self-affirmation theory: an update and appraisal. In *Cognitive Dissonance: Progress on a Pivotal Theory in Social Psychology*, ed. E Harmon-Jones, J Mills, pp. 127–48. Washington, DC: Am. Psychol. Assoc.

Asch S. 1954. *Social Psychology*. Englewood Cliffs, NJ: Prentice-Hall

Baumeister RF, Smart I, Boden JM. 1996. Relation of threatened egotism to violence and aggression: the dark side of high self-esteem. *Psychol. Rev.* 103:5–33

Binning KR, Sherman DK, Cohen GL, Heitland K. 2010. Seeing the other side: reducing political partisanship via self-affirmation in the 2008 presidential election. *Anal. Soc. Issues Public Policy* 10:276–92

Blanton H, Cooper J, Skurnik I, Aronson J. 1997. When bad things happen to good feedback: exacerbating the need for self-justification through self-affirmation. *Personal. Soc. Psychol. Bull.* 23:684–92

Bowen NK, Wegmann KM, Webber KC. 2013. Enhancing a brief writing intervention to combat stereotype threat among middle-school students. *J. Educ. Psychol.* 105:427–35

Briñol P, Petty RE, Gallardo I, DeMarree KG. 2007. The effect of self-affirmation in non-threatening persuasion domains: timing affects the process. *Personal. Soc. Psychol. Bull.* 33:1533–46

Bronfenbrenner U. 1977. Toward an experimental ecology of human development. *Am. Psychol.* 32:513–31

Bryan CJ, Walton GM, Rogers T, Dweck CS. 2011. Motivating voter turnout by invoking the self. *Proc. Natl. Acad. Sci. USA* 108:12653–56

Bugental DB, Ellerson PC, Lin EK, Rainey B, Kokotovic A, O'Hara N. 2002. A cognitive approach to child abuse prevention. *J. Fam. Psychol.* 16:243–58

Burson A, Crocker J, Mischkowski D. 2012. Two types of value-affirmation: implications for self-control following social exclusion. *Soc. Psychol. Personal. Sci.* 3:510–16

Cacioppo JT, Patrick W. 2008. *Loneliness: Human Nature and the Need for Social Connection*. New York: Norton

Carter GL, Clover K, Whyte IM, Dawson AH, D'Este C. 2013. Postcards from the EDge: 5-year outcomes of a randomised controlled trial for hospital-treated self-poisoning. *Br. J. Psychiatry* 202:372–80

Carver R. 1989. A small, good thing. In *Where I'm Calling From*. New York: Random House

Caspi A, Elder GH, Bem DJ. 1987. Moving against the world: life-course patterns of explosive children. *Dev. Psychol.* 23:308–13

Caspi A, Moffitt TE. 1995. The continuity of maladaptive behavior: from description to understanding in the study of antisocial behavior. In *Developmental Psychopathology Vol. 2: Risk, Disorder, and Adaptation. Wiley Series on Personality Processes*, ed. D Cicchetti, DJ Cohen, pp. 472–511. Oxford, UK: Wiley

Čehajić-Clancy S, Effron DA, Halperin E, Liberman V, Ross LD. 2011. Affirmation, acknowledgment of in-group responsibility, group-based guilt, and support for reparative measures. *J. Personal. Soc. Psychol.* 101:256–70

Cent. Disease Control Prev. (CDC). *Smoking and Tobacco Use*. Atlanta, GA: CDC. **http://www.cdc. gov/tobacco/data_statistics/fact_sheets/fast_facts/index.htm**

Chen E, Miller GE. 2012. "Shift-and-persist" strategies: why low socioeconomic status isn't always bad for health. *Perspect. Psychol. Sci.* 7:135–58

Cohen D, Nisbett RE, Bowdle BF, Schwarz N. 1996. Insult, aggression, and the southern culture of honor: an "experimental ethnography." *J. Personal. Soc. Psychol.* 70:945–60

Cohen GL. 2012. Identity, ideology, and bias. In *Ideology, Psychology, and Law*, ed. J Hanson, pp. 385–403. New York: Oxford Univ. Press

Cohen GL, Garcia J. 2008. Identity, belonging, and achievement: a model, interventions, implications. *Curr. Dir. Psychol. Sci.* 17:365–69

Cohen GL, Garcia J, Apfel N, Master A. 2006. Reducing the racial achievement gap: a social-psychological intervention. *Science* 313:1307–10

Cohen GL, Garcia J, Purdie-Vaughns V, Apfel N, Brzustoski P. 2009. Recursive processes in self-affirmation: intervening to close the minority achievement gap. *Science* 324:400–3

Cohen GL, Purdie-Vaughns V, Garcia J. 2012. An identity threat perspective on intervention. In *Stereotype Threat: Theory, Process, and Application*, ed. M Inzlichtt, T Schmader, pp. 280–96. New York: Oxford Univ. Press

Cohen GL, Sherman DK, Bastardi A, Hsu L, McGoey M, Ross L. 2007. Bridging the partisan divide: self-affirmation reduces ideological closed-mindedness and inflexibility in negotiation. *J. Personal. Soc. Psychol.* 93:415–30

Cohen GL, Steele CM, Ross LD. 1999. The mentor's dilemma: providing critical feedback across the racial divide. *Personal. Soc. Psychol. Bull.* 25:1302–18

Cook JE, Purdie-Vaughns V, Garcia J, Cohen GL. 2012. Chronic threat and contingent belonging: protective benefits of values affirmation on identity development. *J. Personal. Soc. Psychol.* 102:479–96

Cornil Y, Chandon P. 2013. From fan to fat? Vicarious losing increases unhealthy eating, but self-affirmation is an effective remedy. *Psychol. Sci.* In press. **http://pss.sagepub.com/content/early/2013/08/07/0956797613481232.long**. doi:10.1177/0956797613481232

Correll J, Spencer SJ, Zanna MP. 2004. An affirmed self and an open mind: self-affirmation and sensitivity to argument strength. *J. Exp. Soc. Psychol.* 40:350–56

Creswell JD, Dutcher JM, Klein WM, Harris PR, Levine JM. 2013. Self-affirmation improves problem-solving under stress. *PLoS ONE* 8:e62593

Creswell JD, Irwin MR, Burklund LJ, Lieberman MD, Arevalo JM, et al. 2012. Mindfulness-based stress reduction training reduces loneliness and pro-inflammatory gene expression in older adults: a small randomized controlled trial. *Brain Behav. Immunol.* 26:1095–101

Creswell JD, Lam S, Stanton AL, Taylor SE, Bower JE, Sherman DK. 2007. Does self-affirmation, cognitive processing, or discovery of meaning explain cancer-related health benefits of expressive writing? *Personal. Soc. Psychol. Bull.* 33:238–50

Creswell JD, Welch W, Taylor SE, Sherman D, Gruenewald T, Mann T. 2005. Affirmation of personal values buffers neuroendocrine and psychological stress responses. *Psychol. Sci.* 16:846–51

Critcher CR, Dunning D, Armor DA. 2010. When self-affirmations reduce defensiveness: timing is key. *Personal. Soc. Psychol. Bull.* 36:947–59

Crocker J, Niiya Y, Mischkowski D. 2008. Why does writing about important values reduce defensiveness? Self-affirmation and the role of positive, other-directed feelings. *Psychol. Sci.* 19:740–47

Dillard AJ, McCaul KD, Magnan RE. 2005. Why is such a smart person like you smoking? Using self-affirmation to reduce defensiveness to cigarette warning labels. *J. Appl. Biobehav. Res.* 10:165–82

Doosje BE, Branscombe NR, Spears R, Manstead AS. 2006. Antecedents and consequences of group-based guilt: the effects of ingroup identification. *Group Process. Intergr. Relat.* 9:325–38

Dunning D. 2005. *Self-Insight: Roadblocks and Detours on the Path to Knowing Thyself.* New York: Psychol. Press

Dweck CS. 2008. Can personality be changed? The role of beliefs in personality and change. *Curr. Dir. Psychol. Sci.* 17:391–94

Eccles J, Lord S, Midgley C. 1991. What are we doing to early adolescents? The impact of educational contexts on early adolescents. *Am. Educ. J.* 99:521–42

Ehret PJ, LaBrie JW, Santerre C, Sherman DK. 2014. Self-affirmation and motivational interviewing: integrating perspectives to reduce resistance and increase efficacy of alcohol interventions. *Health Psychol. Rev.* In press

Elder GH Jr. 1974. *Children of the Great Depression: Social Change in Life Experience.* Chicago: Univ. Chicago Press

Elder GH. 1977. Family history and the life course. *J. Fam. Hist.* 2:279–304

Elder GH. 1998. The life course as developmental theory. *Child Dev.* 69:1–12

Epton T, Harris PR. 2008. Self-affirmation promotes health behavior change. *Health Psychol.* 27:746–52

Finkel EJ, Slotter EB, Luchies LB, Walton GM, Gross JJ. 2013. A brief intervention to promote conflict reappraisal preserves marital quality over time. *Psychol. Sci.* 24:1595–601

Freedman JL, Fraser SC. 1966. Compliance without pressure: the foot-in-the-door technique. *J. Personal. Soc. Psychol.* 4:195–202

Freedom Writers, Gruwell E. 1999. *The Freedom Writers Diary: How a Teacher and 150 Teens Used Writing to Change Themselves and the World Around Them*. New York: Broadway Books

Freund J, Brandmaier AM, Lewejohann L, Kirste I, Kritzler M, et al. 2013. Emergence of individuality in genetically identical mice. *Science* 340:756–59

Fry RB, Prentice-Dunn S. 2005. Effects of coping information and value affirmation on responses to perceived health threat. *Health Comm.* 17:133–47

Fuligni AJ, Telzer EH, Bower J, Cole SW, Kiang L, Irwin MR. 2009. A preliminary study of daily interpersonal stress and C-reactive protein levels among adolescents from Latin American and European backgrounds. *Psychosom. Med.* 71:329–33

Garcia J, Cohen GL. 2012. A social psychological approach to educational intervention. In *Behavioral Foundations of Policy*, ed. E Shafir, pp. 329–50. Princeton, NJ: Princeton Univ. Press

Gilbert DT, Pinel EC, Wilson TD, Blumberg SJ, Wheatley TP. 1998. Immune neglect: a source of durability bias in affective forecasting. *J. Personal. Soc. Psychol.* 75:617–38

Gladwell M. 2008. *Outliers: The Story of Success*. New York: Little, Brown

Gollwitzer PM, Sheeran P. 2006. Implementation intentions and goal achievement: a meta-analysis of effects and processes. *Adv. Exp. Soc. Psychol.* 38:69–119

Gottman JM. 2011. *The Science of Trust: Emotional Attunement for Couples*. New York: Norton

Green D, Shachar R. 2000. Habit formation and political behavior: evidence of consuetude in voter turnout. *Br. J. Polit. Sci.* 30:561–73

Greenberg J, Solomon S, Pyszczynski T. 1997. Terror management theory of self-esteem and cultural worldviews: empirical assessments and conceptual refinements. In *Advances in Experimental Social Psychology*, ed. MP Zanna, 29:61–139. Orlando, FL: Academic

Greenwald AG. 1980. The totalitarian ego: fabrication and revision of personal history. *Am. Psychol.* 35:603–18

Griffin DW, Harris PR. 2011. Calibrating the response to health warnings limiting both overreaction and underreaction with self-affirmation. *Psychol. Sci.* 22:572–78

Grubb WN. 2009. *The Money Myth: School Resources, Outcomes, and Equity*. New York: Sage Found.

Haines J, Neumark-Sztainer D, Wall M, Story M. 2007. Personal, behavioral, and environmental risk and protective factors for adolescent overweight. *Obesity* 15:2748–60

Harackiewicz JM, Canning EA, Tibbetts Y, Giffen CJ, Hyde JS. 2014. Closing the social class achievement gap for first-generation students in undergraduate biology. *J. Educ. Psychol.* In press

Harber KD, Yeung D, Iacovelli A. 2011. Psychosocial resources, threat, and the perception of distance and height: support for the resources and perception model. *Emotion* 11:1080–90

Harris PR, Epton T. 2009. The impact of self-affirmation on health cognition, health behaviour and other health-related responses: a narrative review. *Soc. Personal. Psychol. Compass* 3:962–78

Harris PR, Epton T. 2010. The impact of self-affirmation on health-related cognition and health behaviour: issues and prospects. *Soc. Personal. Psychol. Compass* 4:439–54

Harris PR, Mayle K, Mabbott L, Napper L. 2007. Self-affirmation reduces smokers' defensiveness to graphic on-pack cigarette warning labels. *Health Psychol.* 26:437–46

Harris PR, Napper L. 2005. Self-affirmation and the biased processing of threatening health-risk information. *Personal. Soc. Psychol. Bull.* 31:1250–63

Havranek EP, Hanratty R, Tate C, Dickinson LM, Steiner JF, Cohen GL, Blair IA. 2012. The effect of values affirmation on race-discordant patient-provider communication. *Arch. Intern. Med.* 172:1662–67

Heckman JJ, Lochner L, Taber C. 1998. General equilibrium treatment effects: a study of tuition policy. *Am. Econ. Rev.* 88:381–86

Howell JL, Shepperd JA. 2012. Reducing information avoidance through affirmation. *Psychol. Sci.* 23:141–45

Inzlicht M, Schmader T, eds. 2011. *Stereotype Threat: Theory, Process, and Application*. New York: Oxford Univ. Press

Jaremka LM, Bunyan DP, Collins NL, Sherman DK. 2011. Reducing defensive distancing: self-affirmation and risk regulation in response to relationship threats. *J. Exp. Soc. Psychol.* 47:264–68

Karniol R, Galili L, Shtilerman D, Naim R, Stern K, et al. 2011. Why Superman can wait: cognitive self-transformation in the delay of gratification paradigm. *J. Clin. Child Adolesc. Psychol.* 40:307–17

Kennedy KA, Pronin E. 2008. When disagreement gets ugly: perceptions of bias and the escalation of conflict. *Personal. Soc. Psychol. Bull.* 34:833–48

Keough KA, Markus HR. 1998. The role of the self in building the bridge from philosophy to biology. *Psychol. Inq.* 9:49–53

Kiecolt-Glaser JK, Page GG, Marucha PT, MacCallum RC, Glaser R. 1998. Psychological influences on surgical recovery: perspectives from psychoneuroimmunology. *Am. Psychol.* 53:1209–18

Klein WM, Harris PR. 2009. Self-affirmation enhances attentional bias toward threatening components of a persuasive message. *Psychol. Sci.* 20:1463–67

Klein WM, Harris PR, Ferrer RA, Zajac LE. 2011. Feelings of vulnerability in response to threatening messages: effects of self-affirmation. *J. Exp. Soc. Psychol.* 47:1237–42

Koole SL, Smeets K, van Knippenberg A, Dijksterhuis A. 1999. The cessation of rumination through self-affirmation. *J. Personal. Soc. Psychol.* 77:111–25

Kunda Z. 1990. The case for motivated reasoning. *Psychol. Bull.* 108:480–98

Lakey B, Orehek E. 2011. Relational regulation theory: a new approach to explain the link between perceived social support and mental health. *Psychol. Rev.* 118:482–95

Landau MJ, Greenberg J. 2006. Play it safe or go for the gold? A terror management perspective on self-enhancement and protection motives in risky decision making. *Personal. Soc. Psychol. Bull.* 32:1633–45

Leary MR. 2005. Sociometer theory and the pursuit of relational value: getting to the root of self-esteem. *Eur. Rev. Soc. Psychol.* 16:75–111

Legault L, Al-Khindi T, Inzlicht M. 2012. Preserving integrity in the face of performance threat: self-affirmation enhances neurophysiological responsiveness to errors. *Psychol. Sci.* 23:1455–60

Lejuez CW, Hopko DR, LePage JP, Hopko SD, McNeil DW. 2001. A brief behavioral activation treatment for depression. *Cogn. Behav. Pract.* 8:164–75

Lepper MR, Woolverton M. 2001. The wisdom of practice: lessons learned from the study of highly effective tutors. In *Improving Academic Achievement: Contributions of Social Psychology*, ed. J Aronson, pp. 133–56. Orlando, FL: Academic

Lewin K. 1943. Defining the "field at a given time." *Psychol. Rev.* 50:292–310

Lewin K. 1997/1948. *Resolving Social Conflicts and Field Theory in Social Science*. Washington, DC: Am. Psychol. Assoc.

Logel C, Cohen GL. 2012. The role of the self in physical health. *Psychol. Sci.* 23:53–55

Lyubomirsky S, Della Porta M. 2010. Boosting happiness, buttressing resilience: results from cognitive and behavioral interventions. In *Handbook of Adult Resilience: Concepts, Methods, and Applications*, ed. JW Reich, AJ Zautra, J Hall, pp. 450–64. New York: Guilford

Mancuso CA, Choi TN, Wenn H, Wenderoth S, Hollenberg JP, et al. 2012. Increasing physical activity in patients with asthma through positive affect and self-affirmation. *Arch. Intern. Med.* 172:337–43

Marigold DC, Holmes JG, Ross M. 2007. More than words: reframing compliments from romantic partners fosters security in low self-esteem individuals. *J. Personal. Soc. Psychol.* 92:232–48

Marigold DC, Holmes JG, Ross M. 2010. Fostering relationship resilience: an intervention for low self-esteem individuals. *J. Exp. Soc. Psychol.* 46:624–30

Martens A, Johns M, Greenberg J, Schimel J. 2006. Combating stereotype threat: the effect of self-affirmation on women's intellectual performance. *J. Exp. Soc. Psychol.* 42:236–43

Masten AS, Cicchetti D. 2010. Developmental cascades. *Dev. Psychopathol.* 22:491–95

Masten AS, Obradović J. 2006. Competence and resilience in development. *Ann. N.Y. Acad. Sci.* 1094:13–27

Master SL, Eisenberger NI, Taylor SE, Naliboff BD, Shirinyan D, Lieberman MD. 2009. A picture's worth: Partner photographs reduce experimentally induced pain. *Psychol. Sci.* 20:1316–18

Matsuda KN, Melde C, Taylor TJ, Freng A, Esbensen FA. 2013. Gang membership and adherence to the "code of the street." *Justice Q.* 30:440–48

McCord J. 1978. A thirty-year follow-up of treatment effects. *Am. Psychol.* 33:284–89

McQueen A, Klein WM. 2006. Experimental manipulations of self-affirmation: a systematic review. *Self Identity* 5:289–354

Miller G, Chen E, Cole SW. 2009. Health psychology: developing biologically plausible models linking the social world and physical health. *Annu. Rev. Psychol.* 60:501–24

Miyake A, Kost-Smith LE, Finkelstein ND, Pollock SJ, Cohen GL, Ito TA. 2010. Reducing the gender achievement gap in college science: a classroom study of values affirmation. *Science* 330:1234–37

Moffitt TE, Arseneault L, Belsky D, Dickson N, Hancox RJ, et al. 2011. A gradient of childhood self-control predicts health, wealth, and public safety. *Proc. Natl. Acad. Sci. USA* 108:2693–98

Murray SL, Griffin DW, Rose P, Bellavia G. 2006. For better or worse? Self-esteem and the contingencies of acceptance in marriage. *Personal. Soc. Psychol. Bull.* 32:866–80

Napper L, Harris PR, Epton T. 2009. Developing and testing a self-affirmation manipulation. *Self Identity* 8:45–62

Nickerson C, Schwarz N, Diener E, Kahneman D. 2003. Zeroing in on the dark side of the American dream: a closer look at the negative consequences of the goal for financial success. *Psychol. Sci.* 14:531–36

Norris S. 2008. *Coping with Illness.* Video file. La Jolla: Univ. Calif. Telev. (UCTV). **http://www.uctv.tv/search-details.asp?showID=15400**

Obradović J, Burt KB, Masten AS. 2010. Testing a dual cascade model linking competence and symptoms over 20 years from childhood to adulthood. *J. Clin. Child Adolesc. Psychol.* 39:109–17

Ochsner KN, Bunge SA, Gross JJ, Gabrieli JD. 2002. Rethinking feelings: an fMRI study of the cognitive regulation of emotion. *J. Cogn. Neurosci.* 14:1215–29

Ogedegbe GO, Boutin-Foster C, Wells MT, Allegrante JP, Isen AM, et al. 2012. A randomized controlled trial of positive-affect intervention and medication adherence in hypertensive African Americans. *Arch. Intern. Med.* 172:322–26

Overall NC, Simpson JA, Struthers H. 2013. Buffering attachment-related avoidance: softening emotional and behavioral defenses during conflict discussions. *J. Personal. Soc. Psychol.* 104:854–71

Paluck EL. 2009. Reducing intergroup prejudice and conflict using the media: a field experiment in Rwanda. *J. Personal. Soc. Psychol.* 96:574–87

Pennebaker JW, Chung CK. 2011. Expressive writing: connections to physical and mental health. In *The Oxford Handbook of Health Psychology*, ed. HS Friendman, pp. 417–37. New York: Oxford Univ. Press

Peterson JC, Charlson ME, Hoffman Z, Wells MT, Wong S, et al. 2012. A randomized controlled trial of positive-affect induction to promote physical activity after percutaneous coronary intervention. *Arch. Intern. Med.* 172:329–36

Pietersma S, Dijkstra A. 2012. Cognitive self-affirmation inclination: an individual difference in dealing with self-threats. *Br. J. Soc. Psychol.* 51:33–51

Pratto F, John OP. 1991. Automatic vigilance: the attention-grabbing power of negative social information. *J. Personal. Soc. Psychol.* 61:380–91

Pressman SD, Cohen S. 2007. Use of social words in autobiographies and longevity. *Psychosom. Med.* 69:262–69

Raudenbush, SW. 1984. Magnitude of teacher expectancy effects on pupil IQ as a function of the credibility of expectancy induction: a synthesis of findings from 18 experiments. *J. Educ. Psychol.* 76:85–97

Reardon SF. 2011. The widening academic achievement gap between the rich and the poor: new evidence and possible explanations. In *Whither Opportunity? Rising Inequality and the Uncertain Life Chances of Low-Income Children*, ed. R Murnane, G Duncan, pp. 91–116. New York: Sage Found.

Reed MB, Aspinwall LG. 1998. Self-affirmation reduces biased processing of health-risk information. *Motiv. Emot.* 22:99–132

Robinson TN. 2010. Stealth interventions for obesity prevention and control: motivating behavior change. In *Obesity Prevention: The Role of Brain and Society on Individual Behavior*, ed. L Dube, A Bechara, A Dagher, A Drewnowski, J Lebel, P James, R Yada, pp. 319–28. New York: Elsevier

Rokeach M. 1973. *The Nature of Human Values.* New York: Free Press

Rosenthal R. 1994. Interpersonal expectancy effects: a 30-year perspective. *Curr. Dir. Psychol. Sci.* 3:176–79

Ross LD, Nisbett RE. 2011. *The Person and the Situation: Perspectives of Social Psychology.* London: Pinter & Martin

Sabaté E. 2003. *Adherence to Long-Term Therapies: Evidence for Action.* Geneva: World Health Organ.

Sapolsky RM. 2004. *Why Zebras Don't Get Ulcers: The Acclaimed Guide to Stress, Stress-Related Diseases, and Coping—Now Revised and Updated.* New York: Holt Paperb.

Sapolsky RM. 2010. Foreword. In *Formative Experiences: The Interaction of Caregiving, Culture, and Developmental Psychobiology*, ed. CM Worthman, PM Plotsky, DS Schechter, CA Cummings, pp. xxiii–xxvi. New York: Cambridge Univ. Press

Savitsky K, Epley N, Gilovich T. 2001. Do others judge us as harshly as we think? Overestimating the impact of our failures, shortcomings, and mishaps. *J. Personal. Soc. Psychol.* 81:44–56

Schimel J, Arndt J, Banko KM, Cook A. 2004. Not all self-affirmations were created equal: the cognitive and social benefits of affirming the intrinsic (versus extrinsic) self. *Soc. Cogn.* 22:75–99

Schmeichel BJ, Vohs KD. 2009. Self-affirmation and self-control: affirming core values counteracts ego depletion. *J. Personal. Soc. Psychol.* 96:770–82

Schreier HM, Schonert-Reichl KA, Chen E. 2013. Effect of volunteering on risk factors for cardiovascular disease in adolescents: a randomized controlled trial. *JAMA Pediatr.* 167:327–32

Schulz R. 1976. The effects of control and predictability on the psychological and physical well-being of the institutionalized aged. *J. Personal. Soc. Psychol.* 33:563–73

Schulz R, Hanusa BH. 1978. Long-term effects of control and predictability-enhancing interventions: findings and ethical issues. *J. Personal. Soc. Psychol.* 36:1194–201

Shapiro JR, Williams AM, Hambarchyan M. 2012. Are all interventions created equal? A multi-threat approach to tailoring stereotype threat interventions. *J. Personal. Soc. Psychol.* 104:277–88

Sherman DAK, Nelson LD, Steele CM. 2000. Do messages about health risks threaten the self? Increasing the acceptance of threatening health messages via self-affirmation. *Personal. Soc. Psychol. Bull.* 26:1046–58

Sherman DK. 2013. Self-affirmation: understanding the effects. *Soc. Personal. Psychol. Compass.* In press

Sherman DK, Bunyan DP, Creswell JD, Jaremka LM. 2009. Psychological vulnerability and stress: the effects of self-affirmation on sympathetic nervous system responses to naturalistic stressors. *Health Psychol.* 28:554–62

Sherman DK, Cohen GL. 2006. The psychology of self-defense: self-affirmation theory. In *Advances in Experimental Social Psychology*, ed. MP Zanna, 38:183–242. San Diego, CA: Academic

Sherman DK, Cohen GL, Nelson LD, Nussbaum AD, Bunyan DP, Garcia J. 2009. Affirmed yet unaware: exploring the role of awareness in the process of self-affirmation. *J. Personal. Soc. Psychol.* 97:745–64

Sherman DK, Hartson KA. 2011. Reconciling self-protection with self-improvement: self-affirmation theory. In *The Handbook of Self-Enhancement and Self-Protection*, ed. M Alicke, C Sedikides, pp. 128–51. New York: Guilford

Sherman DK, Hartson KA, Binning KR, Purdie-Vaughns V, Garcia J, et al. 2013. Deflecting the trajectory and changing the narrative: how self-affirmation affects academic performance and motivation under identity threat. *J. Personal. Soc. Psychol.* 104:591–618

Sherman DK, Kim HS. 2005. Is there an "I" in "team?" The role of the self in group-serving judgments. *J. Personal. Soc. Psychol.* 88:108–20

Shnabel N, Purdie-Vaughns V, Cook JE, Garcia J, Cohen GL. 2013. Demystifying values-affirmation interventions: writing about social belonging is a key to buffering against identity threat. *Personal. Soc. Psychol. Bull.* 39:663–76

Silverman A, Logel C, Cohen GL. 2012. Self-affirmation as a deliberate coping strategy: the moderating role of choice. *J. Exp. Soc. Psychol.* 49:93–98

Sivanathan N, Molden DC, Galinsky AD, Ku G. 2008. The promise and peril of self-affirmation in de-escalation of commitment. *Organ. Behav. Hum. Decis. Process.* 107:1–14

Sivanathan N, Pettit NC. 2010. Protecting the self through consumption: status goods as affirmational commodities. *J. Exp. Soc. Psychol.* 46:564–70

Smith A. 1759/2011. *The Theory of Moral Sentiments.* New York: Empire

Stanton AL, Danoff-Burg S, Sworowski LA, Collins CA, Branstetter AD, et al. 2002. Randomized, controlled trial of written emotional expression and benefit finding in breast cancer patients. *J. Clin. Oncol.* 20:4160–68

Steele CM. 1988. The psychology of self-affirmation: sustaining the integrity of the self. In *Advances in Experimental Social Psychology*, ed. L Berkowitz, 21:261–302. New York: Academic

Steele CM. 2010. *Whistling Vivaldi and Other Clues to How Stereotypes Affect Us.* New York: Norton

Steele CM, Southwick LL, Critchlow B. 1981. Dissonance and alcohol: drinking your troubles away. *J. Personal. Soc. Psychol.* 41:831–46

Steele CM, Spencer SJ, Aronson J. 2002. Contending with group image: the psychology of stereotype and social identity threat. In *Advances in Experimental Social Psychology*, ed. MP Zanna, 34:379–440. New York: Academic

Steele CM, Spencer SJ, Lynch M. 1993. Self-image resilience and dissonance: the role of affirmational resources. *J. Personal. Soc. Psychol.* 64:885–96

Stephens NM, Markus, HR, Fryberg SA. 2012. Social class disparities in health and education: reducing inequality by applying a sociocultural self model of behavior. *Psychol. Rev.* 119:723–44

Sterling P. 2004. Principles of allostasis: optimal design, predictive regulation, pathophysiology and rational therapeutics. In *Allostasis, Homeostasis, and the Costs of Adaptation*, ed. J Schulkin, pp. 17–64. Cambridge, UK: Cambridge Univ. Press

Stinson DA, Logel C, Shepherd S, Zanna MP. 2011. Rewriting the self-fulfilling prophecy of social rejection: self-affirmation improves relational security and social behavior up to 2 months later. *Psychol. Sci.* 22:1145–49

Stone J, Aronson E, Crain AL, Winslow MP, Fried CB. 1994. Inducing hypocrisy as a means of encouraging young adults to use condoms. *Personal. Soc. Psychol. Bull.* 20:116–28

Stone J, Whitehead J, Schmader T, Focella E. 2011. Thanks for asking: self-affirming questions reduce backlash when stigmatized targets confront prejudice. *J. Exp. Soc. Psychol.* 47:589–98

Taylor SE. 2007. Social support. In *Foundations of Health Psychology*, ed. HS Friedman, pp. 145–71. New York: Oxford Univ. Press

Taylor SE. 2010. Mechanisms linking early life stress to adult health outcomes. *Proc. Natl. Acad. Sci. USA* 107:8507–12

Taylor VJ, Walton GM. 2011. Stereotype threat undermines academic learning. *Personal. Soc. Psychol. Bull.* 37:1055–67

Thomaes S, Bushman BJ, de Castro BO, Cohen GL, Denissen JJ. 2009. Reducing narcissistic aggression by buttressing self-esteem: an experimental field study. *Psychol. Sci.* 20:1536–42

Thomaes S, Bushman BJ, de Castro BO, Reijntjes A. 2012. Arousing "gentle passions" in young adolescents: sustained experimental effects of value affirmations on prosocial feelings and behaviors. *Dev. Psychol.* 48:103–10

Toma CL, Hancock JT. 2013. Self-affirmation underlies Facebook use. *Personal. Soc. Psychol. Bull.* 39:321–31

Tugade MM, Fredrickson BL. 2004. Emotions: positive emotions and health. In *Encyclopedia of Health and Behavior*, ed. N Anderson, pp. 306–10. Thousand Oaks, CA: Sage

van Koningsbruggen GM, Das E. 2009. Don't derogate this message! Self-affirmation promotes online type 2 diabetes risk test taking. *Psychol. Health* 24:635–49

van Koningsbruggen GM, Das E, Roskos-Ewoldsen DR. 2009. How self-affirmation reduces defensive processing of threatening health information: evidence at the implicit level. *Health Psychol.* 28:563–68

Verghese A, Brady E, Kapur CC, Horwitz RI. 2011. The bedside evaluation: ritual and reason. *Ann. Intern. Med.* 155:550–53

Vohs KD, Park JK, Schmeichel BJ. 2013. Self-affirmation can enable goal disengagement. *J. Personal. Soc. Psychol.* 104:14–27

Wakslak CJ, Trope Y. 2009. Cognitive consequences of affirming the self: the relationship between self-affirmation and object construal. *J. Exp. Soc. Psychol.* 45:927–32

Walton GM, Cohen GL. 2011. A brief social-belonging intervention improves academic and health outcomes of minority students. *Science* 331:1447–51

Walton GM, Spencer SJ. 2009. Latent ability: grades and test scores systematically underestimate the intellectual ability of negatively stereotyped students. *Psychol. Sci.* 20:1132–39

Ward A, Atkins DC, Lepper MR, Ross L. 2011. Affirming the self to promote agreement with another: lowering a psychological barrier to conflict resolution. *Personal. Soc. Psychol. Bull.* 37:1216–28

Wilson TD. 2011. *Redirect: The Surprising New Science of Psychological Change*. New York: Little, Brown

Wilson TD, Linville PW. 1982. Improving the academic performance of college freshmen: attribution therapy revisited. *J. Personal. Soc. Psychol.* 42:367–76

Wood JV, Perunovic WQ, Lee JW. 2009. Positive self-statements: power to some, peril for others. *Psychol. Sci.* 20:860–66

Woolf K, McManus IC, Gill D, Dacre J. 2009. The effect of a brief social intervention on the examination results of UK medical students: a cluster randomised controlled trial. *BMC Med. Educ.* 9:35

Worthman CM, Plotsky PM, Schechter DS, Cummings CA, eds. 2010. *Formative Experiences: The Interaction of Caregiving, Culture, and Developmental Psychobiology*. New York: Cambridge Univ. Press

Yeager DS, Purdie-Vaughns V, Garcia J, Apfel N, Brzustoski P, et al. 2014. Breaking the cycle of mistrust: wise interventions to provide critical feedback across the racial divide. *J. Exp. Psychol.: Gen.* In press. **http://psycnet.apa.org/psycarticles/2013-28213-001.pdf**. doi:10.1037/a0033906

Yeager DS, Walton GM. 2011. Social-psychological interventions in education: they're not magic. *Rev. Educ. Res.* 81:267–301

Zhao X, Peterson EB, Kim W, Rolfe-Redding J. 2012. Effects of self-affirmation on daily versus occasional smokers' responses to graphic warning labels. *Comm. Res.* In press. **http://crx.sagepub.com/content/early/2012/11/09/0093650212465433.full.pdf+html**. doi:10.1177/0093650212465433

Zolnierek KBH, DiMatteo MR. 2009. Physician communication and patient adherence to treatment: a meta-analysis. *Med. Care* 47:826–34

Gender Similarities and Differences

Janet Shibley Hyde

Department of Psychology, University of Wisconsin, Madison, Wisconsin 53706;
email: jshyde@wisc.edu

Annu. Rev. Psychol. 2014. 65:373–98

First published online as a Review in Advance on
June 26, 2013

The *Annual Review of Psychology* is online at
http://psych.annualreviews.org

This article's doi:
10.1146/annurev-psych-010213-115057

Keywords

sex differences, gender similarities hypothesis, intersectionality,
meta-analysis, effect size

Abstract

Whether men and women are fundamentally different or similar has been
debated for more than a century. This review summarizes major theories designed to explain gender differences: evolutionary theories, cognitive social
learning theory, sociocultural theory, and expectancy-value theory. The gender similarities hypothesis raises the possibility of theorizing gender similarities. Statistical methods for the analysis of gender differences and similarities
are reviewed, including effect sizes, meta-analysis, taxometric analysis, and
equivalence testing. Then, relying mainly on evidence from meta-analyses,
gender differences are reviewed in cognitive performance (e.g., math performance), personality and social behaviors (e.g., temperament, emotions,
aggression, and leadership), and psychological well-being. The evidence on
gender differences in variance is summarized. The final sections explore applications of intersectionality and directions for future research.

Contents

INTRODUCTION

For centuries, humans have been fascinated with the idea of psychological gender differences, believing that these differences are both large and immutable. For example, the English clergyman Thomas Gisborne, in his helpful book, *An Enquiry Into the Duties of the Female Sex* (1797), described God's will in creating gender differences.

> The Power who called the human race into being has, with infinite wisdom, regarded, in the structure of the corporeal frame, the tasks which the different sexes were respectively destined to fulfil.... He has adopted with the most conspicuous wisdom, a corresponding plan of discrimination between the mental powers and dispositions of the two sexes. The science of legislation, of jurisprudence; the conduct of government in all its executive functions; the abstruse researches of erudition... assigned chiefly or entirely to men, demand the efforts of a mind endued with close and comprehensive reasoning in a degree in which they are not requisite for the discharge of the customary offices of female duty... to diffuse throughout the family circle the enlivening and endearing smile of cheerfulness, the superiority of the female mind is unrivalled. (Gisborne 1797, pp. 19–22)

Even when formal scientific psychology emerged, around 1879, the consensus remained that psychological gender differences were large (Shields 1975). However, a few researchers, such as Thorndike (1914), Hollingworth (1918), and Woolley (1914), dissented, arguing instead for gender similarities. These debates persist to the present day.

Research on gender differences and similarities is important for several reasons. First, stereotypes about psychological gender differences abound, influencing people's behavior, and it is important to evaluate whether they are accurate. Second, psychological gender differences are often invoked in important policy issues, such as single-sex schooling or explaining why, in 2005, there were no women on the faculty in mathematics at Harvard; it is crucial to have accurate scientific information available to evaluate such policy recommendations and explanations.

Previous *Annual Review* articles have taken up the question of gender. These include Deaux's review, Sex and Gender (1985); Stewart & McDermott's, Gender in Psychology (2004); and Martin & Ruble's, Patterns of Gender Development (2010). In addition, Zahn-Waxler and colleagues' article in the *Annual Review of Clinical Psychology* (2008) addressed gender and psychological disorders in childhood and adolescence, and Hines's (2011) review in the *Annual Review of Neuroscience* evaluated gender development and the human brain. This review does not repeat material from these previous excellent reviews but instead focuses specifically on the question of gender similarities and differences, with the goal of identifying which psychological attributes show large gender differences, which show small differences, and which show no differences.

The gender similarities hypothesis states that males and females are similar on most, but not all, psychological variables (Hyde 2005). Evidence for the hypothesis came from a review of 46 meta-analyses of research on psychological gender differences that were available at the time. The 46 meta-analyses yielded 124 effect sizes (Cohen's *d* equal to the mean score for males minus the mean score for females, divided by the within-groups standard deviation) for gender differences. Strikingly, 30% of the effect sizes were between 0 and 0.10, and an additional 48% were in the range of a small difference, between 0.11 and 0.35. That is, 78% of the gender differences were small or very close to 0. The gender similarities hypothesis provides important input into the current review.

Whenever possible, conclusions in this review are based on the findings of meta-analyses, which are abundant in the field of gender differences. Meta-analyses confer substantial advantages when evaluating gender differences. First, they evaluate whether a particular gender difference is replicable; too often, individual studies reporting a gender difference capture the imagination of the press and scientists and the finding lives on, despite later studies that yield disconfirming results. Meta-analyses assess whether multiple studies find the same result. Second, meta-analyses go beyond the simple yes/no answer to whether there is a gender difference in a particular psychological attribute by estimating the magnitude of the gender difference. Third, meta-analyses can systematically explore moderators, such as social context, that may contribute to the presence or absence of gender differences.

Although this review is intended to be comprehensive, several topics were beyond the scope of it. These include gender differences in the human brain (Hines 2011, Joel 2012); gender and sex hormones; gender differences in physical health; and studies of gender bias, in which gender is studied not as a person variable but rather as a stimulus variable (Marsh et al. 2009, Swim et al. 1989).

In the sections that follow, several major theories of the origins of psychological gender differences are described first. Next, statistical methods for evaluating gender differences and similarities are summarized. The third section reviews research on gender differences and similarities in average scores on a wide array of psychological attributes (e.g., cognitive variables, personality and social psychology measures, and well-being and psychopathology). The question of gender differences in variability or variance is considered in the fourth section. Next the review addresses the concept of intersectionality and its implications for the study of gender similarities and differences. The final section includes a summary of the findings along with suggestions for future research directions.

THEORIES OF THE ORIGINS OF PSYCHOLOGICAL GENDER DIFFERENCES AND SIMILARITIES

A review of all theories and hypothesized causes of psychological gender differences is beyond the scope of this article. Instead, this review focuses on three "grand theories" of differences:

Gender similarities hypothesis: the hypothesis that males and females are similar on most, but not all, psychological variables

Meta-analysis: a statistical technique that allows a researcher to combine the results of many research studies on a given topic

Effect size: in the study of gender differences, a measure of how large the difference is, equal to the mean for males minus the mean for females divided by the standard deviation

Intersectionality: an approach that simultaneously considers multiple categories of identity, difference, and disadvantage, such as gender, race, class, and sexual orientation

STEM: science, technology, engineering, and mathematics

evolutionary theories, cognitive social learning theory, and sociocultural theory. Following that, a more specific theory is presented, expectancy-value theory. Finally, recognizing that most theories have been framed to explain gender differences, I consider the possibility of theorizing gender similarities.

Evolutionary Theories

Evolutionary psychology has focused on how psychological gender differences are the product of evolutionary selection, based on an assumption that different behaviors are adaptive for males compared with females (e.g., Buss & Schmitt 1993). Two concepts are key to the argument: sexual selection and parental investment. Originally proposed by Darwin, sexual selection, which is distinct from natural selection, consists of two processes: (*a*) Members of one gender (usually males) compete among themselves to gain mating privileges with members of the other gender (usually females), and (*b*) members of the other gender (usually females) have preferences for and exercise choice in mating with certain members of the first gender (usually males). Sexual selection can be invoked, for example, to explain gender differences in aggression.

Parental investment refers to behaviors or other investments of the parent with respect to the offspring that increase the offspring's chance of survival but that also cost the parent something (Trivers 1972). Behaviors are adaptive if they help the individual produce many offspring, but then those offspring must also survive and reproduce if the individual's genes are to be successfully passed on to future generations. Gender enters the picture because human females generally have substantially greater parental investment in their offspring than do human males. Women invest a precious egg (compared with the millions of sperm that men can produce every day) and then invest nine months of gestation, which is costly to the body. At birth, then, women have greater parental investment than men do, and it is to the advantage of the person with the greater investment to care for the offspring, making sure that they survive to adulthood. Herein lies the evolutionary explanation for women's greater involvement in child care, which in turn may have enormous repercussions in other domains, such as the explanation for the dearth of women in certain science, technology, engineering, and mathematics (STEM) disciplines.

It is beyond the scope of this article to review all the evidence for and against evolutionary theories. Briefly, the evidence appears to be mixed (Pedersen et al. 2011). As one example, evolutionary psychologists Buss & Schmitt (1993) predicted large gender differences in the desired number of sexual partners and reported that men, on average, over the next 30 years, desire 16 partners, compared with women's desire for 4. This finding is consistent with evolutionary theories insofar as men are said to increase their fitness by having sex with numerous women. Another team, however, collected similar data and reached very different conclusions (Pedersen et al. 2002). Although they found men desiring more partners than women did, the distributions were highly skewed, with a few individuals wanting hundreds of partners, so the mean is not an appropriate statistic, nor are significance tests requiring an assumption of normal distributions appropriate. Taking this into account, the researchers focused on the median, which for both men and women was one partner. Overall, then, their results indicated gender similarities.

Cognitive Social Learning Theory

Cognitive social learning theory is another approach with broad utility in understanding psychological gender differences. As formulated by Bussey & Bandura (1999), the theory holds that both children's and adults' behavior is shaped by reinforcements and punishments. In addition, people imitate or model others in their environment, particularly if the others are powerful or admirable. Abundant evidence exists for the processes specified by social learning theory (Bussey & Bandura 1999).

In the more recent versions of the theory, cognitive components have been added, such as attention, self-regulation, and self-efficacy. For example, as children grow, control of their behavior shifts from externally imposed reinforcements and punishments to internalized standards and self-regulation. In particular, children internalize gender norms and conform their behavior to those norms. Self-efficacy, another cognitive component, refers to a person's belief in her or his ability to accomplish a particular task. Self-efficacy may be important in explaining certain gender effects. For example, although girls' math performance is equal to that of boys, generally there is a wider gender gap in math self-efficacy ($d = 0.33$, Else-Quest et al. 2010). Self-efficacy is important because of its power in shaping people's decisions about whether to take on a challenging task, such as majoring in mathematics.

Sociocultural Theory

Sociocultural theory, also called social role theory or social structural theory, was proposed by Eagly & Wood (1999; Wood & Eagly 2012) as an alternative to evolutionary theorizing about gender differences. The essential argument of the theory is that a society's division of labor by gender drives all other psychological gender differences. Psychological gender differences result from individuals' accommodations or adaptations to the particular restrictions on or opportunities for their gender in their society. The theory acknowledges biological differences between men and women, such as differences in size and strength and women's capacity to bear and nurse children. These differences historically contributed to the division of labor by gender. Men's greater size and strength led them to pursue activities such as warfare, which gave them greater status and wealth, as well as power over women. Once men were in these roles of greater power, their behavior became more dominant, and women's behavior became more subordinate. Women's assignment to the role of child care led them to develop qualities such as nurturance and a facility with relationships.

With a few exceptions (e.g., Schmitt 2005), evolutionary psychologists emphasize cross-cultural universals in patterns of gender differences, resulting from evolution many centuries ago. In contrast, sociocultural theory focuses on variations across cultures in patterns of gender differences. Eagly & Wood (1999) reanalyzed Buss's cross-national data on gender differences in mate preferences. Their hypothesis was that the greater the gender difference in power and status (gender inequality) in a culture, the greater would be the gender differences in mate preferences. Using a United Nations database that indexes gender inequality for participating nations, Eagly & Wood (1999) found strong correlations between gender inequality and the magnitude of gender differences in mate preferences (see also Zentner & Mitura 2012). That is, the nations with the largest gender gaps in power also have the largest gender gaps in mate preferences. These findings are consistent with sociocultural theory and are inconsistent with evolutionary theory.

Other researchers have tested the hypothesis that psychological gender differences should be smaller in nations with more gender equality and larger in nations with more inequality. For example, in a cross-national meta-analysis of gender differences in math performance, the researchers used measures of nations' gender equality to predict the gender gap in math performance (Else-Quest et al. 2010). Some indices of gender equality, such as the Gender Empowerment Measure, are global or are composites of multiple indicators, such as women's share of parliamentary seats and the wage gap. Other indices of gender equality are domain-specific, such as women's share of research positions. The domain-specific indicators were most successful at predicting cross-national variations. For example, women's share of research positions in nations significantly predicted smaller gender gaps in math performance as well as smaller gaps in math self-concept and math self-efficacy.

Sociocultural theory is more recent than the other theories reviewed here. Overall, though, evidence is accumulating in support of it.

Expectancy-Value Theory

Eccles's expectancy-value theory (Eccles et al. 1994, Meece et al. 1982), although not proposed as a grand theory of psychological gender differences, nonetheless has broad utility in accounting for multiple phenomena discussed in this review. According to the theory, two categories of factors contribute to a person's decision to take on a challenging task, such as enrolling in calculus in high school: expectancies (expectations for success at the task) and task values (e.g., interest in the task, usefulness of the task for current or future goals). In turn, many factors influence expectancies and values. For example, an adolescent's expectancy of success in a calculus course may be influenced by her self-concept of math ability, past achievement experiences (grades in past math courses, scores on standardized tests), socializers' beliefs and behaviors (e.g., parents' belief that engineering would be a good career for their daughter), and the broader sociocultural milieu (the gender distribution that she observes in her intended occupation). The model has received abundant empirical support (e.g., Eccles et al. 1994).

Expectancy-value theory is especially helpful in identifying the wide array of factors that contribute to the underrepresentation of women in STEM careers. Moreover, it identifies points at which interventions might be effective. It may also be applicable to understanding phenomena such as gender differences in self-esteem and domain-specific self-concept.

Theories of Gender Similarities

The theories reviewed to this point were designed to explain gender differences. Little or no attention has been devoted to theorizing gender similarities. Several possibilities exist.

In the realm of evolutionary forces, theorists have focused on sexual selection and its capacity to create gender differences. Missing from their analysis is a consideration of natural selection, which should act equally on males and females and therefore should create gender similarities (Hyde 2006). Even at the chromosomal level, humans have 23 pairs of chromosomes, only one of which, the sex chromosomes, differ between males and females. The remaining 22 pairs of autosomes are found in both males and females and pass from fathers to daughters, and from mothers to sons, across generations. The evolutionary psychologists' focus on sexual selection should not obscure the greater force of natural selection, which creates gender similarities.

Cognitive social learning theory, sociocultural theory, and expectancy-value theory, although designed to explain gender differences, can easily be adapted to understanding gender similarities, as well as trends over time toward greater gender similarities in the United States. Using cognitive social learning theory, for example, one might speculate that punishments for gender-role violations have declined over time, allowing boys and girls to behave more similarly to each other. As of this writing, it appears that no direct evidence exists that punishment for gender-role violations has declined over time, but it would be an interesting hypothesis to test. Cognitive social learning theory might also account for the influx of women into the biological sciences and medicine since 1970 as resulting in part from the increasing number of female role models; the entry of more women into a field in turn promotes the entry of more women. This same prediction arises from expectancy-value theory.

Sociocultural theory, with its focus on power inequalities and the division of labor by gender, explains gender differences but can also contribute to an understanding of gender similarities. Gender similarities are expected in nations in which there is gender equality. Moreover, as the division of labor by gender narrows over time, psychological gender similarities should arise. As an example, with the emergence of the women's movement and increased labor force participation of women beginning in the 1970s, family roles have shifted toward equality as least to some extent. A 2001 study found that fathers with an employed wife spent on average 23 hours per week with their children, compared with only 17 hours per week in 1981 (Sandberg & Hofferth 2001). Sociocultural theory predicts that, as men increasingly occupy the child-care role, they will develop more nurturant qualities, reducing the gender gap in nurturance.

Overall, then, an important future research strategy will be to theorize gender similarities. Existing theories may be adapted to this task, yet novel theories may also be needed.

STATISTICAL METHODS FOR THE ANALYSIS OF GENDER SIMILARITIES AND DIFFERENCES

Cohen's d (Cohen 1988), equal to the mean for males minus the mean for females, divided by the pooled within-groups standard deviation, is the most common measure of the magnitude of gender differences in psychological research. Cohen's guidelines for interpreting effect sizes are that $d = 0.20$ is a small difference, 0.50 is moderate, and 0.80 is large. Moreover, Hyde (2005) interprets a d value ≤ 0.10 as being trivial, as being a gender similarity. Other statistics are available, though, and an exploration of them will be helpful in interpreting the magnitude of gender differences.

An important equivalence formula is $d = 2r/\sqrt{(1-r^2)}$. A quick approximation is $d = 2r$. Therefore a d of 0.20, which Cohen interpreted as a small difference, is equivalent to $r = 0.10$. That is, if we computed the correlation between gender (coded 0, 1) and an outcome such as mathematics performance, an r value of 0.10 would yield a d value of 0.20. Similarly, the d value of 0.10, interpreted here as trivial, is equivalent to $r = 0.05$, which most scientists would agree is a trivial relationship.

Cohen (1988) provided another way to understand equivalents of d, in terms of the percent overlap of two distributions at various values of d, assuming that both distributions are normal and have the same variance. For example, for $d = 0.10$, there is 92.3% overlap between the two distributions, and for $d = 0.20$, there is 85.3% overlap. At a very large value of d, 1.0, there is still 44.6% overlap between the distributions. This approach underscores the point that, with small or moderate values of d, within-gender variance is much larger than between-gender variance.

Another equivalence provided by Cohen (1988) assesses the percentage of Group B that will equal or exceed the median for Group A at various values of d, again assuming normal distributions with equal variance. For example, for $d = 0.10$, 52% of Group B (e.g., males) would score above the median for Group A (e.g., females). For $d = 0.20$, 54% of Group B scores above the median for Group A. These equivalencies again support the reasonableness of interpreting $d = 0.20$ as a small effect. For a very large difference, $d = 1.0$, 69% of Group B scores above the median for Group A.

Del Giudice and colleagues (2012) introduced the use of Mahalanobis D to the measurement of the magnitude of gender differences in personality and concluded that the gender similarities hypothesis is incorrect and that there are very large gender differences. A staple of multivariate statistics for decades, D in this application measures the distance between two centroids in multi-variate space. It is a multivariate generalization of the d statistic. What was not made clear in the Del Giudice paper is that D is computed by taking the linear combination of the original variables (scores on emotional stability, dominance, vigilance, and so on) that maximizes the difference between groups. What they showed, then, is that, if one takes a large enough set of psychological measures and then takes a linear combination to maximize differences, one can get a big gender difference. Moreover, this difference or distance is along a dimension in multivariate space that is a linear combination of the original variables, but this dimension is uninterpretable. What does it mean to say that there are large differences in personality, lumping together distinct aspects such as emotional stability, dominance, and vigilance? Certainly contemporary personality theorists do not argue that there is a single dimension to personality. Overall, then, this application of Mahalanobis D produces results that are biased toward finding a large difference because of taking a linear combination that maximizes group differences, and it appears to yield results that are uninterpretable.

Carothers & Reis (2013) introduced another statistical application for the analysis of gender similarities and differences, taxometric methods. These methods allow the researcher to determine whether the latent structure of a construct is dimensional (continuous) or taxonic (categorical). This approach analyzes whether males' and females' psychological attributes differ in categorical ways or dimensional ways. Tapping multiple data sets, the researchers selected psychological variables that typically are quite gender differentiated, such as masculinity/femininity, relational-interdependent self-construal, and science inclination. With only a few exceptions, the constructs showed gender to be dimensional, not taxonic, contrary to stereotypes that hold that males and females are categorically different. These taxometric methods hold great promise for the future.

Ball and colleagues (2013) introduced equivalence testing as another method for analyzing gender similarities and differences. The problem with identifying gender similarities when using traditional significance testing methods is that one is trying to prove the null hypothesis. Equivalence testing reverses the approach, so that a significant result can indicate significant similarities, e.g., whether the male and female means are within 0.20 standard deviations of each other or some other value.

In summary, the effect size d (or Hedges' g) will doubtless continue to be a mainstay in evaluating the magnitude of gender differences. Newer methods are becoming available, including taxometric methods and equivalence testing, and they offer additional leverage in gender analyses.

AVERAGE GENDER SIMILARITIES AND DIFFERENCES

Most gender differences research has examined whether average gender differences exist over a wide array of psychological characteristics. The sections that follow review research on gender differences in cognitive variables (mathematical, spatial, and verbal performance), personality and social psychological variables, and well-being and psychopathology. The final section considers the STEM question: Why are women underrepresented in certain careers in science, technology, engineering, and mathematics?

Cognitive Gender Similarities and Differences

In their important review, Maccoby & Jacklin (1974) concluded that gender differences are reliably found in mathematical, spatial, and verbal abilities, with males outperforming females on mathematical and spatial tests and females outperforming males on verbal tests. This view of cognitive gender differences continues to dominate the field to the present day. Here the evidence on each of these gender differences is reviewed, focusing on the magnitude of the differences.

Mathematical performance. A 1990 meta-analysis reviewed 100 relevant studies representing the testing of more than 3 million persons (Hyde et al. 1990). Overall, the gender difference was trivial in magnitude, $d = -0.05$. However, moderator analyses examining age and cognitive level of the test (from lowest to highest: computation, understanding of math concepts, and complex problem solving) revealed that more substantial differences favoring males emerged in complex problem solving in high school ($d = 0.29$). This gender gap is of concern because complex problem solving is precisely the mathematical skill needed to enter STEM occupations.

Spurred by then-Harvard President Lawrence Summers's 2005 comments that women lack the mathematical ability to succeed at the highest levels of mathematics and science, Hyde and colleagues conducted additional meta-analyses based on contemporary data. These more recent data indicate that, in general, females have reached parity with males in math performance. One meta-analysis synthesized data from state assessments of US children's math skills (Hyde et al. 2008a). Data represented the testing of more than 7 million students in grades 2 through 11. Across grades, effect sizes ranged between -0.02 and $+0.06$, i.e., there was no gender difference at any grade level. Because state assessments generally tap only lower-level math skills, the authors turned to data from the National Assessment of Educational Progress, which does include items assessing complex problem solving. For these items, at grade 12, the average effect size was $d = 0.07$, indicating that girls had reached parity with boys even for complex problem solving at the high school level.

In a second meta-analysis based on contemporary studies, Lindberg and colleagues synthesized data from 242 studies appearing between 1990 and 2007, representing the testing of 1.2 million people (Lindberg et al. 2010). Overall, there was no gender difference ($d = 0.05$). The gender difference in complex problem solving was small ($d = 0.16$).

In a third meta-analysis, Else-Quest and colleagues (2010) examined international data on gender differences in mathematics performance, relating it to measures of gender inequality across nations (see also Nosek et al. 2009). Briefly, the findings indicate great variability across nations in the magnitude and even the direction of the gender difference, as noted in the discussion of sociocultural theory.

Overall, then, it appears that girls have reached parity with boys in mathematics performance, at least in the United States. The gender difference in complex problem solving in high school is smaller than it was in the 1990 meta-analysis and has even disappeared in one analysis of National Assessment of Educational Progress data (Hyde et al. 2008a).

Spatial performance. Spatial abilities are assessed in a variety of ways. This review focuses on a particular spatial skill, three-dimensional (3D) mental rotation, which requires the test taker to mentally rotate an object in three dimensions to determine whether it matches one of several other objects. Although many occupations do not require mental rotation skills, several do, including engineering and architecture, areas in which women are underrepresented.

According to an early meta-analysis, the gender difference in 3D mental rotation is large, favoring males, $d = 0.73$ (Linn & Petersen 1985). In a later meta-analysis, the gender difference was moderate in magnitude, $d = 0.56$ (Voyer et al. 1995). These overall effect sizes, however, mask some complexities. Gender researchers have suspected for some time that, for mathematical and spatial performance, tightly timed tests—which measure speed as much as skill—are advantageous to males, whereas untimed tests or tests with ample time provide more opportunity for females to display their skills. One meta-analysis found that, indeed, with short time limits, the gender difference in mental rotation was large ($d = 1.03$), whereas in tests with no time limits the effect size was only moderate ($d = 0.51$) (Voyer 2011; see also Maeda & Yoon 2013).

There is some evidence from individual studies that a male advantage in mental rotation emerges as early as infancy (Moore & Johnson 2008, Quinn & Liben 2008). However, it is a bit too early to tell exactly what these findings mean.

Others note that a spatial training curriculum is notably absent from the schools, so that the gender difference may result from informal, extracurricular learning based on the different experiences of boys and girls in areas such as sports and video game playing. It is clear that scores on mental rotation tests can be improved with training (Newcombe et al. 2002, Uttal et al. 2013). According to a meta-analysis, the average effect size for the difference between training and control groups was $d = 0.44$ (Uttal et al. 2013). In one experiment, college students were given 10 hours of training on an action video game, Medal of Honor: Pacific Assault; controls played a puzzle game (Feng 2007). Both women and men in the experimental group improved their performance on a mental rotation test. The women improved more than the men, and experimental group women performed as well as control group men. On average, US boys spend 1 hour 37 minutes per day playing video games compared with 49 minutes for girls (Rideout et al. 2010). That is, boys practice with video games about twice as much as girls do, representing a major gender gap in experience relevant to 3D spatial skills.

On the question of the relevance of spatial skills for the underrepresentation of women in engineering, faculty at one college of engineering created multimedia software that provides training in mental rotation (Gerson et al. 2001). Entering students majoring in engineering take the mental rotation training. This training has improved the retention of women in the engineering major from 47% to 77%.

Overall, then, there is a moderate gender difference favoring males in 3D mental rotation. However, this gender difference may result from the absence of spatial training in the schools combined with major gender gaps in relevant out-of-school experiences.

Verbal skills. Contrary to stereotypes that females have better verbal skills than males do, gender differences in verbal skills overall favor females but are quite small, $d = -0.11$ (Hyde & Linn 1988). This overall value, however, masks variations for different types of verbal ability. No gender differences were found for vocabulary ($d = -0.02$), reading comprehension ($d = -0.03$), or essay writing ($d = -0.09$). The largest effect was for verbal fluency, $d = -0.33$.

In an analysis based on well-sampled studies of US adolescents, Hedges & Nowell (1995) computed effect sizes for gender differences in reading comprehension and vocabulary. For reading comprehension, effect sizes ranged from -0.18 (National Longitudinal Survey of Youth data) to $+0.002$ (High School & Beyond data). For vocabulary, effect sizes ranged between -0.06 (National Longitudinal Study of the High School Class of 1972) and $+0.25$ (Project Talent). Again, the differences were not large and did not consistently favor females.

In a recent study, international data were analyzed from the Program for International Student Assessment data set, which samples 15-year-olds in participating nations (Reilly 2012). For reading achievement in the United States, $d = -0.26$, a small average difference favoring girls. However, at the lowest level of performance, boys outnumbered girls by a ratio of 4.5 to 1, leading to the question of whether boys with learning disabilities account for the female advantage. Across all 65 participating nations, the gender difference was larger, $d = -0.44$. In an effort to account for variability in the magnitude of the gender difference across nations, effect sizes were correlated with measures of gender equity across nations and yielded significant effects, a finding that is consistent with sociocultural theory.

Taking these three studies together, it is difficult to reconcile the gender gap found in the Program for International Student Assessment data ($d = -0.26$) with the gaps that are close to zero in the other two studies. If there is a female advantage in reading comprehension and other verbal skills, it is a small one.

Attitudes. Attitudes about cognitive abilities and gender differences in abilities are often as important as actual performance in predicting educational and career outcomes. Attitudes toward mathematics have been studied extensively. According to a meta-analysis, for 15-year-olds in the United States, $d = 0.27$ for the gender difference in math self-confidence and -0.23 for anxiety

(Else-Quest et al. 2010). That is, the gender differences in math self-confidence and math anxiety are larger than the gender difference in actual performance.

Personality and Social Behaviors

This section considers gender differences in a wide array of personality measures and social behaviors. Personality domains reviewed here include temperament, personality, impulsivity, emotion, and interests. Social behaviors include aggression, helping behavior, communication, sexuality, and leadership.

Temperament. A meta-analysis of research on gender differences in temperament included data from children between the ages of 3 months and 13 years (Else-Quest et al. 2006; see also Else-Quest 2012). Temperament can be thought of as biologically based emotional and behavioral consistencies that appear early in life and predict outcomes in domains such as psychopathology and personality. In a sense, temperament represents the earliest indication of the individual's personality. Multiple theoretical models are used in temperament research, leading to different measures, but one can think of three basic temperament factors: effortful control (including attention, effortful control, and persistence), negative affectivity (emotionality, distress to limits, fear) and surgency (activity, impulsivity).

For the effortful control factor, girls scored higher on inhibitory control ($d = -0.41$) and attention ($d = -0.23$) (Else-Quest et al. 2006). These average gender differences are in the small-to-moderate range and contrast to larger gender differences at the tail of the distribution, where boys with attention deficit–hyperactivity disorder (ADHD) outnumber girls by ratios of 2:1 to 9:1 across studies (Rucklidge 2010). This distinction between modest average gender differences and marked gender differences at the tail of the distribution illustrates a common problem in which people infer, from marked gender differences in extreme scores, that differences between girls and boys are categorical—i.e., that all boys are more active than girls—when in fact average gender differences are moderate, representing substantial overlap between the male and female distributions.

For the negative affectivity factor, there was no gender difference for negative affectivity ($d = -0.06$), sadness (-0.10), or emotionality (0.01). These findings are perhaps surprising given the power of negative affectivity to predict later depression (Watson & Clark 1984) and the reliable gender difference in depression, discussed in a later section.

In regard to the surgency factor, gender differences in activity ranged between $d = 0.15$ and 0.33, depending on the measure. For impulsivity, $d = 0.18$.

Personality and the five factors. Feingold (1994) conducted a meta-analysis of gender differences in personality based on US test norming data rooted in the Big Five model of personality (McCrae & Costa 2013). For the neuroticism factor, $d = -0.27$ for anxiety. For the extraversion factor, $d = -0.14$ for gregariousness but $+0.49$ for assertiveness. Openness to experience had an effect size of 0.13, and conscientiousness had -0.07. The largest gender difference was for tender-mindedness, which is part of the agreeableness factor, $d = -1.07$.

Although they did not use formal meta-analytic methods, Costa and colleagues synthesized data from the NEO Personality Inventory for more than 23,000 individuals across 26 cultures (Costa et al. 2001). To facilitate comparison between the Costa findings, which are more recent, and the Feingold (1994) findings, **Table 1** shows effect sizes for comparable scales representing each of the five factors. Costa and colleagues provided data for 26 cultures, but because of space limitations, only data for Americans, Japanese, and black South Africans are shown. **Table 1** shows that the

Table 1 Effect sizes for gender differences in personality across two meta-analyses, based on the Big Five model

Personality factor	Feingold (1994)	Costa et al. (2001) US adults	Costa et al. (2001) Japanese	Costa et al. (2001) Black South Africans
Neuroticism, Anxiety	−0.27	−0.40	−0.09	−0.08
Extraversion, Gregariousness	−0.14	−0.21		
Openness to Ideas	0.13	0.32		
Agreeableness, Tender-mindedness	−1.07	−0.31	−0.39	−0.05
Conscientiousness, Order	−0.07	−0.05		

Costa data for US adults generally agree with the Feingold results for the direction of gender differences, if not the magnitude. However, strikingly, the robust finding of greater neuroticism among women was not found for Japanese or black South Africans, providing evidence of the importance of culture in shaping gender differences in personality.

It should also be noted that the gender differences found by Feingold and by Costa and coworkers for the US sample are highly consistent with gender stereotypes in the United States, where women traditionally have been expected to be more neurotic and tender-minded than men (e.g., Broverman et al. 1972). Yet gender stereotypes and roles can vary across cultures. Costa and colleagues' analysis indicated that gender differences in self-reported personality traits are largest in prosperous cultures where women have many educational opportunities. Neuroticism might seem like a luxury for a black South African woman, erasing a gender difference that is found in the prosperous United States.

Impulsivity. Another meta-analysis examined gender differences in impulsivity, distinguishing among reward hypersensitivity, punishment hyposensitivity, and inadequate effortful control (Cross et al. 2011). Women were more sensitive to punishment ($d = -0.33$), but there was no gender difference in reward sensitivity. Men showed greater sensation seeking on questionnaire measures ($d = 0.41$) and behavioral measures (0.36). Contrary to expectations, there was no gender difference on measures of deficits in effortful control. The impulsivity meta-analysis, however, examined data only from samples of persons aged 11 and older, in contrast to the temperament meta-analysis, which focused on younger children.

Emotions. Emotional experience and expression, too, are the object of gender stereotypes in which anger is more acceptable for men, and most other emotions (e.g., sadness, fear, happiness) are considered more acceptable for women (e.g., Durik et al. 2006). Are these stereotypes consistent with actual behavior?

One meta-analysis examined gender differences in emotion expression in children from birth to adolescence (Chaplin & Aldao 2013). The results indicated trivial gender differences for positive emotions ($d = -0.08$), internalizing emotions such as sadness and anxiety ($d = -0.10$), and externalizing emotions such as anger ($d = 0.09$). However, the magnitude of the gender differences varied as a function of age. For example, the gender gap in positive emotions grew larger with age ($d = -0.20$ in middle childhood and -0.28 in adolescence), perhaps reflecting increasing socialization pressure with age. The magnitude of gender differences also varied with context. For example, when children are alone, $d = -0.03$ for internalizing emotions, but $d = -0.16$ when children are with adults. This meta-analysis again confirms the importance of context in creating or erasing gender differences.

Else-Quest and colleagues (2012) conducted a meta-analysis of gender differences in the self-conscious emotions, which are gender stereotyped in that women are expected to experience more guilt, shame, and embarrassment, whereas men are expected to experience more pride. The results indicated small differences favoring females for guilt ($d = -0.27$) and shame ($d = -0.29$) and, contrary to stereotypes, trivial differences for embarrassment ($d = -0.08$), authentic pride ($d = -0.01$), and hubristic pride ($d = -0.09$).

Overall, then, although stereotypes portray women as the emotional ones and hold that there are large gender differences in emotions such as fear and pride, the data, from both children and adults, indicate that gender differences in emotional experience are small or, in many cases, trivial.

Interests. Su and colleagues (2009) meta-analyzed data on gender differences from 47 interest inventories. The authors summarized their global findings as "Men and Things, Women and People." That is, on the Things–People dimension, the gender difference was large ($d = 0.93$), with women being more interested in people and men more interested in things. Regarding STEM, large gender differences were found for interest in engineering ($d = 1.11$), with more moderate gender differences for interest in science (0.36) and mathematics (0.34).

These findings regarding interests may help to explain the underrepresentation of women in certain STEM fields such as engineering. However, gender differences in interests are not hardwired or immutable. They, too, are shaped by sociocultural factors, a point that is discussed in more detail in the section on STEM.

Aggression. Several meta-analyses are available on gender differences in aggression (Archer 2004, Eagly & Steffen 1986, Hyde 1984). The focus here is on the Archer review because it covers the most recent data.

Gender differences in aggression do appear consistently and are generally moderate in magnitude. For physical aggression, $d = 0.55$ (Archer 2004). Developmentally, this difference appears about as early as children begin playing with one another, around the age of 2 (Alink et al. 2006).

A stereotype about "mean girls" has emerged, implying that, although boys may engage in more physical aggression, girls engage in much more verbal and relational aggression. "Relational aggression" refers to behavior that is intended to hurt others by damaging their peer relationships (Crick & Grotpeter 1995) and is sometimes also called indirect aggression. Contrary to the stereotype, the gender difference is not large, though. According to the Archer meta-analysis, $d = -0.19$ for peer ratings and -0.13 for teacher reports. In both cases, girls score higher, but the difference is small. Boys are quite capable of relational aggression.

It is important to recognize that patterns of gender differences in aggressive behavior are highly context dependent. In one striking experiment, researchers used the technique of deindividuation to produce a situation that removed the influences of gender roles (Lightdale & Prentice 1994). Deindividuation refers to a state in which the person has lost his or her individual identity; that is, the person has become anonymous. Under such conditions, people feel no obligation to conform to social norms such as gender roles. Half the participants were assigned to an individuated condition by having them sit close to the experimenter, identify themselves by name, wear large name tags, and answer personal questions. Those assigned to the deindividuated condition sat far from the experimenter and were simply told to wait quietly. Next, the participants played a video game in which they first defended and then attacked by dropping bombs. The number of bombs dropped was the measure of aggressive behavior. The results indicated that, in the individuated condition, men dropped significantly more bombs than women did, consistent with the gender differences found in meta-analyses. In the deindividuated condition—that is, in the absence of gender roles—there were no significant gender differences, and, in fact, females dropped somewhat more bombs than males did. In short, a significant gender difference in aggression disappeared when the influence of gender roles was removed.

Findings such as these have led some researchers to conclude that the emphasis on gender differences in aggression research is misplaced and that, instead, context plays a far greater role (Richardson & Hammock 2007). Consistent with this view, a meta-analysis by Bettencourt & Kernahan (1997) of experimental studies indicated that, in the context of violent cues but no provocation, a moderate gender difference is found ($d = 0.41$), whereas when violent cues and provocation are both present, the gender difference is eliminated.

Communication. As with other areas, stereotypes about enormous gender differences in communication abound, exemplified by Deborah Tannen's best-selling book, *You Just Don't Understand: Women and Men in Conversation* (1991). Tannen has argued that women's and men's patterns of speaking are so vastly different that men and women essentially belong to different linguistic communities. In particular, it has been said that women use more tentative speech than men do, as indicated by greater use of tag questions (That was a great movie, wasn't it?) and hedges (I'm kind of interested in biology), none of which convey self-confidence and strength.

According to a meta-analysis of studies of tentative speech, however, the gender differences favor women but are small (Leaper & Robnett 2011). For tag questions, $d = -0.23$, and for hedges, $d = -0.15$. Moreover, the magnitude of the gender difference depends on context. It is larger in lab studies ($d = -0.28$) than in naturalistic studies outside the lab ($d = -0.09$).

Helping behavior. Eagly & Crowley (1986; see also Eagly 2009) conducted a meta-analysis of research on gender differences in helping behavior, yielding $d = 0.34$, indicating that males help more. This overall effect, however, masks wide variations in the magnitude and even direction of the gender difference. Moderator analyses, for example, indicated that the gender difference favoring males was especially pronounced when the situation might involve danger, such as stopping to help a motorist with a flat tire. The gender difference was also larger when the helping behavior was observed by others rather than when the person was alone; heroism is part of the male role, but it is hard to be a hero when no one is watching. Other kinds of helping, such as helping a distressed child, are associated with the female role, and here we see less helping by males and more by females.

Sexuality. Sexuality is another area in which stereotypes hold that women and men are vastly different. A meta-analysis by Petersen & Hyde (2010) paints a complex picture. Across 14 distinct sexual behaviors (e.g., number of partners, casual sex, extramarital sex) and 16 sexual attitudes (e.g., attitudes about extramarital sex, attitudes about homosexuality), no gender differences were large. Four were in the moderate range: males were more likely to masturbate ($d = 0.53$), to use pornography ($d = 0.63$), and to have more sexual partners ($d = 0.36$), and males had more favorable attitudes toward casual sex ($d = 0.45$). Many gender similarities were found as well, with effect sizes ≤ 0.10 for oral sex, attitudes about extramarital sex, attitudes about masturbation, attitudes about condom use, and attitudes about lesbians (but attitudes toward gay men showed somewhat more favorable attitudes among women, $d = -0.18$). Moderator analyses indicated that some gender gaps have been narrowing over time, including attitudes about casual sex.

Unlike many of the other domains reviewed here, for which both self-report and behavioral measures are typically available, most sex research is based on self-report. That leads to the question of whether some gender differences, such as the one in number of sexual partners, are actual behavioral differences or merely represent different reporting biases among women and men. Consistent with the double standard (Crawford & Popp 2003), might men exaggerate their number of partners, or might women underreport theirs?

Several experiments by Fisher and colleagues have addressed these questions (Alexander & Fisher 2003, Fisher 2007, Jonason & Fisher 2009). Using the bogus pipeline technique, researchers randomly assigned college students to one of three experimental conditions (Alexander & Fisher 2003). In the bogus pipeline condition, participants were hooked up to a fake polygraph while they were completing the sex questionnaire, and told that the machine could detect untruthful answers, presumably eliciting very honest reporting. In the anonymous condition, the student filled out the sex questionnaire anonymously, as is typical of much sex research, and placed the questionnaire in a locked box when finished. In the exposure threat condition, respondents had to hand their completed questionnaire to the experimenter, who was an undergraduate peer, and the experimenter sat in full view while the respondents completed their questionnaire. For reports of the number of sex partners, the gender difference was largest in the exposure threat condition, males reporting more partners. The gender difference was also present in the anonymous condition; however, the gender difference was erased in the bogus pipeline condition, presumably when participants were giving the most honest answers. This research suggests that some gender differences in sexuality do not represent actual differences in behavior but instead are an artifact of contextual factors that cause reporting biases consistent with gender roles.

Leadership. Eagly and colleagues conducted a series of meta-analyses on gender and leadership. One meta-analysis examined data on gender and the effectiveness of leaders (Eagly et al. 1995). Overall, there was no gender difference in leadership effectiveness, $d = -0.02$, which was true whether objective or subjective measures were used. However, male leaders were somewhat more effective in positions that were consistent with the male role, and female leaders were more effective in positions consistent with the female role. Overall, then, there were no gender differences in leadership effectiveness, but women may be more effective than men in certain situations.

A separate question is whether women and men differ in their leadership styles. The styles that have been studied most are transformational (innovative leadership in which the leader serves as a positive role model based on gaining the trust of the followers), transactional (leadership by administering rewards for good behaviors and punishments or corrections for poor performance), and laissez-faire (the leader is neglectful and uninvolved). Transformational style is a concept that has emerged relatively recently and is seen as admirable. For transformational leadership, $d = -0.10$, i.e., a trivial difference (Eagly et al. 2003). For transactional leadership, women have a slight edge in reward-based approaches, $d = -0.13$, whereas men are more inclined to wait until problems crop up and then address them, $d = 0.27$. Men are also somewhat more likely to engage in laissez-faire leadership, $d = 0.16$.

Overall, then, although leadership is stereotyped as masculine, there is no evidence that women are incompetent as leaders, whether measured by effectiveness or by the use of optimal styles such as transformational leadership.

Well-Being and Psychopathology

Some psychological disorders show lopsided gender ratios (Zahn-Waxler et al. 2008). For example, twice as many women as men are depressed (Kessler et al. 1993). Roughly 90% of anorexics are females (Subst. Abuse Ment. Health Serv. Adm. 2009), and, depending on the study, boys with ADHD outnumber girls by 2:1 to 9:1 (Rucklidge 2010). The focus here is particularly on gender differences in depression, rumination, and self-esteem, because they have been studied extensively.

Depression. In adulthood, twice as many women as men are depressed (Kessler et al. 1993). Although girls are no more depressed than boys in childhood, more girls than boys are depressed by ages 13 to 15 (Hankin et al. 1998, Kessler et al. 1993). Although no comprehensive meta-analysis is available, two more specific meta-analyses have been conducted. Twenge & Nolen-Hoeksema (2002) meta-analyzed studies that had used the Children's Depression Inventory (CDI) and found that, between the ages of 8 and 12, $d = 0.04$, whereas between ages 13 and 16, $d = -0.16$. This gender difference in adolescence is not large, which appears to contrast with statistics on the 2:1 ratio of depressed females to depressed males. A resolution probably lies in the fact that the effect sizes are based on mean differences in community samples, whereas the statistics on depression examine extreme scores at the tail of the distribution. Moreover, the CDI measures symptoms of depression, whereas most studies finding the 2:1 ratio assessed diagnoses of depression. In terms of developmental trends, boys' CDI scores held relatively constant from younger to older ages, whereas girls' scores increased, so that $d = -0.22$ by age 14.

The other available meta-analysis explored gender differences in depression at the other end of the life span, among those 75 and older (Luppa et al. 2012). Gender ratios for prevalence rates ranged between 1.4 and 2.2, suggesting that the preponderance of women with depression is a phenomenon that continues into old age.

Hundreds of studies have attempted to identify the factor or factors that account for the gender difference in depression and why it emerges in adolescence. Synthesizing these studies and previous theoretical models, Hyde and colleagues (2008b) proposed the ABC model of gender differences in depression. According to the model, affective, biological, and cognitive factors converge to create an overall vulnerability to depression. Rooted in a vulnerability $\times$ stress approach, the model holds that negative life events interact with the depressogenic vulnerability, yielding increased levels of depression in adolescence, especially for girls. Biological factors in the model include genetic factors such as the 5HTTLPR polymorphism as well as pubertal hormones and pubertal timing (early, on time, or late). The affective factors are several dimensions of temperament including, especially, negative affectivity. Three aspects of cognitive vulnerability are included in the model: cognitive vulnerability as defined in the hopelessness theory of depression (Abramson et al. 1989); objectified body consciousness (a cognitive process in which individuals become observers and critics of their bodies and appearance, McKinley & Hyde 1996; see also Fredrickson & Roberts 1997); and rumination (the tendency to think repetitively and passively about the negative emotions elicited by negative events, Nolen-Hoeksema 2001). According to the ABC model, it is likely that multiple factors contribute to the gender difference in depression, including gender differences in stress beginning in adolescence, girls' greater vulnerability to the negative effects of early puberty, girls' greater objectified body consciousness, and the adverse effects of peer sexual harassment on girls.

Rumination. As noted, some theorists have argued that gender differences in depression can be accounted for at least in part by gender differences in rumination. The one available meta-analysis found that $d = -0.14$ in child samples and -0.36 in adolescent samples (Rood et al. 2009). Thus the gender difference in rumination widens from childhood to adolescence, in parallel to the emerging gender difference in depression.

Self-esteem. The popular media contend that girls have terrible problems with self-esteem beginning in adolescence and, by implication, that boys do not have self-esteem problems. A 1999 meta-analysis tested these claims (Kling et al. 1999). Averaged over all ages, $d = 0.21$, indicating a small difference favoring males but clearly not the large difference that one might expect based on media reports. The effect size increased from 0.16 in elementary school to 0.23 in middle school and 0.33 in high school, but then declined to 0.18 among college students and 0.10 among adults between the ages of 23 and 59, so that the gender difference was not large for any age group. An analysis by ethnicity for US samples showed that the magnitude of the gender difference was $d = 0.20$ among whites but -0.04 among blacks. That is, the much touted gender difference may be found only among whites and not among ethnic minorities (too few samples of other ethnic minorities were available for analysis).

EMCP: engineering, mathematics, computer science, and physics

The meta-analysis described above synthesized studies that measured global self-esteem. Another approach to studying self-esteem is to measure domain-specific self-esteem or self-concept—for example, self-concept of math ability or self-concept of athletic ability. Another meta-analysis examined studies that had measured domain-specific self-esteem (Gentile et al. 2009). Males scored higher than females on physical appearance ($d = 0.35$), athletic (0.41), and self-satisfaction (0.33) self-esteem, whereas females scored higher on behavioral conduct ($d = -0.17$) and moral-ethical (-0.38) self-esteem. For all other domains, gender similarities were found; effect sizes were close to 0 for academic, social, and family self-esteem.

The STEM Issue

It is well known that women are underrepresented in careers in science, technology, engineering, and mathematics (STEM), although this global statement is not entirely consistent with a more nuanced view of the data. Today, for example, women earn 53% of the PhDs in biology, 48% of the MD degrees, and 78% of the veterinary degrees (Natl. Cent. Educ. Stat. 2012). Those fields display gender similarities, or even a preponderance of women in the case of veterinarians. In contrast, women earn only 18% of the undergraduate degrees in engineering, 31% of the doctoral degrees in mathematics, 22% of the doctoral degrees in computer science, and 19% of the doctoral degrees in physics (Natl. Sci. Found. 2011). It is in these areas that the gender gaps lie.

A variety of explanations have been offered for the gender gaps in engineering, mathematics, computer science, and physics (EMCP, which is a distinct subset of STEM). Then-president of Harvard, Lawrence Summers, famously opined that women lacked the mathematical ability to succeed in these areas, although that argument is contradicted by the evidence for gender similarities in mathematics performance presented previously (but see the discussion of greater male variability below). Other explanations include a chilly institutional climate for women graduate students and faculty in these disciplines (Stewart & LaVaque-Manty 2008); parents' and teachers' gender-stereotyped beliefs and behaviors that discourage girls from these areas (Chhin et al. 2008, Jussim et al. 1996); girls' and women's lack of interest in EMCP and preference for other fields (Ceci & Williams 2011); stereotype threat and lack of a sense of belonging in these fields (Miyake et al. 2010); the distracting effect of romance (Holland & Eisenhart 1990, Park et al. 2011); and women's family roles, which prevent them from working 80 hours per week, or perceptions that these occupations are not family friendly (Frome et al. 2008). A newer and more novel explanation concerns societal values that emphasize self-expressive value systems, prominent in the United States and other postindustrial nations, in which people seek to take courses and find an occupation that is highly interesting and that they will love (Charles & Bradley 2009). In such a societal context, women think that engineering will not be interesting and opt for something that will be. The researchers found that the gender gap in engineering was largest in postindustrial/postmaterialist nations, such as Finland, Germany, Switzerland, and Hong Kong. The gender gap in engineering was smaller in materialist nations with developing economies such as Bulgaria, Colombia, Latvia, and Romania, where the goal is to get a stable job that pays well rather than following one's loves.

It is beyond the scope of this article to review in depth each of these hypotheses and the evidence for them. It is worth noting, though, that the explanation based on women's family roles is inconsistent with the success of women in biology and psychology; surely it takes as many hours of work per week to succeed in those sciences as it does in EMCP. Moreover, recent evidence confirms that bias against women job candidates continues to exist in the sciences, so that discrimination remains a viable hypothesis (Moss-Racusin et al. 2012).

GENDER DIFFERENCES AND SIMILARITIES IN VARIABILITY

The previous section reviewed evidence on gender similarities and differences in average scores. However, another possibility involves gender differences not in means but in variance. The greater male variability hypothesis was originally proposed by Henry Havelock Ellis in 1894 to explain the excess of males among the mentally defective as well as among geniuses (Shields 1975). The idea is that the variance of the distribution of scores for males is larger than the variance for females, creating an excess of males in both the high and low tails of the distribution. It is this hypothesis that Summers apparently had in mind when trying to explain the dearth of women faculty in mathematics at Harvard.

The statistic used to evaluate the greater male variability hypothesis is the variance ratio, equal to the ratio of male variance to female variance. Thus, values greater than 1.0 indicate greater male variance and values less than 1.0 indicate greater female variance.

Several meta-analyses have examined variance ratios for outcomes including mathematics performance (Hedges & Nowell 1995, Hyde et al. 2008a, Lindberg et al. 2010), verbal and spatial performance (Hedges & Nowell 1995), and temperament (Else-Quest et al. 2006). An overview of these findings is provided in **Table 2**.

For mathematics performance, across three meta-analyses and a wide variety of samples, variance ratios consistently range between 1.05 and 1.20. Males display more variability, but the variance ratios are not very far from 1.0, i.e., the variances are not radically different. Similarly, for verbal performance, variance ratios range between 1.03 and 1.16. For temperament, two variance ratios are less than 1.0—for fear and emotionality—indicating greater female variability. However, none of these variance ratios are very far from 1.0, indicating equal variability for males and females.

What is the effect of variance ratios such as these on the number of males and females in the upper tail of the distribution, e.g., the distribution of mathematics performance? Hedges & Friedman (1993) computed the predicted ratio of the number of males to the number of females in the upper tail for various combinations of d and variance ratio values, assuming a normal distribution (which may or may not be accurate for a given data set). For example, for $d = 0.01$ and variance ratio $= 1.05$ (values similar to those shown in **Table 2**), the ratio of males to females above the 95 percentile should be 1.11, i.e., there will be 111 males for every 100 females—not so different from 50–50. At a more extreme point on the upper end of the distribution, the 99.9 percentile, the gender ratio would be 1.33, i.e., 133 males for every 100 females. If we take slightly larger values of d and variance ratio, $d = 0.05$ and variance ratio $= 1.12$, then the gender ratio is 1.34 at the 95 percentile and 2.15 at the 99.9 percentile. Variance ratios such as these cannot begin to explain why only 18% of the undergraduate degrees in engineering go to women, particularly because such a major does not require mathematical skills at the 99.9 percentile.

It is also important to note that, even if there is slightly greater male variability for some cognitive measures, this finding is simply a description of the phenomenon. It does not address the causes of greater male variability, which could be due to biological factors, sociocultural factors, or both (Johnson et al. 2008, 2009).

GENDER SIMILARITIES, DIFFERENCES, AND INTERSECTIONALITY

To this point, this review has described the evidence regarding gender differences and similarities in isolation, neglecting other important social categories such as ethnicity and sexual orientation.

Greater male variability hypothesis: the belief that the variance in the distribution of scores is larger for males than females, on intelligence or other abilities, so that there are more high-scoring males than females, but also more low-scoring males

Variance ratio: the ratio of male variance to female variance, used to test the greater male variability hypothesis

Table 2 Variance ratios (M:F) in meta-analyses of mathematics, verbal, and spatial performance, and temperament

Domain	VR (M:F)
Verbal	
Hedges & Nowell (1995), Project Talent	1.16
Hedges & Nowell (1995), NLS-72	1.03
Hedges & Nowell (1995), NLSY	1.16
Hedges & Nowell (1995), HS&B	1.10
Hedges & Nowell (1995), NELS:88	1.16
Mathematics	
Hedges & Nowell (1995), Project Talent	1.20
Hedges & Nowell (1995), NLS-72	1.05
Hedges & Nowell (1995), NLSY	1.19
Hedges & Nowell (1995), HS&B	1.16
Hedges & Nowell (1995), NELS:88	1.06
Lindberg et al. (2010), NLSY, 2002	1.05
Lindberg et al. (2010), NAEP, 2000	1.18
Hyde et al. (2008a), Grade 2	1.11
Hyde et al. (2008a), Grade 11	1.17
Spatial	
Hedges & Nowell (1995), Project Talent	1.27
Hedges & Nowell (1995), HS&B	1.27
Temperament (Else-Quest et al. 2006)	
Persistence	1.00
Inhibitory control	1.09
Emotionality	0.94
Fear	0.93
Activity	1.00–1.06

Abbreviations: HS&B, High School and Beyond; M:F, ratio of males to females; NAEP, National Assessment of Educational Progress; NELS:88, National Education Longitudinal Study of 1988; NLS-72, National Longitudinal Study of the High School Class of 1972; NLSY, National Longitudinal Survey of Youth; VR, variance ratio (the ratio of male variance to female variance).

Intersectionality is an approach that simultaneously considers multiple categories of identity, difference, and disadvantage, such as gender, race, class, sexual orientation, disability, and religion (Cole 2009). Intersectionality holds that gender effects can never be understood in isolation and must always be examined in context, i.e., in the context of ethnicity and other social identities and categories. One implication is that scientists should not make global statements about gender differences, referring to an entire nation, much less to cross-culturally universal differences. As an example, the case of the intersection of gender and ethnicity is considered in more detail.

In the meta-analysis of gender differences in self-esteem described previously, the magnitude of the gender difference was $d = 0.20$ among whites but -0.04 among blacks (Kling et al. 1999). That is, the small but much publicized gender gap in self-esteem was found for whites but not blacks. Global statements about gender differences in self-esteem miss the mark.

Similarly, an early meta-analysis of research on gender differences in mathematics performance found $d = 0.13$ for whites, but $d = -0.02$ for blacks, 0.00 for Hispanics, and -0.09 for Asian

Americans (Hyde et al. 1990). The male advantage (although very small) was found for whites and was not present for blacks, Hispanics, or Asian Americans.

The meta-analysis of gender differences in self-conscious emotions also found evidence of the intersection of gender and ethnicity (Else-Quest et al. 2012). For example, for shame, $d = -0.32$ for whites but -0.06 for nonwhites. That is, the overall finding of $d = -0.29$ for shame obscured variations in the magnitude of the gender difference across ethnic groups and, in particular, masked the absence of the difference among nonwhites.

Few gender meta-analyses have looked for variations in the magnitude of the gender difference as a function of ethnicity or other potential moderators such as social class. Meta-analysis provides an excellent method for the analysis of the intersection of gender and ethnicity. Future gender meta-analyses should routinely consider ethnicity and social class as potential moderators. Several factors will complicate this effort. First, ethnic groups are specific to nations. The examples given in the previous paragraphs were for US samples. Other nations have different relevant ethnic groups, with different meanings attached to membership in those groups. At the least, meta-analysts can consider ethnicity in US samples and examine it in samples from other nations based on an understanding of relevant ethnic groups in those nations. Second, many researchers are negligent about reporting the ethnicity of their samples, despite American Psychological Association style guidelines that mandate this reporting. For example, in the math meta-analysis, 70 studies reported ethnicity and the remaining 184 did not (Hyde et al. 1990). Moreover, in studies with samples covering multiple ethnicities, the data typically are not analyzed for gender differences separately by ethnicity. If we are to realize the potential of intersectional approaches in psychology, researchers at the least must improve their reporting of the gender and ethnicity of their samples and, ideally, analyze gender × ethnicity interactions.

SUMMARY AND FUTURE DIRECTIONS

Overall, based on the numerous meta-analyses reported here, there is much evidence in support of the gender similarities hypothesis. Domains in which gender differences are small (around $d = 0.20$) or trivial ($d \leq 0.10$) include mathematics performance, verbal skills, some personality dimensions such as gregariousness and conscientiousness, reward sensitivity, the temperament dimension of negative affectivity, relational aggression, tentative speech, some aspects of sexuality (e.g., oral sex experience, attitudes about extramarital sex, attitudes about masturbation), leadership effectiveness, self-esteem, and academic self-concept.

Nonetheless, the gender similarities hypothesis acknowledges exceptions to the general rule. Exceptions to gender similarities, where differences are moderate ($d = 0.50$) or large ($d = 0.80$), include 3D mental rotation, the personality dimension of agreeableness/tender-mindedness, sensation seeking, interests in things versus people, physical aggression, some sexual behaviors (masturbation and pornography use), and attitudes about casual sex.

This review also reveals much evidence of the importance of context in creating or erasing gender differences. For example, deindividuation, which removes the influence of gender roles, erases the gender difference in aggression. Nations with greater gender equality have much smaller gender gaps in mathematics performance and in mate preferences.

Mountains of research have been conducted on psychological gender differences, yielding the patterns of results described above. Given the current state of research, what are the most important directions for future research?

A distinctly different approach holds that the search for gender differences and their causes is not a productive research strategy. For example, in the case of the gender difference in spatial performance, which is moderately large, Newcombe and colleagues (2002) argued that documenting gender differences and their cause was relatively unimportant and that the real goal should be to find training methods or interventions that would maximize everyone's spatial competence. When researchers find a gender difference, they might productively ask themselves, is this important, and why is it important? Are other issues more important?

Nonetheless, research on psychological gender differences will continue for years to come, given many scientists' firm beliefs that such differences exist and are large and the media's insatiable thirst for new findings of gender differences. What, then, are the best directions to take this research? Two approaches seem especially promising: intersectional approaches and contextual approaches.

Intersectional approaches to the study of gender similarities and differences can profitably investigate the intersection of gender and ethnicity and the intersection of gender and social class. Researchers, reviewers, and editors should no longer settle for a report of a gender difference. They must ask about the ethnicity of the sample and whether the gender difference, if found in a predominantly white sample, is also found in ethnic minority samples. Researchers should chart the magnitude and direction of gender differences across different ethnic groups. The same is true for the intersection of gender and social class. With college-student samples, these analyses are difficult because the participants are predominantly middle class. Nonetheless, even in college samples, some individuals are first-generation college students whereas others have parents who are college graduates, giving researchers some leverage in studying the intersection of gender and social class. If samples of youth are recruited from primary or secondary schools, recruiting should occur over a range of schools that vary in the social class of the students, so that researchers can examine the magnitude and direction of gender differences at various social class levels. Meta-analysts should routinely examine race and social class as moderators of the magnitude of gender differences.

Identifying contexts in which gender differences appear or disappear will continue to be an important strategy, both in primary research and in meta-analyses. Eagly & Crowley's (1986) meta-analysis of research on gender differences in helping behavior provides a model. They considered theoretically derived variables that should moderate the gender difference in helping behavior: The male role emphasizes heroic and chivalrous helping, whereas the female role emphasizes nurturant helping. For example, when the helping behavior was observed (encouraging heroic helping), the effect size for the gender difference was large, $d = 0.74$. In contrast, when the helping was not observed, there was no gender difference, $d = -0.02$. Large gender differences can be created and erased by the context. Situational variables such as these must be taken into account in meta-analyses, and they warrant much more primary research, guided by theories such as sociocultural theory, expectancy-value theory, and cognitive social learning theory.

Above all, researchers should keep the possibilities of gender differences and gender similarities in balance as they report and interpret their findings. There are serious costs to an overemphasis on gender differences, such as beliefs that boys and girls are so different that they must be educated in gender-segregated schools or a belief that marital therapy for heterosexual couples cannot succeed because of profound gender differences in communication styles. A nonsignificant gender difference, that is, a gender similarity, is as interesting and important as a gender difference.

SUMMARY POINTS

1. The gender similarities hypothesis states that males and females are similar on most, but not all, psychological variables. The current review found much evidence in support of gender similarities.

2. Meta-analysis is a statistical technique that can be used to synthesize previous studies of gender differences on a particular psychological attribute. It focuses on the effect size, that is, how large the difference between males and females is.

3. Cognitive social learning theory explains psychological gender differences as being a result of females and males receiving different rewards and punishments for their behaviors, people's tendency to imitate same-gender models, and cognitive processes such as attention and self-efficacy.

4. Sociocultural theory argues that contemporary psychological gender differences have their origins in the prehistoric division of labor by gender; once males and females take on different roles, they develop the psychological qualities that equip them for those roles.

5. Contemporary data indicate that girls have reached parity with boys in mathematics performance, from grades 2 through 11.

6. Gender differences persist in spatial performance, in particular three-dimensional mental rotation. A spatial curriculum should be implemented in the schools that would improve the performance of both girls and boys.

7. Intersectionality is a research approach that emphasizes the simultaneous consideration of multiple categories of identity and disadvantage, including gender, ethnicity, social class, and sexual orientation.

DISCLOSURE STATEMENT

The author is not aware of any affiliations, memberships, funding, or financial holdings that might be perceived as affecting the objectivity of this review.

ACKNOWLEDGMENTS

Preparation of this review was supported in part by grants REC 0635444 and DRL 1138114 from the National Science Foundation. Any opinions expressed are those of the author and not the National Science Foundation. I thank Nicole Else-Quest and Amy Mezulis for insightful comments on an earlier draft of this review.

LITERATURE CITED

Abramson LY, Metalsky G, Alloy L. 1989. Hopelessness depression: a theory-based subtype of depression. *Psychol. Rev.* 96:358–72

Alexander MG, Fisher TD. 2003. Truth and consequences: using the bogus pipeline to examine sex differences in self-reported sexuality. *J. Sex Res.* 4:27–35

Alink LR, Mesman J, van Zeijl J, Stolk MN, Juffer F, et al. 2006. The early childhood aggression curve: development of physical aggression in 10- to 50-month-old children. *Child Dev.* 77:954–66

Archer J. 2004. Sex differences in aggression in real-world settings: a meta-analytic review. *Rev. Gen. Psychol.* 8:291–322

Ball LC, Cribbie RA, Steele JR. 2013. Beyond gender differences: using tests of equivalence to evaluate gender similarities. *Psychol. Women Q.* 37:147–54

Bettencourt BA, Kernahan C. 1997. A meta-analysis of aggression in the presence of violent cues: effects of gender differences and aversive provocation. *Aggress. Behav.* 23:447–56

Broverman IK, Vogel SR, Broverman DM, Clarkson FE, Rosenkrantz PS. 1972. Sex role stereotypes: a current appraisal. *J. Soc. Issues* 28:59–78

Buss DM, Schmitt DP. 1993. Sexual strategies theory: an evolutionary perspective on human mating. *Psychol. Rev.* 100:204–32

Bussey K, Bandura A. 1999. Social cognitive theory of gender development and differentiation. *Psychol. Rev.* 106:676–713

Carothers BJ, Reis HT. 2013. Men and women are from earth: examining the latent structure of gender. *J. Personal. Soc. Psychol.* 104:385–407

Ceci SJ, Williams WM. 2011. Understanding current causes of women's underrepresentation in science. *Proc. Natl. Acad. Sci. USA* 108:3157–62

Chaplin TM, Aldao A. 2013. Gender differences in emotion expression in children: a meta-analytic review. *Psychol. Bull.* 139:735–65

Charles M, Bradley K. 2009. Indulging our gendered selves? Sex segregation by field of study in 44 countries. *Am. J. Sociol.* 114:924–76

Chhin CS, Bleeker MM, Jacobs JE. 2008. Gender-typed occupational choices: the long-term impact of parents' beliefs and expectations. In *Gender and Occupational Outcomes*, ed. H Watt, J Eccles, pp. 215–34. Washington, DC: Am. Psychol. Assoc.

Cohen J. 1988. *Statistical Power Analysis for the Behavioral Sciences*. Hillsdale, NJ: Erlbaum. 2nd ed.

Cole ER. 2009. Intersectionality and research in psychology. *Am. Psychol.* 64:170–80

Costa PT, Terracciano A, McCrae RR. 2001. Gender differences in personality traits across cultures: robust and surprising findings. *J. Personal. Soc. Psychol.* 81:322–31

Crawford M, Popp D. 2003. Sexual double standards: a review and methodological critique of two decades of research. *J. Sex Res.* 40:13–26

Crick NR, Grotpeter JK. 1995. Relational aggression, gender, and social psychological adjustment. *Child Dev.* 66:710–22

Cross CP, Copping LT, Campbell A. 2011. Sex differences in impulsivity: a meta-analysis. *Psychol. Bull.* 137:97–130

Deaux K. 1985. Sex and gender. *Annu. Rev. Psychol.* 36:49–81

Del Giudice M, Booth T, Irwing P. 2012. The distance between Mars and Venus: measuring global sex differences in personality. *PLoS ONE* 7:e29265

Durik AM, Hyde J, Marks A, Roy A, Anaya D, Schultz G. 2006. Ethnicity and gender stereotypes of emotion. *Sex Roles* 54:429–45

Eagly AH. 2009. The his and hers of prosocial behavior: an examination of the social psychology of gender. *Am. Psychol.* 64:644–58

Eagly AH, Crowley M. 1986. Gender and helping behavior: a meta-analytic review of the social psychological literature. *Psychol. Bull.* 100:283–308

Eagly AH, Johannesen-Schmidt MC, van Engen ML. 2003. Transformational, transactional, and laissez-faire leadership styles: a meta-analysis comparing women and men. *Psychol. Bull.* 129:569–91

Eagly AH, Karau S, Makhijani M. 1995. Gender and the effectiveness of leaders: a meta-analysis. *Psychol. Bull.* 117:125–45

Eagly AH, Steffen VJ. 1986. Gender and aggressive behavior: a meta-analytic review of the social psychological literature. *Psychol. Bull.* 100:309–30

Eagly AH, Wood W. 1999. The origins of sex differences in human behavior: evolved dispositions versus social roles. *Am. Psychol.* 54:408–23

Eccles JS. 1994. Understanding women's educational and occupational choices: applying the Eccles et al. model of achievement-related choices. *Psychol. Women Q.* 18:585–610

Else-Quest NM. 2012. Gender differences in temperament. In *Handbook of Temperament*, ed. M Zentner, R Shiner, pp. 479–96. New York: Guilford

Else-Quest NM, Higgins A, Allison C, Morton LC. 2012. Gender differences in self-conscious emotional experience: a meta-analysis. *Psychol. Bull.* 138:947–81

Else-Quest NM, Hyde JS, Goldsmith HH, Van Hulle C. 2006. Gender differences in temperament: a meta-analysis. *Psychol. Bull.* 132:33–72

The fundamental statement of cognitive social learning as it applies to gender development.

An explanation of the concept of intersectionality and its applications in psychology.

A complete statement of sociocultural theory together with evidence for it.

A review of research relevant to expectancy-value theory.

Else-Quest NM, Hyde JS, Linn MC. 2010. Cross-national patterns of gender differences in mathematics: a meta-analysis. *Psychol. Bull.* 136:103–27

Feingold A. 1994. Gender differences in personality: a meta-analysis. *Psychol. Bull.* 116:429–56

Feng J. 2007. Playing an action video game reduces gender differences in spatial cognition. *Psychol. Sci.* 18:850–55

Fisher TD. 2007. Sex of experimenter and social norm effects on reports of sexual behavior in young men and women. *Arch. Sex. Behav.* 36:89–100

Fredrickson B, Roberts T. 1997. Objectification theory: toward understanding women's lived experiences and mental health risks. *Psychol. Women Q.* 21:173–206

Frome PM, Alfeld CJ, Eccles JS, Barber BL. 2008. Is the desire for a family-flexible job keeping young women out of male-dominated occupations? In *Gender and Occupational Outcomes*, ed. H Watt, J Eccles, pp. 195–214. Washington, DC: Am. Psychol. Assoc.

Gentile B, Grabe S, Dolan-Pascoe B, Twenge JM, Wells BE, Maitino A. 2009. Gender differences in domain-specific self-esteem: a meta-analysis. *Rev. Gen. Psychol.* 13:34–45

Gerson H, Sorby SA, Wysocki A, Baartmans BJ. 2001. The development and assessment of multimedia software for improving 3-D visualization skills. *Comput. Appl. Eng. Educ.* 9:105–13

Gisborne T. 1797. *An Enquiry Into the Duties of the Female Sex*. London: Cadell & Davies

Hankin BL, Abramson L, Moffitt T, Silva P, McGee R, Angell K. 1998. Development of depression from preadolescence to young adulthood: emerging gender differences in a 10-year longitudinal study. *J. Abnorm. Psychol.* 107:128–40

Hedges LV, Friedman L. 1993. Gender differences in variability in intellectual abilities: a reanalysis of Feingold's results. *Rev. Educ. Res.* 63:94–105

Hedges LV, Nowell A. 1995. Sex differences in mental test scores, variability, and numbers of high-scoring individuals. *Science* 269:41–45

Hines M. 2011. Gender development and the human brain. *Annu. Rev. Neurosci.* 34:69–88

Holland DC, Eisenhart MA. 1990. *Educated in Romance: Women, Achievement, and the College Culture*. Chicago: Univ. Chicago Press

Hollingworth LS. 1918. Comparison of the sexes in mental traits. *Psychol. Bull.* 15:427–32

Hyde JS. 1984. How large are gender differences in aggression? A developmental meta-analysis. *Dev. Psychol.* 20:722–36

Hyde JS. 2005. The gender similarities hypothesis. *Am. Psychol.* 60:581–92

Hyde JS. 2006. Gender similarities still rule. *Am. Psychol.* 61:641–42

Hyde JS, Fennema E, Lamon S. 1990. Gender differences in mathematics performance: a meta-analysis. *Psychol. Bull.* 107:139–55

Hyde JS, Lindberg SM, Linn MC, Ellis A, Williams C. 2008a. Gender similarities characterize math performance. *Science* 321:494–95

Hyde JS, Linn MC. 1988. Gender differences in verbal ability: a meta-analysis. *Psychol. Bull.* 104:53–69

Hyde JS, Mezulis AH, Abramson LY. 2008b. The ABCs of depression: integrating affective, biological and cognitive models to explain the emergence of the gender difference in depression. *Psychol. Rev.* 115:291–313

Joel D. 2012. Genetic-gonadal-genitals sex (3G-sex) and the misconception of brain and gender, or, why 3G-males and 3G-females have intersex brain and intersex gender. *Biol. Sex Differ.* 3:27

Johnson W, Carothers A, Deary IJ. 2008. Sex differences in variability in general intelligence. *Perspect. Psychol. Sci.* 3:518–31

Johnson W, Carothers A, Deary IJ. 2009. A role for the X chromosome in sex differences in variability in general intelligence? *Perspect. Psychol. Sci.* 4:598–621

Jonason PK, Fisher TD. 2009. The power of prestige: why young men report having more sex partners than young women. *Sex Roles* 60:151–59

Jussim L, Eccles J, Madon S. 1996. Social perception, social stereotypes, and teacher expectations: accuracy and the quest for the powerful self-fulfilling prophecy. In *Advances in Experimental Social Psychology*, ed. MP Zanna, 28:281–388. San Diego, CA: Academic

Kessler RC, McGonagle K, Swartz M, Blazer D, Nelson C. 1993. Sex and depression in the National Comorbidity Survey: I. Lifetime prevalence, chronicity and recurrence. *J. Affect. Disord.* 29:85–96

Presents the original formulation of Hyde's gender similarities hypothesis and the evidence for it.

Reviews research on affective, biological, and cognitive factors that contribute to gender differences in depression.

Kling KC, Hyde JS, Showers CJ, Buswell BN. 1999. Gender differences in self-esteem: a meta-analysis. *Psychol. Bull.* 125:470–500

Leaper C, Robnett RD. 2011. Women are more likely than men to use tentative language, aren't they? A meta-analysis testing for gender differences and moderators. *Psychol. Women Q.* 35:129–42

Lightdale JR, Prentice DA. 1994. Rethinking sex differences in aggression: aggressive behavior in the absence of social roles. *Personal. Soc. Psychol. Bull.* 20:34–44

Lindberg SM, Hyde JS, Petersen J, Linn MC. 2010. New trends in gender and mathematics performance: a meta-analysis. *Psychol. Bull.* 136:1123–35

Linn MC, Petersen AC. 1985. Emergence and characterization of sex differences in spatial ability: a meta-analysis. *Child Dev.* 56:1479–98

Luppa M, Sikorski C, Luck T, Ehreke L, Konnopka A, Riedel-Heller SG. 2012. Age- and gender-specific prevalence of depression in latest-life—systematic review and meta-analysis. *J. Affect. Disord.* 136:212–21

Maccoby EE, Jacklin CN. 1974. *The Psychology of Sex Differences.* Stanford, CA: Stanford Univ. Press

Maeda Y, Yoon SY. 2013. A meta-analysis on gender differences in mental rotation ability measured by the Purdue Spatial Visualization Tests: Visualization of rotations (PSVT:R). *Educ. Psychol. Rev.* 25:69–94

Marsh HW, Bornmann L, Mutz R, Daniel H, O'Mara A. 2009. Gender effects in the peer reviews of grant proposals: a comprehensive meta-analysis comparing traditional and multilevel approaches. *Rev. Educ. Res.* 79:1290–326

Martin CL, Ruble DN. 2010. Patterns of gender development. *Annu. Rev. Psychol.* 61:353–81

McCrae RR, Costa P. 2013. Introduction to the empirical and theoretical status of the five-factor model of personality traits. In *Personality Disorders and the Five-Factor Model of Personality*, ed. TA Widiger, PT Costa, pp. 15–27. Washington, DC: Am. Psychol. Assoc. 3rd ed.

McKinley NM, Hyde JS. 1996. The Objectified Body Consciousness Scale: development and validation. *Psychol. Women Q.* 20:181–215

Meece JL, Eccles-Parsons J, Kaczala CM, Goff SB, Futterman R. 1982. Sex differences in math achievement: toward a model of academic choice. *Psychol. Bull.* 91:324–48

Miyake A, Kost-Smith LE, Finkelstein ND, Pollock SJ, Cohen GL, Ito TA. 2010. Reducing the gender achievement gap in college science: a classroom study of values affirmation. *Science* 330:1234–37

Moore DS, Johnson SP. 2008. Mental rotation in human infants. *Psychol. Sci.* 19:1063–66

Moss-Racusin CA, Dovidio JF, Brescoll VL, Graham MJ, Handelsman J. 2012. Science faculty's subtle gender biases favor male students. *Proc. Natl. Acad. Sci. USA* 109:16474–79

Natl. Cent. Educ. Stat. 2012. *Digest of Education Statistics.* Washington, DC: US Dep. Educ., Inst. Educ. Sci. **http://nces.ed.gov/programs/digest/**

Natl. Sci. Found. 2011. *S&E Degrees: 1966–2008.* Arlington, VA: Natl. Sci. Found., Natl. Cent. Sci. Eng. Statist. **http://www.nsf.gov/statistics/nsf11316/pdf/nsf11316.pdf**

Newcombe NS, Mathason L, Terlecki M. 2002. Maximization of spatial competence: more important than finding the cause of sex differences. In *Biology, Society, and Behavior: The Development of Sex Differences in Cognition*, ed. A McGillicuddy-De Lisi, R De Lisi, pp. 183–206. Westport, CT: Ablex

Nolen-Hoeksema S. 2001. Gender differences in depression. *Curr. Dir. Psychol. Sci.* 10:173–76

Nosek BA, Smyth FL, Siram N, Lindner NM, Devos T, et al. 2009. National differences in gender-science stereotypes predict national sex differences in science and math achievement. *Proc. Natl. Acad. Sci. USA* 106:10593–97

Park LE, Young AF, Troisi JD, Pinkus RT. 2011. Effects of everyday romantic goal pursuit on women's attitudes toward math and science. *Personal. Soc. Psychol. Bull.* 37:1259–73

Pedersen WC, Miller LC, Putcha-Bhagavatula AD, Yang Y. 2002. Evolved sex differences in the number of partners desired? The long and the short of it. *Psychol. Sci.* 13:157–61

Pedersen WC, Putcha-Bhagavatula A, Miller LC. 2011. Are men and women really that different? Examining some of sexual strategies theory (SST)'s key assumptions about sex-distinct mating mechanisms. *Sex Roles* 64:629–43

Petersen JL, Hyde JS. 2010. A meta-analytic review of research on gender differences in sexuality: 1993 to 2007. *Psychol. Bull.* 136:21–38

Quinn PC, Liben LS. 2008. A sex difference in mental rotation in young infants. *Psychol. Sci.* 19:1067–70

Reilly D. 2012. Gender, culture, and sex-typed cognitive abilities. *PLoS ONE* 7(7):e39904

Richardson DS, Hammock GS. 2007. Social context of human aggression: Are we paying too much attention to gender? *Aggress. Viol. Behav.* 12:417–26

Rideout VJ, Foehr UG, Roberts DF. 2010. *Generation M²: Media in the Lives of 8- to 18-Year-Olds*. Menlo Park, CA: Kaiser Fam. Found.

Rood L, Roelofs J, Bögels SM, Nolen-Hoeksema S, Schouten E. 2009. The influence of emotion-focused rumination and distraction on depressive symptoms in non-clinical youth: a meta-analytic review. *Clin. Psychol. Rev.* 29:607–16

Rucklidge JJ. 2010. Gender differences in attention-deficit/hyperactivity disorder. *Psychiatr. Clin. N. Am.* 33:357–73

Sandberg JF, Hofferth SL. 2001. Changes in children's time with parents: United States, 1981–1997. *Demography* 38:423–36

Schmitt DP. 2005. Sociosexuality from Argentina to Zimbabwe: a 48-nation study of sex, culture, and strategies of human mating. *Behav. Brain Sci.* 28:247–311

Shields S. 1975. Functionalism, Darwinism, and the psychology of women. *Am. Psychol.* 30:739–54

Stewart A, LaVaque-Manty D. 2008. Advancing women faculty in science and engineering: an effort in institutional transformation. In *Gender and Occupational Outcomes*, ed. H Watt, J Eccles, pp. 299–322. Washington, DC: Am. Psychol. Assoc.

Stewart A, McDermott C. 2004. Gender in psychology. *Annu. Rev. Psychol.* 55:519–44

Su R, Rounds J, Armstrong P. 2009. Men and things, women and people: a meta-analysis of sex differences in interests. *Psychol. Bull.* 135:859–84

Subst. Abuse Ment. Health Serv. Adm. 2009. Results from the 2008 National Survey on Drug Use and Health: National Findings. *Off. Appl. Stud., NSDUH Ser. H-36, HHS Publ. No. SMA 09–4434*. Rockville, MD: SAMHSA

Swim J, Borgida E, Maruyama G, Myers DG. 1989. Joan McKay versus John McKay: Do gender stereotypes bias evaluations? *Psychol. Bull.* 105:409–29

Tannen D. 1991. *You Just Don't Understand: Women and Men in Conversation*. New York: Ballantine

Thorndike EL. 1914. *Educational Psychology*, Vol. 3. New York: Teachers College, Columbia Univ.

Trivers RL. 1972. Parental investment and sexual selection. In *Sexual Selection and the Descent of Man, 1871–1971*, ed. B Campbell, pp. 136–79. Chicago: Aldine

Twenge JM, Nolen-Hoeksema S. 2002. Age, gender, race, socioeconomic status, and birth cohort differences on the Children's Depression Inventory: a meta-analysis. *J. Abnorm. Psychol.* 111:578–88

Uttal DH, Meadow NG, Tipton E, Hand LL, Alden AR, et al. 2013. The malleability of spatial skills: a meta-analysis of training studies. *Psychol. Bull.* 139:352–402

Voyer D. 2011. Time limits and gender differences on paper-and-pencil tests of mental rotation: a meta-analysis. *Psychon. Bull. Rev.* 18:267–77

Voyer D, Voyer S, Bryden MP. 1995. Magnitude of sex differences in spatial abilities: a meta-analysis and consideration of critical variables. *Psychol. Bull.* 117:250–70

Watson D, Clark LA. 1984. Negative affectivity: the disposition to experience aversive emotional states. *Psychol. Bull.* 96:465–90

Wood W, Eagly AH. 2012. Biosocial construction of sex differences and similarities in behavior. *Adv. Exp. Soc. Psychol.* 46:55–123

Woolley HT. 1914. The psychology of sex. *Psychol. Bull.* 11:353–79

Zahn-Waxler C, Shirtcliff EA, Marceau K. 2008. Disorders of childhood and adolescence: gender and psychopathology. *Annu. Rev. Clin. Psychol.* 4:275–303

Zentner M, Mitura K. 2012. Stepping out of the caveman's shadow: Nations' gender gap predicts degree of sex differentiation in mate preferences. *Psychol. Sci.* 23:1176–85

Dehumanization and Infrahumanization

Nick Haslam and Steve Loughnan

School of Psychological Sciences, University of Melbourne, Parkville, Victoria 3010, Australia;
email: nhaslam@unimelb.edu.au, stephen.loughnan@unimelb.edu.au

Annu. Rev. Psychol. 2014. 65:399–423

First published online as a Review in Advance on
June 26, 2013

The *Annual Review of Psychology* is online at
http://psych.annualreviews.org

This article's doi:
10.1146/annurev-psych-010213-115045

Keywords

aggression, power, stereotypes, violence

Abstract

We review early and recent psychological theories of dehumanization and
survey the burgeoning empirical literature, focusing on six fundamental
questions. First, we examine how people are dehumanized, exploring the
range of ways in which perceptions of lesser humanness have been conceptualized and demonstrated. Second, we review who is dehumanized, examining the social targets that have been shown to be denied humanness
and commonalities among them. Third, we investigate who dehumanizes,
notably the personality, ideological, and other individual differences that increase the propensity to see others as less than human. Fourth, we explore
when people dehumanize, focusing on transient situational and motivational
factors that promote dehumanizing perceptions. Fifth, we examine the consequences of dehumanization, emphasizing its implications for prosocial and
antisocial behavior and for moral judgment. Finally, we ask what can be done
to reduce dehumanization. We conclude with a discussion of limitations of
current scholarship and directions for future research.

Contents

INTRODUCTION

To perceive a human being as less than human would seem on the surface to be an extraordinary category mistake. If so, it is a mistake that is remarkably tenacious and widespread. Victims of genocide are labeled as vermin by perpetrators. Slaves are officially adjudged to be worth a fraction of a person. Immigrants are likened to invasive pests or infectious diseases. African players are greeted with monkey noises in European football stadiums. Indigenous people are stereotyped as brute savages, noble or otherwise. Outraged members of the public call sex offenders animals. Psychopaths treat victims merely as means to their vicious ends. The poor are mocked as libidinous dolts. Passers-by look through homeless people as if they were transparent obstacles. Dementia sufferers are represented in the media as shuffling zombies. Degrading pornographers depict women as mindless, pneumatic objects. Exhausted doctors view their patients as inert bodies. Patients feel their individual identities have been stripped away by depersonalized medicine.

Dehumanization is important as a psychological phenomenon because it can be so common and yet so dire in its consequences. It is the most striking violation of our belief in a common humanity: our Enlightenment assumption that we are all essentially one and the same. It can be blatant or subtle; driven by hate, lust, or indifference; collectively organized or intensely personal. Because of its long history, deep ramifications, and wide variety, dehumanization is a crucial topic of study for psychologists.

In this article we review the burgeoning psychological literature on dehumanization, setting aside the smaller but growing body of work in other fields of sociology and genocide studies (e.g., Savage 2013, Smith 2010). We begin with a brief survey of contributions made by pioneering psychologists between the 1970s and the 1990s and then offer a more detailed discussion of the theoretical perspectives that have arisen since then. These theories, which traffic in concepts of infrahumanization, humanness, stereotype content, and mind perception, represent a promising "new look" at the field.

After these historical and theoretical preliminaries, we examine six key questions addressed by recent dehumanization research. First, we ask how people dehumanize, exploring the diverse ways in which people are perceived as less than human. Second, we ask who is dehumanized, examining the range of groups and individuals that have been shown to be the targets of dehumanization. Third, we shift focus to ask who dehumanizes, addressing the personal characteristics of perceivers who are especially prone to dehumanize others. Fourth, we ask when people dehumanize, reviewing research on the transient factors—contextual, emotional, and motivational—that promote dehumanization. Fifth, we ask what the consequences of dehumanization are, exploring research on the outcomes and implications of dehumanizing perceptions. Finally, we ask how we can overcome dehumanization, investigating research on ways to counteract these perceptions.

EARLY THEORIES OF DEHUMANIZATION

Kelman (1976) and Staub (1989) were among the first social psychologists to address dehumanization systematically, examining it in the context of mass violence. Kelman conceptualized the process primarily as a perception of victims that weakens the victimizer's normal restraints on violent behavior. The dehumanizing perception consists of a denial of victims' "identity" and "community," referring respectively to their distinct individuality and their belonging to a network of caring interpersonal relations. When these attributes are denied, victims become a deindividuated mass that lacks the capacity to evoke compassion.

The moral dimension of dehumanization features in two other early accounts. Opotow (1990) discussed dehumanization as one of several forms of moral exclusion in which people are placed "outside the boundary in which moral values, rules, and considerations of fairness apply" (p. 1). Opotow framed dehumanization not as a denial of specific attributes but rather as a categorical act of exclusion from a moral community that makes people indifferent to the suffering and unjust treatment of others. Bandura (1999) emphasized how dehumanization enables a disengagement of the aggressor's moral self-sanctions. Together these accounts show how dehumanization makes the other seem less morally worthy and makes the self less subject to the self-condemnation and empathic distress that might otherwise restrain aggressive behavior.

Two final early perspectives in dehumanization focused exclusively on its role in intergroup conflict. Schwartz & Struch (1989) proposed that people are dehumanized when they are seen as lacking prosocial values or when their values are seen as incongruent with those of the perceiver's in-group. Bar-Tal (1989), in contrast, conceptualized dehumanization as a form of collectively shared delegitimizing belief in which a group is given a subhuman or demonic label. Beliefs of this

Dehumanization: perceiving a person or group as lacking humanness

Infrahumanization: perceiving an out-group as lacking uniquely human attributes relative to an in-group

Humanness: attributes that define what it is to be human

Mind perception: the process of perceiving minds in entities and the consequences of this process sort arise in the context of extreme interethnic conflict and hatred, and they serve to explain the conflict, justify the in-group's aggression, and provide it with a sense of superiority.

These early accounts of dehumanization vary in their emphases but share some common threads. Dehumanization is understood as an extreme phenomenon, observed in conditions of conflict, and it is primarily called upon to explain and enable acts of violence.

THE "NEW LOOK" AT DEHUMANIZATION: FOUR THEORIES

Infrahumanization Theory

A "new look" at dehumanization-related processes was initiated by psychologists in Belgium. Starting with the anthropological insight that ethnic groups often reserve the "human essence" for themselves, Leyens and colleagues (2001) theorized that this form of ethnocentrism may be a general phenomenon. They proposed that people tend to perceive out-group members as less human than in-group members even in the absence of significant intergroup antagonism. Most importantly, Leyens and colleagues argued that this process may be subtle, in contrast to the blatant denials of humanness described by early dehumanization theorists. To emphasize this distinction they coined the term "infrahumanization" to refer to the subtler form.

Leyens and colleagues first sought a working understanding of humanness. An informal survey of laypeople suggested three main attributes that distinguished humans from animals: intelligence, language, and refined emotions (sentiments in French). Focusing on these "secondary" emotions, which are understood to be unique to humans, these researchers reasoned that ascribing fewer secondary emotions to out-group members than to in-group members amounts to a subtle denial of the out-group's humanity; compared to the in-group, the out-group is less human. Because uniquely human emotions may be positive (e.g., joy) or negative (e.g., embarrassment), this ascription of lesser humanness could in principle occur independently of any negative evaluation of the out-group.

Leyens and colleagues established the predicted infrahumanization effect in a large body of research (for reviews, see Leyens et al. 2003, 2007). Their research has demonstrated that the phenomenon is robust across many intergroup contexts, evident in the absence of intergroup conflict, contingent on the existence of meaningful in-group/out-group distinctions, and independent of out-group derogation or in-group favoritism. The phenomenon can be demonstrated in simple judgment tasks, typically involving the attribution of emotions to groups, and also using implicit association methods (e.g., Paladino et al. 2002). It can be shown when humanness is represented by secondary versus primary emotions or by more directly human- and animal-related words (Viki et al. 2006). Infrahumanization has a variety of behavioral implications, and it appears to involve not simply a lack of recognition of the out-group's humanity but also an active reluctance to accept it.

Infrahumanization theory was a major theoretical advance. It recognized that humanness can be denied to others in subtle and commonplace ways, rather than being confined to blatant denials in killing fields and torture chambers. It provided a clear operational definition of humanness as those attributes that distinguish humans from other animals. Infrahumanization researchers also popularized simple methods through which the differential attribution of humanness to in-group and out-group could be tested. All of these innovations made dehumanization-related phenomena tractable for social psychology researchers and relevant to normal intergroup relations in a way that earlier theoretical approaches did not.

The Dual Model of Dehumanization

In an effort to integrate infrahumanization theory with previous work on dehumanization, Haslam (2006) developed a new model. A key conceptual innovation addressed infrahumanization theory's understanding of humanness. Although Leyens had been more explicit than previous theorists in defining humanness as that which is unique to our species (e.g., secondary emotions), Haslam proposed that human uniqueness, and the human-animal distinction on which it rests, is only one of two ways in which humanness might be understood. People also tend to conceptualize humanness in opposition to inanimate objects such as robots and automatons; Haslam designated the distinguishing attributes as human nature. Whereas humans are distinguished from animals on attributes involving cognitive capacity, civility, and refinement, we differ from inanimate objects on the basis of emotionality, vitality, and warmth.

Human uniqueness: attributes that distinguish humans from other animals

Human nature: attributes that are essentially or typically human

Haslam and colleagues found substantial empirical support for the two senses of humanness. Ratings of the extent to which traits reflect human uniqueness and human nature are uncorrelated, and traits that best reflect each sense have different content. Traits that embody human uniqueness are seen as late to develop and believed to differ across cultures, whereas those that embody human nature are seen as essence-like, universal, and emotion related (Haslam et al. 2005). The two sets of characteristics differentiate humans from animals and robots, respectively, as predicted (Haslam et al. 2008), and understandings of them are highly convergent across cultures (Bain et al. 2012, Park et al. 2012).

Haslam (2006) reasoned that if humanness has two distinct meanings, tied to two human-nonhuman contrasts, then two broad varieties of dehumanization should be evident. When individuals are denied human uniqueness, they should be seen as lacking refinement, self-control, intelligence, and rationality, and subtly or overtly likened to animals. A comprehensive review of prior dehumanization scholarship indicated that this "animalistic" form of dehumanization captures phenomena ranging from the most blatant genocidal labeling of people as vermin through to the subtlety of infrahumanization. In contrast, when individuals are denied human nature, they are seen as lacking warmth, emotion, and individuality, and likened to inanimate objects. This "mechanistic" form captures phenomena described by previous writers on dehumanization in the contexts of technology, medicine, and forms of objectification in which people are perceived as inert or instrumental. Research motivated by this dual model of dehumanization has found extensive evidence for both forms in studies that examine perceptions of social groups and individuals and that explore the perceiver's and the target's perspectives.

The dual model is broader than infrahumanization theory in two main ways. First, it extends the concept of humanness by incorporating the human-object distinction alongside the human-animal distinction, thereby encompassing forms of dehumanization that relate to denials of human nature. Second, it aims to encompass the diverse forms of dehumanization—subtle or blatant, animal or object related, intergroup or interpersonal—rather than to pick out a specific phenomenon in group perception. The two theories differ in their reach rather than being in competition. Indeed, infrahumanization can be understood as a specific variant within Haslam's framework.

The Stereotype Content Account

A third theoretical perspective on dehumanization was developed by Harris & Fiske (2006). Their account of "dehumanized perception" is distinctive in several respects. First, unlike infrahumanization theory or Haslam's dual model, it does not proceed from an explicit definition of humanness. Instead, it defines dehumanization as the failure to spontaneously consider another person's mind, or to engage in social cognition when perceiving them. Second, the theory has primarily been examined using social neuroscience methods. Ingeniously, Harris and Fiske argue that dehumanization can be said to occur when the neural network that underpins social cognition (e.g., medial prefrontal cortex, superior temporal sulcus) fails to activate in the normal manner when a human target is perceived. Third, the theory specifies the sorts of target that are most likely to be dehumanized, based on stereotype content.

According to the stereotype content model (SCM; Fiske et al. 2002), group stereotypes vary on the dimensions of warmth and competence. Admired groups (e.g., in-groups) are perceived as high on both dimensions, pitied groups (e.g., the elderly) are seen as warm but incompetent, envied groups (e.g., the rich) are seen as cold but competent, and groups that evoke disgust (e.g., the homeless) are unambivalently seen as low on both dimensions. Harris & Fiske (2006) argue that dehumanizing perceptions target these "lowest of the low" and consistently find that low-low groups fail to engage the social cognition network, instead activating disgust-related structures such as the insula. These groups also fail to elicit spontaneous attributions of mental states compared to groups that fall in the other three quadrants of the SCM (Harris & Fiske 2011). Nevertheless, cold but incompetent groups may also be dehumanized as robot-like, consistent with Haslam's mechanistic form.

The Mind Perception Account

A fourth theoretical approach to dehumanization emerged from recent work on mind perception, the study of attributions of mind to entities of all sorts (Waytz et al. 2010). A surprising finding of this research is that mind is ascribed along two separate dimensions (Gray et al. 2007). "Agency" includes mental capabilities such as thinking, self-control, and communication and distinguishes humans from nonhuman animals, whereas "experience" includes attributes such as emotion, consciousness, and personality and distinguishes humans from robots and inanimate objects. These dimensions show strong affinities with Haslam's model: Agency represents human uniqueness both in content and in its implied contrast (animals), and in the same manner experience represents human nature.

The mind perception framework conceptualizes dehumanization as mind denial or "dementalization" (Kozak et al. 2006). In theory, mind denials could be specific to one dimension or generalized across both. The mind perception framework also enables a widening of theoretical focus, seeing dehumanization not as an exceptional process that must be understood only on its own terms but rather as a phenomenon that is related to the fundamental processes of mind attribution: Too little mind is bestowed on some entities and too much on others (e.g., anthropomorphic perceptions of beloved pets, misbehaving computers, and dreaded deities; Epley et al. 2007). Any factors that influence mind attribution in general, such as the motives that it serves, can help us to understand why people might fail to attribute mind to their fellow humans (Waytz et al. 2010).

HOW DO WE DEHUMANIZE?

We can now begin to answer the six key questions posed at the beginning of this review: in essence, how dehumanization occurs, who experiences it, who perpetrates it, when it occurs, what its consequences are, and how it can be overcome. The first question is prefigured by our review of major theories, which lay out some of the diverse ways in which dehumanization can be conceptualized. Nevertheless, it is valuable to survey the many shades of dehumanization that have been demonstrated within the empirical literature.

The great diversity among forms of dehumanization has a qualitative and a quantitative aspect. The qualitative aspect refers to the nature of the nonhuman entities that dehumanized people are likened to or conversely to the nature of the attributes that are denied to those people. Different theories and ways of assessing dehumanization implicate qualitatively distinct kinds of entity or attribute. The quantitative aspect refers to the differing degrees of blatancy, explicitness, or severity seen in empirical demonstrations of dehumanization.

Qualitative Differences Among Forms of Dehumanization

The theoretical approaches reviewed above suggest that dehumanization can occur in two registers with distinctive psychological content. In Haslam's (2006) model, the animalistic form is defined by the contrast between humans and animals, occurring when people are directly associated with animals or denied uniquely human attributes. The mechanistic form is defined by the contrast between humans and inanimate objects, occurring when people are likened to objects or denied human nature. The two contrasts, closely aligned with the dimensions of Gray et al.'s (2007) mind perception framework, invoke qualitatively different metaphors and attributes, which have been shown to be independent in studies of lay understandings of the respective entities (Haslam et al. 2008). Nevertheless, the contrasts involve dimensions, not mutually exclusive types, so people may be denied attributes on both dimensions simultaneously, as in the wholesale denial of mind that may occur in perceptions of pariah groups (Harris & Fiske 2006).

Quantitative Differences Among Forms of Dehumanization

Dehumanization has been investigated along a spectrum from blatant and severe to subtle and relatively mild. Two main components contribute to this spectrum. First, blatant examples of dehumanization are explicit: The perceiver views the target as less than human in a way that is direct, overt, and consciously accessible to the perceiver. In subtler examples, the lesser humanness of the target is indirect, implicit, and nonconscious. More blatant forms of dehumanization, for example, tend to draw a direct metaphorical link between a person or group and a nonhuman entity, whereas subtler forms ascribe fewer human attributes to a target. Second, more blatant forms of dehumanization make absolute judgments about a particular target, denying its humanity outright, whereas subtler forms merely make relative judgments, seeing one group as less human than another. The following sections review the diverse forms of dehumanization in light of these two components of blatancy.

Explicit Versus Implicit Dehumanization

At the top of the blatancy spectrum are instances of dehumanization that are offensively direct. The most blatant are cases where people directly liken individuals or groups to nonhumans in language. For example, Tileagă (2007, p. 730) observed dehumanizing language in middle-class Romanians' discourse on the Romany (gypsy) minority (e.g., "there is... a block especially built for them and they have eaten it from the ground like rats"), and Haslam and colleagues (2011) demonstrated experimentally that animal metaphors typically signify degradation (e.g., apes, dogs) or disgust (e.g., rats, pigs).

Equally blatant phenomena are revealed by studies that use self-report dehumanization scales to assess perceptions about deviants (e.g., "Some people deserve to be treated like animals"; Bandura et al. 1996), enemies (e.g., "Terrorists are vermin that need to be exterminated"; Jackson & Gaertner 2010), and ethnic groups (e.g., "Native Americans were basically wild creatures before the arrival of the White men"; Castano & Giner-Sorolla 2006) and perceptions of being dehumanized (e.g., "I felt like I was mechanical and cold, like a robot"; Bastian & Haslam 2010). Endorsement of these items reflects an explicit perception of people as less than human but potentially assesses dehumanization merely as a manifestation of antipathy.

Less blatant, but still somewhat explicit, are beliefs that others lack the characteristics that humans possess. This form of dehumanization is typified by classic infrahumanization studies (Leyens et al. 2003), which require participants to select emotion terms that characterize in-group and out-group from a list that includes a mix of primary and secondary emotions. The number of secondary emotions ascribed to a group is a measure of its perceived humanness. Viki et al. (2006) have shown that the same methodology can be employed using words that refer directly to humans (e.g., person, citizen) and animals (e.g., wildlife, mongrel) rather than indirectly to their distinctive attributes, a somewhat more blatant version of the same task. Similar procedures have been used to assess the attribution of human traits (e.g., Haslam & Bain 2007, Heflick & Goldenberg 2009), human suffering (Riva & Andrighetto 2012), and mental capacities (e.g., Waytz & Epley 2012). One advantage of this popular method is that it taps a relatively subtle form of dehumanization. Participants can be unaware that their choice of attributes indicates dehumanization of the target, allowing these methods to be resistant to faking (Eyssel & Ribas 2012). Another advantage is that balancing the list of attributes by valence (i.e., positive and negative emotions or traits) allows subtle dehumanization to be neatly distinguished from antipathy.

Dehumanization can also be observed even more subtly in the implicit associations people hold about social groups. Many studies have used the Go/no-Go Association Task (GNAT) or the implicit association task (IAT) to demonstrate these automatic perceptions. Researchers have examined associations between social groups and nonhuman entities (e.g., Bain et al. 2009, Rudman & Mescher 2012) or, even less directly, associations between groups and human attributes such as traits and emotions (e.g., Martinez et al. 2012). Such studies reveal very subtle, nonconscious forms of dehumanization: In essence, participants are unintentionally revealing a lack of automatic association between persons and the distinctive qualities of persons rather than deliberately expressing an equation between persons and nonpersons, as in the most blatant form of dehumanization.

Subtle, nonconscious forms of dehumanization have also been demonstrated using priming, linguistic, and neuroscience methods. Subliminal presentation of black faces facilitates identification of ape images (Goff et al. 2008), and subliminal presentation of monkey versus human faces facilitates identification of out-group versus in-group names (Boccato et al. 2008). People used relatively few mental-state verbs (e.g., think, feel) when writing about dehumanized targets drawn from the low-low quadrant of the SCM (Harris & Fiske 2011). A small number of neuroimaging studies (Harris & Fiske 2006, 2011) reveal a lack of activation of social cognition networks in the brain when low-low targets are present. Because they do not rely on an explicit, direct, and conscious expression of the lack of humanness of another person, these methods provide another scientific pathway to subtle dehumanization.

Relative Versus Absolute Dehumanization

Explicitness is a major component of blatancy, but another important component is the extent to which a target is denied humanness absolutely or merely by comparison with another. Absolute denials ascribe deficient or absent humanity to a target. Relative denials involve perceptions that one group is less human than another. For example, a study finding that fewer secondary emotions are ascribed to citizens of one country than another demonstrates a relative form of dehumanization, whereas one in which a single group is rated as subhuman demonstrates an absolute form. The basic infrahumanization effect is relative in this sense because it involves the differential attribution of humanness to out-group and in-group. The same is true of most implicit association studies, which usually compare the strength of association of humanness-related stimuli and two different social targets.

Conclusions

Our review shows that researchers have conceptualized dehumanization in qualitatively and quantitatively diverse ways. The quantitative variations represent a spectrum of blatancy, ranging from explicit likenings of people to despised nonhumans to weaker implicit associations of some people with human attributes than others.

The continuum stretching between these extremes poses the terminological challenge of deciding whether or where a semantic line should be drawn between dehumanization proper and subtler phenomena such as infrahumanization. Some readers of the literature favor a narrow, restrictive definition of dehumanization. As Leyens et al. (2007) argued, "people are inclined to perceive members of out-groups as somewhat less human, or more animal-like, than themselves; such a view corresponds to the word infrahumanization.... By contrast, dehumanization of an out-group implies that its members are no longer humans at all" (p. 143). However, if subtlety varies by degrees, it is not possible to draw sharp distinctions along the spectrum between history's paradigm cases of dehumanization (e.g., blatant, explicit, and absolute equations of humans with nonhumans, such as "Jews are vermin"), less blatant but still highly objectionable denials of humanness (e.g., the nonconscious "Africans = apes" association; Goff et al. 2008), and subtler phenomena like infrahumanization.

In recognition of this spectrum, we propose a broad and inclusive definition of dehumanization that encompasses blatant and subtle forms, retaining the term "infrahumanization" to refer to a specific but important variant within the dehumanization spectrum (i.e., one that involves the subtle differential attribution or association of uniquely human attributes to groups). Although our view expands the meaning of dehumanization from earlier usages, it has the virtue of simplicity, avoids conceptual hairsplitting, and recognizes the commonalities among the diverse phenomena explored in recent research. We recommend that researchers conceptualize dehumanization as a broad spectrum whose milder variants have important continuities with its most severe forms.

WHO IS DEHUMANIZED?

Researchers have documented dehumanizing perceptions of a wide variety of target groups and individuals. We begin this section with a survey of these targets before examining whether certain target types are most likely to be dehumanized.

Specific Targets of Dehumanization

A major emphasis of dehumanization research has been the attribution of lesser humanness to particular ethnic groups. These groups have been the primary focus of infrahumanization research given its theoretical claim that infrahumanization is a form of ethnocentrism. Many of the original demonstrations of the effect involved national or ethnic comparisons (e.g., Belgians versus Arabs and Turks, Walloon versus Flemish Belgians, Canarian versus mainland Spaniards, northern versus southern Italians; see Leyens et al. 2003), although ethnicity-based infrahumanization is not invariably found (e.g., Italians did not infrahumanize Germans; Vaes & Paladino 2010). Less subtle forms of ethnic dehumanization have also been demonstrated, notably Boccato and colleagues' (2008) finding that northern Italians automatically associated southern Italians with apes to a greater extent than their fellow northerners.

Other targets of dehumanization may be understood as "racial" rather than ethnic groups in the sense that they exemplify popular conceptions of broad races (e.g., "Asian" or "black" rather than "Japanese" or "Zulu") or ancestry-based subpopulations (e.g., Caucasian Americans and African

Americans). Several researchers have demonstrated dehumanizing perceptions of people of African descent by white perceivers, whether through implicit associations with nonhuman apes (Goff et al. 2008) or the ascription of fewer uniquely human characteristics (Costello & Hodson 2013). Less research has been conducted on perceptions of other "racial" groups, but Bain and colleagues (2009) found that European Australians implicitly associated East Asian faces with machines more than white faces and associated them less with human nature traits. Chinese participants associated white faces less strongly with uniquely human traits than East Asian faces.

Researchers have also explored dehumanizing perceptions of groups that are defined by social or historical predicaments rather than intrinsic ethnicity but that may be ethnically different from perceivers. In Canada, Hodson & Costello (2007) documented a denial of uniquely human traits to immigrant groups, and Esses et al. (2008) demonstrated that refugees were rated as barbaric and lacking in humane values. In Australia, Saminaden et al. (2010) showed that people from a multi-ethnic assortment of traditional societies were more strongly associated with animals and children and less strongly associated with uniquely human traits than equally multiethnic representatives of industrialized societies. In the cases of refugees and traditional peoples, the dehumanizing perception appears to be linked to a belief that the targets are primitive and undeveloped, perhaps reflecting an equation of perceived social development with phylogenetic development.

Several studies have begun to expand the range of dehumanized target groups. Subtle forms of dehumanization have been demonstrated in perceptions of occupational groups (Loughnan & Haslam 2007), people from lower social class backgrounds (Loughnan et al. 2013), medical patients (Lammers & Stapel 2011, Vaes & Muratore 2013), the mentally ill (Martinez et al. 2011), sex offenders (Viki et al. 2012), violent criminals (Bastian et al. 2013a), and asexuals (MacInnis & Hodson 2012). This list heeds Jahoda's (1999) observation, following a discussion of colonial-era dehumanization of non-European "savages," that "Savages... form part of a cluster that includes not only children but also the rural and urban poor, criminals, the mentally ill, and even women" (p. 237).

The possibility that "even women" may be dehumanized has recently been supported by several researchers, who show that dehumanizing perceptions may depend on perceiver characteristics and how women are depicted. Heflick & Goldenberg (2009) and Heflick and colleagues (2011), for example, found that when participants focused on women's appearance rather than their personhood they viewed them as lacking human nature, as well as warmth, morality, and competence. Loughnan et al. (2010b) showed that less mind, moral worth, competence, and capacity to experience pain were attributed to women (and men) when their bodies were sexualized or made visually salient. At a basic and automatic level, Bernard et al. (2012) showed that sexualized women are visually processed as objects rather than people, and Cikara et al. (2011) found that hostile sexist men viewing sexualized images of women showed reduced neural activation in social cognition networks. Sexualized women are implicitly associated with animals by male and female perceivers alike (Vaes et al. 2011), and men who implicitly associate women with animals and objects have a higher propensity for sexual aggression (Rudman & Mescher 2012).

To this point, our review of targets of dehumanization has examined the perceptions of groups or individual members of identified groups. Humanness may also be differentially ascribed to individuals as individuals. There is now a substantial body of work indicating that the self is attributed greater humanness than others and in some circumstances can be, or feel, dehumanized. The finding that people commonly perceive themselves as being more human (i.e., having more human nature) than average was first obtained by Haslam and colleagues (2005). This "self-humanizing" effect is distinct from the more familiar phenomenon of self-enhancement, uncorrelated with self-esteem, and cross-culturally robust (Loughnan et al. 2010c), even in Eastern cultures where self-enhancement is difficult to establish (Park et al. 2013). Arguably the lesser perceived humanness of others reflects the philosophical problem of other minds: the attenuated, merely two-dimensional reality of minds outside our own.

The self may also undergo a perceived loss of humanity under certain conditions. Bastian and Haslam (Bastian & Haslam 2010; see also Bastian et al. 2013b) showed that people who recalled or experienced episodes of social exclusion rated themselves as lacking human nature traits, implying a temporary state akin to the numbed, cognitively deconstructed state previously identified as an outcome of ostracism (Twenge et al. 2003). Bastian and colleagues (2012b) found that players of violent video games rated themselves lower on humanness after playing a violent interactive video game than after playing an equally frustrating and competitive nonviolent game. Different interpersonal experiences may also generate qualitatively different perceptions of having been dehumanized. Whereas people report feeling shame and guilt when they feel they have been abased (i.e., denied uniquely human attributes), they tend to feel numbed, sad, or angry when they feel that they have been rejected, invalidated, or treated instrumentally (i.e., denied human nature) (Bastian & Haslam 2011).

Commonalities Among Targets of Dehumanization

A diverse assortment of groups and individuals appear to be potential targets of dehumanization. Are there are any consistencies among them, such that target types are particularly vulnerable to dehumanization? This question can be systematically examined only in studies that have explored perceptions of multiple groups.

The theoretical claim that dehumanization is most likely for groups stereotyped as lacking both warmth and competence has been supported by two studies. Harris & Fiske (2006) confirmed that the medial prefrontal cortex, a brain structure crucial for social cognition, was deactivated only when perceiving members of groups that fell within the SCM's low-low quadrant (i.e., drug addicts and homeless people). Vaes & Paladino (2010) showed that northern Italians infrahumanized a variety of ethnic out-groups to some degree, but the effect was particularly strong for those stereotyped as cold and incompetent. These studies offer convergent support for the stereotype content account, although Vaes & Paladino's (2010) study suggested that dehumanization is driven by the competence dimension more than by warmth.

The possible primacy of incompetence-related stereotypes is consistent with findings that low-status groups are most readily dehumanized. Capozza and colleagues (2012a) showed that higher-status real and minimal groups implicitly dehumanized lower-status groups, but lower-status groups did not perceive themselves as more human than higher-status groups. This asymmetry implies that intergroup status differentials that are correlated with competence-related stereotypes moderate dehumanization. Status may be especially relevant when dehumanization is defined along the dimension of human uniqueness, given that uniquely human attributes implicate competence and sophistication.

Nevertheless, status has not consistently predicted levels of dehumanization: Rodriguez-Perez and colleagues (2011) found that attribution of secondary emotions to members of 27 national or regional groups was uncorrelated with the perceived status of these groups. Instead, the groups that were ascribed the fewest uniquely human emotions were those seen as the least friendly, similar, and familiar to the Spanish in-group. Although previous infrahumanization research had discounted the role of familiarity in the basic phenomenon, the effect may be stronger for groups that are more socially distant as well as those that are socially subordinate.

Our review of dehumanization's targets indicates that a remarkably broad range of social targets can be perceived to lack humanness. These targets extend far beyond ethnic groups, the focus of most infrahumanization research, to include groups defined by gender, social and sexual deviance, and illness, as well as the self. There is now substantial evidence that the lowest of the low are most vulnerable to dehumanization, especially when humanness is understood as human uniqueness, a vertical dimension of comparison in which being human amounts to being above animals.

However, it is unlikely that all forms of dehumanization fit within this hierarchical framework. Some targets may be seen as lacking humanness in a more horizontal manner, based on distance and disconnection rather than status and domination. For example, dehumanization in the domain of medicine (Lammers & Stapel 2011), where people seek emotional distance from others' suffering, and in self-perception, where people perceive others as less human than they are or feel their own humanness has been sapped by social exclusion, implicates a different kind of humanness than infrahumanization. In these cases, human nature—warmth, depth, and emotionality—is denied as a result of social disconnection rather than human uniqueness being denied as a result of hierarchical thinking.

WHO DEHUMANIZES?

Certain groups and individuals are more likely to be dehumanized than others. Similarly, shifting focus from targets to perceivers, certain people may be more apt to dehumanize than others. Although the capacity to see others as less than human may be universal, apparent even among children (Costello & Hodson 2013, Vezzali et al. 2012), there may be individual differences in the tendency to do so. There is now evidence that individual differences in personality, beliefs, ideologies, and attitudes play a role.

Personality characteristics have been explored in several studies. Hodson & Costello (2007) found that Canadians who scored higher on interpersonal disgust-proneness, the tendency to experience disgust in response to contact with strangers, were more likely to dehumanize immigrants. More narcissistic individuals were especially likely to see others as less human than themselves (Locke 2009), and higher levels of psychopathy and autism were associated with the ascription of less mind to human targets (Gray et al. 2011). Although these four traits are somewhat dissimilar—involving emotional aversion, perceived superiority of the self, callousness, and social disconnection, respectively—they all bear directly on interpersonal relations, and narcissism and psychopathy correlate moderately as elements of personality's "dark triad," alongside Machiavellianism. Tendencies to dehumanize others may be stronger among people who are disagreeable (callous and self-seeking), who experience strong emotional aversion to members of out-groups (perhaps especially in the context of xenophobic perceptions of immigrants), or who have diminished capacity for empathy or mentalizing.

The literature on the role of ideologies in dehumanization is more substantial than the literature on personality. DeLuca-McLean & Castano (2009) found that conservative American participants infrahumanized a Hispanic hurricane victim but liberal participants did not, and Maoz & McCauley (2008) found that Israeli (right-wing) hawks dehumanized Palestinians more than (left-wing) doves. Viki & Calitri (2008) showed that British participants were more likely to infrahumanize Americans if they held nationalistic beliefs (i.e., in the superiority of Britain over other countries) but less likely to do so if they held patriotic beliefs (i.e., positive views of their nation unaccompanied by a belief in superiority). By implication, infrahumanization depends on not just the degree of in-group identification but also on the tendency to derogate out-groups.

The most replicated ideological correlate of dehumanization is social dominance orientation (SDO). Hodson & Costello (2007) found SDO to be their strongest predictor of dehumanization of immigrants, Esses et al. (2008) found it to be associated with dehumanization of refugees, and Jackson & Gaertner (2010) showed it to correlate with dehumanization of enemy war victims. In each of these studies, SDO was more strongly associated with dehumanization than was right-wing authoritarianism, implying that dehumanization of the groups in question rests on a tough-minded striving for dominance rather than on social conformity and an exaggerated perception of threat. Perhaps the most striking finding, from Costello & Hodson (2013), is that white parents' levels of SDO predict their children's tendencies to dehumanize black children.

Costello & Hodson (2010) examined a related belief that is associated with the propensity to dehumanize others. People who perceived a greater divide between humans and other animals were more likely to engage in racial dehumanization. According to the authors' interspecies model of prejudice, the oppression of marginalized human groups is associated with a belief in human supremacy over animals. This vertical differentiation of humans from animals promotes the view that "inferior" humans are bestial and justifies discrimination against them. In this regard, human-animal divide beliefs are akin to SDO: The two correlated ideologies both implicate hierarchical thinking and predict tendencies to dehumanize (see sidebar, Animals, Meat, and Dehumanization). The role of human-animal divide beliefs in dehumanization and prejudice is also supported experimentally by the finding that people show increased moral concern for marginalized groups when similarities between humans and animals are accentuated (Bastian et al. 2012a).

Attitudes represent a final set of individual difference variables that may correlate with dehumanization tendencies, although they have been examined only in relation to perceptions of women. Two studies using divergent methodologies have found that hostile sexism predicts the denial of humanness to female targets. Viki & Abrams (2003) showed that hostile sexists denied uniquely human positive emotions to women, whereas benevolent sexists did the reverse. Cikara et al. (2011) found that male hostile sexists showed reduced neural activation of brain regions associated with mental state attribution when viewing images of sexualized women. However, hostile sexism was not correlated with implicit associations of nonsexualized women with animals or objects (Rudman & Mescher 2012).

There is some consistency among the individual differences associated with the propensity to dehumanize. First, this propensity is associated with hostile and disagreeable characteristics, including psychopathic and narcissistic traits, nationalistic beliefs, and hostile attitudes. Second, it is linked to emotional aversion to unfamiliar persons. Third, it is associated with hierarchical ideological positions, notably SDO and belief in human dominion over animals. Fourth, it may be associated with social disconnection and deficient empathy, given the link to autistic traits. These conclusions suggest that several distinct individual-difference domains are implicated in seeing people as less than human, each potentially having particular relevance to certain kinds or targets of dehumanization.

WHEN DO PEOPLE DEHUMANIZE?

The preceding section reviewed enduring individual differences associated with the tendency to see others as less than human; the "who" of dehumanization. More transient factors determine the "when" of dehumanization: the conditions or circumstances under which it occurs. These factors include emotional, motivational, and cognitive states of the perceiver; aspects of the situation such as threat; and social-structural factors such as power.

Emotion

Research on emotional states linked to dehumanization is scarce. However, consistent with findings that dispositional disgust-proneness is associated with the tendency to dehumanize (Hodson & Costello 2007) and that disgust-inducing groups are most likely to be dehumanized (Harris & Fiske 2006), experienced disgust also promotes dehumanization. Buckels & Trapnell (2013) recently showed that experimentally induced disgust produced stronger implicit associations between an out-group and animals than did induced sadness or neutral mood. The related emotion of contempt, which combines aversion with anger and targets people of perceived low status, has also been linked to dehumanization of refugees (Esses et al. 2008).

Motives

A larger quantity of research has examined the role of motives in dehumanization. Four main motives have been examined: sociality, sexuality, moral equanimity, and group protection. These motives are disparate, and their relevance to dehumanization may be restricted to specific inter-group or interpersonal contexts.

Evidence that the need for social connection plays a role in dehumanization originated in research on anthropomorphism, which showed that people with unmet sociality needs were especially likely to attribute mind to nonhumans (Epley et al. 2008). In a striking extrapolation, Waytz & Epley (2012) reasoned that if unmet needs for connection promote mind attribution, then satiated sociality needs should promote mind denial. They demonstrated experimentally that people who felt more socially connected were more likely to dehumanize distant others. This finding that feeling connected makes one more likely to dehumanize others is intriguing when placed alongside Bastian & Haslam's (2010) finding that people who have been socially excluded feel less than human themselves.

Research on the role of sexual motives in dehumanization is restricted to a single study on the perception of objectified women by Vaes and colleagues (2011). Male perceivers associated sexualized female targets with animals to a greater extent than nonsexualized female (or male) targets, implicating an appetitive sexual motive in the process. It can be argued that an aversive process must operate if dehumanization is said to occur (Cikara et al. 2011), but the finding of Vaes and colleagues satisfies our broad, motivationally agnostic understanding of dehumanization as a denial of humanness, and the woman-animal association can have aversive consequences (Rudman & Mescher 2012).

The desire for moral equanimity also plays a part in some forms of dehumanization. Castano & Giner-Sorolla (2006) found that people were more likely to dehumanize an out-group that had suffered a historical harm when their in-group was assigned responsibility for it. People are motivated to avoid collective guilt and the tarnishing of their in-group's image, and by denying the humanity or moral worth of its historical victims, they can accomplish that goal post hoc.

A group-protective motive outside of the moral domain also plays a part in another dehumanization-related effect. Koval and colleagues (2012) found that people tend to judge their in-group's negative attributes to be human (i.e., human nature) to a greater extent than out-group flaws. This effect of humanizing in-group flaws is independent of the familiar tendency to ascribe more positive attributes to the in-group. The finding that the effect is amplified when in-group identity is threatened and that it is not obtained for positive attributes implies that it is motivated by a desire to protect the image of the in-group. Seeing one's group's failings as only human renders them excusable, and the failure to humanize the out-group's failings constitutes a subtle, motivated form of dehumanization.

Cognitions

Relatively little research has explored cognitive factors that promote the dehumanization of groups. Two factors that may be implicated are suggested by research on moderators of the self-humanizing effect, in which others are seen as less human than the self (Haslam et al. 2005). Haslam & Bain (2007) showed that this effect was diminished when participants' self-focus was disrupted and when their construal of the other was more concrete (i.e., comparing the self to a hypothetical individual or past self rather than to an average person or future self). By implication, egocentrism and abstract construal may promote dehumanization.

Threat

An association between perceived threat and dehumanization has been suggested in several studies. Maoz & McCauley (2008) found greater tendencies to dehumanize Palestinians among Jewish participants who perceived them as a more severe threat, although dehumanization and threat represented partially distinct contributors to support for aggressive policies. Perceived threat also moderates the effect of dehumanization on endorsement of aggression, such that participants who saw Muslims as a greater threat only showed a proclivity to torture Muslim prisoners of war if they also dehumanized them (Viki et al. 2013). The existential threat of mortality has also been implicated in infrahumanization, with terror management theory proposing that people defend against this threat by attempting to transcend their creatureliness. Goldenberg et al. (2009) and Vaes et al. (2010) argued that ascribing uniquely human attributes selectively to the self and the in-group is a plausible way to do so. They demonstrated that reminders of mortality increase infrahumanization. Whereas threat posed by others may increase dehumanization by promoting a more bestial view of the out-group, mortality threat may increase it by promoting a less bestial view of the in-group.

Power

The only social-structural factor that has been investigated as a contributor to dehumanization is power. Lammers & Stapel (2011) found that participants who had a greater personal sense of power tended to ascribe more animalistic traits to a low-status fictitious out-group and that participants induced to feel powerful in a medical decision-making context were more likely to dehumanize a fictitious patient and also to endorse a more painful but effective treatment. The capacity for power to increase dehumanization has been further demonstrated by Gwinn and colleagues (2013), who found that students who were assigned high-power roles within dyads rated their low-power partner as lacking uniquely human traits. Most impressively, this tendency was found in a concrete interaction, in the absence of derogation of the low-power partner, and whether the dyadic activity was cooperative or competitive.

The research reviewed in this section clarifies the diverse factors that determine when dehumanization occurs. These factors include an assortment of stable individual differences, variable psychological states, contextual triggers, and social positions. Empirical support for these factors is thinly spread, but it helps to flesh out our understanding of the range of intrapersonal, interpersonal, and broader social conditions that promote dehumanization.

WHAT ARE THE CONSEQUENCES OF DEHUMANIZATION?

A major impetus for the study of dehumanization is to understand its profoundly negative consequences. Dehumanization of enemies, victims, and colonized peoples has been associated with pogroms, atrocities, and exploitation. Although recent dehumanization research has rarely investigated such extreme events and seldom allows strong inferences that dehumanization causes particular outcomes, it has established a variety of effects that are plausibly interpreted as consequences of dehumanization.

These putative consequences can be divided into four broad groupings. First, dehumanizing perceptions of individuals or groups may reduce prosocial behavior toward them. Second, dehumanizing perceptions may increase antisocial behavior toward their targets. Third, these perceptions may have a variety of implications for moral evaluation of targets. Fourth, dehumanizing perceptions of others may have functional consequences for the perceiver or the target.

Reduced Prosociality

Dehumanizing perceptions of others may be associated with a diminished tendency to respond to them prosocially. Vaes et al. (2002) established that people respond more prosocially to others who express themselves in terms of secondary emotions because, they inferred, these others are tacitly seen as more human. An implication of this finding is that people should discriminate against outgroup members by failing to help, as they are perceived as lacking these uniquely human emotions. Vaes and coworkers (2003) supported this prediction of differential helping: Participants were less likely to help and express solidarity with out-group members who needed assistance than in-group members and indeed were particularly unhelpful to out-group members who violated expectations by expressing secondary emotions. A related effect was obtained by Cuddy and colleagues (2007), who showed that the tendency to deny uniquely human emotions to other-race Hurricane Katrina victims was associated with a lesser likelihood of volunteering to help with relief efforts.

Dehumanization can also diminish collective helping. Zebel and colleagues (2008) found that Dutch participants who perceived Muslims as subtly animal-like were less supportive of reparations being made to the Bosnian Muslim families of victims of an atrocity that Dutch peacekeepers had failed to prevent. In related work, Cehajic et al. (2009) showed that dehumanization of a victim group was associated with diminished empathy for them. Dehumanization of sex offenders has also been shown to predict lack of support for rehabilitation programs (Viki et al. 2013).

Dehumanization may also diminish prosocial behavior by reducing intergroup forgiveness. Tam and colleagues (2007) found that Protestants and Catholics in Northern Ireland were less likely to forgive one another for past violence if they infrahumanized the other community. This effect was independent of anger and out-group attitudes, suggesting that dehumanization is not merely an epiphenomenon of negative evaluation. Infrahumanization may also reduce forgiveness by rendering apologies ineffective. Like Tam and colleagues, Wohl et al. (2012) showed that people tended not to forgive others whom they infrahumanized. In addition, they showed that apologies issued by transgressor groups did not generate forgiveness if they were expressed using secondary emotions. These studies reveal the powerful role that infrahumanization may play in hindering intergroup reconciliation.

Increased Antisociality

Reductions in prosocial behavior toward dehumanized groups represent omissions, but the most well-known consequences of dehumanization involve the commission of antisocial acts. The link between dehumanization, violence, and aggression was emphasized in the early writings of Kelman and Staub on war and genocide, and early work by Bandura and colleagues (1996) firmly established that dehumanization of victims disinhibits violent actions. Subsequent research has revealed the wide variety of forms of aggression with which dehumanization is associated and the multiple mechanisms that account for this association.

Dehumanization is sometimes associated with predatory forms of aggression that are not direct responses to provocation. The tendency to dehumanize others is associated with perpetration of bullying among children (Obermann 2011), consistent with the work of Bandura et al. (1996), who showed that dehumanization-prone children were particularly unlikely to experience anticipatory guilt before and remorse after engaging in aggressive behavior. In a different context, men who implicitly associated women with animals and objects reported greater proclivities to rape and sexually harass them (Rudman & Mescher 2012).

Dehumanization has also been shown to predict forms of aggression that are perceived as reactive and retaliatory—and often righteous—by the perpetrator. Perceiving enemies as less than human is associated with support for war among Americans (Jackson & Gaertner 2010), for torture of Muslim prisoners of war among British Christians (Viki et al. 2013), and for coerced population transfers of Palestinians among Israelis (Maoz & McCauley 2008). Perceiving criminals as less than human predicts harsh and retributive sentencing decisions independently of the moral outrage that their crimes evoke (Bastian et al. 2013a). The special relevance of dehumanization to retributive responses in ongoing conflicts is demonstrated by Leidner et al. (2013), who showed that the more Palestinian and Jewish Israeli participants dehumanized one another in Haslam's mechanistic sense—denial of human nature or "sentience"—the more they supported retributive forms of justice that punished their opponents over restorative forms that sought peace through apologies and affirmation of shared values. This preference for retributive justice was, in turn, associated with support for violence (e.g., bombings) rather than peace deals.

Related effects have been observed among cyber-warriors: Dehumanization of opponents, and of the self, occurs among players of violent video games (Bastian et al. 2012b). The tendency to dehumanize others that these games promoted can increase extragame aggressive behavior, possibly accounting in part for the effects of violent video games on general aggressiveness (Greitemeyer & McLatchie 2011). However, the causal role of dehumanization as an enabling precursor of aggression cannot be established in this research, as the dehumanizing perception can serve as a post-hoc rationalization instead. Perhaps ironically, however, perceiving violence itself as less than human (i.e., animalistic), rather than the enemy, may sometimes reduce support for military aggression (Motyl et al. 2009).

Retaliation in the form of support for punitive treatment of people who violate social norms is also associated with dehumanization. Viki et al. (2012) showed that people who dehumanized sex offenders favored especially harsh punishments. Goff et al. (2008) found that media reports of crimes in Philadelphia contained more dehumanizing jungle imagery when defendants were

African American than when they were white, and this imagery was associated with defendants receiving death sentences. In another study, Goff et al. (2008) showed that white participants who viewed a videotape of police violently subduing a suspect believed the violence to be more justified when the suspect was described as African American and they had been primed with ape-related stimuli. This work suggests that dehumanization may facilitate aggression by promoting an image of feral dangerousness.

The antisocial consequences of dehumanization discussed above involve forms of hostile approach, such as aggressive and punitive actions. A few studies have explored hostile avoidance. Martinez et al. (2011) found that mental illness labels led hypothetical persons to be perceived as animalistic, increasing their perceived dangerousness and intentions to socially reject them. Similarly, Viki et al. (2012) found that participants who dehumanized sex offenders were more likely to support excluding them from society. These links between dehumanization and social exclusion may be especially pertinent for socially deviant groups.

Consequences for Moral Judgment

Another possible consequence of dehumanizing perceptions is to confer diminished moral standing on people (cf. Opotow 1990). Researchers have shown that perceived moral status covaries strongly with attributions of mind and that different kinds of mind denial have different moral implications (Gray et al. 2007). In particular, people who are seen as lacking agentic mental states are judged to be deficient in moral responsibility (moral agency), and those seen as lacking experiential mental states are judged to lack the right to be protected from harm (moral patiency). Bastian et al. (2011) confirmed this pattern in relation to perceived humanness, finding that people seen as lacking uniquely human traits were viewed as less blameworthy and punishable for immoral behavior, whereas people seen as lacking human nature were judged less worthy of protection, less capable of rehabilitation, and less deserving of praise for moral behavior.

Dehumanization's effects on moral standing might help to account for its links to antisocial and diminished prosocial behavior. The finding that people are willing to harm and exclude dehumanized persons, and see them as less worthy of help, forgiveness, and empathy, is consistent with the evidence that a perceived lack of human nature or experience is associated with reduced moral worth. The lesser blame and punishment assigned to people lacking human uniqueness or agency appears to conflict with the substantial evidence that people seen as animal-like are often targeted for punitive treatment. One resolution to this apparent paradox is that this punitiveness is driven not by a perception that the punished are morally responsible for their actions, but rather by perceived dangerousness and threat. Punitive treatment of animalistically dehumanized people may reflect a judgment that they are not moral agents: Coercive treatment is required precisely because they are not amenable to reasoning or capable of controlling themselves.

Functional Consequences

The consequences of dehumanization reviewed above have been unambiguously negative. Two studies conducted in a medical context complicate that generalization. Lammers & Stapel (2011) found that participants who denied human nature traits to a fictitious patient in a medical decision-making scenario were most likely to recommend a treatment that was more painful but ultimately more effective than its alternative. Although this evidence is several steps removed from clinical reality, it implies that under certain conditions medical dehumanization might benefit patients. The possibility that it might also benefit doctors is suggested by Vaes & Muratore (2013), who showed that health workers who were less inclined to humanize the suffering of a fictitious terminal patient showed fewer symptoms of burnout (i.e., exhaustion, poor relationships with patients, disillusionment). These studies imply that dehumanization may sometimes be advantageous in domains such as medicine where tough-minded but prudent decisions must be made on behalf of people who may suffer short-term costs. However, these implications must be weighed against the strong evidence that empathy and humanizing have predominantly positive associations with patient outcomes (Haque & Waytz 2012, Haslam 2007).

HOW CAN WE OVERCOME DEHUMANIZATION?

Recent research has documented the existence of dehumanizing perceptions and their causes, correlates, and consequences. Relatively little attention has been paid to the important practical problem of how these perceptions can be reduced. This problem is likely to be a knotty one. First, many dehumanizing perceptions are rooted in stereotypes and intergroup relations that have long histories. Second, these perceptions are often unconscious and automatic. Third, dehumanizing perceptions are often reinforced by strong motives and biases: They can protect in-group identity (Koval et al. 2012), people actively resist information that challenges them (Vaes et al. 2003), and they can be a moving target because people judge to be human whatever distinguishes their group from others (Paladino & Vaes 2009).

Despite these reasons for pessimism there is evidence that prosocial behavior can be increased by humanizing social targets (Majdandžić et al. 2012) and that dehumanization can be reduced by factors that are well known to social psychologists. One is intergroup contact. Greater or higher-quality contact was associated with less dehumanizing perceptions of (*a*) members of other communities in sectarian Northern Ireland (Tam et al. 2007), (*b*) sex offenders by staff at a rehabilitation center (Viki et al. 2012), and (*c*) immigrants by Italian citizens and southern Italians by northerners (Capozza et al. 2012b). In the only experimental study, an imagined contact intervention reduced infrahumanization of immigrants by Italian children (Vezzali et al. 2012).

A second way to reduce dehumanization is to promote a common or superordinate identity, thereby emphasizing the similarities and shared fate of different subgroups and de-emphasizing their boundaries. In a correlational study, Capozza et al. (2012b) showed that the humanizing effects of contact were partly mediated by the construal of Italians and immigrants as sharing a single identity as town dwellers and of northerners and southerners as sharing a national identity. Albarello & Rubini (2012) experimentally demonstrated reduced dehumanization of blacks when Caucasian Italian participants received human identity primes.

Although superordinate categorization may hold promise in reducing dehumanization, some writers have expressed caution about making human identity salient. Morton & Postmes (2011) argue that groups that have harmed others can use notions of shared humanity to deflect collective responsibility and guilt and to expect unearned forgiveness. Awareness of common humanity can also reduce empathy for victim groups (Greenaway et al. 2012). Making the human category salient can also backfire if it is framed negatively (e.g., human "nature red in tooth and claw"), increasing support for torture and the use of force by in-group members and reducing their associated feelings of guilt. In essence, a sense of common human identity can normalize aggression and excuse the harmful behavior of in-group members as "only human."

There is little evidence for alternative methods of reducing dehumanization besides contact and superordinate identity. One study has shown that emphasizing similarities between humans and animals led to humanized perceptions of immigrants by Canadian participants (Costello & Hodson 2010), and another has shown that multiple categorization of blacks (i.e., supplementing racial labels with information about age, gender, religion, and so on) attenuated dehumanizing perceptions in Italy (Albarello & Rubini 2012). In view of the paucity of work of this type, experimental research on the reduction of dehumanization is an urgent priority.

CONCLUSIONS

This review reveals the vitality of the "new look" at dehumanization that has emerged in the new century. Original theoretical perspectives have driven research programs that have begun to answer many of the key questions in the field. The central message of this work is one of diversity. Recent research shows that dehumanization can take many forms, including subtle variations that extend far beyond the extreme phenomena that provided the focus for early dehumanization scholarship. It shows that dehumanization can involve many themes, from derogation to degradation to disconnection. It demonstrates that the potential targets of dehumanization are many, rather than being confined to combatants and victims of genocide. It indicates that dehumanization is associated with a diverse assortment of individual differences (e.g., personality traits, ideologies, attitudes) and contextual factors (e.g., emotions, motives, threats, social positions) rather than being driven only by hate or hatefulness. It shows the consequences of dehumanization to be disparate: They include many varieties of aggression—the focus of early theory—but stretch to forms of social exclusion, diminished prosociality, moral judgment, and even potentially beneficial outcomes.

Despite this evidence of significant progress, the psychology of dehumanization also faces important challenges. More work is needed to establish that dehumanizing perceptions exert a causal influence on behavior in ecologically valid contexts. Researchers have given insufficient attention to how dehumanization operates in interpersonal relationships and interactions as distinct from perceptions of groups. Ways of reducing dehumanization, or humanizing dehumanized groups, are under-researched. Similarly, it is important to clarify distinctive neural signatures of different forms of dehumanization (e.g., Jack et al. 2013) and to use social neuroscience methods to unpack the conceptual overlaps between dehumanization, empathy, mirroring, and mentalizing. The relationship between subtle and blatant forms of dehumanization remains uncertain, and plausible hypotheses—e.g., subtle forms predispose blatant forms under conditions of conflict—have yet to be examined. More generally, there is a need to establish patterns within the diversity of dehumanization, such as determining whether particular forms of dehumanization have selective associations with particular targets, perceiver characteristics, contextual triggers, and consequences. The delineation of these patterns will help to refine theory on this challenging topic.

Although much remains to be done, the psychology of dehumanization has taken great strides in the past decade. Theorists and researchers have established that perceiving people as less than human is surprisingly common, complex, and broad in its implications for social life, both everyday and *in extremis*. The next decade of work is likely to cement dehumanization as a fundamental process in social perception.

SUMMARY POINTS

1. The study of dehumanization has undergone a renaissance in the past decade.

2. Several new theories offer compelling accounts that make dehumanization-related phenomena empirically tractable.

3. Dehumanization phenomena lie on a spectrum from blatant to subtle and also take different qualitative forms.

4. Although the best-known historical examples of dehumanization involve ethnic or racial groups, research has documented dehumanizing perceptions of many other targets, including the self.

5. Several personality, ideological, and attitudinal factors are associated with the tendency to dehumanize others.

6. Several emotional, motivational, and social-structural factors influence when dehumanization occurs.

7. Many consequences of dehumanization have been demonstrated, extending beyond effects on aggressive behavior to reduced prosociality and some functional consequences.

8. Relatively little research has examined the crucial task of identifying how dehumanizing perceptions can be challenged and overcome.

FUTURE ISSUES

1. What is the range of groups that can be dehumanized, and what are the common elements among them?

2. Can dehumanization be examined as an interpersonal phenomenon, based on the dynamics of interactions and relationships, as well as an intergroup phenomenon?

3. Do different forms of dehumanization have different neural signatures?

4. When do dehumanizing perceptions have causal effects on social outcomes rather than merely being side effects of negative evaluations?

5. What are the implications of dehumanizing perceptions beyond their central consequence of promoting aggression?

6. Can dehumanization be studied in the thick of real-life social conflicts?

7. Can dehumanizing perceptions be studied longitudinally?

8. What are the best ways to humanize targets of dehumanizing perception?

DISCLOSURE STATEMENT

The authors are not aware of any affiliations, memberships, funding, or financial holdings that might be perceived as affecting the objectivity of this review.

LITERATURE CITED

Albarello F, Rubini M. 2012. Reducing dehumanization outcomes towards blacks: the role of multiple categorisation and of human identity. *Eur. J. Soc. Psychol.* 42:875–82

Bain P, Park J, Kwok C, Haslam N. 2009. Attributing human uniqueness and human nature to cultural groups: distinct forms of subtle dehumanization. *Group Process. Intergr. Relat.* 12:789–805

Bain P, Vaes J, Kashima Y, Haslam N, Guan Y. 2012. Folk conceptions of humanness: beliefs about distinctive and core human characteristics in Australia, Italy, and China. *J. Cross-Cult. Psychol.* 43:53–58

Bandura A. 1999. Moral disengagement in the perpetration of inhumanities. *Personal. Soc. Psychol. Rev.* 3:193–209

Bandura A, Barbaranelli C, Caprara G, Pastorelli C. 1996. Mechanisms of moral disengagement in the exercise of moral agency. *J. Personal. Soc. Psychol.* 71:364–74

Bar-Tal D. 1989. Delegitimization: the extreme case of stereotyping. In *Stereotyping and Prejudice: Changing Conceptions*, ed. D Bar-Tal, C Grauman, A Kruglanski, W Stroebe, pp. 169–88. New York: Springer

Bastian B, Costello K, Loughnan S, Hodson G. 2012a. When closing the human-animal divide expands moral concern: the importance of framing. *Soc. Psychol. Personal. Sci.* 3:421–29

Bastian B, Denson T, Haslam N. 2013a. The roles of dehumanization and moral outrage in retributive justice. *PLoS ONE* 8(4):e61842

Bastian B, Haslam N. 2010. Excluded from humanity: ostracism and dehumanization. *J. Exp. Soc. Psychol.* 46:107–13

Bastian B, Haslam N. 2011. Experiencing dehumanization: cognitive and emotional effects of everyday dehumanization. *Basic Appl. Soc. Psychol.* 33:295–303

Bastian B, Jetten J, Chen H, Radke H, Harding J, Fasoli F. 2013b. Losing our humanity: the self-dehumanizing consequences of social ostracism. *Personal. Soc. Psychol. Bull.* 39:156–69

Bastian B, Jetten J, Radke H. 2012b. Cyber-dehumanization: violent video game playing diminishes our humanity. *J. Exp. Soc. Psychol.* 48:486–91

Bastian B, Laham S, Wilson S, Haslam N, Koval P. 2011. Blaming, praising, and protecting our humanity: the implications of everyday dehumanization for judgments of moral status. *Br. J. Soc. Psychol.* 50:469–83

Bastian B, Loughnan S, Haslam N, Radke H. 2012c. Don't mind meat? The denial of mind to animals used for human consumption. *Personal. Soc. Psychol. Bull.* 38:247–56

Bernard P, Gervais S, Allen J, Campomizzi S, Klein O. 2012. Integrating sexual objectification with object versus person recognition: the sexualized body-inversion hypothesis. *Psychol. Sci.* 23:469–71

Bilewicz M, Imhoff R, Drogosz M. 2011. The humanity of what we eat: conceptions of human uniqueness among vegetarians and omnivores. *Eur. J. Soc. Psychol.* 41:201–9

Boccato G, Capozza D, Falvo R, Durante F. 2008. The missing link: ingroup, outgroup, and the human species. *Soc. Cogn.* 26:224–34

Bratanova B, Loughnan S, Bastian B. 2011. Categorization as food reduces moral concern for animals. *Appetite* 57:193–96

Buckels E, Trapnell P. 2013. Disgust facilitates outgroup dehumanization. *Group Process. Intergr. Relat.* In press

Capozza D, Andrighetto L, Di Bernardo G, Falvo R. 2012a. Does status affect intergroup perceptions of humanity? *Group Process. Intergr. Relat.* 15:363–77

Capozza D, Trifiletti E, Vezzali L, Favara I. 2012b. Can intergroup contact improve humanity attributions? *Int. J. Psychol.* 48:527–41

Castano E, Giner-Sorolla R. 2006. Not quite human: infrahumanization in response to collective responsibility for intergroup killing. *J. Personal. Soc. Psychol.* 90:804–18

Cehajic S, Brown R, Gonzalez R. 2009. What do I care? Perceived ingroup responsibility and dehumanization as predictors of empathy felt for the victim group. *Group Process. Intergr. Relat.* 12:715–29

Cikara M, Eberhardt J, Fiske S. 2011. From agents to objects: sexist attitudes and neural responses to sexualized targets. *J. Cogn. Neurosci.* 3:540–51

Costello K, Hodson G. 2010. Exploring the roots of dehumanization: the role of animal-human similarity in promoting immigrant humanization. *Group Process. Intergr. Relat.* 13:3–22

Costello K, Hodson G. 2013. Explaining dehumanization among children: the interspecies model of prejudice. *Br. J. Soc. Psychol.* In press

Cuddy A, Rock M, Norton M. 2007. Aid in the aftermath of hurricane Katrina: inferences of secondary emotions and intergroup helping. *Group Process. Intergr. Relat.* 10:107–18

DeLuca-McLean D, Castano E. 2009. Infra-humanization of ethnic minorities: the moderating role of ideology. *Basic Appl. Soc. Psychol.* 31:102–8

Epley N, Waytz A, Akalis S, Cacioppo J. 2008. When we need a human: motivational determinants of anthropomorphism. *Soc. Cogn.* 19:114–20

Epley N, Waytz A, Cacioppo J. 2007. On seeing human: a three-factor theory of anthropomorphism. *Psychol. Rev.* 114:864–86

Strongest evidence to date that people can perceive themselves as lacking humanness.

Explores the intergenerational and epistemic roots of dehumanization.

Esses V, Veenvliet S, Hodson G, Mihic L. 2008. Justice, morality, and the dehumanization of refugees. *Soc. Justice Res.* 21:4–25

Eyssel F, Ribas X. 2012. How to be good (or bad): on the fakeability of dehumanization and prejudice against outgroups. *Group Process. Intergr. Relat.* 15:804–12

Fiske S, Cuddy A, Glick P, Xu J. 2002. A model of (often mixed) stereotype content: Competence and warmth respectively follow from perceived status and competition. *J. Personal. Soc. Psychol.* 82:878–902

Goff P, Eberhardt J, Williams M, Jackson M. 2008. Not yet human: implicit knowledge, historical dehumanization, and contemporary consequences. *J. Personal. Soc. Psychol.* 94:292–306

Goldenberg J, Heflick N, Vaes J, Motyl M, Greenberg J. 2009. Of mice and men and objectified women: a terror management account of infra-humanization. *Group Process. Intergr. Relat.* 12:763–76

Gray H, Gray K, Wegner D. 2007. Dimensions of mind perception. *Science* 315:619

Gray K, Jenkins A, Heberlein A, Wegner D. 2011. Distortions of mind perception in psychopathology. *Proc. Nat. Acad. Sci. USA* 108:477–79

Greenaway K, Louis W, Wohl M. 2012. Awareness of common humanity reduces empathy and heightens expectations of forgiveness for temporally distant wrongdoing. *Soc. Psychol. Personal. Sci.* 3:446–54

Greitemeyer T, McLatchie N. 2011. Denying humanness to others: a newly discovered mechanism by which violent video games increase aggressive behavior. *Psychol. Sci.* 22:659–65

Gwinn J, Judd C, Park B. 2013. Less power = less human? Effects of power differentials on dehumanization. *J. Exp. Soc. Psychol.* 49:464–70

Haque O, Waytz A. 2012. Dehumanization in medicine: causes, solutions, and functions. *Perspect. Psychol. Sci.* 7:176–86

Harris L, Fiske S. 2006. Dehumanizing the lowest of the low: neuroimaging responses to extreme out-groups. *Psychol. Sci.* 17:847–53

Harris L, Fiske S. 2011. Dehumanized perception: a psychological means to facilitate atrocities, torture, and genocide? *Z. Psychol./J. Psychol.* 219:175–81

Haslam N. 2006. Dehumanization: an integrative review. *Personal. Soc. Psychol. Rev.* 10:252–64

Haslam N. 2007. Humanising medical practice: the role of empathy. *Med. J. Aust.* 187:381–82

Haslam N, Bain P. 2007. Humanizing the self: moderators of the attribution of lesser humanness to others. *Personal. Soc. Psychol. Bull.* 33:57–68

Haslam N, Bain P, Douge L, Lee M, Bastian B. 2005. More human than you: attributing humanness to self and others. *J. Personal. Soc. Psychol.* 89:937–50

Haslam N, Kashima Y, Loughnan S, Shi J, Suitner C. 2008. Subhuman, inhuman, and superhuman: contrasting humans with nonhumans in three cultures. *Soc. Cogn.* 26:248–58

Haslam N, Loughnan S, Sun P. 2011. Beastly: What makes animal metaphors offensive? *J. Lang. Soc. Psychol.* 30:311–25

Heflick N, Goldenberg J. 2009. Objectifying Sarah Palin: evidence that objectification causes women to be perceived as less competent and less fully human. *J. Exp. Soc. Psychol.* 45:598–601

Heflick N, Goldenberg J, Cooper D, Puvia E. 2011. From women to objects: appearance focus, target gender, and perceptions of warmth, morality and competence. *J. Exp. Soc. Psychol.* 47:572–81

Hodson G, Costello K. 2007. Interpersonal disgust, ideological orientations, and dehumanization as predictors of intergroup attitudes. *Psychol. Sci.* 18:691–98

Jack A, Dawson A, Norr M. 2013. Seeing human: distinct and overlapping neural signatures associated with two forms of dehumanization. *NeuroImage* 79:313–28

Jackson L, Gaertner L. 2010. Mechanisms of moral disengagement and their differential use by right-wing authoritarianism and social dominance orientation in support of war. *Aggress. Behav.* 36:238–50

Jahoda G. 1999. *Images of Savages: Ancient Roots of Modern Prejudice in Western Culture*. London: Routledge

Kelman H. 1976. Violence without restraint: reflections on the dehumanization of victims and victimizers. In *Varieties of Psychohistory*, ed. G Kren, L Rappoport, pp. 282–314. New York: Springer

Koval P, Laham S, Haslam N, Bastian B, Whelan J. 2012. Our flaws are more human than yours: ingroup bias in humanizing negative characteristics. *Personal. Soc. Psychol. Bull.* 38:283–95

Kozak M, Marsh A, Wegner D. 2006. What do I think you are doing? Action identification and mind attribution. *J. Personal. Soc. Psychol.* 90:543–55

Establishes the neural underpinnings of dehumanization.

Provides an integrative, psychological account of dehumanization.

Lammers J, Stapel D. 2011. Power increases dehumanization. *Group Process. Intergr. Relat.* 14:113–26

Leidner B, Castano E, Ginges J. 2013. Dehumanization, retributive and restorative justice, and aggressive versus diplomatic intergroup conflict resolution strategies. *Personal. Soc. Psychol. Bull.* 39:181–92

Leyens J-P, Cortes B, Demoulin S, Dovidio J, Fiske S, Gaunt R. 2003. Emotional prejudice, essentialism, and nationalism: the 2002 Tajfel lecture. *Eur. J. Soc. Psychol.* 33:703–17

Leyens J-P, Demoulin S, Vaes J, Gaunt R, Paladino M. 2007. Infra-humanization: the wall of group differences. *J. Soc. Issues Policy Rev.* 1:139–72

Leyens J-P, Rodriguez-Torres R, Rodriguez-Perez A, Gaunt R, Paladino M, et al. 2001. Psychological essentialism and the differential attribution of uniquely human emotions to ingroups and outgroups. *Eur. J. Soc. Psychol.* 81:395–411

Locke K. 2009. Aggression, narcissism, self-esteem, and the attribution of desirable and humanizing traits to self versus others. *J. Res. Personal.* 43:99–102

Loughnan S, Haslam N. 2007. Animals and androids: implicit associations between social categories and nonhumans. *Psychol. Sci.* 18:116–21

Loughnan S, Haslam N, Bastian B. 2010a. The role of meat consumption in the denial of moral status and mind to meat animals. *Appetite* 55:156–59

Loughnan S, Haslam N, Murnane T, Vaes J, Reynolds C, Suitner C. 2010b. Objectification leads to depersonalization: the denial of mind and moral concern to objectified others. *Eur. J. Soc. Psychol.* 40:709–17

Loughnan S, Haslam N, Sutton R, Spencer B. 2013. Dehumanization and social class: animality in stereotypes of "white trash," "chavs," and "bogans." *Soc. Psychol.* In press

Loughnan S, Leidner B, Doron G, Haslam N, Kashima Y, et al. 2010c. Universal biases in self-perception: better and more human than average. *Br. J. Soc. Psychol.* 49:627–36

MacInnis C, Hodson G. 2012. Intergroup bias toward "Group X": evidence of prejudice, dehumanization, avoidance, and discrimination against bisexuals. *Group Process. Intergr. Relat.* 15:725–43

Majdandžić J, Bauer H, Windischberger C, Moser E, Engl E, Lamm C. 2012. The human factor: behavioral and neural correlates of humanized perception in moral decision making. *PLoS ONE* 7:e47698

Maoz I, McCauley C. 2008. Threat, dehumanization, and support for retaliatory aggressive policies in asymmetric conflict. *J. Confl. Resolut.* 52:93–116

Martinez A, Piff P, Mendoza-Denton R, Hinshaw S. 2011. The power of a label: mental illness diagnoses, ascribed humanity, and social rejection. *J. Soc. Clin. Psychol.* 30:1–23

Martinez R, Rodriguez-Bailon R, Moya M. 2012. Are they animals or machines? Measuring dehumanization. *Span. J. Psychol.* 15:1110–22

Morton T, Postmes T. 2011. Moral duty or moral defence? The effects of perceiving shared humanity with the victims of ingroup perpetrated harm. *Eur. J. Soc. Psychol.* 41:127–34

Motyl M, Hart J, Pyszczynski T. 2009. When animals attack: the effects of mortality salience, infrahumanization of violence, and authoritarianism on support for war. *J. Exp. Soc. Psychol.* 46:200–3

Obermann M. 2011. Moral disengagement in self-reported and peer-nominated bullying. *Aggress. Behav.* 37:133–44

Opotow S. 1990. Moral exclusion and injustice: an introduction. *J. Soc. Issues Policy Rev.* 46:1–20

Paladino M, Leyens J-P, Rodriguez-Torres R, Rodriguez-Perez A, Gaunt R, Demoulin S. 2002. Differential association of uniquely and non uniquely human emotions to the ingroup and the outgroup. *Group Process. Intergr. Relat.* 5:105–17

Paladino M, Vaes J. 2009. Ours is human: on the pervasiveness of infra-humanization in intergroup relations. *Br. J. Soc. Psychol.* 48:237–51

Park J, Haslam N, Kashima Y. 2012. Relational to the core: beliefs about human nature in Japan, Korea, and Australia. *J. Cross-Cult. Psychol.* 43:774–83

Park J, Haslam N, Shimizu H, Kashima Y, Uchida Y. 2013. More human than others, but not always better: the robustness of self-humanizing across cultures and interpersonal comparisons. *J. Cross-Cult. Psychol.* 44:671–83

Riva P, Andrighetto L. 2012. "Everybody feels a broken bone, but only we can feel a broken heart": Group membership influences the perception of targets' suffering. *Eur. J. Soc. Psychol.* 42:801–6

Rodriguez-Perez A, Delgado-Rodriguez N, Betancor-Rodriguez V, Leyens J-P, Vaes J. 2011. Infra-humanization of outgroups throughout the world: the role of similarity, intergroup friendship, knowledge of the outgroup, and status. *An. Psicol.* 27:679–87

Rudman L, Mescher K. 2012. Of animals and objects: men's implicit dehumanization of women and likelihood of sexual aggression. *Personal. Soc. Psychol. Bull.* 38:734–46

Saminaden A, Loughnan S, Haslam N. 2010. Afterimages of savages: implicit associations between "primitives," animals and children. *Br. J. Soc. Psychol.* 49:91–105

Savage R. 2013. Modern genocidal dehumanization: a new model. *Patterns Prejudice* 47:139–61

Schwartz S, Struch N. 1989. Values, stereotypes, and intergroup antagonism. In *Stereotypes and Prejudice: Changing Conceptions*, ed. D Bar-Tal, C Grauman, A Kruglanski, W Stroebe, pp. 151–67. New York: Springer-Verlag

Smith D. 2010. *Less than Human: Why We Demean, Enslave, and Exterminate Others*. New York: St. Martin's

Staub E. 1989. *The Roots of Evil: The Origins of Genocide and Other Group Violence*. New York: Cambridge Univ. Press

Tam T, Hewstone M, Cairns E, Tausch N, Maio G, Kenworthy J. 2007. The impact of intergroup emotions on forgiveness in Northern Ireland. *Group Process. Intergr. Relat.* 10:119–36

Tileagă C. 2007. Ideologies of moral exclusion: a critical discursive reframing of depersonalization, delegitimization and dehumanization. *Br. J. Soc. Psychol.* 46:717–37

Twenge J, Catanese K, Baumeister R. 2003. Social exclusion and the deconstructed state: time perception, meaninglessness, lethargy, lack of emotion, and self-awareness. *J. Personal. Soc. Psychol.* 85:409–23

Vaes J, Heflick N, Goldenberg J. 2010. "We are people": in-group humanization as an existential defense. *J. Personal. Soc. Psychol.* 98:750–60

Vaes J, Muratore M. 2013. Defensive dehumanization in the medical practice: a cross-sectional study from a health care worker's perspective. *Br. J. Soc. Psychol.* 52:180–90

Vaes J, Paladino M. 2010. The uniquely human content of stereotypes. *Group Process. Intergr. Relat.* 13:23–39

Vaes J, Paladino M, Castelli L, Leyens J-P, Giovanazzi A. 2003. On the behavioral consequences of infrahumanization: the implicit role of uniquely human emotions. *J. Personal. Soc. Psychol.* 85:1016–34

Vaes J, Paladino M, Leyens J-P. 2002. The lost e-mail: prosocial reactions induced by uniquely human emotions. *Br. J. Soc. Psychol.* 41:521–34

Vaes J, Paladino M, Puvia E. 2011. Are sexualized females complete human beings? Why males and females dehumanize sexually objectified women. *Eur. J. Soc. Psychol.* 41:774–85

Vezzali L, Capozza D, Stathi S, Giovanni D. 2012. Increasing outgroup trust, reducing infrahumanization, and enhancing future contact intentions via imagined intergroup contact. *J. Exp. Soc. Psychol.* 48:437–40

Viki G, Abrams D. 2003. Infra-humanization: ambivalent sexism and the attribution of primary and secondary emotions to women. *J. Exp. Soc. Psychol.* 39:492–99

Viki G, Calitri R. 2008. Infrahuman outgroup or suprahuman ingroup: the role of nationalism and patriotism in the infrahumanization of outgroups. *Eur. J. Soc. Psychol.* 38:1054–61

Viki G, Fullerton I, Raggett H, Tait F, Wiltshire S. 2012. The role of dehumanization in attitudes toward the social exclusion and rehabilitation of sex offenders. *J. Appl. Soc. Psychol.* 42:2349–67

Viki G, Osgood D, Phillips S. 2013. Dehumanization and self-reported proclivity to torture prisoners of war. *J. Exp. Soc. Psychol.* 49:325–28

Viki G, Winchester L, Titshall L, Chisango T, Pina A, Russell R. 2006. Beyond secondary emotions: the infra-humanization of groups using human-related and animal-related words. *Soc. Cogn.* 24:753–75

Waytz A, Epley N. 2012. Social connection enables dehumanization. *J. Exp. Soc. Psychol.* 48:70–76

Waytz A, Gray K, Epley N, Wegner D. 2010. Causes and consequences of mind perception. *Trends Cogn. Sci.* 14:383–88

Wohl M, Hornsey M, Bennett S. 2012. Why group apologies succeed and fail: intergroup forgiveness and the role of primary and secondary emotions. *J. Personal. Soc. Psychol.* 102:306–22

Zebel S, Zimmermann A, Viki G, Doosje B. 2008. Dehumanization and guilt as distinct but related predictors of support for reparation policies. *Polit. Psychol.* 29:193–219

Examines how likening women to animals and objects is associated with a suite of hostile beliefs.

Provides suggestive evidence that dehumanization may be functional in some circumstances.

A thorough and systematic account of the mind perception perspective.

The Sociocultural Appraisals, Values, and Emotions (SAVE) Framework of Prosociality: Core Processes from Gene to Meme

Dacher Keltner,[1] Aleksandr Kogan,[2] Paul K. Piff,[3] and Sarina R. Saturn[4]

[1] Department of Psychology, University of California, Berkeley, California 94720; email: keltner@socrates.berkeley.edu

[2] Department of Psychology, University of Cambridge, Downing Street, Cambridge CB2 3EB, United Kingdom; email: ak823@cam.ac.uk

[3] Department of Psychology, University of California, Berkeley, California 94720; email: ppiff@berkeley.edu

[4] School of Psychological Science, Oregon State University, Corvallis, Oregon 97331; email: sarina.saturn@oregonstate.edu

Annu. Rev. Psychol. 2014. 65:425–60

The *Annual Review of Psychology* is online at http://psych.annualreviews.org

This article's doi: 10.1146/annurev-psych-010213-115054

Keywords

prosociality, altruism, cooperation, trust, elevation, compassion, empathy

Abstract

The study of prosocial behavior—altruism, cooperation, trust, and the related moral emotions—has matured enough to produce general scholarly consensus that prosociality is widespread, intuitive, and rooted deeply within our biological makeup. Several evolutionary frameworks model the conditions under which prosocial behavior is evolutionarily viable, yet no unifying treatment exists of the psychological decision-making processes that result in prosociality. Here, we provide such a perspective in the form of the sociocultural appraisals, values, and emotions (SAVE) framework of prosociality. We review evidence for the components of our framework at four levels of analysis: intrapsychic, dyadic, group, and cultural. Within these levels, we consider how phenomena such as altruistic punishment, prosocial contagion, self–other similarity, and numerous others give rise to prosocial behavior. We then extend our reasoning to chart the biological underpinnings of prosociality and apply our framework to understand the role of social class in prosociality.

Contents

INTRODUCTION

> [Sympathy] will have been increased through natural selection; for those communities, which included the greatest number of the most sympathetic members, would flourish best, and rear the greatest number of offspring. [Darwin 2005 (1871), p. 130]

> How selfish soever man may be supposed, there are evidently some principles in his nature, which interest him in the fortune of others, and render their happiness necessary to him, though he derives nothing from it except the pleasure of seeing it. [Smith 2006 (1759), p. 3]

> All the world faiths insist that true spirituality must be expressed consistently in practical compassion, the ability to feel with the other. (Armstrong 2009, p. 8)

Prosocial behavior—when people act in ways that benefit others—has many forms: altruism, cooperation, caregiving, mutual coordination, and the experience of moral emotions, such as compassion, elevation, and gratitude (de Waal 2008, Penner et al. 2005). Understanding prosocial behavior has long been the provenance of controversy and scientific advance. Evolutionary theorists have sought explanations for why people would behave in ways costly to the self, with treatments of the distal mechanisms, such as inclusive fitness and reciprocal altruism, and proximal forces, including tit-for-tat, altruistic punishment, and status seeking (Axelrod 1984; Fehr & Fischbacher 2003; Hamilton 1964; Hardy & Van Vugt 2006; Henrich 2004; Nowak & Sigmund 2005; Rand et al. 2009; Sober & Wilson 1998; Trivers 1971, 1972). Some of social psychology's most enduring studies are counterintuitive demonstrations of why people fail to act on behalf of those who suffer (e.g., Darley & Batson 1973). Studies within developmental psychology have long grappled with the ontogenetic development and individual variation in prosociality (e.g., Fehr et al. 2008, Warneken & Tomasello 2006). Recent modeling of cooperative behavior suggests that prosociality is evident throughout nature and at many levels of analysis, from genes to multicellular organisms to societies (Nowak 2006). Indeed, cooperation may very well be necessary for complex biological systems to emerge from genomes to the global community.

These lines of inquiry converge on a question that we seek to answer in this article: Why are people good to others? Twenty years ago, social scientists sought to demonstrate rigorously the existence of what might be thought of as selfless prosociality—that is, that people do indeed act on behalf of others independent of the benefits to the self. Batson and colleagues' elegant work demonstrated that even when the most obvious forms of self-interest (social rewards, distress reduction) cannot be gratified, people still help others in need, owing to a state of empathic concern or sympathy (Batson & Shaw 1991). Here, we build on this work, synthesizing different discoveries to home in on a set of core processes—from inside the mind to those distributed across social collectives—that enable prosocial action.

Our review is organized into four parts. We first present briefly an equation for modeling the psychological decision to engage in prosocial behavior. Broadly, our framework encapsulates the sociocultural appraisals, values, and emotions that guide prosocial behavior; as such, we refer to our framework as the SAVE framework of prosociality. After outlining the theoretical components of our framework, we consider how proximal forces at four levels of analysis shape the components of our equation, reviewing intrapsychic, dyadic, group, and sociocultural factors that influence prosociality. Third, we rely on certain components of our framework to review the new science of the neurophysiology of prosociality. We then conclude by summarizing the emerging literature on social class and prosociality as a case study of our framework.

THE SOCIOCULTURAL APPRAISALS, VALUES, AND EMOTIONS FRAMEWORK OF PROSOCIALITY

Evolutionary theorists have proposed several mechanisms by which cooperation and altruism could have evolved, including inclusive fitness, direct reciprocal altruism, indirect reciprocal altruism, genetic group selection, and cultural group selection (Bshary & Bergmüller 2008, Hamilton 1964, Henrich 2004, Nowak 2006, Seyfarth & Cheney 2012, Sober & Wilson 1998, Trivers 1971). Within this scholarship, theorists have developed mathematical frameworks for understanding under which conditions cooperation is evolutionarily advantageous. These models focus primarily on extrapsychic mechanisms—i.e., those outside the individual—that render prosocial behavior biologically sensible and evolutionarily stable over time. Underspecified in such models are the intrapsychic processes—i.e., those inside the mind—that shape the individual's decision to act in prosocial fashion. For instance, why do certain psychological states but not others enable prosocial responding? Why are individuals more likely to behave prosocially when they see that others have done the same? How do social collectives encourage prosocial behavior?

Here, we turn to this task: developing a framework of the core psychological processes that give rise to prosocial behavior. Several theories posit that prosocial behavior follows from cost-benefit analyses in which the individual takes stock of the person in need, the costs of helping, and the immediate or delayed rewards for the self to be derived from prosocial action (e.g., Darley & Batson 1973, Hamilton 1964, Nesse 1990, Nowak 2006, Sober & Wilson 1998, Trivers 1971). Our analysis builds on and extends this foundation, introducing new processes that investigators have discovered over the past 20 years of research to be critical determinants of prosocial behavior.

Our framework focuses on individual-level appraisal processes that give rise to prosocial action, but we model how this intrapsychic cost-benefit analysis is further shaped by dyadic, group, and cultural factors. All components of our equation are conceptualized as perceptions of the giver— the person who acts in prosocial fashion. As such, the components of our equation need not be accurate or rational. Indeed, our equation may yield decisions to act prosocially that contrast with different kinds of rationality: psychological rationality (e.g., is the perception founded on reasonable appraisals of the situation?), economic (e.g., is the cost-benefit analysis appropriate?), and evolutionary (e.g., will the behavior maximize fitness?). Although each component in our framework can be subdivided into subprocesses, to balance parsimony with completeness, we provide an equation whose components capture the complexities of the intrapsychic processes that lead to prosocial behavior:

$$M \times (D \times (1 + B_{self}) + K \times B_{recipient} - C_{inaction}) > C_{action}$$

In our framework, M is what we call the social momentum for acting prosocially (ranging from 0 to infinity). This term represents the degree to which the individual's sociocultural milieu encourages or discourages prosocial action. Social momentum is largely affected at the cultural level in the form of representations of social norms and values relating to prosocial behavior. Values of M ranging from 0 to 1 represent social resistance: a dampening of prosocial behavior. Values of M exactly at 1 capture an absence of social influence. Finally, values ranging from 1 to infinity capture positive social momentum, where social norms and group behavior catalyze prosocial behavior.

The terms within the parentheses build on previous attempts to model the cost-benefit analyses that give rise to prosocial behavior. Two of our components deal first with the giver. A first determinant is B_{self}, the perceived benefit to the self of acting prosocially. Numerous discoveries have emerged regarding the benefits to self for acting prosocially. These benefits come in many forms, as we consider later: positive emotions carrying short- and long-term benefits for the individual; dyadic rewards of reciprocity; and group-based experiences of respect, status, and prestige, reflecting indirect reciprocity (Nowak 2006). Our second term is D, or default, which captures the biases and perceptions a person carries that are independent of the particular person who is in need that make prosocial behavior more or less likely. Most broadly, D captures (*a*) individual differences in prosociality, and (*b*) situational factors that characterize the immediate social context (e.g., features of the physical environment), which shape people's default proclivities to act prosocially independent of the potential recipient of prosocial action. In our formulation, D multiplies by $(1 + B_{self})$, allowing for D to both act independent of benefits to the self (e.g., love of humanity) and also magnify the benefits to self (e.g., highly prosocial people reap greater personal benefits from acting kindly).

Table 1 Prosociality constructs at four levels of analysis

Level	Construct
Intrapsychic	Intuitive bias (D)
	Individual differences (D)
	Giving feels good (B_{self})
	Guilt ($C_{inaction}$)
Dyadic	Reciprocity (B_{self})
	Prosocial detection (K)
	Self-other similarity (K)
Group	Prosocial contagion (D)
	Reputation (B_{self})
	Gossip ($C_{inaction}$)
	Altruistic punishment ($C_{inaction}$)
Cultural	Norms and values (M)
	Religion (M)

Two of our components explicitly address the recipient. $B_{recipient}$ is the perceived benefit to the recipient of a particular prosocial act: It captures changes in the state of the recipient of prosocial action (e.g., enhanced ability to cope, reductions in distress when suffering, increased pleasure of mutual gain through cooperation). K captures the giver's biases and perceptions of the specific recipient, which range from positively valenced preferences (e.g., in-group members) to negative values that reflect adversarial stances toward others (e.g., competition, intergroup biases). We conceptualize K as a modifying factor: It directly influences $B_{recipient}$, which captures the benefit another person can receive from the prosocial action. Processes such as perceptions of self–other overlap, and the recipient's prosocial intentions can amplify the perceived connectedness to the recipient.

Finally, we include two terms to conceptualize the costs that figure into prosocial behavior. C_{action} has received extensive theoretical treatment (e.g., Nowak 2006, Sober & Wilson 1998) and refers to the cost to the self for acting prosocially. For example, prosocial behavior can involve the giving up of a valued resource (e.g., money) to benefit another. $C_{inaction}$ captures distinct sets of cost altogether ignored by past mathematical models of prosocial behavior: the perceived consequences of not acting. This can take the form of guilt at the intrapsychic level. Furthermore, groups and cultures have developed numerous forms of sanctions against noncooperators to promote prosocial norms. These include reputation loss, gossip, altruistic punishment, and legal norms that punish antisocial behavior.

The components of our equation set the stage for the next sections of our review (see **Table 1**). Below, we examine how processes that arise across four levels of analysis—from the intrapersonal and the dyadic to the group and the cultural—inform the terms of our equation. Intrapersonal processes represent individual-level characteristics that can vary from one person to the next (e.g., temperament, personality traits) and are largely independent of the specific context and situation. Dyadic processes capture shifts in the prosocial calculus as a result of interacting with specific targets; they are inherently interpersonal. At the group level, we examine how events occurring within one's immediate social network—that is, others with whom a person interacts—can affect a person's prosocial behavior within the network. Finally, we examine how prosociality is affected by mechanisms at the cultural level, which refers to the broader social context one lives in and identifies with and that includes a group far larger than those any one person can expect to encounter (i.e., not within one's immediate social network).

INTRAPERSONAL PROCESSES AND PROSOCIALITY

The Kindness Instinct: Intuitive Bias Toward Prosociality (D)

The past 20 years have seen startling discoveries that support the supposition that humans have an intuitive, default tendency toward some degree of prosociality. Here is but a sampling. Studies of nonhuman primates yield compelling evidence of altruism and generosity (de Waal 2009, 2012). For example, both chimpanzees and bonobos maintain long-term partnerships with nonkin, routinely sharing resources and the provision of care (de Waal & Lanting 1997, Langergraber et al. 2007). High levels of prosociality are observed cross-culturally. For instance, across numerous studies, when people are asked to split a resource between themselves and a stranger, people typically choose to give between 40% and 50%—high levels of generosity considering that in many of these studies, (*a*) the recipient was anonymous and (*b*) there were no repercussions for keeping the entire resource for oneself (Camerer 2003). Even within small-scale societies, the most common offer is 50%, and the average offer in many societies is above 40% (Henrich et al. 2005). Infants as young as three months show a preference for geometric shapes depicted as helping another (Hamlin et al. 2007, 2010, 2011), and children as young as 14 months and 18 months old actively help others and cooperate in joint tasks (Warneken & Tomasello 2006, 2007). In the United States, more than 30% of the population reported volunteering in 2005–2006 (Omoto et al. 2010), and in 2008, Americans donated on average 4.7% of their income to charity (Gipple & Gose 2012), showing the pervasiveness of prosociality even within societies that emphasize individuality and competition. These empirical examples illustrate that prosociality is likely (*a*) intuitive, (*b*) widespread, and (*c*) deeply engrained in human behavioral tendencies. Kindness, it seems, may very well be a basic instinct.

Recent studies on the prevalence of prosociality align with earlier analyses of the tendency for humans to respond to harm, need, vulnerability, and weakness in others—a response that many have been attributed to the emergence of the need to care for hypervulnerable human offspring (Bowlby 1969, Keltner 2009, Mikulincer & Shaver 2009). More specifically, distress vocalizations, facial displays of sadness, baby-faced facial morphology, submissive posture, and the blush and display of embarrassment increase the likelihood of prosocial response (Goetz et al. 2010, Penner et al. 2005). In fact, a recent fMRI study found that images of suffering and need (e.g., images of physical malnutrition in children) activated a midbrain region known as the periaqueductal gray, which when stimulated in mammalian species triggers caregiving behavior (Simon-Thomas et al. 2012). Within the social psychological literature, cues related to need, harm, vulnerability, and weakness trigger more prosocial tendencies (Penner et al. 2005, Piff et al. 2010).

This intuitive tendency toward prosociality is most clearly brought into focus in recent work by Rand and colleagues (2012). In a series of experiments, participants took part in the public goods game in groups of four. Each participant was given 40¢ and allowed to give some amount, between 0¢ and 40¢, to the group, which was doubled and then split between the four members. In such a game, the best outcome for the group is if everyone contributes everything they started with—in that case, each person will end the game with 80¢. However, for each individual, the best strategy is to keep one's own endowment and free ride—receive the group benefits without incurring any cost. People who made their allocation decisions in ten seconds or less contributed about 65% of their endowment; people who deliberated for longer than ten seconds contributed closer to 50%. Follow-up experiments yielded similar evidence of a default tendency toward prosociality: Causing individuals to make their decisions quickly prompted them to cooperate more with others (by allocating ~67% to the group) than did individuals instructed to deliberate and reflect on their decision (these individuals allocated 50% to the group). These findings indicate that cooperation is a relatively intuitive snap judgment, whereas self-interest may be the product of more deliberative and calculative cognitive processes.

Individual Factors Shaping the Propensity to Act Prosocially (*D*)

Prosociality is one of many basic tendencies humans show toward one another. Yet not all people are equally cooperative and prosocial. Any treatment of prosociality, then, must consider the striking individual differences in prosocial behavior (*D* within our framework). In studies of economic games and social values, some individuals are strongly disposed to cooperate, others to compete (Van Lange 1999), some to give to public goods, others to exploit such resources (Frank 1988). In the literature on adult personality, highly agreeable individuals show high levels of cooperation across different tasks (Graziano et al. 2007), and individuals who are high in openness to experience display greater perspective taking (McCrae & Sutin 2009). Studies find that individuals with other personality profiles, such as Machiavellians, are very likely to exploit others and abandon cooperation in favor of self-interest (Gunnthorsdottir et al. 2002). Fairly novel with respect to formal modeling of prosocial behavior, the *D* component of our framework captures these meaningful, default variations in the individual and how she or he responds to opportunities for prosocial responding.

Where do these individual differences come from? One part of the answer is biologically based temperament. Recent studies highlight several neurotransmitters and their underlying genetics as being related to prosocial behavior, including oxytocin (e.g., Kogan et al. 2011, Kosfeld et al. 2005, Rodrigues et al. 2009b), serotonin (e.g., Crockett et al. 2008, 2010), and dopamine (e.g., Bachner-Melman et al. 2005, Reuter et al. 2011). Other work has linked individual differences in vagus nerve activity to prosociality (e.g., Eisenberg et al. 1995; A. Kogan, C. Oveis, J. Gruber, I.B. Mauss, A. Shallcross, E. Impett, I. Van der Löwe, B. Hui, C. Cheng, and D. Keltner, manuscript under review; Oveis et al. 2009).

Giving Feels Good: Intrinsic Personal Benefits of Prosocial Action (*B*ₛₑₗf)

Previous formulations of prosocial behavior have focused primarily on the costs to the giver and the benefits to the recipient, with little emphasis on the immediate benefits of prosocial acts for the giver. Yet emerging evidence suggests that acting with kindness yields many kinds of benefits for the giver. For example, research has documented that caring for others is linked to greater self-esteem and self-efficacy (Crocker 2008, Piferi & Lawler 2006). In other work, Dunn and colleagues (2008) investigated how spending money on oneself versus others affects happiness. Results from a nationally representative US sample demonstrated a positive link between prosocial spending (e.g., gifts for others, charities) and self-reported happiness. In an experimental follow-up, participants were given $5 or $20 and told to spend the money either on themselves or on someone else by the end of the day. Participants who spent the money on others reported higher levels of happiness than did participants who spent money on themselves. These findings have since been replicated in 136 cultures (Aknin et al. 2013). Kindness and prosociality, it seems, are universally rewarding. In our framework, these sorts of intrinsic rewards associated with prosociality are a central component of the benefits enjoyed by the self (*B*ₛₑₗf) and point to novel hypotheses to guide future research. For instance, given recent evidence suggesting that individuals' desired levels of positive emotion vary (e.g., Diener et al. 2006), future work should explore how this individual difference modulates inclinations toward prosociality.

In still other work on the personal benefits of prosociality, researchers have shown that prosocially disposed people tend to be happier and healthier. Within organizations, employees who are more prosocially inclined tend to be more creative and engage in enhanced problem solving (Grant & Berry 2011). In our own work, we have documented that people with increased tendencies toward prosociality report greater levels of life satisfaction, positive emotions, self-esteem, happier relationships, and more love experiences with close others and even with humanity in their daily lives (Le et al. 2013). People especially motivated to care for their partners experience greater positive emotions and relationship satisfaction when they engage in daily sacrifices for their partners (Kogan et al. 2010)—these findings illustrate the importance of studying the interactions among framework components. In this instance, individual differences toward prosociality (D) appear to amplify the rewards for prosocial action (B_{self}); giving feels good, but particularly for those who are prosocially inclined.

More generally, there appear to be strong emotional benefits to acting prosocially and being prosocially inclined. Prosocial emotions such as compassion (Fredrickson 2001, Goetz et al. 2010, McCullough et al. 2004) may give rise to numerous social and personal benefits, including greater social support and purpose in life (Fredrickson et al. 2008), feelings of being close to friends (Waugh & Fredrickson 2006), relationship satisfaction (Harker & Keltner 2001, Impett et al. 2010), personal success (Lyubomirsky et al. 2005), and life expectancy (Danner et al. 2001). Prosocial behavior also tends to trigger affective responses, such as gratitude, that engage neurophysiological processes known to have beneficial regulatory effects on basic systems such as the immune and cortisol systems, a point to which we return below.

Guilt as Deterrent: Intrapsychic Costs of Inaction ($C_{inaction}$)

Alongside the individual benefits derived from prosocial acts, failures to act prosocially can yield intrapsychic costs. Given that prosociality is a valued group norm, failures to behave prosocially can result in negative self-evaluation and distress that accompany failures to adhere to internal standards (Tangney et al. 2007). Under such circumstances, a particularly significant negative emotion likely to arise is guilt.

Feeling guilt is costly in several ways. It threatens the self and is thus aversive. Guilt is associated with elevated sympathetic autonomic arousal (Strauman 1989) and is metabolically costly. People are motivated to avoid this distress by behaving prosocially and avoiding transgressions. In this way, guilt helps maintain prosocial and other-oriented behavior.

Empirical evidence corroborates this claim. Guilt-prone individuals—who anticipate negative feelings about personal wrongdoing—report greater empathy and perspective taking, and they engage in more communal, ethical, and prosocial patterns of behavior (Cohen et al. 2011, 2013). In situations that are private and confidential, absent pressures to conform to social norms or risks of punishment, the anticipation of guilt promotes prosocial behavior (Cohen et al. 2013). Even when one has not personally transgressed, guilt is a powerful motivator of prosocial behavior. For instance, vicarious feelings of guilt—that is, guilt felt on behalf of another's misdeeds—can motivate prosocial reparative behavior (Brown et al. 2008). These findings converge on the notion that the motivation to avoid feeling guilt can maintain prosocial responding even absent other costs to the self (e.g., punishment).

INTERPERSONAL PROCESSES AND PROSOCIALITY

Thus far, we have seen how the default tendency toward prosociality, the rewards of prosocial action, and the costs of inaction all increase the likelihood of prosocial behavior. In the following section, we focus on the dyadic, face-to-face processes that encourage prosocial responses.

Selective Prosociality: Dyadic Processes that Shape the Propensity to Help a Particular Recipient (K)

Opportunities for prosocial action often arise in the context of face-to-face, dyadic interactions: helping someone in obvious distress, cooperating with a colleague, giving care to someone who is ill, intervening during an emergency. Previous studies focused on how recipient characteristics, such as gender and ethnicity, influence rates of prosocial response (Penner et al. 2005). Building on this prior work, here we consider recent advances in the study of dyadic processes that influence tendencies toward prosociality.

Identifying prosocial recipients. Many analyses of the emergence of prosocial behavior center on what is known as the trust problem (Axelrod 1984, Frank 1988, Nesse 1990, Nowak 2006, Sober & Wilson 1998): How do people selectively engage in relationships with others who are going to cooperate rather than exploit? The costs of prosocial behavior are self-evident—directing resources to others—and the risks are just as clear, from harm to self to varying forms of exploitation.

Given the potential risks of prosocial action, rates of cooperation and altruism are highest when individuals can systematically detect the individuals who are prosocially inclined (e.g., Frank 1988, Nowak 2006). The capacity to detect prosocial tendencies in others allows individuals to strategically enter into cooperative, mutually beneficial relations, and avoid the costs of being exploited. For example, Wedekind & Milinski (2000) and others have found using iterative economic games that once individuals know others' predilection to cooperate or defect, they will preferentially allocate resources to more cooperative group members. Within our framework, we conceptualize this bias toward helping prosocial others as a dyadic process that affects the biases and perceptions toward the specific recipient (K) component of our equation.

A critical step in the process of preferentially helping those who are prosocially inclined is to identify who is likely to be prosocial. Mounting evidence suggests that humans can infer the traits and states of others from thin slices, or brief segments, of behavior (Ambady et al. 2000). For instance, seeing someone for less than one minute is enough to reliably detect at better-than-chance levels people's sexual orientation (Ambady et al. 1999), personality (Borkenau 2004, Oltmanns et al. 2004), and socioeconomic status (Kraus & Keltner 2009). People are also strikingly adept at detecting the prosocial tendencies of others. In one study, interpersonal tendencies associated with psychopathy were detectable from as little as five seconds of facial behavior (Fowler et al. 2009). In our own work, we have shown that naïve perceptions of the prosociality of targets of observers who had viewed 20-second silent video clips mapped onto differences in the rs53576 single-nucleotide polymorphism (SNP) of the target's oxytocin receptor gene (Kogan et al. 2011)—a gene that is related to individual differences in prosocial behavior (Rodrigues et al. 2009b, Tost et al. 2010). Perhaps most strikingly, Albrechtsen and colleagues (2009) showed naïve observers 15-second video clips taken from confession statements of inmates. Some of these confessions were honest and others were lies. On the basis of these brief videos, naïve observers could detect at better-than-chance levels who was lying and who was honest.

Such quick and reliable detection of a target's prosocial motivations depends on the reliable signaling and recognition of behavioral displays of prosocial intention. This issue of whether there are telltale nonverbal signals of prosociality has been investigated in studies we present in **Table 2**. Indeed, evidence suggests that prosociality is signaled through a combination of head tilts, gaze, smiling, head nods, blush, embarrassment displays, oblique eyebrows, and laughter (Bachorowski & Owren 2001; Eisenberg et al. 1989; Feinberg et al. 2012b; Gonzaga et al. 2001, 2006; Kogan et al. 2011). In a related literature, researchers have investigated which behaviors

Table 2   Nonverbal signs of prosocial character

Nonverbal behavior	Significance
Head tilts, gaze, smile[a]	Social engagement
Head nods[b]	Deference, submissiveness
Blush[c]	Concern over social evaluation
Embarrassment display[c]	Desire to appease, reconcile
Oblique eyebrows[d]	Concern for other
Laughter[e]	Warmth, cooperativeness

[a]Gonzaga et al. 2001, 2006; [b]Kogan et al. 2011; [c]Feinberg et al. 2012a; [d]Eisenberg et al. 1989; [e]Bachorowski & Owren 2001.

people use to detect prosocial intent. This literature reveals that observers rely on many of the signals of prosociality to detect those who are more prosocially inclined (Goetz et al. 2010).

These studies establish that the likelihood of a target acting in prosocial fashion—and eliciting such action from another—is reliably signaled in specific patterns of nonverbal behavior. This signaling component is an important dyadic process of prosociality and informs the K of our framework by motivating prosocial behavior (in the presence of prosocial cues) or constraining it (absent such cues). It is important to note there is no single signal of prosocial intention. And the nonverbal displays of prosociality will no doubt have context-specific meaning and will likely signal different dimensions of prosociality. For example, head nods signal respect and an interest in the other's welfare. Embarrassment displays—defined by their gaze aversion, controlled smile, head movements down and away, and occasional face touching—signal a concern over social norms and fear of negative evaluation. As novelists have long known and psychologists are beginning to document, there is a rich nonverbal vocabulary of prosocial intention.

Perceived self–other similarity.   Perceived self–other similarity is a second dyadic process that informs the K component, acting as a motivator of prosocial behavior (in the case of perceived similarity) or constraint (in the case of perceived dissimilarity). Perhaps one of the most dramatic demonstrations of this principle comes from reports of people who helped save Jewish members of their community during the Holocaust; they consistently report a sense of shared humanity and commonality as a powerful motivator for their behavior (Monroe 1996, 2004).

Direct manipulations of similarity between self and other also increase the likelihood of prosocial response. One recent demonstration capitalized on people's tendency to mimic, often unconsciously, the nonverbal behaviors of others. Valdesolo & DeSteno (2011) had participants and confederates sit across from one another and listen with earphones to rhythmic patterns of tones while tapping their fingers to the tones. The participant and confederate either (*a*) listened to the same pattern of tones, and therefore mimicked one another in synchronous tapping, or (*b*) listened to different patterns of tones, and therefore tapped their fingers at different times. Participants whose tapping was mimicked by the confederate later reported feeling more similar to the confederate, had higher levels of compassion, and were more likely to help that person complete a long and uninteresting task later in the study. Much like acts of behavioral synchrony used to induce social cohesion and cooperation among groups in the real world (e.g., coordinated marching in the military), even subtle acts of mimicry in the lab can induce feelings of self–other similarity and enhance prosocial responding.

Give to Receive: Dyadic Benefits of Prosociality (B_{self})

An enduring contribution to the study of prosocial behavior is the notion of reciprocal altruism—that exchanges of generosity and the ensuing rewards for the self outweigh the immediate costs of prosocial behavior, leading altruism to be an evolutionarily viable strategy (Axelrod 1984, Nowak 2006, Trivers 1971). Implied by reciprocal altruism is the notion that individuals are more likely to behave favorably toward others when they expect their favors to be returned. Reciprocity amplifies the perceived benefits of prosocial action (B_{self}) and promotes more prosocial relations. The mutual sharing of resources is a foundation of cooperative bonds among both nonhuman primates (de Waal 2012) and humans (Sussman & Cloninger 2011). In humans, reciprocation in nonverbal behavior—when one person reciprocates a dominance display of another with submissive posture—tends to produce greater interpersonal liking (Tiedens & Fragale 2003). Flynn and colleagues have found that the exchange of favors at work is a powerful mechanism by which individuals build alliances and rise in respect and status (Flynn et al. 2006). In negotiations between counterparts, reciprocated concessions are a pathway to more integrative outcomes that benefit both sides and, by implication, more prosocial outcomes (Thompson 2006). More broadly, in a meta-analysis of more than 180 effect sizes, Balliet and colleagues (2011) found that rewards promoted cooperation across a number of different paradigms and cultures.

Guided by theoretical claims about reciprocal altruism, gratitude brings into focus the benefits to the self for acting in prosocial fashion in at least two ways (McCullough et al. 2004, Nesse 1990, Nesse & Ellsworth 2009). First, the expression of gratitude, in the form of linguistic acts or gifts, rewards the generous acts of others. Algoe and her colleagues (2008) have documented that expressions of gratitude predict increased closeness among group members over time. Within romantic couples, longitudinal data have revealed that feelings of gratitude at time 1 predict greater responsiveness to the partner's needs at time 2 (Gordon et al. 2012). In work settings, managerial expressions of gratitude can enhance feelings of social worth among employees (i.e., causing them to view themselves as viable members of the community) and subsequently increase their prosocial behavior (Grant & Gino 2010).

The manner in which expressions of gratitude by the recipient serve as rewards to the giver is brought into sharp focus by recent discoveries concerning the prosocial functions of touch. The tactile system of hand, skin, and parts of the cortex plays an important role in rewarding prosocial behavior within dyadic interactions. The right kind of touch can trigger activation in reward regions of the frontal lobes (Rolls et al. 2003), as well as oxytocin release (Holt-Lunstad et al. 2008) and activation in the vagus nerve, which is associated with social connection, as we discuss below (Porges 2007). Touch is a primary reinforcer. And recent studies by Hertenstein and colleagues have found that strangers can communicate gratitude (and other prosocial emotions such as sympathy and love) with brief touches to a stranger's arm (Hertenstein et al. 2006, Piff et al. 2012a). Follow-up studies have found that touch can increase cooperation in economic games and in team activities (Kraus et al. 2010, Kurzban 2001). When recipients of prosocial behavior express gratitude to their benefactor through touch, they are providing a powerful reward for prosocial action.

Beyond serving as a reward for acts of kindness, gratitude also influences the default tendency toward prosocial action (D). It produces increased tendencies toward generosity, favors, sacrifices, and expressions of appreciation, which are critical to prosocial relations. As an illustration, participants in studies by DeSteno and colleagues (Bartlett & DeSteno 2006, DeSteno et al. 2010) were helped unexpectedly by a confederate (to fix a computer problem). Being the recipient of generosity led participants to feel gratitude, and in this state, they then proved to be more generous in allocating their time and resources to other strangers. For these and other reasons, gratitude has been considered a moral emotion and a primary determinant of prosocial behavior (McCullough et al. 2001), as it reinforces the self and rewards prosocial action (B_{self}).

GROUP PROCESSES AND PROSOCIALITY

Cooperation has many advantages within groups (e.g., Sober & Wilson 1998). In the most immediate sense, highly adversarial, self-focused individuals—for instance, free riders and hypercompetitive types—undermine group functioning (Felps et al. 2006). By contrast, other-focused individuals, who are relatively more attuned to the needs of others, actually make for more effective problem solving in collective tasks (e.g., Woolley et al. 2010). Cast within an evolutionary framework, groups likewise are invested in more prosocial members, in light of the dependence humans experience vis-à-vis others to accomplish basic tasks of survival and reproduction. These converging lines of reasoning suggest that group-based processes should increase the prosociality of members within a group or social network. Here we focus on recent discoveries related to several group processes and how they alter the terms of our SAVE framework.

Prosocial Contagion: Prosocial Behavior Within the Group Induces Bias Toward Prosociality (*D*)

From laughter, blushing, and voting patterns to destructive health habits, feelings of anxiety, and expressions of gratitude, nearly all manner of social behavior is potentially contagious, spreading to others in rapid, involuntary fashion (for reviews, see Christakis & Fowler 2009, Hatfield et al. 1993). Humans are a highly mimetic species, disposed to imitate and take on the tendencies of others in their surroundings and social networks.

Contagious prosociality—the spreading of altruistic, cooperative intention and action to others—is one means by which members of groups avoid the risks of mutual exploitation and foster cooperation (e.g., Goetz et al. 2010). More specifically, prosocial contagion should bias people toward prosocial behavior in general and thus is a group-level dynamic affecting the bias and perceptions independent of the recipient term (*D*) in our equation.

There is intriguing evidence for contagious prosociality (Nowak & Roch 2007). For example, in a study of charity in organizations, when individuals were transferred to sections of an organization that had higher levels of charity, their levels of charity rose in volume (Christakis & Fowler 2009). Of course, this finding can be interpreted in multiple ways—explicit social norms or pressures may have led to the documented increase in charity—but it is intriguing nonetheless that the degree to which generosity is part of a social milieu can influence in contagious fashion others' generosity. Other studies further bolster the notion of contagious prosociality. In one study, participants who played a dictator game after observing other participants behaving prosocially exhibited more generosity compared with those participants in a baseline condition (Krupka & Weber 2009). In other work, witnessing one person helping another caused participants to engage in more helping behavior in a subsequent task (Jonas et al. 2008). Thus, prosocial actions of others can elicit altruistic tendencies in oneself.

In experimental work, Fowler & Christakis (2010) have demonstrated with greater rigor how prosocial behavior spreads through social networks. In this important study, participants played several rounds of the public goods game (described above) in groups of four, but in this version, each round was played with an entirely new set of participants. In each round of the game, the participant was given 20 money units (MUs) and allowed to give some amount, between 0 and 20, to the group. Each MU the participant gave to the group was translated to an increase of 0.4 MU for each of the four group members; a gift of 1 MU would ultimately cost the giver

0.6 MU personally but benefit each other group member, translating into a collective gain of 1 MU. If participants kept all their MUs, they would end the game with 20 MUs; if they each gave all their MUs to the group, each member would end the game with 32 MUs. In this study, results revealed that for every MU a player gave, his or her partners would give 0.19 MUs more on average to a new set of players in the next round and 0.07 MUs on average to yet another new set of players.

One potential mechanism behind contagious altruism comes in the form of elevation: moral emotion elicited by witnessing the virtuous behavior of others (Algoe & Haidt 2009). In a series of studies, Schnall and colleagues (2010) documented that participants who were induced to feel elevation after seeing another person acting prosocially were more likely to volunteer for another unpaid study and spent double the time helping on a tedious task than did participants who were not induced to feel elevation. In follow-up work, Schnall & Roper (2012) showed that elevation is especially effective in promoting prosocial behavior after people reminded themselves of previous prosocial behavior, suggesting that elevation boosts people's propensity to act on their moral values. Elevation, then, can act as a powerful group-level force that shapes the D component of our framework—boosting the propensity to act prosocially independent of the specific needs and characteristics of the benefactor.

Rewarding the Kind: Reputation as a Group Benefit to Self for Acting Prosocially (B_{self})

Reputation refers to the beliefs, evaluations, and impressions about an individual's character held by group members within a social network (Emler 1994). Reputations differ from impressions of an individual's personality, the temperament-like idiosyncrasies of the individual (Craik 2009). Theoretical analyses of the emergence of prosociality posit that reputation is critically important for the development and sustainability of indirect reciprocity: a system in which people receive reciprocal benefits for their kindness not from the person they helped but from another member of the same group (Fu et al. 2008, Nowak 2006, Nowak et al. 2000). Empirical evidence from numerous domains has documented the pervasiveness of reputation and the benefits people can gain in the form of reputation for their prosocial behavior, which result in group-level benefits for the person acting kindly (B_{self}).

Studies of organizations and residence halls have documented the alacrity with which reputations form and are distributed across group members (Craik 2009). In studies of social networks that arise in financial advising firms, individuals gain reputations for the quality of the work they do and the degree to which they are good team players (Burt et al. 2013). Perhaps more impressively, those reputations travel with the individual as they move to different units in the organization: If one moves to a new unit within an organization, the members of that new group will know his/her reputation. Dovetailing with these observations, in studies of residence hall members and MBA students in working groups, individuals came to acquire a distributed reputation (for example, as someone who is collaborative or someone who routinely free rides) within a week of the group's formation (Anderson et al. 2001, Anderson & Shirako 2008). Group members also reach considerable consensus in their judgments of other group members' reputations, suggesting that individuals within a group share reputational information reliably. For example, the average correlation between two dorm members' judgments of a third dorm member's reputation for influence and status was about $r = 0.70$, a high degree of reliability.

What is the content of a person's reputation? Presently, empirical data are sparse—this is an area in need of empirical inquiry and could be guided by recent formulations of the basic dimensions of person perception, which state that impressions of others, for example, emphasize perceptions of competence and warmth (Fiske et al. 2007). However, some suggestive evidence does exist. For example, the reputation an individual earns within a social network is based on that individual's tendency to cooperate and to be a good community member (Keltner et al. 2008). In this research, members of a residence hall wrote about the reputations of two other members in their residence hall. The reputation stories centered on whether the person was a good member of the community—the degree to which she or he was believed to be considerate, kind, sharing, agreeable.

Recent work has documented that reputation-related processes increase prosocial tendencies within social groups. Computer simulations (Nowak & Sigmund 1998) have repeatedly demonstrated that cooperation can be a viable evolutionary strategy because of the reputational benefits that it affords the cooperator. In effect, cooperating confers the reputation of a valuable community member to the cooperating individual and increases the likelihood that they will be cooperated with in the future. Reputation, in this way, functions in the same way as prosocial detecting at the dyadic level: It solves the commitment problem. In a direct test of the hypothesis, Wedekind & Milinski (2000) provided players knowledge of the other players' past history of cooperation, mirroring the reputation-related conversations about an individual's predilection for prosociality that emerge naturally in groups. They found that participants will readily cooperate and give resources to an interaction partner whom they know to have a history of cooperation, but they will compete and choose not to give resources to interaction partners known to be greedy or competitive (see also Milinski et al. 2001). In a compelling follow-up, Milinski et al. (2002) conducted a laboratory test of whether public displays of prosociality (donations to the relief fund UNICEF) conferred important advantages to the individual. Participants played 16 successive rounds of an economic game in groups in which, for each round, participants decided whether to donate money to a group member and thereafter to charity. During the game, information about each participant's allocation decisions was displayed to the other group members. At the end of the sixteenth round, participants also cast their vote for one group member to represent their group as a potential delegate in the student council. Results revealed that the more money participants gave away in general, the more they received from others. More importantly, the more participants donated to charity, the more money they also received from others, and the more votes they received to represent the group in the student council; thus it appears that individuals are rewarded for prosocial acts even when others did not directly benefit from those acts. These findings indicate that prosocial behavior is rewarded by others via indirect reciprocity and enhanced reputation, and they underscore the very clear benefits (B_{self}) associated with prosociality in social networks and collectives.

The evaluative dimension to a person's reputation captures the esteem that person enjoys within the eyes of group members. Analysis of reputation and the status benefits associated with acting prosocially has led to the competitive altruism hypothesis: Given the rewards associated with reputation and status, social collectives can encourage individuals to act in prosocial fashion in exchange for social status afforded to them by group members (e.g., Milinski et al. 2002). Group members trade resources for social esteem.

Two kinds of empirical study support the competitive altruism thesis. A first concerns who rises in the ranks of social hierarchies. Judge et al. (2002) brought together nearly 75 studies that determined which social traits predict who enjoys elevated status and who emerges as leaders in organizations, schools, and military units. In these studies, prosociality—as captured in self-reports of the trait agreeableness—predicted rises in social standing in school settings (the correlation across studies between social standing and agreeableness in organizations and the military was near zero). In this same meta-analysis, Judge et al. observed that agreeableness predicted the ability to remain in positions of elevated rank across group contexts. Here one might infer that once in positions of power, individuals are indeed trading prosociality for elevated esteem.

Experimental evidence provides a second line of support for the competitive altruism thesis. For example, van Vugt and his colleagues have found that group members will give greater social status and power to other group members who act altruistically (Hardy & Van Vugt 2006). In other research, Willer (2009) asked participants to rank the status of individuals who gave to a public good or did not, and the study found that participants ranked the generous as being of higher status. More recent work suggests that motivations to gain status can cause individuals to behave in costly proenvironmental fashion, but only in situations where such acts are public and observable by others (Griskevicius et al. 2010). Groups conspire to give status and esteem to those who act in prosocial fashion, which in turn motivates prosocial behavior.

Gossip and Altruistic Punishment: Group Mechanisms to Guard Against Inaction ($C_{inaction}$)

Gossip. Gossip is a form of evaluative commentary between two people about the character of a third individual who is not present (Craik 2009; Wert & Salovey 2004a,b). The information spread in gossip is most typically plausible, unverifiable, and potentially damning to the person's reputation. Thus gossip, like teasing, employs many of the linguistic features of off-record communication—forms of exaggeration, humor, indirectness—that suggest that the communicative act is as much hypothetical as rooted in truth. Craik (2009) refers to gossip as a primary form of reputational discourse: It is how group members investigate and arrive at consensus about the reputations of other members of social networks. We suggest that concern over gossip is a powerful check against free riding—that is, gossip is a form of cost for not acting prosocially ($C_{inaction}$) and thereby motivates others to prosocial action.

In keeping with this thesis, new studies using innovative methods are beginning to document how gossip promotes cooperation within social networks. For example, in more ethologically oriented work, Kniffin & Wilson (2005) found that in the banter and badinage of a college rowing crew, the crew members systematically focused their gossip on one member who was not making practices or being a good team member. Our own research focused on how acts of gossip were distributed among members of a sorority house at a Californian university (Keltner et al. 2008). Surveys of the members of the group allowed us to identify who were frequent targets of gossip and to whom the gossip flowed. The frequent targets of gossip in the sorority were well-known and highly visible but not well-liked, and they themselves, in separate surveys, reported that they were cold, aggressive, and highly Machiavellian, willing to backstab and take others down to rise in power. It would seem that gossip targets those individuals who pose the most threat to the cooperative fabric of social groups.

Several recent studies have documented more systematic associations between gossip and increases in prosociality in groups. For example, Beersma & van Kleef (2011) have found that if individuals play an economic game with a person identified as a gossip, they behave in more cooperative fashion. And in still other research, Feinberg and colleagues (2012b) have found that the most prosocial individuals, as captured in the social values inventory, are the most likely to resort to gossip to warn others about free riders in social networks, again attesting to the notion advanced here that gossip is a group-level process that helps increase prosociality.

Altruistic punishment. In addition to gossip, researchers have identified a second group-level process that guards against free riding by increasing the cost of not acting prosocially ($C_{inaction}$): altruistic punishment. Empirical studies suggest that altruistic punishment—that is, punishing free riders at a cost to oneself—is an effective method of preventing free riders from spreading and prevailing within social collectives, and it is also extremely widespread. Within our framework, altruistic punishment serves as both a dyadic and a group-level mechanism to increase the cost of inaction.

At the dyadic level, people with whom one interacts can directly sanction the individual for not acting prosocially. Fehr and colleagues have conducted numerous studies using the ultimatum game to model dyadic altruistic punishment (Fehr & Fischbacher 2003). In the ultimatum game, participant A is given an allotment of MUs (e.g., 10 MUs) and must make a decision of how many of the MUs to share with participant B. Participant B then must decide whether to accept or reject the offer from participant A, in which case both participants get nothing. If participant B is being rationally selfish, he/she will accept any offer greater than 0; however, numerous studies show that people would rather get nothing at all than accept an unfair offer (Fehr & Fischbacher 2003, Güth et al. 1982, Henrich 2001). In fact, most people regularly reject offers that are less than 25% of the total MUs. These findings illustrate that people are more than willing to engage in altruistic punishment—and punish those who take more than their fair share—in the name of upholding fairness and equality, even at a cost to the self. Furthermore, multiple evolutionary analyses of altruistic punishment suggest that punishment is a stable strategy, even with one-time anonymous interactions and within large groups (Boyd et al. 2003, Fehr & Fischbacher 2003, Fowler 2005).

At the group level, people are perhaps even more willing to assume costs to punish free riders for not acting fairly, even with complete strangers. In one telling study, Fehr & Fischbacher (2004) gave participant A 100 MUs, which he/she could share with participant B, who had no ability to reject the offer. Additionally, the game involved a third participant C, who was given 50 MUs and had the ability to punish participant A at a cost—specifically, participant C had to give up 3 MUs for every 1 MU they removed from participant A. Nearly two-thirds of all participant Cs chose to punish participant As for acting unfairly, and the level of punishment increased as a function of how unfair participant A behaved. In another demonstration of group-level altruistic punishment, participants in a study by Fehr & Gächter (2002) played the public goods game (described above). In the key punishment condition in the study, participants were informed of each other's decisions and then allowed to spend between 0 and 10 MUs to punish each specific member of the group—for every 1 MU spent to punish, 3 MUs would be subtracted from the punished participant. Fehr & Gächter found that not only did participants regularly punish other participants who were acting selfishly, but cooperation in fact increased over successive rounds of the game when punishment was allowed. These studies suggest that the threat of punishment from the group is a powerful force to promote prosocial behavior—and is thus a core aspect of the cost of the inaction ($C_{inaction}$) component of our equation.

Recent findings suggest that punishment is not the only route—or even the best route—toward promoting prosocial behavior within groups. Rand and colleagues (2009) had participants partake in an iterative public goods game, playing with the same three others for a series of rounds. After reach round, participants could either punish the free riders who had not contributed to the public investment or reward the virtuous others who acted cooperatively and contributed heavily into the public investment. They found that when participants could both punish and reward, only rewarding led to greater payoffs for the group and higher levels of cooperation; punishment became unrelated to cooperation and actually resulted in lower overall group payoffs. However, this study examined punishment of not acting prosocially; presently, no studies have examined the relative effects of punishment or reward as deterrents for antisocial action (e.g., stealing from the group resource)—an intriguing area for future research. It thus remains to be seen whether altruistic punishment can truly be supplanted by group rewarding or, alternatively, if punishment plays an important role in guarding against antisocial behavior.

CULTURAL VALUES, NORMS, AND PROSOCIALITY

No human societies exist without social norms and values that guide social behavior. In fact, the ability to develop and enforce normative standards of behavior has been argued to be among the most distinguishing features of the human species (e.g., Fehr & Fischbacher 2004). Ethnographies of various cultures around the world provide vivid descriptions of the powerful values and norms that shape behavior in collectives—from norms about participation in group rituals to food sharing to cooperation (e.g., Gurven 2004, Henrich et al. 2004, Sober & Wilson 1998). Given the importance of prosociality to stable human societies, it is not surprising that values about prosociality and altruism are found cross-culturally (Schwartz & Bilsky 1990). A rich literature documents the extent to which prosocial behavior can be influenced by social norms: a person's beliefs about the rules and standards that guide or constrain social behavior in a given situation without the force of laws (Cialdini & Trost 1998). Dozens of studies have documented the extent to which prosocial norms are important impetuses to prosocial behavior (or the lack thereof). With regard to our SAVE framework, prosocial norms can increase or decrease what we have called in our framework the social momentum (M) of prosocial behavior—that is, multiplying the benefits of prosocial behavior in the positive case or potentially nullifying them in the negative case.

The Prosocial Force of Numbers: Norms, Values, and Others' Actions Shape Social Momentum (M)

Empirical studies inevitably document striking variations in levels of prosociality across cultures. Perhaps the most rigorous demonstration of such variation is Henrich and colleagues' study of ultimatum game behavior in 15 different small societies (Henrich et al. 2001, 2005, 2006). In the study, the participants were foragers, slash-and-burn farmers, nomadic herding groups, and individuals in settled, agriculturalist societies in Africa, South America, and Indonesia. On average, across the 15 cultures, participants gave 39% of the good to anonymous strangers. Yet there was significant cultural variation—in particular, according to the extent to which individuals within a culture needed to collaborate with others to gather resources to survive. The more the members of a culture depended on one another to gather food and see to others' survival needs, the more they offered to a stranger when they were allocators in the ultimatum game. For example, the Machiguenga people of Peru rarely collaborate with group members outside their family to produce food. Their average allocation in the ultimatum game was 26% of the resource. The Lamerala of Indonesia, by contrast, fish in highly collaborative groups of individuals from different families. The average gift in this culture, so dependent on cooperation for survival, was 58%.

Cultural values concerning individualism (an orientation toward self-interest and one's own goals) versus collectivism (an orientation toward collective goals and others' interests) can also underlie different patterns of prosociality, both across cultures as well as within them. Cultures vary profoundly in terms of relational style, cooperation, and reciprocity as a function of culturally upheld values of collectivism (for instance, in China) versus individualism (for instance, in the United States; for a review, see Oyserman et al. 2002). Collective versus individual norms also predict important variations in cooperative tendencies within cultures. In one study, individuals who reported more collectivistic values in an organization were more likely to engage in a variety of prosocial acts, including increased helping, to benefit their organization as a whole (Moorman & Blakely 1995). Using an experimental approach, Utz (2004) found that supraliminal primes of collectivistic values using words such as "group" and "together" caused individuals to behave more prosocially in an economic game relative to participants who unscrambled sentences with individualistic-related words such as "individual" and "independent." These studies highlight how culturally upheld values concerning individualism versus collectivism underpin prosocial tendencies (see also Oyserman & Lee 2008).

The activation of social norms—or beliefs about how one should behave in a given context—can also influence prosocial tendencies, including generosity and helping behavior (Cohen et al. 2010, Effron & Miller 2011, Gailliot et al. 2008, Jonas et al. 2008, Schindler et al. 2012). For instance, simply priming participants with prosocial norm-related words such as "equality" and "helping" can cause individuals to help more (Jonas et al. 2008). The effects of prosocial norms are malleable and context specific. In one study, participants were less generous in tasks that were framed as "economic"—which presumably activated beliefs that one should behave in self-interested fashion—compared with participants in tasks framed as noneconomic (Pillutla & Chen 1999). Situation-specific norms and values can significantly influence the extent to which prosocial behavior is perceived to be endorsed by others and, as a consequence, either dampen or accentuate prosocial responding.

Beyond norms concerning how one should behave, beliefs about how others do behave in a given situation can also significantly enhance prosociality. In one illustrative study, Goldstein and colleagues (2008) studied the effects of social norms on proenvironmental behavior among hotel patrons. They randomly assigned patrons of a particular hotel to receive in their rooms a towel reuse card that employed either a descriptive social norm (which stated that the majority of guests reuse their towels at least once) or a standard proenvironmental message ("Help save the environment"). The rate of towel reuse was 9% higher when patrons were exposed to the descriptive norm compared with the plea to save the environment. This evidence indicates that perceptions of what the majority of others do in a given situation can be a driving force in an individual's decision to behave prosocially. The more people there are perceived as exhibiting a particular prosocial act, the more momentum there is perceived to underlie that act (*M*), which, in turn, increases one's own likelihood of behaving in that fashion.

Faith and Kindness: Prosociality Is a Universal Religious Virtue (*M*)

People the world over define themselves in terms of religion—as Muslims, Protestants, Methodists, Unitarians, Jews, Catholics, Mormons, Buddhists, Hindus, or Sikhs (Diener et al. 2011). Religions are a powerful kind of culture (Cohen 2009). The world's major religions are similar in the esteem they attach to compassion, altruism, and treating others, even strangers and adversaries, with kindness (Armstrong 2009). This conduct is seen in such practices as tithing and tending to those who suffer. It is seen in moral codes such as the Golden Rule—that people treat others as they themselves would like to be treated (see **Table 3**).

Survey studies repeatedly find associations between self-reports of increased religious conviction and practice and prosocial tendencies. For instance, a recent survey of charitable giving in the United States found that individuals in religious regions of the country (e.g., the Bible Belt) gave significantly more of their incomes to charity than did individuals in less religious regions (i.e., the Northeast; Gipple & Gose 2012). Religious individuals report that their religious convictions help them to be ethical, fair, helpful, and kind toward others (Woods & Ironson 1999). Religious participants also exhibit increased feelings of "compassionate love" for close others and strangers (Sprecher & Fehr 2005). Moreover, two recent meta-analyses indicate that increased religiosity is associated with increased agreeableness (a trait defined by cooperativeness; Saroglou 2002) and benevolence (a value rooted in desires to help others; Saroglou et al. 2004).

Experimental research yields a similar conclusion: Exposure to religious concepts increases people's tendency to act in more prosocial fashion (Norenzayan & Shariff 2008, Shariff & Norenzayan 2007). In a first study in this research, participants were presented with sequences

Table 3 The Golden Rule across cultures and religions

Source	Statement
Matthew 7:12	"In everything, therefore, treat people the same way you want them to treat you, for this is the Law and the Prophets" (*New American Standard Bible* 1995).
Sextus the Pythagorean	"What you wish your neighbors to be to you, you will also be to them."
Buddhism	"Putting oneself in the place of another, one should not kill nor cause another to kill."
Hinduism (Mahabharata)	"One should never do that to another which one regards as injurious to one's own self."
Muhammad	"Hurt no one so that no one may hurt you."
Taoism	"He is kind to the kind; he is also kind to the unkind."
Dalai Lama	"If you want others to be happy, practice compassion. If you want to be happy, practice compassion."

of five words, randomly arranged, and asked to generate sentences using four of those words. In the religion prime condition, the five words always included at least one word with religious meaning, such as Spirit, divine, God, sacred, and prophet. In a neutral prime condition, participants did the same task of unscrambling sentences, but none of the words had religious meaning. Participants then received ten Canadian dollars and were asked to give some amount away to a stranger. Participants in the neutral prime condition were more than twice as likely to give nothing to a stranger as compared with those in the religion prime condition (36% versus 16%). By contrast, people who were primed with religious concepts were more than four times as likely to treat a stranger as an equal by giving half of the money to the stranger (52% in religious prime versus 12% in control condition). This same line of research documented that secular, nonreligious concepts related to ethical behavior—words such as civic, jury, court, police, and contract—generated similar levels of generosity as the religious words prompted. Social institutions that value prosocial behavior—be they religious or civic—significantly enhance prosocial behavior within collections.

Our conceptual review and the findings we have summarized are in keeping with a broader theme in the literature on the cultural triggers of prosociality: Making prosociality more salient in narratives, stories, conversations, and concepts, as religious practice often does, increases prosociality. Cast within the SAVE framework, we would suggest that such practices, ranging from religious doctrine to family dinner-time conversation, contribute to *M*, the cultural milieu, which influences the proclivity toward prosociality.

TOWARD THE STUDY OF THE PROSOCIAL NERVOUS SYSTEM

In our review, we have highlighted several processes that enable prosocial behavior. Given the many evolutionary arguments for the functions of prosociality, we presuppose that there should be genetically encoded neurophysiological processes, from peripheral nerves to molecules in the brain, which underlie the core mechanisms of prosocial behavior identified in this review.

In the abstract, one might think of these multiple interacting processes as the prosocial nervous system in humans, with parallels in the rudimentary neurobiological architecture of many other mammalian species. This thinking finds theoretical precursors in earlier formulations: claims about the role of the vagus nerve (Porges 2003) and the neuropeptide oxytocin (Carter et al. 2008) in attachment and love, and recent attempts to map empathy networks in the brain (Bernhardt

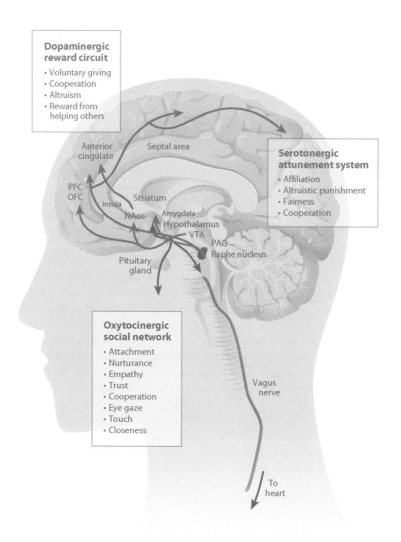

Figure 1

The circuitry underlying the prosocial nervous system. PFC, prefrontal cortex; OFC, orbitofrontal cortex; NAcc, nucleus accumbens; VTA, ventral tegmental area; PAG, periaqueductal gray.

& Singer 2012). Select studies have begun to explore neurophysiological correlates of specific prosocial processes outlined in our SAVE framework (see **Figure 1**).

Here we review evidence concerning biological correlates of prosociality that broadly fall into three classes. A first concerns the systems that promote affiliation, closeness, and ultimately nurturance toward others. We would expect these systems to be active in many acts of prosociality—a thesis garnering increasing support—and to covary with several components of our SAVE framework, most notably the individual's default propensity for prosocial behavior (D) and perceptions of specific others (K). Second, we would expect specific neurophysiological systems to enable experiences of personal reward for acting prosocially, thus carrying the intrinsic benefits of selflessness (B_{self}). Third, we posit that a global system related to behavioral inhibition and the coordination of affective states with actual behavior would also be recruited to guide prosociality. This system is likely to affect several components, including D and $C_{inaction}$, as we discuss below. Three families of neurotransmitters map onto these functions: oxytocin/vasopressin, dopamine, and serotonin.

At the outset, we note that virtually every biological system implicated in prosociality has been linked to numerous other social and nonsocial processes. For instance, oxytocin was originally identified in its role in uterine contractions during birth and lactation (Donaldson & Young 2008). The vagus nerve, in addition to being linked to prosociality, is also involved in attention (Hansen et al. 2003), self-regulation (Bornstein & Suess 2000), exercise (Dixon et al. 1992), respiration (Grossman & Kollai 1993), and sleep (Vanoli et al. 1995). Likewise, serotonin has broad influences on mood, sleep, appetite, and memory (Roth 1994). Furthermore, the dopaminergic system plays roles in addiction (Belin & Everitt 2008) and numerous psychopathologies (Pritchard et al. 2009). These findings underscore that many biological systems are intimately involved in promoting prosociality, but no biological system exclusively exists to promote prosociality.

Neurophysiological Underpinnings of the Kindness Instinct: Oxytocin and Vasopressin

Concern for others—the motivation that guides prosociality—arises from neurophysiological processes that promote attachment and caregiving (Decety & Svetlova 2012, Panksepp 2007) and includes the hypothalamus and its release of the neuropeptides oxytocin and vasopressin. Homologs of oxytocin and vasopressin are seen across the animal kingdom, in species as diverse as worms, hydra, insects, and vertebrates. Oxytocin and vasopressin are thus, not surprisingly, ancient systems, dating back to at least 700 mya (Donaldson & Young 2008). Traditionally known for their roles in reproduction and homeostasis in a variety of species (Carter et al. 2008), more recent studies have shown their pivotal roles in different manifestations of human prosocial behavior (Bartz et al. 2011, Domes et al. 2007b, Kosfeld et al. 2005). Oxytocin and vasopressin double as neurotransmitters and hormones and are projected to various brain areas, as well as ferried to the pituitary gland for peripheral release (Donaldson & Young 2008). Centrally, these neuropeptides exert social influences by targeting key emotional processing areas in the brain, including the amygdala, septal area, and reward circuitry described shortly (Young et al. 2001, Zink & Meyer-Lindenberg 2012). They both also have a strong presence in the periaqueductal gray (Jenkins et al. 1984), which is a key processing area for pain of the self and others, as well as for nurturance (Bartels & Zeki 2004, Simon-Thomas et al. 2012). A link between the prosocial and pain systems also involves other neurochemical players, including prolactin and opioids (Panksepp 2007).

A growing body of work has linked oxytocin to affiliation and closeness, critical processes in prosociality. For example, the strength of romantic ties, as measured by nonverbal displays of romantic love (Gonzaga et al. 2006) and interactive reciprocity (Schneiderman et al. 2012), directly relates to the amount of oxytocin released during dyadic interactions. Oxytocin's involvement in different attachments, including romantic, parental, and filial, have the same underlying mechanisms by promoting biobehavioral synchrony (Feldman 2012). Furthermore, empathy toward strangers relates to natural oxytocin release and more generosity toward strangers in the ultimatum game (Barraza & Zak 2009). Likewise, oxytocin administration promotes trust and cooperation (Kosfeld et al. 2005). These findings converge on the role of oxytocin in influencing the bias and perceptions of specific others (K) component of our framework—that is, the shifts in the oxytocin system in response to specific others promotes prosocial behavior toward them. This specificity is perhaps best seen in work by De Dreu and colleagues (De Dreu et al. 2010, 2011), who have found that intranasal oxytocin promotes prosocial behavior only toward in-group members.

Further supporting this claim, levels of oxytocin also strongly reflect the strength of the mother–infant bond, including eye gaze, affectionate touch, vocalizations, and bonding behaviors.

Moreover, mothers who display more synchronicity of behaviors with their infants' signals show more nucleus accumbens activation and this neural region's correlation with oxytocin release (Atzil et al. 2011). Both maternal and paternal touch and play trigger oxytocin release in parents and activate caregiving circuitry, which includes the prefrontal cortex and nucleus accumbens (Feldman 2012). Interestingly, giving fathers oxytocin artificially induces natural oxytocin increases in their infants (Weisman et al. 2012). Additionally, nonfamilial relationships later in life are related to parenting styles and oxytocin such that more synchronous parenting in infancy influences reciprocity of offspring with their future best friends (Feldman et al. 2013).

Oxytocin and vasopressin are also involved in default, individual differences in prosociality (**D**). In particular, genetic variations of the oxytocin and vasopressin systems, by way of naturally occurring polymorphisms, have also been associated with individual differences in prosociality. For example, variations of the vasopressin receptor AVPR1a are associated with individual differences in the allocation of funds in the dictator game (Knafo et al. 2008) and civic duty (Poulin et al. 2012). Furthermore, an SNP of the oxytocin receptor (OXTR) has been related to a variety of prosocial behaviors, such as compassionate displays toward one's romantic partner (Kogan et al. 2011), trait empathy and empathic accuracy (Rodrigues et al. 2009b), prosocial temperament (Tost et al. 2010), and engagement in charitable activities (Poulin et al. 2012). OXTR SNPs have also been connected to prosocial behaviors in the dictator game and social value orientation (Israel et al. 2009). OXTR variations influence affiliative behavior via neural structure and activation (Tost et al. 2010), as well as through physiological influences on the hypothalamic-pituitary-adrenal (HPA) stress system (Norman et al. 2012, Rodrigues et al. 2009b).

A second pathway for the oxytocin system to affect **D** is through the vagus nerve, a primary branch of the autonomic nervous system. Central release of oxytocin regulates the output of the dorsal motor nucleus of the vagus nerve. Peripherally, the vagus nerve exits the brain stem and contains branches that are involved in modulating the muscles behind behavioral displays of social engagement, including eye gaze, facial expressions, vocal communication (prosody), orientation, and social gestures (Porges 2001, 2007). These branches communicate with the nucleus ambiguous, which interacts with the myelinated vagus and oxytocin to promote calm states via parasympathetic-mediated heart rate decreases (Norman et al. 2012). Therefore, prosociality can be intertwined with powerful calming and soothing experiences via oxytocin and the myelinated vagus (Carter 1998, Porges 2003).

Psychological evidence suggests that greater baseline activity of the vagus nerve—as indexed by respiratory sinus arrhythmia—is associated with numerous processes linked to prosociality, including positive emotions, social connection, emotion regulation, and emotion expressivity (Beauchaine 2001, Butler et al. 2006, Côté et al. 2011, Eisenberg et al. 1995, Fabes & Eisenberg 1997, Kok & Fredrickson 2010, Oveis et al. 2009, Porges 2001). More recently, we have shown that vagus nerve activity is related to self-reports and peer reports of prosociality (A. Kogan, C. Oveis, J. Gruber, I.B. Mauss, A. Shallcross, E. Impett, I. Van der Löwe, B. Hui, C. Cheng, and D. Keltner, manuscript under review). Differences in baseline vagus nerve activity are thought to be relatively stable, reflecting individual differences in the vagus system. Within the SAVE framework, the vagus nerve then affects the individual difference component of prosociality: the default tendency toward prosociality (**D**).

The relationship between vagus nerve activation and prosocial behavior is driven, in part, by a reduction in arousal, which enables a shift in attention to the person in need (A. Kogan, C. Oveis, J. Gruber, I.B. Mauss, A. Shallcross, E. Impett, I. Van der Löwe, B. Hui, C. Cheng, and D. Keltner, manuscript under review). The same appears to be true of oxytocin: Oxytocin can dampen stress reactivity in both the brain and the body (Carter et al. 2008, Gimpl & Fahrenholz 2001, Meyer-Lindenberg 2008) via interactions with the HPA axis and sympathetic nervous system

(Rodrigues et al. 2009a). Circulating levels of oxytocin are associated with lower cardiovascular and sympathetic stress reactivity (Grewen & Light 2011). Oxytocin also robustly decreases amygdala activation and coupling to brain stem regions involved in the coordination of fearful responses (Domes et al. 2007a).

Benefits of Prosociality: Dopamine and the Reward Pathways of the Brain

One of the key components of our SAVE framework is the benefit to self (B_{self}) for acting prosocially. Recent neurological studies support this part of our framework, that giving feels good. Indeed, the dopaminergic reward pathway is central to prosociality owing to reward-pathway inhibition of threat-related responding and the intrinsic rewards that become associated with prosocial acts (Eisenberger & Cole 2012). The reward circuitry includes cortical regions, such as the anterior cingulate cortex and the orbitofrontal cortex of the prefrontal cortex, as well as subcortical structures including the ventral tegmental area and the ventral striatum, which includes the nucleus accumbens. The nearby caudate nucleus, which is part of the dorsal striatum, is important for feedback processing related to social learning associated with rewards, punishments, and cooperation (Delgado 2007; Delgado et al. 2005; Rilling et al. 2002, 2004).

Patterns of activation in this reward circuit provide motivations and incentives for acting on behalf of strangers. Important neuroimaging evidence suggests that both voluntary and mandatory transfers of funds to a charity activate regions of the ventral striatum and nucleus accumbens, which are implicated in the processing of self-relevant rewards, from the prospects of winning money to consuming sweet foods (Harbaugh et al. 2007). The reward system also guides decisions to donate (Moll et al. 2006). Furthermore, a number of studies have illustrated how cooperation and fairness activate reward regions of the brain, as well (Tabibnia & Lieberman 2007). In addition, the prefrontal cortex is involved when altruistic choices prevail over selfish ones (Moll et al. 2006). Decety et al. (2004) also showed that cooperation is socially rewarding and involves the orbitofrontal cortex. Additionally, mutual cooperative outcomes in the prisoner's dilemma are associated with increased activity in the anterior cingulate cortex, striatum, prefrontal cortex, and ventral striatum (Rilling et al. 2002, 2004).

Other studies have examined the activation of the reward circuit when caring for close others. Giving support to a romantic partner by holding their arm while receiving a shock activates reward circuitry, specifically the ventral striatum and septal area. Furthermore, activity in these areas correlates with self-reports of support-giving effectiveness and social connection, as well as reduced amygdala activity. Additionally, septal activity is associated with reduced bilateral amygdala activity (Inagaki & Eisenberger 2012). Dopaminergic reward areas are also activated when mothers view their own infant's face compared with that of an unknown's, implicating a role in perceiving relationship strength (K) (Strathearn et al. 2008). These regions, including ventral tegmental area and caudate nucleus, are also activated during feelings of romantic love (Bartels & Zeki 2004, Fisher et al. 2005). Collectively, these findings demonstrate the powerful role the dopamine-rich reward circuit of the brain plays in prosociality—in particular, by creating the "feeling good" effect of acting kindly (B_{self}).

Individual differences in prosocial tendencies also map onto differential sensitivity within the reward circuitry when acting prosocially. For example, there are distinct neural correlates in social value orientation (SVO), one measure of prosociality, such that in individuals who display more prosocial behavior, the anterior cingulate cortex is more active when reciprocating than when defecting and vice versa for individualistic individuals. Furthermore, insula activation relates to going against one's SVO tendencies. This study also illustrates that those in the prosocial group of SVO have more activity in the ventral striatum and prefrontal cortex than activity in baseline states, whereas those in the individualistic group experience the opposite (Van den Bos et al. 2009).

Spitzer et al. (2007) offer one more example of how differences in proclivities manifest themselves in the brain: Orbitofrontal cortex activity is strongly related to Machiavellian personality characteristics and norm compliance in the dictator game. Moreover, dopaminergic polymorphisms have also been associated with both self-reported and behavioral altruism (Bachner-Melman et al. 2005, Reuter et al. 2011). These findings highlight an interaction between D and B_{self}: Individual differences (captured by D) in sensitivity of the reward circuit boost or dampen the benefit of acting prosocially for the individual (B_{self}), thus shifting people's propensity to act prosocially in general.

Attunement to Others and Emotion Regulation: Serotonin

Prosocial actions require tuning to the needs of others and regulating self-relevant actions. Serotonin (5-HT) is a monoamine neurotransmitter with widespread functions throughout the entire nervous system; these core processes give rise to prosocial behavior. Much like the other neurotransmitters tied to prosociality, the serotonin system is extremely multifunctional and highly conserved among mammals. The serotonin system is active throughout the forebrain and has at least 14 known receptors (by comparison, oxytocin has only one known receptor), making it likely the most complex of the neurotransmitter systems involved in prosociality (Crockett 2009). It helps regulate mood, appetite, libido, sleep, and many cognitive processes. One of serotonin's theorized roles is as a behavioral inhibitor; such a role in orchestrating social cognition and emotional responses (Lesch & Waider 2012) allows it to modulate prosocial behaviors as well. And indeed, empirical data have broadly linked serotonin to a wide variety of prosocial (and antisocial) behaviors.

Serotonin is synthesized from the amino acid tryptophan and many studies have shown that acute tryptophan depletion, an experimental procedure for lowering central serotonin levels, robustly influences neural responses for key brain areas, including the amygdala, prefrontal cortex, and anterior cingulate, involved in social and emotional processes (Evers et al. 2010). Tryptophan depletion reduces the level of cooperation in participants playing an iterated prisoner's dilemma game (Wood et al. 2006). Moreover, lowering serotonin levels also increases altruistic punishment and impulsive choice in the ultimatum game (Crockett et al. 2010). In addition, depletion reduces ventral striatal responses to fairness and increases dorsal striatal responses to punishment, which is accompanied by an increase in the likelihood to punish unfair behavior in the ultimatum game (Crockett et al. 2013).

Likewise, increasing serotonin levels through selective serotonin reuptake inhibitors (SSRI), commonly used as antidepressants, also influences prosociality in "healthy" participants. For instance, SSRI administration increases a behavioral index of social affiliation (Knutson et al. 1998). In addition, enhancing serotonin causes individuals to reduce the points awarded to the self and increases cooperative messages, thereby increasing affiliative behavior and social status in a mixed-motive prisoner's dilemma game (Tse & Bond 2002). Increasing the level of this neurotransmitter also makes participants less likely to reject unfair offers in the ultimatum game. In this same study, Crockett et al. (2010) showed that individuals with high trait empathy displayed stronger effects of SSRI on moral judgment and behavior compared with those low in trait empathy.

Serotoninergic polymorphisms have been associated with individual differences in amygdala activity, vagal control of the heart, and the propensity to develop depressive and anxious symptoms (Caspi et al. 2010). This heightened stress reactivity can influence one's ability to regulate personal distress and tend to others. Indeed, genetic variation in the serotonin system relates to social learning, economic decision making, and attachment anxiety, suggesting that this association would expand to prosocial tendencies (Crişan et al. 2009).

Our SAVE framework of prosociality allows us to contextualize these findings within the broader prosociality literature. First, serotonin is clearly an important factor in shaping D, people's default proclivity toward prosociality. Those with genetic polymorphisms that promote greater levels of serotonin within their systems appear poised to act more prosocially toward people in general, showing greater restraint from aggression. Serotonin also plays a indirect role in affecting $C_{inaction}$. When people experience reductions in serotonin levels, they engage in greater altruistic punishment (Crockett et al. 2008), which suggests that those with low baseline serotonin levels act at least in part as "prosociality enforcers" within society—punishing violators of the fairness norm.

THE POOR GIVE MORE: THE CASE OF SOCIAL CLASS AND PROSOCIAL BEHAVIOR

Our SAVE framework points to several promising lines of inquiry in the study of cultural variations in prosociality. For example, in accounting for cultural variation in prosociality across 15 societies, Henrich and colleagues theorize that it is economic interdependence that gives rise to increased prosociality. We suggest that such interdependence alters the D component of our framework, the local default tendency toward different forms of prosociality. The emergence of certain memes—units of cultural information—such as the Golden Rule (Armstrong 2009) during certain historical periods quite sensibly would alter the M component. Historical changes in privacy, and the extent to which one's behavior is publicly monitored, would change the role of reputation and, in turn, the benefits of acting prosocially (B_{self}) and the costs of inaction ($C_{inaction}$). Technological innovation and trends toward globalization have given rise to increased connections and contact among individuals from different groups and nations, in turn boosting K by increasing people's sense of self–other similarity with an ever-expanding and diverse community of individuals.

Perhaps the most developed literature that fits within our analysis of cultural variations is that on social class. Defined in terms of a person's wealth, education, and prestige of work relative to others in society (Adler et al. 2000, Oakes & Rossi 2003), social class exerts a pervasive influence on people's social cognitive tendencies (for review, see Kraus et al. 2012). In our own research, we have investigated how social class influences prosocial behavior.

In several different studies, we found that upper-class individuals are less altruistic than lower-class individuals. They endorse fewer contributions to charity, share less in economic games, and are less inclined to help those who are in need (Piff et al. 2010). They even behave more unethically—for instance, by cheating in a game—to maximize self-interest (Piff et al. 2012b).

The finding that those with more tend to give less may seem inherently paradoxical. However, a more detailed consideration of the person- and situation-level factors that vary by social class yields deeper insight into the class–prosociality link. Upper-class individuals tend to have more independence and control over others (Adler et al. 2000), and they value their independence over social connection (Piff et al. 2012b, Stephens et al. 2007). By contrast, individuals from lower-class backgrounds are more interdependent: They spend more time taking care of others (Argyle 1994), have stronger extended family ties (Lareau 2002), and are more embedded in social networks that depend on reciprocal aid (Lamont 2000). These findings suggest that among lower-class individuals there exist norms and values that specifically reinforce prosocial behavior and communal relationships (D), and the frequency at which lower-class individuals observe instances of prosocial behavior and helping may be relatively high (the M component of our framework). By contrast, the norms and values of upper-class individuals may be oriented more toward individual achievement and self-interest, and the perceived rates of helping behavior in their social networks and environments may be relatively low.

Individuals from different social class groups also diverge in their perceptions of others (K). Recent studies suggest that lower-class individuals are more empathic and compassionate than their upper-class counterparts across self-report, physiological, and neurological measures of these constructs (Kraus et al. 2010, Stellar et al. 2012). Class differences in perceptions of and sensitivity to others should drive differential levels of prosociality (e.g., Batson & Shaw 1991). Indeed, when individuals from upper-class backgrounds were made to feel compassion via an experimental manipulation, class-based differences in prosocial helping behavior—which were otherwise observable in a control condition—virtually disappeared (Piff et al. 2010).

The perceived costs and benefits of prosocial behavior are also likely to vary as a function of social class. Upper-class individuals have more privacy and freedom from observation, which may reduce the cost of inaction ($C_{inaction}$). Upper-class individuals are also less likely to rely on others for assistance (Piff et al. 2012c), which could undermine the perceived benefits of prosocial behavior (B_{self}). By contrast, selfishness may be more costly for lower-class individuals, who reside in communities in which decency and kindness are central to one's reputation (Lamont 2000). Lower-class individuals also rely more on their relationships to cope (in contrast with upper-class individuals, who prioritize individual forms of coping; Piff et al. 2012c), which should heighten the perceived personal benefits of prosocial action.

$$M^*(D^*(1 + B_{self}) + K^*B_{recipient} - C_{inaction}) > C_{action}$$

Let us now return to our SAVE framework to synthesize the above insights. Lower-class people exist within more prosocial communities, leading to altruistic contagion and other mechanisms that boost D (bias and perceptions independent of the recipient) as well as M (the social momentum for prosocial action). Lower-class people also rely more on others and reputation is more centrally important, making the benefit to self (B_{self}) of prosocial behavior higher than it is for upper-class individuals. Findings also suggest that lower-class individuals experience greater compassion, thus boosting the K component (perceived need and self–other similarity). Thus, although the cost of action (C_{action}) is higher among lower-class people, the factors that promote prosocial behavior on the left side of the equation are higher as well. Given that lower-class individuals have proven to be more prosocial than higher-class individuals across a variety of contexts, the increases on the left side of the equation are likely to be greater—and potentially much greater—than those on the right side for lower-class individuals as compared with upper-class people.

CONCLUSION

Since at least the time of Darwin, scientists have grappled with the question of how, and why, behavior that is costly to the self but beneficial to others can emerge. In our review, we have aimed to synthesize the confluence of psychological factors that shape the individual's inclinations toward prosociality. We have focused our efforts on encapsulating these varied factors within our SAVE framework, capturing the default bias toward prosociality, perceptions of recipients, emotional and reputation benefits to the self for acting prosocially, the potential costs of not acting prosocially, and the social momentum of a prosocial action—all factors that are central to prosocial responding. We have focused our review on emergent studies at four levels of analysis: the individual, dyad, group, and culture. In offering our synthetic SAVE framework, and casting our net broadly across levels of analysis, we hope new studies will continue to examine the proposition that sympathy is one of humanity's strongest instincts.

DISCLOSURE STATEMENT

The authors are not aware of any affiliations, memberships, funding, or financial holdings that might be perceived as affecting the objectivity of this review.

LITERATURE CITED

Adler NE, Epel ES, Castellazzo G, Ickovics JR. 2000. Relationship of subjective and objective social status with psychological and physiological functioning: preliminary data in healthy white women. *Health Psychol.* 19(6):586–92

Aknin LB, Barrington-Leigh CP, Dunn EW, Helliwell JF, Burns J, et al. 2013. Prosocial spending and well-being: cross-cultural evidence for a psychological universal. *J. Personal. Soc. Psychol.* 104(4):635–52

Albrechtsen JS, Meissner CA, Susa KJ. 2009. Can intuition improve deception detection performance? *J. Exp. Soc. Psychol.* 45(4):1052–55

Algoe SB, Haidt J. 2009. Witnessing excellence in action: the "other-praising" emotions of elevation, gratitude, and admiration. *J. Posit. Psychol.* 4(2):105–27

Algoe SB, Haidt J, Gable SL. 2008. Beyond reciprocity: gratitude and relationships in everyday life. *Emotion* 8(3):425–29

Ambady N, Bernieri FJ, Richeson JA. 2000. Toward a histology of social behavior: judgmental accuracy from thin slices of the behavioral stream. *Adv. Exp. Soc. Psychol.* 32:201–71

Ambady N, Hallahan M, Conner B. 1999. Accuracy of judgments of sexual orientation from thin slices of behavior. *J. Personal. Soc. Psychol.* 77(3):538–47

Anderson C, John OP, Keltner D, Kring AM. 2001. Who attains social status? Effects of personality and physical attractiveness in social groups. *J. Personal. Soc. Psychol.* 81(1):116–32

Anderson C, Shirako A. 2008. Are individuals' reputations related to their history of behavior? *J. Personal. Soc. Psychol.* 94(2):320–33

Argyle M. 1994. *The Psychology of Social Class.* London: Routledge

Armstrong K. 2009. *The Case for God: What Religion Really Means.* New York: Knopf

Atzil S, Hendler T, Feldman R. 2011. Specifying the neurobiological basis of human attachment: brain, hormones, and behavior in synchronous and intrusive mothers. *Neuropsychopharmacology* 36(13):2603–15

Axelrod R. 1984. *The Evolution of Cooperation.* New York: Basic Books

Bachner-Melman R, Gritsenko I, Nemanov L, Zohar AH, Dina C, Ebstein RP. 2005. Dopaminergic polymorphisms associated with self-report measures of human altruism: a fresh phenotype for the dopamine D4 receptor. *Mol. Psychiatry* 10(4):333–35

Bachorowski JA, Owren MJ. 2001. Not all laughs are alike: Voiced but not unvoiced laughter readily elicits positive affect. *Psychol. Sci.* 12(3):252–57

Balliet D, Mulder LB, Van Lange PM. 2011. Reward, punishment, and cooperation: a meta-analysis. *Psychol. Bull.* 137(4):594–615

Barraza JA, Zak PJ. 2009. Empathy toward strangers triggers oxytocin release and subsequent generosity. *Ann. N.Y. Acad. Sci.* 1167:182–89

Bartels A, Zeki S. 2004. The neural correlates of maternal and romantic love. *NeuroImage* 21(3):1155–66

Bartlett MY, DeSteno D. 2006. Gratitude and prosocial behavior: helping when it costs you. *Psychol. Sci.* 17(4):319–25

Bartz JA, Zaki J, Bolger N, Ochsner KN. 2011. Social effects of oxytocin in humans: Context and person matter. *Trends Cogn. Sci.* 15(7):301–9

Batson CD, Shaw LL. 1991. Evidence for altruism: toward a pluralism of prosocial motives. *Psychol. Inq.* 2(2):107–22

Beauchaine T. 2001. Vagal tone, development, and Gray's motivational theory: toward an integrated model of autonomic nervous system functioning in psychopathology. *Dev. Psychopathol.* 13(2):183–214

Beersma B, Van Kleef GA. 2011. How the grapevine keeps you in line: Gossip increases contributions to the group. *Soc. Psychol. Personal. Sci.* 2(6):642–49

Belin D, Everitt BJ. 2008. Cocaine seeking habits depend upon dopamine-dependent serial connectivity linking the ventral with the dorsal striatum. *Neuron* 57(3):432–41

Bernhardt BC, Singer T. 2012. The neural basis of empathy. *Annu. Rev. Neurosci.* 35:1–23

Borkenau P, Mauer N, Riemann R, Spinath FM, Angleitner A. 2004. Thin slices of behavior as cues of personality and intelligence. *J. Personal. Soc. Psychol.* 86(4):599–614

Bornstein MH, Suess PE. 2000. Physiological self-regulation and information processing in infancy: cardiac vagal tone and habituation. *Child Dev.* 71(2):273–87

Bowlby J. 1969. *Attachment.* New York: Basic Books

Boyd R, Gintis H, Bowles S, Richerson PJ. 2003. The evolution of altruistic punishment. *Proc. Natl. Acad. Sci. USA* 100(6):3531–35

Brown R, González R, Zagefka H, Manzi J, Cehajic S. 2008. Nuestra culpa: collective guilt and shame as predictors of reparation for historical wrongdoing. *J. Personal. Soc. Psychol.* 94(1):75–90

Bshary R, Bergmüller R. 2008. Distinguishing four fundamental approaches to the evolution of helping. *J. Evol. Biol.* 21(2):405–20

Burt RS, Kilduff M, Tasselli S. 2013. Social network analysis: foundations and frontiers on advantage. *Annu. Rev. Psychol.* 64:527–47

Butler EA, Wilhelm FH, Gross JJ. 2006. Respiratory sinus arrhythmia, emotion, and emotion regulation during social interaction. *Psychophysiology* 43(6):612–22

Camerer CF. 2003. *Behavioral Game Theory: Experiments in Strategic Interaction.* Princeton, NJ: Princeton Univ. Press

Carter CS. 1998. Neuroendocrine perspectives on social attachment and love. *Psychoneuroendocrinology* 23(8):779–818

Carter CS, Grippo AJ, Pournajafi-Nazarloo H, Ruscio MG, Porges SW. 2008. Oxytocin, vasopressin and sociality. *Prog. Brain Res.* 170(8):331–36

Caspi A, Hariri AR, Holmes A, Uher R, Moffitt TE. 2010. Genetic sensitivity to the environment: the case of the serotonin transporter gene and its implications for studying complex diseases and traits. *Am. J. Psychiatry* 167(5):509–27

Christakis NA, Fowler JH. 2009. *Connected: The Surprising Power of Our Social Networks and How They Shape Our Lives.* New York: Little, Brown

Cialdini RB, Trost MR. 1998. Social influence: social norms, conformity, and compliance. In *The Handbook of Social Psychology*, ed. DT Gilbert, ST Fiske, G Lindzey, pp. 151–92. New York: McGraw-Hill. 4th ed.

Cohen AB. 2009. Many forms of culture. *Am. Psychol.* 64(3):194–204

Cohen TR, Panter AT, Turan N. 2013. Predicting counterproductive work behavior from guilt proneness. *J. Bus. Ethics.* 114:45–53

Cohen TR, Wildschut T, Insko CA. 2010. How communication increases interpersonal cooperation in mixed-motive situations. *J. Exp. Soc. Psychol.* 46(1):39–50

Cohen TR, Wolf ST, Panter AT, Insko CA. 2011. Introducing the GASP scale: a new measure of guilt and shame proneness. *J. Personal. Soc. Psychol.* 100(5):947–66

Côté S, Kraus MW, Cheng BH, Oveis C, Van der Löwe I, et al. 2011. Social power facilitates the effect of prosocial orientation on empathic accuracy. *J. Personal. Soc. Psychol.* 101(2):217–32

Craik KH. 2009. *Reputation: A Network Interpretation.* New York: Oxford Univ. Press

Crişan LG, Pana S, Vulturar R, Heilman RM, Szekely R, et al. 2009. Genetic contributions of the serotonin transporter to social learning of fear and economic decision making. *Soc. Cogn. Affect. Neurosci.* 4(4):399–408

Crocker J. 2008. From egosystem to ecosystem: implications for relationships, learning, and well-being. In *Transcending Self-Interest: Psychological Explorations of the Quiet Ego*, ed. HA Wayment, JJ Bauer, pp. 63–72. Washington, DC: Am. Psychol. Assoc.

Crockett MJ. 2009. The neurochemistry of fairness: clarifying the link between serotonin and prosocial behavior. *Ann. N. Y. Acad. Sci.* 1167:76–86

Crockett MJ, Apergis-Schoute A, Herrmann B, Lieberman M, Müller U, et al. 2013. Serotonin modulates striatal responses to fairness and retaliation in humans. *J. Neurosci.* 33(8):3505–13

Crockett MJ, Clark L, Hauser MD, Robbins TW. 2010. Serotonin selectively influences moral judgment and behavior through effects on harm aversion. *Proc. Natl. Acad. Sci. USA* 107(40):17433–38

Crockett MJ, Clark L, Tabibnia G, Lieberman MD, Robbins TW. 2008. Serotonin modulates behavioral reactions to unfairness. *Science* 320:1739

Danner DD, Snowdon DA, Friesen WV. 2001. Positive emotions in early life and longevity: findings from the nun study. *J. Personal. Soc. Psychol.* 80(5):804–13

Darley JM, Batson CD. 1973. "From Jerusalem to Jericho": a study of situational and dispositional variables in helping behavior. *J. Personal. Soc. Psychol.* 27:100–8

Darwin C. 1871. *The Origin of the Species and the Descent of Man*. Chestnut Hill, MA: Adamant Media Corp.

De Dreu CKW, Greer LL, Handgraaf MJJ, Shalvi S, Van Kleef GA, et al. 2010. The neuropeptide oxytocin regulates parochial altruism in intergroup conflict among humans. *Science* 328:1408–11

De Dreu CKW, Greer LL, Van Kleef GA, Shalvi S, Handgraaf MJJ. 2011. Oxytocin promotes human ethnocentrism. *Proc. Natl. Acad. Sci. USA* 108(4):1262–66

De Waal FBM. 2008. Putting the altruism back into altruism: the evolution of empathy. *Annu. Rev. Psychol.* 59:279–300

De Waal FBM. 2009. *Primates and Philosophers: How Morality Evolved*. Princeton, NJ: Princeton Univ. Press

De Waal FBM. 2012. The antiquity of empathy. *Science* 336:874–76

De Waal FBM, Lanting F. 1997. *Bonobo: The Forgotten Ape*. Berkeley/Los Angeles: Univ. Calif. Press

Decety J, Jackson PL, Sommerville JA, Chaminade T, Meltzoff AN. 2004. The neural bases of cooperation and competition: an fMRI investigation. *NeuroImage* 23(2):744–51

Decety J, Svetlova M. 2012. Putting together phylogenetic and ontogenetic perspectives on empathy. *Dev. Cogn. Neurosci.* 2(1):1–24

Delgado MR. 2007. Reward-related responses in the human striatum. *Ann. N.Y. Acad. Sci.* 1104:70–88

Delgado MR, Frank RH, Phelps EA. 2005. Perceptions of moral character modulate the neural systems of reward during the trust game. *Nat. Neurosci.* 8(11):1611–18

DeSteno D, Bartlett MY, Baumann J, Williams LA, Dickens L. 2010. Gratitude as moral sentiment: emotion-guided cooperation in economic exchange. *Emotion* 10(2):289–93

Diener E, Lucas R, Scollon CN. 2006. Beyond the hedonic treadmill: revising the adaptation theory of well-being. *Am. Psychol.* 61:305–14

Diener E, Tay L, Myers DG. 2011. The religion paradox: If religion makes people happy, why are so many dropping out? *J. Personal. Soc. Psychol.* 101(6):1278–90

Dixon EM, Kamath MV, McCartney N, Fallen EL. 1992. Neural regulation of heart rate variability in endurance athletes and sedentary controls. *Cardiovasc. Res.* 26(7):713–19

Domes G, Heinrichs M, Gläscher J, Büchel C, Braus DF, Herpertz SC. 2007a. Oxytocin attenuates amygdala responses to emotional faces regardless of valence. *Biol. Psychiatry* 62(10):1187–90

Domes G, Heinrichs M, Michel A, Berger C, Herpertz SC. 2007b. Oxytocin improves "mind-reading" in humans. *Biol. Psychiatry* 61(6):731–33

Donaldson ZR, Young LJ. 2008. Oxytocin, vasopressin, and the neurogenetics of sociality. *Science* 322:900–4

Dunn EW, Aknin LB, Norton MI. 2008. Spending money on others promotes happiness. *Science* 319:1687–88

Effron DA, Miller DT. 2011. Diffusion of entitlement: an inhibitory effect of scarcity on consumption. *J. Exp. Soc. Psychol.* 47(2):378–83

Eisenberg N, Fabes RA, Miller PA, Fultz J. 1989. Relation of sympathy and personal distress to prosocial behavior: a multimethod study. *J. Personal. Soc. Psychol.* 57(1):55–66

Eisenberg N, Fabes RA, Murphy B, Maszk P, Smith M, Karbon M. 1995. The role of emotionality and regulation in children's social functioning: a longitudinal study. *Child Dev.* 66(5):1360–84

Eisenberger NI, Cole SW. 2012. Social neuroscience and health: neurophysiological mechanisms linking social ties with physical health. *Nat. Neurosci.* 15(5):669–74

Emler N. 1994. Gossip, reputation, and social adaptation. In *Good Gossip*, ed. R Goodman, A Ben-Ze'ev, pp. 117–33. Lawrence: Univ. Kans. Press

Evers EAT, Sambeth A, Ramaekers JG, Riedel WJ, Van der Veen FM. 2010. The effects of acute tryptophan depletion on brain activation during cognition and emotional processing in healthy volunteers. *Curr. Pharm. Des.* 16(18):1998–2011

Fabes RA, Eisenberg N. 1997. Regulatory control and adults' stress-related responses to daily life events. *J. Personal. Soc. Psychol.* 73(5):1107–17

Fehr E, Bernhard H, Rockenbach B. 2008. Egalitarianism in young children. *Nature* 454:1079–83

Fehr E, Fischbacher U. 2003. The nature of human altruism. *Nature* 425:785–91

Fehr E, Fischbacher U. 2004. Social norms and human cooperation. *Trends Cogn. Sci.* 8(4):185–90

Fehr E, Gächter S. 2002. Altruistic punishment in humans. *Nature* 415:137–40

Feinberg M, Willer R, Keltner D. 2012a. Flustered and faithful: embarrassment as a signal of prosociality. *J. Personal. Soc. Psychol.* 102(1):81–97

Feinberg M, Willer R, Stellar J, Keltner D. 2012b. The virtues of gossip: reputational information sharing as prosocial behavior. *J. Personal. Soc. Psychol.* 102(5):1015–30

Feldman R. 2012. Oxytocin and social affiliation in humans. *Horm. Behav.* 61(3):380–91

Feldman R, Gordon I, Influs M, Gutbir T, Ebstein RP. 2013. Parental oxytocin and early caregiving jointly shape children's oxytocin response and social reciprocity. *Neuropsychopharmacology* 38:1154–62

Felps W, Mitchell TR, Byington E. 2006. How, when, and why bad apples spoil the barrel: negative group members and dysfunctional groups. *Res. Organ. Behav.* 27:175–222

Fisher H, Aron A, Brown LL. 2005. Romantic love: an fMRI study of a neural mechanism for mate choice. *J. Comp. Neurol.* 493(1):58–62

Fiske ST, Cuddy AJC, Glick P. 2007. Universal dimensions of social cognition: warmth and competence. *Trends Cogn. Sci.* 11(2):77–83

Flynn FJ, Reagans RE, Amanatullah ET, Ames DR. 2006. Helping one's way to the top: Self-monitors achieve status by helping others and knowing who helps whom. *J. Personal. Soc. Psychol.* 91(6):1123–37

Fowler JH. 2005. Altruistic punishment and the origin of cooperation. *Proc. Natl. Acad. Sci. USA* 102(19):7047–49

Fowler JH, Christakis NA. 2010. Cooperative behavior cascades in human social networks. *Proc. Natl. Acad. Sci. USA* 107(12):5334–38

Fowler KA, Lilienfeld SO, Patrick CJ. 2009. Detecting psychopathy from thin slices of behavior. *Psychol. Assess.* 21(1):68–78

Frank R. 1988. *Passions Within Reason: The Strategic Role of the Emotions*. New York: Norton

Fredrickson BL. 2001. The role of positive emotions in positive psychology. The broaden-and-build theory of positive emotions. *Am. Psychol.* 56(3):218–26

Fredrickson BL, Cohn MA, Coffey KA, Pek J, Finkel SM. 2008. Open hearts build lives: Positive emotions, induced through loving-kindness meditation, build consequential personal resources. *J. Personal. Soc. Psychol.* 95(5):1045–62

Fu F, Hauert C, Nowak M, Wang L. 2008. Reputation-based partner choice promotes cooperation in social networks. *Phys. Rev. E* 78(2):026117

Gailliot MT, Stillman TF, Schmeichel BJ, Maner JK, Plant EA. 2008. Mortality salience increases adherence to salient norms and values. *Personal. Soc. Psychol. Bull.* 34(7):993–1003

Gimpl G, Fahrenholz F. 2001. The oxytocin receptor system: structure, function, and regulation. *Physiol. Rev.* 81(2):629–83

Gipple E, Gose B. 2012. America's generosity divide. *Chron. Philanthr.* Aug. 19. **http://philanthropy.com/article/America-s-Generosity-Divide/133775/**

Goetz JL, Keltner D, Simon-Thomas E. 2010. Compassion: an evolutionary analysis and empirical review. *Psychol. Bull.* 136(3):351–74

Goldstein NJ, Cialdini RB, Griskevicius V. 2008. A room with a viewpoint: using social norms to motivate environmental conservation in hotels. *J. Consum. Res.* 35(3):472–82

Gonzaga GC, Keltner D, Londahl EA, Smith MD. 2001. Love and the commitment problem in romantic relations and friendship. *J. Personal. Soc. Psychol.* 81(2):247–62

Gonzaga GC, Turner RA, Keltner D, Campos B, Altemus M. 2006. Romantic love and sexual desire in close relationships. *Emotion* 6(2):163–79

Gordon AM, Impett EA, Kogan A, Oveis C, Keltner D. 2012. To have and to hold: Gratitude promotes relationship maintenance in intimate bonds. *J. Personal. Soc. Psychol.* 103(2):257–74

Grant AM, Berry J. 2011. The necessity of others is the mother of invention: intrinsic and prosocial motivations, perspective taking, and creativity. *Acad. Manag. J.* 54(1):73–96

Grant AM, Gino F. 2010. A little thanks goes a long way: explaining why gratitude expressions motivate prosocial behavior. *J. Personal. Soc. Psychol.* 98(6):946–55

Graziano WG, Habashi MM, Sheese BE, Tobin RM. 2007. Agreeableness, empathy, and helping: a person x situation perspective. *J. Personal. Soc. Psychol.* 93(4):583–99

Grewen KM, Light KC. 2011. Plasma oxytocin is related to lower cardiovascular and sympathetic reactivity to stress. *Biol. Psychiatry* 87(3):340–49

Griskevicius V, Tybur JM, Van den Bergh B. 2010. Going green to be seen: status, reputation, and conspicuous conservation. *J. Personal. Soc. Psychol.* 98(3):392–404

Grossman P, Kollai M. 1993. Respiratory sinus arrhythmia, cardiac vagal tone, and respiration: within- and between-individual relations. *Psychophysiology* 30(5):486–95

Gunnthorsdottir A, McCabe K, Smith V. 2002. Using the Machiavellianism instrument to predict trustworthiness in a bargaining game. *J. Econ. Psychol.* 23(1):49–66

Gurven M. 2004. Reciprocal altruism and food sharing decisions among Hiwi and Ache hunter/gatherers. *Behav. Ecol. Sociobiol.* 56(4):366–80

Güth W, Schmittberger R, Schwarze B. 1982. An experimental analysis of ultimatum bargaining. *J. Econ. Behav. Organ.* 3(4):367–88

Hamilton WD. 1964. The genetical evolution of social behaviour. *J. Theoret. Biol.* 7(1):1–52

Hamlin JK, Wynn K, Bloom P. 2007. Social evaluation by preverbal infants. *Nature* 450:557–59

Hamlin JK, Wynn K, Bloom P. 2010. Three-month-olds show a negativity bias in their social evaluations. *Dev. Sci.* 13(6):923–29

Hamlin JK, Wynn K, Bloom P, Mahajan N. 2011. How infants and toddlers react to antisocial others. *Proc. Natl. Acad. Sci. USA* 108(50):19931–36

Hansen AL, Johnsen BH, Thayer JF. 2003. Vagal influence on working memory and attention. *Int. J. Psychophysiol.* 48(3):263–74

Harbaugh WT, Mayr U, Burghart DR. 2007. Neural responses to taxation and voluntary giving reveal motives for charitable donations. *Science* 316:1622–25

Hardy CL, Van Vugt M. 2006. Nice guys finish first: the competitive altruism hypothesis. *Personal. Soc. Psychol. Bull.* 32(10):1402–13

Harker L, Keltner D. 2001. Expressions of positive emotion in women's college yearbook pictures and their relationship to personality and life outcomes across adulthood. *J. Personal. Soc. Psychol.* 80(1):112–24

Hatfield E, Cacioppo JT, Rapson RL. 1993. Emotional contagion. *Curr. Dir. Psychol. Sci.* 2(3):96–99

Henrich J. 2004. Cultural group selection, coevolutionary processes and large-scale cooperation. *J. Econ. Behav. Organ.* 53(1):3–35

Henrich J, Boyd R, Bowles S, Camerer C. 2001. In search of homo economicus: behavioral experiments in 15 small-scale societies. *Am. Econ. Rev.* 91(2):73–79

Henrich J, Boyd R, Bowles S, Camerer C, Fehr E, et al. 2005. "Economic man" in cross-cultural perspective: behavioral experiments in 15 small-scale societies. *Behav. Brain Sci.* 28(6):795–815

Henrich J, Boyd R, Bowles S, Camerer CF, Fehr E, Gintis H. 2004. *Foundations of Human Sociality: Economic Experiments and Ethnographic Evidence from Fifteen Small-Scale Societies.* Oxford, UK: Oxford Univ. Press

Henrich J, McElreath R, Barr A, Ensminger J, Barrett C, et al. 2006. Costly punishment across human societies. *Science* 312:1767–70

Hertenstein MJ, Keltner D, App B, Bulleit BA, Jaskolka AR. 2006. Touch communicates distinct emotions. *Emotion* 6(3):528–33

Holt-Lunstad J, Birmingham WA, Light KC. 2008. Influence of a "warm touch" support enhancement intervention among married couples on ambulatory blood pressure, oxytocin, alpha amylase, and cortisol. *Psychosom. Med.* 70(9):976–85

Impett EA, Gordon AM, Kogan A, Oveis C, Gable SL, Keltner D. 2010. Moving toward more perfect unions: daily and long-term consequences of approach and avoidance goals in romantic relationships. *J. Personal. Soc. Psychol.* 99(6):948–63

Inagaki TK, Eisenberger NI. 2012. Neural correlates of giving support to a loved one. *Psychosom. Med.* 74(1):3–7

Israel S, Lerer E, Shalev I, Uzefovsky F, Riebold M, et al. 2009. The oxytocin receptor (OXTR) contributes to prosocial fund allocations in the dictator game and the social value orientations task. *PLoS ONE* 4(5):e5535

Jenkins JS, Ang VTY, Hawthorn J, Rossor MN, Iversen LL. 1984. Vasopressin, oxytocin and neurophysins in the human brain and spinal cord. *Brain Res.* 291(1):111–17

Jonas E, Martens A, Kayser DN, Fritsche I, Sullivan D, Greenberg J. 2008. Focus theory of normative conduct and Terror-Management Theory: the interactive impact of mortality salience and norm salience on social judgment. *J. Personal. Soc. Psychol.* 95(6):1239–51

Judge TA, Bono JE, Ilies R, Gerhardt MW. 2002. Personality and leadership: a qualitative and quantitative review. *J. Appl. Psychol.* 87(4):765–80

Keltner D. 2009. *Born to Be Good: The Science of a Meaningful Life*. New York: Norton

Keltner D, Van Kleef GA, Chen S, Kraus MW. 2008. A reciprocal influence model of social power: emerging principles and lines of inquiry. *Adv. Exp. Soc. Psychol.* 40:151–92

Knafo A, Israel S, Darvasi A, Bachner-Melman R, Uzefovsky F, et al. 2008. Individual differences in allocation of funds in the dictator game associated with length of the arginine vasopressin 1a receptor RS3 promoter region and correlation between RS3 length and hippocampal mRNA. *Genes Brain Behav.* 7(3):266–75

Kniffin KM, Wilson DS. 2005. Utilities of gossip across organizational levels. *Hum. Nat.* 16(3):278–92

Knutson B, Wolkowitz OM, Cole SW, Chan T, Moore EA, et al. 1998. Selective alteration of personality and social behavior by serotonergic intervention. *Am. J. Psychiatry* 155(3):373–79

Kogan A, Impett EA, Oveis C, Hui B, Gordon AM, Keltner D. 2010. When giving feels good: the intrinsic benefits of sacrifice in romantic relationships for the communally motivated. *Psychol. Sci.* 21(12):1918–24

Kogan A, Saslow LR, Impett EA, Oveis C, Keltner D, et al. 2011. Thin-slicing study of the oxytocin receptor (OXTR) gene and the evaluation and expression of the prosocial disposition. *Proc. Natl. Acad. Sci. USA* 108(48):19189–92

Kok BE, Fredrickson BL. 2010. Upward spirals of the heart: Autonomic flexibility, as indexed by vagal tone, reciprocally and prospectively predicts positive emotions and social connectedness. *Biol. Psychol.* 85(3):432–36

Kosfeld M, Heinrichs M, Zak PJ, Fischbacher U, Fehr E. 2005. Oxytocin increases trust in humans. *Nature* 435:673–76

Kraus MW, Côté S, Keltner D. 2010. Social class, contextualism, and empathic accuracy. *Psychol. Sci.* 21:1716–23

Kraus MW, Huang C, Keltner D. 2010. Tactile communication, cooperation, and performance: an ethological study of the NBA. *Emotion* 10(5):745–49

Kraus MW, Keltner D. 2009. Signs of socioeconomic status: a thin-slicing approach. *Psychol. Sci.* 20(1):99–106

Kraus MW, Piff PK, Mendoza-Denton R, Rheinschmidt ML, Keltner D. 2012. Social class, solipsism, and contextualism: how the rich are different from the poor. *Psychol. Rev.* 119(3):546–72

Krupka E, Weber RA. 2009. The focusing and informational effects of norms on pro-social behavior. *J. Econ. Psychol.* 30(3):307–20

Kurzban R. 2001. The social psychophysics of cooperation: nonverbal communication in a public goods game. *J. Nonverbal Behav.* 25(4):241–59

Lamont M. 2000. *The Dignity of Working Men: Morality and the Boundaries of Race, Class, and Immigration*. New York: Russell Sage Found.

Langergraber KE, Mitani JC, Vigilant L. 2007. The limited impact of kinship on cooperation in wild chimpanzees. *Proc. Natl. Acad. Sci. USA* 104(19):7786–90

Lareau A. 2002. Invisible inequality: social class and childrearing in black families and white families. *Am. Sociol. Rev.* 67(5):747–76

Le BM, Impett EA, Kogan A, Webster GD, Cheng C. 2013. The personal and interpersonal rewards of communal orientation. *J. Soc. Personal Relatsh.* 30:694–710

Lesch K-P, Waider J. 2012. Serotonin in the modulation of neural plasticity and networks: implications for neurodevelopmental disorders. *Neuron* 76(1):175–91

Lyubomirsky S, King L, Diener E. 2005. The benefits of frequent positive affect: Does happiness lead to success? *Psychol. Bull.* 131(6):803–55

McCrae RR, Sutin AR. 2009. Openness to experience and its social consequences. In *Handbook of Individual Differences in Social Behavior*, ed. MR Leary, H Hoyle, pp. 257–73. New York: Guilford

McCullough ME, Kilpatrick SD, Emmons RA, Larson DB. 2001. Is gratitude a moral affect? *Psychol. Bull.* 127(2):249–66

McCullough ME, Tsang J-A, Emmons RA. 2004. Gratitude in intermediate affective terrain: links of grateful moods to individual differences and daily emotional experience. *J. Personal. Soc. Psychol.* 86(2):295–309

Meyer-Lindenberg A. 2008. Impact of prosocial neuropeptides on human brain function. *Prog. Brain Res.* 170:463–70

Mikulincer M, Shaver PR, eds. 2009. *Prosocial Motives, Emotions, and Behavior: The Better Angels of Our Nature.* Washington, DC: Am. Psychol. Assoc.

Milinski M, Semmann D, Bakker TC, Krambeck H-J. 2001. Cooperation through indirect reciprocity: image scoring or standing strategy? *Proc. R. Soc. B* 268(1484):2495–501

Milinski M, Semmann D, Krambeck H-J. 2002. Reputation helps solve the "tragedy of the commons." *Nature* 415:424–26

Moll J, Krueger F, Zahn R, Pardini M, De Oliveira-Souza R, Grafman J. 2006. Human fronto-mesolimbic networks guide decisions about charitable donation. *Proc. Natl. Acad. Sci. USA* 103(42):15623–28

Monroe K. 1996. *The Heart of Altruism: Perceptions of a Common Humanity.* Princeton, NJ: Princeton Univ. Press

Monroe K. 2004. *The Hand of Compassion: Portraits of Moral Choice During the Holocaust.* Princeton, NJ: Princeton Univ. Press

Moorman RH, Blakely GL. 1995. Individualism-collectivism as an individual difference predictor of organizational citizenship behavior. *J. Organ. Behav.* 16(2):127–42

Nesse RM. 1990. Evolutionary explanations of emotions. *Hum. Nat.* 1(3):261–89

Nesse RM, Ellsworth PC. 2009. Evolution, emotions, and emotional disorders. *Am. Psychol.* 64(2):129–39

Norenzayan A, Shariff AF. 2008. The origin and evolution of religious prosociality. *Science* 322:58–62

Norman GJ, Hawkley L, Luhmann M, Ball AB, Cole SW, et al. 2012. Variation in the oxytocin receptor gene influences neurocardiac reactivity to social stress and HPA function: a population based study. *Horm. Behav.* 61(1):134–39

Nowak MA. 2006. Five rules for the evolution of cooperation. *Science* 314:1560–63

Nowak MA, Page KM, Sigmund K. 2000. Fairness versus reason in the ultimatum game. *Science* 289:1773–75

Nowak MA, Roch S. 2007. Upstream reciprocity and the evolution of gratitude. *Proc. R. Soc. B* 274(1610):605–9

Nowak MA, Sigmund K. 1998. Evolution of indirect reciprocity by image scoring. *Nature* 393:573–77

Nowak MA, Sigmund K. 2005. Evolution of indirect reciprocity. *Nature* 437:1291–98

Oakes JM, Rossi PH. 2003. The measurement of SES in health research: current practice and steps toward a new approach. *Soc. Sci. Med.* 56(4):769–84

Oltmanns TF, Friedman JN, Fiedler ER, Turkheimer E. 2004. Perceptions of people with personality disorders based on thin slices of behavior. *J. Res. Personal.* 38(3):216–29

Omoto AM, Snyder M, Hackett JD. 2010. Personality and motivational antecedents of activism and civic engagement. *J. Personal.* 78(6):1703–34

Oveis C, Cohen AB, Gruber J, Shiota MN, Haidt J, Keltner D. 2009. Resting respiratory sinus arrhythmia is associated with tonic positive emotionality. *Emotion* 9(2):265–70

Oyserman D, Coon HM, Kemmelmeier M. 2002. Rethinking individualism and collectivism: evaluation of theoretical assumptions and meta-analyses. *Psychol. Bull.* 128(1):3–72

Oyserman D, Lee SWS. 2008. Does culture influence what and how we think? Effects of priming individualism and collectivism. *Psychol. Bull.* 134(2):311–42

Panksepp J. 2007. The neuroevolutionary and neuroaffective psychobiology of the prosocial brain. In *The Oxford Handbook of Evolutionary Psychology*, ed. RIM Dunbar, L Barrett, pp. 145–62. Oxford, UK: Oxford Univ. Press

Penner LA, Dovidio JF, Piliavin JA, Schroeder DA. 2005. Prosocial behavior: multilevel perspectives. *Annu. Rev. Psychol.* 56(1):365–92

Piferi RL, Lawler KA. 2006. Social support and ambulatory blood pressure: an examination of both receiving and giving. *Int. J. Psychophysiol.* 62(2):328–36

Piff PK, Kraus MW, Côté S, Cheng BH, Keltner D. 2010. Having less, giving more: the influence of social class on prosocial behavior. *J. Personal. Soc. Psychol.* 99(5):771–84

Piff PK, Purcell A, Gruber J, Hertenstein MJ, Keltner D. 2012a. Contact high: mania proneness and positive perception of emotional touches. *Cogn. Emot.* 26(6):1116–23

Piff PK, Stancato D, Côté S, Mendoza-Dentona R, Keltner D. 2012b. Higher social class predicts increased unethical behavior. *Proc. Natl. Acad. Sci. USA* 109(11):4086–91

Piff PK, Stancato DM, Martinez AG, Kraus MW, Keltner D. 2012c. Class, chaos, and the construction of community. *J. Personal. Soc. Psychol.* 103(6):949–62

Pillutla M, Chen X. 1999. Social norms and cooperation in social dilemmas: the effects of context and feedback. *Organ. Behav. Hum. Decis. Proc.* 78(2):81–103

Porges SW. 2001. The polyvagal theory: phylogenetic substrates of a social nervous system. *Int. J. Psychophysiol.* 42(2):123–46

Porges SW. 2003. The polyvagal theory: phylogenetic contributions to social behavior. *Physiol. Behav.* 79(3):503–13

Porges SW. 2007. The polyvagal perspective. *Biol. Psychol.* 74(2):116–43

Poulin MJ, Holman EA, Buffone A. 2012. The neurogenetics of nice: receptor genes for oxytocin and vasopressin interact with threat to predict prosocial behavior. *Psychol. Sci.* 23(5):446–52

Pritchard AL, Ratcliffe L, Sorour E, Haque S, Holder R, et al. 2009. Investigation of dopamine receptors in susceptibility to behavioural and psychological symptoms in Alzheimer's disease. *Int. J. Geriatr. Psychiatry* 24(9):1020–25

Rand DG, Dreber A, Ellingsen T, Fudenberg D, Nowak MA. 2009. Positive interactions promote public cooperation. *Science* 325:1272–75

Rand DG, Greene JD, Nowak MA. 2012. Spontaneous giving and calculated greed. *Nature* 489:427–30

Reuter M, Frenzel C, Walter NT, Markett S, Montag C. 2011. Investigating the genetic basis of altruism: the role of the COMT Val158Met polymorphism. *Soc. Cogn. Affect. Neurosci.* 6(5):662–68

Rilling JK, Gutman DA, Zeh TR, Pagnoni G, Berns GS, Kilts CD. 2002. A neural basis for social cooperation. *Neuron* 35(2):395–405

Rilling JK, Sanfey AG, Aronson JA, Nystrom LE, Cohen JD. 2004. Opposing BOLD responses to reciprocated and unreciprocated altruism in putative reward pathways. *NeuroReport* 15(16):2539–43

Rodrigues SM, LeDoux JE, Sapolsky RM. 2009a. The influence of stress hormones on fear circuitry. *Annu. Rev. Neurosci.* 32:289–313

Rodrigues SM, Saslow LR, Garcia N, John OP, Keltner D. 2009b. Oxytocin receptor genetic variation relates to empathy and stress reactivity in humans. *Proc. Natl. Acad. Sci. USA* 106(50):21437–41

Rolls ET, O'Doherty J, Kringelbach ML, Francis S, Bowtell R, McGlone F. 2003. Representations of pleasant and painful touch in the human orbitofrontal and cingulate cortices. *Cereb. Cortex* 13(3):308–17

Roth BL. 1994. Multiple serotonin receptors: clinical and experimental aspects. *Ann. Clin. Psychiatry* 6:67–78

Saroglou V. 2002. Religion and the five factors of personality: a meta-analytic review. *Personal. Individ. Differ.* 32(1):15–25

Saroglou V, Delpierre V, Dernelle R. 2004. Values and religiosity: A meta-analysis of studies using Schwartz's model. *Personal. Individ. Differ.* 37(4):721–34

Schindler S, Reinhard M-A, Stahlberg D. 2012. Mortality salience increases personal relevance of the norm of reciprocity. *Psychol. Rep.* 111(2):565–74

Schnall S, Roper J. 2012. Elevation puts moral values into action. *Soc. Psychol. Personal. Sci.* 3(3):373–78

Schnall S, Roper J, Fessler DM. 2010. Elevation leads to altruistic behavior. *Psychol. Sci.* 21(3):315–20

Schneiderman I, Zagoory-Sharon O, Leckman JF, Feldman R. 2012. Oxytocin during the initial stages of romantic attachment: relations to couples' interactive reciprocity. *Psychoneuroendocrinology* 37(8):1277–85

Schwartz SH, Bilsky W. 1990. Toward a theory of the universal content and structure of values: extensions and cross-cultural replications. *J. Personal. Soc. Psychol.* 58(5):878–91

Seyfarth RM, Cheney DL. 2012. The evolutionary origins of friendship. *Annu. Rev. Psychol.* 63:153–77

Shariff AF, Norenzayan A. 2007. God is watching you: Priming God concepts increases prosocial behavior in an anonymous economic game. *Psychol. Sci.* 18(9):803–9

Simon-Thomas ER, Godzik J, Castle E, Antonenko O, Ponz A, et al. 2012. An fMRI study of caring versus self-focus during induced compassion and pride. *Soc. Cogn. Affect. Neurosci.* 7(6):635–48

Smith A. 2006 (1759). *The Theory of Moral Sentiments*. Mineola, NY: Dover

Sober E, Wilson DS. 1998. *Unto Others: The Evolution and Psychology of Unselfish Behavior*. Cambridge, MA: Harvard Univ. Press

Spitzer M, Fischbacher U, Herrnberger B, Grön G, Fehr E. 2007. The neural signature of social norm compliance. *Neuron* 56(1):185–96

Sprecher S, Fehr B. 2005. Compassionate love for close others and humanity. *J. Soc. Personal Relatsh.* 22(5):629–51

Stellar JE, Manzo VM, Kraus MW, Keltner D. 2012. Class and compassion: Socioeconomic factors predict responses to suffering. *Emotion* 12:449–59

Stephens NM, Markus HR, Townsend SSM. 2007. Choice as an act of meaning: the case of social class. *J. Personal. Soc. Psychol.* 93(5):814–30

Strathearn L, Li J, Fonagy P, Montague PR. 2008. What's in a smile? Maternal brain responses to infant facial cues. *Pediatrics* 122(1):40–51

Strauman TJ. 1989. Self-discrepancies in clinical depression and social phobia: cognitive structures that underlie emotional disorders? *J. Abnorm. Psychol.* 98(1):14–22

Sussman RW, Cloninger CR, eds. 2011. *Origins of Altruism and Cooperation.* New York: Springer

Tabibnia G, Lieberman MD. 2007. Fairness and cooperation are rewarding: evidence from social cognitive neuroscience. *Ann. N. Y. Acad. Sci.* 1118:90–101

Tangney JP, Stuewig J, Mashek DJ. 2007. Moral emotions and moral behavior. *Annu. Rev. Psychol.* 58:345–72

Thompson LL, ed. 2006. *Negotiation Theory and Research.* New York: Psychol. Press

Tiedens LZ, Fragale AR. 2003. Power moves: complementarity in dominant and submissive nonverbal behavior. *J. Personal. Soc. Psychol.* 84(3):558–68

Tost H, Kolachana B, Hakimi S, Lemaitre H, Verchinski BA, et al. 2010. A common allele in the oxytocin receptor gene (OXTR) impacts prosocial temperament and human hypothalamic-limbic structure and function. *Proc. Natl. Acad. Sci. USA* 107(31):13936–41

Trivers RL. 1971. The evolution of reciprocal altruism. *Q. Rev. Biol.* 46(1):35–57

Trivers RL. 1972. Parental investment and sexual selection. In *Sexual Selection and the Descent of Man*, ed. B Campbell, pp. 136–79. Chicago: Aldine

Tse WS, Bond AJ. 2002. Serotonergic intervention affects both social dominance and affiliative behaviour. *Psychopharmacology* 161(3):324–30

Utz S. 2004. Self-activation is a two-edged sword: the effects of I primes on cooperation. *J. Exp. Soc. Psychol.* 40(6):769–76

Valdesolo P, Desteno D. 2011. Synchrony and the social tuning of compassion. *Emotion* 11(2):262–66

Van den Bos W, Van Dijk E, Westenberg M, Rombouts SARB, Crone EA. 2009. What motivates repayment? Neural correlates of reciprocity in the Trust Game. *Soc. Cogn. Affect. Neurosci.* 4(3):294–304

Van Lange PAM. 1999. The pursuit of joint outcomes and equality in outcomes: an integrative model of social value orientation. *J. Personal. Soc. Psychol.* 77(2)337–49

Vanoli E, Adamson PB, Pinna GD, Lazzara R, Orr WC. 1995. Heart rate variability during specific sleep stages: a comparison of healthy subjects with patients after myocardial infarction. *Circulation* 91(7):1918–22

Warneken F, Tomasello M. 2006. Altruistic helping in human infants and young chimpanzees. *Science* 311:1301–3

Warneken F, Tomasello M. 2007. Helping and cooperation at 14 months of age. *Infancy* 11(3):271–94

Waugh CE, Fredrickson BL. 2006. Nice to know you: positive emotions, self-other overlap, and complex understanding in the formation of a new relationship. *J. Posit. Psychol.* 1(2):93–106

Wedekind C, Milinski M. 2000. Cooperation through image scoring in humans. *Science* 288:850–52

Weisman O, Zagoory-Sharon O, Feldman R. 2012. Oxytocin administration to parent enhances infant physiological and behavioral readiness for social engagement. *Biol. Psychiatry* 72(12):982–89

Wert SR, Salovey P. 2004a. A social comparison account of gossip. *Rev. Gen. Psychol.* 8(2):122–37

Wert SR, Salovey P. 2004b. Introduction to the special issue on gossip. *Rev. Gen. Psychol.* 8(2):76–77

Willer R. 2009. Groups reward individual sacrifice: the status solution to the collective action problem. *Am. Sociol. Rev.* 73:23–43

Wood RM, Rilling JK, Sanfey AG, Bhagwagar Z, Rogers RD. 2006. Effects of tryptophan depletion on the performance of an iterated Prisoner's Dilemma game in healthy adults. *Neuropsychopharmacology* 31(5):1075–84

Woods TE, Ironson GH. 1999. Religion and spirituality in the face of illness: how cancer, cardiac, and HIV patients describe their spirituality/religiosity. *J. Health Psychol.* 4(3):393–412

Woolley AW, Chabris CF, Pentland A, Hashmi N, Malone TW. 2010. Evidence for a collective intelligence factor in the performance of human groups. *Science* 330:686–88

Young LJ, Lim MM, Gingrich B, Insel TR. 2001. Cellular mechanisms of social attachment. *Horm. Behav.* 40(2):133–38

Zink CF, Meyer-Lindenberg A. 2012. Human neuroimaging of oxytocin and vasopressin in social cognition. *Horm. Behav.* 61(3):400–9

Deviance and Dissent
in Groups

Jolanda Jetten and Matthew J. Hornsey

School of Psychology, University of Queensland, St. Lucia, Queensland 4072, Australia;
email: j.jetten@psy.uq.edu.au

Annu. Rev. Psychol. 2014. 65:461–85

First published online as a Review in Advance on
June 7, 2013

The *Annual Review of Psychology* is online at
http://psych.annualreviews.org

This article's doi:
10.1146/annurev-psych-010213-115151

Keywords

group processes, black sheep effect, intragroup dynamics, social identity

Abstract

Traditionally, group research has focused more on the motivations that make
people conform than on the motivations and conditions underpinning deviance and dissent. This has led to a literature that focuses on the value that
groups place on uniformity and paints a relatively dark picture of dissent and
deviance: as reflections of a lack of group loyalty, as signs of disengagement,
or as delinquent behavior. An alternative point of view, which has gained
momentum in recent years, focuses on deviance and dissent as normal and
healthy aspects of group life. In this review, we focus on the motivations that
group members have to deviate and dissent, and the functional as well as
the dysfunctional effects of deviance and dissent. In doing so we aim for a
balanced and complete account of deviance and dissent, highlighting when
such behaviors will be encouraged as well as when they will be punished.

Contents

INTRODUCTION AND HISTORICAL OVERVIEW

Classic studies in social psychology have focused on the pervasiveness of conformity and pressures for unanimity. For example, the message of Asch's (1951) line judgment studies is that conformity is a powerful and prevalent force in groups and that nonconformists risk mockery. Social psychological theorizing argues that group members will see deviance and dissent as dangerous for the group; that they threaten people's worldview, create uncertainty, and rob groups of momentum (Festinger 1950). Consistent with this, there is now considerable evidence that deviants are more likely to be rejected than are group members who conform (e.g., Marques & Paez 1994, Tata et al. 1996).

This classic view sometimes obscures the fact that deviance and dissent are also prevalent phenomena within groups (Haslam & Reicher 2012a,b; Jetten & Hornsey 2011, 2012; Reicher & Haslam 2006; see also Moscovici 1976). Even in Asch's original paradigm, only 12% of participants conformed on all trials—a larger percentage (24% of participants) never conformed (Asch 1951). Conformity is not the default in groups, nor is dissent and deviance the exception. Rather, conformity (like dissent and deviance) is observed only under some conditions and in some contexts.

What is more, even though deviants and dissenters are at times perceived as troublemakers, these individuals can also be the most admired members in the group, the people who liven up the group and who contribute most to the achievement of group goals. In sum, a growing body of literature argues that deviance and dissent—although potentially stressful—are normal and healthy aspects of group life and are often recognized as such by group members.

Deviance: the violation of the norms of a group

Dissent: the expression of disagreement with group norms, group action, or a group decision

In this review, we start by defining our key terms and then elaborate on various motives that group members might have for engaging in deviance and dissent. We then review work examining reactions of other group members to deviance and dissent; focus on the value of and tolerance for deviance and dissent for the group; and review the conditions under which deviance and dissent are more or less likely to be punished by others. In our review, we focus mainly on work that has been published in the past 20 years. We only refer to classic work when it is important to understand the origin of ideas and when such background is needed to gain an appreciation of how the field has developed. For reviews of earlier work, we refer the reader to Levine (1989), Levine & Kerr (2007), Moscovici (1976), and Turner (1991). We also confine our review to deviance or dissent in relation to relevant group norms. Therefore, we do not use the word "deviance" to refer to criminality, delinquency, or other stigmatized behavior in society (an approach that is quite common in sociology) and do not review the associated literature on this. Neither do we review research on personal or interpersonal forms of negative and harmful behavior (e.g., bullying, aggression).

Group norms: beliefs about how group members should act within the group

Positive deviants: individuals who deviate by contributing more to the group than the average group member

DEFINITIONS OF DEVIANCE AND DISSENT

We define deviance as the violation of the norms of a group. As such, the likelihood that behavior will be labeled as deviant is always determined in relation to (*a*) the content of a group norm that is salient and (*b*) the contexts in which deviance and dissent are expressed. This means that the same behavior can be perceived both as deviant and normative depending on the group norm and context. For example, for boxers, hitting someone will be normative during a boxing match but not after the match has finished.

What is considered deviant may also change with time. Group norms are dynamic, responsive to contextual changes, and in constant flux. Group members negotiate the content of norms that should guide behavior and may contest their validity when they are no longer seen as appropriate for the group. As a result, behavior that was previously perceived as deviant might become conformist when the majority changes its stance and other behaviors become normative (Blanton & Christie 2003, Chan et al. 2010). In the words of the sociologist Merton: "...the rebel, revolutionary, nonconformist, individualist, heretic and renegade of an earlier time is often the culture hero of today" (1968, p. 237).

Having said that, in social psychological research certain behaviors are regularly interpreted as deviant in group contexts, and these tend to form the basis for operationalizations of deviance in the literature. For example, deviance has been operationalized as possessing qualities or attitudes that differ from the prototype (Hutchison et al. 2011), poor performance in a group task (Marques & Paez 1994), disloyalty (Branscombe et al. 1993), engaging in socially undesirable or antisocial behavior (see, e.g., Marques et al. 2001) or arguing against group interests (see, e.g., Castano et al. 2002).

When we define deviance as the violation of group norms, we need to be open to the possibility that norms can be violated in two ways: Individuals can fail to live up to important group norms or reject group norms (i.e., negative deviants), or individuals can deviate by contributing more to the group than the average group member (i.e., positive deviants). The latter deviants stand out from the group in an objectively positive way, for example by evincing exceptional performance or exceptional integrity (Fielding et al. 2006). Interestingly, and as we outline in greater detail below, it is not the case that acceptance of these positive deviants is necessarily greater than the acceptance of negative deviants.

We define dissent as the expression of disagreement with group norms, group action, or a group decision. In many cases dissent can be considered an example of deviance, which is why

Table 1 Reasons for deviance and dissent in groups

Motivations for deviance and dissent
Motive 1: disengagement, disloyalty, or disrespect for the group
Motive 2: loyalty and concern for the group
Motive 3: moral rebellion—when personal moral convictions take precedence over group norms
Motive 4: desire to express difference, individuality, and uniqueness
Motive 5: tangible rewards and instrumental gain derived from dissent and deviance

deviance and dissent are often referred to in the same breath. But not all groups would see dissent as synonymous with deviance. For example, in academia, being critical and challenging of the status quo is collectively encouraged, and failure to engage in critical dissent might be seen as deviant (Hornsey et al. 2006, McAuliffe et al. 2002). Out of respect for this conceptual difference we avoid using the terms deviance and dissent interchangeably, although we acknowledge that they are related.

REASONS FOR DEVIANCE AND DISSENT

What makes people conform, and what makes them defy group pressure? Traditionally, group members are seen to conform for two reasons (Deutsch & Gerard 1955). First, in the face of uncertainty, people look to others as a guide to reality and as a guide to the appropriate way to behave (that is, they see others as a source of informational influence). Second, people may conform so they fit in, obtain approval from others, or avoid punishment and social isolation (normative influence).

The social identity approach (comprising social identity theory and self-categorization theory) points to the importance of group identification in understanding conformity (Turner 1991). Conformity to norms signifies inclusion in the group, makes members feel good about their group membership, and is a way to express loyalty and commitment (Louis et al. 2005, Sassenberg et al. 2011). In particular, those who are strongly identified with a group will be motivated to conform to norms even when such conformity clashes with their own personal interests (Zdaniuk & Levine 2001).

Because most research has focused on explaining conformity, far less is known about the motives that might lead people to deviate or dissent from groups.[1] In **Table 1** we identify five reasons why people might seek to engage in deviance or dissent. Motive 1 captures the implicit assumption of the majority of the literature: Because it is assumed that conformity is a sign of loyalty, then deviance and dissent are seen to be motivated by disloyalty or disengagement (Blanton & Christie 2003). Indeed, those who are less committed to the group have been found to conform less to salient group norms than those who are more committed (Spears et al. 1997). Packer (2008) has argued that low identifiers' behavior can best be described as passive nonconformity: Those who are less committed to the group do not care about group performance or group functioning, and their disinterest manifests itself as withdrawal, noncompliance, and indifference to group norms. Others have focused on more sinister motives of deviants and dissenters and have associated their

---

[1]Of course not all deviance is motivated: Sometimes people deviate simply because they do not have the ability or awareness to conform to normative requirements (Monin & O'Connor 2011). For example, newcomers may not be sufficiently socialized yet to know the group norms or they may not have acquired the skills to conform. Because of space constraints, we do not discuss these examples of deviance and dissent here.

actions with a motivation to harm or sabotage the group (Warren 2003). In the organizational literature, it has been noted that employees may deviate from norms because they are dissatisfied with the organization, angry about a perceived injustice, or because they enjoy the thrill associated with rebellion (Christian & Ellis 2013, Ferris et al. 2012). In some of those cases, the deviant's rule violation is deliberate, aimed at undermining the group's well-being and functioning (Bennett & Robinson 2000). These motives are particularly relevant when explaining deviance and dissent among low identifiers (Cronin & Smith 2011).

The conflating of conformity with loyalty—and of nonconformity with disloyalty—is so entrenched in the literature that it sometimes obscures the fact that deviance and dissent can be multiply determined. Motive 2 describes the other side of the coin of Motive 1: that dissent and deviance can be motivated by group loyalty. That is, group members may dissent because they care for the group and are concerned about the course of action that other group members are taking. Dissent is then motivated by an attempt to change group norms for the better, a phenomenon that has been variously described as "constructive deviance" (e.g., Galperin 2012) or "constructive patriotism" (Shatz et al. 1999).

The normative conflict model of dissent (Packer 2008, 2011) speaks to this motive. The model focuses on how those with lower and higher levels of identification with the group respond to normative conflict (i.e., a discrepancy between current group norms and a group member's perception of what is right or moral). This model suggests that both lower and higher identifiers might be motivated to dissent, but for different reasons. Whereas those who are less committed to the group dissent or deviate because they disengage from group goals (i.e., Motive 1), highly identified group members dissent because they care about the group. In other words, their dissent is in the service of the group, aimed at changing group norms that they perceive as detrimental.

Because dissent by low and high identifiers is motivated by different concerns, the way in which dissent is expressed will also differ. Low identifiers are more likely to engage in actions that undermine the group (e.g., they might withdraw or aim to exit the group), whereas high identifiers' dissent reflects group engagement and attempts to improve the group. As we elaborate below, because dissent is expressed in such different ways and motivated by different concerns, it is also likely to be responded to differently by other group members.

A growing body of work provides support for predictions derived from the normative conflict model of dissent (Crane & Platow 2010, Packer 2009, Packer & Chasteen 2010, Tauber & Sassenberg 2012; for a review, see Packer 2011). These studies typically involve designs in which group identification is measured and normative conflict is measured or manipulated. When normative conflict is measured, participants are asked to what extent they find a particular group norm harmful for the group (Packer 2009). When normative conflict is manipulated, participants are typically presented with contexts in which group members engage in behavior or hold attitudes that are harmful for the group. For example, among students, normative conflict arises when they reflect on the negative health consequences of binge drinking (Packer & Chasteen 2010). In other conditions, participants are asked to consider the extent to which engagement in these negative behaviors might harm them personally. Consistent with the model, dissent is higher among those who are more strongly committed to the group when participants perceive harmful consequences for the collective (but not when considering personal harm). In contrast, perceptions of collective harm do not affect the responses of those lower in identification, and levels of dissent among these members have been found to be relatively low.

Motive 3 describes the fact that people often have moral convictions that prevent them from following and acting in line with group norms ("moral rebels," see Monin et al. 2008). For example, people might resile from expressing racist comments even though the group demands this, or they might resist harming someone else because that would be inconsistent with personal moral

Constructive deviance: deviance or dissent motivated by a desire to attempt to change group norms for the better

Moral rebels: individuals who give priority to following personal convictions over group norms when individual and group norms clash norms. By way of illustration, participants in Milgram's obedience studies who refused to go to the highest shock levels often referred to moral norms that prevented them from continuing: "I'd like to continue, but can't do that to a man" or "I can't go on with this; no, this is not right" (Milgram 1963, p. 376). For these individuals, nonconformity was less a choice than a moral imperative.

Consistent with this, subsequent work shows that those with moral convictions are less likely to be swayed by group pressure. For example, in two studies examining attitudes toward gay law reform and toward a government apology to Aborigines for past wrongdoing, those who had a strong moral basis for their attitudes were unaffected by the group norm, an effect that was independent of attitude intensity (Hornsey et al. 2003). Indeed, on public behavioral intentions, those with a strong moral basis for their attitude were more likely to act in line with their personal conviction when they felt they were in a minority than when they felt they were in a majority (counter-conformity). Along similar lines, Shamir (1997) found that prevailing government opinion did not affect Israelis' willingness to express their opinion about the Palestinian territories. Presumably this was because the issue was of such personal relevance that concerns about social isolation or punishment for dissenting became irrelevant.

Motive 4 relates to the notion that group members might dissent and deviate because they want to express individuality and uniqueness (Imhoff & Erb 2009). In this sense we agree with Codol (1984, p. 317), who argued that "both conformity and resistance to conformity are fundamentally linked to the image of oneself that one wishes to present to others (and undoubtedly also to oneself)." In some ways, deviance and dissent are ideally suited to help define and clarify that image. Blanton and colleagues (2001) found evidence for this in a study where participants were presented with a social influence attempt (e.g., that it would be a good idea for all students on campus to receive a flu shot). When the behavior was described as the right thing to do, students' intentions to get a flu shot were higher when such behavior was counternormative (i.e., only a minority of students on campus were expected to get a flu shot) than when such behavior was perceived as normative for the group (i.e., it was anticipated that the majority of students on campus would get a flu shot). Consistent with these findings, other research has found that people can endorse a minority position (rather than a majority position) as a way of clarifying their self-concept and communicating to others who they are (Rios Morrison & Wheeler 2010). Particularly when publicly expressed, dissent and deviance might be good ways to enhance individuality and uniqueness in group contexts (Blanton & Christie 2003).

The desire to stand out and be different may be especially pronounced when people attribute the normative consensus to obedience. Conway & Schaller (2005) found that, when an authority explicitly commanded group members to make a particular choice, this enhanced participants' desire to deviate from that group norm (and especially when the authority was still present). The principles of reactance—and the associated desire for control and authenticity of expression—can drive a perverse desire for deviance in precisely the conditions when the explicit pressure for conformity is greatest.

At times the desire to seek out distinctiveness leads an individual to adopt norms, values, and lifestyles that run counter to the mainstream. For example, Jetten and colleagues (2001) found that the motivation to shock others and to differentiate oneself from the mainstream was an important reason for having body piercings. Interestingly, subcultures often emerge whereby all those who want to be different express their difference from the mainstream in a similar way. That is, being different and standing out with the aim of upsetting the mainstream may involve the development of new subcultural norms strictly prescribing how one should rebel (Hornsey & Jetten 2004).

Finally, people might engage in deviance and dissent because norm violations are associated with tangible rewards, making the costs of punishment less of a deterrent (Motive 5). The organizational literature in particular has focused on this motive for deviance: Employees might engage in fraud, steal from the company, or commit crimes because these behaviors are associated with financial gain and success (Bennett & Robinson 2000, Warren 2003).

Another literature that has focused on instrumental gain as a motive for deviance is work on impostorism (Hornsey & Jetten 2003, 2011; Warner et al. 2007). Impostorism is a particular form of deviance and involves individuals breaking group norms by passing themselves off as genuine group members even though they do not meet key criteria for group membership. Impostorism allows people to cross what are normally impermeable group boundaries (e.g., gender, race, or class) and is a way to obtain access to groups, professions, or classes that could not be legitimately claimed otherwise. By resorting to impostorism, people are able to escape prejudice, can run away from persecution, can gain social acceptance, or can pass themselves off as more successful than they really are. For example, to avoid exclusion and prejudice, gays and lesbians may hide their sexual orientation (Warner et al. 2007), and those who are HIV positive might not reveal their illness (Molero et al. 2011).

Group locomotion: the ability of a group to achieve its goals

MOTIVES FOR REJECTING DEVIANCE AND DISSENT

In this section we review literature that has examined the motives for rejecting deviants and dissenters, both for individual group members and for the group as a whole. We identify five distinct motives: rejection of deviance and dissent helps to restore (*a*) threatened group positivity, (*b*) threatened group cohesion, (*c*) threatened group distinctiveness, (*d*) threatened group locomotion, and (*e*) threatened self-image. We discuss these motivations and recent empirical support for them in turn.

Restoring Threatened Group Positivity

The notion that deviance and dissent threaten the positivity of the group—and that rejection of these individuals serves the function of restoring positivity—dominates recent empirical work (e.g., Castano et al. 2002, Hutchison & Abrams 2003). Indeed, this reasoning is at the heart of work on the so-called black sheep effect (Marques et al. 2001). This work centers on two interrelated observations. First, a favorable in-group member (e.g., someone who is likeable, qualified, loyal, attractive) is rated more positively than an out-group member who engages in similarly favorable behavior. Second, the opposite effect occurs when group members are confronted by an unlikeable, incompetent, or disloyal in-group member, such that the deviant in-group member is rated more harshly by fellow group members than is an out-group member who engages in the same behavior. Heightened derogation of the in-group deviant is seen as a form of in-group enhancement, distancing the group from qualities that reflect poorly upon it (Hutchison & Abrams 2003, Marques & Paez 1994).

Two studies by Hutchison and colleagues (2008) provide direct evidence that devaluation serves the function of identity maintenance and protection. Among highly identified group members, descriptions of the in-group were more positive the more these members excluded an undesirable target. Reinforcing the notion that rejection of black sheep serves an identity-enhancing function, making an intergroup context salient increases the derogation of in-group deviants and dissenters (Chekroun & Nugier 2011, Matheson et al. 2003). Similarly, people who criticized their groups faced heightened censure if they made their comments in public or directly to an out-group audience (Elder et al. 2005, Hornsey et al. 2005). It has also been found that deviants are more likely to be derogated (*a*) when the deviant behavior relates to a dimension of comparison that is directly relevant to in-group identity (Abrams et al. 2008b), (*b*) when the group identity is threatened (Branscombe et al. 1993), or (*c*) when the group's position is unstable or challenged (Marques et al. 2001).

In addition to the protection of group identity, derogation of in-group members can also serve the function of protecting the threatened identities of individual group members. Eidelman & Biernat (2003) showed that group members lower their identification with the group after being presented with an in-group deviant. In that way, they dissociate and distance themselves from these deviants and limit the threat of being associatively miscast with the unfavorable in-group member. Chekroun & Nugier (2011) showed that rejection of in-group deviants was positively correlated with the level of shame and embarrassment the deviant invoked.

One might wonder whether the fear that deviants and dissenters damage the positive image of the group is real or imagined. This question has not been examined in great depth, but there is some evidence from the stereotyping literature that the more typical of the in-group the deviant is perceived to be, the more the image of the in-group is negatively affected by the deviant's presence (Castano et al. 2002). There is also evidence that deviants in other groups are perceived as harmful to those groups. For example, Kunda & Oleson (1997) found that an out-group with an extreme deviant in its midst was seen as less favorable than a group that included only moderate deviants.

Restoring Threatened Group Cohesion

The above research speaks to the fact that group members are motivated to see their group in a positive light and so are especially keen to rid the group of members who behave in a dislikeable or incompetent way. But group members are not just motivated to see their group as positive; they also are motivated to see their group as tight, well defined, and cohesive. One reason for this is that cohesive groups offer certainty and structure about what to think and how to behave (Festinger 1950). Thus, censuring of deviance and dissent can be a way of protecting the subjective validity of one's attitudes, beliefs, and worldviews. In extreme cases, divergent attitudes may threaten the very definition of the group, leading to internecine conflict or schisms (Sani & Reicher 2000).

Another reason why cohesion is important is because it offers resilience in the intergroup context. Classic work on minority influence makes the point that consistency and cohesion within minority groups are important preconditions for converting the majority and changing the status quo (Moscovici 1976). Minority groups that are fractured or riven with internal dissent are less likely to challenge the majority's worldview—or indeed to hold together. This might help explain meta-analytical evidence that rejection of deviance increases as the proportionate size of the group decreases (Tata et al. 1996).

Similarly, Janis (1972) makes the point that pressure for cohesion and unanimity is particularly strong when the group faces threat from the outside (e.g., media scrutiny, budgetary crisis, or armed conflict). Indeed, external pressures and excessive cohesion are two important ingredients of the phenomenon of groupthink, one symptom of which is the active censuring of dissenters by self-appointed "mindguards." It is easy to recognize this phenomenon in historical events, for example the normative pressure to silence dissent within the United States and its allies following the two wars with Iraq (Kelman 1995). It can also be detected experimentally: Muslims who criticized their religion in Indonesia faced significantly more personal censure from other Muslims when inter-religious conflict was primed than when it was not (Ariyanto et al. 2010). Furthermore, small-group experiments have found that intergroup conflict increases enforcement of in-group norms, particularly when out-group participation in the conflict is high (Benard 2012).

Restoring Threatened Group Distinctiveness

Deviants and dissenters not only threaten within-group cohesion, their actions may also undermine between-group distinctiveness. That is, deviants' norm breaking might mean that their behavior is more representative of a rival out-group than of their own group, thus reducing the clarity of in-group boundaries. Robbed of intergroup distinctiveness, groups can become fuzzy and poorly defined, diluting their ability to provide meaning and self-definition for their members.

This principle is captured by the model of subjective group dynamics (Abrams et al. 2000), which was established to help account for the black sheep effect described previously. According to the subjective group dynamics model, people evaluate group members' behavior as a function of whether they validate or undermine prescriptive and descriptive group norms, and interactions with deviants are shaped by the desire to enhance or maintain this subjective validity (Frings et al. 2012). Importantly, actions and attitudes are not evaluated in isolation but rather in the context of a salient intergroup comparison. Consistent with this principle, there is now a large body of work showing that deviants who exaggerate intergroup differences are liked more than deviants who dilute them, even when the severity of their group norm violations is identical (e.g., Abrams et al. 2000, 2002; Hichy et al. 2008).

Distinctiveness from relevant out-groups might be particularly important for minority groups. One reason for this is that people use group solidarity as a buffer against the self-esteem consequences of stigma. Thus, distinctiveness helps provide the kind of certainty and definition that can nourish the self-concept and provide meaning. Another reason that distinctiveness might be important for minority groups is that it offers the psychological platform from which groups can work to change the status quo. Work on impostorism in the gay community confirms the importance of distinctiveness for minority groups. Warner and colleagues (2007) presented gay participants with one of two targets who turned out to be impostors: a straight person trying to pass as gay, and a gay person trying to pass as straight. Even though both impostors were disliked more than control targets who had not resorted to impostorism, mediational analysis showed that they were derogated for different reasons. Gay targets who tried to pass as straight were rated as damaging because they were seen to be ashamed about their sexuality. In contrast, a straight person trying to pass as gay was seen to be blurring the boundaries between the in-group and the out-group, and this was associated with greater perceived damage to the group. Schoemann & Branscombe (2011) also found that distinctiveness threat underpinned negative reactions to older people who try to "pass" as young.

Restoring Threatened Group Locomotion

A fourth motive for derogating deviants and dissenters is that these individuals may cause emotional, cognitive, and communicative stress, undermining the ability of group to achieve its goals [what Festinger (1950) described as group locomotion]. Dealing with dissent and divergent opinions can be emotionally and cognitively taxing for a group. For example, when confronted with a deviant group member, those who strongly identified with the group showed reduced recall on an unrelated memory task (Coull et al. 2001). Presumably, cognitive resources are needed to cognitively "fence off" deviant members from the rest of the group.

When facing other stressors, groups can strive for premature closure whereby they seek consensus simply to avoid being exhausted by dissent (Kruglanski & Webster 1996). Dissenters' and deviants' actions are met with frustration when they slow the group down and prevent it from achieving its goals. Derogation then serves the function of excluding those who stand in the way of goal achievement. In line with this reasoning, Kruglanski & Webster (1991) found that dissenters were evaluated more harshly when the group faced deadline pressure or when group members were experiencing cognitive load (e.g., the discussion took place in a noisy environment).

Restoring a Threatened Self-Image

In the research on black sheep and subjective group dynamics, attitudinal deviance tended to be operationalized on the basis of relatively neutral, nonmoral issues: Participants would be told, for example, that participants were deviant in their attitudes about student accommodation (Abrams et al. 2002) or their styles of imagination (Marques et al. 2001). But what might happen if the attitudinal deviance has a clear moral flavor? This is what Monin would call a moral rebel: someone who stands up and takes a conspicuous stance in opposition to a norm, expectation, or convention that they perceive to be immoral. Images of the moral rebel are often heroic and noble: Nelson Mandela's resistance to apartheid; those who participated in the civil rights movement; and the "unknown rebel" who stood in the path of the tanks during the Tiananmen Square massacre (Wolf & Zuckerman 2012). Surely this subset of deviants would be received more positively by rank-and-file group members.

Research by Monin and colleagues suggests otherwise (Monin & O'Connor 2011, Monin et al. 2008). As an example of the type of paradigm they used, participants were asked to take part in a role-playing game that could be interpreted as racist. Somewhat dramatically, a confederate refused to do the experiment on the grounds that it was offensive. Some of the participants were third-party observers who witnessed the event but were doing an unrelated task in the experiment and so were not personally implicated in the moral decision. These participants tended to reward the moral rebel, describing him as more moral, likable, and respected than an obedient participant who participated in the role-play. This effect, however, was reversed for those participants who had previously engaged in the task themselves.

Monin and colleagues concluded that moral rebellion represents a threat to group members on three fronts: (*a*) The rebel's moral stance is seen as an implicit criticism of those who did not take the stance, so group members anticipate condemnation from the rebel; (*b*) the actions of the rebel make you question your own assumptions and attitudes, leading to a dissonance-like state; and (*c*) the rebel strips those of us who conspire in immoral acts from the rationalization that we had no choice. By reminding us of our freedom to act, the rebel makes us confront our own past actions, leading to an existential crisis. In each case, the moral rebel arouses resentment, and a solution to the threat posed by rebels is to derogate them and to deny that they are moral at all.

The moral rebel can be seen as an example of a broader category: the so-called positive deviant (Fielding et al. 2006). Positive deviants can be constructive role models who trigger positive change (e.g., Kraschnewski et al. 2011, Ma & Magnus 2012). However, in some contexts people who perform exceptionally well can also face jealousy and resentment: They might be pressured to reduce their performance, and their failures might elicit schadenfreude (Feather & Sherman 2002, Shoenberger et al. 2012). Parks & Stone (2010) found that group members who were especially unselfish in their behavior were seen by some as setting an undesirable behavioral standard and were downgraded accordingly.

THE VALUE OF DISSENT AND DEVIANCE

Even though social psychologists traditionally have focused on the threatening and dysfunctional aspects of dissent and deviance, there is now a growing body of theorizing and empirical work elaborating how these individuals' actions can leave a positive legacy. Here, we focus on evidence that dissent increases the quality of group decision making and how it is essential for creativity, innovation, and learning. We also discuss how deviance can sharpen the group's understanding of its values and how it can facilitate social change.

The Value of Dissent

The notion that dissent is essential for good group decision making is well developed. Research on minority influence (De Dreu & West 2001, Nemeth 1995, Nemeth & Goncalo 2011; for a meta-analytical overview, see Wood et al. 1994) has shown that dissenting minorities exert influence on the group as a whole because they force the majority to think outside the box. It is also clear from this body of work that minorities influence the group in a different way than do majorities. The influence of minorities is indirect, delayed, and not always visible—when these group members are influential, change is often not attributed to their influence. The value of opinion minorities lies in their ability to guard the group against complacency, to challenge conventional wisdom, and to keep the group sharp and on its toes. In that way, dissenting minorities can change norms or behavioral conventions that have lost their utility. This resonates with classic work on groupthink (Janis 1972), which demonstrated the dangers of having too much convergence and agreement in the group, especially in the early stages of group decision making. The presence of dissent might lead group members to tackle the faults of their group, and the dissenters' critical stance protects the group from suboptimal decision making (Packer 2009). Accordingly, there is evidence that groups that include devil's advocates make higher-quality decisions (Nemeth et al. 2001) and are less prone to classic decision-making mistakes such as escalation of commitment in the face of losses (Greitemeyer et al. 2009).

Dissenting minorities promote higher-quality decisions because they change the way groups think and process information. Researchers working from within the minority influence literature have shown that majorities instigate a narrowing of focus and convergent thinking (Nemeth 1995). This is because group members confronted with a majority position are mostly motivated to corroborate existing views: They believe that because many people in a group say this, they must be right (consensus implies correctness). However, minorities who express views that dissent from the majority are more likely to stimulate divergent thinking, as group members strive to understand why the minority is dissenting. Divergence of opinion also leads to dissonance in groups, and this leads to greater attention to the message, the consideration of multiple perspectives, a reassessment of what the issues are, and a motivation to reduce the negative tension by seeking a new group consensus (Matz & Wood 2005). This work has led some to argue that groups would benefit from adopting norms of critical dissent. For example, Postmes et al. (2001) experimentally induced norms encouraging group members either to seek consensus or to engage critically with the available information. Groups with critical norms were less likely to fall in the trap of focusing on shared information at the expense of unshared information, and they were less likely to display signs of groupthink than were groups with consensus norms. This, in turn, was associated with improved decision quality.

Related to the impact of dissent on the quality of decision making, there is also evidence that dissent—because it stimulates divergent thinking—enhances creativity and innovation in groups (De Dreu & West 2001, Nemeth et al. 2001, Troyer & Youngreen 2009, Van Dyne & Saavedra 1996). For example, instructions encouraging criticism and debate within a group lead to more creative ideas being generated than when groups are instructed to brainstorm (Nemeth et al. 2004), although this link may emerge only in groups where there is a high degree of participation in team decision making (De Dreu & West 2001).

Van Dyne & Saavedra (1996) conducted a 10-week field experiment among natural work groups. They also found evidence that groups including confederates who were instructed to engage in minority influence developed more original products than did control groups. Interestingly, they did not find any evidence that there was more conflict in the minority influence group than in the control condition. This suggests that expressing divergent opinions or even dissent is not necessarily associated with enhanced tension (see also Wood et al. 1994).

There is also evidence that dissent can be beneficial in educational contexts. When working on a task, dissent with one or several others can promote quality of learning (Butera et al. 2011). This is because dissent and exposure to disconfirming information and opposing arguments may stimulate cognitive activity. This might be beneficial for learning because it forces people to critically reflect on the validity of their views and because it enhances openness to other viewpoints.

However, dissent is not always beneficial. Darnon et al. (2007) found that only in contexts where dissent is regulated in an epistemic manner (i.e., dissent and conflict relate to the learning task) did conflict enhance learning outcomes. When conflict was introduced among learners that related to their performance (i.e., the participant's competence was questioned), self-threat was enhanced and learning was reduced.

It is also important to keep in mind that dissent does not always lead to better performance in groups. At times, the presence of dissenters in the group is associated with conflict, and this undermines task focus and performance (Butera et al. 2011, De Dreu 2006). There is a fine balance between dissent that can help a group to move forward and dissent that undermines harmony and group functioning (Jehn et al. 1999). For example, Dooley & Fryxell (1999) found that dissent was associated with better decision making only when group members were committed to the group and therefore wanted the group to do well.

The Value of Deviance

Although recent social psychological theorizing has made important contributions to understanding the value of dissent (see previous section), it has very little to say on the value of deviance within groups. In order to develop a better understanding of why and how group deviants can be beneficial for the group, it is instructive to consider sociological work on deviance in groups (Durkheim 1958, Erikson 1966; see also Ben-Yehuda 2010). At the origin of this theorizing lies the work of Durkheim (1958), who argued for the normality and functionality of deviance.

Durkheim (1958) identified several ways in which groups benefit from having deviants in their midst. First, deviants have an important role to play in affirming group values, clarifying norms, and in helping group members to understand how they are different and distinct from other groups (for a similar point in the organizational context, see Markova & Folger 2012). That is, group members know what is the right thing to do by knowing what is normatively deviant and unacceptable (to be "good" makes sense only in relation to being "bad"; Coser 1962, p. 174). Interestingly, it is clear from this work that it is not only through rejection of the deviant that norms and values become affirmed and strengthened. Indeed, deviance also serves this function when the deviant is not excluded but rather is accepted by the group. That is, by tolerating a deviant or dissenter, group members can show that they act in accordance with their beliefs and values, and this strengthens the social fabric of the group (Coser 1962).

Second, deviance is functional and valuable for groups because it draws attention to alternative forms of behavior and thereby allows for social change (Choi & Levine 2004, Ellemers & Jetten 2013, Hansen & Levine 2009, Prislin & Christensen 2005, Prislin & Filson 2009). For example, Rosa Parks's refusal to give up her bus seat to a white passenger was an important catalyst for the civil rights movement, ultimately leading to the abolishment of segregation laws in the United States. By drawing attention to different viewpoints, by exposing group norms through the process of violating them, by challenging conventional wisdoms, and by creating conflict, tension and debate, deviants are able to move a group forward (see also Moscovici 1976). As Durkheim explains: "It would never have been possible to establish the freedom of thought we now enjoy if the regulations prohibiting it had not been violated before being solemnly abrogated" (1958, p. 67).

TOLERANCE FOR DISSENT AND DEVIANCE

Given the positive contributions of dissenters and deviants to the group, it is not surprising that groups are often remarkably tolerant of these individuals. Indeed, there are many examples where group members treat dissenters and deviants with respect and encourage them to continue to express their views because they contribute in these positive ways to the functioning of the group (Ellemers & Jetten 2013). The importance of dissent is increasingly recognized among management theorists (Amabile 1996), who have turned their attention to the microstrategies that organizations can employ to encourage dissent and fearless expression. Mindful of the benefits of dissent, some groups might create informal roles within their ranks that free people up to engage in dissent. An example is the role of court jesters in the Middle Ages who, perhaps because of their marginal and nonthreatening position, were the only ones who were licensed to openly raise unpleasant truths in the presence of the king or queen. A modern equivalent is the role of the devil's advocate, whose purpose is to question the group's functioning in order to understand the organization's weaknesses. In this section, we review research that has examined tolerance for dissenters and deviants.

Tolerance for Dissent

Contrary to the assumed wisdom that dissenters face personal censure, there is a growing body of work showing that groups can be surprisingly accepting of dissenters within their ranks (Esposo et al. 2013, Hiew & Hornsey 2010, Hornsey et al. 2002, Rabinovich & Morton 2010), and at times dissenters are even liked more than other group members (Van Dyne & Saavedra 1996). In work on group-directed criticism, group members are presented with either an in-group member or an outsider criticizing their group (e.g., Hornsey et al. 2002, Rabinovich & Morton 2010). These studies consistently show that in-group members criticizing the group are downgraded less strongly than outsiders who make exactly the same comments (the intergroup sensitivity effect). A critical message also arouses less emotional sensitivity and is agreed with more strongly when it is delivered by an in-group member. Importantly, the greater acceptance of the in-group message over the out-group message does not emerge when people are presented with positive or neutral statements about the group; the effect seems to be specific to criticisms. Furthermore, evaluations of in-group critics are often comparable to evaluations of in-group members who make positive or neutral comments about the group (Hornsey et al. 2002).

This relative tolerance toward internal critics appears to be rooted in the relatively generous attributions that group members make about their motives. When in-group members criticize the group, they are more likely to be seen to be doing so because they care for the group and want to create constructive change. Darker motivations are assumed to drive criticisms by out-group members—it is assumed they criticize because they intend to undermine, harm, and weaken the group—and it is this attributional bias that mediates the intergroup sensitivity effect (Hornsey & Imani 2004). The work on responses to in-group criticism makes clear that deviance and dissent are not unwelcome by definition. The fact that group members are interested in what a dissenter has to say, and that they consider at length why the dissenter would be saying it, goes against traditional views that have portrayed groups as reflexively intolerant and dogmatic (for a similar point, see Spears 2010).

However, even though there is some evidence that dissenters are tolerated and respected by other group members, this does not necessarily mean that dissenters are always liked and admired by others, even when they bring objective value to the group. Rink & Ellemers (2009) showed that newcomers were more involved in the group task, contributed more unique information during a decision-making task, and impacted more positively on group performance than did old-timers. However, newcomers were also less accepted than old-timers, and their presence dampened group identification levels for all group members. Sometimes the presence of a dissenter can lead to an ironic discrepancy between subjective and objective reality: Nemeth & Ormiston (2007) found that although observers report more innovation and better decision making in groups with dissenters, group members themselves reported lower innovation, cohesion, and task satisfaction (see also Rijnbout & McKimmie 2012a).

Tolerance for Deviance

Groups may also be remarkably tolerant of deviants. Sociologists have even suggested that a group's solidarity benefits from tolerating the deviant because it shows the strength of the group to deal with a plurality of views and behaviors (Coser 1962, Erikson 1966). Rejection of the deviant might actually harm solidarity because it demonstrates the group's rigidity and inability to adapt. Durkheim went as far as to argue that—to keep them vibrant—groups need deviants to such an extent that groups would quickly want to find someone breaking the rules if there were not enough deviant individuals in their midst. Durkheim (1958, pp. 68–69) states:

> Imagine a society of saints, a perfect cloister of exemplary individuals. Crimes, properly so called, will there be unknown; but faults which appear venial to the layman will create there the same scandal that the ordinary defense does in ordinary consciousness. If, then, this society has the power to judge and punish, it will define these acts as criminal and will treat them as such.

Durkheim's reasoning makes clear that deviants and dissenters are an important part of group life and that groups often accept and tolerate these individuals because they might be beneficial for group functioning. Therefore, the emphasis in sociological work is quite different from the focus in social psychological work: Sociology focuses on keeping deviance within bounds, whereas social psychologists focus on how groups aim to eradicate deviance. This suggests that the two disciplines start from two very different assumptions. Whereas sociologists perceive deviants as part of a healthy group, social psychologists perceive deviants as separate from a healthy group. In the latter view, healthy group life can exist only after the deviant has been removed (Jetten & Hornsey 2011).

FACTORS THAT AFFECT GROUP TOLERANCE OF DEVIANCE AND DISSENT

In the review above it is clear that deviants and dissenters may at times be seen to contribute to group functioning, and at other times their presence might be seen to be detrimental to the group. In this section we review conditions and factors that moderate these responses.

Qualities of the Dissenter/Deviant

One factor that affects whether deviants are treated harshly is whether they have engaged in similar deviant behavior in the past. Gollwitzer & Keller (2010) showed that when group members were evaluating a member of their own group, repeat offenders received harsher punishment for their actions than did a first-time offender. Evaluations of out-group members were not affected by whether they had engaged in similar rule breaking before. The authors suggest that ongoing deviance is more of a threat to the group identity when confronted with an in-group member than an out-group member, and this explains the harsher punishment of the former compared to the latter. Other work has shown that negative responses to in-group deviants are affected by the extent to which there is certainty about the guilt of the deviant. People reacted more negatively to in-group than out-group suspects when guilt was certain, but they reacted more negatively to out-group than in-group suspects when guilt was uncertain (van Prooijen 2006). The deviant's actions also matter: Intention to punish diminishes considerably when suspects express remorse (e.g., Carlsmith et al. 2002) and when they are willing to abandon their deviant position (Chan et al. 2010).

Unsurprisingly, the severity of the deviant's actions and the objective harm that is caused to the group affects responses to the deviant. Typically, modest violations of norms are derogated most by high identifiers, who by definition are especially sensitive to the integrity of the group's norms (Castano et al. 2002, Hornsey & Jetten 2003). However, there is evidence that group identification does not affect evaluations when the actions of the deviant are more harmful to the image of the group. For example, high and low identifiers are equally harsh on in-group deviants involved in serious violations such as academic fraud or abuse of Iraqi prisoners (Iyer et al. 2012).

There is also evidence that responses to deviants and dissenters depend on who they are and what their position is in the group. For example, powerful group members are given the freedom to behave in a more idiosyncratic way than nonpowerful members, and even subtle inductions of power can have the effect of increasing minor violations of social norms (Galinsky et al. 2008). Furthermore, dissenters and divergent thinkers within groups are tolerated more when they are prototypical members of the group (Rijnbout & McKimmie 2012b). For leaders, however, the norms are more nuanced. Whereas future leaders appear to be given license to innovate and to question established norms, current and ex-leaders are expected to show more loyalty to the status quo (Abrams et al. 2008a).

There is also evidence that group members are more willing to embrace criticism when the critic has been a member of the group for a long time than when the same criticisms come from a newcomer to the group (Hornsey et al. 2007b). This is consistent with the classic notion of "idiosyncrasy credits": People who have proven their loyalty to their group in the past have the most permission to violate rules and to challenge the group culture (Hollander 1958). The central role of loyalty attributions is evident also in the work on group criticism: In-group members who criticize the group are tolerated only when their message is intended to be constructive and when it is clear that they have the best interests of the group at heart (e.g., Hornsey et al. 2004). Those expressing criticism can signal that their intentions are constructive by using inclusive language emphasizing their commitment to the group ("we have a problem" rather than "they have a problem") or by otherwise emphasizing their "groupy" credentials (Hornsey et al. 2004) or shared group membership (Wirtz & Doosje 2013).

Qualities of the Group

There is some evidence that the stage of group life affects how group members respond to deviance and dissent. There are particularly strong pressures on members to conform in the initial phases when the group has just formed (Agazarian & Gantt 2003, Worchel 1998). In these early stages, groups often adopt a dress code or uniform and design other symbols that identify the group and mark people as being members. Members may be asked to demonstrate their loyalty to the group, and in this phase dissent or independent thinking is more likely to be viewed with suspicion (Rink & Ellemers 2009, Van Dyne & Saavedra 1996).

At other times, the group may strive for greater diversity and heterogeneity. Because dissenters and deviants provide such diversity, they are more accepted by other group members (Hutchison et al. 2011). Broader cultural norms also matter; for example, conformity is greater in collectivist cultures than in individualist cultures (Bond & Smith 1996), presumably because dissent is punished more harshly in groups with collectivist values (Hornsey et al. 2006). It has also been found that group goals affect whether group members attend to dissent. Toma and colleagues (2013) showed that in groups with cooperative goals, initial dissent among group members led to a greater willingness to be influenced by others than when the group held competitive goals. This suggests that disagreeing in a cooperative context can help group members to overcome and address differences of opinion.

A final factor that has been found to be important in moderating evaluations is whether the deviant/dissenter is the only person in the group who does not conform or whether he/she has social support from others. Classic work by Asch (1951) demonstrates that groups are more dismissive of a sole dissenter than of a group of dissenters. Although a sole dissenter can be ridiculed and pressured to get back in line, a group of dissenters and deviants might not be overlooked that easily, making social influence and social change more likely (Haslam & Reicher 2012b).

Group Treatment of the Deviant or Dissenter

The punishment meted out to deviants or dissenters can have ironic effects on how they are subsequently regarded. Eidelman and colleagues (2006) asked Christian participants to evaluate a prolife Christian (a deviant target) either before or after having the opportunity to exclude the target from the group. Evaluations of the target were more positive after exclusion from the group than before. This suggests that the need to further derogate deviants is diminished after exclusion, presumably because they can no longer threaten the group identity. Similar findings were obtained in a paradigm where, over time, a deviant was either reintegrated or remained marginalized and excluded (Chan et al. 2009). Group members who were more strongly committed to the group were most negative toward an excluded deviant who was later reintegrated. In contrast, there was evidence that group members were quite accepting of the deviant who faced continued exclusion. Presumably, this is because actions of the deviant who was evicted from the group no longer represented a threat to the group, with the consequence that group members could open their minds to the deviant and his/her message. In a similar vein, Curseu et al. (2012) found that groups that harbored a dissenter who subsequently left showed greater cognitive complexity than did groups that still had the dissenter within their ranks.

There is some evidence that unless the group changes its position or officially reintegrates the deviant, a rejected deviant will stay rejected even after being subsequently vindicated. Chan and colleagues (2010) manipulated historical facts about Galileo, who was excommunicated and rejected in the seventeenth century for his view—later verified—that the Earth revolves around the Sun. Catholic participants' negativity toward Galileo remained relatively high when they were led to believe that the Church had refused to formally reinstate him. This emphasizes that it is the stance of the group that determines how deviance is perceived and responded to as much as it is the actions of the individual deviant.

Strategic Factors

Previously we made the case that just as there are pressures to show conformity and respect for group norms, there are also countervailing motives to engage in deviance and dissent. People may not be prepared to take the risk of breaking group rules themselves but may be quietly relieved when others do. But what happens when a group member expresses a deviant or group-threatening attitude that you privately agree with? If you actively support the dissenter, you risk facing censure yourself. But if you fail to support the dissenter, you are violating your principles and potentially missing an opportunity to steer the group in a better direction. Managing these competing pressures requires close attention to the possibilities afforded by the context. Group members weigh up a number of strategic considerations: Who is watching? What can be gained? What can be lost?

One well-established principle is that the willingness to confront deviance changes as a function of the status of the audience. For example, in-group critics and other nonnormative members are rated more negatively when evaluations are public than when participants evaluate them privately, a tendency that gets more pronounced when the audience has high status (Hornsey et al. 2007a). Group members tend to be especially strategic in their judgments when they are low identifiers and so have not necessarily internalized the sanctity of the group's norms. For example, low identifiers and newcomers tend to express conformity and to confront rule violations in others only when they are being monitored by a high-status audience (Jetten et al. 2006, 2010). High identifiers and old-timers, in contrast, tend to defend the group norms irrespective of audience.

It is not the case, however, that highly identified group members are never strategic when they consider how to respond to deviance and dissent within their group. Packer (2013) found that highly identified group members were quite sensitive to the intergroup context when expressing dissent. Because highly identified group members are more concerned about the reputation of the group than are low identifiers, they were less likely to "air the group's dirty laundry" when doing so would make the group vulnerable (either because they were communicating to an out-group audience or because intergroup competition was particularly salient). Another recent paper also provides a fascinating twist on the intuitive position that those who are least secure in the group will be most likely to shy away from endorsing deviance and dissent in others. Across four studies, Rios and colleagues (2012) showed that the people who are most likely to express minority attitudes—and to endorse minority attitudes expressed by others—are those people who traditionally are associated with insecurity, vulnerability, and social defensiveness: those with high self-uncertainty and those low in implicit self-esteem. The authors argue that minority opinions can represent strivings for self-definition and defensive attempts to compensate for threats to the self-concept.

Strategic factors also play a role in the evaluation of positive deviants. Positive deviance is more likely to be embraced and celebrated if it helps enhance the reputation of the group; for example, in an intergroup context (Schmitt et al. 2000) or when the positive deviant attributes his/her success to the group (Fielding et al. 2006). Other work has shown that deviance and dissent are tolerated when they fit with the broader goals of the group (Teixeira et al. 2011, 2013). For example, Morton and colleagues (2007) found that partisans' evaluations of an in-group political candidate who expressed normative or deviant opinions depended on the implications of deviance for achieving group goals. High identifiers expressed stronger intentions to vote for a normative candidate over a deviant when public opinion was with the group. But when public opinion was against the group (or when the deviant was attracting high public support), high identifiers gave equal support to normative and deviant candidates. These findings suggest that backing the deviant might be a strategic choice for high identifiers when the deviant has the potential to lift the group's standing in the eyes of relevant third parties.

AN APPRECIATION FOR THE IMPORTANCE OF DEVIANCE AND DISSENT IN GROUPS

In this review we revisited the assumption that deviance and dissent are necessarily counterproductive forces for the group and therefore are perceived as problematic and unwelcome. By focusing on the myriad motivations of deviants and dissenters—and by focusing on the functional as well as the dysfunctional effects of deviance and dissent—we hope to have provided a balanced and complete view of these phenomena.

Unavoidably, by focusing on the functional as well as the dysfunctional impact of deviance and dissent, the picture that emerges is more complex than traditionally assumed: Groups are at times hostile toward deviants and dissenters, but at times they embrace them and are even protective of them. However, to conclude that the picture is more complex than previously assumed will not be satisfying or useful for researchers in the field who want guidance on how this review can inform their research. Therefore, instead of highlighting the complexity of the messages that emerge from recent work, it might be more useful to consider how the research focus needs to be redirected and broadened to enable a greater appreciation of the value of deviance and dissent. Three pointers in particular emerge from this review that might be useful to keep in mind when embarking on further research in this field.

First, the research reviewed here points to the normality and ordinariness of deviance and dissent—as acts that all group members engage in from time to time. The observation that dissent and deviance are not extraordinary behaviors that only a small number of individuals engage in for some unknown or sinister reasons demands a change in the way that we study group processes: The behaviors of deviants and dissenters should be seen and studied as part of group life rather than as separate and distinct from it (Jetten & Hornsey 2011).

Second, as we have outlined, the study of deviance and dissent should be broadened to encompass the diverse motivations that underpin them. Deviants and dissenters at times are troublemakers: Their actions are harmful to the group, and it is understandable that groups will respond negatively to them. At other times, however, dissenters and deviants are indistinguishable from any other group member who has the group's interests at heart. This is because they often engage in such behaviors for constructive reasons: because they wish to improve the group, campaign to change suboptimal group cultures, or simply avoid collective mistakes. In fact, very often the dissenter or deviant and the most loyal group member are the same person. By assuming that deviants and dissenters are acting against the group rather than for the group, we risk ignoring a rich and important ingredient of group life (Packer 2008).

Third, groups do often recognize the value of deviance and dissent. Engaging with the functions and dysfunctions of dissent and deviance teaches us that group life is more than pressures for conformity and striving for sameness. By assuming that groups are mainly motivated to exclude deviants and punish dissent, we fail to acknowledge that deviants and dissenters help keep groups healthy and vibrant and are often appreciated as such.

More than 30 years ago Moscovici (1976) complained that the final goal of researchers always appears to be "the reclamation of deviants." In particular, he argues that researchers in the field have focused on only one set of forces that drive group responses to deviance: "making everybody alike, blurring the particularity and individuality of persons or subgroups" (Moscovici 1976, p. 17; see also Levine 1989). Similar sentiments have been voiced more recently, and it has been argued that an understanding of basic group processes is necessarily impoverished if theorizing does not take account of the group members that conform to group norms as well as those members that challenge them (Ellemers & Jetten 2013; Haslam & Reicher 2012a; Jetten & Hornsey 2011, 2012; Packer 2008). It is only when we integrate research on deviants and dissent with theorizing on group processes more generally that we can develop a more complete, balanced, and refined understanding of deviants and dissenters in groups.

SUMMARY POINTS

1. Within groups, deviance and dissent are common and are often recognized as beneficial to group functioning.

2. Healthy groups have deviants and dissenters in their midst.

3. What is considered deviant and dissenting is contextually determined and may change with time.

4. There are a number of reasons why group members engage in deviance and dissent within groups. Among others, deviance and dissent may be motivated by (*a*) disengagement, disloyalty, or disrespect for the group, (*b*) group loyalty, (*c*) moral reasons, (*d*) a desire to express difference, individuality, and uniqueness, and (*e*) a wish to obtain the tangible rewards that deviance and dissent provide.

5. Rejection of deviance and dissent helps to restore threatened group positivity, threatened group cohesion, threatened group distinctiveness, threatened group locomotion, and threatened self-image.

6. Deviants and dissenters can damage the group but can also contribute in positive ways to group functioning. In particular, under some conditions, dissent increases the quality of group decision making and enhances group creativity, innovation, and learning. Deviance can sharpen the group's understanding of its values and can facilitate social change.

7. Other group members often recognize the value of deviants and dissenters and are therefore often remarkably tolerant of these individuals.

FUTURE ISSUES

1. Whereas classic research examined responses to deviants and dissenters in groups where members interacted over a period of time [e.g., Schachter's (1951) research on rejection, deviance, and communication], recent work has examined responses to deviants and dissenters using scenarios and contexts devoid of interaction. To understand fully the trajectory of responses to deviants and dissenters, more research needs to be conducted examining responses to deviants and dissenters over time in real interacting groups and in different group contexts (e.g., different group goals or different group cultures).

2. We know little about the micro strategies for how group members manage dissent and deviance in live, interactive groups. This would require a more descriptive communication approach to the question of deviance and dissent.

3. There are many different disciplines within the social sciences that examine deviance and dissent. There is a need for a theoretical integration of work on dissent, minority influence, interpersonal deviance, interpersonal aggression, bullying, and criminal behavior.

DISCLOSURE STATEMENT

The authors are not aware of any affiliations, memberships, funding, or financial holdings that might be perceived as affecting the objectivity of this review.

ACKNOWLEDGMENTS

We thank Alex Haslam, John Levine, and Dominic Packer for insightful comments on earlier drafts of this article. This review was supported by a Discovery grant from the Australian Research Council (DP1094034).

LITERATURE CITED

Abrams D, Marques JM, Bown N, Dougill M. 2002. Anti-norm and pro-norm deviance in the bank and on the campus: two experiments on subjective group dynamics. *Group Process. Intergroup Relat.* 5:163–82

Abrams D, Marques JM, Bown N, Henson M. 2000. Pro-norm and anti-norm deviance within in-groups and out-groups. *J. Personal. Soc. Psychol.* 78:906–12

Abrams D, Randsley de Moura G, Marques JM, Hutchison P. 2008a. Innovation credit: When can leaders oppose their group's norms? *J. Personal. Soc. Psychol.* 95(3):662–78

Abrams D, Rutland A, Ferrell JM, Pelletier J. 2008b. Children's judgments of disloyal and immoral peer behavior: subjective group dynamics in minimal intergroup contexts. *Child Dev.* 79(2):444–61

Agazarian Y, Gantt S. 2003. Phases of group development: systems-centered hypotheses and their implications for research and practice. *Group Dyn. Theory Res. Pract.* 7:238–52

Amabile TM. 1996. *Creativity in Context*. Boulder, CO: Westview

Ariyanto A, Hornsey MJ, Gallois C. 2010. United we stand: Intergroup conflict moderates the intergroup sensitivity effect. *Eur. J. Soc. Psychol.* 40:169–77

Asch SE. 1951. Effects of group pressure upon the modification and distortion of judgments. In *Groups, Leadership and Men: Research in Human Relations*, ed. H Guetzkow, pp. 177–90. Pittsburgh, PA: Carnegie Press

Benard S. 2012. Cohesion from conflict: Does intergroup conflict motivate intragroup norm enforcement and support for centralized leadership? *Soc. Psychol. Q.* 75:107–30

Bennett RJ, Robinson SL. 2000. Development of a measure of workplace deviance. *J. Appl. Psychol.* 85:349–60

Ben-Yehuda N. 2010. Positive and negative deviance: more fuel for a controversy. *Deviant Behav.* 11:221–43

Blanton H, Christie C. 2003. Deviance regulation: a theory of action and identity. *Rev. Gen. Psychol.* 7:115–49

Blanton H, Stuart AE, Van den Eijnden RJJM. 2001. An introduction to deviance regulation theory: the effect of behavioral norms on message framing. *Personal. Soc. Psychol. Bull.* 27(7):848–58

Bond R, Smith PB. 1996. Culture and conformity: a meta-analysis of studies using Asch's (1952b, 1956) line judgment task. *Psychol. Bull.* 119:111–37

Branscombe NR, Wann DL, Noel JG, Coleman J. 1993. In-group or out-group extremity: importance of the threatened social identity. *Personal. Soc. Psychol. Bull.* 19:381–88

Butera F, Darnon C, Mugny G. 2011. Learning from conflict. See Jetten & Hornsey 2011, pp. 36–53

Carlsmith KM, Darley JM, Robinson PH. 2002. Why do we punish? Deterrence and just deserts as motives for punishment. *J. Personal. Soc. Psychol.* 83:284–99

Castano E, Paladino M, Coull A, Yzerbyt VY. 2002. Protecting the ingroup stereotype: ingroup identification and the management of deviant ingroup members. *Br. J. Soc. Psychol.* 41:365–85

Chan MKH, Louis WR, Hornsey MJ. 2009. The effects of exclusion and reintegration on evaluation of deviant opinion holders. *Personal. Soc. Psychol. Bull.* 35(12):1619–31

Chan MKH, Louis WR, Jetten J. 2010. When groups are wrong and deviants are right. *Eur. J. Soc. Psychol.* 40:1103–9

Chekroun P, Nugier A. 2011. "I'm ashamed because of you, so please, don't do that!" Reactions to deviance as a protection against a threat to social image. *Eur. J. Soc. Psychol.* 41:479–88

Choi HS, Levine JM. 2004. Minority influence in work teams: the impact of newcomers. *J. Exp. Soc. Psychol.* 40:273–80

Christian JS, Ellis APJ. 2013. The crucial role of turnover intentions in transforming moral disengagement into deviant behavior at work. *J. Bus. Ethics.* In press

Codol J-P. 1984. Social differentiation and non-differentiation. In *The Social Dimension: European Developments in Social Psychology*, ed. H Tajfel, pp. 314–37. Cambridge, UK: Cambridge Univ. Press

A classic text showing the prevalence of dissent despite tremendous conformity pressures.

Conway LG, Schaller M. 2005. When authorities' commands backfire: attributions about consensus and effects on deviant decision making. *J. Personal. Soc. Psychol.* 89:311–26

Coser L. 1962. Some functions of deviant behavior and normative flexibility. *Am. J. Sociol.* 68:172–81

Coull A, Yzerbyt VY, Castano E, Paladino MP, Leemans V. 2001. Protecting the ingroup: motivated allocation of cognitive resources in the presence of threatening ingroup members. *Group Process. Intergroup Relat.* 4:327–39

Crane MF, Platow MJ. 2010. Deviance as adherence to injunctive group norms: the overlooked role of social identification in deviance. *Br. J. Soc. Psychol.* 49:827–47

Cronin T, Smith H. 2011. Protest, exit, or deviance: adjunct university faculty reactions to occupational rank-based mistreatment. *J. Appl. Soc. Psychol.* 41:2352–73

Curseu PL, Schruijer SGL, Boros S. 2012. Socially rejected while cognitively successful: the impact of minority dissent on groups' cognitive complexity. *Br. J. Soc. Psychol.* 51:570–82

Darnon C, Doll S, Butera F. 2007. Dealing with a disagreeing partner: relational and epistemic conflict elaboration. *Eur. J. Psychol. Educ.* 22:227–42

De Dreu CKW. 2006. When too much and too little hurts: evidence for a curvilinear relationship between task conflict and innovation in teams. *J. Manag.* 32:83–107

De Dreu CKW, West MA. 2001. Minority dissent and team innovation: the importance of participation in decision making. *J. Appl. Psychol.* 86:1191–201

Deutsch M, Gerard H. 1955. A study of normative and informational social influences upon individual judgment. *J. Abnorm. Soc. Psychol.* 51:629–36

Dooley RS, Fryxell GE. 1999. Attaining decision quality and commitment from dissent: the moderating effects of loyalty and competence in strategic decision-making teams. *Acad. Manag. J.* 42:389–402

Durkheim E. 1958 [1895]. *The Rules of Sociological Method.* Glencoe: Free Press

Eidelman S, Biernat M. 2003. Derogating black sheep: individual or group protection? *J. Exp. Soc. Psychol.* 39:602–9

Eidelman S, Silvia PJ, Biernat M. 2006. Responding to deviance: target exclusion and differential devaluation. *Personal. Soc. Psychol. Bull.* 32:1153–64

Elder TJ, Sutton RM, Douglas KM. 2005. Keeping it to ourselves: effects of audience size and composition on reactions to criticism of the ingroup. *Group Process. Intergroup Relat.* 8:231–44

Ellemers N, Jetten J. 2013. The many ways to be marginal in a group. *Personal. Soc. Psychol. Rev.* 17:3–21

Erikson KT. 1966. *Wayward Puritans: A Study in the Sociology of Deviance.* New York: Wiley

Esposo SR Hornsey MJ, Spoor JR. 2013. Shooting the messenger: Outsiders critical of your group are rejected regardless of argument quality. *Br. J. Soc. Psychol.* 52:386–95

Feather NT, Sherman R. 2002. Envy, resentment, schadenfreude, and sympathy: reactions to deserved and undeserved achievement and subsequent failure. *Personal. Soc. Psychol. Bull.* 28:953–61

Ferris DL, Spence JR, Brown DJ, Heller D. 2012. Interpersonal injustice and workplace deviance: the role of esteem threat. *J. Manag.* 38:1788–811

Festinger L. 1950. Informal social communication. *Psychol. Rev.* 57(5):271–82

Fielding KS, Hogg MA, Annandale N. 2006. Reactions to positive deviance: social identity and attributional dimensions. *Group Process. Intergroup Relat.* 9:199–218

Frings D, Hurst J, Cleveland C, Blascovich J, Abrams D. 2012. Challenge, threat, and subjective group dynamics: reactions to normative and deviant group members. *Group Dyn. Theory Res. Pract.* 16:105–21

Galinsky AD, Magee JC, Gruenfeld DH, Whitson J, Liljenquist KA. 2008. Social power reduces the strength of the situation: implications for creativity, conformity, and dissonance. *J. Personal. Soc. Psychol.* 95:1450–66

Galperin BL. 2012. Exploring the nomological network of workplace deviance: developing and validating a measure of constructive deviance. *J. Appl. Soc. Psychol.* 42:2988–3025

Gollwitzer M, Keller L. 2010. What you did only matters if you are one of us: Offenders' group membership moderates the effect of criminal history on punishment severity. *Soc. Psychol.* 41:20–26

Greitemeyer T, Schulz-Hardt S, Frey D. 2009. The effects of authentic and contrived dissent on escalation of commitment in group decision making. *Eur. J. Soc. Psychol.* 39:639–47

Hansen T, Levine JM. 2009. Newcomers as change agents: effects of newcomers' behavioral style and teams' performance optimism. *Soc. Influ.* 4:46–61

A classic text emphasizing the functionality of deviance for group life.

Haslam SA, Reicher SD. 2012a. When prisoners take over the prison: a social psychology of resistance. *Personal. Soc. Psychol. Rev.* 16:154–79

Haslam SA, Reicher SD. 2012b. Contesting the "nature" of conformity: what Milgram and Zimbardo's studies really show. *PLoS Biol.* 10(11):e1001426

Hichy Z, Mari S, Capozza D. 2008. Pro-norm and anti-norm deviants: a test of the subjective group dynamics model. *Eur. J. Soc. Psychol.* 148:641–44

Hiew DN, Hornsey MJ. 2010. Does time reduce resistance to out-group critics? An investigation of the persistence of the intergroup sensitivity effect over time. *Br. J. Soc. Psychol.* 49:569–81

Hollander EP. 1958. Conformity, status and idiosyncrasy credit. *Psychol. Rev.* 65:117–27

Hornsey MJ, de Bruijn P, Creed J, Allen J, Ariyanto A, Svensson A. 2005. Keeping it in-house: how audience affects responses to group criticism. *Eur. J. Soc. Psychol.* 35:291–312

Hornsey MJ, Frederiks E, Smith JR, Ford L. 2007a. Strategic defensiveness: public and private responses to group criticism. *Br. J. Soc. Psychol.* 46:697–716

Hornsey MJ, Grice T, Jetten J, Paulsen N, Callan V. 2007b. Group-directed criticisms and recommendations for change: why newcomers arouse more resistance than old-timers. *Personal. Soc. Psychol. Bull.* 32:1620–32

Hornsey MJ, Imani A. 2004. Criticizing groups from the inside and the outside: an identity perspective on the intergroup sensitivity effect. *Personal. Soc. Psychol. Bull.* 30:365–83

Hornsey MJ, Jetten J. 2003. Not being what you claim to be: impostors as sources of group threat. *Eur. J. Soc. Psychol.* 33:639–57

Hornsey MJ, Jetten J. 2004. The individual within the group: balancing the need to belong with the need to be different. *Personal. Soc. Psychol. Rev.* 8:248–64

Hornsey MJ, Jetten J. 2011. Impostors within groups: the psychology of claiming to be something you are not. See Jetten & Hornsey 2011, pp. 158–78

Hornsey MJ, Jetten J, McAuliffe B, Hogg MA. 2006. The impact of individualist and collectivist group norms on evaluations of dissenting group members. *J. Exp. Soc. Psychol.* 42:57–68

Hornsey MJ, Majkut L, Terry DJ, McKimmie BM. 2003. On being loud and proud: non-conformity and counter-conformity to group norms. *Br. J. Soc. Psychol.* 42:319–35

Hornsey MJ, Oppes T, Svensson A. 2002. "It's OK if we say it, but you can't": responses to intergroup and intragroup criticism. *Eur. J. Soc. Psychol.* 32:293–307

Hornsey MJ, Trembath M, Gunthorpe S. 2004. "You can criticize because you care": identity attachment, constructiveness, and the intergroup sensitivity effect. *Eur. J. Soc. Psychol.* 34:499–518

Hutchison P, Abrams D. 2003. Ingroup identification moderates stereotype change in reaction to ingroup deviance. *Eur. J. Soc. Psychol.* 33:497–506

Hutchison P, Abrams D, Gutierrez R, Viki GT. 2008. Getting rid of the bad ones: the relationship between group identification, deviant derogation, and stereotype maintenance. *J. Exp. Soc. Psychol.* 44:874–81

Hutchison P, Jetten J, Gutierrez R. 2011. Deviant but desirable: perceived group variability and reactions to atypical group members. *J. Exp. Soc. Psychol.* 47:1155–61

Imhoff R, Erb H-P. 2009. What motivates nonconformity? Uniqueness seeking blocks majority influence. *Personal. Soc. Psychol. Bull.* 35:309–20

Iyer A, Jetten J, Haslam SA. 2012. Sugaring o'er the devil: Moral superiority and group identification help individuals downplay the implications of ingroup rule-breaking. *Eur. J. Soc. Psychol.* 42:141–49

Janis IL. 1972. *Victims of Groupthink.* Boston, MA: Houghton Mifflin

Jehn K, Northcraft G, Neale M. 1999. Why differences make a difference: a field study of diversity, conflict, and performance in workgroups. *Adm. Sci. Q.* 44:741–63

Jetten J, Branscombe NR, Schmitt MT, Spears R. 2001. Rebels with a cause: group identification as a response to perceived discrimination from the mainstream. *Personal. Soc. Psychol. Bull.* 27:1204–13

Jetten J, Hornsey MJ, eds. 2011. *Rebels in Groups: Dissent, Deviance, Difference and Defiance.* Chichester, UK: Wiley-Blackwell

Jetten J, Hornsey MJ. 2012. Conformity: beyond the Asch line judgment studies. In *Refreshing Social Psychology: Beyond the Classic Studies*, ed. J Smith, SA Haslam, pp. 76–90. London: Sage

Jetten J, Hornsey MJ, Adarves-Yorno I. 2006. When group members admit to being conformist: the role of relative intragroup status in conformity self-reports. *Personal. Soc. Psychol. Bull.* 32:162–73

This chapter outlines the different reasons why people may engage in impostorism.

This edited book includes chapters that show that dissent, difference, deviance, and defiance are just as much a part of group life and as essential for good group functioning as is conformity.

Jetten J, Hornsey MJ, Spears R, Haslam SA, Cowell E. 2010. Rule transgressions in groups: the conditional nature of newcomers' willingness to confront deviance. *Eur. J. Soc. Psychol.* 40:338–48

Kelman HC. 1995. Decision making and public discourse in the Gulf War: an assessment of underlying psychological and moral assumptions. *Peace Confl. J. Peace Psychol.* 1:117–30

Kraschnewski JL, Stuckey HL, Roviniak LS, Lehman EB, Reddy M, et al. 2011. Efficacy of a weight-loss website based on positive deviance: a randomized trial. *Am. J. Prev. Med.* 41:610–14

Kruglanski AW, Webster DM. 1991. Group members' reactions to opinion deviates and conformists at varying degrees of proximity to decision deadline and of environmental noise. *J. Personal. Soc. Psychol.* 61:212–25

Kruglanski AW, Webster DM. 1996. Motivated closing of the mind: "seizing" and "freezing." *Psychol. Rev.* 103:263–83

Kunda Z, Oleson KC. 1997. When exceptions prove the rule: how extremity of deviance determines the impact of deviant examples on stereotypes. *J. Personal. Soc. Psychol.* 72:965–79

Levine JM. 1989. Reaction to opinion deviance in small groups. In *Psychology of Group Influence*, ed. PB Paulus, pp. 187–231. Hillsdale, NJ: Erlbaum

Levine JM, Kerr NL. 2007. Inclusion and exclusion: implications for group processes. In *Social Psychology: Handbook of Basic Principles*, ed. AE Kruglanski, ET Higgins, pp. 759–84. New York: Guilford. 2nd ed.

Louis WR, Taylor DM, Douglas RL. 2005. Normative influence and rational conflict decisions: group norms and cost-benefit analyses for intergroup behaviour. *Group Process. Intergroup Relat.* 8:355–74

Ma P, Magnus JH. 2012. Exploring the concept of positive deviance related to breastfeeding initiation in black and white WIC enrolled first time mothers. *Matern. Child Health J.* 16:1583–93

Markova G, Folger R. 2012. Every cloud has a silver lining: positive effects of deviant coworkers. *Eur. J. Soc. Psychol.* 152:586–612

Marques JM, Abrams D, Serôdio RG. 2001. Being better by being right: subjective group dynamics and derogation of ingroup deviants when generic norms are undermined. *J. Personal. Soc. Psychol.* 81:436–47

Marques JM, Paez D. 1994. The "black sheep effect": social categorization, rejection of ingroup deviates, and perception of group variability. *Eur. Rev. Soc. Psychol.* 5:37–68

Matheson K, Cole B, Majka K. 2003. Dissidence from within: examining intragroup reactions to attitudinal opposition. *J. Exp. Soc. Psychol.* 39:161–69

Matz DC, Wood W. 2005. Cognitive dissonance in groups: the consequences of disagreement. *J. Personal. Soc. Psychol.* 88:22–37

McAuliffe BJ, Jetten J, Hornsey MJ, Hogg MA. 2002. Individualist and collectivist norms: when it's ok to go your own way. *Eur. J. Soc. Psychol.* 33:57–70

Merton RK. 1968. *Social Theory and Social Structure*. New York: Free Press

Milgram S. 1963. Behavioral study of obedience. *J. Abnorm. Soc. Psychol.* 67:371–78

Molero F, Fuster MJ, Jetten J, Moriano JA. 2011. Living with HIV/AIDS: a psychosocial perspective on coping with prejudice and discrimination. *J. Appl. Soc. Psychol.* 41:609–26

Monin B, O'Connor K. 2011. Reactions to defiant deviants: deliverance or defensiveness? See Jetten & Hornsey 2011, pp. 261–79

Monin B, Sawyer PJ, Marquez MJ. 2008. The rejection of moral rebels: resenting those who do the right thing. *J. Personal. Soc. Psychol.* 95(1):76–93

Morton TA, Postmes T, Jetten J. 2007. Playing the game: strategic considerations and responses to normative and deviant group members. *Eur. J. Soc. Psychol.* 37:599–616

Moscovici S. 1976. *Social Influence and Social Change*. New York: Academic

Nemeth C. 1995. Dissent as driving cognition, attitudes and judgments. *Soc. Cogn.* 13:273–91

Nemeth C, Brown K, Rogers J. 2001. Devil's advocate versus authentic dissent: stimulating quantity and quality. *Eur. J. Soc. Psychol.* 31:707–20

Nemeth C, Goncalo JA. 2011. Rogues and heroes: finding value in dissent. See Jetten & Hornsey 2011, pp. 17–35

Nemeth C, Ormiston M. 2007. Creative idea generation: harmony versus stimulation. *J. Exp. Soc. Psychol.* 37:524–35

Nemeth C, Personnaz B, Personnaz M, Goncalo JA. 2004. The liberating role of conflict in group creativity: a study in two countries. *Eur. J. Soc. Psychol.* 34:365–74

This book has become a classic in the field and reveals Moscovici's frustration with the one-sided interest of social psychologists in conformity.

Packer DJ. 2008. On being with us and against us: a normative conflict model of dissent in social groups. *Personal. Soc. Psychol. Rev.* 12:50–72

Packer DJ. 2009. Avoiding groupthink: Whereas weakly identified members remain silent, strongly identified members dissent about collective problems. *Psychol. Sci.* 20:546–48

Packer DJ. 2011. The dissenter's dilemma, and a social identity solution. See Jetten & Hornsey 2011, pp. 281–301

Packer DJ. 2013. On not airing our dirty laundry: Intergroup contexts suppress ingroup criticism among strongly identified group members. *Br. J. Soc. Psychol.* In press

Packer DJ, Chasteen AL. 2010. Loyal deviance: testing the normative conflict model of dissent in social groups. *Personal. Soc. Psychol. Bull.* 36:5–18

Parks G, Stone AB. 2010. The desire to expel unselfish members from the group. *J. Personal. Soc. Psychol.* 99:303–10

Postmes T, Spears R, Cihangir S. 2001. Quality of decision making and group norms. *J. Personal. Soc. Psychol.* 80:918–30

Prislin R, Christensen PN. 2005. Social change in the aftermath of successful minority influence. *Eur. Rev. Soc. Psychol.* 16:43–73

Prislin R, Filson J. 2009. Seeking conversion versus advocating tolerance in the pursuit of social change. *J. Personal. Soc. Psychol.* 97:811–22

Rabinovich A, Morton TA. 2010. Who says we are bad people? The impact of criticism source and attributional content on responses to group-based criticism. *Personal. Soc. Psychol. Bull.* 36:524–36

Reicher SD, Haslam SA. 2006. Rethinking the psychology of tyranny: the BBC Prison Study. *Br. J. Soc. Psychol.* 45:1–40

Rijnbout JS, McKimmie BM. 2012a. Deviance in organizational group decision-making: the role of information processing, confidence, and elaboration. *Group Process. Intergroup Relat.* 15:813–28

Rijnbout JS, McKimmie BM. 2012b. Deviance in group decision making: group-member centrality alleviates negative consequences for the group. *Eur. J. Soc. Psychol.* 42:915–23

Rink F, Ellemers N. 2009. Temporary versus permanent group membership: how the future prospects of newcomers affect newcomer acceptance and newcomer influence. *Personal. Soc. Psychol. Bull.* 35:764–76

Rios K, Wheeler SC, Miller DT. 2012. Compensatory nonconformity: self-uncertainty and low implicit self-esteem increase adoption and expression of minority opinions. *J. Exp. Soc. Psychol.* 48:1300–09

Rios Morrison K, Wheeler SC. 2010. Nonconformity defines the self: the role of minority opinion status in self-concept clarity. *Personal. Soc. Psychol. Bull.* 36:297–308

Sani F, Reicher S. 2000. Contested identities and schisms in groups: opposing the ordination of women as priests in the Church of England. *Br. J. Soc. Psychol.* 39:95–112

Sassenberg K, Matschke C, Scholl A. 2011. The impact of discrepancies from ingroup norms on group members' well-being and motivation. *Eur. J. Soc. Psychol.* 41:886–97

Schachter S. 1951. Deviation, rejection, and communication. *J. Abnorm. Soc. Psychol.* 46:190–207

Schmitt MT, Silvia PJ, Branscombe NR. 2000. The intersection of self-evaluation maintenance and social identity theories: intragroup judgment in interpersonal and intergroup contexts. *Personal. Soc. Psychol. Bull.* 26:1598–606

Schoemann AM, Branscombe NR. 2011. Looking young for your age: perceptions of anti-aging actions. *Eur. J. Soc. Psychol.* 41:86–95

Shamir J. 1997. Speaking up and silencing out in face of a changing climate of opinion. *J. Mass Commun. Q.* 74:602–14

Shatz RT, Staub E, Lavine H. 1999. On the varieties of national attachment: blind versus constructive patriotism. *Polit. Psychol.* 20:151–74

Shoenberger N, Heckert A, Heckert D. 2012. Techniques of neutralization theory and positive deviance. *Deviant Behav.* 33:774–91

Spears R. 2010. Group rationale, collective sense: beyond intergroup bias. *Br. J. Soc. Psychol.* 49:1–20

Spears R, Doosje B, Ellemers N. 1997. Self-stereotyping in the face of threats to group status and distinctiveness: the role of group identification. *Personal. Soc. Psychol. Bull.* 23:538–53

Tata J, Anthony T, Lin H, Newman B, Tang S, et al. 1996. Proportionate group size and rejection of the deviate: a meta-analytic integration. *J. Soc. Behav. Personal.* 11(4):739–52

Tauber S, Sassenberg K. 2012. The impact of identification on adherence to group norms in team sports: Who is going the extra mile? *Group Dyn. Theory Res. Pract.* 16:231–40

Teixeira CP, Demoulin S, Yzerbyt VY. 2011. Choosing the best means to an end: the influence of ingroup goals on the selection of representatives in intergroup negotiations. *J. Exp. Soc. Psychol.* 47:228–34

Teixeira CP, Demoulin S, Yzerbyt VY. 2013. Playing with deviance: typicality assessments of ingroup members as a strategy of outgroup approach. *Eur. J. Soc. Psychol.* 43:32–39

Toma C, Giles I, Butera F. 2013. Strategic use of preference confirmation in group decision making: the role of competition and dissent. *Br. J. Soc. Psychol.* 32:44–63

Troyer L, Youngreen R. 2009. Conflict and creativity in groups. *J. Soc. Issues* 65:409–27

Turner JC. 1991. *Social Influence*. Milton-Keynes, UK: Open Univ. Press

Van Dyne L, Saavedra R. 1996. A naturalistic minority influence experiment: effects of divergent thinking, conflict and originality in work groups. *Br. J. Soc. Psychol.* 35:151–68

Van Prooijen J-W. 2006. Retributive reactions to suspected offenders: the importance of social categorizations and guilt probability. *Personal. Soc. Psychol. Bull.* 32:715–26

Warner R, Hornsey MJ, Jetten J. 2007. Why minority members resent impostors. *Eur. J. Soc. Psychol.* 37:1–18

Warren DE. 2003. Constructive and destructive deviance in organizations. *Acad. Manag. Rev.* 28(4):622–32

Wirtz C, Doosje B. 2013. Reactions to threatening critical messages from minority group members with shared or distinct group identities. *Eur. J. Soc. Psychol.* 43:50–61

Wolf B, Zuckerman P. 2012. Deviant heroes: nonconformists as agents of justice and social change. *Deviant Behav.* 33:639–54

Wood W, Lundgren S, Ouellette JA, Busceme S, Blackstone T. 1994. Processes of minority influence: influence effectiveness and source perception. *Psychol. Bull.* 115:323–45

Worchel S. 1998. A developmental view of the search for group identity. In *Social Identity: International Perspectives*, ed. S Worchel, JF Morales, D Paez, J-C Deschamps, pp. 53–74. Thousand Oaks, CA: Sage

Zdaniuk B, Levine JM. 2001. Group loyalty: impact of members' identification and contributions. *J. Exp. Soc. Psychol.* 37:502–9

Cultural Neuroscience: Biology of the Mind in Cultural Contexts

Heejung S. Kim[1] and Joni Y. Sasaki[2]

[1]Department of Psychological and Brain Sciences, University of California, Santa Barbara, California 93106; email: heejung.kim@psych.ucsb.edu

[2]Department of Psychology, York University, Toronto, Ontario M3J 1P3, Canada; email: jsasaki@yorku.ca

Annu. Rev. Psychol. 2014. 65:487–514

First published online as a Review in Advance on September 11, 2013

The *Annual Review of Psychology* is online at http://psych.annualreviews.org

This article's doi: 10.1146/annurev-psych-010213-115040

Keywords

cultural psychology, genetics, brain imaging, neuroendocrinology, physiological responses

Abstract

This article provides a review of how cultural contexts shape and are shaped by psychological and neurobiological processes. We propose a framework that aims to culturally contextualize behavioral, genetic, neural, and physiological processes. Empirical evidence is presented to offer concrete examples of how neurobiological processes underlie social behaviors, and how these components are interconnected in larger cultural contexts. These findings provide some understanding of how the meanings shared by cultural experiences trigger a neurobiological, psychological, and behavioral chain of events, and how these events may be coordinated and maintained within a person. The review concludes with a reflection on the current state of cultural neuroscience and questions for the field to address.

Contents

INTRODUCTION

At the root of the study of the mind and behavior has always been the question of nature and nurture. Some previous philosophical and scientific inquiries have taken the view that the human mind and its contents are almost entirely acquired (Aristotle and Locke) or almost entirely innate (Plato and Hobbes), and hence, the phrase "nature versus nurture" was coined (Galton 1874). Most contemporary researchers, however, acknowledge both nature and nurture as joint determinants that influence psychological and behavioral outcomes (Plomin & Asbury 2005). Thus, the more productive questions for current scientific inquiries should be, How do nature and nurture work together, and what are the processes through which biology and culture shape the mind?

Cultural psychology is a field that investigates the influence of nurture, or cultural contexts, on human psychological tendencies and behaviors (Fiske et al. 1998, Shweder 1995). Over the last few decades, the field has generated numerous empirical findings that highlight diversity in human behaviors, traits, and psychological processes as products of engagement in specific sociocultural contexts. The specific nature of culture is multidimensional in that it includes shared physical environments, social structures, institutions, interactions, worldviews, and values (Kim & Markus 1999, Kitayama et al. 1997, Miyamoto et al. 2006). Cultural contexts are made up of these products of human minds that are loosely but coherently built on shared basic assumptions about the world (Kitayama 2002). They provide a shared meaning system through which individuals interpret situations and make sense of their experiences, and these meanings that are shared within cultural contexts are at the psychological core of nurture (Bruner 1990).

Although the empirical focus of cultural psychology has been on nurture, researchers recognize that in humans the impact of nature, or biological processes and constraints, at both species and individual levels, should not be ignored and that it is imperative to look at how nature and nurture jointly make up human psychological and behavioral tendencies. The recent emergence of cultural neuroscience attests to such recognition. Cultural neuroscience is a branch of cultural psychology

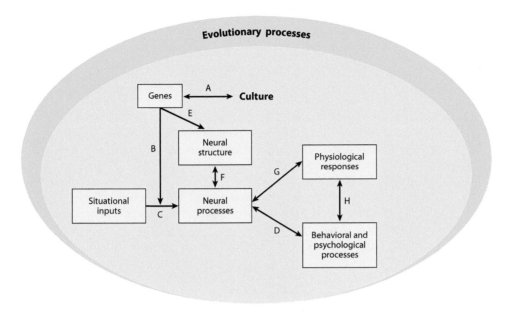

Figure 1

Framework of cultural neuroscience.

that aims to address how cultural and biological factors interact (Chiao & Ambady 2007). It is perhaps an unexpected combination of perspectives—the study of meaning and the study of the neural system—but it is a combination that is essential to gain a fuller understanding of human behaviors and psychological processes. This review focuses on how shared meanings afforded by cultural contexts shape and are shaped by psychological and biological processes.

FRAMEWORK OF CULTURAL NEUROSCIENCE

The field of cultural psychology has flourished and accumulated a large body of literature over the last several decades. Although these empirical investigations began with comparisons between national/ethnic cultures, they later became more inclusive of other sociocultural contexts, such as social class (Snibbe & Markus 2005, Stephens et al. 2007), regions within a country (Kitayama et al. 2006a, Nisbett 1993, Uskul et al. 2008), and religion (Cohen & Hill 2007, Tsai et al. 2007; see Cohen 2009 for a review). In terms of the domains of psychology, researchers have documented cultural variations in just about every aspect of psychological functioning, from the more basic processes, such as emotion (Kitayama et al. 2006b) and cognition (Nisbett et al. 2001) to more complex processes, such as the self (Heine et al. 1999), relationships (Kim et al. 2008), and psychological well-being (Suh 2002).

In this review, we present findings regarding how cultural factors are linked to neurobiological functioning and propose an overarching framework of cultural neuroscience that is inclusive of different levels of analysis (**Figure 1**). The central argument of our framework is that individuals' biological and psychological processes occur within larger cultural contexts and the constraints of evolutionary processes. At present, the existing empirical evidence illuminating these interlocking processes is relatively limited, and some processes, especially the ways in which different levels implicate each other, have yet to be empirically studied. However, it is worthwhile to consider how these biological components work together and are influenced by cultural contexts.

In this review, we present existing evidence in three broad sections to provide concrete examples of how these biological processes occur in larger cultural contexts. The next section, on "Genetics," reviews theories and empirical evidence on how cultural and genetic factors influence each other at a larger societal level through evolutionary processes via gene-culture coevolution (Link A in **Figure 1**) as well as theories and evidence on how cultural factors and genetic factors interact to shape individuals' psychological and behavioral tendencies via gene-culture interaction (Links B → C → D). We speculate that these interactions between genes and culture exist because genes and cultural meanings shape people's interpretation of situations, which in turn implicates psychological and behavioral outcomes via neural structures and responses. The section on "Neural Correlates and Structural Change" addresses neural structures and activity underlying psychological processes primarily by reviewing brain imaging and electroencephalography (EEG) studies. In this section, we discuss how cultural factors influence the way the brain processes information and how the results corroborate cultural differences in behavioral and psychological outcomes (Links C and D). We also review evidence on the cultural shaping of brain structure. We speculate that this occurs through the interaction of genes and culture (Link E) and through culture-specific neural activities (Link F). The section on "Physiological Processes" addresses findings from studies that involve physiological responses. More specifically, we review how culture moderates cardiovascular, neuroendocrine, and immune responses to situational cues (Links C and G). We also review studies that consider these physiological responses as correlates of psychological and behavioral outcomes to speculate on their role in shaping social behaviors that contribute to the maintenance of cultures (Link H).

GENETICS

Because genes are considered one of the potential determinants of behaviors and other psychological outcomes, an important question is how genes and cultural contexts jointly affect human psychology. We argue that cultural factors may influence how genetic predispositions manifest themselves in behavioral and psychological tendencies, and we review several relevant theoretical approaches that aim to explain the possible ways in which genes and culture work together.

The Theory of Dual Inheritance, or Gene-Culture Coevolution

Dual inheritance theory (Boyd & Richerson 1985), also known as gene-culture coevolutionary theory (Chiao & Blizinsky 2010, Feldman & Laland 1996; see also Cavalli-Sforza & Feldman 1981, Fincher & Thornhill 2012, Lumsden & Wilson 1981), posits that just as the process of natural selection acts on genes to transmit genetic information from one generation to the next, cultural traits are adaptive, and cultural selection may simultaneously influence and be influenced by genetic selection. According to this theory, certain genotypes may predispose people to create particular features in their environment, thus influencing cultural selection, or the normative traits and tendencies that are culturally transmitted. Concurrently, aspects of the broader culture may act as environmental pressures that ultimately affect genetic selection, or the types of traits that are genetically selected in that culture (see Odling-Smee et al. 2003 for a discussion of the process of niche construction). By conceptualizing culture as a phenomenon that evolves in interaction with genetic selection processes, dual inheritance theory aims to explain the macrolevel interplay between genes and culture.

Numerous empirical studies have found support for the theory of dual inheritance. For example, in a study of lactose tolerance across Europe, researchers showed that cultures that depend more on milk products tend to support lactose-tolerant human populations, and the cattle in these regions tend to have higher frequencies of milk protein genes (Beja-Pereira et al. 2003). The authors argued that the human fitness advantages of milk consumption led to (*a*) selection of genes for lactose tolerance in humans, (*b*) transmission of cultural practices supporting cattle domestication and milk consumption, and (*c*) selection of milk-protein genes in cattle. The co-occurrence of these events suggests that genes and culture may influence each other in coevolution.

To bridge dual inheritance theory with perspectives from cultural psychology, researchers have studied whether prevalence of certain genotypes is associated with particular cultural tendencies. One study showed that nations with a greater historical prevalence of pathogens also tended to be more collectivistic, and this association may be explained by higher frequencies of the short (S) allele on the promoter region polymorphism (5-HTTLPR) of the serotonin transporter gene *SLC6A4* compared with the long (L) allele (Chiao & Blizinsky 2010; see also Way & Lieberman 2010). Moreover, although the S allele of the 5-HTTLPR polymorphism is linked to greater risk of depression, anxiety, and negative affect at the individual level (Lesch et al. 1996), there is an inverse correlation between the frequency of the S allele and the rate of anxiety and depression at the national level. Given that the cultural value of collectivism may buffer against threats such as pathogen prevalence (Fincher et al. 2008), collectivism may also serve the adaptive function of reducing the risk of environmental stress, which may have led to genetic selection of the S allele of 5-HTTLPR in collectivistic cultures (Chiao & Blizinsky 2010; see also Chiao 2010).

Gene-Environment Interaction

Another model that offers an understanding of how genetic factors influence psychological out-comes of individuals is that of gene-environment interaction. This model theorizes not that genes relate to outcomes directly but rather that genetic influences may be moderated by environmental input (Caspi et al. 2002, 2003). Some people may be genetically predisposed to react to a given environmental influence more strongly than others, and likewise, people with the same genetic predisposition may at times react quite differently depending on differences in the environment. For instance, a study by Caspi et al. (2003) found that the association between adverse life events and degree of depressive symptoms is much stronger among those who carry an S allele of the 5-HTTLPR polymorphism than in those who do not (see Karg et al. 2011 for meta-analytic support for this gene-environment interaction). Gene-environment interactions have also been observed with other genes, such as the dopamine D4 receptor (*DRD4*) gene (Bakermans-Kranenburg et al. 2008, Sasaki et al. 2013) and the monoamine oxidase-A (*MAOA*) gene (Caspi et al. 2002).

Although these previous studies suggest that certain risk genotypes lead to greater vulnerability to negative experiences, further studies showed that they may also be associated with increased benefits from positive social environments (Taylor et al. 2006). Thus, it has been suggested that, rather than genetic risk, these genetic influences may be more accurately described as suscepti-bility to environmental influence (Belsky et al. 2009, Obradović & Boyce 2009, Way & Taylor 2010). The notion of differential susceptibility allows multiple ways of conceptualizing the nature of environment as well as different outcome variables that are implicated in gene-environment interactions. One such framework stemming from this notion is that of gene-culture interaction.

Gene-Culture Interaction

The gene-culture interaction model builds and expands on the gene-environment interaction framework. Gene-environment interaction research is mostly concerned with psychological and physical health outcomes as a way to understand factors that make people vulnerable to health-related risks. Consequently, this research tends to focus on the environment as a factor that varies in the degree to which it causes distress or provides support to individuals. The gene-culture interaction model includes cultural contexts in the notion of environment. Culture differs from the typical conceptualization of environment in at least two ways. First, culture is a form of the environment within which a certain set of loosely but coherently connected values, institutions, and patterns of actions and interactions are collectively shared (Kitayama 2002). Thus, gene-culture interaction studies operationalize the cultural environment as social groups with shared experiences—such as national or regional culture, religion, and social class—that shape specific meaning systems. Second, because divergences across cultures reflect each group's adaptation to their context-specific challenges and goals, the gene-culture interaction model assumes cultural tendencies to be comparably functional within their own contexts and supports investigation of patterns of normative behaviors and psychological tendencies in addition to well-being and health-related outcomes.

The gene-culture interaction model also differs from dual inheritance theory. Dual inheritance theory provides a theoretical framework to understand the macroevolutionary processes involving culture and genes, and thus it is not conceived as a way to explain the process in which genetic and sociocultural factors interact to shape psychological tendencies and behaviors at the individual level (Kim & Sasaki 2012). The gene-culture interaction model posits that there is a genetic basis for the susceptibility to environmental input, and thus the degree to which one engages in culture-specific behaviors may be influenced by these genetic factors. In other words, dual inheritance theory concerns the distribution of specific genes within cultural groups, whereas the gene-culture interaction model concerns culturally moderated associations between specific genes and behavioral and psychological tendencies (Sasaki 2013).

From the gene-culture interaction perspective, genetic influences shape psychological and behavioral predispositions, and cultural influences may shape how these predispositions are manifested in social behaviors and psychological outcomes. Below we review empirical findings that support the model, drawing on evidence from a range of psychological processes, from attention to psychological well-being. A basic assumption in all these studies is that certain genes are associated with the degree of sensitivity to certain aspects of environmental input, building on the idea of differential susceptibility (Belsky et al. 2009, Obradović & Boyce 2009, Way & Taylor 2010). The model predicts that particular genotypes predispose the carriers to respond particularly strongly to environmental input. Thus, when these carriers are engaged in different cultural contexts with divergent patterns and meanings of psychological and behavioral tendencies, they should embody those specific patterns that are expected and rewarded in their respective cultural contexts more closely compared with those who do not carry the same genotypes (Kim & Sasaki 2012). Consequently, the model also predicts that carrying these differential susceptibility genes could at times lead to different and even opposite behavioral outcomes in different cultures.

Cognitive processes. A study of locus of attention examined a serotonin receptor polymorphism and culture as potential interacting determinants of this cognitive tendency (Kim et al. 2010b). Much research has found that the serotonin (5-hydroxytryptamine, or 5-HT) system is involved with several cognitive functions, and in a state of depleted serotonin, people are better able to attend to focal objects (see Schmitt et al. 2006 for a review). In addition, reliable differences have been found in locus of attention between East Asians and North Americans. Whereas Easterners tend to pay greater attention to background and contextual information, Westerners tend to pay greater attention to focal information (Masuda & Nisbett 2001). Thus, we investigated whether the link between attention and serotonin is moderated by cultural factors. We chose a polymorphism (C-1019G) within the promoter region of the serotonin receptor gene *HTR1A* as the target gene in this study and compared the cognitive styles of Koreans and European Americans.

The results showed a significant interaction between the *HTR1A* genotype and culture. Among European Americans, there was a linear pattern such that those homozygous for the guanine (G) allele (which has been previously linked with reduced serotonergic neurotransmission) reported paying less attention to nonfocal, contextual information than those homozygous for the cytosine (C) allele, with those heterozygous reporting an intermediate level of attention. However, this link between *HTR1A* and locus of attention was completely reversed among Koreans: those homozygous for the G allele reported paying more attention to contextual information than those homozygous for the C allele. To help rule out the potential alternative explanation of a gene-gene interaction (Kaufman et al. 2006), or the interaction between the target gene and other unmeasured genes that covary between the two cultural groups, this study used the triangulation method. Specifically, we also included a group of Korean Americans who were born and raised in the United States and thus share a similar genetic composition with their counterparts who were born and raised in Korea but share similar cultural experiences with European Americans. The results showed that the association between *HTR1A* and locus of attention among Korean Americans was the same as that of European Americans but not that of Koreans born and raised in Korea, further supporting the conclusion that the demonstrated interaction was due to cultural factors (Kim et al. 2010b).

Another study used the model of gene-culture interaction with another serotonin system polymorphism, 5-HTTLPR, by investigating cultural differences in perceiving changes in facial expressions and whether 5-HTTLPR modulates these cultural differences (K. Ishii, H.S. Kim, J.Y. Sasaki, M. Shinada, I. Kusumi, unpublished manuscript). In a previous study, Japanese and Americans watched videos of faces with disappearing smiles (i.e., a happy expression gradually morphing into a neutral expression) and judged the point at which the emotional expressions disappeared. Japanese detected the disappearance of smiles more quickly than Americans. The authors maintained that this is because social disapproval carries greater psychological importance in Japanese culture (Ishii et al. 2011). Building on this previous finding, a gene-culture interaction study found that Japanese with the SS genotype, which is theorized to be linked to greater susceptibility to environmental input, detected the disappearance of smiles with greater perceptual efficiency, closely embodying the predominant cultural tendency, compared with Japanese with SL and LL genotypes, whereas Americans did not differ by genotype (K. Ishii, H.S. Kim, J.Y. Sasaki, M. Shinada, I. Kusumi, unpublished manuscript). As in the study on locus of attention described above, Asian Americans who were born and raised in the United States showed a pattern consistent with that of European Americans, whereas the Japanese (those born and raised in Japan) pattern differed from both groups. These results showed that the 5-HTTLPR polymorphism interacts with cultural factors to affect the perception of facial expressions, and those with greater environmental susceptibility seem to heighten their vigilance for culturally emphasized aspects of social cues.

Further evidence in support of the gene-culture interaction model comes from quantitative behavioral genetics. For instance, Turkheimer et al. (2003) examined the heritability of IQ as a function of social class and, interestingly, found that IQ heritability rates were much lower among families from the lowest social class compared with higher social classes. Other studies with large samples of twins (Harden et al. 2007, Tucker-Drob et al. 2011) also showed that genetic influences were significantly weaker among participants from the lowest social class. Social class provides social and physical contexts in which a meaningful degree of shared social experiences occur. Belonging to a particular social class drastically increases one's chances of engaging in a particular set of behaviors and encountering certain physical and social environments that have important implications for behavioral, psychological, and health outcomes (Schreier & Chen 2013). Thus, it appears that people from the lowest social class may come from an impoverished environment that restricts development of genetic potential (see Nisbett et al. 2012 for a review).

Emotional processes. The tendency to suppress one's feelings is an emotion regulation strategy that is more common in East Asian cultures than in the United States (Matsumoto et al. 2008, Tsai & Levenson 1997). In the United States, expression of emotion is encouraged more strongly (Butler et al. 2009, Kim & Chu 2011). Based on these behavioral differences, we conducted a gene-culture interaction study in which Korean and American participants indicated their tendency to regulate their emotions using suppression, and we determined their genotype for an oxytocin receptor gene (*OXTR rs*53576) (Kim et al. 2011). The G allele of *OXTR rs*53576 is associated with more sensitive parenting behavior (Bakermans-Kranenburg & van IJzendoorn 2008), greater sensitivity to infant crying (Riem et al. 2011), more empathic accuracy (Rodrigues et al. 2009), and less loneliness (Lucht et al. 2009) compared with the adenine (A) allele. The results of this study showed the expected interaction between culture and *OXTR* (Kim et al. 2011). Americans with two copies of the G allele (GG genotype, which has been linked to greater socioemotional sensitivity) reported suppressing emotion significantly less than Americans with two copies of the A allele (AA genotype, which has been linked to less socioemotional sensitivity), consistent with the idea that *less* emotional suppression may be the more emotionally sensitive response in mainstream American culture. However, Koreans showed the exact opposite pattern: Those with the GG genotype reported suppressing emotion *more* than those with the AA genotype, which supports past research suggesting that emotional suppression may be the more emotionally sensitive response in East Asian culture. The analysis including Asian Americans who were born and raised in the United States for triangulation purposes, again, showed that the Asian American pattern of association was more similar to that of European Americans than it was to that of Koreans born and raised in Korea.

Interpersonal and prosocial behaviors. To investigate the gene-culture interaction in a more interpersonal domain, we examined the roles of culture and *OXTR rs*53576 in the use of emotional support (Kim et al. 2010a). Previous research has shown that cultures differ in the norms and evaluations of emotional support seeking as a means for coping with stress and that Asians tend to be more cautious than European Americans about seeking support from close others (Kim et al. 2008). Building on these findings, we conducted a study in which Koreans and Americans, including Korean Americans and European Americans who were born and raised in the United States, indicated their current distress level and their social support seeking behaviors. Results again supported the gene-culture interaction model. The relationship between *OXTR* and emotional support seeking was moderated by both culture and distress level. In particular, when under great distress, Americans with either GG or AG genotypes reported relying on emotional support more than Americans with the AA genotype. In contrast, Koreans with GG or AG genotypes did not increase support seeking any more than those with the AA genotype. The same triangulation as used in previously described studies confirmed that for Korean Americans, although the overall level of emotional support seeking was in the middle of the levels of European Americans and Koreans, the pattern of association between OXTR genotypes and emotional support seeking was very similar to that of European Americans but not to that of Koreans. These results, again, show that people with genotypes that are expected to render them more sensitive to the social environment seem to be more strongly influenced by sociocultural expectations than are people without those genotypes.

Taking a somewhat different approach, another study examined how implicit priming of religion would moderate the association between *DRD4* and prosocial behaviors (Sasaki et al. 2013). This study differs from other studies examining the interaction between a gene and sociocultural context in that it incorporated experimental priming of religious thoughts. Certain *DRD4* variants (7-repeat or 2-repeat alleles, depending on ethnicity; Wang et al. 2004) are expected to be associated with greater susceptibility to reward- and punishment-related environmental influences than others. Thus, we theorized that carriers of these alleles would be more susceptible to environmentally triggered religious thoughts that typically encourage prosocial behaviors (Shariff & Norenzayan 2007). Indeed, participants with *DRD4* susceptibility variants behaved in a more prosocial manner when implicitly primed with religious concepts compared with the control condition, whereas participants without *DRD4* susceptibility variants were not affected by priming. This study directly tested the idea of environmental susceptibility, and the findings support a few notable inferences. First, the differential susceptibility gene may influence even how one is affected by fleeting situational cues, such as implicit primes, not just long-term development and socialization. Second, this study demonstrated the directionality of environmental influence. Taken together with the other gene-culture interaction studies, this research suggests that carriers of differential susceptibility genes tend to assimilate to what is expected and fostered by the environment in a systematic way.

Well-being and health. Much research has demonstrated the importance of sociocultural contexts in how given psychological experiences lead to different well-being outcomes (Kitayama et al. 2006b, Suh 2002). Gene-culture interaction findings suggest that genetic factors, in conjunction with sociocultural factors, may also play a role in shaping one's well-being. In fact, Dressler and colleagues (2009) found that, in Brazil, cultural consonance—the extent to which people perceive their family's values as congruent with the values of one's culture—interacted with a serotonin receptor polymorphism (*HTR2A* −1438G-A) in influencing depressive symptoms. Although this study was conducted in the context of a single culture, this finding suggests the psychological importance of the subjective sense that one's life is culturally normative, especially for people with a greater-susceptibility genotype.

In related research, we examined how cultural factors and genetic factors may jointly affect people's psychological well-being, specifically looking at the roles of regional culture, religiosity, and *OXTR*. Previous research has investigated the link between religiosity and psychological and physical well-being and found that the link is generally, but not always, positive (McCullough et al. 2000). One of the ways that religion may benefit individuals is by increasing social affiliation, such as involvement in a fellowship or community (Atran & Norenzayan 2004). Although this may be true universally, the degree to which a religion emphasizes the importance of social affiliation may differ by culture: Religion in an East Asian cultural context tends to place greater emphasis on social affiliation than religion in a North American cultural context (Sasaki & Kim 2011). Given that some individuals may be genetically predisposed to be more socially sensitive than others, the way religion is linked to well-being may depend on cultural context and genetic makeup. A gene-culture interaction study found that Koreans showed a positive relationship between religiosity and psychological well-being, whereas European Americans showed a negative relationship, but these relationships between religiosity and well-being were found only among people who were more genetically predisposed to social sensitivity (i.e., those with an *OXTR* genotype of GG). Interestingly, there was no cultural difference in the relationship between religiosity and psychological well-being for people with other *OXTR* genotypes, who were less genetically predisposed toward social sensitivity. In fact, for people with *OXTR* genotypes associated with less social sensitivity, there seemed to be no relationship between religiosity and well-being, regardless of culture. Thus, although social affiliation may be an important part of religion everywhere, the well-being benefits that occur through religious social affiliation may be particularly strong in certain cultures, such as in East Asia, that provide relatively greater opportunities for social affiliation in religious groups. Furthermore, this cultural difference may occur only for those who are genetically predisposed to be sensitive to social affiliative behaviors in the first place (Sasaki et al. 2011).

Other studies found that genes interact with social class to shape psychological and biological functions (Adler et al. 1994, Miller et al. 2009). To explain health discrepancies between groups, researchers have investigated biological mechanisms that may be implicated by different experiences. For example, one study found that there are detectable changes in gene transcription that occur as a result of early life experiences (Miller et al. 2009). Among people who grew up in low-social-class contexts, genes associated with proinflammatory actions were upregulated, and genes responsive to glucocorticoid receptor–mediated signaling were downregulated. This is a defensive phenotypic pattern that reflects the body's reaction to threatening environments. In particular, this pattern tends to result in heightened immune activation as well as increased cortisol output, which may increase chances of survival in the short term but have negative consequences in the long term. Thus, in addition to showing how gene expression can be moderated by sociocultural inputs, these results suggest important downstream effects on well-being outcomes, including mental and physical health.

Further thoughts on genes and culture. Research investigating the interplay of specific genes and culture in shaping individuals' psychological and behavioral tendencies is still in its infancy. However, the early empirical evidence highlights the mutual influence of genetic and sociocultural factors in shaping processes beyond health and well-being outcomes. Moreover, by examining behavioral tendencies that differ across cultural contexts, these studies point to a systematic pattern of genetic susceptibility within specific cultural contexts in that cultural influences nudge the behaviors and psychological tendencies of those with susceptibility genes in the culturally consonant direction. Moreover, the exact patterns of these interactions may be systematic and informative. In some studies, the interaction is a full crossover interaction; in other studies, the interaction is driven by a significant association in one culture and a lack of association in the other culture. For example, *OXTR* is significantly associated with emotional support seeking in the United States, where people are encouraged to seek emotional support when under distress, but this association is not significant in Korea, where such encouragement is absent. However, *OXTR* is significantly associated with emotion suppression in both Korea and the United States, but in opposite directions. This may be because not only is there a norm of emotion suppression in Korea but there is also a counter-norm of emotion expression in the United States (Butler et al. 2009, Kim & Chu 2011). Similarly, *HTR1A* is associated with locus of attention in opposite ways in Korea and the United States. Perhaps this also is due to the fact that there are opposing loci to which people are encouraged to direct their attention. Given these patterns of results, we suspect that people with greater-susceptibility genotypes are more likely to engage in culturally normative behaviors than are people without those genotypes. Thus, the association between genes and behavioral outcomes may be significant when there is an actively fostered set of behaviors within a cultural context, not merely when such cultural emphasis is absent.

So far these findings suggest that certain target genes increase or decrease susceptibility to specific aspects of the cultural environment. Although the empirical evidence is still quite limited, it appears that oxytocin-related genes may influence sensitivity toward social and emotional cues, and dopamine-related genes may influence sensitivity toward reward and punishment aspects of the environment. This specificity of genes, alone or together with other genes, in terms of their sensitivity to different aspects of environmental inputs, is a topic that will require further research, but at present, we can infer that these genes may not influence sensitivity to cultural norms in general.

Moreover, the relative frequencies of these genes vary within cultural groups (i.e., East Asians and European Americans): Some alleles that confer greater susceptibility (e.g., the G allele of *OXTR*) are more common among European Americans (Kim et al. 2010a, 2011), and other greater-susceptibility alleles (e.g., the S allele of *5-HTTLPR*) are more common among

East Asians (Chiao & Blizinsky 2010). Thus, there probably is not a single gene for cultural conformity per se. Rather, the complex genetic makeup of individuals predisposes them to be particularly sensitive to different aspects of the cultural environment in varied ways, and a person who is susceptible to emotional cues may not necessarily also be susceptible to reward and punishment cues (cf. Na et al. 2010). One should therefore be cautious about overgeneralizing the meaning of each specific gene-culture interaction.

We speculate that the interaction between genes and cultural meanings occurs in the brain. Although no gene-culture interaction studies have been conducted to look at neural activations, it is clearly assumed that neural processes are implicated, and the consideration of studies looking at neural correlates of culture-specific behaviors would suggest different models to consider.

NEURAL CORRELATES AND STRUCTURAL CHANGE

In this section, we present recent studies that used magnetic resonance imaging (MRI), functional MRI (fMRI), and EEG measures to examine structural change and neural correlates of culturally related psychological processes. This particular area within cultural neuroscience has been a subject of very active research, with studies on a wide range of topics that are largely consistent with behavioral and psychological findings and that illuminate the underlying neural mechanisms of these phenomena. Although our review of these studies is not meant to be comprehensive, we discuss some of the seminal corroborating studies in this area and, importantly, highlight studies that capitalize on the unique potential of neuroscientific measures to illuminate the psychological processes themselves.

Representations of Self Versus Others

Culture plays a crucial role in ascribing meaning and value to the self. Many cultural differences in psychology are based on the different ways that people across cultures construe the self. For cultures such as those in North America, the self tends to be seen as more independent, whereas for cultures such as those in East Asia, the self may be understood as more interdependent (Markus & Kitayama 1991). People from cultures that foster more independent self-construals tend to emphasize individual agency, uniqueness, and personal choice (e.g., Iyengar & Lepper 1999, Kim & Markus 1999 for national difference; Snibbe & Markus 2005, Stephens et al. 2007 for social class), while people from cultures that foster more interdependent self-construals tend to focus on maintaining harmony in relationships and fulfilling social obligations (Miller et al. 1990).

The self is also one of the most actively investigated topics in cultural neuroscience, and thus as a whole the topic presents a good collection of methodological approaches, such as cross-national and cross-religious comparisons and priming of cultural concepts. Self-related neural activity in response to different situational and relational stimuli seems to parallel the findings from behavioral studies. For instance, one study found that both Chinese and Western participants showed greater activation in the medial prefrontal cortex (MPFC) when judging traits about the self versus familiar others (i.e., people well known but not close) (Zhu et al. 2007), consistent with past research on the MPFC in relation to self-judgments relative to other-judgments (Kelley et al. 2002, Lieberman et al. 2004). However, in this study only Chinese participants showed greater MPFC activation when thinking about their mother versus familiar others. Compared with British people, Chinese people also tended to show a weaker advantage for recognizing their own face versus familiar faces, as evidenced by reduced N2 amplitude in event-related potentials (ERPs)—a response that has been linked to deeper processing of faces and the ability to differentiate them (Sui et al. 2009).

Aside from ethnic or national differences, religious differences may also be implicated in neural representations of self processes. Two studies found that people who hold Christian or Buddhist beliefs (versus the nonreligious) showed dampened patterns of neural activation in the ventral MPFC (VMPFC), which is associated with labeling stimuli as self-relevant (Northoff et al. 2006), when making self-referential judgments, perhaps because of a religious emphasis on denial of self (Han et al. 2008, 2010). Taken together, these findings appear to corroborate theoretical and empirical studies in cultural psychology that suggest that the conceptualization of self may be more or less overlapping with conceptualization of close others and may have a weaker or greater emphasis based on culturally construed meanings.

Some research has used cultural priming techniques together with neural measures to more effectively address questions surrounding the causal nature of cultural influence. In one study, Chinese participants primed with more independent (versus interdependent) self-construals showed greater activation of the right middle and inferior frontal cortex, which may be linked to self-recognition (Keenan et al. 2000), when viewing their own face compared with a familiar person's face (Sui & Han 2007). Another similar study examined the effect of self-construal priming on ERP responses to one's own face and a friend's face among British and Chinese participants. The results showed that culturally incongruent self-construal priming (i.e., independent self to Chinese and interdependent self to British) weakened the typical culture-specific pattern on the anterior N2 component (Sui et al. 2013). In a study with bicultural participants, priming Western cultural symbols led to increased neural differentiation of close others from the self in the VMPFC, while priming Chinese cultural symbols decreased differentiation (Ng et al. 2010). Other research has found that bicultural people primed with individualistic values exhibited greater MPFC activation to general trait descriptions of the self, whereas bicultural people primed with collectivistic values seemed to show greater MPFC activation to context-specific traits about the self (Chiao et al. 2009). Thus, neural indicators of stimuli discrimination may depend on the salience of cultural information, and similarly, the extent to which the same brain region is activated may vary according to salient cultural information and the way the self is construed in the broader culture.

Cognitive Processes

Cultural differences in cognition can be broadly organized according to two main systems of thought: analytic thinking, which tends to be more prevalent in North American and Western European cultures, and holistic thinking, which tends to be more prevalent in non-Western cultures (Nisbett et al. 2001). Whereas analytic thinking is generally characterized by greater attention to central objects, categorization according to formalized rules, and attributional tendencies that focus on dispositional causes, holistic thinking is characterized by greater attention to the field, categorization according to family resemblance or relational rules, and attributional tendencies based on situational causes (Nisbett et al. 2001).

Foundational research in the area of culture and cognition has been corroborated and extended using approaches from neuroscience. We describe a set of studies that we consider particularly influential because they illuminate ways in which the cognitive processes underlying certain behaviors may actually be different across cultures, even when the behavioral responses appear similar. We believe that these studies exemplify how neuroscientific technology may be used to investigate cultural psychological processes that are difficult to directly access otherwise.

In number processing, for instance, people from two different cultures may arrive at the same response when given the same numerical task, yet the psychological processes leading to that response may differ from each other. In a study by Tang and colleagues (2006), native Chinese and

English speakers engaged different brain regions when performing the same mental arithmetic tasks. There were no differences in the accuracy or reaction times of participants completing this task, yet patterns of brain activation revealed significant differences. In particular, whereas English speakers performing the addition task showed activation in language-related regions, such as the left perisylvian cortices (including the Broca and Wernicke areas), Chinese speakers showed stronger activation in vision- and space-processing regions, including visuo-premotor association areas. The authors of this research argue that these differences are likely shaped by language and other features of the cultural environment, such as education and learning strategies. These findings are consistent with previous research showing that talking aloud interferes with problem solving for Asian Americans, who may rely on language processes less during these tasks compared with European Americans (Kim 2002). The neural evidence on cultural differences in numeric processing, in conjunction with behavioral evidence on language use and problem solving, suggests rather convincingly that even the same response may be supported by quite different psychological processes, depending on culture.

Culture-specific patterns of brain activity are also found with attention-related tasks. East Asians exhibit greater activation in regions associated with attentional control or effort (e.g., frontal and parietal activation) when they are engaged in judgments that involve ignoring the context—a more effortful task in this culture—whereas European Americans show greater activation in the same regions when they are engaged in judgments that involve attending to the context (Hedden et al. 2008). These results show that the same brain regions are activated when people are engaged in culturally incongruent attentional tasks, independent of the actual content of the task (i.e., ignoring the context versus attending to the context). In an ERP study, researchers demonstrated that East Asian Americans showed greater P3 amplitudes, which are thought to index attention to infrequent events, in response to contextually discrepant stimuli, compared with European Americans (Lewis et al. 2008). In a conceptually related study, more interdependent (versus independent) Japanese female participants who listened to words that did not match the spoken vocal tone (e.g., the word "satisfaction" spoken in a negative tone of voice) showed greater N400 ERP activation, which has been shown to indicate detection of semantic incongruity (Ishii et al. 2010).

East Asians and European Americans also seem to reconcile competing strategies for semantic judgments in categorization tasks via distinct brain regions (Gutchess et al. 2010). When they had to categorize stimuli based on a particular rule (i.e., relational or taxonomical) while ignoring the other conflicting rule, East Asians and European Americans performed at similar levels. However, their neural activations differed. East Asians in this study showed activation in frontal-parietal networks as they engaged in top-down controlled processes, whereas European Americans showed activation in the temporal lobes and the cingulate gyrus, indicating semantic information processing, top-down detection of conflict, and monitoring.

Evidence using neural measures also corroborates cultural differences in causal attribution. The processing of contextual information in certain brain regions, such as the left parietal cortex, may be sensitive to cultural information about causality (Han et al. 2011). In addition, European Americans tend to make inferences about a person's disposition more quickly and spontaneously than East Asians. Furthermore, European Americans show a stronger N400 response when judging incongruous versus congruous personal traits, whereas Asian Americans show no such response (Na & Kitayama 2011). A similar pattern of results was found in a study on spontaneous trait inferences among people from middle-class backgrounds (who tend to show more analytic cognitive styles) and people from working-class backgrounds (who tend to show more holistic cognitive styles; Grossmann & Varnum 2011, Kraus et al. 2010), such that middle-class participants exhibited greater N400 signaling to incongruous traits compared with working-class participants (Varnum et al. 2012). Across various neural measures, this research not only corroborates past behavioral research but also suggests that stimuli with particular meanings in one culture versus another may evoke distinct patterns of neural responses, depending on culture.

Emotions and Interpersonal and Group Processes

Culture moderates the process of emotion regulation as well as the way people feel in response to interpersonal and intergroup interactions. In line with past behavioral research demonstrating the cultural shaping of emotion regulation (Matsumoto et al. 2008, Tsai & Levenson 1997), several fMRI studies suggest that these cultural differences emerge at the level of neural activity. In one study, American participants were instructed to suppress emotion while viewing film clips eliciting disgust. Although participants reported experiencing reduced negative affect, they actually showed greater emotion-related responses in the right insula and the right amygdala (Goldin et al. 2008). The dissociation between self-report and brain activation in this study highlights one of the important advantages of neural measures—they can at times reveal responses that might have gone undetected otherwise, particularly for constructs such as emotion that have been somewhat difficult to capture in the past without self-report measures. Interestingly, a similar study conducted with Japanese participants did not find increased activation in the insula or amygdala during emotion suppression (Ohira et al. 2006). Although these studies do not directly compare different cultural groups, the divergent findings within each particular culture are informative for illustrating how similar investigations can yield different neural results, depending on the culture of the participants.

Individual and group interactions are influenced not only by one's own thoughts and emotions but also by what one perceives other people's thoughts or emotions to be. Theory of mind (ToM), or the ability to reason about beliefs, desires, and intentions, may be one mechanism through which people can very quickly and effortlessly make predictions about other people's mental states and then employ that information in social situations (Dennett 1987, Fodor 1987). Recent neural evidence has illuminated interesting differences in ToM processing across cultures. Children aged 8–11 years reading a ToM-relevant story or observing a ToM-relevant cartoon, for instance, showed VMPFC activation regardless of cultural background; however, monolingual American children showed greater activation in the right temporoparietal junction (TPJ), a region associated with mental state inference (Saxe & Kanwisher 2003), compared with bilingual Japanese children (Kobayashi et al. 2007). Similarly, research with American and Japanese adults demonstrated strong activation patterns for both groups in several regions that have been associated with ToM, including the right MPFC, right anterior cingulate cortex, and bilateral TPJ, yet monolingual Americans also showed greater activation in other ToM-related brain regions (e.g., bilateral temporal pole, right insula, and right MPFC) compared with bilingual Japanese (Kobayashi et al. 2006). These studies suggest that there may be some components of ToM that are processed similarly across cultures, whereas other components may be more culture-specific and are potentially underpinned by different neural processes, depending on culture. However, the psychological meaning of these differences is not yet clear.

A related study on the ToM-related experience of empathy—vicariously feeling what another person feels—found that, although both European American and Korean participants showed greater activation in the left TPJ when observing the emotional pain of an in-group versus an out-group member, this effect was stronger for Koreans than European Americans (Cheon et al. 2011). Additionally, research examining the experience of empathy in response to anger expressions showed that Chinese participants instructed to empathize with a person with an angry face showed greater activation in the left dorsolateral prefrontal cortex, a region associated with emotion regulation, whereas German participants showed stronger responses in the right TPJ, right inferior and superior temporal gyri, and left middle insula—regions typically involved in empathy and emotion processing (de Greck et al. 2012). This study is particularly interesting given that it demonstrates that the same information may be processed through different neural paths in different cultures, perhaps leading to different psychological responses. Taking together these studies on ToM and empathy, it seems possible that ToM ability and empathy are underpinned by a variety of psychological processes, as reflected by different patterns of neural activation. Importantly, the degree of neural response to ToM- or empathy-related tasks seemed to vary according to cultural background. These divergences in neural activation raise the possibility that the psychological and neural pathways for social connections with others differ across cultures.

In every culture, social hierarchies are important, yet the way people navigate these social structures can vary depending on the normative values and behaviors within a particular culture. An fMRI study on culture and dominance versus subordination nicely illustrates this point. Participants in this study were shown the outlines of dominant and subordinate body displays, and results showed that American and Japanese participants had selective neural activation in the caudate nucleus and MPFC in response to body displays that were more reinforced in their respective cultures. That is, Americans produced this pattern of activation when viewing dominant displays, whereas Japanese produced the same pattern of activation when viewing subordinate displays (Freeman et al. 2009). The authors suggest that parts of the MPFC may be implicated in retrieval or representation of self-relevant cultural behaviors, such as dominance or subordination, while the caudate may link those behaviors to a culture-bound reward value. By demonstrating that people from different cultures may at times show the same pattern of activation in response to quite different sets of stimuli, this study illustrates the importance of incorporating cultural meanings in neuroscience.

Taken together, these studies demonstrate that the ways culture affects neural responses to social information and stimuli present a fairly complex picture. Sometimes a similar pattern of neural activation may occur in response to different stimuli across cultures, depending on the cultural meaning of the stimulus (e.g., effortful attention; Hedden et al. 2008). Yet at other times, different patterns of neural activation can underlie seemingly similar behavioral outcomes because people from different cultures may produce the same behavior through different psychological processes (e.g., arithmetic task; Tang et al. 2006). We believe that these research areas are likely to lead to greater theoretical advancements and thus warrant future investigation.

Neuroanatomical Differences

Although most studies in cultural neuroscience thus far have examined brain activity using fMRI or EEG measures, some have used structural MRI to address the question of whether neuroanatomical differences reflect cultural influences. In particular, might engagement in different cultural contexts be associated with systematically different brain structures? In fact, some studies suggest that this is the case. For instance, there are anatomical differences in the middle left frontal gyrus, the inferior middle left temporal gyrus, and the superior parietal left lobule of English-speaking Caucasians versus Chinese-speaking Asians (Kochunov et al. 2003) and hemispheric-shape differences between Europeans and Japanese (i.e., hemispheres are relatively shorter and wider for Japanese compared with Europeans; Zilles et al. 2001). Other research shows that Americans not of Asian descent differed from Chinese Singaporeans in the cortical thickness of bilateral frontal, parietal, and medial-temporal polymodal association cortices (Chee et al. 2011), and the authors speculate that one potential explanation for these results is that these structural differences are linked to the use of different cognitive strategies, such as holistic versus analytic thinking. These neuroanatomical differences between cultural groups potentially provide evidence for neural plasticity. Yet, although culture and language are among the possible explanations for the structural differences found in these studies, these cross-ethnic comparisons raise several other potential explanations, including environmental and genetic factors.

One way to isolate the impact of language learning in particular may be to examine the case of second-language acquisition. There is evidence, for instance, of differences in gray matter density between English monolingual subjects and Italian-English bilingual subjects in parietal cortex regions indexing meaning-sound associations (Mechelli et al. 2004). Another study found that Europeans who did not speak Chinese showed differences in gray and white matter density compared with Chinese speakers, and this difference held whether the Chinese speakers were native Chinese monolingual subjects or Europeans who were bilingual in English and Chinese (Crinion et al. 2009; see Green et al. 2007 for a review of linguistic effects on brain structures). Given that language systems may be highly sensitive to culture-specific input, the comparison of different language speakers from similar ethnic or national backgrounds seems to be a particularly effective, systematic way to address the issue of neuroplasticity.

PHYSIOLOGICAL PROCESSES

In this section, we focus on cultural differences in cardiovascular, neuroendocrine, and immune responses, which result from underlying neural processes. Studies in cultural psychology show that there are culturally shared, distinct meaning systems that can lead to divergent outcomes in psychological processes and social behaviors. Central elements of these meaning systems include values, which affect people's sense of good and bad, and norms, which affect people's sense of expectations within the social environment. Thus, one consequence of facing cultural meaning violation through engaging in actions that are discordant with cultural values and expectations may be psychological distress (Heine et al. 2006, Proulx & Heine 2008). In many studies examining physiological functions, the key psychological factors of interest are distress and threats induced by psychological and social causes (Blascovich & Tomaka 1996, Dickerson & Kemeny 2004), and thus, experiencing cultural meaning violation could lead to detectable changes in biological functioning. In the following section, we review findings demonstrating how one's subjective psychological state may affect biological states, and how biological functioning may be implicated in cultural processes.

Social Relationships

One line of research examining how people from different cultures vary in their biological responses to a given situation focuses on the effect of social support use (see Sherman et al. 2009 for a review). Compared with European Americans, Asians/Asian Americans are less willing to seek explicit social support and instead rely more on implicit social support—spending time with or thinking about close others without talking about one's stressor—because they are more concerned about potentially disturbing their social network (Kim et al. 2008, Taylor et al. 2004). Thus, explicitly asking for social support may be a source of distress among Asians/Asian Americans. Taylor et al. (2007) investigated psychological and biological outcomes of seeking explicit and implicit social support. Asian/Asian American and European American participants underwent a lab stressor (Kirschbaum et al. 1993) and were randomly assigned to either an explicit social support condition (i.e., writing a letter asking for advice and support about the stressor from a close other) or an implicit social support condition (i.e., writing about the aspects of a close group that is important to them). The study included both psychological and biological (i.e., salivary cortisol) measures of stress experiences. The results showed that according to both measures, engaging in the culturally discordant form of social support seeking for either cultural group increased stress levels.

Similarly, perceiving that one is lacking a social network from which he or she may draw support has different biological consequences in different cultures. One implication from research on culture and social support seeking is that people from East Asian cultural contexts may not equate positive social relationships with their availability for social support, and consequently they may not experience a great deal of stress if they perceive that their social network provides lower levels of explicit social support. For instance, one study (Chiang et al. 2013) examined the link between proinflammatory cytokines and perception of support availability among Asian Americans and European Americans. Proinflammatory cytokines are part of an innate immune response that is adaptive in the short term but can have long-term negative impacts such as elevated chronic inflammation, which has been implicated in many chronic diseases (Ridker et al. 2000). Specifically looking at the proinflammatory cytokine interleukin-6 (IL-6), this study found that culture was a significant moderator of the link between perceived support availability and the level of IL-6. Among European Americans, having more available social support predicted lower levels of IL-6, indicating lower inflammatory activity, whereas among Asian Americans, this relationship was not statistically significant.

Taking a more experimental approach, one study examining social class as a cultural context found that first-generation college students, who tend to have stronger interdependent relational norms, showed a stronger cortisol response to a lab stressor when the college culture was described as independence focused (i.e., emphasizing personal self-expression and intellectual journey) than when it was described as interdependence focused (i.e., emphasizing community and social connections) (Stephens et al. 2012). Thus, a "culturally mismatched" environment—having to engage in cultural contexts that differ from what one is familiar with—can be a cause of distress.

Cognitive and Emotional Processes

Cultural differences in the biological effects of situational factors are also found in relation to cognitive and emotional processes. East Asians and European Americans who are from cultural contexts with divergent views on the value of verbal expression (Kim & Sherman 2007) differ in how they are affected by verbal expression of thoughts as indicated by their cortisol response. Speaking thoughts aloud decreases cortisol responses to a challenging cognitive task among European Americans, who are from a cultural context that considers verbal expression to be beneficial for thinking, whereas the same action bears no such benefit among East Asian Americans, who are from a cultural context that does not share the value of verbal expression (Kim 2008). Relatedly, these general patterns of cultural differences in the impact of expression extend to emotional expression as well. Butler and colleagues (2009) found that European Americans who suppressed their emotions while watching film clips meant to elicit negative emotions had significantly higher blood pressure than those given instructions allowing expression of their negative emotions, but Asian Americans who suppressed their emotions had marginally lower blood pressure than those who expressed their emotions. These studies demonstrate that cultural expectations and meanings regarding social interactions, specifically how to appropriately engage in social support use, express thoughts, and regulate emotion, lead to culture-specific biological consequences of these actions.

Looking at regional differences between American southern and northern males in their response to insults, Cohen et al. (1996) measured both cortisol and testosterone, a hormone associated with aggression and dominance, and found that southern males, who see insults as a threat to their honor, showed marked increases in cortisol and testosterone when insulted. However, northern males, who are not as concerned about the notion of honor, did not show such responses (Cohen et al. 1996).

Religion also moderates how people physiologically respond to environmental stimuli. Weisbuch-Remington et al. (2005) examined cardiovascular responses to subliminally presented Christian religious symbols that were negative (e.g., image of a demon) or positive (e.g., image of Christ) among Christians and non-Christians. Using the biopsychosocial model of challenge and threat (Blascovich & Tomaka 1996), this study found that religious affiliation moderated how participants' cardiovascular state was affected by the religious symbols. Christians responded to negative images with more threatened cardiovascular reactions compared with their reactions to positive images, whereas non-Christians did not show such a difference.

Taken together, these studies illustrate that experiences in shared sociocultural contexts, such as national, regional, social class, and religious contexts, give rise to the psychological meaning of situations, actions, and objects and thus moderate the relationship between stimuli and psychological and biological outcomes. The reviewed studies show that these biological functions mostly corroborate behavioral findings in that culture moderates the relationships between stimuli and outcomes in consistent and predicted manners. Use of physiological measures could reduce certain methodological concerns common in self-report. Moreover, as physiological functions are associated with numerous health outcomes, such as inflammation or cardiovascular disorders, these investigations may point to important consequences of culture-specific processes.

Neurotransmitters and Social Behaviors

Although the use of biological responses as outcome variables is more common, a small number of studies investigate more mechanistic roles of biological measures in sociocultural processes. Oxytocin, a peptide produced in the hypothalamus that functions as both neurotransmitter and hormone (Hatton 1990), has been the focus of much investigation. An array of prosocial tendencies, such as social bonds, trust, cooperation, affiliation, and positive communication, have been associated with oxytocin, examined as both plasma oxytocin (Feldman et al. 2007) and exogenously administered oxytocin (Ditzen et al. 2009, Kosfeld et al. 2005) in animals and humans (see Meyer-Lindenberg et al. 2011 for a review). Yet recent research suggests that rather than simply promoting prosociality, oxytocin may increase sensitivity to important social cues. For example, in humans oxytocin increases the ability to accurately attribute the emotions and mental states of others (Bartz et al. 2010, Domes et al. 2007), and in rodents it increases the ability to accurately detect disease-infected others (using oxytocin-gene-knockout rodents, Kavaliers et al. 2004; see Kavaliers & Choleris 2011 for a review). Moreover, another study shows that oxytocin may increase in-group bias among humans. Using the experimental method of administering intranasal oxytocin spray, this study found that oxytocin increased the degree to which participants favored in-group others and derogated out-group others (De Dreu et al. 2011; see Bartz et al. 2011, Meyer-Lindenberg et al. 2011, Miller 2013 for relevant reviews).

These psychological tendencies and behaviors associated with oxytocin—empathic accuracy, accuracy in pathogen detection, and ethnocentrism—are crucial elements in the maintenance of sociocultural processes. For instance, empathic accuracy may be a necessary ability to gauge others' reactions and approval/disapproval of one's actions. Sociocultural norms and valuations are often reinforced and maintained through social interactions (Fiske et al. 1998, Na et al. 2013), and thus one's ability to perceive others' intentions may be a crucial psychological mechanism for the maintenance of cultural systems (Kim et al. 2011).

Ethnocentrism, in which people favor familiar in-group others over unfamiliar out-group others, is a basic part of human sociality. This tendency may first be implicated in sociocultural processes in that psychological closed-ness in ethnocentrism would serve to maintain and strengthen culture-specific behaviors. Moreover, it may play a role in shaping certain aspects of cultural diversity. It has been argued that ethnocentric patterns of social behaviors, which are more common in certain cultures than in others, may serve as a pathogen-avoidance mechanism (Fincher et al. 2008, Kavaliers & Choleris 2011, Schaller & Murray 2008). Regions with higher pathogen prevalence tend to develop collectivistic cultures that foster stronger in-group biases than do regions with lower pathogen prevalence (Fincher et al. 2008). Thus, oxytocin, which seems to be causally involved in these social processes, may play an important role in the emergence and maintenance of sociocultural systems. There are likely other neurotransmitters and hormones that are associated with various social behaviors. The case of oxytocin provides one example of how neurotransmitters may have important functions in these larger collective processes and also an example of how the study of mind and culture can incorporate biological processes beyond simply looking at them as outcome measures. This is a particularly exciting and important issue raised by taking the theoretical perspective of the interplay between culture and biology.

INTEGRATION AND FUTURE DIRECTIONS OF CULTURAL NEUROSCIENCE

The studies reviewed herein demonstrate that cultural influences are engaged at many different levels of biological functions. These studies also provide more complete information on the mechanisms of cultural influence, as neural evidence provides researchers with a more precise understanding of how meanings shaped and shared by cultural experiences trigger a neural, psychological, and behavioral chain of events, and of how these events are coordinated and maintained within a person. From a neuroscientific perspective, the study of culture provides valuable information on the ways in which certain neural structures may serve similar functions across cultures while at the same time being malleable in response to cultural inputs.

Following our review of the current state of cultural neuroscience research, we conclude with future directions. In a way, these involve current methodological issues that have limited a causal understanding of the interplay of two main constituent factors: culture and genes. Both are factors that are difficult to study in a true experiment, at least among humans, and thus the field has inherent uncertainty about the causal roles of these factors. Our recommendation is to borrow from the methodological innovations of cultural psychology and cultural neuroscience to increase confidence in the causal role of cultural and biological factors.

First, most of the studies to date with perspectives from cultural neuroscience use cross-sectional designs comparing genetic associations, neural correlates, and physiological responses among different cultural groups. In our view, one of the chief theoretical gains of cultural neuroscience is the demonstration of adaptability and its resultant diversity in biological functioning, along with greater appreciation for the role of biology in psychological and behavioral processes. Although these studies clearly demonstrate cultural diversity in neural functions, they do not necessarily show the process through which cultural factors influence them, and the causal role of cultural experiences is therefore unclear. Thus, we propose that there should be greater empirical efforts in cultural neuroscience research to investigate the psychological consequences of cultural change.

One of the most direct and convincing ways to understand the impact of cultural contexts is to look at change in cultural environments and subsequent changes in behavior. As the cultural contexts in which people are engaged or the meanings construed in cultural contexts change, so too should the way people process information (Kim & Markus 1999), experience emotion (De Leersnyder et al. 2011), and interact with others (Taylor et al. 2004). Moreover, culture-specific psychological processes are quite responsive to situational cues, such as cultural icons (Hong et al.

2000), relational concepts (Kühnen et al. 2001), and language (Ji et al. 2004, see Oyserman & Lee 2008 for a review). Borrowing from these methods, research in cultural neuroscience may focus on people who undergo cultural changes via acculturation (Kim et al. 2010b), or situational malleability, using methods such as experimental priming (Ng et al. 2010, Sasaki et al. 2013). Investigations of both immediate situational shifts as well as slower developmental or stable and long-term changes will complement each other and provide insight into biological malleability.

A second question is how to piece together the findings from different areas within cultural neuroscience into an integrative framework. Integration is required at many levels of analysis. As suggested by Li (2003), there is evidence of cultural influence on cognitive and developmental plasticity at multiple levels, from the more macro level of biological evolution to the more micro levels of neural and genetic change. We posit that a major challenge for researchers now is to demonstrate how changes at one level can lead to changes at another. For example, for greater understanding of the gene-culture interaction model, more research must examine the neural and molecular mechanisms linking cultural and genetic factors to culture-specific behavioral outcomes. Studies investigating gene-environment interactions can inform the mechanisms of the gene-culture interaction model. Studies have shown how environmental input triggers changes in gene expression (Cole et al. 2007) and implicates physiological responses (Rodrigues et al. 2009) and brain reactivity (Pezawas et al. 2005) that may explain psychological and biological outcomes. A similar systematic and mechanistic approach is needed to investigate the influences of culture and genes. In so doing, investigators may attend to the entire chain of neural, physiological, psychological, and behavioral events to gain a more precise understanding of which parts of the chain are affected by culture and genes.

Third, more research should use process-oriented approaches within neural and genetic levels of investigation, as well as between these levels, as suggested above. For instance, it is important to investigate how culture influences processes involving multiple genes or the functional connection of different neural networks. There are novel theoretical perspectives and methodological tools available to address some of these questions, such as pathway analysis in genetics (Zhong et al. 2010) and neural network analysis (Bullmore & Bassett 2010, Butts 2009). These available models will be of great value to further advance understandings of neural processes and pathways that underlie human behaviors and psychological outcomes.

Furthermore, it is important to note that genetic-association studies are ultimately correlational and that the causal role of any given gene is therefore still an open question. One way to address this issue may be through the use of experimental manipulation of exogenous hormones. For instance, as mentioned earlier, studies with intranasal oxytocin administration show that oxytocin can be safely used in experimental settings (MacDonald et al. 2011) and that the administration may increase the salience of social cues (Bartz et al. 2011). Given this evidence, the use of experimentally administered exogenous hormones may be a particularly good way to directly test the mechanistic role of target neurotransmitters. Similar experimental manipulation is possible for serotonin using acute tryptophan depletion, increasing the potential for more causal models. Although these medical drugs should be administered with caution, at least theoretically, such experiments may be useful.

Finally, we consider the most central necessity of the field to be the development of new theories that are specific to cultural neuroscience. Up to this point, most studies have been based on existing theories from behavioral studies in cultural psychology, finding empirical evidence with neural correlates and physiological responses that parallel behavioral and self-report responses. Although this approach has been and is useful for the reasons articulated earlier, there is also a great need for novel theoretical frameworks that will allow researchers to take advantage of the unique potential of neuroscientific methods and generate new research questions.

These possibilities are reminders of the fact that cultural neuroscience is young and thus poses many questions that have yet to be answered. However, its youth also highlights its unique potential in addressing the age-old question of nature and nurture as joint determinants of human behaviors and the question of how these influences come about. Whether through behavioral or neural studies, the field of cultural neuroscience underscores the importance of meaning making as a key factor in psychological and biological processes.

SUMMARY POINTS

1. Cultural neuroscience is a unique combination of perspectives that investigates how culture has implications not only for shared environments, as has historically been shown in cultural psychology, but also for the brain, physiology, and genes, which have generally been within the purview of neuroscience.

2. Genes and culture mutually influence each other and influence psychological tendencies at the macro level, via gene-culture coevolution, and at the micro level, in gene-culture interactions. The same genetic tendency can be manifested differently depending on the cultural context.

3. Theoretical advancement is especially evident from studies demonstrating divergent patterns of neural activation that underlie seemingly similar behavioral outcomes.

4. Violation of cultural meaning can affect cardiovascular and neuroendocrine responses, which has implications for health and well-being.

5. Cultural neuroscience provides cultural psychology with information about the genetic factors interacting with culture, neural mechanisms underlying cultural differences, and physiological responses linked to psychological processes.

6. Cultural neuroscience provides neuroscience with information about how cultural inputs have implications for malleability in genetic expression, neural structure and activity, and physiological responses linked to psychological processes.

7. More cultural neuroscience research should examine cultural change and the resulting psychological consequences with a process-oriented and experiment-based approach.

8. New theories and integration of genetic, physiological, and neural evidence are required for cultural neuroscience to move toward a more holistic understanding of the mind.

DISCLOSURE STATEMENT

The authors are not aware of any affiliations, memberships, funding, or financial holdings that might be perceived as affecting the objectivity of this review.

ACKNOWLEDGMENTS

Preparation of this manuscript was supported by NSF BCS-1124552 to H.S. Kim.

LITERATURE CITED

Adler NE, Boyce T, Chesney MA, Cohen S, Folkman S, et al. 1994. Socioeconomic status and health: the challenge of the gradient. *Am. Psychol.* 49:15–24

Atran S, Norenzayan A. 2004. Religion's evolutionary landscape: counterintuition, commitment, compassion, communion. *Behav. Brain Sci.* 27:713–70

Bakermans-Kranenburg MJ, van IJzendoorn MH. 2008. Oxytocin receptor (*OXTR*) and serotonin transporter (*5-HTT*) genes associated with observed parenting. *Soc. Cogn. Affect. Neurosci.* 3:128–34

Bakermans-Kranenburg MJ, van IJzendoorn MH, Pijlman FT, Mesman J, Juffer F. 2008. Experimental evidence for differential susceptibility: dopamine D4 receptor polymorphism (DRD4 VNTR) moderates intervention effects on toddlers' externalizing behavior in a randomized controlled trial. *Dev. Psychol.* 44:293–300

Bartz JA, Zaki J, Bolger N, Hollander E, Ludwig NN, et al. 2010. Oxytocin selectively improves empathic accuracy. *Psychol. Sci.* 21:1426–28

Bartz JA, Zaki J, Bolger N, Ochsner KN. 2011. Social effects of oxytocin in humans: context and person matter. *Trends Cogn. Sci.* 15:301–9

Beja-Pereira A, Luikart G, England PR, Bradley DG, Jann OC, et al. 2003. Gene-culture coevolution between cattle milk protein genes and human lactase genes. *Nat. Genet.* 35:311–13

Belsky J, Jonassaint C, Pluess M, Stanton M, Brummett B, Williams R. 2009. Vulnerability genes or plasticity genes? *Mol. Psychiatry* 14:746–54

Blascovich J, Tomaka J. 1996. The biopsychosocial model of arousal regulation. In *Advances in Experimental Social Psychology, Vol. 28*, ed. J Blascovich, J Tomaka, pp. 1–51. San Diego, CA: Academic

Boyd R, Richerson PJ. 1985.*Culture and the Evolutionary Process.* Chicago: Univ. Chicago Press

Bruner J. 1990. *Acts of Meaning.* Cambridge, MA: Harvard Univ. Press

Bullmore ET, Bassett DS. 2011. Brain graphs: graphical models of the human brain connectome. *Annu. Rev. Clin. Psychol.* 7:113–40

Butler EA, Lee TL, Gross JJ. 2009. Does expressing your emotions raise or lower your blood pressure? The answer depends on cultural context. *J. Cross-Cult. Psychol.* 40:510–17

Butts CT. 2009. Revisiting the foundations of network analysis. *Science* 325:414–16

Caspi A, McClay J, Moffitt TE, Mill J, Martin J, et al. 2002. Role of genotype in the cycle of violence in maltreated children. *Science* 297:851–54

Caspi A, Sugden K, Moffitt TE, Taylor A, Craig IW, et al. 2003. Influence of life stress on depression: moderation by a polymorphism in the *5-HTT* gene. *Science* 301:386–89

Cavalli-Sforza L, Feldman M. 1981. *Cultural Transmission and Evolution: A Quantitative Approach.* Princeton, NJ: Princeton Univ. Press

Chee MW, Zheng H, Goh JO, Park D. 2011. Brain structure in young and old East Asians and Westerners: comparisons of structural volume and cortical thickness. *J. Cogn. Neurosci.* 23:1065–79

Cheon BK, Im D, Harada T, Kim J, Mathur VA, et al. 2011. Cultural influences on neural basis of intergroup empathy. *NeuroImage* 57:642–50

Chiang JJ, Saphire-Bernstein S, Kim HS, Sherman DK, Taylor SE. 2013. Cultural differences in the link between supportive relationships and proinflammatory cytokines. *Soc. Psychol. Personal. Sci.* 4:511–20

Chiao JY. 2010. Neural basis of social status hierarchy across species. *Curr. Opin. Neurobiol.* 20:803–9

Chiao JY, Ambady N. 2007. Cultural neuroscience: parsing universality and diversity across levels of analysis. In *Handbook of Cultural Psychology*, ed. S Kitayama, D Cohen, pp. 237–54. New York: Guilford

Chiao JY, Blizinsky KD. 2010. Culture–gene coevolution of individualism–collectivism and the serotonin transporter gene (*5-HTTLPR*). *Proc. R. Soc. B* 277:529–37

Chiao JY, Harada T, Komeda H, Li Z, Mano Y, et al. 2009. Neural basis of individualistic and collectivistic views of self. *Hum. Brain Mapp.* 30:2813–20

Cohen AB. 2009. Many forms of culture. *Am. Psychol.* 64:194–204

Cohen AB, Hill PC. 2007. Religion as culture: religious individualism and collectivism among American Catholics, Jews, and Protestants. *J. Personal.* 75:709–42

Cohen D, Nisbett RE, Bowdle BF, Schwarz N. 1996. Insult, aggression, and the Southern culture of honor: an "experimental ethnography." *J. Personal. Soc. Psychol.* 70:945–60

Cole SW, Hawkley LC, Arevalo JM, Sung CY, Rose RM, Cacioppo JT. 2007. Social regulation of gene expression in human leukocytes. *Genome Biol.* 8:R189

Crinion JT, Green DW, Chung R, Ali N, Grogan A, et al. 2009. Neuroanatomical markers of speaking Chinese. *Hum. Brain Mapp.* 30:4108–15

De Dreu CKW, Greer LL, Van Keef GA, Shalvi S, Handgraaf MJJ. 2011. Oxytocin promotes human ethnocentrism. *Proc. Natl. Acad. Sci. USA* 108:1262–66

Applies gene-culture coevolution theory empirically to explain individualism versus collectivism across nations.

Describes finding that oxytocin does not increase prosocial tendencies uniformly; the effect is moderated by group membership.

de Greck M, Shi Z, Wang G, Zuo X, Yang X, et al. 2012. Culture modulates brain activity during empathy with anger. *NeuroImage* 59:2871–82

de Leersnyder J, Mesquita B, Kim HS. 2011. Where do my emotions belong? A study of immigrants' emotional acculturation. *Personal. Soc. Psychol. Bull.* 37:451–63

Dennett DC. 1987. *The Intentional Stance*. Cambridge, MA: MIT Press

Dickerson SS, Kemeny ME. 2004. Acute stressors and cortisol responses: a theoretical integration and synthesis of laboratory research. *Psychol. Bull.* 130:355–91

Ditzen B, Schaer M, Gabriel B, Bodenmann G, Ehlert U, Heinrichs M. 2009. Intranasal oxytocin increases positive communication and reduces cortisol levels during couple conflict. *Biol. Psychiatry* 65:728–31

Domes G, Heinrichs M, Michel A, Berger C, Hepertz SC. 2007. Oxytocin improves "mind-reading" in humans. *Biol. Psychiatry* 61:731–33

Dressler WW, Balieiro MC, Ribeiro RP, Santos JED. 2009. Cultural consonance, a 5HT2A receptor polymorphism, and depressive symptoms: a longitudinal study of gene × culture interaction in urban Brazil. *Am. J. Hum. Biol.* 21:91–97

Feldman MW, Laland KN. 1996. Gene–culture co-evolutionary theory. *Trends Ecol. Evol.* 11:453–57

Feldman R, Weller A, Zagoory-Sharon O, Levine A. 2007. Evidence for a neuroendocrinological foundation of human affiliation: plasma oxytocin levels across pregnancy and the postpartum period predict mother–infant bonding. *Psychol. Sci.* 18:965–70

Fincher CL, Thornhill R. 2012. Parasite-stress promotes in-group assortative sociality: the cases of strong family ties and heightened religiosity. *Behav. Brain Sci.* 35:61–119

Fincher CL, Thornhill R, Murray DR, Schaller M. 2008. Pathogen prevalence predicts human cross-cultural variability in individualism/collectivism. *Proc. R. Soc. B* 275:1279–85

Fiske AP, Kitayama S, Markus HR, Nisbett RE. 1998. The cultural matrix of social psychology. In *The Handbook of Social Psychology*, ed. DT Gilbert, ST Fiske, G Lindzey, pp. 915–81. San Francisco: McGraw-Hill. 4th ed.

Fodor JA. 1987. *Psychosemantics: The Problem of Meaning in the Philosophy of Mind*. Cambridge, MA: MIT Press

Freeman JB, Rule NO, Adams RB, Ambady N. 2009. Culture shapes a mesolimbic response to signals of dominance and subordination that associates with behavior. *NeuroImage* 47:353–59

Galton F. 1874. *English Men of Science: Their Nature and Nurture*. London: Macmillan

Goldin PR, McRae K, Ramel W, Gross JJ. 2008. The neural bases of emotion regulation: reappraisal and suppression of negative emotion. *Biol. Psychiatry* 63:577–86

Green DW, Crinion J, Price CJ. 2007. Exploring cross-linguistic vocabulary effects on brain structures using voxel-based morphometry. *Biling. Lang. Cogn.* 10:189–99

Grossmann I, Varnum MEW. 2011. Social class, culture, and cognition. *Soc. Psychol. Personal. Sci.* 2:81–89

Gutchess AH, Hedden T, Ketay S, Aron A, Gabrieli JDE. 2010. Neural differences in the processing of semantic relationships across cultures. *Soc. Cogn. Affect. Neurosci.* 5:254–63

Han S, Gu X, Mao L, Ge J, Wang G, Ma Y. 2010. Neural substrates of self-referential processing in Chinese Buddhists. *Soc. Cogn. Affect. Neurosci.* 5:332–39

Han S, Mao L, Gu X, Zhu Y, Ge J, Ma Y. 2008. Neural consequences of religious belief on self-referential processing. *Soc. Neurosci.* 3:1–15

Han S, Mao L, Qin J, Friederici AD, Ge J. 2011. Functional roles and cultural modulations of the medial prefrontal and parietal activity associated with causal attribution. *Neuropsychologia* 49:83–91

Harden KP, Turkheimer E, Loehlin JC. 2007. Genotype by environment interaction in adolescents' cognitive aptitude. *Behav. Genet.* 37:273–83

Hatton GI. 1990. Emerging concepts of structure-function dynamics in adult brain: the hypothalamo-neurohypophysial system. *Prog. Neurobiol.* 34:437–504

Hedden T, Ketay S, Aron A, Markus HR, Gabrieli JD. 2008. Cultural influences on neural substrates of attentional control. *Psychol. Sci.* 19:12–17

Heine SJ, Lehman DR, Markus HR, Kitayama S. 1999. Is there a universal need for positive self-regard? *Psychol. Rev.* 106:766–94

Heine SJ, Proulx T, Vohs KD. 2006. The meaning maintenance model: on the coherence of social motivations. *Personal. Soc. Psychol. Rev.* 10:88–111

Hong Y, Morris MW, Chiu C, Benet-Martinez V. 2000. Multicultural minds: a dynamic constructivist approach to culture and cognition. *Am. Psychol.* 55:709–20

Ishii K, Kobayashi Y, Kitayama S. 2010. Interdependence modulates the brain response to word–voice incongruity. *Soc. Cogn. Affect. Neurosci.* 5:307–17

Ishii K, Miyamoto Y, Niedenthal PM, Mayama K. 2011. When your smile fades away: cultural differences in sensitivity to the disappearance of smiles. *Soc. Psychol. Personal. Sci.* 2:516–22

Iyengar S, Lepper M. 1999. Rethinking the value of choice: a cultural perspective on intrinsic motivation. *J. Personal. Soc. Psychol.* 76:349–66

Ji LJ, Zhang Z, Nisbett RE. 2004. Is it culture, or is it language? Examination of language effects in cross-cultural research on categorization. *J. Personal. Soc. Psychol.* 87:57–65

Karg K, Burmeister M, Shedden K, Sen S. 2011. The serotonin transporter promoter variant (*5-HTTLPR*), stress, and depression meta-analysis revisited. *Arch. Gen. Psychiatry* 68:444–54

Kaufman J, Yang BZ, Douglas-Palumberi H, Grasso D, Lipschitz D, et al. 2006. Brain-derived neurotrophic factor–*5-HTTLPR* gene interactions and environmental modifiers of depression in children. *Biol. Psychiatry* 59:673–80

Kavaliers M, Agmo A, Choleris E, Gustafson JA, Korach KS, et al. 2004. Oxytocin and estrogen receptor α and β knockout mice provide discriminably different odor cues in behavioral assays. *Genes Brain Behav.* 3:189–95

Kavaliers M, Choleris E. 2011. Sociality, pathogen avoidance, and the neuropeptides oxytocin and arginine vasopressin. *Psychol. Sci.* 22:1367–74

Keenan JP, Wheeler MA, Gallup GG, Pascual-Leone A. 2000. Self-recognition and the right prefrontal cortex. *Trends Cogn. Sci.* 4:338–44

Kelley WM, Macrae CN, Wyland CL, Caglar S, Inati S, Heatherton TF. 2002. Finding the self? An event-related fMRI study. *J. Cogn. Neurosci.* 14:785–94

Kim H, Markus HR. 1999. Deviance or uniqueness, harmony or conformity? A cultural analysis. *J. Personal. Soc. Psychol.* 77:785–800

Kim HS. 2002. We talk, therefore we think? A cultural analysis of the effect of talking on thinking. *J. Personal. Soc. Psychol.* 83:828–42

Kim HS. 2008. Culture and the cognitive and neuroendocrine responses to speech. *J. Personal. Soc. Psychol.* 94:32–47

Kim HS, Chu TQ. 2011. Cultural variation in the motivation of self-expression. In *Frontiers of Social Psychology: Social Motivation*, ed. DA Dunning, pp. 57–77. New York: Psychology

Kim HS, Sasaki JY. 2012. Emotion regulation: the interplay of culture and genes. *Soc. Personal. Psychol. Compass* 6:865–77

Kim HS, Sherman DK. 2007. "Express yourself": culture and the effect of self-expression on choice. *J. Personal. Soc. Psychol.* 92:1–11

Kim HS, Sherman DK, Mojaverian T, Sasaki JY, Park J, et al. 2011. Gene-culture interaction: oxytocin receptor polymorphism (*OXTR*) and emotion regulation. *Soc. Psychol. Personal. Sci.* 2:665–72

Kim HS, Sherman DK, Sasaki JY, Xu J, Chu TQ, et al. 2010a. Culture, distress and oxytocin receptor polymorphism (*OXTR*) interact to influence emotional support seeking. *Proc. Natl. Acad. Sci. USA* 107:15717–21

Kim HS, Sherman DK, Taylor SE. 2008. Culture and social support. *Am. Psychol.* 63:518–26

Kim HS, Sherman DK, Taylor SE, Sasaki JY, Chu TQ, et al. 2010b. Culture, the serotonin receptor polymorphism (*5-HTR1A*), and locus of attention. *Soc. Cogn. Affect. Neurosci.* 5:212–18

Kirschbaum C, Pirke KM, Hellhammer DH. 1993. The "Trier Social Stress Test"—a tool for investigating psychobiological stress responses in a laboratory setting. *Neuropsychobiology* 28:76–81

Kitayama S. 2002. Culture and basic psychological processes—toward a system view of culture: comment on Oyserman et al. (2002). *Psychol. Bull.* 128:89–96

Kitayama S, Ishii K, Imada T, Takemura K, Ramaswamy J. 2006a. Voluntary settlement and the spirit of independence: evidence from Japan's "northern frontier." *J. Personal. Soc. Psychol.* 91:369–84

Kitayama S, Markus HR, Matsumoto H, Norasakkunkit V. 1997. Individual and collective processes in the construction of the self: self-enhancement in the United States and self-criticism in Japan. *J. Personal. Soc. Psychol.* 72:1245–67

Discusses the finding that the same psychological task can lead to different neuroendocrine responses.

Describes the finding that the association between genes and behaviors may vary between cultures.

Kitayama S, Mesquita B, Karasawa M. 2006b. Cultural affordances and emotional experience: socially engaging and disengaging emotions in Japan and the United States. *J. Personal. Soc. Psychol.* 91:890–903

Kobayashi C, Glover GH, Temple E. 2006. Cultural and linguistic influence on neural bases of 'Theory of Mind': an fMRI study with Japanese bilinguals. *Brain Lang.* 98:210–20

Kobayashi C, Glover GH, Temple E. 2007. Cultural and linguistic effects on neural bases of "theory of mind" in American and Japanese children. *Brain Res.* 1164:95–107

Kochunov P, Fox P, Lancaster J, Tan LH, Amunts K, et al. 2003. Localized morphological brain differences between English-speaking Caucasians and Chinese-speaking Asians: new evidence of anatomical plasticity. *Neuroreport* 14:961–64

Kosfeld M, Heinrichs M, Zak PJ, Fishbacher U, Fehr E. 2005. Oxytocin increases trust in humans. *Nature* 435:673–76

Kraus MW, Côte S, Keltner D. 2010. Social class, contextualism, and empathic accuracy. *Psychol. Sci.* 21:1716–23

Kühnen U, Hannover B, Schubert B. 2001. The semantic–procedural interface model of the self: the role of self-knowledge for context-dependent versus context-independent modes of thinking. *J. Personal. Soc. Psychol.* 80:397–409

Lesch KP, Bengel D, Heils A, Sabol SZ, Greenberg BD, et al. 1996. Association of anxiety-related traits with a polymorphism in the serotonin transporter gene regulatory region. *Science* 274:1527–31

Lewis RS, Goto SG, Kong LL. 2008. Culture and context: East Asian American and European American differences in P3 event-related potentials and self-construal. *Personal. Soc. Psychol. Bull.* 34:623–34

Li S-C. 2003. Biocultural orchestration of developmental plasticity across levels: the interplay of biology and culture in shaping the mind and behavior across the life span. *Psychol. Bull.* 129:171–94

Lieberman MD, Jarcho JM, Satpute AB. 2004. Evidence-based and intuition-based self-knowledge: an fMRI study. *J. Personal. Soc. Psychol.* 87:421–35

Lucht MJ, Barnow S, Sonnenfeld C, Rosenberger A, Grabe HJ, et al. 2009. Associations between the oxytocin receptor gene (*OXTR*) and affect, loneliness and intelligence in normal subjects. *Prog. Neuro-Psychopharmacol. Biol. Psychiatry* 33:860–66

Lumsden CJ, Wilson EO. 1981. *Genes, Mind, and Culture.* Cambridge, MA: Harvard Univ. Press

MacDonald E, Dadds MR, Brennan JL, Williams K, Levy F, Cauchi AJ. 2011. A review of safety, side-effects and subjective reactions to intranasal oxytocin in human research. *Psychoneuroendocrinology* 36:1114–26

Markus HR, Kitayama S. 1991. Culture and the self: implications for cognition, emotion, and motivation. *Psychol. Rev.* 98:224–53

Masuda T, Nisbett RE. 2001. Attending holistically versus analytically: comparing the context sensitivity of Japanese and Americans. *J. Personal. Soc. Psychol.* 81:922–34

Matsumoto D, Yoo SH, Nakagawa S, Multinational Study of Cultural Display Rules. 2008. Culture, emotion regulation, and adjustment. *J. Personal. Soc. Psychol.* 94:925–37

McCullough ME, Hoyt WT, Larson DB, Koenig HG, Thoresen C. 2000. Religious involvement and mortality: a meta-analytic review. *Health Psychol.* 19:211–22

Mechelli A, Crinion JT, Noppeney U, O'Doherty J, Ashburner J, et al. 2004. Neurolinguistics: structural plasticity in the bilingual brain. *Nature* 431:757

Meyer-Lindenberg A, Domes G, Kirsch P, Heinrichs M. 2011. Oxytocin and vasopressin in the human brain: social neuropeptides for translational medicine. *Nat. Rev. Neurosci.* 12:524–38

Miller G. 2013. The promise and perils of oxytocin. *Science* 339:267–69

Miller GE, Chen E, Fok AK, Walker H, Lim A, et al. 2009. Low early-life social class leaves a biological residue manifested by decreased glucocorticoid and increased proinflammatory signaling. *Proc. Natl. Acad. Sci. USA* 106:14716–21

Miller JG, Bersoff DM, Harwood RL. 1990. Perceptions of social responsibilities in India and in the United States: moral imperatives or personal decisions? *J. Personal. Soc. Psychol.* 58:33–47

Miyamoto Y, Nisbett RE, Masuda T. 2006. Culture and the physical environment: holistic versus analytic perceptual affordances. *Psychol. Sci.* 17:113–19

Na J, Choi I, Sul S. 2013. I like you because you think in the "right" way: cultural idealization of thinking style. *Soc. Cogn.* 31:390–404

Explains that different linguistic experiences lead to changes in brain structure.

Na J, Grossmann I, Varnum ME, Kitayama S, Gonzalez R, Nisbett RE. 2010. Cultural differences are not always reducible to individual differences. *Proc. Natl. Acad. Sci. USA* 107:6192–97

Na J, Kitayama S. 2011. Spontaneous trait inference is culture-specific: behavioral and neural evidence. *Psychol. Sci.* 22:1025–32

Ng SH, Han S, Mao L, Lai JCL. 2010. Dynamic bicultural brains: a fMRI study of their flexible neural representation of self and significant others in response to culture priming. *Asian J. Soc. Psychol.* 13:83–91

Nisbett RE. 1993. Violence and US regional culture. *Am. Psychol.* 48:441–49

Nisbett RE, Aronson J, Blair C, Dickens W, Flynn J, et al. 2012. Intelligence: new findings and theoretical developments. *Am. Psychol.* 67:130–59

Nisbett RE, Peng K, Choi I, Norenzayan A. 2001. Culture and systems of thought: holistic versus analytic cognition. *Psychol. Rev.* 108:291–310

Northoff G, Heinzel A, de Greck M, Bermpohl F, Dobrowolny H, Panksepp J. 2006. Self-referential processing in our brain: a meta-analysis of imaging studies on the self. *NeuroImage* 31:440–57

Obradović J, Boyce WT. 2009. Individual differences in behavioral, physiological, and genetic sensitivities to contexts: implications for development and adaptation. *Dev. Neurosci.* 31:300–8

Odling-Smee FJ, Laland KN, Feldman MW. 2003. *Niche Construction: The Neglected Process in Evolution.* Princeton, NJ: Princeton Univ. Press

Ohira H, Nomura M, Ichikawa N, Isowa T, Iidaka T, et al. 2006. Association of neural and physiological responses during voluntary emotion suppression. *NeuroImage* 29:721–33

Oyserman D, Lee SW. 2008. Does culture influence what and how we think? Effects of priming individualism and collectivism. *Psychol. Bull.* 134:311–42

Pezawas L, Meyer-Lindenberg A, Drabant EM, Verchinski BA, Munoz KE, et al. 2005. 5-HTTLPR polymorphism impacts human cingulate-amygdala interactions: a genetic susceptibility mechanism for depression. *Nat. Neurosci.* 8:828–34

Plomin R, Asbury K. 2005. Nature and nurture: genetic and environmental influences on behavior. *Ann. Am. Acad. Polit. Soc. Sci.* 600:86–98

Proulx T, Heine SJ. 2008. The case of the transmogrifying experimenter: affirmation of a moral schema following implicit change detection. *Psychol. Sci.* 19:1294–300

Ridker PM, Rifai N, Stampfer MJ, Hennekens CH. 2000. Plasma concentration of interleukin-6 and the risk of future myocardial infarction among apparently healthy men. *Circulation* 101:1767–72

Riem MME, Pieper S, Out D, Bakermans-Kranenburg MJ, van IJzendoorn MH. 2011. Oxytocin receptor gene and depressive symptoms associated with physiological reactivity to infant crying. *Soc. Cogn. Affect. Neurosci.* 6:294–300

Rodrigues SM, Saslow LR, Garcia N, John OP, Keltner D. 2009. Oxytocin receptor genetic variation relates to empathy and stress reactivity in humans. *Proc. Natl. Acad. Sci. USA* 106:21437–41

Sasaki JY. 2013. Promise and challenges surrounding culture–gene coevolution and gene–culture interactions. *Psychol. Inq.* 24:64–70

Sasaki JY, Kim HS. 2011. At the intersection of culture and religion: a cultural analysis of religion's implications for secondary control and social affiliation. *J. Personal. Soc. Psychol.* 101:401–14

Discusses the possibility that susceptibility to implicit influences on prosocial behavior may have a genetic basis.

Sasaki JY, Kim HS, Mojaverian T, Kelley LD, Park IY, Janušonis S. 2013. Religion priming differentially increases prosocial behavior among variants of dopamine D4 receptor (*DRD4*) gene. *Soc. Cogn. Affect. Neurosci.* 8:209–15

Sasaki JY, Kim HS, Xu J. 2011. Religion and well-being: the moderating role of culture and the oxytocin receptor (*OXTR*) gene. *J. Cross-Cult. Psychol.* 42:1394–405

Saxe R, Kanwisher N. 2003. People thinking about thinking people: the role of the temporo-parietal junction in "theory of mind." *NeuroImage* 19:1835–42

Schaller M, Murray DR. 2008. Pathogens, personality, and culture: disease prevalence predicts worldwide variability in sociosexuality, extraversion, and openness to experience. *J. Personal. Soc. Psychol.* 95:212–21

Schmitt JAJ, Wingen M, Ramaekers JG, Evers EAT, Riedel WJ. 2006. Serotonin and human cognitive performance. *Curr. Pharm. Des.* 12:2473–86

Schreier HM, Chen E. 2013. Socioeconomic status and the health of youth: a multilevel, multidomain approach to conceptualizing pathways. *Psychol. Bull.* 139:606–54

Shariff AF, Norenzayan A. 2007. God is watching you: priming god concepts increases prosocial behavior in an anonymous economic game. *Psychol. Sci.* 18:803–9

Sherman DK, Kim HS, Taylor SE. 2009. Culture and social support: neural bases and biological impact. *Prog. Brain Res.* 178:227–37

Shweder R. 1995. Cultural psychology: What is it? In *The Culture and Psychology Reader*, ed. NR Goldberger, JB Veroff, pp. 41–86. New York: NYU Press

Snibbe AC, Markus HR. 2005. You can't always get what you want: educational attainment, agency, and choice. *J. Personal. Soc. Psychol.* 88:703–20

Stephens NM, Markus HR, Townsend SS. 2007. Choice as an act of meaning: the case of social class. *J. Personal. Soc. Psychol.* 93:814–30

Stephens NM, Townsend SS, Markus HR, Phillips LT. 2012. A cultural mismatch: independent cultural norms produce greater increases in cortisol and more negative emotions among first-generation college students. *J. Exp. Soc. Psychol.* 48:1389–93

Suh EM. 2002. Culture, identity consistency, and subjective well-being. *J. Personal. Soc. Psychol.* 83:1378–91

Sui J, Han S. 2007. Self-construal priming modulates neural substrates of self-awareness. *Psychol. Sci.* 18:861–66

Sui J, Hong Y, Liu CH, Humphreys GW, Han S. 2013. Dynamic cultural modulation of neural responses to one's own and friend's faces. *Soc. Cogn. Affect. Neurosci.* 8:326–32

Sui J, Liu CH, Han S. 2009. Cultural difference in neural mechanisms of self-recognition. *Soc. Neurosci.* 4:402–11

Tang YY, Zhang WT, Chen KW, Feng SH, Ji Y, et al. 2006. Arithmetic processing in the brain shaped by cultures. *Proc. Natl. Acad. Sci. USA* 103:10775–80

Taylor SE, Sherman DK, Kim HS, Jarcho J, Takagi K, Dunagan MS. 2004. Culture and social support: Who seeks it and why? *J. Personal. Soc. Psychol.* 87:354–62

Taylor SE, Way BM, Welch WT, Hilmert CJ, Lehman BJ, Eisenberger NI. 2006. Early family environment, current adversity, the serotonin transporter promoter polymorphism, and depressive symptomatology. *Biol. Psychiatry* 60:671–76

Taylor SE, Welch WT, Kim HS, Sherman DK. 2007. Cultural differences in the impact of social support on psychological and biological stress responses. *Psychol. Sci.* 18:831–37

Tsai JL, Levenson RW. 1997. Cultural influences on emotional responding: Chinese American and European American dating couples during interpersonal conflict. *J. Cross-Cult. Psychol.* 28:600–25

Tsai JL, Miao FF, Seppala E. 2007. Good feelings in Christianity and Buddhism: religious differences in ideal affect. *Personal. Soc. Psychol. Bull.* 33:409–21

Tucker-Drob EM, Rhemtulla M, Harden KP, Turkheimer E, Fask D. 2011. Emergence of a gene × socioeconomic status interaction on infant mental ability between 10 months and 2 years. *Psychol. Sci.* 22:125–33

Turkheimer E, Haley A, Waldron M, D'Onofrio B, Gottesman II. 2003. Socioeconomic status modifies heritability of IQ in young children. *Psychol. Sci.* 14:623–28

Uskul AK, Kitayama S, Nisbett RE. 2008. Ecocultural basis of cognition: farmers and fishermen are more holistic than herders. *Proc. Natl. Acad. Sci. USA* 105:8552–56

Varnum ME, Na J, Murata A, Kitayama S. 2012. Social class differences in N400 indicate differences in spontaneous trait inference. *J. Exp. Psychol.: Gen.* 141:518–26

Wang E, Ding Y-C, Flodman P, Kidd JR, Kidd KK, et al. 2004. The genetic architecture of selection at the human dopamine receptor D4 (*DRD4*) gene locus. *Am. J. Hum. Genet.* 74:931–44

Way BM, Lieberman MD. 2010. Is there a genetic contribution to cultural differences? Collectivism, individualism and genetic markers of social sensitivity. *Soc. Cogn. Affect. Neurosci.* 5:203–11

Way BM, Taylor SE. 2010. Social influences on health: Is serotonin a critical mediator? *Psychosom. Med.* 72:107–12

Weisbuch-Remington M, Mendes WB, Seery MD, Blascovich J. 2005. The nonconscious influence of religious symbols in motivated performance situations. *Personal. Soc. Psychol. Bull.* 31:1203–16

Notes that self-construal priming leads to differences in neural responses in regions linked to self-recognition.

Discusses finding that differences in brain activation between people from different cultures occur even when the goal of processing is the same.

Zhong H, Yang X, Kaplan LM, Molony C, Schadt EE. 2010. Integrating pathway analysis and genetics of gene expression for genome-wide association studies. *Am. J. Hum. Genet.* 86:581–91

Zhu Y, Zhang L, Fan J, Han S. 2007. Neural basis of cultural influence on self-representation. *NeuroImage* 34:1310–16

Zilles K, Kawashima R, Dabringhaus A, Fukuda H, Schormann T. 2001. Hemispheric shape of European and Japanese brains: 3-D MRI analysis of intersubject variability, ethnical, and gender differences. *NeuroImage* 13:262–71

A Phenotypic Null Hypothesis for the Genetics of Personality

Eric Turkheimer,[1] Erik Pettersson,[2] and Erin E. Horn[1]

[1]Department of Psychology, University of Virginia, Charlottesville, Virginia 22904;
email: ent3c@virginia.edu

[2]Department of Medical Epidemiology and Biostatistics, Karolinska Institute,
SE-171 77 Stockholm, Sweden

Annu. Rev. Psychol. 2014. 65:515–40

First published online as a Review in Advance on
September 18, 2013

The *Annual Review of Psychology* is online at
http://psych.annualreviews.org

This article's doi:
10.1146/annurev-psych-113011-143752

Keywords

behavior genetics, twins, genomics

Abstract

We review the genetically informed literature on the genetics of personality. Over the past century, quantitative genetic studies, using identical and fraternal twins, have demonstrated that differences in human personality are substantially heritable. We focus on more contemporary questions to which that basic observation has led. We examine whether differences in the heritability of personality are replicable across different traits, samples, and studies; how the heritability of personality relates to its reliability; and how behavior genetics can be employed in studies of validity, and we discuss the stability of personality in genetic and environmental variance. The appropriate null hypothesis in behavior genetics is not that genetic or environmental influence on personality is zero. Instead, we offer a phenotypic null hypothesis, which states that genetic variance is not an independent mechanism of individual differences in personality but rather a reflection of processes that are best conceptualized at the phenotypic level.

Contents

INTRODUCTION

Personality and behavior genetics have a special relationship. The scientific origin of both fields is in the nineteenth century, and they came of age at the same time, after World War II, as human personality was distinguished from cognitive ability on the one hand and psychopathology on the other and as behavior genetics embarked on its modern empirical programs of experimental studies of model organisms and quantitative genetic studies of humans. Both personality psychology and behavior genetics were spurred by the development of modern factor analysis and the computational power that supported it.

Another reason for this special relationship is even more important. The nineteenth-century roots of behavior genetics involved the classical questions of nature and nurture formulated by Francis Galton, questions that are still important to this field. However, for personality, as opposed to other phenotypes such as intelligence and psychopathology, the so-called nature-nurture debate was never an issue. For thousands of years, animal breeders had been selecting domesticated livestock for behavioral traits; any farm owner, never mind any dog owner, knew perfectly well that behavioral traits with strong analogs to human personality could be transmitted genetically in lower animals, even prior to any scientific knowledge about what "genetic" transmission entailed.

The earliest research known as behavior genetics involved transmission and breeding of temperamental traits in dogs. The first article about behavior genetics in this journal (Fuller 1960) extensively covered the genetics of temperament in *Drosophila*, mice, and dogs, with scarcely any consideration of nature and nurture or genes and environment; in the experimental studies of breeding at that time, the unity of nature and nurture was taken for granted. Had the behavior genetics of personality remained focused on experimental studies of temperament in mice and dogs, the field's history would not be nearly as fraught as we find it today. Investigators inevitably decided to extend the incontrovertible research on the genetics of personality in lower animals to the analogs of those temperamental traits in humans. Although traits such as aggression and activity level translate fairly transparently from dogs to humans, the breeding and cross-fostering studies that had been employed to study them do not, so investigators had to turn to other methods, namely the twin and adoption studies that eventually came to be the hallmark of modern behavior genetics.

BASICS OF BEHAVIOR GENETICS

The goal of this article is to go beyond the assertions and denials of heritability that have traditionally characterized the genetics of behavior. A very brief review is necessary, however, to introduce

Phenotype: the observable characteristics of an organism, as opposed to their genetic or environmental origins

Heritability: the proportion of variance in phenotype that is associated with variation in genotype

some terms and abbreviations that are used in the remainder of the article. In the classical twin model, phenotypic variances and covariances of pairs of identical or fraternal twins are partitioned into three components: the additive effects of multiple genes (A), of which 100% are shared in identical twins and 50% in fraternal twins; the shared environmental effects that make siblings raised together in the same family similar (C); and the remainder (E), sometimes termed the nonshared or unique environment, which comprises everything that makes twins raised together different, including measurement error. Some elaborations of this basic design are introduced below.

The assumptions—both statistical and biological—of the classical twin model have been hotly contended for as long as twin studies have existed, and disagreement about them has not abated (Joseph 2004, Charney 2012). We do not use our limited space debating these issues, for several reasons. They have, of course, been debated many times already. In addition, objections to the assumptions of twin studies are most relevant when the goal of the studies is to compute the heritability of one trait or another, and our explicit goal is to avoid doing so. We have made the case elsewhere (Turkheimer 1998, 2000; Turkheimer & Harden 2013) that the numerical values of heritability coefficients do not matter very much anyway, other than by differing from zero or one. Moreover, some recent DNA-based statistical methods that do not require twins or any assumptions about them have reached conclusions very similar to those from the classical twin studies (Turkheimer 2011, Yang et al. 2011).

With that in mind, we now turn to the question of whether differences in human personality are heritable. We can be mercifully brief: yes. Every review of the genetics of personality, from the early reports from Cattell (1981) and Eysenck (1990) to modern summaries by Plomin & Caspi (1990), Bouchard & Loehlin (2001), and Krueger & Johnson (2008), has concluded that identical twins are more similar for personality traits than are fraternal twins and that the personalities of adopted children are more similar to the personalities of their biological parents than to those of their adoptive parents. Personality is not alone in this regard; indeed, Turkheimer (2000) has long argued that all human traits are heritable, referring to the universality of heritability as the First Law of Behavior Genetics.

The other two laws of behavior genetics pertain to the two environmental components of the classical model: the shared and nonshared environment, and there are some basic results regarding them that should be discussed before proceeding to other questions. The Second Law of Behavior Genetics, which states that the shared environmental component of human individual differences is small, is usually true for most traits, but the situation is somewhat starker for personality. It is remarkable, in surveying the genetically informed personality literature in a very wide context, how completely absent the shared environment is. In fact, it is often the case that identical twins are more than twice as similar as fraternal twins, a violation of the classical twin model that, if uncorrected, produces negative estimates for shared environmental variance. In this review, the near-unanimous absence of shared environmental effects provides a useful simplifying assumption that allows us to focus on genetic effects (which we sometimes refer to simply as A) and nonshared environmental ones (E) (see sidebar Why Are There No Shared Environmental Effects on Personality?).

The Third Law of Behavior Genetics states that even identical twins raised in the same home are not perfectly correlated for anything, especially behavior and certainly not personality. Uncorrelated variance between members of an identical twin pair is known as the unique or nonshared environment, and although we use the latter term here it is misleading in many ways (Turkheimer & Waldron 2000). We prefer to consider the nonshared environment in more concrete terms, as the phenotypic variance within identical twin pairs raised together, especially as an alternative to thinking of it as some unspecified set of environmental agents that cause members of identical twin pairs to differ from each other. We apply this distinction to the analysis of validity studies in the remainder of this review, and hopefully its utility will become apparent.

WHY ARE THERE NO SHARED ENVIRONMENTAL EFFECTS ON PERSONALITY?

One possibility is that complex genetic interactions [epistasis, or what Lykken (1982) has referred to more broadly as emergenesis] produce configural effects that increase the similarity of identical twin pairs compared with all other types of relationships. Loehlin and colleagues (2003) have shown that analyses including half-siblings demonstrate surplus similarity in identical twins relative to other relationship types. One must also consider the possibility, however, that families simply do not contribute much common systematic variance to the personalities of children raised together. In the domain of cognitive ability, hypotheses about the absence of family effects are fraught with controversy, for good reasons. Intelligence is a directional trait; in general it is always good to have more of it, and parents invest extraordinary resources in the cognitive abilities of their children. One of the most important social institutions in modern civilization—the educational system—is dedicated to increasing cognitive ability in children, and varies mostly at the level of families (i.e., children raised in the same family are usually exposed to the same schools). Personality traits, in contrast, are bidirectional, with positive and negative traits at both ends, and there is nothing analogous to the educational system dedicated to changing them.

VARIABILITY OF HERITABILITY

Are some personality traits more heritable than others? This would seem to be a foundational issue of behavior genetics as it has traditionally been formulated. If the goal of behavior genetics is to answer nature-nurture questions, then one would expect the answers to the questions to differ, trait by trait. Unfortunately, this particular issue suffers from widely acknowledged but frequently ignored limitations inherent in the concept of heritability itself. We recently discussed this issue at length (Turkheimer & Harden 2013) and do so only briefly here. Reviews of the heritability concept always include the caveat that a heritability coefficient applies only to the population in which it was computed, but the most important implications of this limitation are not generally acknowledged.

A heritability coefficient represents the proportion of phenotypic variability that is associated with variability in genotype. As such, it is an effect size, a variance ratio, an R^2 coefficient; and like any variance ratio it is sensitive to characteristics of the population in ways that means are not. In particular, variance ratios depend crucially on the variability of both the predictor and the outcome. For example, the question, "How much of the variance in college performance is explained by differences in SAT scores?" has no meaningful answer, other than, "It depends on the variability of SAT scores and other factors at the institutions where the study is conducted." The dependence of standardized correlation coefficients on their variability is a direct consequence of their presumed advantage, which is that they are unit free. Correlations between x and y are not expressed in units of x and units of y; they are expressed in standard deviations of x and standard deviations of y, and the value of the correlation changes as those standard deviations change. This consideration was the basis of Tukey's (1954) famous opposition to correlation coefficients, as summarized in Turkheimer & Harden (2013).

Notwithstanding these concerns, there is a considerable literature on what is usually termed the differential heritability of personality traits. This literature was initiated by a review by Thompson & Wilde (1973). Thompson was a founder and later president of the Behavior Genetics Association. After reviewing the experimental and animal literature in a manner typical for the time, these authors turned to twin studies, and then to twin studies of personality. In reviewing the extant literature, they noted a number of attempts to "replicate" heritabilities across the genders or ages of twins, and to their apparent surprise the results were uniformly unsuccessful. Rank-order

Genotype:
a collective term for the genetic characteristics of an organism

correlations among heritabilities across gender and age ranged from 0.06 to 0.29, did not reach statistical significance, and were as likely to be negative as positive. Dismayed by these results, these authors reached generally negative conclusions about the genetics of personality and the prospects for twin studies in general. The review appears to have spurred the twin research community to take a serious look at the problem, largely in the form of a 30-year research program conducted by Loehlin. Beginning with the classic book *Heredity, Environment, and Personality*, Loehlin & Nichols (1976) conducted an exhaustive analysis of California Psychological Inventory (CPI) scores in a sample of 850 pairs of twins who had taken the National Merit Scholarship Qualification Test (NMSQT).

Loehlin and Nichols's decisive answer was that the relative magnitudes of heritabilities did not replicate. The authors divided the sample by gender, divided the male and female samples into two random subsamples, computed the difference between the identical and fraternal twin correlations in each of the four subsamples, and compared the rank differences from lowest to highest. The pairwise Spearman rank correlations between the subsamples ranged from -0.22 to $+0.30$; none of them were significantly different from zero. To test whether this result might have occurred because of inadequacies in the CPI scales, these authors constructed their own by using a cluster analysis to create 70 small groupings of three or four items. The results for these scales were no different. They concluded, "In short, for personality and interests, as for abilities, the existing twin literature appears to agree with our own finding that while identical-twin pairs tend to be more similar than fraternal-twin pairs. . . . [t]he difficulty is in showing that trait X is more heritable that trait Y" (Loehlin & Nichols 1976, p. 46).

The subsequent literature did little to change Loehlin and Nichols's conclusion. Carey et al. (1978) reexamined Loehlin and Nichols's results in combination with other samples and demonstrated that monozygotic (MZ) twin correlations were more stable than dizygotic (DZ) ones but that both displayed some detectable stability across samples and that extraversion scales appeared to have slightly higher heritabilities than others. However, as Loehlin (1978) pointed out, the consistencies of the heritabilities were still zero in Carey et al.'s data, just as they were for Loehlin & Nichols (1976).

Loehlin (1982) then returned to the problem, armed with two new tools: a much larger sample (13,000 Swedish twin pairs with measures of extraversion and instability) and structural equation modeling, the application of which to twin studies Loehlin pioneered. Analyses of the Swedish sample suggested that genetic and shared environmental parameters were not equal across the male and female samples or across the three birth cohorts included in the full sample. This apparent success led to another problem, one that continues to be important below: With sufficiently large samples, null hypotheses are always wrong (Meehl 1967). The goal of conducting hypothesis tests in individual studies is not simply to reject or fail to reject hypotheses one at a time but rather, through replication, to build individual hypotheses into cumulative theories that explain the phenomena of interest; the latter goal is much more difficult to achieve than the former. Statistical significance notwithstanding, what is one to make of the finding that the heritability of extraversion in males changes from 0.50 in the earliest-born cohort to 0.36 in the second cohort to 0.66 in the third? And why is the heritability of instability higher for females than for males in two cohorts, but equal in the third?

Loehlin's (1982) other finding in the Swedish sample was that the heritabilities of extraversion and instability could not be differentiated, and that led him to formulate a new hypothesis in the NMSQT sample. Extraversion and neuroticism are the two largest factors in the personality domain, and if their heritabilities are equal, then their relative dominance in the factor matrix could mask differences on less important traits. Returning to the NMSQT data, Loehlin created item clusters, factor-analyzed them, and rotated the first two factors to extraversion and neuroticism.

The remaining factors (stereotyped masculinity, intolerance of ambiguity, persistence, cynical attitudes, and intellectual interests) showed significant (although, once again, not especially systematic) gender differences and significant differences among the traits. In particular, intolerance of ambiguity and stereotyped masculinity showed lower heritabilities than did other traits, as well as stronger shared family influence.

Several years later, Loehlin (1985) returned to the problem again, this time combining the NMSQT sample with the Veterans Administration Twin Sample (Horn et al. 1976) and adoption data from the Texas Adoption Project. Loehlin analyzed whether identical biometric parameters could be fit to all 18 of the CPI subscales and found fairly decisively that they could not. Once again, it proved difficult to theorize about what the nature of those differences might be. Loehlin (1985, p. 217) concluded, "One could pursue matters further by continuing to fit models on an ad hoc scale-by-scale basis, but in doing so one would presumably be running an increasing risk of merely fitting to idiosyncrasies in the data, so it is perhaps prudent to stop at this point." A further analysis of high- and low-heritability items from the NMSQT showed no consistency with a similar analysis conducted by Horn et al. (1976).

Finally, 30 years after he began this research, Loehlin (2012) revisited the problem in a sample of 2,600 Australian twin pairs, using his original methodology of comparing MZ and DZ twin correlations across male and female pairs divided into two random subsamples. As before, Loehlin cluster-analyzed the items, deriving 11 clusters, including 1 extraversion cluster, 2 neuroticism-like clusters, and various narrower clusters. This time, he found substantial consistency in MZ-DZ differences across the four groups. The biometric results did not vary much across scales; shared environmental terms were zero throughout, and the genetic terms ranged from 0.48 to 0.20. Loehlin noted that the greatest differences in heritability were observed, as before, for the traits that load most highly on broad factors of extraversion and neuroticism, which did not differ from each other.

What can we make of these attempts to find differential heritability of personality traits? The most reliable traits—the ones that account for the most variance in the covariance matrix of personality responses—are the traits for which heritability is least variable. Less reliable traits that account for less variance in the personality matrix are more variable, and thus more likely to differ from each other, but rarely systematically. This pattern of results is typical for all of behavioral genomics. One can identify broad dimensions of behavior; quantify their relation to a broad spectrum of genes; and obtain consistent, replicable results that fail to differentiate among behaviors and become uninteresting once they are established. Under most circumstances, both extraversion and neuroticism are heritable at approximately 0.4, and there is little more to be said. Alternatively, one can focus on narrow domains of behavior or (as in the section titled Genomics of Personality below) the relations of behavior to specific as opposed to agglomerated genetic variance, and obtain results that appear to differentiate among traits or genes but fail to replicate in the next study.

HERITABILITY AND RELIABILITY

Personality assessment is inherently hierarchical. In the Five Factor Model (FFM), each major trait is subdivided into facets. In most classical research on the structure of personality, the facets, and often even the factors themselves, were measured by simply summing responses to individual items. Correspondence between items and scales was determined by (*a*) classical psychometric theory and coefficient alpha, (*b*) a priori groupings of items known as testlets, or (*c*) cluster-analytic methods such as those used by Loehlin. With the advent of item response theory and categorical factor analytic models on the one hand, and increased computational power on the other, however, there is no reason for the factor-analytic process not to begin with the items themselves, organized hierarchically into facets that are in turn organized hierarchically into traits. In the other direction, the FFM traits are often analyzed into two broader factors, alpha and beta (Digman 1997, DeYoung 2006), and beyond that even into a single general factor of personality (GFP) (Rushton et al. 2008; however, see Pettersson et al. 2012 for a skeptical view of the substantive basis of the GFP).

We characterize this process as one of reliability because the core question, about how personality items group together into traits, is essentially psychometric. Reliability refers to the tendency for multiple measures of a single personality trait to covary. In classical twin models, just as one can partition the variance of a single trait into biometric components, one can also decompose the covariances among multiple traits, the common factors that those covariances define, and the residual variances (error variance, in classical psychometrics; uniqueness, in factor-analytic terminology) of the items after the common variance has been accounted for. The reliability coefficients of classical psychometric theory involve the ratio of the variance of the common factor to the full variances of the items. The behavior genetic question is about the biometric composition of the common factor and the residuals.

Loehlin et al. (1998) investigated common and unique variance in three different measures of the FFM. In this case, common variance in each facet represents multimethod variance among three methods employed in the NMSQT study: self-rating scales, personality inventory items, and adjective checklists. As expected, the common variance in the FFM traits consisted of A and E. The variance unique to the methods had significant but substantially lower heritabilities and was generally more unstable; even the shared environmental term occasionally appeared. Kandler et al. (2010) reported similar results for common and unique variance among self- and peer ratings of personality.

Jang et al. (1998) analyzed common and unique variance among the FFM facets composing the FFM traits and showed that the five main traits of the FFM were heritable at approximately 0.5, whereas the heritabilities of the unique variances of the facets were once again lower but significant. When the components of unique variances were corrected for unreliability, they were indistinguishable from the traits. Jang et al. (2002) administered the NEO PI-R (Neuroticism-Extroversion-Openness Personality Inventory, Revised) and analyzed common and unique variance at the factor and facet levels. For the set of six facets belonging to the same factor, they fit two common A and two common E factors and also partitioned the unique variance of each facet into A and E. Results showed that all traits are around 50% heritable; approximately half the variability in facets is shared with the common factors; shared and nonshared (A and E) variance exists at all levels of the factor hierarchy; more of the common variance is shared in comparison to the unique variance (the heritability of the common variance is higher); and conversely, more of the shared variance is common. In the other direction, by examining higher-level common factors of the FFM, Jang et al. (2006) showed that the higher-order factors of the FFM, alpha and beta, fit the same pattern: Heritabilities are somewhat higher at the facet level than at the trait level but are still substantially lower than unity.

In summary, biometric models of the psychometric structure of personality show that there is heritable variance all the way down to the item level and nonshared environmental variance all the way up to the most general level. The proportion of genetic variance increases as one moves up the psychometric hierarchy, as more and more error of measurement is eliminated, but when reliability is accounted for, the proportion of heritable variance does not seem to vary substantially by level of analysis.

VALIDITY

We have written extensively about the role behavior genetics can play in the assessment of validity (Turkheimer & Harden 2013). The central problem in assessing the validity of personality measures in humans is the evaluation of causal hypotheses, as well as the limitations placed on causal inference by the impossibility of random assignment to experimental conditions. Suppose one hypothesizes that extraversion is a risk factor for illicit drug use, and observes a correlation between measures of the two traits in the general population. Obviously, one cannot conclude from such data that extraversion causes drug use, and most of the experimental tools that might be available with nonhuman participants—everything from cross-fostering studies to random assignment, to drug exposure, to genetic knockouts—are not available to a researcher concerned with humans.

There are two main threats to the validity of causal inferences based on phenotypic associations. The first is direction of causation, the possibility that drug use causes extraversion instead of the other way around. Although there are behavior genetic models that can discriminate direction of causation, at least in theory (Heath et al. 1993), they have proven difficult to apply in practice. Other quasi-experimental methods, particularly longitudinal designs (which, of course, can be combined with genetically informative data), are more practical for concerns about direction of causation. In the remainder of this section, we assume that it is reasonable to presume that the direction of causation flows from personality to some outcome in another domain.

The other kind of threat to causal inferences about phenotypic associations between personality variables and other outcomes involves third-variable confounds. Returning to the example of extraversion and drug use, the genetic background that contributes to extraversion may also contribute to propensity for drug use. If the phenotypic association between extraversion and drug use is mediated genetically, then there is no reason for the more extraverted member of an MZ pair to be more prone to drug use than her introverted cotwin. If, however, extraversion actually causes drug use there is no reason the process would not occur just as clearly within twin pairs as between them. It is crucial to understand that, in this context, genetic correlations between drug use and extraversion are an alternative to a causal hypothesis.

We reach two conclusions from this analysis. First, the causal relationships of interest to psychologists are almost always phenotypic in nature. If extraversion causes drug use, it matters little how the two phenotypes may be divided into biometric variance components; our hypothesis is that phenotypic extraversion causes phenotypic drug use. Second, the nonshared environment has a special role to play in the assessment of causal hypotheses within genetically informed designs. It is useful to consider the nonshared environment in concrete terms, as the difference in phenotype between a pair of identical twins reared in the same family. If, within pairs of identical twins, the twin who is more extraverted is also the twin more likely to use drugs, then the association cannot be mediated by genes, because the twins are genetically identical; it cannot be mediated by a family variable such as neighborhood, because the twins were raised together.

There are many ways to analyze bivariate family designs in which a personality variable is evaluated as a possible cause of an outcome (Turkheimer & Harden 2013). The most straightforward (**Figure 1**) is the so-called bivariate Cholesky decomposition, which corresponds to a biometric regression model in which the phenotypic regression between an outcome and a predictor is decomposed into separate regressions in the ACE domains. We (Turkheimer & Harden 2013) have demonstrated that when the biometric components of the predictor are appropriately (i.e., not) standardized, and when the predictor causes the outcome and is not confounded by uncontrolled A and C processes, then the three regression coefficients, b_A, b_C, and b_E, are equal to one another and to the hypothetical unstandardized structural regression coefficient, b_P (**Figure 1**), expressed as

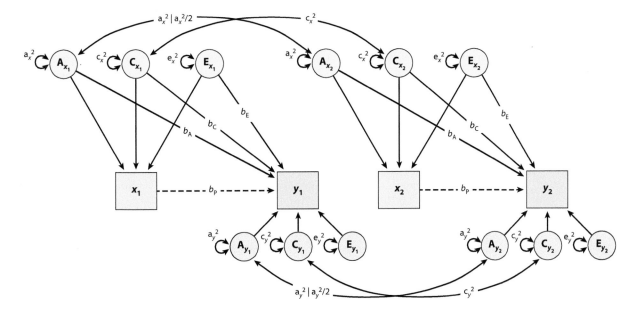

Figure 1

Unstandardized bivariate Cholesky model, representing a genetically informed regression of an outcome on a predictor. The three regressions, b_A, b_C, and b_E, estimate the phenotypic quasi-causal regression b_P, plus genetic and shared environmental confounds. Abbreviations: A, genetic effects; C, shared environmental effects; E, nonshared environmental effects.

phenotypic units of y per phenotypic unit of x. If there are genetic and shared environmental confounds, and if we assume that the nonshared environmental effect is unconfounded (the crucial assumption of the model), then the nonshared environmental regression continues to estimate b_P; b_A and b_C are equal to b_P plus the magnitude of the genetic and environmental confounds, respectively.

The genetically informed literature on validity in personality is vast and unfocused, encompassing everything with which personality might plausibly be related. We focus on the key issue of the relationship between personality and psychopathology and on the smaller set of studies that report results in three substantive areas in a form similar enough to our unstandardized genetically informed bivariate regression model to allow us to compute the relevant parameters. Klump et al. (2002) analyzed relations between Multidimensional Personality Questionnaire (MPQ) scores [negative emotionality (NE), positive emotionality (PE), and constraint] and disordered eating behaviors [Minnesota Eating Disorders Inventory (M-EDI)] in a sample of twins from the Minnesota Twin Family Study. They reported results in the most commonly used format, a standardized bivariate regression model, in which the regression coefficients have been standardized by fixing the variances of the latent biometric variances of the predictors (in this case, the MPQ scores) to unity. We prefer unstandardized models because the standardized models confound the magnitude of the quasi-causal unstandardized coefficient with the magnitudes of the ACE variances in the predictor (Turkheimer & Harden 2013), but Klump et al. (2002, tables 2 and 3) report the twin correlations in sufficient detail to estimate the unstandardized regressions from the values they report. We describe the results for relations between two higher-order factors of the MPQ (NE and PE; results were not reported for constraint, because the phenotypic relation with M-EDI was not significant) and the total score of the M-EDI.

For NE, a regression of the M-EDI on NE without genetically informative controls shows that a unit of change in NE is associated with 0.28 units of change in the MDI. When the genetic regression is included in the model, however, we observe that much of the observed association is attributable to shared genetic background: The unstandardized genetic regression coefficient is 0.79 units of MDI per unit of NE, and the E regression, estimating the phenotypic effect, is 0.08 units, which does remain significant at $p < 0.05$. For PE, the A regression was equal to -0.24 units of M-EDI per unity of PE, which is highly significant and in the same direction as the phenotypic effect; the E regression was actually in the opposite direction (0.09) and, in our reanalysis based on summary statistics, significantly so ($p = 0.03$). These results suggest that the phenotypic results for the relation between PE and eating disorders are potentially misleading. Twin pairs who, on average, have higher PE scores have lower M-EDI scores; but within twin pairs, the twin with the higher PE score has, if anything, higher M-EDI scores.

Klump et al. (2002, p. 387) concluded, "In general, results suggested that common genetic factors contribute more to relationships between personality and disordered eating attitudes and behaviors than common nonshared environmental factors." This statement is true as far as it goes, but it misses an important point: The "nonshared environmental factors" the authors are discounting are not unknown and unmeasured environmental events, but rather the phenotypic causal effects of personality itself. If differences in PE cause differences in eating, one would expect to observe the effect both between and within pairs. Having observed that PE is associated with eating behavior only between pairs, the most useful conclusion is that the observed association is probably not phenotypically causal but is, instead, the result of a shared genetic background (in the absence of shared environmental variance) between PE and eating.

This pattern of findings is broadly characteristic of the genetically informed literature examining the validity of personality as a predictor of psychopathology. One of the better-established relationships is between neuroticism and depression. Fanous et al. (2002) administered the short form of the Eysenck Personality Questionnaire (EPQ) to obtain neuroticism scores and a structured interview for lifetime depression according to DSM-III criteria for a large sample of male and female twins from the Virginia Twin Registry. These authors report parameters from standardized Cholesky decompositions; once again, we use the reported twin correlations to compute the unstandardized parameters. The phenotypic effect of neuroticism on depression was 0.50 in males and 0.33 in females; both had $p < 0.05$. Once the genetic relationship between the two was accounted for, however, the effects were reduced to 0.30 in males and 0.20 in females; again, both had $p < 0.05$.

Kendler et al. (2006) conducted a similar study of neuroticism and depression in a large sample of Swedish twins. The unstandardized phenotypic regression of depression on neuroticism (recomputed from their published results) was 0.39 in females and 0.40 in males. Once the common genetic background of neuroticism and depression was controlled, the corresponding regression coefficients were 0.13 in males and 0.06 in females.

STRUCTURE

Since the beginning of factor-analytic personality research, investigators have endeavored to combine psychometric methodologies with biometric analyses. The simplest way to combine them is to factor-analyze personality items to derive a latent personality structure (e.g., by using the FFM) and then decompose the resulting latent variables into their biometric components. This methodology has led to the usual conclusions, as we review above in the section titled Heritability and Reliability: Personality factors are more or less equally heritable, shared effects of families are hard to find, and the nonshared environment accounts for a substantial proportion of variance (although a somewhat lower one at the latent level because unreliability of measurement has been eliminated).

A more interesting method of combining psychometric and biometric analyses of personality responses is to reverse the order of the analyses: One may use a twin design to obtain a biometric partitioning of variation and covariation among personality items in genetic and environmental covariance matrices, and then model the psychometric structure separately in the three domains. The empirical investigation of this possibility once again starts with Loehlin, the NMSQT sample, and the CPI. Loehlin (1987) created 31 item clusters in the same way he had when investigating differential heritability. He then employed standard formulas to compute twin correlations for each cluster, used these to compute the ACE correlation matrices for the 31 clusters, and submitted them separately to exploratory factor analysis. In the A and E domains, Loehlin's (1987) results seemed to accord fairly closely with portions of the (at that time not fully developed) FFM. The genetic factors included versions of extraversion, neuroticism, conscientiousness, and openness. The E factors were less well defined but seemed to include a neuroticism factor and (more weakly) extraversion and conscientiousness factors. As usual, there was not a great deal of C variance in these data, but Loehlin managed to extract two factors, one of which was a somewhat artifactual gender factor that arose because only same-sex pairs were analyzed. As a result, any variation due to gender varied only between pairs, equally, for MZ and DZ twins, so gender effects were counted as C.

Loehlin then replicated these analyses in the Veterans Administration Twin Sample (Horn et al. 1976) and the Texas Adoption Project, rotating the factors from the replication samples to maximum congruence to the NMSQT. The FFM-type factors in the A and E domains replicated fairly well; the C factors, especially the gender factor, did not, because the Veteran twins included opposite-sex DZ pairs. Finally, the A factors in the replication samples could be rotated to at least modest concordance with the A factor from the NMSQT. The conclusion, which is typical of the studies that followed, is quite surprising: Personality structure in the ACE domains seems to be mostly a reflection of phenotypic personality structure, which is to say that some version of the FFM fits fairly well in all three.

Carey & Dilalla (1994) conducted a similar analysis on the same data and reached the same conclusion: "[T]he loadings from the three [A, C and E] matrices are remarkably similar and, moreover, parallel the first three phenotypic factors of the CPI." Heath et al. (1994, p. 770) concluded, "The patterns of loadings . . . were remarkably consistent for Genetic and Environmental Factors 1–4 and quite consistent with what would have been predicted from the observed phenotypic correlations." Livesley et al. (1998), analyzing personality disorders using the Dimensional Assessment Personality Disorder Basic Questionnaire, found concordance coefficients greater than 0.95 for pairs of A, E, and phenotypic factors. Krueger (2000) analyzed 11 scales from the MPQ in a sample of 2,490 pairs of twins from the Minnesota Twin Family Study. He conducted principal components analysis on the phenotypic, A, and E correlation matrices; obtained scores for the sets of principal components; and compared them. All the correlations between phenotypic and genetic components were greater than 0.95, and all the correlations between phenotypic and nonshared environmental components were at least 0.87.

McCrae et al. (2001) collected NEO-PI scores from 1,150 German and Canadian twins. They analyzed biometric structure by using the original Loehlin method and found the usual result of equality across the A, C, and E loadings, which they referred to as the puzzle of parallel structure. Jang et al. (2006) showed what appears to be very high factor concordance between the higher-order structure of the phenotypic, A, and E matrices in the Canadian and German twin samples, plus an additional twin sample from Japan. Yamagata et al. (2006) presented similar results at the facet level; all the correspondence coefficients between phenotypic and A matrices and between phenotypic and E matrices were greater than 0.95. Yamagata et al. (2006, p. 994) concluded, "These results suggest that . . . the phenotypic five-factor structure is reflective of not only genetic structure, but also environmental structure." However, it may be simpler to conclude that it is the other way around: The genetic and environmental structures of personality are a reflection of phenotypic structure, with little evidence to support differences between genetic and environmental structure or etiology.

Loehlin (2011) returned to his cross-validated cluster analytic methods using data from the Australian Twin Data. Three cross-validated A clusters (emotionality, confidence, reserve) emerged, all of which were repeated in the five cross-validated E clusters. Of the three additional E clusters that cross-validated, one (unscrupulousness) was very similar to an A cluster that just missed the cross-validation standard. Two additional E clusters (with only three items each) did not appear in the A clusters. Loehlin & Martin (2013) used factor analysis of A and E matrices to extract broad factors from seven scales from a combination of the EPQ and the MPQ. The factors were rotated to a general factor (cf. Pettersson et al. 2012) and two supplementary factors that were identified as social conformity and other-dependence. These authors (Loehlin & Martin 2013, p. 761) concluded that "the structure of personality is inherent in the evolved phenotype, and is not the immediate consequence of either genetic or environmental organizing factors."

STABILITY

Lifetime developmental trends have attracted considerable interest in recent nongenetic studies of personality (Caspi et al. 2005), and various aspects of stability and change in the genetics of personality have been examined for some time. There are two main phenotypic issues in the genetics of personality that are usually characterized as changes in the mean and in the rank order of personality traits. Questions about changes in the mean of a trait involve trends in the population mean as a function of age; behavior genetics, with its emphasis on individual differences, has little to offer on this question other than the unsurprising conclusion that variation in slopes of change across age has a genetic component. Rank-order changes refer to analyses of stability, that is, whether individuals who score relatively high on a trait at one age continue to do so later in life. Caspi et al. (2005, p. 466) summarized the phenotypic literature on the stability of personality as follows:

> Test-retest correlations over time (a) are moderate in magnitude, even from childhood to early adulthood. Furthermore, rank-order stability (b) increases with age. Test-retest correlations (unadjusted for measurement error) increased from 0.41 in childhood to 0.55 at age 30, and then reached a plateau around 0.70 between ages 50 and 70. Rank-order stability (c) decreases as the time interval between observations increases, and does not vary markedly (d) across the Big Five traits nor (e) according to assessment method (i.e., self-reports, observer ratings, and projective tests), or (f) by gender.

There are many ways to model longitudinal stability in genetically informative models. We prefer state-trait-error (STE) (Kenny & Zautra 1995) models, which allow partitioning of longitudinal effects into stable effects that are constant over time intervals, simplex effects that have a structured relation with time, and random effects that are uncorrelated in time. **Figure 2** shows a schematic path diagram of an STE model for genetic and nonshared environmental influences on a trait. The trait terms are stable common factors, similar to the intercept term in a growth model, representing constant variation in a trait. The state term is represented by a simplex process, in which the value of the trait at time k is linearly related to the trait at time $k + 1$, with coefficient b generally less than 1.0. Over longer intervals spanning multiple simplex paths, therefore, the state-based stability declines exponentially as b_k.

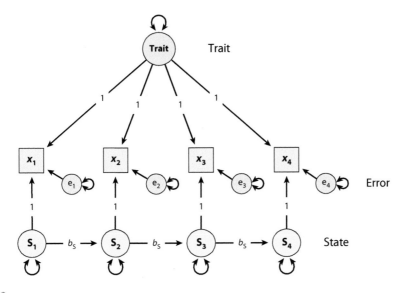

Figure 2

State-trait-error model representing stability in a phenotype as a sum of two components: a stable trait and a simplex state, which decays with time.

The stability of genetic and environmental influences on personality varies as a function of age and the interval between measurement occasions. Similar to most of the other effects reviewed in this article, they do not differ systematically in terms of the trait under study, at least within the domains of the major personality traits from the EPQ, FFM, and Minnesota-based systems. Because the most important determinant appears to be age, we organize our discussion into three sections: childhood and adolescence, early adulthood and mid-adulthood, and old age. We describe genetic and nonshared environmental correlations among measurement occasions for each study. Shared environment, as is typical, is mostly absent.

There are fewer genetically informed longitudinal studies of children than there are of adults. The youngest participants to be studied repeatedly are a sample of German twins described by Spengler et al. (2012), who describe self-report data from a sample of German children on a childhood version of the FFM at two measurement occasions at mean ages of 9 and 13 years. Genetic correlations between ages 9 and 13 were 0.72 for neuroticism, 0.32 for openness, and unity for the other FFM traits. Nonshared environmental correlations were 0.3 for neuroticism, 0.18 for extraversion, 0.28 for agreeableness, 0.31 for conscientiousness, and zero for openness. De Fruyt and colleagues (2006) examined Neuroticism and Extraversion scores in a sample of 548 Belgian children at a three-year interval starting at age 9. A correlations were close to unity, whereas E correlations ranged from 0.57 to 0.67. Gillespie et al. (2004) fit simplex models to EPQ scores obtained from a sample of Australian adolescent twins at ages 12, 14, and 16 years. Approximations of the longitudinal A and E correlations can be recovered from their simplex results. Genetic correlations ranged from 0.7 to unity, and E correlations ranged from 0.2 to 0.5. Bratko & Butkovic (2007) reported on a sample of Croatian twins tested with the EPQ at 17 and 21 years of age. The A correlations between the two ages were 0.87 for extraversion and 0.83 for neuroticism; the E correlations were 0.36 and 0.38.

Proceeding to early adulthood, the first extensive longitudinal twin study to be reported was that by McGue et al. (1993), which involved a small sample of 127 twin pairs from the Minnesota Twin Family Study who were tested with the MPQ twice at an average 10-year interval, at an

Twin study:
a comparison of the similarity of identical and fraternal twins, used to estimate genetic and environmental variance

average age of 19.8 years at time 1 and 29.6 years at time 2. Results showed considerable phenotypic stability over time, which was largely attributable to genetic effects. For the three higher-order traits of PE, NE, and constraint, the genetic correlations between ages 20 and 30 were 0.81, 0.72, and 0.80, respectively. The corresponding E correlations were 0.30, 0.47, and 0.32. Viken et al. (1994) described a very large sample of Finnish twins who were measured twice for extraversion and neuroticism at an interval of 6 years. The twins varied in age at first testing from 18 to 48. Genetic correlations between measurements for both traits were at least 0.80 for the youngest (age 18) cohort and quickly rose to 1.0 thereafter. Nonshared environmental longitudinal correlations were approximately 0.3 for the 18-year-olds and slowly increased to approximately 0.5 for oldest cohort.

Blonigen et al. (2008) reported the MPQ scores of Minnesota twins tested at a 7-year interval, at ages 17 and 24. A third measurement occasion, at age 29, was added by Hopwood et al. 2011; we give only the results from the latter report. For the major MPQ dimensions of agentic and communal PE, NE, and constraint, A correlations increased from around 0.7 between ages 17 and 24 to 0.95 and greater between ages 24 to 29, but did not show a strong relation to length of interval. E correlations increased from approximately 0.35 between ages 17 and 24 to approximately 0.6 between ages 24 and 29.

Bleidorn et al. (2009) examined three measurement occasions of FFM data for the Bielefeld Longitudinal Study of Adult Twins (BiLSAT) sample in Germany, at mean ages 31, 36, and 40, although there was also considerable age variability within the cohort. Results were reported in the form of latent growth models. There was significant A and E variation in both the level (mean) and slope (also a source of stability) parameters for all of the FFM model traits and most of the facets; unfortunately, the residual terms uncorrelated with level were not ACE parameterized, making it impossible to compute the stability and instability of the A and E terms. Fortunately, Kandler et al. (2010) reported results from an expanded version of the BiLSAT sample. There were three measurement occasions in two cohorts, one at ages 23, 29, and 35 and the other at ages 39, 47, and 54. Genetic stability was nearly perfect throughout. Nonshared environmental stability was 0.37 at the earliest retest, between ages 23 and 29, and increased to 0.94 at the latest, between ages 47 and 54.

The literature also includes two interesting longitudinal studies conducted beginning in middle age. Johnson et al. (2005) described results for twins in late adulthood at two occasions, at average ages of 59 and 64. For the three broad domains of PE, NE, and constraint, the genetic correlations were 0.97, 1.0, and 0.93, respectively; the corresponding E correlations were 0.73, 0.71, and 0.64. Read et al. (2006) measured a sample of elderly twin pairs at three occasions with the EPQ, at ages 82, 84, and 86. Controls for mortality were included. All the genetic correlations were unity for both extraversion and neuroticism. E correlations ranged from 0.5 to 0.6 for extraversion and from 0.4 to 0.5 for neuroticism.

The results of studies of the stability of genetic and environmental variance in personality variables are difficult to interpret individually because of their joint dependence on the age at which the data were collected and the interval between the measurements. To examine the results in more depth, we recorded the A and E correlations between measurement occasions for all studies reporting more than one occasion of measurement for either neuroticism or extraversion. **Table 1** provides the recorded data. Notably omitted from the table is the study by Wray et al. (2007), who reported sophisticated analyses of genetic and environmental stability but used a design that included parents and children as well as twin pairs, making their sample impossible to characterize in terms of age. (All the genetic correlations were above 0.8, even at the 22-year interval, and did not show any systematic relationship to the length of the interval; E correlations ranged from 0.24 to 0.53, varying inversely with length of interval.) For studies reporting results separately for males and females, we computed the mean correlation. We included results for

Table 1 Genetic and unique environment correlations across time

Study	Trait	Age1	Interval	rA	rE
Bratko & Butkevic (2007)	E	17	4	0.87	0.36
	N	17	4	0.83	0.38
De Fruyt et al. (2006)	E	9	3	0.94	0.57
	N	9	3	1.00	0.67
Gillespie et al. (2004)	N	12	2	0.81	0.32
		12	4	0.74	0.24
		14	2	0.84	0.27
	E	12	2	0.88	0.32
		12	4	0.88	0.18
		14	2	0.96	0.39
Hopwood et al. (2011)	N	17	7	0.75	0.36
		17	12	0.86	0.32
		24	5	0.99	0.62
	E	17	7	0.73	0.38
		17	12	0.71	0.38
		24	5	0.96	0.57
Johnson et al. (2005)	NE	59	5	1.00	0.71
	PE	59	5	0.97	0.73
Kandler et al. (2010)	N	23	6	1.00	0.37
		23	12	1.00	0.25
		29	6	1.00	0.73
		41	7	1.00	0.58
		41	14	1.00	0.47
		48	7	1.00	0.94
	E	23	6	1.00	0.50
		23	12	1.00	0.28
		29	6	1.00	0.80
		41	7	1.00	0.82
		41	14	1.00	0.67
		48	7	1.00	0.89
Read et al. (2006)	N	82	2	1.00	0.48
		82	2	1.00	0.44
		84	2	1.00	0.40
	E	82	2	1.00	0.51
		82	2	1.00	0.57
		84	2	1.00	0.54
Spengler et al. (2012)	N	9	3	0.72	0.30
		9	3	1.00	0.18
Viken et al. (1994)	N	21	6	0.83	0.25
		27	6	1.00	0.35
		33	6	0.84	0.47
		39	6	1.00	0.35

(Continued)

Table 1 (*Continued*)

Study	Trait	Age1	Interval	rA	rE
		45	6	1.00	0.48
		51	6	1.00	0.47
	E	21	6	0.87	0.35
		27	6	1.00	0.44
		33	6	1.00	0.51
		39	6	1.00	0.50
		45	6	1.00	0.52
		51	6	1.00	0.48
McGue et al. (1993)	NE	20	10	0.72	0.47
	PE	20	10	0.81	0.30
Wray et al. (2007)	N	—	9	0.91	0.53
			19	0.93	0.38
			22	0.95	0.24
			10	0.95	0.44
			13	0.88	0.42
			3	0.82	0.48

Abbreviations: Age1, age at assessment occasion one; N, neuroticism; E, extraversion; NE, negative emotionality; PE, positive emotionality; rA, genetic correlation; rE, nonshared environment correlation.

PE with extraversion and NE with neuroticism. Kandler (2012) conducted a similar analysis of personality stability as a function of age but not interval between measurements. Our results suggest that it is difficult to understand the results of one without including the other.

Figure 3 illustrates the univariate relationships of age and interval as predictors of stability for A and C. For A (Figure 3*a*), stability rises quickly through early adulthood, reaching 1.0 by the mid-twenties. The stability of E is lower in general, also rises through middle age, and appears to drop off in old age. Genetic stability does not show a clear relationship with the interval

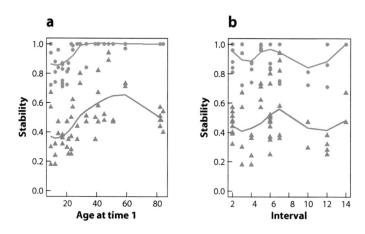

Figure 3

Univariate relation between genetic (*red circles*) and shared environmental (*blue triangles*) test-retest correlations and (*a*) age at first measurement and (*b*) interval between testings.

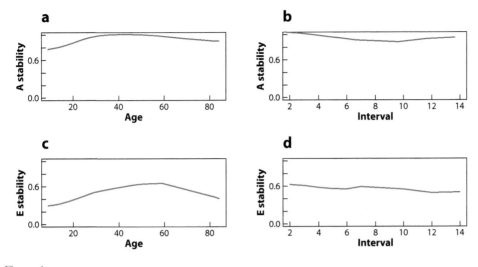

Figure 4

(*a,b*) Results of generalized additive model of genetic and (*c,d*) nonshared environmental stabilities as a function of age (*a,c*) and (*b,d*) interval between measurements. Abbreviations: A, genetic effects; E, nonshared environmental effects.

between measurements, whereas E stability appears to diminish at longer intervals. The univariate relationships between age and interval on the one hand and stability on the other are difficult to discern in the univariate plots, however, because age and interval are themselves correlated. Studies starting with younger participants have longer intervals of measurement. We therefore analyzed the joint effect of age and interval.

For several reasons, we analyzed these results as nonparametrically as possible. First, the observations are not independent, with multiple coefficients reported from individual studies. Second, correlation coefficients as an outcome variable are not normally distributed, and many of these are closely bounded by 1.0. Third, there is good reason to expect the relationship between stability and both age and interval to be nonlinear. For all of these reasons, we decided to fit a generalized additive model (GAM) (Hastie & Tibshirani 1990) to the genetic and nonshared environmental stabilities. A GAM model fits nonlinear smooth functions to the relations between multiple predictors and the outcome; the effect of each predictor is conditional on the other predictors. These smooth functions can then be added together, in a nonlinear smoothing-based analog of multiple regressions, to produce a nonlinear multivariate predictor of the outcome.

Figure 4 shows the results. There were no differences in stability between neuroticism and extraversion, so the results are reported together. Genetic stability increases rapidly through the mid-twenties and remains close to unity throughout the life span, decreasing only slightly in old age; no relationship between genetic stability and the interval between the measurements is apparent. In contrast, nonshared environmental stability increases gradually through midlife and then drops off substantially in old age. Nonshared environmental stability also shows a strong relationship with the interval between the measurements. After early adulthood, genetic influences on personality are nearly perfectly stable and time independent; nonshared environmental influences decrease slowly over time with exponentially decreasing effects and become unstable in old age.

Consider a hypothetical pair of identical twins whose personalities develop throughout the life span. In the usual absence of shared environmental effects, their pair-average score on personality traits is highly, even perfectly, stable relative to the average of other pairs, largely as an expression of their genetic endowment. At the same time, within-pair differences between twins show environmental influences that come and go, systematically but temporarily, from childhood through late middle age. At any given point in time, something might happen to make one member of the pair more extraverted or more neurotic; then, as time goes by, the within-pair difference decays, and the twins return to their genetically influenced mean. Finally, in old age, new differential processes appear to be established that make within-pair differences much less stable over time.

A PHENOTYPIC NULL HYPOTHESIS

Loehlin & Martin (2013), at the end of their paper that marks the conclusion of Loehlin's long investigation of personality structure in genetic and environmental domains, remark that personality appears to be a "phenotypic process." What do they mean by that? In some sense, of course, everything psychological is a phenotypic process, in that we observe it at the level of the phenotype. But not everything is phenotypic in the same way. Suppose we observe a patient with Huntington's disease, exhibiting the writhing choreiform movements and cognitive disabilities that are characteristic of the disorder. Those symptoms are phenotypic, but we would not say that Huntington's disease itself is a phenotypic process, and we would not seek psychological or social explanations of the co-occurrence of choreiform movement and dementia. Why not? Because we know that a circumscribed, theoretically coherent explanation of the Huntington's phenotype exists at the genetic level. The Huntington's genotype explains the Huntington's phenotype. We could say, following Meehl (1977), that Huntington's disease has a specific genetic etiology.

By way of contrast, consider marital status. Divorce is heritable (Johnson et al. 2004), but do we really expect that intensive twin studies of marital processes will lead us to a genetic explanation of divorce? Presumably not, although twin studies can be informative about marriage in other important ways, especially as quasi-experimental tests of causal hypotheses, in the manner of the validity studies reviewed above. For marriage and divorce, we recognize that the observed phenotypic structure as it exists in our culture is the result of psychological- and social-level (that is, phenotypic) forces. The point is not that they are environmental as opposed to genetic; indeed, as we cannot emphasize enough, marriage, divorce, and whatever may cause them are just as heritable as anything else. The heritability of marriage is a by-product of the universal, nonspecific, genetic pull on everything, not an indication that divorce is a biological process awaiting genetic analysis. Marriage and divorce are heritable, but they do not have a specific genetic etiology. For marriage and divorce, genotypic variation is phenotypic variation observed at a different level of analysis.

The laws of behavior genetics are not actual laws, and calling them that may have led to some misunderstandings of what was originally intended. In particular, although the First Law of Behavior Genetics has sometimes been considered an endorsement of a hereditarian view of behavior (e.g., Pinker 2003), the universality of heritability is best interpreted as a *reductio ad absurdum* of these very distinctions—as a way of observing that the endeavor of figuring out how genetic or environmental a trait is, let alone declaring that it is exclusively one or the other, is pointless. The laws of behavior genetics are collectively a null hypothesis and were described as such the first time they were mentioned (Turkheimer & Gottesman 1991). An updated version of the laws taking these multivariate findings into account, which we propose to call the phenotypic null hypothesis of behavior genetics, can be stated simply as follows: All traits are heritable, and the multivariate structure of the biometric components of behavior does not differ from the phenotypic structure.

The phenotypic null hypothesis is a statement of the simplest and most general reason that a phenotype would be heritable, the simplest version of what we already know, a standard against which the novelty of new hypotheses can be judged. In its original form, the First Law was an acknowledgment that we already knew on the basis of univariate behavior genetics: Behavior is heritable; $h^2 > 0$; and as such there is little point in either demonstrating heritability over and over or trying to argue it away. The phenotypic null hypothesis integrates what we have learned from multivariate behavior genetics: Until demonstrated otherwise, complex heritable behavioral traits should be the result of psychological processes defined at a high level of analysis, rather than at the level of genes or neurons. Although such complex traits are never independent of genetic variation, they cannot be defined by genetic processes. Genes and behavior are a single entity, a single organism observed at two levels of analysis. Some traits are better understood using low-level concepts (genes, neurons, structures), whereas others require high-level constructs (organizations, algorithms, beliefs). Personality, for the first time in the history of genetically informed scientific psychology, has turned out to be a clear instance of the latter case.

The remarkable finding that the multivariate structure of personality is not detectably different across biometric domains is actually a direct prediction from the phenotypic null hypothesis. "The puzzle of parallel structures" (McCrae et al. 2001, p. 515) is a puzzle only because of our ingrained expectation that the heritability of the traits of the FFM implies the existence of genetic mechanisms, which somehow are more biological than the psychological and phenotypic patterning of behavior that we actually observe. The phenotypic null hypothesis can be considered in another way in the analysis of genetic and environmental stability in personality. Nonshared environmental effects on personality are modest but detectable, and they exist in time: Something happens to make one twin more extraverted than the other at a measurement occasion, and at some later point in time the same twin will still be more extraverted but less so, with the difference continuing to decay as more time passes. Genetic effects do not operate in this way. If a pair of identical twins is, on average, more extraverted than another pair, they will tend to remain so regardless of the length of time that passes before they are assessed again. Genetic differences in adults are almost perfectly stable, as one would expect if genes were exerting a steady but nonspecific pull on the phenotype.

The phenotypic null hypothesis plays out somewhat differently in validity studies. We suggest that, when studying relations between personality variables and differences in other domains of behavior, our scientific hypotheses are usually phenotypic in nature. When we hypothesize that an extraverted personality predisposes individuals to externalizing problems, for example, the causal hypothesis itself is from extraverted phenotype to externalizing phenotype, and the possibility that the phenotypic association between the two is the result of a shared genetic background is an alternative to the causal hypothesis. It is not surprising, then, that this is the area in which the phenotypic null hypothesis is most frequently rejected, because genuine causal relations between one domain and another are very hard to find. Most of the time, the reason differences in behavior are correlated across domains is that they share a general unsystematic genetic background. That is not the same as saying that there is a specific genetic mechanism that links them; the most we can say is that their nonspecific genetic backgrounds overlap.

GENOMICS OF PERSONALITY

As was the case for both the early experimental research on temperament in dogs and the large-scale twin studies of the past century, personality has played a central role in our understanding of the genetics of behavior as the sequencing of the human genome has been completed and it has become possible to assess genomic variation directly in the DNA. The still-brief history of molecular genetic studies of personality comes in three distinct phases: (*a*) an anticipatory phase that looked to estimates of heritability from the quantitative genetics of personality as a guide to expectations for the success of molecular genetics (Martin et al. 1997), (*b*) a period of considerable empirical optimism as early linkage and association studies produced multiple significant effects

Linkage analysis: association between DNA and a phenotype as they are transmitted within a family for various personality traits, and (*c*) an extended period of frustration as most of the reported discoveries either turned out to be very small or failed to replicate at all.

Two relatively simple methods prevailed in the early days of the molecular genetics of personality. Linkage analysis is a technique that looks for within-family cosegregation between a trait of interest and a genetic marker. Candidate gene association studies are even simpler: They are no more than correlational analyses of relations between identified genes and either categorical or continuous outcomes. Linkage and association studies have complementary strengths and weaknesses. Association studies are vulnerable to population stratification, meaning that there are many possible causal pathways that could explain a correlation between a gene and a personality trait, many of which are obviously spurious (Hamer & Sirota 2000). If members of one ethnic group are more extraverted than members of another, then in an ethnically mixed sample any gene that differs between the groups for any reason will be correlated with extraversion (Turkheimer 2012). Linkage studies similarly control for population stratification by focusing on within-family relationships that cannot be accounted for by environmental or cultural confounds varying at the level of family or culture. The inferential benefit comes with a price in statistical power because linkage studies require not only multiple family members but also family members who differ on the outcome of interest.

Despite these difficulties, early reports of linkage and association suggested that the optimism about the potential for a molecular genetics of personality would be borne out. Several reports of associations between the D4 receptor gene (*DRD4*) and sensation seeking (Benjamin et al. 1996), and between the serotonin transporter gene (*SLC6A4*) and anxiety-related traits (Lesch et al. 1996), were met with considerable enthusiasm and cited widely. As the literature evolved, however, it became more and more difficult to establish a clear replication of the early findings, at least at anything close to the large effect sizes that had been reported in the early papers. A series of meta-analyses conducted by Munafò et al. (2003, 2008, 2009) established quite clearly that the associations, if they differed from zero at all, were vanishingly small. The most recent review (Munafò & Flint 2011, p. 395) is very gloomy in outlook: "The first candidate gene studies of human personality promised much but, in the fifteen years since their publication, have delivered little in the way of clear evidence for the contribution of specific genetic variants to observed variation in personality traits."

Ironically, the most recent developments in genomic technology have worked against confidence in the magnitude of the findings from linkage and candidate gene association studies. The rapid development of genomewide association studies (GWASs) has enabled the inexpensive assessment of variation of initially hundreds of thousands and, later, millions of single-nucleotide polymorphisms (SNPs). GWASs enabled the testing of associations with hundreds of thousands of loci at low cost, but they introduced obvious problems of multiple hypothesis testing. The broader genomics community responded by abandoning theoretically driven selection of candidate gene hypotheses in favor of extremely stringent ($p < 10^{-8}$) hurdles for genomewide significance, which, in the face of ever-smaller effect sizes, demanded larger and larger samples (Lander & Schork 1994).

Although GWASs have produced some notable successes in medicine [and it is fair to say that the jury is still out on neuropsychiatry (Visscher & Montgomery 2009)], in personality it is difficult to point to any successes at all from GWASs. It is not that statistical significance, even genomewide statistical significance, has never been achieved. Indeed, most GWASs report one or two associations at or close to genomewide significance, which then are not replicated in the next study. No GWAS of personality variables has ever reported an association accounting for as much as 0.05% of the variance. None of the classic loci from the early era of candidate gene association studies have ever surpassed or even approached genomewide significance.

Candidate gene association: a statistical association between a gene and a phenotype, usually across families

Genomewide association study (GWAS): a relatively inexpensive method to assess associations with as many as one million SNPs and a phenotype in large samples

Single-nucleotide polymorphism (SNP): a single unit of DNA that takes only two values across people

In the most comprehensive GWAS of personality conducted to date, de Moor et al. (2010) combined results from 10 independent samples constituting a total of 17,375 adults, and withheld five additional samples, with 3,294 adults, for replication. All participants were of European ancestry and had been administered the NEO-PI, and information on 2.4 million SNPs was available. These authors calculated results in the individual discovery samples, combined using meta-analytic procedures and replicated in the withheld samples. Two SNPs showed genomewide association with openness and one with conscientiousness. Each of the three SNPs accounted for a little more than 0.2% of the variation in the corresponding personality trait. The effects did not replicate in the withheld samples; no external replication attempts have yet been reported.

The difficulties encountered in the molecular genetics of personality are a reflection of the phenotypic null hypothesis operating at a genomic level of organization. The question of whether there were associations to be found between individual genes or SNPs and variation in personality was settled on the day it was agreed that identical twins were more correlated for neuroticism than were fraternal twins. If one accepts that neuroticism is heritable, what mechanisms are available other than the cumulative effects of genes at multiple loci? However, the causal structure, as opposed to the mere existence, of molecular genetic associations with personality is exactly as would be predicted by the phenotypic null hypothesis. The more similar people are in genotype, the more similar they are in personality, but genotypic similarity appears to be carried across many—by current indications, uncountable—genes with effects that are both tiny and unsystematic, beyond their cumulative effect of making people who share them similar in general.

CONCLUSION

Null hypotheses cannot be confirmed, but the conclusion of this review is that in the genetics of personality, a paradoxical outcome that has been looming for a long time has finally come to pass: Personality is heritable, but it has no genetic mechanism. The prospect of this outcome has haunted the nature-nurture debate from its inception, as both sides of the old debate were led to a dead end of thinking that the point of the debate was to evaluate the separate effects of genes and environment. It became clear long ago that neither genes nor environment could be discounted for anything important, a conclusion that stalled the discussion either in intransigent hereditarian and environmentalist positions or in an unsatisfying interactionist middle ground.

Although the search for genetic mechanisms of human personality, in our view, will never bear fruit, it is nevertheless possible to construct a genetically informed phenotypic science of behavior. Behavior genetic methods will not provide a mechanism in such a science; instead, they will provide a means of establishing quasi-experimental control over familial associations that otherwise confound associations among human variables in nonexperimental settings. The heritability of personality has one important consequence that cannot be restated often enough: Uncontrolled correlations between the behaviors of genetically related individuals are not necessarily causal, let alone environmental. If extraverted mothers have extraverted children, it is not necessarily the case that the children are learning to be extraverted by modeling their parents' behavior. This caveat remains in effect no matter how the genetics of extraversion actually works; it remains in effect if there is no more of a genetic mechanism for extraversion than there is for divorce. Genetically informed research designs can partially, imperfectly, control for the genetic and shared environmental confounds that otherwise cloud causal interpretation of associations like these, and they have been extraordinarily successful at doing so. The quantification of heritability itself is unimportant in such analyses, except as a node in statistical models that control for genetic pathways in nonexperimental studies.

Perhaps because the results of GWASs of personality appear so bleak, the personality field has largely avoided the most common conclusion reached on the basis of the almost-as-discouraging results that have emerged from the molecular genetics of other behavioral traits like intelligence or psychopathology. GWASs, it is said, have demonstrated that the effects of individual genes are universally small; even the largest accounts for less than 1% of the variance. Therefore, we will need ever-larger studies, consortia of studies, and meta-analyses of consortia to detect the vanishingly small effects of individual genes. We are skeptical that this strategy will be successful for personality in the long run. Can one point to a field of science that has been successful by stringing together the multiple effects of such tiny associations? The phenotypic null hypothesis suggests that the foundational idea that there are individual causal genetic variants for personality, however small, is itself flawed. Except in the weakest statistical sense, there actually is not a large set of neuroticism genes, each with small effect; there is merely a nonspecific genetic background to phenotypic neuroticism, and to its phenotypic causes and effects.

When Galton first formulated the nature-nurture debate in the nineteenth century, the alternative to "genetic" was supposed to be "environmental." That classical version of the behavior genetic analysis of personality has finally reached a clear conclusion. Both genes and environments matter, but neither genetic nor environmental effects can be broken down into discrete and specifiable mechanisms at a lower level of analysis. The establishment of genetic and environmental variance in personality has answered important questions, but as the genes-versus-environment version of the debate has reached its end, it has turned out that another question, about the existence of lower-level mechanisms for observed phenotypic behavior, constituted a large part of what we wanted to know all along. In observing, again and again, the heritability and environmentality of behavior in general and personality in particular, we have assumed that the causal (or at least the explanatory) arrows must be directed from the bottom up. The phenotypic null hypothesis suggests that the explanatory direction is exactly the reverse: Phenotypic variation explains the genetic structure of behavior. If the failure to reject the phenotypic null hypothesis for the genetics of personality represents a victory for any particular mode of explanation, the winner is not naïve environmentalism but rather biologically informed psychological explanation; the loser is not genetics but rather poorly informed and superficial biologism.

SUMMARY POINTS

1. All personality traits are heritable, and equally so. To the limited extent it is possible to specify numerical values of heritability at all, all personality traits are heritable at about $h^2 \approx 0.4$. Narrow traits in sufficiently large samples sometimes show significant differences, but these do not replicate from one study to another.

2. The heritability of personality exists at all levels of its hierarchical structure. Personality items are heritable, narrow facets are heritable, the traits of the FFM of personality and other systems are heritable, and high-order traits are heritable. The only systematic differences among the levels involve the progressive elimination of measurement error.

3. The multivariate structures of the three genetic and environmental biometric components of personality do not differ from each other and, therefore, do not differ from the phenotypic structure of personality that they jointly compose.

4. Most observed associations among personality differences and other variables are a combination of a noncausal shared genetic background and a smaller, plausibly causal phenotypic remainder that operate within pairs of identical twins raised together.

5. The developmental structure of phenotypic personality stability as a function of age is a combination of (*a*) genetic differences that become nearly perfectly stable in early adulthood and do not decay over time and (*b*) environmental differences that also become more stable, but are generally less so, become more unstable in late life and decay slowly over time.

6. DNA-based studies have shown that the heritability of human personality is based on the accumulated action of a very large number of genes. Attempts to specify individual genes causing differences in personality traits have not been successful.

FUTURE ISSUES

1. Larger and larger GWASs are being conducted, allowing researchers to detect smaller and smaller associations between SNPs and personality traits with genomewide significance. Whether such associations, which will almost certainly be smaller than $r = 0.02$, will have meaningful psychological or biological content remains to be determined.

2. Genomic technology is proceeding rapidly. In particular, it will soon be possible to obtain the full genetic sequence on large numbers of people, which will provide more information than can be obtained from SNPs and GWASs. Whether full-genome sequencing will provide a more detailed account of genetic mechanisms underlying human personality remains to be seen.

3. Some new technologies, such as genomic complex-trait analysis, focus more on predicting personality from the full genome rather than on finding individual genes that are associated with specific traits. Currently, the ability to predict personality from genomic data is quite low. It is not known how much higher it can get.

4. If it ever became possible to predict personality from genomic data alone, there would be profound ethical issues involved in the use of the data for reproductive decision making or scientific purposes.

DISCLOSURE STATEMENT

The authors are not aware of any affiliations, memberships, funding, or financial holdings that might be perceived as affecting the objectivity of this review.

LITERATURE CITED

Benjamin J, Li L, Patterson C, Greenberg BD, Murphy DL, Hamer DH. 1996. Population and familial association between the D4 dopamine receptor gene and measures of novelty seeking. *Nat. Genet.* 12:81–84

Bleidorn W, Kandler C, Riemann R, Angleitner A, Spinath FM. 2009. Patterns and sources of adult personality development: growth curve analyses of the NEO PI-R scales in a longitudinal twin study. *J. Personal. Soc. Psychol.* 97:142–55

Blonigen DM, Carlson MD, Hicks BM, Krueger RF, Iacono WG. 2008. Stability and change in personality traits from late adolescence to early adulthood: a longitudinal twin study. *J. Personal.* 76:229–266

Bouchard TJ Jr, Loehlin JC. 2001. Genes, evolution, and personality. *Behav. Genet.* 31:243–73

Bratko D, Butkovic A. 2007. Stability of genetic and environmental effects from adolescence to young adulthood: results of Croatian longitudinal twin study of personality. *Twin Res. Hum. Genet.* 10:151–57

Carey G, DiLalla DL. 1994. Personality and psychopathology: genetic perspectives. *J. Abnorm. Psychol.* 103:32–43

Carey G, Goldsmith HH, Tellegen A, Gottesman II. 1978. Genetics and personality inventories: the limits of replication with twin data. *Behav. Genet.* 8:299–313

Caspi A, Roberts BW, Shiner RL. 2005. Personality development: stability and change. *Annu. Rev. Psychol.* 56:453–84

Cattell RB, Rao DC, Schuerger JM, Vaughan DS. 1981. Unitary personality source traits analyzed for heritability. *Hum. Hered.* 31(5):261–75

Charney E. 2012. Behavior genetics and postgenomics. *Behav. Brain Sci.* 35:331–58

De Fruyt F, Bartels M, Van Leeuwen KG, De Clercq B, Decuyper M, Mervielde I. 2006. Five types of personality continuity in childhood and adolescence. *J. Personal. Soc. Psychol.* 91(3):538–52

de Moor MH, Costa PT, Terracciano A, Krueger RF, De Geus EJC, et al. 2010. Meta-analysis of genome-wide association studies for personality. *Mol. Psychiatry* 17:337–49

DeYoung CG. 2006. Higher-order factors of the Big Five in a multi-informant sample. *J. Personal. Soc. Psychol.* 91:1138–51

Digman JM. 1997. Higher-order factors of the Big Five. *J. Personal. Soc. Psychol.* 73:1246–56

Eysenck HJ. 1990. Genetic and environmental contributions to individual differences: the three major dimensions of personality. *J. Personal.* 58(1):245–61

Fanous A, Gardner CO, Prescott CA, Cancro R, Kendler KS. 2002. Neuroticism, major depression and gender: a population-based twin study. *Psychol. Med.* 32:719–28

Fuller JL. 1960. Behavior genetics. *Annu. Rev. Psychol.* 11:41–70

Gillespie NA, Evans DE, Wright MM, Martin NG. 2004. Genetic simplex modeling of Eysenck's dimensions of personality in a sample of young Australian twins. *Twin Res.* 7:637–48

Hamer D, Sirota L. 2000. Beware the chopsticks gene. *Mol. Psychiatry* 5:11–13

Hastie T, Tibshirani R. 1990. *Monographs on Statistics and Applied Probability*, vol. 43: *Generalized Additive Models*. New York: Chapman & Hall

Heath AC, Cloninger CR, Martin NG. 1994. Testing a model for the genetic structure of personality: a comparison of the personality systems of Cloninger and Eysenck. *J. Personal. Soc. Psychol.* 66:762–75

Heath AC, Kessler RC, Neale MC, Hewitt JK, Eaves LJ, Kendler KS. 1993. Testing hypotheses about direction of causation using cross-sectional family data. *Behav. Genet.* 23:29–50

Hopwood CJ, Donnellan MB, Blonigen DM, Krueger RF, McGue M, et al. 2011. Genetic and environmental influences on personality trait stability and growth during the transition to adulthood: a three-wave longitudinal study. *J. Personal. Soc. Psychol.* 100:545–56

Horn JM, Plomin R, Rosenman R. 1976. Heritability of personality traits in adult male twins. *Behav. Genet.* 6:17–30

Jang KL, Livesley WJ, Ando J, Yamagata S, Suzuki A, et al. 2006. Behavioral genetics of the higher-order factors of the Big Five. *Personal. Individ. Differ.* 41:261–72

Jang KL, Livesley WJ, Angleitner A, Riemann R, Vernon PA. 2002. Genetic and environmental influences on the covariance of facets defining the domains of the five-factor model of personality. *Personal. Individ. Differ.* 33:83–101

Jang KL, McCrae RR, Angleitner A, Riemann R, Livesley WJ. 1998. Heritability of facet-level traits in a cross-cultural twin sample: support for a hierarchical model of personality. *J. Personal. Soc. Psychol.* 74:1556–65

Johnson W, McGue M, Krueger RF. 2005. Personality stability in late adulthood: a behavioral genetic analysis. *J. Personal.* 73:523–52

Johnson W, McGue M, Krueger RF, Bouchard TJ Jr. 2004. Marriage and personality: a genetic analysis. *J. Personal. Soc. Psychol.* 86:285–94

Joseph J. 2004. *The Gene Illusion: Genetic Research in Psychiatry and Psychology Under the Microscope*. New York: Algora

Kandler C. 2012. Nature and nurture in personality development. The case of neuroticism and extraversion. *Curr. Dir. Psychol. Sci.* 21(5):290–96

Kandler C, Bleidorn W, Riemann R, Spinath FM, Thiel W, Angleitner A. 2010. Sources of cumulative continuity in personality: a longitudinal multiple-rater twin study. *J. Personal. Soc. Psychol.* 98:995–1008

Kandler C, Riemann R, Spinath FM, Angleitner A. 2010. Sources of variance in personality facets: a multiple-rater twin study of self-peer, peer-peer, and self-self (dis)agreement. *J. Personal.* 78:1565–94

Kendler KS, Gatz M, Gardner CO, Pedersen NL. 2006. Personality and major depression: a Swedish longitudinal, population-based twin study. *Arch. Gen. Psychiatry* 63:1113–20

Kenny DA, Zautra A. 1995. The trait-state-error model for multiwave data. *J. Consult. Clin. Psychol.* 63:52–59

Klump KL, McGue M, Iacono WG. 2002. Genetic relationships between personality and eating attitudes and behaviors. *J. Abnorm. Psychol.* 111:380–89

Krueger RF. 2000. Phenotypic, genetic, and nonshared environmental parallels in the structure of personality: a view from the Multidimensional Personality Questionnaire. *J. Personal. Soc. Psychol.* 79:1057–67

Krueger RF, Johnson W. 2008. Behavioral genetics and personality: a new look at the integration of nature and nurture. *Handb. Personal. Theory Res.* 3:287–310

Lander ES, Schork NJ. 1994. Genetic dissection of complex traits. *Science* 264:2037–48

Lesch KP, Bengel D, Heils A, Sabol SZ, Greenberg BD, et al. 1996. Association of anxiety-related traits with a polymorphism in the serotonin transporter gene regulatory region. *Science* 274:1527–31

Livesley WJ, Jang KL, Vernon PA. 1998. Phenotypic and genetic structure of traits delineating personality disorder. *Arch. Gen. Psychiatry* 55:941–48

Loehlin JC. 1982. Are personality traits differentially heritable? *Behav. Genet.* 12:417–28

Loehlin JC. 1978. Are CPI scales differently heritable? How good is the evidence? *Behav. Genet.* 8:381–82

Loehlin JC. 1985. Fitting heredity-environment models jointly to twin and adoption data from the California Psychological Inventory. *Behav. Genet.* 15:199–221

Loehlin JC. 1987. Heredity, environment, and the structure of the California Psychological Inventory. *Multivar. Behav. Res.* 22:137–48

Loehlin JC. 2011. Genetic and environmental structures of personality: a cluster-analysis approach. *Personal. Individ. Differ.* 51:662–66

Loehlin JC. 2012. The differential heritability of personality item clusters. *Behav. Genet.* 42:500–7

Loehlin JC, Martin NG. 2013. General and supplementary factors of personality in genetic and environmental correlation matrices. *Personal. Individ. Differ.* 54:761–66

Loehlin JC, McCrae RR, Costa PT, John OP. 1998. Heritabilities of common and measure-specific components of the Big Five personality factors. *J. Res. Personal.* 32:431–53

Loehlin JC, Neiderhiser JM, Reiss D. 2003. The behavior genetics of personality and the NEAD study. *J. Res. Personal.* 37(5):373–87

Loehlin JC, Nichols RC. 1976. *Heredity, Environment, and Personality: A Study of 850 Sets of Twins*. Austin: Univ. Tex. Press

Lykken DT. 1982. Research with twins: the concept of emergenesis. *Psychophysiology* 19:361–72

Martinl N, Boomsma D, Machin G. 1997. A twin-pronged attack on complex traits. *Nat. Genet.* 17:387–92

McGue M, Bacon S, Lykken DT. 1993. Personality stability and change in early adulthood: a behavioral genetic analysis. *Dev. Psychol.* 29:96–109

McCrae RR, Jang KL, Livesley WJ, Riemann R, Angleitner A. 2001. Sources of structure: genetic, environmental, and artifactual influences on the covariation of personality traits. *J. Personal.* 69:511–35

Meehl PE. 1967. Theory-testing in psychology and physics: a methodological paradox. *Philos. Sci.* 34:103–15

Meehl PE. 1977. Specific etiology and other forms of strong influence: some quantitative meanings. *J. Med. Philos.* 2:33–53

Munafò MR, Clark TG, Moore LR, Payne E, Walton R, Flint J. 2003. Genetic polymorphisms and personality in healthy adults: a systematic review and meta-analysis. *Mol. Psychiatry* 8:471–84

Munafò MR, Clark T, Flint J. 2004. Does measurement instrument moderate the association between the serotonin transporter gene and anxiety-related personality traits? A meta-analysis. *Mol. Psychiatry* 10:415–19

Munafò MR, Brown SM, Hariri AR. 2008. Serotonin transporter (5-HTTLPR) genotype and amygdala activation: a meta-analysis. *Biol. Psychiatry* 63:852–57

Munafò MR, Flint J. 2011. Dissecting the genetic architecture of human personality. *Trends Cogn. Sci.* 15:395–400

Munafò MR, Freimer NB, Ng W, Ophoff R, Veijola J, et al. 2009. 5-HTTLPR genotype and anxiety-related personality traits: a meta-analysis and new data. *Am. J. Med. Genet. B* 150:271–81

Pinker S. 2003. *The Blank Slate: The Modern Denial of Human Nature*. New York: Penguin

Pettersson E, Turkheimer E, Horn EE, Menatti AR. 2012. The general factor of personality and evaluation. *Eur. J. Personal.* 26:292–302

Plomin R, Caspi A. 1990. Behavioral genetics and personality. *Handb. Personal. Theory Res.* 2:251–76

Read S, Vogler GP, Pedersen NL, Johansson B. 2006. Stability and change in genetic and environmental components of personality in old age. *Personal. Individ. Differ.* 40:1637–47

Rushton JP, Bons TA, Hur YM. 2008. The genetics and evolution of the general factor of personality. *J. Res. Personal.* 42:1173–85

Spengler M, Gottschling J, Spinath FM. 2012. Personality in childhood—a longitudinal behavior genetic approach. *Personal. Individ. Differ.* 53:411–16

Tukey JW. 1954. Causation, regression, and path analysis. In *Statistics and Mathematics in Biology*, ed. O Kempthorne, TA Bancroft, JW Gowen, JL Lush, pp. 35–66. Ames: Iowa State Univ. Press

Thompson WR, Wilde GJS. 1973. Behavior genetics. In *Handbook of General Psychology*, ed. BB Wolman, pp. 206–29. Englewood Cliffs, NJ: Prentice-Hall

Turkheimer E. 1998. Heritability and biological explanation. *Psychol. Rev.* 105:782–91

Turkheimer E. 2000. Three laws of behavior genetics and what they mean. *Curr. Dir. Psychol. Sci.* 9:160–64

Turkheimer E. 2011. Still missing. *Res. Hum. Dev.* 8:227–41

Turkheimer E. 2012. Genome wide association studies of behavior are social science. In *Philosophy of Behavioral Biology*, ed. KS Plaisance, TAC Reydon, pp. 43–64. New York: Springer

Turkheimer E, Gottesman II. 1991. Is $H^2 = 0$ a null hypothesis anymore? *Behav. Brain Sci.* 14:410–11

Turkheimer E, Harden KP. 2013. Behavior genetic research methods: testing quasi-causal hypotheses using multivariate twin data. In *Handbook of Research Methods in Personality and Social Psychology*, ed. HT Reis, CM Judd. Cambridge Univ. Press. 2nd ed. In press

Turkheimer E, Waldron M. 2000. Nonshared environment: a theoretical, methodological, and quantitative review. *Psychol. Bull.* 126:78–108

Viken RJ, Rose RJ, Kaprio J, Koskenvuo M. 1994. A developmental genetic analysis of adult personality: extraversion and neuroticism from 18 to 59 years of age. *J. Personal. Soc. Psychol.* 66:722–22

Visscher PM, Montgomery GW. 2009. Genome-wide association studies and human disease. *JAMA* 302:2028–29

Wray NR, Birley AJ, Sullivan PF, Visscher PM, Martin NG. 2007. Genetic and phenotypic stability of measures of neuroticism over 22 years. *Twin Res. Hum. Genet.* 10:695–702

Yamagata S, Suzuki A, Ando J, Ono Y, Kijima N, et al. 2006. Is the genetic structure of human personality universal? A cross-cultural twin study from North America, Europe, and Asia. *J. Personal. Soc. Psychol.* 90:987–98

Yang J, Manolio TA, Pasquale LR, Boerwinkle E, Caporaso N, et al. 2011. Genome partitioning of genetic variation for complex traits using common SNPs. *Nat. Genet.* 43:519–25

Environmental Psychology Matters

Robert Gifford

Department of Psychology, University of Victoria, Victoria V8W 3P5, Canada;
email: rgifford@uvic.ca

Annu. Rev. Psychol. 2014. 65:541–79

First published online as a Review in Advance on
September 11, 2013

The *Annual Review of Psychology* is online at
http://psych.annualreviews.org

This article's doi:
10.1146/annurev-psych-010213-115048

Keywords

proenvironmental behavior, climate change, nature, place attachment, built
environments, interventions, virtual environments

Abstract

Environmental psychology examines transactions between individuals and
their built and natural environments. This includes investigating behaviors that inhibit or foster sustainable, climate-healthy, and nature-enhancing
choices, the antecedents and correlates of those behaviors, and interventions
to increase proenvironmental behavior. It also includes transactions in which
nature provides restoration or inflicts stress, and transactions that are more
mutual, such as the development of place attachment and identity and the
impacts on and from important physical settings such as home, workplaces,
schools, and public spaces. As people spend more time in virtual environments, online transactions are coming under increasing research attention.
Every aspect of human existence occurs in one environment or another, and
the transactions with and within them have important consequences both
for people and their natural and built worlds. Environmental psychology
matters.

Contents

THE BEHAVIORAL SCIENCE OF HUMAN TRANSACTIONS WITH AND WITHIN BUILT AND NATURAL ENVIRONMENTS

Wherever you go, there you are—and it matters. This is the fundamental premise of environmental psychology: We are always embedded in a place. In fact, we are always nested within layers of place, from a room, to a building, to a street, to a community, to a region, to a nation, and to the world. If, instead, we happen to be in a vehicle, an urban park, on the water, or in a wilderness, we are still somewhere. Person-place influences are both mutual and crucial. We shape not only buildings but also the land, the waters, the air, and other life forms—and they shape us.

Environmental psychology includes theory, research, and practice aimed at improving human relations with the natural environment and making the built environment more humane. Considering the enormous investment society makes in developing and shaping the physical environment, and the huge current and potential costs of misusing nature and natural resources, environmental psychology is a key component of human, animal, and environmental welfare. It is essential for policy-making (Vlek 2000). Environmental psychology matters (Gifford 2002).

Environmental psychologists continue to investigate fundamental psychological processes such as environmental perception, spatial cognition, social space, human development, and personality as they filter and structure interactions with the environment. The traditional emphasis of the field on the built environment has remained stable (Giuliani & Scopelliti 2009), and the recent growth of the field stems from investigations of proenvironmental behavior, climate change, interactions with nature, and attachment to place.

Environmental psychology began half a century ago because psychology had rarely extended its concern to the physical setting of behavior; for the most part, the discipline proceeded in its investigations as if people acted and interacted nowhere, in a black void. By implication, the physical locus of existence did not matter, but in reality, of course it does. Obvious as this fundamental premise may be, and even though the first *Annual Review of Psychology* survey of the field appeared 41 years ago (Craik 1973), in operational terms the discipline as a whole still does not fully accept it: Most departments of psychology in 2014 do not include even one environmental psychologist. Those with two or more faculty members who are primarily dedicated to the field probably can be counted on one's fingers.

Despite this severe shortage of landed scientists, research in environmental psychology has somehow managed to flourish. Two comprehensive handbooks have appeared (Bechtel & Churchman 2002, Clayton 2012), and a third is in preparation. The number of submissions to the *Journal of Environmental Psychology* (JEP) quadrupled from 2002 to 2012. This explosion of interest is partially rooted in the global development in the field; *JEP* received submissions from over 40 countries in 2012. The 2008 American Psychological Association Presidential Address was devoted to psychology's contribution to a sustainable environment (Kazdin 2009).

Perhaps this is because the wider society gradually has awakened to the importance of the natural environment over approximately the same half-century as the lifespan of environmental psychology, including its fragility and vulnerability to human actions and its potential for enhancing human life. Over the same period, the ability of environmental psychology to contribute ideas and solutions to the design of the built environment has been realized. One gets the feeling that, perhaps more than in some other areas of psychology, environmental psychologists are driven by personal conviction to a cause.

This article focuses on key developments in environmental psychology over the past decade or so, but it does not refrain from reaching further back where necessary. The last broadband *ARP* survey of the field was 18 years ago (Sundstrom et al. 1996), which forces the present attempt to update readers to be much more selective than its author would wish.

PROENVIRONMENTAL CONCERN AND BEHAVIOR

Many environmental problems are rooted in human behavior and can thus be solved by understanding behavior.[1] Proenvironmental behavior matters. Influences on proenvironmental behavior include childhood experience; knowledge and education; personality; perceived behavioral control; values, attitudes, and worldviews of various kinds; felt responsibility and moral commitment; place attachment; norms and habits; goals; affect; and many demographic factors.[2] These influences also quite likely combine to determine behavioral outcomes; that is, they interact. Thus, one important challenge is to learn more about how these influences moderate and mediate one another.

A second challenge is to learn which domains of environment-related behaviors (i.e., the big five related to energy conservation, transportation, food, waste disposal, and material purchases) are more or most influential in which social domains: private (e.g., at home), public (e.g., writing letters or attending meetings), organizational (at work or school), or activist (Stern 2000).

A third challenge is to widen and deepen the field's consideration of how society works in terms of the production and consumption of goods and services and how broader social and political influences contribute to the formation of values, attitudes, and behavior (Uzzell & Räthzel 2009).

The many influences on environmental concern and behavior are considered next.

Childhood Experience

Children who spend time in nature are more likely to engage in proenvironmental behavior as adults (Cheng & Monroe 2012); this is more true when the time is spent in "wilder" than in "domesticated" nature (Wells & Lekies 2006). They are also more likely to spend time in nature as adults (Thompson et al. 2008).

Knowledge and Education

A recent summary of 15 knowledge surveys concluded that Americans are quite knowledgeable about some environmental problems (e.g., what renewable resources are, where garbage goes, and

---

[1] Of course, influences at other levels of analysis also influence proenvironmental choices, such as structural barriers, economic and political factors, and technological advances (Gifford 2008b).

[2] Finally, but importantly, we must note that environment-friendly behavior is often undertaken for nonenvironmental reasons, such as to save money or to improve one's health (cf. Whitmarsh 2009). In engaging in behavior choices like these, individuals have been called "honeybees" because, like those insects pollinating fruit trees in the pursuit of a nonenvironmental, self-interested goal, they inadvertently provide important environmental benefits (Gifford 2011).

what causes habitat destruction) but less knowledgeable about others (e.g., climate change, energy production, and water quality) (Robelia & Murphy 2012). Making informed proenvironmental choices obviously depends on having correct knowledge. Even self-reported knowledge, fallible as it may be, seems to predict proenvironmental behavior reasonably well (Fielding & Head 2012).

Education is also important. Individuals with more education in general are more concerned about the environment. Education alone often does not lead to more proenvironmental behavior, but it serves as a priming agent. For example, reading classic environmental books such as Rachel Carson's *Silent Spring* has been associated with more frequent environmental behavior (Mobley et al. 2010). Some forms of education, such as by peers in a workplace (Carrico & Riemer 2011), in a classroom where the desired behavior is proximate (Werner et al. 2012), or in teaching people how to reduce the smoke from their woodstoves (Hine et al. 2011), have been shown to be effective.

Personality

The Big Five personality factors represent much of the normal personality domain. Openness has been related to more proenvironmental activities (Fraj & Martinez 2006) and to more frequent proenvironmental behaviors, but this relation was fully mediated by environmental attitudes and connection to nature (Markowitz et al. 2012). In a German study, greater openness and greater agreeableness and, to a lesser extent, more conscientiousness and less emotional stability were associated with greater environmental concern (Hirsh 2010). Openness, agreeableness, and conscientiousness were strongly linked to environmental engagement across both persons and nations (Milfont & Sibley 2012). Agreeableness, conscientiousness, and less Machiavellianism were related to more recycling (Swami et al. 2011).

Consideration of future consequences—the tendency to establish and achieve goals and to plan strategies for meeting long-term obligations—was positively related to engaging in sustainable behaviors (Corral-Verdugo & Pinheiro 2006, Milfont & Gouveia 2006), including choosing public transport more often (Joireman et al. 2004).

Internal locus of control and self-efficacy have been associated with stronger proenvironmental intentions and behavior, including less use of cars for commuting (Abrahamse et al. 2009), more recycling in mainland China (Tang et al. 2011) and in Spain (Tabernero & Hernández 2011), and less electricity use among Danish consumers (Thøgersen & Grønhøj 2010). Locus of control also seems to moderate the link between one's values and proenvironmental behavior (Engqvist Jonsson & Nilsson 2013). In order for values to be expressed in proenvironmental behavior, people apparently must believe they have some control over events.

Values and Worldviews

Schwartz's (1992) value theory has been modified to fit environmental issues (e.g., Stern et al. 1993), and support for the categorization of values into biospheric, egocentric, and altruistic dimensions has been reported (e.g., de Groot & Steg 2007). Associations between values and environmental concern seem, at least in a study that included six widely dispersed nations, to be quite consistent (Schultz et al. 2005). Not surprisingly, persons who hold more altruistic, prosocial, and biospheric values report favoring environmental preservation, whereas those who see the environment as a source of resources to be consumed tend to hold self-enhancement values (Kaiser & Byrka 2011, Milfont & Gouveia 2006, Nilsson et al. 2004, Nordlund & Garvill 2002), and these egoistic values result in less environmental concern (de Groot & Steg 2010).

However, their relations with proenvironmental behavior typically are weak, so moderating and mediating variables such as personal norms and beliefs are needed to satisfactorily predict behavior from values (Nordlund & Garvill 2003).

These environmental values are related to the ways that individuals construe themselves. People with independent self-construal (i.e., individuals who differentiate themselves from others) tend to have egoistic values and to report being competitive about managing resources; those with interdependent self-construal (i.e., people who relate to others) tend toward sharing resources; and those with meta-personal self-construal (i.e., individuals who feel fundamentally interconnected with all living things) tend to have biospheric values and to report they would cooperate more in a commons dilemma (Arnocky et al. 2007). Despite these self-reports, in a commons dilemma microworld, participants with prosocial and proself orientations made similar resource management choices (Hine et al. 2009). However, their motives may differ: Proselfs may view harvesting restraint by others as a chance to maximize their own profit, whereas prosocials may be trying to maximize the group's outcome by compensating for what they think might be too much restraint by others. This was supported in that proselfs responded to overharvesting by others by increasing their own harvests, whereas prosocials' harvesting did not increase in response to others' lack of restraint.

In terms of political, economic, and technological values, individuals who value free-market principles, view technology as the solution to environmental problems, and believe that economics is the best measure of progress tend to have less environmental concern (Heath & Gifford 2006).

Postmaterialist values typically are held by more affluent citizens who have fewer worries about the necessities of life; they tend to be concerned with higher-level goals and actions such as self-improvement, personal freedom, and providing direct input to government. Holding postmaterialist values and political competence is related to an increased interest in environmental political action (e.g., Oreg & Katz-Gerro 2006), probably because these values are associated with environmental concern and perceived threat, which when combined with these individuals' sense of control, leads to a willingness to sacrifice and thus causes the adoption of proenvironmental behaviors.

Beliefs about the nature of nature are related to one's environmental concern. Those who believe that nature is ephemeral (that it is delicate and fragile and even small disturbances will have drastic consequences) are most concerned; those who hold nature-benign worldviews (that nature is very capable of adapting) are least concerned (Poortinga et al. 2003). Another widespread worldview held by individuals is that threats to the environment are weaker in their own area than in distant places (Gifford et al. 2009). Egalitarians believe this more strongly, and individualists believe it less strongly (Lima & Castro 2005).

However, relations between values and environmental attitudes may not be as simple as some of these findings imply. People have multiple values, and the relations between values must be considered. For example, appeals to environmental values are more effective in increasing proenvironmental behavior than are appeals to self-interest (financial) values (Bolderdijk et al. 2013) or even appeals to the combination of environmental and financial values (Evans et al. 2013). When two values conflict, the difference between the pre-existing level of endorsement of the two values predicts one's environmental attitudes better than the endorsement level of either single value (Howes & Gifford 2009). Moreover, values may combine with motivational style to more strongly predict proenvironmental intentions; for example, the more people hold altruistic and biospheric values and are self-determined as a motivational style, the more they act proenvironmentally (de Groot & Steg 2010).

Felt Responsibility, Moral Concerns, and Commitment

As one might expect, feeling responsible is an important part of environmental concern. This feeling of responsibility apparently stems largely from a sense of guilt (Ferguson & Branscombe 2010). The discourse on environment in such places as newspaper editorials and public service announcements tends to evoke harm and care as the moral foundations for action. These concerns tend to resonate more with liberals, which may be why liberals usually have more proenvironmental attitudes. However, when proenvironmental messages are framed in terms of purity as a moral foundation, conservatives' attitudes toward the environment move much closer to those of liberals (Feinberg & Willer 2013). Finally, making a small symbolic commitment, such as to reuse towels in a hotel, can lead to a considerable (25%–40%) increase in towel reuse and towel hanging (Baca-Motes et al. 2013).

Frugality, Diversity, and Empowerment Attitudes

Three other attitudes appear to assist in the understanding of proenvironmental concern and behavioral intentions. Positive attitudes toward frugality predict intentions to reduce energy choices (Fujii 2006). Positive attitudes toward sociocultural diversity and biodiversity also predict proenvironmental behavior (Corral-Verdugo et al. 2009). If one expects to feel empowered—that is, to develop a sense of self-efficacy and solidarity—one is more likely to participate in the development of a proenvironmental program (Maeda & Hirose 2009).

Place Attachment

If individuals have a strong attachment to a place, they probably want to protect it (Scannell & Gifford 2013). In one study, adding place attachment to the standard values-beliefs-norms (VBN) model doubled the predictability of whether people would conserve native plants (Raymond et al. 2011). However, place attachment comes in multiple varieties, and not all are equally related to proenvironmental behavior: Natural place attachment but not civic place attachment appears to have that connection (Scannell & Gifford 2010a).

Norms, Habits, and Defaults: Behavioral Momentum

Much of today's behavior simply follows from yesterday's behavior. This has been investigated in terms of norms, habits, and defaults, but perhaps an encompassing term for this is behavioral momentum. In terms of norms, if one believes that the "usual thing to do" is to recycle (a descriptive norm), one is likely to recycle. Personal norms represent one's sense of moral obligation toward taking action, for example, to oppose nuclear energy (de Groot & Steg 2010), to reduce car use (Abrahamse et al. 2009), or to conserve water (Corral-Verdugo & Frías 2006). Subjective or injunctive norms represent one's sense that significant others expect a certain pattern of behavior. For example, parents can create norms in young children to recycle and reuse paper (Matthies et al. 2012). Local norms are based on physical proximity; they seem particularly relevant for behaviors that occur in a specific proximate location (Fornara et al. 2011).

Evidence about the influence of norms is strangely mixed. One study reports that in a survey normative influence was a better predictor of proenvironmental behavior than other beliefs, and in a field study norms produced the greatest behavior change, although participants in both studies claimed that norms were the least influential factor (Nolan et al. 2008). In contrast, a recent meta-analysis that examined a variety of social influences (block leaders, public commitment, modeling, group feedback, social comparison feedback, and social norms) across 29 studies found that norms were the least potent influence on behavior (W. Abrahamse & L. Steg, manuscript under review).

Perhaps this is because the norm-behavior link is not as straightforward as it appears. For example, what happens if a person is faced with multiple norms, and the norms conflict? When an injunctive norm conflicts with a descriptive norm, behavior intentions weaken (Smith et al. 2012). However, other work suggests that norm conflict can actually strengthen perceived environmental effectiveness if the person has a positive attitude toward the issue (McDonald et al. 2013). Nevertheless, when people see evidence of counter-norm behavior (e.g., litter) in the presence of information proscribing that behavior, such as a "Do Not Litter" sign, they often will engage in antinorm behavior, that is, add to the litter (Keizer et al. 2008).

Norms can become habits, a second form of behavioral momentum. Unfortunately, the obvious approach to measuring habit—asking about a person's past behavior—may not be an adequate way of measuring it (Knussen & Yule 2008). Assessing habits may not be as straightforward as it appears. A third form of behavioral momentum is choosing the default. Often, people will say they prefer the green alternative but in fact they often tend to (passively) "choose" whichever default is offered to them (Pichert & Katsikopoulos 2008). Clearly, the policy strategy implied by this finding is to make the green option the default.

Affect

Emotions play a role in proenvironmental concern and behavior. For example, a Swedish study reports that worry, hope, and joy play a role in recycling (Ojala 2008). Having an affective connection to nature significantly predicts the intention to engage with it (Hinds & Sparks 2008). Anticipating unpleasant emotions predicts the desire to engage in proenvironmental actions (Carrus et al. 2008). On the other hand, positive affect toward one's pollution-emitting device weakens one's support for policy measures that would restrict its use and for the willingness to switch to a less-polluting device (Hine et al. 2007).

Demographic Factors

Age, gender, wealth, religion, urban-rural residence, and identification with a group have been related to environmental concern. Older people generally report more proenvironmental concern or behavior than younger people (e.g., Grønhøj & Thøgersen 2009), but not always (e.g., Sardianou 2007).

Gender differences are inconsistent. In some studies, women report stronger environmental attitudes, concerns, and behaviors than men (e.g., Scannell & Gifford 2013). However, in China, women are more engaged than men in domestic environmental behaviors (e.g., recycling), but outside the home (e.g., environmental organization donations) no gender differences are exhibited, and women express lower levels of concern than men (Xiao & Hong 2010). A possible reason for this pattern is that health and safety, which are threatened by problematic environments are more important to women, particularly women with children at home (see, e.g., Dietz et al. 2002).

One generalization is that environmentalists tend to be middle-class or upper-middle-class individuals. Environmental concern also appears to be related to wealth on the global scale; it has a clear positive relation with national gross domestic product per capita (Franzen 2003). Of course, not everyone in wealthier places is environmentally concerned; for example, conservative white males in the United States clearly are less concerned, on average, than are other US demographic groups (McCright & Dunlap 2012). Meanwhile, some research concludes that citizens of developing countries have as much, or more, environmental concern as do those of developed countries (Mostafa 2012). Perhaps the resolution of these apparently contradictory findings is that citizens of poorer countries are more concerned about local environmental problems because the problems are salient to them, whereas citizens of wealthy countries are more concerned about global problems because they can afford a more cosmopolitan perspective, given that they have fewer local environmental problems.

The hypothesis that environmental concern is rooted in religious beliefs and values has often been debated. One view within the Judeo-Christian religious tradition is that the Earth was created for people to master and use; the associated implicit belief is that humans are separate from nature, and that belief enables people to exploit nature's resources for their own benefit. However, others within the Judeo-Christian tradition hold stewardship of nature as an ethic. The stewardship ethic also applies in principle for Muslims; humans, according to Islam, are merely a part of the holistic system of life created by Allah, and although humans have the right to survive, they have been given the role of responsible leadership on earth.

Empirical research on this issue remains divided. One recent study found that no differences exist between Christians and non-Christians in the perception of general environmental threats and that Christians judged the threat of genetically modified crops to be more serious than did non-Christians (Biel & Nilsson 2005). Another study found that Islamic religious teachings are associated with proenvironmental behavior, thus lending support to the theory that an Islamic environmental ethic exists (Rice 2006).

People who live in rural areas experience the environment in very different ways from their urban counterparts; doubtless most inhabitants of rural areas are more in touch with nature. Does that result in greater or lesser environmental concern or behavior? Again, the results are mixed. In China, residents of larger cities are more likely to engage in proenvironmental behaviors than are residents of smaller cities (Chen et al. 2011). However, students in the United Kingdom who had grown up in rural areas report more positive orientations toward the natural environment than do urban-raised students (Hinds & Sparks 2008). The anthropocentric beliefs of rural residents seem consistent with their more direct use of natural resources for human ends.

Finally, and perhaps less intuitive than some of the results discussed above, is the finding that individuals with a stronger sense of identification with a group report engaging in more proenvironmental behavior (Dono et al. 2010). However, this depends on which sort of group one identifies with.

Measures

Many tools for measuring environmental attitudes have been proposed. One compilation includes 14 such measures (Gifford 2007a, chapter 3). Perhaps the most comprehensive recent measure, built from numerous existing measures, is the Environmental Attitudes Inventory (Milfont & Duckitt 2010). The Environmental Attitudes Inventory is a multidimensional instrument that captures the hierarchical nature of environmental attitudes; it is composed of 12 scales that appear to represent most or all of the main constructs tapped by earlier measures. These include enjoyment of nature, support for interventionist conservation policies, intentions of personal environmental activism, support for conservationism if it provides human benefits, confidence that science and technology can solve environmental problems, fear of ecological collapse, support for using nature for development, self-report of personal conservation behaviors, beliefs that humans are meant to dominate nature, beliefs that humans should use nature, beliefs that nature is valuable for its own sake, and support for population control policies.

Another instrument recently created with the specific purpose of combining and building upon earlier measures is the New Human Interdependence Paradigm scale (Corral-Verdugo et al. 2008). However, the most widely used measure so far is the revised New Ecological Paradigm scale (Dunlap et al. 2000).

MAJOR AND MACRO THEORETICAL APPROACHES

At least seven major theoretical approaches have guided work by environmental psychologists across their range of interests, from the built environment to the natural environment and proenvironmental behavior (Gifford 2007a). These include (*a*) stimulation theories, which conceptualize the physical environment as a crucial source of sensory information; (*b*) control theories that emphasize the importance of an individual's real, perceived, or desired control over stimulation; (*c*) ecological psychology, which emphasizes a dynamic-system approach to person-environment relations; (*d*) integral approaches such as interactionism, transactionalism, and organismic theory that attempt to describe the full, complex interrelationship of persons and settings; (*e*) operant approaches, which adopt a direct problem-solving approach that employs behavior modification techniques; (*f*) environment-centered theories, such as the spiritual-instrumental model and ecopsychology, which emphasize the environment's own welfare; and (*g*) theories that include such elements as goals, norms, intentions, values, and attitudes. Most of the above might be called macro approaches; the last are more specific meso-scale approaches.

Within the zone of proenvironmental attitudes and behavior, recent theories vary in scope, from the meso to the macro. One such macro-scale proposal is the general model of social dilemmas (Gifford 2006, 2008b). It posits that impactful behavior choices made by individuals (including those who head organizations as well as the average citizen) often have a geophysical influence (e.g., weather, extent and accessibility of the resource), occur within a regulatory context (e.g., policies and pricing), and are influenced by technological developments (e.g., new drilling methods, factory fishing boats) as well as psychological elements (motivations, cognitions, norms, interpersonal influences, and decision-making strategies). The general model of social dilemmas includes downstream consequences of these decisions for (*a*) the decision maker (and significant others), (*b*) the community, and (*c*) the environment. Finally, the model recognizes that these outcomes feed their consequences back upstream, influencing the regulatory context (in particular) but also sometimes influencing the other upstream factors— geophysical (such as climate impacts), technological, and social factors—in a continuing dynamic cycle of influence. However inclusive it might be, such a theory is difficult to test, at least as a whole (although its individual links can and should be tested).

MESO THEORIES

With fewer constructs, meso-scale theories are far easier to investigate. Among these are the theory of planned behavior (TPB) (Ajzen 2005), VBN theory (Stern 2000), and goal-framing theory (Lindenberg & Steg 2007). Other, less-specified, notions include the reasonable person model (Kaplan & Kaplan 2009) and the human interdependence paradigm (Gärling et al. 2002).

These meso-scale theories propose attractively parsimonious accounts of behavior and therefore are eminently investigable (e.g., Kaiser & Gutscher 2003). The TPB, for example, proposes that attitudes toward a behavior, subjective norms, and perceived behavioral control predict behavioral intention, which predicts actual behavior. However, many studies have identified personal and social factors that enhance the TPB's predictive validity, including habit, descriptive norms, self-identity, and place attachment (e.g., Bamberg & Schmidt 2003, Chen & Tung 2010, Fielding et al. 2008, Heath & Gifford 2002, Hinds & Sparks 2008, Raymond et al. 2011, Whitmarsh & O'Neill 2010). Structural inadequacies, such as a lack of availability of recycling facilities[3] or public transport, also constrain proenvironmental behavior (e.g., Heath & Gifford 2002, Steg & Gifford 2005). Assuming these factors are useful additions to the understanding and prediction of proenvironmental behavior, they tend to push theoretical thinking back toward the macro scale.

The VBN theory (Stern 2000) predicts, in a chain-like sequence, that one's values (altruistic, biocentric, and not egocentric) cause one to espouse an ecological worldview, which leads one to believe that adverse consequences to the environment can occur, which increases one's perceived ability to reduce threats to the environment, which leads to a sense of obligation to act in a proenvironmental manner, which culminates in four kinds of proenvironmental behavior (activism such as participating in public demonstrations, nonactivist behaviors in the public sphere such as letter writing, private-sphere behaviors such as recycling at home, and behaviors within organizations such as lobbying for double-sided printing). This sequence has been supported for climate-relevant behaviors such as the acceptability of household energy-saving policies (Steg et al. 2005), and parts of it have been verified in terms of values and awareness of consequences (Hansla et al. 2008). That is, researchers have shown that each link in VBN's chain of hypothesized constructs is indeed predicted by its predecessor.

Goal-framing theory (Lindenberg & Steg 2007) posits that three types of goals influence the way people process information and act upon it: hedonic (pleasure oriented), gain (self-interest), and normative (what others are thought to be doing). At any given time, one goal is presumed to be focal while the others are in the background and might increase or decrease the strength of the focal goal.

The reasonable person model (Kaplan & Kaplan 2009) proposes that understanding people's informational needs in particular settings has the potential to make it easier for people to help themselves. People are unreasonable when a place does not support their needs for information and are more likely to be reasonable in environments that do.

The human interdependence paradigm (Gärling et al. 2002) emphasizes the tension between the drive for human development, which tends to require unsustainable use of resources, and concern for the environment, which usually implies preservationist or at least sustainable use of resources. This paradigm reflects the central conflict in commons dilemmas between self-interest and that of a common resource pool, which has been the subject of dozens of studies (cf. Biel et al. 2008, Kopelman et al. 2002) that often have used microworld simulations (e.g., Gifford & Gifford 2000) to investigate the 30 or more influences on cooperation in the commons (Gifford 2007a, chapter 14).

Each of these meso theories certainly includes a part of the truth about proenvironmental behavior, and their relatively few components allow for convenient testing. However, the price of simplicity is incompleteness, and excluded influences undoubtedly play a role.[4]

PROENVIRONMENTAL BEHAVIOR IS STILL INSUFFICIENT: WHY?

The need for more proenvironmental behavior is very widely recognized, but in most built and natural places too little of it is occurring to ensure sustainability. In common dilemma terms, our

---

[3] One disturbing recent finding deserves further research attention. When participants in two different contexts had structural facilities available for recycling, they used more paper than when facilities were not available (Catlin & Wang 2013).

[4] See Footnote 2.

species is "defecting," that is, extracting resources faster than they can replenish. The responsibility for this can be placed with the individuals, households, and organizations whose actions are contributing to the problem, but environmental psychology as a science can support those whose job is to create more effective policy by developing improved theory, focusing on the barriers experienced by people, and conducting studies that emphasize behavior change over self-reports.

The Main Theories Are Too Exclusive or Too Inclusive

The meso-scale theories cover important explanatory territory, but they do not overcome the problem that their predictive strength, although often of moderate magnitude, usually does not account for the bulk of the variance in proenvironmental concern or behavior. A further related and longstanding problem is the gap between stated intentions and objective behavior, although some have argued that the attitude-behavior gap is an empirical chimera that does not exist at all, if the phenomenon is considered from Donald Campbell's (1963) perspective that verbal statements and overt acts both stem from one root behavioral disposition (Kaiser et al. 2010). If the attitude-behavior gap does exist, as most believe it does, it probably occurs in part from the dampening influence of structural barriers (one cannot take public transport if it does not exist in one's community) and psychological barriers.

A problem with macro-scale theories is that although they are inclusive about the drivers of human behavior, they are difficult to investigate as a whole through conventional empirical study. They do, however, serve as big-picture reminders of the human and nonhuman antecedents and consequences of environment-impactful behavior and therefore can assist policy makers in understanding more about the antecedents and consequences of their policies.

In sum, one reason that proenvironmental behavior remains a challenge may be that meso theories are too narrow for policy makers to effectively utilize and macro theories are too broad for scientists to test. If so, one goal for environmental psychology should be to develop an intermediate-sized theory that incorporates most of the impactful drivers of behavior but remains manageable in size and parsimonious.

Psychological Barriers to Proenvironmental Behavior

Researchers have begun to identify and categorize psychological barriers to proenvironmental behavior (e.g., Gifford 2008a, Lorenzoni et al. 2007). The most exhaustive account of psychological barriers to behavior change organizes about 30 separate "dragons of inaction" into seven conceptual categories: limited cognition, ideologies and worldviews, social influences, sunk costs, discredence, perceived risks, and limited behavior, that is, engaging in a few low-impact actions and rationalizing that contribution to be sufficient (Gifford 2011). These barriers certainly matter, and they present an important research challenge. Whose proenvironmental behavior is constrained by which barriers, and how can they best be overcome?

Self-Reports Do Not Change Behavior

Another problem that impedes understanding of objective proenvironmental behavior is researchers' reliance on self-reports. After all, to be blunt, not concern for the environment, not felt responsibility, not subjective norms, not attitude toward the behavior, not goals, and not even behavioral intentions solve environmental problems. Only actual behavior will bring a resolution.

Even self-reported proenvironmental behavior does not match actual proenvironmental behavior particularly well. A recent meta-analysis (C. Kormos & R. Gifford, manuscript submitted) found the association between self-reported and actual proenvironmental behavior to be about $r = 0.45$, which is to say that these two constructs, which purport to cover the same territory, share only about 20% of their variance. This gap can be caused in part by imperfect memory, social desirability bias, and the lack of opportunity to observe others' behavior (e.g., in reporting household energy use, the reporter will not always have observed the actions of others in the household). Attempts have been made to overcome this problem by using Rasch models (Kaiser et al. 2007), although the proposed solution itself depends on self-reports of one's past behavior, which may not escape the problem.

Four Ways Forward

How might these problems be overcome? First, because macro contextual factors such as climate, geography, technology, economic trends, and the political slant of one's government often constrain or encourage proenvironmental behavior, they should be considered more often. Environmental psychologists should work with experts in technical and other social science fields; such teams will have a better grasp on the big picture. Second, increased understanding of how the psychological barriers operate is essential. Third, improved measurement of self-reports is needed, and self-reports should only be relied upon only when objective behavior measurements cannot be made. Fourth, more meta-analyses that examine the relative potency of the many drivers of proenvironmental behavior are needed; each individual study is useful but almost always is limited at least in generalizability resulting from relatively small or localized samples. At least in principle, meta-analyses reveal something closer to the truth of relations between constructs.

Fortunately, four pertinent meta-analyses have been conducted. The first considered 315 relevant studies and concluded that proenvironmental behavior was most strongly predicted by knowledge of the issues, knowledge of action strategies, locus of control, attitudes, verbal commitment, and sense of responsibility (Hines et al. 1986–1987). A second meta-analysis, performed 20 years later, confirmed those results for the most part but also concluded that the intention to engage in proenvironmental behavior mediates the impact of the other personal and social influences, that personal norms influence this intention, and that problem awareness is a significant indirect influence on proenvironmental intention; the impact of problem awareness appears to be mediated by moral and social norms, guilt, and attribution processes (Bamberg & Möser 2007).

A third meta-analysis focused on individuals' commitment to action; the findings confirmed that commitment can be effective but called for further examination of the reasons that it works (Lokhorst et al. 2013). A fourth reported on the relative value of different treatments or interventions for promoting proenvironmental behavior; it concluded that the most effective approaches employed cognitive dissonance, goal setting, social modeling, and prompts, although as might be expected, different treatments are more effective for different proenvironmental behaviors, and combined approaches often work better than single approaches (Osbaldiston & Schott 2012).

In sum, an important goal for environmental psychology is to find a theoretical framework that is more parsimonious than the macro approaches but more inclusive and therefore more predictive of environmental behavior than the meso approaches. This model should include more contextual (extrapsychological) factors, attend to the psychological barriers between concern and action, and make greater use of objective measures of behavior. Given the bewildering plethora of influences on environmental concern, intentions, and behavior, more cooperation with other experts is called for, and more meta-analyses are needed to clarify connections among the constructs and thereby to contribute to a more viable and powerful account of proenvironmental behavior.

CLIMATE CHANGE AND HUMAN BEHAVIOR

Climate change is not new; the earth's temperature and climate have varied considerably over millions of years. However, in the past century, greenhouse gas (GHG)-emitting human activities have caused the Earth's temperature to rise higher than it has been since civilization developed 10,000 years ago (Intergov. Panel Climate Change 2007). Worldwide GHG emissions continue to rise despite official efforts to raise awareness and many citizens' efforts to change. Further climate change probably will result not only in higher maximum temperatures (and therefore more heat-related deaths), but also in more frequent extreme weather events, a rise in sea levels, an increase in widespread infectious diseases, and decreases in crop yields and water quality. Climate change matters.

Current climate change is primarily driven by GHG-emitting human behaviors and therefore may be largely mitigated by changes to human behavior. However, human behavior is the least understood aspect of the climate change system (Intergov. Panel Climate Change 2007). Thus, unfortunately, the main cause of the problem is its least understood element. Understanding behavior at the psychological level of analysis therefore is essential, given that the cumulative impact of individuals' decisions and behaviors is the key factor driving climate change (Gifford et al. 2011a).

Fortunately, some environmental psychologists have been working on the problem for more than 30 years (Fischhoff & Furby 1983); they have learned much about different behaviors with different impacts and are actively developing interventions (Gifford 2008a, Spence et al. 2008). The pace of research has accelerated recently, including the American Psychological Association (2010) task force report and subsequent special issue (Swim et al. 2011). At the same time, recognition that the wider political and social context must be considered when interpreting the meaning of attitudes in places with different dominant political ideologies (Räthzel & Uzzell 2009) can and should be integrated with the climate change models and efforts by other disciplines.

Mitigative and Adaptive Responses

Human responses to climate change can take two basic approaches. Mitigation refers to proactive efforts to prevent further climate change, and adaptation refers to reactive responses to events caused by climate change. Both can take many forms, but an important distinction in the latter is that for nonpsychologists, adaptation usually means structural changes, such as building seawalls, whereas for psychologists, adaptation means the more personal responses such as cognitions, emotions, decision processes, and coping strategies (e.g., Reser & Swim 2011).

As the threat of climate change impacts becomes urgent, a focus on psychological adaptation is needed. Apart from quite salient impacts that are already evident in some northern regions, few opportunities are yet available for studying psychological adaptation to clear and present impacts of climate change. Events that quite probably are climate related include the huge storm that struck the New York and New Jersey areas in October 2012. Until more climate-related events occur, research on individual and collective responses to earlier weather-related disasters such as Hurricane Katrina (e.g., Adeola 2009) can be informative.

Individuals may prepare for the expected increase in climate-related threats such as more extreme weather events and sea-level rise in both behavioral and emotional ways. The former involves precautions to prevent damage and injury; the latter refers to intraindividual awareness, anticipation, and readiness, reflected in one's capacity to psychologically respond in an emergency. Individuals, households, and communities may or may not have resilience, that is, the "inner strengths and coping resources for necessary adaptation to situational demands" (Am. Psychol. Assoc. 2010, p. 117), or experience vulnerability, the extent to which individuals and communities are at risk and are unable to cope with the adverse impacts of climate change (e.g., Smit & Wandel 2006). The more resilience and the less vulnerability that individuals and communities have, the greater their adaptive capacity. Psychology can help with both forms of adaptation; the former by helping to build public understanding and support for necessary infrastructure improvements, and the latter through its expertise in ameliorating stress and facilitating coping (Swim et al. 2011).

High- Versus Low-Impact Mitigation Behaviors

Distinguishing among environment-relevant behaviors is important because these behaviors can have different psychological and contextual determinants (Stern 2000) and because they vary in environmental impact. Some actions (e.g., recycling) that have relatively little environmental impact tend to be influenced by attitudes, personal norms, and values. In contrast, high-impact behaviors (e.g., driving) tend to be more important to people and are entrenched in habit; the behaviors more often are primarily driven by contextual factors (e.g., commuting distance) and therefore are more difficult to change (Gardner & Stern 2002). Low-impact behaviors have received more attention to date, but given finite resources, high-impact behaviors should receive more attention (Gardner & Stern 2008).

One hope is that people will gravitate from low- to high-impact behaviors, a progression called the spillover effect, via low-impact catalyst behaviors such as recycling. Some evidence for spillover exists (e.g., Thøgersen & Ölander 2003, Whitmarsh & O'Neill 2010), but sometimes action in one behavioral domain actually leads to less action in others so that no net positive effect occurs (Herring & Sorrell 2008).

Impact-Oriented Versus Intent-Oriented Mitigation Behaviors

Whether a behavior is high or low in impact differs from whether a person intends to act proenvironmentally or not. Impact refers to an action's objective impact on the climate; intent refers to a person's intention to act in a way that will have a positive impact on the environment or climate. The two may coincide ("I intend to help by engaging in a high-impact behavior by moving to a plant-based diet"; food choices objectively make an important difference in GHG emissions) or not ("I intend to help by returning plastic bags to the grocery store"; recycling plastic bags, although helpful, has a much less important impact). Intent-oriented environmental actions probably are driven more by one's attitudes, whereas impact-oriented behaviors probably are driven more by motivations, contextual influences (e.g., pricing), and demographic variables. For example, actual household energy use (an impact-oriented behavior) is most strongly related to nonattitude factors such as income, household size, age, health, and convenience (Gatersleben et al. 2002).

In a UK survey, the energy conservation levels of respondents who said they engaged in behaviors to help mitigate climate change surprisingly did not significantly differ from those who did not report engaging in such behaviors (Whitmarsh 2009). Furthermore, a marked discrepancy was observed between the percentage of respondents who stated that they engaged in an action specifically out of concern about climate change (31%) and the percentage who reported actually engaging in energy conservation behavior (96%) (Whitmarsh 2009).

Curtailment Versus Efficiency Behaviors

Curtailment behaviors reduce consumption (e.g., turning off a light); efficiency behaviors are one-time choices to adopt an efficient technology (e.g., installing more insulation or solar panels). Curtailment behaviors have a large potential impact; one study suggests that in households that have not already taken any of 27 curtailment actions in their transport and in-home behaviors, cumulative energy savings could exceed 60% of energy used (Gardner & Stern 2008). That being said, efficiency behaviors may have greater energy-saving potential (Gardner & Stern 2002) mainly because they do not require consistent, long-term maintenance of the target behavior (Lehman & Geller 2004): Once the change is made, the savings are automatic or behavior free. However, efficiency behaviors may be more subject to losses caused by the rebound effect, the tendency to overspend energy as a psychological compensation for making a climate-virtuous choice.

INTERVENTION SCIENCE

All the knowledge so far gained can be used in another of environmental psychology's key roles: the development, evaluation, and implementation of interventions that target direct and indirect sustainability and climate-impactful behaviors. Intervention science is not as simple as turning a switch; in order to accomplish its ultimate goal of behavior change, it must take the social, political, economic, and cultural context into account; help to design climate-related policies and regulations; create effective public messages; predict public reactions to proposed policies; provide explanations for the public acceptance or rejection of new technologies, and comprehend how risks associated with climate change are understood. Interventions matter.

In order to be effective, intervention scientists should make several careful decisions in their work plans (e.g., Steg & Vlek 2009). They should carefully consider the behavior in question. Targeted behaviors should have large and negative demonstrated impacts but be amenable to change. The demographics of the key group for that behavior must be taken into account. The type of intervention (see below) must be carefully selected. Resources must be used efficiently. Psychologically important aspects of the targeted behaviors should be considered, such as perceived costs and benefits, norms and habits, and emotional and moral dimensions. The expected outcomes also need to be considered: These can include change in the behavior itself, improvements to the environment, and changes to the person's own quality of life.

Informational and Communication Strategies

Many interventions focus mainly on informational communication. Although this approach is relatively inexpensive, it has not been very effective in the ultimate goal of behavior change (Abrahamse et al. 2005). However, communication does at least set the stage for action, and without it there would not be the widespread awareness of climate change that currently exists. Nevertheless, communication about climate change is challenging because for most people the phenomenon is not immediately sensed, which naturally leads them to question its existence (cf. Moser 2010).

However, certain communication strategies work better than others in turning awareness into the willingness or intention to act. For example, informing the public that scientists aim to educate people about the consequences of climate change, as opposed to suggesting that people take a particular course of action, results in stronger willingness to act (Rabinovich et al. 2012). Messages framed with motivational or empowering statements (e.g., "We help solve climate change when we take transit, compost, or buy green energy") produce greater perceived competence to deal with climate change, climate change engagement, and some climate-relevant behavioral intentions than do sacrifice messages (e.g., "I am going to have to get used to driving less, turning off the lights, and turning down the heat") (Gifford & Comeau 2011).

Antecedent Versus Consequence Strategies

Interventions that aim to change the drivers of a selected behavior before it is performed employ antecedent strategies. The most common antecedent strategy is the information campaign, although the "information deficit" model on which such campaigns are based (that people simply need to become more aware or possess more facts) has been widely criticized (e.g., Kolmuss & Agyeman 2002). A second antecedent strategy is modeling, in which a key player enacts the desired behavior so as to influence proximate others to follow suit (e.g., Sussman et al. 2013). A third such strategy is to obtain behavioral commitments from individuals or organizations (e.g., Baca-Motes et al. 2013). A fourth antecedent strategy uses prompts to change behavior, for example, by posting a sign at an exit door directing individuals to turn off unused lights (e.g., Sussman & Gifford 2012).

Consequence strategies aim to change behavior after it has occurred in order to influence its future occurrence. This family of strategies, including giving people feedback (e.g., new desktop wireless devices tell householders how much energy they are using at the moment), rewards (e.g., rebates for saving energy), and punishment (e.g., fines or even jail for overfishing or poaching), aims to influence the selected behavior after its performance.

Informational Versus Structural Strategies

The goal of informational strategies is to change the (internal) psychological precursors (e.g., attitudes, knowledge, and motivation) of proenvironmental behavior. The goal of structural strategies is to change the (external) physical, technical, legal, or pricing circumstances surrounding the proenvironmental behavior.

Informational approaches appear to be best suited for easier (i.e., low cost in terms of effort, money, or social disapproval) behaviors with few barriers (Steg & Vlek 2009). They are somewhat effective for (a) prompting and eliciting proenvironmental behavioral commitments (Abrahamse et al. 2005); (b) social marketing, in which an intervention is carefully tailored to the needs and barriers of a particular group (Abrahamse et al. 2007, McKenzie-Mohr 2000, Thøgersen 2007); (c) implementation intention strategies, which ask people not only to commit to some behavior change but also how they plan to do so (see, e.g., Bamberg 2002); and (d) the provision of descriptive norm information, that is, telling people what other proximate individuals, such as neighbors or other hotel guests, are doing for the environment (e.g., Schultz et al. 2007). They may also be effective in campaigns to increase public acceptance of structural strategies, such as policies designed to reduce car use (Gärling & Schuitema 2007).

Structural strategies seem to be more effective for changing less-convenient and higher-cost behaviors (Steg & Vlek 2009), often so that the incentives (or disincentives) render the behavior more (or less) attractive (Thøgersen 2005). Among the main structural strategies (physical design changes that make the desired behavior easier or more obvious, pricing, rewards, and punishments), rewards often are most effective (Geller 2002). However, reward-based structural strategies sometimes last only as long as the rewards are offered, and often they are only effective in conjunction with a person's existing behavior-change goals (Gärling & Loukopoulos 2007). Like efficiency behaviors, to which they are similar, physical forms of structural changes, such as putting a recycling bin in every office instead of down the hall, have the advantage of changing behavior in a more permanent way.

Policy versions of structural strategies for increasing proenvironmental behavior (especially price increases or restrictive changes such as a reduced speed limit) are more acceptable when they are perceived to be fair, when they are effective, and when they do not seriously infringe on individual freedom. They are more acceptable to individuals with strong environmental values, those who are more aware of the problem, and those who feel morally obligated to ease the problem. Policies that can make proenvironmental behavior seem more attractive are likely to be evaluated as more effective and acceptable. Finally, policies that promote the adoption of energy-efficient equipment are preferred to those that seek to reduce the use of existing equipment (Gifford et al. 2011b).

The most effective interventions are tailored to the individual (or household) and to the specific behavior, take into account the particular barriers, and employ mixed strategies. Combinations of strategies, such as implementing information, feedback, and social interaction in a group often are the most effective and durable. In implementing one such combination, 19 of 38 household behaviors in the Netherlands were changed, and the changes were maintained or increased two years later (e.g., Staats et al. 2004). In another Dutch study, a combination of tailored information, goal setting, and tailored feedback was used to encourage households to reduce their gas, electricity, and fuel use (Abrahamse et al. 2007). After five months, intervention households used 5.1% less energy, whereas control households used 0.7% more.

NATURE: THE CAPRICIOUS RESTORATIVE AGENT

Nature matters. Like the Hindu god Shiva, the natural environment both gives and takes away. It has mainly been studied by environmental psychologists as a force for restoring depleted cognitive capacities (e.g., Kaplan 1995, Ulrich 1984), but its destructive power also compels the study of human coping, adaptation, and resilience (e.g., Adeola 2009).

To a lesser extent, nature has been considered as a complex environment to which humans have a variety of hard-wired orientations (e.g., Ornstein & Ehrlich 2000), as a focus of aesthetic appreciation and inspiration (e.g., Williams & Harvey 2001), as the setting for child development (e.g., Korpela et al. 2002), as our basic life-support system that absolutely requires conservation (e.g., Schmuck & Schultz 2002), and as a fount of design ideas (e.g., Joye 2007). Consideration of the natural environment in planning and design is important for human health, well-being, and restoration (e.g., Hartig & Staats 2003).

Measuring the Connection

Seven tools for measuring the human-nature relation have been developed recently. Five focus on nature connectedness or relatedness (Davis et al. 2009, Dutcher et al. 2007, Mayer & Frantz 2004, Nisbet et al. 2009), including one designed to measure children's connections with nature (Cheng & Monroe 2012). The sixth employs a behavior-based measure of the need for recovery among office workers (Smolders et al. 2012). Another was developed to measure six forms of incompatibility, that is, a poor fit between what one would like to do and what is actually happening in a setting, which leads to mental fatigue (and thus a need for restoration). The six forms of incompatibility are being distracted, being in need of information, being on duty, deceiving others, having difficulty, and being in danger (Herzog et al. 2011).

Causes and Consequences of the Connection

Perhaps some people can be connected to both self and nature, but the evidence suggests that this is not typical. Implicit connections to nature are negatively correlated with egoistic concerns (Schultz et al. 2004). When objective self-awareness is heightened in people with lower levels of environmental values, their connection to nature declines (Frantz et al. 2005). In contrast, principled moral reasoning, the most advanced level of moral development, correlates positively with ecocentrism, that is, belief in the intrinsic importance of nature (Karpiak & Baril 2008).

Not surprisingly, being psychologically connected to nature is associated with proenvironmental concern and behavior (Davis et al. 2009, Dutcher et al. 2007). Living near greenery is associated with less reported crime (Kuo & Sullivan 2001), and more social activity occurs in green spaces than in spaces that are less green (Sullivan et al. 2004).

Nature Restores

Abundant evidence favors the straightforward proposition that nature is restorative (Kaplan 1995). Nature improves cognitive functioning, productivity, mood, vitality, connectivity with nature, and speed of recovery in hospital, and it reduces stress and anger. These trends hold for actually being in nature (e.g., Berman et al. 2008), for merely having some nature (e.g., plants) in a room (e.g., Raanaas et al. 2011), for seeing a poster image of nature in one's room or office—at least for males (Kweon et al. 2008), or even for seeing nature through one's window (Ulrich 1984). More-fatigued people report greater restoration than less-fatigued people from walking in a forest (Hartig & Staats 2006). Green spaces improve the functioning of children with attention deficit disorder (Taylor et al. 2001).

In some ways, people seem to realize these effects and to expect even more of them. When asked why they engage in nature activities, individuals report doing so for 10 reasons: They believe that nature activities will facilitate a sense of cognitive freedom, allow them to simply experience nature, enhance their ecosystem connectedness, escape from stress, offer a physical challenge, foster personal growth, provide an opportunity to guide others, heighten their sense of self-control, renew social connections, and improve their health (Gifford 2007a).

People rate murals of nature scenes as more restorative than murals of indoor scenes, particularly nature scenes that include water (Felsten 2009). At the same time, even as they report being happier after a walk in nature than after a walk indoors, they underestimate the hedonic benefit they received (Nisbet & Zelenski 2011). This suggests that support for the conservation of nature, and for spending time in it, would be greater if people realized that they benefit from it more than they think.

Restoration Is Not Limited to Nature

However, restoration appears to be achievable in nonnatural settings, too (Scopelliti & Giuliani 2004). For example, visiting a house of worship seems to have many of the same benefits (e.g., Herzog et al. 2010), and an indoor simulation of a natural setting may have many of the same stress-reducing properties as the real thing (Kjellgren & Buhrkall 2010). The role of water is intriguing as a kind of cross-modal influence: Scenes that include water, whether in natural or built settings, elicit stronger ratings of restorativeness than do scenes without water in them (White et al. 2010).

Nature Is Not Always Nice

Nature is far from restorative when it delivers storms, wildfires, temperature extremes, earthquakes, tsunamis, volcanic eruptions, and meteors. It is not restorative or perceived as such when it harbors potential danger, such as a possible stalker (Herzog & Rector 2009) or other threats (van den Berg & ter Heijne 2005).

Given nature's destructive side, environmental psychologists have investigated factors that influence disaster preparedness (e.g., Mishra et al. 2010); the immediate response to disasters, such as prior experience or social connections (e.g., Adeola 2009); and the longer-term consequences of disasters (e.g., Caia et al. 2010).

PLACE ATTACHMENT AND IDENTITY

Place attachment and identity matter. Becoming bonded to a place is psychologically important in itself, but it also has implications for important external issues, including sustainability and climate change. The psychology of place, in a variety of guises, has been a very active topic recently in environmental psychology. Some efforts have focused on defining it, some on discovering its correlates, some on its antecedents, and some on its consequences. Phenomenologist approaches emphasize the meaning of place (e.g., Seamon 2012). Theory in the area is developing but remains uncrystalized (Lewicka 2011).

Place attachment has most often been described as an emotional connection to a place (e.g., Brown et al. 2003). For the most part, it is portrayed as a multifaceted concept that characterizes the bonding between individuals and their important places (e.g., Giuliani 2003). Obviously, place attachment is rarely attained instantly; residents need to spend time in a place, to hear stories, or to be part of a spiritual quest centered there (Hay 1998). One grows attached to settings where memorable or important events occurred (Manzo 2005).

Place identity is most often defined in terms of an overlap with one's sense of self. It develops when individuals experience similarities between self and place and incorporate cognitions about the physical environment (memories, thoughts, values, preferences, and categorizations) into their self-definitions. It has been viewed as stemming from the development of three processes: congruity between self and place, fit with the environment, and self-extension (Droseltis & Vignoles 2010).

One view of the relation between place attachment and place identity is that the former evolves, with time, into the latter (Clayton 2003). Consistent with this idea, natives of a place tend to have both place attachment and place identity, but people who move to a new place tend to report more place attachment than place identity (Hernandez et al. 2007), which suggests that attachment precedes identity.

A few other constructs bear some similarity to place attachment and place identity: sense of community, place dependence, and environmental identity. Some suggest that sense of place encompasses the subconcepts of place identity, place attachment, and place dependence (e.g., Jorgensen & Stedman 2001) or that it includes ancestral ties, feeling like an insider, and a desire to stay in the place (Hay 1998).

Person, Place, and Process

One approach to defining place attachment is to conceptualize it as having three primary dimensions: persons, places, and processes (Scannell & Gifford 2010b). In terms of persons, some researchers show that attachment to a place means attachment to the persons who live there and the social interactions that the place affords (e.g., Hidalgo & Hernández 2001).

Second, place attachment obviously is also about the physical place. The types of places that individuals find meaningful include a broad range of physical settings, from built environments such as houses, streets, buildings, and nonresidential indoor settings such as a retail store (Ng 2003), to natural environments such as lakes, parks, trails, forests, and mountains (Manzo 2003, 2005), or a place's climate (Knez 2005). Certain neighborhood forms, such as New Urbanism (characterized by narrow streets, houses close together on small lots with narrow setbacks, often with picket fences and front porches, often facing a central common green, with local amenities), seem to promote more of a sense of community than others, such as the conventional suburban form (characterized by wide streets, larger lots, and fewer porches, picket fences, or proximate amenities) (e.g., Kim & Kaplan 2004, Pendola & Gen 2008).

Place attachment can exist at multiple spatial levels. One might be attached to a chair, a room, a residence, a neighborhood, a park, a town or city, a region, a state or province, a nation, or the world. The strength of attachment differs depending on the level of analysis: Greater place attachment emerged for the home and city levels than for the middle-scale neighborhood level

(Hidalgo & Hernández 2001, Lewicka 2010). The social dimension of place attachment (feeling attached to the people in the place) may be stronger than the physical dimension (feeling attached to the built and natural elements of the place), although physical and social attachments both influenced the overall bond (Lewicka 2010).

Place attachment may be civic or natural. Civic place attachment is focused on one's community (e.g., Vorkinn & Riese 2001); natural place attachment is focused on nature (Scannell & Gifford 2010a). Civic and natural place attachments can, and do, predict outcomes differently, which reinforces the notion that they are distinct constructs (Scannell & Gifford 2010a). The identity analog of the relation to nature is environmental identity, the inclusion of nature in one's self-concept (Clayton 2003).

Other researchers focus on the meaning that a place has for a person. The meaning-mediated model of place attachment (Stedman 2003) proposes that individuals do not become directly attached to the physical features of a place but rather to the meaning that those features represent. In this view, a developed area may symbolize community or an underdeveloped area may symbolize wilderness. The physical aspects are said to constrain the possible meanings a place may adopt and, therefore, physically based place attachment rests in these symbolic meanings.

Places also become meaningful from personally important experiences, such as place-based revelations (e.g., religious epiphanies in a sacred place) or secular realizations of connectedness to nature in a wilderness, milestones (e.g., where I first met my lover), or experiences of personal growth: "[I]t is not simply the places themselves that are significant, but rather what can be called 'experience-in-place' that creates meaning" (Manzo 2005, p. 74). Place attachment seems to develop from experiences and emotional bonds first established with a place in childhood (Morgan 2010).

Place attachment can be faith based. Through religion, the meanings of certain places become elevated to the status of sacred (Mazumdar & Mazumdar 2004). Revered places such as Mecca or Jerusalem or, on a smaller scale, churches, temples, shrines, burial sites, or sacred places, are central to many religions, and their spiritual meanings are shared among worshippers.

Third, place attachment is about the processes it involves. Five processes can be distinguished: Place-related distinctiveness is about knowing one is from A, not B; place-referent continuity is about perceived similarity between one's current place and an earlier place to which one was attached, often one's childhood home; place-congruent continuity refers to the similarity of the current place's climate with that of one's childhood; place-related self-esteem is about feeling good in a place, or proud to be living there; and place-related self-efficacy occurs if the place supplies all or most of one's needs (Knez 2005).

The Functions of Place Attachment

Presumably, place attachment develops because it serves one or more functions, but what might those be? One is to provide a sense of security (e.g., Giuliani 2003). Attachment to one's neighborhood has been associated with fewer perceived incivilities (e.g., drug dealing, gang activity, and traffic) and less fear of crime (Brown et al. 2003). A second function is to facilitate a sense of belongingness: the feeling that one is in the right place, a place where one fits in (Giuliani 2003). Third, place attachment provides a sense of continuity (Scannell & Gifford 2010a). Fourth, it fosters restoration: In studies of children's favorite places, place-visit experiences tend to have a restorative theme (Korpela et al. 2002). Restoration within a favorite place appears to improve self-regulatory processes by providing a secure, comfortable environment conducive to self-reflection, problem solving, and stress relief. Fifth, attachment facilitates the successful pursuit of one's goals (e.g., Kyle et al. 2004b).

How Place Matters

Place attachment influences attitudes and behavior beyond itself. For example, it seems to lead to increased civic activity, at least as long as one also has neighborhood social ties (Lewicka 2005). Individuals with greater place attachment tend to be more prepared for floods (Mishra et al. 2010).

Although place attachment clearly matters, it does not always do so in supportive or positive ways (e.g., Brown et al. 2012). For example, Norwegian residents who were strongly attached to specific areas of a municipality tended to express more opposition to a proposed hydro power plant development, but those who were especially attached to the municipality as a whole tended to favor the development (Vorkinn & Riese 2001).

Place attachment may reduce climate change engagement if climate-positive actions appear to threaten existing place meanings, as demonstrated in a sample of UK residents who opposed proposals to build wind farms in their local area (Devine-Wright & Howes 2010). It can be associated with less, as well as more, proenvironmental behavior (e.g., Uzzell et al. 2002, Vaske & Kobrin 2001). Perhaps the resolution of this lies in the recent finding that natural place attachment appears to foster proenvironmental behavior, but civic place attachment does not (Scannell & Gifford 2013).

The physical aspects of a place may suffer if people cling to place meanings that are incompatible with place preservation or in cases where NIMBY (not in my backyard)-ism is retrogressive, that is, when it hinders desirable social goals or the normal evolution of architectural style, or positive forms of development that would accomplish these things. However, when planning incorporates or enhances elements that are central to the meaning of the place, it will be better received (e.g., Manzo & Perkins 2006).

Different forms of place relationships have different outcomes. Hikers with a greater sense of place identity viewed problems (such as crowding, litter, or noise) along a trail to be more important, but those with a greater sense of place dependence perceived problems to be less important (Kyle et al. 2004a), perhaps because these problems tended to be by-products of their own place use.

Emotional relationships with place usually are positive, but they can include fear, hatred, and ambivalence (Manzo 2005). For example, unhappy or traumatic experiences in a childhood home may well create what might be called negative place attachment. If place attachment did not exist, neither would homesickness—but it does; it causes problems for people who are forced by circumstance to leave a place to which they are attached, such as students who leave home for their education (e.g., Scopelliti & Tiberio 2010).

Finally, the loss of a place to which one is attached can result in grief and distress. Individuals who have been absent from their homes for an extended period of time often express a great desire to return to or visit the place, and at times, the return can involve much effort or cost.

SOCIAL DESIGN

In many ways, social design is where environmental psychology began (e.g., Osmond 1957; Sommer 1969, 1983). Social design matters. According to a famous dictum, architectural form is supposed to follow function, but for too many buildings, it does not seem to (Nasar et al. 2005). Public participation in design is an important part of the design process (e.g., Churchman 2012). However, now that public participation has become a routine part of architectural practice—at least nominally—less effort has been expended on it in recent years by academic or science-oriented environmental psychologists.

Nevertheless, environmental psychology–oriented design research and thinking continues (e.g., Peponis et al. 2007). For example, which office design features foster creativity? Green hues seem to facilitate creativity (Lichtenfeld et al. 2012). In one study, a positive social climate and a lack of environmental distractions predicted perceived creativity in offices (Stokols et al. 2002), but in another, perceived creativity was associated with more complexity and less use of cool colors, as well as views of natural environments and less use of manufactured or composite surface materials (McCoy & Evans 2002). Importantly, only the second of these studies compared perceptions of creativity with objective creative performance; greater creativity was found in an office with more of the attributes examined (views and less manufactured materials) than in an office with fewer of those features.

More broadly, which workplace features help to support the growing cadre of knowledge-oriented employees? The work engagement of employees is influenced by their aesthetic judgments and mood, which in turn are influenced by how they appraise the lighting in their workspace (Veitch et al. 2011). Lighting that employees are able to adjust for themselves at their own workstation is better than overhead lighting: Employees find their workstation more satisfying and pleasurable, the environment as a whole more satisfying, and their job more satisfying. They report being more committed to their organization, express less intention to change jobs, and report fewer and less intense symptoms of physical illness (Veitch et al. 2010).

Employees believe a workplace offers more support for collaboration when the distance from their workstation to a meeting space is shorter, the distance to a kitchen or coffee area is longer, and the percentage of floor space that is dedicated to shared services and amenities is larger (Hua et al. 2011). Research contradicts the common belief that open-plan designs produce more collaboration, even when the occupants judge the space favorably (Lansdale et al. 2011).

Others have examined which office forms are more satisfying or are associated with better health and job satisfaction (e.g., Danielsson & Bodin 2008). The lowest health status was found among employees in medium-sized and small open-plan offices; the best in cell offices (four-walls and window) and flex offices (shared open space with machines, no assigned workspaces). Workers in these office forms and in shared-room offices also had the highest job satisfaction. Lowest job satisfaction was in "combi" offices (in which employees have their own workstations, but more than 20% of their time is spent in teamwork away from one's own desk), followed by medium-sized open-plan offices. Not surprisingly, open-plan office workers are more satisfied next to a window, especially if they also have reasonably tall partitions around them (Yildirim et al. 2007), but windows apparently do not guarantee better work performance (Wang & Boubekri 2010).

The effects of building elements on their users are rarely simple; they can and do interact with influences external to the building. For example, school buildings in poor condition matter for student achievement, but this interacts with student mobility (the frequency with which a school's students change schools), so that poor condition plus mobility hinder achievement apart from either influence alone (Evans et al. 2010).

A challenge for social design is that the aesthetic preferences of architects and laypersons often diverge (e.g., Douglas & Gifford 2001). Some buildings are admired by laypersons but not architects, some by architects but not laypersons, some by both groups, and some by neither (Gifford et al. 2000). Researchers have begun to isolate the specific building features that result in these differences (e.g., Brown & Gifford 2001, Gifford et al. 2002). Fortunately, strategies are now being developed to find ways to reconcile the preferences of the two groups (e.g., Fawcett et al. 2008).

Social design as a construct might be enlarged to include broader societal benefits, such as constructing green buildings. To the extent that such buildings have technical benefits such as reduced energy or water use, they are valuable. A further reasonable assumption might be that green buildings are beneficial for their occupants (e.g., Joye 2007). However, what seems reasonable is not always the case: In one study of 15 buildings that varied in objective greenness, employee engagement and attitudes did not increase with increasing greenness, and, in fact, employees' impressions of their offices were negatively correlated with increasing greenness (McCunn & Gifford 2012).

HOME AND NEIGHBORHOOD

One's residence is the most important physical setting for most people. It can be inadequate, loved, threatening, satisfactory, restorative, a sanctuary, or gone (in the case of mobility, disaster, or homelessness). Its role in providing comfort, security, and pleasure is part of place attachment, as described previously. Many proenvironmental behavior choices are made in the home—from heating and cooling, to food choices and other purchasing decisions, to being the site from which commuting begins—and all these directly or indirectly influence sustainability and GHG emissions. The worldwide growth in cars and driving, in parallel to the growth of suburban living, is not sustainable and has very mixed effects on the quality of life (e.g., Gifford & Steg 2007). Therefore, home can be a behavioral wedge in the effort to improve overall sustainability (Stern 2008). Home matters.

Inadequate or poor-quality housing harms the physical and socioemotional health of children and adults (Evans et al. 2000, Gifford 2007c, Gifford & Lacombe 2006). Prolonged high indoor population density often impairs mental and physical health, task performance, child development, and social interaction (e.g., Evans & Saegert 2000). When low-income residents are moved to better housing, their psychological distress can decline. When it does, careful analyses suggest that the specific basis for this is reduced crowding (Wells & Harris 2007). Moving low-income individuals to better housing benefits them, but higher rates of mobility tend to be related to lower levels of well-being for most people (Oishi 2010).

Homes are threatened and sometimes destroyed by natural and technological forces. The psychological impacts include, for example, anxiety and depression associated with local air pollution (Marques & Lima 2011). However, residential threats and risks are not always directly related; for example, place attachment mediated the relation between proximity to a nuclear plant and perceived risk from it (Venables et al. 2012).

Communication after a disaster matters. If the communication between policy makers and the public is top-down, public understanding and support of policies and its trust of government decline; at the same time, perceived risk and noncompliance to policies increase (García Mira et al. 2006).

Home—at least urban residences—can pose threats, too. Although cities have some glorious benefits, mood and anxiety problems and the incidence of schizophrenia are more frequent in city dwellers, and recent functional magnetic resonance imaging research suggests that neural processes may mediate these problems through the processing of social stress (Lederbogen et al. 2011).

Housing satisfaction usually includes neighborhood elements such as trees and green spaces, cleanliness, distance to amenities, general appearance, and low levels of traffic and crime (e.g., Hur & Morrow-Jones 2008). Fear of crime is an important component of life in some neighborhoods, but those that are designed in accordance with defensible space principles (e.g., clearly marked residential territories and good surveillability of the street from residences as physical crime-deterrence features) usually have lower crime rates (e.g., Marzbali et al. 2012). Unfortunately, once disorder—in the form of vandalism, litter, or broken windows—begins, it tends to grow because residents begin to accept disorder as the norm (Keizer et al. 2008).

Documented interventions to improve disordered neighborhoods are relatively rare. Fortunately, quality-of-life research and methods are receiving much-needed attention (e.g., Marans & Stimson 2011). One such effort engaged residents of a low- and moderate-income neighborhood in adding amenities such as kiosks, benches, trellises for hanging gardens, and artwork, and it resulted in many residents reporting that the neighborhood was better and a good place to live, with more social interaction and participation, and that they had an increased sense of place (Semenza & March 2009).

VIRTUAL ENVIRONMENTS

The very world in which people in industrialized societies live has profoundly changed. Distance has disappeared. We experience far-off places and people through screens. For video gamers, reality is animated. Although the "screen revolution" has been going on since the advent of television, the difference now is that individuals have much more power to decide where to go and with whom to interact, rather than being limited to the offerings of a few major networks and receiving little opportunity to interact with the content. At the same time, physically proximate people and environments are allocated less time because of that spent on screens. The pace of technological change has greatly increased, and many people have what I call change overload disorder.

Environmental psychologists have been examining what these changes might mean (e.g., Stokols & Montero 2002) and how they might affect human functioning, behavior settings (i.e., theoretical entities that capture the essence of the relation between a standing pattern of behavior—such as the usual actions of football players, referees, and the audience—and the milieu within which it occurs, the stadium), and transactions between humans and the natural environment. Putting screens between ourselves and the actual physical and social worlds changes our connections with them in fundamental ways (e.g., Levi & Kocher 1999). The new reality will require a very different understanding of environmental transactions and new ways of thinking about how people perceive and represent the world (e.g., Heft 2001).

One challenge for an environmental psychology that matters, therefore, is to understand the import of dividing our time between the proximate and the distant and virtual worlds. For example, spatial discounting means that although individuals may be more aware of problems in distant environments through watching news stories on television or online, they may be less concerned about local problems (e.g., Gifford et al. 2009, Uzzell 2000). Will this blending of the near, the far, and the unreal lead to increased assistance for victims when disaster strikes far away, or will it cause numbness to their plight resulting from awareness of too many far-flung disasters?

Environmental psychologists are still struggling with the boundaries and definitions of the physical and social environments (Heft 1998, Kaplan & Kaplan 2009), but understanding them better, including new ways of conceptualizing the intertwined nature of the real and the virtual worlds we live in, is crucial (Stokols et al. 2009).

BASIC PSYCHOLOGICAL PROCESSES AND THE ENVIRONMENT

All human existence is related to environmental psychology. This includes such fundamental processes as how we see the world, find our way around in it, deal with noise, manage the space between us, and engage—or not—in healthy levels of movement.

Environmental Perception and Evaluation

Obviously, how individuals receive and process information from the everyday world matters. Environmental psychologists emphasize understanding how individuals respond to complex everyday settings and scenes. Work in the phenomenological tradition continues (e.g., Graumann 2002, Wells & Baldwin 2012). The ecological approach, which stresses that a complete understanding of perception must include its embeddedness in a sociocultural and historical web, remains an important perspective (e.g., Heft 2012).

Recent research clarifies how people experience aspects of their world. For example, one's level of awareness, degree of adaptation, and necessary selectiveness in attending to environmental cues within complex real scenes mean that people sometimes miss important elements of a scene, resulting in negative consequences for their health or safety (e.g., Stamps 2005). For example, perceived safety in outdoor places depends in part on (greater) perceived enclosure, that is, whether the scene is experienced as having wall-like elements, which in turn depends in part on atmospheric permeability, that is, the distance that one can see (Stamps 2010). Fog—and presumably thick smog—reduces atmospheric permeability, which makes places appear more open, which implies to perceivers that they are less safe (Stamps 2012).

In interiors, warm colors are not only more attractive, but they seem to be better remembered (Hidayetoglu et al. 2012). Putting more credentials on the wall makes a therapist appear more qualified (Devlin et al. 2009), and dim lighting also seems to elicit more favorable impressions from their clients (Miwa & Hanyu 2006). Other work suggests that certain long-held assumptions may not be tenable. For example, older research reported that humans prefer savannah-like landscapes, but we may prefer forest views instead (Han 2007).

Spatial Cognition and Wayfinding

What is new in the environmental psychology of finding one's way around? In keeping with the societal trends in technology, researchers have been asking whether virtual wayfinding (on a computer) produces the same results as real-world wayfinding, and some evidence suggests that it does (e.g., Jansen-Osmann & Berendt 2002).

Some findings are consistent with older research. Males often wayfind better than females, and this was recently confirmed in a virtual context. Males tend to use cartographic-like search strategies more often, whereas females tend to use local cues (Coluccia et al. 2007) and landmarks more often (Jansen-Osmann & Wiedenbauer 2004).

In complex, multifloor buildings, people might use one of three strategies to find their way: the central-point strategy employs the best-known parts of the building, the direction strategy relies on heading toward the horizontal location of the place sought, and the floor strategy focuses on heading for the floor on which the location is to be found (Hölscher et al. 2006). The latter strategy yielded the best wayfinding performance and was preferred by people with more experience in the building.

Other findings might be considered counterintuitive. For example, one might reasonably assume that Global Positioning System (GPS) devices help people wayfind, but even after being trained to use the devices, people who used the GPS system traveled longer and made more stops than did those who used traditional paper maps (Ishikawa et al. 2008). Although one might assume that individuals use proximate cues for wayfinding that have nothing to do with cartographic considerations, new evidence suggests that north is always used as the wayfinder's main and most accurate frame of reference (Frankenstein et al. 2012).

The foregoing studies show that wayfinding and the cognitive maps that people use are complex and subject to numerous immediate and antecedent influences. Beyond that, understanding these influences requires widening the picture to take into account sociocultural factors that, for example, do not always operate from within Western or industrialized cultural traditions (Heft 2013).

Wayfinding is an especially important problem for people with dementia. Not infrequently these individuals become disoriented within a building and sometimes wander outside and become lost. Those who have tried to optimize building design to reduce confusion report that interiors (*a*) should not be monotonously uniform, (*b*) should have a series of distinct local cues and as much visual access to the destination as possible, and (*c*) should have good signage so that navigation can proceed from point to point with fewer errors (Passini et al. 2000).

Responses to Noise

The global sound level is rising, and more people are exposed to greater sound levels. For example, the European Union estimates that 30% of its citizens are exposed to road traffic sound levels greater than those recommended by the World Health Organization. Although the normal assumption is that loud sounds are broadly detrimental, the history of noise research includes examples of null effects, and a few examples of increased performance exist (see Gifford 2007b, chapter 12). For example, somewhat loud sound may increase physiological arousal, which can speed the performance of easy, routine, or well-learned tasks.

Some results confirm the more expected outcomes. For example, louder noise is more annoying (Pierrette et al. 2012). Road traffic noise impairs children's reading speed and basic mathematics (Ljung et al. 2009). Irrelevant speech affects cognitive tasks and increases mental workload levels of open-plan office workers (Smith-Jackson & Klein 2009). Louder sound affects the memory, motivation to work, and tiredness of open-plan office workers (Jahncke et al. 2011).

Some researchers are moving toward finer-grained analyses to identify (*a*) which kinds of noise result in annoyance or detrimental effects on (*b*) which kinds of human responses in (*c*) which kinds of settings for (*d*) which sorts of persons. In one example of this approach, aircraft noise was associated with elevated hyperactivity scores in children, and road noise was associated with lower scores on a behavior problems scale, but neither type of noise was associated with a broadband measure of the children's mental health (Stansfeld et al. 2009).

Among other examples of finer-grained results, speech noise was more harmful than aircraft noise to the prose memory of adolescent students (Sörqvist 2010). Nature sounds appear to not harm memory, but when they are combined with voices or ground traffic, memory does suffer (Benfield et al. 2010). Street noise seems to harm the executive functioning of urban boys but not girls (Belojevic et al. 2012). Clearly, noise matters (Stewart et al. 2011), but much more research is needed to determine just how and when it does—and does not—have negative impacts.

Social Space

Personal space, crowding, territoriality, and privacy clearly are important parts of everyday functioning; social space matters. However, some might argue that enough is already known about these topics or that they do not have the societal-level importance of some topics covered previously. Research on social space has slowed to a trickle as efforts on topics deemed more important have increased.

Recent work confirms some expected outcomes, such as that being forced to sit close to others on public transport results in adverse reactions (Evans & Wener 2007). People who prefer seats at the end of long tables have a greater need to define their own territory (Kaya & Burgess 2007). Children who have been abused need more personal space around them (Vranic 2003). High density in a room alters preschoolers' choice of activities and time spent on off-task activities.

However, some less-predictable outcomes have also been reported, suggesting that despite the slowdown in social space research, not everything is known about how people use social space after all. For example, one might expect that territorial intrusions would result in faster responses by men than women, but at least in one context (a very large religious gathering) the reverse was true (Ruback & Kohli 2005). Technology is changing social space usage: Headphone wearers choose larger interpersonal distances (Lloyd et al. 2009). Finally, who would guess that spatially confined shoppers react by making more varied and unique product choices (Levav & Zhu 2009)? Social space matters.

Physical Activity

Around the world, whether waistlines a few years ago were relatively small or relatively large, they are now expanding. Getting people to move at all, and without the aid of GHG-producing machines, is a challenge both for human health and climate change mitigation. Physical activity matters.

Efforts have been made to make neighborhoods more walkable, schoolyards more encouraging of physical activity, and stairs more enticing. Walkable neighborhoods obviously include sidewalks, shops, and amenities, natural features such as trees and parks, and high residential density (e.g., Brown et al. 2007). Less obviously, walkable neighborhoods include slopes and stairs, moderate traffic volume, and public transportation stops (Borst et al. 2008).

Drawing attention to stairs, which too often are relegated to a dark side corner of a building's lobby, helps encourage their use. For example, when text encouraging the use of stairs was placed directly on four successive stair risers at eye level, stair use increased (Eves et al. 2009).

CONCLUSION

Scientific psychology began in the nineteenth century, but not until the middle of the twentieth century was psychology's range extended in any serious way to the physical environment. From the vantage point of the early twenty-first century, the psychology that attempted to understand persons in a physical vacuum is now revealed as woefully inadequate. Environmental psychology completes the picture by including the built and natural settings within which all humans exist. It is therefore essential not only to a complete understanding of human thought and behavior, but also for a full account of every other psychological process and for every application of psychology to the improvement of everyday life. Environmental psychology matters.

DISCLOSURE STATEMENT

The author is not aware of any affiliations, memberships, funding, or financial holdings that might be perceived as affecting the objectivity of this review.

LITERATURE CITED

Abrahamse W, Steg L, Gifford R, Vlek C. 2009. Factors influencing car use for commuting and the intention to reduce it: a question of self-interest or morality? *Transport. Res. Part F: Psychol. Behav.* 12:317–24

Abrahamse W, Steg L, Vlek C, Rothengatter T. 2005. A review of intervention studies aimed at household energy conservation. *J. Environ. Psychol.* 25:273–91

Abrahamse W, Steg L, Vlek C, Rothengatter T. 2007. The effect of tailored information, goal setting, and tailored feedback on household energy use, energy-related behaviors, and behavioral antecedents. *J. Environ. Psychol.* 27:265–76

Adeola F. 2009. Katrina cataclysm: Does duration of residency and prior experience affect impacts, evacuation, and adaptation behavior among survivors? *Environ. Behav.* 41:459–89

Ajzen I, ed. 2005. *Attitudes, Personality and Behavior*. Milton-Keynes, UK: McGraw-Hill

Am. Psychol. Assoc. 2010. *Psychology and Global Climate Change: Addressing a Multifaceted Phenomenon and set of Challenges. Report of the American Psychological Association Task Force on the Interface Between Psychology and Global Climate Change.* **http://www.apa.org/science/about/publications/climate-change.aspx**

Arnocky S, Stroink M, DeCicco T. 2007. Self-construal predicts environmental concern, cooperation, and conservation. *J. Environ. Psychol.* 27:255–64

Baca-Motes K, Brown A, Gneezy A, Keenan EA, Nelson LD. 2013. Commitment and behavior change: evidence from the field. *J. Consum. Res.* 39:1070–84

Bamberg S. 2002. Effects of implementation intentions on the actual performance of new environmentally friendly behaviors—results of two field experiments. *J. Environ. Psychol.* 22:399–411

Bamberg S, Möser G. 2007. Twenty years after Hines, Hungerford, and Tomera: a new meta-analysis of psycho-social determinants of pro-environmental behaviour. *J. Environ. Psychol.* 27:14–25

Bamberg S, Schmidt P. 2003. Incentives, morality, or habit? Predicting students' car use for university routes with the models of Ajzen, Schwartz and Triandis. *Environ. Behav.* 35:264–85

Bechtel RB, Churchman A, eds. 2002. *Handbook of Environmental Psychology.* New York: Wiley

Belojevic G, Evans GW, Paunovic K, Jakovljevic B. 2012. Traffic noise and executive functioning in urban primary school children: the moderating role of gender. *J. Environ. Psychol.* 32:337–41

Benfield JA, Bell PB, Troup LJ, Soderstrom N. 2010. Does anthropogenic noise in national parks impair memory? *Environ. Behav.* 42:693–706

Berman MG, Jonides J, Kaplan S. 2008. The cognitive benefits of interacting with nature. *Psychol. Sci.* 19:1207–12

Biel A, Eek D, Gärling T, Gustafsson M, eds. 2008. *New Issues and Paradigms in Research on Social Dilemmas.* New York: Springer

Biel A, Nilsson A. 2005. Religious values and environmental concern: harmony and detachment. *Soc. Sci. Q.* 86:178–91

Bolderdijk JW, Steg L, Geller ES, Lehman PK, Postmes T. 2013. Comparing the effectiveness of monetary versus moral motives in environmental campaigning. *Nat. Clim. Change* 3:413–16

Borst HC, Miedema HME, de Vries SI, Graham JMA, van Dongen JEF. 2008. Relationships between street characteristics and perceived attractiveness for walking reported by elderly people. *J. Environ. Psychol.* 28:353–61

Brown BB, Altman I, Werner CM. 2012. Place attachment. In *The International Encyclopedia of Housing and Home,* ed. M Pareja-Eastaway, pp. 183–88. Oxford, UK: Elsevier

Brown BB, Perkins DD, Brown G. 2003. Place attachment in a revitalizing neighborhood: individual and block levels of analysis. *J. Environ. Psychol.* 23:259–71

Brown BB, Werner CM, Amburgey JW, Szalay C. 2007. Walkable route perceptions and physical features: converging evidence for en route walking experiences. *Environ. Behav.* 39:34–61

Brown G, Gifford R. 2001. Architects predict lay evaluations of large contemporary buildings: whose conceptual properties? *J. Environ. Psychol.* 21:93–99

Caia G, Ventimiglia F, Maass, A. 2010. Container vs. dacha: the psychological effects of temporary housing characteristics on earthquake survivors. *J. Environ. Psychol.* 30:60–66

Campbell DT. 1963. Social attitudes and other acquired behavioral dispositions. In *Psychology: A Study of a Science,* Vol. 6, ed. S Koch, pp. 94–172. New York: McGraw-Hill

Carrico AR, Riemer M. 2011. Motivating energy conservation in the workplace: an evaluation of the use of group-level feedback and peer education. *J. Environ. Psychol.* 31:1–13

Carrus G, Passafaro P, Bonnes M. 2008. Emotions, habits and rational choices in ecological behaviours: the case of recycling and use of public transportation. *J. Environ. Psychol.* 28:51–62

Catlin JR, Wang Y. 2013. Recycling gone bad: when the option to recycle increases resource consumption. *J. Consum. Psychol.* 23:122–27

Chen M-F, Tung P-J. 2010. The moderating effect of perceived lack of facilities on consumers' recycling intentions. *Environ. Behav.* 42:824–44

Chen X, Peterson MN, Hull V, Lu C, Lee GD, et al. 2011. Effects of attitudinal and sociodemographic factors on pro-environmental behaviour in urban China. *Environ. Conserv.* 38:5–52

Cheng JCH, Monroe MC. 2012. Connection to nature: children's affective attitude toward nature. *Environ. Behav.* 44:31–49

Churchman A. 2012. Public participation around the world: introduction to the special theme issue. *J. Archit. Plan. Res.* 29:1–4

Clayton S. 2003. Environmental identity: conceptual and operational definition. In *Identity and the Natural Environment: The Psychological Significance of Nature*, ed. S Clayton, S Opotow, pp. 45–65. Cambridge, MA: MIT Press

Clayton S, ed. 2012. *The Oxford Handbook of Environmental and Conservation Psychology*. New York: Oxford Univ. Press

Coluccia E, Iosue G, Brandimonte MA. 2007. The relationship between map drawing and spatial orientation abilities: a study of gender differences. *J. Environ. Psychol.* 27:135–44

Corral-Verdugo V, Bonnes M, Tapia-Fonllem C, Fraijo-Sing B, Frías-Armenta M, Carrus G. 2009. Correlates of pro-sustainability orientation: the affinity towards diversity. *J. Environ. Psychol.* 29:34–43

Corral-Verdugo V, Carrus G, Bonnes M, Moser G, Sinha JBP. 2008. Environmental beliefs and endorsement of sustainable development principles in water conservation: towards a New Human Interdependence Paradigm Scale. *Environ. Behav.* 40:703–25

Corral-Verdugo V, Frías-Armenta M. 2006. Personal normative beliefs, antisocial behavior, and residential water conservation. *Environ. Behav.* 38:406–21

Corral-Verdugo V, Pinheiro JQ. 2006. Sustainability, future orientation and water conservation. *Rev. Eur. Psychol. Appl.* 56:191–98

Craik KH. 1973. Environmental psychology. *Annu. Rev. Psychol.* 24:403–22

Danielsson CB, Bodin L. 2008. Office type in relation to health, well-being, and job satisfaction among employees. *Environ. Behav.* 40:636–68

Davis JL, Green JD, Reed A. 2009. Interdependence with the environment: commitment, interconnectedness, and environmental behavior. *J. Environ. Psychol.* 29:173–80

de Groot JIM, Steg L. 2007. Value orientations and environmental beliefs in five countries. *J. Cross-Cult. Psychol.* 38:318–32

de Groot JIM, Steg L. 2010. Relationship between value orientations, self-determined motivational types and pro-environmental behavioural intentions. *J. Environ. Psychol.* 30:368–78

Devine-Wright P, Howes Y. 2010. Disruption to place attachment and the protection of restorative environments: a wind energy case study. *J. Environ. Psychol.* 30:271–80

Devlin AS, Donovan S, Nicolov A, Nold O, Packard A, Zandan G. 2009. "Impressive?" Credentials, family photographs, and the perception of therapist qualities. *J. Environ. Psychol.* 29:503–12

Dietz T, Kalof L, Stern PC. 2002. Gender, values, and environmentalism. *Soc. Sci. Q.* 83:353–64

Dono J, Webb J, Richardson B. 2010. The relationship between environmental activism, pro-environmental behavior and social identity. *J. Environ. Psychol.* 30:178–86

Douglas D, Gifford R. 2001. Evaluation of the physical classroom by students and professors: a lens model approach. *Educ. Res.* 43:295–309

Droseltis O, Vignoles VL. 2010. Towards an integrative model of place identification: dimensionality and predictors of intrapersonal-level place preferences. *J. Environ. Psychol.* 30:23–34

Dunlap RE, Van Liere KD, Mertig AG, Jones ER. 2000. Measuring endorsement of the new ecological paradigm: a revised NEP scale. *J. Soc. Issues* 56:425–42

Dutcher DD, Finley JC, Luloff AE. 2007. Connectivity with nature as a measure of environmental values. *Environ. Behav.* 39:474–93

Engqvist Jonsson A-K, Nilsson A. 2013. Exploring the relationship between values and pro-environmental behavior: the influence of locus of control. *Environ. Values.* In press

Evans GW, Saegert S. 2000. Residential crowding in the context of inner city poverty. In *Theoretical Perspectives in Environment-Behavior Research: Underlying Assumptions, Research Problems, and Relationships*, ed. S Wapner, J Demick, H Minamik, T Yamamoto, pp. 247–68. New York: Plenum

Evans GW, Wells NM, Chan HE, Saltzman H. 2000. Housing quality and mental health. *J. Consult. Clin. Psychol.* 68:526–30

Evans GW, Wener RE. 2007. Crowding and personal space invasion on the train: Please don't make me sit in the middle. *J. Environ. Psychol.* 27:90–94

Evans GW, Yoo MJ, Sipple J. 2010. The ecological context of student achievement: School building quality effects are exacerbated by high levels of student mobility. *J. Environ. Psychol.* 30:239–44

Evans L, Maio GR, Corner A, Hodgetts CJ, Ahmed S, Hahn U. 2013. Self-interest and pro-environmental behavior. *Nat. Clim. Change* 3:122–25

Eves FF, Olander EK, Nicoll G, Puig-Ribera A, Griffin C. 2009. Increasing stair climbing in a train station: the effects of contextual variables and visibility. *J. Environ. Psychol.* 29:300–3

Fawcett W, Ellingham I, Platt S. 2008. Reconciling the architectural preferences of architects and the public: the ordered preference model. *Environ. Behav.* 40:599–618

Feinberg M, Willer R. 2013. The moral roots of environmental attitudes. *Psychol. Sci.* 24:56–62

Felsten G. 2009. Where to take a study break on the college campus: an attention restoration theory prospective. *J. Environ. Psychol.* 29:160–67

Ferguson MA, Branscombe NR. 2010. Collective guilt mediates the effect of beliefs about global warming on willingness to engage in mitigation behavior. *J. Environ. Psychol.* 30:135–42

Fielding KS, Head BW. 2012. Determinants of young Australians' environmental actions: the role of responsibility attributions, locus of control, knowledge and attitudes. *Environ. Educ. Res.* 18:171–86

Fielding KS, McDonald R, Louis WR. 2008. Theory of planned behaviour, identity and intentions to engage in environmental activism. *J. Environ. Psychol.* 28:318–26

Fischhoff B, Furby L. 1983. Psychological dimensions of climatic change. In *Social Science Research and Climate Change*, ed. RS Chen, E Boulding, SH Schneider, pp. 183–203. Dordrecht, Neth.: Reidel

Fornara F, Carrus G, Passafaro P, Bonnes M. 2011. Distinguishing the sources of normative influence on pro-environmental behaviours: the role of local norms in household waste recycling. *Group Proc. Intergroup Relat.* 5:623–35

Fraj E, Martinez E. 2006. Influence of personality on ecological consumer behaviour. *J. Consum. Behav.* 5:167–81

Frankenstein J, Mohler BJ, Bülthoff HH, Meilinger T. 2012. Is the map in our head pointed north? *Psychol. Sci.* 23:120–25

Frantz CM, Mayer FS, Norton C, Rock M. 2005. There is no "I" in nature: the influence of self-awareness on connectedness to nature. *J. Environ. Psychol.* 25:427–36

Franzen A. 2003. Environmental attitudes in international comparison: an analysis of the ISSP surveys 1993 and 2000. *Soc. Sci. Q.* 84:297–308

Fujii S. 2006. Environmental concern, attitude toward frugality, and ease of behavior as determinants of pro-environmental behavior intentions. *J. Environ. Psychol.* 26:262–68

García Mira R, Real JE, Uzzell D, San Juan C, Pol E. 2006. Coping with a threat to quality of life: the case of the "Prestige" disaster. *Eur. Rev. Appl. Psychol.* 56:53–60

Gardner GT, Stern PC. 2002. *Environmental Problems and Human Behavior.* Boston, MA: Pearson. 2nd ed.

Gardner GT, Stern PC. 2008. The short list: the most effective actions U.S. households can take to curb climate change. *Environment* 50:12–25

Gärling T, Biel A, Gustafsson M. 2002. The new environmental psychology: the human interdependence paradigm. See Bechtel & Churchman 2002, pp. 85–94

Gärling T, Loukopoulos P. 2007. Effectiveness, public acceptance, and political feasibility of coercive measures for reducing car traffic. See Gärling & Steg 2007, pp. 313–24

Gärling T, Schuitema G. 2007. Travel demand management targeting reduced private car use: effectiveness, public acceptability and political feasibility. *J. Soc. Issues* 63:139–53

Gärling T, Steg L, eds. 2007. *Threats to the Quality of Urban Life from Car Traffic: Problems, Causes, and Solutions.* Amsterdam: Elsevier

Gatersleben B, Steg L, Vlek C. 2002. Measurement and determinants of environmentally significant consumer behavior. *Environ. Behav.* 34:335–62

Geller ES. 2002. The challenge of increasing proenvironmental behavior. See Bechtel & Churchman 2002, pp. 525–40

Gifford R. 2002. Making a difference: some ways that environmental psychology has made a difference. See Bechtel & Churchman 2002, pp. 323–34

Gifford R. 2006. A general model of social dilemmas. *Int. J. Ecol. Econ. Stat.* 5:23–40

Gifford R. 2007a. *Environmental Psychology: Principles and Practice.* Colville, WA: Optimal Books. 4th ed.

Gifford R. 2007b. Environmental psychology and sustainable development: expansion, maturation, and challenges. *J. Soc. Issues* 63:199–212

Gifford R. 2007c. The consequences of living in high-rise buildings. *Arch. Sci. Rev.* 50:2–17

Gifford R. 2008a. Psychology's essential role in alleviating the impacts of climate change. *Can. Psychol.* 49:273–80

Gifford R. 2008b. Toward a comprehensive model of social dilemmas. In *New Issues and Paradigms in Research on Social Dilemmas*, ed. A Biel, D Eek, T Gärling, M Gustafsson, pp. 265–79. New York: Springer

Gifford R. 2011. The dragons of inaction: psychological barriers that limit climate change mitigation. *Am. Psychol.* 66:290–302

Gifford R, Comeau L. 2011. Message framing influences perceived climate change competence, engagement, and behavioral intentions. *Global Environ. Change* 21:1301–7

Gifford J, Gifford R. 2000. FISH 3: A microworld for studying social dilemmas and resource management. *Behav. Res. Methods Instrum. Comput.* 32:417–22

Gifford R, Hine DW, Muller-Clemm W, Reynolds DJ, Shaw KT. 2000. Decoding modern architecture: understanding the aesthetic differences of architects and laypersons. *Environ. Behav.* 32:163–87

Gifford R, Hine DW, Muller-Clemm W, Shaw KT. 2002. Why architects and laypersons judge buildings differently: cognitive and physical bases. *J. Archit. Plan. Res.* 19:131–48

Gifford R, Kormos C, McIntyre A. 2011a. Behavioral dimensions of climate change: drivers, responses, barriers, and interventions. *WIREs Clim. Change.* doi:10.1002/wcc.143

Gifford R, Lacombe C. 2006. Housing quality and children's socioemotional health. *J. Hous. Built Environ.* 21:177–89

Gifford R, Scannell L, Kormos C, Smolova L, Biel A, et al. 2009. Temporal pessimism and spatial optimism in environmental assessments: an 18-nation study. *J. Environ. Psychol.* 29:1–12

Gifford R, Steg L. 2007. The impact of automobile traffic on quality of life. See Gärling & Steg 2007, pp. 33–51

Gifford R, Steg L, Reser JP. 2011b. Environmental psychology. In *IAAP Handbook of Applied Psychology*, ed. P Martin, F Cheung, M Kyrios, L Littlefield, M Knowles, B Overmier, JP Prieto, pp. 440–70. Chichester, UK: Wiley Blackwell

Giuliani MV. 2003. Theory of attachment and place attachment. In *Psychological Theories for Environmental Issues*, ed. M Bonnes, T Lee, M Bonaiuto, pp. 137–70. Aldershot, UK: Ashgate

Giuliani MV, Scopelliti M. 2009. Empirical research in environmental psychology: past, present, and future. *J. Environ. Psychol.* 29:375–86

Graumann CF. 2002. The phenomenological approach to people-environment studies. See Bechtel & Churchman 2002, pp. 95–113

Grønhøj A, Thøgersen J. 2009. Like father, like son? Intergenerational transmission of values, attitudes, and behaviours in the environmental domain. *J. Environ. Behav.* 29:414–21

Han K-T. 2007. Responses to six major terrestrial biomes in terms of scenic beauty, preference, and restorativeness. *Environ. Behav.* 39:529–56

Hansla A, Gamble A, Juliusson A, Gärling T. 2008. The relationships between awareness of consequences, environmental concern, and value orientations. *J. Environ. Psychol.* 28:1–9

Hartig T, Staats H. 2003. Guest editors' introduction: restorative environments. *J. Environ. Psychol.* 23:103–7

Hartig T, Staats H. 2006. The need for psychological restoration as a determinant of environmental preferences. *J. Environ. Psychol.* 26:215–26

Hay R. 1998. Sense of place in developmental context. *J. Environ. Psychol.* 18:5–29

Heath Y, Gifford R. 2002. Extending the theory of planned behavior: predicting the use of public transportation. *J. Appl. Soc. Psychol.* 32:2154–85

Heath Y, Gifford R. 2006. Free-market ideology and environmental degradation. *Environ. Behav.* 38:48–71

Heft H. 1998. Essay review: the elusive environment in environmental psychology. *Br. J. Psychol.* 89: 519–23

Heft H. 2001. *Ecological Psychology in Context: James Gibson, Roger Barker, and the Legacy of William James's Radical Empiricism.* Mahwah, NJ: Erlbaum

Heft H. 2012. The foundations of ecological psychology. In *The Oxford Handbook of Environmental and Conservation Psychology*, ed. S Clayton, pp. 1–40. New York: Oxford

Heft H. 2013. Environment, cognition, and culture: reconsidering the cognitive map. *J. Environ. Psychol.* 33:14–25

Hernandez D, Hidalgo MC, Salazar-Laplace E, Hess S. 2007. Place attachment and place identity in natives and non-natives. *J. Environ. Psychol.* 27:310–19

Herring H, Sorrell S, eds. 2008. *Energy Efficiency and Sustainable Consumption: Dealing with the Rebound Effect.* Basingstoke, UK: Palgrave Macmillan

Herzog TR, Hayes LJ, Applin RC, Weatherly AM. 2011. Incompatibility and mental fatigue. *Environ. Behav.* 43:827–47

Herzog TR, Ouellette P, Rolens JR, Koenigs AM. 2010. Houses of worship as restorative environments. *Environ. Behav.* 42:395–419

Herzog TR, Rector AE. 2009. Perceived danger and judged likelihood of restoration. *Environ. Behav.* 41:387–401

Hidalgo MC, Hernández B. 2001. Place attachment: conceptual and empirical questions. *J. Environ. Psychol.* 21:273–81

Hidayetoglu ML, Yildirim K, Akalin A. 2012. The effects of color and light on indoor wayfinding and the evaluation of the perceived environment. *J. Environ. Psychol.* 32:50–58

Hinds J, Sparks P. 2008. Engaging with the natural environment: the role of affective connection and identity. *J. Environ. Psychol.* 28:109–20

Hine DW, Bhullar N, Marks ADG, Kelly P, Scott JG. 2011. Comparing the effectiveness of education and technology in reducing wood smoke pollution: a field experiment. *J. Environ. Psychol.* 31:282–88

Hine DW, Gifford R, Heath Y, Cooksey R, Quain P. 2009. A cue utilization approach for investigating harvest decisions in commons dilemmas. *J. Appl. Soc. Psychol.* 39:564–88

Hine DW, Marks ADG, Nachreiner M, Gifford R, Heath Y. 2007. Keeping the home fires burning: the affect heuristic and wood smoke pollution. *Environ. Psychol.* 27:26–32

Hines JM, Hungerford HR, Tomera AN. 1986–1987. Analysis and synthesis of research on responsible environmental behavior: a meta-analysis. *J. Environ. Educ.* 18:1–8

Hirsh JB. 2010. Personality and environmental concern. *J. Environ. Psychol.* 30:245–48

Hölscher C, Meilinger T, Vrachliotis G, Brösamle M, Knauff M. 2006. Up the down staircase: wayfinding strategies in multi-level buildings. *J. Environ. Psychol.* 26:284–99

Howes Y, Gifford R. 2009. Stable or dynamic value importance?: The interaction between value endorsement level and situational differences on decision-making in environmental issues. *Environ. Behav.* 41:549–82

Hua Y, Loftness V, Heerwagen JH, Powell KM. 2011. Relationship between workplace spatial settings and occupant-perceived support for collaboration. *Environ. Behav.* 43:807–26

Hur M, Morrow-Jones H. 2008. Factors that influence residents' satisfaction with neighborhoods. *Environ. Behav.* 40:619–35

Intergov. Panel Climate Change. 2007. Intergovernmental Panel on Climate Change (IPCC) Summary for Policymakers. 2007. *Climate Change 2007: The Physical Science Basis. Contribution of Working Group I to the Fourth Assessment Report of the Intergovernmental Panel on Climate Change.* Cambridge, UK/New York: Cambridge Univ. Press

Ishikawa T, Fujiwara H, Imai O, Okabe A. 2008. Wayfinding with a GPS-based mobile navigation system: a comparison with maps and direct experience. *J. Environ. Psychol.* 28:74–82

Jahncke H, Hygge S, Halin N, Green AM, Dimberg K. 2011. Open-plan office noise: cognitive performance and restoration. *J. Environ. Psychol.* 31:373–82

Jansen-Osmann P, Berendt B. 2002. Investigating distance knowledge using virtual environments. *Environ. Behav.* 34:178–93

Jansen-Osmann P, Wiedenbauer G. 2004. The representation of landmarks and routes in children and adults: a study in a virtual environment. *J. Environ. Psychol.* 24:347–57

Joireman JA, Van Lange PAM, Van Vugt M. 2004. Who cares about the environmental impact of cars? *Environ. Behav.* 36:187–206

Jorgensen BS, Stedman RC. 2001. Sense of place as an attitude: lakeshore owners attitudes toward their properties. *J. Environ. Psychol.* 21:233–48

Joye Y. 2007. Architectural lessons from environmental psychology: the case of biophilic architecture. *Rev. Gen. Psychol.* 11:305–28

Kaiser FG, Byrka K. 2011. Environmentalism as a trait: gauging people's prosocial personality in terms of environmental engagement. *Int. J. Psychol.* 46:71–79

Kaiser FG, Byrka K, Hartig T. 2010. Reviving Campbell's paradigm for attitude research. *Personal. Soc. Psychol. Rev.* 14:351–67

Kaiser FG, Gutscher H. 2003. The proposition of a general version of the theory of planned behavior: predicting ecological behavior. *J. Appl. Soc. Psychol.* 33:586–603

Kaiser FG, Oerke B, Bogner FX. 2007. Behavior-based environmental attitude: development of an instrument for adolescents. *J. Environ. Psychol.* 27:242–51

Kaplan S. 1995. The restorative benefits of nature: towards an integrative framework. *J. Environ. Psychol.* 15:169–82

Kaplan S, Kaplan R. 2009. Creating a larger role for environmental psychology: the reasonable person model as an integrative framework. *J. Environ. Psychol.* 29:329–39

Karpiak CP, Baril GL. 2008. Moral reasoning and concern for the environment. *J. Environ. Psychol.* 28:203–8

Kaya N, Burgess B. 2007. Territoriality: seat preferences in different types of classroom arrangements. *Environ. Behav.* 36:859–76

Kazdin AE. 2009. Psychological science's contributions to a sustainable environment: extending our reach to a grand challenge of society. *Am. Psychol.* 64:339–56

Keizer K, Lindenberg S, Steg L. 2008. The spreading of disorder. *Science* 322:1681–85

Kim J, Kaplan R. 2004. Physical and psychological factors in sense of community: new urbanist Kentlands and nearby Orchard Village. *Environ. Behav.* 36:313–40

Kjellgren A, Buhrkall H. 2010. A comparison of the restorative effect of a natural environment with that of a simulated natural environment. *J. Environ. Psychol.* 30:464–72

Knez I. 2005. Attachment and identity as related to a place and its perceived climate. *J. Environ. Psychol.* 25:207–18

Knussen C, Yule F. 2008. "I'm not in the habit of recycling": the role of habitual behavior in the disposal of household waste. *Environ. Behav.* 40:683–702

Kolmuss A, Agyeman J. 2002. Mind the gap: Why do people act environmentally and what are the barriers to pro-environmental behavior? *Environ. Educ. Res.* 8:239–60

Kopelman S, Weber JM, Messick DM. 2002. Factors influencing cooperation in commons dilemmas: a review of experimental psychological research. In *The Drama of the Commons*, ed. E Ostrom, T Dietz, N Dolšak, PC Stern, S Stonich, EU Weber, pp. 113–56. Washington, DC: Natl. Acad. Press

Korpela K, Kytta M, Hartig T. 2002. Restorative experience, self-regulation, and children's place preferences. *J. Environ. Psychol.* 22:387–98

Kuo FE, Sullivan WC. 2001. Environment and crime in the inner city: Does vegetation reduce crime? *Environ. Behav.* 33:343–67

Kweon BS, Ulrich RS, Walker VD, Tassinary LG. 2008. Anger and stress: the role of landscape posters in an office setting. *Environ. Behav.* 40:355–81

Kyle GT, Graefe A, Manning R, Bacon J. 2004a. Effect of activity involvement and place attachment on recreationists' perceptions of setting density. *J. Leisure Res.* 36:209–31

Kyle GT, Mowen AJ, Tarrant M. 2004b. Linking place preferences with place meaning: an examination of the relationship between place motivation and place attachment. *J. Environ. Psychol.* 24:439–54

Lansdale M, Parkin P, Austin S, Baguley T. 2011. Designing for interaction in research environments: a case study. *J. Environ. Psychol.* 31:407–20

Lederbogen F, Kirsch P, Haddad L, Streit F, Tost H, et al. 2011. City living and urban upbringing affect neural social stress processing in humans. *Nature* 474:498–501

Lehman PK, Geller ES. 2004. Behavior analysis and environmental protection: accomplishments and potential for more. *Behav. Soc. Issues* 13:13–32

Levav J, Zhu R. 2009. Seeking freedom through variety. *J. Consum. Res.* 36:600–10

Levi D, Kocher S. 1999. Virtual nature: the future effects of information technology on our relationship to nature. *Environ. Behav.* 31:203–26

Lewicka M. 2005. Ways to make people active: the role of place attachment, cultural capital, and neighborhood ties. *J. Environ. Psychol.* 25:381–95

Lewicka M. 2010. What makes neighborhood different from home and city? Effects of place scale on place attachment. *J. Environ. Psychol.* 30:35–51

Lewicka M. 2011. Place attachment: How far have we come in the last 40 years? *J. Environ. Psychol.* 31:207–30

Lichtenfeld S, Elliot AJ, Maier MA, Pekrun R. 2012. Fertile green: Green facilitates creative performance. *Personal. Soc. Psychol.* 38:784–97

Lima ML, Castro P. 2005. Cultural theory meets the community: worldviews and local issues. *J. Environ. Psychol.* 25:23–35

Lindenberg S, Steg L. 2007. Normative, gain and hedonic goal frames guiding environmental behavior. *J. Soc. Issues* 63:117–37

Ljung R, Sörqvist P, Hygge S. 2009. Effects of road traffic noise and irrelevant speech on children's reading and mathematical performance. *Noise Health* 11:1 94–98

Lloyd DM, Coates A, Knopp J, Oram S, Rowbotham S. 2009. Don't stand so close to me: the effect of auditory input on interpersonal space. *Perception* 38:617–20

Lokhorst AM, Werner C, Staats H, van Dijk E, Gale JL. 2013. Commitment and behavior change: a meta-analysis and critical review of commitment-making strategies in environmental research. *Environ. Behav.* 45:3–34

Lorenzoni I, Nicholson-Cole S, Whitmarsh L. 2007. Barriers perceived to engaging with climate change among the UK public and their policy implications. *Glob. Environ. Change* 17:445–59

Maeda H, Hirose Y. 2009. Expectation of empowerment as a determinant of citizen participation in waste management planning. *Jap. Psychol. Res.* 51:24–34

Manzo LC. 2003. Beyond house and haven: toward a revisioning of emotional relationships with places. *J. Environ. Psychol.* 23:47–61

Manzo LC. 2005. For better or worse: exploring multiple dimensions of place meaning. *J. Environ. Psychol.* 25:67–86

Manzo LC, Perkins DD. 2006. Neighborhoods as common ground: the importance of place attachment to community participation and development. *J. Plan. Lit.* 20:335–50

Marans RW, Stimson R, eds. 2011. *Investigating Quality of Urban Life: Theory, Methods, and Empirical Research.* Dordrecht, Neth.: Springer

Markowitz EM, Goldberg LR, Ashton MC, Lee K. 2012. Profiling the "pro-environmental individual": a personality perspective. *J. Personal.* 80:81–111

Marques S, Lima ML. 2011. Living in grey areas: industrial activity and psychological health. *J. Environ. Psychol.* 31:314–22

Marzbali MH, Abdullah A, Razak NA, Tilaki MJM. 2012. The influence of crime prevention through environmental design on victimisation and fear of crime. *J. Environ. Psychol.* 32:79–88

Matthies E, Selge S, Klöckner CA. 2012. The role of parental behaviour for the development of behaviour specific environmental norms—the example of recycling and re-use behaviour. *J. Environ. Psychol.* 32:277–84

Mayer FS, Frantz CM. 2004. The connectedness to nature scale: a measure of individuals' feeling in community with nature. *J. Environ. Psychol.* 24:503–15

Mazumdar S, Mazumdar S. 2004. Religion and place attachment: a study of sacred places. *J. Environ. Psychol.* 24:385–97

McCoy JM, Evans GW. 2002. The potential role of the physical environment in fostering creativity. *Creat. Res. J.* 14:409–26

McCright AM, Dunlap RE. 2012. Bringing ideology in: the conservative white male effect on worry about environmental problems in the USA. *J. Risk Res.* 16:211–26

McCunn LJ, Gifford R. 2012. Do green offices affect employee engagement and environmental motivation? *Archit. Sci. Rev.* 55:128–34

McDonald RI, Fielding KS, Louis WR. 2013. Energizing and de-motivating effects of norm conflict. *Personal. Soc. Psychol.* 39:57–72

McKenzie-Mohr D. 2000. Fostering sustainable behaviour through community-based social marketing. *Am. Psychol.* 55:531–37

Milfont TL, Duckitt J. 2010. The Environmental Attitudes Inventory: a valid and reliable measure to assess the structure of environmental attitudes. *J. Environ. Psychol.* 30:80–94

Milfont TL, Gouveia VV. 2006. Time perspective and values: an exploratory study of their relations to environmental attitudes. *J. Environ. Psychol.* 26:72–82

Milfont TL, Sibley CG. 2012. The big five personality traits and environmental engagement: associations at the individual and societal level. *J. Environ. Psychol.* 32:187–95

Mishra S, Mazumdar S, Suar D. 2010. Place attachment and flood preparedness. *J. Environ. Psychol.* 20:187–97

Miwa Y, Hanyu K. 2006. The effects of interior design on communication and impressions of a counselor in a counseling room. *Environ. Behav.* 38:484–502

Mobley C, Vagias WM, DeWard SL. 2010. Exploring additional determinants of environmental behavior: the role of environmental literature and environmental attitudes. *Environ. Behav.* 42:420–47

Morgan P. 2010. Towards a developmental theory of place attachment. *J. Environ. Psychol.* 30:11–22

Moser SC. 2010. Communicating climate change: history, challenges, process and future directions. *WIRES Clim. Change* 1:31–53

Mostafa MM. 2012. Does globalisation affect consumers' pro-environmental intentions? A multilevel analysis across 25 countries. *Int. J. Sustain. Dev. World Ecol.* 19:1–9

Nasar JL, Stamps AE, Hanyu K. 2005. Form and function in public buildings. *J. Environ. Psychol.* 25:159–65

Ng CF. 2003. Satisfying shoppers' psychological needs: from public market to cyber-mall. *J. Environ. Psychol.* 23:439–55

Nilsson A, von Borgstede C, Biel A. 2004. Willingness to accept climate change strategies: the effect of values and norms. *J. Environ. Psychol.* 24:267–77

Nisbet EK, Zelenski JM. 2011. Underestimating nearby nature: affective forecasting errors obscure the happy path to sustainability. *Psychol. Sci.* 22:1101–6

Nisbet EK, Zelenski JM, Murphy SA. 2009. The nature relatedness scale: linking individuals' connection with nature to environmental concern and behavior. *Environ. Behav.* 41:715–40

Nolan JM, Schultz PW, Cialdini RB, Goldstein NJ, Griskevicius V. 2008. Normative social influence is underdetected. *Personal. Soc. Psychol. Bull.* 34:913–23

Nordlund AM, Garvill J. 2002. Value structures behind proenvironmental behavior. *Environ. Behav.* 34:740–56

Nordlund AM, Garvill J. 2003. Effects of values, problem awareness and personal norm on willingness to reduce personal car use. *J. Environ. Psychol.* 23:339–47

Oishi S. 2010. The psychology of residential mobility: implications for the self, social relationships, and well-being. *Perspect. Psychol. Sci.* 5:5–21

Ojala M. 2008. Recycling and ambivalence: quantitative and qualitative analyses of household recycling among young adults. *Environ. Behav.* 40:777–97

Oreg S, Katz-Gerro T. 2006. Predicting proenvironmental behavior cross-nationally. *Environ. Behav.* 38:462–83

Ornstein R, Ehrlich P. 2000. *New World New Mind.* Malor Books

Osbaldiston R, Schott JP. 2012. Environmental sustainability and behavioral science: meta-analysis of proenvironmental behavior experiments. *Environ. Behav.* 44:257–99

Osmond H. 1957. Function as the basis of psychiatric ward design. *Ment. Hosp. (Archit. Suppl.)* 8:23–30

Passini R, Pigot H, Rainville C, Tétreault M-H. 2000. Wayfinding in a nursing home for advanced dementia of the Alzheimer's type. *Environ. Behav.* 32:684–710

Pendola R, Gen S. 2008. Does "Main Street" promote sense of community? A comparison of San Francisco neighbourhoods. *Environ. Behav.* 40:535–74

Peponis J, Bafna S, Bajaj R, Bromberg J, Congdon C, et al. 2007. Designing space to support knowledge work. *Environ. Behav.* 39:815–40

Pichert D, Katsikopoulos KV. 2008. Green defaults: information presentation and pro-environmental behaviour. *J. Environ. Psychol.* 28:63–73

Pierrette M, Marquis-Favre C, Morel J, Rioux L, Vallet M, et al. 2012. Noise annoyance from industrial and road traffic combined noises: a survey and a total annoyance model comparison. *J. Environ. Psychol.* 32:178–86

Poortinga W, Steg L, Vlek C. 2003. Myths of nature and environmental management strategies. A field study on energy reductions in traffic and transport. In *People, Places, and Sustainability*, ed. G Moser, E Pol, Y Bernard, M Bonnes, J Corraliza, pp. 280–90. Ashland, OH: Hogrefe & Huber

Raanaas RK, Evensen KH, Rich D, Sjostrom G, Patil C. 2011. Benefits of indoor plants on attention capacity in an office setting. *J. Environ. Psychol.* 31:99–105

Rabinovich A, Morton M, Birney ME. 2012. Communicating climate science: the role of perceived communicator's motives. *J. Environ. Psychol.* 32:11–18

Räthzel N, Uzzell, D. 2009. Changing relations in global environmental change. *Glob. Environ. Change* 19:326–35

Raymond CM, Brown G, Robinson GM. 2011. The influence of place attachment, and moral and normative concerns on the conservation of native vegetation: a test of two behavioural models. *J. Environ. Psychol.* 31:323–35

Reser JP, Swim JK. 2011. Adapting and coping with the threat and impacts of climate change. *Am. Psychol.* 66:277–89

Rice G. 2006. Pro-environmental behavior in Egypt: Is there a role for Islamic environmental ethics? *J. Bus. Ethics* 65:373–90

Robelia B, Murphy T. 2012. What do people know about key environmental issues? A review of environmental knowledge surveys. *Environ. Educ. Res.* 18:299–321

Ruback RB, Kohli N. 2005. Territoriality at the Magh Mela: the effects of organizational factors and intruder characteristics. *Environ. Behav.* 37:178–200

Sardianou E. 2007. Estimating energy conservation patterns of Greek households. *Energy Policy* 35:3778–91

Scannell L, Gifford R. 2010a. The relations between natural and civic place attachment and pro-environmental behavior. *J. Environ. Psychol.* 30:289–97

Scannell L, Gifford R. 2010b. Defining place attachment: a tripartite organizing framework. *J. Environ. Psychol.* 30:1–10

Scannell L. Gifford R. 2013. The role of place attachment in receptivity to local and global climate change messages. *Environ. Behav.* 45:60–85

Schmuck P, Schultz WP, eds. 2002. *Psychology of Sustainable Development.* Dordrecht, Neth.: Kluwer Acad.

Schultz PW, Gouveia VV, Cameron LD, Tankha G, Schmuck P, Franek M. 2005. Values and their relationship to environmental concern and conservation behavior. *J. Cross-Cult. Psychol.* 36:457–75

Schultz PW, Nolan JM, Cialdini RB, Goldstein NJ, Griskevicius V. 2007. The constructive, destructive, and reconstructive power of social norms. *Psychol. Sci.* 18:429–34

Schultz PW, Shriver C, Tabanico JL, Khazian AM. 2004. Implicit connections with nature. *J. Environ. Psychol.* 24:31–42

Schwartz SH. 1992. Universals in the content and structures of values: theoretical advances and empirical tests in 20 countries. In *Advances in Experimental Psychology*, Vol. 25, ed. M Zanna, pp. 1–65. Orlando, FL: Academic

Scopelliti M, Giuliani MV. 2004. Choosing restorative environments across the lifespan: a matter of place experience. *J. Environ. Psychol.* 24:423–37

Scopelliti M, Tiberio L. 2010. Homesickness in university students: the role of multiple place attachment. *Environ. Behav.* 42:335–50

Seamon D. 2012. Place, place identity, and phenomenology. In *The Role of Place Identity in the Perception, Understanding, and Design of the Built Environment*, ed. H Casakin, F Bernardo, pp. 3–21. London: Bentham

Semenza JC, March TL. 2009. An urban community-based intervention to advance social interactions. *Environ. Behav.* 41:22–42

Smit B, Wandel J. 2006. Adaptation, adaptive capacity and vulnerability. *Glob. Environ. Change* 16:282–92

Smith JR, Louis WR, Terry DJ, Greenaway KH, Clarke MR, Cheng X. 2012. Congruent or conflicted? The impact of injunctive and descriptive norms on environmental intentions. *J. Environ. Psychol.* 32:353–61

Smith-Jackson TL, Klein KW. 2009. Open-plan offices: task performance and mental workload. *J. Environ. Psychol.* 29:279–89

Smolders KCHJ, de Kort YAW, Tenner AD, Kaiser FG. 2012. Need for recovery in offices: behaviour-based assessment. *J. Environ. Psychol.* 32:126–34

Sommer R. 1969. *Personal Space: The Behavioral Basis of Design.* Englewood Cliffs, NJ: Prentice-Hall

Sommer R. 1983. *Social Design: Creating Buildings With People in Mind.* Englewood Cliffs, NJ: Prentice-Hall

Sörqvist P. 2010. Effects of aircraft noise and speech on prose memory: what role for working memory capacity? *J. Environ. Psychol.* 30:112–18

Spence A, Pidgeon N, Uzzell D. 2008. Climate change: psychology's contribution. *Psychologist* 22:108–11

Staats H, Harland P, Wilke HAM. 2004. Effecting durable change: a team approach to improve environmental behavior in the household. *Environ. Behav.* 36:341–67

Stamps AE. 2005. Enclosure and safety in urbanscapes. *Environ. Behav.* 37:102–33

Stamps AE. 2010. Effects of permeability on perceived enclosure and spaciousness. *Environ. Behav.* 42:864–86

Stamps AE. 2012. Atmospheric permeability and perceived enclosure. *Environ. Behav.* 44:427–46

Stansfeld SA, Clark C, Cameron RM, Alfred T, Head J, et al. 2009. Aircraft and road traffic noise exposure and children's mental health. *J. Environ. Psychol.* 29:203–7

Stedman RC. 2003. Is it really just a social construction? The contribution of the physical environment to sense of place. *Soc. Natural Resour.* 16:671–85

Steg L, Dreijerink L, Abrahamse W. 2005. Factors influencing the acceptability of energy policies: a test of VBN theory. *J. Environ. Psychol.* 25:415–25

Steg L, Gifford R. 2005. Sustainable transportation and quality of life. *J. Transp. Geogr.* 13:59–69

Steg L, Vlek C. 2009. Encouraging pro-environmental behaviour: an integrative review and research agenda. *J. Environ. Psychol.* 29:309–17

Stern PC. 2000. Toward a coherent theory of environmentally significant behavior. *J. Soc. Issues* 56:407–24

Stern PC. 2008. Environmentally significant behavior in the home. In *The Cambridge Handbook of Psychology and Economic Behaviour*, ed. A. Lewis, pp. 363–82. Cambridge, UK: Cambridge Univ. Press

Stern PC, Dietz T, Kalof L. 1993. Value orientations, gender, and environmental concern. *Environ. Behav.* 25:322–48

Stewart J, McManus F, Rodgers N, Weedon V, Bronzaft A. 2011. *Why Noise Matters: A Worldwide Perspective on the Problems, Policies and Solutions.* London: Routledge

Stokols D, Clitheroe C, Zmuidzinas M. 2002. Qualities of work environments that promote perceived support for creativity. *Creativ. Res. J.* 14:137–47

Stokols D, Misra S, Runnerstrom MG, Hipp JA. 2009. Psychology in an age of ecological crisis: from personal angst to collective action. *Am. Psychol.* 64:181–93

Stokols D, Montero M. 2002. Toward an environmental psychology of the Internet. See Bechtel & Churchman 2002, pp. 661–75

Sullivan WC, Kuo FE, DePooter SF. 2004. The fruit of urban nature: vital neighborhood spaces. *Environ. Behav.* 36:678–700

Sundstrom E, Bell PA, Busby PL, Asmus C. 1996. Environmental psychology 1989–1994. *Annu. Rev. Psychol.* 47:485–512

Sussman R, Gifford R. 2012. Please turn off the lights: the effectiveness of visual prompts. *Appl. Ergon.* 43:596–603

Sussman R, Greeno M, Gifford R, Scannell L. 2013. The effectiveness of models and prompts on waste diversion: a field experiment on composting by cafeteria patrons. *J. Appl. Soc. Psychol.* 43:24–34

Swami V, Chamorro-Premuzic T, Snelgar R, Furnham A. 2011. Personality, individual differences, and demographic antecedents of self-reported household waste management behaviours. *J. Environ. Psychol.* 31:21–26

Swim JK, Stern PC, Doherty TJ, Clayton S, Reser JP, et al. 2011. Psychology's contributions to understanding and addressing global climate change. *Am. Psychol.* 66:241–50

Tabernero C, Hernández B. 2011. Self-efficacy and intrinsic motivation guiding environmental behavior. *Environ. Behav.* 43:658–75

Tang Z, Chen X, Luo J. 2011. Determining socio-psychological drivers for rural household recycling behavior in developing countries. *Environ. Behav.* 43:848–77

Taylor AF, Kuo F, Sullivan WC. 2001. Coping with ADD: the surprising connection to green play settings. *Environ. Behav.* 33:54–77

Thøgersen J. 2005. How may consumer policy empower consumers for sustainable lifestyles? *J. Consum. Policy* 28:143–78

Thøgersen J. 2007. Social marketing of alternative transportation modes. See Gärling & Steg 2007, pp. 367–81

Thøgersen J, Grønhøj A. 2010. Electricity saving in households—a social cognitive approach. *Energy Policy* 38:7732–43

Thøgersen J, Ölander F. 2003. Spillover of environment-friendly consumer behaviour. *J. Environ. Psychol.* 23:225–36

Thompson CW, Aspinall P, Montarzino A. 2008. The childhood factor: adult visits to green places and the significance of childhood experience. *Environ. Behav.* 40:111–43

Ulrich RS. 1984. View through a window may influence recovery from surgery. *Science* 224:420–21

Uzzell D, Pol E, Badenas D. 2002. Place identification, social cohesion, and environmental sustainability. *Environ. Behav.* 34:26–53

Uzzell D, Räthzel N. 2009. Transforming environmental psychology. *J. Environ. Psychol.* 29:340–50

Uzzell DL. 2000. The psycho-spatial dimensions of global environmental problems. *J. Environ. Psychol.* 20:307–18

van den Berg AE, ter Heijne M. 2005. Fear versus fascination: an exploration of emotional responses to natural threats. *J. Environ. Psychol.* 25:261–72

Vaske JJ, Kobrin KC. 2001. Place attachment and environmentally responsible behavior. *J. Environ. Educ.* 32:16–21

Veitch JA, Newsham GR, Mancini S, Arsenault CD. 2010. Lighting and office renovation effects on employee and organizational well-being. *Rep. IRC-RR-306*. Ottawa, Can.: Natl. Res. Counc. Inst. Res. Constr.

Veitch JA, Stokkermans MGM, Newsham GR. 2011. Linking lighting appraisals to work behaviors. *Environ. Behav.* 45:198–214

Venables D, Pidgeon NF, Parkhill KA, Henwood KL, Simmons P. 2012. Living with nuclear power: sense of place, proximity, and risk perceptions in local host communities. *J. Environ. Psychol.* 32:371–83

Vlek C. 2000. Essential psychology for environmental policy making. *Int. J. Psychol.* 35:153–67

Vorkinn M, Riese H. 2001. Environmental concern in a local context: the significance of place attachment. *Environ. Behav.* 33:249–63

Vranic A. 2003. Personal space in physically abused children. *Environ. Behav.* 35:550–65

Wang N, Boubekri M. 2010. Investigation of declared seating preference and measured cognitive performance in a sunlit room. *J. Environ. Psychol.* 30:226–38

Wells JC, Baldwin ED. 2012. Historic preservation, significance, and age value: a comparative phenomenology of historic Charleston and the nearby new-urbanist community of I'On. *J. Environ. Psychol.* 32:384–400

Wells NM, Harris JD. 2007. Housing quality, psychological distress, and the mediating role of social withdrawal: a longitudinal study of low-income women. *J. Environ. Psychol.* 27:69–78

Wells NM, Lekies KS. 2006. Nature and the life course: pathways from childhood nature experiences to adult environmentalism. *Child. Youth Environ.* 16:1–24

Werner CM, Cook S, Colby J, Lim HJ. 2012. "Lights out" in university classrooms: Brief group discussion can change behaviour. *J. Environ. Psychol.* 32:418–26

White M, Smith A, Humphryes K, Pahl S, Snelling D, Depledge M. 2010. Blue space: the importance of water for preference, affect, and restorativeness ratings of natural and built scenes. *J. Environ. Psychol.* 30:482–93

Whitmarsh L. 2009. Behavioural responses to climate change: asymmetry of intentions and impacts. *J. Environ. Psychol.* 29:13–23

Whitmarsh L, O'Neill S. 2010. Green identity, green living? The role of pro-environmental self-identity in determining consistency across diverse pro-environmental behaviours. *J. Environ. Psychol.* 30:305–14

Williams K, Harvey D. 2001. Transcendent experience in forest environments. *J. Environ. Psychol.* 21:249–60

Xiao C, Hong D. 2010. Gender differences in environmental behaviors in China. *Popul. Environ.* 32:88–104

Yildirim K, Akalin-Baskaya A, Celebi M. 2007. The effects of window proximity, partition height, and gender on perceptions of open-plan offices. *J. Environ. Psychol.* 27:154–65

Socioecological Psychology

Shigehiro Oishi

Department of Psychology, University of Virginia, Charlottesville, Virginia 22904;
email: soishi@virginia.edu

Annu. Rev. Psychol. 2014. 65:581–609

First published online as a Review in Advance on
August 26, 2013

The *Annual Review of Psychology* is online at
http://psych.annualreviews.org

This article's doi:
10.1146/annurev-psych-030413-152156

Keywords

social ecology, culture, physical environments, interpersonal environments,
economic environments, political environments

Abstract

Socioecological psychology investigates humans' cognitive, emotional, and
behavioral adaption to physical, interpersonal, economic, and political environments. This article summarizes three types of socioecological psychology
research: (*a*) association studies that link an aspect of social ecology (e.g.,
population density) with psychology (e.g., prosocial behavior), (*b*) process
studies that clarify why there is an association between social ecology and
psychology (e.g., residential mobility → anxiety → familiarity seeking), and
(*c*) niche construction studies that illuminate how psychological states give
rise to the creation and maintenance of a social ecology (e.g., familiarity
seeking → dominance of national chain stores). Socioecological psychology
attempts to bring the objectivist perspective to psychological science, investigating how objective social and physical environments, not just perception
and construal of the environments, affect one's thinking, feeling, and behaviors, as well as how people's thinking, feeling, and behaviors give rise to
social and built environments.

Contents

WHAT IS SOCIOECOLOGICAL PSYCHOLOGY?

Socioecological psychology is an area within psychology that investigates how mind and behavior are shaped in part by their natural and social habitats (social ecology) and how natural and social habitats are in turn shaped partly by mind and behavior (Oishi & Graham 2010). The main goal of this approach is to illuminate how individuals and social ecologies define each other.

Most psychological research, including social psychology, investigates how an individual's perception and construal of the environment affect one's thinking, feeling, and behavior (Dweck 2006, Wilson 2011). In one sense, the focus on subjective, intrapsychic phenomenology, such as one's perception, representation, and mindset, is the hallmark of psychology and indeed what makes psychology different from other social sciences—most notably sociology—that attend to objective, social structural factors.

The dominant view in psychological science is that human emotion, cognition, and behavior can be understood once the processes within an individual (e.g., internal representation, the activation of a particular brain region) are understood (e.g., Adolphs 2010, Mitchell 2009). The exclusive emphasis on intrapsychic phenomenology, however, has some drawbacks. Most notably, this view neglects the fact that people most often think, feel emotions, and act in reaction to, and in the presence of, other people (Berscheid & Reis 1998) and in certain physical (Barker 1968), climatic (Anderson 2001), political (Inglehart 1997), economic (Diener et al. 1995), demographic (Taylor 1998), and cultural conditions (Markus & Kitayama 1991).

Despite the rise of relationship, cultural, and evolutionary psychologies in the past 30 years, mainstream psychological science has remained deeply intrapsychic and subjectivist (for critiques, see Cartwright 1979, Rozin 2001, Sampson 1981, Smith & Semin 2004). Socioecological psychology attempts to bring the objectivist perspective to psychological science, investigating how objective social and physical environments, not just perception and construal of the environments, affect one's thinking, feeling, and behaviors, as well as how people's thinking, feeling, and behaviors give rise to built environments (human-made surroundings such as buildings and parks) and social environments. In other words, socioecological psychology combines the previous attempts to bring environments and daily contexts to psychology (e.g., Barker 1968, Bronfenbrenner 1977, Lewin 1939, Milgram 1970) while maintaining its focus on the mutual constitution of objective macroenvironments and psyche.

There are three types of socioecological psychology research (see **Table 1**). The first type is the association study, which sheds light on the association between social ecology and a target

Social ecology: natural and social habitats, including physical, interpersonal, economic, and political environments

Physical environments: physical factors and surroundings such as climate, weather, landscapes, buildings, roads, and green spaces

Table 1 Three types of socioecological psychology research

1. **Association study**: shows that an aspect of social ecology is associated with a particular cognition, emotion, and/or action (e.g., population density → less helping).
2. **Process study**: identifies a psychological mediator of the association between an aspect of social ecology and a particular cognition/emotion/action (e.g., population density → diffusion of responsibility/information overload → less helping).
3. **Niche construction study**: shows that a particular cognition/emotion/action gives rise to the creation of a niche (e.g., information overload → creation of formal institutions such as a department of welfare to take care of people in need of help).

cognition, emotion, or behavior (e.g., a hot climate → more violent crime). The second type of socioecological psychology research is the process study, which goes a step further to demonstrate that a particular feature of social ecology evokes a psychological state, which in turn gives rise to the target cognition, emotion, or behavior (e.g., a hot climate → hostility/crankiness → aggression). The process study aims to identify and elucidate the psychological mechanisms underlying the association between the social ecology and the target cognition, emotion, or behavior. The third type of socioecological research is the niche construction study (Odling-Smee et al. 2003, Yamagishi 2011), which aims to explain how a particular psychological state might give rise to the establishment and maintenance of a particular form of social ecology (e.g., hostility/crankiness → self-defense and permissive gun ownership laws).

Although socioecological psychology is similar to sociology in that both attend to objective, macro factors, socioecological psychology is different from sociology in its focus on psychological mechanisms underlying the association between social ecology and human cognition, emotion, and behavior. As stated by Milgram (1970), sociologists tend to focus on sociological facts (e.g., population density) that are external to individuals, whereas psychologists (here, socioecological psychologists) pay attention to psychological mechanisms that link the individual's experience to his/her social ecology. Many sociologists, epidemiologists, demographers, and other social scientists conduct almost exclusively association studies (for exceptions, see Cook et al. 1983, Vasi & Macy 2003; for a review on experiments in sociology, see Jackson & Cox 2013); in contrast, socioecological psychologists conduct association, process, and niche construction studies.

Socioecological psychology is similar to ecological psychology (Barker 1968), environmental psychology (Craik 1973, Stokols 1978), and community psychology (Kelly 1971, Reppucci et al. 1999) in its interests in everyday environments. A main difference is that socioecological psychology uses experimental as well as observational and survey methods, whereas ecological, environmental, and community psychologies rely almost exclusively on observational and survey methods. Socioecological psychology is similar to cultural psychology (Kitayama & Cohen 2007) in its interests in distal, macroenvironmental factors. Far more similarities than differences exist between them. As detailed in Oishi & Graham (2010), however, one key difference is that cultural psychology explores how psychological processes are grounded in culture (e.g., cultural practices, rituals, and symbols), whereas socioecological psychology explores how psychological processes are grounded in objective, concrete, macro conditions (e.g., green space, sex ratio, and income inequality) as well as cultural contexts.

Socioecological psychology is also similar to behavioral ecology, which investigates how organisms survive and reproduce by adapting to their environments (Davies et al. 2012), in the sense that both take organisms' adaptation to their habitats as a central theme. Behavioral ecologists often start their investigation from the observation of animal/plant behaviors in their natural habitats. For instance, the prominent biologist Masakazu Konishi (1994) observed that songbirds start

Sex ratio: the proportion of males to females in a given area

Income inequality: the degree to which a small proportion of the population owns societal wealth

Table 2 Research strategies of socioecological psychology

1. Observe the behaviors of humans in their natural habitats (e.g., observe that people go to Starbucks in an unfamiliar town, even those who do not usually go to Starbucks in their own neighborhoods).
2. Form and test hypotheses regarding the relation between an aspect of social ecology and a particular cognition/emotion/action (association study): Are Starbucks stores more popular in tourist towns? Are Starbucks stores more popular in mobile cities than in stable cities?
3. Test whether there is a causal effect of the social ecology on the target cognition/emotion/action: e.g., unfamiliar town → familiarity seeking?
4. Form and test hypotheses regarding why a particular social ecology causes a particular cognition/emotion/action (process study): e.g., unknown town → anxiety → familiarity seeking?
5. Form and test hypotheses regarding what kinds of man-made environments a particular cognition/emotion/action might give rise to (niche construction study): e.g., unknown town → anxiety → familiarity seeking → dominance of national chain stores in mobile cities?

singing in spring and asked why. He hypothesized that the number of daylight hours might be a reason and recorded the daylight (photoperiod) as well as other weather conditions in the field. These systematic observations showed a strong correspondence between the number of daylight hours and singing. He went back to the laboratory and manipulated the photoperiod, and he showed that the photoperiod indeed had a causal effect on singing behavior. Furthermore, he analyzed the brain of the songbird before and after it started singing and realized that testosterone was significantly higher in singing birds than in not-yet-singing birds. He then manipulated the amount of testosterone via injection and found that the amount of testosterone had a causal effect on singing behavior. I believe that the research strategy of behavioral ecologists should be a model for socioecological psychologists (see **Table 2**). That is, socioecological psychologists should start their research from the observation of humans in their natural, social habitats and eventually test the causal effect of environments in a controlled laboratory setting (for an example in behavioral ecology, see Moore et al. 2004).

In addition, many topical overlaps exist between socioecological psychology and behavioral ecology, such as crowding behavior, mating, aggression, cooperation, and group behaviors. A major difference is that most behavioral ecologists explain organisms' adaptation to environments in terms of survival values from an evolutionary perspective, whereas socioecological psychologists are more interested in psychological mechanisms that are evoked by such environmental pressures (e.g., envy and jealousy) rather than the biological mechanisms per se (e.g., testosterone) underlying the link between ecology and behavior.

In short, socioecological psychology illuminates how humans adapt to distal yet important macro factors, such as physical, interpersonal, economic, and political environments, and delineates how humans actively modify existing environments or create new niches to improve living conditions. The present review provides a selective summary of recent as well as classic socioecological psychology studies and outlines future directions for research (for historical antecedents of socioecological psychology, see Oishi & Graham 2010, Oishi et al. 2009).

Political environments: the environmental factors that affect human political activities such as political system, dominant political ideology, welfare policies, and taxation

PHYSICAL ENVIRONMENTS

The role of physical environments, such as green space, landscape, and climate, in human mind, emotion, and behavior has been examined extensively. A large longitudinal study, for instance, found that people reported higher levels of life satisfaction and lower levels of psychological distress when living in areas with more green space than when living in areas with less green space (White et al. 2013). Most readers would not be surprised by the finding that a walk in a park improved one's mood to a greater extent than a walk along an urban street (Johansson et al. 2011). What is more surprising, however, is that a walk in a park also improved one's performance in an attention task to a greater degree than did a walk in an urban street. Similarly, a wide variety of studies found that natural environments (e.g., green space, a view of nature) improved performance in memory and learning tasks as well as self-regulation tasks, such as impulse control (for a review, see Kaplan & Berman 2010).

But why should green space increase performance in memory and learning tasks? According to Kaplan & Berman (2010), natural environments evoke "soft fascination" or capture involuntary attention without requiring any immediate actions. The soft fascination evoked by natural environments, then, is thought to help restore mental capacities. In contrast, urban environments evoke directed, voluntary attention (e.g., to traffic lights, cars, and bikes) that requires some actions and thus depletes mental capacities. A recent neuroimaging study found support for the idea that urban environments increase stress sensitivity. Specifically, individuals currently living in an urban area showed significantly greater activation in the amygdala during a stress task than did those living in a nonurban area (Lederbogen et al. 2011). Consistent with the attention restoration theory (Kaplan & Berman 2010), a recent field experiment showed that not all natural environments are equal in their effects on well-being. A walk in a tended (tamed) forest increased positive moods and decreased negative moods more than did a walk in a wild forest (Martens et al. 2011), presumably because a wild forest would elicit more alertness than a tended forest. Collectively, these studies demonstrate not only the link between natural environments and well-being/performance, but also how features of natural environments affect one's well-being and cognitive performance.

Physical environments include not only natural environments but also buildings and other built environments, such as roads, bridges, and signs. In today's large cities, there are many high-rise buildings that rarely existed 100 years ago. Most rural areas in the developing world do not have many tall buildings. In addition, there are far more decorative moldings in European homes than in African homes. Segall et al. (1963) speculated that differences in built environments should give rise to different types of susceptibility to visual illusion. Consistent with their predictions, Americans who were surrounded by tall buildings and rooms with moldings were much more susceptible to Müller-Lyer and Sander parallelogram illusions than were Africans. In contrast, Africans were more vulnerable to horizontal-vertical illusion tasks than were Americans.

Foreign travelers would notice stark differences in landscapes from their home country, not just major monuments such as the Great Wall and Eiffel Tower, but also cafes, movie theaters, game arcades, and the smell, noise, and feel of the street. Some cities are extremely easy to navigate owing to clear signs and logical layouts (e.g., Manhattan), whereas other cities are much more difficult for foreigners because of the overwhelming amount of information and the lack of simple structures (e.g., Hong Kong and Tokyo). Miyamoto et al. (2006) showed that well-known cultural differences in thought style (American = analytic; Japanese = holistic) are due in part to different landscapes. The main figures are much easier to detect in American landscapes than in Japanese landscapes. Then, people living in a clear figure-ground landscape learn to pay attention primarily to an important central visual element, whereas people living in a complex figure-ground landscape must learn to pay attention to both figures and grounds. In addition, recent studies demonstrate the niche construction process such that individuals who have a tendency to pay attention to a central, visual element draw portraits and take photos, even create websites dominated by the central figure, whereas individuals who have a tendency to pay attention to both the figure and ground tend to draw portraits, take photos, and create websites that are *not* dominated by a central figure (Masuda et al. 2008, Wang et al. 2012).

Pathogen
prevalence: the
degree to which
infectious agents such
as viruses and bacteria
are present in a given
area

Whereas green space provides benevolent physical environments for humans, pathogens provide a variety of threats to humans. Pathogens, such as malaria and tuberculosis, are contagious. In general, regions near the equator tend to have more pathogens than regions more distant from the equator. To avoid or minimize this environmental threat, humans are thought to have devised various defense mechanisms. For instance, in a region with a lot of pathogens, individuals must avoid contact with strangers who may carry potential infectious diseases. In such a region, residents should make a sharp ingroup-outgroup distinction (collectivism) and should not be overly sociable (low extraversion) or adventurous (low openness). Indeed, people living in a nation with a historically high level of pathogens are more likely to hold collectivist values (Fincher et al. 2008) and to be less extraverted and less open to experiences than those living in a nation with a historically low level of pathogens (Schaller & Murray 2008).

Recent studies also found that people living in a nation with a historically high level of pathogens endorse the value of family ties and religiosity (Fincher & Thornhill 2012) (see **Figure 1**) and ingroup loyalty, authority, and purity (van Leeuwen et al. 2012). A study of 33 nations also showed that historical pathogen prevalence was associated with tightness (stricter rules regarding acceptable behaviors in a given situation; Gelfand et al. 2011). Subsequent experiments showed that the cues associated with pathogens evoked more conformity, demonstrating the causal effect of an environmental threat on conformity (Murray & Schaller 2012). Thus, the prevalence of pathogens seems to evoke a specific set of behavioral reactions in humans, ranging from conformity to a sharp ingroup-outgroup distinction to introversion and to a lack of openness (for an implication for prejudice, see Schaller & Neuberg 2012).

Like pathogens, climate and weather present some challenges to humans. The most well-known program of research in this area is concerned with the link between heat and violence (Anderson 2001). Researchers have long noted the association between heat and violence. Anderson et al. (2000) found that US cities with higher average temperatures had higher violent crime rates than those with lower average temperatures. This was true even when researchers controlled for various other factors, such as population size and median income. Furthermore, violent crime rates were higher in months with higher average temperatures than in months with lower average temperatures within the same city over time (Bushman et al. 2005, Cohn & Rotton 1997). More strikingly, even within a day, temperature played a role in predicting the prevalence of violent crimes. A series of laboratory experiments also showed that heat has a causal effect on violence. Furthermore, Anderson (2001) identified the psychological process, such that heat evokes crankiness, which in turn produces violence.

In addition to the link between climate and antisocial behaviors, researchers have found a link between climate and prosocial behavior. For example, in two studies, Cunningham (1979, p. 1947) tested Joni Mitchell's famous lyric, "So many things I would have done, but clouds got in my way" (from the song "Both Sides Now"). In support of Mitchell's lyric, pedestrians in Minneapolis were more willing to help the survey interviewer on sunny days than on cloudy days, on cooler days in summer, and on warmer days in winter. In the second study, Cunningham obtained the records of how much servers at a restaurant in a suburb of Chicago earned in tips over three months (April, May, and June) and found that diners left more in tips on sunny days than on cloudy days and on pleasant spring/summer days than on hot spring/summer days [see, however, Flynn & Greenberg (2012) for null effect]. In subsequent field experiments, Rind (1996) manipulated the information regarding weather and showed that customers tipped more when they believed that the weather was sunny versus cloudy (for replication, see Rind & Strohmetz 2001). Whereas the behaviors assessed by Cunningham and Rind were deliberate, Guéguen & Lamy (2013) examined a spontaneous helping behavior. Specifically, they found that pedestrians were more likely to pick

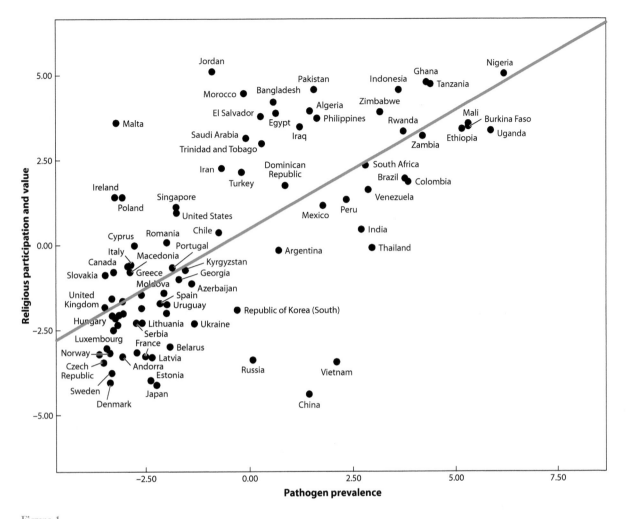

Figure 1

The association between pathogen prevalence (combined parasite stress) and religiosity across 89 nations. The red line is the regression line ($r = 0.70$, $p < 0.001$). Figure adapted from Fincher & Thornhill (2012).

up a dropped glove by a confederate on sunny days than on cloudy days. These studies demonstrate that both prosocial and antisocial behaviors are affected by weather.

Similar to the link between heat and pro-/antisocial behaviors, researchers have found that climates are associated with emotional expressiveness (Pennebaker et al. 1996). In most nations, people living in a colder region self-reported being less emotionally expressive and were also perceived to be less emotionally expressive than those living in a warmer region. McCrae et al. (2007) tested Montesquieu's (1748/1989) famous hypothesis that warm weather makes individuals lazy, pleasure seeking, and impulsive. These researchers examined data from 49 cultures and found that the mean annual temperature was positively associated with participants' perception of how extraverted and open people in their culture typically are. Mostly consistent with Montesquieu's hypothesis, the facet level analyses showed that those living in a warm nation were perceived to be warm ($r = 0.54$), gregarious ($r = 0.36$), excitement seeking ($r = 0.28$), and less orderly ($r = -0.30$).

The link between weather and pro-/antisocial behavior is somewhat intuitive, as predicted by many people including Montesquieu and Joni Mitchell. Recently, researchers have also identified more subtle and somewhat surprising effects of weather. For instance, people thought that global warming was real and a more severe concern when they completed a survey on a day warmer than usual than on a day colder than usual (Li et al. 2011, Risen & Critcher 2011). A laboratory experiment (Risen & Critcher 2011, study 2) also established a causal effect of the temperature on the belief in global warming.

In a similar vein, Simonsohn (2010) analyzed the college enrollment decisions of 1,284 high school seniors and found that students who visited the campus of a university known for academic strengths and recreational weaknesses on a cloudy day were significantly more likely to be enrolled there. This happened presumably because students were more likely to focus on academic matters on a cloudy day than on a sunny day.

Whereas the effect of climate and weather on violence and prosocial behaviors is well replicated, the association between climate and mood is surprisingly mixed. Many studies find that people feel more negative affect on cold, dark, and/or windy days in winter and on hot and humid days in summer. In contrast, few studies have found an effect of various weather and climatic conditions on positive affect and life satisfaction. For instance, seasonal affective disorder is ignited by the shorter photoperiod (the length of light exposure during the day; Young et al. 1997). Interestingly, Swedes consumed more selective serotonin reuptake inhibitors, a medication used to treat depression, in colder summers than in warmer summers (Hartig et al. 2007). Thus, the link between weather and depression has been demonstrated not only by self-report but also by an objective behavioral index. In a diary study of more than 1,200 participants in Germany, Denissen et al. (2008) also found that people reported less negative affect on a sunny day. However, this study found no association between various climatic variables and positive affect (see also Watson 2000). Likewise, Lucas & Lawless (2013) recently found no association between weather and life satisfaction in a sample with more than 1 million participants [however, Connolly (2013) found a weather effect on life satisfaction among women but not among men]. Although people think that good weather is an important predictor of happiness, people living in a pleasant climate (e.g., Californians) are typically no happier than those living in a harsh climate (e.g., Midwesterners) (Schkade & Kahneman 1998). Overall, then, strong wind and the lack of sunlight are associated with negative moods, whereas climatic variables have surprisingly small or no associations with positive moods [see, however, Golder & Macy (2011) for the link between changes in daylight and positive affect].

Another line of research has examined the association between climate and subjective well-being for high- and low-income nations. The basic idea is that climatic demands (deviation from 22°C or 72°F) are inversely associated with well-being in poor nations, where people do not have resources to fend off the demanding weather. In contrast, climatic demands should be unrelated to well-being in wealthy nations because people in wealthy nations have resources to fend off the demanding weather. Van de Vliert (2009) found initial support for this hypothesis in suicide rates and self-reported happiness and health. Fischer & Van de Vliert (2011) replicated the same hypothesis on anxiety, depression, job burnout, and health complaints. These findings suggest that the link between climate and well-being might be moderated by the wealth of nations (e.g., access to air conditioning and supermarkets) and that the null findings regarding the link between weather and mood in the United States (e.g., Lucas & Lawless 2013) could be that in a wealthy nation such as the United States, the effect of weather is minimized by various amenities. If the resource moderation hypothesis is correct, then the effect of photoperiod should be larger on people's moods and well-being than that of temperature and wind (because photoperiod is harder to control than are temperature and wind).

INTERPERSONAL ENVIRONMENTS

Besides physical environments, such as green space and climate, markers of interpersonal environments, such as population density, residential mobility, and sex ratio, affect the human mind, cognition, and behavior. For instance, research has consistently found that population density is negatively associated with prosocial behavior (e.g., Levine et al. 1994). That is, people living in nonurban communities are more likely to help strangers than are those living in urban communities (for a meta-analysis, see Steblay 1987). Similarly, people living in less densely populated areas were more likely to vote in a presidential election than were those living in more densely populated areas, controlling for a host of variables (Preuss 1981).

But why might this be the case? Milgram (1970) postulated the overload hypothesis: Urbanites help others less than rural residents because urbanites come into contact with a far larger number of individuals than rural counterparts on a daily basis, and therefore urbanites need to conserve psychological energies by limiting the number of people with whom they interact. In an elegant experiment, Darley & Latané (1968) demonstrated that population density reduces helping behavior, presumably due to diffusion of responsibility. Thus, Darley, Latané, and Milgram identified the psychological mechanisms underlying the association between social ecology and human behavior. It is also noteworthy that Milgram had already postulated how the urban overload would give rise to social structures (the third type of socioecological psychology): Urban overload would result in the formation of specialized institutions, such as departments of welfare and housing that deal with individuals who need help in an urban community.

Biologists have repeatedly found that population density causes aggression in nonhominids, ranging from trout (Titus 1990) to mice (Greenberg 1972) to brown jays (Williams et al. 1994) to Zebra Finches (Poot et al. 2012). Interestingly, however, population density does not seem to automatically cause aggression in hominids. For instance, Judge & de Waal (1997) found that male rhesus monkeys in a densely populated habitat increased affiliative behaviors, such as grooming to curve aggressive encounters. Not surprisingly, then, human reactions to population density vary widely, ranging from aggression to withdrawal (Regoeczi 2003). This is perhaps one of the many examples of the superior human power of niche construction. People living in a densely populated area have developed the propensity to create more private space in and outside of the home via various technologies and methods (e.g., partitions, headphones), thereby attenuating the potentially adverse effect of population density on aggression. A recent study of 33 nations also found that historically dense nations have a much tighter culture than do sparsely populated nations (Gelfand et al. 2011). In a densely populated nation, it would be easier to regulate the potential issues related to density (e.g., aggression, resource allocation) if there were tighter norms.

Interpersonal environments: the environmental factors that affect human relations, such as population size, population density, residential mobility, and sex ratio

Residential mobility: the degree to which people in a given area change residence in a given period of time

Sex Ratio

Closely related to population density, the sex ratio in a population has a profound impact on human mating behaviors. It is well known in behavioral ecology that the local sex ratio affects aggression and mating behaviors in a wide variety of animals (Davies et al. 2012). This is also true in humans. For instance, a city with a male-biased sex ratio (more men) has higher rates of violence than does a city with a female-biased sex ratio (Barber 2003). Women were more selective in a US state with a male-biased sex ratio than were women living in a state with a female-biased sex ratio (Pollet & Nettle 2008). Specifically, in a more "competitive" US state, where there were more unmarried men than women, men of high socioeconomic status (SES) were more likely to be married than were low-SES men. In contrast, in a noncompetitive US state, the SES of men was not associated with marriage. Likewise, polygamous marriages were more common in the region of Uganda with

Figure 2

Dollar amount people expect men to spend on three different mating-related products as a function of sex ratio (with standard error bars). From Griskevicius et al. (2012, study 4). The financial consequences of too many men: sex ratio effects on saving, borrowing, and spending. *Journal of Personality and Social Psychology* 102:69–80. Adapted with permission from the American Psychological Association.

a female-biased sex ratio (more unmarried women than men) than in the region of Uganda with a male-biased sex ratio (more unmarried men than women; Pollet & Nettle 2009). Although the local sex ratio is not easily apparent to residents, the data show that American men's chance of marriage and Ugandan men's chance of polygynous marriage are in part related to the local sex ratio.

The local sex ratio has a surprisingly wide range of implications. For example, men living in a city with a male-biased sex ratio had more credit card debt than did men living in a city with a women-biased sex ratio (Griskevicius et al. 2012, study 1). This was supposedly because intrasex competition is tougher for men living in a city with a male-biased sex ratio than in a city with a female-biased sex ratio. In a tough mating condition, men show financial impatience and try to spend more money on conspicuous consumption of products to attract women (Griskevicius et al. 2012, studies 2–4) (see **Figure 2**). Even a career choice seems to be affected by local sex ratios. In a city with a tough intrasex competition (more women), women are likely to choose career over family presumably because they must be more independent in such a city due to the lower chance of getting married (Durante et al. 2012). Thus, the local sex ratio seems to have a profound impact on interpersonal environments of human behaviors ranging from aggression to consumption to career choice.

Demographic Diversity

Interpersonal environments are quite different depending on the cities/towns in which individuals live. In New York City, San Francisco, and Miami, many neighborhoods are characterized by a particular racial/ethnic group, such as Chinatown and Little Havana. In 2010, more than 50% of Washington, DC residents were African American, whereas only 2.5% of Fargo, North Dakota residents were African American. Sociologist Marylee Taylor (1998) analyzed the 1990 General Social Survey data that were linkable to respondents' residence (metropolitan statistical areas). After controlling for a host of variables, such as age cohort, education, and occupation, she found that white participants living in a city with more African Americans showed greater prejudice toward African Americans than did those living in a city with fewer African Americans. Interestingly, this effect was present only in the Northern states. Taylor examined the role of economic and political threat as potential mediators; however, none of these threat variables explained the link between living in a city with more African Americans and negative attitudes toward African Americans.

Political scientist Robert Putnam (2007) analyzed Social Capital Community Benchmark Survey data from more than 30,000 respondents living in 40 communities in the United States and found that residents of homogeneous cities (e.g., Bismarck, North Dakota and Lewiston, Maine) were more trusting of not just others in general, but also of neighbors and people of different ethnicities compared to residents of heterogeneous cities (e.g., San Francisco and Houston). Putnam speculated that heterogeneous contexts seem to encourage white residents to "hunker down" like a turtle, whereas homogeneous contexts encourage white residents to bond with others.

Putnam's findings have been replicated by large independent samples in the United States and Canada (Stolle et al. 2008), where residents living in more heterogeneous cities trusted others less than did those living in homogeneous cities. It is interesting to note, however, that the inverse association between racial heterogeneity and general trust was not present when the Census tract-level[1] racial/ethnic heterogeneity was assessed (Oliver & Wong 2003). Portes & Vickstrom (2011) provided a persuasive critique on Putnam's social capital work and pointed out the possibility that the inverse relation between heterogeneity and trust could be spurious, due to other third variables such as economic inequality and percent Scandinavian-origin population. In addition, the inverse relationship between racial/ethnic diversity and general trust was present among European Americans but not among African Americans. Indeed, African Americans living in a heterogeneous neighborhood of Detroit were more trusting of others than were African Americans living in a homogeneous neighborhood (Marschall & Stolle 2004).

Seder & Oishi (2009) examined the racial composition of participants' Facebook networks and found that European Americans whose Facebook friends were predominantly European Americans were more satisfied with their lives than were those whose Facebook friends included many nonwhite people. This was true even when controlling for religiosity and political orientation. Similar to the findings of Marschall & Stolle (2004), the life satisfaction of nonwhite participants was not associated with homogeneity of the friendship network.

Residential Mobility

Residential mobility is another factor that determines one's interpersonal environments. In a residentially mobile area, one cannot expect to have the same group of friends for an extended period of time. In a residentially stable area, in contrast, one can expect to be with the same group of friends (and enemies) for an extended period of time. Recent studies have elucidated the ways in which the residential mobility and stability of neighborhoods are associated with various cognitions, emotions, and behaviors (for reviews, see Oishi 2010, Oishi & Talhelm 2012). For instance, Sampson et al. (1997) documented that crime rates were lower in residentially stable neighborhoods than in mobile neighborhoods in the city of Chicago. Furthermore, they discovered that the association between residential stability and low crime rate was due in part to higher levels of collective efficacy in stable neighborhoods where neighbors are willing to intervene and monitor neighborhood issues. Likewise, residents of stable neighborhoods in Madison, Wisconsin were more engaged in community affairs than were residents of mobile neighborhoods (Kang & Kwak 2003).

---

[1]On average, 4,000 residents live in one Census tract.

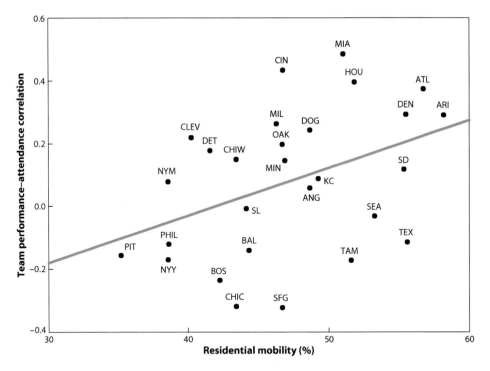

Figure 3

Residential mobility and conditional community support. The *x*-axis indicates the five-year residential mobility (percentage of residents in the year 2000 who were not living in their current residence five years before). The *y*-axis indicates the within-team correlation between team performance and attendance. A higher correlation means more conditional community support (the better the performance of the team, the greater the attendance). Each dot represents a Major League Baseball team. The red line is the regression line ($r = 0.41$, $p < 0.05$). From Oishi et al. (2007, study 2). The socioecological model of procommunity action: the benefits of residential stability. *Journal of Personality and Social Psychology* 93:831–44. Adapted with permission from the American Psychological Association.

Residents of stable neighborhoods in Minneapolis/St. Paul were also more likely to buy Critical Habitat License Plates, which include an extra fee that goes to the preservation of natural habitats in Minnesota (Oishi et al. 2007, study 1). Furthermore, residents of stable cities, such as Pittsburgh and Boston, attended home baseball games regardless of their home teams' performance (unconditional identification), whereas residents of mobile cities such as Atlanta and Phoenix attended home baseball games much more when their home teams were winning (conditional identification; Oishi et al. 2007, study 2) (see **Figure 3**). A parallel regional variation was observed in Japan (Oishi et al. 2009): Home game attendance was less conditional in stable Japanese cities (e.g., Osaka and Tokorozawa) than in mobile cities (e.g., Fukuoka and Sendai).

Although a great deal of evidence supports the association between residential stability and prosocial action, the studies summarized above were cross sectional as opposed to longitudinal. To examine the effect of neighborhood stability more clearly, O'Brien et al. (2012) followed middle school students in Binghamton, New York over three years. These researchers found that students who moved to a stable neighborhood showed a significant increase in prosociality whereas students who moved to a mobile neighborhood showed a decrease in prosociality between 2006 (time 1) and 2009 (time 2). Considering that middle school students' moves are driven by their caretakers and not by themselves, the selection bias is less of a concern than in the previous cross-sectional studies.

Although most studies cited above statistically controlled for various third variables, such as median income, racial composition, and dominant political ideology, stable communities could be different from mobile communities in numerous other ways. The most serious concern is a selection bias: Procommunity, prosocial people are more likely to decide to live in and move to a stable neighborhood than are anticommunity, antisocial individuals.

A more stringent test of the causal effect of residential stability on prosocial behavior is an experiment. In order to test whether residential stability has a causal effect on procommunity action, Oishi et al. (2007, study 3) conducted a laboratory experiment in which participants were randomly assigned to a mobile or a stable "community." Residential mobility and stability were manipulated such that participants in the mobile condition completed three group tasks in three different groups, whereas participants in the stable condition completed the three group tasks in the same group. In a fourth task, participants played Trivial Pursuit for 10 minutes. The participants were told beforehand that the top scorer in the game would receive a $10 reward. Thus, we created a situation in which helping others would directly impede the participants' own self-interest. To assess their prosocial, unselfish action, we had one confederate in each group who sighed and looked clueless. We also videotaped and coded participants' helping behaviors toward the confederate and toward other group members. Consistent with the correlational studies summarized above, participants in the stable condition helped the confederate as well as other group members significantly more often than did those in the mobile condition. Furthermore, we demonstrated that the effect of residential stability on prosocial behavior was mediated by identification with the community; that is, residential stability increased identification with the community, which in turn resulted in greater prosocial action.

Residential mobility affects not just one's relationships with one's community but also one's relationships with other people (for reviews, see Oishi 2010, Yuki & Schug 2012). Americans are more trusting of strangers than are Japanese (Yamagishi & Yamagishi 1994). Using an agent-based computer model, Macy & Sato (2002) showed that this cultural difference was explained by residential mobility. That is, it is more adaptive for people living in a mobile area to be trusting of strangers. Similarly, Americans are much more open and self-disclosing to others than are Japanese. This cultural difference was explained by relational mobility, which is the general degree to which individuals in a society have opportunities to form new relationships and terminate old ones (Schug et al. 2010). Namely, people in a relationally mobile society seem to be self-disclosing to others because self-disclosure is likely to result in the formation of a new relationship. In contrast, people in a relationally nonmobile society seem to avoid disclosing too much because the self-disclosure could backfire later. By self-disclosing, people in a relationally mobile society can find others who share their interests. Thus, residents of a mobile society should have friends whose interests are similar to their own. Indeed, previous cross-cultural studies showed that Americans have more similar friends than do Japanese (Heine & Renshaw 2002). Schug et al. (2009) showed that this cultural difference was explained by relational mobility. In the United States, students in a larger, relationally mobile university had friends who were more similar to them in comparison with students in a smaller, relationally nonmobile university (Bahns et al. 2012).

In addition to social relations, residential mobility appears to be associated with consumer behaviors. For instance, there are more national chain stores, such as Home Depot, Target, and Whole Foods, in mobile US states (e.g., Nevada and Florida) than in stable states (e.g., Pennsylvania and New York). This is true even after controlling for the population size and median income. But why should there be more national chain stores in mobile states than in stable states? Oishi et al. (2012) reasoned that a mobile lifestyle is exciting but also anxiety provoking.

Thus, people in a mobile context might prefer a familiar product more than would those in a stable context. Indeed, in a series of experiments, the thought of a mobile lifestyle increased familiarity liking. Moreover, the effect of residential mobility on familiarity liking was explained by relationship anxiety (anxiety over having a reliable social network). That is, the thought of a mobile lifestyle evoked more relationship anxiety, which explained why people in a mobile condition preferred familiar objects more than did those in a stable condition. More generally, these findings imply that national chain stores are a psychological reaction and a niche construction for individuals living in a mobile but stressful environment.

Related to residential mobility, several theorists construed the concept of early environmental unpredictability, which consists of residential moves as well as employment changes and changes in a parental figure during the first five years of life (Belsky et al. 2012). Longitudinal studies found that people who grew up in an unpredictable condition were more likely to engage in sexual behaviors developmentally earlier than those who grew up in a predictable condition (Simpson et al. 2012). This is in all probability because the chance of reproductive success is smaller for those who grow up in an unpredictable condition than for those who grow up in a predictable condition. Thus, it is more advantageous to engage in sexual behaviors earlier in an unpredictable condition.

ECONOMIC ENVIRONMENTS

Economists, sociologists, and other social scientists have documented the effects of economic conditions on various human behaviors, ranging from consumer spending (Katona 1968) to criminal activities (Rosenfeld & Fornango 2007) to voting (Kramer 1971). The links are fairly straightforward—such as the finding that people do not spend as much money on nonessential items during a recession as they do during an economic boom—and do not require much psychological analysis. However, recent psychological research showed more distal, nonintuitive links between economic conditions and human behaviors. For instance, in a harsh economic condition, women have their first baby at an earlier age than do women living in a favorable economic condition (Low et al. 2008, Wilson & Daly 1997), which is presumably because reproductive success is lower overall in an economically harsh condition than in a favorable condition. Even more intriguingly, although people spend less money on furniture, electronics, and leisure during an economic recession, people spend more money on personal care products and cosmetics (Hill et al. 2012, study 1). In subsequent experiments, Hill and colleagues showed that women who were primed with an economic recession indicated a greater desire to purchase beauty products than did women in a control condition. This was because women in a recession condition preferred mates with greater resources, which in turn made them desire beauty products, presumably to enhance their attractiveness for mates with resources.

Psychologists have long known that economic conditions have implications not just for economic behaviors but also for noneconomic behaviors. For instance, Hovland & Sears (1940) tested whether economic conditions were associated with the frequency of lynching. Analyzing the lynching data from a 49-year period (1882 to 1930), they found that the deviation from the expected economic conditions (e.g., per-acre value of cotton that was higher or lower than expected from the regression equation) was indeed strongly and inversely associated with the frequency of lynching, in particular, the lynching of African Americans ($r = -0.61$ to -0.72). Later experiments also showed a link between economic threats and greater prejudice. For instance, when primed with an economic threat, non-Asian American college students showed greater prejudice toward Asians (their main economic threat) than did those in the control condition (Butz & Yogeeswaran 2011). Not surprisingly, this link was explained by the heightened level of anxiety in the economic threat condition.

Economic conditions are also associated with authoritarianism. For instance, during an economic recession more people joined authoritarian churches, such as the Roman Catholic Church, than nonauthoritarian churches, such as the Presbyterian Church (Sales 1972). In contrast, during an economic boom more people joined nonauthoritarian churches than authoritarian churches. Likewise, the analysis of comic strips revealed that the main characters were more likely to be described as powerful (authoritarian) during an economic recession than during an economic boom (Sales 1973). Finally, the experimental manipulation of threat evoked the endorsement of authoritarianism (Sales & Friend 1973). Thus, macroeconomic conditions present important backgrounds for human cognition, emotion, and action.

Economic conditions are also known to be associated with subjective well-being (life satisfaction, positive affect, and relative lack of negative affect). Numerous international surveys showed that residents of wealthy nations reported having higher levels of life satisfaction and experiencing more positive affect than those living in poor nations (e.g., Deaton 2008, Diener et al. 1995). Interestingly, however, gross domestic product (GDP) per capita was not associated with the frequency in which residents felt worried, angry, or sad (Oishi & Schimmack 2010a). Furthermore, residents of poor nations were more likely to report having a meaning or purpose in life than were residents of wealthy nations (S. Oishi & E. Diener, manuscript under review). The inverse correlation between GDP per capita and meaning in life was explained by religiosity; namely, residents of poor nations were more likely to be religious than were residents of wealthy nations, and religiosity was associated with meaning in life.

In addition to surveying the wealth of nations, scholars have also examined the role of economic inequality. In social epidemiology, numerous studies have shown that residents of economically unequal nations and regions have more health problems and indeed have higher mortality risks than do those living in more equal nations (Wilkinson & Pickett 2006). The evidence ranges from mortality and homicide to obesity and cardiovascular disease rates. However, it is unclear why residents of unequal societies are not as healthy as those of equal societies. Some scholars have demonstrated that interpersonal trust is lower in unequal societies than in equal societies (Kawachi et al. 1997). Social psychological experiments also have shown that an uneven distribution of resources reduces general trust (e.g., Cozzolino 2011). Still, it is conceptually unclear why the lack of trust and other psychological consequences of inequality should be associated with mortality and illness (for a thoughtful critique, see Deaton 2003).

Compared to the link with physical health, the potential link between inequality and happiness seems to be more straightforward. Conceptually, income inequality could evoke a sense of unfairness and make people less trustful of others, in particular, persons in power. The evidence showing the association between income inequality and unhappiness, however, is surprisingly tenuous. For instance, most international data show an inverse correlation between Gini coefficients and the mean level of life satisfaction across nations. However, once GDP per capita is statistically controlled, the association often disappears (Diener et al. 1995, Oishi 2012). A cross-nation study has a major problem of third variables because equal nations, such as Denmark and Sweden, are different from unequal nations, such as Sierra Leone and Brazil, in many dimensions other than income inequality. Thus, it is important to examine one nation that experienced a large change in the degree of income inequality over time. The United States is such a nation. In the 1940s and 1950s, the United States had more income equality than most European nations. Yet, since the 1980s, US income inequality has grown to a level almost equal to that of Latin America today. A cross-temporal analysis within the United States from 1972 to 2008 showed that indeed, Americans were on average happier in the years of more income equality than in the years of inequality (Oishi et al. 2011). This was particularly true among low-income Americans. Finally, the link between income equality and happiness was mediated by perceived fairness and general trust. In the years of income equality, Americans felt there was more fairness and trusted others more than in the years of income inequality.

Despite the well-known discontent of income inequality, such as the Occupy Wall Street movement and people's general preference for an equal society over an unequal society (Norton & Ariely 2011), many nations are moving toward greater inequality. What psychological mechanisms might give rise to the tolerance of economic inequality? One intriguing possibility is the value of meritocracy and personal choice. People who are tolerant for inequality tend to be conservative and think that one's life conditions are determined largely by one's talent and efforts (Jost et al. 2004). Experimental studies also found that priming individuals with personal choice increased victim blaming (Savani et al. 2011) and tolerance for income inequality (Savani & Rattan 2012). Another possibility is system justification, or the rationalization of the status quo (Jost et al. 2004). Indeed, residents of unequal nations appear to rationalize the status quo in part by holding ambivalent attitudes (e.g., competent but cold) toward the groups in power (Durante et al. 2013).

In addition to economic conditions, the type of economic activities is also known to be associated with human mind and behavior. Using data from a field study of four East African tribes (within each tribe, roughly half were farmers and the other half were pastoralists; see Edgerton 1965 for the research design), well-known anthropologist Walter Goldschmidt (1971) compared farmers with pastoralists and observed that pastoralists were far more independent than farmers, even within the same tribe. He attributed this difference to economic independence and dependence. Pastoralists are not dependent on others in raising their animals: "When conflict arises, they find it possible simply to move away from it" (Goldschmidt 1971, p. 135). In contrast, farmers cannot simply move away from a conflict, as they are attached to their farmlands. Most importantly, Goldschmidt notes that pastoralists' independence is "not merely a matter of personal choice, but is necessitated by environmental circumstances—i.e., it is an ecological adjustment" (p. 136). These findings indicate that people adapt to the local ecology to maximize their success in local environments. Indeed, Goldschmidt further observed that socialization processes vary across different occupational groups, probably because of the costs and benefits of being independent.

In psychology, John Berry (1979) explicitly theorized and tested the role of ecological settings in psychological differentiation, in particular, in perceptual differentiation, termed field dependence and independence. Consistent with the findings from East Africa by Goldschmidt (1971) and Edgerton (1965), Berry's research on Indian tribes in northern Canada showed that hunters who were mobile and low in food accumulation were more perceptually independent than those who stayed in one region and engaged in marine agriculture (catching salmon and shellfish; Berry & Annis 1974). More recently, Uskul et al. (2008) found that within the same region of Turkey, herders were more perceptually independent than were fishermen and tea farmers. Within agriculture, rice farming requires far more cooperation with neighbors (due to irrigation needs) than does wheat farming. Talhelm and colleagues (T. Talhelm, X. Zhang, S. Oishi, C. Shimin, & D. Duan, manuscript under review) indeed found that Chinese who grew up in a rice farming area were more perceptually interdependent than were those who grew up in a wheat farming area.

Dominant economic activities were also shown to be associated with the norm for violence. The culture of honor (i.e., tolerance for violence against honor violations) in the southern part of the United States is thought to have originated from multiple factors, including the dominant economy being herding (Nisbett & Cohen 1996). Herders must defend their livestock from others because livestock are relatively easy to steal and are far more valuable than crops. In addition, the southern part of the United States had an insufficient police force when herders initially populated the area. Thus, a strong norm for self-defense emerged as herders adapted to the local ecology.

The dominant form of economic activities is also shown to be associated with prosociality. Henrich and colleagues (2005) administered the ultimatum, the dictator, and the public goods games in 15 small-scale societies. Tribes engaging in whaling or large-scale farming benefit from cooperation in their daily lives and were far more prosocial than were those engaging in horticulture and other activities, who did not benefit from cooperation. Another important predictor of prosociality was market integration. Those engaging in market exchanges were more prosocial in comparison with those who did not engage in such exchanges. These studies show that the degree of interdependence in daily economic activities is associated with such basic psychological processes as perception and prosociality.

To our knowledge, however, there is no experimental research on the degree of interdependence in daily economic activities. Thus, the causal direction might be of question. Furthermore, economic interdependence often involves both task interdependence and reward interdependence. For instance, whaling requires many fishermen and multiple roles, such as navigator and harpooner. A great degree of task interdependence exists because fishermen have to coordinate with others to capture a whale. In addition, their reward is highly interdependent, as their pay is dependent on the total yield for the whole ship. Wageman & Baker (1997) manipulated both task and reward interdependence and assessed the degree of cooperation in multiple measures, including observers' ratings and actual time spent helping the partner. They found that the task interdependence (engaging in a task that requires mutual dependence) increased the degree of cooperation in all outcome measures, whereas reward interdependence did not (for a replication, see Allen et al. 2003).

The importance of task interdependence rather than reward interdependence in cooperation makes a great deal of sense in light of recent work on coordination. For instance, Wiltermuth & Heath (2009) found that participants randomly assigned to a synchronized walking condition (experiment 1) and a coordinated singing and moving condition (experiment 2) were significantly more likely to feel connected with other group members and to cooperate with others than were participants in the noncoordination conditions (see also Valdesolo et al. 2010). Overall, then, task interdependence and coordinated actions in daily economic activities seem to be important ecological conditions for prosociality and other important social behaviors.

POLITICAL ENVIRONMENTS

In their classic work, *The Civic Culture*, political scientists Almond & Verba (1963) analyzed survey data from five nations and found that residents of democratic nations (the United States and the United Kingdom) trusted others more and were more confident in their governments' abilities to improve citizens' welfare than were residents of nations where democracy was still young (Mexico and Italy). These findings were later confirmed in a much larger survey (e.g., Inglehart 1997). Furthermore, people living in democratic nations (operationalized as having more civil rights) reported being happy and more satisfied with their lives than did those living in nondemocratic nations (Diener et al. 1995). However, once GDP per capita was statistically controlled, the association between democracy and subjective well-being disappeared.

Because the cross-national analysis has third-variable problems, Inglehart et al. (2008) analyzed the World Values Survey and European Values Study 1981 to 2007 data. The data from the late 1980s to 1990s provide an interesting natural experiment because many former Soviet Union and communist nations went through democratization during that period. Although several post-Soviet nations, such as Moldova and Ukraine, enjoyed a boost in happiness and life satisfaction, other nations, such as Hungary, Romania, and Lithuania, did not show any noticeable increase. Indeed, Inglehart and colleagues found that the level of democracy was negatively associated with the mean levels of life satisfaction and happiness at time 2 after controlling for time 1 well-being and other variables including GDP per capita. Helliwell & Huang (2008) replicated this finding using two objective indicators of democracy (voice/accountability and political stability).

It is important to note that the level of democracy is not necessarily associated with the quality of governance. Corruption is rampant in some democratic nations. Helliwell & Huang (2008) indeed found that the quality of governance (e.g., regulatory quality, rule of law, and lack of corruption) was positively associated with the life satisfaction and happiness of residents. Thus, the objective indicators of democracy do not seem to be associated with subjective well-being. Rather, it is the objective indicators of government efficiency that seem to matter to people's daily lives. Interestingly, Inglehart et al. (2008) found that nations whose citizens reported an increase in a subjective sense of free choice also experienced an increase in subjective well-being over time. It might be, then, that the rule of law, regulatory quality, and meritocracy (the lack of corruption) are more closely associated with a subjective sense of freedom than are electoral stability and democracy per se.

However, it is difficult to discern why some aspects of political climates are associated with trust, happiness, and other psychological processes solely on the basis of surveys and social indicators. To this end, Kurt Lewin and colleagues' classic laboratory experiments on democratic leadership are informative. Lewin and colleagues (1939, 1945) manipulated the political climate via leadership style and found that children were friendly to one another and less aggressive in democratic groups than in autocratic and laissez-faire groups. Subsequent experiments also showed that an autocratic political climate gave rise to group instability due to members' departure relative to a democratic political climate (Van Vugt et al. 2004). In these experiments, democratic leaders encouraged fairness and active participation in decision-making processes. Although not directly measured, then, these experimental findings, combined with the survey results summarized above, suggest that democracy increases trust and civility to fellow citizens to the extent that it guarantees fairness and freedom. These mediational processes need to be tested explicitly in the future.

Social welfare is another important political environment. In general, it is believed that residents living in nations with generous unemployment benefits and pensions are happier and more satisfied with their lives than are those living in nations with less generous benefits. Pacek & Radcliff's (2008a) analysis of 18 nations from 1980 to 2000 in the World Values Survey data revealed that residents of nations with generous unemployment benefits, disability benefits, and pensions were indeed more satisfied with their lives and happier than were those of nations with less generous welfare. Pacek & Radcliff (2008b) replicated the basic findings from the World Values Survey in 11 nations in the Eurobarometer data (however, for the null finding see Veenhoven 2000). It is also reassuring that Radcliff and colleagues showed that residents of US states with more liberal welfare spending were more satisfied with their lives than were those of states with more stringent welfare spending, controlling for various individual-level variables (Alvarez-Díaz et al. 2010). Moreover, Flavin & Radcliff (2009) found that the suicide rate was lower in US states with higher per capita public assistance expenditure. Thus, the positive association between social welfare and well-being is observed both at the cross-national and cross-state levels of analyses.

Large welfare spending is associated with "big" government. Are the residents of a country with big government more satisfied with their lives than residents living under a small government? Bjornskov et al. (2007) analyzed data from 70 nations and found that although welfare spending was positively associated with the life satisfaction of nations, the total government spending per GDP was negatively associated with the life satisfaction of nations (for a replication, see Oishi et al. 2012). In light of Helliwell & Huang's (2008) findings, it appears that what matters to residents' subjective quality of life is not how much of the budget the government spends on its residents, but rather how efficiently it spends.

Taxation is another policy that creates an important political environment for residents. Opinions are divergent on what a fair tax system is. Many conservatives feel that a flat tax is the fairest system, as everyone pays the same percentage of income. In contrast, many liberals feel that a progressive tax is the fairest system. A cross-national study of 54 nations (Oishi et al. 2012) showed that residents of countries with progressive taxation (e.g., Sweden and Denmark) were more satisfied with their lives and reported experiencing more positive emotions than did residents of countries with less progressive taxation (e.g., Hong Kong and Russia). The association between progressive taxation and the mean levels of subjective well-being was mediated by satisfaction with public goods. That is, residents of nations with more progressive taxation were more satisfied with public transportation, education, health care, highways, clean water, and clean air, which explained why these residents were happier and more satisfied with their lives in general than were residents of nations with less progressive taxation.

In the United States, political environments are quite diverse as a result of different state laws. For instance, as of January 2013, same-sex marriage was legal in Connecticut, Iowa, Maine, Maryland, Massachusetts, New Hampshire, New York, Vermont, Washington state, and Washington, DC. Hatzenbuehler et al. (2010) analyzed longitudinal, nationally representative data and found that psychiatric disorders increased between time 1 (2001–2002) and time 2 (2004–2005) among lesbian, gay, and bisexual (LGB) individuals living in the states that banned same-sex marriage. In contrast, LGBs living in the states that had legalized same-sex marriage did not show any significant change between times 1 and 2. A follow-up study also showed that LGB youths living in Oregon counties with higher percentages of same-sex couples, more registered Democrats, gay-straight alliances in schools, and school policies banning anti-LGB bullying were less suicidal than were LGB youths living in Oregon counties with lower percentages of same-sex couples, fewer registered Democrats, no gay-straight alliances, or no anti-LGB bullying policies in schools (Hatzenbuehler 2011). These findings demonstrate the profound role of political climate on the mental health of sexual minorities in the United States.

As the US political climate has become more divisive over the past few decades (Jost 2006), researchers have begun investigating the psychology of political minorities. For example, political minorities (liberals living in a conservative city; conservatives living in a liberal city) are more likely to move to a city whose dominant politics match theirs than are political majorities (Motyl et al. 2013). Furthermore, subsequent experiments showed that the political misfit between participants and their local community caused a greater intention to move away, and the political minority's tendency to move to a new city was explained by the low level of belonging in the original community.

Progressive taxation: taxation in which a tax rate becomes progressively higher in higher income brackets

Economic environments: the environmental factors that affect human economic activities such as gross domestic product (GDP), unemployment rate, and inflation rate

SUMMARY AND FUTURE DIRECTIONS

The perception and construal of the world (e.g., the perceptions of inequality, climate) are clearly important in one's thinking, feeling, and action. This subjectivist approach is well represented in mainstream psychological science (Dweck 2006, Wilson 2011). Socioecological psychology attempts to bring the objectivist perspective to psychological science, investigating how objective physical environments (e.g., green space, climate, pathogen prevalence), interpersonal environments (e.g., sex ratio, population density, residential mobility), economic environments (e.g., wealth, income inequality, dominant economic activities), and political environments (e.g., democracy, welfare spending)—not just perception and construal of the environments—affect one's thinking, feeling, and behaviors. Socioecological psychology aims to elucidate the psychological mechanisms underlying the links between aspects of physical, interpersonal, economic, and political environments and human cognition, emotion, and action. Finally, socioecological psychology attempts to illuminate how particular psychological tendencies (e.g., familiarity seeking) give rise to a niche construction (e.g., shopping malls). In other words, socioecological psychology brings into mainstream psychology the concerns of Lewin (1939), Barker (1968), Bronfenbrenner (1977), and other pioneers for the macro environment.

Although socioecological psychology provides an important perspective on psychological science, it has some limitations that need to be addressed. First, most of the socioecological psychology research summarized above has been either an association study or a process study, that is, either a study that demonstrates the association between social ecology and human cognition, emotion, and action or a study that demonstrates the psychological processes underlying the association between them. The third type of study, the niche construction study, has been rare.

Even earthworms are known to modify their soils or relocate themselves (a bit) closer to better soils to increase their fitness (Odling-Smee et al. 2003). It is clear that humans modify and create new environments significantly more than do earthworms and that socioecological psychologists need to document this important human endeavor more in the future. In terms of environmental choice, however, some research exists. Personality psychologists have long noted that people not only are influenced by their situations but also actively choose certain situations (Allport 1937). More recently, some personality psychologists extended the "situation" choice to include larger contexts, such as cities and nations. For instance, extraverted young adults living in a rural area are more likely to move to a larger city than are introverted young adults living in a rural area (Jokela et al. 2008). Interestingly, extraverted young adults already living in an urban area are unlikely to move. Over a long period, a selection bias like this will give rise to the concentration of extraverts in urban areas and introverts in rural areas.

The active processes by which people choose where to live must then result in distinct regional clustering of personality. Indeed, Rentfrow et al. (2008) found that residents of Washington, DC, New York, and Oregon were the highest in openness to experiences among residents of the 50 US states, whereas residents of North Dakota and Minnesota were the most agreeable. Park & Peterson (2010) also found systematic variation across US cities in character strengths. For instance, residents of San Francisco, Los Angeles, and Oakland were the highest in curiosity and creativity, whereas residents of El Paso and Miami were the highest in forgiveness and honesty. Within Japan, Kitayama et al. (2006) found that Japanese in Hokkaido (a northern island that was settled largely by the former samurai class in the late 1800s) showed more individualistic tendencies than did Japanese in Kyoto.

The move of samurais to Hokkaido was driven largely by the Meiji government's policy. In contrast, the residential mobility of North Americans today is largely driven by their own decisions. What might be causing the regional clustering of personality? Job opportunities, climates, recreational opportunities, and images of the city are obviously important factors in choosing where to live. Economist Richard Florida (2002) argued that creative people move to a creative city and that the fate of the city depends in part on whether it can attract creative individuals. He showed that the cities that attracted more creative people (e.g., Austin and Seattle) in the 1990s saw a large economic growth, whereas the cities that could not attract creative people (e.g., Pittsburgh and Cleveland) saw an economic decline.

A recent study also confirmed that Americans' stereotypes about various regions of the United States are quite accurate (Rogers & Wood 2010). For instance, people have a generally accurate image of New York as an open place. Thus, people might move to New York City because they accurately perceive it to be an open city. The communities populated by open people are likely to create museums and various art and music venues and are likely to adopt liberal policies (e.g., same-sex marriage), creating a niche that fits its residents.

Socioecological psychologists must formally examine the cycle of self-selection and niche construction processes. For instance, it is important to test whether the concentration of open people will give rise to higher per capita museum and music venues and the adoption of liberal policies, and whether this in turn attracts even more open-minded people. To this end, David Sloan Wilson and colleagues' field intervention project in Binghamton (e.g., O'Brien et al. 2012) is instructive. It combines urban planning with behavioral scientific methods to empirically test the role of parks, community gardens, and other amenities in prosociality (Harris 2011). These researchers created new parks and community gardens and conducted community interventions. In addition, researchers are following residents' prosociality using multiple methods (e.g., the dropped letter method, which measures the percentage of the stamped letters dropped in various neighborhoods that are eventually mailed back). A project like this will help explicate the effect of physical environments on psychology (e.g., whether the creation of community gardens increases procommunity action), self-selection process (e.g., who is attracted and who is not attracted to new amenities), and community-level force (e.g., emergent properties of a community). Such knowledge will in turn help us understand why some communities react better than others to an emergency situation (e.g., drought).

Second, a major limitation of socioecological psychology is a lack of a unified theory. Evolutionary psychology has thrived recently thanks in part to a unified theory based on natural and sexual selection (Gangestad & Simpson 2007). In contrast, socioecological psychology does not yet have such a theory. In the long term, the advancement of socioecological psychology might depend on the creation of a unified theory. In particular, socioecological psychology covers a wide range of topics that are typically studied in different disciplines. A unified theory would provide the critical glue to hold the divergent programs of research together.

In the short run, socioecological psychology can make progress by building midrange theories that are specific to some aspects of social ecology. For instance, pathogen prevalence theory (Schaller & Neuberg 2012) has generated quite a bit of excitement in the literature on cultural values, individualism/collectivism, and stereotypes in part because germs and diseases are major life challenges to which humans have created various defense mechanisms. Residential mobility theory (Oishi 2010, Oishi & Talhelm 2012) has also generated various specific hypotheses regarding a wide range of psychological phenomena, from self-concepts to happiness to social networking strategies to procommunity action. This type of theorizing can start with the question, "What kind of psychological reaction does a particular social ecology evoke?" The answer given by pathogen prevalence theorists was fear. The answer given by residential mobility theorists was excitement, anxiety, and uncertainty. Socioecological psychologists need to ask these questions to generate process-oriented hypotheses and eventually build a theory about a particular social ecology.

The third limitation of socioecological psychology is that so far the majority of socioecological psychology relies on simple, correlational design. More rigorous methods should be incorporated in future research. For instance, Harden et al. (2009) used a behavioral genetics (twins) method to test the link between population density and psychopathology. By controlling for genes and other individual differences, they were able to test the effect of population density in isolation. The genetically informative design is one way to address the third-variable problems. In addition, experimental methods (e.g., Oishi et al. 2007), field experiments (e.g., Johansson et al. 2011), and longitudinal methods (e.g., Hatzenbuehler et al. 2010) should be utilized more often in socioecological psychology.

The final limitation of socioecological psychology is that moderators have not yet been extensively explored. Psychological reactions to a particular social ecology could be quite different across individuals with different values, personalities, and cultural backgrounds. For instance, introverts react to relocation much more negatively than do extraverts (Oishi & Schimmack 2010b). Likewise, conservatives are not as much bothered by income inequality as liberals are (Napier & Jost 2008). Drivers of a car with air conditioning do not honk on a hot day as violently as do drivers of a car without air conditioning (Kenrick & MacFarlane 1984). Finally, the effect of harsh climates is more adverse in poor nations than in rich nations (Fischer & Van de Vliert 2011). Thus, specific moderators need to be identified to add nuanced understanding to socioecological psychology.

CONCLUSION

Homo sapiens is an extraordinary species, successfully inhabiting most parts of the world today. Humans can adapt to most physical environments because they devise defense mechanisms against natural environments, actively modify existing environments, and relocate to better environments. Using a variety of methods, socioecological psychology aims to advance our understanding of how humans adapt to physical, interpersonal, economic, and political environments. In other words, socioecological psychology attempts to bring the objectivist perspective to psychological science by investigating how objective social and physical environments affect people's thinking, feeling, and behaviors on the one hand, and how people's thinking, feeling, and behaviors give rise to social and built environments on the other. By concretely illuminating the mutual influence of person and environment, socioecological psychology connects the past (e.g., Bronfenbrenner 1977, Lewin 1939) with the present (e.g., new research methods, multilevel analysis) and broadens the scope and knowledge of psychological science.

SUMMARY POINTS

1. Socioecological psychology attempts to bring the objectivist perspective to psychological science.

2. Socioecological psychology illuminates how objective physical environments (e.g., green space, climate, and pathogen prevalence), interpersonal environments (e.g., sex ratio, population density, and residential mobility), economic environments (e.g., wealth, income inequality and dominant economic activities), and political environments (e.g., democracy and welfare spending)—not just perception and construal of the environments—affect one's thinking, feeling, and behaviors.

3. Socioecological psychology aims to elucidate the psychological mechanisms underlying the links between aspects of physical, interpersonal, economic, and political environments and human cognition, emotion, and action.

4. Finally, socioecological psychology attempts to shed light on how particular psychological tendencies (e.g., familiarity seeking) give rise to a niche construction (e.g., proliferation of national chain stores).

FUTURE ISSUES

1. A grand, unified theory is still missing in socioecological psychology.

2. The niche construction process (how humans adapt to their natural and social habitats by creating new technologies, norms, and environments) needs to be studied more.

3. Behavioral genetics and experimental designs need to be incorporated to discern the causal role of social ecology.

DISCLOSURE STATEMENT

The author is not aware of any affiliations, memberships, funding, or financial holdings that might be perceived as affecting the objectivity of this review.

ACKNOWLEDGMENTS

I thank Jordan Axt, Kelly Hoffman, and Matt Motyl for their invaluable comments on earlier versions of this manuscript. I thank Corey Fincher and Vladas Griskevicius for providing the original versions of **Figures 1** and **2**, respectively.

LITERATURE CITED

Adolphs R. 2010. Conceptual challenges and directions for social neuroscience. *Neuron* 65:752–67

Allen BC, Sargent LD, Bradley LM. 2003. Differential effects of task and reward interdependence on perceived helping behavior, effort, and group performance. *Small Group Res.* 34:716–40

Allport GW. 1937. *Personality: A Psychological Interpretation.* New York: Holt

Almond GA, Verba S. 1963. *The Civic Culture.* Boston, MA: Little Brown

Alvarez-Díaz A, González L, Radcliff B. 2010. The politics of happiness: on the political determinants of quality of life in the American states. *J. Polit.* 72:894–905

Anderson CA. 2001. Heat and violence. *Curr. Dir. Psychol. Sci.* 10:33–38

Anderson CA, Anderson KB, Dorr N, DeNeve KM, Flanagan M. 2000. Temperature and aggression. *Adv. Exp. Soc. Psychol.* 32:63–133

Bahns AJ, Pickett KM, Crandall CS. 2012. Social ecology of similarity: big schools, small schools and social relationships. *Group Process. Intergroup Relat.* 15:119–31

Barber N. 2003. The sex ratio and female marital opportunity as historical predictors of violent crime in England, Scotland, and the United States. *Cross-Cult. Res.* 37:373–92

Barker RC. 1968. *Ecological Psychology: Concepts and Methods for Studying the Environment of Human Behavior.* Stanford, CA: Stanford Univ. Press

Belsky J, Schlomer GL, Ellis BJ. 2012. Beyond cumulative risk: distinguishing harshness and unpredictability as determinants of parenting and early life history strategy. *Dev. Psychol.* 48:662–73

Berry JW. 1979. A cultural ecology of social behavior. *Adv. Exp. Soc. Psychol.* 12:177–206

Berry JW, Annis RC. 1974. Ecology, culture and psychological differentiation. *Int. J. Psychol.* 9:173–93

Berscheid E, Reis HT. 1998. Attraction and close relationships. In *The Handbook of Social Psychology*, ed. DT Gilbert, ST Fiske, G Lindzey, pp. 193–281. New York: McGraw-Hill. 4th ed.

Bjornskov C, Dreher A, Fischer JAV. 2007. The bigger the better? Evidence of the effect of government size on life satisfaction around the world. *Public Choice* 130:267–92

Bronfenbrenner U. 1977. Toward an experimental ecology of human development. *Am. Psychol.* 32:513–31

Bushman BJ, Wang MC, Anderson CA. 2005. Is the curve relating temperature to aggression linear or curvilinear? Assaults and temperature in Minneapolis reexamined. *J. Personal. Soc. Psychol.* 89:62–66

Butz DA, Yogeeswaran K. 2011. A new threat in the air: Macroeconomic threat increases prejudice against Asian Americans. *J. Exp. Soc. Psychol.* 47:22–27

Cartwright D. 1979. Contemporary social psychology in historical perspective. *Soc. Psychol. Q.* 42:82–93

Cohn EG, Rotton J. 1997. Assault as a function of time and temperature: a moderator-variable time-series analysis. *J. Personal. Soc. Psychol.* 72:1322–34

Connolly M. 2013. Some like it mild and not too wet: the influence of weather on subjective well-being. *J. Happiness Stud.* 14:457–73

Cook KS, Emerson RM, Gillmore MR, Yamagishi T. 1983. The distribution of power in exchange networks: theory and experimental results. *Am. J. Sociol.* 89:275–305

Cozzolino PJ. 2011. Trust, cooperation, and equality: a psychological analysis of the formation of social capital. *Br. J. Soc. Psychol.* 50:302–20

Craik KH. 1973. Environmental psychology. *Annu. Rev. Psychol.* 24:403–22

Cunningham MR. 1979. Weather, mood, and helping behavior: quasi experiments with the sunshine Samaritan. *J. Personal. Soc. Psychol.* 37:1947–56

Darley JM, Latané B. 1968. Bystander intervention in emergencies: diffusion of responsibility. *J. Personal. Soc. Psychol.* 8:377–82

Davies NB, Krebs JR, West SA. 2012. *Introduction to Behavioral Ecology.* West Sussex, UK: Wiley

Presents a comprehensive summary of the heat hypothesis of aggression.

Deaton A. 2003. Health, inequality, and economic development. *J. Econ. Lit.* 41:113–58

Deaton A. 2008. Income, health, and well-being around the world: evidence from the Gallup World Poll. *J. Econ. Perspect.* 22:53–72

Denissen JJA, Butalid L, Penke L, van Aken MA. 2008. The effects of weather on daily mood: a multilevel approach. *Emotion* 8:662–67

Diener E, Diener M, Diener C. 1995. Factors predicting the subjective well-being of nations. *J. Personal. Soc. Psychol.* 69:851–64

Durante F, Fiske ST, Kervyn N, Cuddy AJC, Akande A, et al. 2013. Nations' income inequality predicts ambivalence in stereotype content: how societies mind the gap. *Br. J. Soc. Psychol.* In press

Durante KM, Griskevicius V, Simpson JA, Cantú SM, Tybur JM. 2012. Sex ratio and women's career choice: Does a scarcity of men lead women to choose briefcase over baby? *J. Personal. Soc. Psychol.* 103:121–34

Dweck CS. 2006. *Mindset*. New York: Random House

Edgerton RB. 1965. "Cultural" versus "ecological" factors in the expression of values, attitudes, and personality characteristics. *Am. Anthropol.* 67:442–47

Fincher CL, Thornhill R. 2012. Parasite-stress promotes in-group assortative sociality: the cases of strong family ties and heightened religiosity. *Behav. Brain Sci.* 35(2):39–59

Fincher CL, Thornhill R, Murray DR, Schaller M. 2008. Pathogen prevalence predicts human cross-cultural variability in individualism/collectivism. *Proc. R. Soc. B* 275:1279–85

Fischer R, Van de Vliert E. 2011. Does climate undermine subjective well-being? A 58-nation study. *Personal. Soc. Psychol. Bull.* 37:1031–41

Flavin P, Radcliff B. 2009. Public policies and suicide rates in the American states. *Soc. Indic. Res.* 90:195–209

Florida R. 2002. *The Rise of the Creative Class*. New York: Basic Books

Flynn SM, Greenberg AE. 2012. Does weather actually affect tipping? An empirical time-series data. *J. Appl. Soc. Psychol.* 42:702–16

Gangestad SW, Simpson JA. 2007. *The Evolution of Mind: Fundamental Questions and Controversies*. New York: Guilford

Gelfand MJ, Raver JL, Nishii L, Leslie LM, Lun J, et al. 2011. Differences between tight and loose cultures: a 33-nation study. *Science* 332:1100–4

Golder SA, Macy MW. 2011. Diurnal and seasonal mood vary with work, sleep, and daylength across diverse cultures. *Science* 333:1878–81

Goldschmidt W. 1971. Independence as an element in pastoral social systems. *Anthropol. Q.* 44:132–42

Greenberg G. 1972. The effects of ambient temperature and population density on aggression in two inbred straints of mice, *Mus musculus. Behaviour* 42:119–30

Griskevicius V, Tybur JM, Ackerman JM, Delton AW, Robertson TE, White AE. 2012. The financial consequences of too many men: sex ratio effects on saving, borrowing, and spending. *J. Personal. Soc. Psychol.* 102:69–80

Guéguen N, Lamy L. 2013. Weather and helping: additional evidence of the effect of the sunshine Samaritan. *J. Soc. Psychol.* 153(2):123–26

Harden KP, D'Onofrio BM, Van Hulle C, Turkheimer E, Rodgers JL, et al. 2009. Population density and youth antisocial behavior. *J. Child Psychol. Psychiatry* 50:999–1008

Harris E. 2011. Darwin's city: David Sloan Wilson is using the lens of evolution to understand life in the struggling city of Binghamton, New York. *Nature* 474:146–49

Hartig T, Catalano R, Ong M. 2007. Cold summer weather, constrained restoration, and the use of antide-pressants in Sweden. *J. Environ. Psychol.* 27:107–16

Hatzenbuehler ML. 2011. The social environment and suicide attempts in lesbian, gay, and bi-sexual youth. *Pediatrics* 127:896–903

Hatzenbuehler ML, McLaughlin KA, Keyes KM, Hasin DS. 2010. The impact of institutional discrimination on psychiatric disorders in lesbian, gay, and bisexual populations: a prospective study. *Am. J. Public Health* 100:452–59

Heine SJ, Renshaw K. 2002. Interjudge agreement, self-enhancement, and liking: cross-cultural divergences. *Personal. Soc. Psychol. Bull.* 28:578–87

Helliwell JF, Huang H. 2008. How's your government? International evidence linking good government and well-being. *Br. J. Polit. Sci.* 38:595–619

Represents one of the first studies to link pathogen prevalence with individualism/collectivism.

Provides an exemplary socioecological study on cultural norms.

Describes a series of studies showing the surprising power of the sex ratio in financial decision making and consumer behavior.

Henrich J, Boyd R, Bowles S, Camerer C, Fehr E, Gintis H, et al. 2005. Economic man in cross-cultural perspective: behavioral experiments in 15 small-scale societies. *Behav. Brain Sci.* 28:795–855

Hill SE, Rodeheffer CD, Griskevicius V, Durante K, White AE. 2012. Boosting beauty in an economic decline: mating, spending, and the lipstick effect. *J. Personal. Soc. Psychol.* 103:275–91

Hovland CI, Sears RR. 1940. Minor studies of aggression: VI. Correlation of lynchings with economic indices. *J. Psychol. Interdiscip. Appl.* 9:301–10

Inglehart R. 1997. *Modernization and Post-Modernization: Cultural, Economic, and Political Change in 43 Societies.* Princeton, NJ: Princeton Univ. Press

Inglehart R, Foa R, Peterson C, Welzel C. 2008. Development, freedom, and rising happiness: a global perspective (1981–2007). *Perspect. Psychol. Sci.* 3:264–85

Jackson M, Cox DR. 2013. The principles of experimental design and their application in sociology. *Annu. Rev. Sociol.* 39:27–49

Johansson M, Hartig T, Staats H. 2011. Psychological benefits of walking: moderation by company and outdoor environment. *Appl. Psychol.: Health Well-Being* 3:261–80

Jokela M, Elovainio M, Kivimäki M, Keltikangas-Järvinen L. 2008. Temperament and migration patterns in Finland. *Psychol. Sci.* 19:831–37

Jost JT. 2006. The end of the end of ideology. *Am. Psychol.* 61:651–70

Jost JT, Banaji MR, Nosek BA. 2004. A decade of system justification theory: accumulated evidence of conscious and unconscious bolstering of the status quo. *Polit. Psychol.* 25:881–919

Judge PG, de Waal FBM. 1997. Rhesus monkey behaviour under diverse population densities: coping with long-term crowding. *Anim. Behav.* 54:643–62

Kang N, Kwak N. 2003. A multilevel approach to civic participation: individual length of residence, neighborhood residential stability, and their interactive effects with media use. *Commun. Res.* 30:80–106

Kaplan S, Berman MG. 2010. Directed attention as a common resource for executive functioning and self-regulation. *Perspect. Psychol. Sci.* 5:43–57

Katona G. 1968. Consumer behavior: theory and findings on expectations and aspirations. *Am. Econ. Rev.* 58:19–30

Kawachi I, Kennedy BP, Lochner SM, Prothrow-Stith D. 1997. Social capital, income inequality, and mortality. *Am. J. Public Health* 87:1491–98

Kelly JG. 1971. Qualities for the community psychologist. *Am. Psychol.* 26:897–903

Kenrick DT, MacFarlane SW. 1984. Ambient temperature and horn-honking: a field study of the heat/aggression relationship. *Environ. Behav.* 18:179–91

Kitayama S, Cohen D. 2007. *Handbook of Cultural Psychology.* New York: Guilford

Kitayama S, Ishii K, Imada T, Takemura K, Ramaswamy J. 2006. Voluntary settlement and the spririt of independence: Evidence from Japan's "Northern Frontier." *J. Personal. Soc. Psychol.* 91:369–84

Konishi M. 1994. *Why Do Songbirds Sing?* Tokyo: Iwanami-Shinsho

Kramer GH. 1971. Short-term fluctuations in U.S. voting behavior, 1896–1964. *Am. Polit. Sci. Rev.* 65:131–43

Lederbogen F, Kirsch P, Haddad L, Streit F, Tost H, et al. 2011. City living and urban upbringing affect neural social stress processing in humans. *Nature* 474:498–501

Levine RV, Martinez TS, Brase G, Sorenson K. 1994. Helping in 36 U.S. cities. *J. Personal. Soc. Psychol.* 67:69–82

Lewin K. 1939. Field theory and experiment in social psychology: concepts and methods. *Am. J. Sociol.* 44:868–96

Lewin K, French JRP Jr, Hendry C, Deets LE, Zander A, et al. 1945. The practicality of democracy. In *Human Nature and Enduring Peace: Third Yearbook for the Society for the Psychological Study of Social Issues,* ed. M Gardner, pp. 295–347. Boston, MA: Houghton Mifflin

Lewin K, Lippitt R, White RK. 1939. Patterns of aggressive behavior in experimentally created "social climates." *J. Soc. Psychol.* 10:271–99

Li Y, Johnson ER, Zaval L. 2011. Local warming: daily temperature change influences belief in global warming. *Psychol. Sci.* 22:454–59

Low BS, Hazel A, Parker N, Welch KB. 2008. Influences on women's reproductive lives: unexpected ecological underpinnings. *Cross-Cult. Res.* 42:201–19

Represents a seminal socioecological paper on cooperation and fairness.

Lucas RE, Lawless NM. 2013. Does life seem better on a sunny day? Examining the association between daily weather conditions and life satisfaction judgments. *J. Personal. Soc. Psychol.* 104:872–84

Macy MW, Sato Y. 2002. Trust, cooperation, and market formation in the U.S. and Japan. *Proc. Natl. Acad. Sci. USA* 99:7214–20

Markus HR, Kitayama S. 1991. Culture and the self: implications for cognition, emotion, and motivation. *Psychol. Rev.* 98:224–53

Marschall MJ, Stolle D. 2004. Race and the city: neighborhood context and the development of generalized trust. *Polit. Behav.* 26:125–53

Martens D, Gutscher H, Bauer N. 2011. Walking in "wild" and "tended" urban forests: the impact on psychological well-being. *J. Environ. Psychol.* 31:36–44

Masuda T, Gonzalez R, Kwan L, Nisbett RE. 2008. Culture and aesthetic preference: comparing the attention to context of East Asians and European Americans. *Personal. Soc. Psychol. Bull.* 34:1260–75

McCrae RR, Terracciano A, Realo A, Allik J. 2007. Climatic warmth and national wealth: some culture-level determinants of national character stereotypes. *Eur. J. Personal.* 21:953–76

Milgram S. 1970. The experience of living in cities. *Science* 167:1461–68

Mitchell JP. 2009. Social psychology as a natural kind. *Trends Cogn. Sci.* 13(6):246–51

Miyamoto Y, Nisbett RE, Masuda T. 2006. Culture and the physical environment. *Psychol. Sci.* 17:113–19

Montesquieu CLS. 1748/1989. *Montesquieu: The Spirit of the Laws.* Cambridge, UK: Cambridge Univ. Press

Moore IT, Wingfield JC, Brenowitz EA. 2004. Plasticity of the avian song control system in response to localized environmental cues in an equatorial songbird. *J. Neurosci.* 24:10182–85

Motyl M, Iyer R, Oishi S, Trawalter S, Nosek B. 2013. *How Moral Migration Geographically Segregates and Polarizes Groups.* Charlottesville: Univ. Va.

Murray DR, Schaller M. 2012. Threat(s) and conformity deconstructed: perceived threat of infectious disease and its implications for conformist attitudes and behavior. *Eur. J. Soc. Psychol.* 42:180–88

Napier JL, Jost JT. 2008. Why are conservatives happier than liberals? *Psychol. Sci.* 19:565–72

Nisbett RE, Cohen D. 1996. ***The Culture of Honor: The Psychology of Violence in the South.*** **Denver, CO: Westview**

Norton MI, Ariely D. 2011. Building a better America—one wealth quintile at a time. *Perspect. Psychol. Sci.* 6:9–12

O'Brien DT, Gallup AC, Wilson DS. 2012. Residential mobility and prosocial development within a single city. *Am. J. Community Psychol.* 50:26–36

Odling-Smee J, Laland KN, Feldman MW. 2003. *Niche Construction: The Neglected Process in Evolution.* Princeton, NJ: Princeton Univ. Press

Oishi S. 2010. The psychology of residential mobility: implications for the self, social relationships, and well-being. *Perspect. Psychol. Sci.* 5:5–21

Oishi S. 2012. *The Psychological Wealth of Nations: Do Happy People Make a Happy Society?* Malden, MA: Wiley-Blackwell

Oishi S, Graham J. 2010. Social ecology: lost and found in psychological science. ***Perspect. Psychol. Sci.*** **5:356–77**

Oishi S, Ishii K, Lun J. 2009. Residential mobility and conditionality of group identification. *J. Exp. Soc. Psychol.* 45:913–19

Oishi S, Kesebir S, Diener E. 2011. Income inequality and happiness. *Psychol. Sci.* 22:1095–100

Oishi S, Kesebir S, Snyder BH. 2009. Sociology: a lost connection in social psychology. *Personal. Soc. Psychol. Rev.* 13:334–53

Oishi S, Miao F, Koo M, Kisling J, Ratliff KA. 2012. Residential mobility breeds familiarity-seeking. *J. Personal. Soc. Psychol.* 102:149–62

Oishi S, Rothman AJ, Snyder M, Su J, Zehm K, et al. 2007. The socioecological model of procommunity action: the benefits of residential stability. *J. Personal. Soc. Psychol.* 93:831–44

Oishi S, Schimmack U. 2010a. Culture and well-being: a new inquiry into the psychological wealth of nations. *Perspect. Psychol. Sci.* 5:463–71

Oishi S, Schimmack U. 2010b. Residential mobility, well-being, and mortality. *J. Personal. Soc. Psychol.* 98(6):980–94

Describes an amazing program of research on the social ecology of violence. An epitome of socioecological psychology with methodological rigor and creativity.

Reviews the historical antecedents of socioecological psychology.

Oishi S, Schimmack U, Diener E. 2012. Progressive taxation and the subjective well-being of nations. *Psychol. Sci.* 23:86–92

Oishi S, Talhelm T. 2012. Residential mobility: what psychological research reveals. *Curr. Dir. Psychol. Sci.* 21:425–30

Oliver JE, Wong J. 2003. Intergroup prejudice in multiethnic settings. *Am. J. Polit. Sci.* 47:567–82

Pacek A, Radcliff B. 2008a. Welfare policy and subjective well-being across nations: an individual-level assessment. *Soc. Indic. Res.* 89:179–91

Pacek A, Radcliff B. 2008b. Assessing the welfare state: the politics of happiness. *Perspect. Polit.* 6:267–77

Park N, Peterson C. 2010. Does it matter where we live? The urban psychology of character strengths. *Am. Psychol.* 65:535–47

Pennebaker JW, Rime B, Blankenship VE. 1996. Stereotypes of emotional expressiveness of Northerners and Southerners: a cross-cultural test of Montesquieu's hypotheses. *J. Personal. Soc. Psychol.* 70:372–80

Pollet TV, Nettle D. 2008. Driving a hard bargain: sex ratio and male marriage success in a historical US population. *Biol. Lett.* 4:31–33

Pollet TV, Nettle D. 2009. Market forces affect patterns of polygyny in Uganda. *Proc. Natl. Acad. Sci. USA* 106:2114–17

Poot H, ter Maat A, Trost L, Schwabl I, Jansen RF, Gahr M. 2012. Behavioural and physiological effects of population density on domesticated Zebra Finches (*Taeniopygia guttata*) held in aviaries. *Physiol. Behav.* 105:821–28

Portes A, Vickstrom E. 2011. Diversity, social capital, and cohesion. *Annu. Rev. Sociol.* 37:461–79

Preuss GG. 1981. The effects of density and urban residence on voter turnout. *Popul. Environ.: Behav. Soc. Issues* 4:245–65

Putnam RD. 2007. *E pluribus unum*: diversity and community in the twenty-first century. The 2006 Johan Skytte prize lecture. *Scand. Polit. Stud.* 30:137–74

Regoeczi WC. 2003. When context matters: a multilevel analysis of household and neighborhood crowding on aggression and withdrawal. *J. Environ. Psychol.* 23:457–70

Rentfrow PJ, Gosling SD, Potter J. 2008. A theory of the emergence, persistence, and expression of geographic variation in psychological characteristics. *Perspect. Psychol. Sci.* 3:339–69

Reppucci ND, Woolard JL, Fried CS. 1999. Social, community, and preventive interventions. *Annu. Rev. Psychol.* 50:387–418

Rind B. 1996. Effect of beliefs about weather conditions on tipping. *J. Appl. Soc. Psychol.* 26:137–47

Rind B, Strohmetz D. 2001. Effect of beliefs about future weather conditions on restaurant tipping. *J. Appl. Soc. Psychol.* 31:260–64

Risen JL, Critcher CR. 2011. Visceral fit: While in a visceral state, associated states of the world seem more likely. *J. Personal. Soc. Psychol.* 100:777–93

Rogers KH, Wood D. 2010. Accuracy of United States regional personality stereotypes. *J. Res. Personal.* 44:704–13

Rosenfeld R, Fornango R. 2007. The impact of economic conditions on robbery and property crime: the role of consumer sentiment. *Criminology* 45:735–69

Rozin P. 2001. Social psychology and science: some lessons from Solomon Asch. *Personal. Soc. Psychol. Rev.* 5:2–14

Sales SM. 1972. Economic threat as a determinant of conversion rates in authoritarian and nonauthoritarian churches. *J. Personal. Soc. Psychol.* 23:420–28

Sales SM. 1973. Threat as a factor in authoritarianism: an analysis of archival data. *J. Personal. Soc. Psychol.* 28:44–57

Sales SM, Friend KE. 1973. Success and failure as determinants of level of authoritarianism. *Behav. Sci.* 18:163–72

Sampson EE. 1981. Cognitive psychology as ideology. *Am. Psychol.* 36:730–43

Sampson RJ, Raudenbush SW, Earls F. 1997. Neighborhoods and violent crime: a multilevel study of collective efficacy. *Science* 277:918–24

Savani K, Rattan A. 2012. A choice mind-set increases the acceptance and maintenance of wealth inequality. *Psychol. Sci.* 23:796–804

Describes groundbreaking work on geographical variation in personality.

Savani K, Stephens NM, Markus HR. 2011. The unanticipated interpersonal consequences of choice: victim blaming and reduced support for the public good. *Psychol. Sci.* 22:795–802

Schaller M, Murray DR. 2008. Pathogens, personality and culture: Disease prevalence predicts worldwide variability in sociosexuality, extraversion, and openness to experience. *J. Personal. Soc. Psychol.* 95:212–21

Schaller M, Neuberg SL. 2012. Danger, disease, and the nature of prejudice(s). *Adv. Exp. Soc. Psychol.* 46:1–54

Schkade DA, Kahneman D. 1998. Does living in California make people happy? A focusing illusion in judgments of life satisfaction. *Psychol. Sci.* 9:340–46

Schug J, Yuki M, Horikawa H, Takemura K. 2009. Similarity attraction and actually selecting similar others: how cross-societal differences in relational mobility affect interpersonal similarity in Japan and the United States. *Asian J. Soc. Psychol.* 12:95–103

Schug J, Yuki M, Maddux WW. 2010. Relational mobility explains between- and within-culture differences in self-disclosure toward close friends. *Psychol. Sci.* 21:1471–78

Seder JP, Oishi S. 2009. Racial homogeneity in college students' Facebook friendship network and subjective well-being. *J. Res. Personal.* 43:438–43

Segall MH, Campbell DT, Herskovits MJ. 1963. Cultural differences in the perception of geometric illusions. *Science* 139:769–71

Simonsohn U. 2010. Weather to go to college. *Econ. J.* 120:270–80

Simpson JA, Griskevicius V, Kuo SI-C, Sung S, Collins WA. 2012. Evolution, stress, and sensitive periods: the influence of unpredictability in early versus late childhood on sex and risky behavior. *Dev. Psychol.* 48:674–86

Smith ER, Semin GR. 2004. The foundations of socially situated action: socially situated cognition. *Adv. Exp. Soc. Psychol.* 36:53–117

Steblay NM. 1987. Helping behavior in rural and urban environments: a meta-analysis. *Psychol. Bull.* 102:346–56

Stokols D. 1978. Environmental psychology. *Annu. Rev. Psychol.* 29:253–95

Stolle D, Soroka S, Johnston R. 2008. When does diversity erode trust? Neighborhood diversity, trust, and the mediating effect of social interactions. *Polit. Stud.* 56:57–75

Taylor MC. 1998. How white attitudes vary with the racial composition of local populations: Numbers count. *Am. Sociol. Rev.* 63:512–35

Titus RG. 1990. Territorial behavior and its role in population regulation of young brown trout (*Salmo trutta*): new perspectives. *Ann. Zool. Fennici* 27:119–30

Uskul AK, Kitayama S, Nisbett RE. 2008. Ecocultural basis of cognition: Farmers and fishermen are more holistic than herders. *Proc. Natl. Acad. Sci. USA* 105:8552–56

Valdesolo P, Ouyang J, DeSteno D. 2010. The rhythm of joint action: Synchrony promotes cooperative ability. *J. Exp. Soc. Psychol.* 46:693–95

Van de Vliert E. 2009. *Climate, Affluence, and Culture*. New York: Cambridge Univ. Press

Van Leeuwen F, Park JH, Koenig BL, Graham J. 2012. Regional variation in pathogen prevalence predicts endorsement of group-focused moral concerns. *Evol. Hum. Behav.* 33:429–37

Van Vugt M, Jepson SF, Hart CM, De Cremer D. 2004. Autocratic leadership in social dilemmas: a threat to group stability. *J. Exp. Soc. Psychol.* 40:1–13

Vasi IB, Macy M. 2003. The mobilizer's dilemma: crisis, empowerment, and collective action. *Soc. Forbes* 81:979–98

Veenhoven R. 2000. Well-being in the welfare state: Level not higher, distribution not more equitable. *J. Comp. Policy Anal.* 2:91–125

Wageman R, Baker G. 1997. Incentives and cooperation: the joint effect of task and reward interdependence on group performance. *J. Organ. Behav.* 18:139–58

Wang H, Masuda T, Ito K, Rashid M. 2012. How much information? East Asian and North American cultural products and information search performance. *Personal. Soc. Psychol. Bull.* 38:1539–51

Watson D. 2000. *Mood and Temperament*. New York: Guilford

White MP, Alcock I, Wheeler BW, Depledge MH. 2013. Would you be happier living in a green urban area? A fixed-effects analysis of panel data. *Psychol. Sci.* 24:920–28

Represents a bold theoretical paper on the social ecology of stereotypes and prejudices.

Wilkinson RG, Pickett KE. 2006. Income inequality and population health: a review and explanation of the evidence. *Soc. Sci. Med.* 62:1768–84

Williams DA, Lawton MF, Lawton RO. 1994. Population growth, range expansion, and competition in the cooperatively breeding brown jay, *Cyanocorax morio*. *Anim. Behav.* 48:309–22

Wilson M, Daly M. 1997. Life expectancy, economic inequality, homicide, and reproductive timing in Chicago neighborhoods. *Br. Med. J.* 314:1271–74

Wilson TD. 2011. *Redirect: The Surprising New Science of Psychological Change*. New York: Little, Brown

Wiltermuth SS, Heath C. 2009. Synchrony and cooperation. *Psychol. Sci.* 20:1–5

Yamagishi T. 2011. Micro-macro dynamics of the cultural construction of reality: a niche construction approach. In *Advances in Culture and Psychology, Vol. 1*, ed. MJ Gelfand, C-y Chiu, Y-y Hong, pp. 251–308. New York: Oxford Univ. Press

Yamagishi T, Yamagishi M. 1994. Trust and commitment in the United States and Japan. *Motiv. Emot.* 18:129–66

Young MA, Meaden PM, Fogg LF, Cherin EA, Eastman CI. 1997. Which H_2O_2 environmental variables are related to the onset of seasonal affective disorder? *J. Abnorm. Psychol.* 106:554–62

Yuki M, Schug J. 2012. Relational mobility: a socio-ecological approach to personal relationships. In *Relationship Science: Integrating Evolutionary, Neuroscience, and Sociocultural Approaches*, ed. O Gillath, GE Adams, AD Kunkel, pp. 137–52. Washington, DC: Am. Psychol. Assoc.

Social Class Culture Cycles: How Three Gateway Contexts Shape Selves and Fuel Inequality

Nicole M. Stephens,[1] Hazel Rose Markus,[2] and L. Taylor Phillips[3]

[1] Kellogg School of Management at Northwestern University, Evanston, Illinois 60201; email: n-stephens@kellogg.northwestern.edu

[2] Department of Psychology, and [3] Graduate School of Business, Stanford University, Stanford, California 94305

Annu. Rev. Psychol. 2014. 65:611–34

First published online as a Review in Advance on September 25, 2013

The *Annual Review of Psychology* is online at http://psych.annualreviews.org

This article's doi: 10.1146/annurev-psych-010213-115143

Keywords

social class, culture, education, inequality, intervention

Abstract

America's unprecedented levels of inequality have far-reaching negative consequences for society as a whole. Although differential access to resources contributes to inequality, the current review illuminates how ongoing participation in different social class contexts also gives rise to culture-specific selves and patterns of thinking, feeling, and acting. We integrate a growing body of interdisciplinary research to reveal how social class culture cycles operate over the course of the lifespan and through critical gateway contexts, including homes, schools, and workplaces. We first document how each of these contexts socializes social class cultural differences. Then, we demonstrate how these gateway institutions, which could provide access to upward social mobility, are structured according to middle-class ways of being a self and thus can fuel and perpetuate inequality. We conclude with a discussion of intervention opportunities that can reduce inequality by taking into account the contextual responsiveness of the self.

Contents

INTRODUCTION

A growing social class divide characterizes the contemporary American experience (Murray 2013, Pickety & Saez 2003). In the past 50 years, economic gains in American society have been heavily concentrated at the very top of the income distribution. For example, in 2008 the top 1% of Americans held 21% of the total income compared to 9% in the 1970s, a twofold increase from three decades earlier (Saez 2010). As a result, people at the bottom of the social class hierarchy are increasingly disconnected from the material resources, skills, and life experiences needed to thrive (Duncan & Murnane 2011, Stephens et al. 2012a). This staggering social class divide predicts a wide range of important life outcomes. For example, 74% of students at the 146 top-ranked colleges come from families with earnings in the top income quartile whereas only 3% come from the bottom quartile (Carnevale & Rose 2004).

To explain why social class so powerfully shapes important life outcomes (e.g., attaining a college degree), social scientists often point to resources as the answer. A common approach is to consider how differential access to resources (e.g., money, power, status) creates opportunity gaps that constrain what people are able to do and, in turn, produces inequality (e.g., Bertrand et al. 2004, Kraus et al. 2011, Shah et al. 2012). Material resources, power, and status have a powerful influence on behavior, but they are only the beginning of the story. Life in different social class contexts also affords people different selves. These selves provide culture-specific answers to foundational questions such as "Who am I?" and "How should someone like me act?" Social class experience shapes the type of self that one is likely to become and defines the behaviors that are likely to be experienced as normative.

We use the term self to refer to the continually developing sense of agency or "me" at the center of one's experience (Markus & Conner 2013, Markus & Kitayama 2010, Oyserman & Markus 1993). Selves are interpretive frameworks or schemas that lend meaning to people's experiences and thus provide the mechanism through which contexts shape behavior. Selves are not fixed characteristics of individuals but are instead highly malleable psychological states—ways of being. They emerge in response to the requirements of the multiple and intersecting contexts with which people interact in the course of a given day or over a lifetime. Although people tend to have some continuity in how they think about themselves across time and place, everyone has multiple selves that can arise or be activated in different situations. For example, depending on the situation, most people can behave both independently (focusing on themselves and their preferences) and interdependently (focusing on others and adjusting to the requirements of relationships). One powerful way in which sociocultural contexts—including nation, gender, religion, race/ethnicity, and social class—influence behavior is by fostering the elaboration of one self more than other selves.

The current review integrates a growing body of research from psychology, sociology, organizational behavior, anthropology, and education to illuminate the social class culture cycles, in which selves are both shaped by and shapers of the cultures—i.e., the ideas, interactions, and institutions—of their social class contexts. To accomplish this goal, the review contains two sections. The first provides an overview of research that characterizes the culture-specific behavioral patterns and psychological tendencies that selves in different American social class contexts are likely to afford.

The second section provides an in-depth review of research illuminating how social class culture cycles operate over the lifespan and through three critical contexts—the home, school, and workplace. Following Ridgeway & Fisk (2012), we call these gateway contexts because they are both psychologically formative (i.e., afford particular selves) and function as key access points to future opportunities and valued life outcomes. To reveal how these cycles operate, we first highlight how each gateway context can foster social class cultural differences. Second, we illuminate how mainstream institutions are structured to reflect and reinforce mostly middle-class ways of being a self. Through these dual processes of differential socialization and the institutionalization of middle-class norms, these gateway contexts can fuel and perpetuate inequality.

Earlier accounts of social class cultural differences left the impression that working-class cultures consisted of a constellation of individual attitudes, values, and behaviors that were largely fixed and therefore passed on from one generation to the next (e.g., Moynihan 1965).[1] The past few decades of social psychological research on selves, identities, and cultures, however, reveals that selves are far more dynamic and malleable than was previously theorized (Chen et al. 2001, Hong et al. 2000, Lee & Tiedens 2001, Markus & Hamedani 2007, Markus & Kitayama 2010). For example, since selves are highly contingent on their supporting sociocultural contexts, they change quickly in response to different contextual conditions. Moreover, because individuals actively contribute to their culture cycles, people can change their cultures over time by challenging the ideas, practices, and institutions that constitute them. Taking into account the contextual responsiveness of the self, we conclude this review with a discussion of potential interventions that could reduce the production of inequality.

Throughout this review, we focus on variation in selves that emerge in different social class contexts. To cover a large interdisciplinary literature on social class and behavior, we use the terms middle class and working class as relative terms to organize a broad literature across disciplines in which social class is defined differently (e.g., in terms of educational attainment, household income, or occupational status). Specifically, we use the term working class to refer to individuals in contexts on the bottom half of the social class divide, including people who have attained less

---

[1] The argument was that people in poverty were so socially and economically isolated that they became disorganized, developed low aspirations, and turned away from middle-class values. Once this culture of poverty was in place, the argument went, it was transmitted to the next generation even if the social conditions changed. In the ensuing debates, people cast culture as an internal force that was located within individuals (e.g., in attributes and values), whereas structure (e.g., resources and institutions) was cast as an external force located outside of individuals and their actions. Much research in the past half century, however, has questioned this distinction and now regards culture and structure as interdependent forces that interact to influence each other in a bidirectional, ongoing cycle termed mutual constitution (see Stephens et al. 2012c).

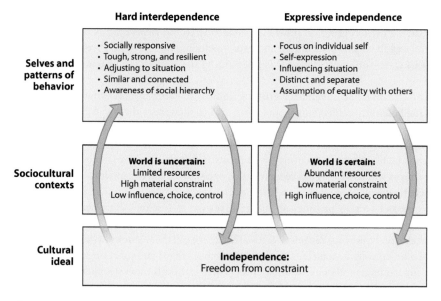

Hard interdependence　　　　　　**Expressive independence**

Selves and patterns of behavior

- Socially responsive
- Tough, strong, and resilient
- Adjusting to situation
- Similar and connected
- Awareness of social hierarchy

- Focus on individual self
- Self-expression
- Influencing situation
- Distinct and separate
- Assumption of equality with others

Sociocultural contexts

World is uncertain:
Limited resources
High material constraint
Low influence, choice, control

World is certain:
Abundant resources
Low material constraint
High influence, choice, control

Cultural ideal

Independence:
Freedom from constraint

Figure 1

US American social class culture cycles.

than a four-year college degree[2] or who have relatively lower incomes or lower-status occupations. We use the term middle class to refer to individuals in contexts on the top half of the social class divide, including people who have attained at least a four-year college degree or who have relatively higher incomes or higher-status occupations.

DIFFERENT SELVES: EXPRESSIVE INDEPENDENCE VERSUS HARD INTERDEPENDENCE

Understanding how social class shapes selves requires attention to both the material resources (e.g., income, access to high-quality education) and the social resources (e.g., relationships with family and friends) that organize people's experiences in different social class contexts. It also requires considering how the availability of these resources shapes behavior over time as well as the resulting cultural norms. For example, how much and what type of influence do people have over their experience in a given situation? Does the situation encourage or allow for the expression of personal preferences, ideas, and opinions? Over time and across situations that afford certain behavior patterns, how people are able to act in turn shapes how people understand what it means to act as a normatively appropriate person (Bourdieu 1977, Correll 2004).

How, then, do repeated experiences in different social class contexts shape what behaviors are possible and the type of self that one is likely to become? To answer this question, it is first necessary to recognize that people's local social class contexts are embedded in a larger national context. As shown in **Figure 1**, in American contexts, all people are exposed to the foundational cultural ideal of independence (e.g., the American Dream, the Protestant Work Ethic). In an

---

[2]We use the term middle class to refer to individuals with a four-year degree or more and the term working class to refer to individuals with less than a four-year degree because these are the modal self-descriptions among individuals with these levels of educational attainment (Lareau & Conley 2008).

effort to achieve this shared cultural ideal, most Americans strive to be free from constraint (see Bellah et al. 1985, Hochschild 1996). This shared independent ideal is not only a metaphor for how one ought to live one's life, but it is also built into and promoted by the social machinery—law, politics, employment, education, media, and healthcare—of mainstream American society (cf. Wilson 2009). Despite the shared aspiration of independence, social class contexts provide unequal opportunities to realize this cultural ideal.

Middle-class American contexts promote and scaffold the American cultural ideal of independence. They provide greater access to economic capital, higher power and status, more geographic mobility, and greater opportunities for choice, influence, and control than do working-class contexts (Day & Newburger 2002, Kohn 1969, Pascarella & Terenzini 1991, Pattillo-McCoy 1999). In response to contexts that can be characterized as relatively stable, predictable, and safe (e.g., higher job security, safer neighborhoods; Bernstein 1974, Kohn 1969), people need to worry far less about making ends meet or overcoming persistent threats than in working-class contexts. Instead, middle-class contexts enable people to act in ways that reflect and further reinforce the independent cultural ideal—expressing their personal preferences, influencing their social contexts, standing out from others, and developing and exploring their own interests.

Life in middle-class contexts tends to afford an understanding of the self and behavior as independent from others and the social context. As shown in **Figure 1**, the broader cultural mandate to be free from constraint, coupled with the wealth of opportunities to act according to this ideal in middle-class contexts, promotes selves and patterns of behavior that are both individual focused and self-expressive. As an example, when a parent asked a middle-class child why he changed his mind, he asserted, "This is America. It's my prerogative to change my mind if I want to" (Lareau 2003, p. 130). We call this way of being expressive independence to distinguish it from the self-protective form of strength and toughness that working-class contexts are more likely to afford.

Although working-class contexts also tend to promote the American cultural ideal of independence, they less often scaffold and institutionalize it. Working-class American contexts are characterized by less access to economic capital, lower power and status, more geographic mobility constraints, and fewer opportunities for choice, control, and influence than middle-class contexts (Lachman & Weaver 1998, Pattillo-McCoy 1999). In response to contexts that can be characterized as relatively chaotic, unpredictable, and risky, people have less freedom to chart their own course and to express themselves than in middle-class contexts. Instead, responding effectively to the conditions of working-class contexts requires a different set of behaviors—adjusting to the social context, being aware of one's position in social hierarchy, and relying on others for material assistance and support (Kohn 1969, Lareau 2003). Notably, however, in working-class contexts, adjusting, responding, and overcoming challenges is often coupled with a sense of toughness, strength, and resilience.

With higher levels of material constraints and fewer opportunities for influence, choice, and control, working-class contexts tend to afford an understanding of the self and behavior as interdependent with others and the social context. As shown in **Figure 1**, the broader cultural ideal of freedom from constraint, coupled with the requirement to adjust to the needs of others and the demands of the social context, promotes selves and patterns of behavior that are both socially responsive and self-protective. We call this way of being hard interdependence[3] because it affords

---

[3]The interdependence that develops in relatively low-resourced, working-class American contexts is different from the style of interdependence common in many East Asian or South Asian contexts. Interdependence in East or South Asian contexts is part of the dominant discourse and is fostered by the mainstream practices and institutions of the larger society (e.g., Tsai et al. 2007), whereas interdependence in American working-class contexts is afforded primarily by holding a relatively low

not only an awareness of the influence of social contexts (Kraus et al. 2009, 2012; Stephens et al. 2007, 2011) but also a focus on strength and toughness (Chen & Miller 2012, Kusserow 2004, Stephens et al. 2009). For example, a college student from a working-class background described how confronting and overcoming adversity had fostered a sense of resilience: "I've been through a lot in my life and that defines who I am now. It gave me a perspective that made college a lot easier to tackle. Midterms and papers are hard, but at the same time they seem like another drop in the bucket" (N.M. Stephens, M.G. Hamedani, & M. Destin, manuscript under review).

In sum, the conditions of different social class contexts give rise to culture-specific selves and corresponding patterns of behavior. The selves that emerge through ongoing participation in middle-class contexts tend to reflect and promote cultural norms of expressive independence, whereas selves in working-class contexts tend to reflect and promote norms of hard interdependence. Each of these ways of being enables people to adapt to their local social class contexts. Furthermore, both expressive independence and hard interdependence can be highly functional even beyond the local social class contexts in which they emerge. However, as we illuminate in the next section, gateway American institutions often translate these social class differences into inequality. They do so by institutionalizing middle-class cultural norms as the cultural ideal and by devaluing the hard interdependence that is prevalent in many working-class contexts.

THE SOCIAL CLASS CULTURE CYCLE: THREE GATEWAY CONTEXTS

In this section, we describe how three gateway contexts—home, school, and workplace— contribute to social class culture cycles. In doing so, we specify two key processes through which the cycle operates: (*a*) socializing social class cultural differences and (*b*) institutionalizing middle-class norms.

The Role of Families

Families are an important gateway context that often provides access to critical resources such as financial and social support, education, and health care (Chen 2004, Evans 2004). For example, early childhood family environments have long-term impacts on children's physical health outcomes (Repetti et al. 2002) and academic achievement (Reardon 2011). Families have such a formative influence, in part, because they provide the initial platform through which children learn how to act as culturally appropriate people in the world (e.g., Lareau 2003). Below we describe the initiation of the social class culture cycle as it emerges in middle-class and working-class families.

Socializing different selves. Local family contexts tend to socialize culture-specific selves and patterns of behavior that will enable individuals to effectively respond to the conditions of those contexts. For example, parents often encourage children to engage in activities and to develop the types of specialized skills that will prepare them to be successful in the different types of worlds that they anticipate their children are likely to encounter in the future.

Middle-class families often prepare their children for a world that is relatively materially unconstrained and thus more stable, predictable, and safe (e.g., higher job security, safer neighborhoods; Bernstein 1974, Kohn 1969). To thrive in contexts with these conditions, children need to develop selves that orient their behavior toward expressive independence. For example, in a series of

---

status within the larger social hierarchy and needing to protect the self against environmental threats and adjust to and attend to others. The style of interdependence common in working-class contexts reflects the foundational American ideal to be free from constraint (e.g., including some expressions of independence through its normative emphasis on strength and toughness) but is tempered by the ongoing requirement to be socially responsive.

interviews, Kusserow (2004) found that parents in middle-class families assume that their children possess soft selves that are like "delicate flowers" and that need to be cultivated to grow and reach their potential. Likewise, parents use words like "bloom" to describe the careful and gentle process of child development (e.g., Kusserow 2012, Lareau 2003). Guided by these assumptions about the nature of the self, parents often encourage their children to prioritize their individual needs, to express themselves, and to influence the world.

In contrast, working-class families often prepare their children for a world that is relatively materially constrained and thus more unstable, unpredictable, and risky (e.g., lack of access to healthcare, lack of an economic safety net). To thrive in contexts with these conditions, children need to develop selves that orient their behavior toward hard interdependence. Kusserow (2004) found that working-class families assume that their children possess hard fortress-like selves that need to be self-protective, tough, strong, and resilient so that children are not easily beaten down and are able to persist in the face of adversity. Parents use words like "keeping your pride" to describe the fortifying process of child development (Kusserow 2012). Guided by these assumptions about the nature of the self, parents often encourage their children to prioritize others' needs over their own, to be attentive to the requirements of the context, and to be strong by standing up for themselves.

Communication styles. These efforts to craft different selves can be seen in how parents interact with their children. Parents may implicitly or explicitly develop these ways of being, for example, through their styles of communication. Middle-class contexts afford and even require the expression of personal desires, beliefs, and opinions, as well as a consideration of how rules can be changed. Parents in middle-class contexts foster norms of expressive independence by immersing their children in what Lareau (2003) calls "a steady stream of speech" or constant conversation in which they encourage their children to share what they are thinking, feeling, and learning (Hart & Risley 1995, Lareau & Calarco 2012, Phillips 2011). Moreover, in the classic book *Class, Codes, and Control* (1974), Basil Bernstein finds that speech patterns in middle-class contexts are characterized by complex grammatical constructions that are often abstract and involve frequent counterfactuals or conditional statements. For example, if a child does or says something inappropriate, parents may ask an indirect question: "Do you really think you should be saying that right now?" or "What do you think will happen if you continue to do that?" (Bernstein 1974, Kusserow 2004). This style of indirect questioning promotes expressive independence by encouraging children to explore their own thoughts and beliefs and to reach their own conclusions.

In contrast, working-class contexts often have less of a safety net than do middle-class contexts, and breaking the rules or stepping out of line can have more severe consequences. Parents in working-class contexts therefore display far less tolerance for breaking the rules and leave little room for error in communicating with their children. Bernstein (1974) finds that speech patterns in working-class contexts are characterized by simple grammatical constructions that are concrete and involve few counterfactuals or conditional statements. For example, when a child does something inappropriate, working-class parents often issue direct commands, such as "Do not say that" or "Never do that again." Such direct commands promote hard interdependence by communicating the importance of being tough and strong and adjusting to the rules.

Storytelling. Parents' efforts to cultivate different selves are also evident in the cultural practice of storytelling. Storytelling is an important medium through which parents can model the "right" way to think, feel, and act as a person in the world. Middle-class contexts, with their built-in safety net, afford ample opportunities for exploration, optimism, and self-expression. When telling stories, parents in middle-class contexts tend to highlight the positive elements of the story while encouraging their children to ask questions and consider alternative realities. For example, if a child tries to rewrite a story by insisting that Santa Claus comes at Easter, a parent may ask: "Really, does he? Tell me about it? How does that work?" This style of storytelling can foster expressive independence by encouraging children to prioritize their own views, to see the world as their oyster, and to challenge the status quo.

In contrast, working-class contexts, with a stronger imperative to avoid errors given the lack of safety net, often require consideration of facts and a close attention to the potential costs of breaking the rules. As a result, parents in working-class contexts tend to dramatize the negative aspects of the story while emphasizing the facts to ensure that their children get the right answers (Miller & Sperry 1987, 2012; Miller et al. 2005). For example, if a child in a working-class context were to insist that Santa Claus visits at Easter, a parent might challenge the child's statement by saying "No, he doesn't, don't be crazy." This style of storytelling can foster hard interdependence by conveying to children that you can't always get what you want and that the world is not theirs for the making.

Activities and play. How children spend their time also fosters different selves. In middle-class contexts, which often require and reward individuality, parents frequently engage in what Lareau (2003) calls concerted cultivation. They provide a range of enrichment activities (e.g., play dates, creative classes) that will help their children develop and explore their personal interests (Vincent & Ball 2007). For example, parents are likely to ask questions and give their children choices: "Would you prefer to try art or sports camp this summer?" In the course of answering such questions, parents tend to encourage their children to elaborate their preferences as well as to consider what those preferences signal about who they are. Parents then further scaffold their children's interactions with their instructors in these activities, helping to ensure good experiences while also teaching their children to voice their likes and dislikes to authority figures (see Lareau & Weininger 2003). For example, a parent might say, "If you don't like the way Mr. Thompson is arranging the teams, you should tell him." Engaging in structured and individually tailored activities can promote expressive independence by showing children the importance of pursuing their own passions, expressing themselves through their actions, and influencing the world to reflect their preferences.

In working-class contexts, which are more likely to require an awareness of the importance of others' needs and preferences, parents more often adhere to what Lareau (2003) calls a natural growth model. In other words, parents are less likely to create structured activity schedules to meet their children's personal interests. Instead, they more often trust that their children will develop naturally—through frequent social interactions with others and with limited parental intervention. For example, a parent might tell a child to go outside to play with siblings and neighborhood friends and would expect the child to figure out how to entertain herself. Parents are less likely to scaffold these interactions with peers. For example, if neighborhood children were to have a dispute, a parent might emphasize the importance of resolving the problem on their own. Encouraging children to engage in unstructured activities without parental intervention can foster hard interdependence by instilling the value of getting along with others and teaching children how to stand their ground and negotiate their social interactions for themselves.

The Role of Schools

Schools are a critical gateway context that can provide access to valuable financial assets, social networks, and future educational and job opportunities (Lareau & Weininger 2003). For example, in the US economy today most jobs that provide a living wage and basic benefits require at least a four-year college degree, and college graduates can expect to earn 84% more money than high school graduates earn (Carnevale et al. 2011).

Although education is an increasingly important arbiter of who has access to valued life opportunities, schools are not neutral spaces. Instead, the ideas, practices, and standards of evaluation prevalent in educational settings both reflect and promote culture-specific norms for how to be a good student. Schools can promote these norms by providing students with educational experiences that encourage the development of specialized skills and patterns of behavior, which will help them to effectively navigate their future occupations (Bowles & Gintis 1976, Oakes 1982). In doing so, schools can either continue to foster the selves that children develop in the home or they can provide a pathway to becoming bicultural and thereby interrupt the social class culture cycles that are often initiated in the home.

Schools in working-class, low-income communities often reflect and promote the norms of hard interdependence that are common in many working-class families. Given the low rates of social mobility in American society compared to other industrialized nations (OECD 2010), many educators in working-class schools assume that most working-class students will not migrate to the middle class but rather that they need to be prepared for the conditions of the low-wage, blue-collar jobs they are likely to hold in the future. If students from working-class families attend schools in their local working-class communities, they are often socialized by the schools and their teachers in a way that will continue to develop patterns of behavior that reflect hard interdependence. At the same time, they rarely get the opportunity to develop the norms of expressive independence that are institutionalized in many mainstream American settings.

On the other hand, schools in middle-class or mixed-social-class communities often represent a potential access point to opportunities to attain higher education and thus upward social mobility in American society. These schools tend to offer greater resources (e.g., new textbooks, Internet access) and higher-quality teachers (Darling-Hammond 2006, Phillips & Chin 2004). They also tend to foster the norms of expressive independence that are institutionalized and taken for granted in many university settings and in high-status, professional occupations (Stephens et al. 2012a). Many educators in these schools assume that students need to be prepared to excel in university classrooms and to navigate the high-wage professional or managerial jobs that they will likely hold in the future.

Middle-class students who attend these schools have an opportunity, then, to strengthen the norms of expressive independence that are often cultivated in family contexts. In contrast, working-class students who attend middle-class schools (or who defy the odds and make it to universities) have an opportunity to develop additional selves that orient behavior toward expressive independence. However, if educators do not provide the additional time and resources that many working-class students need during this challenging transition, then the exclusive focus on expressive independence in middle-class schools can create barriers to working-class students' success. For example, even before students have the opportunity to learn how to enact expressive independence, many educators rely on these norms as the cultural standard through which they interpret and evaluate students' behavior (Fryberg & Markus 2007, Greenfield 1997, Kim 2002, Li 2003). Moreover, the exclusion of norms of hard interdependence can inadvertently signal to working-class students that school is not a place for students like them and, as a result, lead them to struggle both socially and academically.

Schools in working-class contexts socialize hard interdependence. Schools in working-class communities often continue to foster the norms of hard interdependence that many working-class families begin to cultivate in the home. Schools promote these ways of being because they tend to assume that their mostly working-class students will go straight from high school to the workforce to obtain a low-wage, blue-collar job.[4] Blue-collar jobs present relatively few opportunities for choice and control, little substantive complexity, and a high degree of routinization and supervision (Kohn & Schooler 1969, 1973). To effectively navigate jobs with these expectations, workers need to be familiar with and know how to enact hard interdependence, including being tough and strong and cooperating with and adjusting to others.

To cultivate the skills and values that many students will need in working-class occupations, working-class schools often present a classroom experience that resembles the military (Anyon 1980, MacLeod 2009). For instance, the classroom experience is characterized by relatively limited individual freedom, restricted access to class materials and supplies, more routine and structured activities throughout the day, and stricter rules. To convey the importance of deference to authority and following the rules, teachers often evaluate students' homework based on whether they followed the instructions rather than whether they get the right answer. These conditions tend to foster hard interdependence by emphasizing the importance of solidarity, knowing one's place in the hierarchy, and recognizing that "it's not all about you."

Schools in middle-class contexts socialize expressive independence. Schools in middle-class or mixed-social-class communities often continue to foster the norms of expressive independence that many middle-class families cultivate in the home. Teachers in middle-class schools tend to assume that their students will go from high school to college and afterward obtain a high-wage professional or managerial job. Both colleges and managerial or professional occupations require relatively high levels of autonomy, substantively complex work, and a nonroutinized flow of tasks (Kohn & Schooler 1969, 1973). To effectively navigate contexts with these expectations, students need to develop expressive independence—to be confident in their abilities, promote their interests, and express their ideas and opinions.

To cultivate the skills and values that many students will need in high-wage, professional occupations, middle-class schools provide an academic experience closer to that of a university setting. For instance, the classroom experience is characterized by ample individual freedom, open access to class materials (e.g., art supplies), complex and varied tasks, and freedom of movement and activities (e.g., a choice among tasks; Anyon 1980). To instill independent thinking when solving problems, teachers focus not on following the rules but rather on the importance of understanding the logic behind the process of answering a question (Anyon 1980, Heath 1982). They also emphasize the value of independent work, encourage students to ask questions, and place greater emphasis on creativity and challenging assumptions. These conditions tend to foster expressive independence by promoting a sense of ownership, an awareness of opportunities for choice and self-expression, and a desire to promote individual accomplishments.

Producing disadvantage: working-class students in middle-class schools. As described in the section above, working-class students who attend low-income, working-class schools are often further socialized with hard interdependence, whereas middle-class students in middle-class schools often gain additional expertise with expressive independence. These differences are not inherently problematic, as both of these ways of being are responsive to the conditions of the contexts in which they emerge. The reality, however, is that important gateway institutions in American society, which serve as key access points to valued resources and upward mobility, institutionalize expressive independence as the norm and therefore evaluate and treat people on the

---

[4]Given income-based residential segregation, middle-class students rarely live in working-class neighborhoods. If they do, they often attend private schools instead of local working-class public schools (cf. Reardon 2011).

basis of these middle-class expectations. As a result, the continued socialization of hard interdependence can limit working-class students' access to subsequent opportunities (e.g., college or professional jobs).

Many working-class students, however, do have the opportunity to attend middle-class schools and to gain access to higher education. These students have a chance to become bicultural, developing norms of expressive independence that are often required to excel in middle-class university settings and beyond. Yet, as we document in the sections that follow, these students are still disadvantaged because middle-class schools tend to take it for granted that expressive independence is the only "right" way to be a student. Additionally, teachers rarely harness the norms of hard independence—a sense of strength and resilience, an awareness of others' needs, and an ability to adjust oneself to the social context—that many students from working-class contexts bring with them to school settings. As a result, the school culture can inadvertently signal to working-class students that they do not belong and are unlikely to be successful there. These experiences can disadvantage working-class students and prevent them from fully realizing their potential.

Institutional interactions. Middle-class American schools and university settings tend to reflect and promote expressive independence as the standard against which students' and parents' behavior is interpreted and evaluated. This focus on expressive independence guides administrators' and educators' assumptions about how students should learn, be motivated, and interact with peers and professors. For example, in a survey of administrators at research universities and liberal arts colleges, we found that the vast majority reported that their institutions expect students to enact norms of expressive independence—to pave their own paths, to challenge norms and rules, to express their personal preferences, and to work independently (Stephens et al. 2012b).

For students from middle-class backgrounds, expressive independence is likely experienced as a seamless continuation of their previous experiences at home. As a result, they are not only equipped with the "rules of the game" needed to excel, but they are also likely to take it for granted that they belong and know how to fully realize their academic potential. Yet, for many working-class students, who are more often guided by norms of hard interdependence, expressive independence is often disconnected from their previous experiences at home, and thus they are less likely to feel comfortable in these settings and to have the skills needed to enact the expected behaviors. For example, college students from working-class backgrounds, who are more accustomed to schools with highly structured curricula and clear rules, report difficulty choosing a major or planning out their schedules to manage multiple and often competing demands on their time (e.g., papers and exams). As a result of such difficulties, working-class students are often disadvantaged. They experience more stress and perform worse academically than do their middle-class peers (Stephens et al. 2012b,d).

Student-teacher interactions. Teachers in mainstream schools often assume that good students are those who exemplify norms of expressive independence. For example, Calarco (2011) finds that teachers expect students to be proactive learners—to go out of their way to ask questions, take charge of their educational experience, and express their needs to the teacher. If students demand the help that they require, teachers often view this behavior as indicating a motivated, thoughtful, and intellectually curious student. Yet, if students sit quietly, try to figure things out on their own, and do not speak up when they need help, teachers may assume either that students do not need help or that they do not have the drive, talent, or imagination necessary to excel.

Middle-class students, guided by norms of expressive independence, often learn how to prioritize their own needs and tend to assume they are on equal footing with the teacher. As a result, they have more comfort and familiarity expressing these needs and are thus more likely than working-class students to approach the teacher, raise their hand to ask questions, and even interrupt the teacher in the middle of class. On the other hand, working-class students, guided by norms of hard interdependence, more often learn the importance of "hanging in there" and of showing respect and deference to authority figures. As a result, students from working-class contexts often seek to avoid burdening the teacher and thus are less likely to proactively ask questions of the teacher or request assistance when they need it (Calarco 2011; see also Kim & Sax 2009).

Because norms of expressive independence guide teachers' responses to students, middle-class students who enact these norms are given an educational leg-up on their working-class peers. Not only do teachers more often help their middle-class students, but they also respond more positively to them, given that they are likely to fit their assumptions about what it means to be a good student. Teachers offer middle-class students more attention, more frequent praise, and higher levels of responsiveness (Calarco 2011, Rist 1970). However, working-class students, who more often enact norms of hard interdependence, are less likely to fit with teachers' normative views of a good student. They therefore receive less ongoing support than their middle-class peers, which places them at a distinct academic disadvantage.

Parent-teacher interactions. Just as teachers assume that students should be proactive learners, they assume that good parents are those who are highly involved, informed, assertive, and advocate for their children. Teachers and administrators (who are often middle class themselves) expect parents to take charge of and influence their children's educational experience—that is, they expect parents to act as partners with the teacher. If parents act according to these expectations, then teachers tend to assume that these parents are highly committed to their children's education and are therefore more attentive to the parents' demands. If parents are less involved, however, teachers tend to assume that parents are either satisfied with their children's academic experience and progress or that they simply do not care about their children's education.

Middle-class parents, guided by norms of expressive independence, often take on the role of educational expert, as they tend to assume that they are equals with the teacher and know what is best for their child academically (Reay 1998). As a result, middle-class parents are more likely than working-class parents to challenge the rules, question the judgments of school officials, and take charge of their children's educational experience in a way that promotes learning and growth (Horvat et al. 2003). For example, if a teacher gives a child negative feedback that threatens the child's sense of self-esteem, a parent might set up a meeting with the teacher to discuss how the teacher can provide more sensitive feedback in the future (see Lareau & Weininger 2003). In contrast, many working-class parents, guided by norms of hard interdependence, often assume that the teacher is the expert who should be primarily responsible for their child's education. Because they are aware of their lower rank in the social hierarchy in relation to the teacher as well as their own limited experience navigating the educational system, they may feel uncomfortable interacting with the teacher and be less equipped to initiate discussions with the teacher about their children's progress.

Norms of expressive independence guide teachers' responses to parents, and thus middle-class parents are more often successful advocates for their children, securing them additional help, academic opportunities, and individually tailored learning experiences. Middle-class students reap the benefits of their parents' advocacy and efforts to promote their academic interests. For example, students from affluent families are more likely to receive accommodations for learning disabilities on college entrance exams such as the SAT and ACT than are students from low-income families (Calif. State Audit. 2000). Additionally, when the result of a test does not produce the desired outcome (e.g., admission into the gifted program), middle-class parents are more likely to have their children retested and to ask school officials to make an exception to the rule (Lareau & Weininger 2003).

On the other hand, although working-class parents are often equally committed to fighting for their children, they are less likely to have the resources or knowledge required to effectively advocate on their children's behalf. As a result, working-class students are often disadvantaged because they less often receive the intervening parental support that would produce more positive academic outcomes and greater access to opportunities. Additionally, if teachers assume that middle-class parents' greater involvement indicates that they are more committed to their children's educational success than are working-class parents, then teachers are likely to respond more positively to their interactions with both the middle-class parents and their children (Lareau 1987).

The Role of the Workplace

Workplaces provide access to income, health insurance, and other valuable resources that help employees provide for their families, send children to college, and save for retirement. Thus, the workplace is yet another important gateway context that can either continue to foster the selves that are initiated in the home and often perpetuated in schools or that can interrupt and change the course of these social class culture cycles. Like the institution of education, however, workplaces are not neutral spaces but instead reflect culture-specific norms and assumptions about how to be a good employee or coworker. Just as teachers prepare students for different anticipated life trajectories, so too do employers socialize workers to be effective in different types of occupations (Acker 2006). The occupations typically held in middle-class contexts are those that require a college degree, are managerial or professional in nature, and involve nonmanual labor (often called white-collar jobs). In contrast, the occupations typically held in working-class contexts often require a high school diploma or less, provide hourly wages, and involve manual labor or low-skill service work (called blue- or pink-collar jobs).

Working-class occupations often reflect and promote the norms of hard interdependence that are common in many working-class families and schools. If students go straight from high school to work rather than attending college, then their managers and coworkers will often assume these individuals will remain in these working-class jobs and need to be prepared for work that is generally routinized, monotonous, and team-oriented. Thus, these workers tend to be socialized by their managers and coworkers in a way that will continue to develop patterns of behavior that reflect hard interdependence. On the other hand, middle-class occupations often represent a potential access point to increasingly high-status positions and secure, higher incomes. Many managers in middle-class workplaces reasonably assume that their employees will remain in the middle class and need to be prepared to eventually work as independent managers, innovators, and even power brokers. Thus, they tend to foster the norms of expressive independence that are taken for granted in many middle-class homes and schools.

Those employees from working-class backgrounds who defy the odds to attend college and then gain access to middle-class jobs likely will have accumulated some experience and comfort with norms of expressive independence. In university settings, they will have been exposed to these norms and may have attained some level of fluency in expressive independence (as well as hard interdependence) and therefore have become bicultural. Nevertheless, these students still have far less experience with and knowledge about how to enact the particular norms of expressive independence required in elite, high-status professions (e.g., consulting or investment banking) compared to their peers, who have inhabited middle-class worlds for their entire lives. Thus, on the path to career success, the exclusive focus on expressive independence is likely to create obstacles for employees from working-class backgrounds.

Working-class occupations socialize hard interdependence. Working-class occupations (e.g., machine technicians) continue to foster the norms of hard interdependence that employees are often previously exposed to both in the home and at school. These occupations promote these ways of being because they often require interdependence with others (e.g., working together to fight a fire), involve close monitoring by one's superiors, and have a relatively routinized set of tasks and procedures (Kohn & Schooler 1969, 1973). Work settings characterized by these conditions also tend to offer employees relatively few opportunities to influence the type of work that they do, decide how they spend their time, or express themselves.

To navigate working-class jobs effectively, workers need to follow the rules, cooperate with others, show discipline, and be deferential to their superiors (Berg et al. 2010, Wrzesniewski & Dutton 2001). These behavioral requirements reflect and foster norms of hard interdependence. For instance, workers are often socialized through workplace interactions to value social relations, coworkers, and security (Cooke & Rousseau 1998, Friedlander 1965, Lamont 2000, Salzinger 2003, Urtasun & Núñez 2012). For example, Barker (1993) finds that both supervisors and coworkers in a working-class manufacturing company emphasize that job success relies on cooperating with fellow workers and being responsive to social norms. Work teams in this setting are organized to stick together over time, and these ongoing relationships are meant to enhance group solidarity, enforce rules, and increase productivity. Additionally, because working-class jobs are often physically strenuous and produce tangible, concrete outputs (e.g., building a house or fixing a sink; Torlina 2011, Williams 2012), employees are often socialized to view work as means to an end or as a functional activity necessary to support one's family (Lamont 2000).

Middle-class occupations socialize expressive independence. Middle-class occupations (e.g., managers) continue to foster the norms of expressive independence that their workers are often previously exposed to both in the home and in schools. Middle-class occupations focus on these ways of being because they often require independence from others (e.g., writing a memo on one's computer), are relatively cognitively demanding, and involve a specific outcome goal coupled with the personal freedom to decide how and in what manner one wants to pursue that goal. Such work often focuses on personal freedom and choice and offers employees the opportunity to job craft or to have the ability to influence their job to meet their needs (Berg et al. 2010). For example, software engineers at Google are offered the option of using 20% of their day to work on a task of their choosing (Wojcicki 2011).

To navigate middle-class jobs effectively, workers need to be creative, express themselves, and experiment with different strategies. These behavioral requirements further reflect and foster norms of expressive independence. For instance, workers are often socialized through workplace interactions to value independence and freedom (Bacon & Storey 1996, Cooke & Rousseau 1998, Friedlander 1965, Hyman 1994, Lamont 2000, Urtasun & Núñez 2012). For example, Sutton & Hargadon (1996) found that IDEO (a professional product-design firm) emphasizes to employees that job success relies on challenging and breaking rules, expressing personal views, and being independent thinkers. To ensure that people remain independent and creative in their thinking, project work teams are regularly reorganized so as to disrupt the emergence of strong group norms. Furthermore, because the products of labor in middle-class jobs are often based on ideas (e.g., a presentation), employees are socialized to view work not as a means to an end (e.g., to pay the bills) but instead as a valuable end in and of itself (e.g., a source of self-expression or personal fulfillment; Williams 2012).

Producing disadvantage: working-class employees in middle-class workplaces. As described in the section above, working-class employees in working-class occupations are often further socialized with hard interdependence whereas middle-class employees in middle-class occupations continue to accumulate additional expertise with expressive independence. Again, these cultural differences can be beneficial in their respective contexts, as they can help people to respond to the expectations and requirements of different types of occupations. At the same time, however, given that expressive independence is the American cultural ideal and standard against which gateway institutions evaluate employees' competence or success, the continued development of hard interdependence in working-class occupations can also function as an obstacle to upward mobility. For example, working-class employees who enact hard interdependence may seem less qualified for a promotion or for additional opportunities in the future than comparably qualified employees who enact expressive independence.

Some employees from working-class backgrounds manage to defy the odds to earn college degrees and gain entry to middle-class workplaces. These employees have an opportunity to continue on the path to becoming bicultural (and achieving upward mobility) by further developing the norms of expressive independence to which they are often exposed in educational settings. Yet, as we document in the sections that follow, working-class employees are often still disadvantaged in middle-class workplaces because expressive independence is left unmarked as the only "right" way to be an employee and is taken for granted as the norm. Managers often judge potential employees according to these middle-class norms and, at the same time, fail to leverage the norms of hard interdependence that many working-class employees bring with them to occupational settings. As a result, the workplace culture can signal to working-class employees that that they do not belong and prevent them from fully realizing their potential.

Hiring interactions. Managers and employers in mainstream American workplaces (who are themselves mostly middle class) expect and prioritize the norms of expressive independence that pervade many middle-class contexts. For instance, they expect job applicants to ask questions, to express their preferences, and to take risks. These expectations can guide decisions about hiring or promotion (Cooke & Rousseau 1998, England 1967, Mills 2002, Urtasun & Núñez 2012). For example, Rivera (2012) finds that during important decisions about hiring, these expectations for potential employees can manifest themselves in managers' desire to feel a connection or sense of fit with the applicants. Perceptions of fit can, in turn, shape how managers assess applicants' qualifications for a position at an organization (e.g., the merit of their previous experience) as well as their judgment of whether that person is likely to get along with coworkers and bosses.

Throughout the hiring process for these middle-class jobs, many applicants from middle-class backgrounds communicate norms of expressive independence, emphasizing control, choice, and nonconformity. Middle-class applicants also tend to call attention to the numerous, and often expensive, activities and hobbies they enjoy. Managers' familiarity and comfort with applicants who demonstrate cultural fit—through shared norms and extracurricular interests—enables them to view these applicants as successful employees at their organization. For instance, in evaluating one applicant's résumé, a manager noted the importance of identifying hires who would fit in with other employees at the organization: "With his lacrosse and her squash, they'd really get along . . . on the trading floor" (Rivera 2012, p. 1009). As a result, applicants from middle-class backgrounds are advantaged because they are more likely to fit with managers' assumptions about what it means to be an ideal employee and coworker (Ridgeway & Fisk 2012, Rivera 2012).

In contrast, when applicants from working-class backgrounds participate in the hiring process for middle-class occupations, they have had fewer of the life experiences that foster and promote the cultural ideal of expressive independence. Instead, they are more likely to enact norms of hard interdependence, emphasizing social responsivity and toughness in their interactions with potential managers or employers. To make matters worse, working-class applicants also have a more difficult time signaling their cultural fit with the organization by discussing ski weekends or tennis lessons (Ridgeway & Fisk 2012). As a result, hiring managers often view applicants from working-class backgrounds as less well equipped to be successful or to fit in with the company culture of expressive independence (Ridgeway & Fisk 2012, Rivera 2012). Similar to the case in schools, applicants from working-class backgrounds are disadvantaged compared to their middle-class counterparts: Managers assume that working-class applicants do not fit their expectations about what it means to be an ideal employee or coworker.

Workplace interactions. Little empirical research has directly examined how workers from different social class backgrounds respond to a predominantly middle-class workplace culture of expressive independence. We expect, however, that workers' experiences and responses would be quite comparable to those of students. For example, workers from middle-class backgrounds, who have been socialized with expressive independence at home and in schools, would likely be more familiar and comfortable with a workplace culture of expressive independence and thus have a relative advantage.

Yet, for many workers from working-class backgrounds who have likely been socialized with hard interdependence at home and in schools, a focus on expressive independence could reduce their sense of belonging and additionally render it more difficult for them to fit in with and adapt to workplace expectations (cf. Stephens et al. 2012b,d). This mismatch between working-class employees and their middle-class colleagues and institutions could also reduce employees' job security and satisfaction, continuing the cycle of disadvantage for working-class employees.

GENERAL DISCUSSION

The current review synthesizes a growing interdisciplinary literature on social class and behavior to reveal how three gateway contexts—home, school, and workplace—contribute to social class culture cycles. We reveal how these cycles operate through the two key processes of socialization and institutional disadvantage. First, social class contexts characterized by different conditions foster different ways of being a person, student, and worker. Second, middle-class schools and workplaces, which serve as gateway institutions to valued resources and upward social mobility, can create barriers to success for many Americans from working-class backgrounds. They do so by institutionalizing expressive independence as the cultural standard for measuring success. These processes often work in tandem to create, maintain, and reproduce a growing social class divide in access to valued resources, life experiences, and outcomes.

If left unchecked, this social class divide in American society will continue to grow. This divide threatens foundational American ideals, including the American Dream, or the belief that with hard work and effort people can improve their social standing in society. An emerging body of research further suggests that this divide has far-reaching negative consequences for society as a whole. For example, nations with higher levels of inequality are less economically competitive than those with lower levels of inequality (Barro 2001). More unequal nations can also expect to have higher levels of a wide range of social ills, including crime, drug use, school dropouts, depression, anxiety, and early deaths (Kawachi & Kennedy 2002). In the face of higher levels of income inequality, all members of society can expect to live shorter lives, to suffer from higher rates of chronic illnesses, and to be less happy and less trusting of one another than when income inequality is lower (Oishi et al. 2011, Wilkinson 2002).

Sites of Change: Reducing Social Class Inequality

Given the negative individual and societal consequences of this social class divide, a pressing issue for researchers and practitioners alike is understanding its sources and developing the tools to reduce its pernicious effects. As we have illuminated in the current review, the dual processes of socialization and institutional disadvantage are indeed strong forces of social reproduction. The continued growth of social class inequality is, however, not inevitable. In fact, the first step toward halting or even reducing inequality is making visible the largely unseen processes through which social class cycles operate to produce inequality. Although the social class culture cycles operate through both individuals and institutions, interventions need not target all elements of the cycles simultaneously. Rather, the current review suggests that interventions can productively target the constituent elements of culture cycles (e.g., individuals, institutions) in a way that will influence other elements of the cycle and thus become self-sustaining.

Diversifying institutional norms. Institutional norms are one important site of change. Institutions are not neutral but instead promote particular middle-class understandings of how to be an effective person, student, or worker. Institutional norms reflect middle-class perspectives, in part, because the people (e.g., university administrators or managers) who hold the power to create these institutions and define institutional rules and standards of success are typically from middle-class backgrounds. Thus, even in the absence of discriminatory intentions, people in these positions of power often build institutions to reflect their own cultural norms and assumptions about the right way to be a person. And, as we have shown, students and employees from different social class backgrounds not only have differential access to these institutionalized middle-class norms but they also experience these norms quite differently. This is a process that can generate and perpetuate inequality.

Although most gateway contexts reflect middle-class cultural norms, emerging research from social psychology suggests that broadening institutional norms can promote a more inclusive environment and reduce inequality in the process (Davies et al. 2005, Markus et al. 2000, Oyserman et al. 2007, Purdie-Vaughns et al. 2008). For example, our own research with working-class college students demonstrates that even small changes to the norms communicated in cultural products can make a difference. Specifically, reframing welcome letters to make them more inclusive of interdependent selves improved working-class students' college experience (i.e., reduced stress; Stephens et al. 2012d) and their performance on academic tasks (Stephens et al. 2012b). If institutions were to make their cultures more inclusive, then people from diverse social class backgrounds may be able to leverage different aspects of their selves on the pathway to success. For instance, working-class individuals could capitalize on the strength and social responsiveness associated with hard interdependence. At the same time, middle-class individuals could continue to leverage the rule challenging and self-expression associated with expressive independence. In other words, multiple paths to success could be made available to people from different backgrounds.

Another way to diversify institutional norms might be to increase awareness of social class cultural differences and how they are likely to matter for people's experiences in schools or workplaces. Raising awareness in this way might enable power brokers to see the advantages of both hard interdependence and expressive independence and thereby encourage them to be more accepting of different ways of being a student or employee. Awareness of the potential for bias can sometimes diminish the bias itself (see Apfelbaum et al. 2010, Castilla & Benard 2010, Devine et al.

2012). For example, in a typical gateway interaction, a student from a working-class background may be interviewing for a management job with a middle-class supervisor. To the extent managers are unaware of social class differences, they are likely to implicitly value and prioritize expressive independence over the hard interdependence that the potential hire is likely to demonstrate. But to the extent that managers are aware of such social class differences, as well as the potential advantages of hard interdependence, they may be able to work to overcome some of their normative preferences for expressive independence. In turn, these efforts may serve to reduce some of the disadvantage faced by applicants from working-class backgrounds.

Empowering selves. A second site of change is to empower selves in gateway institutions and thereby afford some of the ways of being that are prioritized in important gateway contexts. Supporting the potential effectiveness of such an approach, a growing literature on power, resources, and status indicates that even a single situational experience of having or lacking resources can shift the self and behavior immediately and quite dramatically (e.g., Shah et al. 2012, Vohs et al. 2006). For example, individuals assigned to a high-power role or asked to imagine having power in a single situation view themselves as more independent from others and also display behaviors that are often aligned with norms of expressive independence (Lee & Tiedens 2001). Specifically, they show greater confidence, attend less to others and the social context, are more emotionally expressive, and focus more on pursuing their own goals (Anderson & Berdahl 2002, Gruenfeld et al. 2008, Guinote 2008).

Given the central roles of power, resources, and status in changing selves and behavior in the immediate situation, interventions might seek to provide people with a more enduring sense of psychological empowerment. One route to such empowerment might be to provide individuals with additional knowledge, understanding, or cultural capital. For example, in our own intervention, by exposing students to the stories of successful college students from different social class backgrounds, we empowered working-class students with an understanding of how their backgrounds can make a difference for the college experience—in terms of obstacles, strengths, and strategies for success. Through this experience, students learned that their struggles were an expected part of being a working-class college student with a different background, rather than an indication that they did not belong or could not do well in college. Equipped with this understanding, working-class students also learned and were empowered to enact the behavioral strategies (e.g., asking for help from professors) that students "like them" needed to improve their academic performance (N.M. Stephens, M.G. Hamedani, & M. Destin, manuscript under review; see also Gurin et al. 2013).

Another approach to empowering selves is to educate students directly about the expectations of the dominant culture and the "rules of the game" needed to operate within that culture. For example, an intervention might teach students about the assumptions embedded in the university culture: How do teachers expect students to behave both inside and outside of the classroom? And what is the logic underlying these assumptions? For example, if students from working-class backgrounds understand that professors expect them to voice their ideas and opinions and take the initiative to ask for help, then they may be better equipped to adjust themselves to these expectations of the college culture. Another possibility is that students could be provided "cultural training" sessions in which they would be taught and given a chance to practice the rules for how to interact with professors or peers.

Future Directions

Future research is needed to disentangle the immediate situational effects of power, status, or resources from the more enduring or chronic experiences of social class (see Stephens & Townsend

2013). For example, how might the cultural norms that emerge from repeated or chronic experiences of social class—e.g., interacting with particular ideas, practices, and institutions over time—diverge from those produced by situational manipulations of power? And how do previous experiences in different social class contexts shape how people respond to the presence or absence of resources? For example, Shah and colleagues (2012) reveal that stripping the rich of resources in a single situation can cause them to display behavioral tendencies (e.g., overborrowing) common among the poor. If provided resources, however, would the poor have access to the appropriate cultural scripts or rules for how to display the behavioral tendencies common among the rich? Findings from studies on the manipulation of power and control suggest that the poor will immediately shift in some behaviors but that people's social class backgrounds will also moderate their responses to the acquisition of resources, power, or status.

Future work is also needed to examine the psychological consequences of repeatedly navigating within and across social class boundaries.[5] For example, how do working-class individuals who ascend the social class hierarchy manage the competing and often contradictory demands of school and family life? And how do their selves and behaviors change in responses to these experiences? Moreover, as students adjust to the predominantly middle-class culture of education and work, to what extent do they shed their working-class ways of being versus become bicultural, or fluent in both cultures? Research that illuminates the dynamic nature of self and identity suggests that students from working-class backgrounds are shaped by their ongoing interactions in middle-class schools and workplaces. Yet to what extent and how they are shaped are open questions. Further, research on biculturalism suggests that people who learn middle-class ways of being and also retain working-class ways will have higher levels of psychological well-being and be better prepared to thrive in diverse settings than those who do not (cf. LaFromboise et al. 1993). For example, in middle-class workplaces, elements of hard interdependence may help students from working-class backgrounds to overcome adversity or to adjust to their roles in the organizational hierarchy.

CONCLUSION

Everyday life in American society—from what people watch on television to how they interact with and educate their children—is more stratified along social class lines than ever before. These social class divides not only shape the nature and content of people's everyday lives but also inform the types of experiences to which people have access, as well as the selves and patterns of behavior that people have an opportunity to develop. As America becomes more experientially and culturally divided by social class, individuals who have spent their lives in working-class communities will have an even harder time gaining access to the skills, knowledge, and resources needed to successfully navigate opportunities in a middle-class world. In turn, they will have a harder time accessing the educational credentials and job opportunities that are increasingly necessary to earn a living wage.

Despite the magnitude of these social class divides and their myriad negative consequences for the nation as a whole, American society has been slow to recognize their significance. This blindness to class inequality has been difficult to overcome because social class itself—especially the idea that social class shapes one's life chances and outcomes—runs counter to the idea of America as the land of equal opportunity. Recognizing the influence of these divides further threatens the middle-class belief that success is the result of individual effort or merit alone. For people with middle-class standing, these social class culture cycles afford access to the accumulation of

---

[5]Future work should consider in greater depth how the contextual experiences, as well as the culture-specific selves and patterns of behavior they afford, vary within the working and middle classes.

the experiences, skills, and resources required for success. Moreover, the criteria used to define merit are actively constructed by the people who have the power to define institutional rules and therefore reflect middle-class perspectives. In other words, these cycles and the selves and patterns of behavior that they afford are produced and malleable rather than natural and fixed. With these insights in mind, researchers and practitioners alike will be better equipped to intervene in and change the course of the social class culture cycles and, in doing so, create a more educated, healthy, and productive citizenry.

DISCLOSURE STATEMENT

The authors are not aware of any affiliations, memberships, funding, or financial holdings that might be perceived as affecting the objectivity of this review.

ACKNOWLEDGMENT

We thank Stephanie Fryberg for her comments on earlier versions of this article.

LITERATURE CITED

Acker J. 2006. Inequality regimes: gender, class, and race in organizations. *Gend. Soc.* 20:441–64

Anderson C, Berdahl JL. 2002. The experience of power: examining the effects of power on approach and inhibition tendencies. *J. Personal. Soc. Psychol.* 83:1362–77

Anyon J. 1980. Social class and the hidden curriculum of work. *J. Educ.* 162:67–92

Apfelbaum EP, Pauker K, Sommers SR, Ambady N. 2010. In blind pursuit of racial equality? *Psychol. Sci.* 21:1587–92

Bacon N, Storey J. 1996. Individualism and collectivism and the changing role of trade unions. In *The New Workplace and Trade Unionism*, ed. P Ackers, C Smith, P Smith, pp. 41–76. London: Routledge

Barker JR. 1993. Tightening the iron cage: concertive control in self-managing teams. *Admin. Sci. Q.* 38:408–37

Barro RJ. 2001. Human capital and growth. *Am. Econ. Rev.* 91:12–17

Bellah RN, Madsen R, Sullivan WM, Swidler A, Tipton SM. 1985. *Habits of the Heart*. Berkeley: Univ. Calif. Press

Berg JM, Wrzesniewski A, Dutton JE. 2010. Perceiving and responding to challenges in job crafting at different ranks: when proactivity requires adaptivity. *J. Org. Behav.* 31:158–86

Bernstein B. 1974. *Class, Codes and Control. Volume 3: Towards a Theory of Educational Transmissions*. New York: Routledge

Bertrand M, Mullainathan S, Shafir E. 2004. A behavioral-economics view of poverty. *Am. Econ. Rev.* 94:419–23

Bourdieu P. 1977. *Outline of a Theory of Practice*. London: Cambridge Univ. Press

Bowles S, Gintis H. 1976. *Schooling in Capitalist America: Educational Reform and the Contradictions of Economic Life*. New York: Basic Books

Calarco JM. 2011. "I need help!" Social class and children's help-seeking in elementary school. *Am. Sociol. Rev.* 76:862–82

Calif. State Audit. 2000. *Standardized tests: Although some students may receive extra time on standardized tests that is not deserved, others may not be getting the assistance they need.* Rep. 2000-108. Sacramento: Calif. State Audit.

Carnevale AP, Rose SJ. 2004. Socioeconomic status, race/ethnicity, and selective college admissions. In *America's Untapped Resource: Low-Income Students in Higher Education*, ed. RD Kahlenberg, pp. 101–56. New York: Century Found.

Carnevale A, Rose SJ, Cheah B. 2011. *The College Payoff: Education, Occupations, Lifetime Earnings*. Washington, DC: Georgetown Univ. Cent. Educ. Workforce

Castilla EJ, Benard S. 2010. The paradox of meritocracy in organizations. *Admin. Sci. Q.* 55:543–76

Chen E. 2004. Why socioeconomic status affects the health of children: a psychosocial perspective. *Curr. Dir. Psychol. Sci.* 13:112–15

Chen E, Miller GE. 2012. "Shift-and-persist" strategies: why low socioeconomic status isn't always bad for health. *Personal. Psychol. Sci.* 7:135–58

Chen S, Lee-Chai AY, Bargh JA. 2001. Relationship orientation as a moderator of the effects of social power. *J. Personal. Soc. Psychol.* 80:173–87

Cooke RA, Rousseau DM. 1998. Behavioural norms and expectations: a quantitative approach to the assessment of organizational culture. *Group Organ. Stud.* 13:245–73

Correll SJ. 2004. Constraints into preferences: gender, status, and emerging career aspirations. *Am. Sociol. Rev.* 69:93–113

Darling-Hammond L. 2006. Securing the right to learn: policy and practice for powerful teaching and learning. *Educ. Res.* 35:13–24

Davies PG, Spencer SJ, Steele CM. 2005. Clearing the air: Identity safety moderates the effects of stereotype threat on women's leadership aspirations. *J. Personal. Soc. Psychol.* 88:276–87

Day JC, Newburger EC. 2002. *The Big Payoff: Educational Attainment and Synthetic Estimates of Work-Life Earnings.* Washington, DC: US Census Bur. **http://www.census.gov/prod/2002pubs/p23-210.pdf**

Devine PG, Forscher PS, Austin AJ, Cox WTL. 2012. Long-term reduction in implicit race bias: a prejudice habit-breaking intervention. *J. Exp. Soc. Psychol.* 48:1267–78

Duncan GJ, Murnane RJ. 2011. *Whither Opportunity? Rising Inequality, Schools, and Children's Life Chances.* New York: Sage Found.

England GW. 1967. Personal value systems of American managers. *Acad. Manag. J.* 10:53–68

Evans GW. 2004. The environment of childhood poverty. *Am. Psychol.* 59:77–92

Fiske ST, Markus HR. 2012. *Facing Social Class: How Societal Rank Influences Interaction.* New York: Sage Found.

Friedlander F. 1965. Comparative work value system. *Pers. Psychol.* 18:1–20

Fryberg SA, Markus HR. 2007. Cultural models of education in American Indian, Asian American and European American contexts. *Soc. Psychol. Educ.* 10:213–46

Greenfield PM. 1997. You can't take it with you: why ability assessments don't cross cultures. *Am. Psychol.* 52:1115–24

Gruenfeld DH, Inesi ME, Magee JC, Galinsky AD. 2008. Power and the objectification of social targets. *J. Personal. Soc. Psychol.* 95:111–27

Guinote A. 2008. Power and affordances: when the situation has more power over powerful than powerless individuals. *J. Personal. Soc. Psychol.* 95:237–52

Gurin P, Nagda BA, Zuniga X. 2013. *Dialogue Across Difference: Practice, Theory, and Research on Intergroup Dialogue.* New York: Sage Found.

Hart B, Risley TR. 1995. *Meaningful Differences in the Everyday Experience of Young American Children.* Baltimore, Md.: Brookes Publ.

Heath SB. 1982. What no bedtime story means: narrative skills at home and school. *Lang. Soc.* 11:49–76

Hochschild JL. 1996. *Facing Up to the American Dream: Race, Class, and the Soul of the Nation.* Princeton, NJ: Princeton Univ. Press

Hong YY, Morris M, Chiu CY, Benet-Martínez V. 2000. Multicultural minds: a dynamic constructivist approach to culture and cognition. *Am. Psychol.* 55:709–20

Horvat EM, Weininger EB, Lareau A. 2003. From social ties to social capital: class differences in the relations between schools and parent networks. *Am. Educ. Res. J.* 40:319–51

Hyman R. 1994. Anomaly or artifact? Comments on Bern and Honorton. *Psychol. Rev.* 115:19–24

Kawachi I, Kennedy E. 2002. *The Health of Nations: Why Inequality Is Harmful to Your Health.* New Press

Kim HS. 2002. We talk, therefore we think? A cultural analysis of the effect of talking on thinking. *J. Personal. Soc. Psychol.* 83:828–42

Kim YK, Sax LJ. 2009. Student-faculty interaction in research universities: differences by student gender, race, social class, and first-generation status. *Res. High. Educ.* 50:437–59

Kohn ML. 1969. *Class and Conformity: A Study in Values.* Homewood, Ill.: Dorsey

Kohn ML, Schooler C. 1969. Class, occupation, and orientation. *Am. Sociol. Rev.* 34:659–78

Kohn ML, Schooler C. 1973. Occupational experience and psychological functioning: an assessment of reciprocal effects. *Am. Sociol. Rev.* 38:97–118

Kraus MW, Piff PK, Keltner D. 2009. Social class, sense of control, and social explanation. *J. Personal. Soc. Psychol.* 97:992–1004

Kraus MW, Piff PK, Keltner D. 2011. Social class as culture: the convergence of resources and rank in the social realm. *Curr. Dir. Psychol. Sci.* 20:246–50

Kraus MW, Piff PK, Mendoza-Denton R, Rheinschmidt ML, Keltner D. 2012. Social class, solipsism, and contextualism: how the rich are different from the poor. *Psychol. Rev.* 119:546–72

Kusserow A. 2004. *American Individualisms: Child Rearing and Social Class in Three Neighborhoods*. New York: Palgrave Macmillan

Kusserow A. 2012. When hard and soft clash: class-based individualisms in Manhattan and Queens. See Fiske & Markus 2012, pp. 195–215

Lachman ME, Weaver SL. 1998. The sense of control as a moderator of social class differences in health and well-being. *J. Personal. Soc. Psychol.* 74:763–73

LaFromboise T, Coleman HL, Gerton J. 1993. Psychological impact of biculturalism: evidence and theory. *Psychol. Bull.* 114:395–412

Lamont M. 2000. *The Dignity of Working Men: Morality and the Boundaries of Race, Class, and Immigration*. Cambridge, Mass.: Harvard Univ. Press

Lareau A. 1987. Social class differences in family-school relationships: the importance of cultural capital. *Sociol. Educ.* 60:73–85

Lareau A. 2003. *Unequal Childhoods: Race, Class, and Family Life*. Berkeley: Univ. Calif. Press

Lareau A, Calarco JM. 2012. Class, cultural capital, and institutions: the case of families and schools. See Fiske & Markus 2012, pp. 61–86

Lareau A, Conley D. 2008. *Social Class: How Does It Work?* New York: Sage Found.

Lareau A, Weininger E. 2003. Cultural capital in educational research: a critical assessment. *Theory Soc.* 32:567–606

Lee F, Tiedens LZ. 2001. Is it lonely at the top? The independence and interdependence of power holders. *Res. Org. Behav.* 23:43–91

Li J. 2003. US and Chinese cultural beliefs about learning. *J. Educ. Psychol.* 95:258–67

MacLeod J. 2009. *Ain't No Makin' It: Aspirations and Attainment in a Low-Income Neighborhood*. Boulder, Colo.: Westview. 3rd ed.

Markus HR, Conner A. 2013. *Clash! 8 Cultural Conflicts That Make Us Who We Are*. New York: Hudson St. Press

Markus HR, Hamedani MG. 2007. Sociocultural psychology: the dynamic interdependence among self systems and social systems. In *Handbook of Cultural Psychology*, ed. S Kitayama, D Cohen, pp. 3–39. New York: Guilford

Markus HR, Kitayama S. 2010. Cultures and selves: a cycle of mutual constitution. *Perspect. Psychol. Sci.* 5:420–30

Markus HR, Steele CM, Steele DM. 2000. Colorblindness as a barrier to inclusion: assimilation and nonimmigrant minorities. *Daedalus* 129:233–59

Miller P, Sperry LL. 1987. The socialization of anger and aggression. *Merrill-Palmer Q.* 33:1–31

Miller PJ, Cho GE, Bracey JR. 2005. Working-class children's experience through the prism of personal storytelling. *Hum. Dev.* 48:115–35

Miller PJ, Sperry DE. 2012. Déjà vu: the continuing misrecognition of low-income children's verbal abilities. See Fiske & Markus 2012, pp. 109–30

Mills CW. 2002. *White Collar: The American Middle Classes*. New York: Oxford Univ. Press

Moynihan DP. 1965. *The Negro Family: The Case for National Action*. Washington, DC: Off. Policy Plan. Res., US Dep. Labor

Murray P. 2013. *Coming Apart: The State of White America, 1960–2010*. New York: Crown

Oakes J. 1982. Classroom social relationships: exploring the Bowles and Gintis hypothesis. *Sociol. Educ.* 55:197–212

Oishi S, Kesebir S, Diener E. 2011. Income inequality and happiness. *Psychol. Sci.* 22:1095–100

Org. Econ. Coop. Dev. (OECD). 2010. *A Family Affair: Intergenerational Social Mobility Across OECD Countries.* Paris: OECD. **http://www.oecd.org/tax/public-finance/chapter%205%20gfg%202010.pdf**

Oyserman D, Fryberg S, Yoder N. 2007. Identity-based motivation and health. *J. Personal. Soc. Psychol.* 93:1011–27

Oyserman D, Markus HR. 1993. The sociocultural self. In *The Self in Social Perspective*, ed. J. Suls, 7:187–220. Hillsdale, NJ: Erlbaum

Pascarella ET, Terenzini PT. 1991. *How College Affects Students: Findings and Insights from Twenty Years of Research.* San Francisco: Jossey-Bass

Pattillo-McCoy M. 1999. *Black Picket Fences: Privilege and Peril Among the Black Middle Class.* Chicago: Univ. Chicago Press

Phillips M. 2011. Parenting, time wise, and disparities in academic outcomes. See Duncan & Murnane 2011, 10:207–28

Phillips M, Chin T. 2004. School inequality: what do we know? In *Social Inequality*, ed. KM Neckerman, 12:467–519. New York: Sage Found.

Pickety T, Saez E. 2003. Income inequality in the United States, 1913–1998. *Q. J. Econ.* 118:1–39

Purdie-Vaughns V, Steele CM, Davies PG, Ditlmann R, Randall-Crosby J. 2008. Social identity contingencies: how diversity cues signal threat or safety for African-Americans in mainstream institutions. *J. Personal. Soc. Psychol.* 4:615–30

Reardon SF. 2011. The widening academic achievement gap between the rich and the poor: new evidence and possible explanations. See Duncan & Murnane 2011, 5:91–116

Reay D. 1998. *Class Work: Mothers' Involvement in Their Children's Primary Schooling.* London: Univ. Coll. Lond. Press

Repetti RL, Taylor SE, Seeman TE. 2002. Risky families: family social environments and the mental and physical health of offspring. *Psychol. Bull.* 128:330–66

Ridgeway CL, Fisk SR. 2012. Class rules, status dynamics, and "gateway" interactions. See Fiske & Markus 2012, pp. 131–51

Rist R. 1970. Student social class and teacher expectations: the self-fulfilling prophecy in ghetto education. *Harv. Educ. Rev.* 40:411–51

Rivera L. 2012. Hiring as cultural matching: the case of elite professional service firms. *Am. Sociol. Rev.* 77:999–1022

Saez E. 2010. *The Evolution of Top Incomes in the United States (Updated with 2008 Estimates).* Berkeley: Univ. Calif. Press

Salzinger L. 2003. *Genders in Production: Making Workers in Mexico's Global Factories.* Berkeley: Univ. Calif. Press

Shah AK, Mullainathan S, Shafir E. 2012. Some consequences of having too little. *Science* 338:682–85

Stephens NM, Fryberg SA, Markus HR. 2011. When choice does not equal freedom: a sociocultural analysis of agency in working-class American contexts. *Soc. Psychol. Personal. Sci.* 2:33–41

Stephens NM, Fryberg SA, Markus HR. 2012a. It's your choice: how the middle-class model of independence disadvantages working-class Americans. See Fiske & Markus 2012, pp. 87–106

Stephens NM, Fryberg SA, Markus HR, Johnson C, Covarrubias R. 2012b. Unseen disadvantage: How American universities' focus on independence undermines the academic performance of first-generation college students. *J. Personal. Soc. Psychol.* 102:1178–97

Stephens NM, Hamedani MG, Markus HR, Bergsieker HB, Eloul L. 2009. Why did they "choose" to stay? Perspectives of Hurricane Katrina observers and survivors. *Psychol. Sci.* 20:878–86

Stephens NM, Markus HR, Fryberg SA. 2012c. Social class disparities in health and education: reducing inequality by applying a sociocultural self model of behavior. *Psychol. Rev.* 119:723–44

Stephens NM, Markus HR, Townsend, SSM. 2007. Choice as an act of meaning: the case of social class. *J. Personal. Soc. Psychol.* 93:814–30

Stephens NM, Townsend SSM. 2013. Rank is not enough: why we need a sociocultural perspective to understand social class. *Psychol. Inq.* 24:126–30

Stephens NM, Townsend SSM, Markus HR, Phillips LT. 2012d. A cultural mismatch: Independent cultural norms produce greater increases in cortisol and more negative emotions among first-generation college students. *J. Exp. Soc. Psychol.* 48:1389–93

Sutton RI, Hargadon AB. 1996. Brainstorming groups in context: effectiveness in a product design firm. *Admin. Sci. Q.* 41:685–718

Torlina J. 2011. *Working Class: Challenging Myths About Blue-Collar Labor*. Boulder, Colo.: Lynne Rienner Publ.

Tsai JL, Miao FF, Seppala E. 2007. Good feelings in Christianity and Buddhism: religious differences in ideal affect. *Personal. Soc. Psychol. Bull.* 33:409–21

Urtasun A, Núñez I. 2012. Work-based competences and careers prospects: a study of Spanish employees. *Pers. Rev.* 41:428–49

Vincent C, Ball SJ. 2007. "Making up" the middle-class child: families, activities, and class dispositions. *Sociology* 41:1061–77

Vohs KD, Mead NL, Goode MR. 2006. The psychological consequences of money. *Science* 314:1154–56

Wilkinson RG. 2002. *Unhealthy Societies: The Afflictions of Inequality*. New York: Routledge

Williams JC. 2012. The class culture gap. See Fiske & Markus 2012, pp. 39–58

Wilson WJ. 2009. *More Than Just Race: Being Black and Poor in the Inner City (Issues of Our Time)*. New York: Norton

Wojcicki S. 2011 (July). The eight pillars of innovation. *Think Q.* **http://www.google.com/think/articles/8-pillars-of-innovation.html**

Wrzesniewski A, Dutton JE. 2001. Crafting a job: revisioning employees as active crafters of their work. *Acad. Manag. Rev.* 26:179–201

(Un)Ethical Behavior in Organizations

Linda Klebe Treviño,[1] Niki A. den Nieuwenboer,[2,*] and Jennifer J. Kish-Gephart[3,*]

[1] Smeal College of Business, The Pennsylvania State University, University Park, Pennsylvania 16802; email: ltrevino@psu.edu

[2] Leavey School of Business, Santa Clara University, Santa Clara, California 95053; email: ndennieuwenboer@scu.edu

[3] Sam M. Walton College of Business, University of Arkansas-Fayetteville, Arkansas 72701; email: jgephart@uark.edu

Annu. Rev. Psychol. 2014. 65:635–60

First published online as a Review in Advance on July 3, 2013

The *Annual Review of Psychology* is online at http://psych.annualreviews.org

This article's doi: 10.1146/annurev-psych-113011-143745

*Authors contributed equally.

Keywords

organizational ethics, ethical decision making, ethical leadership, moral identity, ethical infrastructures

Abstract

This review spotlights research related to ethical and unethical behavior in organizations. It builds on previous reviews and meta-analyses of the literature on (un)ethical behavior in organizations and discusses recent advances in the field. The review emphasizes how this research speaks to the influence of the organizational context on (un)ethical behavior, proceeding from a more macro to a more micro view on (un)ethical behavior and covering ethical infrastructures, interpersonal influences, individual differences, and cognitive and affective processes. The conclusion highlights opportunities for future research.

Contents

INTRODUCTION

Starting in the 1980s, the systematic study of (un)ethical behavior in organizations—often referred to as behavioral ethics in organizations or as organizational ethics (Treviño et al. 2006)—began to take shape. Over the years, a series of ethical debacles has only increased the salience of this area of study for practitioners and researchers alike. Indeed, as a testament to the growing interest among researchers, a number of literature reviews have appeared in recent years—including several qualitative reviews (O'Fallon & Butterfield 2005, Tenbrunsel & Smith-Crowe 2008, Treviño et al. 2006), a meta-analysis of research on the sources of unethical choice in organizations (Kish-Gephart et al. 2010), a meta-analysis of the ethical climate literature (Martin & Cullen 2006), and a meta-analysis of the whistleblowing literature (Mesmer-Magnus & Viswesvaran 2005). The meta-analytic reviews, in particular, represent a major advance, showing that enough research has been conducted for investigators to undertake such statistical reviews.

In this review, the term "ethical behavior" is used broadly to include both ethical and unethical behavior. Ethical behavior in organizations refers to the study of ethical and unethical decisions and behavior in an organizational context, especially in a work context. Drawing on an earlier review by Treviño and colleagues (2006), behavioral ethics researchers have, for the most part, studied three types of related outcomes: unethical behavior that is contrary to accepted moral norms in society (e.g., lying, cheating, stealing); routine ethical behavior that meets the minimum moral standards of society (e.g., honesty, treating people with respect); and extraordinary ethical behavior that goes beyond society's moral minima (e.g., charitable giving, whistleblowing). Here, we focus primarily on the former two outcomes. In addition, following Tenbrunsel & Smith-Crowe (2008), our review assumes that actions need not be intentional in order to qualify as ethical or unethical. Finally, it is important to note that, although research on ethical behavior in organizations rests upon a social scientific base, the study of ethical behavior in organizations is far from value free. Most research in the field begins with the premise that ethical behavior in organizations is good and unethical behavior is bad, and that understanding the predictors of each can help organizations produce more of the former and less of the latter.

Some overlap exists in the above definitions of outcome variables with organizational behavior research on extrarole behavior (e.g., helping, voice) and deviance (e.g., theft). Although more work is needed to bring these overlapping literatures together (Treviño et al. 2006), the major distinction between these topic areas is that research on (un)ethical behavior focuses on behavior that is consistent or inconsistent with societal norms whereas the research on extrarole behavior and deviance focuses on behavior that is consistent or inconsistent with organizational norms. For example, behavior may be considered deviant (contrary to organizational norms) while being consistent with societal norms (e.g., external whistleblowing), or a behavior may be consistent with an organizational norm while being inconsistent with societal norms (e.g., deceiving customers).

Because readers can find in-depth and historical reviews in the papers cited above and other reviews to be cited below, our emphasis here is on work published within the past five to seven years. This review also is not exhaustive. Instead, we emphasize major areas of development and discuss significant and exemplary work within those areas. To develop a list of the most influential recent work, we supplemented our own search of the literature with recommendations of literature that we solicited from more than 20 experts in the field.

THEORETICAL HISTORY AND STAGE SETTING

Before moving to the detailed review, we highlight some of the major theories that have guided organizational ethics research in the past. This brief overview will not only help readers to understand why studying (un)ethical behavior "in organizations" is important, but it will also help set the stage for understanding the recent discussion about how ethical decisions are made, which is currently guiding many of the types of questions that are being asked and the methodologies that are being used.

Why is studying (un)ethical behavior "in organizations" significant? The assumption is that something very important changes when we examine (un)ethical behavior in an organizational context. People who are acting and making decisions in organizations are doing so within power and authority structures and under organizational, leader, and peer influences and constraints. According to Treviño's (1986) person-situation interactionist model of ethical decision making in organizations, for instance, organizations are influential in large part because people rely on others when they are determining how to think about an ethical dilemma. This model emphasized the importance of cognitive moral development theory (Kohlberg 1969) for understanding organizational ethics. On the basis of Lawrence Kohlberg's work on moral reasoning, we understand that most adults are at what he termed the conventional level of cognitive moral development, meaning that they are looking outside themselves for guidance when making ethical decisions. When applied to organizations, this theory explains the powerful influence of peers, leaders, significant others, rules, laws, and codes, all of which can guide employees' ethical decision making and behavior.

An important ongoing and overarching conversation in the field is related to the process of ethical decision making. Important in this respect has been Rest's (1986) rational and deliberative four-stage model of individual ethical decision making. According to the model, individuals facing an ethical dilemma first experience moral awareness: They recognize that the issue being faced is an ethical issue. Next, they engage in moral judgment, or the process of deciding what is right and wrong. They then form a moral motivation or intention, and finally, they take action. Since the introduction of the model, many organizational ethics studies have examined the effects of select individual-, situational-, and organizational-level factors on one or more of the four stages (O'Fallon & Butterfield 2005). Accordingly, much of the earlier work in this field has (implicitly or explicitly) assumed that individual ethical decision making operates in this highly deliberative, step-by-step fashion (Treviño et al. 2006).

In recent years, following a trend in moral psychology, behavioral ethics research has advanced the idea that ethical decision making is not always rational and deliberative but can also be affective, intuitive, and impulsive. The moral psychologist Jonathan Haidt (2001) is generally credited with offering the most significant challenge to the traditional deliberative approach, arguing that people react emotionally and automatically to ethically charged situations (e.g., with disgust or other emotions) and form instant judgments of right and wrong that are later rationalized.

This work has inspired the development of several models within the behavioral ethics literature that take a more intuitive approach. Reynolds (2006), for instance, proposed a neurocognitive model of ethical decision making, arguing that ethical decision making involves both a conscious deliberative process and a more automatic pattern-matching approach based on cognitive prototypes. He argued that people either first behave and then rationalize, or first make an active moral judgment and then behave. Around the same time, Sonenshein (2007) proposed a sensemaking intuition model, which argues that issues are not inherently ethical or unethical, but rather that, in response to the equivocal and uncertain environments that constitute work organizations, organizational members socially construct ethical issues through a process of sensemaking. Individuals then make quick intuitive judgments about these ethical issues, and finally, they justify these judgments to others. We point interested readers to a review of the literature on intuitive ethical decision making by Weaver and colleagues (2013).

In the following sections, we begin by discussing the organizational-level factors—representing organizations' ethical infrastructures—that researchers have examined as influencers in ethical decision making and behavior. We then move to the interpersonal level, where we discuss peer and leader influences. We continue with the individual level, focusing first on relatively stable individual differences and next on the cognitive and affective processes that can be triggered within individuals. We conclude with future directions for the field.

ETHICAL INFRASTRUCTURE: CODES, PROGRAMS, CLIMATE, AND CULTURE

Because of the "in organizations" emphasis of this review, we begin with the ethical context in organizations. Tenbrunsel & Smith-Crowe (2008) referred to the organizational context as the organization's ethical infrastructure. The aspects of the infrastructure that are most commonly studied include ethics codes, ethics programs, ethical climate, and ethical culture.

Ethics Codes and Programs

Ethics codes typically identify the organization's conduct standards, the types of ethical and legal issues employees are likely to face in their organization, and the organization's core values. Although more and more organizations adopt such codes, research on the impact of code existence has produced mixed results, and a recent meta-analytic review found no significant independent effect of code existence on unethical choice (Kish-Gephart et al. 2010). It did find a negative effect of code enforcement (i.e., employees' perception that the existing code is enforced) on unethical behavior. The meta-analysis also found that when perceived code enforcement and other organizational variables (e.g., ethical culture and ethical climate) are taken into account simultaneously, code existence has a small positive effect on unethical behavior. This suggests that in the presence of these other factors, employees can view the mere existence of a code as a negative sign that the code represents window dressing only, thus producing a cynical response that leads to more unethical behavior. Organizations may therefore need to rethink their approach to codes and insure that, if they have codes, code adherence is closely tied to the performance management structure of the organization and to other organizational routines and is not viewed by employees as mere window dressing.

Although little recent academic research exists on codes, we point to one study that is tangentially related to ethics codes in organizations and adds an interesting twist to thinking about code signing. Many organizations require employees to sign the code of conduct annually. By signing the code, employees are purportedly attesting to the fact that they have read the code and that they agree to abide by it. In a recent study, Shu and colleagues (2012) altered the placement of a "pledge" to be honest—the pledge was placed either before the activity (at the top of a form) or after the activity (at the bottom of a form). In the laboratory as well as in a naturalistic setting (i.e., an insurance company where customers had to report their odometer mileage), the authors found that a pledge to be honest is more effective (cheating is lower) when it is placed at the beginning of an activity rather than at the end, as is often done. By making ethics salient before the activity, attention is directed to the self; thoughts of morality are activated and accessible at the right time. In contrast, placing the pledge after the activity allows for self-interested motivations and mental justifications to take over. This simple but powerful finding may apply to other pledges as well, including honor code pledges on exams or a pledge to adhere to a code of conduct at work. For example, it is unclear whether employees have read and understood the code when they are asked to attest that they have done so. The research by Shu and colleagues (2012) suggests that managers may find it worthwhile to ask employees to sign a form before important events, such as at the beginning of the annual compliance process, stating that employees will read the code and will answer compliance questions truthfully. If they are required to do that, they may be less likely to dishonestly sign an attestation at the end saying that they did read it and agree to abide by it when they did not read the code.

In sum, researchers need to know much more about the effect of ethics codes on attitudes and behavior. Although gaining access to organizational contexts presents many challenges, this is a necessary step to further understand when and why codes of conduct are effective. Indeed, organizations do not usually develop just a code and nothing more, suggesting the importance of studying codes not just on their own but as a part of a broader organizational context with other elements of formal ethics and compliance programs.

In addition to the code of conduct, a formal ethics and compliance program often includes training programs, telephone lines for those seeking guidance or avenues to (anonymously) report issues, investigation processes, and performance management systems that incorporate legal compliance standards and that discipline wrongdoers. Although the role of formal ethics and compliance programs, especially in large organizations, has grown considerably in the past 20 years, academic study in this field has remained scant. Though more practitioner focused, the Ethics Resource Center's National Business Ethics Survey (Ethics Resour. Cent. 2012) regularly surveys employees from a wide variety of regions who work in different types of US organizations. According to recent results, comprehensive ethics programs (that include multiple elements) are associated with important outcomes such as reductions in felt pressure to compromise standards, observed misconduct, and perceived retaliation for reporting as well as increases in the reporting of misconduct. Future work should consider these ethics program components separately to determine whether some of them are more important and effective than others, or when and why combining some of them may produce the best results. For example, organizations spend millions of dollars on annual ethics training for their employees with little information about whether the training improves ethical decision making and/or behavior. Research that investigates new approaches to training (such as the giving-voice-to-values program that emphasizes the development of employees' voice efficacy; Gentile 2010) is needed to direct organizations' attention to training and its effects. Further, research attention to how ethics and compliance programs are managed, by whom, and with what effects, would also be helpful.

Ethical Climate

Victor & Cullen (1988, p. 101) defined ethical climate as "the prevailing perceptions of typical organizational practices and procedures that have ethical content" and "those aspects of work climate that determine what constitutes ethical behavior at work." Since the introduction of the ethical climate construct (Victor & Cullen 1988), studies have measured ethical climate almost exclusively as an individual perception rather than as an aggregated group-level construct. The related literature has been reviewed in both a meta-analysis (Martin & Cullen 2006) and a qualitative review (Simha & Cullen 2012). Most of the reviewed research supports the existence of five of the nine originally proposed climates that describe what people in the organization consider when they are faced with an ethical dilemma. In the instrumental or self-interested climate, people consider the self-interest of the organization or the individual. In a caring climate, people think about care and concern for others. In the independence climate, the individual makes decisions based on his or her own principles. In a rules climate and in a laws and codes climate, individuals consider either the organization's rules or society's laws and standards, respectively, when making decisions.

In Martin & Cullen's (2006) meta-analytic review of the ethical climate research, the authors found support for positive relationships between a caring climate and employee attitudes such as commitment and satisfaction, and a negative relationship between a caring climate and dysfunctional employee behavior. This research found the opposite relationships with self-interested climate. Similarly, Kish-Gephart and colleagues' (2010) meta-analysis studied the influences of three types of ethical climate (egoistic, benevolent, and principled) on unethical choice (intentions and behaviors) in organizations and found that egoistic climates were positively associated with unethical choice, whereas benevolent and principled climates were negatively associated with unethical choice.

Although less research exists on the antecedents of ethical climate, one study (Schminke et al. 2005) found that the leader's level of cognitive moral development positively influences employee perceptions of ethical climate and other employee attitudes. This work suggests that leader selection and development may be important for creating and sustaining an ethical climate and points to the potential importance of studying other antecedents of ethical climate.

More recently, Arnaud & Schminke (2012) demonstrated that the effects of ethical climate on reducing unethical behavior can be significantly enhanced if one takes into account moral emotion and moral efficacy. In particular, the relationship between employees' ethical climate perceptions (at the unit level) and work unit unethical behavior was enhanced by collective emotion (a shared sense of empathic concern in a department) and collective ethical efficacy (a shared belief that those in the department are capable of executing ethical action). Thus, this study explores the effects of ethical climate in a more complex way by demonstrating the conditions under which a climate is likely to be more effective at influencing behavior. These authors relied upon Schminke's 16-item measure of ethical climate that conceptualizes ethical climate along two dimensions, self-focused and other-focused. In contrast to most ethical climate studies that have focused on the organizational level, this study demonstrated that subunit ethical climate also plays a significant role. More research will be needed to clarify the dimensionality of ethical climate (e.g., whether researchers should be using two, three, or five dimensions going forward). Research is also needed to better understand whether and when ethical climate is best studied at the organization or unit level (or both).

Ethical Culture

Treviño's (1986) ethical decision-making model, reviewed previously, emphasized the importance of the organizational context by introducing the notion of ethical culture as a moderator of the relationship between cognitive moral development and (un)ethical behavior. She later elaborated on the meaning of the ethical culture construct (Treviño 1990), suggesting that ethical culture is a subset of organizational culture and represents the interplay among the ethics-related formal (e.g., rules and policies, performance management systems) and informal (e.g., norms, language, rituals) organizational systems that influence employee ethical and unethical behavior. Similar to ethical climate research, survey research on ethical culture and its effects has treated ethical culture as an individual's perception of the organizational context rather than an aggregated group-level construct (e.g., Schaubroeck et al. 2012).

Although a meta-analysis found support for a negative relationship between ethical culture and unethical choices when studied independently, this relationship disappeared when other organization environment characteristics (three ethical climate dimensions and code existence and enforcement) were studied simultaneously (Kish-Gephart et al. 2010). This effect likely occurred because ethical culture was highly correlated with code enforcement as well as all three ethical climate dimensions. These findings indicate a need to determine whether and when ethical culture has a role to play in future research and what that role will be. For example, perhaps ethical culture precedes perceptions of ethical climate such that having a strong ethical culture influences employees' ethical climate perceptions.

Few recent studies have been conducted on ethical culture. A notable exception is Schaubroeck and colleagues' (2012) study of the effects of unit-level ethical culture on observed unethical behavior. Drawing on a sample of US Army soldiers in a study conducted across three levels of US Army units in Iraq, the researchers found that unit-level ethical culture mediated the relationship between ethical leadership and (un)ethical behavior, including transgressions against noncombatants and intentions to report misconduct. Similar to work on ethical climate, researchers need to better understand when organizational-level ethical culture may be important compared to unit-level ethical culture because, until recently, almost all ethical context work has measured individuals' perceptions of their organization's overall culture. Yet within the same organization, subunits may vary in terms of the ethical culture and climate environments they create.

Important components of ethical culture at the organization level are formal systems, including decision-making processes, organizational structure, and performance management systems. Because people in organizations pay such close attention to what is rewarded and what is disciplined, the performance management system—including setting goals and tying rewards to those goals—is particularly important. The role of goal setting in producing unethical behavior is being debated. Ordóñez and colleagues (2009a) claimed that goal setting may cause systematic harm when implemented without care, including increasing unethical behavior. They relied on their own work (e.g., Schweitzer et al. 2004) and on the research of others to propose a number of mechanisms by which this might occur, including focusing attention too narrowly on bottom-line goals to the exclusion of other ethical considerations, increasing risk taking, and increasing unethical behavior by motivating people to misrepresent performance in order to meet the goal. Locke & Latham (2009) criticized this work, citing an article of their own (Latham & Locke 2006) in which they outlined goal setting's potential pitfalls and possible antidotes. This article was followed by a rebuttal by the original authors (Ordóñez et al. 2009b). Although entering this debate is beyond the scope of our review, we note that more research is needed to understand when and how goal setting, as part of a broader performance management system, may contribute to unethical behavior. More research on other aspects of the performance management system is also needed. For example, how important is disciplining rule violators, and what are the effects of keeping that information private versus making it public in some way?

Taking a step back from the research on infrastructure, we note that researchers have rarely addressed how such organizational influences may fit into a conversation about ethical decision making as more automatic versus more deliberative. As an exception, Reynolds (2006) made some suggestions about how his neurocognitive model may be applied to understanding failures of organizational culture. For example, shared cognitive prototypes may be mislabeled, or the culture may emphasize a moral rule that is inappropriate. We would also expect that, over time, an organization's culture or climate is likely to become ingrained and internalized by organizational members, making it likely that certain behaviors may become automatic, simply becoming part of "the way we do things around here." In a strong ethical culture, for example, a salesperson should be less likely to lie to a customer because not lying "is" the way things are done, and the salesperson doesn't need to deliberate about that decision. Unfortunately, the opposite may also be true in organizations where lying to customers is the norm.

Our review of the recent research on organizational infrastructures finds that much more needs to be done to understand the relationships between and among its parts such as ethics programs (including codes), ethical climates, and ethical culture. We can say with certainty that the ethical infrastructure matters. But, what parts of it matter most—separately and together? And, how can we best characterize and measure ethical infrastructure? Answers to these questions are likely to provide valuable practical implications for organizations.

INTERPERSONAL INFLUENCES

In this section, we review research on another type of key contextual influence on (un)ethical behavior in organizations: the interpersonal influences of others in the work context, including peers as well as leaders. We also discuss the role of fair treatment by managers.

Peer Influence

For the traditional employee, coworkers are an important part of the everyday work experience. As such, peers represent a potentially powerful influence on (un)ethical behavior (Bandura 1986, Kohlberg 1969, Robinson & O'Leary-Kelly 1998). As Moore & Gino (2013) argue, peers "help to establish a standard for ethical behavior through their actions or inaction." Research on in-group member effects finds that when an in-group member cheats, other in-group members are also more likely to cheat (e.g., Gino et al. 2009a). According to a study by Gino & Galinsky (2012), this might be related to psychological closeness and feeling connected to someone who behaves unethically, as this "can create distance from one's own moral compass" (p. 15) and increase one's propensity to copy that unethical behavior as well as to engage in moral disengagement (discussed below).

One particularly interesting field study asked whether people adapt their level of unethical behavior based on local organizational norms. In a study of the behavior of vehicle emission testing inspectors, Pierce & Snyder (2008) found that when working across different facilities (i.e., switching job locations), inspectors adjusted their level of unethical behavior not gradually but almost immediately to conform to the local organizational norm of unethical behavior—which in this case meant allowing vehicles to pass the inspection despite failing the inspection criteria. However, as Pitesa & Thau (2013) found, not everyone is equally susceptible to such social influences. Because of a tendency to focus more on oneself than on others, people who are higher in power ignore (un)ethical social influences more easily and are less likely to copy others' (un)ethical behavior.

The influence of out-group members on unethical behavior is more complex. Out-group members who cheat influence people's unethical behavior, but less so than do in-group members (Gino et al. 2009a). In addition, in situations where another in-group member exhibits unethical behavior, the presence of an out-group member (observer) may trigger compensatory (overly ethical) behavior. Gino and colleagues (2009b) found that being observed by an out-group member induced guilt in in-group members, leading in-group members to compensate for their peer's unethical behavior.

Research also suggests that unethical behavior may be attenuated when peers make ethics salient by simply talking about it. Work by Gino and colleagues (2009a), for example, suggests that when a peer asks whether unethical behavior is acceptable or not, people cheat less. Other research similarly supports the salutary effects of discussing ethics with coworkers. Gunia and colleagues (2012) found that, compared to making quick choices, giving individuals the opportunity to have an ethics-directed conversation with a colleague influenced them to make more ethical decisions. However, having a conversation focused on self-interest produced more unethical decisions. Thus, employees should be encouraged to converse about ethical issues with peers. Such conversations must focus on ethics and not on self-interest.

What seems clear from this research is that peers do influence (un)ethical behavior, a finding with significant implications for organizations. Future research should aim to understand how groups of individuals collectively develop norms that support (un)ethical behavior.

Leader Influence

In addition to examining the role of peers, recent organizational ethics research has focused a great deal on systematically studying the role of leadership on (un)ethical behavior. In the context of organizational ethics, leadership is an especially important topic because leaders play a key role as authority figures and role models, and they influence subordinates' attitudes and behaviors.

Drawing on social learning theory (Bandura 1986), Brown and colleagues (2005) introduced the ethical leadership construct and developed a reliable survey measure. They defined ethical leadership as "the demonstration of normatively appropriate conduct through personal actions and interpersonal relationships, and the promotion of such conduct to followers through two-way communication, reinforcement, and decision making" (p. 120). According to the authors, employees attend to the behavior and messages of ethical leaders because of their attractiveness, credibility, and legitimacy as models as well as their status in the organization and power to affect employee outcomes. Their study found that ethical leadership is positively associated with followers' job satisfaction and voice. For other reviews on ethical leadership, we refer readers to Brown & Treviño (2006) and Brown & Mitchell (2010).

Research related to the antecedents of ethical leadership has just begun. Prior work on personality as an antecedent has demonstrated support for a relationship with conscientiousness but has produced mixed results related to agreeableness and neuroticism (Kalshoven et al. 2011).

Mayer and colleagues (2012) found support for a relationship between the leader's moral identity and employee perceptions of ethical leadership. Jordan and colleagues (2011) found that higher levels of leader cognitive moral development are related to employee perceptions of ethical leadership. Given the importance of ethical leadership for organizational outcomes (as discussed next), more work is needed to study both individual differences and contextual antecedents of ethical leadership (Brown & Treviño 2006).

Most ethical leadership research has examined the outcomes of this type of leadership, finding that ethical leadership improves employee attitudes, such as job satisfaction, affective commitment, and work engagement, and reduces turnover intentions (Brown et al. 2005, Kim & Brymer 2011, Neubert et al. 2009, Ruiz et al. 2011, Tanner et al. 2010). Research has also focused on positive behavioral outcomes, including citizenship behavior (Avey et al. 2011, Kacmar et al. 2011, Piccolo et al. 2010), voice (Brown & Treviño 2006, Walumbwa & Schaubroeck 2009), and job performance (Piccolo et al. 2010, Walumbwa et al. 2011). The study by Walumbwa and colleagues was conducted in Mainland China and suggests that the ethical leadership construct may also be valid in non-Western cultures.

Ethical leadership has also been found to reduce deviance and unethical behavior (e.g., Mayer et al. 2009). Mayer and colleagues (2012) found significant relationships between ethical leadership and reduced work group conflict and unethical behavior. However, Detert and colleagues (2007) found that ethical leadership in restaurant managers was not related to counterproductive work behavior, measured as actual food loss in their restaurants. The authors speculated that ethical leadership may be less influential in contexts that employ low-level, low-paid workers for whom fair treatment and close supervision (which were significantly related to counterproductive work behavior) may be more important than ethical leadership.

The multilevel nature of ethical leadership has also been considered. Mayer and colleagues (2009) studied the effects of different levels of ethical leadership (executive and supervisory) and showed that top managers' ethical leadership influenced supervisory-level ethical leadership and that the effect on citizenship and deviance flowed through the supervisory-level leader. Both levels of ethical leadership had direct influences on those outcomes. Their mediation hypothesis was supported, suggesting a trickle-down effect of executive ethical leadership.

In a series of studies, Mayer and colleagues (2013) further hypothesized and found that leader influence does not operate in a vacuum but rather interacts with peer influence to affect the reporting of misconduct. Employees are more likely to feel safe reporting misconduct if they believe they have the support of both peers and leaders. These findings suggest that future research should examine how ethical leadership fits within a broader context of peers, leaders, and other potential social influences.

Ethical leaders are not the only leaders who may influence (un)ethical behavior. Transformational leadership (Bass & Avolio 1990) has an ethical component, as do authentic leadership (Avolio & Gardner 2005) and leader behavioral integrity (Bauman 2013, Simons 2002). Negative leadership styles such as abusive supervision (Tepper 2000) are also relevant. Abusive supervision is defined as "subordinates' perception of the extent to which their supervisors engage in the sustained display of hostile verbal and nonverbal behaviors, excluding physical contact" (Tepper 2000, p. 178), and it has long been associated with employee deviance (see Tepper et al. 2007). Recent work has shown that its effects can trickle down from managers to supervisors as well (Mawritz et al. 2012). Hannah and colleagues (2013) connected abusive supervision to increased unethical behavior in a study of military personnel. This study demonstrated that abuse by supervisors increases the likelihood that followers will engage in unethical actions and reduces the likelihood that they will report misconduct. Other types of unethical leadership may also be an issue (Brown & Mitchell 2010), but reducing abusive supervision seems particularly important for organizations that wish to decrease follower unethical behavior.

Just and Unjust Treatment by Managers

Just and unjust treatment by managers has been associated with a wide variety of outcomes relevant to behavioral ethics, including prosocial and antisocial or deviant behaviors such as employee theft and other unethical behaviors (e.g., Greenberg 1990, Weaver & Treviño 1999). Although organizational justice is one of the most studied topics in organizational behavior, until fairly recently justice researchers did not explicitly make the connection to behavioral ethics (Cropanzano & Stein 2009). Organizational justice researchers have traditionally treated employee reactions as instrumental and based upon self- or group interest only (Tyler & Blader 2000). Noting that normative foundations of justice (e.g., Rawls 1971) had been largely forgotten in the organizational justice literature, Folger and colleagues (2005) proposed the concept of deontic justice, arguing that people are morally motivated to care about fairness for its own sake and not just for instrumental reasons. The authors noted, for example, that people react retributively to the unfair treatment of others simply because they see it as unfair and not because it harms them or their group. They are even willing to harm their own self-interest in reacting retributively. Accordingly, Rupp & Bell (2010) found that subjects who expressed retributive cognitions against a transgressor who had not behaved fairly in the past were more likely to sacrifice their own resources to punish that transgressor.

Skarlicki & Rupp (2010) brought a dual-processing (Chaiken & Trope 1999) perspective to understanding these reactions. They proposed that reactions might differ depending on the decision-processing frame and that these frames could be primed (decision frames are discussed in more detail below). Experiential processing is less conscious and more automatic, quick, and emotional, whereas rational processing is more conscious and deliberative. The researchers found that subjects primed to use experiential processing (to be open to their feelings and intuitions) were more retributive toward individuals who treated others unfairly than were subjects primed to use rational processing. Further, those high in moral identity (also discussed below) tended to be more retributive regardless of the primes because morality is so important to their identity and self-concept. This research is important for organizations that wish to support ethical conduct via fair treatment. Employees care not just about the fair treatment of themselves and their group, but as observers, when they learn that unrelated others are treated unfairly, they are likely to take retributive action as well.

So, what do we know about interpersonal influences on (un)ethical behavior in organizations? We know that peers and leaders matter a great deal, alone and in combination. Employees are more likely to be unethical in the presence of unethical colleagues, abusive leaders, or unfair treatment, but they are more likely to be ethical when they are led by ethical leaders at multiple levels, feel supported by ethical colleagues, and are fairly treated.

INDIVIDUAL DIFFERENCES

Although individual differences are not strictly organizational, we cannot ignore the role of these variables as influencers on (un)ethical behavior in organizations. In this section, we focus on individual differences that have been recently introduced to the literature, with an eye toward highlighting the extent to which they may be important to organizational ethics. Readers interested in other individual differences historically studied in behavioral ethics research (e.g., locus of control, cognitive moral development) are referred to Kish-Gephart and colleagues' (2010) meta-analytic review.

Moral Attentiveness

Drawing on social cognitive theory (Bandura 1986), Reynolds (2008) proposed the moral attentiveness construct, or "the extent to which one chronically perceives and considers morality and moral elements in his or her experiences" (p. 1028). Reynolds distinguishes moral attentiveness from moral sensitivity and moral awareness in that the latter two require the existence of a particular moral issue whereas moral attentiveness does not. One's degree of moral attentiveness is believed to color how one perceives and interprets incoming morality-related information. In addition to developing a scale to measure moral attentiveness, Reynolds proposed and found that perceptual moral attentiveness (how information is colored as it is received) was positively related to both the recall and reporting of ethics-related behaviors and to moral awareness. Reynolds also argued that organizations might be able to influence moral attentiveness. For example, he proposed that moral attentiveness may increase with certain types of experiences and, thus, organizations may want to shape ethics initiatives with moral attentiveness in mind.

Moral Conation

Researchers have traditionally focused much of their attention on moral judgment, leaving open questions about moral motivation. Therefore, some researchers are delving more deeply into the motivational aspect of ethical decision making. In this context, Hannah and colleagues (2011a) developed the moral conation construct, or "the capacity to generate responsibility and motivation to take moral action in the face of adversity and persevere through challenges" (p. 664). Moral conation is theorized to encompass three components—moral courage, moral efficacy, and moral ownership—which are associated with the last two stages of Rest's (1986) model (i.e., moral motivation and moral action).

Research has furthermore argued and shown that the three components of moral conation are related to (un)ethical behavior. Hannah et al. (2011b), for instance, found that moral courage—a malleable character strength that enables one to act on moral principles in the face of danger—is positively related to prosocial and ethical behavior outcomes and that it can be influenced by authentic leadership. When it comes to moral ownership, Hannah and colleagues (2011a) argued that those higher in moral ownership will take more responsibility for their own and others' actions because they are unable to "turn a blind eye" (p. 675) to unethical actions. The ascription of responsibility to the self has long been considered important to ethical decision making (e.g., Schwartz 1968), and recent research reviewed by Dana and colleagues (2012) suggests that increasing one's personal accountability for ethical behavior by decreasing moral "wiggle room" (p. 218) is extraordinarily important. Finally, moral efficacy, or one's belief in one's ability to do what is necessary to take moral action, contributes to self-regulatory processes that support the person doing the right thing even when it is difficult to do so.

Although Hannah and colleagues (2011a) conceptualize moral conation as an individual difference, the authors also argue that moral conation can be developed through social learning, training, ethical role models, and other means. These propositions await future research. In addition, future testing will be required to determine whether moral conation is best treated as three separate constructs or as one overarching one. Finally, it remains unclear to what extent moral conation involves conscious deliberation. Moral ownership invokes responsibility, which would seem to be accompanied by deliberation. But those who are high on moral efficacy may act more intuitively because they feel they have the expertise to do so. Moral courage may be associated with behavior that looks intuitive and impulsive but may come from deliberation and practice, leading to behavior that is automatized over time.

Moral Identity

Moral identity is rooted in social identity theory (Ashforth & Mael 1989) as well as in the self-regulatory assumptions of social cognitive theory (Bandura 1986). According to Aquino & Reed (2002), moral identity can be defined as "a self-conception organized around a set of moral traits" (p. 1424). They noted that moral identity represents a component of one's social self-schema and complements moral development theory. That is, while cognitive moral development (Kohlberg 1969) relies on sophistication of moral reasoning to explain moral action, moral identity motivates moral action because individuals see certain moral traits as being integral to their self-concept or identity.

Shao and colleagues (2008) reviewed the research on moral identity and reported significant positive relationships with prosocial behaviors such as volunteering and charitable donations and significant negative relationships with unethical behavior such as cheating. The authors also noted that moral identity interacts with contextual variables such that individuals with stronger moral identities are more sensitive to a number of contextual cues such as certain types of leadership behaviors and the organization's culture.

Moral identity, when combined with the individual difference, moral judgment, has also been found to influence people's ethical behavior. In two studies, Reynolds & Ceranic (2007) combined specific types of moral judgment (consequentialism and formalism) with moral identity and found that ethical behavior (charitable giving) and unethical behavior (cheating) are influenced by both, as well as by their interaction.

DeCelles and colleagues (2012) found that a strong moral identity can protect against self-interested behavior in those who have the psychological experience of feeling powerful (via either trait power or manipulated power). The implication is that organizations should consider the moral identity of people they promote to powerful positions because those who have weak moral identities can be expected to engage in more self-serving behavior. For those already in positions of power and who are also high in trait power, organizations should consider interventions that might help them develop their moral identities.

In a conceptual piece, O'Reilly & Aquino (2011) elucidated the role of moral identity in a person's intuitive reactions to injustice. According to their model, the centrality of one's moral identity increases the likelihood that a person will see mistreatment as a moral violation and increases the likelihood that she/he will experience anger and justice cognitions as a result. Furthermore, Aquino and colleagues (2011) found that those who score higher in moral identity experience a state of moral elevation (a warm or pleasant emotional experience) after exposure to others' acts of "uncommon goodness." This feeling of moral elevation mediated the relationship between moral identity and prosocial behaviors. Although conducted in the laboratory, the latter studies have organizational implications. For instance, organization members who observe a leader or coworker engage in particularly helpful behavior may experience moral elevation and be motivated to do the same.

Aquino & Freeman (2012) make the connection to the business context particularly salient. They offer a social-cognitive model of moral identity that conceptualizes moral identity as both an individual difference and a mental construct that can be activated by situational influences ranging from subtle primes to a variety of other business-relevant contextual cues. For example, they propose that financial rewards (which trigger a business frame) may weaken the power of a strong moral identity, instead making salient a material identity. They also discuss how group norms and role models can support or suppress moral identity. They present evidence for the priming of moral identity (Reed et al. 2007) and for the influence of financial incentives (Aquino et al. 2009), among other research supportive of their ideas.

COGNITION AND COGNITIVE PROCESSES

The above discussion involves individual differences that are mostly cognitive in nature. In this section, we move to literature that emphasizes cognitive processes more explicitly. We begin with moral disengagement—a concept that has been treated primarily as an individual difference but is consistent with a broader literature that includes related cognitive processes. We then discuss research that explores the influence of decision frames on cognition and unethical behavior.

Moral Disengagement

According to Bandura's (1986) social cognitive theory, people internalize behavioral standards via socialization, and these standards guide behavior. If the opportunity to engage in unethical behavior arises, the theory proposes that moral standards are activated, and self-regulatory mechanisms (e.g., guilt and self-censure) subsequently prevent the individual from engaging in that behavior. However, this self-regulatory process is not always successful. In an extension of his social cognitive theory, Bandura's (1999) moral disengagement theory suggests that self-regulatory processes can be deactivated by the use of moral disengagement techniques, such as diffusing responsibility, displacing responsibility, blaming the victim, or claiming that the action is warranted because it serves a higher purpose (for a recent review, see Moore et al. 2012). These techniques help to disengage self-regulatory processes, thus preventing self-censure or guilt and rendering the unethical behavior unproblematic for one's conscience. In presenting eight types of cognitive distortion mechanisms, Bandura's theory helps to theoretically unify the rationalization techniques (also referred to as moral justifications or neutralizations) identified by other researchers (e.g., Ashforth & Anand 2003, Kelman & Hamilton 1989, Sykes & Matza 1957, Tenbrunsel & Messick 1999).

Behavioral ethics researchers have drawn upon this work to help explain (un)ethical behavior in the workplace. Studies taking the individual differences approach have shown that an individual's general propensity to morally disengage is related to increased unethical behavior, even after accounting for alternative individual differences (Aquino et al. 2007, Bandura et al. 2001, Detert et al. 2008). Moore and colleagues (2012) developed a reliable eight-item measure of the propensity to morally disengage and found that it is positively associated with unethical behaviors including self-reported unethical behavior, fraud decisions, self-serving decisions, and the reporting of others' unethical behavior. Research has also found relationships between an individual's propensity to morally disengage and other individual traits such as cynicism, locus of control, moral identity, and moral personality (Detert et al. 2008, Duffy et al. 2005).

In addition to conceptualizing moral disengagement as an individual difference, recent research suggests that certain situations may influence the use of justifications and thus the incidence of unethical behavior (Bersoff 1999, Mazar et al. 2008, Shalvi et al. 2012). Much of this research draws on the idea that people desire not only to benefit themselves but also to appear as good and moral people (Kunda 1990, Tsang 2002). As such, unethical behavior is argued to occur more often in situations that provide opportunities to "legitimately" justify unethical behavior (via rationalizations) while maintaining the appearance of being moral. Wiltermuth (2011) referred to this phenomenon as "moral camouflage." Across four laboratory studies, he found that people were more likely to cheat in situations that allowed participants to justify their cheating as helping others and not just themselves. Although these studies did not directly measure rationalization techniques, participants likely rationalized their behavior by suggesting that their actions also served others, and thus the good helps to offset the bad (i.e., "the metaphor of the ledger," Ashforth & Anand 2003, p. 21). Umphress and colleagues (2010, 2011) similarly argued and found that employees use neutralization techniques to justify unethical behavior that they believe benefits the organization. Lastly, recent work suggests that when primed by a situation to think creatively or to experience positive affect, employees may be more innovative in finding ways to justify self-serving behavior (Gino & Ariely 2012, Vincent et al. 2013).

The empirical research examining the situational use of justifications has been primarily conducted in the laboratory. Nevertheless, some theoretical work suggests a connection between this research and the workplace (e.g., Liu et al. 2012). Beu & Buckley (2004), for instance, argued that savvy leaders are able to induce employee unethical behavior by framing situations to help employees morally disengage. Although empirical research is needed to test Beu & Buckley's arguments, future research should also consider preventive measures for moral disengagement more generally—that is, how can educators or managers influence moral disengagement such that people recognize its occurrence and engage in it less? For example, can individuals be taught to see red flags when they hear certain phrases, such as "It's not our responsibility" or "Everyone else is doing it"?

Decision Frames

Research is also beginning to demonstrate the powerful influence of decision frames on how individuals think about situations and respond with (un)ethical behavior. A number of studies have explored framing issues similar to those in Kahneman & Tversky's (1979) prospect theory. For example, Kern & Chugh (2009) conducted a direct test of the effects of a loss versus a gain frame on unethical behavior. Their study confirmed that when situations are framed as a potential loss (e.g., not being able to make a sale and lose out on commission), participants are more likely to engage in unethical behavior compared to when that same situation is framed as a gain. Interestingly, though, this effect disappeared if participants were explicitly instructed to take their time. These results suggest again that taking time to make a decision reduces unethical behavior, perhaps because it lessens risk-seeking biases related to loss aversion.

Greenbaum and colleagues (2012) introduced what might be considered another kind of decision frame, referred to as bottom-line mentality (BLM) or "one-dimensional thinking that revolves around securing bottom-line outcomes to the neglect of competing priorities" (p. 344). In some organizations, situations are framed mostly in terms of how decisions and behaviors affect the financial bottom line. Such BLM thinking can be passed on from the supervisor to the subordinate through social learning processes (Bandura 1977) and can cause people to focus solely on the bottom line at the expense of other considerations (such as ethics or quality). In a field study, the authors found that BLM had a positive relationship with social undermining behavior because more BLM thinking invites a win-lose approach and fosters adversarial behavior among employees. What may actually be at the root of the problem are the mental models that are invoked by the idea of money, as Kouchaki and colleagues (2013) showed. In a series of lab studies, Kouchaki and colleagues found that the mere exposure to money triggered a business decision frame, which in turn led to a greater likelihood of unethical behavior and intentions (cf. Gino & Pierce 2009a, described in detail below). Similarly, Molinsky and colleagues (2012) found that triggering economic-oriented decision schema also reduced people's compassion.

The economic frame—argued by many to be *the* frame adopted by most business organizations (Ghoshal 2005)—also influences how people talk about social issues at work. Sonenshein (2006) advanced the idea of issue crafting, which he described as a tactic that people can use to increase the legitimacy of social issues, thereby influencing the audience to take the issue more seriously. Sonenshein found that individuals use more economic and less normative language when talking about social issues, even when they privately would do the opposite. Other work by Sonenshein (2009) suggests that individuals frame issues in different ways, with potential consequences for behavior. He found that some employees craft strategic business issues as having an ethical component, whereas other employees do not. Those who do craft issues in this way tend to adopt what he calls an employee welfare frame, where they reinterpret the strategic issue as having a deontological (e.g., infringing on a person's rights) or utilitarian (e.g., having negative outcomes) impact. In this way, people's own issue framing can lead them to perceive certain issues as ethical while others do not.

In a recent review of the ethical decision-making literature, Tenbrunsel & Smith-Crowe (2008) offered a model and typology that emphasized the role of cognitive decision frames and their influence on intentionality (or lack thereof). In their model, if decision makers are aware that they are facing an ethical decision (i.e., moral awareness), they make an ethical or unethical decision intentionally. However, if they are unaware, their decision falls into the amoral domain, and their ethical or unethical decision is classified as unintended. The authors use the terms "bounded ethicality" and "ethical fading" to refer to the psychological processes that contribute to the absence of ethical awareness and interfere with people doing what is right in a conscious manner (Tenbrunsel et al. 2010, p. 154). One factor that influences how a decision is framed, and thus one's moral awareness, is time. Tenbrunsel and colleagues (2010) argued that in the short term, the "want" self (hotheaded and focused on immediate outcomes) often prevails over the "should" self. However, when looking back on the unethical action later, the "should" self reemerges and motivates a more positive (ethical) framing of the past behavior. A comprehensive review of this "ethical fading" perspective is available in Bazerman & Tenbrunsel's (2011) book, *Blind Spots*.

Organizations may be manipulating decision frames unintentionally. Yet, research suggests that decision frames can have a powerful impact on behavior. Training managers to be more aware of the decision frames they utilize and impose on others (intentionally or unintentionally) should help to avoid the use of decision frames that lead to unethical behavior and perhaps support framing issues in ways that support ethical behavior.

EMOTIONS AND AFFECTIVE PROCESSES

Behavioral ethics researchers have also begun to consider the effects of affective processes on unethical behavior. Early work by Damasio (1994) helped jump-start this area of interest through studies of brain regions that regulate emotions in moral decision making and behavior. Gaudine & Thorne (2001) later argued against the prevailing assumption in organizational studies that emotions have no place in a "rational" ethical decision-making process and advanced a theoretical framework that linked emotional arousal and negative or positive feeling states to Rest's (1986) four-stage model (reviewed above). More recently, behavioral ethics researchers have begun to consider discrete emotions, with a particular interest in the social emotion of envy.

Envy is an interpersonal emotion triggered by "social comparisons with advantaged others in domains of personal relevance" (Hill et al. 2011, p. 653). Neuroscience research using functional magnetic resonance imaging technology suggests that envy activates parts of the brain related to social pain, similar to the distress that accompanies social exclusion (Takahashi et al. 2009). This social pain, in turn, motivates people to engage in behavior aimed at alleviating the envious feelings (Tai et al. 2012). One option, for example, is to look for ways to undermine or otherwise humble the envied other. As Polman & Ruttan (2012) point out, envy motivates a person "to better oneself or to worsen the situation of another" (p. 135).

Empirical research supports the idea that envy motivates unethical behavior, including deception (Moran & Schweitzer 2008) and dishonesty (Gino & Pierce 2009a,b, 2010). Gino & Pierce (2009a), for instance, have conducted multiple studies examining the effects of inequity on triggering episodic envy and subsequent unethical behavior and even demonstrated that the presence of material items (e.g., stacks of money in a room) may influence people's experience of envy and induce cheating behavior as a response.

Focusing on the organization more directly, Duffy and colleagues (2012) examined when and why envy influences social undermining behavior at work. The authors found support for the effect of situational envy, or "a general envy of others in an environment" (Duffy et al. 2012, p. 645), on social undermining via the mediating influence of moral disengagement. However, two variables—identification with the victims (high social identification) and being part of a team that does not tend to engage in undermining (low undermining of group norms)—weakened the relationship between envy and moral disengagement. The authors argued that high identification with teammates likely made it more difficult to dehumanize or displace responsibility onto teammates, and low team norms for undermining made it more difficult to argue that the behavior was for the greater good of the team (moral justification). The results suggest that managers can take steps to minimize the negative implications of envy by fostering an environment with clear ethical norms and close connections with coworkers. Given that workplaces tend to foster social comparisons and are thus potential breeding grounds for envy, future research should examine additional organizational factors that may attenuate the negative effects or harness the positive effects of that emotion.

Although envy has recently received much attention in the literature, comparatively less behavioral ethics research has focused on the effects of other discrete emotions such as shame, anger, or fear (for exceptions, see Gino et al. 2009b, Kish-Gephart et al. 2009, Polman & Ruttan 2012, Umphress & Bingham 2011). We expect the study of the role of affect in ethical decision making to increase, especially for those emotions that might be triggered by common interpersonal situations in the workplace and that have strong implications for organizational ethics. For example, empathy has long been associated with prosocial behavior (see Eisenberg & Miller 1987). If the organization can increase decision makers' empathy for stakeholders who risk being harmed by an action under consideration, the decision may be altered to reduce that risk. Organizations may also wish to support feelings of anger or moral outrage that can move an employee to overcome fear and stop unethical behavior from taking place (Kish-Gephart et al. 2009).

An additional consideration for researchers is how emotions influence moral reasoning or the approach a person uses to solve an ethical dilemma. For example, Greene's (2009) dual-process theory of moral judgment argues that more automatic negative emotional responses are related to deontological-type judgments (e.g., disapproval of a decision to kill one human being to save multiple others), whereas more controlled processes are related to utilitarian-type judgments (approval of the same decision because saving multiple people serves the greater good).

Although the influence of affective processes on unethical behavior may at times appear straightforward, emotions are complex, and their effects are likely to be contingent on the situational context. Guilt, for example, is believed to reduce the incidence of unethical behavior (Agnihotri et al. 2012, Cohen 2010). Yet, individuals who experience guilt can also become so focused on rectifying the guilt that other individuals are unintentionally hurt in the process (De Hooge et al. 2011). Similarly, although empathy may motivate prosocial behavior, research suggests that people may be more willing to help others in a dishonest manner when they experience empathy rather than envy (Gino & Pierce 2009b, 2010). Such findings suggest that much remains to be learned about the complex effects of emotions and even more about what these effects mean for (un)ethical behavior in organizations.

EGO DEPLETION AND SELF-REGULATION PROCESSES

In the preceding sections, we described research that demonstrates how certain cognitive and affective processes influence (un)ethical behavior. A related topic involves understanding how cognitive self-regulation processes—the cognitive processes that prevent people from engaging in unethical behavior when the opportunity arises—break down when people experience a deficit in self-control. Self-control can be defined as "the capacity to alter or override dominant response tendencies, and to regulate behavior, thoughts, and emotions" (De Ridder et al. 2012, p. 77). Individuals use self-control to resist unwanted behaviors, such as stealing office supplies or using unprofessional language to respond to an abusive supervisor. But ego depletion theory (Baumeister & Heatherton 1996) suggests that self-control is a finite resource that can be depleted in the short term, like a muscle can be fatigued. Linking this theory to unethical behavior, Gino and colleagues (2011) found that when a person's self-control was depleted by a prior act that required self-control, the likelihood of unethical behavior increased. However, in support of an interactionist view of unethical behavior, this was less true for those with a stronger moral identity. Relying on similar theoretical arguments, Barnes and colleagues (2011) found that lack of sleep was associated with unethical behavior in three studies. Moreover, Christian & Ellis (2011) found that sleep deprivation was associated with theft and interpersonal deviance.

Understanding that those whose self-regulatory resources are depleted are more likely to engage in unethical behavior has significant organizational implications. Christian & Ellis (2011) recommend potential organizational responses. For example, managers should call attention to ethical issues, remove temptations (if possible), develop less stressful work climates, provide opportunities for naps, help employees to develop their self-control resources, reduce demands that would interfere with sleep (e.g., extended shifts), and monitor those who may be depleted. Hopefully, by understanding that the depletion of self-control resources leads to unethical behavior, concerned managers can take action to reduce it.

FUTURE RESEARCH

This review documents the thriving research interest in the behavioral ethics domain. In this section, we discuss some additional thoughts about where the field is and should be going in terms of future research, including topics, opportunities for theory development, and the use of different methodologies.

Topics for Future Research

Despite the buzz of research activity, a number of noteworthy topics have received little attention. Here, we note a few that have not yet been mentioned in our review. For example, the role of new work arrangements should be considered because work is increasingly being accomplished across wide distances and through technological interfaces (e.g., email, Web applications, instant messaging, video conferencing). In today's distributed organizations, teams are often dispersed across different locations, including in homes or in offices in different cities or countries. These work arrangements are likely to present organizations with unique ethics management challenges. Recent research already suggests that people are more willing to lie when communicating through email versus when communicating through pen and paper (Naquin et al. 2010). And the importance of observers and witnesses (even in the form of out-group members) as highlighted in previous parts of this review, suggests that the absence of physical observers when working through a technological interface or from home may further increase the likelihood of unethical behavior. Because monitoring is more challenging when people are working remotely, these new work arrangements may also increase people's opportunity to engage in unethical behavior. Furthermore, they may change the way employees think about ethical issues. For example, working remotely and virtually may mute potential harm to stakeholders, thus lessening the moral intensity or lessening the opportunity for ethical dialogue.

In a related vein, little research attention has been given to group-level ethical decision making or behavior despite the fact that many decisions in organizations are made in a group context, and most work involves groups. It seems reasonable to expect that unethical behavior will be higher in groups because of moral disengagement (e.g., diffusion of responsibility) or that certain members of groups may have more or less influence on (un)ethical decisions.

The potential effect of structural features of organizations has also been neglected, specifically those features that are either explicitly designed to improve employees' ethical behavior or that may contribute to unethical behavior. For example, aside from conceptual work (Hoffman 2010), we know little about ethics and compliance officers in organizations, such as how they do their work and what makes them and their work effective or ineffective. This seems important given their role in managing ethics programs and ethical climates and cultures, and encouraging ethical and discouraging unethical behavior in organizations.

The role of authority structures and systems also remains underexplored. For example, indirect agency involves perpetrating unethical behavior through someone else, such as when a manager suggests that a subordinate accomplish a task by unethical means. Although indirect agency has been associated with unethical behavior in the past (Milgram 1974, Paharia et al. 2009), future research should extend beyond the idea of authority dynamics to better understand the scope, mechanisms, triggers, and outcomes of indirect agency in organizations.

Continuing Theory Development

In conducting this review, we noted the many references to various aspects of Bandura's (1986) social cognitive theory. This work has guided multiple areas of study, from moral attentiveness, to moral conation, to moral disengagement, to moral identity, to ethical leadership, and to abusive supervision (via social learning). Therefore, it seems important to acknowledge the theory's continuing relevance in many areas of study of (un)ethical behavior in organizations. Social cognitive theory is a broad theory that can accommodate a variety of different approaches to the study of behavioral ethics in organizations. The theory allows for the study of successful self-regulation but also the study of failures to self-regulate (i.e., moral disengagement). More thought should be given to social cognitive theory as a potential umbrella theory that can explain multiple relevant ethical and unethical outcomes. But, because social cognitive theory assumes forethought and takes a distinctly cognitive view, future research should consider how to supplement social cognitive theory with theories that better account for the less conscious intuitive and affective processes that are so important, especially theories that can do so in the context of complex organizational life.

Although much progress has been made in expanding our understanding of the deliberative and intuitive characteristics of ethical decision making, more empirical and theoretical research is necessary to sort out the processes and outcomes. For example, future research is needed to understand when ethical decision making in organizations is more intuitive versus more deliberative and when one may be more desirable over the other. As described above, Gunia and colleagues (2012) found that, compared to making quick choices, giving individuals the opportunity to engage in contemplation or to have a conversation with an ethical colleague influences them to make decisions that are more ethical. In contrast, Zhong (2011) found that contemplation reduced people's ethical behavior compared to decisions that were based on feeling or intuition. In his study, deliberative decision making increased unethical behaviors and reduced altruistic motives. Future research needs to offer theory that can help to resolve the apparent contradiction in these studies.

Methodological Issues

Researchers are utilizing a variety of methodologies to conduct behavioral ethics research, with survey and, more recently, laboratory research predominating. Laboratory experiments can help us to understand psychological processes and mechanisms because of the high amounts of control afforded to the researcher. Therefore, it makes sense that this methodology is being used to help understand the role of cognition and affect in ethical decision making and behavior. New perspectives have been gained through the use of functional magnetic resonance imaging technology that allows researchers to observe the effects of various influences on the brain during the ethical decision-making process. We refer readers to a review by Salvador & Folger (2009) for more on this approach and its findings. However, given our "in organizations" perspective, we wish to emphasize that the realities of working inside an organization are difficult to capture with the aforementioned methodologies. For example, replicating authority relations, group dynamics, or the role of identification with and commitment to the organization is challenging in experimental settings. Therefore, we encourage researchers to extend the results of laboratory research to field methodologies to insure generalizability of the findings to complex organizational environments.

Given the prominence of research related to intuitive and automatic processes, it is important to note the recent use of subtle priming studies and the Implicit Association Test (IAT). In one example, Reynolds and colleagues (2010) developed an implicit measure of "an individual's assumption that business is inherently moral" (p. 753). The study showed that people's implicit assumptions about the morality of business influenced their unethical decisions (beyond explicit attitudes) and interacted with subtle contextual cues (about competition) to influence behavior. Another recent study using the IAT suggests that occupational identities may have moral implications. Leavitt and colleagues (2012) discuss "situated identities" that are associated with one's occupation (in this case, Army medics). The authors demonstrated that occupational identities can be primed with subtle cues and that these identities subsequently predict ethical judgments. Overall, the IAT seems to be a promising methodology for studying the less conscious side of ethical decision making. Readers interested in such methods more generally should consult a recent review by Uhlmann and colleagues (2012).

A limitation related to both traditional experiments and survey research is that, by design, they test models that have been theorized and conceptualized up front. Qualitative research has the potential to address this limitation (Lee 1999), especially in areas of organizational ethics that are currently poorly understood. For example, recent work by Gehman and colleagues (2013) used grounded theory methods to advance the idea of "values work," a process that underscores the challenge of bringing values practices to life in organizations and sustaining them over time. Potential future research areas include investigating the complexities of managing ethical climates, cultures, and infrastructures in organizations; understanding the ways in which organization members respond to ethics initiatives; and learning how messages about ethics are passed upward, downward, and around the organization.

CONCLUSION

The blossoming research on (un)ethical behavior in organizations is welcome and much needed given contemporary events. We hope the research reviewed here will help inspire future investigations that expand our understanding of and ability to encourage ethical behavior as well as prevent unethical behavior in the workplace.

DISCLOSURE STATEMENT

The authors are not aware of any affiliations, memberships, funding, or financial holdings that might be perceived as affecting the objectivity of this review.

LITERATURE CITED

Agnihotri R, Rapp A, Kothandaraman P, Singh RK. 2012. An emotion-based model of salesperson ethical behaviors. *J. Bus. Ethics* 109:243–57

Aquino K, Freeman D. 2012. Moral identity in business situations: a social-cognitive framework for understanding moral functioning. In *Moral Personality, Identity, and Character*, ed. D Narvaez, DK Lapsley, pp. 375–95. New York: Cambridge Univ. Press

Aquino K, Freeman D, Reed A, Lim VK, Felps W. 2009. Testing a social-cognitive model of moral behavior: the interactive influence of situations and moral identity centrality. *J. Personal. Soc. Psychol.* 97:123–41

Aquino K, McFerran B, Laven M. 2011. Moral identity and the experience of moral elevation in response to acts of uncommon goodness. *J. Personal. Soc. Psychol.* 100:703–18

Aquino K, Reed A. 2002. The self-importance of moral identity. *J. Personal. Soc. Psychol.* 83:1423–40

Aquino K, Reed A, Thau S, Freeman D. 2007. A grotesque and dark beauty: how moral identity and mechanisms of moral disengagement influence cognitive and emotional reactions to war. *J. Exp. Soc. Psychol.* 43:385–92

Arnaud A, Schminke M. 2012. The ethical climate and context of organizations: a comprehensive model. *Organ. Sci.* 23:1767–80

Ashforth BE, Anand V. 2003. The normalization of corruption in organizations. *Res. Organ. Behav.* 25:1–52

Ashforth BE, Mael F. 1989. Social identity theory and the organization. *Acad. Manag. Rev.* 14:20–39

Avey J, Palanski M, Walumbwa F. 2011. When leadership goes unnoticed: the moderating role of follower self-esteem on the relationship between ethical leadership and follower behavior. *J. Bus. Ethics* 98:573–82

Avolio BJ, Gardner WL. 2005. Authentic leadership development: getting to the root of positive forms of leadership. *Leadersh. Q.* 16:315–38

Bandura A. 1977. *Social Learning Theory*. Englewood Cliffs, NJ: Prentice-Hall

Bandura A. 1986. *Social Foundations of Thought and Action: A Social Cognitive Theory*. Englewood Cliffs, NJ: Prentice-Hall

Bandura A. 1997. *Self-Efficacy: The Exercise of Control*. New York: Freeman

Bandura A. 1999. Moral disengagement in the perpetuation of inhumanities. *Personal. Soc. Psychol. Rev.* 3:193–209

Bandura A, Caprara GV, Barbaranelli C, Pastorelli C, Regalia C. 2001. Sociocognitive self-regulatory mechanisms governing transgressive behavior. *J. Personal. Soc. Psychol.* 80:125–35

Barnes CM, Schaubroeck J, Huth M, Ghumman S. 2011. Lack of sleep and unethical conduct. *Organ. Behav. Hum. Decis. Process.* 115:169–80

Bass BM, Avolio BJ. 1990. Developing transformational leadership: 1992 and beyond. *J. Eur. Ind. Train.* 14:21–27

Bauman C. 2013. Leadership and the three faces of integrity. *Leadersh. Q.* 24:414–26

Baumeister RF, Heatherton TF. 1996. Self-regulation failure: an overview. *Psychol. Inq.* 7:1–15

Bazerman MH, Tenbrunsel AE. 2011. *Blind Spots: Why We Fail To Do What's Right and What To Do About It*. Princeton, NJ: Princeton Univ. Press

Bersoff DM. 1999. Why good people sometimes do bad things: motivated reasoning and unethical behavior. *Personal. Soc. Psychol. Bull.* 25:28–39

Beu DS, Buckley MR. 2004. This is war: how the politically astute achieve crimes of obedience through the use of moral disengagement. *Leadersh. Q.* 15:551–68

Develops a measure and conducts validity tests on the self-importance of moral identity.

One of the first attempts to explain how corruption can become normal and spread within organizations.

Brown ME, Mitchell MS. 2010. Ethical and unethical leadership: exploring new avenues for future research. *Bus. Ethics Q.* 20:583–616

Brown ME, Treviño LK. 2006. Ethical leadership: a review and future directions. *Leadersh. Q.* 17:595–616

Brown ME, Treviño LK, Harrison DA. 2005. Ethical leadership: a social learning perspective for construct development and testing. *Organ. Behav. Hum. Decis. Process.* 97:117–34

Chaiken S, Trope Y. 1999. *Dual-Process Theories in Social Psychology.* New York: Guilford

Christian MS, Ellis APJ. 2011. Examining the effects of sleep deprivation on workplace deviance: a self-regulatory perspective. *Acad. Manag. J.* 54:913–34

Cohen TR. 2010. Moral emotions and unethical bargaining: the differential effects of empathy and perspective taking in deterring deceitful negotiation. *J. Bus. Ethics* 94:569–79

Cropanzano R, Stein JH. 2009. Organizational justice and behavioral ethics: promises and prospects. *Bus. Ethics Q.* 19:193–233

Damasio A. 1994. *Descartes' Error: Emotion, Reason, and the Human Brain.* New York: Putnam

Dana J, Loewenstein G, Weber R. 2012. Ethical immunity: how people violate their own moral standards without feeling they are doing so. In *Behavioral Business Ethics: Shaping an Emerging Field*, ed. D DeCremer, AE Tenbrunsel, pp. 201–19. New York: Routledge

DeCelles KA, DeRue DS, Margolis JD, Ceranic TL. 2012. Does power corrupt or enable? When and why power facilitates self-interested behavior. *J. Appl. Psychol.* 97:681–89

De Hooge IE, Nelissen RM, Breugelmans SM, Zeelenberg M. 2011. What is moral about guilt? Acting "prosocially" at the disadvantage of others. *J. Personal. Soc. Psychol.* 100:462–73

De Ridder DT, Lensvelt-Mulders G, Finkenauer C, Stok FM, Baumeister RF. 2012. Taking stock of self-control: a meta-analysis of how trait self-control relates to a wide range of behaviors. *Personal. Soc. Psychol. Rev.* 16:76–99

Detert JR, Treviño LK, Burris ER, Andiappan M. 2007. Managerial modes of influence and counterproductivity in organizations: a longitudinal business-unit-level investigation. *J. Appl. Psychol.* 92:993–1005

Detert JR, Treviño LK, Sweitzer VL. 2008. Moral disengagement in ethical decision making: a study of antecedents and outcomes. *J. Appl. Psychol.* 93:374–91

Duffy MK, Aquino K, Tepper BJ, Reed A, O'Leary-Kelly AM. 2005. *Moral disengagement and social identification: When does being similar result in harm doing?* Presented at annu. meet. Acad. Manag., Honolulu, Hawaii

Duffy MK, Scott KL, Shaw JD, Tepper BJ, Aquino K. 2012. A social context model of envy and social undermining. *Acad. Manag. J.* 55:643–66

Eisenberg N, Miller PA. 1987. The regulation of empathy to pro-social and related behaviors. *Psychol. Bull.* 101:91–119

Ethics Resour. Cent. 2012. *2011 National Business Ethics Survey: Workplace Ethics in Transition.* Arlington, VA: Ethics Resour. Cent.

Folger R, Cropanzano R, Goldman B. 2005. What is the relationship between justice and morality? In *Handbook of Organizational Justice*, ed. J Greenberg, JA Colquitt, pp. 215–45. Mahwah, NJ: Erlbaum

Gaudine A, Thorne L. 2001. Emotion and ethical decision-making in organizations. *J. Bus. Ethics* 31:175–87

Gehman J, Treviño LK, Garud R. 2013. Values work: a process study of the emergence and performance of organizational values practices. *Acad. Manag. J.* 56:84–112

Gentile M. 2010. *Giving Voice to Values: How to Speak Your Mind When You Know What's Right.* New Haven, CT: Yale Univ. Press

Ghoshal S. 2005. Bad management theories are destroying good management practices. *Acad. Manag. Learn. Educ.* 4:75–91

Gino F, Ariely D. 2012. The dark side of creativity: Original thinkers can be more dishonest. *J. Personal. Soc. Psychol.* 102:445–59

Gino F, Ayal S, Ariely D. 2009a. Contagion and differentiation in unethical behavior: the effect of one bad apple on the barrel. *Psychol. Sci.* 20:393–98

Gino F, Galinsky AD. 2012. Vicarious dishonesty: when psychological closeness creates distance from one's moral compass. *Organ. Behav. Hum. Decis. Process.* 119:15–26

Gino F, Gu J, Zhong CB. 2009b. Contagion or restitution? When bad apples can motivate ethical behavior. *J. Exp. Soc. Psychol.* 45:1299–302

Introduces a widely used measure of ethical leadership and establishes its validity.

Examines the effects of situational envy on moral disengagement and social undermining at work.

Shows that unethical behavior depends on the norms implied by others' behavior, not on cost-benefit analyses.

Gino F, Pierce L. 2009a. The abundance effect: unethical behavior in the presence of wealth. *Organ. Behav. Hum. Decis. Process.* 109:142–55

Gino F, Pierce L. 2009b. Dishonesty in the name of equity. *Psychol. Sci.* 20:1153–60

Gino F, Pierce L. 2010. Robin Hood under the hood: wealth-based discrimination in illicit customer help. *Organ. Sci.* 21:1176–94

Gino F, Schweitzer ME, Mead NL, Ariely D. 2011. Unable to resist temptation: how self-control depletion promotes unethical behavior. *Organ. Behav. Hum. Decis. Process.* 115:191–203

Greenbaum RL, Mawritz MB, Eissa G. 2012. Bottom-line mentality as an antecedent of social undermining and the moderating roles of core self-evaluations and conscientiousness. *J. Appl. Psychol.* 97:343–59

Greenberg J. 1990. Employee theft as a reaction to underpayment inequity—the hidden cost of pay cuts. *J. Appl. Psychol.* 75:561–68

Greene JD. 2009. Dual-process morality and the personal/impersonal distinction: a reply to McGuire, Langdon, Coltheart, and Mackenzie. *J. Exp. Soc. Psychol.* 45:581–84

Gunia BC, Wang L, Huang L, Wang JW, Murnighan JK. 2012. Contemplation and conversation: subtle influences on moral decision making. *Acad. Manag. J.* 55:13–33

Haidt J. 2001. The emotional dog and its rational tail: a social intuitionist approach to moral judgment. *Psychol. Rev.* 108:814–34

Introduces the social intuitionist model of moral judgment as an alternative to a rationalist model.

Hannah S, Schaubroeck J, Peng C, Lord R, Treviño LK, et al. 2013. Joint influences of individual and work unit abusive supervision on ethical intentions and behaviors: a moderated mediation model. *J. Appl. Psychol.* 98:579–92

Hannah ST, Avolio BJ, May DR. 2011a. Moral maturation and moral conation: a capacity approach to explaining moral thought and action. *Acad. Manag. Rev.* 36:663–85

Hannah ST, Avolio BJ, Walumbwa FO. 2011b. Relationships between authentic leadership, moral courage, and ethical and pro-social behaviors. *Bus. Ethics Q.* 21:555–78

Hill SE, DelPriore DJ, Vaughan PW. 2011. The cognitive consequences of envy: attention, memory and self-regulatory depletion. *J. Personal. Soc. Psychol.* 101:653–66

Hoffman WM. 2010. Repositioning the corporate ethics officer. *Bus. Ethics Q.* 20:744–45

Jordan J, Brown ME, Treviño LK, Finkelstein S. 2011. Someone to look up to: executive–follower ethical reasoning and perceptions of ethical leadership. *J. Manag.* 39:660–83

Kacmar KM, Bachrach DG, Harris KJ, Zivnuska S. 2011. Fostering good citizenship through ethical leadership: exploring the moderating role of gender and organizational politics. *J. Appl. Psychol.* 96:633–42

Kahneman D, Tversky A. 1979. Prospect theory: analysis of decision under risk. *Econometrica* 47:263–91

Kalshoven K, Den Hartog DN, De Hoogh AHB. 2011. Ethical leader behavior and big five factors of personality. *J. Bus. Ethics* 100:349–66

Kelman HC, Hamilton VL. 1989. *Crimes of Obedience*. New Haven, CT: Yale Univ. Press

Kern MC, Chugh D. 2009. Bounded ethicality: the perils of loss framing. *Psychol. Sci.* 20:378–84

Kim WG, Brymer RA. 2011. The effects of ethical leadership on manager job satisfaction, commitment, behavioral outcomes, and firm performance. *Int. J. Hospitality Manag.* 30:1020–26

Kish-Gephart JJ, Detert JR, Treviño LK, Edmondson AC. 2009. Silenced by fear: the nature, sources, and consequences of fear at work. *Res. Organ. Behav.* 29:163–93

Kish-Gephart JJ, Harrison DA, Treviño LK. 2010. Bad apples, bad cases, and bad barrels: meta-analytic evidence about sources of unethical decisions at work. *J. Appl. Psychol.* 95:1–31

Provides a meta-analytic review of prominent individual-, situational-, and organizational-level variables in the field.

Kohlberg L. 1969. Stage and sequence: the cognitive developmental approach to socialization. In *Handbook of Socialization Theory and Research*, ed. DA Goslin, pp. 347–480. Chicago: Rand McNally

Kouchaki M, Smith-Crowe K, Brief AP, Sousa C. 2013. Seeing green: Mere exposure to money triggers a business decision frame and unethical outcomes. *Organ. Behav. Hum. Decis. Process* 121:53–61

Kunda Z. 1990. The case for motivated reasoning. *Psychol. Bull.* 108:480–98

Latham GP, Locke EA. 2006. Enhancing the benefits and overcoming the pitfalls of goal setting. *Organ. Dyn.* 35:332–40

Leavitt K, Reynolds SJ, Barnes CM, Schilpzand P, Hannah ST. 2012. Different hats, different obligations: plural occupational identities and situated moral judgments. *Acad. Manag. J.* 55:1316–33

Lee TW. 1999. *Using Qualitative Methods in Organizational Research*. Thousand Oaks, CA: Sage

Liu Y, Lam LWR, Loi R. 2012. Ethical leadership and workplace deviance: the role of moral disengagement. *Adv. Glob. Leadersh.* 7:37–56

Locke EA, Latham GP. 2009. Has goal setting gone wild, or have its attackers abandoned good scholarship? *Acad. Manag. Perspect.* 23:17–23

Martin KD, Cullen JB. 2006. Continuities and extensions of ethical climate theory: a meta-analytic review. *J. Bus. Ethics* 69:175–94

Mawritz MB, Mayer DM, Hoobler JM, Wayne SJ, Marinova SV. 2012. A trickle-down model of abusive supervision. *Pers. Psychol.* 65:325–57

Mayer DM, Aquino K, Greenbaum RL, Kuenzi M. 2012. Who displays ethical leadership, and why does it matter? An examination of antecedents and consequences of ethical leadership. *Acad. Manag. J.* 55:151–71

Mayer DM, Kuenzi M, Greenbaum R, Bardes M, Salvador R. 2009. How low does ethical leadership flow? Test of a trickle-down model. *Organ. Behav. Hum. Decis. Process.* 108:1–13

Mayer DM, Nurmohamed S, Treviño LK, Shapiro DL, Schminke M. 2013. Encouraging employees to report unethical conduct internally: it takes a village. *Organ. Behav. Hum. Decis. Process.* 121:89–103

Mazar N, Amir O, Ariely D. 2008. The dishonesty of honest people: a theory of self-concept maintenance. *J. Market. Res.* 45:633–44

Mesmer-Magnus JR, Viswesvaran C. 2005. Whistleblowing in organizations: an examination of correlates of whistleblowing intentions, actions, and retaliation. *J. Bus. Ethics* 62:277–97

Milgram S. 1974. *Obedience to Authority: An Experimental View*. New York: Harper & Row

Molinsky AL, Grant AM, Margolis JD. 2012. The bedside manner of *homo economicus*: how and why priming an economic schema reduces compassion. *Organ. Behav. Hum. Decis. Process.* 119:27–37

Moore C, Detert JR, Treviño LK, Baker VL, Mayer DM. 2012. Why employees do bad things: moral disengagement and unethical organizational behavior. *Pers. Psychol.* 65:1–48

Moore C, Gino F. 2013. Ethically adrift: how others pull our moral compass from true north and how we can fix it. *Res. Organ. Behav.* 33:In press

Moran S, Schweitzer ME. 2008. When better is worse: envy and the use of deception. *Negot. Confl. Manag. Res.* 1:3–29

Naquin CE, Kurtzberg TR, Belkin LY. 2010. The finer points of lying online: e-mail versus pen and paper. *J. Appl. Psychol.* 95:387–94

Neubert MJ, Carlson DS, Kacmar KM, Roberts JA, Chonko LB. 2009. The virtuous influence of ethical leadership behavior: evidence from the field. *J. Bus. Ethics* 90:157–70

O'Fallon MJ, Butterfield KD. 2005. A review of the empirical ethical decision-making literature: 1996–2003. *J. Bus. Ethics* 59:375–413

Ordóñez LD, Schweitzer ME, Galinsky AD, Bazerman MH. 2009a. Goals gone wild: the systematic side effects of overprescribing goal setting. *Acad. Manag. Perspect.* 23:6–16

Ordóñez LD, Schweitzer ME, Galinsky AD, Bazerman MH. 2009b. On good scholarship, goal setting, and scholars gone wild. *Acad. Manag. Perspect.* 23:82–87

O'Reilly J, Aquino K. 2011. A model of third parties' morally motivated responses to mistreatment in organizations. *Acad. Manag. Rev.* 36:526–43

Paharia N, Kassam KS, Greene JD, Bazerman MH. 2009. Dirty work, clean hands: the moral psychology of indirect agency. *Organ. Behav. Hum. Decis. Process.* 109:134–41

Piccolo RF, Greenbaum R, Den Hartog DN, Folger R. 2010. The relationship between ethical leadership and core job characteristics. *J. Organ. Behav.* 31:259–78

Pierce L, Snyder J. 2008. Ethical spillovers in firms: evidence from vehicle emissions testing. *Manag. Sci.* 54:1891–903

Pitesa M, Thau S. 2013. Compliant sinners, obstinate saints: how power and self-focus determine the effectiveness of social influences in ethical decision making. *Acad. Manag. J.* 56:635–58

Polman E, Ruttan RL. 2012. Effects of anger, guilt and envy on moral hypocrisy. *Personal. Soc. Psychol. Bull.* 38:129–39

Rawls J. 1971. *A Theory of Justice*. Cambridge, MA: Harvard Univ. Press

Develops an eight-item measure of moral disengagement and demonstrates its predictive validity in multiple studies.

Reed A, Aquino K, Levy E. 2007. Moral identity and judgments of charitable behaviors. *J. Mark.* 71:178–93

Rest JR. 1986. *Moral Development: Advances in Research and Theory.* New York: Praeger

Reynolds SJ. 2006. A neurocognitive model of the ethical decision-making process: implications for study and practice. *J. Appl. Psychol.* 91:737–48

Reynolds SJ. 2008. Moral attentiveness: Who pays attention to the moral aspects of life? *J. Appl. Psychol.* 93:1027–41

Reynolds SJ, Ceranic TL. 2007. The effects of moral judgment and moral identity on moral behavior: an empirical examination of the moral individual. *J. Appl. Psychol.* 92:1610–24

Reynolds SJ, Leavitt K, DeCelles KA. 2010. Automatic ethics: the effects of implicit assumptions and contextual cues on moral behavior. *J. Appl. Psychol.* 95:752–60

Robinson SL, O'Leary-Kelly AM. 1998. Monkey see, monkey do: the influence of work groups on the antisocial behavior of employees. *Acad. Manag. J.* 41:658–72

Ruiz P, Ruiz C, Martinez R. 2011. Improving the "leader-follower" relationship: top manager or supervisor? The ethical leadership trickle-down effect on follower job response. *J. Bus. Ethics* 99:587–608

Rupp DE, Bell CM. 2010. Extending the deontic model of justice: moral self-regulation in third-party responses to injustice. *Bus. Ethics Q.* 20:89–106

Salvador R, Folger RG. 2009. Business ethics and the brain. *Bus. Ethics Q.* 19:1–31

Schaubroeck JM, Hannah ST, Avolio BJ, Kozlowski SWJ, Lord RG, et al. 2012. Embedding ethical leadership within and across organization levels. *Acad. Manag. J.* 55:1053–78

Schminke M, Ambrose ML, Neubaum DO. 2005. The effect of leader moral development on ethical climate and employee attitudes. *Organ. Behav. Hum. Decis. Process.* 97:135–51

Schwartz SH. 1968. Words, deeds and perception of consequences and responsibility in action situations. *J. Personal. Soc. Psychol.* 10:232–42

Schweitzer ME, Ordonez L, Douma B. 2004. Goal setting as a motivator of unethical behavior. *Acad. Manag. J.* 47:422–32

Shalvi S, Eldar O, Bereby-Meyer Y. 2012. Honesty requires time (and lack of justifications). *Psychol. Sci.* 23:1264–70

Shao RD, Aquino K, Freeman D. 2008. Beyond moral reasoning: a review of moral identity research and its implications for business ethics. *Bus. Ethics Q.* 18:513–40

Shu LL, Mazar N, Gino F, Ariely D, Bazerman MH. 2012. Signing at the beginning makes ethics salient and decreases dishonest self-reports in comparison to signing at the end. *Proc. Natl. Acad. Sci. USA* 109:15197–200

Simha A, Cullen JB. 2012. Ethical climates and their effects on organizational outcomes: implications from the past and prophecies for the future. *Acad. Manag. Perspect.* 26:20–34

Simons T. 2002. Behavioral integrity: the perceived alignment between managers' words and deeds as a research focus. *Organ. Sci.* 13:18–35

Skarlicki DP, Rupp DE. 2010. Dual processing and organizational justice: the role of rational versus experiential processing in third-party reactions to workplace mistreatment. *J. Appl. Psychol.* 95:944–52

Sonenshein S. 2006. Crafting social issues at work. *Acad. Manag. J.* 49:1158–72

Sonenshein S. 2007. The role of construction, intuition, and justification in responding to ethical issues at work: the sensemaking-intuition model. *Acad. Manag. Rev.* 32:1022–40

Sonenshein S. 2009. Emergence of ethical issues during strategic change implementation. *Organ. Sci.* 20:223–39

Sykes GM, Matza D. 1957. Techniques of neutralization: a theory of delinquency. *Am. Sociol. Rev.* 22:664–70

Tai K, Narayanan J, McAllister D. 2012. Envy as pain: rethinking the nature of envy and its implications for employees and organizations. *Acad. Manag. Rev.* 37:107–29

Takahashi H, Kato M, Matsuura M, Mobbs D, Suhara T, Okubo Y. 2009. When your gain is my pain and your pain is my gain: neutral correlates of envy and schadenfreude. *Science* 323:938–39

Tanner C, Brugger A, Van Schie S, Lebherz C. 2010. Actions speak louder than words: the benefits of ethical behaviors of leaders. *Z. Psychol. J. Psychol.* 218:225–33

Tenbrunsel AE, Diekmann KA, Wade-Benzoni KA, Bazerman MH. 2010. The ethical mirage: a temporal explanation as to why we are not as ethical as we think we are. *Res. Organ. Behav.* 30:153–73

Uses knowledge of brain functioning to understand ethical decisions as less deliberate and reasoned.

Combines social psychological and organizational literature to advance a model of intuitive ethical decision making.

Tenbrunsel AE, Messick DM. 1999. Sanctioning systems, decision frames, and cooperation. *Adm. Sci. Q.* 44:684–707

Tenbrunsel AE, Smith-Crowe K. 2008. Ethical decision making: where we've been and where we're going. *Acad. Manag. Ann.* 2:545–607

Tepper BJ. 2000. Consequences of abusive supervision. *Acad. Manag. J.* 43:178–90

Tepper BJ, Moss SE, Lockhart DE, Carr JC. 2007. Abusive supervision, upward maintenance communication, and subordinates' psychological distress. *Acad. Manag. J.* 50:1169–80

Treviño LK. 1986. Ethical decision making in organizations: a person-situation interactionist model. *Acad. Manag. Rev.* 11:601–17

Treviño LK. 1990. A cultural perspective on changing and developing organizational ethics. In *Research on Organizational Change and Development*, ed. RW Passmore, pp. 195–230. Greenwich, CT: JAI

Treviño LK, Weaver GR, Reynolds SJ. 2006. Behavioral ethics in organizations: a review. *J. Manag.* 32:951–90

Tsang J. 2002. Moral rationalization and the integration of situational factors and psychological processes in immoral behavior. *Rev. Gen. Psychol.* 6:25–50

Tyler T, Blader SL. 2000. *Cooperation in Group: Procedural Justice, Social Identity, and Behavioral Engagement.* Philadelphia, PA: Psychol. Press

Uhlmann EL, Leavitt K, Menges JL, Koopman J, Howe MD, Johnson RE. 2012. Getting explicit about the implicit: a taxonomy of implicit measures and guide for their use in organizational research. *Organ. Res. Methods* 15:553–601

Umphress EE, Bingham JB. 2011. When employees do bad things for good reasons: examining unethical pro-organizational behaviors. *Organ. Sci.* 22:621–40

Umphress EE, Bingham JB, Mitchell MS. 2010. Unethical behavior in the name of the company: the moderating effect of organizational identification and positive reciprocity beliefs on unethical pro-organizational behavior. *J. Appl. Psychol.* 95:769–80

Victor B, Cullen JB. 1988. The organizational bases of ethical work climates. *Adm. Sci. Q.* 33:101–25

Vincent LC, Emich KJ, Goncalo JA. 2013. Stretching the moral gray zone: positive affect, moral disengagement, and dishonesty. *Psychol. Sci.* 24:595–99

Walumbwa FO, Mayer DM, Wang P, Wang H, Workman K, Christensen AL. 2011. Linking ethical leadership to employee performance: the roles of leader-member exchange, self-efficacy, and organizational identification. *Organ. Behav. Hum. Decis. Process.* 115:204–13

Walumbwa FO, Schaubroeck J. 2009. Leader personality traits and employee voice behavior: mediating roles of ethical leadership and work group psychological safety. *J. Appl. Psychol.* 94:1275–86

Weaver GR, Reynolds SJ, Brown ME. 2013. *Moral intuition: connecting current knowledge to future research and organizational practice.* Work. Pap., Dep. Bus. Admin., Univ. Del., Newark

Weaver GR, Treviño LK. 1999. Compliance and values oriented ethics programs: influences on employees' attitudes and behavior. *Bus. Ethics Q.* 9:315–35

Wiltermuth SS. 2011. Cheating more when the spoils are split. *Organ. Behav. Hum. Decis. Process.* 115:157–68

Zhong C. 2011. The ethical dangers of deliberative decision making. *Adm. Sci. Q.* 56:1–25

Beyond Motivation: Job and Work Design for Development, Health, Ambidexterity, and More

Sharon K. Parker

The University of Western Australia, Crawley, Perth, Western Australia 6009, Australia; email: sharon.parker@uwa.edu.au

Annu. Rev. Psychol. 2014. 65:661–91

First published online as a Review in Advance on September 6, 2013

The *Annual Review of Psychology* is online at http://psych.annualreviews.org

This article's doi: 10.1146/annurev-psych-010213-115208

Keywords

job design, autonomy, job enrichment, job characteristics, self-managing teams

Abstract

Much research shows it is possible to design motivating work, which has positive consequences for individuals and their organizations. This article reviews research that adopts this motivational perspective on work design, and it emphasizes that it is important to continue to refine motivational theories. In light of continued large numbers of poor-quality jobs, attention must also be given to influencing practice and policy to promote the effective implementation of enriched work designs. Nevertheless, current and future work-based challenges mean that designing work for motivation is necessary but insufficient. This review argues that work design can be a powerful vehicle for learning and development, for maintaining and enhancing employees' physical and mental health, and for achieving control and flexibility simultaneously (for example, in the form of ambidexterity); all these outcomes are important given the challenges in today's workplaces. The review concludes by suggesting methodological directions.

Contents

INTRODUCTION

Ten hours (a day) is a long time just doing this. . . . I've had three years in here and I'm like, I'm going to get the hell out. . . . It's just the most boring work you can do.

                    —*Ford autoworker*

I love my job. . . . I've learned so much. . . . I can talk with biochemists, software engineers, all these interesting people. . . . I love being independent, relying on myself. . . . I just do whatever works, it's exciting.

                    —*Corporate headhunter*

We see about a hundred injuries a year and I'm amazed there aren't more. The main causes are inexperience and repetition. . . . People work the same job all the time and they stop thinking.

                    —*Slaughterhouse human resources director*

These quotations, from a book in which Americans talk about their jobs (Bowe et al. 2000, pp. 38, 12, and 52, respectively), highlight the diverse outcomes one's work design can cause. Work design, or the content and organization of one's work tasks, activities, relationships, and responsibilities, has been linked to almost every end goal that is of concern in an organization—safety, performance, and innovation, to name a few. Work design also matters for individuals; it affects their sense of meaning, their health, and their development. On the global front, the importance of work design is exemplified by the International Labor Organization's Decent Work Agenda, which focuses not just on obtaining work for all but on ensuring quality work that provides "better prospects for personal development and freedom for people to express their concerns, organize and participate in the decisions that affect their lives" (**http://www.ilo.org/global/topics/decent-work/lang–en/index.htm**). On the theoretical front, Miner (2003) rated work design theory as one of the few theories in the field of organizational behavior that are simultaneously important, valid, and useful.

Despite its salience for practice and policy, and its sound theoretical underpinning, work design has not received the research attention that is warranted (Humphrey et al. 2007), especially given radical shifts in work organization (Grant & Parker 2009). As an example, work design has not been the focus of any previous Annual Reviews article. The goal of this article is thus, unashamedly, to help promote work design research as a distinct area of psychological inquiry. The review has two parts. First, it discusses dominant motivational approaches to work design. Contemporary challenges mean that designing work for motivation is necessary but insufficient, so the second part of the review identifies three goals of work design that are central given enhanced complexity in many workplaces: work design for learning and development, work design for health and well-being, and work design for the dual outcomes of control and flexibility. In both parts, the focus of this review is on more recent research and new theoretical directions [for further advances, see also the special issue of the *Journal of Organizational Behavior*, with an introduction by Grant et al. (2010)]; for reviews of earlier work, the reader is referred to the online reference list (follow the Supplemental Material link from the Annual Reviews home page at **http://www.annualreviews.org**). In addition, this review uses the term work design instead of job design to reflect that the topic is concerned not only with employees' prescribed technical tasks within a fixed job but also with employee engagement in emergent, social, and self-initiated activities within flexible roles (Morgeson & Campion 2003, Parker & Wall 1998).

Definition and Brief History

Imagine designing the role of a police officer. Illustrative work design decisions include the following: Which activities should be grouped together to form a meaningful job? Which decisions should be made by officers and which by their supervisors? Should individual jobs be grouped together into a team? Can one build in routine tasks amid complex ones to ensure officers are not overwhelmed by demands? These decisions about the content and organization of officers' tasks, activities, relationships, and responsibilities will affect outcomes at multiple levels, including individual officers, such as how engaged they feel or their level of strain; the wider organization, such as whether the police service achieves its targets; and society, such as how effectively crime is detected and prevented.

Historically, interest in the topic of work design arose in response to the wide-scale adoption of scientific management principles in the design of early industrial jobs. A key principle is job simplification, in which mental work is allocated to the managers while workers perform only the manual work. The negative consequences of job simplification, such as turnover, strikes, and absenteeism, prompted interest in redesigning work. At the group level, the application of sociotechnical systems theory led to the design of autonomous work groups, which are still popular today. At the individual level, job rotation, job enlargement, and job enrichment emerged as motivational antidotes to simplified jobs; job enrichment is the most important of these approaches because of its emphasis on increasing employees' autonomy. The theory underpinning these and related work redesigns, and research regarding their effects, is discussed next.

PART 1: MOTIVATIONAL WORK DESIGN PERSPECTIVES

Unsurprisingly, given that work design emerged from studies of alienating and meaningless jobs, psychological research on the subject has motivation at its core (Campion 1988). The first section of Part 1 describes established motivational perspectives on work design. The second section reviews expanded motivational perspectives on work design. The third section discusses the embedding of motivational work design principles into policy and practice.

Established Motivational Perspectives: The Job Characteristics Model, Elaborations, and Group Work Design

The dominant motivational model of work design is the job characteristics model (JCM). This section reviews the JCM as well as elaborations to this model and its extension to groups.

Scientific management: a theory of management focused on achieving efficiency by analyzing work and breaking it down into simplified tasks. Employees carry out the simplified tasks while managers make decisions and engage in mental work

Sociotechnical systems theory: the idea that the technical and social aspects of work should be jointly optimized when designing work

Autonomous work group: a group of interdependent members that have collective autonomy over day-to-day aspects of their work

Job rotation: rotating employees from one job to another job

Job enlargement: expanding the content of jobs to include additional tasks

Job enrichment: increasing employees' autonomy over the planning and execution of their own work

Job characteristics model. Hackman & Oldham (1976) proposed in the JCM that work should be designed to have five core job characteristics (job variety, job autonomy, job feedback, job significance, and job identity), which engender three critical psychological states in individuals— experiencing meaning, feeling responsible for outcomes, and understanding the results of their efforts. In turn, these psychological states were proposed to enhance employees' intrinsic motivation, job satisfaction, and performance, while reducing turnover. Although some more specific propositions of the JCM have not been consistently supported (such as the idea that individuals with a high need for growth will benefit most from the core job characteristics), the central proposition that work characteristics affect attitudinal outcomes has been well established in several meta-analyses. The most recent meta-analysis (Humphrey et al. 2007), of 259 studies, showed that all or most of the five core work characteristics relate to the JCM outcomes of job satisfaction, growth satisfaction, and internal work motivation, as well as to other outcomes such as organizational commitment, coworker satisfaction, burnout, and role perceptions. In addition, experienced meaning was the key psychological state that mediated the relationship between job characteristics and outcomes. These meta-analytic findings—based mostly on studies with cross-sectional research designs—are supported by longitudinal and quasi-experimental studies showing positive effects of job enrichment on attitudes and affective reactions (see the review by Parker & Wall 1998). Longitudinal studies also show that low autonomy and low support increase absence, and that job enrichment can reduce employee turnover.

Meta-analyses show clear links between work characteristics and subjective job performance, although when objective job performance is considered, only job autonomy is important (Humphrey et al. 2007). Several quasi-experimental and longitudinal studies also show positive performance effects of motivating work characteristics, although a smaller set of other studies have failed to show performance effects (Kopelman 2006), which suggests that the relationship between enrichment and performance is moderated, as discussed in the next section.

An issue that has long dogged the JCM is the use of job incumbents' perceptions to assess job characteristics. For instance, critics have argued that individuals' perceptions of their job characteristics are constructions that arise from social influences, such as the attitudes of their peers. However, although social cues do affect perceptions of work characteristics, there is plenty of evidence that using perceptions to assess job characteristics is valid in most situations (see Daniels 2006, Morgeson & Campion 2003).

Elaborated job characteristics approaches. The JCM's core elements have been expanded. For example, the elaborated job characteristics model proposed the need to extend the core work characteristics, moderators, outcomes, mechanisms, and antecedents of work design (Parker et al. 2001; see also Morgeson & Humphrey 2008), as discussed below.

First, there are important job features beyond the JCM's five core job characteristics. Over the years, much attention has been given to social characteristics such as task interdependence (Langfred 2005). Further job characteristics have become salient as a result of changes in work organization. For example, the rise of dual working parents highlights the need to consider autonomy over working hours; the growth in service work identifies the need to consider emotional job demands; the rise of individuals working from home highlights the role of social contact during work; and changes in career structures bring to the fore opportunities for skill development. In their Work Design Questionnaire, Morgeson & Humphrey (2006) distinguished 21 job characteristics covering four categories: task motivation (i.e., the five JCM characteristics), knowledge motivation (e.g., problem-solving demands), social characteristics (e.g., social support), and contextual characteristics (e.g., work conditions). In Humphrey et al.'s (2007) meta-analysis, motivational work characteristics explained 34% of the variance in job satisfaction;

Job variety: the degree to which a job involves a variety of activities and uses a number of different skills

Job significance: the degree to which a job has a substantial impact on the lives or work of others

Job feedback: the degree to which a job incumbent obtains clear information about his or her effectiveness in performing the job

Job identity: the degree to which a job requires completion of a whole job, from beginning to end

Job autonomy: the degree to which a job provides discretion over daily work decisions, such as when and how to do tasks

Job demands: aspects of jobs that require sustained and/or high levels of physical, mental, or emotional effort (e.g., time pressure, emotional demands)

social and contextual characteristics explained a further 17% and 4%, respectively. Besides expanding what work characteristics are considered, it is important to consider interactions between them, such as the balance between individual autonomy and group autonomy (Langfred 2000).

A second extension is to consider outcomes of work design beyond those specified in the JCM. In some cases, the outcomes are extensions of established ones—for example, going beyond increased effort and productivity as the key indicators of performance to examine performance outcomes such as customer loyalty and employee creativity. In other cases, outcomes have been extended to reflect changes in the nature of work or the workforce. For example, the increasing number of employed women means it is important to consider how work design affects family functioning (see, e.g., Kelly et al. 2011), and interest in social responsibility raises questions about how poor-quality work might lead individuals to seek out enriching volunteer opportunities (Grant 2012a). Additional work design outcomes are further considered in Part 2 of this article (see also reviews such as Demerouti & Bakker 2011, Morgeson & Humphrey 2008).

Third, scholars have identified mechanisms by which work design might affect job attitudes and behaviors beyond the JCM's critical psychological states. Some of these expanded mechanisms are motivationally oriented, such as self-efficacy (Parker 1998) and psychological empowerment (Morgeson & Campion 2003). Other mechanisms are nonmotivational. For example, employees with autonomy can often respond to problems faster than specialists can (Wall & Jackson 1995), and they can often make better decisions than supervisors can because they can access unique information that is only available to those doing the work (Langfred & Moye 2004). Job enrichment can promote learning and more effective coping, mechanisms considered further in the second part of this review.

Fourth, scholars have considered an elaborated set of moderators of how work characteristics affect outcomes. When it comes to individual differences, the concept of fit suggests that which work characteristics are valued varies according to individual preferences, desires, and demographics. Individual differences do moderate work design effects, although these findings are rather inconsistent (Morgeson & Campion 2003). Moreover, there is no basis for expecting that any single individual difference variable will moderate all work characteristic–outcome relationships, because the processes underpinning these links vary according to the work characteristic and the outcome. A theoretical approach will help move this area forward, such as Raja & Johns's (2010) study that drew on trait activation theory (which predicts that people behaviorally express their traits in situations that cue those traits) to understand the link between personality, job scope, and performance. Several theoretical predictions remain untested, such as Fried et al.'s (2007) proposal that simplified jobs might not cause adverse effects early in one's career if a job is seen as a stepping stone for future enriched jobs.

The most consistent contextual moderator of work design is uncertainty. Job enrichment appears to most enhance performance when operational uncertainty is high rather than low (see Wall & Jackson 1995). This is probably because, in unpredictable situations, knowledge is incomplete and flexible responses are required, and autonomy facilitates both the speed and quality of decision making. Scholars have also argued that enriched work design is most effective when it aligns with organizational and human resource systems (Cordery & Parker 2007), a perspective that concurs with the high-performance work systems perspective that bundles of aligned practices enhance organizational performance (see, e.g., Combs et al. 2006). In contrast to these arguments, Morgeson et al. (2006) found that autonomous work groups are effective only when reward, feedback, and information systems are poor. Although studies have considered national cultural influences on work design, there is no clear overall picture of cultural effects (Erez 2010), which is a salient void in the context of globalization.

Interdependence: the degree to which individuals need to work closely with others to carry out their roles

Social support: the provision of emotional or instrumental help, typically from a peer or supervisor

Empowerment (psychological): an individual's experience of meaning, impact, competence, and self-determination

Empowerment
(structural):
structures, policies,
and practices designed
to delegate power and
authority

A fifth elaboration of the JCM has been to consider individual and contextual factors that shape, influence, and/or constrain work characteristics. Regarding individual factors, job incumbents can proactively craft their own job designs (see Expanded Motivational Theories, below). Regarding contextual factors, variables such as institutional regimes, organizational design, leadership, occupational context, and organizational practices (e.g., structural empowerment, lean production, temporary employment, downsizing, teleworking) can directly affect or generate work characteristics or exert a cross-level influence on work characteristics (see Motivational Work Design in Practice, below). An implication of these findings is that work can be redesigned not only by direct manipulation of job characteristics but also, for example, by developing empowering leaders or by restructuring. A further implication is that work design should be proactively considered when new technologies and strategies are introduced (although, unfortunately, work design is often disregarded). Occupations can also shape or constrain work characteristics (Dierdorff & Morgeson 2013), and the relationship between broader practices and work design can be reciprocal, for example, a positive leader-member exchange relationship between a manager and the job incumbent might contribute to more enriched work that, in turn, reinforces and enhances the positive relationship between the manager and the job incumbent.

Altogether, the JCM has been expanded in useful ways. It can, and should, be expanded further to reflect changes in work in general (e.g., a growth in virtual work, changes in employment contracts, and an increase in service and knowledge work) and changes in the nature of the workforce (e.g., aging, more women, increased diversity as a result of migration patterns).

Group work design. Group work design is appropriate when individual roles are interdependent and there is a need for collective working. Sociotechnical systems principles were early influences on group work design. Scholars (see, e.g., Campion et al. 1993) extended these ideas, proposing input-process-output models of team effectiveness. Inputs include group-level work design, contextual influences, and group composition; processes include intermediary group states or attributes such as group norms; and outputs include team-level performance and team-member affective reactions. Subsequent team research expanded these models in various ways, although the work design characteristics focused on are still primarily group-level versions of the JCM, with the additional inclusion of interdependence.

Most attention has been given to group autonomy, which is when team members are allocated collective responsibility for their work. There is encouragingly consistent evidence across studies of autonomous work groups, team effectiveness, and team empowerment that group autonomy is associated with positive team member job attitudes and reactions, such as job satisfaction and organizational commitment (Maynard et al. 2012, Parker & Wall 1998). One dent in this positive picture is the question of whether team autonomy can operate as an insidious form of control. Barker's (1993, p. 432) ethnographic study showed that in self-managing teams, workers imposed values on themselves in an increasingly rigid way, such that initially enthusiastic participants became "strained and burdened." Such findings might not be generalizable. For example, Gaille (2013) reported for a large sample of UK workers that, although individual autonomy was more strongly correlated with well-being and satisfaction than participation in a semiautonomous work group was, the latter had no negative effect on well-being and had a positive effect on learning.

Just as for individual-level work design and performance, the story for performance and behavioral outcomes of group autonomy is more complex (Cohen & Bailey 1997). Reviews and meta-analyses identify positive performance and behavioral effects of group autonomy (see, e.g., Cohen & Bailey 1997), for example, via psychological empowerment (Maynard et al. 2012). However, at least a few rigorous studies have shown nonsignificant or mixed effects (see Parker & Wall 1998). Null effects might be partly explained by a mismatch between group autonomy and team member task interdependence: Group work does not make sense if team members have low task interdependence. Consistent with this premise, Langfred (2005) reported that teams with high task interdependence perform better with high levels of team autonomy, whereas low-interdependence teams perform better with high levels of individual autonomy. Likewise, a meta-analysis by Burke et al. (2006) showed that empowering leadership predicts team productivity most strongly when interdependence in the team is high rather than low.

Beyond interdependence, other moderators of group autonomy effects have been identified; for example, self-managing teams have more positive effects when team members are not isolated from external influences (Haas 2010), when task uncertainty is high (Cordery et al. 2010), and when teams engage in conceptual tasks for which the means-ends is not clear rather than simpler behavioral tasks (Stewart & Barrick 2000). Virtuality also appears important: Kirkman et al. (2004) showed that team empowerment is a stronger predictor of team effectiveness when teams meet face to face less often; their explanation for this finding is that empowerment is especially important for facilitating learning within a challenging virtual context.

Another question concerns the higher-level effects of group autonomy. A case study showed that autonomous group work design can enhance intrateam performance while hampering interteam coordination because of the high team ownership experienced by team members (Ingvaldsen & Rolfsen 2012). Similarly, in a simulation study, decentralized planning was associated with increased team member proactivity and aspiration, but also with coordination problems across teams, resulting in net negative effects on multisystem performance (Lanaj et al. 2013).

A broader literature on concepts such as high-performance work systems (HPWSs) typically considers self-management of teams to be one of the important practices, alongside other elements such as incentive compensation and extensive training. HPWSs are associated with organizational performance, and the link is stronger when a system of practices is considered rather than one single practice (Combs et al. 2006). One would anticipate that these positive organization-level effects are partly accounted for by the positive effects of individual or group work design at lower levels of analysis, although most studies have not examined these pathways.

Expanded Motivational Theories: Proactive, Prosocial, and Other Perspectives

This section extends beyond intrinsic motivation to consider the effect of work design on proactive and prosocial forms of motivation (see also Grant & Parker 2009), as well as on other forms of motivation.

Proactive perspectives on work design. The JCM is relatively passive in terms of the type of outcomes it considers as well as the presumed causes of work design.

Regarding outcomes, job satisfaction is one of the most popular outcomes of work design, yet satisfaction can be experienced as a form of passive contentment. Likewise, task performance concerns carrying out expected tasks well, but more active types of performance, such as taking initiative and proactively introducing improvements, are considered increasingly important in today's dynamic workplaces. Consequently, scholars have increasingly become concerned with how work design can facilitate more proactive attitudes and behaviors. Parker et al. (2010) argued that work design can promote "can do," "reason to," and "energized to" motivational states that in turn stimulate proactivity. Thus, varied and challenging tasks provide employees the opportunity for enactive mastery, which, in turn, cultivates self-efficacy beliefs that they can take charge of their environment (Parker 1998). Enriched jobs also enhance individuals' reason to be proactive, for example, by giving individuals a better appreciation of the impact of their work (Grant 2007) and by promoting flexible role orientations in which individuals feel ownership for broader work goals

Job resources:
aspects of a job that
help employees to
achieve their work
goals, to develop
personally, and to deal
with job demands

(Parker et al. 2001). Interestingly, time pressure and situational constraints—which are typically considered to be stressors in work settings—can also generate a reason to be proactive. From a control theory perspective, these stressors signal a mismatch between a desired and an actual situation, which stimulates employees to want to proactively rectify the situation (Fay & Sonnentag 2002). Finally, enriched jobs can promote "energized to" states, such as feelings of enthusiasm and vigor (Parker et al. 2009). A meta-analysis by Tornau & Frese (2013) highlighted the importance of job control and social support in predicting proactive work behavior.

A second proactive perspective relates to the causes of work design. The traditional work design approach assumes that others (e.g., managers) design jobs, or that work design derives from broader organizational and technological choices. However, individuals mold their work characteristics to fit their individual abilities or personalities. Much recent attention has been given to how individuals redesign their own work, for example, through job crafting, proactive work behavior, or obtaining personalized employment arrangements in the form of idiosyncratic deals (Grant & Parker 2009). Groups can also initiate work design change (see, e.g., Leana et al. 2009). Training individuals to proactively craft their work might increase the effectiveness of top-down work redesign efforts by equipping job incumbents with the skills and attitudes to realize the opportunities offered. Knowledge and professional workers might particularly benefit from redesigning their own work, because these individuals typically have more autonomy, higher education, and higher aspiration for career progression and are increasingly subjected to excessive work demands that might require crafting to be manageable (see below). Theoretically, although scholars recognize that individuals' proactivity can shape their work design, the mechanisms by which this process occurs have barely been considered (Grant & Parker 2009).

The above proactive perspectives come together in the idea of a positive spiral, in which work design promotes proactive attitudes and behaviors that, in turn, lead individuals to shape their work design, causing further development of proactive attitudes and behaviors, ad infinitum. In support of such a spiral, Frese et al. (2007) showed that autonomy and job complexity predict control orientation (a motivational state that includes self-efficacy), which predicts personal initiative, which in turn leads to perceptions of autonomy and complexity. Research on the job demands–resources model (see below) is similarly concerned with positive spirals between job resources and personal resources (Demerouti & Bakker 2011). One issue to explore further is how work design might, via such positive spirals, contribute to positive organization-level outcomes, such as organizational innovation or corporate entrepreneurship.

Prosocial motivation and relational work design. Attention to social and relational aspects of work design has recently gathered pace, in part because of shifts in practice, such as a greater level of collaboration across intra- and interorganizational boundaries (Grant & Parker 2009). A key advance is the relational job design perspective, which focuses on how work structures can provide more or fewer opportunities for employees to interact with others, which in turn affect their motivation, attitudes, and job performance (Grant 2007). In an extension of research on task significance, Grant (2007) argued that when jobs are structured such that incumbents have contact with those who benefit from their work (i.e., beneficiaries, such as clients, customers, and patients), job incumbents empathize with the beneficiaries, which encourages incumbents' effort, persistence, and helping behavior.

A series of studies by Grant and colleagues has supported and extended these ideas. In a field experiment in a call center, callers were given brief contact with a beneficiary—in this case, a scholarship recipient who benefited from funding raised by callers. Compared with controls, these callers spent significantly more time on calls over the next month and vastly increased their average weekly revenue (Grant et al. 2007). In another study, nurses who volunteered to help assemble surgical kits for use in disadvantaged countries met and heard vivid stories from beneficiaries (in this case, health care practitioners who had previously used surgical kits in former war zones). Compared with controls, these nurses had increased prosocial motivation and assembled more kits (Bellé 2013), an effect that was even stronger for individuals high in prosocial motivation at the outset. The positive effects of relational work design are boosted by transformational leadership (Grant 2012b).

A key theoretical contribution of the relational perspective is that work design can activate employees' prosocial motivation, that is, their desire to bring benefit to others. This contrasts with the traditional emphasis on designing work to enhance intrinsic interest in the job. Practically, relational work design can be a path for increasing work meaning when enriched types of work redesign are impossible or politically untenable. It is also likely that different forms of relational work design will suit different contexts. For a sample of doctors who already had frequent contact with patients, structural support was a powerful form of relational work design, albeit one focused on enhancing relationships among employees rather than between employees and their beneficiaries (Parker et al. 2012).

Self-determination theory, regulatory focus, and goal regulation. Parker & Ohly (2008) incorporated recent developments in motivation theory into their theorizing about work design. One contribution of their model derives from the application of self-determination theory (SDT; see Gagné & Deci 2005) to work design. From a SDT perspective, an individual can experience an unenjoyable task (or task that is not intrinsically motivating) as meaningful because the task is seen as important (identified motivation) and/or because the task is congruent with the individual's values (integrated regulation). Integrated and identified motivation occur when individuals take in external values or regulations through a process of internalization, which is in turn aided by their needs for relatedness and social processes (Gagné & Deci 2005). Work designs such as self-managing teams and relational work design likely exert some of their performance effects via identified and integrated motivation, yet such processes have not been explicitly considered (Parker & Ohly 2008). A further issue relates to the meaning of autonomy. In SDT, autonomy refers to an internalized sense of choice (Gagné & Deci 2005); in the JCM, in contrast, job autonomy refers to actual freedom of choice and discretion in one's job (Hackman & Oldham 1976). As discussed below (see Enabling Bureaucracy), some scholars argue that employees can be motivated even if they lack job autonomy so long as they have a sense of choice through participation in decision making, a concept consistent with the SDT perspective.

Parker & Ohly (2008) proposed several further neglected motivational pathways by which work design might exert its effects, such as activating individuals' regulatory focus (Higgins 1998). For example, enriched work design increases control, which enhances the salience of internal forces of behavior and activates a promotion focus, which in turn is associated with creativity (Meyer et al. 2004). Work design can also affect the goals people choose or set (goal generation), as well as how they regulate effort during goal pursuit (goal striving; see Kanfer 1990). In terms of the former, job enrichment should result in individuals setting more difficult goals (job enrichment enhances commitment, which leads to setting challenging goals); more creative goals (job enrichment increases positive affect, which broadens thinking), and more long-term goals (feedback from a customer promotes internalization of customer goals, resulting in wanting to satisfy customers). Likewise, goal striving involves processes that are likely enhanced by work design. For example, staying on track with a goal requires resolving discrepancies between current performance and the desired goal state (Kanfer 1990), a process that occurs only if individuals see factors that affect their performance as controllable, a belief affected by job enrichment. Successful self-regulation is also aided by having tasks with attentional pull or tasks that feel important or interesting (Beal et al. 2006), which again is likely fostered by job enrichment.

Relational work design: designing roles to enhance opportunities for employees to interact positively with others, such as the beneficiaries of their work

Goal generation and striving processes might also be affected by work design via unconscious mechanisms (Parker & Ohly 2008). When goal-directed behaviors are repeated consistently in a similar situation with positive reinforcement, they can become habitual (Bargh & Chartrand 1999). For example, a job with little autonomy might reduce self-efficacy and promote a prevention focus, which leads an individual to avoid difficult goals. Over time, avoiding difficult goals might become a habitual response that involves little conscious processing. Thus, work characteristics potentially create situational cues, which people respond to in habitual ways or with automatic routines. Such a possibility has yet to be explored.

Motivational Work Design in Practice

How relevant are motivation perspectives in today's workplaces? Listening to the rhetoric about highly skilled jobs in the knowledge economy, one could be forgiven for assuming that most jobs these days are complex and enriched. Certainly this is true for some sectors and some jobs. However, there continues to be a large (and in some cases growing) number of low-wage, low-quality jobs in advanced and developing economies (Osterman & Shulman 2011). Indeed, evidence in the United States suggests an increasing polarization of job quality—more "good jobs" and more "bad jobs," with a growing gap between them (Kalleberg 2011). The fifth European Working Conditions Survey, conducted in 2010, of 44,000 workers across 34 European countries, identified more than one-fifth of jobs as having poor intrinsic quality. Examples of poor contemporary work design abound, even in new jobs. For example, weatherization jobs (making houses more energy efficient) in the United States have primarily been designed as low-wage, poor-quality jobs with little opportunity for development (Osterman & Shulman 2011).

Why do poor-quality work designs continue to exist when there is clear evidence about the negative individual consequences of job simplification, as well as considerable evidence about the negative organizational consequences, such as poor performance, absence, and turnover? One could argue that enriched jobs, which have greater compensation and training requirements, are prohibitive in industries in which efficiency and cost effectiveness are key. However, whether deskilled jobs are the optimal economic option in these industries is highly debatable, especially taking into account turnover, absenteeism, and other such costs. Moreover, the long-run social and health costs of these jobs "are real and quantifiable, and they are paid by families and communities" (Osterman & Shulman 2011, p. 144).

The forces that perpetuate job simplification and poor-quality work reside at many levels, which suggests that changing the situation will require insights and action from multiple stakeholders. Globally, the rise of poor-quality jobs is driven by changes in technology and other macroeconomic and social forces (Davis 2010). For example, owing to increased competitive pressure coupled with the decline of unions, organizations can use outsourcing and contingent contracts to design work in ways they might not otherwise have been able to (Osterman & Shulman 2011). Likewise, technology has eradicated many middle-level jobs, leaving low-skilled jobs that cannot be computerized.

Work design is also affected by national policies, regulation, and institutions (Holman 2013). In regard to the weatherization jobs referred to above, although various advocacy groups pushed for quality jobs, this goal was held back by other stakeholders' competing goals as well as by complex political pressures. In this vein, Payne & Keep (2003) argued that the United Kingdom has adopted a "low road" set of competitive strategies, such as low-cost production, that are less conducive to enriched job designs with high-level skill use. In contrast, the Nordic countries are considered world leaders in supporting high-quality work designs; in the fifth European Working Conditions Survey, their jobs were of the highest quality. Norway has a long history of industrial democracy, underpinned by a long-term agreement between the key employers' organization and the key trade union. Likewise, whereas low-wage retail jobs exist in Germany, these jobs are broader and more interesting than those in the United States as a result of Germany's strong vocational training system (Osterman & Shulman 2011). Thus, although unions, business associations, academics, and community groups can shape job quality, redesigning work on a large scale likely requires supportive government policy. The Norwegian model of involving social scientists in changing practice might enable academics to play a more active role in shaping work design policy. Policy would also be aided by systematic tracking of work characteristics at a national level, as is carried out by the large-scale European work survey.

At the level of the organization, poor-quality work design sometimes represents a continuation of traditional practice, with insufficient knowledge or motivation on the part of CEOs, managers, engineers, or other job designers to create better jobs (similar issues apply to the take-up of high-performance work systems). Many managers continue to maintain the "enduring cultural frame of Taylorism" (Vidal 2013, p. 604). Even if organizations attempt work redesign, there is no guarantee of success. Davis (2010) drew on new institution theory to suggest that organizations copy what others are doing in order to reduce uncertainty, but whether an initiative works or is well implemented is of less concern, and the result is that business fads come and go. Davis urged scholars to investigate organizations' motives for work redesign (e.g., mimicry, legitimacy) prior to evaluating it because the motive will likely affect success. Work redesign is also more difficult to copy effectively than are other interventions such as technology and training because it involves the redistribution of power and challenges implicit assumptions about control and leadership (Parker & Wall 1998). From this perspective, the development of evidence-based tools, case studies, processes, and guidance will help practitioners and managers to analyze and successfully redesign work.

Considering the level of the individual work designer, scholars need to revisit why those responsible for work design tend to design and implement simplified jobs. Campion & Stevens's (1991) study of naive job designers (MBA students) showed that there is a dominant logic of work design focused around simplification and efficiency, although this logic can be changed with training. We need more research to understand whether this logic still exists among today's job designers and, if so, what biases, attitudes, or knowledge bases drive this logic and how these might be altered.

PART 2: EXPANDED WORK DESIGN PERSPECTIVES

Motivational theories of work design have dominated psychological approaches to work design. A continued focus by psychologists on motivation is justified given the prevalence of demotivating jobs, as noted above. However, advances in technology, a growth in knowledge work, and other such forces mean that many jobs are becoming more complex. There has been a growth in abstract tasks, or jobs that are difficult to computerize, as well as a rise in expectations for job quality and flexibility as a result of a more educated workforce, an increasing number of women in the work place, and a change in the mind-sets of young people (Kalleberg 2011). This heterogeneity in work design practice needs to be matched by theoretical heterogeneity. We need to expand the criterion space beyond motivation, not just by adding extra dependent variables to empirical studies but by exploring when, why, and how work design can help to achieve different purposes.

To address increased complexity, work should be designed to achieve three key outcomes. First, work design as a vehicle for learning and development is important at the aggregate level, because of projected global skills shortages, and at the individual level, because skill development is needed for effectiveness within a complex environment. Second, the level of demands and the pace of change, combined with the pressures of dual-career families, bring to the foreground the role of work design in facilitating health and well-being. Third, because organizations are under pressure to meet the needs of multiple stakeholders, scholars must consider how to design work that promotes more than one outcome at the same time—for example, control and flexibility.

Designing Work for Learning and Development

The idea that work design affects individual development is a long-standing one. In 1957, Argyris argued that bureaucratic jobs can result in adults becoming infantlike—that is, passive, dependent on others, and focused on the short term. Since then, scholars have argued that enriched work designs promote positive forms of development in which an individual "changes the world through work actions and thereby changes him or herself" (Frese & Zapf 1994, p. 86). Nevertheless, the role of work design as a vehicle for learning and development has mostly been advanced by industrial sociologists and European organizational researchers. The time is ripe for this perspective to become more mainstream.

At a global level, as a result of technological and economic change, there is an increasing premium on highly skilled employees (Manyika et al. 2012). The traditional solution to this challenge is to improve the supply of skills, for example, through better education. But attention must also be given to the demand side: Organizations need to be encouraged to design work that both requires greater skill utilization and facilitates skill development (Osterman & Shulman 2011, Payne & Keep 2003). Promoting learning and development is also important at the individual level. Individuals need to develop sufficient cognitive, self, social, and affective complexity in order to interact adaptively in dynamic and unpredictable environments (Lord et al. 2011). The development of this complexity also facilitates their career effectiveness in a context that demands adaptive capabilities for success (Hall & Heras 2010).

This section considers how work design might promote job incumbents' learning and development. Development is distinct from learning or change in that it involves structural transformation—that is, moving to a qualitatively distinct state that is progressive as well as internally directed (Moshman 1998). For example, acquiring knowledge about a topic is cognitive change, whereas increasing structural complexity in the organization of knowledge is cognitive development. Much development occurs in childhood as a result of biology and maturation, but development also occurs in adulthood as a result of experience, especially work. Next the article considers how work design can shape cognitive, identity, and moral processes in the short term and cognitive, identity, and moral development in the long term. The final section proposes that work design can also speed up individuals' learning and development.

Cognitive processes and development. Influenced by the German action theory principle that all actions involve goal setting, planning, decision making, monitoring, and feedback, Frese & Zapf (1994, p. 43) argued that lower levels of job control and lower job complexity inhibit learning because individuals engage in an incomplete action sequence. From this perspective, job control is important because control means it is possible to choose adequate strategies to deal with a situation, resulting in feedback and learning. Complexity in a job also promotes learning because, although work on a challenging task must initially be regulated at the highest intellectual level, with practice the actions become more automatized and can be regulated at lower, less conscious levels. Over time, skills become routinized, freeing up resources for learning yet more skills. For example, if a job frequently involves long-range goal setting, individuals will increasingly routinize this metacognitive skill.

In a similar vein, Wall & Jackson (1995) in the United Kingdom argued that when individuals have the autonomy to control variance at the source, they obtain immediate feedback about the effects of their actions, which promotes the development of elaborated mental models. In addition, when problem rectification is under their control, individuals can observe cause and effect, and thus develop anticipatory knowledge that enables them to prevent problems. In support of these ideas, a series of innovative studies have shown that job autonomy reduces machine downtime because operators learn to prevent faults (see, e.g., Leach et al. 2003). Further studies have identified moderators of these learning effects; for example, work design promotes more learning for individuals who are able to control their attention via psychological flexibility (Bond & Flaxman 2006).

Over the longer term, work design might promote changes in the structure and organization of knowledge (i.e., cognitive development). Building on earlier work, Schooler et al. (2004) reported that, controlling for levels of these variables assessed 20 years prior, having complex work with low supervision predicted employees' later intellectual flexibility, including the ability to deal with complex cognitive problems. Although these findings are not lagged effects, this study supports the premise that enriched work design affects adult cognitive development. Related evidence comes from studies showing that complex, intellectually demanding occupations are associated with better cognitive functioning in later life (Karp et al. 2009). Indeed, a study of more than 10,000 twins concluded that "greater complexity of work, and particularly complex work with people, may reduce the risk of Alzheimer's disease" (Andel et al. 2005, p. 257).

One critical cognitive aspect that can develop during adulthood is epistemic cognition, that is, how one thinks about knowledge. Development of epistemic cognition involves moving from a dualist, objectivist view of knowledge to a more relativist and contextualized view—for example, by being less black and white in one's thinking. One pathway by which enriched jobs might promote epistemic cognition is through increasing individuals' tendency to adopt others' perspectives (Parker & Axtell 2001). Another pathway is through affecting epistemic motivation, or the desire to hold well-informed conclusions about the world, which in turn affects epistemic cognition. Epistemic motivation is enhanced by accountability but reduced by time pressure and fatigue, suggesting that autonomous jobs that are not overly demanding might facilitate epistemic motivation and, ultimately, more complex ways of thinking.

Identity processes and development. It is unsurprising that work affects individuals' role identities as well their occupational identities. For example, the introduction of new technology reduces purchasers' job autonomy and their opportunity to interact with suppliers, which damages their sense of professional identity (Eriksson-Zetterquist et al. 2009, Johns 2010). Perhaps more interesting is that work design can potentially affect an individual's personal identity, that is, how one perceives the entirety of oneself—such as one's goals, traits, and characteristics—in relation to the environment (Oyserman 2001). Bosma & Kuunen (2001) identified three facilitators of identity development, all of which are potentially affected by work design: opportunities for growth, successful development experiences, and openness to experience. Challenging, enriched jobs obviously can provide the first of these two elements. In regard to openness to experience, prior evidence shows that enriched jobs promote self-efficacy for more proactive and interpersonal tasks (Parker 1998), which, aggregated over long periods, potentially translates into openness to experience. Consistent with this reasoning, the Schooler et al. (2004) study referenced above showed that individuals in complex jobs develop a more self-directed orientation (see also Frese et al. 2007), and Xanthopoulou et al. (2007) reported that job resources such as autonomy and support result in higher levels of personal resources (self-efficacy, optimism, and organization-based self-esteem) that potentially lead to greater openness to experience.

One mechanism that might explain the development of one's self-concept as a result of work design is need fulfillment. From a self-determination perspective, autonomy-supporting and need-satisfying environments satisfy one's basic needs of autonomy, relatedness, and achievement and thereby promote identity development (Grolnick et al. 1997). In contrast, controlling social environments, such as bureaucratic job structures, detract from internalization, that is, the process by which identity-relevant explorations are brought into alignment with the self. Thwarted needs also foster a fragile self-esteem, which is less conducive to growth, whereas meeting basic needs fosters a secure self-esteem in which individuals like and accept themselves, "warts and all," and thereby develop their identity (Kernis 2000).

An uninvestigated mechanism underpinning the link between work design and identity development is that enriched jobs might allow individuals to explore and experiment with different identities, or try out what Ibarra (1999) referred to as provisional selves (Hall & Heras 2010). For example, in self-managing teams, members have the opportunity to try out supervisory tasks that are distributed throughout the team and to potentially develop a leader identity. Once individuals have a leader identity, they will then behave in identity-congruent ways that lead them to engage in yet more leadership activities (Oyserman 2001). Work design likely also facilitates a form of identity development argued to be important for effective leadership, which is a shift in focus from an individual identity (me) to a relational identity (you and me) or a collective identity (all of us) (Lord et al. 2011). For example, members of self-managing teams have shared accountability for team outcomes. The outcome dependencies, as well as the need for cooperation in self-managing teams, motivate team members to engage in intrateam perspective taking, which likely fosters a stronger relational identity orientation.

Moral processes and development. Moral processes include recognizing a moral issue, engaging in moral reasoning to identify the ideal behavior, being motivated to focus on moral concerns, and then carrying out the chosen moral action (see Treviño et al. 2014). Individuals in narrow, deskilled jobs might not identify an issue as a moral concern because they lack an understanding of the bigger picture and/or are unable to see the perspectives of others (Parker & Axtell 2001). Because of their restricted jobs, they may have little understanding of the consequences of their actions and may not even realize ethical implications. Thus, poor-quality work designs might impede recognition of a moral issue, the first step in the moral process.

Individuals with poor job designs might also lack the motivation to focus on moral concerns. That is, even if one recognizes a moral concern and is able to identify what should be done, moral temptations require one to have the self-regulatory capacity to resist one action in favor of another action (Hannah et al. 2011). Deskilled jobs can result in narrow, "not my job" role orientations, reduced perspective taking, and lowered self-efficacy, which suggests that employees in deskilled jobs often lack ownership of, and self-efficacy for, addressing moral issues. As an example, in the well-known aircraft brake scandal, in which brakes designed by Goodrich engineers subsequently failed, an employee made the following note in regard to diagrams that he knew had been falsified: "After all, we're just drawing some curves and what happens to them after they leave here—well we're not responsible for that" (Vandivier 1972; cited in Jones & Ryan 1998, p. 438). Excessive bureaucracy and overly narrow jobs appeared in this case to result in diffused responsibility; that is, no individuals take ownership of the decisions. In addition, work designs that keep group members isolated from other members isolate individuals from the big picture and therefore render them unable to compare notes on moral problems (Jones & Ryan 1998). Cross-functional teams, in which individuals have access to information from multiple parties, can reduce feelings of isolation and increase self-efficacy and motivation to address a moral issue.

Even when individuals have recognized a moral issue and are motivated to act ethically, they still need to take action. Moral action is affected by self-regulation: Unethical behaviors are more likely when individuals' self-regulatory resources are depleted after mentally taxing activities (Gino et al. 2011), which suggests the need to carefully manage the level of work demands in any job with significant moral temptation. In addition, moral action is likely affected by autonomy. As with all behavior, the implementation of moral action is likely constrained in low-autonomy situations because of the lack of opportunity to act. However, this link also means that if individuals are motivated to behave unethically, autonomy allows them the latitude to do so, as occurs, for example, in the case of rogue traders. Thus, autonomy might be an important moderator of the effects of moral motivation on action.

A further influence on ethical behavior is an individual's level of moral reasoning. Treviño (1986) argued that individuals at higher stages of moral reasoning development are less susceptible to external temptations and are more likely to take moral action or to self-select out of unethical situations. This brings us to the potential role of work design in fostering moral development. Similarly to cognitive development, the development of moral reasoning is facilitated by exposure to new situations that cannot be understood using existing schemas, therefore necessitating the development of new schemas. Social experiences involving role taking, such as educational experiences, are especially powerful: "Faced with the 'unique' other, the individual is constantly challenged to rise to a more general perspective that preserves the unique perspectives of both self and other" (Wilson et al. 1992, p. 32). Treviño (1986) proposed that jobs in which individuals are required to engage in complex role taking, such as democratic leadership roles in which the leader needs to be sensitive to others' views, can help individuals to develop advanced moral reasoning. As an illustration, self-managing team members make complex decisions, manage colleagues' poor performance, and engage in other self-directed activities; all of these actions involve consulting with peers and navigating dynamic hierarchies of influence. Such complex role taking should, over time, expand moral reasoning complexity.

To date, little empirical research links job design to moral reasoning development, although Wilson et al. (1992) reported in a 10-year longitudinal study that, over and above occupational and educational attainment, individuals' career fulfillment predicts moral reasoning development. These authors recommended further consideration of work variables in promoting moral reasoning. The role of autonomy is especially intriguing. As noted above, on the one hand, autonomy allows individuals who want to act unethically the opportunity to do so (autonomy as a moderator), but on the other hand, autonomy with other enriched work characteristics might facilitate awareness and ownership of moral issues as well as, in the longer term, more complex moral reasoning (autonomy as an antecedent).

Accelerating learning and development. In the field of leadership development, experiences that accelerate learning include assessment, challenge, and support (Day et al. 2009). Assessment provides feedback that motivates individuals to close skill gaps, challenge motivates individuals to try new behaviors, and support helps individuals to cope with setbacks. Work design is a powerful source of assessment, challenge, and support because these elements can be embedded into the work design, yielding continuous rather than single development opportunities. In contrast, challenge in leadership programs is often achieved via participation in temporary stretch projects. Theories of learned industriousness and adaption-level theory suggest that having a sustained opportunity to adapt to high demands can promote the development of resources to aid in self-regulation. Converse & DeShon (2009) showed that exposure to two demanding tasks can lead to adaption effects, whereas exposure to one demanding task results in depletion. One would predict that work design allows more adaptation, and potentially greater self-regulatory capacity, relative to one-off development opportunities.

Evidence also suggests that learning is accelerated when challenge occurs within an individual's "zone of proximal development" rather than adopting a sink-or-swim approach (Day et al. 2009,

p. 29). Work redesign is recommended to be incremental, with job enrichment expanding as the capability of the individual or team grows (Parker & Wall 1998). Social support, a key job design resource, also increases an individual's zone of proximal development (Day et al. 2009). A further important facilitator of accelerated learning is developmental readiness—that is, receptiveness to challenge, feedback, and support—which is shaped by the interaction of learning orientation, self-efficacy, and metacognitive ability. As discussed above, work design can influence these elements, so enriched work design potentially facilitates developmentally ready employees.

Designing Work for Mental and Physical Health

The World Health Organization (WHO) defined health as a "state of complete physical, mental, and social well-being, and not merely the absence of disease of infirmity" (World Health Organ. 1948, p. 100). Consistent with this definition, Parker et al. (2003) reviewed evidence that work design affects distress, strain, and injury, as well as indicators of active mental and physical health such as aspiration, self-efficacy, engagement, and safe working. Because outcomes related to active mental health are covered above, this section focuses on designing work to prevent or mitigate strain and other negative health outcomes.

The incorporation of work design into policy in some countries indicates its relevance for health. For example, Sweden has explicitly built work design principles into occupational health statutes. Nevertheless, the increased complexity in many jobs, the pressures associated with dual-parent working, and heightened concerns about health issues in society all highlight the need for more attention to the design of healthy work. As observed in the fifth European Working Conditions Survey (see also Holman 2013), the average level of work intensity of jobs has increased; almost half of jobs are identified as potentially unhealthy due to their poor intrinsic quality and/or their poor working-time quality.

Strain arises as a result of an individual's interaction with the work environment. According to Spector (1998), if situations and events are appraised as a threat (a stressor), negative emotions arise that can lead to psychological strain such as anxiety, physical strain such as heart disease, and/or behavioral strain such as smoking. Reverse paths can also occur, for example, when an individual who is feeling anxious is more likely to appraise a situation as threatening. Individual differences in characteristics such as coping style affect paths in this model, for example, when different individuals place themselves into different environments, appraise different events as stressors, and respond differently when negative emotions arise.

Job demands–control model. Work characteristics are important features of the external environment that are appraised by individuals, especially the levels of job demands and job control (or job autonomy). The influential demand-control model (Karasek 1979) proposes that high job demands and low job control cause psychological strain and, in the long term, stress-related illnesses such as heart disease. A unique element of the model is the interaction hypothesis that high job demands cause strain when accompanied by low decision latitude (i.e., low job control and low skill discretion), but if demands occur in the presence of high decision latitude—a so-called active job—then strain will not accrue. Instead, an active job leads to feelings of mastery and confidence, which, in turn, help the person to cope with further job demands, promoting more learning, and so on, in a positive spiral (Karasek & Theorell 1990).

Like the JCM, the demand-control model has received many criticisms, including its focus on a narrow set of work characteristics. Nevertheless, also like the JCM, the demand-control model has spurred much research. Support for the model is strongest in regard to the negative strain effects of excess job demands. In a review on 19 longitudinal studies, De Lange et al.

(2003) reported that two-thirds of the studies showed negative strain effects of high job demands, especially on psychological well-being and sickness/absence. However, the effects of demand on absence are complex; there is some evidence that higher demands result in lower absence, perhaps because these individuals have more pressure to attend (Smulders & Nijhuis 1999) or perhaps because the demands are experienced as a challenge. High demands combined with low control have also been shown to affect cardiovascular disease in a series of rigorous studies, particularly for men (Belkic et al. 2004); an explanation for this effect is that these jobs promote psychological strain, hypertension, and/or physical risk factors like smoking, which then increase the likelihood of heart disease. A handful of intervention studies support these conclusions. Excess job demands can also reduce safety (Nahrgang et al. 2011); for example, when employees face heightened production goals, they are more likely to ignore safety procedures to get the job done.

Job control can affect the strain process through several pathways. Scholars have argued that individuals have a need for control, so if this need is unfulfilled, negative strain effects arise (Gagné & Deci 2005). Control also promotes active coping, which leads to learning and mastery and thus to reduced strain (Karasek 1979). Consistent with these predictions, Daniels et al. (2013) showed that changing work activities in order to solve problems, a process the authors conceptualized as enacting job control, subsequently reduced employees' negative affect, cognitive failure, and fatigue. In terms of strain outcomes, many cross-sectional studies show that a lack of perceived job control relates to anxiety, depression, burnout, excess alcohol consumption, and other such outcomes, although the results are more mixed in longitudinal studies. In their review, De Lange et al. (2003) reported that only approximately one-half of the longitudinal studies showed a main effect of job control on subsequent health outcomes. The strain-reducing effects of job autonomy likely depend on individual differences or contextual variables (Warr 2007).

Although the main effect of job control on health has been investigated, there has been even more interest in whether the negative strain effects of demand can be buffered by high job control, as implied in the demand-control model (Karasek 1979) and the job demands–resources model (see below) and as demonstrated in laboratory studies (Sonnentag & Frese 2003). This interaction hypothesis is of practical value because it suggests that high demands are not negative for health so long as they are accompanied by high control. Multiple reviews have concluded that support for this interaction effect is not convincing (see, e.g., De Lange et al. 2003, Van der Doef & Maes 1999), although reviews of this research tend to conclude that conceptual and methodological imprecision has made interactive effects difficult to detect (Sonnentag & Frese 2003). For example, interactions have been observed in studies that use an unconfounded measure of job control or multilevel approaches or that take into account moderators such as self-efficacy (Schaubroeck et al. 2000). Multilevel studies allow the opportunity to separate the variance of job demands and job control into individual-level and group-level components. Future studies must also pay more attention to mechanisms and their timing. For example, if the positive effects of control depend on an individual learning how to use this control to cope with the demands, buffering effects of control will be realized only after sufficient time.

Extensions to the demand-control model. There are further models of strain that relate to work design (see Sonnentag & Frese 2003). The job demands–resources model (Bakker & Demerouti 2007) identifies a broader set of job resources beyond autonomy and skill discretion that includes career opportunities and participation in decision making. One of the most important resources is social support, which can fulfill basic needs for belongingness and facilitate achievement of work goals, thereby promoting both motivational outcomes (e.g., engagement) and alleviating strain (Demerouti & Bakker 2011). Much evidence suggests that receiving social support from supervisors and peers matters for employees' health (De Lange et al. 2003, Van der Doef & Maes 1999). Intriguingly, the act of giving support also appears to have health benefits (Brown et al. 2003), likely because of the positive affect that helping generates, which suggests that structuring jobs so that individuals have the opportunity to help others could facilitate better health. Extensions of the job demands–resources model include the concepts that job resources are especially important for motivation when demands are high and—similar to the learning and development perspective above—that job resources shape, and are shaped by, personal resources such as self-efficacy and optimism (Demerouti & Bakker 2011).

The conservation of resources theory (Hobfoll 1989) proposed that resource loss is especially salient, and loss prompts two distinct strategies by which individuals seek to maintain or secure resources. When an individual's psychological resources are threatened with loss, the recovery of lost resources becomes a central motivating force, so individuals use external resources to protect themselves (a protection mechanism). In contrast, when individuals are not threatened by resource loss, they are motivated to use external resources in order to further enrich their resource pool (an accumulation mechanism). In a quasi-experimental study of junior doctors, Parker et al. (2013) showed that a social support intervention led to reduced workload for those doctors experiencing high resource loss (i.e., suffering from anxiety and depression), consistent with a protection mechanism, whereas the support intervention boosted proactivity and skill development for doctors not experiencing resource loss, consistent with an accumulation mechanism. This study suggests that support matters for health, although how it is mobilized and used depends on individual differences.

In a further extension of the demand-control model, scholars have differentiated challenge demands from hindrance demands (LePine et al. 2005). Challenge demands create the opportunity for development and achievement, such as job scope, whereas hindrance demands are seen as obstacles to achievement and growth, such as role ambiguity. Meta-analyses support this distinction and have shown that both types of demands are associated with strain; however, hindrance stressors are also associated with turnover and withdrawal, whereas challenge stressors are positively related to motivation and performance (Crawford et al. 2010). Hindrance demands arguably trigger negative emotions and passive coping, whereas challenge demands trigger positive emotions and cognitions and active coping. This stream of research is consistent with studies that show that demands can sometimes promote active health outcomes (for example, time pressure predicts proactive behavior at work).

The challenge-hindrance approach provides a more nuanced approach to demands. However, rather than categorizing some demands as challenges and others as hindrances, it may ultimately be more useful to integrate appraisal theory to consider how demands are appraised by an individual (see Ohly & Fritz 2009). An appraisal-based approach can assess why someone might perceive a particular demand as a challenge, whereas someone else perceives the same demand as a hindrance. One could consider primary appraisals of the demand (e.g., is it irrelevant, benign, or harmful?), attributions about the demand (e.g., is it controllable?), and secondary appraisals of the demand (e.g., can I cope?). Appraisals will also vary within individuals according to the situation, and this variation has consequences for momentary experiences of strain. For example, in a within-person study, Fisher et al. (2013) showed how, for individuals with high performance goal orientation, appraisals of task importance were associated with negative emotions.

Even with challenge stressors, there might be a tipping point at which excess or sustained levels are damaging. On the basis of earlier observations of U-shaped relationships between job demands and health, Johns (2010) observed that some jobs can be too rich. Bunderson & Thompson (2009,

p. 50) likewise reported how zookeepers who conceptualized their work as a calling experienced that work as a source of meaning and identity but also as "unbending duty, sacrifice, and vigilance."

Strategies for designing healthy work. On the basis of the above analysis, the most obvious strategy is to directly change work characteristics, using approaches such as reducing strain-inducing demands and/or increasing job resources. For example, increased scheduling control over work hours and location leads to improved work-family fit (Kelly et al. 2011). Such a strategy is a primary stress intervention because it changes the environment. Scholars now need to extend this research to consider how to redesign work to support employee health across a range of contemporary work situations, such as working from home, in virtual teams, or on temporary employment contracts.

A further primary intervention strategy is to design jobs in a way that prevents the emergence of strain-inducing demands in the first place. For example, allowing customer agents the authority to deal with complaints on the spot speeds up service and reduces customer anger. Dealing with angry customers likely requires considerable emotional regulation on the part of the employee, and such self-control is highly depleting of one's regulatory resources (Muraven & Baumeister 2000). A related strategy is to design work in a way that enables and motivates individuals to proactively reduce job demands and/or increase job resources themselves. For example, Elsbach & Hargadon (2006, p. 471) proposed that, to avoid professional work becoming "relentlessly mindful and stress inducing," each workday should be designed with bouts of undemanding tasks inserted between challenging tasks. Job autonomy allows individuals to implement this type of strategy, or indeed any other coping strategy they find valuable. A variant of this strategy is to design jobs that promote positive feelings and meaning, such as jobs with the opportunity to support others, which might counteract stress reactions.

Secondary stress-intervention strategies involve changing individuals, including how they perceive and react to the environment. Stress-management training is an example. Yet, as argued in this article, work design can shape an individual's motivation (e.g., self-efficacy), behavior (e.g., proactivity), and emotional and cognitive capabilities, all of which can affect how individuals perceive and react to stressors in the work environment. For example, self-efficacious individuals are likely to perceive demands as less threatening and are more likely to take up any proactive job-crafting opportunities to reduce demands (Parker et al. 2001). Tertiary interventions are concerned with treatment and rehabilitation processes, such as counseling, for individuals who are experiencing strain. Yet again, work design might play a role. Scholars have examined how work design can promote recovery inside and outside of work. For example, individuals who have higher levels of control in their job, and lower demands, feel less need for recovery in the evening (Sonnentag & Zijlstra 2006). Work design can also potentially protect and enhance regulatory resources and facilitate their replenishment, for example, by allowing timing autonomy so employees can rest when required.

Secondary and tertiary interventions are often more popular than primary interventions because changing the individual is seen as more palatable and straightforward than changing the environment. However, secondary and tertiary interventions can have effects that are short term because they do not address the root cause of strain. Work design might be a powerful and more enduring intervention precisely because it changes both the environment and the individual. As Hackman (2009, p. 316) observed, "humans are 'wired up' for both adaption and growth": Redesigning work can promote growth, whereas individually oriented interventions such as stress-management training promote adaption. Hackman urged scholars to go beyond a focus on individual interventions to "explore ways to develop and exploit the structural features of the social systems within which people live and work," a perspective supported in this review.

Designing Work for Control and Flexibility: Ambidexterity, Enabling Bureaucracy, and High-Reliability Organizing

Thus far, this article has focused on work design for separate outcomes such as motivation, learning, and health. However, increased environmental complexity, pressures to satisfy many stakeholders, and globalized competition mean that multiple outcomes are often desired at the same time. Work design that promotes multiple outcomes likely differs from that which promotes a single outcome (Johns 2010), especially if the outcomes are recognized as competing—for example, achieving both exploitation and exploration, both efficiency and innovation, or both safety and productivity.

Many of these competing outcomes can be summarized as a tension between control and flexibility (Quinn & Rohrbaugh 1983). Whereas control is about achieving consistency and efficiency (internal control, e.g., via standardization procedures) and achieving alignment with the mission (external control, e.g., via feedback systems), flexibility focuses on achieving responsiveness via job enrichment and related practices (internal flexibility) and achieving adaptability within a changing environment (external flexibility). It is typically assumed that practices to achieve control and flexibility are incompatible. For example, bureaucratic controls like standardization and hierarchy enable efficiency but impede the opportunity for mutual adjustment that enables flexibility. In the work design literature, scholars have observed that autonomy has benefits for flexibility and creativity but drawbacks for efficiency and coordination (Lanaj et al. 2013). Likewise, Biron & Bamberger (2010, p. 168) stated that a key challenge of structural empowerment is reconciling "the potential loss of control inherent in sharing authority with the potential motivation and productivity benefits that often accompany empowerment."

The question of how to achieve control and flexibility simultaneously is especially pertinent in professional sectors that have traditionally emphasized flexibility. Controls are increasingly being introduced into these sectors in the quest for consistency and cost efficiency. Examples include detailed guidelines that specify sentences judges should impose, standardized protocols for doctors to follow in diagnosis and treatment, and the specification of content and pedagogies for teachers (Davis 2010). Is it possible to introduce such controls and retain high levels of job enrichment, and the associated benefits for flexibility and creativity? Or is the introduction of these controls "perverse because professionals are the people we rely on to make wise decisions in uncertain circumstances" (Oldham & Hackman 2010, p. 467)? Understanding how to reconcile this tension between control and flexibility is an issue that will likely become more pressing in the future, given the projected growth in knowledge work. For example, it will be a particular challenge in large-scale collaborative creativity activities, such as the design of a new aircraft, involving several thousand engineers, in which the tasks are highly interdependent (requiring control) but also uncertain and complex (requiring flexibility and creativity) (Adler & Chen 2011).

The traditional contingency theory solution to the tension between control and flexibility is that bureaucratic structures (emphasizing control) should be in place when tasks are stable, whereas organic structures (emphasizing flexibility) should be preferred in dynamic, uncertain situations (Burns & Stalker 1961). However, this trade-off approach has been criticized. Both control and flexibility are increasingly required in many situations, and paradox perspectives suggest that it is possible to achieve seemingly contradictory outcomes simultaneously (Smith & Lewis 2011). This section reviews three perspectives relevant to achieving the dual outcomes of control and flexibility, with a focus on the implications of each for work design.

Ambidexterity. Scholars (e.g., O'Reilly & Tushman 2007) have argued that successful organizations are ambidextrous, both exploiting current capabilities (a control-oriented perspective) and exploring new possibilities (a flexibility-oriented perspective). Although external strategies for achieving these dual outcomes, such as outsourcing, have been suggested, ambidextrous organizations achieve a focus on exploration and exploitation simultaneously through internal strategies (Raisch & Birkinshaw 2008).

One internal structural solution is that different business units carry out different activities; for example, one unit may focus on innovation while the other focuses on manufacture (O'Reilly & Tushman 2007). The work design implications of structural solutions have rarely been discussed, but one would expect that business units pursuing exploration require job enrichment to stimulate creativity and innovation, whereas units pursuing exploitation would tend to be more bureaucratic with lower job enrichment. Nevertheless, questions arise. For example, is some degree of enrichment important for units designed to exploit capabilities? Research reviewed in this article suggests that at least moderate enrichment is preferable for most outcomes. Perhaps some types of autonomy (i.e., over when and how to do things) are appropriate for exploitation units, whereas members of exploration units should have broader autonomy (i.e., over what to do)? Some work characteristics (such as job feedback) might be important for both exploration and exploitation, whereas others (such as connecting with end users) might be more important for exploration than for exploitation. In addition, the top management team plays a central role in coordinating activities across the different types of units (O'Reilly & Tushman 2007), but perhaps there are also work design options, such as job rotation or joint membership of project teams, that complement the leader-oriented approach.

A second strategy for ambidexterity is one in which leaders create a supportive context that builds the whole business unit's capacity to be ambidextrous, thereby alleviating the coordination issues between subunits that can exist with structural solutions. Individual or group work design is central to this strategy of contextual ambidexterity: Scholars argue that it is achieved when individuals are empowered to judge for themselves how to best divide their time between the conflicting demands of exploration and exploitation (Gibson & Birkinshaw 2004). Besides a high level of autonomy, work characteristics one might expect to see in contextually ambidextrous organizations include task variety (employees engage in both exploration and exploitation tasks), task identity (employees don't just execute tasks but also improve them), and task significance (employees can have more impact through implementing improvements). Such an enriched work design likely promotes not only creativity, as a result of intrinsic motivation, but also proactivity, citizenship, and employee learning and development; all these outcomes should support the dual goals of exploration and exploitation. In addition, Gibson & Birkinshaw (2004) argued that individuals working in ambidextrous contexts need high levels of behavioral and cognitive complexity, which this article proposes can be facilitated by enriched jobs that involve challenge, feedback, and support. Altogether, enriched work design potentially plays a central role in achieving contextual ambidexterity, although this proposition is untested.

Nevertheless, enriched work design likely needs to be complemented with forms of control in order to ensure alignment, albeit not necessarily traditional forms of internal control such as standardization and monitoring. Informal forms of control, such as leadership and culture, potentially help employees work out the right way to behave without stifling flexible behavior. Gibson & Birkinshaw (2004) argued that, in addition to job enrichment, behaviorally complex leaders and a shared vision combine to inspire employees to deliver results, ensure the discipline to meet standards, and provide the stretch to induce ambitious goals. In a similar vein, Bledow et al. (2009) proposed that transformational leaders' intellectual stimulation and individual consideration promote creativity and exploration, whereas leaders' vision and inspirational motivation

Ambidexterity: an individual, team, or organization that simultaneously exploits current capabilities and explores new possibilities assist in alignment and integration. Careful selection, training, and compensation practices can also be used to limit opportunistic behavior on the part of enriched employees.

Enabling
bureaucracy:
organizational design
that combines
formalization and
other controls with an
enabling and
supportive context

Additional work design features beyond enrichment might be important in enabling organization-level and team-level ambidexterity. For example, connecting individuals with end users or beneficiaries potentially provides an important source of external information that can stimulate innovation. At the team level, Haas (2010) showed teams high in both group autonomy and external knowledge were most effective for achieving both operational and strategic performance, but only when knowledge content was scarce and the source of knowledge was nonorganizational. Switching from exploration to exploitation tasks is also likely to be cognitively demanding; scholars have observed that these processes require very distinct learning processes. One would therefore expect to find high levels of cognitive demands in jobs in ambidextrous organizations, which creates a need to consider how to design work to support effective self-regulation and protect against health risks. Exactly how work design supports and enables organizational ambidexterity is a topic worthy of empirical investigation, especially given the existing dearth of studies in this domain.

Enabling bureaucracy. A different approach for reconciling the tension between control and flexibility is that put forward by Adler and colleagues. Rather than establishing cultural controls to balance job autonomy, these scholars advocated limiting job autonomy and instead creating an enabling context that combines employee participation with motivating formal control systems. A classic example of an enabling bureaucracy is New United Motor Manufacturing, Inc. (NUMMI), a Toyota car manufacturing facility that previously operated in California (Adler & Borys 1996). In a Tayloristic manufacturing plant, repair and improvement are separated from routine production, whereas at NUMMI, employees could repair and solve breakdowns. Rather than following set procedures designed by engineers, NUMMI workers could help to design and standardize their own work methods. Adler & Borys (1996) characterized such practices as participative centralization: participation in that employees can contribute to important decisions, and centralization in the form of standardization and hierarchical authority.

Importantly, in this system, motivation arguably does not come from job autonomy; rather, employees are motivated by participative leadership, extensive training, employment security, engagement in continuous improvement, and other such positive features of the work context. The enabling context, combined with a clear understanding of the organization's mission, allows employees to experience identified motivation, that is, the internalization of values (Adler & Borys 1996, p. 80). A strong level of identification means that employees see formal controls such as standardized procedures as an effective way of achieving valued goals rather than as a coercive control mechanism. Clear organizational goals and values, enabling rules and procedures, and high trust are also argued to help foster interdependent self-concepts among employees, rather than solely independent self-concepts, which further aids coordination (Adler & Chen 2011).

In an analysis of lean production, Treville & Antonakis (2006) similarly argued that a lack of autonomy over work timing and methods can be compensated for by other positive aspects of work design, including high levels of accountability (because employees can influence decisions), high skill variety and task identity (because employees are involved in repair and improvement), high levels of feedback (because employees have access to information), and high work facilitation (because lean production emphasizes the removal of obstacles to help performance). These authors draw on ideas of gestalt cognition, that individuals store, process, and recall information in a configural or schematic form (Fiske & Taylor 1991), to suggest that employees working in lean systems experience motivation not by "summing their isolated evaluations of individual practices;" they instead "make a complex and holistic evaluation by giving each job characteristic meaning from the other practices with which it occurs" (Treville & Antonakis 2006, p. 115). In essence, the overall positive work design configuration under lean production is argued to be motivating despite low job autonomy.

Altogether, these perspectives raise an intriguing set of questions about the motivational properties of job designs in an enabling bureaucracy. Adler (2012, p. 248) has argued that these systems can be motivating, although in a study of enabling bureaucracy among software developers, some embraced the approach ("In this business, you've got to be exact, and the process ensures that we are. You have to get out of hacker mode!") whereas other developers felt alienated by the bureaucracy ("Programmers like to program. They never like to document."). Research is needed to understand whether, how, and which employees are motivated under enabling bureaucracy forms, or whether and how creativity, proactivity, and other outcomes are jeopardized by the high level of formal control in these systems. Studies of lean production have shown varied results (see Cullinane et al. 2013), from mixed effects on work characteristics with no net impact on strain (Jackson & Mullarkey 2000) to outright negative effects on both work characteristics and strain (Parker 2003). No clear conclusions can be drawn, but the question of whether a supportive context can substitute for autonomy is a critical one.

High-reliability organizing: an approach to obtaining nearly error-free operations within a complex and hazardous environment

High-reliability organizing. Yet another way to resolve the tension between control and flexibility is high-reliability organizing. Classic examples of high reliability organizations (HROs) are nuclear power plants, air traffic control systems, and space shuttles. In these environments, the tension between control and flexibility often manifests as a tension between safety and service.

Scholars (e.g., Roberts 1990) have identified various elements that are essential for effective HROs, including a strategic focus on safety, careful attention to procedures, limited trial-and-error learning, continuous training, and strong safety cultures. From a work design perspective, Weick et al. (2008) proposed the importance of the underspecification of structures for aiding flexibility. Underspecification of structures refers to the subordination of hierarchical authority structures during critical events, such that decisions can be made by whoever has the expertise rather than whoever has the highest rank. For example, on the flight deck of an aircraft carrier out at sea, when an aircraft is landing or departing, any person on the deck "can call it foul" and make decisions (Roberts et al. 1994, p. 622).

A further example of HROs is the effective incident command systems in which public safety professionals such as firefighters manage the temporary control systems for dealing with emergencies (Bigley & Roberts 2001). These systems are highly bureaucratic, with extensive rules and procedures, functional division of labor, specialized job roles, and a clear hierarchy of positions. The incident commander is the highest-ranking position, and the person in this role is responsible for all activities that take place at an incident. Nevertheless, this high-control system can also be extremely flexible and enable reliable performance under challenging circumstances. Flexibility is enabled by the structure that develops at the scene. The incident commander is the first person to arrive, and this individual builds the structure from that point. In the words of one chief, "I go in. I've got my hat on. I'm the incident commander. I'm also the operations chief and also the division supervisor. And until that thing gets big enough to where I'm dividing it, I wear all those hats" (Bigley & Roberts 2001, p. 1287). The structure can then change over time as higher-ranking officers arrive. In addition, because roles are clear and well defined, it is easy for individuals to engage in role switching according to needs during an incident. A further element that supports flexibility is that supervisors transfer authority to those with the expertise and allow individuals with sufficient experience to improvise or depart from standard procedures when required. Shared mental models among members are also important: Dysfunction can occur when individuals are empowered to improvise yet lack the knowledge of or concern for bigger-picture perspectives (Bigley & Roberts 2001).

A related example of a clear hierarchy of roles that nonetheless allows flexibility in the moment is described in Klein et al.'s (2006) analysis of emergency medical teams. These teams face unpredictable patient demands and constantly changing team composition, yet they also need to achieve highly reliable performance and to train and develop novices. Control and flexibility are achieved when clearly designated leaders dynamically delegate the leadership role to junior leaders but also withdraw the leadership role according to the urgency and novelty of the situation. Dynamic delegation is supported by shared routines and values among team members.

Achieving control and flexibility via HROs involves a work design that changes quite dramatically according to the situation. Theories of work design, as well as the dominant methodological approaches, do not currently cater to such dynamism.

METHODOLOGICAL DIRECTIONS

A strength of research in this field is that quasi-experiments and field experiments have often been used to evaluate work redesign. Rigorous evaluation studies continue to be important for informing practice and policy: It is one thing to demonstrate a causal relationship between variables, and another to show that work redesign can be successfully implemented with positive outcomes. Also important are true longitudinal studies (in which all variables are assessed at each time wave) to investigate reverse causality, reciprocal effects, and the timing of processes (Parker et al. 2014). To understand whether work design has consequences for individual development, very long term studies are also required.

Thus far, with the exception of a burgeoning number of within-person diary studies, multi-level processes have not been well articulated or investigated in the work design literature. As noted by Morgeson & Campion (2003), work design theory tends to focus on a job, yet studies are typically operationalized at the level of an individual. Multilevel approaches can be used to identify job-level versus individual-level sources of variation in job perceptions. For example, aggregating perceived work characteristics across job incumbents in the same job can help to reduce idiosyncratic individual influences on job perceptions. A further important multilevel approach is to examine the top-down processes by which individuals' perceptions of work characteristics are formed, which will allow the opportunity to better understand the role of context. Researchers also need to assess the effects of work design at higher levels to identify possible unintended consequences (Johns 2010), such as team autonomy improving team performance but impairing overall system performance. Related to this point is the need to understand the potential role of work design in facilitating higher-level organizing, for example, how team-level autonomy might enhance organization-level ambidexterity.

A related methodological direction is to consider units of analysis other than a whole job, such as work design at the daily level, work design at the event level, work design at the project level, and even work design across a career. For example, in high-reliability contexts, it might be that team effectiveness is most strongly determined by individuals' autonomy during critical events rather than by their general or average level of job autonomy.

Applying a configuration approach is likely a fruitful way forward in studies of work design (Johns 2010, Treville & Antonakis 2006). From this perspective, work designs can be understood as bundles of interconnected work characteristics, rather than discrete job aspects, that cause particular outcomes. The assumption is that the bundle accounts for more variance (and possibly different outcomes) than discrete job aspects do, perhaps because the elements co-occur or operate together in meaningful ways, or perhaps because individuals perceive work design in a holistic way rather than as separate elements. For example, high significance–low autonomy configurations might occur because autonomy is reduced when a job is so important that the cost of error is very high, as occurs when firewalls are introduced to prevent employees from having direct contact with customers (Johns 2010). Regression approaches do not allow for the possibility that job characteristics might have different meanings depending on what attributes they co-occur with. Configurational approaches also allow for the possibility of equifinality; for example, work design research has tended to assume there is one optimal sociotechnical systems design—the autonomous work group—but it might be that different configurations of social and technical systems are compatible with different types of organizational strategies. A configuration approach is also likely a useful way to examine work organization archetypes or combinations of work design and broader organizational systems (Cordery & Parker 2007).

Finally, Barley & Kunda (2001) argued that there are insufficient data on what people actually do in their work. Ethnographic studies, participant observation, and rich qualitative studies that provide detailed contextualized accounts of work in situ, such as that by Klein et al. (2006), will likely be especially helpful in understanding what actually happens in contemporary jobs.

SUMMARY AND CONCLUSION

Work design as a field of theoretical inquiry was largely developed as a response to the technically oriented design of demotivating and alienating jobs that emerged after the industrial revolution. As such, it is unsurprising that work design research has predominantly focused on motivation. Indeed, the dominant work design model, the JCM, was articulated in a paper entitled "Motivation Through the Design of Work: Test of a Theory" (Hackman & Oldham 1976). Work design continues to feature in the motivation section of articles [for example, job design is labeled as a first-generation motivation theory in Miner's (2003) review of organizational theories]. As outlined in this article, motivational work design theory has been extended in various ways, such as by employing proactive and relational approaches to designing work (Grant & Parker 2009), and can be extended further, such as by investigating how work design might affect goal generation, goal striving, and self-regulation. Importantly, beyond refining theory, more needs to be done to embed the core principles of motivational work design in policy and practice. Large numbers of simplified, deskilled jobs still exist, and the gap between "good jobs" and "bad jobs" continues to grow.

But designing work for motivation is not enough. In the context of globalization and rapid technological change, we are witnessing an increase in challenge and complexity in many jobs. The second part of this article argues that work design for other critical ends warrants mainstream attention. First, it is important to give more attention to how work design can support individuals' cognitive, identity, and moral development. The analysis of work design as a vehicle for learning and development hopefully illustrates the untapped potential of work design. The nature and organization of individuals' work roles may have profound consequences, maybe even as extreme as reducing individuals' chance of dementia as they age or, at the aggregate level, helping nations to meet projected skill gaps.

Second, although considering work design from a health perspective has a long history, we need to extend this perspective given the demands many employees increasingly face in their work lives. Work redesign might promote physical and mental health in more ways than hitherto considered, serving not only as a primary intervention but also as a secondary intervention that boosts employees' active coping and as a tertiary intervention that facilitates recovery. Hackman's (2009) plea for scholars to focus on changing the situation and thereby promoting individual growth, instead of solely changing the individual and thereby promoting adaptation, reiterates the importance of work design for health and well-being.

Third, this article considers how we might design work for control and flexibility at the same time. Different possibilities exist, from combining enriched work designs with informal control mechanisms (contextual ambidexterity); to combining low job autonomy with positive work characteristics, participation in decision making, and a supportive context (enabling bureaucracy); to creating a bureaucratic structure with roles that can be flexibly deployed and dynamically altered (high-reliability organizing). The pros and cons of these different work design options across various situations are currently unexplored. The need to understand how to design jobs that support the dual outcomes of control and flexibility will become more pressing given the growing application of bureaucratic principles to professional settings such as health care.

In the final section, beyond the frequent plea for rigorous, multilevel longitudinal studies, this article recommends the consideration of units of analysis other than a whole job, a configurational approach to work design, and contextualized studies of contemporary jobs. Work design research has a long and important history. It also has a bright future, but we need to go beyond the dominant motivational paradigm.

DISCLOSURE STATEMENT

The author is not aware of any affiliations, memberships, funding, or financial holdings that might be perceived as affecting the objectivity of this review.

ACKNOWLEDGMENTS

I sincerely appreciate the helpful feedback on this article from my colleagues, who are also some of the shining stars in the field of work design: Michael Frese, Adam Grant, Gary Johns, Fred Morgeson, and Yitzhak Fried. I am also grateful to my academic mentors and role models: John Cordery, who launched my interest in this field, and Toby Wall, whose passion for making jobs better inspired me to turn this interest into a career.

LITERATURE CITED

Adler PS. 2012. Perspective—the sociological ambivalence of bureaucracy: from Weber via Gouldner to Marx. *Org. Sci.* 23:244–66

Adler PS, Borys B. 1996. Two types of bureaucracy: enabling and coercive. *Admin. Sci. Q.* 41:61–89

Adler PS, Chen CX. 2011. Combining creativity and control: understanding individual motivation in large-scale collaborative creativity. *Account. Organ. Soc.* 36:63–85

Andel R, Crowe M, Pedersen NL, Mortimer J, Crimmins E. 2005. Complexity of work and risk of Alzheimer's disease: a population-based study of Swedish twins. *J. Gerontol.* 60:251–58

Argyris C. 1957. *Personality and Organization: The Conflict Between System and the Individual.* Oxford, UK: Harpers

Bakker AB, Demerouti E. 2007. The job demands–resources model: state of the art. *J. Manag. Psychol.* 22:309–28

Bargh JA, Chartrand TL. 1999. The unbearable automaticity of being. *Am. Psychol.* 54:462–79

Barker JR. 1993. Tightening the iron cage: concertive control in self-managing teams. *Admin. Sci. Q.* 38:408–37

Barley SR, Kunda G. 2001. Bringing work back in. *Organ. Sci.* 12:76–95

Beal DJ, Trougakos JP, Weiss HM, Green SG. 2006. Episodic processes in emotional labor: perceptions of affective delivery and regulation strategies. *J. Appl. Psychol.* 91:1053–65

Belkic KL, Landsbergis PA, Schnall PL, Baker D. 2004. Is job strain a major source of cardiovascular disease risk? *Scand. J. Work Environ. Health* 30:85–128

Bellé N. 2013. Experimental evidence on the relationship between public service motivation and job performance. *Public Admin. Rev.* 73:143–53

Bigley GA, Roberts KH. 2001. The incident command system: high-reliability organizing for complex and volatile task environments. *Acad. Manag. J.* 44:1281–99

Biron M, Bamberger P. 2010. The impact of structural empowerment on individual well-being and performance: taking agent preferences, self-efficacy and operational constraints into account. *Hum. Relat.* 63:163–91

Bledow R, Frese M, Anderson N, Erez M, Farr J. 2009. A dialectic perspective on innovation: conflicting demands, multiple pathways, and ambidexterity. *Ind. Organ. Psychol.* 2:305–37

Bond FW, Flaxman PE. 2006. The ability of psychological flexibility and job control to predict learning, job performance, and mental health. *J. Organ. Behav. Manag.* 26:113–30

Bosma HA, Kuunen ES. 2001. Determinants and mechanisms in ego identity development: a review and synthesis. *Dev. Rev.* 32:307–88

Bowe J, Bowe M, Streeter S. Murphy D, eds. 2000. *Gig: Americans Talk About Their Jobs at the Turn of the Millennium*. New York: Random House

Brown SL, Nesse RM, Vinokur AD, Smith DM. 2003. Providing social support may be more beneficial than receiving it: results from a prospective study of mortality. *Psychol. Sci.* 14:320–27

Bunderson S, Thompson JA. 2009. The call of the wild: zookeepers, callings, and the double-edged sword of deeply meaningful work. *Admin. Sci. Q.* 54:32–57

Burke CS, Stagl KC, Klein C, Goodwin GF, Salas E, Halpin SM. 2006. What type of leadership behaviors are functional in teams? A meta-analysis. *Leadersh. Q.* 17:288–307

Burns T, Stalker GM. 1961. *The Management of Innovation*. London: Tavistock

Campion MA. 1988. Interdisciplinary approaches to job design: a constructive replication with extensions. *J. Appl. Psychol.* 73:467–81

Campion MA, Medsker GJ, Higgs AC. 1993. Relations between work group characteristics and effectiveness: implications for designing effective work groups. *Pers. Psychol.* 46:823–50

Campion MA, Stevens MJ. 1991. Neglected questions in job design: how people design jobs, task-job predictability, and influence of training. *J. Bus. Psychol.* 6:169–91

Cohen SG, Bailey DE. 1997. What makes teams work: group effectiveness research from the shop floor to the executive suite. *J. Manag.* 23:239–90

Combs J, Liu Y, Hall A, Ketchen D. 2006. How much do high-performance work practices matter? A meta-analysis of their effects on organizational performance. *Pers. Psychol.* 59:501–28

Converse PD, DeShon RP. 2009. A tale of two tasks: reversing the self-regulatory resource depletion effect. *J. Appl. Psychol.* 94:1318–24

Cordery JL, Morrison D, Wright BM, Wall TD. 2010. The impact of autonomy and task uncertainty on team performance: a longitudinal field study. *J. Organ. Behav.* 31:240–58

Cordery J, Parker SK. 2007. Work organization. In *Oxford Handbook of Human Resource Management*, ed. P Boxall, J Purcell, P Wright, pp. 187–209. Oxford, UK: Oxford Univ. Press

Crawford ER, LePine JA, Rich BL. 2010. Linking job demands and resources to employee engagement and burnout: A theoretical extension and meta-analytic test. *J. Appl. Psychol.* 95:834–48

Cullinane SJ, Bosak J, Flood PC, Demerouti E. 2013. Job design under lean manufacturing and its impact on employee outcomes. *Organ. Psychol. Rev.* 3:41–61

Daniels K. 2006. Rethinking job characteristics in work stress research. *Hum. Relat.* 59:267–90

Daniels K, Beesley N, Wimalasiri V, Cheyne A. 2013. Problem solving and well-being: exploring the instrumental role of job control and social support. *J. Manag.* 39:1016–43

Davis GF. 2010. Job design meets organizational sociology. *J. Organ. Behav.* 31:302–8

Day DV, Harrison MM, Halpin S. 2009. *An Integrative Approach to Leader Development: Connecting Adult Development, Identity, and Expertise*. New York: Routledge

De Lange AH, Taris TW, Kompier MA, Houtman I, Bongers PM. 2003. The very best of the millennium: longitudinal research and the demand-control-(support) model. *J. Occup. Health Psychol.* 8:282–305

Demerouti E, Bakker AB. 2011. The job demands–resources model: challenges for future research. *J. Ind. Psychol.* 37:1–9

Dierdorff EC, Morgeson FP. 2013. Getting what the occupation gives: exploring multilevel links between work design and occupational values. *Pers. Psychol.* 66:687–721

Elsbach KD, Hargadon AB. 2006. Enhancing creativity through "mindless" work: a framework of workday design. *Organ. Sci.* 17:470–83

Erez M. 2010. Culture and job design. *J. Organ. Behav.* 31:389–400

Eriksson-Zetterquist U, Lindberg K, Styhre A. 2009. When the good times are over: professionals encountering new technology. *Hum. Relat.* 62:1145–70

Fay D, Sonnentag S. 2002. Rethinking the effects of stressors: a longitudinal study on personal initiative. *J. Occup. Health Psychol.* 7:221–34

Fisher CD, Minbashian A, Beckmann N, Wood RE. 2013. Task appraisals, emotions, and performance goal orientation. *J. Appl. Psychol.* 98:364–73

Fiske ST, Taylor SE. 1991. *Social Cognition.* New York: McGraw-Hill

Frese M, Garst H, Fay D. 2007. Making things happen: reciprocal relationships between work characteristics and personal initiative in a four-wave longitudinal structural equation model. *J. Appl. Psychol.* 92:1084–102

Frese M, Zapf D. 1994. Action as the core of work psychology: a German approach. In *Handbook of Industrial and Organizational Psychology*, ed. MD Dunnette, HC Triandis, LM Hough, pp. 271–340. Palo Alto, CA: Consult. Psychol. 2nd ed.

Fried Y, Grant A, Levi A, Hadani, Slowik LH. 2007. Placing the job characteristics model in context: the contributing role of time. *J. Organ. Behav.* 28:911–27

Gagné M, Deci EL. 2005. Self-determination theory and work motivation. *J. Organ. Behav.* 26:331–62

Gaille D. 2013. Direct participation and the quality of work. *Hum. Relat.* 66:453–73

Gibson CB, Birkinshaw J. 2004. The antecedents, consequences, and mediating role of organizational ambidexterity. *Acad. Manag J.* 47:209–26

Gino F, Schweitzer ME, Mead NL, Ariely D. 2011. Unable to resist temptation: how self-control depletion promotes unethical behavior. *Organ. Behav. Hum. Decis. Proc.* 115:191–203

Grant AM. 2007. Relational job design and the motivation to make a prosocial difference. *Acad. Manag. Rev.* 32:393–417

Grant AM. 2012a. Giving time, time after time: work design and sustained employee participation in corporate volunteering. *Acad. Manag. Rev.* 37:589–615

Grant AM. 2012b. Leading with meaning: beneficiary contact, prosocial impact, and the performance effects of transformational leadership. *Acad. Manag. J.* 55:458–76

Grant AM, Campbell EM, Chen G, Cottone K, Lapedis D, Lee K. 2007. Impact and the art of motivation maintenance: the effects of contact with beneficiaries on persistence behavior. *Organ. Behav. Human Decis. Proc.* 103:53–67

Grant AM, Fried Y, Parker SK, Frese M. 2010. Putting job design in context: introduction to the special issue. *J. Organ. Behav.* 31:145–57

Grant AM, Parker SK. 2009. Redesigning work design theories: the rise of relational and proactive perspectives. *Acad. Manag. Ann.* 3:317–75

Grolnick WS, Deci EL, Ryan RM. 1997. Internalization within the family: the self-determination theory perspective. In *Parenting and Children's Internalization of Values: A Handbook of Contemporary Theory*, ed. JE Grusec, L Kuczynski, pp. 135–61. New York: Wiley

Haas MR. 2010. The double-edged swords of autonomy and external knowledge: analyzing team effectiveness in a multinational organization. *Acad. Manag. J.* 53:989–1008

Hackman JR. 2009. The perils of positivity. *J. Organ. Behav.* 2:309–19

Hackman JR, Oldham GR. 1976. Motivation through the design of work: test of a theory. *Organ. Behav. Hum. Perform.* 16:250–79

Hall DTT, Heras ML. 2010. Reintegrating job design and career theory: creating not just good jobs but smart jobs. *J. Organ. Behav.* 31:448–62

Hannah ST, Avolio BJ, May DR. 2011. Moral maturation and moral conation: a capacity approach to explaining moral thought and action. *Acad. Manag. Rev.* 36:663–85

Higgins ET. 1998. Promotion and prevention: regulatory focus as a motivational principle. *Adv. Exp. Soc. Psychol.* 30:1–46

Hobfoll SE. 1989. Conservation of resources: a new attempt at conceptualizing stress. *Am. Psychol.* 44:513–24

Holman D. 2013. Job types and job quality in Europe. *Hum. Relat.* 66:475–502

Humphrey SE, Nahrgang JD, Morgeson FP. 2007. Integrating motivational, social, and contextual work design features: a meta-analytic summary and theoretical extension of the work design literature. *J. Appl. Psychol.* 92:1332–56

Ibarra H. 1999. Provisional selves: experimenting with image and identity in professional adaptation. *Admin. Sci. Q.* 44:764–91

Ingvaldsen JA, Rolfsen M. 2012. Autonomous work groups and the challenge of inter-group coordination. *Hum. Relat.* 65:861–81

Jackson PR, Mullarkey S. 2000. Lean production teams and health in garment manufacture. *J. Occup. Health Psychol.* 5:231–45

Johns G. 2010. Some unintended consequences of job design. *J. Organ. Behav.* 31:361–69

Jones TM, Ryan LV. 1998. The effect of organizational forces on individual morality: judgment, moral approbation, and behavior. *Bus. Ethics Q.* 8:431–45

Kalleberg AL. 2011. *Good Jobs, Bad Jobs: The Rise of Polarized and Precarious Employment Systems in the United States, 1970s to 2000s.* New York: Russell Sage Found.

Kanfer R. 1990. Motivation and individual differences in learning: an integration of developmental, differential and cognitive perspectives. *Learn. Individ. Differ.* 2:221–39

Karasek RA Jr. 1979. Job demands, job decision latitude, and mental strain: implications for job redesign. *Admin. Sci. Q.* 24:285–308

Karasek RA, Theorell T. 1990. *Healthy Work: Stress, Productivity, and the Reconstruction of Working Life.* New York: Basic

Karp A, Andel R, Parker MG, Wang HX, Winblad B, Fratiglioni L. 2009. Mentally stimulating activities at work during midlife and dementia risk after age 75: follow-up study from the Kungsholmen Project. *Am. J. Geriatr. Psychiatry* 17:227–36

Kelly EL, Moen P, Tranby E. 2011. Changing workplaces to reduce work-family conflict schedule control in a white-collar organization. *Am. Sociol. Rev.* 76:265–90

Kernis MH. 2000. Substitute needs and the distinction between fragile and secure high self-esteem. *Psychol. Inq.* 11:298–300

Kirkman BL, Rosen B, Tesluk PE, Gibson CB. 2004. The impact of team empowerment on virtual team performance: the moderating role of face-to-face interaction. *Acad. Manag. J.* 47:175–92

Klein KJ, Ziegert JC, Knight AP, Xiao Y. 2006. Dynamic delegation: shared, hierarchical, and deindividualized leadership in extreme action teams. *Admin. Sci. Q.* 51:590–621

Kopelman RE. 2006. Job redesign and productivity: a review of the evidence. *Natl. Product. Rev.* 4:237–55

Lanaj K, Hollenbeck J, Ilgen D, Barnes C, Harmon S. 2013. The double-edged sword of decentralized planning in multiteam systems. *Acad. Manag. J.* 56:735–57

Langfred CW. 2000. The paradox of self-management: individual and group autonomy in work groups. *J. Organ. Behav.* 21:563–85

Langfred CW. 2005. Autonomy and performance in teams: the multilevel moderating effect of task interdependence. *J. Manag.* 31:513–29

Langfred CW, Moye NA. 2004. Effects of task autonomy on performance: an extended model considering motivational, informational, and structural mechanisms. *J. Appl. Psychol.* 89:934–45

Leach DJ, Wall TD, Jackson PR. 2003. The effect of empowerment on job knowledge: an empirical test involving operators of complex technology. *J. Occup. Organ. Psychol.* 76:27–52

Leana C, Appelbaum E, Shevchuk I. 2009. Work process and quality of care in early childhood education: the role of job crafting. *Acad. Manag. J.* 52:1169–92

LePine JA, Podsakoff NP, LePine MA. 2005. A meta-analytic test of the challenge stressor-hindrance stressor framework: an explanation for inconsistent relationships among stressors and performance. *Acad. Manag. J.* 48:764–75

Lord RG, Hannah ST, Jennings PL. 2011. A framework for understanding leadership and individual requisite complexity. *Organ. Psychol. Rev.* 1:104–27

Manyika J, Lund S, Auguste B, Ramaswamy S. 2012. *Help wanted: the future of work in advanced economies.* Disc. Pap., McKinsey Glob. Inst., New York

Maynard MT, Gilson LL, Mathieu JE. 2012. Empowerment—fad or fab? A multilevel review of the past two decades of research. *J. Manag.* 38:1231–81

Meyer JP, Becker TE, Vandenberghe C. 2004. Employee commitment and motivation: a conceptual analysis and integrative model. *J. Appl. Psychol.* 89:991–1007

Miner JB. 2003. The rated importance, scientific validity, and practical usefulness of organizational behavior theories: a quantitative review. *Acad. Manag. Learn. Educ.* 2:250–68

Morgeson FP, Campion MA. 2003. Work design. In *Handbook of Psychology*, Vol. 12: *Industrial and Organizational Psychology*, ed. WC Borman, DR Ilgen, RJ Klimoski, IB Weiner, pp. 423–52. Hoboken, NJ: Wiley

Morgeson FP, Humphrey SE. 2006. The Work Design Questionnaire (WDQ): developing and validating a comprehensive measure for assessing job design and the nature of work. *J. Appl. Psychol.* 91:1321–39

Morgeson FP, Humphrey SE. 2008. Job and team design: toward a more integrative conceptualization of work design. In *Research in Personnel and Human Resources Management*, Vol. 27, ed. JJ Martocchio, pp. 39–92. Bingley, UK: Emerald

Morgeson FP, Johnson MD, Campion MA, Medsker GJ, Mumford TV. 2006. Understanding reactions to job redesign: a quasi-experimental investigation of the moderating effects of organizational context on perceptions of performance behavior. *Pers. Psychol.* 59:333–63

Moshman D. 1998. Cognitive development beyond childhood. In *Handbook of Child Psychology*, Vol. 2: *Cognition, Perception and Language*, ed. W Damon, D Kuhn, RS Siegler, pp. 947–78. New York: Wiley. 5th ed.

Muraven M, Baumeister RF. 2000. Self-regulation and depletion of limited resources: does self-control resemble a muscle? *Psychol. Bull.* 126:247–59

Nahrgang JD, Morgeson FP, Hofmann DA. 2011. A meta-analytic investigation of the link between job demands, job resources, burnout, engagement, and safety outcomes. *J. Appl. Psychol.* 96:71–94

Ohly S, Fritz C. 2009. Work characteristics, challenge appraisal, creativity, and proactive behavior: a multilevel study. *J. Organ. Behav.* 31:543–65

Oldham GR, Hackman JR. 2010. Not what it was and not what it will be: the future of job design research. *J. Organ. Behav.* 31:463–79

O'Reilly C, Tushman M. 2007. *Ambidexterity as a dynamic capability: resolving the innovator's dilemma.* Res. Pap. 1963, Grad. Sch. Bus., Stanford Univ. **http://ssrn.com/abstract=978493**

Osterman P, Shulman B. 2011. *Good Jobs America: Making Work Better for Everyone.* New York: Russell Sage Found.

Oyserman D. 2001. Self-concept and identity. In *Blackwell Handbook of Social Psychology*, ed. A Tesser, N Schwarz, pp. 499–517. Malden, MA: Blackwell

Parker SK. 1998. Enhancing role breadth self-efficacy: the roles of job enrichment and other organizational interventions. *J. Appl. Psychol.* 83:835–52

Parker SK. 2003. Longitudinal effects of lean production on employee outcomes and the mediating role of work characteristics. *J. Appl. Psychol.* 88:620–34

Parker SK, Andrei D, Li W. 2014. An overdue overhaul: revamping work design theory from a time perspective. In *Time and Work*, Vol. 1, ed. AJ Shipp, Y Fried. East Sussex, UK: Psychol. Press. In press

Parker SK, Axtell CM. 2001. Seeing another viewpoint: antecedents and outcomes of employee perspective taking. *Acad. Manag. J.* 44:1085–100

Parker SK, Bindl U, Strauss K. 2010. Making things happen: a model of proactive motivation. *J. Manag.* 36:827–56

Parker SK, Johnson A, Collins C, Nguyen H. 2013. Making the most of structural support: moderating influence of employees' clarity and negative affect. *Acad. Manag. J.* 56:867–92

Parker SK, Ohly S. 2008. Designing motivating jobs: an expanded framework for linking work characteristics and motivation. In *Work Motivation: Past, Present and Future*, ed. R Kanfer, G Chen, RD Pritchard, pp. 233–84. New York/Abingdon, UK: Routledge

Parker SK, Turner N, Griffin MA. 2003. Designing healthy work. In *Health and Safety in Organizations: A Multilevel Perspective*, ed. DA Hofmann, LE Tetrick, pp. 91–130. San Francisco: Jossey-Bass

Parker SK, Wall T. 1998. *Job and Work Design: Organizing Work to Promote Well-Being and Effectiveness.* London: Sage

Parker SK, Wall TD, Cordery JL. 2001. Future work design research and practice: towards an elaborated model of work design. *J. Occup. Organ. Psychol.* 74:413–40

Payne J, Keep E. 2003. Re-visiting the Nordic approaches to work re-organization and job redesign: lessons for UK skills policy. *Policy Stud.* 24:205–25

Quinn RE, Rohrbaugh J. 1983. A spatial model of effectiveness criteria: towards a competing values approach to organizational analysis. *Manag. Sci.* 29:363–77

Raisch S, Birkinshaw J. 2008. Organizational ambidexterity: antecedents, outcomes, and moderators. *J. Manag.* 34:375–409

Raja U, Johns G. 2010. The joint effects of personality and job scope on in-role performance, citizenship behaviors, and creativity. *Hum. Relat.* 63:981–1005

Roberts KH. 1990. Some characteristics of high reliability organizations. *Organ. Sci.* 1:160–77

Roberts KH, Stout SK, Halpern JJ. 1994. Decision dynamics in two high reliability military organizations. *Manag. Sci.* 40:614–24

Schaubroeck J, Lam SS, Xie JL. 2000. Collective efficacy versus self-efficacy in coping responses to stressors and control: a cross-cultural study. *J. Appl. Psychol.* 85:512–25

Schooler C, Mulatu MS, Oates G. 2004. Occupational self-direction, intellectual functioning, and self-directed orientation in older workers: findings and implications for individuals and societies. *Am. J. Sociol.* 110:161–97

Smith W, Lewis M. 2011. Toward a theory of paradox: a dynamic equilibrium model of organizing. *Acad. Manag. Rev.* 36:381–403

Smulders PG, Nijhuis FJ. 1999. The job demands–job control model and absence behaviour: results of a 3-year longitudinal study. *Work Stress* 13:115–31

Sonnentag S, Frese M. 2003. Stress in organizations. In *Handbook of Psychology*, Vol. 12: *Industrial and Organizational Psychology*, ed. WC Borman, DR Ilgen, RJ Klimoski, IB Weiner, pp. 453–91. Hoboken, NJ: Wiley

Sonnentag S, Zijlstra FRH. 2006. Job characteristics and off-job activities as predictors of need for recovery, well-being, and fatigue. *J. Appl. Psychol.* 91:330–50

Spector PE. 1998. A control model of the job stress process. In *Theories of Organizational Stress*, ed. CL Cooper, pp. 153–69. Oxford, UK: Oxford Univ. Press

Stewart GL, Barrick MR. 2000. Team structure and performance: assessing the mediating role of intrateam process and the moderating role of task type. *Acad. Manag. J.* 43:135–48

Tornau K, Frese M. 2013. Construct clean-up in proactivity research: a meta-analysis on the nomological net of work-related proactivity concepts and their incremental validities. *Appl. Psychol.* 62:44–96

Treville S, Antonakis J. 2006. Could lean production job design be intrinsically motivating? Contextual, configurational, and levels-of-analysis issues. *J. Oper. Manag.* 24:99–123

Treviño LK. 1986. Ethical decision making in organizations: a person-situation interactionist model. *Acad. Manag. Rev.* 11:601–17

Treviño LK, den Nieuwenboer NA, Kish-Gephart JJ. 2014. (Un)ethical behavior in organizations. *Annu. Rev. Psychol.* 65:In press

Vandivier K. 1972. The aircraft brake scandal. *Harper's Mag.* 244:45–52

Van der Doef M, Maes S. 1999. The job demand-control (-support) model and psychological well-being: a review of 20 years of empirical research. *Work Stress* 13:87–114

Vidal M. 2013. Low-autonomy work and bad jobs in post-Fordist capitalism. *Hum. Relat.* 66:587–612

Wall TD, Jackson PR. 1995. New manufacturing initiatives and shopfloor work design. In *The Changing Nature of Work*, ed. A Howard, pp. 139–74. San Francisco: Jossey-Bass

Warr PB. 2007. *Work, Happiness, and Unhappiness.* New York: Routledge

Weick KE, Sutcliffe KM, Obstfeld D. 2008. Organizing for high reliability: processes of collective mindfulness. *Crisis Manag.* 3:81–123

Wilson KL, Rest JR, Boldizar JP, Deemer DK. 1992. Moral judgment development: the effects of education and occupation. *Soc. Justice Res.* 5:31–48

World Health Organ. 1948. *Preamble to the Constitution of the World Health Organization as adopted by the International Health Conference, New York, 19–22 June, 1946.* Signed 22 July 1946 by represent. 61 states (Off. Records World Health Organ., No. 2, p. 100). Entered into force 7 April 1948

Xanthopoulou D, Bakker AB, Demerouti E, Schaufeli WB. 2007. The role of personal resources in the job demands–resources model. *Int. J. Stress Manag.* 14:121–41

A Century of Selection

Ann Marie Ryan[1] and Robert E. Ployhart[2]

[1]Department of Psychology, Michigan State University, East Lansing, Michigan 48824;
email: ryanan@msu.edu

[2]Darla Moore School of Business, University of South Carolina, Columbia, South Carolina
29208; email: ployhart@moore.sc.edu

Annu. Rev. Psychol. 2014. 65:693–717

First published online as a Review in Advance on
September 11, 2013

The *Annual Review of Psychology* is online at
http://psych.annualreviews.org

This article's doi:
10.1146/annurev-psych-010213-115134

Keywords

employee selection, validation, technology and selection, selection
constructs, selection methods

Abstract

Over 100 years of psychological research on employee selection has yielded
many advances, but the field continues to tackle controversies and challenging problems, revisit once-settled topics, and expand its borders. This
review discusses recent advances in designing, implementing, and evaluating
selection systems. Key trends such as expanding the criterion space, improving situational judgment tests, and tackling socially desirable responding are
discussed. Particular attention is paid to the ways in which technology has
substantially altered the selection research and practice landscape. Other areas where practice lacks a research base are noted, and directions for future
research are discussed.

Contents

INTRODUCTION

Whereas the scientific study of employee selection is now a century old, the practice of selecting employees is much more ancient. One of the first books on employee selection was published in 1913[1]: Hugo Munsterberg's *Psychology and Industrial Efficiency*, which described the selection of streetcar motormen, ship officers, and telephone switchboard operators. Perhaps because of its age, the study of employee selection is easily thought of as a mature research area. A vast number of studies on the topic have been published in addition to books, handbooks, and reviews; many psychologists are engaged full time in thriving practices associated with designing, implementing, and evaluating selection practices; and laws and professional guidelines direct the appropriate conduct of employee selection practice. With a century of research and psychologically driven practice, one may wonder: What is left to uncover? Haven't all the "big" questions been resolved?

What is fascinating and motivating to us is that plenty is going on. The area was last reviewed in the *Annual Review of Psychology* six years ago (Sackett & Lievens 2008). Today, the field of selection research is

(*a*) full of controversies, such as:

- Is the validity of integrity testing overstated (Ones et al. 2012, Van Iddekinge et al. 2012)?
- Are content validation strategies useful (Binning & LeBreton 2009, Murphy 2009, Murphy et al. 2009, Thornton 2009)?

(*b*) actively engaged in revisiting many "settled" questions, such as:

- Does differential validity exist for cognitive ability tests (Aguinis et al. 2010, Berry et al. 2011, Meade & Tonidandel 2010)?

---

[1] The German language version was published in 1912 and the English language version in 1913.

- What are the magnitudes of subgroup differences on commonly used predictors (Bobko & Roth 2013, Dean et al. 2008, Foldes et al. 2008, Whetzel et al. 2008)?
- Is there value in considering specific abilities above g in predicting job performance (Lang et al. 2010, Mount et al. 2008)?
- Are vocational interests of any value in selecting employees (Van Iddekinge et al. 2011a)?

(c) still working on major "intractable" challenges, such as:

- Can we reduce adverse impact in cognitive ability testing without sacrificing validity (DeCorte et al. 2010, Kehoe 2008, Ployhart & Holtz 2008, Pyburn et al. 2008)?
- Can we design personality tools for selection use that are not fakeable, or can we otherwise prevent or detect faking (Fan et al. 2012, van Hooft et al. 2012)?
- How can we convince stakeholders of the need to move away from subjectivity in hiring (Highhouse 2008, Kuncel 2008, O'Brien 2008)?

(d) expanding into literatures and organizational levels far removed from those historically investigated, including:

- How do we link selection methods and constructs to indices of unit-level outcomes (performance, turnover) (Van Iddekinge et al. 2009)?
- How might psychological research connect to firm-level strategy, economics-derived research on human capital resources, or competitive advantage (Ployhart & Moliterno 2011)?

(e) constantly being pushed by those in practice, who continually are confronting questions to which researchers have not yet produced answers (or haven't even begun to study!).

- Is unproctored, Internet testing appropriate, or are there major problems with this practice (e.g., unstandardized testing environments, cheating) (Beaty et al. 2011, Tippins 2009 and ensuing commentaries)?
- How well do prototypical assessment tools generalize globally (Ryan & Tippins 2009)?
- How can we design psychometrically sound tools to leverage new technological advances (e.g., immersive simulations) (Scott & Lezotte 2012)?
- How can we best measure knowledge, skills, abilities, and other characteristics (KSAOs) that have taken on increased importance in a rapidly changing work environment (e.g., adaptability, cross-cultural competence) (Inceoglu & Bartram 2012)?

So, as a mature field, selection research is not in a rocking chair in a retirement home but is more akin to a highly active senior who has not been slowed down by age.

Since the last *Annual Review of Psychology* article on this topic, multiple comprehensive handbooks on selection have been published (e.g., Farr & Tippins 2010, Schmitt 2012), new text editions specifically on the topic have emerged (e.g., Guion 2011), volumes have summarized knowledge of specific major topics (e.g., adverse impact, Outtz 2010; technology and selection, Tippins & Adler 2011), and high-quality review articles have been produced (Breaugh 2009, Macan 2009, Thornton & Gibbons 2009). Thus, there are many new summaries of the state of research, and producing a summary of the summaries would not be a useful contribution. Instead, we set our goal for this review to be more forward looking than backward looking and to zero in on those specific questions and topics that are currently of great interest as well as those that are likely to occupy research attention in the decade ahead. To base these predictions on the scholarly literature is a fairly obvious task. However, given the applied nature of selection research, we undertook a short survey of selection "practice leaders" (i.e., a dozen organizational psychologists whose full-time focus is on employee selection and who are viewed as influential in this arena). We mention views of these practice leaders throughout in discussing what is missing in the literature.

To provide some structure to our review, we have organized our discussion of research into the three areas of designing, implementing, and evaluating selection systems. To be sure, research covered in one section often has implications for the others, but some organizing structure is required.

DESIGNING SELECTION SYSTEMS

Selection researchers have long focused on two key questions in designing selection processes: What should be assessed? How should we assess it? In this section we review advances in considering what should be assessed (definitions and measures of desired outcomes of selection as well as constructs of focus in selection) and how it is assessed (methods of assessment). Although decisions regarding what to assess are based on job analysis, competency modeling, and other types of needs assessment, those topics have recently been reviewed in another *Annual Review of Psychology* article (Sanchez & Levine 2012) and thus are not discussed here.

Outcomes of Selection

For a number of years, selection researchers have noted the importance of "expanding the criterion space" (see Campbell 1990) or the need to define success at work more broadly than just task performance. In recent years, we have seen continued discussion of the need for expansion but also some action in terms of studying criteria other than task performance. There are several themes to this research.

First, more studies have looked at broadening the criterion space at the individual level. For example, predicting turnover with selection tools has been a greater focus (e.g., Barrick & Zimmerman 2009, Maltarich et al. 2010), and meta-analyses have examined relations between personality and organizational citizenship behavior and counterproductive work behavior (Chiaburu et al. 2011, Le et al. 2011, O'Boyle et al. 2012). However, given the focus on adaptive performance in today's workplace (Dorsey et al. 2010), it is surprising how little selection-related work has occurred. Therefore, although we see some expansion in what criteria are being studied by selection researchers, a continued expansion in the decade ahead is needed to improve predictive accuracy.

Second, selection researchers have begun to predict performance at unit and organizational levels rather than just at the individual level. **Figure 1** illustrates how multilevel considerations factor into selection research, with an indication of the amount of research in various areas. Units that hire more employees using valid selection scores show more effective training, customer service performance, and financial performance over time than units that do not (Ployhart et al. 2011, Van Iddekinge et al. 2009). Ployhart and colleagues (2009) found that positive changes in unit-level service-orientation KSAO scores generated corresponding positive changes in unit-level financial performance over time, but with diminishing returns. A meta-analysis by Crook and colleagues (2011) found that unit-level KSAOs are related to a number of unit-level performance metrics. This research is demonstrating that the tools and KSAOs used in selection may also relate to higher levels of financial performance, but the relationships may be more variable (contextualized) than found at the individual level. As the push for demonstrating the value of selection tools is likely to be as strong as ever in the years ahead, we anticipate work on the value of selection to higher-level outcomes to continue to emerge as an important area of research focus. Also, as the practice leaders we surveyed noted, our move away from a focus on the "job" as the unit of analysis and the dynamic nature of work role boundaries should push us to new and better ways of defining the desired outcomes of selection processes.

Third, we see some efforts to align selection systems with organizational strategy. One example of this would be cases where competency modeling processes are used to align selection

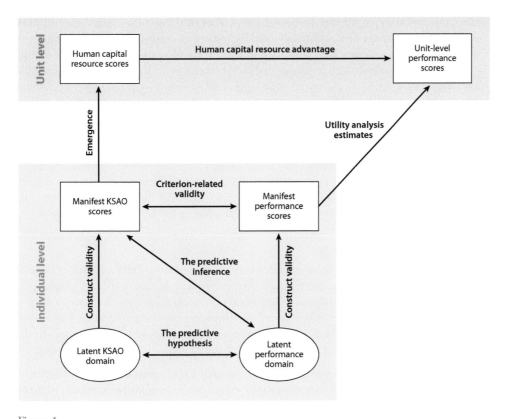

Figure 1

Illustration of multilevel relationships investigated in selection research. Abbreviation: KSAO, knowledge, skills, abilities, and other characteristics.

systems with other human resource (HR) systems and with the overall direction of the organization (Campion et al. 2011, Schippman 2010). Another example would be decisions regarding outsourcing of selection practices (Ordanini & Silvestri 2008). A final area links the KSAOs that are the target or focus of selection systems with an organization's human capital resources that underlie competitive advantage (Ployhart & Moliterno 2011, Wright & McMahan 2011). Human capital resources may generate firm-level competitive advantage because they are heterogeneous and difficult to imitate. Because KSAOs comprise the microfoundation of these human capital resources, selection may thus have a strong influence on a firm's ability to generate strategic competitive advantage (Coff & Kryscynski 2011).

What are we not doing? Cleveland & Collela (2010) argue that we are still limited in definitions of success and should include concepts such as employee health and well-being and nonwork criteria such as levels of work-family conflict. These constructs have been of interest to other psychologists, and even economists, for a long time, yet have not seemed to penetrate the criterion barrier in the selection field. At the same time, Cleveland & Collela (2010) note that the use of health status or family satisfaction as measures for selecting employees might create issues related to employee privacy and discrimination. We suggest a step back from a definition of success as including nonwork outcomes to a focus on work behaviors that lead to those outcomes. As an example, rather than attempting to develop selection tools to predict work-nonwork conflict, which could lead to assessment of "inappropriate" constructs (marital status, relationship stability), selection designers might attempt to map out predictors of ability to set boundaries on work assignments, time management, and decision making in contexts of competing demands. Although these are not the only factors that contribute to work-nonwork conflict, they are ones that an employer might reasonably seek to predict and might be able to do so without straying outside what is acceptable.

As has been noted in selection reviews for most of the century of research, the "criterion problem" (Guion 2011) persists: Poor quality, contaminated, and mis- or underspecified measures of performance hinder our capacity to advance understanding of the true importance of individual differences as predictors. Although more data are now tracked by organizations (e.g., big data) on individual performance, we are still limited in our capacity to predict because of the challenge of obtaining accurate and complete assessments of individual behavior at work. However, with more different types of data available, it may be possible to assemble validity evidence based on multiple types of criteria, so that the limitations of one type are offset by the benefits of another type.

Constructs

Selection is essentially a predictive hypothesis, where one proposes that certain KSAOs of individuals are related to certain outcome(s) of interest to the organization (Guion 2011). This generally lends itself to looking at the prototypical individual differences (cognitive abilities, personality traits) studied in all areas of psychology as well as job-specific knowledge and skills. Rather than reviewing every study on specific KSAOs, we summarize the trends in what is assessed. In the next section we focus more specifically on the how, or the methods used to do that assessing.

Cognitive constructs. For many years, research on cognitive ability has been almost devoid in the selection area because it has been so firmly established as a predictor of job performance. As noted above, one ongoing development is that some researchers have questioned the blanket dismissal of the value of assessing specific abilities in conjunction with g (Lang et al. 2010, Mount et al. 2008) and are delineating contextual factors that might indicate when such a focus would be useful.

Scherbaum et al. (2012) recently argued that applied researchers need to give greater consideration to the developments in cognitive psychology and intelligence research more generally; others have suggested that the field is moving forward and is not missing much (Oswald & Hough 2012, Postlethwaite et al. 2012). Our own view is that there is room for expanding our focus from g to incorporating other cognitive psychology research into assessment. For example, there has been some interest in improving assessments of procedural knowledge, although most of this work is focused less on knowledge constructs and more on the methods used to assess this knowledge (see the section below on Situational Judgment Tests). Similarly, declarative knowledge assessment is not an area of research focus [for an exception, see Lievens & Patterson's (2011) examination of incremental validity of simulations over a declarative knowledge assessment]. The practice leaders we surveyed noted that they are often engaged in developing and implementing job knowledge assessments (e.g., programming, skilled trade knowledge), yet a lag exists in bringing findings from cognitive research on knowledge acquisition, situated cognition, and similar concepts (e.g., Breuker 2013, Compton 2013) into selection research. As another example, cognitive psychology work on multitasking and related concepts has yet to be broadly applied in selection contexts (for exceptions, see Colom et al. 2010 and Kantrowitz et al. 2012).

Noncognitive constructs. Active research is ongoing in the long-studied areas of personality and interest measurement, with a recent focus on the assessment of emotional intelligence, social skills, and integrity.

Personality. Over time, personality research in selection contexts has evolved from examinations of a hodgepodge of traits to a clear focus on the five-factor model constructs and, more recently, to a focus on using facets of the five-factor model for selection and/or looking at compound traits (e.g., proactivity, customer orientation) (for a review, see Hough & Dilchert 2010). Although recent studies have examined specific traits (e.g., affective orientation; Sojka & Deeter-Schmelz 2008) and nonlinear relationships between traits and outcomes (Le et al. 2011), selection-related personality research of late has a greater focus on how to assess than on what to assess, as we discuss below in the section on Self-Report Measures.

Interests. The value of vocational interests for use in employee selection has been reconsidered, and researchers have moved from prior views that interests are useful for occupational selection but that their range would be restricted and their value limited when selecting for specific jobs in specific organizations. Recent research suggests the usefulness of interests above and beyond personality measures (e.g., Van Iddekinge et al. 2011a) and for predicting both performance and turnover (Van Iddekinge et al. 2011b). We anticipate that this renewed attention to interests will result in valuable research in the next several years.

Emotional intelligence. A specific construct of focus in recent years has been emotional intelligence. Researchers have worked to better define and conceptualize emotional intelligence (Cherniss 2010, Harms & Crede 2010, Riggio 2010), to establish the predictive value of emotional intelligence (Blickle et al. 2009, Christiansen et al. 2010), and to document the relative roles of emotion perception, emotion understanding, and emotion regulation in predicting job performance (Joseph & Newman 2010, Newman et al. 2010). We anticipate that continued research will focus on social and emotional skills measurement in selection contexts for two reasons: Technology now allows for innovative and efficient ways of assessing these constructs, and much like personality inventories, these constructs are susceptible to socially desirable responding, making the design of useful tools a challenge (Lievens et al. 2011).

Integrity. Integrity test validity has been a focus of debate. Van Iddekinge and colleagues (2012) produced an updated meta-analysis of integrity test score criterion-related validities, finding them to be considerably smaller than prior research suggested. The findings from this study were in turn challenged for not being sufficiently comprehensive (Ones et al. 2012). At present it appears that integrity test score validities are large enough that they can be useful for selection, but the specific magnitude of these validities depends on which assumptions one is willing to make and which data sources one is willing to accept (Sackett & Schmitt 2012).

This debate has cast attention on definitions of rigor in primary study validation efforts as well as in meta-analyses and on how the goals of science and the commercial uses of science do not always align (Banks et al. 2012, Kepes et al. 2012). These are issues with broader implications for all of applied science, not just selection researchers. Although our practice survey participants did not single out integrity assessment as an area of research need, the focus in the business world on ethics (e.g., Drover et al. 2012) translates into a continued need to improve methods of integrity assessment. Much like with personality assessment, key challenges remain related to how to do so, given the issue of socially desirable responding in selection contexts.

Other constructs. One final note as to constructs of interest is the practice demand for tools that assess culture fit or person-organization fit. Although there is active research on person-organization fit (e.g., Meyer et al. 2010) and organizations adopting fit assessment tools, we have not seen published work on the use of such fit assessments in selection contexts. This may reflect that many of these assessments are uniquely designed for particular organizations and their cultures, or it may indicate that they are simply personality and value instruments with a different label.

Methods

Arthur & Villado (2008) make the point that selection researchers compare apples and oranges by comparing research on a construct (e.g., conscientiousness, cognitive ability) with research on a method [e.g., interview, situational judgment test (SJT), biodata]. One emerging trend is greater attention to multiconstruct methods, particularly interviews, assessment centers, and SJTs; we discuss each of these in turn. Although little novel research specifically on biodata has been undertaken (however, see interesting work on elaboration by Levashina et al. 2012 and on scoring by Cucina et al. 2012), researchers continue to investigate ways to improve the use of personality assessment, which has applicability to all self-report inventories, including biodata measures. We discuss the issue of socially desirable responding and self-report measures as well.

Interviews. As the most commonly used selection tool, interviews are likely to be a target of research. At the time of the Sackett & Lievens (2008) review, there was an active research focus on interview structure and on what constructs interviews measure. Within the past six years, there actually has not been much research activity beyond some studies on acceptance and improving the value of structured interviews (Chen et al. 2008, Klehe et al. 2008, Melchers et al. 2011) and some focus on what constructs interviews measure (Huffcutt 2011). Research has instead shifted to impression management in the interview, with researchers emphasizing that impression management is not just a bias but is a contributor to the criterion-related validity of the interview (Barrick et al. 2009, 2010; Kleinmann & Klehe 2011; Swider et al. 2011). Research has also focused on the factors that influence initial impressions in the interview and how these initial impressions affect interview scores (Stewart et al. 2008).

Where should interview research head? In a review paper, Macan (2009) argued that we need to understand what constructs are measured best via the interview versus other methods, and we echo that as an important research need. Although our practice survey did not indicate demands from the field for interview research, given the increased use of technology in interviewing to reduce costs (Skype, videoconferencing; Baker & Demps 2009), research on these forms of interviewing is needed. Our personal experiences suggest that, much like with Internet testing, giving applicants responsibility for their own assessment environment does not mean they will make wise choices (e.g., how close to get to the camera, what angle to sit at, what is visible in the background) or have good environmental control (e.g., noise, interruptions), and these factors can negatively affect evaluations. In our experience, many firms have used the interview to assess fit with the company's culture and values. However, the fit with values rarely factors into interview selection research, so there is a missed opportunity to more directly influence interview practice.

Assessment Centers. Assessment centers are predictor methods that present the applicant with a variety of activities or exercises (e.g., inbox, role play, leaderless group projects) designed to assess multiple KSAOs. Despite several decades of activity, research on assessment center construct validity continues to sort through questions of what assessment centers actually measure and how to enhance their value (Dilchert & Ones 2009, Gibbons & Rupp 2009, Hoffman & Meade 2012, Hoffman et al. 2011, Jones & Born 2008, Meriac et al. 2009, Putka & Hoffman 2013; see also a 2008 series of articles in the journal *Industrial and Organizational Psychology: Perspectives on Science* *and Practice*). One interesting result of this scrutiny is a better recognition of the ability to assess situational demands as a potentially important predictor of performance on a number of selection tools (e.g., assessment centers, interviews, SJTs; Jansen et al. 2012). Other suggestions emerging for practice are to use role-player prompts (Schollaert & Lievens 2012), reduce demands on assessors (Melchers et al. 2010), construct parallel forms of exercises (Brummel et al. 2009), and use technology for assessment exercise delivery (Lievens et al. 2010). We conclude that assessment center research remains vibrant and that many of the products of this effort have applicability to other selection methods (e.g., one can have parallel versions of interviews or SJTs, the demands on evaluators in interviews have similar influences as those on assessors, and construct validity questions similarly occur for SJTs and interviews).

Situational Judgment Tests. SJTs are predictor methods that present candidates with work-related situations and then assess how they might respond to those situations. Research interest in SJTs has grown to the point where there is now a reasonably large literature and corresponding narrative reviews (e.g., Lievens et al. 2008, Whetzel & McDaniel 2009). The majority of research published on SJTs since 2008 has followed three major themes.

First, there continues to be interest in examining the factors that may influence the criterion-related validity of SJTs. Several studies have demonstrated that SJT scores manifest validity across different high-stakes contexts (Lievens & Patterson 2011, Lievens & Sackett 2012). Other studies have examined the impact of response instructions on validity with Lievens et al. (2009) and have found no meaningful differences between two response instructions (what one would do versus what one should do) for predicting medical school performance. McDaniel and colleagues (2011) found that score adjustments that affect scatter and elevation can actually enhance validity. Motowidlo & Beier (2010) presented an alternative scoring system and found that scores based on this approach produced validity based on implicit trait policies and the knowledge facet of KSAOs.

Second, research continues to explore the nature of constructs assessed by SJTs. The construct validity of SJT scores has posed something of a mystery: Although scores on SJTs predict job performance, they do not fall into homogeneous groupings that correspond to existing KSAOs. A meta-analysis by Christian and colleagues (2010) classified SJT constructs into four broad categories: knowledge and skills, applied social skills (including interpersonal, teamwork, and leadership skills), basic tendencies (including personality), and heterogeneous composites of multiple KSAOs. Their review suggests most SJTs are intended to measure interpersonally related KSAOs, primarily social skills, teamwork, and leadership. One-third of the studies they reviewed failed to report the nature of any constructs measured by the SJT. Importantly, they found that matching the constructs assessed by the SJT to the nature of performance in a given context can enhance criterion-related validity. Other research has extended SJTs to measure different construct domains, including personal initiative (Bledow & Frese 2009) and team role knowledge (Mumford et al. 2008). In a different examination of construct validity, MacKenzie and colleagues (2010) found that the construct validity of SJT scores may be affected by whether the scores are obtained in applicant versus incumbent contexts. Finally, Westring et al. (2009) examined the systematic variance attributable to KSAO and situational factors and found that situations explained three times as much SJT score variance as did KSAO factors.

The final area of research has examined the magnitude of subgroup differences on SJT scores. Whetzel and colleagues (2008) found that whites perform better than African Americans, Asians, and Hispanics, and women perform better than men. Not surprisingly, the racial subgroup differences are larger when the SJT is more cognitively loaded. Bobko & Roth (2013) reported larger white/African American subgroup differences for SJTs than was found in previous research;

the disparities were credited to their consideration of constructs, context (applicant versus incumbent), and statistical artifacts.

Overall, research on SJTs continues to expand into new directions. SJTs have clearly established themselves as viable predictors of outcomes in a number of contexts. We suspect the next wave of this research will extend these findings into new areas, including predicting performance in other outcome domains (e.g., citizenship behaviors, turnover), employing SJTs in new cultural contexts, using SJTs to assess different constructs, and examining the effects of faking or applicant perceptions on SJT scores. Research that examines ways of enhancing the validity, reducing subgroup differences, or increasing efficiency will continue to be popular. Technology and SJTs are on a collision course, as most of the digital hiring simulations are in many ways more elaborate SJTs. At the same time, there are areas that have probably seen enough research. At present these areas include the effects of response instructions on SJT scores, and criterion-related validity studies in commonly examined contexts.

Self-report measures and socially desirable responding. The persistent problem of socially desirable responding or faking in applicant settings has continued to capture research attention. Some voices continue to call for a shift in focus from "faking" to developing broader theories of self-presentation or motivation (Ellingson & McFarland 2011, Griffith & Peterson 2011, Marcus 2009, Tett & Simonet 2011) that do not assume that such behaviors by applicants are illegitimate or have no positive value for prediction. There continue to be studies that address whether faking is a problem (Komar et al. 2008) and that examine the detection and magnitude of faking effects (Berry & Sackett 2009, LaHuis & Copeland 2009), but researchers have moved on to tackle the more thorny issue of how to reduce or eliminate faking. Approaches to reduction include warnings during testing (Fan et al. 2012, Landers et al. 2011) and eye tracking (van Hooft & Born 2012). Some of the most interesting work has revolved around variations on forced choice methods (Converse et al. 2008, 2010); for example, the US Army has adopted a multidimensional item response theory approach to personality assessment to address faking concerns (Stark et al. 2012). We expect the search for ways to use self-report tools more effectively in selection contexts will continue, as these tools are often cost effective and efficient for screening and add incremental validity, despite problems with socially desirable responding. However, without a common theory or even a definition of faking, these approaches will likely be piecemeal and incomplete.

Other methods. One method that seldom gets much research focus is the use of individual psychological assessment. Although some commentary has been generated recently around the need for more research on this practice area (see Silzer & Jeanneret 2011 and accompanying commentaries), there is not much to report in the way of empirical research on individual assessment. The validity of credit scores was supported by Bernerth and colleagues (2012), and some work has been done on what inferences are made in resume screening (Derous et al. 2009, 2012; Tsai et al. 2011). With the rise of e-portfolios (collections of evidence documenting competencies) for use in selection in certain sectors (e.g., education; Ndoye et al. 2012) and video resumes (Eisner 2010), investigation of what is being assessed by these methods as well as how to bring standardization to these evaluations is needed. Talk of using neuroimaging, genetic testing, and other methods that represent advances in other areas of psychology remains just talk (Zickar & Lake 2011); their application to selection is likely to remain hypothetical because of concerns with acceptability, particularly with regard to privacy, ethicality, and legality.

From a practice perspective, there needs to be more comparative research on method variations. SJT research on scoring provides a good example of how "going into the weeds" on topics such as instructions and scoring of response options may provide insight into what works best. A few years back similar scrutiny was given to how to ask interview questions (e.g., behavior description versus situational description; Klehe & Latham 2005) and what different elements of interview structure are essential (e.g., Chapman & Zweeg 2005), resulting in improved advice on best practices in interview design. From a practice perspective, differences in instructions, item wording, response formats, and the like are changes that can be implemented with relative ease, and their "value" is therefore easy to sell to organizational decision makers. Yet, we seldom investigate their effects on validity, adverse impact, efficiency, and applicant reactions—we can and should do more. However, for this research on method variations to be published, it will be vital for researchers to develop a solid theoretical basis for proposing any differences and then to follow through on programmatic research using designs that strongly test the theory.

Combining Assessments

One final design topic relates to how one puts it all together. That is, besides deciding what to measure and how to measure it, selection system designers decide how those measures will be combined and implemented (whether compensatory or noncompensatory use; single or multi-stage; and any sequencing, weighting, and cut score decisions; DeCorte et al. 2011). There has been considerable revisiting of prior thinking in this area as well. For example, Hattrup (2012) summarized how ways of forming predictor composites are shifting as our view of the criterion space is expanding. Finch and colleagues (2009) considered how predictor combinations in multistage selection affect expected performance and adverse impact. DeCorte and colleagues (2011) provided tools for using pareto-optimal methods to determine the best ways to combine and use predictors with considerations of validity and adverse impact as well as cost and time constraints.

In sum, recent research on combinations and decisions has shown that simple mechanistic ideas for how to address adverse impact (e.g., add a noncognitive predictor, change the order of assessment administration) have deepened appreciation for the complexity of selection system design. Further work on why decisions are enacted the way they are (e.g., stakeholder assumptions, timeliness of hiring concerns) can point to the directions most in need of research. We suspect, as has been true for the past decade, that efficiency plays a major role in choices that employers make, and any research that addresses ways to improve efficiency is of as much practical value as that focused on effectiveness.

IMPLEMENTING SELECTION SYSTEMS

Since the Sackett & Lievens (2008) review, the major topics in research on implementation have been the use of technology (which certainly is part of design as well), globalization, and retesting.

Technology

In several previous reviews, the use of technology in selection has received mention, but since 2008, there truly has been an explosion in how technology has changed and continues to change selection practice. Computerized assessments are now fairly mainstream for big organizations, and off-the-shelf computerized assessment tools are used by smaller organizations. International guidelines for computer-based and Internet-delivered testing are providing some direction for best practices (Bartram 2009). Applicant tracking systems are standard and affect the choices organizations make about what tools can be implemented. The use of technology in recruitment continues to expand (for a review, see Maurer & Cook 2011). However, our survey of practice leaders suggested that a greater examination of the usefulness and validity of these high-tech and multimedia methods vis-à-vis more traditional formats is still strongly needed to better understand their utility. Potosky (2008) provided a conceptual framework for considering how media attributes (transparency, social bandwidth, interactivity, and surveillance) might affect the psychometric properties of measures; research using this or other theoretical frameworks might enable us to make more significant strides in understanding and best utilizing technological advances in selection contexts.

Perhaps the most controversial area related to technology and selection has been whether using unproctored Internet testing is appropriate (for a good overview of the issues, see Tippins 2009 and accompanying commentaries). Unproctored Internet testing and proctored tests seem to evidence similar validities (Beaty et al. 2011) and similar levels of cheating or response distortion (Arthur et al. 2010). Many organizations have advocated that computer adaptive testing be used when going unproctored, as this will allow for less item exposure and less likelihood of cheating. Others have advocated for the use of a proctored verification or score confirmation test for presumed passers whenever an initial unproctored test is used. However, surprisingly little has been published on these emerging practices (see Kantrowitz et al. 2011 on computer adaptive tests; Scott & Lezotte 2012 for a general review of web-based assessments). Our surveyed practice leaders clearly felt there was not enough research: They said they want to see more data on the validities of UITs and the pros and cons of verification testing as well as research on the next generation of technology delivery (e.g., mobile testing), and we have to agree. However, for this research to make a broad scientific contribution, it will be vital for investigators to demonstrate the construct validity of their assessments, use field experiments or quasi-experiments, and/or develop a solid theoretical explanation for why differences should (or should not) exist between the administration modes.

There is no question that social media is causing a revolution in recruiting. Social media refers generically to Internet-based platforms (e.g., LinkedIn, Facebook) that connect people and organizations synchronously and asynchronously. Social media offers a potentially powerful mechanism for sourcing active and passive candidates, and although it has been primarily discussed as a recruiting tool, it is also being used in hiring decisions. Brown & Vaughn (2011), Davison et al. (2011), and Kluemper & Rosen (2009) discussed a number of concerns with using social media for employee selection purposes. The major conclusion is that although social media platforms may offer some opportunities for enhancing the speed, efficiency, or effectiveness of selection tools and processes, a number of legal (e.g., discrimination, privacy) and scientific (e.g., validity) issues must be carefully considered (Zickar & Lake 2011). This is an area where practice far outpaces research, and to date there is no published research that examines the validity, subgroup differences, or stakeholder opinions of using social media for hiring decisions. We hope this will change dramatically by the time of the next review on selection.

The value of technology for assessment is mentioned in a number of areas, but little empirical work exists to help guide innovative use. For example, although automated item-generation and test-assembly methods have taken hold in the educational testing literature (Gutl et al. 2011, Luecht 2000), we do not see published work on their viability or use in selection, although we know some practice leaders are engaged in deploying such methods to reduce the challenges of maintaining uncompromised, high-quality item pools, particularly in the cognitive ability domain. We hear discussions of how useful computational approaches to content analysis could be, such as latent semantic analysis (examining the relative positions of units of text in a semantic space of N dimensions) and data mining (automated approaches to identifying patterns in data) (see Indulska et al. 2012 for a comparative presentation on these); however, we do not see any examples of their applicability in selection systems in the published literature. Virtual role-plays and other immersive simulations are being marketed for employee selection use, but the published literature offers little information on them (e.g., McNelly et al. 2011 on web-based management simulations,

Oostrom et al. 2012 on computerized in-baskets). Indeed, "gamification," or the use of computer simulation games for business-related purposes (including recruiting and selection), is emerging as a stable industry yet gives little to no attention to the scientific literature on psychometrics or assessment. So although we hear talk about how crowdsourcing and other advances from the use of algorithms in Internet searches and in financial circles will make their way into making predictions about job applicants, we have yet to see published work on their application in this context (for an example of crowdsourcing to develop assessments in educational contexts, see Zualkernan et al. 2012). These are the research frontiers at the moment, and they are areas that investigators must examine or else the field runs the risk of being marginalized by gaming and technology-focused developers.

Globalization

Our survey of practice leaders indicated that globalization of selection systems is a top concern in need of research, particularly with regard to cross-cultural equivalence of tools, cross-cultural acceptability of practices, and navigation of selection environments (e.g., legal and social norms) when taking a process global. Although a sizeable literature exists on selection for international assignments (for a review, see Caligiuri et al. 2009), there has been a surprising lack of published research on globalizing selection systems (for a review, see Carey et al. 2010). Reserves of talent do not exist equally around the globe, as birthrates are declining or slowing in many Western countries, whereas developing countries have increasing populations (see, e.g., PriceWaterhouseCoopers 2010). Economic and labor pressures in many developed countries have led their organizations to source talent in developing countries, where the labor is often cheaper. Although historically this sourcing was limited to nontechnical jobs, currently it is increasing for professional occupations as well (e.g., engineering, accounting). Yet only limited selection research considers cross-cultural issues (for a review, see Caligiuri & Paul 2010).

Specific papers appear here and there on the use of global versus local norms (e.g., Bartram 2008), on cross-cultural equivalence of specific measures (e.g., Bartram 2013), on validity generalization across cultures (e.g., Ones et al. 2010), and on applicant reactions across cultures (e.g., Ryan et al. 2009). Almost all of this work points positively to the cross-culture transportability of methods, with some tweaks and adjustments for cultural context, yet it seems those in practice feel that the research base is still lacking. Ryan & Tippins (2009) provide an overview and specific guidance for the design, conduct, and implementation of global selection systems. Their recommendations outline a number of directions for future research that need to be addressed if the scientific literature is to better guide practice.

One other point related to globalization came from our survey of practice leaders, who noted that language proficiency assessment seems to be outside the expertise of most selection researchers, and thus its implementation into selection systems, validation, adverse impact, etc., does not get the same research scrutiny as other selection tools do, although it should.

Retesting

One implementation question that has drawn quite a lot of attention in the past few years is retesting. Researchers have looked at whether retesting (or even simply reapplying) affects performance (Matton et al. 2011), faking (Landers et al. 2010), validity (Lievens et al. 2007), adverse impact (Dunleavy et al. 2008, Schleicher et al. 2010), and applicant reactions (Schleicher et al. 2010). In general, this research suggests a need for caution in how data from retested applicants are considered in research as well as careful consideration of retesting policies by organizations because of score elevation, accompanying effects on validity, and potential problematic effects on adverse impact. We view this spate of attention to an implementation issue as a positive development; practitioners often lament that there is not a lot of guidance in the selection literature on assessment policy issues and what are truly best practices.

EVALUATING SELECTION SYSTEMS

With regard to the evaluation of selection methods, continued discussion of ways to gather validation evidence and to reduce adverse impact and bias were major topics in the past few years, along with a focus on the attitudes and opinions of selection systems stakeholders, including hiring managers, HR professionals, and applicants.

Validation

One would think that the validation of selection procedures would be a ho-hum, or routine, topic after so many years of research and the establishment of various sets of professional guidelines. However, research guidance on how to conduct criterion validation studies continues to grow (for a review, see Van Iddekinge & Ployhart 2008). As noted previously, we continue to see debate around the usefulness of content validation strategies for supporting selection tool use (see Murphy 2009 and the accompanying set of commentary articles). We also see renewed discussion of the usefulness of synthetic validation methods (see Johnson et al. 2010 and accompanying commentaries). Although there is some practical guidance for conducting transportability studies and for documenting the appropriate use of validity generalization results (Gibson & Caplinger 2007, McDaniel 2007), no empirical work exists on comparisons of practices in this area.

Subgroup Differences and Predictive Bias

Evaluation work also continues on how to reduce subgroup differences (i.e., mean differences between different groups, such as race or sex) and adverse impact (i.e., differences in hiring rates between different subgroups) (Outtz 2010). A closely related topic is how to enhance or change the diversity of the selected workforce (Newman & Lyon 2009). In a recent review, Ryan & Powers (2012) described how many of the choices made in recruitment, in choosing selection system content, and in how selection systems are implemented may make small differences in the diversity of those hired, but when considered in aggregation might have appreciable effects on the adverse impact of hiring processes. However, there still remains a lot of variability in how adverse impact is actually assessed (Biddle & Morris 2011, Cohen et al. 2010, Murphy & Jacobs 2012) and a desire among our practice leaders for further investigation and guidance.

As noted previously, there has been a shift in views regarding predictive bias. Although the received wisdom was once that there is no differential validity with cognitive ability tests, a "revival" of this research (Aguinis et al. 2010, Meade & Tonidandel 2010) has suggested the need to reconsider those conclusions (Berry et al. 2011). One concern with this focus is whether it is a chase of fairly small effects, evidenced only with large sample sizes, and whether renewed research will ultimately result in conclusions different from those of the past. One point raised, however, certainly could change that thinking: whether context moderates the likelihood of finding predictive bias. For example, might the organization's diversity climate, affirmative action policy, selection ratio, and targeted recruiting efforts factor into both who is hired and how they are evaluated once on the job? We expect to see some of this type of work emerging over the next several years.

Stakeholder Goals and Perceptions

We separate our discussion of internal stakeholders from external stakeholders. Internal stakeholders include incumbent employees and managers who must live with the results of the selection hires, selection managers who own responsibility for the design of the selection system, and HR managers who must align the selection system with the organization's strategic goals and economic realities. External stakeholders include applicants affected by the selection system.

Internal stakeholders. Understanding what leads to the adoption and support of selection systems is always a practical concern. Some research effort has been devoted to understanding what influences internal stakeholder perceptions of selection procedures (Furnham 2008, König et al. 2010). Research on utility analysis models, which are intended to provide information on the financial returns from different selection practices, appears to have waned dramatically from its popularity in the 1980s (Cascio & Aguinis 2008). It is not that interest in demonstrating return on investment (ROI) is less important (in fact, given current economic realities, quite the opposite is true). There are still researchers who use traditional utility analysis procedures in an attempt to value employee selection (e.g., Le et al. 2007), but these estimates are usually met with skepticism and concern (e.g., Schmitt 2007). Rather, researchers have focused on better integrating what we know about decision making and persuasion from cognitive and social psychology into methods of presenting cases for changing selection processes. For example, Winkler and colleagues (2010) present a multiattribute supply chain model of ROI that managers may find more persuasive. Similarly, Boudreau (2010) has argued that efforts to convey ROI must be based on existing decision-making models and methods that practicing managers accept and are familiar with. Other research has followed a different approach, adopting methods in strategic human resources, to examine the direct dollar consequences of acquiring higher-quality aggregate KSAOs or using more valid selection practices on unit-level performance (e.g., Ployhart et al. 2009, Van Iddekinge et al. 2009). Examining this issue from a different perspective, Highhouse (2008) noted that managers are frequently resistant to use or be persuaded by validity information of a technical nature, preferring instead to rely on intuition and heuristic judgments. Work on how best to present the case for use of selection tools is likely to continue in the next few years, particularly as new technologies entice stakeholders to use unproven methods and raise concerns over development costs.

External stakeholders. Applicant reactions research has fizzled a bit from a period of strong activity to studies on specific methods less investigated (e.g., reactions to emotional intelligence measures, Iliescu et al. 2012; reactions to credit checks, Kuhn 2012), country-specific investigations (e.g., Saudi Arabia, Anderson et al. 2012; Vietnam, Hoang et al. 2012; Greece, Nikolaou 2011), comparisons of internal and external candidate views (e.g., Giumetti & Sinar 2012), and summaries (Anderson et al. 2010, Truxillo et al. 2009 on explanations). Ryan & Huth (2008) argued that much of the research results in platitudes (e.g., treat people with respect) and therefore has little value for those in practice who are seeking specific guidance on how to improve reactions. We also believe research often focuses on the wrong outcomes, as reactions are unlikely to have much influence on test scores or validity given the typical strong demands and consequences present in a selection system. Rather, we suspect the consequences of reactions are much more subtle, such as spreading negative information about the company, affecting consumer behavior, or harming the company's brand or reputation. These more subtle outcomes may still be quite important from the broader perspective of the business, but they are harder to investigate (i.e., most research simply looks at intentions and not behavior).

Table 1 Forecasted shifts in the selection research base

Globalization
Shift from Western-centric view to multicultural view. Knowledge, skills, abilities, and other characteristics (KSAO) composites, assessments, and selection systems for multicultural competencies (e.g., willingness to work with others from different cultures) become more prominent. In the past, much selection research has been framed within the US legal system. Other countries have very different systems. Further, even within the United States, attitudes are changing, and demographics are changing (e.g., whites are projected to no longer be the majority by 2050). Although adverse impact research has been prominent for the past 50 years (since the US Civil Rights Act of 1964), one would think it might start to decline

Technology
Internet and social media platforms continue to change approaches to assessment and assessment content
Large vendors hold the assessment data on millions of candidates, essentially becoming placement offices where companies can come to them to source viable candidates. This might lead to a revival of placement research, and a very different—and vital—role for vendors

Changes in the nature of work
Increased use of teams and workgroups means a greater focus on relevant interpersonal KSAOs (e.g., teamwork)
Work requires greater knowledge (e.g., growth of professional service industry, high-knowledge jobs), and job knowledge testing becomes more common and sophisticated (e.g., complex simulations)
Working for organizations without homogeneous identities (e.g., limited liability corporations, firms that collaborate in some industries but compete in others, part-time or project-based work) leads to less focus on culture fit and more focus on adaptability
Increased focus on prediction of performance for older workers as those from the baby-boom generation begin to work part time to balance professional and personal preferences

What we need less of:
Demonstrating that small effects "could" occur (i.e., differential prediction/differential validity research)
Continued reestimation of the size of subgroup differences
Predictor-criterion correspondence validity studies (i.e., match the predictor construct with the criterion construct)
Arguing about narrow versus broad predictor usefulness
Demonstrating that applicants can fake
Describing applicant reactions without links to behavioral or objective outcomes

What we need more of:
Theoretically directed research on technologically sophisticated assessments
Psychometrics, scoring, and validity of gamified systems
Prediction of criteria that exist at unit or multiple levels
How to select for company fit, values, and culture
Predicting a broader range of criteria (e.g., adaptive, longitudinal, turnover)
Connecting selection research into the broader talent life cycle
Design, implementation, and evaluation of global selection systems
Greater conceptual specification and investigation of the role of context in selection
Investigation of internal stakeholder perceptions, reactions, judgments, and decision-making processes

CONCLUSIONS

With the scientific field of employee selection turning 100, it is interesting to speculate on what a selection review conducted 100 years from now might look like. Such an exercise is not purely academic but speaks to what is the core of this profession and what we believe is lasting about it. We believe the following questions are worth considering.

- One hundred years from now, will criterion-related validity still be the central question within selection? The predictive hypothesis has remained the core hypothesis in selection research for the past 100 years (Guion 2011)—could it possibly not be the core question for the next 100 years?

■ There is every reasonable expectation that organizations will still need to hire employees in the next century, but does this practical need guarantee the life of employee selection research? For example, could the day come when selection research moves entirely into practice or technical functions? Might selection research be conducted entirely by vendors, in the service of their products and services? Ironically, it is the heavy emphasis on psychometrics that makes selection researchers unique, but this is also the kind of research that has been slowly eroding from the applied psychology journals, being seen as too narrow and too atheoretical. Will the assessment of KSAOs in the future bear any resemblance to the KSAOs of interest today? For example, might selection research evolve into the study of biological or genetic individual differences? If so, would the KSAO measurement methodologies of today be seen as akin to the "introspection" methods from 100 years ago?

■ Who will most strongly shape the future of selection research? To date, most of this research has occurred within the United States, and is largely shaped by Western culture. Business already operates in a global economy, and the study of selection will likewise be pulled into this broader context.

Standing on approximately 100 years of employee selection research finds the field in a curious position. While there is great sophistication in selection procedures, methodologies, and practices, the basic question that is of interest to selection researchers—namely, the predictive hypothesis—remains largely unchanged. Some have argued this suggests that selection research has remained invariant, perhaps even indifferent, to changes in the broader world (e.g., Cascio & Aguinis 2008). Others have argued that selection research has shown impressive advancements and remains a vibrant area of research (e.g., Sackett & Lievens 2008). We offer yet a third perspective: that traditional selection research will remain active and engaging, but the broader challenges facing the field will push selection research into exciting new areas and in turn attract a broader array of scientist-practitioners. **Table 1** offers a glimpse of some of those directions and what are likely to be areas of emphasis and de-emphasis in research. Selection research will expand to consider a broader range of criteria (within and across levels), in different cultures and contexts, and in an ever-expanding array of practical applications. Viva selection!

DISCLOSURE STATEMENT

The authors are not aware of any affiliations, memberships, funding, or financial holdings that might be perceived as affecting the objectivity of this review.

LITERATURE CITED

Aguinis H, Culpepper SA, Pierce CA. 2010. Revival of test bias research in pre-employment testing. *J. Appl. Psychol.* 95:648–80

Anderson N, Ahmed S, Ana CC. 2012. Applicant reactions in Saudi Arabia: organizational attractiveness and core-self evaluation. *Int. J. Sel. Assess.* 20(2):197–208

Anderson N, Salgado JF, Hulsheger UR. 2010. Applicant reactions in selection: comprehensive meta-analysis into reaction generalization versus situational specificity. *Int. J. Sel. Assess.* 18:291–304

Arthur W, Glaze RM, Villado AJ, Taylor JE. 2010. The magnitude and extent of cheating and response distortion effects on unproctored internet-based tests of cognitive ability and personality. *Int. J. Sel. Assess.* 18:1–16

Arthur W, Villado AJ. 2008. The importance of distinguishing between constructs and methods when comparing predictors in personnel selection research and practice. *J. Appl. Psychol.* 93:435–42

Baker E, Demps J. 2009. Videoconferencing as a tool for recruiting and interviewing. *J. Bus. Econ. Res.* 7(10):9–14

Banks GC, Kepes S, McDaniel MA. 2012. Publication bias: a call for improved meta-analytic practice in the organizational sciences. *Int. J. Sel. Assess.* 20:182–96

Barrick MR, Shaffer JA, DeGrassi SW. 2009. What you see may not be what you get: a meta-analysis of the relationship between self-presentation tactics and ratings of interview and job performance. *J. Appl. Psychol.* 94:1394–411

Barrick MR, Swider B, Stewart GL. 2010. Initial evaluations in the interview: relationships with subsequent interviewer evaluations and employment offers. *J. Appl. Psychol.* 95:1037–46

Barrick MR, Zimmerman RD. 2009. Hiring for retention and performance. *Hum. Resour. Manag.* 48:183–206

Bartram D. 2008. Global norms: towards some guidelines for aggregating personality norms across countries. *Int. J. Test.* 8(4):315–33

Bartram D. 2009. The international test commission guidelines on computer-based and internet-delivered testing. *Ind. Organ. Psychol.: Perspect. Sci. Pract.* 2(1):11–13

Bartram D. 2013. Scalar equivalence of OPQ32: Big Five profiles of 31 countries. *J. Cross-Cult. Psychol.* 44(1):61–83

Beaty JC, Nye CD, Borneman MJ, Kantrowitz TM, Drasgow F, Grauer E. 2011. Proctored versus unproctored Internet tests: Are unproctored noncognitive tests as predictive of job performance? *Intl. J. Sel. Assess.* 19:1–10

Bernerth JB, Taylor SG, Walker HJ, Whitman DS. 2012. An empirical investigation of dispositional antecedents and performance-related outcomes of credit scores. *J. Appl. Psychol.* 97(2):469–78

Berry CM, Clark MA, McClure TK. 2011. Racial/ethnic differences in the criterion-related validity of cognitive ability tests: a qualitative and quantitative review. *J. Appl. Psychol.* 96(5):881–906

Berry CM, Sackett PR. 2009. Faking in personnel selection: tradeoffs in performance versus fairness resulting from two cut-score strategies. *Pers. Psychol.* 62(4):835–63

Biddle DA, Morris SB. 2011. Using Lancaster's mid-P correction to the Fisher's exact test for adverse impact analyses. *J. Appl. Psychol.* 96(5):956–65

Binning JF, Lebreton JM. 2009. Coherent conceptualization is useful for many things, and understanding validity is one of them. *Ind. Organ. Psychol.: Perspect. Sci. Pract.* 2(4):486–92

Bledow R, Frese M. 2009. A situational judgment test of personal initiative and its relationship to performance. *Pers. Psychol.* 62:229–58

Blickle G, Momm TS, Kramer J, Mierke J, Liu Y, Ferris GR. 2009. Construct and criterion-related validation of a measure of emotional reasoning skills: a two-study investigation. *Int. J. Sel. Assess.* 17:101–18

Bobko P, Roth PL. 2013. Reviewing, categorizing, and analyzing the literature on black–white mean differences for predictors of job performance: verifying some perceptions and updating/correcting others. *Pers. Psychol.* 66:91–126

Boudreau JW. 2010. *Retooling HR.* Boston, MA: Harv. Bus. Sch. Publ.

Breaugh JA. 2009. The use of biodata for employee selection: past research and future directions. *Hum. Resour. Manag. Rev.* 19:219–31

Breuker J. 2013. A cognitive science perspective on knowledge acquisition. *Int. J. Hum. Comput. Stud.* 71(2):177–83

Brown V, Vaughn E. 2011. The writing on the (Facebook) wall: the use of social networking sites in hiring decisions. *J. Bus. Psychol.* 10:11–21

Brummel BJ, Rupp DE, Spain SM. 2009. Constructing parallel simulation exercises for assessment centers and other forms of behavioral assessment. *Pers. Psychol.* 62(1):135–70

Caligiuri P, Paul KB. 2010. *Selection in Multinational Organizations.* New York: Routledge/Taylor & Francis

Caligiuri P, Tarique I, Jacobs R. 2009. Selection for international assignments. *Hum. Resour. Manag. Rev.* 19:251–62

Campbell JP. 1990. *Modeling the Performance Prediction Problem in Industrial and Organizational Psychology.* Palo Alto, CA: Consult. Psychol. Press

Campion MA, Fink AA, Ruggeberg BJ, Carr L, Phillips GM, Odman RB. 2011. Doing competencies well: best practices in competency modeling. *Pers. Psychol.* 64(1):225–62

Carey T, Herst D, Chan W. 2010. Global selection: selection in international contexts. In *Going Global: Practical Applications and Recommendations for HR and OD Professionals in the Global Workplace*, ed. K Lundby, pp. 143–74. San Francisco, CA: Jossey-Bass

Cascio WF, Aguinis H. 2008. Research in industrial and organizational psychology from 1963 to 2007: changes, choices, and trends. *J. Appl. Psychol.* 93:1062–81

Chapman DS, Zweig DI. 2005. Developing a nomological network for interview structure: antecedents and consequences of the structured selection interview. *Pers. Psychol.* 58(3):673–702

Chen YC, Tsai WC, Hu C. 2008. The influences of interviewer-related and situational factors on interviewer reactions to high structured job interviews. *Int. J. Hum. Resour. Manag.* 19:1056–71

Cherniss C. 2010. Emotional intelligence: towards clarification of a concept. *Ind. Organ. Psychol.: Perspect. Sci. Pract.* 3:110–26

Chiaburu DS, Oh I, Berry CM, Li N, Gardner RG. 2011. The five-factor model of personality traits and organizational citizenship behaviors: a meta-analysis. *J. Appl. Psychol.* 96(6):1140–66

Christian MS, Edwards BD, Bradley JC. 2010. Situational judgment tests: constructs assessed and a meta-analysis of their criterion-related validities. *Pers. Psychol.* 63:83–117

Christiansen ND, Janovics JE, Siers BP. 2010. Emotional intelligence in selection contexts: measurement method, criterion-related validity, and vulnerability to response distortion. *Int. J. Sel. Assess.* 18:87–101

Cleveland JN, Colella A. 2010. *Criterion Validity and Criterion Deficiency: What We Measure Well and What We Ignore*. New York: Routledge/Taylor & Francis

Coff R, Kryscynski D. 2011. Drilling for micro-foundations of human capital–based competitive advantages. *J. Manag.* 37:1429–43

Cohen DB, Aamodt MG, Dunleavy EM. 2010. *Technical Advisory Committee Report on Best Practices in Adverse Impact Analyses*. Washington, DC: Cent. Corp. Excell.

Colom R, Martínez-Molina A, Shih PC, Santacreu J. 2010. Intelligence, working memory, and multitasking performance. *Intelligence* 38(6):543–51

Compton P. 2013. Situated cognition and knowledge acquisition research. *Int. J. Hum. Comput. Stud.* 71(2):184–90

Converse PD, Oswald FL, Imus A, Hedricks C, Roy R, Butera H. 2008. Comparing personality test formats and warnings: effects on criterion-related validity and test-taker reactions. *Int. J. Sel. Assess.* 16:155–69

Converse PD, Pathak J, Quist J, Merbedone M, Gotlib T, Kostic E. 2010. Statement desirability ratings in forced-choice personality measure development: implications for reducing score inflation and providing trait-level information. *Hum. Perform.* 23(4):323–42

Crook TR, Todd SY, Combs JG, Woehr DJ, Ketchen DJ Jr. 2011. Does human capital matter? A meta-analysis of the relationship between human capital and firm performance. *J. Appl. Psychol.* 96(3):443–56

Cucina JM, Caputo PM, Thibodeaux HF, Maclane CN. 2012. Unlocking the key to biodata scoring: a comparison of empirical, rational, and hybrid approaches at different sample sizes. *Pers. Psychol.* 65(2):385–428

Davison HK, Maraist CC, Bing MN. 2011. Friend or foe? The promise and pitfalls of using social networking sites for HR activities. *J. Bus. Psychol.* 26:153–59

Dean MA, Roth PL, Bobko P. 2008. Ethnic and gender subgroup differences in assessment center ratings: a meta-analysis. *J. Appl. Psychol.* 93(3):685–91

DeCorte W, Sackett P, Lievens F. 2010. Selecting predictor subsets: considering validity and adverse impact. *Int. J. Sel. Assess.* 18(3):260–70

DeCorte W, Sackett PR, Lievens F. 2011. Designing pareto-optimal selection systems: formalizing the decisions required for selection system development. *J. Appl. Psychol.* 96(5):907–26

Derous E, Nguyen H, Ryan AM. 2009. Hiring discrimination against Arab minorities: interactions between prejudice and job characteristics. *Hum. Perform.* 22(4):297–320

Derous E, Ryan AM, Nguyen HD. 2012. Multiple categorization in resume screening: examining effects on hiring discrimination against Arab applicants in field and lab settings. *J. Organ. Behav.* 33(4):544–70

Dilchert S, Ones DS. 2009. Assessment center dimensions: individual differences correlates and meta-analytic incremental validity. *Int. J. Sel. Assess.* 17:254–70

Dorsey DW, Cortina JM, Luchman J. 2010. *Adaptive and Citizenship-Related Behaviors at Work*. New York: Routledge/Taylor & Francis

Drover W, Franczak J, Beltramini RF. 2012. A 30-year historical examination of ethical concerns regarding business ethics: Who's concerned? *J. Bus. Ethics* 111(4):431–38

Dunleavy EM, Mueller LM, Buonasera AK, Kuang DC, Dunleavy DG. 2008. On the consequences of frequent applicants in adverse impact analyses: a demonstration study. *Int. J. Sel. Assess.* 16:334–44

Eisner S. 2010. E-employment? College grad career building in a changing and electronic age. *Am. J. Bus. Educ.* 3(7): 25–40

Ellingson JA, McFarland LA. 2011. Understanding faking behavior through the lens of motivation: an application of VIE theory. *Hum. Perform.* 24:322–37

Fan J, Gao D, Carroll SA, Lopez FJ, Tian TS, Meng H. 2012. Testing the efficacy of a new procedure for reducing faking on personality tests within selection contexts. *J. Appl. Psychol.* 97(4):866–80

Farr JL, Tippins NT. 2010. *Handbook of Employee Selection: An Introduction and Overview*. New York: Routledge/Taylor & Francis

Finch DM, Edwards BD, Wallace JC. 2009. Multistage selection strategies: simulating the effects on adverse impact and expected performance for various predictor combinations. *J. Appl. Psychol.* 94:318–40

Foldes HJ, Duehr EE, Ones DS. 2008. Group differences in personality: meta-analyses comparing five U.S. racial groups. *Pers. Psychol.* 61(3):579–616

Furnham A. 2008. HR professionals' beliefs about, and knowledge of, assessment techniques and psychometric tests. *Int. J. Sel. Assess.* 16(3):300–5

Gibbons AM, Rupp DE. 2009. Dimension consistency as an individual difference: a new (old) perspective on the assessment center construct validity debate. *J. Manag.* 35:1154–80

Gibson WM, Caplinger JA. 2007. Transportation of validation results. In *Alternative Validation Strategies: Developing New and Leveraging Existing Validity Evidence*, ed. SM McPhail, pp. 29–81. New York: Wiley

Giumetti GW, Sinar EF. 2012. Don't you know me well enough yet? Comparing reactions of internal and external candidates to employment testing. *Int. J. Sel. Assess.* 20(2):139–48

Griffith RL, Peterson MH. 2011. One piece at a time: the puzzle of applicant faking and a call for theory. *Hum. Perform.* 24:291–301

Guion RM 2011. *Assessment, Measurement, and Prediction for Personnel Decisions*. New York: Routledge

Gutl C, Lankmayr K, Weinhofer J, Hofler M. 2011. Enhanced Automatic Question Creator—EAQC: concept, development and evaluation of an automatic test item creation tool to foster modern e-education. *Electron. J. e-Learn.* 9(1):23–38

Harms PD, Crede M. 2010. Remaining issues in emotional intelligence research: construct overlap, method artifacts and lack of incremental validity. *Ind. Organ. Psychol.: Perspect. Sci. Pract.* 3:154–58

Hattrup K. 2012. Using composite predictors in personnel selection. See Schmitt 2012, pp. 297–319

Highhouse S. 2008. Stubborn reliance on intuition and subjectivity in employee selection. *Ind. Organ. Psychol.: Perspect. Sci. Pract.* 1(3):333–42

Hoang TG, Truxillo DM, Erdogan B, Bauer TN. 2012. Cross-cultural examination of applicant reactions to selection methods: United States and Vietnam. *Int. J. Sel. Assess.* 20(2):209–19

Hoffman BJ, Meade A. 2012. Alternate approaches to understanding the psychometric properties of assessment centers: an analysis of the structure and equivalence of exercise ratings. *Int. J. Sel. Assess.* 20(1):82–97

Hoffman BJ, Melchers KG, Blair CA, Kleinmann M, Ladd RT. 2011. Exercises and dimensions are the currency of assessment centers. *Pers. Psychol.* 64(2):351–95

Hough L, Dilchert S. 2010. Personality: its measurement and validity for employee selection. In *Handbook of Employee Selection*, ed. J Farr, N Tippins, pp. 299–319. New York: Routledge/Taylor & Francis

Huffcutt AI. 2011. An empirical review of the employment interview construct literature. *Int. J. Sel. Assess.* 19:62–81

Iliescu D, Ilie A, Ispas D, Ion A. 2012. Emotional intelligence in personnel selection: applicant reactions, criterion, and incremental validity. *Int. J. Sel. Assess.* 20(3):347–58

Inceoglu I, Bartram D. 2012. Global leadership: the myth of multicultural competency. *Ind. Organ. Psychol.: Perspect. Sci. Pract.* 5(2):216–18

Indulska M, Dirk SH, Recker J. 2012. Quantitative approaches to content analysis: identifying conceptual drift across publication outlets. *Eur. J. Inf. Syst.* 21(1):49–69

Jansen A, Melchers KG, Lievens F, Kleinmann M, Brändli M, et al. 2012. Situation assessment as an ignored factor in the behavioral consistency paradigm underlying the validity of personnel selection procedures. *J. Appl. Psychol.* 96:326–41

Johnson JW, Steel P, Scherbaum CA, Hoffman CC, Jeanneret PR, Foster J. 2010. Validation is like motor oil: Synthetic is better. *Ind. Organ. Psychol.* 3:305–28

Jones RG, Born M. 2008. Assessor constructs in use as the missing component in validation of assessment center dimensions: a critique and directions for research. *Int. J. Sel. Assess.* 16:229–38

Joseph DL, Newman DA. 2010. Emotional intelligence: an integrative meta-analysis and cascading model. *J. Appl. Psychol.* 95(1):54–78

Kantrowitz TM, Dawson CR, Fetzer MS. 2011. Computer adaptive testing (CAT): a faster, smarter, and more secure approach to pre-employment testing. *J. Bus. Psychol.* 26(2):227–32

Kantrowitz TM, Grelle DM, Beaty JC, Wolf MB. 2012. Time is money: polychronicity as a predictor of performance across job levels. *Hum. Perform.* 25(2):114–37

Kehoe JF. 2008. Commentary on pareto-optimality as a rationale for adverse impact reduction: What would organizations do? *Int. J. Sel. Assess.* 16(3):195–200

Kepes S, Banks GC, McDaniel MA, Whetzel DL. 2012. Publication bias in the organizational sciences. *Organ. Res. Methods* 15:624–62

Klehe UC, Konig CJ, Richter GM, Kleinmann M, Melchers KG. 2008. Transparency in structured interviews: consequences for construct and criterion-related validity. *Hum. Perform.* 21:107–37

Klehe UC, Latham GP. 2005. The predictive and incremental validity of the situational and patterned behavior description interviews for team playing behavior. *Int. J. Sel. Assess.* 13(2):108–15

Kleinmann M, Klehe UC. 2011. Selling oneself: construct and criterion-related validity of impression management in structured interviews. *Hum. Perform.* 24:29–46

Kluemper DH, Rosen PA. 2009. Future employment selection methods: evaluating social networking web sites. *J. Manag. Psychol.* 24(6):567–80

Komar S, Brown DJ, Komar JA, Robie C. 2008. Faking and the validity of conscientiousness: a Monte Carlo investigation. *J. Appl. Psychol.* 93:140–54

König CJ, Klehe U, Berchtold M, Kleinmann M. 2010. Reasons for being selective when choosing personnel selection procedures. *Int. J. Sel. Assess.* 18:17–27

Kuhn K. 2012. The controversy over credit checks in selection: using public discourse to gain insight into divergent beliefs, concerns, and experiences. *J. Manag. Inq.* 21(3):331–47

Kuncel NR. 2008. Some new (and old) suggestions for improving personnel selection. *Ind. Organ. Psychol.: Perspect. Sci. Pract.* 1(3):343–46

LaHuis DM, Copeland D. 2009. Investigating faking using a multilevel logistic regression approach to measuring person fit. *Organ. Res. Methods* 12(2):296–319

Landers RN, Sackett PR, Tuzinski KA. 2011. Retesting after initial failure, coaching rumors, and warnings against faking in online personality measures for selection. *J. Appl. Psychol.* 96(1):202–10

Lang JWB, Kersting M, Hulsheger UR, Lang J. 2010. General mental ability, narrower cognitive abilities, and job performance: the perspective of the nested-factors model of cognitive abilities. *Pers. Psychol.* 63:595–640

Le H, Oh IS, Robbins SB, Ilies R, Holland E, Westrick P. 2011. Too much of a good thing: curvilinear relationships between personality traits and job performance. *J. Appl. Psychol.* 96(1):113–33

Le H, Oh IS, Shaffer JA, Schmidt FL. 2007. Implications of methodological advances for the practice of personnel selection: how practitioners benefit from recent developments in meta-analysis. *Acad. Manag. Perspect.* 21(3):6–15

Levashina J, Morgeson FP, Campion MA. 2012. Tell me some more: exploring how verbal ability and item verifiability influence responses to biodata questions in a high-stakes selection context. *Pers. Psychol.* 65(2):359–83

Lievens F, Klehe U, Libbrecht N. 2011. Applicant versus employee scores on self-report emotional intelligence measures. *J. Pers. Psychol.* 10(2):89–95

Lievens F, Patterson F. 2011. The validity and incremental validity of knowledge tests, low-fidelity simulations, and high-fidelity simulations for predicting job performance in advanced-level high-stakes selection. *J. Appl. Psychol.* 96(5):927–40

Lievens F, Peeters H, Schollaert E. 2008. Situational judgment tests: a review of recent research. *Pers. Rev.* 37:426–41

Lievens F, Reeve CL, Heggestad ED. 2007. An examination of psychometric bias due to retesting on cognitive ability tests in selection settings. *J. Appl. Psychol.* 92(6):1672–82

Lievens F, Sackett PR. 2012. The validity of interpersonal skills assessment via situational judgment tests for predicting academic success and job performance. *J. Appl. Psychol.* 97(2):460–68

Lievens F, Sackett PR, Buyse T. 2009. The effects of response instructions on situational judgment test performance and validity in a high-stakes context. *J. Appl. Psychol.* 94:1095–101

Lievens F, Van Keer E, Volckaert E. 2010. Gathering behavioral samples through a computerized and standardized assessment center exercise: Yes, it is possible. *J. Pers. Psychol.* 9(2):94–98

Luecht RM. 2000. *Implementing the computer-adaptive sequential testing (CAST) framework to mass produce high quality computer-adaptive and mastery tests.* Paper presented at Annu. Meet. Natl. Counc. Meas. Educ., New Orleans, La., April 25–27

Macan T. 2009. The employment interview: a review of current studies and directions for future research. *Hum. Resour. Manag. Rev.* 19:203–18

MacKenzie WI, Ployhart RE, Weekley JA, Ehlers C. 2010. Contextual effects on SJT responses: an examination of construct validity and mean differences across applicant and incumbent contexts. *Hum. Perform.* 23:1–21

Maltarich MA, Nyberg AJ, Reilly G. 2010. A conceptual and empirical analysis of the cognitive ability–voluntary turnover relationship. *J. Appl. Psychol.* 95:1058–70

Marcus B. 2009. "Faking" from the applicant's perspective: a theory of self-presentation in personnel selection settings. *Int. J. Sel. Assess.* 17:417–30

Matton N, Vautier S, Raufaste E. 2011. Test-specificity of the advantage of retaking cognitive ability tests. *Int. J. Sel. Assess.* 19:11–17

Maurer SD, Cook DP. 2011. Using company web sites to e-recruit qualified applicants: a job marketing based review of theory-based research. *Comput. Hum. Behav.* 27(1):106–17

McDaniel MA. 2007. Validity generalization as a test validation approach. In *Alternative Validation Strategies: Developing New and Leveraging Existing Validity Evidence*, ed. SM McPhail, pp. 159–80. New York: Wiley

McDaniel MA, Psotka J, Legree PJ, Yost AP, Weekley JA. 2011. Toward an understanding of situational judgment item validity and group differences. *J. Appl. Psychol.* 96:327–36

McNelly T, Ruggeberg BJ, Hall CR. 2011. Web-based management simulations: technology-enhanced assessment for executive-level selection and development. In *Technology-Enhanced Assessment of Talent*, ed. NT Tippins, S Adler, pp. 253–66. San Francisco, CA: Jossey-Bass

Meade AW, Tonidandel S. 2010. Not seeing clearly with Cleary: what test bias analyses do and do not tell us. *Ind. Organ. Psychol.: Perspect. Sci. Pract.* 3(2):192–205

Melchers KG, Kleinmann M, Prinz MA. 2010. Do assessors have too much on their plates? The effects of simultaneously rating multiple assessment center candidates on rating quality. *Int. J. Sel. Assess.* 18(3):329–41

Melchers KG, Lienhardt N, von Aarburg M, Kleinmann M. 2011. Is more structure really better? A comparison of frame-of-reference training and descriptively anchored rating scales to improve interviewers' rating quality. *Pers. Psychol.* 64:53–87

Meriac JP, Hoffman BJ, Woehr DJ, Fleisher MS. 2008. Further evidence for the validity of assessment center dimensions: a meta-analysis of the incremental criterion-related validity of dimension ratings. *J. Appl. Psychol.* 93(5):1042–52

Meyer JP, Hecht TD, Gill H, Toplonytsky L. 2010. Person-organization (culture) fit and employee commitment under conditions of organizational change: a longitudinal study. *J. Vocat. Behav.* 76(3):458–73

Motowidlo SJ, Beier ME. 2010. Differentiating specific job knowledge from implicit trait policies in procedural knowledge measured by a situational judgment test. *J. Appl. Psychol.* 95:321–33

Mount MK, Oh I, Burns M. 2008. Incremental validity of perceptual speed and accuracy over general mental ability. *Pers. Psychol.* 61(1):113–39

Mumford TV, Van Iddekinge CH, Morgeson FP, Campion MA. 2008. The team role test: development and validation of a team role knowledge situational judgment test. *J. Appl. Psychol.* 93:250–67

Munsterberg H. 1913. *Psychology and Industrial Efficiency*. Boston, MA/New York: Houghton Mifflin

Murphy KR. 2009. Content validation is useful for many things, but validity isn't one of them. *Ind. Organ. Psychol.: Perspect. Sci. Pract.* 2:465–68

Murphy KR, Dzieweczynski JL, Zhang Y. 2009. Positive manifold limits the relevance of content-matching strategies for validating selection test batteries. *J. Appl. Psychol.* 94(4):1018–31

Murphy KR, Jacobs RR. 2012. Using effect size measures to reform the determination of adverse impact in equal employment litigation. *Psychol. Public Policy Law* 18(3):477–99

Ndoye A, Ritzhaupt AD, Parker MA. 2012. Use of ePortfolios in K-12 teacher hiring in North Carolina: perspectives of school principals. *Int. J. Educ. Policy Leadersh.* 7(4):1–10

Newman DA, Joseph DL, MacCann C. 2010. Emotional intelligence and job performance: the importance of emotion regulation and emotional labor context. *Ind. Organ. Psychol.: Perspect. Sci. Pract.* 3:159–64

Newman DA, Lyon JS. 2009. Recruitment efforts to reduce adverse impact: targeted recruiting for personality, cognitive ability, and diversity. *J. Appl. Psychol.* 94:298–317

Nikolaou I. 2011. Core processes and applicant reactions to the employment interview: an exploratory study in Greece. *Int. J. Hum. Resour. Manag.* 22(10):2185–201

O'Boyle EH, Forsyth DR, Banks GC, McDaniel MA. 2012. A meta-analysis of the dark triad and work behavior: a social exchange perspective. *J. Appl. Psychol.* 97(3):557–79

O'Brien J. 2008. Interviewer resistance to structure. *Ind. Organ. Psychol.: Perspect. Sci. Pract.* 1(3):367–69

Ones DS, Dilchert S, Viswesvaran C, Salgado JF. 2010. Cognitive abilities. In *Handbook of Employee Selection*, ed. JL Farr, NT Tippins, pp. 255–76. Mahwah, NJ: Erlbaum

Ones DS, Viswesvaran C, Schmidt FL. 2012. Integrity tests predict counterproductive work behaviors and job performance well: comment on Van Iddekinge, Roth, Raymark, and Odle-Dusseau 2012. *J. Appl. Psychol.* 97(3):537–42

Oostrom JK, Bos-Broekema L, Serlie AW, Born MP, Van der Molen HT. 2012. A field study of pretest and posttest reactions to a paper-and-pencil and a computerized in-basket exercise. *Hum. Perform.* 25(2): 95–113

Ordanini A, Silvestri G. 2008. Recruitment and selection services: efficiency and competitive reasons in the outsourcing of HR practices. *Int. J. Hum. Resour. Manag.* 19:372–91

Oswald FL, Hough L. 2012. I-O 2.0 from intelligence 1.5: staying (just) behind the cutting edge of intelligence theories. *Ind. Organ. Psychol.* 5:172–75

Outtz JL, ed. 2010. *Adverse Impact: Implications for Organizational Staffing and High Stakes Selection*. New York: Routledge/Taylor & Francis

Ployhart RE, Holtz BC. 2008. The diversity-validity dilemma: strategies for reducing racioethnic and sex subgroup differences and adverse impact in selection. *Pers. Psychol.* 61(1):153–72

Ployhart RE, Moliterno TP. 2011. Emergence of the human capital resource: a multilevel model. *Acad. Manag. Rev.* 36:127–50

Ployhart RE, Van Iddekinge C, MacKenzie W. 2011. Acquiring and developing human capital in service contexts: the interconnectedness of human capital resources. *Acad. Manag. J.* 54:353–68

Ployhart RE, Weekley JA, Ramsey J. 2009. The consequences of human resource stocks and flows: a longitudinal examination of unit service orientation and unit effectiveness. *Acad. Manag. J.* 52:996–1015

Postlethwaite BE, Giluk TL, Schmidt FL. 2012. I-O psychologists and intelligence research: active, aware, and applied. *Ind. Organ. Psychol.* 5:186–88

Potosky D. 2008. A conceptual framework for the role of the administration medium in the personnel assessment process. *Acad. Manag. Rev.* 33(3):629–48

PriceWaterhouseCoopers. 2010. *Talent Mobility 2020: The Next Generation of International Assignments*. http://www.pwc.com/gx/en/managing-tomorrows-people/future-of-work/pdf/talent-mobility-2020.pdf

Putka DJ, Hoffman BJ. 2013. Clarifying the contribution of assessee-, dimension-, exercise-, and assessor-related effects to reliable and unreliable variance in assessment center ratings. *J. Appl. Psychol.* 98(1):114–33

Pyburn KM, Ployhart RE, Kravitz DA. 2008. The diversity-validity dilemma: overview and legal context. *Pers. Psychol.* 61(1):143–51

Riggio RE. 2010. Before emotional intelligence: research on nonverbal, emotional and social competencies. *Ind. Organ. Psychol.: Perspect. Sci. Pract.* 3:178–82

Ryan AM, Boyce AS, Ghumman S, Jundt D, Schmidt G, Gibby R. 2009. Going global: cultural values and perceptions of selection procedures. *Appl. Psychol.* 58(4):520–56

Ryan AM, Huth M. 2008. Not much more than platitudes? A critical look at the utility of applicant reactions research. *Hum. Resour. Manag. Rev.* 18(3):119–32

Ryan AM, Powers C. 2012. Workplace diversity. See Schmitt 2012, pp. 814–31

Ryan AM, Tippins N. 2009. *Designing and Implementing Global Selection Systems.* West Sussex, UK: Wiley-Blackwell

Sackett PR, Lievens F. 2008. Personnel selection. *Annu. Rev. Psychol.* 59:419–50

Sackett PR, Schmitt N. 2012. On reconciling conflicting meta-analytic findings regarding integrity test validity. *J. Appl. Psychol.* 97:550–56

Sanchez J, Levine E. 2012. The rise and fall of job analysis and the future of work analysis. *Annu. Rev. Psychol.* 63:397–425

Scherbaum C, Goldstein H, Yusko K, Ryan R, Hanges PJ. 2012. Intelligence 2.0: reestablishing a research program on *g* in I-O psychology. *Ind. Organ. Psychol.* 5:128–48

Schippman JS. 2010. Competencies, job analysis, and the next generation of modeling. In *Handbook of Workplace Assessment*, ed. JC Scott, DH Reynolds, pp. 197–231. San Francisco, CA: Jossey-Bass

Schleicher DJ, Van Iddekinge CH, Morgeson FP, Campion MA. 2010. If at first you don't succeed, try, try again: understanding race, age, and gender differences in retesting score improvement. *J. Appl. Psychol.* 95(4):603–17

Schmitt N. 2007. The value of personnel selection: reflections on some remarkable claims. *Acad. Manag. Perspect.* 21:19–23

Schmitt N. 2012. *The Oxford Handbook of Personnel Assessment and Selection.* New York: Oxford Univ. Press

Schollaert E, Lievens F. 2012. Building situational stimuli in assessment center exercises: Do specific exercise instructions and role-player prompts increase the observability of behavior? *Hum. Perform.* 25(3):255–71

Scott JC, Lezotte DV. 2012. Web-based assessments. See Schmitt 2012, pp. 485–513

Silzer R, Jeanneret R. 2011. Individual psychological assessment: a practice and science in search of common ground. *Ind. Organ. Psychol.* 4:270–96

Sojka JZ, Deeter-Schmelz D. 2008. Need for cognition and affective orientation as predictors of sales performance: an investigation of main and interaction effects. *J. Bus. Psychol.* 22(3):179–90

Stark S, Chernyshenko OS, Drasgow F, White LA. 2012. Adaptive testing with multidimensional pairwise preference items: improving the efficiency of personality and other noncognitive assessments. *Organ. Res. Methods* 15(3):463–87

Stewart GL, Darnold T, Barrick MR, Dustin SD. 2008. Exploring the handshake in employment interviews. *J. Appl. Psychol.* 93:1139–46

Swider BW, Barrick MR, Harris TB, Stoverink AC. 2011. Managing and creating an image in the interview: the role of interviewee initial impressions. *J. Appl. Psychol.* 96:1275–88

Tett RP, Simonet DV. 2011. Faking in personality assessment: a "multisaturation" perspective on faking as performance. *Hum. Perform.* 24(4):302–21

Thornton GC. 2009. Evidence of content matching is evidence of validity. *Ind. Organ. Psychol.: Perspect. Sci. Pract.* 2(4):469–74

Thornton GC, Gibbons AM. 2009. Validity of assessment centers for personnel selection. *Hum. Resour. Manag. Rev.* 19:169–87

Tippins NT. 2009. Internet alternatives to traditional proctored testing: Where are we now? *Ind. Organ. Psychol.: Perspect. Sci. Pract.* 2(1):2–10

Tippins NT, Adler S. 2011 *Technology-Enhanced Assessment of Talent.* San Francisco, CA: Jossey-Bass

Truxillo DM, Bodner TE, Bertolino M, Bauer TN, Yonce CA. 2009. Effects of explanations on applicant reactions: a meta-analytic review. *Int. J. Sel. Assess.* 17(4):346–61

Tsai W, Chi N, Huang T, Hsu A. 2011. The effects of applicant résumé contents on recruiters' hiring recommendations: the mediating roles of recruiter fit perceptions. *Appl. Psychol.* 60(2):231–54

van Hooft EAJ, Born MP. 2012. Intentional response distortion on personality tests: using eye-tracking to understand response processes when faking. *J. Appl. Psychol.* 97(2):301–16

Van Iddekinge CH, Ferris GR, Perrewe PL, Perryman AA, Blass FR, Heetderks TD. 2009. Effects of selection and training on unit-level performance over time: a latent growth modeling approach. *J. Appl. Psychol.* 94:829–43

Van Iddekinge CH, Ployhart RE. 2008. Developments in the criterion-related validation of selection procedures: a critical review and recommendations for practice. *Pers. Psychol.* 61(4):871–925

Van Iddekinge CH, Putka DJ, Campbell JP. 2011a. Reconsidering vocational interests for personnel selection: the validity of an interest-based selection test in relation to job knowledge, job performance, and continuance intentions. *J. Appl. Psychol.* 96(1):13–33

Van Iddekinge CH, Roth PL, Putka D, Lanivich SE. 2011b. Are you interested? A meta-analysis of relations between vocational interests and employee performance and turnover. *J. Appl. Psychol.* 96:1167–94

Van Iddekinge CH, Roth PL, Raymark PH, Odle-Dusseau H. 2012. The criterion-related validity of integrity tests: an updated meta-analysis. *J. Appl. Psychol.* 97(3):499–530

Westring AJF, Oswald FL, Schmitt N, Drzakowski S, Imus A, et al. 2009. Estimating trait and situational variance in a situational judgment test. *Hum. Perform.* 22:44–63

Whetzel DL, McDaniel MA. 2009. Situational judgment tests: an overview of current research. *Hum. Resour. Manag. Rev.* 19:188–202

Whetzel DL, McDaniel MA, Nguyen NT. 2008. Subgroup differences in situational judgment test performance: a meta-analysis. *Hum. Perform.* 21(3):291–309

Winkler S, König CJ, Kleinmann M. 2010. Single attribute utility analysis may be futile, but this can't be the end of the story: causal chain analysis as an alternative. *Pers. Psychol.* 63:1041–65

Wright PM, McMahan GC. 2011. Exploring human capital: putting human back into strategic human resource management. *Hum. Resour. Manag. J.* 21:93–104

Zickar MJ, Lake CJ. 2011. Practice agenda: innovative uses of technology-enhanced assessment. In *Technology-Enhanced Assessment of Talent*, ed. NT Tippins, S Adler, pp. 394–417. San Francisco, CA: Jossey-Bass

Zualkernan IA, Raza A, Karim A. 2012. Curriculum-guided crowd sourcing of assessments in a developing country. *J. Educ. Technol. Soc.* 15(4):14–26

Personality, Well-Being, and Health*

Howard S. Friedman[1] and Margaret L. Kern[2]

[1]Department of Psychology, University of California, Riverside, California 92521;
email: Howard.Friedman@ucr.edu

[2]Department of Psychology, University of Pennsylvania, Philadelphia, Pennsylvania 19104;
email: mkern@sas.upenn.edu

Annu. Rev. Psychol. 2014. 65:719–42

The *Annual Review of Psychology* is online at
http://psych.annualreviews.org

This article's doi:
10.1146/annurev-psych-010213-115123

*The authors contributed equally to this article.

Keywords

lifespan perspective, trajectories, conscientiousness

Abstract

A lifespan perspective on personality and health uncovers new causal pathways and provides a deeper, more nuanced approach to interventions. It is unproven that happiness is a direct cause of good health or that negative emotion, worry, and depression are significant direct causes of disease. Instead, depression-related characteristics are likely often reflective of an already-deteriorating trajectory. It is also unproven that challenging work in a demanding environment usually brings long-term health risks; on the contrary, individual strivings for accomplishment and persistent dedication to one's career or community often are associated with sizeable health benefits. Overall, a substantial body of recent research reveals that conscientiousness plays a very significant role in health, with implications across the lifespan. Much more caution is warranted before policy makers offer narrow health recommendations based on short-term or correlational findings. Attention should be shifted to individual trajectories and pathways to health and well-being.

Contents

INTRODUCTION

Although the relationships among personality, well-being, and health have been studied for millennia—since the days of the bodily humors proposed by Hippocrates and Galen—the field remains riddled with conceptual confusion, method artifacts, and misleading conclusions. When inferences drawn from this field are based on incomplete models, they lead to wasteful and even harmful interventions and treatments. Scientists and laypersons alike may overgeneralize from short-term personality correlates of health and overlook long-term causal processes.

There is nevertheless excellent evidence that individual characteristics from earlier in life are reliable predictors and likely causal elements of health later in life. An especially striking finding to emerge in recent years is that a host of characteristics and behaviors associated with the broad personality dimension of conscientiousness is predictive of health and longevity, from childhood through old age. The reasons for these associations are complex and sometimes appear paradoxical, as there are multiple simultaneous causal links to health. The modern study of personality, however, provides many of the concepts, tools, and models necessary for a deeper and more accurate understanding of health, well-being, and long life.

In particular, there is considerable misapprehension concerning the pathways to good health. In this article, we review many of the causes and consequences of the associations among personality, behavior, well-being, and health and longevity. We do this in the context of expanded models and perspectives. Because much of the confusion in the area of personality and health arises from ambiguous definitions, weak measurement, and overlapping constructs of health, we begin with health outcomes. We then review and scrutinize the connections among happiness and health, and among depression, worry, and disease, which likely are not what they first appear to be. Finally, we explain and evaluate the emerging consensus on the significance of conscientiousness across the lifespan and offer suggestions for health interventions.

OUTCOMES

Study of personality—an individual's relatively stable predispositions and patterns of thinking, feeling, and acting—and its relationships to well-being and health continues to be plagued by an overreliance on self-report measures. This is a special problem because many of the questions (or items) used to assess personality are the same questions used to assess health and well-being. Much better assessment strategies are needed.

Outcome measures of well-being may ask individuals how good they feel, how well they cope, and how satisfied they are with life. These are very similar to personality measures of low neuroticism ("am relaxed most of the time"; "am calm"; "am not angry or depressed") and high agreeableness ("am on good terms with others"; "am warm and sympathetic"). Thus it is not surprising that people who report having a joyful, cheerful, relaxed, and agreeable personality also report life satisfaction, emotional thriving, and well-being. Such correlations have little to say about achieving well-being. Relatedly, studies of patient populations often suffer from personality selection artifacts (biases) because neurotic individuals are more likely to report symptoms (such as chest pain) and to seek medical care than nonneurotics, even when there is little or no discernable organic disease. Although such serious measurement artifacts have been recognized for decades (Watson & Pennebaker 1989), erroneous causal deductions are still common.

Analogous issues plague self-report measures of physical health. The commonly used multipurpose Short-Form (36) Health Survey (SF-36), or the closely related RAND 36-Item Health Survey (RAND-36), can be very useful for assessing overall disease burden. However, the SF-36 contains multiple dimensions, including behavioral dysfunction, objective reports, subjective rating, and distress and well-being (Ware 2004). So employing the full SF-36—without sufficient attention to its components—as an outcome measure of health in studies of personality and health again confounds the predictor with the outcome because individuals who report a neurotic, distressed personality also report pain, feeling sick, and a poor sense of well-being. Sometimes this flaw is obfuscated by invoking the significant well-established finding that self-rated health predicts mortality risk (Idler & Benyamini 1997). That is, the argument asserts that self-reported personality predicts self-reported health, and self-reported health predicts mortality, and so therefore a study of self-reported personality and self-reported health is really a study of personality and physical health. A valuable scientific approach, however, necessitates multimethod assessments of personality and behavior coupled with more objective measures of health outcomes.

Longevity

Longevity is, for most purposes, the single best measure of health. First, it is highly reliable and valid. Although there is some unreliability of public records such as birth certificates and death certificates, it is generally the case that if a death certificate shows that a man died on April 15, 2013 at age 80 from septicemia, then it is very likely that he lived eight decades. It is also very likely that he is currently in terrible "health," and so health validity is strong. Life expectancy is thus one of the key measures of public health used worldwide.

Second, using longevity as the outcome helps avoid what we call the "all-cause dilemma" artifact. These are cases in which a person has a disease such as cancer, and, for example, the prostate or breast is removed, and then soon after the individual dies not of cancer but of something else. If the focus of the study is on cancer survival (as a function of personality, coping, and treatment), the death may not be picked up; that is, the cancer did not progress and/or the person did not die of cancer. The patient is considered to be "cured" of cancer even if the patient dies of a different cause. In other words, much research on personality and health is limited and even distorted by the still-common focus on single-disease conditions, with insufficient attention to overall outcomes, especially overall mortality risk.

Relatedly, it is misleading to speak of personality traits or coping styles that predict cancer risk or heart disease risk (e.g., type A personality) if such factors equally predict (are equally relevant to) other diseases. And, in fact, the basic five-factor personality dimensions (particularly conscientiousness, neuroticism, and extraversion, but also often agreeableness and openness) do predict multiple diseases (Friedman 2007, Goodwin & Friedman 2006). This issue was noted many years ago (Friedman & Booth-Kewley 1987), but studies of personality predictors of particular diseases, without sufficient regard for the broader context, are still common. Rigorous research programs on personality, well-being, and health would do better to employ multidimensional assessments of both personality and health and, whenever possible, to include follow-ups to measure all-cause mortality or multiple hard outcomes of disease.

Quality of Life

General health is well captured by longevity because the people who live the longest usually are not those who have been struggling with diabetes, cancer, heart disease, and other chronic disorders. But measures that also directly consider the quality of life—such as the number of years that one lives without significant impairment—are of increasing interest. The World Health Organization uses healthy life expectancy (HALE), defined as years lived without significant impairment from disease or injury. The European Union has developed an indicator of disability-adjusted life expectancy ("Healthy Life Years"). Health psychologists such as Robert Kaplan (2002) have advocated for health-related quality-of-life measures that take into account years of life and the amount of disability while minimizing the value of any "benefits" that come from curing one disease only to have it be replaced by another. Such robust measures include rigorous definitions of disability—such as inability to work, walk, dress, converse, and remember—rather than simply self-report measures of how one feels.

Multiple Outcomes

Consistent with the World Health Organization's definition of health as composed of physical, mental, and social components, we have found (in our own research) that it is empirically and heuristically useful to distinguish and use at least five core health outcomes in addition to longevity (Friedman et al. 2010, Friedman & Martin 2011; see also Aldwin et al. 2006, Baltes & Baltes 1990, Rowe & Kahn 1987). In brief, they encompass the following:

(*a*) Physical health (the ability and energy to complete a range of daily tasks; either diagnosed or not diagnosed with organic disease such as heart disease or cancer). Physical health is defined by an evaluation or evidence-based judgment by a health professional, such as an exam that might be used to qualify for medical treatment or disability payments. (*b*) Subjective well-being (positive mood; life satisfaction). Subjective well-being is often seen as having both an emotional component (frequency of positive and negative emotions) and a cognitive component of self-perceived life satisfaction (Diener et al. 2013). (*c*) Social competence (successful engagement in activities with others). Social competence includes the ability to maintain close relationships, to have a supportive social and/or community network, and to support others. (*d*) Productivity (continued achievement; contributing to society). Productivity involves work that has potentially monetary/economic (paid) value or contributions of recognizable artistic, intellectual, or humanitarian value. With an aging population in many countries, productivity is taking on new meanings and importance (Fried 2012). (*e*) Cognitive function (the ability to think clearly and remember) is defined in terms of mental processes involved in symbolic operations, such as memory, perception, language, spatial ability, decision making, and reasoning. (*f*) Longevity (see Longevity section above). As needed and when possible, some of these outcomes can be multiplied by years to produce quality-of-life-years measures.

These different outcomes are usually correlated (and sometimes highly correlated) with each other. However, a key research challenge is to ascertain the causes of these outcomes and the causal roles, if any, that are played by each of these factors in the others, and the answers will require both independent multimethod assessment and appropriate research designs.

Limits of Biomarkers as Outcomes

A related conundrum that often bedevils research on personality, well-being, and health involves screening, biomarkers, and overdiagnosis (Welch et al. 2011). Many examples exist of interventions that affect a biomarker of disease risk (sometimes termed a surrogate endpoint) but that do not improve quality of life or mortality risk because the causal links are not as expected. In fact, many medical interventions decrease quality of life for many while improving it for only a few, even though short-term biomarkers look better. The US Food and Drug Administration (FDA) now requires that any new class of drug must have studies with hard disease or mortality outcomes, because evaluating only the intermediate outcomes such as blood biomarkers has led to problematic or dangerous treatments in the past (cf. DeMets 2013). For example, lipid levels (especially cholesterol) are very good predictors of cardiovascular-relevant mortality risk, and niacin improves lipid levels, but taking niacin does not decrease mortality risk. Homocysteine (an amino acid) is a good predictor of heart disease, and B vitamins lower homocysteine levels, but B vitamins do not in turn lower disease risk (for an Institute of Medicine report on surrogate endpoints, see Micheel & Ball 2010). Screening for prostate cancer with the prostate-specific antigen (PSA) biomarker is probably the most notorious case of causing significant harm to patients: Most men with elevated PSA levels will never develop symptoms of prostate cancer, but many will face morbidity if treated; overdiagnosis is common in other cancer screens as well (Welch & Black 2010, Welch et al. 2011). What all this means for research on personality and health is that limited-time measurements of outcomes such as cortisol level, vagal tone, and immune markers do not necessarily provide indicators of future long-term health and longevity, especially since biomarkers naturally fluctuate as the body maintains or reestablishes homeostasis.

Biomarkers (particularly aggregations of biomarkers as an indication of chronic physiological dysfunction) become very important when they are studied as mediators of relations in fully specified models, such as if the progression of cancer can be shown to have slowed as a function of a psychosocial intervention that boosts the immune system. Biomarkers can best serve to elucidate the mediating mechanisms of personality-to-disease processes that are discovered in longer-term studies, but at present, such longitudinal mediation studies are quite rare.

HAPPINESS, SUBJECTIVE WELL-BEING, AND HEALTH

Some people thrive, stay generally healthy, recover quickly from illness, and live long, whereas other individuals of the same age, gender, and social class are miserable, often ill, and at higher risk of premature death. Personality, well-being, and physical health are intimately connected but not necessarily simply connected. The core question is sometimes thought to be, "Why do people become sick?" when it is really, "Who becomes sick and who stays well?"

Despite the fact that an individual's sense of well-being is fairly stable across time, a number of clever positive psychology interventions have been developed that increase happiness and the sense of well-being, even in depressed populations (Lyubomirsky & Layous 2013, Sin & Lyubomirsky 2009). But will such interventions also make people healthier? This is a very important issue for both conceptual and practical reasons. On the conceptual side, it matters how we think about the nature of psychological and physical health and the causal models we endorse (often implicitly) or construct. On the practical side, the true causal links between health and happiness impact what scientists, doctors, patients, public health programs, and societies can and should do to promote health. If happiness causes health, then positivity interventions will result in health and long life and thus have public health importance. However, health is highly complex, and as it turns out, multiple causal processes are simultaneously at work in preserving health or promoting disease, although not in the ways often assumed.

Power of Positive Emotion?

A popular model is the one made famous several decades ago by Norman Cousins, commentator and editor of the influential *Saturday Review* (Cousins 1979). Diagnosed with a paralyzing degenerative disease, Cousins checked himself out of the hospital and into a hotel room and treated himself with laughter. Against the odds, he recovered and thereafter publicized creativity and humor as being essential to medical treatment; this was a cultural turning point that spurred greater attention to how the mind could heal the body. An upshot of this work was the popular reemergence in health care of the idea that distress, grief, and psychological tension play key and direct roles in illness and that laughter and good cheer could and should be a core part of a cure. Watching films that you find funny, as Cousins did, will indeed make you feel happier, but should this be a central ingredient of medical care and health promotion?

This development was followed by a number of best-selling popular books, such as Bernie Siegel's *Love, Medicine and Miracles* (1986), and *Peace, Love and Healing* (1990), that were advertised as full of inspiring true stories of healing, gratitude, and love. At their best, such books provide help in relieving the distress of coping with serious illness and can encourage some patients and their families to follow prescribed treatment regimens and try to live healthier lives. At worst, they provide quack treatments for wishing away one's cancer or they blame illness upon personality defects. Despite years of published rebuttals of feel-good "cures," these errant beliefs still permeate discussions of personality and health.

Richard Sloan (2011) has traced this mind-over-matter, virtue-over-disease argument throughout twentieth-century American thought, from unconscious hostile impulses (supposedly causing ulcers, asthma, and more) to the best-selling book, *The Secret* (Byrne 2006), which teaches that you can "think" your way to health and wealth through cosmic energy. He notes, "Negative characteristics—anger, resentment, fear—were always associated with poorer health outcomes. One can search the literature in vain for diseases associated with positive characteristics" (Sloan 2011, p. 896). Whereas in Freud's time and thereafter, the ill were said to be repressed, conflicted, and hostile, today they are viewed as lacking joy, compassion, spirituality, and forgiveness. Despite such warnings as Sloan's, there is recurrent popular advice that a "be happy" mindset is a key to good health.

There is no doubt that subjective well-being and related concepts such as positive emotions are associated with better self-reported health, lower morbidity, less pain, and longevity (Chida & Steptoe 2008, Diener & Chan 2011, Howell et al. 2007, Lyubomirsky et al. 2005, Pressman & Cohen 2005, Veenhoven 2008). An analysis across 142 nations found that positive emotions predict better self-rated health around the world, with positive emotion trumping hunger, shelter, and safety in predictive value (Pressman et al. 2013). A premature conclusion is that by shifting the population to greater levels of happiness, health will thereby improve. Diener & Chan (2011) propose that there is good evidence "that subjective well-being causally influences health and longevity" (p. 21), but this is an empirical question that has not yet been resolved. We believe the truth is much more complex and that more inclusive models need to be specified. Progress in this field will depend on the construction of a complete nomological network and the testing of more elaborate causal pathways.

Actions or interventions that improve well-being might indirectly improve a person's physical function but not act directly. This is an important distinction. To take some obvious examples, people can feel happier by watching TV comedies, eating sugary foods, riding a Ferris wheel, taking cocaine, or partying. But they would not be healthier. On the other hand, taking long walks through the park each day, thriving at work, and maintaining high-quality intimate relationships with loved ones probably will have long-term impacts on both happiness and physical health. But these are much more difficult patterns to establish and maintain. Personality often underlies such broader lifestyle patterns in concert with genetic predispositions, environmental influences, and social relations. Further, as noted in the "Outcomes" section above, shifting people's perceptions of their health from "very good" to "excellent" is an analysis of subjective well-being, not health. We need broader causal models of the relevant relationships, such as the one shown in **Figure 1**.

General "life satisfaction" offers a more stable cognitive evaluation of life than does positive emotion alone. Satisfaction items have been answered by millions of people around the world over the past two decades. As with the simple (emotional well-being → health) model, life satisfaction predicts health and longevity, lower suicide risk, college and job retention, and marital success (Diener et al. 2013). But deeper analyses reveal that a simple causal model is incomplete. For example, in an eight-year study with over 900 individuals, cross-lagged relations between health and life satisfaction found that poor health predicted subsequent life dissatisfaction, but satisfaction did not prospectively predict changes in health (Gana et al. 2013). Moreover, it is now well documented that subjective well-being or happiness is adaptive in some contexts but maladaptive in others (see Ford & Mauss 2014, Gruber et al. 2011, Hershfield et al. 2013).

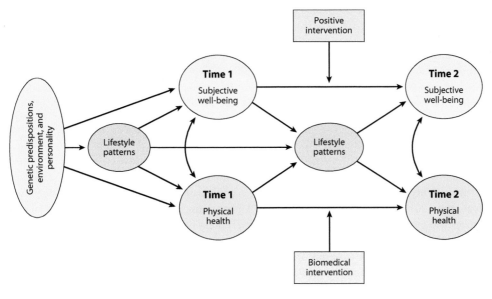

Figure 1

Correlated outcomes model. An example of a broader, more comprehensive causal model of relationships among personality, mediators and moderators, and correlated outcomes.

Meaning and Purpose

Beginning in the early 1960s, work by Viktor Frankl and others proposed that people function best when they have a sense of life purpose (cf. Steger 2009; see also Antonovsky 1979). From a eudaimonic perspective (which originated in debates about Aristotelian ethics), well-being comes not from positive emotion or happiness but rather from fulfilling one's potential, having a sense of meaning or purpose in life, having mastery over one's environment, experiencing spirituality, engaging in life, and maintaining positive relationships with others. Many scholars have argued persuasively that a meaningful life is not necessarily a happy one (Baumeister et al. 2013, King 2001, Ryff & Singer 2009). For example, holocaust survivor and Nobel Prize winner Elie Wiesel has written dozens of books and won dozens of distinguished humanitarian awards, but his is not a life of happiness, laughter, and positive emotion.

Considerable cross-sectional evidence links sense of purpose to various subjective well-being measures, including life satisfaction, self-esteem, ego resilience, and positive perceptions of the world (Steger 2012a). It is correlated with higher levels of agreeableness, extraversion, conscientiousness, and openness to experience, and with lower levels of neuroticism, depression, and psychoticism. Having a sense of purpose facilitates active life engagement, goal setting, and goal pursuit, so it is not surprising that some evidence suggests links between greater meaning/greater purpose and better physical health. For example, over a five-year period, purpose in life was associated with reduced mortality risk (Boyle et al. 2009; see also Ryff et al. 2004). But here again, fuller causal models are needed. That is, although some researchers propose that eudaimonic well-being enables optimal physiological functioning (Ryff & Singer 1998), a limited (well-being → health) model is typically applied, and almost all evidence is correlational or short term in nature. Further, Steger (2012b) notes that "there have been no tests of whether the way the brain strives to restore meaning in low-stakes lab experiments is sufficient to account for the kind of meaning and purpose in life that Frankl argued inspired his survival of Nazi concentration camps" (p. 382).

Some theories include meaning as a critical component of well-being and flourishing (e.g., Ryff & Keyes 1995, Seligman 2011), whereas others see sense of meaning as a motivating factor that leads to greater well-being. Ryan and colleagues (2006) note that rather than focusing on the outcome of feeling good, "eudaimonic conceptions focus on the *content* of one's life, and the *processes* involved in living well" (p. 140). Overall, although strong empirical support is currently lacking for sense of meaning as a vital factor in future health, it is a promising direction, especially because there is considerable evidence that persistent, planful striving for meaningful accomplishment is indeed a key pathway to health and longevity (see sections below titled Challenge and Health and Conscientiousness, Maturity, and Longevity).

Optimism

Optimism—characterized by a tendency toward positive expectations for the future and confidence in one's ability to cope with challenges—has been consistently linked to better health (Boehm & Kubzansky 2012, Carver & Connor-Smith 2010). Here again, caution is needed: When full models are spelled out, there is no good evidence for the healing power of positive thought (as a causal relationship). That is, there is little evidence that optimistic thinking will mobilize an immune system and cause tumors to shrink and increase longevity (Coyne & Tennen 2010). However, optimistic individuals set goals and persist longer despite challenges and setbacks (Carver et al. 2010, Lench 2011). Optimism can function as a self-regulating mechanism, with optimistic people more likely to persevere and engage toward a goal (Carver et al. 2010). Behavioral change programs that include goal-setting strategies can build self-efficacy and confidence for future challenges, creating resilience through challenge. Optimism can provide the motivation to move forward, if tempered by a realistic assessment of when to let go. And optimism can help individuals face the challenges of recuperation from disease.

In summary, although there are many ways to increase one's sense of well-being, only some of them will increase health. This is a critical distinction that becomes clearer with an examination of neuroticism, depression, and disease.

NEUROTICISM, DEPRESSION, WORRY, AND DISEASE

Are individuals who are worrying, tense, anxious, depressed, and emotionally labile more likely to face serious illness and premature death? Overall, the mixed findings concerning neuroticism and health are so striking and jumbled as to call into doubt the viability of further simple studies of these relationships. Instead, more sophisticated causal models are needed that include personality facets, multiple causal mechanisms, interactions with other variables, and consideration of biopsychosocial contexts.

Assumptions that neuroticism leads to disease have existed since ancient medicine, with excessive melancholic and phlegmatic humors believed to cause depression, cancer, rheumatism, fevers, and other disease (Friedman 2007). In reality, the ancients were simply (but insightfully) observing the same correlations seen today. With the discovery of hormones and the introduction of Walter Cannon's (1932) fight or flight model, the focus shifted toward physiological reactions to stress (hormonal instead of humoral explanations), but the hypothesized causal model did not change much.

According to this model, neuroticism leads to or facilitates chronic overactivation of the autonomic nervous system, disturbing homeostatic balance, in turn leading to pathological breakdown, chronic illness, and early mortality (Graham et al. 2006, McEwen 1993). The problem is that advice is then given to stop worrying, slow down, and relax. But a "healthy neuroticism" (Friedman 2000) is often a good thing, as an individual is vigilant about his or her health. For example, in the Terman Life Cycle Study, neuroticism (measured decades earlier) was protective against mortality risk for bereaved men (Taga et al. 2009). A study of over 11,000 Germans compared expected and actual life satisfaction across an 11-year period (Lang et al. 2013), finding that many individuals grew more pessimistic about their future satisfaction with increasing age, and this pessimism was associated with lower morbidity and mortality risk. Such pessimism may reflect a flexible, realistic adaptation to loss at older age (Baltes & Smith 2004).

Neuroticism is highly correlated with negative feelings (DeNeve & Cooper 1998) and, as noted, with health complaints and lower perceptions of health, but its causal role in health and well-being is complex and far from understood (Yap et al. 2012). Most importantly, neuroticism inconsistently predicts mortality risk, with some studies finding higher risk (Abas et al. 2002, Denollet et al. 1996, Schulz et al. 1996, Wilson et al. 2004) and many other studies finding null (Almada et al. 1991, Huppert & Whittington 1995, Iwasa et al. 2008, Mosing et al. 2012) or protective effects (Korten et al. 1999, Taga et al. 2009, Weiss & Costa 2005). Across four decades of adulthood in the Terman Life Cycle Study, neuroticism was most predictive of subjective well-being but least predictive of longevity (the most objective measure of health) (Friedman et al. 2010). The explanation for these findings is that personality trajectories and personality interactions with life events also matter, which strongly suggests that a simple neuroticism-to-poor-health model is incomplete (Chapman et al. 2010, Löckenhoff et al. 2009, Mroczek & Spiro 2007).

Depression

In a meta-analysis of psychological factors in heart disease published over 25 years ago, Booth-Kewley & Friedman (1987) uncovered the then-surprising fact that depression was an excellent

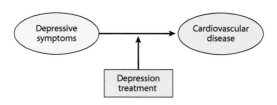

Figure 2

Simple depression and disease model. An overly simple, and generally ineffective, approach to treatment based on the stable correlation between depression and cardiovascular disease.

predictor of cardiovascular disease, although the focus at that time was on type A behavior as a predictor. Subsequent research has confirmed this discovery (Grippo & Johnson 2002, Miller et al. 1996, Rugulies 2002, Smith & Gallo 2001, Suls & Bunde 2005, Wulsin & Singal 2003) and has launched a series of efforts to prevent disease by treating depression—the model represented in **Figure 2**.

The American Heart Association recommends screening of patients for depression in cardiovascular care. Depressed patients with heart disease do indeed often have high levels of biomarkers associated with atherosclerosis (Lichtman et al. 2008), but claims that depression causes illness can confound predictors and outcomes if a full causal model is not specified. An important randomized study found that treating depression in recent heart attack patients did not reduce the risk of death or second heart attack (Berkman et al. 2003; see also Friedman 2011b, Thombs et al. 2013). A Cochrane database review of randomized trials of psychological interventions in adults with coronary heart disease found effects on depression, supporting the success of treating psychological symptoms (Whalley et al. 2011). But there was little evidence that the interventions affected the disease process, with no reduction in the total occurrence of nonfatal infarction or death. A recent meta-analysis of mental health treatments (antidepressants and psychotherapies) for improving secondary event risk and depression among patients with coronary heart disease again showed mental health treatments did not reduce total mortality (absolute risk reduction = −0.00), although there was a minor influence on coronary heart disease events (Rutledge et al. 2013). A French study with over 14,000 individuals found that although depression and mortality risk were strongly related (over the subsequent 15 years), this association was confounded by hostility (hostile ways of thinking), which is known to be relevant to injury (suicide, homicide, accidents) and to a host of unhealthy behaviors (Lemogne et al. 2010). Although there is no doubt that many diseases are associated with higher levels of anxiety and depression, the causal pathways have never been fully elucidated.

A lifespan perspective offers a better way of thinking about these matters by focusing attention on processes that develop over time, with predictors, pathways, and outcomes fully specified. For example, common symptoms in the days or weeks following a serious concussion (traumatic brain injury) are irritability, concentration difficulties, sleep disturbances, and depression. These are also core symptoms of posttraumatic stress disorder. It is also the case that these same symptoms can result from infections and other sources of immune system disruptions with increases of proinflammatory cytokines—as happens when an individual contracts the flu and suffers irritability, disordered sleep, anhedonia, and lethargy (Kemeny 2011). After menopause, not only the odds of heart disease but also the odds of depression for women are significantly increased (Bromberger et al. 2011). In all of these cases, depression and/or anxiety are not only significant correlates of illness but are also significant results of illness or of challenges to homeostasis.

The National Institute of Mental Health states that depression and anxiety are serious illnesses—that is, they are outcomes. In the classification of major depressive disorder in the *Diagnostic and Statistical Manual of Mental Disorders, Fourth Edition* (Am. Psychiatr. Assoc. 1994),

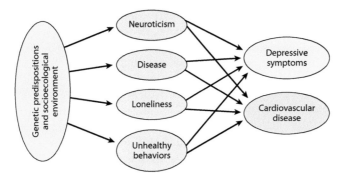

Figure 3

Elaborated depression and disease model. An evidence-based, more complete model that separates personality, social environment, genetics, behaviors, and disease, allowing for more comprehensive examination of causality. This figure is an example of promising directions, not a fully established inclusive model.

symptoms fall into categories of unhealthy thoughts (persistent sadness or empty feelings, worthlessness, helplessness, difficulty concentrating, thoughts of suicide), unhealthy behaviors (overeating or undereating, insomnia or excessive sleeping), unhealthy social relations (loss of interest in hobbies or activities including sex, withdrawal from others), and somatic symptoms (aches and pains, digestive problems, fatigue and decreased energy). Taking into account the genetic influences on depression and the fact that many anxious or depressed individuals self-medicate with cigarettes, mood-altering drugs, or alcohol, we have almost the full panoply of biopsychosocial factors in health and illness. Just as the typical (well-being → health) model is incomplete, the simple (depression → disease) model likely is wrong or at least incomplete. The depression-mortality relationship is confounded by personality, social environments, unhealthy behaviors, and genetic predispositions. A conclusion that depression is a direct cause of disease is unjustified. A more comprehensive model is illustrated in **Figure 3**.

Psychotherapy or advice to cheer up will not stop the progression of cancer or cardiovascular disease (Coyne & Tennen 2010, Thombs et al. 2013), but if a psychosocial treatment helps the person eat better, get out of bed, attend medical appointments, and connect with other people, it may indeed improve health. The precise causal links are very important because if the associations are not a function of mood induction, then interventions to improve positive mood or subjective well-being may be useless. There are no well-controlled studies showing that interventions to improve the chronic mood of neurotics result in direct physiological changes and consequent improvements in progression of cancer or risk of death. To the extent that depression is a result of the disruption of homeostasis rather than the cause of the disruption, many interventions to treat depression in an attempt to improve later health will be futile. Such weak approaches will also undermine the promise of positive psychology to encourage better ways of thinking about depression, subjective well-being, and health.

Of course, if an intervention happens to affect the underlying causes of both health and depression for an individual, health will be improved. Increasing physical activity—changing someone from an inactive to an active person—is a likely candidate in this realm (Carek et al. 2011, Pedersen & Saltin 2006, Ströhle 2009).

Challenge and Health

Despite the common perception that very hard workers (workaholics) put their health at risk through nervous tension, work and health are intricately related, often in a positive way. Work can provide a sense of identity and purpose, stable social connections with others, and of course a source of income for meeting needs for good food, safe shelter, and competent health care. Unemployment is a well-established correlate of disability, illness, depression, health care utilization, and mortality risk, often in vicious cycles (Roelfs et al. 2011). For example, data from the US Panel Study of Income Dynamics showed that job loss predicted increased risk of a new health condition over the next year, with significantly higher risk if no reemployment occurred (Strully 2009). And in England during the 2008–2010 recession, suicides and injury rates rose (Barr et al. 2012). Not surprisingly, deteriorating health also influences work, with the US Panel study finding that poor health predicted subsequently being fired or leaving a job voluntarily. Negative cycles often occur, in which the sick or injured worker loses his or her job, forfeits income for self-care, and faces further deteriorating health; absence from work is a good predictor of subsequent long-term disability and unemployment.

Since the type A behavior pattern was proposed (during the 1950s economic boom) as a cause of heart disease—along with warnings against trying to accomplish increasingly more in less time (Chesney & Rosenman 1985)—there has been concern that busy workplaces are unhealthy. Certainly, a workplace can be excessively challenging, with unreasonably heavy physical work, chemical exposure, violence, or psychological overload (World Health Organ. 1994). But health psychologists have long recognized that challenge is not necessarily harmful (McEwen 2000). The term stress properly refers to a significant physiological disruption that compromises the internal regulatory processes that maintain physiological balance within an organism. The human body is adept at responding to internal and external change. However, when the physiological system is chronically disturbed, resources become depleted and regulatory processes are often affected (Cacioppo & Berntson 2011). It is usually through chronic processes, over time, that negative psychoemotional and behavioral reaction patterns play a role in disrupting metabolism, immune function, and physiological rhythms (including sleep), thereby increasing susceptibility to illness and general breakdown (Kemeny 2011, McEwen 2006). Such disruption is a long-term process that occurs through an interaction of internal and external forces as part of an individual's long-term trajectory, and it cannot be captured in a single measurement or experiment. Challenge and a heavy workload can be healthy or unhealthy, depending on the person, the context, and the person-situation interaction. In a longitudinal analysis of elderly participants in the Terman Life Cycle Study, the continually motivated and productive men and women (who were still working for pay, pursuing new educational opportunities, or seeking new achievements) went on to live much longer than their more laid-back comrades, and this productive orientation mattered much more to longevity than did their sense of happiness and well-being (Friedman et al. 2010).

It has long been recognized that challenge is a key precursor of well-being. For example, flow—very high levels of psychological engagement—emerges when challenge and skill meet (Csikszentmihalyi 1997). Engaged workers approach their jobs with vigor, interest, and absorption and have enthusiasm both for the task at hand and for the organization as a whole (Lepine et al. 2005, Schaufeli et al. 2006). Many studies of "hardiness" show strong beneficial effects of challenge, especially when the individual has a sense of self-control and a commitment to something meaningful (Maddi 2002). In global areas with high concentrations of centenarians (Buettner 2012), most long-lived individuals have remained physically and socially active, embracing rather than avoiding challenge. Much research shows an association between early retirement and increased mortality risk, even after adjusting for various selection artifacts (Bamia et al. 2008, Carlsson et al. 2012).

Outside of the formal work environment, psychological engagement and productivity are again important components of health and successful aging. Individuals who are involved and maintain a sense of personal control sustain a better quality of life (Bambrick & Bonder 2005,

Brown et al. 2009, Pruchno et al. 2010, Schaie & Willis 2011). On the other hand, seeking emotional happiness per se may impede well-being by setting oneself up for disappointment or narcissism (Mauss et al. 2011, Twenge 2006). Modern personality theories help explain how these enduring trajectories emerge. Personality influences the events that are experienced (i.e., situation selection), the elicitation (or provocation) of responses by others, cognitive interpretations of challenges, emotional reactions to experiences, coping responses, and resulting actions. Personality predicts risk exposure to key life stressors such as marriage and divorce, career success and failure, and crime and safety (Bolger & Zuckerman 1995, Caspi et al. 2005, Magnus et al. 1993, Shanahan et al. 2013, Vollrath 2001). About one-third of all crimes happen to the same (repeat) victims, whereas most people face no criminal victimization at all, even after controlling for neighborhood risks (Tseloni 2000, Tseloni & Pease 2003, Tseloni et al. 2004). Children who are both low on conscientiousness and high on neuroticism (that is, who are impulsive and emotional) are more likely to react with distress and anger during peer conflict, reactions which in turn are related to higher levels of victimization (Bollmer et al. 2006; see also De Bolle & Tackett 2013). As is discussed below, it is not the emotional lability (neuroticism) itself that is crucial, but rather the impulsivity (unconscientiousness).

Overall, we believe that it is a misdirection of resources and attention to focus on positive moods as direct causes of good health, or on worrying, hard work, and depression as significant causes of poor health. Instead, a remarkable body of new research suggests that certain aspects of personality do indeed play a significant, and likely causal, role in patterns of living that lead to thriving, health, and longevity. The core trait is usually termed conscientiousness.

CONSCIENTIOUSNESS, MATURITY, AND LONGEVITY

Perhaps the most exciting recent discovery to emerge in the area of personality, well-being, and health is the lifelong importance of conscientiousness. Individuals who are conscientious—that is, prudent, dependable, well organized, and persistent—stay healthier, thrive, and live longer. The size of this effect is equal to or greater than that of many known biomedical risk factors.

Although it has long been known in the social sciences that individuals who are impulsive and low on self-control are prone to face troubles and failures on many fronts, such matters were mostly overlooked in the vast research on personality and health of the past half century. Fortunately, it has also long been known that children, teenagers, and young adults can age out of or be drawn away from delinquent patterns (Steinberg & Morris 2001), often through the development of increased self-monitoring, better social relationships, and more benign environments.

Extensive research following up the initial startling finding of two decades ago (Friedman et al. 1993) that childhood conscientiousness is a strong predictor of longevity has revealed that conscientiousness is a very strong and reliable lifelong predictor of healthy pathways and of health and longevity (Friedman et al. 2013, Goodwin & Friedman 2006, Shanahan et al. 2013). A meta-analysis (of 20 independent samples of approximately 9,000 participants) clearly links higher levels of conscientiousness to the key outcome of lower mortality risk (Kern & Friedman 2008). This finding has been repeatedly confirmed in more recent studies as well (Chapman et al. 2010, Fry & Debats 2009, Hill et al. 2011, Iwasa et al. 2008, Taylor et al. 2009, Terracciano et al. 2008). For example, in a 17-year follow-up in the Whitehall II cohort study ($N = 6,800$), low conscientiousness in midlife was an important risk factor for all-cause mortality, an association that was partly but not fully accounted for by health behaviors and certain other disease risks (Hagger-Johnson et al. 2012).

Conscientiousness predicts reduced disease development (Chapman et al. 2007, Goodwin & Friedman 2006), better coping (Connor-Smith & Flachsbart 2007), fewer symptoms, and various sorts of social competence and productivity (Bogg & Roberts 2013). Finally, low conscientiousness also predicts Alzheimer's disease and related cognitive problems (for a prospective study, see Wilson et al. 2007). It is thus relevant to the full range of core health outcomes we described at the beginning of this review.

Given the multiplicity of influences on health and well-being, how could one personality dimension be so important across so many years? Emerging evidence suggests the relevance of conscientiousness to a number of core biopsychosocial processes. First, conscientious individuals engage in a variety of important healthier behaviors—for example, they smoke less, eat healthier foods, and wear seat belts (Bogg & Roberts 2004, Lodi-Smith et al. 2010, Sutin et al. 2011). Second, conscientiousness affects situation selection. That is, conscientious individuals choose healthier environments, create or evoke healthier situations, and select and maintain healthier friendships and more stable marriages (Kern & Friedman 2011, Lüdtke et al. 2011, Shiner & Masten 2012, Taylor et al. 1997). Third and relatedly, conscientious individuals are more likely to have more successful, meaningful careers, better educations, and higher incomes, all of which are known to be relevant to health, well-being, and longer life (Hampson et al. 2007, Ozer & Benet-Martinez 2006, Poropat 2009, Roberts et al. 2003). For example, rank in high school class ($N = 10,317$ high school graduates), which depends heavily not only on intelligence but also on conscientiousness, was found to be a much better predictor of longevity than was IQ (Hauser & Palloni 2011).

Fourth, conscientiousness often interacts with unhealthy stressors and with other unhealthy personality traits, moderating their detrimental effects. For example, conscientiousness can attenuate the health risk of career failures (Kern et al. 2009). And although being low on conscientiousness and high on neuroticism appears to be a particularly dangerous combination (with individuals who are impulsive, disorganized, anxious, and emotional at very high risk), detrimental effects of anxiety and emotionality are reduced in individuals who are also conscientious (Chapman et al. 2010, Parkes 1984, Terracciano & Costa 2004, Turiano et al. 2013, Vollrath & Torgersen 2002). One reason for this pattern may involve better emotion regulation ability; for example, one study of middle-aged adults found conscientiousness predicted better recovery from negative emotional challenges (Javaras et al. 2012).

Fifth, conscientiousness may be encouraged by certain genetic patterns—and gene-by-environment interactions—that are also related to subsequent health. Serotonin levels in the central nervous system are known to have a genetic basis, change with new circumstances, affect personality (including conscientiousness), and work to regulate core bodily functions (including sleep) necessary for good health (Carver et al. 2011, Caspi et al. 2010, Cicchetti et al. 2012; see also Mõttus et al. 2013 regarding inflammation).

Models of conscientiousness, well-being, and health are conceptually simple at their core but become quite complex in practice because human lives across time are quite complex. For example, at a young age, conscientious children face fewer self-control and school problems; in adolescence, conscientious individuals are less likely to try smoking, alcohol, and illegal drugs; and in adulthood, conscientious people are more likely to connect with other conscientious people—personally, socially, and at work—and to place themselves in healthier social and physical environments (Hampson 2012). Conscientious individuals are more likely to achieve a good education (Poropat 2009), which in turn is helpful in creating more prudent, better-organized, and forward-thinking adults (Vaillant 2012).

Conscientiousness likely also operates to promote health through reduction of very small risks. Prudent, persistent, planful individuals make a myriad of decisions each day that minimize risk. Whether it is carrying a raincoat, packing an extra set of medications, double locking their doors, minimizing germ exposure (through hand-washing or other sanitary practices), or staying off the golf course when thunderstorms are predicted, conscientious individuals slightly lower their risks of injury and disease each day. The individual effect of each behavior is tiny (and hard to document), but taken together and compounded over decades, a substantial effect may emerge. For example, the odds of being struck by lightning in one's lifetime is only one in 10,000 for Americans (National Weather Service; **http://www.lightningsafety.noaa.gov/medical.htm**), but for every 10,000 highly conscientious individuals, one likely avoids this fate. Substantial effects may arise when hundreds of such small risks are taken into account, but there is little research evaluating the overall cumulative impact of such factors. Much more research is needed.

A number of studies suggest that high neuroticism combined with low conscientiousness is particularly risky for poor health outcomes (Chapman et al. 2007, 2010; Terracciano & Costa 2004; Vollrath & Torgersen 2002). On the other hand, a high degree of self-control and grit, coupled with prudent planning and thinking ahead is especially healthy (Duckworth 2011, Moffitt et al. 2011). This pattern, together with a general cluster of conscientiousness-relevant characteristics, is sometimes termed maturity (cf. Vaillant 1971, 2012).

Early Life Influences

When an association between conscientiousness and health is discovered, the usual tendency is to look for the mediators. For example, to what extent is the association between conscientiousness and longevity mediated by health behaviors such as smoking and drinking? A life course perspective, however, also encourages a look back at common predecessor influences. In particular, early life experiences and biological predispositions (including genes, in utero hormones, nutrition, toxins, and postpartum and early infant attachment and environmental challenge) can influence both personality and later health (McEwen 1993, 2006; Puig et al. 2013; Taylor et al. 1997). That is, personality traits, sense of well-being, and many diseases have some genetic or perinatal basis, thus leading to later associations between personality and health that are caused in part by underlying biosocial third variables.

Nevertheless, many of the influences of the genetic code and its expression result from alterations caused by the environment, sometimes in understandable ways and sometimes randomly. One study of large numbers of monozygotic twins found minimal predictive ability for individual health (Roberts et al. 2012), and even these may be overestimates of direct biological effects, as genetic predispositions play a role in situation selection and evocation. For example, Swedish twin studies suggest that core health-relevant social relations such as stable, happy marriages can be partly predicted by genetic variation (Walum et al. 2008; see also Mosing et al. 2012). When the genetic code and early-life stress are viewed as an initial step in a long-term trajectory—in other words, in terms of personality and development—then the model becomes much more powerful as health risks cumulate. It would be a mistake to think of research on personality, well-being, and health as a holding pattern that awaits definitive biological stress research. It may be better to conceive of genetic and perinatal research as one of the developing pieces necessary for a more complete understanding of personality and health.

CONCLUSION: IMPLICATIONS FOR INTERVENTIONS

One of the primary reasons for studying personality and health is to understand ways to improve health and reduce mortality risk. We have argued that a more complete lifespan perspective (with expanded causal models) reveals that certain common assumptions about health and well-being are untenable and some common interventions are unjustified. Nonetheless, hints of effective interventions are emerging. Fuller models of personality and health help clarify causality and offer likely points for successful intervention.

Some elements of the pursuit of happiness may very well result in increased health, but over-simplification of the strong correlations between subjective well-being and physical health can lead to the "no worries" approach to life, with goals of seeking positive emotions and laughter, avoiding "stress," taking it easy, retiring from work, and avoiding commitment. And it also leads to the unconscionable blaming of disease victims. Analogously, a misinterpretation of the correlations of depression with disease can result in the targeting of the wrong behavioral patterns for intervention. For example, there may be advice involving ways to cheer up or overprescription of medication for mild anxiety or depression. Further, the misunderstanding of the role of worrying may lead to minimization of sober, thoughtful, conscientious life patterns now known to be health protective.

Personality is also highly relevant to who completes the research study. Individuals higher on positive emotions, agreeableness, and conscientiousness are much more likely to stay in ongoing studies, thus creating differential attrition and distorting findings (Czajkowski et al. 2009, Friedman 2011b). For example, in a study of medication after a myocardial infarction, being conscientious enough to fully cooperate with treatment (even if with a placebo) emerged as a more important predictor of mortality risk than the medication (Horwitz et al. 1990). A fuller understanding and more comprehensive causal models of personality, health, and well-being would make these sorts of artifacts less likely.

Some of the solutions to these research challenges are well established in the fields of epidemiology and randomized clinical trials but too often are overlooked, or are avoided because they are viewed as too complicated, in the study of personality, health, and well-being. The first solution is to sample randomly from the full relevant population, preferably an initially healthy population. (Sometimes, use of a healthy control group is a reasonable and the only feasible alternative in a study of patients.) Second, employ independent, valid, multidimensional measures of personality and personality change. Third, use the best possible experimental or quasi-experimental design with the proper control groups, including placebo control groups. Fourth, employ intent-to-treat analyses in which everyone is included in the data analyses (including those who did not complete or were not fully exposed to the treatment). And fifth, use multiple outcome measures, both subjective and objective, including all-cause mortality.

These recommendations are difficult to put into practice. Often, longitudinal observational studies and quasi-experimental research designs are necessary and informative, coupled with shorter-term experiments. Fortunately, with the increasing number of long-term data sets, more rigorous information is now emerging (Friedman et al. 2013). Further, new analytic techniques allow integration of extant studies to test lifespan models (Kern et al. 2013, Picinnin & Hofer 2008). Multiple causal links to health exist, and models of the hypothesized full long-term pathways should be spelled out in all research in this field, even when the full model is not being investigated in a particular study (for a discussion of causal inference in personality psychology, see Lee 2012).

In summary, a key contribution of modern personality research to understanding health and well-being is the focus on healthy patterns, clusters of predictors, and what we like to call pathways to health and longevity. One of the most striking and important surprise conclusions of the eight-decade "Longevity Project" studies of the Terman Life Cycle Study (Friedman & Martin 2011) is the extent to which health risk factors and protective factors do not occur in isolation but rather bunch together. For example, the unconscientious boys in the Terman sample—even though very bright—were more likely to grow up to achieve less education, have unstable marriages, drink and smoke more, and be unsuccessful at work, all of which were relevant to dying at younger ages. Such health risks and relationship challenges (e.g., divorce or job loss, loneliness and social isolation) are usually studied as independent health threats. But attention to personality can broaden and sharpen research approaches because it is stable and slow changing, and it is tied to a full range of biopsychosocial influences. Fundamental attention to the individual person across time draws consideration to the deeper causal processes.

Although the evidence for widely effective interventions is not yet available, more comprehensive models point toward core patterns that may indeed emerge as efficacious policies in promoting a well-organized, healthy, productive, long life. For example, the three elements of healthy lifestyles described in the following paragraph all involve long-term patterns, are potentially modifiable, and are known to be highly relevant to good health and well-being and to reestablishing homeostasis in the face of environmental challenges. They are deserving of increased research attention.

First, individuals with good ties to social networks and who are well integrated into their communities tend to be happier and healthier (Hawkley & Cacioppo 2010, Taylor 2011). And, the degree and quality of such relations can be changed. Second, people who are physically active—doing things—tend to have better mental and physical health. Although physical activity levels (not formal exercise per se) are somewhat stable over time, they too can be modified, and increased activity usually produces beneficial effects (Bouchard et al. 2012, Mutrie & Faulkner 2004, Pedersen & Saltin 2006). Third, self-controlled, conscientious individuals who live and work with purpose and are involved with helping others appear to thrive across the long term (Friedman & Martin 2011). This third factor may be the most important because it plays a role in the first two as well. One of the biggest but most promising challenges of health psychology, of positive psychology, and indeed of public health is to understand and develop interventions at the individual level, the social (interpersonal) level, the community level, and the societal level to help launch individuals on these healthy pathways, to help them maintain and deepen adherence to these pathways, and to help them recover when they stumble or are forced off these roads to health and well-being.

Isn't this the same as promoting happiness, reducing work challenge, and treating depression? Not at all. One could argue that increasing physical activity, strengthening social ties, and developing a meaningful sense of purpose are all established elements of treating depression. The problem is that many other approaches to treating depression and subjective well-being likely are not very relevant to health. Further, such approaches often do not consider long-term lifespan trajectories and the understanding of context.

There is no longer a need for studies that simply correlate personality with health and subjective well-being, or that correlate happiness and health, or even that involve simple predictive studies of personality and later health outcomes. Instead, the field is ready for longitudinal studies of mediators and moderators, and for intervention studies of how, when, and why changes in individual character affect health and well-being. Individual differences earlier in life are reliable predictors and likely causes of well-being and health status later in life, and a fuller understanding of the causal pathways and how they can be altered holds the promise of significant value to individuals and to society.

DISCLOSURE STATEMENT

The authors are not aware of any affiliations, memberships, funding, or financial holdings that might be perceived as affecting the objectivity of this review.

LITERATURE CITED

Abas M, Hotopf M, Prince M. 2002. Depression and mortality in a high-risk population. 11-Year follow-up of the Medical Research Council Elderly Hypertension Trial. *Br. J. Psychiatry* 181:123–28

Aldwin CM, Spiro A, Park CL. 2006. Health, behavior, and optimal aging: a life span developmental perspective. In *Handbook of the Psychology of Aging*, ed. JE Birren, KW Schaie, pp. 85–104. New York: Elsevier. 6th ed.

Almada SJ, Zonderman AB, Shekelle RB, Dyer AR, Daviglus ML, et al. 1991. Neuroticism and cynicism and risk of death in middle-aged men: the Western Electric Study. *Psychosom. Med.* 53:165–75

Am. Psychiatr. Assoc. 1994. *Diagnostic and Statistical Manual of Mental Disorders, Fourth Edition*. Arlington, VA: Am. Psychiatr. Assoc.

Antonovsky A. 1979. *Health, Stress, and Coping*. San Francisco: Jossey-Bass

Baltes PB, Baltes MM. 1990. *Successful Aging: Perspectives from the Behavioral Sciences*. New York: Cambridge Univ. Press

Baltes PB, Smith J. 2004. Lifespan psychology: from developmental contextualism to developmental biocultural co-constructivism. *Res. Hum. Dev.* 1:123–44

Bambrick P, Bonder B. 2005. Older adults' perceptions of work. *Work* 24:77–84

Bamia C, Trichopoulou A, Trichopoulos D. 2008. Age at retirement and mortality in a general population sample. The Greek EPIC study. *Am. J. Epidemiol.* 167:561–69

Barr B, Taylor-Robinson D, Scott-Samuel A, McKee M, Stuckler D. 2012. Suicides associated with the 2008–10 economic recession in England: time trend analysis. *Br. Med. J.* 345:e5142–49

Baumeister RF, Vohs KD, Aaker JL, Garbinsky EN. 2013. Some key differences between a happy life and a meaningful life. *J. Posit. Psychol.* In press

Berkman LF, Blumenthal J, Burg M, Carney RM, Catellier D, et al. 2003. Effects of treating depression and low perceived social support on clinical events after myocardial infarction: the Enhancing Recovery in Coronary Heart Disease Patients (ENRICHD) randomized trial. *J. Am. Med. Assoc.* 289:3106–16

Boehm JK, Kubzansky LD. 2012. The heart's content: the association between positive psychological well-being and cardiovascular health. *Psychol. Bull.* 138:655–91

Bogg T, Roberts BW. 2004. Conscientiousness and health-related behaviors: a meta-analysis of the leading behavioral contributors to mortality. *Psychol Bull.* 130:887–919

Bogg T, Roberts BW. 2013. The case for conscientiousness: evidence and implications for a personality trait marker of health and longevity. *Ann. Behav. Med.* 45:278–88

Bolger N, Zuckerman A. 1995. A framework for studying personality in the stress process. *J. Personal. Soc. Psychol.* 69:890–902

Bollmer JM, Harris MJ, Milich R. 2006. Reactions to bullying and peer victimization: narratives, physiological arousal, and personality. *J. Res. Personal.* 40:803–28

Booth-Kewley S, Friedman HS. 1987. Psychological predictors of heart disease: a quantitative review. *Psychol. Bull.* 101:343–62

Bouchard C, Blair SN, Haskell WL. 2012. *Physical Activity and Health*. Champaign, Ill.: Hum. Kinet. 2nd ed.

Boyle PA, Barnes LL, Buchman AS, Bennett DA. 2009. Purpose in life is associated with mortality among community-dwelling older persons. *Psychosom. Med.* 71:574–79

Bromberger JT, Kravitz HM, Chang YF, Cyranowski JM, Brown C, Matthews KA. 2011. Major depression during and after the menopausal transition: Study of Women's Health Across the Nation (SWAN). *Psychol. Med.* 41:1879–88

Brown SL, Smith DM, Schulz R, Kabeto MU, Ubel PA, et al. 2009. Caregiving behavior is associated with decreased mortality risk. *Psychol. Sci.* 20:488–94

Buettner D. 2012. *The Blue Zones: Lessons for Living Longer from the People Who've Lived the Longest*. Washington, DC: Natl. Geogr. Soc. 2nd ed.

Byrne R. 2006. *The Secret*. New York: Atria Books

Cacioppo JT, Berntson GG. 2011. The brain, homeostasis, and health: balancing demands of the internal and external milieu. See Friedman 2011a, pp. 121–37

Cannon WB. 1932. *Wisdom of the Body*. New York: Norton

Carek PJ, Laibstain SE, Clark SE. 2011. Exercise for the treatment of depression and anxiety. *Int. J. Psychiatr. Med.* 41:15–28

Carlsson S, Andersson T, Michaëlsson K, Vågerö D, Ahlbom A. 2012. Late retirement is not associated with increased mortality, results based on all Swedish retirements 1991–2007. *Eur. J. Epidemiol.* 27:483–86

Carver CS, Connor-Smith J. 2010. Personality and coping. *Annu. Rev. Psychol.* 61:679–704

Carver CS, Johnson SL, Joormann J, Kim Y, Nam JY. 2011. Serotonin transporter polymorphism interacts with childhood adversity to predict aspects of impulsivity. *Psychol. Sci.* 22:589–95

Carver CS, Scheier MF, Segerstrom SC. 2010. Optimism. *Clin. Psychol. Rev.* 30:878–89

Caspi A, Hariri AR, Holmes A, Uher R, Moffitt TE. 2010. Genetic sensitivity to the environment: the case of the serotonin transporter gene and its implications for studying complex diseases and traits. *Am. J. Psychiatry* 167:509–27

Caspi A, Roberts BW, Shiner RL. 2005. Personality development: stability and change. *Annu. Rev. Psychol.* 56:453–84

Chapman BP, Duberstein PR, Lyness JM. 2007. The distressed personality type: replicability and general health associations. *Eur. J. Personal.* 21:911–29

Chapman BP, Fiscella K, Kawachi I, Duberstein PB. 2010. Personality, socio-economic status, and all-cause mortality in the United States. *Am. J. Epidemiol.* 171:83–92

Chesney MA, Rosenman RH. 1985. *Anger and Hostility in Cardiovascular and Behavioral Disorders.* Washington, DC: Hemisphere Publ.

Chida Y, Steptoe A. 2008. Positive psychological well-being and mortality: a quantitative review of prospective observational studies. *Psychosom. Med.* 70:741–56

Cicchetti D, Rogosch FA, Thibodeau EL. 2012. The effects of child maltreatment on early signs of antisocial behavior: genetic moderation by tryptophan hydroxylase, serotonin transporter, and monoamine oxidase-A genes. *Dev. Psychopathol.* 24:907–28

Connor-Smith JK, Flachsbart C. 2007. Relations between personality and coping: a meta-analysis. *J. Personal. Soc. Psychol.* 93:1080–107

Cousins N. 1979. *Anatomy of an Illness.* New York: Norton

Coyne JC, Tennen H. 2010. Positive psychology in cancer care: bad science, exaggerated claims, and unproven medicine. *Ann. Behav. Med.* 39:16–26

Csikszentmihalyi M. 1997. *Finding Flow: The Psychology of Engagement with Everyday Life.* New York: Basic Books

Czajkowski SM, Chesney MA, Smith AW. 2009. Adherence and placebo effect. In *The Handbook of Health Behavior Change*, ed. SA Shumaker, JK Ockene, KA Riekert, pp. 713–34. New York: Springer. 3rd ed.

De Bolle M, Tackett JL. 2013. Anchoring bullying and victimization in children within a five-factor model based person-centered framework. *Eur. J. Personal.* 27:280–89

DeMets DL. 2013. The role and potential of surrogate outcomes in clinical trials: Have we made any progress in the past decade? In *Proc. Fourth Seattle Symp. Biostat.: Clin. Trials, Lect. Notes Stat.*, pp. 3–19. New York: Springer Sci.

DeNeve KM, Cooper H. 1998. The happy personality: a meta-analysis of 137 personality traits and subjective well-being. *Psychol. Bull.* 124:197–229

Denollet J, Sys SU, Stroobant N, Rombouts H, Gillebert TC, Brutsaert DL. 1996. Personality as independent predictor of long-term mortality in patients with coronary heart disease. *Lancet* 347:417–21

Diener E, Chan M. 2011. Happy people live longer: Subjective well-being contributes to health and longevity. *Appl. Psychol.: Health Well-Being* 3:1–43

Diener E, Inglehart R, Tay L. 2013. Theory and validity of life satisfaction scales. *Soc. Indic. Res.* 112:497–527

Duckworth AL. 2011. The significance of self-control. *Proc. Natl. Acad. Sci. USA* 108:2639–40

Ford BQ, Mauss IB. 2014. The paradoxical effects of pursuing positive emotion: when and why wanting to feel happy backfires. In *Positive Emotion: Integrating the Light Sides and Dark Sides*, ed. J Gruber, J Moskowitz. Oxford Univ. Press. In press

Fried LP. 2012. What are the roles of public health in an aging society? In *Public Health for an Aging Society*, ed. TR Prohaska, LA Anderson, RH Binstock, pp. 26–52. Baltimore, MD: John Hopkins Univ. Press

Friedman HS. 2000. Long-term relations of personality, health: dynamisms, mechanisms, and tropisms. *J. Personal.* 68:1089–107

Friedman HS. 2007. Personality, disease, and self-healing. In *Foundations of Health Psychology*, ed. HS Friedman, RC Silver, pp. 172–99. New York: Oxford Univ. Press

Friedman HS, ed. 2011a. *Oxford Handbook of Health Psychology.* New York: Oxford Univ. Press

Friedman HS. 2011b. Personality, disease, and self-healing. See Friedman 2011a, pp. 215–40

Friedman HS, Booth-Kewley S. 1987. The "disease-prone personality": a meta-analytic view of the construct. *Am. Psychol.* 42:539–55

Friedman HS, Kern ML, Hampson SE, Duckworth AL. 2013. A new lifespan approach to conscientiousness and health: combining the pieces of the causal puzzle. *Dev. Psychol.* In press. doi:10.1037/a0030373

Friedman HS, Kern ML, Reynolds CA. 2010. Personality and health, subjective well-being, and longevity as adults age. *J. Personal.* 78:179–216

Friedman HS, Martin LR. 2011. *The Longevity Project: Surprising Discoveries for Health and Long Life from the Landmark Eight-Decade Study.* New York: Hudson St. Press

Friedman HS, Tucker JS, Tomlinson-Keasey C, Schwartz JE, Wingard DL, Criqui MH. 1993. Does childhood personality predict longevity? *J. Personal. Soc. Psychol.* 65:176–85

Fry PS, Debats DL. 2009. Perfectionism and the five-factor personality traits as predictors of mortality in older adults. *J. Health Psychol.* 14:513–24

Gana K, Bailly N, Saada Y, Joulain M, Trouillet R, et al. 2013. Relationship between life satisfaction and physical health: a longitudinal test of cross-lagged and simultaneous effects. *Health Psychol.* 32:896–904

Goodwin RG, Friedman HS. 2006. Health status and the five factor personality traits in a nationally representative sample. *J. Health Psychol.* 11:643–54

Graham JE, Christian LM, Kiecolt-Glaser JK. 2006. Stress, age, and immune function: toward a lifespan approach. *J. Behav. Med.* 29:389–400

Grippo AJ, Johnson AK. 2002. Biological mechanisms in the relationship between depression and heart disease. *Neurosci. Biobehav. Rev.* 26:941–62

Gruber J, Mauss IB, Tamir M. 2011. A dark side of happiness? How, when, and why happiness is not always good. *Perspect. Psychol. Sci.* 6:222–33

Hagger-Johnson G, Sabia S, Nabi H, Brunner E, Kivimaki M, et al. 2012. Low conscientiousness and risk of all-cause, cardiovascular and cancer mortality over 17 years: Whitehall II cohort study. *J. Psychosom. Res.* 73:98–103

Hampson SE. 2012. Personality processes: mechanisms by which personality traits "get outside the skin." *Annu. Rev. Psychol.* 63:315–39

Hampson SE, Goldberg LR, Vogt TM, Dubanoski JP. 2007. Mechanisms by which childhood personality traits influence adult health status: educational attainment and healthy behaviors. *Health Psychol.* 26:121–25

Hauser RM, Palloni A. 2011. Adolescent IQ and survival in the Wisconsin Longitudinal Study. *J. Gerontol. B Psychol. Sci. Soc. Sci.* 66B(Suppl. 1):i91–101

Hawkley LC, Cacioppo JT. 2010. Loneliness matters: a theoretical and empirical review of consequences and mechanisms. *Ann. Behav. Med.* 40:218–27

Hershfield HE, Scheibe S, Sims TL, Carstensen LL. 2013. When feeling bad can be good: Mixed emotions benefit physical health across adulthood. *Soc. Psychol. Personal. Sci.* 4:54–61

Hill PL, Turiano NA, Hurd MD, Mroczek DK, Roberts BW. 2011. Conscientiousness and longevity: an examination of possible mediators. *Health Psychol.* 30:536–41

Horwitz RI, Viscoli CM, Berkman L, Donaldson RM, Horwitz SM, et al. 1990. Treatment adherence and risk of death after a myocardial infarction. *Lancet* 336:542–45

Howell R, Kern ML, Lyubomirsky S. 2007. Health benefits: meta-analytically determining the impact of well-being on objective health outcomes. *J. Health Psychol.* 13:1092–104

Huppert FA, Whittington JE. 1995. Symptoms of psychological distress predict 7-year mortality. *Psychol. Med.* 25:1073–86

Idler EL, Benyamini Y. 1997. Self-rated health and mortality: a review of twenty-seven community studies. *J. Health Soc. Behav.* 38:21–37

Iwasa H, Masui Y, Gondo Y, Inagaki H, Kawaai C, Suzuki T. 2008. Personality and all-cause mortality among older adults dwelling in a Japanese community: a five-year population-based prospective cohort study. *Am. J. Geriatr. Psychiatry* 16:399–405

Javaras KN, Schaefer SM, Van Reekum CM. 2012. Conscientiousness predicts greater recovery from negative emotion. *Emotion* 12:875–81

Kaplan R. 2002. Quality of life: an outcomes perspective. *Arch. Phys. Med. Rehabil.* 83:S44–50

Kemeny ME. 2011. Psychoneuroimmunology. See Friedman 2011a, pp. 138–61

Kern ML, Friedman HS. 2008. Do conscientious individuals live longer? A quantitative review. *Health Psychol.* 27:505–12

Kern ML, Friedman HS. 2011. Personality and pathways of influence on physical health. *Soc. Personal. Psychol. Compass* 5:76–87

Kern ML, Friedman HS, Martin LR, Reynolds CA, Luong G. 2009. Conscientiousness, career success, and longevity: a lifespan analysis. *Ann. Behav. Med.* 37:154–63

Kern ML, Hampson SE, Goldberg LR, Friedman HS. 2013. Integrating prospective longitudinal data: modeling personality and health in the Terman Life Cycle and Hawaii Longitudinal studies. *Dev. Psychol.* In press. doi:10.1037/a0030874

King LA. 2001. The hard road to the good life: the happy, mature person. *J. Humanist. Psychol.* 41:51–72

Korten AE, Jorm AF, Jiao Z, Letenneur L, Jacomb PA, et al. 1999. Health, cognitive, and psychosocial factors as predictors of mortality in an elderly community sample. *J. Epidemiol. Community Health* 53:83–88

Lang FR, Weiss D, Gerstorf D, Wagner GG. 2013. Forecasting life satisfaction across adulthood: benefits of seeing a dark future? *Psychol. Aging* 28:249–61

Lee JJ. 2012. Correlation and causation in the study of personality. *Eur. J. Personal.* 26:372–90

Lemogne C, Nabi H, Zins M, Courdier S, Ducimetière P, et al. 2010. Hostility may explain the association between depressive mood and mortality: evidence from the French GAZEL cohort study. *Psychother. Psychosom.* 79:164–71

Lench HC. 2011. Personality and health outcomes: making expectations a reality. *J. Happiness Stud.* 12:493–507

Lepine JA, Podsakoff NP, Lepine MA. 2005. A meta-analytic test of the challenge stressor–hindrance stressor framework: an explanation for inconsistent relationships among stressors and performance. *Acad. Manag. J.* 48:764–75

Lichtman JH, Bigger T Jr, Blumenthal JA, Frasure-Smith N, Kaufmann PG, et al. 2008. Depression and coronary heart disease: recommendations for screening, referral, and treatment. *Circulation* 118:1768–75

Löckenhoff CE, Terracciana A, Patriciu NS, Eaton WW, Costa PT Jr. 2009. Self-reported extremely adverse life events and longitudinal changes in five-factor model personality traits in an urban sample. *J. Trauma Stress* 22:53–59

Lodi-Smith JL, Jackson JJ, Bogg T, Walton K, Wood D, et al. 2010. Mechanisms of health: education and health-related behaviors partially mediate the relationship between conscientiousness and self-reported physical health. *Psychol. Health* 25:305–19

Lüdtke O, Roberts BW, Trautwein U, Nagy G. 2011. A random walk down university avenue: life paths, life events, and personality trait change at the transition to university life. *J. Personal. Soc. Psychol.* 101:620–37

Lyubomirsky S, King LA, Diener E. 2005. The benefits of frequent positive affect: Does happiness lead to success? *Psychol. Bull.* 131:803–55

Lyubomirsky S, Layous K. 2013. How do simple positive activities increase well-being? *Curr. Dir. Psychol. Sci.* 22:57–62

Maddi SR. 2002. The story of hardiness: twenty years of theorizing, research, and practice. *Consult. Psychol. J.: Pract. Res.* 54:173–85

Magnus K, Diener E, Fujita F, Pavot W. 1993. Extraversion and neuroticism as predictors of objective life events: a longitudinal analysis. *J. Personal. Soc. Psychol.* 65:1046–53

Mauss IB, Tamir M, Anderson CL, Savino NS. 2011. Can seeking happiness make people unhappy? Paradoxical effects of valuing happiness. *Emotion* 11:807–15

McEwen BS. 1993. Stress, adaptation, and disease: allostasis and allostatic load. *Ann. N. Y. Acad. Sci.* 840:33–44

McEwen BS. 2000. The neurobiology of stress: from serendipity to clinical relevance. *Brain Res.* 886:172–89

McEwen BS. 2006. Protective and damaging effects of stress mediators: central role of the brain. *Dialogues Clin. Neurosci.* 8:283–93

Micheel C, Ball J. 2010. *Institute of Medicine (U.S.). Committee on Qualification of Biomarkers and Surrogate Endpoints in Chronic Disease. Evaluation of Biomarkers and Surrogate Endpoints in Chronic Disease.* Washington, DC: Natl. Acad. Press

Miller TQ, Smith TW, Turner CW, Guijarro ML, Hallet AJ. 1996. Meta-analytic review of research on hostility and physical health. *Psychol. Bull.* 119:322–48

Moffitt TE, Arseneault L, Belsky D, Dickson N, Hancox RJ, et al. 2011. A gradient of childhood self-control predicts health, wealth, and public safety. *Proc. Natl. Acad. Sci. USA* 108:2693–98

Mosing MA, Medland SE, McRae A, Landers JG, Wright MJ, Martin NG. 2012. Genetic influences on life span and its relationship to personality: a 16-year follow-up study of a sample of aging twins. *Psychosom. Med.* 74:16–22

Mõttus R, Luciano M, Starr JM, Pollard MC, Deary IJ. 2013. Personality traits and inflammation in men and women in their early 70s: the Lothian Birth Cohort 1936 study of healthy aging. *Psychosom. Med.* 75:11–19

Mroczek DK, Spiro A III. 2007. Personality change influences mortality in older men. *Psychol. Sci.* 18:371–76

Mutrie N, Faulkner G. 2004. Physical activity: positive psychology in motion. In *Positive Psychology in Practice*, ed. PA Linley, S Joseph, pp. 146–64. Hoboken, NJ: Wiley

Ozer DJ, Benet-Martinez V. 2006. Personality and the prediction of consequential outcomes. *Annu. Rev. Psychol.* 57:401–21

Parkes KR. 1984. Smoking and the Eysenck personality dimensions: an interactive model. *Psychol. Med.* 14:825–34

Pedersen BK, Saltin B. 2006. Evidence for prescribing exercise as therapy in chronic disease. *Scand. J. Med. Sci. Sports* 16(S1):3–63

Picinnin AM, Hofer SM. 2008. Integrative analysis of longitudinal studies on aging: collaborative research networks, meta-analysis, and optimizing future studies. In *Handbook of Cognitive Aging: Interdisciplinary Perspectives*, ed. SM Hofer, DF Aldwin, pp. 446–76. Los Angeles: Sage

Poropat AE. 2009. A meta-analysis of the five-factor model of personality and academic performance. *Psychol. Bull.* 135:322–38

Pressman SD, Cohen S. 2005. Does positive affect influence health? *Psychol. Bull.* 131:925–71

Pressman SD, Gallagher MW, Lopez SJ. 2013. Is the emotion-health connection a "first-world problem"? *Psychol. Sci.* 24:544–49

Pruchno RA, Wilson-Genderson M, Rose M, Cartwright F. 2010. Successful aging: early influences and contemporary characteristics. *Gerontologist* 5:821–33

Puig J, Englund MM, Simpson JA, Collins WA. 2013. Predicting adult physical illness from infant attachment: a prospective longitudinal study. *Health Psychol.* 32:409–17

Roberts BW, Caspi A, Moffitt T. 2003. Work experiences and personality development in young adulthood. *J. Personal. Soc. Psychol.* 84:582–93

Roberts NJ, Vogelstein JT, Parmigiani G, Kinzler KW, Vogelstein B, Velculescu VE. 2012. The predictive capacity of personal genome sequencing. *Sci. Transl. Med.* 4:133ra58

Roelfs DJ, Shor E, Davidson KW, Schwartz JE. 2011. Losing life and livelihood: a systematic review and meta-analysis of unemployment and all-cause mortality. *Soc. Sci. Med.* 72:840–54

Rowe JW, Kahn RL. 1987. Human aging: usual and successful. *Science* 237:143–49

Rugulies R. 2002. Depression as a predictor for coronary heart disease: a review and meta-analysis. *Am. J. Prev. Med.* 23:51–61

Rutledge T, Redwine LS, Linke SE, Mills PJ. 2013. A meta-analysis of mental health treatments and cardiac rehabilitation for improving clinical outcomes and depression among patients with coronary heart disease. *Psychosom. Med.* 75:335–49

Ryan RM, Huta V, Deci EL. 2006. Living well: a self-determination theory perspective on eudaimonia. *J. Happiness Stud.* 9:139–70

Ryff CD, Keyes CLM. 1995. The structure of psychological well-being revisited. *J. Personal. Soc. Psychol.* 69:719–27

Ryff CD, Singer B. 1998. The contours of positive human health. *Psychol. Inq.* 9:1–28

Ryff CD, Singer B. 2009. Understanding healthy aging: key components and their integration. In *Handbook of Theories of Aging*, ed. VL Bengston, D Gans, NM Pulney, M Silverstein, pp. 117–44. New York: Springer. 2nd ed.

Ryff CD, Singer BH, Love GD. 2004. Positive health: connecting well-being with biology. *Philos. Trans. R. Soc. B* 359:1383–94

Schaie KW, Willis SL, eds. 2011. *Handbook of the Psychology of Aging*. New York: Elsevier. 7th ed.

Schaufeli WB, Bakker AB, Salanova M. 2006. The measurement of work engagement with a short questionnaire: a cross-national study. *Educ. Psychol. Meas.* 66:701–16

Schulz R, Bookwala JB, Knapp JE, Scheier MF, Williamson GM. 1996. Pessimism, age, and cancer mortality. *Psychol. Aging* 11:304–9

Seligman MEP. 2011. *Flourish*. New York: Simon & Schuster

Shanahan MJ, Hill PL, Roberts BW, Eccles J, Friedman HS. 2013. Conscientiousness, health, and aging: the life course of personality model. *Dev. Psychol.* In press. doi: 10.1037/a0031130

Shiner RL, Masten AS. 2012. Childhood personality as a harbinger of competence and resilience in adulthood. *Dev. Psychopathol.* 24:507–28

Siegel BS. 1986. *Love, Medicine and Miracles. Lessons Learned About Self-Healing from a Surgeon's Experience with Exceptional Patients*. New York: HarperCollins

Siegel BS. 1990. *Peace, Love and Healing. Bodymind Communication and the Path to Self-Healing: An Exploration*. New York: HarperCollins

Sin NL, Lyubomirsky S. 2009. Enhancing well-being and alleviating depressive symptoms with positive psychology interventions: a practice friendly meta-analysis. *J. Clin. Psychol.* 65:467–87

Sloan RP. 2011. Virtue and vice in health and illness: the idea that wouldn't die. *Lancet* 377:896–97

Smith TW, Gallo LC. 2001. Personality traits as risk factors for physical illness. In *Handbook of Health Psychology*, ed. A Baum, T Revenson, J Singer, pp. 139–72. Hillsdale, NJ: Erlbaum

Steger MF. 2009. Meaning in life. In *Oxford Handbook of Positive Psychology*, ed. SJ Lopez, pp. 679–87. Oxford, UK: Oxford Univ. Press. 2nd ed.

Steger MF. 2012a. Experiencing meaning in life: optimal functioning at the nexus of spirituality, psychopathology, and well-being. In *The Human Quest for Meaning*, ed. PTP Wong, pp. 165–84. New York: Routledge. 2nd ed.

Steger MF. 2012b. Making meaning in life. *Psychol. Inquiry* 23:381–85

Steinberg L, Morris AS. 2001. Adolescent development. *Annu. Rev. Psychol.* 52:83–101

Ströhle A. 2009. Physical activity, exercise, depression, and anxiety disorders. *J. Neural Transm.* 116:777–84

Strully KW. 2009. Job loss and health in the U.S. labor market. *Demography* 46:221–46

Suls J, Bunde J. 2005. Anger, anxiety, and depression as risk factors for cardiovascular disease: the problems and implications of overlapping affective dispositions. *Psychol. Bull.* 131:260–300

Sutin AR, Ferrucci L, Zonferman AB, Terracciano A. 2011. Personality and obesity across the adult lifespan. *J. Personal. Soc. Psychol.* 101:579–92

Taga KT, Friedman HS, Martin LR. 2009. Early personality predictors of mortality risk following conjugal bereavement. *J. Personal.* 77:669–90

Taylor MD, Whiteman MC, Fowkes GR, Lee AJ, Allerhand M, Deary IJ. 2009. Five Factor Model personality traits and all cause mortality in the Edinburgh Artery Study cohort. *Psychosom. Med.* 71:631–41

Taylor SE. 2011. Social support: a review. See Friedman 2011a, pp. 189–214

Taylor SE, Repetti RL, Seeman T. 1997. Health psychology: What is an unhealthy environment and how does it get under the skin? *Annu. Rev. Psychol.* 48:411–47

Terracciano A, Costa PT Jr. 2004. Smoking and the five-factor model of personality. *Addiction* 99:472–81

Terracciano A, Löckenhoff CE, Zonderman AB, Ferrucci L, Costa PT. 2008. Personality predictors of longevity: activity, emotional stability, and conscientiousness. *Psychosom. Med.* 70:621–27

Thombs BD, Roseman M, Coyne JC, de Jonge P, Delisle VS, et al. 2013. Does evidence support the American Heart Association's recommendation to screen patients for depression in cardiovascular care? An updated systematic review. *PLoS ONE* 8:e52654

Tseloni A. 2000. Personal criminal victimization in the United States: fixed and random effects of individual and household characteristics. *J. Quant. Criminol.* 16:415–42

Tseloni A, Pease K. 2003. Repeat personal victimization: boosts or flags? *Br. J. Criminol.* 43:196–212

Tseloni A, Witterbrood K, Farrell G, Pease K. 2004. Burglary victimization in England and Wales, the United States, and the Netherlands: a cross-national comparative test of routine activities and lifestyle theories. *Br. J. Criminol.* 44:66–91

Turiano NA, Mroczek DK, Moynihan J, Chapman BP. 2013. Big 5 personality traits and interleukin-6: evidence for "healthy neuroticism" in a US population sample. *Brain Behav. Immun.* 28:83–89

Twenge JM. 2006. *Generation Me: Why Today's Young Americans Are More Confident, Assertive, Entitled—And More Miserable Than Ever Before.* New York: Free Press

Vaillant GE. 1971. Theoretical hierarchy of adaptive ego mechanisms: a 30 year follow-up of 30 men selected for psychological health. *Arch. Gen. Psychiatry* 24:107–18

Vaillant GE. 2012. *Triumphs of Experience: The Men of the Harvard Grant Study.* Cambridge, MA: Belknap

Veenhoven R. 2008. Healthy happiness: effects of happiness on physical health and the consequences for preventative health care. *J. Happiness Stud.* 9:449–69

Vollrath M. 2001. Personality and stress. *Scand. J. Personal.* 42:335–47

Vollrath M, Torgersen S. 2002. Who takes health risks? A probe into eight personality types. *Personal. Individ. Differ.* 32:1185–97

Walum H, Westberg L, Henningsson S, Neiderhiser JM, Reiss D, et al. 2008. Genetic variation in the vasopressin receptor 1a gene (*AVPR1A*) associates with pair-bonding behavior in humans. *Proc. Natl. Acad. Sci. USA* 105:14153–56

Ware JE Jr. 2004. SF-36 health survey update. In *The Use of Psychological Testing for Treatment Planning and Outcomes Assessment: Volume 3: Instruments for Adults*, ed. ME Maurish, pp. 693–718. Mahwah, NJ: Erlbaum

Watson D, Pennebaker JW. 1989. Health complaints, stress, and distress: exploring the central role of negative affectivity. *Psychol. Rev.* 96:234–54

Weiss A, Costa PT. 2005. Domain and facet personality predictors of all-cause mortality among Medicare patients aged 65 to 100. *Psychosom. Med.* 67:724–73

Welch HG, Black WC. 2010. Overdiagnosis in cancer. *J. Natl. Cancer Inst.* 102:605–13

Welch HG, Schwartz L, Woloshin S. 2011. *Overdiagnosed: Making People Sick in the Pursuit of Health.* Boston, MA: Beacon

Whalley B, Rees K, Davies P, Bennett P, Ebrahim S, et al. 2011. Psychological interventions for coronary heart disease. *Cochrane Database Syst. Rev.* 8:CD002902

Wilson RS, Mendes de Leon CF, Bienias JL, Evans DA, Bennett DA. 2004. Personality and mortality in old age. *J. Gerontol. B Psychol. Sci. Soc. Sci.* 59:P110–16

Wilson RS, Schneider JA, Arnold SE, Bienias JL, Bennett DA. 2007. Conscientiousness and the incidence of Alzheimer disease and mild cognitive impairment. *Arch. Gen. Psychiatry* 64:1204–12

World Health Organ. 1994. *Global Strategy on Occupational Health For All: The Way to Health at Work.* Geneva, Switz.: World Health Organ. **http://www.who.int/occupational_health/publications/globstrategy/en/index1.html**

Wulsin LR, Singal BM. 2003. Do depressive symptoms increase the risk for the onset of coronary disease? A systematic quantitative review. *Psychosom. Med.* 65:201–10

Yap SC, Anusic I, Lucas RE. 2012. Does personality moderate reaction and adaptation to major life events? Evidence from the British Household Panel Survey. *J. Res. Personal.* 46:477–88

Properties of the Internal Clock: First- and Second-Order Principles of Subjective Time

Melissa J. Allman,[1] Sundeep Teki,[2] Timothy D. Griffiths,[2,3] and Warren H. Meck[4]

[1] Department of Psychology, Michigan State University, East Lansing, Michigan 48823; email: mjallman@msu.edu

[2] Wellcome Trust Center for Neuroimaging, University College London, London, WC1N 3BG United Kingdom; email: s.teki@fil.ion.ucl.ac.uk

[3] Institute of Neuroscience, The Medical School, Newcastle University, Newcastle-upon-Tyne, NE2 4HH United Kingdom; email: tim.griffiths@newcastle.ac.uk

[4] Department of Psychology and Neuroscience, Duke University, Durham, North Carolina 27701; email: meck@psych.duke.edu

Annu. Rev. Psychol. 2014. 65:743–71

First published online as a Review in Advance on September 11, 2013

The *Annual Review of Psychology* is online at http://psych.annualreviews.org

This article's doi:
10.1146/annurev-psych-010213-115117

Keywords

timing, time perception, clock speed, thought speed, memory translation constant, attentional time-sharing, cerebral cortex, basal ganglia, cerebellum

Abstract

Humans share with other animals an ability to measure the passage of physical time and subjectively experience a sense of time passing. Subjective time has hallmark qualities, akin to other senses, which can be accounted for by formal, psychological, and neurobiological models of the internal clock. These include first-order principles, such as changes in clock speed and how temporal memories are stored, and second-order principles, including timescale invariance, multisensory integration, rhythmical structure, and attentional time-sharing. Within these principles there are both typical individual differences—influences of emotionality, thought speed, and psychoactive drugs—and atypical differences in individuals affected with certain clinical disorders (e.g., autism, Parkinson's disease, and schizophrenia). This review summarizes recent behavioral and neurobiological findings and provides a theoretical framework for considering how changes in the properties of the internal clock impact time perception and other psychological domains.

Contents

INTRODUCTION

Time shapes many aspects of our daily lives (Allan 1979, Buhusi & Meck 2005, Meck et al. 2013): The reader may have set aside a certain amount of objective (clock) time (Bisson & Grondin 2013) to read this article before moving onto other activities, which may themselves need to be performed at or for specific times. We rely heavily on external timekeepers and temporal organizers (clocks, calendars) to keep track of the temporal properties of events (i.e., when and for how long an event will occur), but we are also quite adept at keeping track of time on our own given the appropriate circumstances (Nobre & Coull 2010). The challenge, therefore, is to identify the clock inside our heads, something referred to as the "internal clock" (Church 1984). As in other animals, our ability to time external events in the seconds to minutes range (interval timing) allows us to subjectively experience the passage of physical time and allows us to integrate action sequences, thoughts, and behavior and to detect emerging trends and anticipate future outcomes (Bechara et al. 1996, Kotz et al. 2009, Nussbaum et al. 2006). This temporal yardstick (internal clock) can also be both typically and atypically distorted by a variety of sensory, psychological, and physiological factors (e.g., arousal, modality, and pharmacological treatments; see Allman & Meck 2012, Paule et al. 1999, Vatakis & Allman 2013). Perhaps parsimoniously related to the internal clock is our ability to temporally structure our use of language and other cognitive processes such that past events serve as agents for current events (e.g., episodic memory) and for planning and sequencing our intended behaviors toward events in the future (e.g., executive function and prospective memory), which although perhaps uniquely human may not necessarily be so (Allman et al. 2013, Diedrichsen et al. 2003, Nyberg et al. 2010, Schirmer 2004, Siegel et al. 2012, Suddendorf et al. 2009, Ullman 2004, Ullman & Pierpont 2005).

Most researchers agree that there is no single neurological locus that serves as the core (master) clock in the brain, although the primordial circadian clock in the suprachiasmic nucleus can regularly and persistently modulate a variety of species' sleep-wake to day-night cycles (even in conditions devoid of light-dark cues). However, to account for interval timing ability, which has been unequivocally demonstrated, some sort of general-purpose, cognitively controlled internal clock is required (Agostino et al. 2011a; Allman & Meck 2012; Freestone et al. 2013; Guilhardi & Church 2009; Hinton & Meck 1997a,b; Lewis & Meck 2012; Lewis & Miall 2003; Matell &

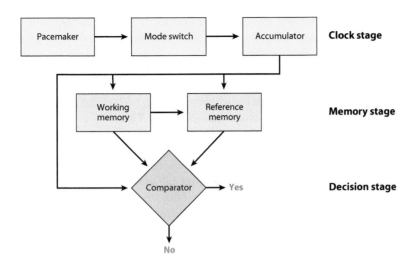

Figure 1

The information-processing model of interval timing as specified by scalar timing theory and other internal clock theories of psychological time. Adapted from Church (1984), Gibbon et al. (1984), Meck (1984), and Treisman (1963, 1984).

Meck 2000; Meck 1984; Treisman 1963, 1984, 2013). The primary goal of this review is to specify the forms this internal clock may take, i.e., psychological, biological, and formal.

As originally proposed, the internal clock (Church 1984, Gibbon et al. 1984, Treisman 1963) is composed of a three-process model (see **Figure 1**). At the onset of a to-be-timed event (stimulus), a pacemaker emits pulses that are gated into an accumulator by attention. The current pulse tally (in working memory) is compared with a previously stored value (in reference memory) for that particular event duration. When the two values match closely enough, a decision rule operates to produce an estimate of time, which can be influenced by feedback. Much like a stopwatch, this system can be started (run mode), paused (stop mode), and reset (repeat mode) to time specific events or multiple events occurring at the same time (Buhusi & Meck 2009b, Meck & Church 1983).

As revealed by psychophysical methods used to quantify sensory responses to physical stimuli (see Gescheider 1997), timing and time perception have a variety of features (indices derived from psychophysical functions) that must be accounted for by all plausible models of the internal clock, regardless of the differences in their proposed mechanisms (Buhusi et al. 2002, 2005; Matell & Meck 2000; Penney et al. 2008; Wencil et al. 2010). For not only is the intensity of the internal perception linearly related to the magnitude of external stimulation (subjective time increases with physical time), but also increases in the magnitude of a physical stimulus produce proportional increases in the variance of the perception (it is more difficult to time precisely for longer durations)—referred to as scalar variance or Weber's law (see Allan 1998). Thus interval timing ability shares many characteristic hallmarks with sensory perception (like vision and hearing; see Fraisse 1984). Considerable progress has been made in specifying the basic operating principles (Wearden 2005) and identifying the behavioral mechanisms and neural substrates involved in interval timing. Indeed models of interval timing have been called "the most successful [models] in the whole of psychology" (Wearden 2001, 2003).

Although neural-network states may be utilized to time subsecond durations without the need for a dedicated clock (Karmarkar & Buonomano 2007, Laje & Buonomano 2013), the timing of suprasecond durations on the order of seconds to minutes appears to involve a number of first- and second-order principles that can be used to classify (within- and between-) individual differences in interval timing ability (for details, see Buhusi & Meck 2005, Gibbon et al. 1984, Meck 2003). These principles define how the internal clock works and how it can be manipulated by sensory, psychological, and physiological factors. First-order principles are those that can be applied to individual event durations and typically involve the accuracy and precision with which the criterion duration is timed. These include differences in (*a*) how fast the subjective clock is ticking—clock speed (α, the rate of pulse accumulation; see **Figure 1**); and (*b*) how the breadth of durations is subjectively stored and compared with ongoing (present) durations—associated memory translation parameter (k^*, comparing the current pulse count to the stored pulse count). Second-order principles compare multiple durations with each other in terms of (*c*) timescale invariance, that is, explaining why it is easier to detect one additional increment in stimulus value (i.e., brightness, duration) between high-intensity events compared with those of low intensity— the scalar property. The influence of nontemporal factors on interval timing also needs to be considered, such as (*d*) why auditory events of a given physical duration are judged subjectively as being longer than visual events—modality effects and memory mixing; (*e*) how our interval timing ability appears intimately related to our sensitivity to organizing rhythms—beat-based versus duration-based timing; and (*f*) how our subjective sense of time can be influenced by how much we are thinking about the temporal quality of events (e.g., the notion that a watched pot never boils)—attentional time-sharing. Of course, perhaps the most compelling challenge, and evidence, for the existence of the internal clock is in its neurobiological instantiation as described in the sections below (Allman & Meck 2012, Coull et al. 2011, Merchant et al. 2013, Salvioni et al. 2013, Teki et al. 2012).

William James (1890) first asked, "To what cerebral process is the sense of time due?" Experimental findings heavily implicate the cerebral cortex (Buonomano & Laje 2010; Durstewitz & Deco 2008; Harrington et al. 1998, 2004, 2010, 2011b; Ivry & Spencer 2004; Ivry & Schlerf 2008; Karmarkar & Buonomano 2007; Koch et al. 2009; Kotz & Schwartze 2010, 2011; Livesey et al. 2007; Matell et al. 2003, 2011; Meck et al. 2008; Van Rijn et al. 2013; Wiener et al. 2010a,b), along with the basal ganglia and cerebellum (motor and cognitive sequencing centers). The oscillatory properties of cortical neurons appear to produce the internal clock ticks and, hence, provide a distinct pattern of activity (ticks) to represent a given duration (cf. accumulator in **Figure 1**), which appear to be detected by striatal medium spiny neurons tuned to trigger an action potential to a target duration by detecting coincident oscillatory patterns (cf. memory processes; see Brody et al. 2003; Kaufman et al. 2005; Lustig et al. 2005; Treisman et al. 1990, 1994). There also appears to be a general form of ordinal (e.g., how much?) analog representation of magnitude (time, space, and number) within the parietal cortex (Bueti & Walsh 2009; Cordes et al. 2007; Meck & Church 1983; Walsh 2003a,b). These various contributions of the cerebral cortex to the properties of the internal clock are outlined in **Table 1**.

The overall strategy of this review is to discuss first- and second-order principles of the internal clock with an emphasis on their neurobiological bases (Allman & Meck 2012, Claassen et al. 2013, Jones et al. 2011, Meck 2005, Merchant et al. 2013, Tregellas et al. 2006, Teki et al. 2012, van Rijn et al. 2011). We examine animal models; typical and atypical individual differences in human timing behavior, such as those affected by certain clinical disorders (e.g., autism, Parkinson's disease, and schizophrenia); drug and lesion effects; and candidate neural substrates for the internal clock (i.e., corticostriatal and cortico-cerebellar circuits). The goal is to provide the basis for a unified model of interval timing based on our current understanding of its underlying psychological and neural mechanisms (Allman & Meck 2012, Buhusi et al. 2013, Claassen et al. 2013, Cope et al. 2013, Jones & Jahanshahi 2013, Jones et al. 2011, Meck 2005, Merchant et al. 2013, Tregellas et al. 2006, Teki et al. 2012).

Table 1 Summary of cortical contributions to interval timing

Cortical area(s)	Technique(s)	Species	Findings	Reference(s)
Neocortex	Decortication by pial stripping	Rat	Rightward shift of timing functions consistent with a change in k^*	Jaldow et al. (1989, 1990)
Lateral AFC/primary motor cortex	Single-unit recording	Rat	Units demonstrate peaks of activity centered around the appropriate signal durations	Matell et al. (2003)
Medial AFC	Single-unit recording	Rat	Units demonstrate a heterogeneous population code of ramps, peaks, and troughs as a function of signal duration	Matell et al. (2011)
Lateral AFC	Aspiration lesion	Rat	Rightward shift of timing functions consistent with a change in k^*	Meck et al. (1987)
Lateral AFC	Aspiration lesion	Rat	Reduced clock speed effect of DA agonists and antagonists	Meck (2005)
Lateral AFC	Aspiration lesion	Rat	Impairments in STP	Olton et al. (1988)
Lateral AFC/primary motor cortex	Single-unit recording	Rat	Units respond to compound stimuli in an STP task	Pang et al. (2001)
PFC, presupplementary, and SMA	Single-unit recording	Monkey	Units code specific target durations by temporal filtering	Mita et al. (2009), Oshio et al. (2008)
PFC, Area 9	Single-unit recording	Monkey	Units respond in perceptual recognition and during the internal generation of a target duration	Yumoto et al. (2011)
Dorsolateral PFC, posterior inferior parietal cortex, basal ganglia, and posterior cingulate cortex	PET	Monkey	Local application of bicuculline resulted in selective impairments in timekeeping within the identified neural networks	Onoe et al. (2001)
Hippocampal structures	Dorsal hippocampal, fimbria-fornix, or medial septal area lesions	Rat/mouse	Leftward shift and sharpening of timing functions consistent with a change in k^*	Balci et al. (2009), Meck (1988), Meck et al. (1984, 1987, 2013), Olton et al. (1988), Yin & Meck (2013), Yin et al. (2010)
Medial temporal lobe	Left or right temporal lobe resection	Human	Left temporal lobe resection leads to a leftward shift of timing functions consistent with a change in k^*. Right resection leads to increased variability	Melgire et al. (2005), Vidalaki et al. (1999)
Left inferior parietal cortex	fMRI	Human	Left-hemispheric bias for implicit timing	Coull & Nobre (2008), Wiener et al. (2010a)
Right dorsolateral PFC	fMRI and TMS in normal controls as well as in patients with right PFC lesions	Human	Right-hemispheric bias for explicit timing with underestimation of duration following TMS and timing deficits in PFC patients	Coull & Nobre (2008), Harrington et al. (1998), Koch et al. (2002), Meck & Malapani (2004), Wiener et al. (2010b)
Left posterior parietal, striatal, and bilateral inferior frontal regions	fMRI	Human	Attending to time	Coull & Nobre (2008), Coull et al. (2003, 2008, 2011), Wencil et al. (2010)

(Continued)

Table 1   (*Continued*)

Cortical area(s)	Technique(s)	Species	Findings	Reference(s)
Left inferior frontal, superior temporal, and SMA regions	fMRI	Human	Accumulator component of timing	Wencil et al. (2010)
Inferior frontal cortices bilaterally	fMRI	Human	Comparator component of timing	Coull et al. (2008), Teki et al. (2011), Wencil et al. (2010)
Frontostriatal circuits: includes presupplementary motor area and right frontal operculum	fMRI	Human	Three areas of a timing network that survive a task-difficulty manipulation have been identified: inferior gyrus, anterior insula, left supramarginal gyrus, and putamen	Coull et al. (2003, 2008, 2011), Harrington et al. (2010), Hinton & Meck (2004), Livesey et al. (2007), Meck et al. (2008), Rao et al. (2001)
Right parietal cortex	fMRI in normal controls and brain-damaged patients with spatial neglect	Human	Cortical involvement of sensorimotor transformations with regard to space, time, and other magnitudes	Bueti & Walsh (2009), Danckert et al. (2007)
SMA, left premotor cortex, and left insula	fMRI	Human	Beat-based perceivers showed greater activation in comparison with duration-based perceivers	Grahn & McAuley (2009); see also Teki et al. (2011)
Left posterior superior, middle temporal gyri, and right premotor cortex	fMRI	Human	Duration-based perceivers showed greater activation in comparison with beat-based perceivers	Grahn & McAuley (2009); see also Teki et al. (2011)
Right superior temporal gyrus	TMS	Human	Impaired auditory temporal processing	Bueti et al. (2008a,b)
Auditory cortex	TMS	Human	Impaired auditory and visual temporal processing	Kanai et al. (2011)
Visual cortex	TMS	Human	Impaired visual temporal processing only	Kanai et al. (2011)

Abbreviations: AFC, agranular frontal cortex; DA, dopamine; fMRI, functional magnetic resonance imaging; k^*, memory translation constant; PET, positron emission tomography; PFC, prefrontal cortex; SMA, supplementary motor area; STP, simultaneous temporal processing; TMS, transcranial magnetic stimulation.

FIRST-ORDER PRINCIPLES OF SUBJECTIVE TIME

Clock Speed/Thought Speed

The rate at which subjective time grows as a function of elapsing physical time is thought to be influenced by clock speed, which is reflected by the number of clock ticks or oscillations per unit time (Church 1984, Maricq et al. 1981, Meck 1983, Treisman 2013). This concept of clock speed and the subjective experience of time can be shown to be logically related to formulations of thought speed, which is independent of thought content but dependent on the level of arousal, mood, and the frequency of environmental events (Pronin 2013, Pronin et al. 2008, Pronin & Jacobs 2008, Pronin & Wegner 2006). Thus, the first-order principle of clock speed can accommodate the second-order principle of the influence of nontemporal features (i.e., modality, arousal, affect) on interval timing. Changes in clock speed (e.g., via arousal, emotion) lead to proportional changes in the representation of event durations, through the rate at which the criterion number of pacemaker pulses (clock ticks) is accumulated. Various pharmacological and psychiatric conditions appear to modify clock speed, and changes in mean clock speed can be modeled either as a within- or between-trials phenomenon, although the convention is to rely on between-trial variation (Gibbon & Church 1984, 1990, 1992; Matell & Meck 2004; Meck 1983). Changes in clock speed are typically measured relative to a baseline condition, and absolute measures (of pulse accumulation) are difficult to obtain (Williamson et al. 2008).

How might we attempt to measure the absolute speed of an internal clock? One strategy would be to attempt to synchronize the time base with a repetitive signal (e.g., visual flicker or auditory click trains) presented at a known frequency (Treisman et al. 1990; Wearden et al. 1999, 2009; but see Repp et al. 2013). This process is referred to as entrainment, and assumptions must be made about the underlying frequencies of these putative oscillatory processes (see Lustig et al. 2005, Matell & Meck 2004, Treisman et al. 1994). Once participants have been entrained to this external metronome, they could then be released into a free-run condition and allowed to return to their normal (clock speed) state. Differences in the horizontal placement of their psychophysical timing functions under these two conditions (entrainment versus free run) would allow investigators to determine their natural oscillation frequency or clock speed (Treisman 2013).

Conventionally, when compared relative to a nondrug baseline (assigned a nominal value of 1.0 in the model), administration of indirect dopamine agonists—including drugs of abuse such as cocaine, methamphetamine, and nicotine—increases clock speed as indexed by a leftward shift in the position of timing functions (i.e., 20% faster; a value of 1.2 in the model; Cheng et al. 2006, 2007; Maricq et al. 1981; Matell et al. 2004, 2006; Meck 1983, 2007). In contrast, dopamine receptor antagonists such as haloperidol and raclopride produce proportional rightward shifts in functions that are interpreted as reflecting a decrease in clock speed (and assigned multiplicative constants <1.0 in the model; Buhusi & Meck 2002; MacDonald & Meck 2004, 2005, 2006; Maricq & Church 1983; Meck 1983, 1986, 1996). In the internal-clock model, increases and decreases in clock speed produce a multiplicative change in the stored clock reading associated with a particular event duration.

Such pharmacological challenges (e.g., methamphetamine and haloperidol) have been coupled with excitotoxic lesions of cholinergic cell bodies in the medial septal area and the nucleus basalis magnocellularis, as well as with radiofrequency lesions of the fimbria-fornix and aspiration lesions of the frontal cortex, to investigate control of the internal clock (Meck 1996, 2006a; Meck et al. 1986, 1987). Lesions of the nucleus basalis magnocellularis (which contains cholinergic cell bodies that project to the frontal cortex), as well as lesions of the frontal cortex itself, selectively reduce the pharmacological modification of clock speed. This ability suggests that clock speed is likely mediated by dopamine receptors located on corticostriatal neurons in the nigrostriatal pathway (recall that cortical oscillations likely serve as the time base of the internal clock coincidence detected by medium spiny neurons in the striatum). Such combined lesion/genomic/pharmacological studies provide a crucial foundation for understanding how the oscillatory properties of corticostriatal circuits subserve clock ticks and the memory processes used in duration discrimination (Agostino et al. 2013; Balci et al. 2012; Buhusi & Oprisan 2013; Meck 1996, 2001; Meck et al. 2012; Oprisan & Buhusi 2011). The selectivity of this cortical control of clock speed is supported by recent findings showing that dopamine in the nucleus accumbens (mesolimbic pathway) plays a crucial role in motivation/incentive salience but not in the regulation of clock speed (Kurti & Matell 2011).

The fact that time can subjectively pass by faster or slower under various conditions (i.e., low/high arousal and/or drug effects) may also account for the pace of behavioral and social interactions involving impulsivity (Wittmann et al. 2011, Wittmann & Paulus 2008). Various clinical populations, considered to have impairments in internal clock–related abilities, have the potential to provide absolute measures of clock speed, including individuals with abnormal and normal aging, attention-deficit/hyperactivity disorder (ADHD), autism, schizophrenia, Parkinson's disease, and drug abuse (Allman 2011; Allman & Meck 2012; Cheng et al. 2011; Kotz et al. 2009; Lustig & Meck 2001, 2005; Grahn & Brett 2009; Malapani et al. 1998; Meck 2006a,b,c; Meck & Benson 2002; Penney et al. 2005; Smith et al. 2007; Wittmann et al. 2007).

Memory Translation Constant

Researchers assume that the accumulation (current tally) of pacemaker pulses grows in a linear fashion as physical duration increases but may not necessarily be stored (remembered) veridically. The difference between the current duration (clock reading) and the encoded duration stored in reference memory is reflected by a memory translation constant (see Church 1984; Gibbon et al. 1984; MacDonald et al. 2007; Meck 2002a,b). That is, the number of pacemaker pulses is transferred from the accumulator to reference memory at some modifiable baud rate that ultimately influences the quantitative aspects of the represented signal duration (e.g., Meck 1983, 1996).

In a modified version of the original timing model, known as scalar timing theory (e.g., Gibbon et al. 1984; Gibbon & Church 1984, 1990, 1992), memory translation has formally been referred to as the k^* parameter, which is a multiplicative constant (Church 2003, Meck 1983). An individual would consistently expect the end of an event to occur later than the programmed time (i.e., if its memory storage constant was greater than 1.0) or earlier (i.e., if its memory storage constant was less than 1.0). The remembered duration of an event is based on the amount of time required to transfer the clock reading (e.g., oscillation vector or number of pulses in the accumulator) into reference memory. Transfer time would be directly proportional to the size of the oscillation vector or the number of pulses in the accumulator and the speed of transfer (i.e., baud rate). Pulse accumulation essentially functions as an up counter and memory transfer functions as a down counter, with the additional assumption that neural networks can function as look-up or conversion tables (Dali & Zemin 1993, Kimura & Hayakawa 2008).

If the speed of this memory storage process were to deviate from normal values, then it would be possible for proportionally shorter or longer values to be represented in memory. Unlike changes in clock speed, changes in memory storage speed would not self-correct, even in the case where individuals were surprised by the mismatch between their clock readings and a value sampled from reference memory. This lack of flexibility is because any updating of memory in this case would lead to the continued distortion of stored values for as long as the modification in memory storage speed remained in effect, i.e., as long as k^* was greater than or less than 1.0 (e.g., Meck 1983, 1996, 2002a).

Derived k^* parameters have been obtained from various typical and atypical populations. For example, principled computer modeling (Wearden 2001) of time-perception (temporal generalization) data in children reveals that the k^* parameter (and hence, memory distortion) quantifiably improves across childhood (Droit-Volet et al. 2001, Lustig & Meck 2011), and this typical trend in k^* is not observed in a broader age range of individuals with autism (Allman 2011, Allman et al. 2011). Damage to hippocampal and cortical circuits produces distortions in temporal memory that are proportional to the physical durations of the events being timed; hippocampal-related damage produces underproductions and cortical-related damage produces overproductions of target durations (Coull et al. 2011; Harrington et al. 1998; Jaldow et al. 1989, 1990; Koch et al. 2003; Meck 1988; Meck et al. 1984, 1987, 2013; Olton et al. 1988; Vidalaki et al. 1999; Yin & Meck 2013; Yin & Troger 2011; Yin et al. 2010). Moreover, the relationship between the magnitude of the error in the content of temporal memory and activity in the frontal cortex and hippocampus has been examined in mature (10- to 16-month-old) and aged (24- to 30-month-old) rats (Meck 2002a,b, 2006c). Regression analyses indicated that neural activity in the frontal cortex of both mature and aged rats, and in the hippocampus only for aged rats, is proportional to the absolute error in the content of temporal memory. The observed changes in neural activity were dependent on the predictability of the programmed time of feedback and age-related changes in memory encoding and retrieval.

SECOND-ORDER PRINCIPLES OF SUBJECTIVE TIME

Scalar Property

The scalar property of interval timing is a form of Weber's law that is shared with the other senses (Gescheider 1997, Gibbon 1977). It is characterized by proportionality between the standard deviation of a response distribution and the target duration being timed, reflected in the linearity of the relationship between timing variability and duration magnitude (Church 1984, 1989; Church et al. 1994; Gibbon 1977, 1991; Gibbon et al. 1984; Malapani & Fairhurst 2002; Piras & Coull 2011). This notion suggests that the coefficient of variation (CV; ratio between the standard deviation and the mean of the sample) should be constant across a range of durations; multiple timescales may also be identified that reflect timing mechanisms with different levels of precision, such as subsecond and suprasecond timing (Cordes & Meck 2013, Gibbon et al. 1997; but see Lewis & Miall 2009 for an alternative view of violations of the scalar property). Moreover, a strong form of Weber's law applied to interval timing can be evaluated by plotting the entire response function obtained from the timing task, e.g., peak-interval or temporal bisection procedures, on a relative timescale, i.e., normalized by the obtained peak time or the point of subjective equality as illustrated in **Figures 2**, **3**, **4**, and **5**. The superimposition of the entire psychometric function for

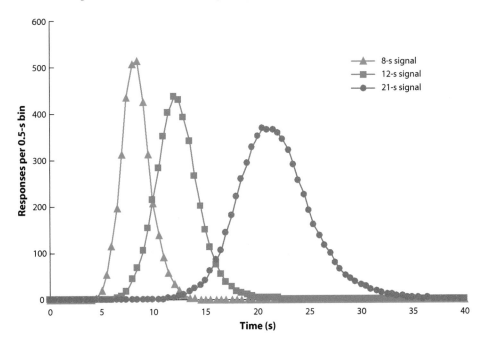

Figure 2

Human peak-interval timing functions for 8-, 12-, and 21-s target durations. Mean keyboard responses per 0.5 s plotted as a function of duration (seconds) for a visual (*blue square*) signal. Data are replotted from Rakitin et al. (1998) with permission.

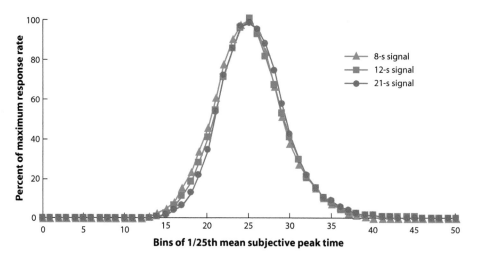

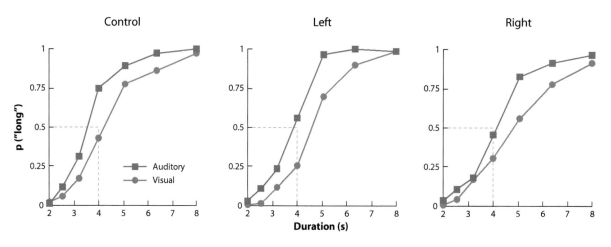

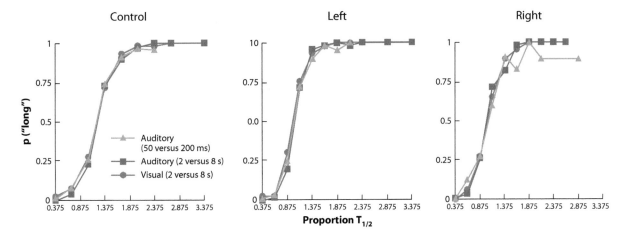

Figure 5

Scalar property. Superimposition plot of temporal bisection functions in control participants and patients with either left or right temporal lobe resection. These rescaled response functions from the data in **Figure 4** were created in three steps. First, for each participant and condition, the probe durations were divided by the corresponding point of subjective equality in order to normalize the data. Second, the resulting proportion $T_{1/2}$ values were rank-ordered across participants by condition and grouped in bins of 0.25 unit width. Third, the probability long response, p ("long"), values corresponding to the $T_{1/2}$ values in a given relative time bin, were averaged for that bin. Note that for these plots the values in the end time bins are less reliable than those in the central bins because fewer p ("long") values are likely to contribute to the end bin averages because not all participants will show the same range of proportion $T_{1/2}$ scores. Data for auditory and visual signal durations are replotted from Melgire et al. (2005) with permission. See Allan & Gibbon (1991) for additional details on this method for evaluating superimposition in the temporal bisection procedure.

Superimposition has been equally consistent for human temporal production and reproduction using the peak-interval procedure with durations ranging from 8 to 21 s (Rakitin et al. 1998) and from 8 to 24 s (Hinton & Rao 2004). Moreover, identification of brain regions showing the scalar property in the hemodynamic response associated with the timing of 11- and 17-s durations in an fMRI experiment is a powerful technique for studying corticostriatal circuits and isolating the perceptron component of the neural representation of time in the putamen and other areas of the dorsal striatum (Coull et al. 2008, 2011; Forstmann et al. 2010; Hinton & Meck 2004; Jin et al. 2009; MacDonald et al. 2012; Matell & Meck 2004; Meck & Malapani 2004). The scalar property (i.e., Weber's law) as applied to the mismatch negativity in event-related potentials (ERPs) associated with temporal deviants has also been used as a marker to study the development and preattentive aspects of interval timing in preverbal infants and in healthy adults (Brannon et al. 2004, 2008).

Violations of the scalar property frequently result from procedural issues (Buhusi et al. 2009, Wearden & Lejeune 2008) or data analysis considerations, i.e., whether the CV should be calculated for peak-interval data based on the distribution of peak times from single-trial analysis or from the mode and spread of the mean response function (e.g., Church et al. 1994, Gibbon & Church 1990, Rakitin et al. 1998). When individual differences are observed in the scalar property, it is important to investigate whether some participants are employing a chronometric counting strategy to improve their accuracy and precision for longer durations (Hinton & Rao 2004). Altered variance patterns have also been observed following damage to the underlying timing mechanisms in the basal ganglia in both Huntington's and Parkinson's diseases (e.g., Aparicio et al. 2005, Artieda et al. 1992, Hinton et al. 2007, Malapani et al. 1998). Consequently, individual differences in the scalar property can be diagnosed and classified according to their variance properties. If participants are counting rather than timing, and count at similar rates for all durations, their count totals will be proportional to the durations that they are instructed to time. In this case, the standard deviations of their counting distributions will be proportional to the square root of the duration rather than to the target duration itself as required for scalar timing. Explicit counting improves the precision of timing performance as reported by Rakitin et al. (1998) and modeled by Killeen (1991) and Killeen & Weiss (1987). Chronometric counting of this sort involves the participant subdividing a given duration into a series of smaller intervals that are counted. Nevertheless, the variability of these subintervals typically displays the scalar property over the range of 0.5–1.3 s (Hinton & Rao 2004).

Damage to and/or pharmacological blockade of corticostriatal circuits impairs the regulation of clock speed as a function of the target duration (MacDonald & Meck 2004, 2005, 2006; Meck 1986, 1996, 2006a,b). This limitation is important because timescale invariance is thought to result from the clock reading increasing monotonically within trials at a rate that depends on the duration of the interval (see Almeida & Ledberg 2010, Killeen & Fetterman 1988). As a consequence, diminished control over this systematic increase in clock speed would result in a violation of the scalar property such that longer intervals will be timed more precisely than shorter intervals owing to the loss of the scalar source of variability in clock speed (assuming that the default is Poisson variability; see Gibbon 1992). Weakened regulation of clock speed in Parkinson's disease can also lead to the coupling or migration of multiple target durations such that the shorter duration is overproduced and the longer duration is underproduced (Jones et al. 2008, Koch et al. 2008, Malapani et al. 1998, Shea-Brown et al. 2006).

Furthermore, the scalar property is also demonstrated in the quality of parent-infant interactions (including gaze and vocalizations); specifically, their coordination alternates between scalar and absolute timing patterns in delicate arrangements (see Jaffe et al. 2001). As noted above, the scalar property is also evidenced in the ERPs of infant brains on a passive duration deviation task employing several different ratios of deviants (1:4; 2:3) to regular 375- to 1,500-ms interstimulus intervals, as the amplitude of the deviant-triggered ERP varied according to the stimulus ratio used (Brannon et al. 2008). These improvements in timing sensitivity correspond to critical periods for the development of other cognitive and behavioral abilities. The steepness of children's temporal generalization functions generally increases across childhood (between 3 and 8 years of age; Droit-Volet et al. 2001, Droit-Volet & Wearden 2001). Characteristic differences in the Weber ratio and quality of superimposition have been observed in the temporal bisection performance of children with a developmental disability or autism (Allman et al. 2011) and in adults at high genetic risk for schizophrenia or major affective disorder (Penney et al. 2005).

Observed deviations in the scalar property of interval timing (e.g., the standard deviation of temporal estimates is proportional to the mean of the interval being timed) are often idiosyncratic, and no principled explanation has been offered for when or at what durations they should occur (except for a hypothesized boundary or transition from one type of timing mechanism to another around 1–3 s; see Gibbon et al. 1997, Grondin 2010). Moreover, most quantitative theories of timing incorporate the scalar property because without it they would fail to account for the vast majority of published data. A number of timing theories implicitly assume that the amount of training or experience with specific durations will reduce the variability in their detection/production, hence providing a basis for a lower coefficient of variation for those particular durations compared with durations that are less well trained (Matell & Meck 2004). These factors, of course, are likely to vary as a function of the task demands and other details specific to the individual participants. At present, it does not seem useful to make a laundry list of exceptions to the scalar property when it is clearly a dominant factor in both the perception and production of durations in the millisecond-to-minutes range. Also, scalar timing theory (Gibbon et al. 1984) is based on the assumption of a Poisson (nonscalar) pacemaker/accumulator that is dominated by scalar sources of variance from memory and/or decision mechanisms. Implicit in this quantitative model is the idea that if the scalar sources of variability could be reduced by practice and/or other factors, then the nonscalar timing mechanism would be revealed. Hence, temporal discrimination is the result of a combination of different stages of information processing (e.g., clock, memory, and decision), each with a unique form of variance, the balance of which produces the scalar property of interval-timing behavior. Evaluation of the scalar property also depends on which response measures are used [e.g., measure of central tendency and variance of a distribution of temporal estimates versus the form of the entire distribution as determined by the degree of superimposition of different response functions (see Allan & Gibbon 1991, figures 10, 11)].

Modality Effects/Memory Mixing

The original internal clock model (Church 1984) has been used to investigate the phenomenon that sounds of a given duration are judged longer than lights of the same duration. This modality difference in the subjective experience of time highlights the roles of attention and memory mixing in duration judgments (see Allan 1998, Penney et al. 1998). It is typically easier (improved performance) to discriminate differences in time with auditory rather than visual events; transfer from visual to auditory events is greater than from auditory to visual events; and although the attribute of duration may be used independently of stimulus modality, modality-specific information is also encoded and available for use in temporal accumulator models of interval timing (Bartolo & Merchant 2009, Bueti & Macaluso 2011, Gibbon et al. 1984, Gilaie-Dotan et al. 2011, Hass et al. 2012, Meck & Church 1982).

If both modalities are presented within the same experimental session, and with the same criterion duration (in temporal bisection), individuals are more likely to give "long" judgments to auditory rather than to visual intermediate durations (Cheng et al. 2008; Meck 1991; Penney et al. 1998, 2000; Wearden et al. 1998). This difference in perceived duration may occur because auditory stimuli capture and hold attention relatively automatically, whereas attending to visual stimuli requires controlled attention (Meck 1984); for instance, older adults show an exaggerated modality effect compared with young adults, consistent with age-related reductions in attentional control (Cheng et al. 2008, 2011; Lustig & Meck 2001). Within the context of the model (Church 1984), pacemaker pulses (clocks ticks) for auditory stimuli are more efficiently accumulated, allowing larger pulse accumulations and less uncertainty in the stimulus duration (see Cicchini et al. 2012). If relatively small visual and relatively large auditory pulse tallies are intermixed and stored together as a reference memory for that criterion duration, then ongoing pulse tallies (in working memory) for auditory events have an increased probability of being judged long, relative to the reference memory randomly drawn from the sample (vice versa for visual events).

Large individual differences in memory mixing as explained by Bayesian models of optimization have been observed in time-perception experiments (temporal bisection, generalization, and reproduction) using children and young adults (e.g., Acerbi et al. 2012; Burr et al. 2013; Cicchini et al. 2012; Droit-Volet et al. 2007; Jazayeri & Shadlen 2010; Ogden et al. 2010; Penney et al. 2000; Shi et al. 2010, 2013a,b). The amount of memory mixing can be influenced by both positive and negative feedback (e.g., Gu & Meck 2011), by neurodegenerative conditions such as Parkinson's disease (Gu et al. 2013, Smith et al. 2007), by psychiatric illnesses such as schizophrenia (e.g., Carroll et al. 2008, Penney et al. 2005), and by temporal lobe resection as a treatment for epilepsy (Melgire et al. 2005). Differences in the temporal bisection functions for auditory and visual signal durations for control participants and patients following left or right temporal lobe resection are illustrated in **Figures 4** and **5**.

Various cortical areas are involved in the timing of both auditory and visual stimuli (Bueti et al. 2008a, N'Diaye et al. 2004). Moreover, intrasensory timing can be distinguished from intersensory timing, in part by decreased striatal and increased superior parietal activation (Harrington et al. 2011a). Combined electroencephalography and magnetoencephalography studies have revealed contributions from both auditory and visual cortices in terms of sustained sensory responses, whereas prefrontal and parietal regions appear to integrate modalities in terms of representing event durations (N'Diaye et al. 2004).

With respect to the neurological basis for the phenomenon that sounds are judged longer than lights, there appears to be an interesting asymmetry in how events in different modalities are timed: The right posterior parietal cortex is involved in the timing of both auditory and visual stimuli, whereas visual areas MT/V5 are involved only in the timing of visual events (Bueti et al. 2008b). Disruption of the auditory cortex using transcranial magnetic stimulation (TMS) impaired timing not only for auditory events, but also for visual events (Kanai et al. 2011). In contrast, TMS administered over the primary visual cortex impaired timing performance only for visual events. These results suggest a superiority of the auditory cortex in temporal precision; likewise, they corroborate the proposal that the temporal dimensions of both auditory and visual events are rapidly encoded in the auditory cortex, thereby contributing to the supramodal role for auditory modalities in timing and time perception (see Bueti 2011, Bueti & Macaluso 2010). In contrast, visual events are encoded in the visual cortex in a more selective and controlled (less automatic) fashion (Kanai et al. 2011; see also Meck 1984, Penney et al. 1996). This asymmetry is consistent with findings from cross-modal transfer of duration studies in which discrimination performance is typically better for auditory than for visual events and transfer from visual to auditory events is greater than from auditory to visual events, and although the attribute of duration may be used independently of stimulus modality, modality-specific information is also encoded and available for use in temporal accumulator models of interval timing (Bueti & Macaluso 2011, Gibbon et al. 1984, Gilaie-Dotan et al. 2011, Hass et al. 2012, Meck & Church 1982).

Beat-Based Versus Duration-Based Timing

An intriguing principle of the internal clock, as it relates to its scope, is highlighted by the large and striking individual differences in sensitivity to an implied beat (much like being able to dance to a tune in a coordinated fashion). The question is whether beat perception and interval timing are mediated by different neural circuits: In essence, are they component processes of a broader internal clock, or are they two separate timing systems? Beat perception has been investigated by presenting participants with ambiguous tone sequences; a periodic 600-ms beat is implied but not explicitly emphasized, and participants are required to judge whether the sequences are speeding up or slowing down at the end (Grahn & McAuley 2009, McAuley & Henry 2010). Individuals who did not detect the implied beat perceived the sequences ending with intervals between 300 and 600 ms to be slowing down, whereas individuals who did detect the implied beat perceived the same sequences to be speeding up. Grahn & McAuley (2009) developed an index of the nature of the decision process and its application to the ambiguous sequence paradigm (termed a temporal contrast metric), which determines whether an individual tends toward or against beat-based or duration-based timing and is based on the general theoretical framework of previous dynamic systems models developed by McAuley and colleagues (e.g., McAuley & Jones 2003, McAuley & Miller 2007). The required speeding up or slowing down judgments are assumed to involve the simultaneous consideration of two temporal referents corresponding to different interstimulus intervals or beats. Neuroimaging during this task revealed higher levels of activity in the supplementary motor area, the left premotor cortex, the left insula, and the left inferior frontal gyrus for the strong-beat group as compared with the weak-beat group. In contrast, the weak-beat group showed higher levels of activity in the right premotor cortex and the left posterior superior and middle temporal gyri. No regions of activation were associated with years of musical experience, and researchers found no evidence that duration-based timing was less accurate or precise than beat-based timing.

Various findings support the proposal that the cerebellum may subserve absolute timing of subsecond intervals (Diedrichsen et al. 2003; Grube et al. 2010a,b; Teki et al. 2011), whereas corticostriatal circuits are involved in the relative timing of longer intervals as well as rhythmic sequences with a regular beat (Coull et al. 2011; Grahn & Brett 2009; Grahn & McAuley 2009; Grahn & Rowe 2012; Meck 2005; Schwartze et al. 2011, 2012a,b; Teki et al. 2011). Other conceptions have stressed the importance of task difficulty; the cerebellum plays a critical role in basic timing and corticostriatal circuits are recruited in a load-dependent manner (Livesey et al. 2007, Tregellas et al. 2006). How stimulus factors, attention and task factors, and development and training factors mediate the strength of beat-based timing is currently under investigation. The assumption is that beat-based timing is engaged only within a limited range of durations, corresponding to an entrainment region that is influenced by the precision of oscillator synchronization and the resetting of coincidence-detection mechanisms at the beginning of a sequence (Coull et al. 2011, Matell & Meck 2004, McAuley et al. 2006).

Understanding the degree to which individuals engage in a beat-based versus duration-based timing mode is critically important for a better characterization of temporal-processing deficits implicated with various developmental disorders (e.g., autism spectrum disorder and ADHD) as well as neurological (e.g., Huntington's and Parkinson's diseases) and psychiatric disorders (e.g., ADHD, schizophrenia) as outlined by Allman & Meck (2012), Conners et al. (1996), Levin et al. (1996), Meck (2005), and Noreika et al. (2013). An underlying propensity to engage in beat-based timing may somehow be related to, or manifested in, the timing of other behavioral tendencies, such as the rhythmical nature of many certain repetitive behaviors performed by those with certain sensory processing disorders (e.g., autism, schizophrenia). Beat-based timing shares a similar neurological basis with stereotypic behavior (of the type also expressed by nonhuman animals), specifically the basal ganglia (and striatum) and action on the D2 receptor. The length and complexity of behavioral habits have been posited to correspond to the nature of fixed routines in autism and may function as forms of a compensatory behavioral clock (Allman & DeLeon 2009, Boucher 2001). It remains to be seen if clinical populations with severe repetitive behaviors are more or less susceptible to beat-based timing; this notion is currently being investigated in autism (Allman et al. 2012, Falter et al. 2012).

Attentional Time-Sharing

As noted above, in the internal clock model the accumulated number of pacemaker pulses depends on attentional resources allocated to interval timing (Meck 1984). When an individual attends to a second task, or when intruder/distractor events are presented, estimated durations are shorter, presumably owing to resources being diverted from timing (Champagne & Fortin 2008, Fortin et al. 2010, Grondin 2010, Macar et al. 1994, Macar & Vidal 2009, Penney et al. 2013). Investigators have recently extended this time-sharing hypothesis by proposing that resource reallocation is proportional to the perceived contrast, both in temporal and nontemporal features, between intruders and the timed events. Experimental findings support this extension by showing that the effect of an intruder/distractor is dependent on the relative duration of the intruder to the intertrial interval (Buhusi & Meck 2006, 2009a,b).

Individual differences in the probability of attending to separate events (e.g., multiple to-be-timed signals presented simultaneously, dual-task components, distractors, and contextual stimuli) can be monitored during an experimental session to evaluate factors governing fatigue and vigilance (e.g., Buhusi & Meck 2006; Meck 1987; Meck & Williams 1997a,b); an overview of the importance of simultaneous temporal processing to the general architecture of the internal clock is provided by Church (1984) and Meck & Church (1982, 1984). Differences in the ability to reproduce previously experienced auditory and visual target durations either in isolation (focused attention) or concurrently (divided attention) have been reported in young adults who typically produce trained criterion durations equally well in either condition and also in older adults who often exhibit an age-related increase in timing variability in divided attention conditions and simultaneous temporal processing (e.g., Bherer et al. 2007, Lustig & Meck 2001, McAuley et al. 2010, Pang et al. 2001). Age-related impairments are often associated with a decrease in working memory span, and the relationship between working memory and timing performance is usually largest for visual targets in divided attention conditions. Moreover, time-of-day effects are frequently observed such that younger adults show better timing performance in the evening, and older adults show better performance in the morning; performance at the optimal time of day for each age group was relatively similar, but the performance for aged adults at the nonoptimal time of day was the most impaired (Lustig & Meck 2001). How these time-of-day effects emerge as a function of normal aging is uncertain, but the circadian modulation of interval timing as well as the associated genetic and molecular bases of individual differences in timing are currently topics of considerable interest (Agostino et al. 2011a,b; Balci et al. 2009).

This second-order principle is also evidenced by behavioral and neurobiological data (e.g., Bherer et al. 2007; Buhusi & Meck 2000, 2006, 2009a,b; Fortin et al. 2009; Gooch et al. 2009; Henry & Herrmann 2013; McAuley et al. 2010). Brain circuits engaged by timekeeping comprise not only those primarily involved in pulse accumulation, but also those involved in the maintenance of attentional and memory resources for timing as well as in the monitoring and reallocation of those resources among tasks (Buhusi & Meck 2009a, Van Rijn et al. 2011). This view is consistent with dynamic attending theory, which proposes that attention can be modeled as a self-sustained oscillation capable of entrainment to the relevant temporal sequence of events (Large & Jones 1999).

Neuroimaging studies in humans suggest that timekeeping tasks engage brain circuits typically involved in attention and working memory (Coull et al. 2008, 2011; Coull & Nobre 2008; Livesey et al. 2007; Lustig et al. 2005; Meck & N'Diaye 2005). Studies with unilateral neglect patients have shown a dramatic underestimation of time for durations up to 60 s (Danckert et al. 2007, Merrifield et al. 2010). These findings have been extended to normal participants who indicate an increased sensitivity to the duration of events presented in left visual space as a result of the right parietal cortex being more dominant in the allocation of attentional resources required for temporal integration (Allman & Danckert 2005). Many behavioral, pharmacological, lesion, and electrophysiological studies in animals support this time-sharing hypothesis as well (Meck et al. 2008).

SUMMARY AND DESCRIPTION OF A UNIFIED MODEL OF TEMPORAL INTEGRATION

Although our sense of time is necessarily subjective and varies according to context (Agostino et al. 2008, Droit-Volet et al. 2013, Droit-Volet & Meck 2007, Wittmann 2013), fundamental properties of interval timing ability have been identified, some of which are common to the perception of other senses. These first- and second-order principles of the internal clock provide diagnostic criteria with which to assess typical and atypical individual differences in timing and time perception (see Coull et al. 2013, Gilaie-Dotan et al. 2011, Lake & Meck 2013). Examining the nature of both individual and population-level differences in interval timing is an exciting prospect to better understand our awareness of subjective time and how time plays such a central role in our physical and mental lives (see Tulving 2002).

Our goal has been to provide the basis for a unified model of the internal clock. For instance, Teki et al. (2012) have recently proposed a timing system within core regions of the motor network such as the cerebellum, the inferior olive, the basal ganglia, the presupplementary motor areas, and the premotor cortex, as well as higher-level areas such as the prefrontal cortex (as illustrated in **Figure 6**). In this manner, Teki et al. (2012) have built on previous proposals by Allman & Meck (2012) and Meck (2005) to show how corticostriatal and cortico-cerebellar systems can subserve different aspects of a perceptual and motor timing system. Previous work

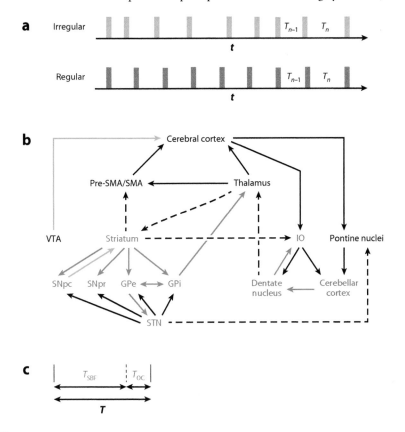

Figure 6

(*a*) Absolute and relative timing task. Irregular: A sequence of clicks with an average of 15% jitter was used to study absolute, duration-based timing. Participants were required to compare the duration of the final interval, T_n, to the penultimate interval, T_{n-1}, where T_n incorporates a difference (ΔT) of 30% of the interonset interval (range: 440–560 ms) from that of the preceding interval such that $T_n = T_{n-1} \pm \Delta T$ 30%. Regular: A sequence of clicks with no jitter is used to study relative, beat-based timing. Participants were required to compare the duration of the final interval, T_n, to the penultimate interval, T_{n-1}, where T_n incorporates a difference (ΔT) of 15% of the interonset interval from that of the preceding interval such that $T_n = T_{n-1} \pm \Delta T$ 15% (see Teki et al. 2011 for further details). (*b*) A unified model of time perception. The striatal network (*blue*) and the olivocerebellar network (*green*) are connected to each other via multiple loops, and with the thalamus, pre-SMA/SMA, and the cerebral cortex. Dopaminergic pathways are shown in orange, inhibitory projections in red, excitatory and known anatomical connections in solid and dashed black lines, respectively. Abbreviations: GPe, globus pallidus external; GPi, globus pallidus internal; IO, inferior olive; SMA, supplementary motor area; SNpc, substantia nigra pars compacta; SNpr, substantia nigra pars reticulate; STN, subthalamic nucleus; VTA, ventral tegmental area. (*c*) Timing mechanism underlying the unified model. To estimate an interval of duration T, both the striato-thalamo-cortical (SBF) networks and olivocerebellar (OC) networks act in parallel to produce timing signals T_{SBF} and T_{OC}, respectively, such that the combined output of the system approximates the length of the criterion time interval, T. Adapted from Meck (2005) and Teki et al. (2011).

by this research group established that olivocerebellar circuits support absolute, duration-based timing and that striato-thalamo-cortical circuits support relative, beat-based timing (Teki et al. 2011). Moreover, recent neuroimaging studies indicate that the timing functions of these circuits are codependent (Jahanshahi et al. 2010). Hence, we have proposed an integrative view of time perception based on coordinated activity in the core striatal and olivocerebellar networks, which are interconnected with each other and with the cerebral cortex through multiple synaptic pathways. Timing in this unified model may involve serial beat-based striatal activation followed by absolute olivocerebellar timing mechanisms (Allman & Meck 2012, Cope et al. 2013, Teki et al. 2012; see also Merchant et al. 2013).

FUTURE DIRECTIONS

The properties and nature of the internal clock can be investigated in many ways, and the strengths of the psychophysical approach coupled with well-specified psychological models and neurobiological mechanisms provide a fertile ground for timing research. In the context first posed by William James, future studies will need to address the degree to which the prefrontal cortex can self-generate multisecond time intervals in the absence of an external to-be-timed event (Lustig et al. 2005, Matell et al. 2011, Mita et al. 2009, Yumoto et al. 2011). Evidence of this type of temporal representation would demonstrate the successful disengagement of cortical circuits from the striatal mechanisms initially required for beat detection and entrainment to external stimuli (see Grahn & Brett 2009, Grahn & McAuley 2009, Grahn & Rowe 2012, Gu et al. 2011). Moreover, the involvement of the prefrontal and parietal cortices may need to be reconsidered in terms of understanding how the basal ganglia can train multiple cortical areas to recognize and/or produce specific sequences of durations in the manner of actor-critic models (e.g., Hampshire et al. 2011, Joel et al. 2002, O'Reilly & Frank 2006). The quest for the internal clock (translating objective time into subjective time) and its neurological basis, which is modifiable by nontemporal stimuli and pharmacological states and which reveals typical and atypical differences in various populations (individuals with neurological, psychiatric, and psychological disorders), is perhaps the elusive key to understanding consciousness in the mind and brain (Smythies et al. 2012).

DISCLOSURE STATEMENT

The authors are not aware of any affiliations, memberships, funding, or financial holdings that might be perceived as affecting the objectivity of this review.

ACKNOWLEDGMENTS

Preparation of this review was supported, in part, by a Eunice Kennedy Shriver National Institute of Child Health and Human Development career development award (K99 HD058698) to M.J.A.

LITERATURE CITED

Acerbi L, Wolpert DM, Vijayakumar S. 2012. Internal representations of temporal statistics and feedback calibrate motor-sensory interval timing. *PLoS Comput. Biol.* 8(11):e1002771

Agostino PV, Cheng RK, Williams CL, West AE, Meck WH. 2013. Acquisition of response thresholds for timed performance is regulated by a calcium-responsive transcription factor, CaRF. *Genes Brain Behav.* 12:633–44

Agostino PV, Golombek DA, Meck WH. 2011. Unwinding the molecular basis of interval and circadian timing. *Front. Integr. Neurosci.* 5:64

Agostino PV, Nascimento MD, Bussi IL, Eguia MC, Golombek DA. 2011. Circadian modulation of interval timing in mice. *Brain Res.* 1370:154–63

Agostino PV, Peryer G, Meck WH. 2008. How music fills our emotions and helps us keep time. *Behav. Brain Sci.* 31:575–76

Allan LG. 1979. Perception of time. *Percept. Psychophys.* 26:340–54

Allan LG. 1998. The influence of the scalar timing model on human timing research. *Behav. Process.* 44:101–17

Allan LG, Gibbon J. 1991. Human bisection at the geometric mean. *Learn. Motiv.* 22:39–58

Allman A, Danckert J. 2005. Time flies when you're having fun: temporal estimation and the experience of boredom. *Brain Cogn.* 59:236–45

Allman MJ. 2011. Deficits in temporal processing associated with autistic disorder. *Front. Integr. Neurosci.* 5:2

Allman MJ, DeLeon IG. 2009. No time like the present: time perception in autism. In *Causes and Risks for Autism*, ed. AC Giordano, VA Lombardi, pp. 65–76. New York: Nova Sci.

Allman MJ, DeLeon IG, Wearden JH. 2011. A psychophysical assessment of timing in individuals with autism. *Am. J. Intellect. Dev. Disabil.* 116:165–78

Allman MJ, Meck WH. 2012. Pathophysiological distortions in time perception and timed performance. *Brain* 135:656–77

Allman MJ, Pelphrey KA, Meck WH. 2012. Developmental neuroscience of time and number: implications for autism and other neurodevelopmental disabilities. *Front. Integr. Neurosci.* 6:7

Allman MJ, Yin B, Meck WH. 2013. Time in the psychopathological mind. In *Subjective Time: An Anthology of the Philosophy, Psychology, and Neuroscience of Temporality*, ed. D Lloyd, V Arstila. Cambridge, MA: MIT Press. In press

Almeida R, Ledberg A. 2010. A biologically plausible model of time-scale invariant interval timing. *J. Comp. Neurosci.* 28:155–75

Aparicio P, Diedrichsen J, Ivry RB. 2005. Effects of focal basal ganglia lesions on timing and force control. *Brain Cogn.* 58:62–74

Artieda J, Pastor MA, Lacruz F, Obeso JA. 1992. Temporal discrimination is abnormal in Parkinson's disease. *Brain* 115:199–210

Balci F, Meck WH, Moore H, Brunner D. 2009. Timing deficits in aging and neuropathology. In *Animal Models of Human Cognitive Aging*, ed. JL Bizon, A Woods, pp. 161–201. Totowa, NJ: Humana

Balci F, Wiener M, Çavdaroğlu B. 2012. Epistasis effects of dopamine genes on interval timing and reward magnitude in humans. *Neuropsychologia* 51:293–308

Bartolo R, Merchant H. 2009. Learning and generalization of time production in humans: rules of transfer across modalities and interval durations. *Exp. Brain Res.* 197:91–100

Bechara A, Tranel D, Damasio H, Damasio AR. 1996. Failure to respond autonomically to anticipated future outcomes following damage to prefrontal cortex. *Cereb. Cortex* 6:215–25

Bherer L, Desjardins S, Fortin C. 2007. Age-related differences in timing with breaks. *Psychol. Aging* 22:398–403

Bisson N, Grondin S. 2013. Time estimates of internet surfing and video gaming. *Timing Time Percept.* 1:39–64

Boucher J. 2001. "Lost in a sea of time": time parsing and autism. In *Time and Memory*, ed. C Hoerl, T McCormack, pp. 111–35 Oxford, UK: Oxford Univ. Press

Brannon EM, Libertus ME, Meck WH, Woldorff MG. 2008. Electrophysiological measures of time processing in infant and adult brains: Weber's law holds. *J. Cogn. Neurosci.* 20:193–203

Brannon EM, Wolfe L, Meck WH, Woldorff M. 2004. Timing in the baby brain. *Cogn. Brain Res.* 21:227–33

Brody CD, Hernández A, Zainos A, Romo R. 2003. Timing and neural encoding of somatosensory parametric working memory in macaque prefrontal cortex. *Cereb. Cortex* 13:1196–207

Bueti D. 2011. The sensory representation of time. *Front. Integr. Neurosci.* 5:34

Bueti D, Bahrami B, Walsh V. 2008a. Sensory and association cortex in time perception. *J. Cogn. Neurosci.* 20:1054–62

Bueti D, Macaluso E. 2010. Auditory temporal expectation modulates activity in visual cortex. *NeuroImage* 51:1168–83

Bueti D, Macaluso E. 2011. Physiological correlates of subjective time: evidence for the temporal accumulator hypothesis. *NeuroImage* 57:1251–63

Bueti D, van Dongen EV, Walsh V. 2008b. The role of superior temporal cortex in auditory timing. *PLoS ONE* 3(6):e 2481

Bueti D, Walsh V. 2009. The parietal cortex and the representation of time, space, number and other magnitudes. *Philos. Trans. R. Soc. B* 364:1831–40

Buhusi CV, Aziz D, Winslow D, Carter RE, Swearingen JE, Buhusi MC. 2009. Interval timing accuracy and scalar timing in C57BL/6 mice. *Behav. Neurosci.* 123:1102–13

Buhusi CV, Meck WH. 2000. Timing for the absence of a stimulus: the gap paradigm reversed. *J. Exp. Psychol. Anim. Behav. Process.* 26:305–22

Buhusi CV, Meck WH. 2002. Differential effects of methamphetamine and haloperidol on the control of an internal clock. *Behav. Neurosci.* 116:291–97

Buhusi CV, Meck WH. 2005. What makes us tick? Functional and neural mechanisms of interval timing. *Nat. Rev. Neurosci.* 6:755–65

Buhusi CV, Meck WH. 2006. Interval timing with gaps and distracters: evaluation of the ambiguity, switch, and time-sharing hypotheses. *J. Exp. Psychol. Anim. Behav. Process.* 32:329–38

Buhusi CV, Meck WH. 2009a. Relative time sharing: new findings and an extension of the resource allocation model of temporal processing. *Philos. Trans. R. Soc. B* 364:1875–85

Buhusi CV, Meck WH. 2009b. Relativity theory and time perception: single or multiple clocks? *PLoS ONE* 4(7):e6268

Buhusi CV, Oprisan SA. 2013. Time-scale invariance as an emergent property in a perceptron with realistic, noisy neurons. *Behav. Process.* 95:60–70

Buhusi CV, Perera D, Meck WH. 2005. Memory for timing visual and auditory signals in albino and pigmented rats. *J. Exp. Psychol. Anim. Behav. Process.* 31:18–30

Buhusi CV, Sasaki A, Meck WH. 2002. Temporal integration as a function of signal/gap intensity in rats (*Rattus norvegicus*) and pigeons (*Columba livia*). *J. Comp. Psychol.* 116:381–90

Buhusi M, Scripa I, Williams CL, Buhusi CV. 2013. Impaired interval timing and spatial-temporal integration in mice deficient in CHL1, a gene associated with schizophrenia. *Timing Time Percept.* 1:21–38

Buonomano DV, Laje R. 2010. Population clocks: motor timing with neural dynamics. *Trends Cogn. Sci.* 14:520–27

Burr D, Rocca ED, Morrone MC. 2013. Contextual effects in interval-duration judgements in vision, audition and touch. *Exp. Brain Res.* 230:87–98

Carroll CA, Boggs J, O'Donnell BF, Shekhar A, Hetrick WP. 2008. Temporal processing dysfunction in schizophrenia. *Brain Cogn.* 67:150–61

Champagne J, Fortin C. 2008. Attention sharing during timing: modulation by processing demands of an expected stimulus. *Percept. Psychophys.* 70:630–39

Cheng RK, Ali YM, Meck WH. 2007. Ketamine "unlocks" the reduced clock-speed effect of cocaine following extended training: evidence for dopamine-glutamate interactions in timing and time perception. *Neurobiol. Learn. Mem.* 88:149–59

Cheng RK, Dyke AG, McConnell MW, Meck WH. 2011. Categorical scaling of duration as a function of temporal context in aged rats. *Brain Res.* 1381:175–86

Cheng RK, MacDonald CJ, Meck WH. 2006. Differential effects of cocaine and ketamine on time estimation: implications for neurobiological models of interval timing. *Pharmacol. Biochem. Behav.* 85:114–22

Cheng RK, Meck WH. 2007. Prenatal choline supplementation increases sensitivity to time by reducing non-scalar sources of variance in adult temporal processing. *Brain Res.* 1186:242–54

Cheng RK, Scott AC, Penney TB, Williams CL, Meck WH. 2008. Prenatal choline availability differentially modulates timing of auditory and visual stimuli in aged rats. *Brain Res.* 1237:167–75

Church RM. 1984. Properties of the internal clock. *Ann. N.Y. Acad. Sci.* 423:566–82

Church RM. 1989. Theories of timing behavior. In *Contemporary Learning Theories: Instrumental Conditioning Theory and the Impact of Biological Constraints on Learning*, ed. SB Klein, RR Mowrer, pp. 41–71. Hillsdale, NJ: Erlbaum

Church RM. 2003. A concise introduction to scalar expectancy theory. See Meck 2003, pp. 3–22

Church RM, Deluty MZ. 1977. Bisection of temporal intervals. *J. Exp. Psychol. Anim. Behav. Process.* 3:216–28

Church RM, Meck WH, Gibbon J. 1994. Application of scalar timing theory to individual trials. *J. Exp. Psychol. Anim. Behav. Process.* 20:135–55

Church RM, Miller KD, Meck WH, Gibbon J. 1991. Symmetrical and asymmetrical sources of variance in temporal generalization. *Anim. Learn. Behav.* 19:207–14

Cicchini GM, Arrighi R, Cecchetti L, Giusti M, Burr DC. 2012. Optimal encoding of interval timing in expert percussionists. *J. Neurosci.* 32:1056–60

Claassen DO, Jones CR, Yu M, Dirnberger G, Malone T, et al. 2013. Deciphering the impact of cerebellar and basal ganglia dysfunction in accuracy and variability of motor timing. *Neuropsychologia* 51:267–74

Conners CK, Levin ED, Sparrow E, Hinton SC, Erhardt D, et al. 1996. Nicotine and attention in adult attention deficit hyperactivity disorder (ADHD). *Psychopharmacol. Bull.* 32:67–73

Cope TE, Grube M, Singh B, Burh DJ, Griffiths TD. 2013. The basal ganglia in perceptual timing: timing performance in multiple system atrophy and Huntington's disease. *Neuropsychologia* 83:e1

Cordes S, Meck WH. 2013. Ordinal judgment in the rat: an understanding of longer and shorter for suprasecond, but not subsecond, durations. *J. Exp. Psychol. Gen.* In press

Cordes S, Williams CL, Meck WH. 2007. Common representations of abstract quantities. *Curr. Direct. Psychol. Sci.* 16:156–61

Coull JT, Cheng RK, Meck WH. 2011. Neuroanatomical and neurochemical substrates of timing. *Neuropsychopharmacology* 36:3–25

Coull JT, Hwang HJ, Leyton M, Dagher A. 2013. Dopaminergic modulation of motor timing in healthy volunteers differs as a function of baseline DA precursor availability. *Timing Time Percept.* 1:77–98

Coull JT, Nazarian B, Vidal F. 2008. Timing, storage, and comparison of stimulus duration engage discrete anatomical components of a perceptual timing network. *J. Cogn. Neurosci.* 20:2185–97

Coull J, Nobre A. 2008. Dissociating explicit timing from temporal expectation with fMRI. *Curr. Opin. Neurobiol.* 18:137–44

Coull JT, Vidal F, Nazarian B, Macar F. 2003. Functional anatomy of the attentional modulation of time estimation. *Science* 303:1506–8

Dali Y, Zemin L. 1993. A multilayer feedforward neural network with adaptive lookup table weight. *Circuit. Sys. IEEE* 4:2411–14

Danckert J, Ferber S, Pun C, Broderick C, Striemer C, et al. 2007. Neglected time: impaired temporal perception of multisecond intervals in unilateral neglect. *J. Cogn. Neurosci.* 19:1706–20

Diedrichsen J, Ivry RB, Pressing J. 2003. Cerebellar and basal ganglia contributions to interval timing. See Meck 2003, pp. 457–83

Droit-Volet S, Clément A, Wearden JH. 2001. Temporal generalization in 3- to 8-year-old children. *J. Exp. Child Psychol.* 80:271–88

Droit-Volet S, Fayolle S, Lamotte M, Gil S. 2013. Time, emotion and the embodiment of timing. *Timing Time Percept.* 1:99–126

Droit-Volet S, Meck WH. 2007. How emotions colour our perception of time. *Trends Cogn. Sci.* 11:504–13

Droit-Volet S, Meck WH, Penney TB. 2007. Sensory modality and time perception in children and adults. *Behav. Process.* 74:244–50

Droit-Volet S, Wearden JH. 2001. Temporal bisection in children. *J. Exp. Child Psychol.* 80:142–59

Durstewitz D, Deco G. 2008. Computational significance of transient dynamics in cortical networks. *Eur. J. Neurosci.* 27:217–27

Falter CM, Noreika V, Wearden JH, Bailey AJ. 2012. More consistent, yet less sensitive: interval timing in autism spectrum disorders. *Q. J. Exp. Psychol.* 65:2093–107

Forstmann BU, Anwander A, Schäfer A, Neumann J, Brown S, et al. 2010. Cortico-striatal connections predict control over speed and accuracy in perceptual decision making. *Proc. Natl. Acad. Sci. USA* 107:15916–20

Fortin C, Fairhurst S, Malapani C, Morin C, Towey J, Meck WH. 2009. Expectancy in humans in multisecond peak-interval timing with gaps. *Atten. Percept. Psychophys.* 71:789–802

Fortin C, Schweickert R, Gaudreault R, Viau-Quesnel C. 2010. Timing is affected by demands in memory search but not by task switching. *J. Exp. Psychol. Hum. Percept. Perform.* 36:580–95

Fraisse P. 1984. Perception and estimation of time. *Annu. Rev. Psychol.* 35:1–36

Freestone DM, MacInnis MLM, Church RM. 2013. Response rates are governed more by time cues than contingency. *Timing Time Percept.* 1:3–20

Gescheider GA. 1997. *Psychophysics: The Fundamentals.* Mahwah, NJ: Erlbaum

Gibbon J. 1977. Scalar expectancy and Weber's law in animal timing. *Psychol. Rev.* 84:279–325

Gibbon J. 1991. Origins of scalar timing theory. *Learn. Motiv.* 22:3–38

Gibbon J. 1992. Ubiquity of scalar timing with a Poisson clock. *J. Math. Psychol.* 35:283–93

Gibbon J, Church RM. 1984. Sources of variance in an information processing theory of timing. In *Animal Cognition*, ed. HL Roitblat, TG Bever, HS Terrace, pp. 465–88. Hillsdale, NJ: Erlbaum

Gibbon J, Church RM. 1990. Representation of time. *Cognition* 37:23–54

Gibbon J, Church RM. 1992. Comparison of variance and covariance patterns in parallel and serial theories of timing. *J. Exp. Anal. Behav.* 57:393–406

Gibbon J, Church RM, Meck WH. 1984. Scalar timing in memory. *Ann. N.Y. Acad. Sci.* 423:52–77

Gibbon J, Malapani C, Dale CL, Gallistel CR. 1997. Toward a neurobiology of temporal cognition: advances and challenges. *Curr. Opin. Neurobiol.* 7:170–84

Gilaie-Dotan S, Kanai R, Rees G. 2011. Anatomy of human sensory cortices reflects inter- individual variability in time estimation. *Front. Integr. Neurosci.* 5:76

Girardi G, Antonucci G, Nico D. 2013. Cueing spatial attention through timing and probability. *Cortex* 49:211–21

Gooch CM, Stern Y, Rakitin BC. 2009. Evidence for age-related changes to temporal attention and memory from the choice time production task. *Aging Neuropsychol. Cogn.* 16:285–310

Grahn JA, Brett M. 2009. Impairment of beat-based rhythm discrimination in Parkinson's disease. *Cortex* 45:54–61

Grahn JA, McAuley JD. 2009. Neural bases of individual differences in beat perception. *NeuroImage* 47:1894–903

Grahn JA, Rowe JB. 2012. Finding and feeling the musical beat: striatal dissociations between detection and prediction of regularity. *Cereb. Cortex* 23:91–21

Grondin S. 2010. Timing and time perception: a review of recent behavioral and neuroscience findings and theoretical directions. *Atten. Percept. Psychophys.* 72:561–82

Grube M, Cooper FE, Chinnery PF, Griffiths TD. 2010a. Dissociation of duration-based and beat-based auditory timing in cerebellar degeneration. *Proc. Natl. Acad. Sci. USA* 107:11597–601

Grube M, Lee K-H, Griffiths TD, Barker AT, Woodruff PW. 2010b. Transcranial magnetic theta-burst stimulation of the human cerebellum distinguishes absolute, duration-based from relative, beat-based perception of subsecond time intervals. *Front. Psychol.* 1:171

Gu B-M, Jurkowski AJ, Lake JI, Malapani C, Meck WH. 2013. Bayesian models of interval timing and distortions in temporal memory as a function of Parkinson's disease and dopamine-related error processing. See Vatakis & Allman 2013. In press

Gu B-M, Meck WH. 2011. New perspectives on Vierordt's law: memory-mixing in ordinal temporal comparison tasks. In *Multidisciplinary Aspects of Time and Time Perception*, ed. A Vatakis, A Esposito, M Giagkou, F Cummins, G Papadelis, pp. 67–78. Lect. Notes Comp. Sci. Ser. Vol. 6789. Berlin: Springer

Gu BM, Cheng RK, Yin B, Meck WH. 2011. Quinpirole-induced sensitization to noisy/sparse periodic input: temporal synchronization as a model of obsessive-compulsive disorder. *Neuroscience* 179:143–50

Guilhardi P, Church RM. 2009. The generality of empirical and theoretical explanations of behavior. *Behav. Process.* 81:205–15

Hampshire A, Thompson R, Duncan J, Owen AM. 2011. Lateral prefrontal cortex subregions make dissociable contributions during fluid reasoning. *Cereb. Cortex* 21:1–10

Harrington DL, Boyd LA, Mayer AR, Sheltraw DM, Lee RR, et al. 2004. Neural representation of interval encoding and decision making. *Cogn. Brain Res.* 21:193–205

Harrington DL, Castillo GN, Fong CH, Reed JD. 2011a. Neural underpinnings of distortions in the experience of time across senses. *Front. Integr. Neurosci.* 5:32

Harrington DL, Castillo GN, Greenberg PA, Song DD, Lessig S, et al. 2011b. Neurobehavioral mechanisms of temporal processing deficits in Parkinson's disease. *PLoS ONE* 6(2):e17461

Harrington DL, Haaland K, Knight R. 1998. Cortical networks underlying mechanism of time perception. *J. Neurosci.* 18: 1085–95

Harrington DL, Zimbelman JL, Hinton SC, Rao SM. 2010. Neural modulation of temporal encoding, maintenance, and decision processes. *Cereb. Cortex* 20:1274–85

Hass J, Blaschke S, Herrmann JM. 2012. Cross-modal distortion of time perception: demerging the effects of observed and performed motion. *PLoS ONE* 7(6):e38092

Henry MJ, Herrmann B. 2013. Low-frequency neural oscillations support dynamic attending in temporal context. *Timing Time Percept.* In press

Hinton SC, Meck WH. 1997a. How time flies: functional and neural mechanisms of interval timing. In *Time and Behaviour: Psychological and Neurobiological Analyses*, ed. CM Bradshaw, E Szabadi, pp. 409–57. New York: Elsevier

Hinton SC, Meck WH. 1997b. The "internal clocks" of circadian and interval timing. *Endeavour* 21:82–87

Hinton SC, Meck WH. 2004. Frontal-striatal circuitry activated by human peak-interval timing in the supra-seconds range. *Cogn. Brain Res.* 21:171–82

Hinton SC, Paulsen JS, Hoffmann RG, Reynolds NC, Zimbelman JL, Rao SM. 2007. Motor timing variability increases in preclinical Huntington's disease patients as estimated onset of motor symptoms approaches. *J. Int. Neuropsychol. Soc.* 13:1–5

Hinton SC, Rao SM. 2004. "One-thousand one ... one-thousand *two* ...": Chronometric counting violates the scalar property in interval timing. *Psychon. Bull. Rev.* 11:24–30

Hoerl C, McCormack T, eds. 2001. *Time and Memory: Issues in Philosophy and Psychology*. Oxford, UK: Clarendon

Ivry RB, Schlerf JE. 2008. Dedicated and intrinsic models of time perception. *Trends Cogn. Sci.* 12:273–80

Ivry RB, Spencer RMC. 2004. The neural representation of time. *Curr. Opin. Neurobiol.* 14:225–32

Jaffe J, Beebe B, Feldstein S, Crown C, Jasnow M. 2001. *Rhythms of Dialogue in Infancy: Monographs for the Society for Research and Child Development*. Serial No. 265, Vol. 66. Boston, MA: Blackwell

Jahanshahi M, Jones CR, Zijlmans J, Katsenschlager R, Lee L, et al. 2010. Dopaminergic modulation of striato-frontal connectivity during motor timing in Parkinson's disease. *Brain* 133:727–45

Jaldow EJ, Oakley DA, Davey GC. 1989. Performance of decorticated rats on fixed interval and fixed time schedules. *Eur. J. Neurosci.* 5:461–70

Jaldow EJ, Oakley DA, Davey GC. 1990. Performance on two fixed-interval schedules in the absence of neocortex in rats. *Behav. Neurosci.* 104:763–77

James W. 1890. The perception of time. In *The Principles of Psychology*, Vol. 1. New York: Holt

Jazayeri M, Shadlen MN. 2010. Temporal context calibrates interval timing. *Nat. Neurosci.* 13:1020–26

Jin, DZ, Fujii N, Graybiel AM. 2009. Neural representation of time in cortico-basal ganglia circuits. *Proc. Natl. Acad. Sci. USA* 106:19156–61

Joel D, Niv Y, Ruppin E. 2002. Actor-critic models of the basal ganglia: new anatomical and computational perspectives. *Neural Netw.* 15:535–47

Jones CR, Claassen DO, Yu M, Spies JR, Malone T, et al. 2011. Modeling accuracy and variability of motor timing in treated and untreated Parkinson's disease and healthy controls. *Front. Integr. Neurosci.* 5:81

Jones CRG, Jahanshahi M. 2013. Contributions of the basal ganglia to temporal processing: evidence from Parkinson's disease. *Timing Time Percept.* In press

Jones CRG, Malone TJL, Dirnberger G, Edwards M, Jahanshahi M. 2008. Basal ganglia, dopamine and temporal processing: performance on three timing tasks on and off medication in Parkinson's disease. *Brain Cogn.* 68:30–41

Kanai R, Lloyd H, Bueti D, Walsh V. 2011. Modality-independent role of the primary auditory cortex in time estimation. *Exp. Brain Res.* 209:465–71

Karmarkar UR, Buonomano DV. 2007. Timing in the absence of clocks: encoding time in neural network states. *Neuron* 53:427–38

Kaufman J, Csibra G, Johnson MH. 2005. Oscillatory activity in the infant brain reflects object maintenance. *Proc. Natl. Acad. Sci. USA* 102:15271–74

Killeen PR. 1991. Counting the minutes. In *Time, Action, and Cognition: Towards Bridging the Gap*, ed. F Macar, V Pouthas, WJ Friedman, pp. 203–14. Dordrecht: Kluwer

Killeen PR, Fetterman JG. 1988. A behavioral theory of timing. *Psychol. Rev.* 95:274–95

Killeen PR, Weiss NA. 1987. Optimal timing and the Weber function. *Psychol. Rev.* 94:455–68

Kimura D, Hayakawa Y. 2008. Reinforcement learning of recurrent neural network for temporal coding. *Neurocomputing* 71:3379–86

Koch G, Costa A, Brusa L, Peppe A, Gatto I, et al. 2008. Impaired reproduction of second but not millisecond time interval in Parkinson's disease. *Neuropsychologica* 46:1305–13

Koch G, Oliveri M, Caltagirone C. 2009. Neural networks engaged in milliseconds and seconds time processing: evidence from transcranial magnetic stimulation and patients with cortical or subcortical dysfunction. *Philos. Trans. R. Soc. B* 364:1907–18

Koch G, Oliveri M, Carlesimo GA, Caltagirone C. 2002. Selective deficit of time perception in a patient with right prefrontal cortex lesion. *Neurology* 59:1658–59

Koch G, Oliveri M, Torriero S, Caltagirone C. 2003. Underestimation of time perception after repetitive transcranial magnetic stimulation. *Neurology* 60:1844–46

Kotz SA, Schwartze M. 2010. Cortical speech processing unplugged: a timely subcortico-cortical framework. *Trends Cogn. Sci.* 14:392–99

Kotz SA, Schwartze M, Schmidt-Kassow M. 2009. Non-motor basal ganglia functions: a review and proposal for a model of sensory predictability in auditory language perception. *Cortex* 45:982–90

Kotz SAE, Schwartze M. 2011. Differential input of the supplementary motor area to a dedicated temporal processing network: functional and clinical implications. *Front. Integr. Neurosci.* 5:86

Kurti AN, Matell MS. 2011. Nucleus accumbens dopamine modulates response rate but not response timing in an interval timing task. *Behav. Neurosci.* 125:215–25

Laje R, Buonomano DV. 2013. Robust timing and motor patterns by taming chaos in recurrent neural networks. *Nat. Neurosci.* 16:925–33

Lake JI, Meck WH. 2013. Differential effects of amphetamine and haloperidol on temporal reproduction: dopaminergic regulation of attention and clock speed. *Neuropsychologia* 51:284–92

Large EW, Jones MR. 1999. The dynamics of attending: how we track time-varying events. *Psychol. Rev.* 106:119–59

Levin ED, Conners CK, Sparrow E, Hinton SC, Erhardt D, et al. 1996. Nicotine effects on adults with attention-deficit/hyperactivity disorder. *Psychopharmacology* 123:55–63

Lewis PA, Meck WH. 2012. Time and the sleeping brain. *Psychologist* 25:594–97

Lewis PA, Miall RC. 2003. Distinct systems for automatic and cognitively controlled time measurement: evidence from neuroimaging. *Curr. Opin. Neurobiol.* 13:250–55

Lewis PA, Miall RC. 2009. The precision of temporal judgement: milliseconds, many minutes, and beyond. *Philos. Trans. R. Soc. B* 364:1897–905

Livesey AC, Wall MB, Smith AT. 2007. Time perception: manipulation of task difficulty dissociates clock functions from other cognitive demands. *Neuropsychologia* 45:321–31

Lustig C, Matell MS, Meck WH. 2005. Not "just" a coincidence: frontal-striatal synchronization in working memory and interval timing. *Memory* 13:441–48

Lustig C, Meck WH. 2001. Paying attention to time as one gets older. *Psychol. Sci.* 12:478–84

Lustig C, Meck WH. 2005. Chronic treatment with haloperidol induces working memory deficits in feedback effects of interval timing. *Brain Cogn.* 58:9–16

Lustig C, Meck WH. 2011. Modality differences in timing and temporal memory throughout the lifespan. *Brain Cogn.* 77:298–303

Macar F, Grondin S, Casini L. 1994. Controlled attention sharing influences time estimation. *Mem. Cogn.* 22:673–86

Macar F, Vidal F. 2009. Timing processes: an outline of behavioural and neural indices not systematically considered in timing models. *Can. J. Exp. Psychol.* 63:227–39

MacDonald CJ, Cheng R-K, Meck WH. 2012. Acquisition of "start" and "stop" response thresholds in peak-interval timing is differentially sensitive to protein synthesis inhibition in the dorsal and ventral striatum. *Front. Integr. Neurosci.* 6:10

MacDonald CJ, Cheng R-K, Williams CL, Meck WH. 2007. Combined organizational and activational effects of short and long photoperiods on spatial and temporal memory in rats. *Behav. Process.* 74:226–33

MacDonald CJ, Meck WH. 2004. Systems-level integration of interval timing and reaction time. *Neurosci. Biobehav. Rev.* 28:747–69

MacDonald CJ, Meck WH. 2005. Differential effects of clozapine and haloperidol on interval timing in the supraseconds range. *Psychopharmacology* 182:232–44

MacDonald CJ, Meck WH. 2006. Interaction of raclopride and preparatory-interval effects on simple reaction-time performance. *Behav. Brain Res.* 175:62–74

Malapani C, Fairhurst S. 2002. Scalar timing in animals and humans. *Learn. Motiv.* 33:156–76

Malapani C, Rakitin B, Meck WH, Deweer B, Dubois B, Gibbon J. 1998. Coupled temporal memories in Parkinson's disease: a dopamine-related dysfunction. *J. Cogn. Neurosci.* 10:316–31

Maricq AV, Church RM. 1983. The differential effects of haloperidol and methamphetamine on time estimation in the rat. *Psychopharmacology* 79:10–15

Maricq AV, Roberts S, Church RM. 1981. Methamphetamine and time estimation. *J. Exp. Psychol. Anim. Behav. Process.* 7:18–30

Matell MS, Bateson M, Meck WH. 2006. Single-trials analyses demonstrate that increases in clock speed contribute to the methamphetamine-induced horizontal shifts in peak-interval timing functions. *Psychopharmacology* 188:201–12

Matell MS, King GR, Meck WH. 2004. Differential adjustment of interval timing by the chronic administration of intermittent or continuous cocaine. *Behav. Neurosci.* 118:150–56

Matell MS, Meck WH. 2000. Neuropsychological mechanisms of interval timing behaviour. *BioEssays* 22:94–103

Matell MS, Meck WH. 2004. Cortico-striatal circuits and interval timing: coincidence-detection of oscillatory processes. *Cogn. Brain Res.* 21:139–70

Matell MS, Meck WH, Nicolelis MAL. 2003. Interval timing and the encoding of signal duration by ensembles of cortical and striatal neurons. *Behav. Neurosci.* 117:760–73

Matell MS, Shea-Brown E, Gooch C, Wilson AG, Rinzel J. 2011. A heterogeneous population code for elapsed time in rat medial agranular cortex. *Behav. Neurosci.* 125:54–73

McAuley JD, Henry MJ. 2010. Modality effects in rhythm processing: Auditory encoding of visual rhythms is neither obligatory nor automatic. *Atten. Percept. Psychophys.* 72:1377–89

McAuley JD, Jones MR. 2003. Modeling effects of rhythmic context on perceived duration: a comparison of interval and entrainment approaches to short-interval timing. *J. Exp. Psychol. Hum. Percept. Perform.* 29:1102–25

McAuley JD, Jones MR, Holub S, Johnston HM, Miller NS. 2006. The time of our lives: lifespan development of timing and event tracking. *J. Exp. Psychol. Gen.* 135:348–67

McAuley JD, Miller NS. 2007. Picking up the pace: effects of global temporal context on sensitivity to the tempo of auditory sequences. *Percept. Psychophys.* 69:709–18

McAuley JD, Wang M, Miller JP, Pang KCH. 2010. Dividing time: concurrent timing of auditory and visual events. *Exp. Aging Res.* 36:306–24

Meck WH. 1983. Selective adjustment of the speed of internal clock and memory processes. *J. Exp. Psychol. Anim. Behav. Process.* 9:171–201

Meck WH. 1984. Attentional bias between modalities: effect on the internal clock, memory, and decision stages used in animal time discrimination. *Ann. N.Y. Acad. Sci.* 423:528–41

Meck WH. 1986. Affinity for the dopamine D_2 receptor predicts neuroleptic potency in decreasing the speed of an internal clock. *Pharmacol. Biochem. Behav.* 25:1185–89

Meck WH. 1987. Vasopressin metabolite neuropeptide facilitates simultaneous temporal processing. *Behav. Brain Res.* 23:147–57

Meck WH. 1988. Hippocampal function is required for feedback control of an internal clock's criterion. *Behav. Neurosci.* 102:54–60

Meck WH. 1991. Modality-specific circadian rhythmicities influence mechanisms of attention and memory for interval timing. *Learn. Motiv.* 22:153–79

Meck WH. 1996. Neuropharmacology of timing and time perception. *Cogn. Brain Res.* 3:227–42

Meck WH. 2001. Interval timing and genomics: What makes mutant mice tick? *Int. J. Comp. Psychol.* 14:211–31

Meck WH. 2002a. Choline uptake in the frontal cortex is proportional to the absolute error of a temporal memory translation constant in mature and aged rats. *Learn. Motiv.* 33:88–104

Meck WH. 2002b. Distortions in the content of temporal memory: neurobiological correlates. In *Animal Cognition and Sequential Behavior: Behavioral, Biological, and Computational Perspectives*, ed. SB Fountain, MD Bunsey, JH Danks, MK McBeath, pp. 175–200. Boston, MA: Kluwer Acad.

Meck WH. 2003. *Functional and Neural Mechanisms of Interval Timing*. Boca Raton, FL: CRC Press

Meck WH. 2005. Neuropsychology of timing and time perception. *Brain Cogn.* 58:1–8

Meck WH. 2006a. Frontal cortex lesions eliminate the clock speed effect of dopaminergic drugs on interval timing. *Brain Res.* 1108:157–67

Meck WH. 2006b. Neuroanatomical localization of an internal clock: a functional link between mesolimbic, nigrostriatal, and mesocortical dopaminergic systems. *Brain Res.* 1109:93–107

Meck WH. 2006c. Temporal memory in mature and aged rats is sensitive to choline acetyltransferase inhibition. *Brain Res.* 1108:168–75

Meck WH. 2007. Acute ethanol potentiates the clock-speed enhancing effects of nicotine on timing and temporal memory. *Alcohol. Clin. Exp. Res.* 31:2106–13

Meck WH, Benson AM. 2002. Dissecting the brain's internal clock: how frontal-striatal circuitry keeps time and shifts attention. *Brain Cogn.* 48:195–211

Meck WH, Cheng RK, MacDonald CJ, Gainetdinov RR, Caron MG, Çevik MÖ. 2012. Gene-dose dependent effects of methamphetamine on interval timing in dopamine-transporter knockout mice. *Neuropharmacology* 62:1221–29

Meck WH, Church RM. 1982. Abstraction of temporal attributes. *J. Exp. Psychol. Anim. Behav. Process.* 8:226–43

Meck WH, Church RM. 1983. A mode control model of counting and timing processes. *J. Exp. Psychol. Anim. Behav. Process.* 9:320–34

Meck WH, Church RM. 1984. Simultaneous temporal processing. *J. Exp. Psychol. Anim. Behav. Process* 10:1–29

Meck WH, Church RM, Matell MS. 2013. Hippocampus, time, and memory—a retrospective analysis. *Behav. Neurosci.* In press

Meck WH, Church RM, Olton DS. 1984. Hippocampus, time, and memory. *Behav. Neurosci.* 98:3–22

Meck WH, Church RM, Wenk GL. 1986. Arginine vasopressin inoculates against age-related increases in sodium-dependent high affinity choline uptake and discrepancies in the content of temporal memory. *Eur. J. Pharmacol.* 130:327–31

Meck WH, Church RM, Wenk GL, Olton DS. 1987. Nucleus basalis magnocellularis and medial septal area lesions differentially impair temporal memory. *J. Neurosci.* 7:3505–11

Meck WH, Malapani C. 2004. Neuroimaging of interval timing. *Cogn. Brain Res.* 21:133–37

Meck WH, N'Diaye K. 2005. Un modèle neurobiologique de la perception et de l'estimation du temps. *Psychol. Fr.* 50:47–63

Meck WH, Penney TB, Pouthas V. 2008. Cortico-striatal representation of time in animals and humans. *Curr. Opin. Neurobiol.* 18:145–52

Meck WH, Vatakis A, van Rijn H. 2013. Timing & time perception enters a new dimension. *Timing Time Percept.* 1:1–2

Meck WH, Williams CL. 1997a. Characterization of the facilitative effects of perinatal choline supplementation on timing and temporal memory. *Neuroreport* 8:2831–35

Meck WH, Williams CL. 1997b. Simultaneous temporal processing is sensitive to prenatal choline availability in mature and aged rats. *Neuroreport* 8:3045–51

Melgire M, Ragot R, Samson S, Penney TB, Meck WH, Pouthas V. 2005. Auditory/visual duration bisection in patients with left or right medial-temporal lobe resection. *Brain Cogn.* 58:119–24

Merchant H, Harrington DL, Meck WH. 2013. Neural basis of the perception and estimation of time. *Annu. Rev. Neurosci.* 36:313–36

Merrifield C, Hurwitz M, Danckert J. 2010. Multimodal temporal perception deficits in a patient with left spatial neglect. *J. Cogn. Neurosci.* 1:244–53

Mita A, Mushiake H, Shima K, Matsuzaka Y, Tanji J. 2009. Interval timing coding by neurons in the presupplementary and supplementary motor areas. *Nat. Neurosci.* 12:502–7

N'Diaye K, Ragot R, Garnero L, Pouthas V. 2004. What is common to brain activity evoked by the perception of visual and auditory filled durations? A study with MEG and EEG co-recordings. *Cogn. Brain Res.* 21:250–68

Nobre K, Coull J. 2010. *Attention and Time.* Oxford, UK: Oxford Univ. Press

Noreika V, Falter CM, Rubia K. 2013. Timing deficits in attention-deficit/hyperactivity disorder (ADHD): evidence from neurocognitive and neuroimaging studies. *Neuropsychologia* 51:235–66

Nussbaum S, Liberman N, Trope Y. 2006. Predicting the near and distant future. *J. Exp. Psychol. Gen.* 135:152–61

Nyberg L, Kim AS, Habib R, Levine B, Tulving E. 2010. Consciousness of subjective time in the brain. *Proc. Natl. Acad. Sci. USA* 107:22356–59

Ogden RS, Wearden JH, Jones LA. 2010. Are memories for duration modality specific? *Q. J. Exp. Psychol.* 63:65–80

Olton DS, Wenk GL, Church RM, Meck WH. 1988. Attention and the frontal cortex as examined by simultaneous temporal processing. *Neuropsychologia* 26:307–18

Onoe H, Komori M, Onoe K, Takechi H, Tsukada H, Watanabe Y. 2001. Cortical networks recruited for time perception: a monkey positron emission tomography (PET) study. *NeuroImage* 13:37–45

Oprisan SA, Buhusi CV. 2011. Modeling pharmacological clock and memory patterns of interval timing in a striatal beat-frequency model with realistic, noisy neurons. *Front. Integr. Neurosci.* 5:52

O'Reilly RC, Frank MJ. 2006. Making working memory work: a computational model of learning in the prefrontal cortex and basal ganglia. *Neural Comp.* 18:283–328

Oshio K, Chiba A, Inase M. 2008. Temporal filtering by prefrontal neurons in duration discrimination. *Eur. J. Neurosci.* 28:2333–43

Pang KCH, Yoder RM, Olton DS. 2001. Neurons in the lateral agranular frontal cortex have divided attention correlates in a simultaneous temporal processing task. *Neuroscience* 103:615–28

Paule MG, Meck WH, McMillan DE, McClure GYH, Bateson M, et al. 1999. The use of timing behaviors in animals and humans to detect drug and/or toxicant effects. *Neurotoxicol. Teratol.* 21:491–502

Penney TB, Allan LG, Meck WH, Gibbon J. 1998. Memory mixing in duration bisection. In *Timing of Behavior: Neural, Psychological and Computational Perspectives*, ed. DA Rosenbaum, CE Collyer, pp. 165–93. Cambridge, MA: MIT Press

Penney TB, Gibbon J, Meck WH. 2000. Differential effects of auditory and visual signals on clock speed and temporal memory. *J. Exp. Psychol. Hum. Percept. Perform.* 26:1770–87

Penney TB, Gibbon J, Meck WH. 2008. Categorical scaling of duration bisection in pigeons (*Columba livia*), mice (*Mus musculus*), and humans (*homo sapiens*). *Psychol. Sci.* 19:1103–9

Penney TB, Holder MD, Meck WH. 1996. Clonidine-induced antagonism of norepinephrine modulates the attentional processes involved in peak-interval timing. *Exp. Clin. Psychopharmacol.* 4:82–92

Penney TB, Meck WH, Roberts SA, Gibbon J, Erlenmeyer-Kimling L. 2005. Interval-timing deficits in individuals at high risk for schizophrenia. *Brain Cogn.* 58:109–18

Penney TB, Yim ENK, Ng KK. 2013. Distractor expectancy effects on interval timing. *Timing Time Percept.* In press

Piras F, Coull JT. 2011. Implicit, predictive timing draws upon the same scalar representation of time as explicit timing. *PLoS ONE* 6(3):e18203

Pronin E. 2013. When the mind races: effects of thought speed on feeling and action. *Curr. Dir. Psychol. Sci.* 22:282–88

Pronin E, Jacobs E. 2008. Thought speed, mood, and the experience of mental motion. *Perspect. Psychol. Sci.* 3:461–85

Pronin E, Jacobs E, Wegner DM. 2008. Psychological effects of thought acceleration. *Emotion* 8:597–612

Pronin E, Wegner DM. 2006. Manic thinking: independent effects of thought speed and thought content on mood. *Psychol. Sci.* 17:807–13

Rakitin BC, Gibbon J, Penney TB, Malapani C, Hinton SC, Meck WH. 1998. Scalar expectancy theory and peak-interval timing in humans. *J. Exp. Psychol. Anim. Behav. Process.* 24:15–33

Rao SM, Mayer AR, Harrington DL. 2001. The evolution of brain activation during temporal processing. *Nat. Neurosci.* 4:317–23

Repp BH, Mendlowitz HB, Hove MJ. 2013. Does rapid auditory stimulation accelerate an internal pacemaker? Don't bet on it. *Timing Time Percept.* 1:65–76

Salvioni P, Murray MM, Kalmbach L, Bueti D. 2013. How the visual brain encodes and keeps track of time. *J. Neurosci.* 33:12423–29

Schirmer A. 2004. Timing speech: a review of lesion and neuroimaging findings. *Cogn. Brain Res.* 21:269–87

Schwartze M, Keller PE, Patel AD, Kotz SA. 2011. The impact of basal ganglia lesions on sensorimotor synchronization, spontaneous motor tempo, and the detection of tempo changes. *Behav. Brain Res.* 216:685–91

Schwartze M, Rothermich K, Kotz SA. 2012a. Functional dissociation of pre-SMA and SMA-proper in temporal processing. *NeuroImage* 60:290–98

Schwartze M, Tavano A, Schroger E, Kotz SA. 2012b. Temporal aspects of prediction in audition: cortical and subcortical neural mechanisms. *Int. J. Psychophysiol.* 83:200–7

Shea-Brown R, Rinzel J, Rakitin BC, Malapani C. 2006. A firing rate model of Parkinsonian deficits in interval timing. *Exp. Brain Res.* 1070:189–201

Shi Z, Chen L, Müller HJ. 2010. Auditory temporal modulation of the visual Ternus effect: the influence of time interval. *Exp. Brain Res.* 203:723–35

Shi Z, Church RM, Meck WH. 2013a. Bayesian optimization of time perception. *Trends Cogn. Sci.* In press

Shi Z, Ganzenmüller S, Müller HJ. 2013b. Reducing bias in auditory duration reproduction by integrating the reproduced signal. *PLoS ONE* 8:e62065

Siegel JJ, Kalmbach B, Chitwood RA, Mauk MD. 2012. Persistent activity in a cortical-to-subcortical circuit: bridging the temporal gap in trace eyelid conditioning. *J. Neurophysiol.* 107:50–64

Smith JG, Harper DN, Gittings D, Abernethy D. 2007. The effects of Parkinson's disease on time estimation as a function of stimulus duration range and modality. *Brain Cogn.* 64:130–43

Smythies J, Edelstein L, Ramachandran V. 2012. Hypotheses relating to the function of the claustrum. *Front. Integr. Neurosci.* 6:53

Suddendorf T, Addis DR, Corballis MC. 2009. Mental time travel and the shaping of the human mind. *Philos. Trans. R. Soc. B* 364:1317–24

Teki S, Grube M, Griffiths TD. 2012. A unified model of time perception accounts for duration- based and beat-based timing mechanisms. *Front. Integr. Neurosci.* 5:90

Teki S, Grube M, Kumar S, Griffiths TD. 2011. Distinct neural substrates of duration-based and beat-based auditory timing. *J. Neurosci.* 31:3805–12

Tregellas JR, Davalos DB, Rojas DC. 2006. Effect of task difficulty on the functional anatomy of temporal processing. *NeuroImage* 32:307–15

Treisman M. 1963. Temporal discrimination and the indifference interval: implications for a model of the "internal clock." *Psychol. Monogr.* 77(13):1–31

Treisman M. 1984. Temporal rhythms and cerebral rhythms. *Ann. N.Y. Acad. Sci.* 423:542–65

Treisman M. 2013. The information-processing model of timing (Treisman, 1963): its sources and further history. *Timing Time Percept.* In press

Treisman M, Cook N, Naish PL, MacCrone JK. 1994. The internal clock: electroencephalographic evidence for oscillatory processes underlying time perception. *Q. J. Exp. Psychol. A* 47:241–89

Treisman M, Faulkner A, Naish PLN, Brogan D. 1990. The internal clock: evidence for a temporal oscillator underlying time perception with some estimates of its characteristic frequency. *Perception* 19:705–43

Tulving E. 2002. Chronesthesia: awareness of subjective time. In *Principles of Frontal Lobe Function*, ed. DT Stuss, RC Knight, pp. 311–25. New York: Oxford Univ. Press

Ullman MT. 2004. Contributions of memory circuits to language: the declarative/procedural model. *Cognition* 92:231–70

Ullman MT, Pierpont EI. 2005. Specific language impairment is not specific to language: the procedural deficit hypothesis. *Cortex* 41:399–433

van Rijn H, Gu B-M, Meck WH. 2013. Dedicated clock/timing-circuit theories of interval timing. In *Neurobiology of Interval Timing*, ed. H Merchant, V de Lafuente. New York: Springer-Verlag. In press

van Rijn H, Kononowicz TW, Meck WH, Ng KK, Penney TB. 2011. Contingent negative variation and its relation to time estimation: a theoretical evaluation. *Front. Integr. Neurosci.* 5:91

Vatakis A, Allman MJ. 2013. *Time Distortions in Mind: Temporal Processing in Clinical Populations*. Leiden, The Neth.: Brill. In press

Vidalaki VN, Ho M-Y, Bradshaw CM, Szabadi E. 1999. Interval timing performance in temporal lobe epilepsy: differences between patients with left and right hemisphere foci. *Neuropsychologia* 37:1061–70

Walsh V. 2003a. A theory of magnitude: common cortical metrics of time, space and quantity. *Trends Cogn. Sci.* 7:483–88

Walsh V. 2003b. Time: the back-door of perception. *Trends Cogn. Sci.* 7:335–38

Wearden JH. 2001. Internal clocks and the representation of time. See Hoerl & McCormack 2001, pp. 37–58

Wearden JH. 2003. Applying the scalar timing model to human time psychology: progress and challenges. In *Time and Mind II: Information Processing Perspectives*, ed. E Helfrich, pp. 21–39. Germany: Hogrefe & Huber

Wearden JH. 2005. Origins and development of internal clock theories of psychological time. *Psychol. Fr.* 50:7–25

Wearden JH, Edwards H, Fakhri M, Percival A. 1998. Why "sounds are judged longer than light:" application of a model of the internal clock in humans. *Q. J. Exp. Psychol. Comp. Physiol. Psychol.* 51B:97–120

Wearden JH, Lejeune H. 2008. Scalar properties in human timing: conformity and violations. *Q. J. Exp. Psychol.* 61:569–87

Wearden JH, Philpott K, Win T. 1999. Speeding up and (...relatively...) slowing down an internal clock in humans. *Behav. Process.* 46:63–73

Wearden JH, Smith-Spark JH, Cousins R, Edelstyn NM, Cody FW, O'Boyle DJ. 2009. Effect of click trains on duration estimates by people with Parkinson's disease. *Q. J. Exp. Psychol.* 62:33–40

Wencil EB, Coslett HB, Aguirre GK, Chatterjee A. 2010. Carving the clock at its component joints: neural bases for interval timing. *J. Neurophysiol.* 104:160–68

Wiener M, Turkeltaub PE, Coslett HB. 2010a. Implicit timing activates the left inferior parietal cortex. *Neuropsychologia* 48:3967–71

Wiener M, Turkeltaub PE, Coslett HB. 2010b. The image of time: a voxel-wise meta-analysis. *NeuroImage* 49:1–15

Williamson LL, Cheng RK, Etchegaray M, Meck WH. 2008. "Speed" warps time: methamphetamine's interactive roles in drug abuse, habit formation, and the biological clocks of circadian and interval timing. *Curr. Drug Abuse Rev.* 1:203–12

Wittmann M. 2013. The inner sense of time: how the brain creates a representation of duration. *Nat. Rev. Neurosci.* 14:217–23

Wittmann M, Leland DS, Churan J, Paulus MP. 2007. Impaired time perception and motor timing in stimulant-dependent subjects. *Drug Alcohol Depend.* 90:183–92

Wittmann M, Paulus MP. 2008. Decision making, impulsivity and time perception. *Trends Cogn. Sci.* 12:7–12

Wittmann M, Simmons AN, Flagan T, Lane SD, Wackermann J, Paulus MP. 2011. Neural substrates of time perception and impulsivity. *Brain Res.* 1406:43–58

Yin B, Meck WH. 2013. Comparison of interval timing behaviour in mice following dorsal or ventral hippocampal lesions with mice having δ opioid receptor gene deletion. *Philos. Trans. R. Soc. B.* In press

Yin B, Troger AB. 2011. Exploring the 4th dimension: hippocampus, time, and memory revisited. *Front. Integr. Neurosci.* 5:36

Yin B, Yin HH, Meck WH. 2010. Dorsal hippocampal lesions lead to double leftward shifts of peak time in a bi-peak procedure in mice. *Soc. Neurosci. Abstr.* 98.20

Yumoto N, Lu X, Henry TR, Miyachi S, Nambu A, et al. 2011. A neural correlate of the processing of multi-second time intervals in primate prefrontal cortex. *PLoS ONE* 6(4):e19168

RELATED RESOURCES

Berry AS, Li X, Lin Z, Lustig C. 2013. Shared and distinct factors driving attention and temporal processing across modalities. *Acta Psychol.* In press

Broadway JM, Engle RW. 2011. Individual differences in working memory capacity and temporal discrimination. *PLoS ONE* 6(10):e25422

Filippopoulos PC, Hallworth P, Lee S, Wearden JH. 2013. Interference between auditory and visual duration judgements suggests a common code for time. *Psychol. Res.* In press

Gaudreault R, Fortin C. 2013. To count or not to count: the effect of instructions on expecting a break in timing. *Atten. Percept. Psychophys.* 75:588–602

Matthews WJ. 2013. How does sequence structure affect the judgment of time? Exploring a weighted sum of segments model. *Cogn. Psychol.* 66:259–82

Penney TB, Brown GDA, Wong JKL. 2013. Stimulus spacing effects in duration perception are larger for auditory stimuli: data and a model. *Acta Psychol.* In press

Cumulative Indexes

Contributing Authors, Volumes 55–65

Cosmides L, 64:201–30
Craighead WE, 65:267–300
Crano WD, 57:345–74
Crosby FJ, 57:585–611
Cudeck R, 58:615–37
Curran PJ, 62:583–619
Curry SJ, 60:229–55

D

Deary IJ, 63:453–82
Delicato LS, 55:181–205
den Nieuwenboer NA, 65:635–60
Derrington AM, 55:181–205
de Waal FBM, 59:279–300
Diamond A, 64:135–68
Dickel N, 62:391–417
Diefendorff JM, 61:543–68
Diehl RL, 55:149–79
Dijksterhuis A, 61:467–90
Dishion TJ, 62:189–214
DiZio P, 56:115–47
Domjan M, 56:179–206
Donnellan MB, 58:175–99
Doss AJ, 56:337–63
Dovidio JF, 56:365–92
Dudai Y, 55:51–86
Dunkel Schetter C, 62:531–58
Dunlop BW, 65:267–300
Dunlosky J, 64:417–44
Dunn EW, 55:493–518
Dupré KE, 60:671–92

E

Eby LT, 61:599–622
Echterhoff G, 63:55–79
Ehrhart MG, 64:361–88
Einarsson E, 61:141–67
Elliot AJ, 65:95–120
Emery NJ, 60:87–113
Erez M, 58:479–514
Evans GW, 57:423–51
Evans JSBT, 59:255–78

F

Faigman DL, 56:631–59
Fairchild AJ, 58:593–614
Fanselow MS, 56:207–34
Farah MJ, 63:571–91

Federico CM, 60:307–37
Federmeier KD, 62:621–47
Fingerhut AW, 58:405–24
Finniss DG, 59:565–90
Fivush R, 62:559–82
Folkman S, 55:745–74
Fouad NA, 58:543–64
Fox NA, 56:235–62
French DC, 59:591–616
Fried I, 63:511–37
Friedman HS, 65:719–42
Friston KJ, 56:57–87
Frith CD, 63:287–313
Frith U, 63:287–313
Fritz MS, 58:593–614
Furman W, 60:631–52

G

Gaissmaier W, 62:451–82
Gallistel CR, 64:169–200
Gallo LC, 62:501–30
Gazzaniga MS, 64:1–20
Geisler WS, 59:167–92
Gelfand MJ, 58:479–514
Gelman SA, 60:115–40
Gerhart B, 56:571–600
Gervain J, 61:191–218
Ghera MA, 56:235–62
Gifford R, 65:541–79
Gigerenzer G, 62:451–82
Glimcher PW, 56:25–56
Glück J, 62:215–41
Goethals GR, 56:545–70
Goldin-Meadow S, 64:257–84
Goldstein NJ, 55:591–621
Golomb JD, 62:73–101
Gonzalez CM, 59:329–60
Goodman GS, 61:325–51
Gorman-Smith D, 57:557–83
Gottesman II, 56:263–86
Gould E, 61:111–40
Graber D, 55:545–71
Graham JW, 60:549–76
Graham S, 65:159–85
Green DP, 60:339–67
Griffiths TD, 65:743–71
Gross JJ, 58:373–403
Grotevant HD, 65:235–65
Grusec JE, 62:243–69
Gunia BC, 61:491–515
Gunnar M, 58:145–73

H

Hall RJ, 61:543–68
Hampson SE, 63:315–39
Han S, 64:335–60
Hanson DR, 56:263–86
Hardt O, 61:141–67
Harring JR, 58:615–37
Haslam N, 65:399–423
Hauser M, 61:303–24
Hawkins EH, 60:197–227
Hawley KM, 56:337–63
Healey MP, 59:387–417
Heatherton TF, 62:363–90
Heil SH, 55:431–61
Heine SJ, 60:369–94
Hen R, 57:117–37
Henderson HA, 56:235–62
Hennessey BA, 61:569–98
Henry D, 57:557–83
Herek GM, 64:309–34
Higgins ET, 59:361–85
Higgins ST, 55:431–61
Hirst W, 63:55–79
Hochman KM, 55:401–30
Hodgkinson GP, 59:387–417
Hollenbeck JR, 56:517–43
Hollins M, 61:243–71
Hollon SD, 57:285–315
Holsboer F, 61:81–109
Holt LL, 55:149–79
Holyoak KJ, 62:135–63
Horn EE, 65:515–40
Hornsey MJ, 65:461–85
Huston AC, 61:411–37
Hwang E, 61:169–90
Hyde JS, 65:373–98

I

Iacoboni M, 60:653–70
Ilgen DR, 56:517–43
Ising M, 61:81–109
Iyer A, 57:585–611
Izard CE, 60:1–25

J

Jetten J, 65:461–85
Johnson EJ, 60:53–85
Johnson M, 56:517–43
Joiner TE Jr, 56:287–314
Jonides J, 59:193–224

P

Palmer SE, 64:77–108
Paluck EL 60:339–67
Park DC, 60:173–96
Parke RD, 55:365–99
Parker LA, 64:21–48
Parker SK, 65:661–91
Parks L, 56:571–600
Peissig JJ, 58:75–96
Penn DC, 58:97–118
Penner LA, 56:365–92
Pennington BF, 60:283–306
Peplau LA, 58:405–24
Peretz I, 56:89–114
Pettersson E, 65:515–40
Phelps EA, 57:27–53
Phillips DA, 62:483–500
Phillips LA, 59:477–505
Phillips LT, 65:611–34
Piff PK, 65:425–60
Piliavin JA, 56:365–92
Pinder CC, 56:485–516
Pittman TS, 59:361–85
Ployhart RE, 65:693–717
Podsakoff NP, 63:539–69
Podsakoff PM, 63:539–69
Posner MI, 58:1–23
Poulos AM, 56:207–34
Povinelli DJ, 58:97–118
Pratte MS, 63:483–509
Price DD, 59:565–90
Prislin R, 57:345–74
Proctor RW, 61:623–51

Q

Quas JA, 61:325–51
Quevedo K, 58:145–73
Quirk GJ, 63:129–51

R

Rabinowitz AR, 65:301–31
Rausch JR, 59:537–63
Rauschecker AM, 63:31–53
Recanzone GH, 59:119–42
Reuter-Lorenz P, 60:173–96
Revenson TA, 58:565–92
Rhodes G, 57:199–226
Rick S, 59:647–72
Rilling JK, 62:23–48

Rissman J, 63:101–28
Robbins P, 63:81–99
Roberts BW, 56:453–84
Roberts RD, 59:507–36
Roediger HL III, 59:225–54
Rothbart MK, 58:1–23
Rubin KH, 60:141–71
Ruble DN, 61:353–81
Runco MA, 55:657–87
Ryan A, 65:693–717
Rynes SL, 56:571–600

S

Sackett PR, 59:419–50
Salmon DP, 60:257–82
Salthouse T, 63:201–26
Sammartino J, 64:77–108
Samuel AG, 62:49–72
Sanchez JI, 63:397–425
Sandler IN, 62:299–329
Sanfey AG, 62:23–48
Sargis EG, 57:529–55
Saribay SA, 59:329–60
Sarkissian H, 63:81–99
Sasaki JY, 65:487–514
Saturn SR, 65:425–60
Saxe R, 55:87–124
Schall JD, 55:23–50
Schaller M, 55:689–714
Schippers MC, 58:515–41
Schloss KB, 64:77–108
Schmidt AC, 61:543–68
Schneider B, 64:361–88
Schoenfelder EN, 62:299–329
Schroeder DA, 56:365–92
Schultz W, 57:87–115
Serbin LA, 55:333–63
Seyfarth RM, 63:153–77
Shadish WR, 60:607–29
Shanks DR, 61:273–301
Shaywitz BA, 59:451–75
Shaywitz SE, 59:451–75
Sherman DK, 65:333–71
Sherry DF, 57:167–97
Shevell SK, 59:143–66
Shi J, 65:209–33
Shiffrar M, 58:47–73
Shiner RL, 56:453–84
Shors TJ, 57:55–85
Siegel JM, 55:125–48
Sincharoen S, 57:585–611

Skinner EA, 58:119–44
Skitka LJ, 57:529–55
Smetana JG, 57:255–84
Snyder DK, 57:317–44
Sobel N, 61:219–41
Sommers T, 63:81–99
Sporer AK, 60:229–55
Stanton AL, 58:565–92
Staudinger UM, 62:215–41
Stephens NM, 65:611–34
Sternberg RJ, 65:1–16
Stewart AJ, 55:519–44
Stewart MO, 57:285–315
Stickgold R, 57:139–66
Stone AA, 64:471–98
Strunk D, 57:285–315
Stuewig J, 58:345–72
Sue S, 60:525–48
Sutter ML, 59:119–42

T

Tangney JP, 58:345–72
Tarr MJ, 58:75–96
Tasselli S, 64:527–48
Teki S, 65:743–71
Tennen H, 58:565–92
Thau S, 60:717–41
Thompson LL, 61:491–515
Thompson RF, 56:1–23
Tindale RS, 55:623–55
Tipsord JM, 62:189–214
Tolan P, 57:557–83
Tomasello M, 64:231–56
Tong F, 63:483–509
Tooby J, 64:201–30
Tourangeau R, 55:775–801
Treviño L, 65:635–60
Trickett EJ, 60:395–419
Turk-Browne NB, 62:73–101
Turkheimer E, 65:515–40
Tyler TR, 57:375–400

U

Uleman JS, 59:329–60
Uskul AK, 62:419–49

V

Vaish A, 64:231–56
van Knippenberg D, 58:515–41

Varnum MEW, 64:335–60
Vogeley K, 64:335–60
Vohs KD, 62:331–61
Volkmar F, 56:315–36
Vu KL, 61:623–51

W

Wagner AD, 63:101–28
Walker BM, 58:453–77
Walker E, 55:401–30
Walker MP, 57:139–66
Walumbwa FO, 60:421–49
Wanberg CR, 63:369–96
Wandell BA, 63:31–53
Wang J, 61:491–515

Wang M, 65:209–33
Wang S, 61:49–79
Ward J, 64:49–76
Weber EU, 60:53–85
Weber TJ, 60:421–49
Weinman J, 59:477–505
Weisz JR, 56:337–63
Welsh DP, 60:631–52
Wexler BE, 64:335–60
Whisman MA, 57:317–44
Williams KD, 58:425–52
Wilson TD, 55:493–518
Wingate LR, 56:287–314
Winne PH, 61:653–78
Winter DA, 58:453–77
Wixted JT, 55:235–69
Wolchik SA, 62:299–329

Wolf M, 63:427–52
Wood J, 61:303–24

Y

Yeatman JD, 63:31–53
Yeshurun Y, 61:219–41
Yuille A, 55:271–304

Z

Zane N, 60:525–48
Zatorre RJ, 56:89–114
Zhang T, 61:439–66
Zimmer-Gembeck MJ,
    58:119–44

Article Titles, Volumes 55–65

Vision

See SENSORY PROCESSES